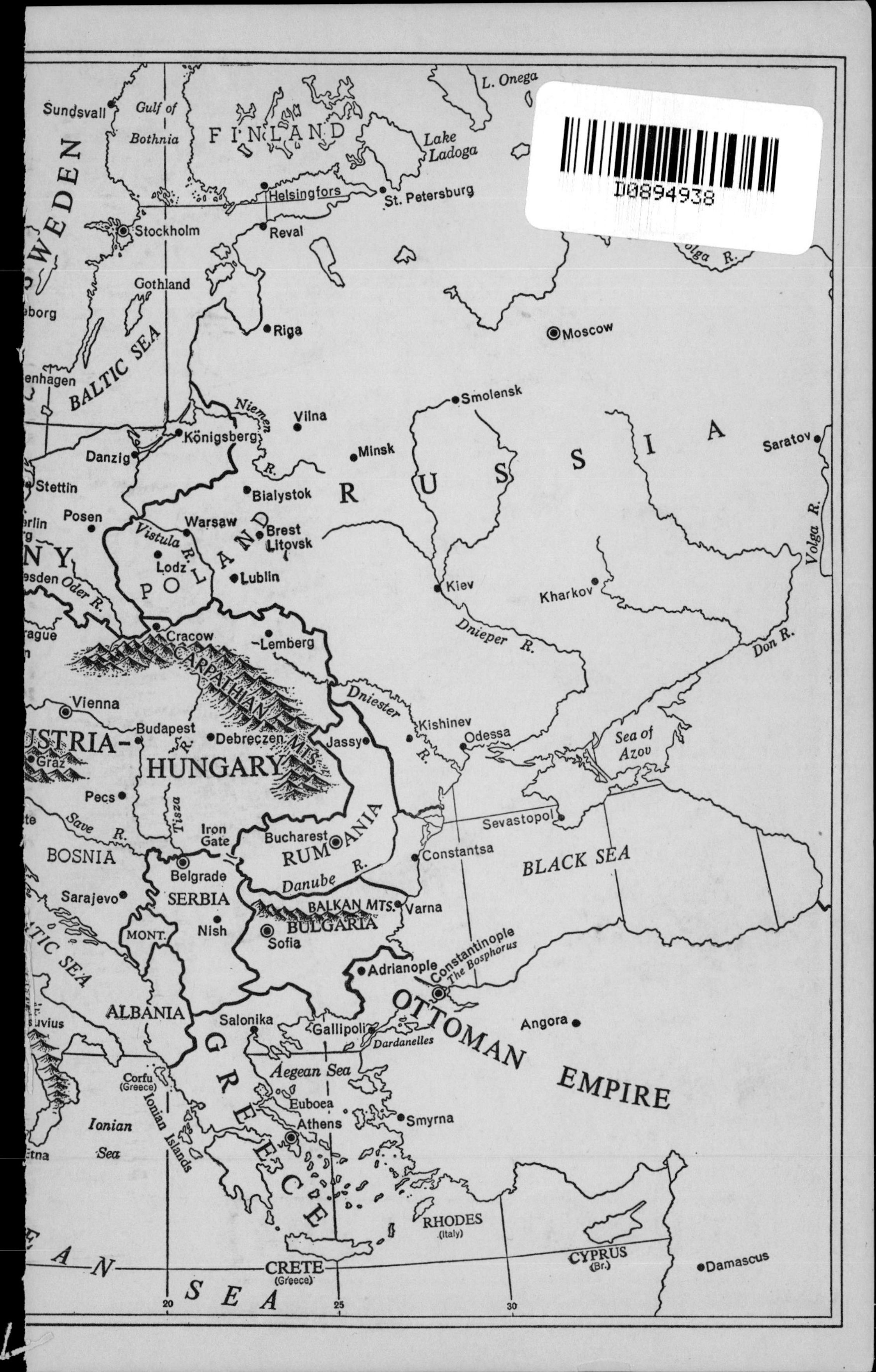

L. Onega
Sundsvall
Gulf of Bothnia
FINLAND
Lake Ladoga
SWEDEN
Helsingfors
St. Petersburg
Stockholm
Reval
Volga R.
Gothland
Riga
Moscow
BALTIC SEA
Smolensk
Niemen R.
Vilna
Königsberg
Minsk
Danzig
R U S S I A
Saratov
Stettin
Bialystok
Posen
Warsaw
Brest Litovsk
Vistula R.
POLAND
Lodz
Lublin
Kiev
Kharkov
Volga R.
Oder R.
Dnieper R.
Cracow
Lemberg
Don R.
CARPATHIAN MTS.
Dniester R.
Vienna
Budapest
Debreczen
Jassy
Kishinev
Odessa
Sea of Azov
HUNGARY
Graz
Pecs
Tisza R.
Save R.
Iron Gate
Bucharest
RUMANIA
Sevastopol
BOSNIA
Belgrade
Constantsa
BLACK SEA
Danube R.
Sarajevo
SERBIA
BALKAN MTS.
Varna
MONT.
Nish
BULGARIA
Sofia
Constantinople
The Bosphorus
Adrianople
ALBANIA
Salonika
Gallipoli
OTTOMAN EMPIRE
Angora
Dardanelles
GREECE
Corfu (Greece)
Aegean Sea
Ionian Islands
Ionian Sea
Euboea
Athens
Smyrna
Etna
RHODES (Italy)
CYPRUS (Br.)
CRETE (Greece)
Damascus
SEA
20
25
30

J. V.

Modern Europe in World Perspective

1914 to the Present

Rinehart Books in European History

Eugene N. Anderson	Modern Europe in World Perspective: 1914 to the Present
Eugene N. Anderson	European Issues in the Twentieth Century
Richard M. Brace	The Making of the Modern World: From the Renaissance to the Present
Wallace E. Caldwell	The Ancient World
Stewart C. Easton	The Heritage of the Past: From the Earliest Times to 1500
Stewart C. Easton	The Heritage of the Past: From the Earliest Times to 1715
Loren C. MacKinney	The Medieval World
L. S. Stavrianos	The Balkans Since 1453

Modern Europe in World Perspective

1914 to the Present

Eugene N. Anderson

University of California at Los Angeles

Rinehart & Company, Inc., New York

CARTOGRAPHY: *Vincent Kotschar*

Printed in the United States of America

Library of Congress Catalog Card Number: 58-6429

To E. N. A., Jr.

Preface

The fundamental experience of Europe in this century has come from war and revolution, from the application of science in technology to create an industrial society, and from economic crisis. The results have been political, social, and economic changes of unprecedented speed and magnitude. Among the states and among the people within a particular state, conditions have varied so greatly that in order to portray their diversity the historian must endeavor to analyze the total culture. He must discuss not merely the international, imperial, and national activities of a few great powers but also the achievements of the many small states. The members of this vigorous continent have not excelled solely in war; some of them, especially certain of the small nations, have set a model for good living in social harmony and international peace. Europe contains peoples at various stages of historical development; Spain, for example, remains in the Old Regime, whereas Sweden is one of the most progressive countries in the world. All have been subjected to common action.

Under the pressure of violent forces since 1914 the structure of European life has to a large extent given way to extensive experimentation in political and social organization. With liberal democracy have appeared socialism, communism, fascism, and other forms of authoritarianism that cannot be readily labeled. At the same time, organization and methods of the United States have strongly influenced Europe. New standards of economic and social achievement have been introduced, with new conceptions of the relations between government and people. Some nations possessed institutions and traditions which enabled them to contend more effectively than others with the cultural impact of the cataclysmic forces. In this time of nationalism none appears to have been prepared for the sudden revelation of the interdependence of states.

If the ideals of the United Nations are taken as criteria, this has not been a successful age. The student of history, however, is offered a range of human endeavor which for so short a span of time has few parallels. No one individual has the capacity to understand or the wisdom to judge all that these recent decades have brought to Europe. I have selected from the wealth of material what seemed most revealing of the total character of European life.

Throughout this book I have tried to emphasize the impact of war and revolution, of technological change, and of economics—without in any way minimizing the importance of political and diplomatic history. The achievements of small states are given due attention, as is the influence of ideology. Two separate chapters on cultural advances are included. Finally, and perhaps most important, I have attempted at all times to place European history "in world perspective." The major points raised in this text are exemplified in a short accompanying book of readings and documents, entitled *European Issues in the Twentieth Century*.

The bibliographies contain a small number of titles from the thousands available. I consider these few particularly useful in pursuing further the analysis in the text, either as expansion of subject matter or as criticism of the present treatment. They will open the way to numerous other works of special interest.

The publishers sent the manuscript to Professors Albert W. Gendebien of Lafayette College and Franklin D. Scott of Northwestern University for review. Their criticism has been of great value in correcting details and improving perspective. I wish to thank them and at the same time relieve them from responsibility for the text. My wife has helped in so many ways that I am unable to acknowledge her contribution.

EUGENE N. ANDERSON

Santa Monica, California
January, 1958

Contents

Part Two · Europe in the 1920's

Part Five · The Cultural Expression

Illustrations

Maps and Charts

Part I

Europe 1914-1919

Chronological Preview

1882
Formation of Triple Alliance

1894
Formation of Dual Alliance

1898
Germany inaugurates naval program

1899–1902
Boer War

1904
Formation of Entente Cordiale

1904–1905
Russo-Japanese War

1905
Russian Revolution
First Moroccan Crisis
Separation of church and state in France

1907
British-Russian Agreement

1908
Bosnian Crisis

1909–1911
Lloyd George budget and constitutional conflict

1911
Second Moroccan Crisis

1912–1913
Balkan Wars

1912
Social Democrats become largest party in Germany

1914
June 28. Assassination of Archduke Francis Ferdinand and wife
July 28. Austria-Hungary declares war on Serbia
Aug. 1. Germany declares war on Russia
Aug. 3. Germany declares war on France
Aug. 4. Great Britain declares war on Germany
Sept. Battle of the Marne
Sept. Battle of Tannenberg

1915
Japan submits Twenty-one Demands to China
May. Treaty of London–Italy enters the war
Sept. Bulgaria declares war on Allies
Dec. Allied defeat at Gallipoli
Oct. Conquest of Serbia

1916
Greece declares war against Central Powers
Battle of Verdun
Hindenburg and Ludendorff assume supreme command
May. Battle of Jutland
Aug. Romania declares war against Central Powers
Dec. Conquest of Romania
Dec. Lloyd George becomes prime minister

1917
Feb. Germany renews submarine warfare
March. Russian Revolution
April 17. United States declares war
July. German *Reichstag* passes peace resolution
Nov. Bolshevik Revolution in Russia
Nov. Clemenceau becomes premier

1918
Jan. Wilson states the "Fourteen Points"
March. Treaty of Brest Litovsk
Nov. German Revolution and establishment of German Republic
Nov. 11. Armistice with Germany

1919
Jan.-June. Peace Conference at Versailles
June. Treaty of Versailles with Germany
Sept. Treaty of St. Germain with Austria
Nov. Treaty of Neuilly with Bulgaria

1920
June. Treaty of Trianon with Hungary
Aug. Treaty of Sèvres with Turkey

1923
Treaty of Lausanne with Turkey

Chapter 1 · Origins of World War I

Three different levels of action must be explored in order to understand the origins of World War I. Ultimate causes are not to be found in the diplomatic negotiations which led directly to the outbreak of hostilities. Soon after World War I Winston Churchill described the shortcomings of this explanation as follows:

> When one looks at the petty subjects which have led to wars between great countries and to so many disputes, it is easy to be misled by the idea that wars arise out of the machinations of secret diplomacy. But of course such small matters are only the symptoms of the dangerous disease, and are only important for that reason. Behind them lie the interests, the passions, and the destiny of mighty races of men; and long antagonisms express themselves in trifles.[1]

To understand this "dangerous disease" one must analyze the forces that lay behind diplomatic maneuvers. First, one must examine the international state system to learn whether its intrinsic nature was such as to incline Europe toward war. Second, one must discuss the ideals of nationalism, imperialism, and militarism, prompted by fear, pride, and acquisitiveness, as motive forces. Finally, one must learn whether or not the political and social conditions inside the states involved in the crisis encouraged the use of war as an instrument of policy. The analysis will provide background for the two subsequent chapters, where the military and economic strength of the belligerents, and the achievement of each state in Armageddon, will be discussed.

DIPLOMATIC BACKGROUND

Serbian Nationalism Erupts

At Sarajevo on June 28, 1914, Gavrilo Printsip, an Austro-Hungarian subject of Serb nationality, assassinated the heir to the Austro-Hungarian throne, Archduke Francis Ferdinand, and his wife. This single act initiated diplomatic and military maneuvers which led directly to the outbreak of

[1] Quoted in G. Lowes Dickinson, *The International Anarchy,* 1904–1914 (New York: The Century Company, 1926), p. 37.

World War I. An explanation of how the murder of two persons could touch off a global holocaust must be sought in history.

Printsip was carrying out the orders of one of the secret patriotic societies devoted to the union of all Serbs into a national state. This group, "Union or Death," was guided by a central committee with headquarters

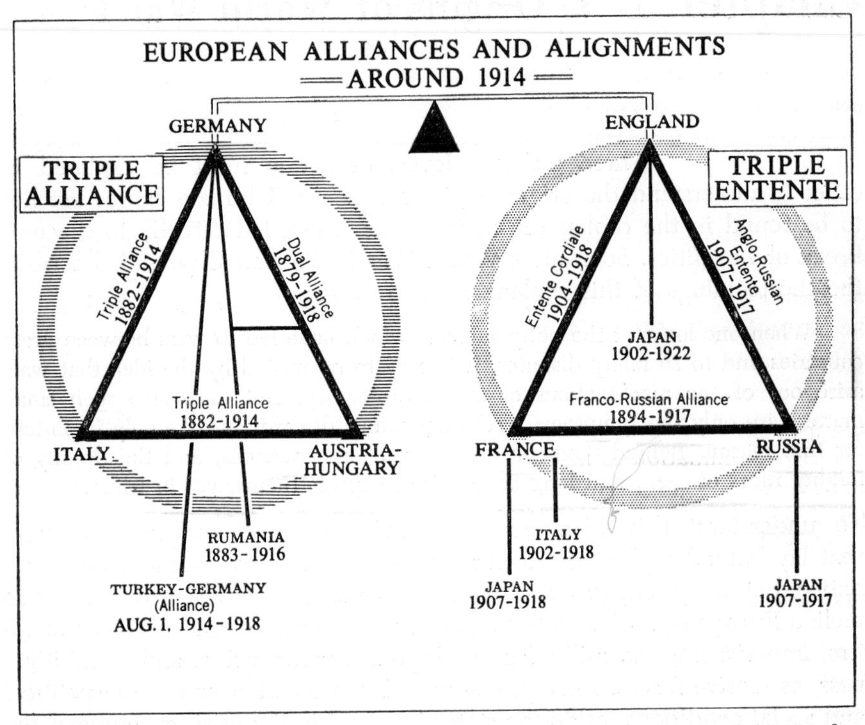

From *The Making of the Modern World* by Richard M. Brace (New York: Rinehart & Company, Inc., 1955).

in Belgrade. According to its statutes it preferred "terrorist action to intellectual propaganda." The membership of the societies consisted largely of students, young army officers, and state employees, groups which in areas of low standard of living and high rate of illiteracy supported ardent nationalism. In spreading sedition among the Serbs in Austria-Hungary the societies enjoyed the clandestine aid of Serbian officials. Premier Nikola Pašić of Serbia had known beforehand about the plot to assassinate the Archduke, but he had taken inadequate preventive measures. All Serbs were taught, as the Serb Minister of Education has written, "to look out for evil in everything that Austria did, no matter how or where." Serbian leaders considered it entirely moral to risk a European or a world war in order to break up the Austro-Hungarian Empire and so unite with Serbia the few million South Slavs in Bosnia, Herzegovina, and other Hapsburg territories.

Unfriendly relations with the empire had persisted almost from 1878, when the little state had acquired independence from the Turks. The accession of Peter I to the Serbian throne after the assassination in 1903 by army officers of the reigning king and queen opened a period of growing hostility. Peter enjoyed popularity among the Slavs in the Austrian provinces of Bosnia and Herzegovina, as well as among his own people. In 1906 a tariff war between Serbia and Austria showed the small Slav country that it needed to acquire Bosnia and Herzegovina in order to have an outlet to the sea. When Austria, in actual control of the two provinces since 1878, formally annexed them in 1908, Serbian leaders correctly interpreted the act as hostile to their state. They began to retaliate in kind. In 1912 Serbia, Bulgaria, Greece, and Montenegro successfully went to war against Turkey. Serbia seized the upper valley of the Vardar, the Sanjak of Novi Pazar, and the northern part of Albania, nearly doubling the size of her territory. The great powers intervened, Austria-Hungary being mainly responsible for preventing Serbia from acquiring a coast line in northern Albania. In the Second Balkan War (1913), fought between Bulgaria on the one hand and Romania, Greece, and Serbia on the other over the division of spoils from the first war (Turkey also participated to regain territory), Bulgaria was quickly defeated. Serbia emerged with increased power and prestige and the determination to achieve her ambition of a "Greater Serbia." Printsip's shots, fired on a patriotic anniversary, concluded years of plotting for the objective.

Austria-Hungary Reacts

Upon news of the terrorist act in 1914 the Austro-Hungarian government determined at once to stop Serbia from being a source of further trouble. It interpreted the assassination as a major effort to destroy the Austrian state; it knew that success of one nationality in securing independence would encourage other nationalities within the polyglot empire to revolt. Believing that it had just cause, the Austrian government decided upon war, not to annex Serbia, but to control her behavior. The Hungarian government, as distinct from that of the Austro-Hungarian Empire as a whole, disliked the proposed action on two counts: it might cause a general war, and it might add more Slavs to the empire. The Magyars in Hungary dominated the other nationalities within the Hungarian state, just as the Germans dominated in Austria; but unlike the Germans, the Magyars felt confident of being able to maintain the ascendancy. They recognized, however, that an empire when threatened would seek to preserve itself. Thus they acquiesced in the Hapsburg strategy of controlling Serbia sufficiently to eliminate it as a disruptive force.

The ultimatum which the Hapsburg government sent to Serbia on July 23 was drawn in such a way that it made acceptance impossible. It stated in detail the measures which the Serbian government must take with respect to the press, the schools, the bureaucracy, and the secret societies, in order to suppress all anti-Austrian propaganda or activity. It culminated in the demand that the government "agree to the cooperation in Serbia of the organs of the Imperial and Royal Government in the suppression of the subversive movement directed against the integrity of the Monarchy," and that Serbia "institute a judicial inquiry against every participant in the conspiracy of the twenty-eighth of June who may be found in Serbian territory; the organs of the Imperial and Royal Government delegated for the purpose will take part in the proceedings held for this purpose." The Serbian government in reply apparently acquiesced in some of the points but rejected other essential demands as an infringement of sovereignty. Austria-Hungary thereupon declared war.

German-Russian Rivalry

As the Serbs well knew, Russia harbored imperialistic ambitions in the Balkans and had propagated Pan-Slav doctrines too long to allow Serbia to suffer a diminution of sovereignty. In the revolutionary period of 1848–1849 the Russian czar had sent troops to Austria to help suppress the rebellion and to restore Hapsburg autocracy. During the years of Bismarck's ascendancy in European international relations, the Russian czar had joined his colleagues in Germany and Austria-Hungary in the League of the Three Emperors to defend conservative, monarchical power against Western liberalism and republicanism. After the fall of Bismarck in 1890, Russia had turned away from the league and followed national interest and the balance of power as guiding principles in her relations with both Germany and Austria. In 1894 autocratic Russia had formed the Dual Alliance with republican France, primarily because France lay on the other side of Germany and was eager to help Russia offset the power of the alliance between Germany and Austria-Hungary.

The progress of Germany's influence in the Balkans and the Near East steadily increased Russia's concern. The Berlin-to-Bagdad Railway, sponsored by Germany, threatened the Russian policy of helping the Ottoman Empire to its death. The despatch in 1913 of a German military mission to Constantinople to reform the Ottoman army alarmed Russia even more. The sudden annexation of Bosnia and Herzegovina by Austria-Hungary in 1908 indicated to Russia that both Central Powers had become imperialistic in a region which for more than a century Russia had considered an area of potential expansion for herself. The wide spread of pan-Slavism in Russia in the course of the nineteenth century had popularized the official policy of acting as friend and protector of the South Slav peoples, particularly the Serbs. Pan-Slavism supported the traditional Russian ambition of controlling the Dardanelles, sole outlet from the Black Sea to the Mediterranean. The Austro-Hungarian ultimatum to Serbia seemed to threaten Russia's ambitions, and the czarist government took alarm. "If

Austria-Hungary devours Serbia," declared the Russian Foreign Minister Sazonov to the German ambassador on July 25, 1914, "we will go to war with her."

The Russian government offered several proposals for a peaceful solution: one, to submit the issue to the European powers for settlement; two, to refer it to a third party like the king of Italy or the king of Great Britain; three, to have Austria eliminate the demands which infringed upon Serbian sovereignty and be content with Serbia's acceptance of the others. Once each of these proposals was rejected, the Russian government began to mobilize for war. It prepared to protect by arms a nation which in eleven years had produced two sets of regicides and which the Russian foreign minister declared might quickly become "an anarchist witches' cauldron."

Upon learning of the assassination, the German government approved the Austrian intention to march into Serbia and urged quick action before the other powers could intervene. As the crisis threatened to become general, the German government sought to restrain Austria-Hungary and advised her, after she had occupied Belgrade, to negotiate with the powers. Germany, however, did not press this proposal and the events continued toward catastrophe. Although the German government did not seek a European war, in order to save Austria-Hungary from disintegration it was willing to take the risks believed necessary.

In 1890, by refusing to continue a defensive treaty of 1887 with Russia, the government of Kaiser William II had destroyed a pillar of Bismarck's system of alliances for preserving the hegemony of Germany. This treaty secured Russia against attack by Germany should Austria-Hungary attack Russia, and assured Germany against a Russian attack should France take the aggressive role against Germany. By this so-called Reinsurance Treaty Bismarck had blocked a possible alliance between Russia and France; he had kept the leadership in international relations by holding the balance of power between Austria-Hungary and Russia; and he had made it useful to Italy and Great Britain to maintain Germany's cooperation.

William II's advisers had found the system complicated, but by dropping the Reinsurance Treaty they opened a road to changes in the diplomatic system such as they had not anticipated. Russia became deeply concerned over her isolated position and inclined to alliance with France. The importance of Austria-Hungary to Germany grew, a fact that tended to give the Hapsburg empire initiative in ways not always approved by Germany. Since Italy, the third member of the Triple Alliance, was known to be unreliable and actually hostile to Austria-Hungary, Germany had to protect her only trustworthy ally, particularly against irredentist efforts, like those of Serbia, to disrupt the empire. The Kaiser had already, in the Bosnian crisis of 1908, publicly assured his ally that he would stand by its side like "a knight in shining armor," although his government recognized the danger of Austria's annexation of the two Slavic provinces. Again in July, 1914, the Kaiser presented Austria-Hungary with a "blank check," that is, an expression of approval of its policy before knowing what that policy would lead to and exactly how it would be executed. Germany had no direct interest in the Serbian affair, but she dared not refuse aid.

German Imperialist Ambitions

The irony of Germany's position vis-a-vis Austria-Hungary lay in the fact that the Kaiser and his government had in the 1890's launched a program of imperialism, priding themselves on being more astute than any other power. They shared the views of the German middle classes, particularly of the intellectuals, that as the nineteenth had been Great Britain's century the twentieth would be Germany's. They expected to take over the British Empire and become the greatest, most powerful state in the world. As they considered the change inevitable, they expected Great Britain and the other countries to acquiesce. In order to assure the outcome, the Kaiser publicly declared, "Our future lies on the sea," "the trident is in our hands," and he demanded "a place in the sun." In 1898 under the guidance of Admiral Alfred von Tirpitz, he introduced a naval program advertised as enabling Germany to hold her own in a conflict with any naval power, and Germany set out to gain overseas colonies. Territorial acquisitions were few, but the effects of the program of *Weltpolitik* upon Germany's international position proved disastrous. By 1914, Germany, the wealthiest, the most powerful, materially the most progressive, and certainly the most ambitious country in Europe, had allowed herself to slip into the position of following the lead of a weak ally. She had to enter a war, not in order to advance her own imperialistic interests, but to preserve the integrity of a decadent ally.

France—Tied to Russia

The Third French Republic took a simple and straightforward position in the crisis. Aleksandr Izvolski, the Russian ambassador in Paris, wrote to his foreign minister, July 27, 1914, "Altogether, I am struck by the way the Minister of Justice and his colleagues correctly understand the situation and how firm and calm is their decision to give us the most complete support and to avoid the least appearance of divergence of view between us." The French government, ready to fulfill the terms of the alliance with Russia, left the diplomatic initiative almost entirely to its autocratic ally. The fatal decision of peace or war for France was taken by default. The French people joined a war which began over something of no intrinsic significance to their country.

When the French government faced the crisis of 1914, the experience of several centuries of history affected the thoughts of the nation. The glory of French supremacy in Europe in the days of Louis XIV and Napoleon, the disastrous defeat of 1870–1871, the loss of Alsace-Lorraine, the decline in power and prestige before the rising might of Germany, the haunting fear of further German attacks—these memories had cemented the Franco-Russian Alliance of 1894 and kept France on call. Prince Otto von Bismarck had endeavored to divert attention from the Rhenish frontier by encouraging France to acquire colonies. He had approved of France's establishment of a protectorate over Tunisia in 1882, but, when France sought in 1905 and 1911 to round out her control of Northwest Africa by adding Morocco to her dependencies, Bismarck's successors directly challenged the action. They tried to gain part of Morocco for Germany or at least to force France to grant compensation elsewhere. The revival of the threat of war prevented the French people from forgetting the potential menace of their eastern neighbor. Aware of the enormous growth of Germany in population, industry, and wealth after 1870, contrasted with their own country, 40 million Frenchmen clung to the Russian alliance as a bulwark of strength against 66 million Germans. Although France would not have started a war for the recovery of Alsace-Lorraine, the French people were willing to fight in one forced upon them, and the government refused to risk the disruption of the alliance by checking Russia.

Britain—Fearful of Isolation

British policy at the time of the July crisis was somewhat complicated by a split within the cabinet between those who wished to remain aloof from European affairs and those who favored aligning the country closely with France and Russia. Among the latter was Sir Edward Grey, the secretary for foreign affairs. By initiating negotiations for a peaceful solution either between the two immediate participants or among the powers, Grey strove to prevent the Austro-Serbian conflict from reaching the stage of military action. In pursuing this policy he refused either to restrain Germany by definitely joining Russia and France or to hold aloof from the Franco-Russian Alliance. He tried to act as an unprejudiced mediator, but his mistrust of Germany and his moral commitment to Russia and France defeated the attempt. Britain was forced by events to enter the war on the side of France and Russia.

Great Britain's policy in 1914 of informal, tentative commitment to the Dual Alliance had emerged from almost two decades of experience. The British government had traditionally kept away from continental entanglements and sought a balance of power in Europe. Subsequent to the Napoleonic period the country as the industrial pioneer had developed such enormous strength that prior to the rise of Germany it had been free from any major threat from a continental state. Secure with respect to Europe, Britain had expanded her power into colonial areas, where she had come into conflict with Russia and France. The emergence of Germany's *Weltpolitik,* modestly begun in the eighties and accelerated with a flourish in the next decade, had forced Great Britain to settle her colonial conflicts and acquire continental friends as insurance against the new rival. German naval expansion, openly aimed at competing with Great Britain, created a source of danger far greater than that of Russia and France in the colonies. As an island dependent upon overseas food and raw material to maintain its 45 million people, Great Britain dared not remain isolated while an expansionist neighbor across the North Sea built a navy large enough to block her oceanic life lines. "The dilemma of Great Britain," wrote the American Admiral Mahan in 1902, "is that she cannot help commanding the approaches to Germany by the very means essential to her own existence as a state of the first order."

Great Britain had first become aware of the danger of isolation at the time of the Boer War (1899–1902). Her imperialist aggression in South Africa had angered all other peoples to such an extent that the British government began to seek allies. It had first suggested an alliance to Germany in 1898. Rebuffed there, Britain drew closer to the United States. Next, in 1902, she secured protection for her interests in the Far East by allying with Japan. Then she began to approach France and Russia for a settlement. Whereas in 1898 she and France had almost come to blows at Fashoda over the question of control of the Upper Nile, by 1904 they were ready to compromise their colonial ambitions. Great Britain gave France freedom of action in Morocco, except for a small part in the north to go to Spain, and France reciprocated for Great Britain in Egypt. In the same year Britain concentrated a strong naval force in the North Sea and in 1905 laid keels for the first dreadnaughts. When Germany challenged France's control of Morocco, Great Britain loyally supported her new friend. In 1906 Germany passed a third navy law expanding her fleet by six new capital ships. In 1907 the British and Russian governments resolved their imperial differences, the main item being the partition of Persia into a northern sphere under Russian influence, a southern one under British domination, and an intermediate free zone. The next year Germany initiated the construction of dreadnaughts; since this type of ship was so powerful that it rendered previous battleships obsolete, Great Britain faced the fact that because of one technical improvement in shipbuilding her naval strength and that of Germany were far more equal than she had anticipated. In 1908 the British nation experienced a naval panic, a feeling of fear of a sudden German attack, which Germany's refusal to consider any proposals for reduction of naval armaments enhanced.

The British, French, and Russian governments now drew steadily closer together. Although colonial agreements did not constitute an alliance, they laid the basis for an Entente Cordiale, that under German pressure assumed many of the characteristics of an alliance. In 1912 the British and French governments agreed secretly that the French fleet should be concentrated in the Mediterranean and the British fleet in the North Sea and the English Channel. Each assumed responsibility in its area toward the other in case of war. The general staffs of their armies began likewise to confer on cooperation in the event of war. In the spring of 1914 the Russian government proposed that the Triple Entente be transformed into an alliance. The British refused, but they approved naval and military conversations with Russia similar to those with France. Sir Edward Grey's statement in June, 1914, to the German ambassador that "though we were not bound by engagement [to France and Russia] as allies, we did from time to time talk as intimately as allies," foreshadowed British policy during the crisis. In the event of war Grey intended to remain loyal to Britain's friends. Not to do so would alienate both France and Russia and isolate Great Britain more than ever. Fortunately for this policy, Germany invaded Belgium in violation of an international agreement which Great Britain had signed. The British government, determined to prevent any great power from acquiring Belgium, considered of vital significance for British security, thereby gained moral justification for entering the war.

Italy—Irredentism and Opportunism

Italy, attempting to associate as an equal with the great states, disliked both the Central Powers and those of the Entente Cordiale. National unification (1859–1870) had not satisfied popular claims for territory considered historically and culturally Italian. From Austria-Hungary Italy coveted the Trentino and the eastern coast of the Adriatic; from France she hoped to acquire Nice and Savoy, Corsica, and Tunisia. Italian policy therefore remained opportunistic. When in 1882 France had seized Tunisia, Italy had allied with Germany and Austria-Hungary to form the Triple Alliance. By 1898 she had become mistrustful of Austria-Hungary; she signed a secret agreement with France nullifying the main terms of the Triple Alliance. In 1911 she opened war against the Ottoman Empire and seized Tripoli, the Dodecanese Islands, and Rhodes. She secured the acquiescence in her conquests of the powers, but her action was not approved. When the crisis of July, 1914, occurred, Italy refused to support either side, waiting to see which way the advantage for her would lie.

Who Were the Guilty?

The question of guilt for the outbreak of the war concerns, first, whether in the name of nationalism Serbia was justified in seeking to unite all the South Slavs by breaking up the Austro-Hungarian Empire, or whether the latter empire was justified in taking the aggressive for the sake of self-preservation. The way in which the question is answered will decide whether Germany, supporting Austria-Hungary, or Russia, assisting Serbia, was in the wrong, and whether France and Great Britain were justified in defending Russia. The only great power that actually wished war was Austria-Hungary, and she hoped that the conflict would remain restricted to a minor engagement with Serbia. All states regarded war as a standard method of conducting international relations; none had much if any sense of collective European responsibility. The leading statesmen of all countries appreciated the tragedy of the situation, and each avowed the innocence of his government. Germany blamed France and Great Britain for not restraining Russia; France and Great Britain blamed Germany for not curbing Austria-Hungary.

The fact that at the time and subsequently Germany received the major blame for starting the war can be attributed to the speed with which she opened hostilities. Austria-Hungary declared war on Serbia on July 28 but did not order total mobilization until July 31. Russia had begun to mobilize on July 25 and ordered total mobilization on July 30. Germany did not follow suit until August 1, at the same time that France did. Political astuteness on Germany's part would have left to Russia the initiative for the fatal declaration of war. Reasons of military strategy induced the German government to act otherwise. Interpreting the Russian mobilization as an intolerable menace, Germany declared war against Russia on August 1 and against France on August 3. Military exigencies were also offered by the Germans as excuse for invading Belgium, an act which led to the only declaration of war on the Allied side, that of Great Britain against Germany on August 4. Thus Germany turned diplomatic maneuvers into a European war. "War," the German strategist Karl von Clausewitz had written a century earlier, "is the extension of diplomacy into action." All the powers agreed with that statement; but once diplomacy had failed to bridge this most recent of Europe's recurring crises Germany was most precipitate in putting it into practice.

THE INTERNATIONAL STATE SYSTEM AND ITS MOTIVE FORCES

An international system and certain general forces conditioned the diplomatic action of all powers. Their contribution to the outbreak of war must now be examined.

The international state system has functioned in modern times in a way characterized as one of anarchy. Indeed, one may support the thesis that whenever in history a number of sovereign states of more or less equal strength have been closely associated they have always competed with each other by arms. Since the essence of a state is to assert supreme power, physical if necessary, over the people, the government is inclined to use force not merely against individuals within the political community but against other states. The British statesman Lord Salisbury remarked toward the end of the nineteenth century, "Let those take who have the power, let those keep who can, is practically the only rule of [Russia's] policy; wherein I am bound to add she does not differ widely from many other civilised States." To acquire additional territory has always been considered a legitimate objective, even a duty of a state. The international state system of the pre-1914 period adhered essentially to the practices described by Machiavelli and perfected by the absolute monarchs of the seventeenth and eighteenth centuries. Reasons of state were advanced to justify any claim or any action in international relations which a government saw fit to defend.

The competitive states were supposed to be kept at peace by the workings of the principle of the balance of power. According to this principle, whenever certain states allied for predatory purposes, other states would form a counteralliance. The result was expected to be a balance of power to preserve peace. Unfortunately for the theory, each group competed with the other in the effort to increase its power. In fact, each state within an alliance competed with the others. Because an impartial judge was lacking, neither group, and no state within a group, felt secure unless it constantly increased its strength, and each alliance attempted to gain some advantage at the other's expense. Such was true of the competition between the Triple Entente and the Triple Alliance. Neither trusted the other; each strove to get the better of the balance of power. As an Austrian statesman said a short time before World War I, because Russia was working for war, "the only possibility to avoid a European conflict lay in redressing the balance of power between the Triple Alliance and the Triple Entente, to the advantage of the Middle European Group." At about the same time, a Russian statesman asserted a similar view, except that he mistrusted Germany and Austria-Hungary and sought to preserve peace by "redressing the balance" in favor of the Triple Entente. Each side feared that the other would strike the first blow, for, as a German historian remarked, "It is impossible to calculate whether and when the other Power will hold that the moment has come for that first blow." Tension and mistrust increased with each crisis and reached the point of explosion in July, 1914.

Nationalism supplied the major ideal driving the states to competitive action. It affected nations like Poland that as yet lacked political unity and those like France and Britain that had enjoyed political unity for centuries. It claimed that peoples should be organized politically in national states, that the individual and society could fulfill their purpose only within the framework of national political unity, and that life, property, and traditional morality itself must be sacrificed if necessary to the achievement of this vital objective. Four empires persisted in Europe—the German, the Austro-Hungarian, the Russian, and the Ottoman—which contained subject nationalities in violation of this ideal, and the action of Printsip exemplified in extreme form the reaction of subject nationalities toward imperial rule. The nationalists believed that once the national state was formed the individual would be free, self-respecting, self-dependent, and creative, devoted to the welfare of the others of his nation, content with life, and at peace with all other nations. The behavior of those nations that were politically united belied the ideal, but the popular faith flourished among all Western peoples and was to guide President Wilson and others in the effort to stabilize peace after World War I.

Nationalism stimulated nations to risk the use of war. Separating each nation from all others, it encouraged each to set its own standards of international conduct, and it caused each to be sensitive to threats to its interests or to affronts to its honor. Lloyd George, member of the Liberal government in Britain, during the Moroccan crisis in 1911, gave a classic example of the shift from self-interest to honor, then to bellicosity. "If a situation were to be forced upon us," he said, "in which peace could only be preserved by the surrender of the great and beneficent position Britain has won by centuries of heroism and achievement, by allowing Britain to be treated, when her interests were vitally affected, as if she were of no account in the Cabinet of Nations, then I say emphatically that peace at that price would be a humiliation intolerable for a great country like ours to endure. National honour is no party question." At the time of the July crisis of 1914 Russia justified the mobilization of her army against Austria in asserting that she was "offended in her honor as a Great Power and compelled to take corresponding measures." The Austrian General Conrad von Hoetzendorff later commented on this statement: "What the honor of Russia had to do with the Austro-Serbian conflict is not comprehensible; very strange is the suggestion that Austria-Hungary should not have felt wounded in her honor as a Great Power by the criminal conduct of Serbia." These reactions express what Churchill called "the passions, and the destiny of mighty races of men." Working through the competitive international state system already inclined toward extreme measures, nationalism drove the peoples of Europe to war.

Imperialism existed as a motive force in international affairs long before the nineteenth century, but in the fifty years or so before the outbreak of World War I it combined with nationalism to seek the aggrandizement of states. Expansion occurred in the colonial world; territorial ambitions in Europe proper, although in 1914 very much alive, were for the time frustrated. Using the cant of international speech, the French minister Joseph Caillaux in 1919 justified France's prewar colonial conquests as "the complement and buttress of the general policy of French governments." "It gave France," he continued, "the material power, the weight necessary for her affirmations of Right in Europe." That is to say, France acquired Tunisia, Morocco, Indochina, and other territories to augment her national power in Europe. The British preached the white man's burden, but they, the Germans, and the other imperialist states all aimed by colonial acquisition to augment the resources of the mother country. That the same colonial territory would be sought by more than one power is evident from the account of the prewar crises. The gain of these territories in themselves would scarcely have been acknowledged as justifying a major war, but disputes over colonies immediately involved questions of national honor and power and were automatically transferred to the European scene.

The *pan* movements pertained primarily to Germans and Slavs. Pan-Germanism lacked any significant support before the war, but Pan-Slavism had begun to be powerful in the 1870's. At the time there had appeared the most popular and influential of the Pan-Slav writings, Danilewski's *Russia and Europe.* The author had preached the irreconcilability of Russia and the rest of the world and the superiority of Russian culture over that of Europe. He had claimed that Russia should unite the Slavs under her hegemony and make Constantinople the capitol of the Russian Empire and the Slavic federation. Russia could do so only by war, in which Danilewski believed that the Graeco-Slavic civilization would triumph over that of the decadent Germano-Roman peoples. These ideals lay back of Russia's defense of Serbia in 1914.

The danger to peace of competitive armaments, of militarism and navalism, which has to some extent always existed, was gravely augmented in the decades before World War I by the magnitude and the speed of industrial productivity and by the creation of the mass army. Under modern conditions of transportation and communication the armed forces of a nation constituted a far more serious immediate danger to opponents than they had in the centuries of travel by foot, in horse-drawn vehicles, or in sailboats. The vast size of the forces made, not merely an absolute monarch and a few aristocrats, as in the Old Regime, but the entire nation fear that they might be conquered. In a world of competitive states, of nationalism and imperialism, the recurring diplomatic crises, however petty the occasion, accentuated the demand for ever-increasing armaments. No power could feel secure. Military and naval leaders could not win governmental approval of preventive war; but as the crisis of July, 1914, approached, the influence of technicians of conflict upon foreign policy increased. The plans for Anglo-French, Anglo-Russian, and Franco-Russian naval cooperation were all negotiated by them; after initial acquiescence, diplomats looked the other way, preferring not to think about the moral commitments involved should a crisis arise. Chancellor Theobald Bethmann-Hollweg apparently knew about the German army's plan to invade Belgium upon the outbreak of war with France, but he had not considered the effects of the action upon foreign policy. The Russian foreign minister, Sazonov, in 1914 did not grasp the fact that a partial mobilization of the Russian army as proposed at the time could not be executed under existing military plans and would be considered by the Germans and Austrians as a cover for total mobilization. The German general staff pressed the government to be the first to declare war so that it would outdistance the other powers in speed of mobilization. In the crisis, arguments of military and naval advantage profoundly affected political policy. The influence was greatest in Russia, Germany, and Austria-Hungary, the three surviving authoritarian powers. It was not lacking in France and Great Britain.

An Austrian historian wrote on the eve of the July crisis: "Questions like that of Serbia must be settled not at the green table, but on the battlefield; not with the pen, but with the sword; not with ink, but with blood. Every historical result is, let me repeat it, in the last resort nothing but the bloody reflection of the gleam of victorious bayonets and swords." The international state system and the forces operating through it accepted war as the ultimate test of their effectiveness. They encouraged recourse to power. "The old diplomacy did its best to render harmless the small things," Winston Churchill wrote in 1923; "it could not do more."

POLITICAL AND SOCIAL CONDITIONS WITHIN THE MAJOR POWERS

In so far as forces existed prior to World War I that made for the preservation of peace, they are to be found in the political and social conditions within the separate states. They may have been similar, but they differed in each in degree of influence. On balance, Austria-Hungary and Russia had graver internal reasons for not risking war than had the other powers, but responsible leaders in these empires appear to have been little aware of them. All governments in the crisis of 1914 paid slight if any attention to the question of whether their people were prepared for war. Statesmen in authoritarian countries had in a few instances since 1870 deliberately provoked international crisis in order to win popular support for an internal measure or in order to overcome party differences. As diplomatic crises became more frequent and more acute after 1900 leaders in these countries, acting in the tradition of absolutism, ignored the conditions of the people, and those in states of free governments knew that the gravity of the crisis would consolidate national unity.

Russia—Revolution and Reaction

A decade before 1914 Russia had been disastrously defeated by Japan. Incompetent leadership, out-of-date equipment, inadequate services, and poor administration throughout the government explained to a large extent the debacle. The Russian people almost *en masse* condemned such a system of government and society and demanded the reforms which in most of the large and small countries of the Western world had become commonplace. A national conference of zemstvos, or county councils, composed of the kinds of individuals who in Great Britain or Germany would have formed the bulwark of moderate, patriotic opinion, unanimously requested in November, 1904, freedom of speech, press, assembly, conscience, person, education, equal civil rights irrespective of religion or nationality, local self-government based on equal electoral rights, reforms for workers and peasants. A majority advocated the introduction of an elective national assembly that should exercise legislative authority; a minority was content to have it receive only advisory power. The associations of lawyers, doctors, and other professions supported the program, including the request for a legislative assembly.

When in the Revolution of 1905 a modicum of political activity became possible, the upper-class groups and their followers divided into two main political parties. The most liberal called themselves the Constitutional Democrats or Cadets, led by Professor Pavel Milyukov. The more moderate reformers took the name of the Octobrists, from the month in which they organized; they produced some able political leaders, among them Aleksandr Guchkov, the grandson of a serf and son of a wealthy Moscow merchant. The two parties differed mainly over the extent to which, for tactical reasons, they would cooperate with a hostile government. The peasants expressed their program in wide areas, especially in the south and southeast, by invading estates, often escorting the owner to the nearest railroad station, and seizing the land. They introduced orderly peasant self-government in the localities and ran affairs to their own satisfaction. The Social Revolutionary party acted as their self-appointed spokesmen. Composed predominantly of intellectuals, it was deeply concerned with the question of governmental reform and strove to keep the peasant behind the program of freedom with the slogan, "All the land for the peasants."

In industrial towns and cities the workers, or proletariat, struck in favor of the program of the zemstvos, organizing soviets, or associations, in their places of work or assembly. The soviets, like the town governments of the settlers in the United States, appeared as a natural response to a political need. They elected representatives, who were then able to cooperate in smaller soviets for the common good. The soviets tended to fall under the control of Marxian Socialists, organized in the Social Democratic party. The latter split into two hostile groups. The Mensheviks believed in the use of persuasion, of evolutionary and moderate tactics for winning the people to socialism, and accepted as coworkers and as members of the party any non-Marxians willing to cooperate for the general improvement of the workers and through them of society. The Bolsheviks, of whom the most famous was Vladimir Ilyich Ulyanov, called Lenin, the future leader of the Russian Revolution of October, 1917, demanded that the party be revolutionary, that it use violence to overthrow the existing society, and that it constitute the disciplined shock troops of revolution. The Bolsheviks believed that the dictatorship of the proletariat, guided by a small group of Communists like Lenin, was essential for success; they aimed to infiltrate the amorphous soviets and lead them to violent action. Neither faction had time in the Revolution of 1905 to test its efficiency; but the Mensheviks were able subsequently to maintain a party, whereas the handful of Bolsheviks was driven underground. By 1914 the retarded development of industry was reflected in the small size of not merely the middle class but the proletariat. Russia lacked a mass basis for socialism or communism.

The government reacted to the revolution by making as few concessions as were necessary to quiet the moderate reformers and re-establish order. It created a national assembly called the Duma, with legislative powers; but as soon as the police and the bureaucracy regained control of the country the government arbitrarily dissolved the Duma in July, 1906, issued a new election decree curtailing suffrage, and ordered new elections. The second Duma, proving less docile than the first, was illegally dismissed after a few weeks, and an even more restrictive electoral decree was tried. This one produced the third Duma, which although critical of government action was sufficiently discreet to last out its term of five years. The fourth Duma, elected in 1912, consisted of about the same kind of deputies as its predecessor. The legislative functions of the body, at first unlimited, had in 1906 been drastically restricted. Parts of the budget were exempt from the Duma's jurisdiction; the minister of finance retained exclusive authority over loans and currency; the crown reserved responsibility for everything that pertained to the army and navy; the government could issue decrees at will while the Duma was not in session; and ministers were responsible, not to the Duma, but to the czar.

Czar Nicholas II appointed as ministers a mixed group of reactionaries and conservatives. The ablest and most influential of the latter, Pëtr Stolypin, operated on two fronts. He had revolutionaries speedily court-martialed and hanged. He tried to stabilize the countryside by enabling the peasants to change from a system of collective ownership and responsibility in the village, or mir, to one of individual peasant farms. In village after village the peasants approved of the new freedom, and on the family holdings agricultural methods greatly improved. Stolypin next made it possible for peasants to be elected to the zemstvos and to become eligible for any position in the governmental bureaucracy.

The reforms proved inadequate, for the peasants were always conscious of the fact that the electoral law introduced in the rural districts the unpopular system of indirect elections, which subordinated them to the political power of a few gentry. Making education available for all and increasing the salaries of teachers did not compensate for the failure to satisfy the overwhelming majority of the population, the peasantry. The Duma failed to achieve any significant reforms in the defense forces or in the bureaucracy or to mitigate harsh official policies toward the Finns, the Poles, and other subject nationalities. It supported the few well-intentioned ministers, however conservative, but it could make little headway against the incompetent reactionaries that the czar, determined to preserve autocracy, mainly appointed to office. Guchkov's appeal to the grand dukes in 1908 to show devotion to the country by resigning their positions in the army pleased the public, but angered the royal family. After Stolypin was assassinated in September, 1911, by a revolutionary, probably with the connivance of the reactionaries, the government drifted. The limited reforms of the Stolypin period ceased. There was no reason to believe that Russia would perform better in another major war than she had in that against Japan, and a few persons understood that another war would bring disaster. The people could not share in any decision, and the government acted as autocracy had acted for centuries. In defense of national honor it challenged the Central Powers.

Austria-Hungary—Conflict of Nationalities

Austria-Hungary differed from the other two continental empires, the Russian and the German, in that she had a crucial nationality problem. The monarchy had been reorganized by the Compromise of 1867, which made Austria and Hungary equal states within an empire held together by the house of Hapsburg, by common ministries for foreign relations and for war, and by the establishment of a customs union, which had to be renewed every ten years. Austria and Hungary were each to handle her own internal affairs, the assumption being that the Germans would dominate the other nationalities in Austria; the Hungarians, or Magyars, the other nationalities in Hungary. Every ten years the Compromise was subjected to a crisis; for the Magyars, a minority in their country, were torn between the longing for national independence and the need of support by Austria and the German *Reich* in order to maintain themselves in a sea of nationalities. The grain-growing Magyar nobility wished to hold the Austrian market until the national economy could absorb Hungary's surplus. The rising industries demanded tariff protection against Austrian competitors. Since all aimed at ultimate economic independence, at each renewal of the customs agreement a quarrel with Austria over terms ensued. The policy toward the army was similarly ambivalent. The Magyars desired complete control of their army; but they knew that achievement of this happy objective would severely diminish Austro-Hungarian strength, a result which they dared not attain. Hence they quarreled over the terms of the Compromise from time to time, weakening but not destroying military unity. On foreign policy comparable disputes occurred, none of them so serious as the others. In 1914 people questioned how much longer the agreement of 1867 would survive.

The critical sources of disruption of the monarchy were found in the relations of the nationalities within each part. Ruling over Slovaks and Ruthenians in the north, Romanians in the east, Serbs and Croats in the south, not to mention Germans and Jews scattered in the various parts of the kingdom, the Magyars in the latter half of the nineteenth century introduced an intensive program of Magyarization of these peoples. They forced all to learn Magyar in the private as well as in the public schools; they prohibited the use of non-Magyar languages in public life, and banned patriotic manifestation of any kind other than that of the Magyars. They

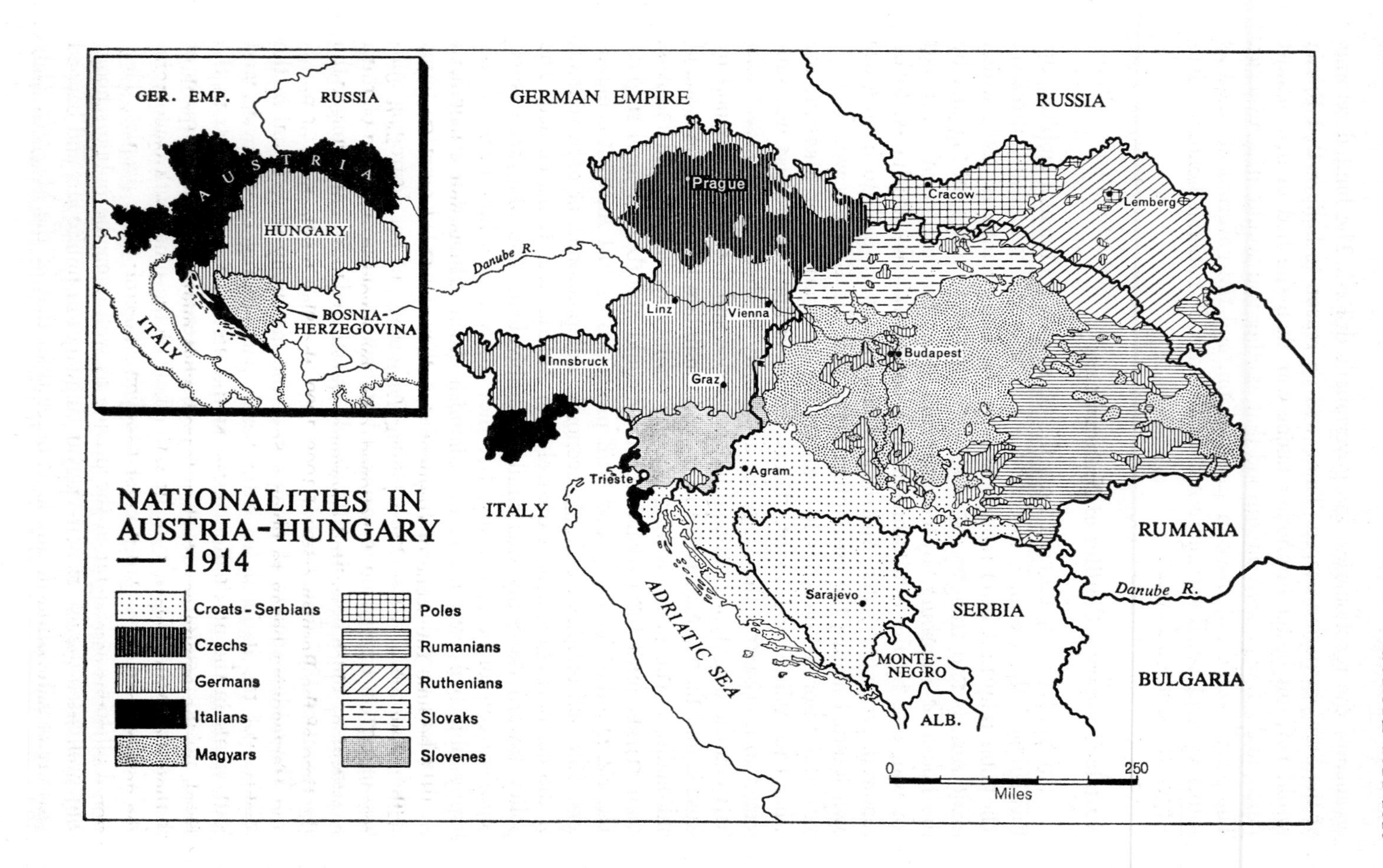
GER. EMP.
RUSSIA
A U S T R I A
HUNGARY
BOSNIA-
HERZEGOVINA
ITALY
GERMAN EMPIRE
RUSSIA
Prague
Cracow
Lemberg
Danube R.
Linz
Vienna
Innsbruck
Budapest
Graz
Trieste
Agram
ITALY
RUMANIA
Danube R.
Sarajevo
SERBIA
ADRIATIC SEA
MONTE-
NEGRO
BULGARIA
ALB.
0
250
Miles
NATIONALITIES IN
AUSTRIA-HUNGARY
— 1914
Croats-Serbians
Czechs
Germans
Italians
Magyars
Poles
Rumanians
Ruthenians
Slovaks
Slovenes

succeeded in considerably increasing the number of people who used Magyar, but antagonized the intellectuals of the Slavic minorities and embittered the Romanians. In 1914, however, the leader of the Magyar gentry, Count Stephen Tisza, could still assert as an attainable goal that "our citizens of the non-Magyar tongue must, in the first place, become accustomed to the fact that they belong to the community of a nation-state, of a state which is not a conglomerate of various races."

In Austria relations among the nationalities were much more complex, because the government tolerated the free growth of national cultures. The Slovenes in the south, a quiet peasant folk, and the Poles in Galicia lived in relatively homogeneous national districts. Apart from their well-known desire for national unity with their fellows in Germany and Russia, the Poles in 1914 caused far less trouble than the Czechs, many of whom lived among Germans. The Czechs had advanced during the nineteenth century to the cultural level of the Germans. They possessed a national university at Prague and, like the other nationalities, free use of their language in private life; they were rapidly growing in economic and political importance and social ambition.

The bitterest clashes with the Germans arose over whether Czech should be placed on par with German as an official language of the state. The Czechs in 1897 obtained that recognition with respect to Bohemia and Moravia, only to lose it two years later. The angry Germans, feeling far superior to the Czechs whom they had dominated for centuries, denounced the language decree as an insult. By its terms they would either have to learn Czech or lose all prospects of a public career. The Czechs, they said, learned German anyway as the superior cultural language. The decree therefore would mean in fact granting the Czechs a monopoly of official positions. The Czechs countered with the assertion that their language compared with the German in every respect, that not to recognize it officially as such was a national insult.

The Austrian *Reichsrat,* or parliament, for a decade and a half prior to 1914 became the scene of frequent riots between Czechs and Germans, with a few other nationalities joining from time to time for their own reasons. The government functioned only by invoking Article 14 of the constitution, which permitted emergency decrees to be issued. When about the time of the Bosnian crisis of 1908–1909, the Slav intellectuals of Bosnia and Herzegovina began to favor a South Slav federation grouped around Serbia, the Hapsburg government became alarmed over the outlook in both north and south of the empire. Nationality leaders did not incline to break up the empire as yet; they feared what might be in store for them if they did. Nonetheless, immediately upon entering war in August, 1914, the government suspended the *Reichsrat.* The institution of popular expression was in this case rightly considered a threat to efficient conduct of war. Although its emperor, Francis Joseph, a man nearly eighty-four years of age, asked only to die in peace, this polyglot empire conformed to tradition; in going to war it tried to settle nationality questions by force of arms.

Two decades previously the governor of the Austrian province of Galicia had denounced war as "an impossibility" for Austria. "Should we be attacked," he had written, "we must accept the situation with God's help, but an aggressive war on account of Constantinople or some other Balkan question is madness. A State of nationalities can make no war without danger to itself. Among a conglomeration of nations victory or defeat causes almost equal difficulty." The argument was not heeded.

Germany—The Bismarckian System and Its Critics

The dominant groups in Germany, that is, the monarchy, the aristocracy, and the upper bourgeoisie, asserted in prewar days that their country set a model for others in form of government and structure of society. Between 1866 and 1871 Bismarck had unified the *Reich* and given it a written constitution, which preserved an authoritarian monarchy. He had created a *Reichstag*, composed of representatives elected by universal manhood suffrage, and made the chief executive, the chancellor, independent of that body. He had continued intact the authoritarian government of Prussia, largest state in the *Reich*, and he had made the Prussian army the main force for defending the empire. The ruling groups argued that by adapting traditional institutions to modern needs Bismarck had founded a government that combined responsiveness to the legitimate desires of the people, with power of initiative and action on the part of the leaders. This type of government, they said, was essential for a state situated in the center of Europe, surrounded by actual or potential enemies; but, they continued, it likewise reflected the ideal social organization. The elite must lead, the masses must follow. The hierarchal distribution of function conformed to nature and to the tenets of the Christian religion. "Render unto Caesar the things that are Caesar's."

From the beginning the Bismarckian system aroused criticism; opposition spread, particularly after the dismissal of the Iron Chancellor in 1890. It came in the main from two groups, the liberal or democratic elements among the middle class, and the Social Democratic workers, who agreed on many points of reform. They advocated the introduction of true parliamentary government by making the chancellor responsible to the *Reichstag*. They wished the ministry in Prussia and in all other German states to be similarly subject to parliamentary control. They denounced the three-class system of voting in Prussia as an anachronism. By this system the voters of Prussia were divided into three groups, according to the amount of taxes they paid. Thus those who paid one third of the taxes in an electoral district had the right to elect one third of the electors; those who paid the second third of the taxes could elect another third of the electors; and the masses elected a final third. The electors then came together and chose the representatives in the parliament. The system manifestly fulfilled its intention of discriminating in favor of aristocratic landlords and wealthy bourgeoisie. It enabled these social groups to rule Prussia, and since Prussia constituted three fifths of the *Reich* area and population, it formed the greatest obstacle to reform in the *Reich* government and society. The liberals and the Social Democrats therefore demanded that this electoral law be replaced by one like that of the *Reich*. They further requested that in both Prussia and the *Reich* the electoral districts, the one unchanged since 1861, the other since 1871, conform to the shift in population. The increase in population, by one third or more, had benefited the towns and cities; redistricting would therefore greatly augment the liberal and especially the Social Democratic vote, as the ruling classes well knew.

With these constitutional and political demands, the reformers sought to abolish or reduce the influence upon society of militarism, evident in the exclusion of officers of bourgeois origin from the elite regiments, in the general toadying to all officers of whatever class but especially of the nobility, and in the authoritarian way of handling strikes. In trying to diminish the prestige of the military the critics intended, not to break Germany's military power, but to make the army a national institution of social equality and civilian rule.

The German Social Democrats nursed additional grievances peculiar to the working class. The proletariat was relegated to the lowest rank in a hierarchal society and in 1914 was still treated as second-class citizens. To the discrimination against it by the electoral laws was added that of the educational system, which offered one type of schooling for the upper classes and another type for the proletariat, closing to them institutions of higher education and preparation for the professions. The Social Democrats knew that the ruling classes mistrusted their loyalty to the state and used compulsory military training to instill mass obedience. They heard about Kaiser William II's speech to certain regiments in the 1890's containing the order to shoot their own people, if necessary, for the defense of the throne. They considered the suspicion unjustified. Since Bismarck's departure from power they had developed the strongest trade-unions in the world. The workers' standard of living had risen steadily with industrialism. The *Reich* system of social insurance introduced by Bismarck, although the sums paid were small, gave some security. The Social Democratic party still discussed the revolutionary introduction of socialism, but in practice it sought the peaceful achievement of its goals through parliamentary methods. In spite of the resistance of the ruling classes, the workers were becoming loyal members of the community, proud of their German heritage. Between 1890 and 1912 the popular vote for the party increased from 1½ to 4¼ millions, and in the latter year the Social Democratic bloc of 110 deputies formed the largest party in the *Reichstag*.

The political and social reforms which both liberals and Social Democrats supported would in time no doubt have been achieved. Bismarck's successors lacked his ability and prestige; thus the power of the *Reichstag* with respect to the executive had somewhat increased. The people criticized the Kaiser for indiscreet remarks that unnecessarily angered other nations and for similar signs of his emotional instability, but the Hohenzollerns seemed assured of indefinite rule. The nationality issue played a relatively minor part. The few Danes in North Schleswig hoped for peaceful return of their region to Denmark; the people of Alsace-Lorraine were being better treated than under Bismarck, and economic prosperity was reconciling them to continuation in the *Reich*. The Poles persisted in their aim to restore an independent national state, and the Germans remained equally determined to prevent them. The question was not acute.

Germany stood in 1914 undoubtedly as the most powerful state on the continent. Hard-working, affluent, ambitious, self-confident, her people seemed as little inclined to revolution as a nation could be. It required four years of fighting against most of the world in the most exhausting war Europe had ever experienced to transform German governmental, and to some extent social, organization.

Great Britain—Indian Summer of Liberalism

On the eve of the conflict of 1914 Great Britain was enjoying the Indian summer of liberalism. She continued to act on the basis of the belief expressed a half century before by Lord Palmerston, "It is by comparing opinions–by a collision of opinions–by rubbing one man's opinions against those of another and seeing which are the hardest and will bear the friction best–that men, in or out of office, can most justly arrive at the knowledge of what is most advantageous to the interests of the whole community." Her political life was organized to facilitate that "rubbing." She was turning away from the crude practice of laissez faire, of using government primarily as an agent for keeping order and of relying upon the laws of nature to harmonize individual action with social good. In the last quarter of the nineteenth century and during the years of the twentieth before 1914 the functions of government in all aspects of life had expanded. A new sense of responsibility for public welfare inspired both the Liberal and the Conservative parties and stimulated the founding of the Labor party. British society had become overwhelmingly urban and sought forms of assistance which its rural predecessor had not thought necessary.

The evidence of change may be taken from many aspects of national life. The law on compulsory public education was actually implemented in the nineties, and was accompanied by the founding of municipal colleges. Recruiting for the army during the Boer War (1899–1902) disclosed shocking physical conditions among the masses. In consequence, the state began to support school lunches and free medical inspection and treatment of school children. The civil service expanded so rapidly that it could not find enough trained personnel. Town and county governments were reorganized in order to supply the increased urban population with public services, gas, electricity, sewage disposal, transportation, libraries, and the like.

In the period of slow economic growth that began with the new century and continued to the outbreak of war, the role of labor in politics expanded to protect workers' interests. Trade-union membership of more than 2 million in 1900 supported political participation in order to protect the unions against such acts as the Taff Vale decision of 1903, which made them liable for damages during strikes. In the election of 1906 labor won twenty-nine seats and formally organized a political party. The Liberal party returned a large majority in that election and, inspired by political figures like David Lloyd George, defended workers' interests. The new government reversed the Taff Vale decision by act of parliament. When three years later the House of Lords, sitting as a judicial body, denied the right to trade-unions to spend any of their money for political purposes, a decision which would have destroyed the Labor party, the Liberal government in 1913 restored the right. Supported by Labor, the Liberal government between 1906 and 1914 introduced old-age pensions, created Trade Boards to prevent sweated labor by fixing minimum wages, established a system for insuring the working class against sickness, and in certain industries provided for unemployment insurance. This was liberalism with a social conscience, a new means for securing "the greatest happiness of the greatest number." The "invisible hand," so dear to believers in laissez faire, was receiving palpable guidance.

Expansion of public responsibility in social legislation took place simultaneously with the rapid demand for increased naval forces and for creating a small expeditionary army to safeguard Great Britain against the challenge of Germany. The dreadnaught program was particularly expensive. To meet the twofold demand the government shifted the financial burden to direct taxes, which struck the wealthy. In 1874 the government had derived 33 per cent of its revenue from direct taxes and 67 per cent from indirect, which hit most severely the masses. In 1913, the order was almost reversed, 60 per cent and 40 per cent, respectively. Chancellor of the Exchequer Lloyd George began the change in the budget of 1907 by taxing unearned incomes more severely than earned ones. Two years later he proposed a "supertax" on incomes of more than £5,000, an increase in inheritance taxes, and a tax on unearned increment of the value of land. The Liberals and Labor in the House of Commons passed the budget, but the Conservative House of Lords rejected it and demanded that the government submit the issue to the country in an election. The government challenged the constitutional right of the Lords to reject a finance bill, and in two elections in 1910 won public support. The House of Lords, forced to pass the Parliament Bill of 1911, lost all control over finance bills, and could delay passage of any other bill for only two years. Unwittingly the financial reforms placed the government on a sound basis for contending with the problems of public finance in the impending war.

The Liberal government courageously proposed to heal two dangerous sores in British imperial relations. In 1909, seven years after defeating the Boers in a bitter war, the British government approved a constitution for the newly created Union of South Africa. Success depended upon cooperation between the Boers and their recent enemies, the English inhabitants of the states involved. A greater display of confidence in humanity could hardly have been made. Three years later the Liberals sought to solve the century-old Irish question. Returning to a policy of Gladstone, their most distinguished leader during the nineteenth century, they proposed to grant the Irish home rule. The Conservatives in the House of Commons and in the House of Lords fought the bill as bitterly as they had the tax reforms. Although World War I was in sight, one noble lord urged the House of Lords not to approve the army budget for such a government, and passage of the Irish Home Rule Bill was delayed until September, 1914. Unfortunately, the outbreak of the war led to postponement in executing the law until the re-establishment of peace.

By an irony of fate the same government that brought Great Britain into the vanguard of social reform and of improvement of imperial relations led the country into World War I. Lord John Morley, one of the most distinguished Liberals, and another member resigned from the cabinet in protest against Sir Edward Grey's having involved the country in such diplomatic tangles. The nation, however, united against Germany. For two decades it had exhibited signs of tension and irritability, zest of the urban middle class for safe, vicarious danger, an angry tone in the battles of political parties, jingoism in a catchy tune. Underneath the bravado, the nation deplored chauvinism and war, and shared the views which on the first day of the conflict Mr. J. L. Garvin expressed in the *Pall Mall Gazette*, "We have to do our part in killing a creed of war. Then at last, after a rain of blood, there may be set the greater rainbow in the Heavens before the vision of the souls of men. And after Armageddon war, indeed, may be no more."

France—The Third Republic and Its Opponents

The French people in 1914 awaited in fear the German attack. They determined to honor international commitments and to defend themselves; but, in addition to being aware of Germany's great superiority in man power and industrial resources, they had no heart for war. Experience since 1870 had shown that military officers were untrustworthy republicans. Building up national defense in time of peace only strengthened those groups hostile to the ideals of liberty, equality, and fraternity. Under the pressure of international crises, particularly those caused by the German threat in the Moroccan affairs, the factions of the French nation grudgingly drew together, increased the defense budget, and in 1913 lowered the age of military service from twenty-one to twenty, extending at the same time the two-year term of compulsory training to three years.

To understand French reluctance to go to war requires analysis of the background of social and political conflict. The royalists and the leaders of the Catholic church in France had never acquiesced in the establishment of the Third Republic. Their reactionary views were shared by the army officers, who headed resistance to the new government and society. They believed in authoritarian rule, sharp class distinctions, discipline, and order. They denounced as sinful the French Revolution and its ideals. Having failed under Marshal MacMahon to prevent the founding of the republic, the reactionaries supported in the late eighties General Boulanger, in the hope that he would destroy the hated government. When he disappointed their expectations, in the next decade they exploited the Dreyfus affair. Captain Alfred Dreyfus, a Jew, was accused of betraying military secrets to the Germans. He was tried by secret court-martial, convicted. and condemned to imprisonment. It soon developed that not he but his accuser, a Captain Esterhazy, was the guilty person; but the army, supported by the Catholic Church and anti-Semitic groups, denounced the efforts to clear Dreyfus as a radical attack upon the honor of army and nation. The conflict, another in the long line of struggles over control of the French nation, ended once more in republican victory.

The outcome of the Dreyfus affair affected the Catholic Church much more deeply than it did the army. Captain Dreyfus was exonerated and the army compelled to reinstate him, but the officer corps escaped a purge and the generals remained hostile to republican ideals and practices. The church, on the other hand, had to atone for its support of an unjust cause. The government passed a number of major anticlerical laws. The Association Act of 1901 permitted the government to close and expropriate the property of monastic orders which were not authorized by the state and performed no socially useful service. In 1904 the government severed diplomatic relations with the Vatican, and in the next year it separated church and state. It broke with the practice, confirmed by the Concordat of 1801, whereby the state subsidized the church and shared with the papacy the responsibility for selecting bishops. The government recommended a candidate for a bishopric; the pope, if he approved, appointed him. If he did not approve, the two authorities negotiated a compromise. By the law of 1905 the state relinquished this power, and for the first time in centuries transferred complete control over the French church to the papacy. Church property was henceforth to belong to the state, but the buildings were placed in the custody of local associations for religious use. The total expense of the church was to be borne by private contributions.

The prorepublican ministry believed that in modern society secular forces were sufficiently strong to withstand any expansion of church influence, so that the loss of state support would actually reduce the power of Catholicism. It expected the decline in church prestige to weaken the authoritarian monarchists, the military, the hypernationalists and anti-Semites, and the other antirepublican elements. The government went to another extreme, just as the French church had adhered to the extreme of combating the republic. Government and church did not reach a middle ground of mutual respect for a decade, but the republic emerged from the Dreyfus affair much stronger than it had been. Charles Maurras' organization, the *Action Française,* and various groups like the *Camelots du Roi,* arose during the conflict. Their monarchism, militarism, and extreme nationalism, their brutal action, and insulting language had little popular appeal. The movements lived from subsidies supplied by a few wealthy reactionaries. By 1914 nationalism and strong military defense had declined in popularity by being associated with these rightist groups.

Pacifism had spread widely among middle class, peasants, and workers since the 1880's. The system of state education developed at that time contributed to this attitude; while inculcating Christian ethics and devotion to national culture, it trained the students in anticlericalism and antimilitarism. The school teachers in particular, occupying a low economic and social position in the nation, as advocates of the new gospel trained the young people in town and country to abhor war. They received aid from socialists and trade-union members. Since France lagged far behind Great Britain and Germany in industrialization, her workers lacked the facilities which big industries provided for mass organization. The General Confederation of Workers was not founded until 1902, and a decade later not more than one tenth of the workers and small-salaried employees belonged to trade-unions. The Socialist party in France polled by 1914 proportionately far fewer votes than the comparable party in Germany; but because of better electoral districting, its 1½ million votes returned almost as many deputies (102) to the French parliament as Germany's 4¼ million votes did to the *Reichstag.* The organized workers advocated either syndicalism, which used the general strike as its main weapon to transfer control of industry to the workers, or Marxian socialism, with its slogan, "Workers of the world, unite." The Socialist leader, Jean Jaurès, as late as 1914, defended the proposal to replace the standing army by a national militia. Legislation pertaining to workers' social insurance, limitation of hours of work, factory inspection, and the like did not approach that in Great Britain or Germany. When Clemenceau as prime minister in 1906 laid down a program of social reform, he failed on every count to achieve it; the peasants and tax-conscious bourgeoisie refused to support the expense of such measures.

The German menace compelled the government to devote more money to military purposes; but not until the war began did the French parliament approve, in principle, an income tax to help pay for defence. Even then it kept the tax low, allowed numerous generous exceptions, and prevented a government check on the accuracy of tax declarations. Except for some writers like Maurice Barrès and politicians like Raymond Poincaré, the French people had lost interest in Alsace-Lorraine. Because of fear of Germany, they were willing to respect their international commitments; but they would have preferred to avoid war.

Italy—Nationalism or Pacifism

Italy did not declare war until May, 1915. She was no better prepared by then, politically and socially, than the other powers had been ten months earlier. Unified late into a national state (1859–1870), Italy had introduced a parliamentary system, but because of the highly centralized method of local government the politicians exploited their power for political purposes. Giovanni Giolitti, the most astute of the politicians between 1903 and 1913, perfected the system of controlling deputies in parliament by dispensing, in return for votes, government contracts, tariff protection, and other items of interest. The practice corrupted political life so thoroughly that it repelled large parts of the public. Since Giolitti upheld neutrality, many of his opponents in 1915 advocated Italy's declaring war in order to prevent the hated spoilsman from arranging a new combination of parties that would return him to power.

The turn to war is the more extraordinary in that the Italian people overwhelmingly favored pacifism. Official party attitude, on the other hand, was divided. The socialists, growing in strength since the nineties, and the clerical party formed the bulwark of the opposition, both to war and to Giolitti; but the socialists, the liberals, and democrats favored the Allied cause over that of the Central Powers. The nationalists, among whom was the writer Gabriele d'Annunzio, a few rebel socialists like Mussolini, the editor of the leading party paper, and many liberals denounced the pacifists and Giolitti. Since the nationalists and liberals were in power in 1915, they bargained with the belligerents in accordance with the ideal of *sacro egoismo* and joined the Allies. They knew that economically the country was utterly unprepared, and that the high rate of illiteracy prevented the people from understanding the issues. Strikes were numerous among both industrial and agricultural workers as an expression of economic grievances and of class conflict. Anarchism and syndicalism had many followers. King Humbert had been assassinated by an anarchist in 1900; his successor, Victor Emmanuel III, carried a revolver. The beginnings of a system of social insurance, state aid to cooperatives, and the extension of the franchise in 1911 to practically all adult males failed to unify the nation. Political bitterness amounting to sabotage of national action continued after entry into the war, until disaster in the battle of Caporetto in October, 1917, forced the parties for a time to subordinate differences to national defense.

IMPERIAL RELATIONS

Study of the maps will show the extent of Europe's domination of the world in 1914. Modern industrialism applied to means of transportation and communication and to the instruments of war had enabled a few European states, relatively small in size of land mass and of population, to seize within the span of a few decades almost all of Africa, many islands in the Pacific, and many regions of Southeast Asia, and to establish spheres of influence in China and the Near and Middle East. Great Britain and France had gained most. Germany had acquired a few Pacific islands and Togoland, part of the Cameroons, and two large but relatively poor areas in southern Africa, plus concessions from China in the Shantung Peninsula and some economic concessions in the Ottoman Empire—not a booty commensurate with the legitimate expectations of the strongest European power. Italy's excursion into imperialism had been even less successful. She had seized Eritrea, Tripoli, and a piece of Somaliland, and had taken possession of the Dodecanese Islands and Rhodes. She had tried to conquer Ethiopia but, when the natives defeated a small Italian force in 1896, had relinquished the attempt. Russia had expanded by land into Korea, Manchuria, and Mongolia, but in the Russo-Japanese War of 1904–1905 she had lost to Japan the extensive rights which she had forced from China. Her only imperial gain lay in northern Persia, which she had assured by agreement in 1907 with Great Britain. Portugal kept the remains of her great empire of the sixteenth century, solely because Great Britain had refused to allow Germany to take them by diplomatic pressure. Spain had lost most of her possessions in the Spanish-American War of 1898; she kept only a few small areas in or off the coast of Africa. The Netherlands' possessions in the East and West Indies and in South America were not as yet endangered, nor was Belgium's possession of the Congo Free State. One extra-European power, Japan, was beginning to compete with the great industrial powers, but her interests extended only to Korea and to China. The United States, in spite of the victory over Spain, continued as a former colony to be hostile to imperialism and strove, unsuccessfully, to preserve the integrity of China against predators.

The significance of the dependencies to the mother country differed widely among the imperialist states. Portugal and Spain did almost nothing to develop their territories. The Spanish army used the constant fighting against the tribes in northern Morocco more or less to occupy the excessive number of officers and to justify the large proportion of the state budget allocated to military purposes. The Netherlands drew large profits from the East Indies, whereas Belgium, which took over the Congo from the private possession of King Leopold I in 1908, lacked time before World War I to take any constructive colonial measures. Germany's dependencies in Africa added financial burdens to the *Reich* budget and entailed an expensive and unpopular war against the natives in Southwest Africa. The Pacific Islands committed the country to naval defence; the acquisitions in China had a similar effect but did at least assure Germany of access to the trade of the Oriental market. *Reich* permission from the Sultan to construct a railway through his empire to Bagdad and exploit resources in the stretch

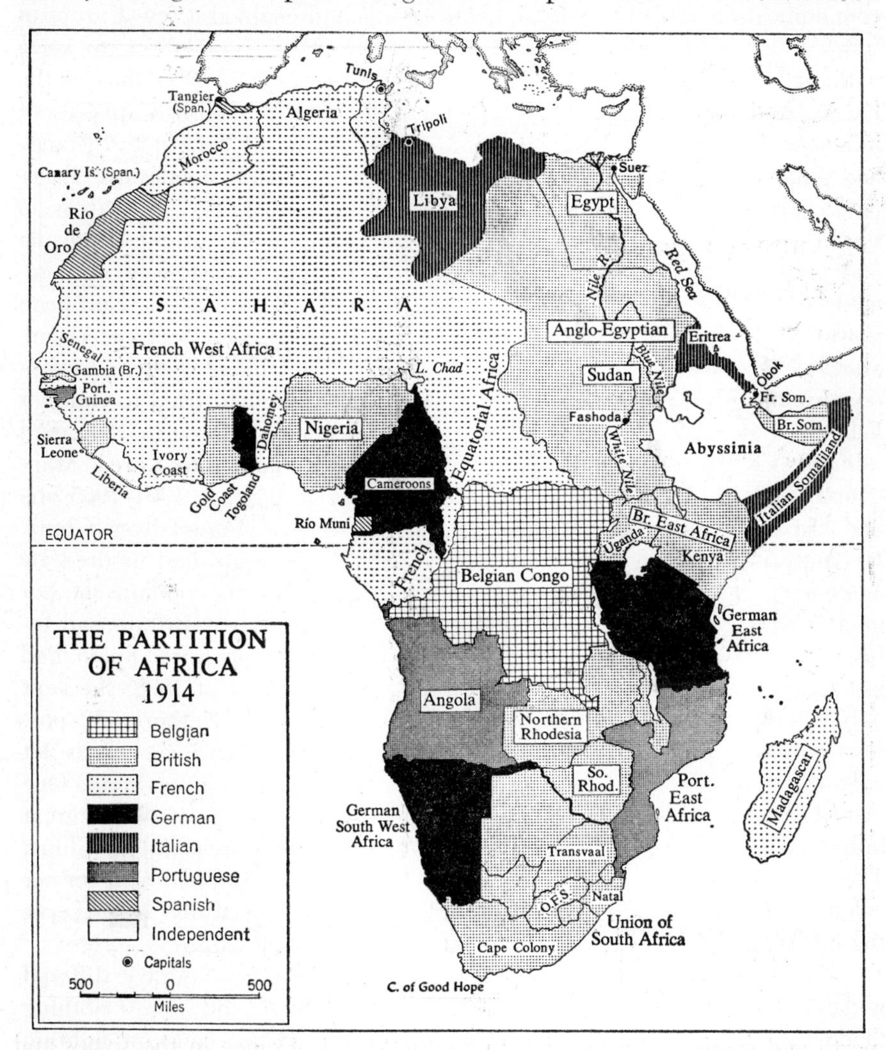

of territory on either side meant present expense and offered vague prospect of gain. Italy's possessions in Africa justified one poor country in expanding its defense budget in order to protect much poorer dependencies. Few Italians, which the homeland exported by the hundreds of thousands each year, could live in the colonies, either because of the heat or, as in Tripoli, because of the scarcity of tillable land. Of the great powers France and Great Britain benefited most and deserve special attention.

The action of the two states in committing themselves to govern new dependencies must rank as one of the most daring in history. Both were imperialistic in China, Southeast Asia, the Near or Middle East, and Africa. In China France concentrated upon gaining economic rights in the south, Great Britain mainly in the Yangtze Valley, although she was active in the

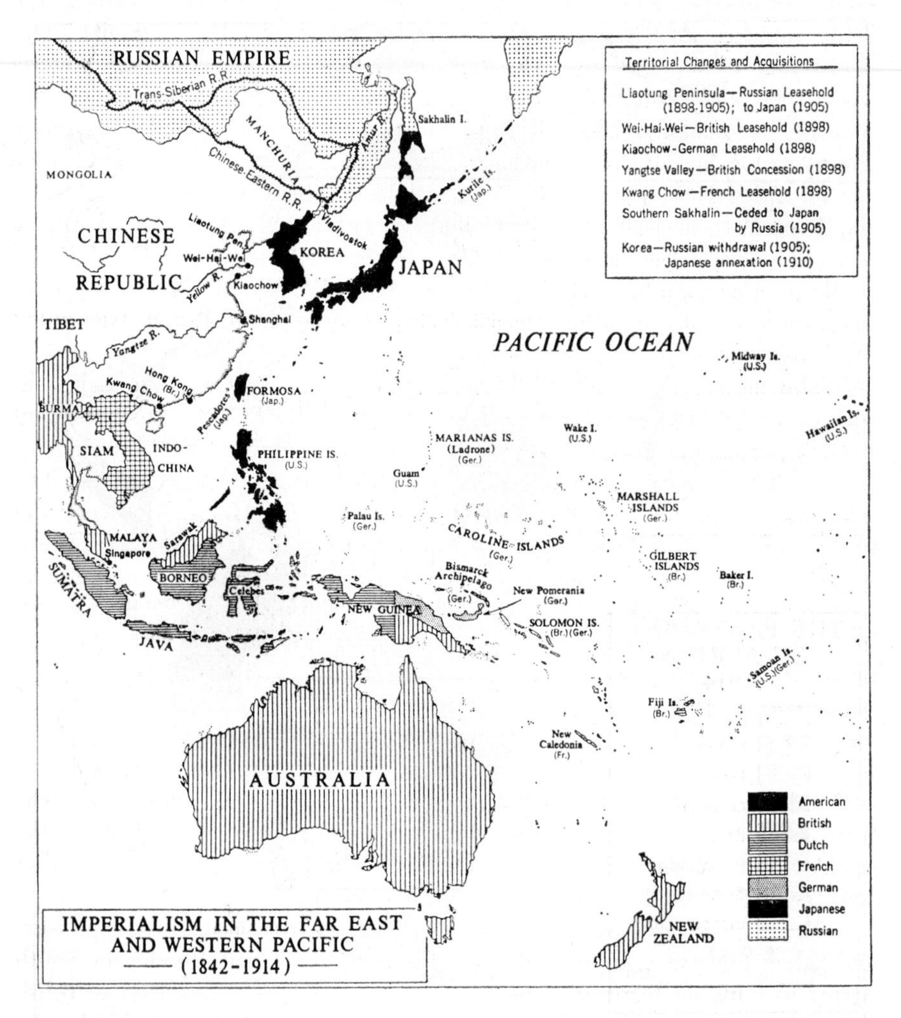

IMPERIALISM IN THE FAR EAST AND WESTERN PACIFIC (1842–1914)

north and south center as well. In Southeast Asia France in the sixties and the eighties took Indochina. Great Britain at about the same time brought North Borneo, part of New Guinea, and Upper Burma under control, and on the other side of India added Baluchistan to the Indian Empire and reduced Afghanistan to a sphere of influence. The Anglo-Russian partition of Persia has already been noted. France tried to acquire Syria, but was repulsed. She made up for the reverse by the magnitude of her conquests in Africa, a continent which she and Great Britain practically divided.

The Third French Republic took Madagascar on the eastern side but was blocked by the British at Fashoda in 1898 from penetrating into the upper Nile Valley; it therefore concentrated on seizing most of Africa west of Egypt and the Sudan and north of the Belgian Congo. A few British conquests in West Africa—Nigeria and the Gold Coast being the most significant—the independent state of Liberia, a couple of German colonies, and some small Spanish colonies were surrounded on the land side by areas of French rule; along the Mediterranean France had possessed Algeria since 1830 and had added Tunisia in 1882 and Morocco, except for the Spanish segment, in 1905–1911. Great Britain acquired in 1875 enough shares in the Suez Canal Company to control the vital waterway. In 1882 she occupied Egypt and began to expand into the Sudan. By the close of the Boer War in 1902, she controlled, except for German East Africa, a solid block of territories extending from Cairo to the Cape of Good Hope. As the mother country of India, Canada, Australia, New Zealand, and other possessions of long standing, the 45 million people of the British Isles ruled more lives than any power in history.

The motive force behind French imperial expansion in the half century before World War I differed from that of the British. An indifferent French parliament and nation were reluctantly committed to the conquests by ambitious army officers, government officials, and missionaries. The officers and officials found in Indochina, Equatorial Africa, Morocco, and elsewhere an outlet for energy which at home the cautious, peaceful bourgeois republic did not offer. At Fashoda, for example, a young officer named Marchand, as leader of a French expedition, who, if he had remained at home, would have died unknown, suddenly became famous. Once involved by these intrepid adventurers, the French government advanced to take over the region. It had no policy of colonial development and did not create a ministry of the colonies until 1894. As the threat of German attack increased, the government thought seriously about training colonial man power to defend France in Europe. By 1914, however, apart from using freely the word "assimilation" of the colonials with France, the country as a whole had scarcely considered the future relations of mother country and dependencies.

The British government participated actively in imperialist expansion and when necessary supported entrepreneurs like Cecil Rhodes in South Africa in winning territory. The new urban population appeared to relish the excitement of reading about the glorious deeds that always added more red color to the map. It thrilled vicariously to this adventure, and some members planned careers in the colonial service or in businesses that engaged in imperial trade. The British were acutely conscious of the power which the possessions gave them throughout the world. The government saw as well the obligations which empire entailed, and when, in 1895, Joseph Chamberlain became head of the Colonial office he tried to draw the empire into working unity. The British had recognized since the lesson taught by the loss of the American colonies that as dependencies matured they must be given self-government. Beginning in 1887 the government conferred at fairly regular intervals with representatives of the colonies, and at the conference in 1907 it substituted with respect to the most advanced of them—Canada, Australia, New Zealand—the term "Dominion"

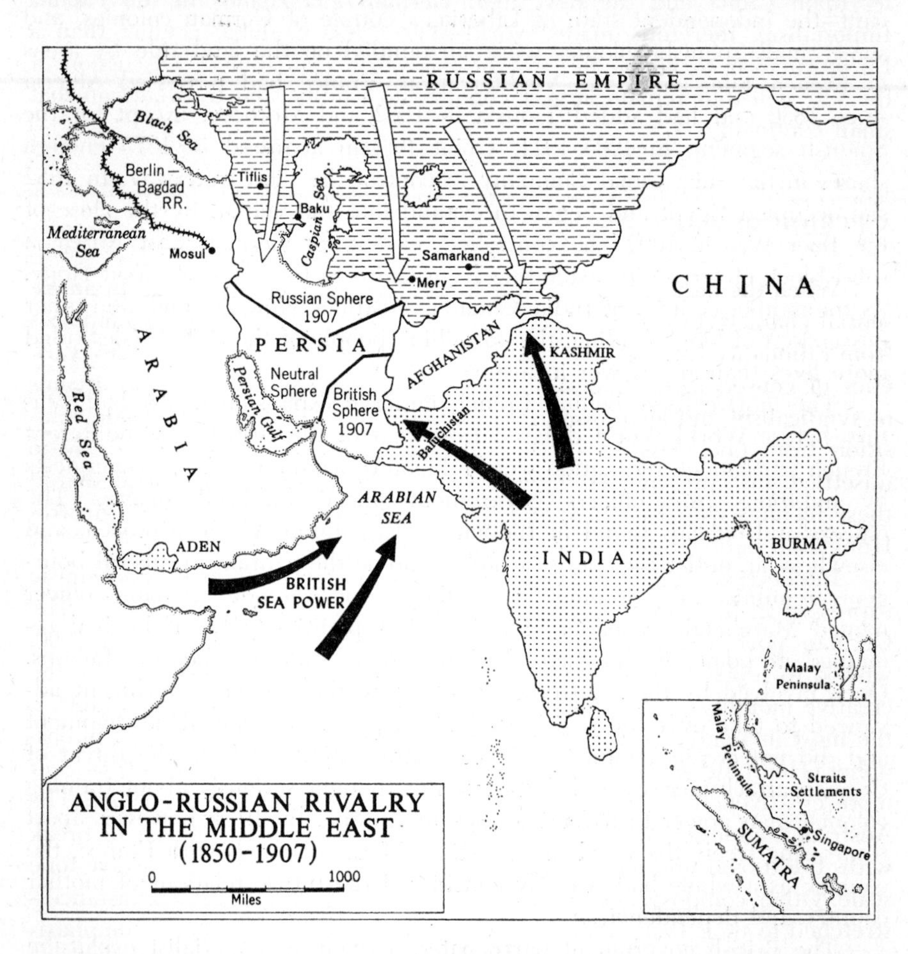

for that of "Colony." By 1914 imperial relations remained in an unorganized stage, depending upon cordial cooperation, free trade relations, and the defensive power of the British navy for preservation. Foreign policy and defense were still planned in London, and Britain definitely thought of herself as occupying an international position somewhere between the European continent and the rest of the world. She felt confident of being the greatest world power, able to obstruct the policy of any state. But the global potential of the empire was rapidly being focused upon the threat from Germany to the British Isles themselves.

When the war of July, 1914, opened it involved vast areas of the rest of the world by virtue of the expanse primarily of British and French territorial holdings. However, unlike World War II, the main imperial powers were all on the Allied side and the conflict affected predominantly the European continent. Japan offered the exception; but she concentrated activity upon China and the few small German-held islands in the Pacific. Imperialism, therefore, made World War I less a global conflict than a European war to which the rest of the world contributed. Discussion of the war will thus remain largely confined to Europe and to events on that small continent.

A PERIOD OF RAPID TRANSITION

When the nations went to war in 1914 they were conforming to an essential characteristic of the life of the period, that of shifting the emphasis from rationality to emotionalism. Competition among ideals, the many varieties of conservatism, liberalism, and socialism, together with the dreams of syndicalism and anarchism, divided society. As industrialism made transition from one class to another increasingly possible, individuals were unsettled, insecure, and excitable. A people as stable as the British shared these feelings with Russian peasants and bourgeoisie and with the Austro-Hungarian nationalities.

Intellectuals and creative persons in the arts, literature, and music expressed in their work the characteristics of an age of swift change. The German poet and philosopher, Friedrich Nietzsche, who died in 1900, wished to replace what he called the slave morality of Christianity by the creative morality of the superman. In his work *Creative Evolution* (1907), the most influential serious book of the prewar decade, the French philosopher, Henri Bergson (1859–1941), described the mind as guided to ever more creativeness by a mystical genetic impulse called the *élan vital.* The Austrian composer, Arnold Schönberg, during the nineties began to break with traditional musical forms to develop the use of the twelve-tone scale. Other composers—Gustav Mahler and Richard Strauss, for instance—stretched to their limits the romantic idiom and forms. Note their emphasis on large orchestras and chorus, and extreme subtlety in the use of musical instruments and the human voice. Their work aroused opposition among young composers, who then sought to return to the elementals of their medium.

Artists were still struggling to break with traditional subject matter and form as laid down by the impressionists. The Belgian painter, Maurice de Vlaminck, wrote soon after the new century began, "I transposed into an orchestration of pure colors all the feelings of which I was conscious. I was a barbarian, tender and full of violence. I translated by instinct, without any method, not merely an artistic truth but above all a human one." Sensitive persons were reacting to an age that was losing its traditional values and had not yet developed new ones. Vlaminck and others turned for guidance to emotion; they became barbarians. Creative writers like Marcel Proust portrayed a part of society in decadence, or like Maurice Maeterlinck chose subjects of exquisite sensitivity, clothing them in rich symbolic language. Some writers attempted to promote or depict a culture expressive of the proletariat, crude, vulgar, elemental in subject matter, which proved repulsive alike to the proletariat and to the upper classes.

Successful in science and technology, the age prior to World War I lagged in applying to social and political life a balance between rationalism and intuition. The creative arts clearly revealed the excessive emotionalism from which people were suffering. Europe had not developed the resources to handle international affairs by peaceful means. She had weathered a number of crises without the use of force; yet the overcoming of each crisis, far from being the start of a genuine detente, set up new tensions. Although all Europe realized that war could solve none of the problems, recourse to violence expressed the psychological character of this period of rapid transition.

Suggestions for Further Reading

ALBRECHT-CARRIÉ, RENÉ. *Italy from Napoleon to Mussolini.* New York: Columbia University Press, 1950. Useful survey.

BROGAN, DENIS. *France under the Republic, 1870–1939.* New York: Harper & Brothers, 1940. Basic work on the subject.

BRUCK, W. F. *Social and Economic History of Germany, 1888–1938.* New York: Oxford University Press, 1938. One of the most revealing books on modern Germany.

DICKINSON, G. LOWES. *The International Anarchy, 1904–1914.* New York: Appleton-Century-Crofts, Inc., 1926. Brilliant. Even though written before the publication of many sources, it is still worth reading.

FAY, SIDNEY B. *The Origins of the World War.* 2nd ed.; 2 vols. New York: The Macmillan Company, 1943. The standard work on the diplomatic background of World War I.

JASZI, OSCAR. *The Dissolution of the Habsburg Monarchy.* Chicago: University of Chicago Press, 1929. One of the finest volumes on any European country.

LATOURETTE, KENNETH SCOTT. *A Short History of the Far East.* 3rd ed. New York: The Macmillan Company, 1957. Interesting and judicious survey, with emphasis on the past hundred years.

PARES, BERNARD. *The Fall of the Russian Monarchy.* New York: Alfred A. Knopf, Inc., 1939. By a scholar with an intimate knowledge of Russia.

THOMSON, DAVID. *England in the Nineteenth Century, 1815–1914.* Baltimore: Penguin Books, Inc., 1950. An excellent brief account extending to 1914.

Chapter 2 · World War I, 1914-1917

STRATEGIC PLANS FOR A SHORT WAR

When World War I began, the authorities in every participating nation had laid strategic plans for a short conflict. Military and civilian leaders alike thought that a nation could not support the economic or the psychological burden of a long war. General Alfred von Schlieffen, chief of staff of the German army, had written less than a decade before, that since nations depended upon continuous industrial development, long wars were not possible.

Forced by the law of competition, all staffs except the British had based their planning upon the use of the modern mass army. All had to take into account a war on two fronts, the western and the eastern, with a minor one in the southeast. The strategy of the German and French army staffs for gaining victory, however, differed radically.

General von Schlieffen, as German chief of staff, had in 1905 drafted the basic plan of operation for his army. He proposed to assume the defensive toward Russia and to throw the overwhelming body of troops against France. Russia, with her vast unfortified spaces, he argued, would fight an evasive war, and a quick, decisive victory over that country would be impossible. France was close and small enough to permit speedy annihilation, and her immediate defeat would deprive Great Britain of a base of operations and keep her out of the war. He considered it good strategy to attack at once the major military opponent and to leave the lesser forces to mopping-up operations. Because of the mountainous and wooded nature of the Franco-German frontier he planned to invade France by way of the coastal plain, including that of Belgium, where indispensable roads and railroads were most numerous and the level space would permit deployment of a mass army. The German troops were to move over this plain in such numbers and with such speed as to outflank the French army, expose it to attack from the north and west as well, and roll the enemy into the Vosges Mountains and Switzerland. Success depended upon the striking power of the German right wing.

The French plan of campaign was simple and clear. Since 1911 a military school in favor of the offensive had come into power. Colonel de

Grandmaison, its leading spokesman, said that the French army must destroy the enemy by bayonet charges. The price would be bloody, but he maintained that the offensive alone was in keeping with "the very nature of war." A French major stated that trench battles like those at Plevna or Mukden would not occur in a war with a French army. And a French general added that a war would be short, rapid in movements, that battles would be fought mainly by infantry, and that artillery would act as "an accessory arm." The French planned to attack northeastward between the Vosges Mountains and the little state of Luxembourg, and to station one army facing the Franco-Belgian frontier. The plan of the French chief of staff in 1911 which had accurately anticipated the German strategy was scrapped in favor of this one of pure offense. Once the war began, the French Plan XVII for attacking Germany collapsed immediately. General Sir Frederick Maurice subsequently wrote that Britain and France suffered for four years from the initial mistakes of this plan.

STATE OF PREPAREDNESS

The following figures indicate the amount of effort of each great power in preparing for war in 1914.

Armies 1914

COUNTRY	POPULATION	ARMY	PERCENTAGE OF ARMY TO POPULATION	COST
Germany	65,000,000	actual 761,000	1.17	$218,000,000
		planned 830,000	1.3	
British and French estimates		870,000		
France, incl. Algeria & Tunis	47,000,000	821,000 *	1.77	241,000,000
Austria-Hungary	51,000,000	479,000	.94	156,000,000
Italy	35,000,000	305,000	.87	94,000,000
Russian Empire	164,000,000	1,445,000 †	.8	399,000,000
German estimate for Russia in Europe alone		1,539,000		
Great Britain	45,000,000	187,000	.4	139,000,000
including colonial garrisons		248,000		

* Term of service raised in 1913 to 3 years.
† Term of service raised in 1913 to 3½ years.

Navies 1914

	OLDER BATTLE-SHIPS	DREAD-NAUGHTS	CRUISERS	DE-STROYERS	SUB-MARINES	COST
Great Britain	40	31	118	362	85	$255,000,000
France	21	7	31	253	76	97,500,000
Russia	10	4	23	103	14	120,000,000
Germany	20	21	47	199	37	120,000,000
Austria-Hungary	12	4	12	88	6	15,250,000
Italy	11	4	22	131	25	55,000,000
United States	24	12	26	69	34	143,500,000
Japan	16	4	33	86	13	47,500,000

SOURCE: Bernadotte E. Schmitt, *Triple Alliance and Triple Entente.* By permission of Henry Holt and Company, Inc., copyright 1934. Appendix. Professor Schmitt adds the following explanatory note: "The tables are based on the Statesman's Year Book, and in order to facilitate comparisons, have been simplified as much as possible; all figures are given in round numbers, and currencies have been converted into dollars at the pre-war rates of exchange. 'Cost' is the budget estimate. As the budgets of different countries do not always include the same items, it is difficult to calculate exactly the expenditure per head of population. The British volunteer army was paid at a much higher rate than Continental soldiers, hence the high cost in proportion to size."

The defense departments of the great powers had prior to 1914 enjoyed from one to two decades of intensive spending. It was a truism in military and naval strategy that, a French military writer stated in 1912, "The great transformations of combat and war and their evolution are due to the progress of arms or, more generally, to all the material objects of which use is made in combat." [1] Had the military and naval leaders by 1914 prepared the fighting forces with the kind of equipment which modern industrialism had made possible? Had they developed strategic plans in accordance with these new materials?

The German army was generally regarded as the most effective in the world. During the previous half century it had adjusted organization and strategy to the existence of railroads. Speedy transportation enabled the general staff to converge hundreds of thousands of troops on a small area or spread them over a large region. Schlieffen had developed the strategy for conquering France around the use of the railroad and to a lesser extent the all-season road, and his successor, General Helmuth von Moltke, continued the practice. Nevertheless, the Schlieffen plan failed in 1914 primarily because of the neglect to prepare adequate facilities for transportation and communication. The German troops moved to the French and Belgian frontiers by railway; after that they had to walk, or if horse-drawn or horse-carried—and few of them were—the horses had to stand the strain. Troops were so tired that many could not keep up. At the farthest advance

[1] Alfred Vagts, *A History of Militarism* (New York: W. W. Norton & Company, Inc., 1937), p. 236.

of the army the horses had slowed to a walk. The automobile was reserved for higher officers; no one had projected its use for the transportation of troops. The same deficiency characterized communications. Against the vigorous resistance of many officers, Schlieffen had created a signal corps; but in 1914 this branch of service proved inadequate. The high command remained many miles behind the front lines so that the Kaiser could be present in safety. In consequence, the general staff was frequently out of touch with action. Connections were maintained by motorcycle, automobile, and telephone; but the service proved to be so slow and haphazard that major decisions had to be left to corps commanders or to lower staff officers sent out with blanket power as special emissaries.

By 1914 the German army was well prepared in railroad engineering and in mobile heavy artillery, and it used the machine gun extensively; but it continued deficient in technical innovations. The outstanding example was the airplane. Whereas France between 1909 and 1912 spent 30,610,000 francs for military planes, the Germans devoted one fourth as much. The French army in 1912 possessed 390 planes and 234 pilots; the German army had only 100 planes and 90 pilots. Neither army had devised effective ways to employ the plane. The French army had expended its funds largely upon man power. When, during the war, deputies from the French Chamber inquired about the supply of artillery, the director of that branch of service replied that the breasts of French infantrymen would gain the victory. The army was actually strong in artillery, but it had scarcely improved the quality of the guns since 1870. The uniforms also continued to be like those of the Franco-Prussian War. Gaily bedecked, encumbered with 65 pounds on his back and a long bayonet on the end of his rifle, the French infantryman in 1914 advanced to the slaughter. A German battalion had eight machine guns to two for the French, and the French high command ignored the fact that since 1870 fire power had increased fourfold.

Among the other three major powers entering the war in 1914, the preparations of Austria-Hungary had not reached the German standard, but at the time they seemed adequate for the kind of enemies to be faced. Great Britain had since 1908 established an expeditionary force of 150,000 men, which was as well armed, except for reserves, as the Germans, particularly in machine guns. It lacked heavy artillery, expecting to use that already available on the continent, and it was trained according to the drill book in use at the time of the Crimean War (1854–1856). It proved by comparison to be an efficient force. The Russian army lacked supplies. In 1914 it possessed 60 heavy batteries to 381 for the German army. A Russian division, equipped with half the guns of a German one, was strong in bayonets, weak in fire power. Russian medical and transport services hardly existed, and the supply of ammunition was low.

In spite of the vast sums of money expended for military purposes over the preceding decade or two, the armies of the major powers were inadequately prepared for conducting even the kind of war for which they had planned. They had not changed their conception of warfare in accordance with the new instruments that modern industry was producing. The gasoline motor, the airplane, the motorized truck, the caterpillar tractor, the light machine gun were all present at the outbreak of war, but military experts did not know how to use them to the advantage of the offensive. One may ask whether any fighting organization, whose purpose is to kill the enemy, can ever be adequately prepared beforehand. As we shall see, the aid of civilians became necessary during the conflict to adjust the military establishments and practices to the potentialities of modern economy and society.

FIRST PHASE

Western Front: Trench Warfare

When in September, 1914, the French army under General Joseph Joffre, aided by the small British expeditionary force on its left, halted the Germans at the Marne River and forced them to retreat, the only phase of the war which had been planned beforehand came to an end. Henceforth the war in the west assumed an unforeseen character. It became a war of position, fought from trenches. Many of the leading officers in each army were replaced; the cavalry, useless on the western front, was transformed; because of the improvements in fire power, defense gained superiority over offense, dooming millions of men for four years to kill each other methodically as opportunity presented itself from cuts in the earth a few yards apart.

From October, 1914, to March, 1918, neither the Allies nor the Germans were able to advance the front line more than ten miles. In 1917 the Germans voluntarily shortened their front by withdrawing to the position fortified in depth known as the Hindenburg Line. From time to time an artillery barrage often lasting several days and followed by infantry charge attempted in vain to tear a hole in the enemy's defense. In February, 1915, the French attacked in Champagne, with a loss of nearly a quarter of a million men in a month. In April they lost 100,000 men in the St. Mihiel sector. In the autumn the French and the British again attacked in Champagne and in Artois, where in six weeks of fighting the French lost 190,000, the British 60,000, and the Germans 140,000 men, or a ratio of attackers' loss to defenders' loss of more than five to three. In the next year, 1916, the Germans took the aggressive against Verdun. That attack in the spring and early summer cost the Germans about 280,000 casualties, the defending French 460,000—a reversal of the ratio—but the Allied line held. In the summer and autumn the Allies attacked on the Somme, where the casualties continued to be so great that by November, 1916, the French had, from the beginning of the war, lost 900,000 men, the British about half as many,

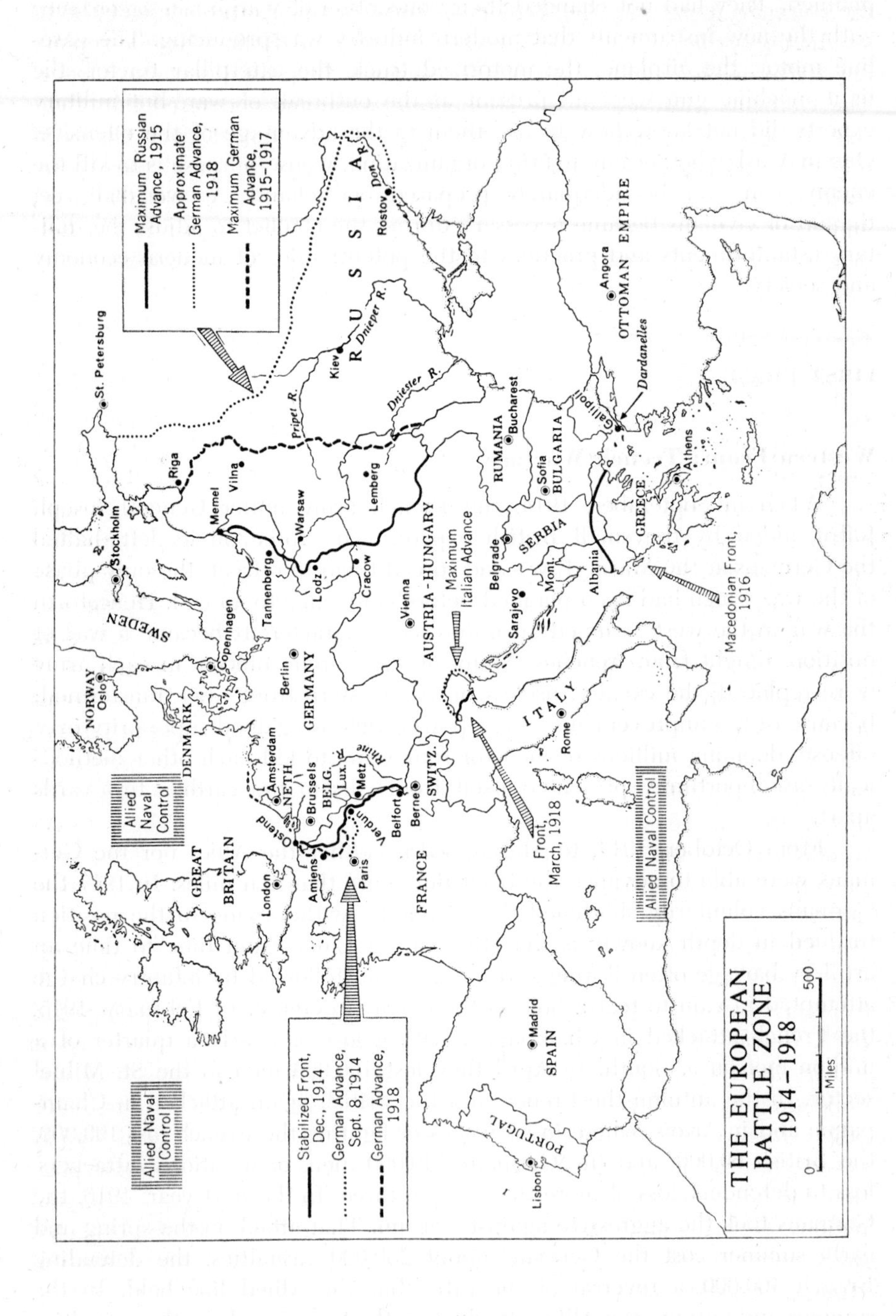
THE EUROPEAN BATTLE ZONE 1914–1918
0
500
Miles
Stabilized Front, Dec., 1914
German Advance, Sept. 8, 1914
German Advance, 1918
Maximum Russian Advance, 1915
Approximate German Advance, 1918
Maximum German Advance, 1915–1917
Allied Naval Control
Allied Naval Control
Allied Naval Control
Macedonian Front, 1916
Front, March, 1918
Maximum Italian Advance
GREAT BRITAIN
London
Paris
Amiens
Ostend
Verdun
Belfort
Berne
SWITZ.
FRANCE
NETH.
Amsterdam
Brussels
BELG.
Lux.
Metz
Rhine R.
DENMARK
NORWAY
Oslo
SWEDEN
Stockholm
Copenhagen
GERMANY
Berlin
Tannenberg
Memel
Riga
Vilna
Warsaw
Lodz
Cracow
Lemberg
Vienna
AUSTRIA-HUNGARY
St. Petersburg
RUSSIA
Pripet R.
Kiev
Dnieper R.
Dniester R.
Rostov
Don R.
RUMANIA
Bucharest
BULGARIA
Sofia
SERBIA
Belgrade
Sarajevo
Mont.
Albania
GREECE
Athens
Gallipoli
Dardanelles
OTTOMAN EMPIRE
Angora
ITALY
Rome
SPAIN
Madrid
PORTUGAL
Lisbon

the Germans more than 800,000, or an Allied-German ratio of about ten to six. In the spring of 1917 the French, with General Robert Nivelle replacing Joffre as commander, struck the Germans in several sectors at once. The Germans withdrew to the Hindenburg Line and countered the offensive. By May the French attack had stopped, with some French troops in mutiny against the slaughter. The British continued to pound the enemy in the north, where from June to December they lost about 300,000 dead and wounded, without capturing the German submarine bases in the Belgian ports. By the end of the year 1917 the line remained unbroken.

Eastern Front: Confused Strategy

The fighting on the other fronts was subsidiary to that in the west. In the German army two groups of high officers fought for precedence of their respective views, one in favor of concentrating strength on the western front and first knocking out France, the other preferring to throw the major force to the east in order to conquer Russia. The first school consistently won, but the western emphasis did not detract from a continuing concern about victory against the Russians, even at the expense of weakening the army in the west. Since Germany held the inside position, she was able to shift troops and supplies from east to west and vice versa according to need. She suffered in her fighting in the east from the inefficiency of Austria-Hungary and from the political unreliability of the Slavic troops in that army. As the war progressed, she had to assume increasing responsibility for the military duties of her ally and to bolster Austro-Hungarian morale by merging the troops and command of the two armies. The conflict in the east remained one of movement, in which the Hapsburg forces usually lost and the Germans won. The emphasis upon the war in the west prevented the Germans from ever following up these victories by a knockout blow.

The strategy on the eastern front was about as confused as the fighting. The vast distances to be covered and the paucity of railroads and all-weather roads made the concentration of troops difficult and the campaigns fairly restricted. Despatch riders and bodies of troops could easily become lost on the Polish plain, and sometimes a battle might be engaged or not, depending upon whether the opposing armies could or wished to find each other. Russia had not begun to fortify her Polish territory until shortly before the war, in spite of the fact that that area offered a favorable position for an immediate attack upon the Bohemian and Silesian industrial regions, Berlin and central Germany. In the event of war Russia expected the Central Powers to cut off this Polish sector at once, and indeed Austria-Hungary's first campaign was aimed northeast from Galicia.

Germany preferred to remain on the defensive in East Prussia; and not until two Russian armies broke into that province in August, 1914, did the high command detach two army corps from the right wing of the army invading France and send them to the east. Prior to the arrival of these reinforcements the new eastern commanders, Hindenburg and Ludendorff, used the available forces in September to destroy one of the Russian armies at Tannenberg, and with it the bulk of Russia's heavy artillery, and to drive the other precipitously back into Russia. While the Austrian forces in the south of Poland met with setbacks and retreated, Hindenburg followed up his success at Tannenberg by a campaign into central Poland against Warsaw and Lodz, where he gained nothing of significance. In the spring of 1915 the Russians were defending their positions and in March forced the surrender of the fortress of Przemyśl with 150,000 Austrian troops, many of them disaffected Slavs. At that moment the eastern faction in the German command succeeded in gaining enough influence to send General August von Mackensen with a force well equipped with artillery into Galicia. The Russians opposed him with almost no heavy artillery and little ammunition and defended themselves mainly with the bayonet. By August, 1915, they had been driven completely out of Russian Poland. Russian losses for the first ten months of the war amounted to 3,800,000 men.

The Russian army revived sufficiently by the winter of 1915–1916 to resume the offensive. The supply of ammunition increased somewhat, and in the summer of 1916 General Brusilov broke the Austrian line, swept into Galicia, and stormed hill after hill in the Carpathians. His losses were enormous, but the Austrian Slavic troops deserted in great numbers.

Southeast Front: Diplomacy

Unlike the conflicts on the western and the eastern fronts, that in the southeast was intimately associated with diplomacy. The two sets of great powers bid for allies among the small Balkan states. Montenegro sided with Serbia almost at once and shared its fate. Turkey had been politically, militarily, and economically aligned with Germany for some years, and, being afraid of Russia's designs on the Straits, joined the Central Powers in October, 1914, and bombarded the Russian ports on the Black Sea. In February, 1915, British and Australian troops began to attack the Dardanelles. Control of the Straits would enable France and Great Britain to ship munitions and other supplies to Russia at all times and to receive in turn food and raw materials. The conflict concentrated on the Gallipoli Peninsula, which the Allies tried throughout the year to take. Turkish defence, assisted by the Germans, withstood the offensive, and in December the Allies abandoned the campaign.

Austria-Hungary attacked Serbia twice in 1914 without appreciable success. At the end of the year the country remained independent, for the Austrian troops had been shifted to the Russian front. In the autumn of 1915 the Central Powers finally turned their attention to Serbia in earnest, hoping thereby to bring other Balkan states into the conflict on their side. They promised Bulgaria territory in Serbian Macedonia, and Turkey ceded to her a small piece of land. In September, 1915, Bulgaria accepted the offer of the Central Powers to join them. A month later she participated in the campaign of the Germans and Austrians in which Serbia, too far away from her allies to be helped, was crushed.

The next Balkan example of war as "the extension of diplomacy into action" concerned Romania and Greece. The former country feared Russia and wished to obtain Bessarabia from her. At the same time it hoped to acquire Bucovina and Transylvania from Austria-Hungary, and it nursed a long feud with Bulgaria over the possession of the Dobruja. Before the war hostility to Russia had been greater than that to Austria-Hungary, and Romania had allied with the Central Powers. When the war began, it had remained neutral. Overestimating the effectiveness of Russia's campaign in the summer of 1916, Romania declared war in August of that year on the Hapsburg empire. The Russian offensive gave out, the Germans invaded Romania, and, with Bulgarian troops also participating, occupied almost all of the country by December. The Romanian army escaped to attach itself to the Russian forces.

Greek policy was split between the pro-German views of King Constantine, himself a German in origin, whose wife was a sister of the Kaiser, and the pro-Allied stand of the leading statesman, Eleutherio Venizelos. The king tried to keep the country neutral; Venizelos wished it to join the Allies. He and his supporters were particularly hostile to Turkey, where many Greeks lived. Both the Central Powers and the Allies intrigued in Greece; but in October, 1915, with the aid of the clever Venizelos, the Allies were able by means of their superior sea power to establish a military base at Salonika. In 1916 the Venizelos government declared war on the Central Powers; the army advanced north and took the important town of Monastir, and in June, 1917, the pro-German king was forced to abdicate. The war in this region continued to be a minor affair.

Italian Front

Italy delayed and bargained with the two sets of powers over the terms of her entry. Although Italy was a member of the Triple Alliance the Central Powers were handicapped in this diplomatic game by the fact that Austria-Hungary would have to pay the price of territory in the Trentino and along the east coast of the Adriatic. The Hapsburg monarchy was willing to make some concessions but not to grant all Italy asked. It preferred to have that country as an enemy rather than to give in at once. The Allies, however, were able to accede to Italy's demands, since these were at the expense of Austria-Hungary and of Turkey; thus in May, 1915, Italy declared war against the Central Powers.

The fighting on the Italian front in the Trentino and along the Isonzo proved to be as insignificant for the ultimate outcome of the war as that in Greece. Much of it was conducted in the Alps, where the shooting from peak to peak and particularly the warfare in winter offered diversion from the drab life in trenches. The glamour, however, did not compensate for the ineffectiveness. Up to the latter part of 1917 eleven battles were fought, only one of which, the Austrian push in 1916 in the direction of Padua and Venice, was serious. That neither combatant shared the military efficiency of its respective ally or allies was revealed in October, 1917, when the Germans combined with the Austrians to attack. At Caporetto, within a few days, they crumbled the front. The Italian troops fled over the Venetian plain, but enough rallied along the Piave River just north of Venice to avert a disaster. Lack of transportation facilities for bringing up supplies once more deprived the Central Powers of possible victory, and by the end of 1917 the war on this front remained indecisive.

Participation of Italy on the Allied side enabled the latter to control the Mediterranean route for supplies from Western and Southern Asia and the Far East. The Suez Canal remained in British hands without much difficulty. A British and Indian force in 1914 seized Basra on the Persian Gulf to assure the flow of Persian oil for the British navy in the East; but it failed to take Bagdad and, besieged in Kut-al-Amara in 1916, surrendered to the Turks. These engagements did not affect the outcome of the war any more than did Russia's capture in 1916 of small strategic areas in Turkish Armenia. In Africa British and French forces easily occupied the German colonies of Togoland and the Cameroons; the Union of South Africa, with some British aid, took German Southwest Africa; a small German army held out in German East Africa until the end of the war. Being secure against attack outside Europe, the French brought colonial troops to Europe to fight; and Indians, Canadians, Australians, and New Zealanders, a few South Africans, and small contingents from other dependencies helped the British on the western front. The greatest advantage derived by the Allies from their dependencies was in the form of economic aid. Food and raw materials, scarce metals, oil, and some manufactures made essential contributions.

Far East

The Far East became an important area of conflict primarily because of Japan's entry into the war (August, 1914). The German island possessions in the Pacific quickly fell victims to the Allies, Australia and New Zealand taking those south of the Equator, Japan those to the north. The Allies were troubled by German naval raiders on commerce, which served more as a nuisance than a menace and in time were for the most part driven off the sea. Japan took the occasion of war to invade neutral China and to seize the German holdings in the Shantung Peninsula. With world attention concentrated on Europe, she subjected China in 1915 to twenty-one demands, among which were the assurance of the Shantung Peninsula as a Japanese sphere of influence, extensive rights of control and exploitation in Southern Manchuria and eastern Inner Mongolia, joint control of the largest iron industry in Central China, the promise of refusal of concessions on the coast to any third power, the employment of Japanese "advisers in political, financial, and military affairs," and dependence upon Japan for most of China's military supplies. Acceptance of the terms would have reduced China to the status of a Japanese protectorate. Unable to protect herself by arms, China accepted some demands but delayed in fulfilling her promises and in acquiescing in others. Early in 1917 the position of the Allies seemed so grave that Japan won the secret approval of Great Britain, France, and Russia for retaining after the war the German possessions in Shantung. Only the United States, still neutral, strove, always by diplomatic means, to support the Chinese against Japanese imperialism. China's declaration of war against Germany in August, 1917, did not change the situation. By opening the floodgates of Japanese imperialism, the war in Europe made certain that another continent would henceforth practice the cupidity and power politics that were bringing the western powers to disaster.

DEMANDS OF TRENCH WARFARE

When the armies in the west dug themselves into trenches and the war became one of attrition, the participating nations were immediately forced to adjust their economic, social, and governmental organization to the insatiable demands of trench warfare. Involved in a conflict of unforeseeable duration, each mass army became the fighting front of a nation in arms. The continuing struggle tested the efficiency of the entire life of each participating people, disclosing sources of strength and weakness that in peacetime were overlooked. Since the nations were fighting a common war, they tended to imitate each other's innovations. Some encountered more difficulty in doing so than did others, and the extent of their ability to keep up with the improvements of the most efficient nations decided their fate in the war.

Almost at once the governments perceived that they would need more soldiers. When trench warfare began, France was already losing 150,000 men a month, of whom one third were killed or taken prisoners. Five hundred miles of trenches had to be manned; and, given the undeviating strategy of frequent frontal attacks, the requirements increased. Each side staked its quantity of human flesh and blood against that of the other. When the United States added its 100,000,000 people to those of the Allies, the scales tilted decidedly against the Central Powers. The latter still demanded proof, especially after Russia's withdrawal from the war following the Bolshevik Revolution in 1917, and the war continued for another year and a half. By the end of that time the Central Powers had exhausted their reserves of man power and were compelled to surrender.

The numbers mobilized during the war were as follows:

CENTRAL POWERS		ALLIED POWERS	
Germany	13,250,000	Russia	*ca.* 19,000,000
Austria-Hungary	9,000,000	Great Britain and Dominions	9,500,000
Turkey	*ca.* 1,800,000	France	8,200,000
Bulgaria	*ca.* 1,000,000	Italy	5,600,000
		Romania	1,000,000
		Belgium	380,000
		Serbia and Montenegro	*ca.* 800,000
		Greece	*ca.* 400,000
		Portugal	*ca.* 53,000
		United States	3,900,000
Total	*ca.* 25,050,000	Total	*ca.* 49,000,000

BLOCKADE AND SEA WARFARE

The relative strength of the two sides in raw materials and food was comparable to that in man power. The Allies in the west drew upon the larger supply as long as they could maintain control of the seas and as long as they had purchasing power. With the closing of the Straits into the Baltic and into the Black Sea, Russia was practically isolated. Her trouble arose, not from a shortage of materials, but from lack of facilities for manufacturing and transporting them. The Central Powers fought under the handicap of encirclement. Overseas connections in the north and in the Mediterranean were blocked by the British and French fleets, and the Allied governments exerted intense economic pressure, such as blacklisting, to prevent firms in neutral countries from doing business with the Central Powers. Some concessions had to be made to the Netherlands, Switzerland, and the Scandinavian countries, too close to Germany and too dependent upon certain German commodities, coal especially, to risk stoppage of all trade.

Germany tried to break the sea blockade primarily by the use of raiders and submarines. The single raiders, until destroyed or forced into internment in neutral harbors, damaged considerable Allied shipping, but they were prevented by the Allied mine belt in the North Sea and Mediterranean and by patrolling fleets from bringing supplies into home ports. German submarines were too few in number and the government was too fearful of antagonizing neutral powers, especially the United States, to employ them consistently in the first period of the war. During a burst of activity in 1915 the submarines sank, among other ships, the British liners the "Lusitania" and the "Arabic," and in 1916 the "Sussex," but the loss of

American lives on these ships aroused such vigorous protests from the United States government against violation of neutral rights that for a time Germany curtailed the use of underwater boats. The vaunted German navy came out of security in North Sea ports on only two occasions. In the winter of 1914–1915 it skirmished several times with the British fleet in the North Sea before running for cover. On May 31, 1916, the two fleets clashed in the battle of Jutland. The German fleet under Admiral Scheer proved technically superior and inflicted twice as much damage on the British force under Admiral Jellicoe as it received; but it retreated homeward, leaving the British in undisputed domination.

The land frontier of the Central Powers on the east, west, and south was closed by fighting. Germany, Austria-Hungary, and their lesser allies had to depend upon their own resources or those they could capture. They possessed plenty of coal, to which they added by conquest 40 per cent of the French resources. Although somewhat short of iron ore, they controlled the supplies in Lorraine, which they soon increased by capturing 90 per cent of those in France, and they were favorably situated for purchasing the rich Swedish ore. From Upper Silesia they extracted some lead and zinc, and by conquest they gained the copper ore of Serbia and the oil of Romania. Except for chrome from Turkey, they lacked all the other nonferrous and steel-hardening metals, and they grew short of oil. Textile raw materials, rawhides, and other items of clothing likewise proved to be in short supply, particularly in the latter half of the war, and except in small quantities all colonial products were unobtainable. In foodstuffs Bulgaria had normally exported small amounts and continued to do so. Hungary and Galicia had supplied grain and meat and Bohemia sugar to Austria, and had had some left over for export. Germany was short of grain and fodder, which she had imported in order to devote more area than otherwise to growing intensively cultivated crops and to raising livestock and dairy herds. All in all, the Central Powers were deficient in raw materials and food to an extent which enabled a blockade to be effective. The question was whether they could compensate for the short supply by the economic utilization of the resources which their central geographic position made possible—whether they had enough to hold out while their armies gained victory.

Important as the supply of materials was, a country could not maintain itself in the war without a well-developed industrial plant. The small countries lacked practically all the industries necessary for sustaining their armies with munitions. Where they did possess a steel plant, they depended upon the importation of the essential materials. When these materials were not supplied by one of the major powers, their munitions soon gave out. Among the industrial powers, the following figures on the percentage distribution of the world's manufacturing production reveal their relative strength:

COUNTRY	PERCENTAGE 1913
United States	35.8
Germany	15.7
United Kingdom	14.0
France	6.4
Russia	5.5
Italy	2.7
Canada	2.3
Belgium	2.1
Japan	1.2

In the production of pig iron (1913) Germany led the continental powers with 16,700,000 tons, to which should be added Austria-Hungary's 2,400,000 tons. The combined resources of Great Britain (10,400,000 tons), France (5,300,000 tons), and Russia (4,500,000 tons) were necessary to counterbalance this amount. In 1914 Germany seized the pig iron of Belgium and Luxembourg (5,000,000 tons) and captured 95 of France's 125 blast furnaces. She had particularly developed heavy industries, machine and machine tools, electrical equipment and chemicals. She had no peer in Europe in these fields, and she indirectly affected the fighting power of other countries by her ability to withhold these materials from them. Although her industrial capacity was not much greater than that of the United Kingdom, it had been developing faster. Her equipment was much more modern, and it enjoyed the strategic advantage of being compactly situated in the center of the continent. Nonetheless, percentages on the average annual increase in manufacturing per head of the population, which indicate the rate of development in the use of mechanical means for production, disclose the fact that Germany had by no means advanced industrially to the point of assured victory. The United Kingdom in the period 1900 to 1913 was lagging far behind (0.7 per cent) in the rate of annual increase, but France (3.3), Italy (3.6), and the United States (3.2) were all ahead of Germany (2.5).

As soon as the war began the armies cried for shells and guns and men, for food, medical aids, clothes, transportation, everything. The demands increased with the fighting. Ammunition was at first particularly in short supply. The French national arsenals in September, 1914, produced 36,000 shells a day, enough to meet the need of a single army corps. General Joffre demanded 70,000 shells a day for his 75's (the main French cannon) alone; in December he received only 30,000 per day. British heavy artillery scarcely existed. In the arsenal at Woolwich several months after the outbreak of hostilities, Minister Lloyd George found stacks of empty shells being slowly filled by hand. Germany, the nation best prepared for war, possessed initially an adequate supply. In Russia everything was lacking except man power and courage. The French ambassador in St. Petersburg, Maurice Paleologue, recorded the lamentations in July 1915 of the chief of staff of the Russian ministry of war. Russia was producing not more than 24,000 shells a day, the general said, and rifles were even more scarce. In some regiments of infantry one third of the soldiers lacked guns and had to wait for the opportunity to pick up the rifles of those killed. The general marveled that the soldiers had not fled in panic. They were still willing to fight bravely, he declared, but as artillery and infantry ran out of munitions the army was "drowning in its own blood."

PLANNING A LONG WAR

Since the problems of production and distribution were common to all belligerents, the solutions attempted were similar. The effectiveness in coping with these difficulties varied according to the level of social achievement; but in all countries some civilians in addition to the military at the front quickly understood that time had become the essence of things and that the crisis could be met only by governmental planning in close cooperation with the entire society. The more individual initiative supplemented governmental direction of the war, the greater the success would be. If, as in Germany, government and industry were already closely allied in an authoritarian regime, the war strengthened the cooperation and the government exploited the full resources of the country until exhaustion brought defeat and overthrow of the existing system. If the government was subject to popular control, as in France and Great Britain, it was compelled by the public to dismiss incompetent persons and to use the total ability of its people. If the government did not trust its people, as in Austria-Hungary and Russia, it could not utilize the resources and its military effort would collapse.

In transforming a capitalistic economy and society into a military machine Germany acted first. Almost as soon as hostilities opened, the German industrialist Walter Rathenau advised preparation for a long war. He suggested that stock be taken of materials on hand and of future needs. The government immediately responded, and by the spring of 1915, with the assistance of committees of business men, it had surveyed the field and created the machinery for administering an approved plan. A War Raw Materials Department was set up in the Prussian Ministry of War, under which worked an array of War Industries Companies. These latter resembled joint-stock companies and were staffed by business and professional men, but they were government-controlled and made no profits. They allocated raw materials to companies at set prices and in fixed quantities for fulfilling government contracts. As a parallel, the government created the Central Purchasing Company to negotiate all purchases and sales abroad, securing thereby, on the most favorable terms, the materials essential for the conduct of the war. It could force down the prices for dairy products from Denmark, iron ore from Sweden, and so on, and it could prevent or restrict to a minimum the return sale to foreign countries of commodities like chemicals, iron and steel, and potash, which Germany required urgently at home. In these ways and by the ultilization of the extensive research laboratories, both public and private, for developing new or substitute products—one thinks especially of the Haber-Bosch process of extracting nitrogen from the air for use in explosives and in agriculture—the government was able to build new plants, open new industries, and shift the economy into war production. Consumers' goods industries that could not be converted to military purposes received short rations or were closed. The system worked well as long as materials were available. From 1916 on, when Hindenburg and Ludendorff took over the supreme command, Germany increasingly felt the truth of the fact that administrative efficiency and military dictatorship could not compensate for essential shortages.

Whereas in Germany the *Reichstag*, the popularly elected representative assembly, scarcely influenced the adjustment to the war, in France and Great Britain the parliament took an active part in forcing a speedy pace. The committees of the French Chamber of Deputies constantly prodded the ministry and kept alert for the correction of any shortcomings. The government placed a socialist, Albert Thomas, in charge of the provision of munitions, on the assumption that an able and patriotic representative of the workers would stir the latter to maximum exertion. In Great Britain Parliament passed, in March, 1915, the Defence of the Realm Act, which allowed the government to seize any factory or plant for the manufacture of war materials, to transfer a plant from one place to another, to take over empty housing for workmen, and to give contracts for war production priority over any other commitment. It set up the new Ministry of Munitions in May, 1915, and the government streamlined its own action by forming a War Council of ministers directly concerned with the conduct of the war.

Since neither France nor Great Britain had prepared for war on the scale of Germany's efforts, they fought for a time against heavy odds. The immediate loss of the industrial resources of her northeastern departments crippled France so severely that by way of replacement during the next four years she carried through practically a second industrial revolution. She succeeded so well in rebuilding her industries that, among the Allies, she became the leading producer of aircraft and artillery and at first supplied the United States Expeditionary Force with these articles. She built a chemical and an electric ferro-alloy industry to supply materials formerly obtained from Germany, and she expanded the production of hydroelectric power to replace lost coal. She introduced methods of mass production, hitherto scarcely used in France, into her munitions plants, thereby creating the basis for some postwar big industry. Under the energetic guidance of Lloyd George as minister of munitions, Great Britain followed suit, more slowly and with more emphasis upon private initiative, but just as effectively. Her large industrial capacity permitted a considerable transfer from the production of civilian articles to that of military supplies. She continued to turn out goods for export in order to preserve foreign markets and help pay the cost of the war, but she utilized her foreign investments in order to purchase essential goods directly. In this way she, and France and Italy as well, tapped the resources of the free world.

Although Austria-Hungary and Russia fought as enemies, their economic and governmental conditions were in many respects similar. Each had progressed in industrial production during the preceding decade or two at a rate faster than that of Germany, but in total capacity each lagged far behind that country. Much more serious were the incompetence of the government and the indifference and the increasing antagonism of the people toward the war effort.

In Austria-Hungary the nationalities were at first held together in sentiment by the tradition of Hapsburg rule, but the government did not dare to ask of them the sacrifices that were normal in a national state. Both government and peoples lacked the moral will necessary for a long, grueling conflict. Crises were not met with initiative and courage. Affairs were allowed more or less to drift. The actual military dictatorship set up at the outbreak of war continued until the death of Emperor Francis Joseph in November, 1916. Civil liberties were curtailed, martial law was introduced in large areas and ruthlessly enforced, as the army created a government paralleling the civilian bureaucracy and wielding more power. In Austria the *Reichsrat* had ceased to function for more than a decade before the war and was not convened from March, 1914, to May, 1917. During this period the government saw no advantage in convoking a body in which representatives of the different nationalities shouted at each other in nine different languages or dialects and sometimes engaged in fights. In Austria, therefore, the public was excluded from the conduct of the war. In Hungary, the government set its own conditions for cooperation with its Austrian counterpart. Count Tisza as premier ran affairs to his own taste, supported in the main by a Diet elected by the vote of only 6 per cent of the population; the rest of the Hungarians were not enfranchised. Ten million were landless peasants in a country where one third of the land was owned by a few hundred families. Notwithstanding the loyalty of the Magyar soldiers, these were not ideal conditions to make a war popular. In Austria the German population continued its bureaucratic, somewhat lethargic ways, and waited for governmental guidance. The Czechs and Poles in the north and their fellow Slavs in the south became increasingly unreliable as soldiers and as civilian subjects. The government and the army never knew whether the soldiers would fight or desert, and many deserted. That these soldiers would manifest great heroism in defence of the empire was more than the government could expect. In Hungary the subject Romanians, Slovaks, and Croats behaved with equal indifference.

In Russia the autocratic czar and his reactionary government so feared and hated the Duma that they convoked it rarely and allowed it to sit for only a few hours or a few days. Patriotic business men offered their services at once and the Union of the Zemstvos, or provincial governments, and the Union of Towns volunteered to organize and direct the medical services for the army. The bureaucracy and the czar met their proposals with hostility: an autocratic government could not admit that anything was amiss. The czar feared for his power; his wife, more autocratic than he was, hated these critical volunteers as enemies to her husband, her son, and the will of God. The minister of war, an indolent, irresponsible old aristocrat with a gift for smooth alibis, covered personal expenses from divers sources, signed statements about the availability of nonexistent munitions, and clung to his position. The bureaucrats did in time permit the Union of the Zemstvos and the Union of the Towns to assume a vast amount of responsibility for the care of the wounded and sick, for their families, even for providing military supplies; but they did so grudgingly. Special councils of officials and private individuals, exemplified by the War Industries Committee of industrialists, trade-unionists, and bureaucrats, were set up to increase production, and they did bring about some improvement. Nonetheless, autocracy preferred to try to preserve its authority rather than to allow the people the power to organize for a mass war. Engaged in a major conflict even as allies of well-organized, productive industrial powers, these two backward empires, Russia and Austria-Hungary, were unable to meet the competition, and in the order named they were the first to disintegrate.

Suggestions for Further Reading

ALBRECHT-CARRIÉ, RENÉ. *Italy from Napoleon to Mussolini.* See the Readings for Chapter 1.

ARON, RAYMOND. *Century of Total War.* Boston: The Beacon Press, 1955. Useful brief analysis of the impact of the world wars on society.

BROGAN, DENIS. *France under the Republic, 1870–1939.* See the Readings for Chapter 1.

CHAMBERS, FRANK P. *The War behind the War, 1914–1918.* London: Faber & Faber, Ltd., 1939. Indispensable for understanding political, social, and economic conditions.

CRUTTWELL, C. R. M. F. *A History of the Great War, 1914–1918.* Oxford: The Clarendon Press, 1934. Standard military history.

JASZI, OSCAR. *The Dissolution of the Hapsburg Monarchy.* See the Readings for Chapter 1.

LATOURETTE, KENNETH SCOTT. *A Short History of the Far East.* See the Readings for Chapter 1.

LENCZOWSKI, GEORGE. *The Middle East in World Affairs.* Ithaca, N. Y.: Cornell University Press, 1956. Standard survey of the history of the region from Egypt to Iran in the present century.

PARES, BERNARD. *The Fall of the Russian Monarchy.* See the Readings for Chapter 1.

ROSENBERG, ARTHUR. *The Birth of the German Republic, 1871–1918.* New York: Oxford University Press, 1931. Based on the evidence obtained by the German parliamentary committee investigating the causes of Germany's defeat in World War I. Excellent.

Chapter 3 · The End of World War I: The Revolutions

The outcome of World War I showed that a modern war is in the long run most effectively fought by people with a popular government able to repudiate incompetent personnel and inept policies in favor of effective ones. A nation under authoritarian rule cannot check on the efficiency of its government in the conduct of war. If it rebels against the rulers, it assures the defeat of the country. If it does not, it acquiesces in the continuation of war under leaders whose mistakes will bring about the same unhappy finale.

COLLAPSE OF RUSSIA

Russia's collapse, the first among the major belligerents, occurred simultaneously at the fighting front, on the home front, and in the government, and its aspects will be considered in that order.

It is estimated that at the end of 1914 Russia had under arms 6½ million men; a year later, 11½ million; at the end of 1916, 14½ million, and a year later 15½ million. The army lost, every six months, a million men killed and wounded, and half a million as prisoners. In 1916 the front army required a replacement of 300,000 men each month. Even for a country of 175,000,000 people this drain was unendurable. By the latter half of 1915 most infantry units had lost from 80 to 90 per cent of their officers. Command personnel had to be obtained from the ranks and recruited among the nonmilitary middle class. Since the soldiers required careful guidance, the decline in quality of the officers' corps proved to be a major source of weakness. The continued military hardships and disasters called for political explanation, which neither the professional nor the parvenu officers were trained to give. The amount of munitions increased in 1916, but General Brusilov was forced to cease the successful campaign against Austria-Hungary, in which the latter lost 1,500,000 men, because of exhaustion of supplies. The Allies shipped munitions and guns to Archangel and Vladivostok, only to learn months afterward that inadequate facilities for transportation had prevented their use. Desertion became common.

The home front felt the shortage as desperately as the soldiers and lacked the pressure of front-line responsibility to keep up its morale. The peasants did not understand the reasons for the war. Ignorance in general, and ignorance in particular of politics, because of the autocratic society, severely handicapped the preservation of morale. Propaganda for morale building was outlawed as contrary to the spirit of paternal rule. When the peasants received pay for their foodstuffs and other raw materials in paper roubles of declining value, they lost interest in producing for the market. When supplies of consumers' goods declined radically and the peasants found little or nothing to purchase, many grew food mainly for their own needs. The mobilization of man power and draft horses created shortages which especially crippled agricultural production. In this rich agricultural country, food became so scarce in the towns and cities that from 1915 on hunger riots broke out. Factory workers struck, not for political, but for economic reasons: they needed clothes and fuel and especially food. Although soldiers and officers at the front frequently sent food home to their relatives, the government was not able to obtain enough even for the army. Food was believed to be plentiful, and stories were current of its spoiling because of neglect; however, the system of transportation had decayed so rapidly that stocks could not be shipped to places of need. The government introduced some general measures of rationing but, being incapable of carrying out a program, it shifted this national responsibility to the municipalities. These could not possibly meet the need. The food queues grew longer and longer, the supplies less and less.

When Czar Nicholas II went to the front in August, 1915, to serve in person as commander in chief, he transferred his own incompetence from the capital to the field. The spirit in which he decided upon the move may be inferred from his remarks, "Perhaps a sin-offering is needed to save Russia. I shall be the victim. God's will be done!" He left the czarina at Petrograd in charge of the government. Her only son suffered from hemophilia, and in her anxiety to save his life she succumbed to the promises of charlatans. The last of these impostors, arriving at court in 1907, claimed to be a man of God. From his early behavior he had received the name of Rasputin, meaning "debaucheé"; his rule of conduct was, "Sin that you may repent." He did not learn to sign his name until he was an adult; his education came from experience. Canny about judging persons and situations, infinitely brazen in bearing, endowed with an iron constitution, he used hypnotism to stop the bleeding of the heir apparent and established control over the czarina. The increase of her power in 1915 meant that Rasputin ruled Russia. Since his notoriously evil ways repelled all persons of independent mind, whether liberals or conservatives, he strengthened the czarina in her aversion to anyone except devoted reactionary followers of the czar.

The czarina soon found her choice of high officials restricted to the least trusted and the least competent persons, men like Baron Stürmer, who was popularly believed to be pro-German and to be willing to betray his country, and Count Protopopov, who was suffering from mental derangement. This strange person handled a hunger strike in state munition factories in 1916 by sending some workers to the front and subjecting the others to military discipline. When criticized personally in the Duma, he threatened to dissolve that body and send the deputies to the front. Mikhail Rodzianko, the liberal deputy in the Duma, told the czar on New Year's Day, 1917, that there was not an honest or reliable man left in his entourage, that the rear of the army was full of rumors of treason. The czarina did not inform the czar of her action, Rodzianko said, and placed in authority incompetent and inexperienced persons. She was hated increasingly throughout the country and was believed even among the common people to be Germany's champion. When the czar asked, "Is it possible that for twenty-two years I have tried to act for the best, and that for twenty-two years I have done wrong?", Rodzianko replied, "Yes, Your Majesty, for twenty-two years you have done wrong."

March Revolution

When the revolution struck early in 1917, every class in Russia participated in it to some extent, as the people spontaneously repudiated their government. On the night of December 29, 1916, Prince Felix Yusupov, Purushkevitch, a Duma deputy of the extreme right, and the Grand Duke Dmitry killed Rasputin and threw his body in the Neva River. Persons in the highest circles, civilian and military, discussed openly the possibility of a palace revolution and the dethronement and assassination of the czar. When the Duma convened on February 27, 1917, the deputies demanded responsible government. The workers in the factories began to riot, the city mobs to surge. The peasants took to looting and seizing the property of the large estates. The soldiers and sailors in garrisons rebelled against the authority of their officers; many lower-rank officers turned against their superiors. When the news of trouble reached the front lines, soldiers deserted to start for home. Officers who tried to control them were frequently shot. When troops were sent to suppress the riots in the cities, most of them either disappeared en route or refused to oppose the rebels; some even joined them. The conditions of near-chaos forced in quick succession the abdication of the czar in March, the fall of the dynasty, and the establishment of a provisional government of mild conservatives and liberals under the premiership of Prince Lvov.

The provisional government was unprepared to rule. It came from the fourth Duma, elected in 1912 by a small body of voters and discredited in the eyes of the public by its feeble record. Although it drafted a program that provided for fulfilling international commitments by continuing the war and that called for a constitutional assembly elected by universal manhood suffrage, the members of the ministry had almost no experience in governing. They made disastrous mistakes; for example, they abolished the hated police without any replacement. Being opposed to authoritarian rule and uncertain about policies necessary to preserve national unity, they delegated responsibility to officials in charge of local administration. Deprived of the flow of orders from the capital, bureaucrats had no idea what to do, and the country began to disintegrate.

The government from its inception faced competition in the Soviet of Workers and Soldiers Deputies. This organization of March, 1917, was composed of left-wing representatives in the Duma, the labor members of the War Industries Committee, and delegates from cooperatives and trade-unions, invited from factories and regiments in Moscow to a conference. It claimed to speak for the masses, and it immediately began to assume functions which the provisional government left unattended. It regulated the food supply, organized a workers' militia to take the place of the police, and issued an order entrusting the control and use of arms to elected committees of soldiers and sailors. By these means it undermined the instruments of authority, because the workers and soldiers trusted the Soviet rather than the Duma.

Although the Soviet did not intend to usurp central power, it was pushed by events in that direction. Dominated by Mensheviks (moderate Socialists who believed in parliamentary government under freedom) and Social Revolutionaries (advocates of nationalization of the soil), it wished to support the provisional government in continuing the war and in executing democratic reforms. At the same time it had to heed the demands of the people for food and for peace, and of the peasants for land. A vice-president of the Soviet, the Social Revolutionary Alexander Kerensky, became minister of justice in the provisional government, against the wishes of his Socialist colleagues, but he could not draw the two bodies into agreement. Under pressure of mass demonstrations against the war, Prince Lvov in May, 1917, reorganized the ministry, including in it three Social Revolutionaries and two Mensheviks, and in July greater disorder caused Kerensky to become prime minister. His government faced the multiple task of continuing the war, restoring order, providing food especially in the cities, and at the same time of reforming the government and society, transferring land to the peasants, and bringing peace. It tried to cooperate with liberals and democrats in achieving moderate change instead of radical transformation. When it did not act speedily to bring reform, the revolution turned to the radical Bolshevik group.

An example of conditions may be offered by citing the attempt of General Kornilov in August to replace the government by military dictatorship. Kornilov planned to march on Petrograd with Caucasian, Cossack, and other divisions thought to be loyal. He ignored a decree of dismissal, issued by Kerensky against him. When the general ordered the advance, he met difficulty. The railway workers sabotaged the trains carrying his troops; the telegraph operators refused to send staff messages; and agitators mingled in his divisions, persuading the troops not to fight. The attempt to restore the prerevolutionary regime collapsed. It was evident not merely that the officers had lost control of the troops but that the legal government under Kerensky lacked military support. The final battle for Russia would be fought between the popular forces of the moderate Socialists and the Bolsheviks, or minority radicals.

Bolsheviks Seize Power

During the first weeks of the revolution the Bolsheviks, since their numbers were few, pursued a cautious policy. They were led by persons like Lev Kamenev, who believed that, according to Marxian dogma, the bourgeoisie must first revolt against autocracy and introduce a liberal form of government and society. The Communists were to wait until this step had been completed before staging the proletarian revolution. Kamenev interpreted the events of March, 1917, as a capitalist transformation: as capitalism grew it would create a proletariat, which would provide the social basis for a true Socialist revolt and creation of a Communist society. Then in April, 1917, Lenin arrived in Russia. The German government had permitted him to cross Germany from Switzerland in a sealed train, counting on his increasing disorder in Russia, which in turn would relieve pressure on the eastern front.

Lenin denounced Kamenev's strategy and offered his own interpretation of events. "The peculiarity of the present situation in Russia," he stated, "is that it represents a *transition* from the first stage of the revolution, which, because of the inadequate organization and insufficient class-consciousness of the proletariat, led to the assumption of power by the bourgeoisie—to its second stage which is to place power in the hands of the proletariat and the poorest strata of the peasantry." "To that extent," he asserted, "the bourgeois, or the bourgeois-democratic, revolution in Russia is *completed*." In the Soviet of Workers and Soldiers Deputies, he said, "you have 'revolutionary-democratic dictatorship of the proletariat and peasantry' already realized in life." "Theory," he said to Kamenev, "is grey, but green is the eternal tree of life." The Bolshevik party came over to this view, whereupon Lenin initiated a program for gaining majority support in the soviets in Petrograd, Moscow, and elsewhere, and for using these to destroy the provisional government.

The conditions suited ideally Bolshevik machinations. Almost all the leaders had lived for years in exile and could not have returned without the March revolution. They formed the only group with a definite objective and a concrete plan for action. Their initial goal was to seize power;

their strategy called for a relatively small, absolutely disciplined party of fanatics taking advantage of the chaos to gain control. They stood for a program of three points: peace at any price; factories to the workers; land to the peasants. The slogans were simple and understandable and could be executed at once by popular action. The soldiers could stop fighting, shoot their officers, and fraternize with the enemy; the workers could seize the factories, the peasants the land. Before the revolution the entire Russian Social Democratic party, then composed of moderate Mensheviks and radical Bolsheviks, had possessed only 40,000 active members. Factory workers, that is, the proletariat, supposedly the backbone of the Marxian movement everywhere, had numbered only 1½ million of a population of 175 million. The membership of the party increased during the year 1917 to merely half a million; but it included the toughest, the best disciplined, and the most ruthless of all political activists. It contained many soldiers and sailors with guns in hand, and the party understood how to manipulate mobs. In November, 1917, Lenin's group overthrew the Kerensky government and assumed power. A small corps of determined radicals, practically unknown except to the police, had performed what even to its members seemed a miracle. Seated precariously in his post of unexpected eminence, Lenin said, "I feel dizzy."

MILITARY RULE IN GERMANY

Writing toward the end of 1917, the German General Erich Ludendorff explained the Russian Revolution, and through inference forecast the ultimate outcome of the war in his own country, by calling the revolution an inevitable consequence of the way of conducting the war. He contrasted former wars fought by armies with the present war fought by peoples. Since defeat now means conquest not merely of armies but of people, he said, the government receives the blame and is overthrown; where, as in Russia, the entire system is rotten, collapse becomes universal. At the time Ludendorff did not apply the theory to his own country. He as quartermaster general of the German armies and Paul von Hindenburg as the commander in chief intimately associated politics with strategy, however, when from 1916 on they organized the country for total war. Neither general understood the nature of politics. The elderly Hindenburg had lived exclusively in the army, lacked imagination about problems of society, and was noted for his limited mentality and his matter-of-fact reactions. In 1914 he said, "It [the war] agrees with me like a visit to a health resort." His inseparable partner, the tense and cocksure commoner, Ludendorff, showed himself irascible and impatient.

Upon their appointment to the high command, Hindenburg and Ludendorff immediately demanded that the full strength of the nation be concentrated on the war. They contrasted the ability of the enemy to dispose of the factories and man power of the neutral world with the Central Powers' restriction to local resources. In order to win victory, they declared, the production of agriculture and industry must be devoted exclusively to war purposes. The whole nation must serve the Fatherland; all other matters must be subordinated to the struggle for the survival of the state and the independence, welfare and future of the people. The army drafted the Hindenburg Plan and in December, 1916, forced the *Reichstag* to approve it in the form of the Auxiliary Service Act. This law ordered the compulsory employment at home of all males between the ages of seventeen and sixty years not in combat forces; it concentrated employment in certain occupations; and it authorized a special body of the war ministry known as the Supreme War Office, assisted by an advisory committe of the *Reichstag*, to administer the program. Women and children were encouraged in every way to work; industries not contributing to the war effort were closed down; trade-union rights were restricted; the rights of assembly and of free speech were curbed; transportation was rationed. By May, 1917, German industry was producing three times the munitions of the previous year. Critics argued that the regimentation was superfluous, that it could not compensate for absolute shortages; but the army obtained supplies for two more years of war.

Strategy for Total Victory

With the economy and man power placed under military control, the high command outlined its strategy for total victory. It considered the western front decisive and advocated the starvation of Great Britain by unrestricted submarine warfare. The stalemate in the military operations on land was to be broken by naval success. With 120 submarines of the most modern type, the Admiralty expected to sink 600,000 tons of shipping a month and within six months force Great Britain to surrender. The civilian ministers opposed the plan as certain to bring the United States into the conflict against Germany. The military and naval command belittled the importance of the American country, arguing that the people would be reluctant to fight and slow to prepare and in any event unable against the submarines to land a soldier in France. On February 1, 1917, Germany loosed the submarines against shipping, and on April 17 the United States declared war. Many other nations followed suit.

The unpolitical thinking of the military command may be seen from the fact that it undertook intensive submarine warfare just at the time when revolution weakened Russia. With the eastern front collapsing, one may ask why Germany risked war with the largest neutral power in the world. The explanation seems to lie in the self-confidence of the high command, its ignorance of the material and especially the moral reserves of free peoples, and its determination to expand German territory in Eastern Europe. The generals shared the war objectives of the most imperialistic groups in Germany, namely, the Pan-German League, the big agrarians, the big industrialists. They all sought to maintain the existing authoritarian form of government and society. The agrarians wished the annexation or domination of vast areas in Poland and Russia, to gain space for more big estates to augment the power of the Junkers, or landed nobility. The big industrialists sought to control the industrial resources of Belgium and northeastern France. Thereby the power of agrarian and industrial forces in Germany would remain balanced. At the same time German military potential would become impregnable. The *Reich* would dominate the continent; it would acquire sufficient new wealth easily to pay the costs of the war and to reward the people for their sufferings. Germany would continue on a vaster, militarily more secure scale than before, to act as an authoritarian country dominated by Junkers, paternalistic industrialists, and militarists. For these reasons the German high command kept a million soldiers in the east after the revolution had knocked out Russia as a military power, and in the west ran the political risk of submarine warfare.

Constitutional Reform and Peace Objectives

The attitude of the dominant military figures and of their civilian supporters may be seen in the handling of two crucial issues that came up in the *Reichstag,* that of constitutional reform and that of peace objectives, including the negotiation of the treaty of Brest Litovsk with Bolshevik Russia. The two issues were connected in that it was the advocates of constitutional reform who demanded a peace of understanding, whereas the opponents of reform were the imperialists.

In the first months of the war all parties represented in the *Reichstag* had accepted a political truce. The Social Democrats voted for the war credits, and the first *Reichstag* deputy in the army to be killed happened to be a Social Democrat. In spite of their supposed Marxian internationalism, the Socialists proved loyal patriots, their stand being made easier for them by hostility to autocratic Russia. The radical wing of the party quickly broke with this policy as un-Marxian. As the war continued, the parties of the left and center, that is, the Social Democrats, the Progressives, and the Catholic Centrists, began to question the government about peace objectives and constitutional reforms. By 1916 they were pressing the government to open negotiations for peace. In the spring of 1917 they advocated a peace of understanding and denounced as imperialists those who would continue the war. In July 1917, discouraged over the results of submarine warfare, a majority in the *Reichstag* passed a resolution in favor of a peace of lasting reconciliation among nations. With such a peace, it said, forcible acquisition of territory and political, economic, or financial coercion were irreconcilable. It rejected all plans for economic isolation after the war, called for freedom of the seas, and urged the creation of international judicial organizations. "As long, however, as the enemy governments will not enter upon such a peace," it declared, "as long as they threaten Germany and her allies with conquest and coercion, the German people will stand together as a man, unflinchingly persevere, and fight until their own and their allies' right to life and development are secured." The high command opposed such negotiations and brought about the fall of Chancellor Bethmann-Hollweg, in favor of the appointment of a nonentity, a lesser official named Michaelis, who buried the peace resolution with the remark, "as I understand it." In other words, he would interpret it as he pleased.

The high command's kind of peace was revealed in the treaty of Brest Litovsk with Bolshevik Russia in March, 1918. Russia had to recognize the independence of Finland, the Baltic provinces, Poland, and the Ukraine, and to cede to Turkey the territories of Kars, Ardahan, and Batum. Whereas Finland was expected to preserve her independence while leaning on Germany, the Ukraine was tied to the Central Powers by a commercial treaty which was expected to assure them a steady and continuing flow of food. As for the Baltic provinces, Chancellor von Hertling, who had replaced the inept Michaelis, declared in the *Reichstag* that they should come under the protection of the German Empire. Almost the same statement applied to Poland. These vast areas should be politically and economincally dependent upon Germany and open to German economic and cultural development. Such was the reply of the military to the *Reichstag*'s peace resolution of the previous July; yet the same *Reichstag* overwhelmingly approved the treaty of Brest Litovsk. The left-wing Independent Socialists alone voted against it; the right-wing Majority Socialists avoided responsibility by not voting.

The question of constitutional reform included a multitude of issues, but two in particular aroused most discussion and, in the popular mind, symbolized the rest. One concerned the introduction of ministerial responsibility in the *Reichstag*. The Constitution of 1871, without stating to what or whom, declared the chancellor to be responsible. In consequence, he had been able to wield a large amount of personal authority by playing off the Kaiser against the *Reichstag*. By 1917, and especially in the last year of the war, the liberal, the Catholic, and the left-wing parties were discussing the possibility of introducing into Germany parliamentary control over the executive as exercised in Great Britain and France. The second issue involved the election law in Prussia, which assured the political domination of the upper classes and gave advantage especially to the Conservative party. As the war continued, an increasing number of people began to question the morality of the system. They declared that the masses sacrificing their lives for the fatherland should be rewarded by the introduction of equal manhood suffrage and the secret ballot, both of which the empire as a whole already enjoyed. The justice of the claim impressed the Emperor William II, who in 1917 promised reform. But since the Conservatives, especially the Junkers, and indeed most of the upper classes, depended largely upon this election system to preserve their political power and thereby many economic advantages, they rejected the reform, and the high command supported them. The Prussian election law remained unchanged until the loss of the war brought down the entire system of government.

THE DISMEMBERMENT OF RUSSIA AT BREST LITOVSK—(1918)

Except during the winter of 1916–1917, the German people did not suffer severely from lack of nourishment. They became short of fats and milk, and the supply of staples diminished; but the government early introduced a rationing system that distributed food and essential materials equitably and at fair prices. Agricultural production suffered from lack of fertilizer, man power, and draft animals, and the hope of obtaining food from the Ukraine failed to materialize. Food scarcity, however, exerted far less effect upon morale than the fact that the people saw no end to the sacrifices demanded. Insight into popular thinking may be gained from the list of demands put forth by the strikers in munitions plants in Berlin in January, 1918.

(1) The speedy bringing about of peace without annexations or indemnities, on the basis of the self-determination of peoples. . . . (2) Delegates of the workers of all countries to be invited to participate in the peace negotiations. As regards Germany in particular: (3) More liberal food supply by the control of food stocks in places of production and in warehouses, for the purpose of insuring an even distribution among all classes of the people. (4) The immediate revocation of the state of siege. The complete restoration of the right of assembly as well as that of free discussion in the press and at public meetings. The restoration, without delay, of the laws for the protection of women and children. The cancellation of all measures of the military authorities which interfere with the activity of trade unions and the prohibition of all fresh restrictions. (5) The abolition of the military control of industrial undertakings. (6) The immediate release of all persons convicted or arrested for political action. (7) The drastic democratization of the entire state organism in Germany, beginning with the introduction of the general, equal, direct, and secret vote for all men and women of over 20 years for the Prussian Diet.[1]

The program of reforms might have come from any group of democratic middle-class citizens as well as from workers. The high command handled the Berlin strike and similar strikes elsewhere by refusing to negotiate with the participants, prohibiting any meetings of the strikers' delegates, suspending *Vorwärts,* the official journal of the Social Democratic party, placing the factories in Berlin under military control and the city under a state of siege, and calling into military service the men who refused to return to work. The military command had one solution for all problems —the use of physical force whether in combating the foreign enemy or in handling workers of its own nation who wanted food, peace, and equal suffrage.

DISINTEGRATION OF AUSTRIA-HUNGARY

The accession to the throne of the Emperor Charles in November, 1916, made no actual difference in the situation of Austria-Hungary. The new ruler was willing to sacrifice some Hapsburg autocratic power for his people, but he inherited difficulties beyond his capacity to overcome. Foreign Minister Count Ottokar Czernin wrote him on April 12, 1917 that the empire was exhausted. It lacked both material and human resources. Undernourishment had caused despair among all classes, and there was danger of revolution. The easy overthrowal of the Russian monarchy

[1] Ralph Haswell Lutz, ed., *Fall of the German Empire, 1914–1918* (2 vols.; Stanford, Calif.: Stanford University Press, 1932), II, 233.

alarmed him, for the same course of events could take place in Germany and Austria-Hungary. The Hapsburg Empire was particularly susceptible to influence from the Russian Revolution because of the kinship of the Slavic peoples. Believing that Germany would also have to make peace within the next few months or succumb to revolution, the count urged the emperor to withdraw from the war.

Count Czernin's prediction proved to be essentially correct. As the war continued, Austria-Hungary showed less and less ability to sustain the effort. The government called together the *Reichsrat* in Austria on May 30, 1917, in the faint hope that by allowing the representatives a part in the war effort it might arouse a sentiment of loyalty. Thereupon a Czech deputy read a manifesto demanding "that the Hapsburg-Lorraine Monarchy be converted into a federation of free and equal national states" and requesting "the union of all branches of the Czechoslovak race in a democratic Czech State." A Yugoslav deputy called for the creation of an autonomous democratic state of the Serbs, Croats, and Slovenes under Hapsburg rule. The convocation of the *Reichsrat* provided the nationality leaders with a public forum for spreading revolutionary demands, and a political amnesty granted by the Austrian government at the time turned loose more agitators for the same cause. Representatives in exile of each major nationality group, the Poles, the Czechs, and Slovaks, the South Slavs, set up a committee to further the cause of national independence among the Allied powers. The polyglot empire was being pulled to pieces.

The elimination of Count Tisza as Hungarian premier in May, 1917, scarcely improved relations of the two parts of the empire. Hungary, normally a food exporter, continued to withhold supplies from Austria, unless compensated in manufactured goods, and to quarrel over the employment of troops. In both Austria and Hungary the bureaucracies were incapable of holding down the price of food and other essentials. Townsmen suffered especially, for wages and salaries lagged far behind the price level. Either from lack of courage or from want of efficiency, the government instituted no universal system of rationing and left that responsibility to local officials. In the winter of 1917–1918 near-starvation reigned in the Austrian towns and cities. Workers received a ration of 1,100 grams of bread a week, and the townspeople of Hungary fared little better. As the year 1918 opened, workers struck and sailors on the ships in the Adriatic mutinied. Picked troops were stationed in the interior of the empire to suppress rebellions. Although the peasants produced food and ate it in plentiful quantities, and although other goods like clothing were available, the black market absorbed the supplies. The end of the war found the administration of both parts of the empire in a state of collapse.

SUPERIORITY OF THE ALLIED SYSTEM OF CIVILIAN RULE

As long as the stalemate on the western front continued, each side used approximately the same strategy and tactics as the other. The opponents differed markedly, however, in the organization of the civilian front. Whereas Germany fitted all civilian participation into the framework of the military and civil bureaucracies, the Allies adapted their organization and habits of self-government to the situations that developed. The contrast helps to explain the meaning of the Allied objective to "make the world safe for democracy."

The German system of government proved to be inflexible. The chancellorship, which could not expand the popular base of its power, lost prestige to the high command. In 1916 Hindenburg and Ludendorff took over supreme civil as well as military authority. In France and Great Britain ministries were changed, and in both countries coalition governments were formed. In France the socialists contributed to the ministries the key figure, Albert Thomas, and in Great Britain several members of the Labor party joined their Liberal and Conservative colleagues in giving the government a national character. Prime Minister Herbert Asquith began the process in Great Britain and Lloyd George, his successor in December, 1916, continued it. In France the cabinets of Aristide Briand, Alexandre Ribot, and Georges Clemenceau, to mention the most important, all sought to be broadly representative.

Democratic adaptation may be seen in the relations between the civil and the military authorities. The French and British, and one may add the Italian, governments were strong enough to hold the generals in check. In Great Britain the cabinet contained so many able civilians that the main difficulty lay in preserving teamwork. The military and naval chiefs grumbled and growled at civilian direction, but they were unable to prevent the ministers from interfering even in questions of strategy. General Joffre, from 1914 to 1917 commander in chief of the French army, succeeded better than his British colleagues in keeping an upper hand. In the first year of the war he made military headquarters into a second government, with its own bureaucracy for directing the economy. He extended the geographical area of martial law until it included a great part of the country. He refused to supply the government with any information relative to operations. When in 1915 information reached the government criticizing the adequacy of the defenses around Verdun, Joffre replied in December to the ministry, "I cannot be party to soldiers under my command bringing before the government, by channels other than the hierarchic channel, complaints or protests concerning the execution of my orders. . . . It is calculated to disturb profoundly the spirit of discipline in the army." He could not maintain independence very long. The ministers and the committees of the French parliament attacked the expansion of military authority, until in 1916 they regained control. When in November, 1917, Clemenceau became premier, the generals confronted a fighter, a man seventy-six years of age and trained (for fifty years) in ruthless political battle. "War," he said, "is too serious a business to be left to the generals."

Defeat of Submarine War

The advantage of the Western method is shown in the story of oceanic shipping, particularly with respect to Great Britain. Trying to conduct the war with a policy of "Business as usual," the British did not introduce until 1917 other than rather haphazard control of shipping. German submarine warfare forced radical change. British losses averaged 51,000 tons a month in 1914; 74,000 tons a month in 1915; 103,000 tons a month in 1916. In February, 1917, the British lost 310,868 tons, and British, Allied, and neutral losses amounted to 532,000 tons. In March the respective figures reached 352,344 tons and 599,000 tons, and in April 526,447 tons and 869,000 tons. First Sea Lord Admiral Jellicoe saw no solution, but Prime Minister Lloyd George immediately met the emergency. He established a new ministry of shipping, placed the experience shipper, Sir Joseph Maclay, in charge, started a program of building more than a million tons a year, purchased ships abroad, and cooperated closely with Britain's allies. Over the strenuous opposition of Admiral Jellicoe and of most naval chiefs, the government introduced the system of shipping in convoys escorted by destroyers and other vessels of war. By these means the British and their allies thwarted the submarine. From the middle of 1917 until November, 1918, 16,657 ships reached or left British shores in convoy with a loss of 0.71 per cent. When American soldiers were transported to France, not a single ship was sunk.

Control of the Economy

The British government hesitated to introduce state control of the economy and of man power. Not until May, 1916, did it pass a Universal Military Service Act; but by the end of the year every able-bodied male served in the army or navy, in industry, agriculture, transport, or the essential professions. As the shortage of man power grew, women and young people to an increasing extent were drawn into the economy. In February, 1917, the Restricted Occupations Order was promulgated, like its German counterpart of 1916, giving priority to occupations essential to the war effort. The government could shut down industries, transfer plants, build new ones, move labor from one place to another; in other words, it exercised the power necessary to meet the emergency of war.

That this was a people's war became evident from the relations between government and labor. The officials and the trade-union leaders in

Britain instituted very early a program of popular education to persuade the workers that they must temporarily give up some of their trade-union rights. Time and man power were both so short that the unionists recognized the necessity of placing nonunion workers on jobs normally filled by unionists, of using less skilled workers in the positions of skilled ones, of shifting essential workers to plants in other localities. The trade-unionists knew that labor's bargaining power had greatly increased with the war shortages, but they patriotically sacrificed their advantage. The Munitions of War Act of 1915 had created a system of compulsory arbitration, and the government formed Commissions of Enquiry which settled grievances before they led to strikes. Strikes were not forbidden; they were handled by persuasion. In 1917 the country showed less labor trouble than in any year in its history. Pacifism was almost completely absent. When the international socialists called a conference at Stockholm in 1917 to try to bring about peace, the government approved attendance of delegates from the Labor party; but the Seamen's Union refused to man the ship to carry the delegation. France dealt with her labor problems in about the same way. Public opinion kept most workers on the job, but in neither country was a worker who asked for a higher wage or who went on strike *ipso facto* regarded as a traitor.

Food shortages occurred in both France and Great Britain. In the former country they were met early by official rationing. Great Britain depended upon private initiative to supply the food, until in 1916 shortages on a considerable scale began to be felt. Then the government rapidly assumed control. It encouraged agriculture to increase production, it took over the purchase and shipping of food from abroad in bulk, bought that produced at home, fixed prices, and attended to just distribution. It appointed fifteen food commissioners in the main centers of the country, forming local food committees "composed of persons well acquainted with conditions and possessing the confidence of the public" to assist in local distribution. In time 94 per cent of everything eaten and drunk in Great Britain was subject to government regulation. Food lines vanished as the people obtained sufficient food at prices within their means.

Morale

In April and May, 1917, there occurred in France one of those near catastrophes, the handling of which tests the character of a nation. French Commander in Chief General Nivelle had directed an offensive against the German lines. Repulsed with huge losses, French soldiers in the sector of the action expressed disapproval of the strategy by insubordination and even mutiny. For several days only two reliable divisions stood between Soissons and Paris. The soldiers were angry, not at their officers, but at "the drinkers of blood" at headquarters and in the government who, they said, senselessly ordered them against German machine guns and barbed

Trench warfare in World War I: the war of attrition. —Bettmann Archive Photo.

Duels between one-man pursuit planes, a French invention, characterized World War I aerial combat. The use of airplanes for observation was introduced by the Germans in 1914, and tactical bombing and strafing were begun by the Americans in the fall of 1918. —Bettmann Archive photo.

French whippet tanks in the Argonne. The military tank was introduced by the British in 1916. —Bettmann Archive photo.

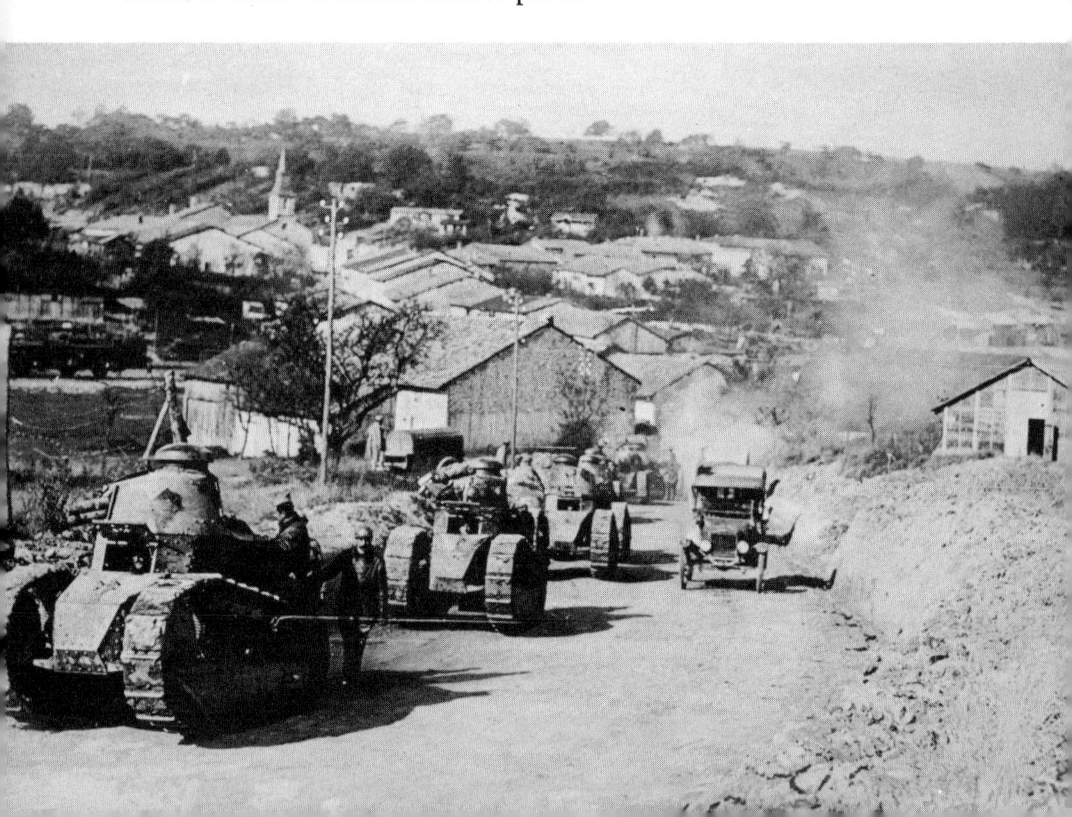

A torpedo boat, seen from a German man-of-war. —Brown Bros. photo.

The U.S.S. Narwhal, commissioned in 1909, was the first submarine equipped with diesel engines and a radio. —Official U.S. Navy photo.

Types of German war prisoners. —Brown Bros. photo.

A munitions dump of barbed wire shells is tended by Italian soldiers; their horses (not yet replaced by more modern means of transportation) are corralled in background. —Brown Bros. photo.

A captive balloon. From its vantage point, 300 yards above the ground, an observer could direct artillery fire by telephone. —Brown Bros. photo.

Royalty by divine right: Czar Nicholas II of Russia and his son. —Brown Bros. photo.

Lenin, addressing a group in Petrograd, 1918. He appealed for a revolution to accelerate the Marxian dialectical process and overthrow capitalism. —Brown Bros. photo.

Adviser to royalty: the inspired Rasputin—mystic, healer, charlatan. —Brown Bros. photo.

Street scene in Petrograd, 1917. A workers' demonstration is suppressed by the police of the Kerensky government. —Sovfoto.

ERNST BARLACH, *Head* (detail, from the War Monument in the Cathedral of Güstrow, Germany), 1927. The memorial is in the form of an angel suspended from the ceiling in a horizontal position. —The Museum of Modern Art, New York; gift of Edward M. M. Warburg.

The Big Four at the Versailles Conference of 1919: Orlando of Italy, Lloyd George of Great Britain, Clemenceau of France, and Wilson of the United States. —Underwood & Underwood photo.

wire. Finding no cause for alarm among the workers and no outside agitation among the soldiers, the government stopped the attack and replaced Nivelle by Henri Pétain. General Pétain put only twenty-three mutineers to death, and instead of imposing further severe sentences he visited the trenches, took a personal interest in the soldiers, instructed the officers to associate more closely with their men than before, and arranged for informal lectures and pamphlets about the purpose of the war. The army recovered, and parading troops in Paris were heartily cheered.

History has shown that wars tend to enhance popular concern about government and political life. People who are asked to sacrifice their lives want to know why. In Germany the military and the authoritarian government succeeded in preventing reform. In France and Great Britain the election system had already returned popularly elected deputies to responsible parliaments, but the system needed some improvement. The French waited until 1919 to introduce a new election law, but the British passed one early in 1918. The law sharply reduced plural voting and introduced women's suffrage. The House of Commons approved the innovation by a vote of seven to one.

UNITED STATES DECLARES WAR

The United States and many other neutral countries ultimately entered the conflict primarily because of the nature of the war. Trench fighting and a contest in attrition forced the neutrals with food, materials, and services for sale to become major objects of attention on the part of the belligerents. Each side soon declared a blockade of the other, which it sought to enforce by physical action. The British and the French used the navy as well as their multifarious trade connections; the Germans, realizing that their navy was too small to compete with that of the Allies, relied upon submarines. Being in command of the seas, the Allies declared almost everything, including food, destined for enemy ports to be contraband, and seized such cargoes. German submarines fought silently from under water, depended for success essentially upon surprise, and torpedoed the opposing ships. Both contraband goods and passengers sank; and as passenger liners frequently carried materials of use for war and as no submarine captain was able to investigate the cargoes of the ships he attacked, the German blockade, in contrast to that of the British and French, involved the loss of lives, not only of enemies but of neutrals as well. For this reason the sinking of Allied liners aroused the anger of the United States. The Germans protested that the British and French blockade affected the lives of women and children and was more inhuman than the German sinking of ships, but such arguments failed to impress the neutral public. The Allies, in control of the transoceanic cable lines, censored the news from Germany that reached the United States. Their propaganda emphasizing common democratic ideals proved more effective than the German. The Allies borrowed $2 billion from American private interests and stimulated the expansion of production of manufactures and food for their open and ravenous markets. By gearing the American and other neutral economies to their needs, the Allies created a material interest in their victory.

The sincerity of the United States effort to keep out of the war showed in 1916 in the outcome of the presidential campaign. Woodrow Wilson won over Charles Evans Hughes primarily on the slogan, "He kept us out of war." The victory was gained by a narrow margin, however, and Wilson doubted his ability to preserve neutrality. He had spoken so sharply to the Germans in the preceding spring that they had called off their submarine campaign. When on February 1, 1917, they suddenly revived it, the President lost no time in preparing for war. He clothed his war message to Congress on April 2 in high moral terms about defending democracy, but his exalted language also expressed American interest in preventing Germany from controlling Europe and upsetting the European and in turn the Atlantic balance of power. A warning of the probable results of German domination over Europe had been supplied a month earlier by the German offer of an alliance to Mexico, with the acquisition of Texas, New Mexico, and Arizona held out as bait. The proposal became known immediately to the United States government and people. On April 6, 1917, the United States declared war on Germany, and later in the year on the other Central Powers except Bulgaria. A conflict between nationalistic Serbs and Austro-Hungarian imperialists had now reached global dimensions.

Although the United States had been producing goods for the Allies, the outbreak of war caught the country unprepared. It lacked army trucks; it depended largely upon the Allies for airplanes and tanks, upon Britain in particular for heavy artillery, and upon France for many smaller guns. It expected the war to continue for some years and aimed at peak production in 1919. Nine and one-half billion dollars credit was now extended to the Allies, and materials continued to pour in to Europe. The American Selective Service Act was immediately passed, and the first 12,000 troops reached France in June, 1917. A year later 10,000 men were shipped across daily, and by the end of 1918 the United States army was 3,600,000 strong, with 2,086,000 in the European theater.

The entry of the United States on the side of the Allies occurred at approximately the time of the liberal revolution in Russia. It counterbalanced the loss to the Allies of Russia by the Bolshevik Revolution and of the severe defeat of Italy at Caporetto in the autumn of that year. The collapse of Russia has already been discussed; but a comparison between the situation of that country and that of Italy will help to explain why, in spite of defeats, the latter state remained in the war. Italy had not been much more competent than Russia about playing its expected part in the war. Each of the two states lacked materials and morale for the grueling competition. Because Russia was so large and so isolated she could be aided very little by the Allies. By contrast, Italy, although far poorer in raw materials and in military potential, could be reached and assisted with materials, troops, and morale builders. The effects of poverty and the activity of a large pacifist party, the Socialists, could be countered, particularly since the Italian front did not figure as one of major operations. When the Germans joined the Austrians in the attack at Caporetto to throw the Italian army back to the Piave River with a loss of 6,000 square miles of territory and 600,000 men, the combined resources of a shocked Italy and of the Allies stalled the enemy and kept the country in the war.

INTER-ALLIED COUNCILS

The year 1917 marked a change in the organization of Allied cooperation. Joint international action on economic and military problems had up to that time been confined to individual arrangements. The recognition in 1917 that victory required the joint use of resources, especially those of the United States, caused the establishment of a large number of inter-Allied councils, on Maritime Transport, on War Purchases and Finance, on Munitions, on Food, on Railway Transportation, and on other problems. One concerned itself with rationing the neutrals and pressing them economically to reduce their trade with the Central Powers and to employ their ships and materials for the cause of the Allies. The council on maritime transport allocated shipping space. Composed of representatives of the relevant departments in each government, it remained in permanent session and sanctioned the shipping of every ton of food and munitions, of every man—in fact, of everything transported by sea. The other councils were organized in a similar way. Each country received attention according to an approved plan; prices were kept down by price fixing and by the substitution of government purchases for haphazard competition.

The system of civilian cooperation set an example which the military leaders were finally induced to follow. In November, 1917, a loosely organized Supreme War Council was set up. In April of the next year, under the urging particularly of the irrepressible Lloyd George and under the even more effective teaching of the disaster at Caporetto and a renewed German offensive, the Allies appointed the French General Foch commander in chief of the Allied Forces in France. The Allies never unified the planning and execution of the war as a whole, however, and Foch's authority suffered from decided limitations. He was to direct strategy, but tactical authority remained with the commander in chief of each national army. Each commander could appeal to his government "if, in his opinion, his army is endangered by reason of instructions received from General Foch." Foch was dissatisfied with the restrictions, and the national commanders disliked the arrangement for the opposite reason. The system worked sufficiently well in the remaining months of the war to secure victory.

ALLIED IMPERIALIST OBJECTIVES

The few gestures during the war toward a negotiated peace were so feeble that they only deserve slight mention. The pope in 1916 and President Wilson prior to the entry of the United States into the war tried to mediate, without success. Neither Germany nor the Allies would consider any conclusion short of total victory. After the accession to the throne of the Emperor Charles in 1916, the Austro-Hungarian government put out feelers, but the Allies ignored them.

As Clemenceau said after the war, in 1914 all the powers had been imperialistic. The opportunities and obligations of combat whetted their appetite. As for Germany, we have seen that two broad groups emerged, one favoring a peace of understanding, the other demanding a peace of conquest. On the Allied side during the first years of the war statesmen spoke in imperialistic terms. Particularly in 1917 and after, President Wilson, statesmen from the British dominions, and numerous prominent individuals and important groups in the European countries began to denounce imperialism and to demand a just and definitive peace. Both programs were to be represented among the Allied statesmen at the peace making.

Until exposed by the Bolsheviks in 1917–1918, the imperialist ambitions among the Allies were kept secret. Japan had declared war against the Central Powers in the expectation of acquiring the German-controlled Pacific islands and territory in China and of expanding her power over other regions of China and elsewhere in the Far East. In the European sphere of war the Russian foreign minister as early as September, 1914, told the French and the British governments his ideas about a postwar settlement. They included the following: German power should be broken. Territorial frontiers should be modified according to the principle of nationality. Russia should obtain "the lower course of the Nieman and the eastern part of Galicia," and Eastern Posnania (Poznán) and Silesia and the western part of Galicia should go to the kingdom of Poland, which Russia would continue to control. France should recover Alsace-Lorraine and add part of Rhenish Prussia and of the Palatinate. Belgium should increase her territory and Denmark should regain Schleswig-Holstein. Hannover should be restored as a kingdom, and Austria should become a triple monarchy, consisting of the empire of Austria, the kingdom of Bohemia, and the kingdom of Hungary. The kingdom of Bohemia should include present-day Bohemia and Slovakia. The kingdom of Hungary should come to "an understanding with Roumania on the subject of Transylvania." Serbia should take Bosnia, Herzegovina, Dalmatia, and northern Albania, and in return for these gains should compensate Bulgaria in Macedonia. The rest of Albania should go to Greece, except for Vlona, which Italy should receive. England, France, and Japan should share the German colonies, and Germany and Austria pay a war indemnity.

The French foreign minister expressed his personal approval of Russia's claims, defining his own country's objectives as the return of Alsace-Lorraine, the abolition of international restrictions upon France's dominance in Morocco, "the rectification of several colonial frontiers" in Africa, and, as "the essential aim," "the destruction of the German Empire and the greatest possible weakening of the military and political power of Prussia." "It is essential," he continued, as reported by the Russian ambassador, "to act in such a way that the separate German states shall be themselves interested in this aim." France approved Russia's claim to freedom of the Straits leading from the Black Sea to the Mediterranean. In March, 1915, the Russian foreign minister wrote to his ambassador in Paris that the British government approved Russia's claim to annex the Straits and Constantinople, subject to security for British economic interests and provided Russia did as much for Britain elsewhere.

One of the main sources of imperialism in the war proved to be competition on the international political market. Italy and Romania may be cited as examples. In 1915 the Allies offered Italy more than the Central Powers did and won her to the cause of democracy. The secret treaty of London of that year granted Italy the prospect of gaining the Trentino, Cisalpine Tyrol, Trieste, the counties of Gorizia and Gradisca, Istria, and a large number of islands along the Dalmatian coast, the province of Dalmatia, Vlona, the island of Saseno, and enough neighboring coastal territory to assure defense. Parts of Albania were to be awarded to Montenegro, Serbia, and Greece, and Italy was to control Albanian foreign affairs. Should there be a partition of Turkey, Italy was assured a large area in Asia Minor, including Adalia (Antalya) and Smyrna, and she was promised an equitable increase in territory in Africa if France and Great Britain augmented their possessions there. As for Romania, the territorial gain was to be similarly large—the Banat, Transylvania up to the Theiss (Tisza), and Bucovina up to the Pruth (Prut).

In 1915 and 1916 Britain, France, Russia, and Italy planned among themselves the partition of the Turkish Empire, either by outright acquisition or as zones of influence. The governments secretly agreed that Mesopotamia should go to Britain, Cilicia and Syria to France, Armenia and Kurdistan to Russia, and a region around Adalia to Italy. Territory between the British and French shares would become part of an Arabian empire but would be divided into a British and a French zone of influence. The distribution satisfied long-standing interests or aspirations of each state.

British commitments did not stop at this point. Britain furnished the troops, money, and leadership in winning Arab support for the Allied side in the war, and during the first year of fighting she had left the impression upon the mind of the Sherif of Mecca, later King Hussein of Hedjaz, that she would support him in founding a united Arabian empire with Damascus as capital. To the inconsistency between this seeming commitment and that of 1916 among the Allies was added the Balfour Declaration of 1917 about Palestine: "His Majesty's Government," Balfour stated to the House of Commons, "view with favour the establishment in Palestine of a national home for the Jewish people, and will use its best endeavours to facilitate the achievement of this object, it being clearly understood that nothing shall be done which may prejudice the civil and religious rights of existing non-Jewish communities in Palestine or the rights and political status enjoyed by Jews in any other country." Since 90 per cent of the inhabitants of Palestine at the time were not Jews but Arabs, the declaration angered Arab leaders, whose support Britain was seeking to win.

The conquest of Damascus in October, 1918, by Arab troops accompanied by the British Colonel T. E. Lawrence, and the occupation of Syria by British forces at the end of the war, aroused French mistrust. And as if to enhance the confusion of intentions, the British and French governments on November 7, 1918, declared their aim with respect to the peoples freed from Ottoman rule to be "the establishment of National Governments and administrations deriving their authority from the initiative and free choice of the indigenous populations." This last policy supported President Wilson's ideal of national self-determination for all peoples.

In 1917 the French appetite in Europe increased. In February the French and Russian governments agreed that France should annex Alsace-Lorraine, with France setting the frontier of Lorraine "so as to provide for the strategical needs and for the inclusion in French territory of the entire iron district of Lorraine and of the entire coal district of the Saar Valley." In addition, the territory of Germany on the left bank of the Rhine was to be formed into "an autonomous and neutral state," to be occupied by French troops "until such time as the enemy States have completely satisfied all the conditions and guarantees indicated in the Treaty of Peace."

If imperialism is defined as the domination of alien peoples by physical force, with very few exceptions, like that of Alsace-Lorraine, the Allied secret objectives seem to have been of the same imperialist nature as those of the Central Powers. The states involved in war saw opportunities for gain which might not recur. As one might expect of statesmen brought up in the tradition of power politics, each government sought to reward the people for the travail of fighting and to augment state power by territorial gain.

WAR TO END WAR

As the war continued it evoked a profound sense of the need for morality in politics. The endless slaughter aroused leaders and social groups in each European state to a sense of the futility of battle as a means of solving international problems. Socialists and labor leaders, liberals and conservatives, churchmen and teachers, idealists from every occupation began to organize in support of a peace to end all wars. Each country showed such increasing numbers of these people that tough realists like Lloyd George and Clemenceau had to pay them some respect. The most noted advocates came from the countries which had in the past century or two emancipated themselves from the imperialism of the European states and which by tradition had imbued international relations with a moral sense. President Wilson spoke most eloquently for these forces. The new-world idealism and a revived and strengthened idealism in the old world animated the President's speeches. In one of January, 1918, he set forth fourteen points as a basis for peace; these will be discussed in the next chapter. He aimed thereby to induce Germany and her allies to surrender and to commit his own allies to the kind of peace he advocated. In July of the same year he offered one of the noblest statements of these conditions. It read as follows:

> 1. The destruction of every arbitrary power anywhere that can separately, secretly, and of its single choice disturb the peace of the world; or, if it cannot be presently destroyed, at least its reduction to virtual impotence.
>
> 2. The settlement of every question, whether of territory, or sovereignty, of economic arrangement, or of political relationship, upon the basis of the free acceptance of that settlement by the people immediately concerned, and not upon the basis of the material interest or advantage of any other nation or people which may desire a different settlement for the sake of its own exterior influence or mastery.
>
> 3. The consent of all nations to be governed in their conduct towards each other by the same principles of honour and of respect for the common law of civilized society that govern the individual citizens of all modern states in their relations with one another; to the end that all promises and covenants may be sacredly observed, no private plots or conspiracies hatched, no selfish injuries wrought with impunity, and a mutual trust established upon the handsome foundation of a mutual respect for right.
>
> 4. The establishment of an organization of peace which shall make certain that the combined power of free nations will check every invasion of right and serve to make peace and justice the more secure by affording a definite tribunal of opinion to which all must submit and by which every international readjustment that cannot be amicably agreed upon by the peoples directly concerned shall be sanctioned.

"The moral climax of this the culminating and final war for human liberty," he declared, "has come." These ideals and not the prospect of imperialist gain steeled the people of the Allied countries to persevere to victory.

DEFEAT OF THE CENTRAL POWERS

The decisive military campaign opened in March, 1918, with a German offensive. Generals Hindenburg and Ludendorff expressed confidence in victory if permitted 1,250,000 casualties. By reducing the forces on all other battlefields they amassed in the west 3½ million men and disposed of a reserve of forty-four divisions. They planned a series of attacks along a wide front and had worked out new offensive tactics, for which they exercised the German troops in secrecy. Infantry and artillery moved into position at the last moment in such a way that complete surprise was insured. The initial bombardment was intense but lasted not longer than four hours. Gas was spread ahead of the German infantry, and high explosives destroyed the barbed wire and other obstructions just before the attack. The assaulting infantry was equipped with small mobile trench mortars and other guns to use against nests of machine guns. The forward infantry units infiltrated as far and as fast as they could; they were followed by others whose duty was to spread out, widen the gap, and surround and destroy pockets of resistance. For the first of the series of assaults the high command concentrated on the 45-mile front between Arras and La Fère a total of 62 divisions, 1,700 batteries of artillery and more than 1,000 airplanes. There were twenty to thirty batteries to every kilometer of the front. It was an unprecedented massing of men and material.

Fortunately for the Allies, the enemy had not developed the tank as a weapon. Although gaining more ground than at any time since 1914, the Germans were stopped short of a breakthrough. Under Foch's leadership the Allies developed a system of defense in depth, allowing the German spearhead to advance and then attacking the sides, closing the gap, and pinching off the advance units. In July, when the Germans tried the last of their five big assaults, Ludendorff was still confident of victory; yet victory remained elusive.

In the campaign of 1918 the German high command misjudged not merely the efficacy of its new strategy but the potential of the Allies and the sagging morale of the German people and troops. The high officers did not understand the latent fighting power of civilian peoples. Many German civilian officials perceived the mistake but lacked prestige effectively to negate the military prejudice. The Allied troops continued to fight and American troops to pour onto the continent. Ludendorff could not comprehend that the German people were tired out, that fatigue had reached the front, that many soldiers felt like the one who in 1917 had written:

> Russia might be dearer to one than the Fatherland. Messrs. Pan-Germans sit on the high horse. But they may be glad that we don't pull them off their big estates one of these days. Another fifteen billions of war loans and Germany is pawned to her rich. Europe is a huge insane asylum. Starvation makes me whistle: *Hunger "über alles in der Welt."* [2]

By June the high command felt sufficiently uncertain to acknowledge

[2] Alfred Vagts, *A History of Militarism* (New York: W. W. Norton & Company, Inc., 1937), p. 267.

privately that diplomacy might supplement arms for winning the war. Acting upon this cue, Richard von Kühlmann, secretary of state for foreign affairs, declared in the *Reichstag* that "an absolute end to the War by military decisions alone, without an exchange of ideas and without diplomacy, is not to be expected." The statement contained the first official intimation that the war would not lead to complete German victory; but before acknowledging any such concession in public the military still needed the convincing argument of the Allies' August offensive.

In early June the Prussian minister of war had announced in the *Reichstag*, "Foch's army no longer exists." In August the Allied offensive began to roll when British and Australian divisions at Amiens, aided by 450 tanks, overwhelmed their opponents. At long last the tank provided the offensive weapon that could conquer trenches. From then on the Allied attack did not cease. For the first time in the war German troops surrendered in large numbers. In August Ludendorff temporarily lost his nerve and declared to the government that the war must be concluded. He quickly recovered his self-confidence; but by the end of September Bulgaria had collapsed, Austria-Hungary was trying to make peace, the *Reichstag* was fearful and restless, and the German army, having lost a million men since March, was finding that casualties were catching up with replacements. Americans and British tanks were swarming over the front. The high command acknowledged that Germany must seek peace; it advised the government to establish contact with President Wilson and insisted that a parliamentary government be introduced. The Kaiser took steps to carry out a "revolution from above" by asking the liberal Prince Maximilian of Baden to become chancellor. Although gravely reluctant, the prince accepted the heavy responsibility.

Prince Maximilian urged the high command to hold for a few days, but the latter replied that a truce was needed at once. Although later the military were to deny the fact, at that time they acknowledged that the army was completely defeated. The new chancellor called upon President Wilson to take the negotiations for peace in hand and accepted the terms laid down in the Fourteen Points and in other public statements. Prince Maximilian re-formed the government to include members of the Center party, the Progressive party, and the Social Democrats. In late October and early November sailors rioted in Kiel and other ports, soldiers not on front-line duty rebelled, mobs formed and demanded the overthrow of the Kaiser. When pressure from Wilson and from the German parties then in power was added, the chancellor on November 9 forced the abdication of the House of Hohenzollern. Ludendorff had fled to Sweden; but Hindenburg remained at his post, and approved the measures. Prince Maximilian promised the reforms for which the discontented parties had asked. He strove to convince the Allies and the German people that a new regime had begun. The "revolution from above" had gone further than its initiators had expected. German resistance had ceased; on November 11 the government acquiesced in an armistice. A trade-unionist, Friedrich Ebert, became acting president of a new German republic, and a cabinet led by Social Democrats took office. The country awaited the verdict of the victorious Allies.

The war on the other fronts continued to be subsidiary; the outcome can be rapidly sketched. Bulgaria fell first. She had fought two years in the Balkan Wars (1912–1914) and four years in the present war. She had mobilized 1¼ million of her 5 million people, leaving the farm work of this peasant state to the women and children. Almost all the German reinforcements had been withdrawn for Ludendorff's offensive. Left to their own devices, the Bulgarian soldiers began to desert the front to go home. In June a pro-German premier was supplanted by the pro-Allied Malinov; King Ferdinand left for Austria, ostensibly for his health. When in September the Allies under General Franchet d'Esperey attacked from Macedonia and moved into Bulgaria, the army surrendered and on September 29 signed an armistice. The king abdicated in favor of his son, and a new regime began. Turkey came next. With Allied armies advancing successfully in Syria and in Mesopotamia, with her connections to Germany severed by the defection of Bulgaria, with her people exhausted and her fighting power in disorder and troops deserting, Turkey sought an armistice. On October 31 hostilities ceased.

The Austro-Hungarian Empire disintegrated, with each of the two parts taking its own way of doing so. Emperor Charles offered a plan on October 16 by which the Austrian part would be transformed into a federal state organized into four subkingdoms, a German-Austrian, a Czech, a Yugoslav, and a Ukrainian one. He did not mention Poland. The Hungarian government in the other half of the Dual Monarchy refused to the bitter end all concessions to its rebellious national minorities. In September Count Tisza told a Yugoslav delegation, "It may be that we shall be ruined, but we shall still have strength enough to crush you." By declaring Hungary independent of Austria the leaders expected to avoid the effects of being on the losing side. Not until October 17 did Tisza admit that Hungary had lost the war.

The last days of the Austro-Hungarian Empire ran along expected lines. In January, 1918, Wilson had declared in favor of preserving Austria-Hungary as a triple monarchy, but he had since become persuaded that the nationalities of the empire must be permitted to decide their own future. The Allied governments had recognized the independence movements of the Poles, Czechoslovaks, and Yugoslavs, and the right of Romanians in Transylvania to join the state of their nationality. In October national councils were formed among each of the peoples, including the Hungarians, and each of these, except the last named, cooperated freely and closely with its counterpart abroad. The transition from Hapsburg rule to an independent Austria, Czechoslovakia, Poland, and Yugoslavia progressed as smoothly as was to be expected. Only in Hungary did the change lead to rioting and revolutionary action. Soldiers and workers set up soviets in Budapest, and a mob invaded Tisza's palace and murdered that haughty magnate. The Austro-Hungarian army disappeared. Hungarian troops in particular started for home, rifle in hand, each man determined to defend his country on his own doorstep. Fighting ceased on the Italian front; by November 6 the Allied army based on Salonika reached Belgrade. An armistice was signed, and on November 11 Emperor Charles abdicated, a Social Democratic government taking control. The Hohenzollerns had ruled for five hundred years, the Hapsburgs for six hundred; now they passed into history after defeat in a war of their own making.

World War I forms the watershed between the nineteenth and twentieth centuries. Many people looked back to the years before 1914 as those of happiness and prosperity, the last experience of normal life. Others, like the Poles, the Czechs and Slovaks, and the South Slavs, associated them with uncertainty and striving for achievement of a distant goal of national freedom. War changed profoundly the life of belligerents and nonbelligerents alike. It accelerated transformation begun in the preceding century to the point of giving old problems a new and startling shape—the reform of the German government, for example. It created difficulties—financial inflation, for instance—unknown in 1914. The succeeding chapters of this book treat the effects of these four years of hatred and destruction. The historian is perhaps the sole person to derive profit from war, not as a moral being but purely as an analyst of the past: he is supplied a unified theme, war and its aftermath. As the reader proceeds he may from time to time let his mind wander, as that of many an older European has done, to the fanciful question of how the continent and the world would have developed had Serbs and Austrians compromised their difficulty, had World War I never occurred.

Suggestions for Further Reading

See the Readings for Chapter 2.

Chapter 4 · The Peace Settlement

RANGE OF PROBLEMS

When the peace conference opened at Versailles in January, 1919, it confronted problems of unprecedented variety and magnitude. The conflict had involved all the great powers and several dozen minor ones. The civilians of the participating countries had shared actively in the conflict. The total deficit of population during the war amounted to over 48 million people, of which 8½ million were military losses and the rest were losses from excess civilian deaths or from decline in the normal birth rate. The direct expenditures for war purposes amounted for the Allies to $156 billion and for the Central Powers to $63 billion. Four historic empires, the Russian, the German, the Austro-Hungarian, and the Ottoman, lay in ruins. Three major dynasties had toppled, together with lesser rulers. New states had appeared in Eastern and Southeastern Europe and in the Near and Middle East. The Communist party had seized Russia and threatened the peoples to the west. A political and social revolution had occurred in Germany and Bulgaria and was taking place in Hungary. Both civil and international wars continued in a great part of Eastern Europe, among Poles, Russians, Communists, German troops not yet repatriated, and peoples of the new Baltic states. Plagues spread through that chaotic area and threatened to move westward. Hunger marked the course of war and disease; and, as the Allies continued to blockade Germany until the peace treaty was signed, the people of that country suffered more from lack of food than they had during the actual conflict. War left problems affecting not merely the military and foreign relations but the entire society.

PERSONNEL AT THE PEACE CONFERENCE

The leading figures at the peace conference, President Wilson, Prime Minister Lloyd George, Premier Clemenceau, Premier Orlando of Italy, and Premier Kimmochi Saionji of Japan, restricted their deliberations largely to international relations. Except for the subject of reparations and a few general economic matters, they ignored economic, social, and gov-

Estimated Population Deficits as Result of World War I

(000's Omitted)

COUNTRIES (PREWAR BOUNDARIES)	1914 POPULATION	MILITARY LOSSES	EXCESS CIVILIAN DEATHS OVER AGE 1	DEFICIT OF BIRTHS	REDUCTION OF INFANT DEATHS	TOTAL DEFICIT OF POPULATION NUMBER	TOTAL DEFICIT OF POPULATION PER CENT
United Kingdom	46,085	744	402	709	67	1,788	3.9
France	39,800	1,320	240	1,686	172	3,074	7.7
Belgium	7,662	40	102	311	37	416	5.4
Italy	35,859	700	800	1,426	191	2,735	7.6
Serbia and Montenegro	3,400	325	450	336	47	1,064	31.3
Romania	7,771	250	430	505	97	1,088	14.0
Greece	4,732	25	100	200	30	295	6.2
Portugal	6,155	4	157	121	18	264	4.3
Germany	67,790	2,000	737	3,158	459	5,436	8.0
Austria-Hungary	53,018	1,100	963	3,600	600	5,063	9.5
Bulgaria	4,852	70	98	317	41	444	9.2
Norway	2,486	..	26	..	..	26	1.0
Sweden	5,680	..	57	26	2	81	1.4
Denmark	2,866	..	18	1	..	19	.7
Netherlands	6,240	..	86	8	1	93	1.5
Switzerland	3,897	..	23	59	5	77	2.0
Spain	20,578	..	321	133	20	434	2.1
Europe (excl. U.S.S.R.)	318,871	6,578	5,010	12,596	1,787	22,397	7.0
U.S.S.R.	140,405	1,500-2,000	..	..	..	26,000	18.5

SOURCE: Frank W. Notestein, and others, *The Future Population of Europe and the Soviet Union* (Population Projections 1940–1970; Geneva; League of Nations, 1944), p. 75.

ernmental issues and negotiated a political treaty. They sought to protect Europe in future from the resurgence of the defeated and exhausted enemy rather than to assist a new Europe to arise. Apart from aid by way of the reparations clauses they did nothing to help the new states to overcome their mountainous difficulties. When compelled by circumstances to maintain peace and administer some kind of law in confused regions of the world, they did so on an emergency basis, expecting the national states to assume these responsibilities as soon as possible. They did not assist the new social and political forces released within the conquered states to establish a democratic regime.

The peace conference was composed of delegates from all twenty-seven states except Russia that had been at war or had severed relations with Germany. The Bolshevik government in Russia sought to be represented, but the Allies refused to recognize it as legitimate authority. Representatives of nonbelligerent countries and of several formerly suppressed nationality groups likewise attended. Everyone with a political axe to grind appeared at Versailles. The official delegates met in plenary session about half a dozen times. The work was done and the issues decided by the representatives of the major powers, each aided by a large body of experts. The delegates of the defeated nations were present in the city, but in contrast to the action of all previous peace conferences in modern times, because of popular hatred they were kept semi-incarcerated and uninformed until the Allies agreed upon terms. After a few changes in detail, the Allies forced acceptance of the following: in June, 1919, the Treaty of Versailles with Germany; in September, 1919, the Treaty of St. Germain with Austria; in November, 1919, the Treaty of Neuilly with Bulgaria; in June, 1920, the Treaty of Trianon with Hungary (ratification was delayed by the revolution in Hungary); and in August, 1920, the Treaty of Sèvres with Turkey.

In organizing the conference Wilson planned to have representatives of all the Allied and Associated nations convene and apply the Fourteen Points, but the resulting body proved too large. Therefore a Council of Ten, composed of heads of government of the United States, France, Great Britain, Italy, and Japan with the foreign ministers, assumed responsibility for deciding issues and drafting terms. The Council appointed fifty-two commissions to study special problems and report on them. By March 24 the Council, attended as it was by numerous advisers, experts, and interpreters, was discontinued as unwieldy. Since Saionji, the Japanese delegate, preferred to participate only in discussions of Far Eastern questions, the Big Four—Wilson, Clemenceau, Lloyd George, and Orlando—now met in secret session, sometimes with one secretary, sometimes with none, to settle the main points of the peace. They held power which permitted them to determine the fate of the world. In December, 1918, Clemenceau had explained to the French Chamber of Deputies his program for concluding peace and had received a favorable vote of four to one. A coalition government headed by Lloyd George emerged overwhelmingly victorious from the British election of December, 1918, the first since 1910. He and his party had promised to "hang the Kaiser" and make Germany bear the whole cost of the war. Orlando occupied a less secure position than the above two, and in the United States the Democratic party had lost control of the Senate in the elections of 1918, so that Wilson's position was shaky. What were the four statesmen like?

Although the war had been fought by young men, the four peacemakers were old. Lloyd George was 56; Orlando, 59; Wilson, 63; and, Clemenceau 78. Lloyd George and Wilson spoke only their native language; Orlando knew French. Clemenceau, who was acquainted with English, negotiated without the aid of an interpreter, an advantage for French interests. As experienced politicians, all had formed their basic views of life well before 1914. The war had demonstrated the limitations of state sovereignty; nevertheless, the four posited a world of national states, independent of one another and fully sovereign. None understood the theory and practice of economics, particularly as applied to the sphere of international economic relations. None had grasped a lesson of the war, namely, that politics and economics are inextricably interwoven, that political decisions have economic consequences, often of crucial significance, and that economic forces may render the political decisions unworkable.

Clemenceau appears to have been least ignorant with respect to the interdependence of economic and political affairs, since he wished reparations and economic handicaps placed upon Germany to weaken that state; but neither he nor the others understood the economic implications for Europe of the reparations clauses. The four statesmen represented democracy at the peak of its power; but their democracy comprehended little of the economic and social ideals of the lower income groups—workers and salaried employees—in an industrial society, or of soldiers who had lived through the cooperative social enterprise of war. Orlando was the least influential among them, as befitted the lesser role of his country in the war. A lawyer by profession, a politician of long standing, he held his office insecurely and dared not recede from any Italian claim. He proved to be more nationally minded, more dubious about the possibility of preserving peace by international organization than was Clemenceau. Lloyd George, a Welshman with a mobile mind and a persuasive tongue, knew how to adapt his views to the currents of the time. During the last months of the war he had talked the language of idealism about peacemaking, but he had also roared as much Jingoism against Germany as the sensationalist press of Lord Northcliffe. Although uncertain about his ultimate demands on the defeated powers, he was determined to protect British and Dominion interests as he understood them. His ignorance of Europe was probably greater than that of any of his three colleagues. At the same time he was a warm-hearted individual, who had never forgotten his own modest background; when confronted with human misery, even among a defeated enemy, he instinctively responded with sympathy.

Woodrow Wilson, son of a Presbyterian minister in western Virginia, had been university professor of history and government and president of Princeton University. Having entered politics first as governor of New Jersey, he had become in 1912 President of the United States. In both offices he had introduced economic and social reforms of general value to the country. A man of deep convictions and of a profound sense of responsibility to society, he transferred the traditional American ideals of government and society to the field of international relations. He knew little about the social and economic aspects of the postwar world and little about Europe. When he found that his American standards, for example, in the matter of national self-determination, did not fit European conditions, he allowed compromises in their application. As long as his ideals were verbally respected, he could be "bamboozled," as Clemenceau expressed it. If he understood the contradiction between principles and their application, he refused to give way. Lloyd George and Clemenceau handled him deftly; Orlando lacked the touch.

Clemenceau remembered the time when in the reign of Louis Napoleon his father had been exiled for political radicalism to one of the French penal colonies. He had hated persons of political power all his life; he had hated and feared Germany most of his life. His courageous action had made enemies numerous and respectful. It was said that to Clemenceau any club was a satisfactory weapon for beating a ministry to death. He interpreted history as a ceaseless interchange of peace and war, peace being a state of preparation for war. He believed himself free from illusions about the future. Since France sat among the victors and Germany was defeated, France should use every means to keep herself on top as long as possible. He accepted international idealism, provided it was buttressed by power politics, alliances, military superiority, and physical restrictions upon the enemy. Aware of the vicissitudes of political life, he expected the conclusion of the peace treaties to be his last great service to France.

THE "FOURTEEN POINTS"

The most specific statement of the terms on which the Allies would make peace had been given in Wilson's Fourteen Points. Six of these referred to general conditions which should apply to victor and vanquished alike—"Open covenants of peace, openly arrived at," "Absolute freedom of navigation upon the seas . . . alike in peace and in war," "The removal, so far as possible, of all economic barriers and the establishment of an equality of trade conditions," reduction of armaments, adjustment of colonial claims which will heed the interests of both the sovereign state and of the colonial peoples, and the creation of a "general association of nations" to afford "mutual guarantees of political independence and territorial integrity to great and small states alike."

The other points dealt with particular countries, and by the time the peace conference was convened some were out of date. Article 6 stated that Russia should be left alone to determine its own "political development and national policy." By Article 7 Belgium and by Article 8 France's invaded territory should be restored and France should regain Alsace-Lorraine. Article 9 promised the readjustment of Italy's frontiers along the lines of nationality, a limitation unsatisfactory to Italy. Article 10 called for the preservation of Austria-Hungary with "the freest opportunity of autonomous development" for the nationalities, a policy that by 1919 was already outmoded by the disintegration of that empire. Article 11 formulated a program for the Balkans. "Rumania, Serbia, and Montenegro should be evacuated; occupied territories restored; Serbia accorded free and secure access to the sea; and the relations of the several Balkan states to one another determined by friendly counsel along historically established lines of allegiance and nationality; and international guarantees of the political and economic independence and territorial integrity of the several Balkan States should be entered into." Wilson had manifestly not anticipated the merging of Serbia and Montenegro into Yugoslavia. His proposal of "friendly counsel" and of "international guarantees" likewise came to nought. Article 12 demanded the breakup of the Ottoman Empire along lines of nationality and the free passage of the Dardanelles. Article 13 stated that Poland should be restored, assured free access to the sea, and its independence and territorial integrity "guaranteed by international covenant." On the surface the program expressed the most advanced thinking about how to achieve peace that the time afforded; its ideals were widely acclaimed.

Plans for a League of Nations

Wilson thought that the most important point was the establishment of a "general association of nations," or, as it came to be called, a League of Nations. He and his advisers, particularly Colonel Edward House, had worked for more than a year on a draft constitution. They had profited from the report of a committee appointed by the British government for the same purpose, and later they were to borrow suggestions from a pamphlet by General Jan Smuts of South Africa entitled *The League of Nations: A Practical Suggestion.* A report on the subject by a French committee went unheeded by the American government and by the French ministry that had requested it to be made. Wilson wished the Peace Conference to place the creation of a league first on the agenda, and to his surprise he found the Allied governments agreeable. On January 25 Lloyd George proposed a resolution, approved by the five major powers, to found a League of Nations "to promote international co-operation, to ensure the fulfillment of accepted international obligations and to provide safeguards against war." The League should be "an integral part of the general Treaty of Peace." It should be "open to every civilized nation which can be relied upon to promote its object," a stipulation that for a time would exclude enemy states from membership. It should meet periodically in international conference and have a permanent organization and a secretariat. General Smuts spoke for Wilson and himself in stating that "in the vast multiplicity of territorial, economic and other problems with which the Conference will find itself confronted it should look upon the setting up of a League of

Nations as its primary and basic task, and as supplying the necessary organ by means of which most of those problems can find their only stable solution. Indeed, the Conference should regard itself as the first or preliminary meeting of the League, intended to work out its organization, functions, and programme."

Representatives of both small and large nations, though not of the defeated countries, drafted the League Covenant within eleven days. After some revision, the conference in plenary session adopted this draft. To insure its acceptance the document was incorporated into each of the peace treaties. Whenever President Wilson was forced to retreat in treaty making from his ideals he consoled himself with the expectation that the League would in time achieve any necessary adjustments.

Conflicting Conceptions of Peace Settlement

Allied leaders accepted the Fourteen Points with reluctance. They mistrusted the President's moral tone and feared that the implementation of Wilsonian ideals would prevent their restraining Germany. Nonetheless they committed themselves to the program, with two exceptions: the British refused to approve Point II, guaranteeing freedom of the seas; Points VII and VIII, freeing and restoring the invaded territory of France and Belgium, were extended to include compensation from Germany for "all damage done to the civilian population of the Allies and their property by the aggression of Germany by land, by sea and from the air." The principle of compensation contrasted with Wilson's statement that "the impartial justice meted out must involve no discrimination between those to whom we wish to be just and those to whom we do not wish to be just. It must be a justice that plays no favorites and knows no standard but the equal rights of the several peoples concerned."

The German government placed itself squarely behind Wilson's principles and offered to join the Allies "in rebuilding that which has been destroyed, in making good whatever wrong has been committed, above all the injustice to Belgium, and in showing mankind new goals of political and social progress." It considered the principal problem to be that of restoring "the broken strength of all the nations which took part in the war, . . . by providing international protection for the welfare, health, and freedom of the working classes." [1] The Germans and their former allies sought a peace not dictated by one party but negotiated between equals. They used this strategy as the best way to reduce the severity of the terms, but they were likewise desirous of being treated as a civilized nation, on a par with others. The German delegation to the peace conference claimed to represent a new, peace-loving country, a democracy and a republic.

[1] Alma Luckau, *The German Delegation at the Paris Peace Conference* (New York: Columbia University Press, 1941. Reprinted by permission of The Carnegie Endowment for International Peace), pp. 220-222.

"The return to a form of government under which the will of the German people could be disregarded, is utterly out of the question," argued the delegates. Militarism had been destroyed; a league of nations was to be created, and the Allies were urged to accept the new Germany as a partner in making a world of justice, peace, and harmony.[2]

Clemenceau replied for the Allies to the German argument. The German delegation, he said, seemed to think "'that Germany has only to make sacrifices in order to attain peace,' as if this were but the end of some mere struggle for territory and power." Germany should receive justice, he said; but "it must be justice for all. There must be justice for the dead and wounded and for those who have been orphaned and bereaved that Europe might be freed from Prussian despotism. There must be justice for the peoples who now stagger under war debts which exceed £30,000,000,000 that liberty might be saved. There must be justice for those millions whose homes and land, ships and property German savagery has spoliated and destroyed." Justice required that Germany be punished and taught not to expose the world to "fresh calamities." He welcomed the German revolution, but he asserted that the people had not transformed their government until the war was lost and all hope of profiting from conquests had ceased. He questioned whether the revolutionary change would be permanent, and he refused to deflect the course of justice "for the sake of convenient peace."[3]

The Germans emphasized the fundamental difference between the new and the old Germany. The Allies, especially Clemenceau and the French, saw little evidence of change and feared the survival of the old order. The Germans wished to start afresh with an international policy of equality and reciprocity; they looked to the future. The Allies could not forget the past; they wished expiation of past wrongs before they would admit equality for the future. The Germans were unwittingly applying to international relations the standards of psychiatry and social reform: help the offender to recover by trusting him. The Allies were acting according to criminal law.

The difference between the conceptions of the Allies and the Germans for a proper treaty may be partly explained by the contrary views about the origins of the war. In Article 231 of the Treaty of Versailles the Allies wrote:

> The Allied and Associated governments affirm and Germany accepts the responsibility of Germany and her allies for causing all the loss and damage to which the Allied and Associated Governments and their nationals have been subjected as a consequence of the war imposed upon them by the aggression of Germany and her allies.

A similar clause was inserted in the treaty with each of the other former enemies. Clemenceau was more explicit in a communication to the German

[2] *Ibid.*, p. 376. [3] *Ibid.*, pp. 411 ff.

delegation in the name of the Allies: "Germany's responsibility, however, is not confined to having planned and started the war. She is no less responsible for the savage and inhuman manner in which it was conducted." [4] This ascription of guilt to Germany on the part of the Allies was used to justify the onerous terms of the treaty. It was absolutely rejected by the entire German nation. Count Ulrich von Brockdorff-Rantzau, speaking for the German people to the peace conference on May 7, 1919, declared: "The demand is made that we shall acknowledge that we alone are guilty of having caused the war. Such a confession in my mouth would be a lie." He maintained that all the powers shared in the responsibility, with Russia having been most to blame because of her early mobilization. He acknowledged that Germany had erred on the side of severity in the conduct of the war, but he added that under the stress of war all belligerents had committed similar acts. He accused the Allies of "coolly and deliberately" starving hundreds of thousands of noncombatants by imposing after November 11 a food blockade. "Remember that," he said, "when you speak of guilt and atonement." [5] He urged that an impartial commission be created to decide the question of war guilt. The Allies refused. The German government condemned the peace treaty as an "act of violence" aimed to "deprive the German people of their honor." It bowed to "overpowering might" and signed the treaty, but it "in no wise" abandoned its conviction that "these conditions of peace represent injustice without parallel." [6]

It is doubtful whether so soon after a bitter war a just peace, a peace of understanding, could have been reached. The Allied governments had spoken of the war as "imposed upon them by the aggression of Germany and her Allies." The German government denounced the peace treaty as "imposed" upon its people. An accusation of war guilt by one side was followed by an accusation of peace guilt by the other. The ideal of a war to end war through a peace of understanding was remote. The animosities of World War I were perpetuated in the peace treaties and led to a more devastating conflict twenty years later.

THE TREATIES

Since the treaties all conformed to a pattern, they can best be analyzed, not separately, but as a group. The terms of all the documents expressed Allied decisions, and disputes in drafting the clauses occurred, not between victors and vanquished, but among the victors. In general, Wilson tried to adhere to the ideals which he had formulated for making the peace. Lloyd George shifted between these ideals and the views of the continental Allies and tried to lessen the differences between them. Clemenceau aimed at one objective, to weaken Germany. Orlando approved or disapproved of proposals, irrespective of the subject, according to their possible effect upon

[4] *Ibid.*, p. 412. [5] *Ibid.*, pp. 220-221. [6] *Ibid.*, p. 482.

Italy's claims arising out of the Treaty of London. If the proposals set a precedent by which he could uphold those claims, he approved them. If they provided arguments against Italy's claims, he opposed them. If they were not relevant to Italy, he tended to be indifferent.

Territorial settlements in a peace treaty differ from any others in that

they cause a definitive loss or gain, as the case may be. Whereas economic or military restrictions can in time be lifted or overcome, territorial losses are almost never recovered. Since the Allies sought to prevent a recurrence of German militarism, they pared as much territory from the country as principle and expediency would allow. The western frontier suffered less change than the east. Alsace and Lorraine were restored to France immediately as a long-overdue satisfaction of what the Allies called the wrong of 1871. France sought to obtain the Saar, a small territory of 650,000 Germans, whose importance lay in the presence of rich coal mines. France claimed this territory on the strength of having owned it between 1792 and 1815 and of needing the coal to compensate for the wartime destruction of many of her own mines by the Germans. President Wilson refused the French claims for permanent possession, arguing the right of national self-determination. A commission composed of a Harvard professor of medieval history, an English historian, and a French politician, André Tardieu, was appointed to work out a settlement. The final result of weeks of tenacious bickering by the French satisfied no one but proved to have the merit of working. The Saar remained a part of Germany; the coal mines were given to France; the territory was administered by the League of Nations; at the end of fifteen years a plebiscite was to be held in the area; should the people vote to return to Germany, the latter could purchase the mines from the French.

Germany's Frontiers

General Foch, supported by Clemenceau as far as he dared, demanded that the German territory on the west bank of the Rhine be controlled directly by France or made an autonomus state. Foch regarded the Rhine as the essential line of defence, and he wished in one way or another to dominate the area up to that natural frontier. This attitude offers one of many examples of the ideas held by leaders in 1919 about the relation between natural frontiers and military defense. These leaders, both military and civilian, had just been fighting with airplanes and tanks, guns that could shoot across the English Channel, and with other instruments of mobility and speed; yet possession or control of a stream a few yards wide seemed to them to afford sufficient security to justify the violation of the right of self-determination of another nation and the perpetuation of enmity. Wilson and Lloyd George refused to allow the French to make this mistake and disregarded feeble efforts of French agents to set up an autonomous state in that region. The other territorial change on the western frontier was slight, the transfer of three small areas—Malmédy and Eupen by a sort of plebiscite, and Moresnet outright—to Belgium. Like Alsace-Lorraine, these were situated along the frontier of two cultures, French and German, and contained a population largely of no very strong national loyalty. On the north, Denmark refused an outright accession of the northern part of Schleswig-Holstein but agreed to accept the results of a plebiscite. In 1920 the northern area containing many Danish-speaking people voted to join Denmark; the southern voted to remain with Germany.

Whereas the western frontier line for Germany could be drawn without great difficulty, that on the east proved to be a major source of friction from that day to the present. The cultural and political demarcation between France and Germany was fairly clear; that between Germany and the new states of Eastern Europe was confused by centuries of fighting, of intermarriage, of cultural interpenetration, and of shifts in political fortune between Slavic and Germanic peoples. In the far north of Germany the port of Memel and its immediate hinterland contained about an equal number of Germans and of Lithuanians. Upon becoming independent of Russia in 1918, Lithuania, desiring an outlet to the sea, claimed Memel. France was eager to sever this territory from the German body, but the peace conference, aware that Prussia had possessed the area since the Middle Ages, retained international control of the little area of 976 square miles, pending future settlement. By force of arms in 1923 the Lithuanian state seized and kept it.

The establishment of the boundary with Poland aroused most anger. The Poles asked for large parts of East Prussia on the ground that it was inhabited by their people. The remainder of East Prussia, the Polish delegate Roman Dmowski suggested, should be made into a republic with Königsberg as capital. West Prussia, taken by Prussia during the first partition of Poland (1772), should go to Poland on both ethnic and historical grounds. Dmowski claimed that the majority of its population remained Polish. As for Danzig, the main city and port, he countered the German statistics showing only 3 per cent of the population to be Polish by his own figures that claimed at least 40 per cent for his nation. His bold assertion and the Allied promise to the Poles in the Fourteen Points of an outlet to the sea constituted the basis of Poland's claim to Danzig. The Poles also asked for the province of Posen, a Prussian acquisition during the partition of Poland in the last quarter of the eighteenth century, and Upper Silesia, which Poland had last possessed in the fourteenth century. Since a historic justification for Upper Silesia did not exist, the Poles mustered an economic argument. The territory, they declared, contained the iron ore, coal, and other minerals and the industries which were essential to make Poland economically a sovereign state.

France supported the claims; Italy went along. Wilson agreed on most points, but he and Lloyd George forced a plebiscite to be held in certain disputed regions. In East Prussia the Polish-speaking people in Allenstein and Marienwerder voted so overwhelmingly to remain in Germany that the Polish demand had to be dropped. In 1921 the plebiscite conducted in Upper Silesia resulted in a vote of 707,605 for Germany, with a majority in 844 communes, to a vote of 479,359 for Poland, with a majority in 675 communes. An international committee responsible to the Council of the League of Nations drew a frontier by dividing towns, property, streetcar lines, houses, anything immobile that happened to be in the way.

The necessity of individuals to declare their nationality caused difficulty. A person might have a German name but speak only Polish, or vice versa; he might be a Pole married to a German and have bilingual children. What were they by nationality? The people had to choose one way or another, even though the example of Danzig offered an alternative solution.

The British in particular rebelled at the thought of transferring the old free Hanseatic city of Danzig, German for centuries, to Poland. A settlement was reached whereby Danzig became a self-governing free city under a high commissioner appointed by the League of Nations; Poland was guaranteed special harbor rights; the territory was placed within the Polish customs system, and its foreign relations were handled by Poland. Posen, West Prussia, and certain small areas passed to Poland. As a result, Poland received a German minority of about 1½ million, and Germany was left with a somewhat smaller number of Poles.

With considerable coercion the Allies had applied the principle of national self-determination. Germany was deprived of 13 per cent of her prewar population and 13 per cent of her prewar area, in which in 1913 she had produced in value 15.7 per cent of her coal and 48.2 per cent of her iron ore. The lost area had contained 19 per cent of the German iron and steel industry, 59 per cent of the zinc ore and smelting, 24 per cent of the lead ore and smelting, and 12 per cent of the sulphur. In addition, Germany was deprived of her colonies and lost almost all her foreign investments, amounting in value in 1913 to $7 billion, or nearly 10 per cent of the estimated national wealth. Justice was not "deflected for the sake of convenient peace."

Breakup of Austria-Hungary: Rival Claims

In the breakup of Austria-Hungary each little successor state seized the opportunity, which it might never again have, to claim territory. The demands were large and buttressed by arguments, some sensible, some preposterous, almost all sympathetically received by the Big Four. Difficulty arose in the main only when two or more states contended for the same piece of land. The arguments advanced by Romania, Poland, Czechoslovakia, and Yugoslavia varied in detail but were identical in substance. Wherever possible each government asserted the right of former historical possession. Since the preponderant historical claim lay with the enemy, this argument had to be employed with caution, particularly since a new state might wish to include territory to which it had no such right (Slovakia and Ruthenia, for example, had never been politically associated with Bohemia). Each stood on firmer ground when it could appeal to the principle of national self-determination and buttress the appeal with statistics on ethnic composition. Each side adduced its own figures, real or plausible, and questioned the accuracy of any others. The peace conference often had no means for learning the truth. It sent committees of experts into the field, but these were frustrated by the absence of reliable statistics and other data and by the fact that in many countries the people were not sufficiently conscious of their nationality. Knowing that the argument of common nationality would not apply to all the coveted areas, the representatives of the new governments advanced the defensive necessity to possess strategic natural frontiers.

Czechoslovakia considered the Danube an indispensable southern boundary, even though the acceptance of it meant the inclusion of 700,000 Hungarians in the new state. In order to obtain the whole of the Banat, Romania asserted with equal conviction that the Danube should mark the frontier with Yugoslavia. Czechoslovakia was willing to include Ruthenia as a federated state in order to prevent Russia from extending south of the Carpathian Mountains. Sometimes the strategic argument was used to gain possession of a valley or a pass in order to prevent the enemy from again coming through that opening. It could be reinforced by a variety of others. The Banat, for example, contained a mixture of Serbs, Germans, Magyars, and Romanians in disputed proportions. The Romanians asserted that the people would be happier if left together and incorporated in their country. Ion Brătianu of Romania and Beneš of Czechoslovakia tried with good effect the argument of complementary regions: a mountain and a plains area with interdependent economy should be kept together. Thus the plains of Slovakia, although inhabited by large numbers of Magyars, should continue to be united with the northern mountains; and in the Banat the Serb plainsmen should remain together with the Romanian mountaineers, for the benefit of each. Frequently a claim for territory was justified by the country's need for a railway line or an entire system of communication that lay within the disputed region. As a last resort came the realistic assertion that if the country did not receive the territory there would be future trouble. A state not allowed to annex a territory outright reluctantly tolerated a plebiscite. All of them pressed for speedy and definitive settlement in order to keep out bolshevism.

Lack of clarity on principles prevented the Allies from reaching a satisfactory solution when two of their friends requested the same territory. Teschen and the smaller regions, Spis and Orava, became the objects of controversy and actual fighting between Czechoslovakia and Poland. The value of the areas derived from their rich coal deposits, to a lesser extent from their railway connections. Since they contained a mixed population of Czechs, Poles, and Germans, they could be legitimately claimed by either of the first two peoples. The Germans, of course, did not count. The Allies proposed a plebiscite but, since fighting continued, finally in 1920 had recourse to partition. Each contestant was awarded a part of Spis and Orava, and in Teschen Czechoslovakia gained most of the mines and the railway, and Poland the town of Teschen and undeveloped coal deposits.

A judgment similar to the one in the instance of Teschen was applied to the Banat, claimed by Romania and Yugoslavia. Yugoslavia was willing to divide it if she obtained the regions occupied by Serbs. That more Germans and Magyars lived in these districts than Serbs did not matter. Romania asked for the entire area, but Serbia, having a better war record than her rival, won Allied support. In the partition each state acquired a minority of the other's nationals.

Elsewhere in the region the Allies decided to transfer to Austria the Burgenland, inhabited largely by German Austrians but historically a part of Hungary. The Austrian government was apathetic, preferring to live on good terms with its neighbor; Hungary protested and gained the right of a plebiscite for Sopron and its region. The plebiscite turned out favorable to Hungary; the rest of the Burgenland went to Austria and continued as before to supply food to Vienna and Wiener Neustadt. In the Klagenfurt region, where native Austrians and Slovenes were fighting for possession, the Allies intervened and in 1920 held a plebiscite in the southern part. When the vote went in favor of Austria, the Allies restored the entire region to the new Austrian republic.

The most acute boundary quarrel occurred between Italy and Yugoslavia. Italy received the line she wished in the Austrian Tyrol, but she met opposition upon demanding territory on the eastern shore of the Adriatic. Orlando used the treaty of London of 1915 as far as he could to support his claims; thereby he kept the French and the British delegates loyal to their pledge, even though Lloyd George felt reluctant to honor it. Orlando knew that the United States and the other belligerents who had joined the Allies since 1915 were not bound by the treaty; nor could he rely upon that document altogether, for the Italian appetite had increased. Contrary to the terms of the treaty of 1915, he now demanded in the name of "reason" and "justice" possession of Fiume. Orlando mustered the time-honored arguments of strategic interest, natural frontier, and ethnic affinity. When these failed to persuade the Allies, he sought to justify Italy's demand for exceptions to the Wilsonian principles by citing the precedent of boundary making for Poland and other states. Italy must dominate the Adriatic for self-protection; to dominate it she must own the islands and the land to the top of the mountain range on the mainland. This area was inhabited by Italians, who, even if not in a majority, were at least as large a proportion of the population as the Poles had been in German areas given to Poland.

As Wilson refused to approve the transfer to Italy of territory predominantly Slavic in population, Orlando accused him of exceptional hostility to Italy. When Wilson stood for the inclusion of Fiume in Yugoslavia as the port for the Slavic, Hungarian, and Austrian hinterland, Orlando denounced him for violating his own principles. Fiume, Orlando said, was Italian in population and should go to Italy. When Wilson suggested that hostile Austria-Hungary would be replaced by the friendly ally Yugoslavia in the Adriatic, the Italian statesmen privately denounced the distinction as nonsensical and publicly demanded satisfaction for Italy's territorial claims. Wilson declared that membership in the League of Nations and disarmament, particularly the nonfortification of the eastern littoral of the Adriatic, would afford Italy complete protection. But Orlando and Sonnino, his foreign minister, believed that any state on the eastern shore of the Adriatic constituted an enemy. When Wilson appealed to the Italian people over the heads of their representatives, the Italian delegation quitted the peace conference in anger and did not return until the treaty with Germany was approved. Orlando fell from power, but his successor continued in the same demands. The dispute was settled in November, 1920, by a treaty between Italy and Yugoslavia. Fiume remained a free city, but Italy received more than she had been promised by the treaty of London—islands, the port of Zara, the entire Istrian Peninsula, and other territory on the mainland. In 1922 the Fascists seized Fiume, and two years later the two countries signed another treaty, by which Fiume remained Italian with special harbor facilities accorded Yugoslavia, and the latter given control of Porto Baros. The conflict between Wilson and Orlando revealed sharply the difference between the diplomacy of idealism and that of power politics. In this instance the latter won.

Hungarian Reaction to Peace Treaty

After the distribution of the Hapsburg territories, the Austrian remnant, 26½ per cent of the former area, scarcely retained the will to live. For a time the provinces threatened to fall apart, and almost the entire population wished to join Germany, an action which the peace treaty forbad. In Hungary the fire of ambition continued to flame, and the peace treaty was absolutely condemned. Count Apponyi, the president of the Hungarian peace delegation, asked with respect to the treaty the rhetorical question, "Should she [Hungary] commit suicide simply in order to escape a natural death?" He denounced the severity of the terms as out of all proportion to Hungary's share of responsibility for the war. "It is a case," he said to the Allied representatives, "of Hungary losing two-thirds of her territory and almost two-thirds of her population, and of the remaining Hungary being deprived of almost every condition of her economic development. For this unfortunate country, i.e. the centre of the country, severed from its peripheries, would be deprived of the greatest part of its coal—ore—and saltmines; of its timber for building, its oil and natural gas-springs, a great part of its labour; it would be deprived of its Alpine pastures, which nourished the stock of cattle; this unfortunate centre of the country would be deprived of all sources and instruments of economic development at the very moment in which it is required to enhance its production."

Apponyi declared that 35 per cent of the population to be severed from Hungary were Hungarians and that 10 per cent were Germans. "From a racial point of view," he added, "they ['the states aggrandized on the ruins of Hungary'] will be split into parts to the same degree, or even a higher degree, than Hungary formerly was." National hegemony, he said, would be transferred to races "at present mostly occupying a lower grade of culture." He predicted that the new states "would be undermined by the irredentism of nations feeling not only the rule of a foreign power but also the hegemony of a nation of a civilisation inferior to their own." This condition, he maintained, was "organically impossible," and he expected the Hungarian remnant and the newly created little states alike to stagnate and probably to decay.

The Hungarian government did not find expressed in the treaty the principles for which the Allies claimed to have fought. Count Apponyi urged that they build the peace not upon force but upon their "great moral influence." "We believe in the power of the moral factors," he concluded, "with which we identify our cause, and I wish you, gentlemen, that the glory of victorious arms should be presented by you to the whole of humanity." [7]

The moral eloquence of Count Apponyi differed from the bitter denunciation used by the German delegation, but it proved to be no more effective. The Allies cut more from Hungary than they had intended, for the total loss was reached by adding up the approved requests of three friendly governments. Beneš of Czechoslovakia had introduced the demands of his country by calling them "prudent, reasonable and just." [8] The Romanians and the Yugoslavs had all employed the same righteous language. When the treaty was submitted to the Hungarian National Assembly, that body denounced it as "based on false data, unjust and contrary to the interests of humanity . . . imposed on us by alien force." [9]

Minorities and Mandates Replace Imperialism

In reorganizing Europe for permanent peace, the Allied statesmen soon discovered that their guiding principle of national self-determination did not fit the regions of Eastern and Southeastern Europe. By the breakup of four great empires, 100 million people were assigned to new states, of whom from 20 to 25 millions became minority groups. As a leading student of the subject has written, "If the principle of national self-determination and homogeneity had been carried to the extreme, minorities would have been forced either to renounce their language and nationality, to emigrate from their homes, or else to live in the expectation that a neighboring state of their own nationality would conquer the territory in which they lived." [10] In an effort to make their ideal work, the Allied statesmen required the small states to accept a treaty of guarantee of minority rights. Poland, Yugoslavia, Czechoslovakia, Romania, Greece, Austria, Bulgaria, Hungary, Turkey, Estonia, Finland (with respect to the Aland islands), Latvia, Lithu-

[7] Francis Deák, *Hungary at the Paris Peace Conference* (New York: Columbia University Press, 1942), pp. 539-549.

[8] *Ibid.*, p. 389. [9] *Ibid.*, p. 337.

[10] Jacob Robinson and others, *Were the Minorities Treaties a Failure?* (New York: Institute of Jewish Affairs, 1943), p. 40.

ania, and Iraq signed such treaties. The provisions were frequently exact quotations from the great documents of human freedom, the English Bill of Rights, the American Declaration of Independence, the Preamble and certain amendments of the American Constitution, and the Declaration of the Rights of Man of the French Revolution. Protection of life and property, freedom of speech, press and assembly, equality before the law, freedom of worship, equal rights of citizenship, the right officially and privately to use one's own language, and similar rights were guaranteed in the treaties irrespective of "birth, nationality, language, race or religion." The governments accepted the treaties often under strenuous protest. Most of the states would like to have imitated Italy, who repelled the intimation that she should sign such a document. The fact that the treaties were to be executed under the auspices of the League of Nations did not diminish the sense of humiliation.

The European Allies had decided during the war to take the dependent areas from Germany and the Ottoman Empire and had secretly agreed among themselves on a division of spoils. The decline in prestige of imperialism as the war continued aided President Wilson, General Jan Smuts of South Africa, and many other idealists to seek a new and just way to solve an old problem. The Allies were not prepared to substitute for annexation the principle of direct international administration; but General Smuts offered an intermediate solution, that the German and Ottoman dependencies become mandates administered by designated states under the supervision of the League of Nations. The proposal was accepted and written into the Covenant of the League. The peace treaties stripped the two empires of their dependencies on two counts, inhumanity to the natives and use of the areas for military or naval bases against the Allies. The Germans flatly denied the accusations, and requested that the colonies be restored to them as mandates. When the Allies refused, dividing the responsibility among themselves, the Germans denounced their action as disguised imperialism.

Economic Terms

The economic clauses were of the same nature in each of the treaties with the defeated powers. The amounts demanded in reparations differed according to the economic condition of the state in question. The Allies recognized that Bulgaria was unable to pay much in reparations and set the sum due from her at $450,000,000 payable over a period of thirty-eight years. Some immediate deliveries of livestock, coal, and certain other materials were also required. Austria and Hungary were treated in the same manner as Bulgaria, with Allied reparations commissions fixing the amounts. Foodstuffs were taken from Austria while people in Vienna were starving, and Allied relief supplies had to be imported. The main attention focused on Germany as the most powerful and the wealthiest of the vanquished states. She was burdened with reparations payments while subjected to severe economic handicaps.

The Allies established the legal basis for exacting reparations in the United States note to Germany of November 5, 1918, which stated that compensation would be made by Germany "for all damage done to the civilian population of the Allies and their property by the aggression of Germany by land, by sea and from the air." Wilson had also demanded that the Central Powers "restore" Belgium, France, Romania, Serbia, and Montenegro. French and British statesmen, particularly Lloyd George, had promised their electorates that Germany would be forced to pay the entire cost of the war. A little postelection thinking made clear that no country could assume such a burden. The Allies soon concentrated upon extracting from Germany as much in reparations as possible. Since Great Britain, in contrast to France and Belgium, had suffered little physical injury, she wished the claim for damage to the civilian population to include war pensions. Wilson's acceptance of this item in the definition of civilian damage has been called one of the crucial decisions of the peace conference; it greatly increased the reparations claims, and it struck the Germans and a considerable number of Allied citizens as unjust.

Ignorant of the amount of damage which the war had caused them or of the amount of reparations which Germany could pay, the Allies split over the question of whether to fix a definite sum. The French favored leaving the final sum uncertain and collecting over an indefinite period as much as could be obtained. The British and the Americans objected to this plan as politically impossible of fulfillment. It would mean, they argued, forcing Germany to work for the Allies and depriving her of the prospect of economic recovery and independence. When the French reluctantly retreated from their position, the Allies appointed a commission of Allied experts to report by 1921 on the sum which Germany could provide. The commission was further empowered to collect the reparations. It had the authority to explore any relevant aspect of the German economy and to recommend action to the Allies. The reparations payments took precedence over all other claims upon the German economy; and the commission was to see that Germany sincerely endeavored to meet these payments and managed her economy in such a way as to do so. For example, it had to be certain "that the German taxation system should impose in general on the taxpayer at least as great a burden as that prevailing in the most heavily burdened of the states represented on the Reparations Commission."[11] Germany governed herself on sufferance.

Supplementing the reparations burdens were numerous economic restrictions and direct deprivations. The Allied argument ran as follows:

> Germany must submit for a few years to certain special disabilities and arrangements. Germany has ruined the industries, the mines, and the machinery

[11] Luckau, *op. cit.*, p. 444.

of neighboring countries, not during battle, but with the deliberate and calculated purpose of enabling her industries to seize their markets before their industries could recover from the devastation thus wantonly inflicted upon them. Germany has despoiled her neighbors of everything she could make use of or carry away. Germany has destroyed the shipping of all nations on the high seas, where there was no chance of rescue for their passengers and crews. It is only justice that restitution should be made and that these wronged people should be safeguarded for a time from the competition of a nation whose industries are intact and have even been fortified by machinery stolen from occupied territories. . . . Somebody must suffer for the consequences of the war. Is it to be Germany, or only the peoples she has wronged? [12]

Germany would have to prove to the world that she had reformed her ways before she would be restored to the international community. Until that time and until she had been admitted to membership in the League of Nations "'the equitable treatment for the commerce of all members of the League,'" stipulated in the Covenant of that organization, "requires that Germany should temporarily be deprived of the right she claims to be treated on a footing of complete equality with other nations." [13]

The Allies admitted that the recovery of German industry was to their own interest as well. They therefore declared that

. . . they will not withhold from Germany commercial facilities without which this resumption [of German industry] cannot take place, but that, subject to conditions and within limits, which cannot be laid down in advance, and subject also to the necessity for having due regard to the special economic situation created for Allied and Associated countries by German aggression and the war, they are prepared to afford to Germany facilities in these directions for the common good.[14]

The Allies devoted one half of the treaty to the economic clauses. A summary of the main provisions will indicate the nature of them all. Germany was required to pay $5 billion in cash or kind by May 1, 1921, but the Reparations Commission could remit portions necessary to buy essential food and raw materials. She should immediately turn over an additional $10 billion in bearer bonds, and the Reparations Commission could demand double that amount if it thought Germany was able to pay the sum. She should deliver to France 7 million tons of coal per year for ten years, plus an additional amount of not over 20 million tons for each of five years and 8 million tons for each of the next five years to compensate for the German destruction of French mines. She should provide Belgium with 8 million tons annually for ten years, Italy an amount rising from 4½ million tons to 8½ million tons for ten years, and Luxembourg an unspecified sum. In each case the price should not exceed that of British or, in the case of Belgium, Dutch export coal.

Germany should restore or replace animals, machinery, equipment, tools, and like articles of a commercial character seized, consumed, or destroyed "in direct consequence of military operations," plus reconstruction

[12] *Ibid.*, p. 414. [13] *Ibid.*, p. 452. [14] *Ibid.*, p. 447.

materials. Until 1925 the Reparations Commission could demand up to 25 per cent of the German production of dye stuffs and chemical drugs. German oceanic cables were confiscated; state property and the property, rights, and interests of her nationals in Allied countries were seized. All shipping vessels of 1,600 tons or more, half of her ships of between 1,000 and 1,600 tons, one fourth of her fishing boats, and a large portion of her river fleet were to be turned over to the Allies. Germany should build for transfer to the Reparations Commission ships of any kind desired not to exceed 200,000 gross tonnage for each of five years. All her rivers in which another country could claim a legitimate interest were placed under international commissions. On any one of the commissions Germany could be outvoted.

All Germany's special privileges acquired abroad were canceled; all her treaties were declared null and void except those which any Allied and Associated power proposed to retain for itself. Czechoslovakia was given a free zone for her commerce in the ports of Hamburg and Stettin. Special tariff provisions against Germany were allotted to France, Poland, and Luxembourg. Germany had to agree in advance to any further international arrangements concerning postal, telegraphic, and radio-telegraphic communications. Her ports, canals, and railways came in for intensive regulation in Allied favor. The sampling should indicate that the Treaty of Versailles afforded the legal basis for thorough curtailment of the German economy and for control of what remained.

German Conception of Economic Peace Terms

The German government denounced the economic terms as a violation of the conditions on which it had accepted a truce.

> A Germany, thus partitioned and weakened, [it asserted] must, though the payment of war expenditures has expressly been given up, declare herself ready to bear the weight of all the expenditures of her adversaries, which amount to twice the national and individual wealth of Germany. . . . The limit will be indicated by the capacity of payment of the German people, the degrees contemplated do not depend on the conditions of its existence but solely on the possibility in which it will find itself to satisfy the demands of its enemies by its work. The German people would thus be condemned to perpetual slavery.[15]

The government accused the Allies of using the treaty provisions "to stamp out German commercial competition"; for, it said, many of the economic clauses had absolutely no relation to reparations.[16] It predicted that reparations payments would cause ruinous inflation. And it warned:

> The idea of extracting the enormous indemnities stipulated in the draft of the peace treaty from what would be left of Germany according to the draft, is impossible. A Germany, in whose population any delight in work would be killed

[15] *Ibid.*, p. 303. [16] *Ibid.*, p. 347.

at the very outset by the despair of the present and the hopelessness of the future, cannot even be counted upon in the question of the payment of indemnities.[17]

Immediately after the Armistice the German government had begun to work on proposals for a peace treaty in harmony with Wilson's ideals. It now brought these forward as an expression of the results, not of dictation, but of negotiation and understanding. The government recommended that a reparations commission with a neutral chairman be created. It proposed that an international coal commission be set up to assure fair and equitable distribution of that commodity. It promised coal to France, provided it received Lorraine iron ore in return. It asked for an international pooling of oceanic shipping to take care of the emergency without the loss of ships to German ownership. It offered participation in German industries and mines by foreign owners whose plants or mines had been damaged or destroyed in the course of the military action. In lieu of the international commissions for the rivers and the loss of Danzig and West Prussia to Poland, it promised Czechoslovakia and Poland full rights of river transportation and use of ports. It agreed to help reconstruct the devastated regions of France and Belgium, not of the other countries; but, it added, "we cannot accomplish it without the technical and financial participation of the victor nations, and they could accomplish it only with our coöperation. Impoverished Europe must desire to bring about this reconstruction as successfully, but at the same time at as little cost as possible." [18]

The German government went further and advised the victorious powers to "agree to render active assistance to Germany in the reconstruction of her economic life." [19] For, it argued,

> It is not Germany alone that at present needs credit on a most extensive scale in order to replenish her exhausted stores, to procure the absolutely indispensable amounts of food stuffs and raw materials, and to consolidate the great floating debts, but almost all the belligerent countries of Europe must resume their normal economic life under the most difficult conditions. To concentrate all the forces of the world upon this problem and to give to all peoples the chance of continued existence is the first and most pressing task. Only when that is accomplished will Germany be in a position to discharge the heavy obligations for reparations assumed by her. . . . This is based upon the assumption, however, that Germany shall be allowed to preserve that territorial integrity which the armistice promises, that we keep our colonial possessions and merchant ships, even those of large tonnage; that we have the same freedom of action both in our own country and in the world at large as other peoples; that all war laws shall be abrogated at once; and that all infringements of our economic rights in German private property, etc., which were suffered during the war, shall be settled according to the principle of reciprocity.[20]

Except for a few minor details, the German counterproposals were rejected.

[17] *Ibid.*, p. 379. [18] *Ibid.*, p. 222. [19] *Ibid.*, p. 377. [20] *Ibid.*, pp. 388-389.

Disarmament and War Criminals

The disarmament clauses caused least difficulty of any of the major terms in the treaties. In this field the Allies performed a straightforward, clear duty which had been well advertised beforehand. Since the changes in government in the enemy states had brought to power the social and political groups that also disliked militarism, the demands aroused at the time no major objections. The Allies made the terms palatable to the defeated peoples by stating that at some future date the victors would likewise disarm. They chose three main means for assuring the military weakness of the enemy. They restricted the numerical size of the army (Germany, 100,000 men, and each of the lesser states 30,000 to 35,000 men, with Turkey allowed 50,000). They required the enlisted and noncommissioned personnel to serve for twelve years and the officers for twenty to twenty-five years (the latter term for Germany), thereby aiming to prevent short-term training of large bodies of men, a system the Prussians had contrived after 1806 to hoodwink Napoleon. They deprived the services of the equipment particularly useful on offense—the airplane, poison gas, tanks, and armored cars. The amount of munitions allowed was precisely limited, the munitions production restricted to designated factories under Allied supervision. The famed general staff was abolished. Apart from being permitted to keep these forces of value only for internal purposes, the countries were disarmed. As for German territory, France put through a stipulation that the entire German area west of the Rhine and a strip 50 kilometers wide east of the Rhine were to be demilitarized. The other border countries of Germany did not receive such favor. The navy was limited on a comparable scale. Germany was permitted to possess six battleships, six light cruisers, twelve destroyers, and twelve torpedo boats, and a personnel of 15,000 men recruited for a long term of service. She was forbidden to have any submarines, as was landlocked Austria. The Allies set up a Disarmament Commission in each country, with full authority to oversee the execution of the terms. The system appeared to be ironclad, and as long as it was enforced it proved to be effective.

The Allies half-heartedly introduced into the peacemaking the idea that certain persons among the enemy should be judged war criminals. This new conception, for which Wilson could find no justification in international law, emerged mainly as a by-product of democratic politics. Hatred had been so aroused, accusations of war crimes had been made so freely, that the new conception became popular. Lloyd George, who had promised the British electorate to hang the Kaiser, took the initiative, and each peace treaty included articles recognizing the right of the Allies to try war criminals. For Germany the Allies provisionally listed 900 names; but when the Netherlands government refused to extradite the Kaiser, the plan lost momentum. At the time of peacemaking the German government had been willing to refer the question to an impartial international commission. After the treaty was accepted, the insecure Weimar Republic dared not alienate its public by turning over the accused to the Allies, and a counteroffer to try them in German courts was accepted. Twelve were finally brought up; six were convicted and given light sentences by German judges. The attempt ended in complete fiasco.

Allocation of the German dependencies as mandates caused no particular difficulty. These will be discussed in Chapter 5, on political international relations. Allied disposition of the possessions of the Ottoman Empire led to renewal of war in the region and delay in peacemaking until 1923 or later.

Ottoman Settlement

The clash between the old diplomacy of secret agreements and imperialism, on the one hand, and Wilsonian ideals, on the other, made itself felt in dealing with the Ottoman settlement. The Allies had to decide, regarding Turkey, whether to honor policies laid down in secret treaties or to try to apply Wilsonian principles. Lloyd George sought to repudiate secret agreements and respect the promise to the Arabs for a free state. The French and Italian representatives demanded satisfaction of their imperialist claims. Premier Venizelos of Greece at the peace conference persuaded the British and French to allow Greece to occupy Smyrna and her hinterland. The Italians, angry over the intrusion into their promised area and having withdrawn temporarily from the conference upon denial of their claims for territory across the Adriatic, now faced an accomplished fact. With British and French aid, Greek forces occupied Smyrna in May, 1919, and advanced toward the interior. Wilson refused to acknowledge the validity of a secret treaty; but since Smyrna and the coastal area contained a large Greek population, he favored Venizelos' request. Delay in settling terms with Turkey automatically eliminated United States influence, and the Treaty of Sèvres in August, 1920, deprived Turkey of Arabia, Palestine, Syria, Mesopotamia, and Armenia. Turkey gave up all rights in Africa and the Mediterranean islands, granted autonomy to Kurdistan, and recognized that Smyrna and the hinterland should be under Greek administration for five years and should then decide by plebiscite to whom they wished to belong.

The peace with Turkey coincided with the breaking of the peace. Although in a defeated European power a revolutionary change of government did not deter the Allies from imposing terms, with Turkey the situation was different. The revolution there, led by the army officer Mustafa Kemal, had begun in the middle of 1919; by the time of the Treaty of Sèvres it was in full swing. A year later the Italians prudently decided to retire from Asia, and in the course of 1922 the revived Turks routed the Greek army and occupied Smyrna, whence they threatened to expel the small Allied force protecting the Straits. The French and Italians early came to terms with the new Turkish movement, and in 1923 at Lausanne the Allies negotiated a peace treaty with Mustafa Kemal—the only treaty achieved on terms of equality. The Turkish rebels had overthrown the sultan's government and established a republic. With the change they had

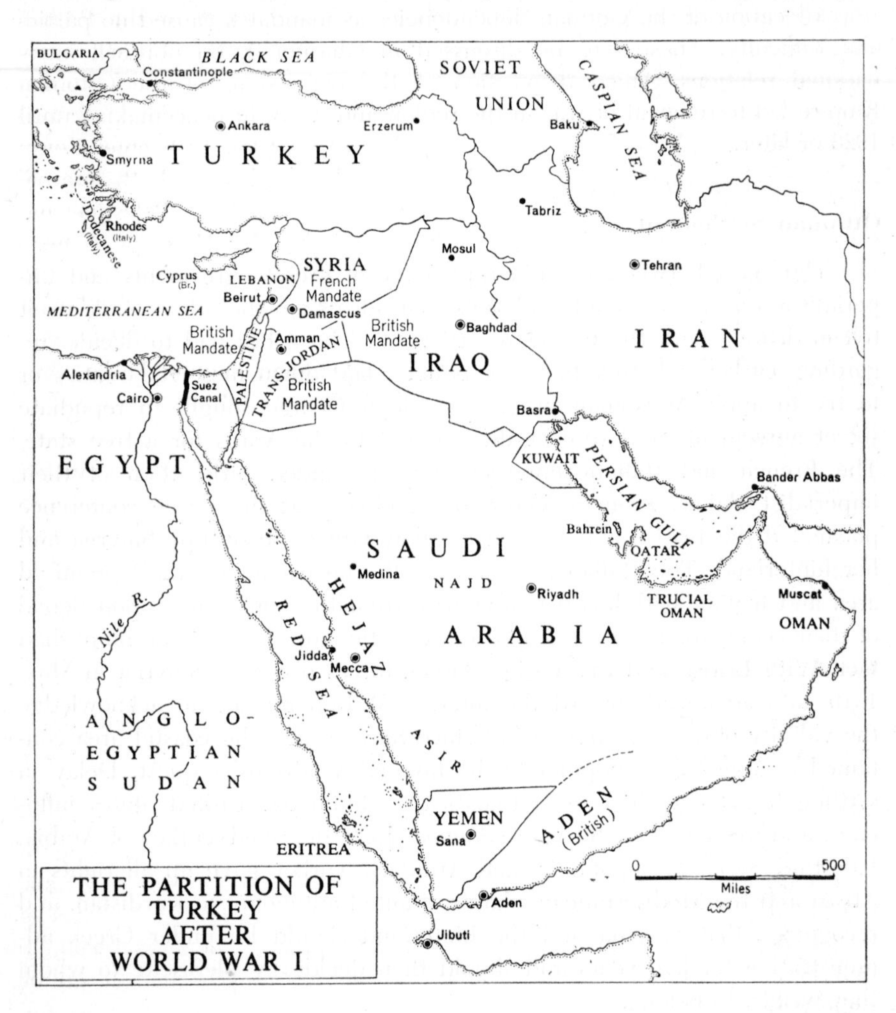

THE PARTITION OF TURKEY AFTER WORLD WAR I

renounced claims to imperial rule over Arabs and had formed a Turkish national state. Their decision eased the way to agreement at Lausanne, for the British were able to retain Iraq and Palestine as mandates, and the French took Syria and Lebanon. Independence for Egypt from Turkey was legally recognized, and the Straits were placed under a commission of the League of Nations with a Turk as permanent chairman. The Straits were declared free to commercial vessels except when Turkey was at war, their use by war vessels was restricted, and the shores were demilitarized.

The terms satisfied every state except Greece, whose hope of empire collapsed and who lost Eastern Thrace as well to Turkey.

Having freed the subject peoples from Turkish domination, the British and French governments sought to introduce a satisfactory form of political life. French power was restricted to Syria and Lebanon, where a nationalist uprising in favor of independence occupied the attention of the French emancipators from Ottoman misrule. By July, 1920, the French army crushed the revolt and organized the mandates after the French model. The other peoples came under British guidance. In Mesopotamia Britain created the kingdom of Iraq with the able and popular Arab chief Feisal as king, but retained important influence on the conduct of both internal and foreign affairs. The British separated Transjordan from Palestine and established Abdullah, son of the prominent Arab ruler Hussein, as head of the state. Along the periphery of Arabia they aided a number of small chiefs to become independent rulers, and they furthered the ambitions of the chieftain Ibn Saud to control the body of the peninsula. After overcoming a rebellious nationalist movement under Saad Zaghlul Pasha, they agreed in 1922 to end the protectorate over Egypt, subject, however, to the continued right of defense of British strategic and commercial interests in Egypt in general and in the Suez Canal in particular, and to the retention of British control over the Sudan. Since in most of the territories in the Near and Middle East nationalist sentiment had affected only a few intellectuals, a peace settlement of more or less disguised imperialism after World War I was temporarily still possible in the area.

Far East: Japanese and Chinese Claims

Peacemaking continued the effects of the war in augmenting the interdependence of events in the Far East and the West. In the Far East there was left a legacy of trouble greater than that in the Near and Middle East. Entitled to attend the Versailles Conference, China seized the occasion to try to reacquire the German holdings in the Shantung Peninsula and to obstruct Japan's imperialist ambitions. The United States supported China, but Great Britain and France, committed by secret treaty and desirous of possessions elsewhere for themselves, favored Japan. Their side won, in that Japan temporarily was to retain in Shantung the German economic rights and the privilege of establishing a Japanese settlement at Tsingtao; she promised ultimately to hand back the territory to China. Fearing the worst interpretation of this agreement, the Chinese government refused to approve the treaty of Versailles; it made a separate treaty whereby Germany did give up the German properties and privilege in China, and the Chinese people began a boycott of Japanese goods. By signing the Austrian treaty, China became a member of the League of Nations, and henceforth she strove to muster the support of that predominantly European body against her Oriental opponent.

Treaties Evaluated

The Allied statesmen were well pleased with their achievement. The treaties, they said, provided "the basis upon which the peoples of Europe can live together in friendship and equality."[21] President Wilson found the German treaty "in entire conformity with the Fourteen Points." Lloyd George approved it in similar terms. Tardieu spoke of "the moderation of her [France's] peace demands"; the treaty, he said, was bound to be good, for "It was France who taught the world justice. And to justice she remains faithful."[22] Clemenceau's reaction expressed his experience and standards. "Life is but a struggle," he told the French parliament after the peace was made. "That struggle you can never get rid of. My idea of life is a perpetual conflict whether in war or in peace. I think it was Bernhardi who said: 'War is but politics pursued in another manner.' We can reverse the aphorism and say: 'Peace is but war pursued in another manner.' . . . If you have thought for a moment that we have been able to make a peace which will do away with the need for watchfulness between the nations of Europe which only yesterday were shedding their blood without stint upon every front, well then it means that you are unable to understand us!"[23]

The peace treaties set the framework within which the European and the Near and Middle-Eastern states functioned during the next twenty years. They posed the problems with which statesmen were to contend. The treaties defined the first peace made by states with responsible, democratic governments, the first major one in which both European and recent colonial powers like the United States and the Union of South Africa participated. It cannot be said that the democracies made a peace of understanding; on the contrary, they incorporated the popular passions of nations at war into the peace treaties, thus compromising Europe's future. The non-European powers did not succeed in eliminating or even lessening the century-old animosities among the European nations. In one sense their presence gave to the peace a world character; in so far they worked in harmony with the unifying forces of modern industrialism. At the same time Europe was not restored as a regional unit with a state system of its own. Russia had to be left out of consideration because of the disinclination of the peace conference to contend with the chaos there. The greatest shortcoming of the work of the conference lay in the fact that after a total war demanding intensive international cooperation, the Allied statesmen switched abruptly to a program of peacemaking—one cannot call it recovery—based on extreme nationalism, the absolute opposite of international cooperation. The peace for this "brave new world" turned out to be the terms of a twenty-year truce.

[21] *Ibid.*, p. 419.

[22] André Tardieu, *The Truth about the Treaty* (Indianapolis: Bobbs-Merrill Company, Inc., 1921), pp. 435, 445.

[23] *Ibid.*, p. 434.

Suggestions for Further Reading

ALBRECHT-CARRIÉ, RENÉ. *Italy at the Paris Peace Conference.* New York: Columbia University Press, 1938. Historical introduction and documents. The documents in this volume, as in those listed below in the same series, are particularly interesting.

ALMOND, NINA, and R. H. LUTZ, eds. *The Treaty of St. Germain: A Documentary History.* Stanford, Calif.: Stanford University Press, 1935.

BAILEY, THOMAS A. *Woodrow Wilson and the Lost Peace.* New York: The Macmillan Company, 1944. Analysis of Wilson's part in the peacemaking.

DEÁK, FRANCIS. *Hungary at the Paris Peace Conference.* New York: Columbia University Press, 1942. Historical introduction and documents.

KEYNES, JOHN MAYNARD. *The Economic Consequences of the Peace.* New York: Harcourt, Brace & Company, Inc., 1920. One of the most influential books of the century. A vigorous condemnation of the peacemaking.

LUCKAU, ALMA. *The German Delegation at the Paris Peace Conference.* New York: Columbia University Press, 1941. Historical introduction and documents.

NICOLSON, HAROLD. *Peacemaking, 1919.* New York: Harcourt, Brace & Company, Inc., 1939. By a wise British diplomat and student of many aspects of life who participated in the peacemaking.

NOWAK, KARL FRIEDRICH. *Versailles.* New York: Payson and Clark, 1929. Work by an indignant German author.

Part II

Europe in the 1920's

Chronological Preview

1918–1920
Civil War in Russia

1919
Béla Kun regime in Hungary
D'Annunzio seizes Fiume
Weimer Constitution adopted in Germany
British Constitution for India–Dyarchy

1920
Poland seizes Vilna
War between Russia and Poland
Kapp *Putsch*

1920–1921
Formation of Little Entente

1920–1922
Greco-Turkish War

1920–1923
Stamboliski rule in Bulgaria

1921
Ireland receives Dominion status
Persian-Russian Treaty

1921–1922
Washington Naval Conference

1921–1927
New Economic Policy in Russia

1922
Franco-Polish Alliance
Treaty of Rapallo
Iraq becomes free state
Fascists gain power in Italy

1923
German inflation
Occupation of the Ruhr
Establishment of U.S.S.R.
Lithuania seizes Memel

1923 (Cont.)
Draft Treaty of Mutual Assistance
Corfu Incident
Primo de Rivera becomes dictator in Spain

1924
Britain's first Labor government
Geneva Protocol
Franco-Czechoslovakian Alliance
First Labor government in Denmark
Dawes Plan
Evacuation of the Ruhr
Death of Lenin

1925
Locarno Agreements
Britain restores the gold standard
Election of von Hindenburg as president of Germany

1926
Murder of Radić
Stabilization of French franc
General strike in Great Britain
Pilsudski seizes power in Poland
Treaty of Berlin between Germany and U.S.S.R.
Germany enters the League of Nations
British Imperial Conference

1927
International Economic Conference at Geneva
British Trades Disputes Act
Geneva Disarmament Conference
Stabilization of Italian lira

1928
Fascist electoral law in Italy
Kellogg-Briand Pact

1929
Stalin gains control of U.S.S.R.
Young Plan for Germany

Chapter 5 · International Organization and Relations—Political

The "war to end war" and the peace of justice, but not of understanding, left behind a Europe far different from that of 1914. Total war had created problems which had both international and internal aspects, and which in varying degrees existed alike among victors, vanquished, and neutrals. The way these problems were met in the 1920's laid the foundation for events at least until World War II. The first two chapters in this part will consider international affairs in the twenties, a record of general failure; subsequent chapters will deal with the national matters, during the decade, that proved to be beyond the capacity of individual states to handle.

ENFORCEMENT OF PEACE TREATIES

Once the peace treaties were signed, they had to be enforced. The small defeated states—Austria, Hungary, and Bulgaria—were too weak to resist the terms, although Hungary tried to do so. The main obstruction to execution arose, as was to be expected, in Germany, the geographic as well as the political and economic center of European affairs, and potentially still the greatest military power in Europe. All major problems in European international relations in the interwar period revolved around this state. Every political party in Germany made public its refusal to acquiesce in the loss of territory in the east. The powerful right-wing National party avowed its hope to recover territory also in the west. All parties hated reparations, the war guilt clause, the inequality in treatment with respect to disarmament, and many other parts of the treaty. The world could expect that Germany would constantly strive to revise the settlement.

In countering Germany, the Allies were divided on policy. In the United States the small isolationist wing of the Republican party in the Senate, led by Senator Henry Cabot Lodge, controlled the Foreign Relations Committee and proved so adept at opposing Wilson that the Senate refused to ratify the peace treaties. The action included the repudiation of the proposed treaty between the United States, Great Britain, and France guaranteeing the Franco-German frontier; thus France was deprived of one of her major means of security against Germany. The United States made a separate peace with each of the enemy states. In these agreements it obtained all the rights of signers of the regular treaties without assuming any of the responsibilities. The fact that the United States had joined the war for reasons of national defense was forgotten. The Senate refused to recognize that the treaties would require enforcement. For the next two decades the United States, the greatest power in the world, kept aloof from continental entanglements and benefited from the temporary protection provided by France and her continental allies against a revival of German military power.

British Criticism

The British attitude toward Germany changed rapidly to one of endeavoring to revive international cooperation. Before negotiations on the treaty of Versailles were completed, Lloyd George began to regret his violent promises about the treatment of Germany, and in the course of the year 1919 British criticism of the treaty became vigorous and widespread. Apart from the effects of a few Zeppelin raids, the British Isles had escaped the direct ravages of war. Great Britain had never been a military nation; as soon as the war ceased and before the peace treaties were concluded, the British began to demobilize their army. By 1920 the country had only 300,000 men under arms, most of whom were scattered over the world and only about one third in Great Britain itself. The British no longer feared Germany; to prevent a recurrence of war they advocated the reintegration of Germany with the family of nations. They wished particularly to prevent the continent from dividing into two hostile camps, with the two pariahs, Germany and Russia, joining forces against the others.

The British criticized the terms of the treaty of Versailles on two essential issues, the drawing of the eastern frontiers and the imposition of the reparations burden. They felt the impact of scholarly research which showed that Germany should not bear the exclusive responsibility for the outbreak of the war. The effects of change were evident in official policy. The British refused to enforce the peace treaty with respect to the eastern German frontier. They felt that the terms about Danzig, West Prussia, and the Sudetenland and the prohibition against the union of Germany and Austria all violated the right of national self-determination. They harbored some similar doubts about Upper Silesia. They feared that the new German republic had been treated in a way suitable to the imperial *Reich* but not to a young democracy struggling against reactionary forces.

Under the stimulus of the economist John Maynard Keynes, whose book *The Economic Consequences of the Peace* appeared in the latter half of 1919, the British came to accept the following theses: that the economic prosperity of Europe mainly depended upon that of Germany, that the purpose of the treaty of Versailles was to destroy the German economic system as it had existed before the war, and that until the treaty was revised the German economy and therefore the European economy could not recover. By February, 1920, the opposition in the House of Commons moved an amendment to the Address of the Throne expressing regret that "Your Majesty's Ministers have not recognized the impracticability of the fulfillment by our late enemies of many of the terms of the Peace Treaties." And Reginald McKenna, Liberal and former chancellor of the exchequer, said, "The economic restoration of Europe should today be our first concern. If we neglect it, our whole foreign trade will contract and decay. . . . What Europe needs at the present time is Peace! Not merely the peace of pacts and treaties, but peace born of the spirit of peace, when the nations 'shall beat their swords into plough-shares.'" As a trading nation, Great Britain wished the economic revival of her important German markets; but in addition she adhered to the liberal moral tradition of believing that all men were essentially decent and reasonable and that one could live with other nations in peace and good will.

French Fear of Germany

When the Treaty of Versailles was submitted to the French parliament for approval, the Socialist deputy Albert Thomas asked how this "sum total of insufficiency . . . [could] constitute a solid security for the country." How many Frenchmen felt that the peace was too soft cannot be estimated. The Parliament ratified the treaty with grave misgivings. A few years later, the French Minister Herriot, one of the most internationally minded leaders of his nation, said to the British Laborite, Ramsay MacDonald, "If there is another war, France will be wiped off the map"; and to the Conservative Austen Chamberlain, British foreign secretary, he declared, "I look forward with terror to her [Germany's] making war upon us again in ten years."

The French knew that in the past half century Germany had grown into a much stronger power than France. As against their 39 million people in 1920, Germany could show 61 million and a consistently higher birth rate. The French loss of 1,359,000 men in the war could not be recouped so quickly and so easily as Germany's loss of 1,885,000 men. For at least a generation France would be very short of men of fighting age, whereas Germany could easily muster a force with which again to attack France. The war had revealed that France lacked the industrial capacity and technology to compete with her enemy. General Foch believed that the German republic preserved the militarism of the old *Reich*. He and his countrymen sought means to prevent the Germans from again seeking to assert their superiority in numbers and resources. They understood that the French position rested upon the victory of a coalition, but they determined to maintain France's dominance as long as they could. Particularly after the United States killed the proposed Anglo-American guarantee of the Franco-German frontier, the French regarded the peace treaties, especially that of Versailles, as the foundation of their power, and they condemned any and all proposals for revision. They feared that relaxation of the terms would endanger the organization of the new Europe. What country, particularly in Eastern and Southeastern Europe, they asked, would then feel safe?

ALLIED CONTROL OF GERMANY

If the Allies could have agreed to enforce the terms, the treaty of Versailles afforded ample legal basis for indefinite control of Germany. In Part XIV, for example, in order to obtain fulfillment of the treaty, the Allies had provided for occupying the territory west of the Rhine and the bridgeheads for fifteen years. If Germany faithfully carried out all terms, the Allies agreed to evacuate the area by district at five-year intervals. If at the end of fifteen years "the guarantees against unprovoked aggression by Germany are not considered sufficient by the Allied and Associated Governments, the evacuation of the occupying troops may be delayed to the extent regarded as necessary for the purpose of obtaining the required guarantees." The same stipulation applied to the reparations clauses. That Germany would not execute the 440 articles of the treaty to the letter, that she would try secretly to increase her military power, that she would attempt to avoid paying reparations, might have been expected. The French strove to implement the guarantees, but the British objected. Since policy toward Germany had to be approved by a coalition, French severity alternated with grudging acquiescence in concessions to Germany. The result was most unfortunate. Franco-German animosity was kept alive, and the successive concessions forced by the British undermined Allied power over the country without gaining its good will and cooperation. A policy either of harshness or of softness consistently executed would have been preferable to indecision. It soon became apparent that Germany would have to be coerced into abiding by the treaty, or continuous revision would be necessary. Allied contradictions furthered the revival of power politics and the prospects of another world war.

The Allies did not lack extensive machinery to control Germany. The Supreme Council, an outgrowth of the Supreme War Council, consisted of ministers of the major Allies. It met intermittently and mainly expressed in public the British and French differences over high policy. In January, 1920, the Allies formed the Conference of Ambassadors to supervise the execution of the treaties. Under the presidency of the French representative, the conference met in Paris; it consisted of the British, Italian, and Japanese ambassadors accredited to France (and a Belgian representative, when Belgian affairs were discussed). The German minister Stresemann called it "a sort of penal committee established against Germany."

The Military, Naval, and Air Commissions of Control created by the Allies were to oversee the reduction of the German army and navy and the abolition of the German air force. These commissions worked harmoniously and on the whole effectively. German violations of the disarmament terms, such as the provision of secret funds for the manufacture of forbidden articles of war and the re-creation of the old general staff in fact, though not in name, usually became known to the Allies; but they amounted to little in the scale of preparation necessary for a modern war. Until Adolf Hitler came to power (1933) Germany remained disarmed.

The third political agency, the Inter-Allied Rhineland High Commission, provided civilian authority in the area occupied by British, French, Belgian, and United States troops. Since the United States would not participate, the commission consisted of representatives of the other three powers. It proved to be a complete failure. Each commissioner worked only in the region occupied by the troops of his country, and the military commander continued to be the important person. Commissioners were poorly, or not at all, informed about the state of affairs in the others' area; and in the event of direct conflict of policy, such as occurred at the time of the French occupation of the Ruhr, the British refused to enforce the French decrees in their district. The office of High Commission is mainly of interest as a forerunner of the institutions tried after World War II.

Reparations and War Debts

The Reparations Commission was created to assume the most important and the most difficult responsibility with respect to Germany—the execution of the reparations clauses. It began its career by recommending after investigation a total reparations bill to Germany of 132 billion marks, with the mark valued at 4.20 to the dollar. The Allies accepted this proposal and agreed to divide the sum into two parts. Payments on the C bonds, totaling 82 billion marks, were not to start immediately. Payments on the rest, covered by A and B bonds to the extent of 12 and 38 billion marks, respectively, should begin immediately, with Germany providing 1 billion marks within twenty-six days and thereafter 2 billion marks a year. In addition, she should pay 26 per cent of the proceeds from German exports, but the sum total of her annual payments should not exceed 3 billion marks. These payments should be made quarterly for a period of thirty years. The Reparations Commission had the power of final decision on matters other than the total amount of reparations to be collected. When the United States withdrew, however, the commission lost the driving force to make it a body of nonpolitical, independent experts. The French government appointed a politician as its member, and the commission became a place of political quarrels over reparations. The British government soon sought to by-pass it in favor of direct Allied negotiations with Germany.

From the beginning reparations became directly related to inter-Allied war debts. At the close of hostilities the various Allies owed the United States more than $7 billion; Great Britain, an almost equal amount; France, $2¼ billion; and the other states, smaller sums. The amounts, especially the sums owed the United States, were increased during the succeeding months. The European peoples considered the money to have been used in the conduct of a common war. They argued that they had borne the brunt of the fighting, whereas the United States had in the main contributed money. The one contribution should balance the other; the war debts should be canceled. The governments expressed willingness to try to repay them if necessary; but they manifestly shared the popular view. The United States Congress regarded these debts as business commitments: the money had been borrowed; it should be repaid. The European Allies replied that reparations would have to be collected in order to pay war debts. The French and Belgians claimed, in addition, enough reparations to cover the cost of reconstructing the devastated areas.

As early as 1922 the British government intimated that it would collect from Germany and from the Allies just enough to pay its war debts to the United States, a plan that would have eliminated three fourths of the continental war debt to Great Britain. At about the same time Prime Minister Raymond Poincaré of France proposed that the C bonds be canceled in return for the cancellation of the Inter-Allied war debts and of the European debts to the United States. The United States Congress rejected the idea as an attempt to make the United States pay for the war. The American government insisted that the full sum be paid, but it varied the amount of interest according to the condition of the debtor country and allowed the obligations to be amortized over a period of 62 years, Great Britain being hardest hit. The British, French, and Italian governments all reduced substantially both interest and principal of the loans which they had made to Allies during the war. Their policy proved to be the wiser one. In spite of its efforts the United States was able to collect only about 25 per cent.

As soon as Germany began to pay reparations, the value of her money declined. Although the French accused the Germans of deliberately sabotaging the reparations payments, the true explanation lacks such simplicity. It is doubtful whether a government would have willfully caused the dangerous fall in the value of its money on the small chance that thereby its armed creditors would pity the financial plight of its 61 million enterprising people and forgive and forget reparations. The government of the Weimar Republic lacked the strength to place its finances in order; it could not count on sufficient popular support, especially from the big industrialists and the big agrarians, to reform the tax system, reduce governmental expenditures, and make government income cover outlay. The reparations payments added an excessive burden to a government already struggling to maintain itself, for Germany had to make payments in the currencies of the recipient countries or in gold, both of which she had to earn in foreign trade. In addition, she required foreign currencies in order to purchase essential imports of food and raw materials so that she could produce exports. Without such import-export trade the standard of living of the German people, already reduced by the war, would further decline. Thus reparations payments competed with the standard of living for the profit earned by selling manufactured goods abroad. Since Germany was at the time unpopular in the world, she was handicapped by the lack of foreign markets to enable her to earn the necessary foreign exchange. As she paid out the available gold and foreign exchange, she destroyed the customary backing for her monetary and credit system. With each payment of reparations the value of money declined, and more money had to be printed in order to cover governmental expenses. An unbalanced budget and reparations payments in gold and foreign currencies led to an increasing disproportion between the amount of goods available and the amount of money in circulation. Rapid inflation ensued.

The British quickly appreciated the difficulty about paying reparations. Their leaders saw that reparations depended upon the ability of Germany to pay and could not be collected by bayonets. They placed trade and economic recovery first; the French emphasized the requirement for money. They needed money to reconstruct the war areas; they wanted few if any German goods, except those like coal, of which they were short. The French politicians understood very little about the problem of transferring marks into francs or about the recovery of world trade. They concentrated upon French interest.

When the victor states endeavored to press reparations on a defeated enemy, the difficulty of collection became paramount. To obtain reparations for a period of thirty years required far more machinery of enforcement than the Allies had set up. Article 248 of the treaty placed German public finance, and hence the German economy, at the disposal of the Allies. Actually, the French and British governments disagreed over the implementation of the article. The British and the Americans objected to interfering in the internal financial affairs of a defeated enemy. They anticipated failure and heavy cost to the Allies themselves. British opinion favored scaling down reparations to an amount which Germany could pay and would pay without coercion. The French demanded direct control of sufficient German sources of revenue to cover the reparations payments, and in 1921 and 1922 the Allies tried this system. With an Allied Committee on Guarantees established to assume responsibility for collection, the Allies first fixed on export and import duties as a source. When these did not supply enough and the German mark continued to decline in value, the Allies under French pressure demanded that the government impose new taxes, reduce expenditures, take effective measures to prevent the flight of capital, and publish adequate financial and economic statistics.

Occupation of the Ruhr

This action, however, did not produce reparations and stop the German inflation; therefore the French government under Poincaré decided late in 1922 to use force. Over the vigorous protests of the British government, French and Belgian troops and technicians in January, 1923, occupied the Ruhr, the industrial heart of Germany. They claimed the authority to do so under a clause in the treaty of Versailles which read:

> The measures which the Allied and Associated Powers shall have the right to take, in case of voluntary default by Germany, and which Germany agrees not to regard as acts of war, may include economic and financial prohibitions and reprisals and in general such other measures as the respective Governments may determine to be necessary in the circumstances. (Part VIII, Annex II, paragraph 18.)

The French and Belgian seizure proved no more successful than the previous endeavors. Given whole-hearted financial and moral support by their government, the Germans in the Ruhr, employers, employees, and workers, went on a general strike. The invading powers confiscated the available supplies of coal and industrial stocks, placed a customs barrier around the Ruhr and collected duties, and tried to run the railroads. By September, 1923, the results of the action had proved to be disastrous for the Germans and disappointing, to say the least, to the French. The German government printed paper money to pay for the support of the striking Ruhr people, and the mark quickly became worthless.

The invaders were likewise not faring well. They obtained no reparations; they incurred heavy expenses in the attempt, and they aroused the severe criticism of the British and other friendly powers. Upon the cessation of German passive resistance, the French and Belgian governments signed agreements, not with the German government, but with private industries in the Ruhr, whereby the latter promised to pay the reparations. The Ruhr thus became a kind of "reparations province" taken from the control of the German government for this purpose and subordinated to France and Belgium. That this system severely weakened Germany made it even more attractive to Poincaré. It did not offer much assurance of continuing reparations, however, and it upset international financial relations so severely that international bankers began to turn against France.

Dawes Plan

While carrying on passive resistance to the occupation of the Ruhr the German government urged the appointment of an international committee of experts to report on Germany's capacity to pay. The French and Belgian governments reluctantly agreed, and on November, 1923, the committee, headed by the Chicago banker General Charles Dawes, set to work. The report of the committee, made in April, 1924, proved to be one of the most successful achievements of the interwar years. It incorporated the wisdom gained from the experience with reparations up to that date; and, although it failed to satisfy everyone on every point, as long as it lasted, until 1929, it took the reparations problem out of international political quarrels and provided the basis for five years of peace and prosperity, the only period of that nature during the interwar years.

The Dawes plan considered the problems of German budgetary equilibrium and currency stabilization in connection with reparations. The committee lacked the authority to recommend a reduction in the total amount of reparations, but it introduced a limited and reasonable schedule of payments; that in the first year was practically covered by an Allied loan, but the standard annuity of 2,500 million marks was not to be reached for five years. These payments should include not merely reparations proper but the cost of military occupation and any other charges levied upon Germany. A prosperity index was to be formulated to determine whether after 1928–1929 Germany was able to pay a larger amount of reparations annually, a provision that pleased the French because of the prospect of more funds and satisfied the Germans because it offered an objective standard by which to judge whether increased payments were possible.

The plan took over from French policy the earmarking of definite sources of revenue for reparations payments and the creation of Allied machinery to supervise the administration of these sources. The revenue from customs receipts, beer, tobacco, and sugar taxes and the alcohol monopoly were to be paid directly to the Allied Commissioner of Controlled Revenue. This revenue supplied half of the standard annuity; it proved so productive that the commissioner was able to return large amounts to the German treasury. The transport tax on the gross revenue of the railroad system was similarly pre-empted, although from 1926 on it was paid to the German Finance Ministry, which then turned the funds over to the Agent General for Reparations Payments. It covered 11.6 per cent of the standard annual payment of reparations. Industry was required to bear a mortgage of 5,000 million marks, the proceeds of which should supply 12 per cent of the reparations. The German railroads took on a similar mortgage of 11,000 million marks for that purpose. The Dawes Commission argued that German industry and railroads could afford to pay these sums because they had been relieved of all indebtedness by the inflation. The railroads, hitherto government owned, were placed in the hands of a joint-stock company under German management and Allied supervision. Altogether, including the transport tax, the railroads bore 38 per cent of the annual payment. The allocation of revenue sources for reparations thus in fact took from the German government the responsibility of finding the necessary funds in the general budget. Both it and the Allies knew what to expect; and, although Article 248 of the Treaty of Versailles remained in force, it was never applied.

In order to protect the value of the German currency against renewed inflation the Dawes plan introduced two new measures. It separated the *Reichsbank*, or German central bank, from government control, giving it exclusive authority to issue bank notes. The maximum amount of its loans to the government was limited to 100 million marks for not longer than three months, and all government debts to the bank had to be paid by the end of the fiscal year. The *Reichsbank* remained in German hands, but half the membership of the board of directors was to be composed of foreigners. In this way the Dawes plan took precautions against inflation by preventing indiscriminate government borrowing and an unbalanced national budget. It likewise protected the value of the mark by imposing upon the Agent General in Germany the responsibility for transferring marks into the currencies of the reparations recipients. Receiving the payments in marks, this official, with the aid of a Transfer Committee, had to obtain the necessary foreign exchange without hurting the German economy to the point of new inflation. If at any time the value of the mark became endangered, the Transfer Committee could postpone the exchange into other currencies. Actually no major transfer difficulty arose before 1929, primarily because the foreign loans made to Germany in these years amply provided her with funds.

The Dawes plan reconciled for the time the interests of all parties and gave each a stake in the success of the venture. The appointment of an American as Reparations Agent and the creation within Germany of administrative machinery of foreign experts for executing the plan assured impartial, nonpolitical procedure. The Dawes loan made to Germany in connection with the plan was placed in Allied countries, neutral states, and the United States and served as a harbinger of better times. By 1929 the next step was possible, namely, that of reducing the total amount of reparations to a manageable sum (less than one third of the original bill), of abolishing all foreign control of reparations, and of making Germany responsible for the transfer of the annual payments into foreign currencies. A Bank of International Settlement was founded in Basel to receive the German payments and distribute the funds among the creditors. These terms, recommended by a committee of international experts under the chairmanship of the American Owen D. Young, lasted for two years, when the world economic depression almost completely wiped out both reparations and war debts. The amount which Germany paid in reparations was disputed; Germany claimed that she had paid more than four times as much as the Reparations Commission asserted it had received. The difference is explained as the result of divergent valuations placed on goods and divergent views about whether certain goods should be called reparations. Objective investigators state that Germany paid about $6 billion, a sum roughly midway between that set by the German government and that put forward by the Reparations Commission.

THE LEAGUE OF NATIONS

The story of the quarrels over the enforcement of the peace treaties reveals the conditions under which the League of Nations came into being. The Covenant of the League had been incorporated in the treaties as a means of assuring approval by the powers; but, except where expressly stipulated, the League of Nations was excluded from any participation in the execution of their terms. Thus it could not consider the sources of the major problems troubling Europe. For example, as long as Franco-German relations growing out of the Treaty of Versailles were barred from its action, the League was restricted to lesser matters and to those of such long range that they were scarcely visible.

The background of the League of Nations must be sought far more in the nonofficial than in the official relations of the peoples of the world. If considered in the light of political precedents alone, the Covenant belongs among the most original documents of history. Except for theoretical plans of idealists like William Penn and Immanuel Kant, it lacked forerunners. By 1914 approximately thirty official international organizations existed, among which were the Universal Postal Union, the International Institute of Agriculture, and the Danube Commission; but none of these wielded any political authority. Between 1815 and 1900 two hundred international disputes had been arbitrated, none of political importance. The international conference at The Hague in 1899 created a Permanent Court of Arbitration, which was neither permanent nor a court but a panel of competent individuals on whom states might call. The court was mainly used for minor cases; and the second international conference at The Hague in 1907 did not lead to improvement. The conduct of official international relations continued to be that of the age of Machiavelli.

The changes that made possible a League of Nations had occurred in the private sector of life, primarily under the impact of modern industrialism. The methods of production and distribution of a machine economy driven by internal combustion motors and electricity were creating an interdependent world economy. The numerous private international associations, many in the field of business and many in science, labor, literature, sport, and all the other aspects of life, showed the response of private individuals to the opportunities for international cooperation. New facilities for transportation and communication and the improvement in the standard of living made this cooperation possible. When the war revealed the destructiveness of the instruments of industrialism, people in every country began to plan an international instrument to stop such holocausts. As a

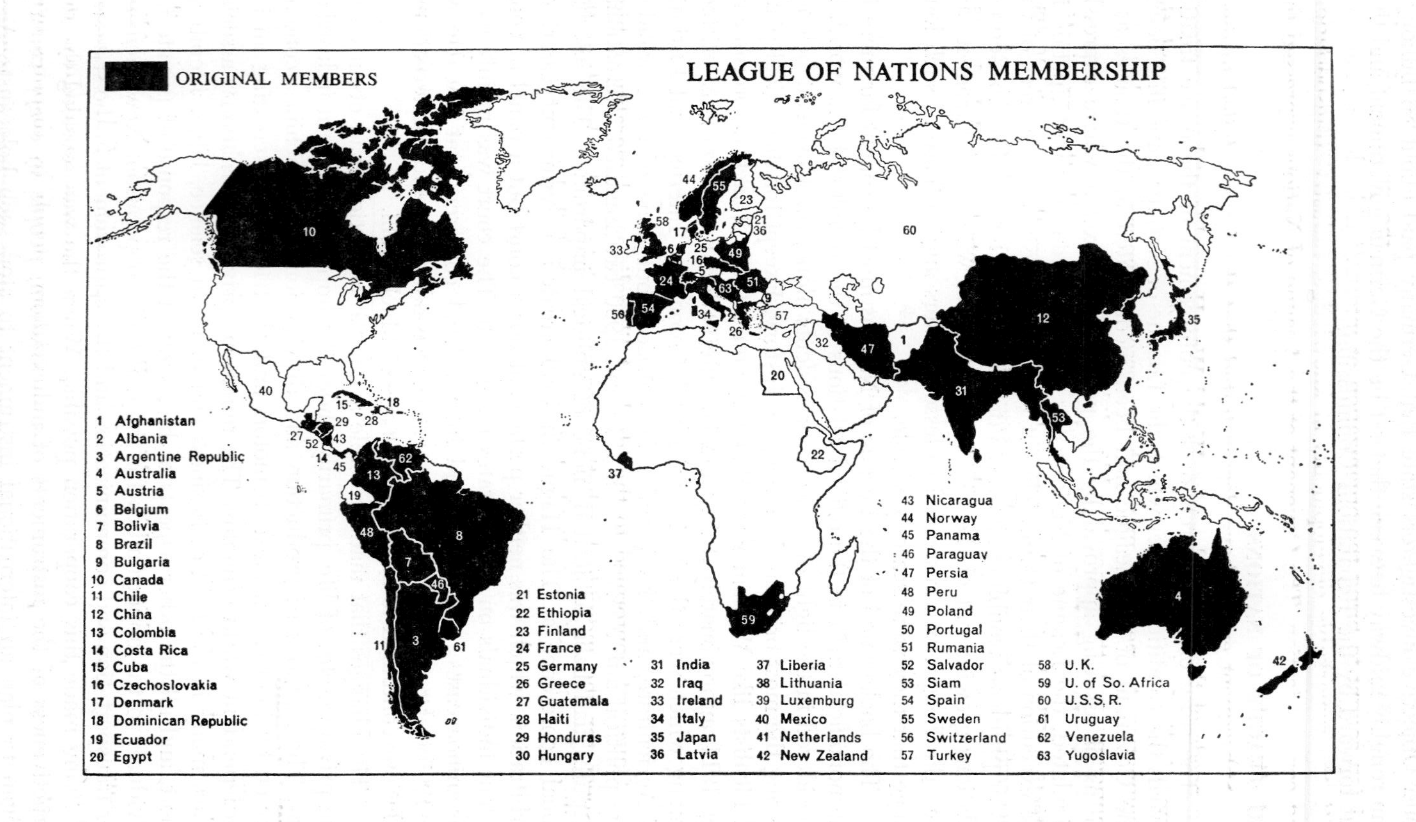
LEAGUE OF NATIONS MEMBERSHIP
ORIGINAL MEMBERS
1 Afghanistan
2 Albania
3 Argentine Republic
4 Australia
5 Austria
6 Belgium
7 Bolivia
8 Brazil
9 Bulgaria
10 Canada
11 Chile
12 China
13 Colombia
14 Costa Rica
15 Cuba
16 Czechoslovakia
17 Denmark
18 Dominican Republic
19 Ecuador
20 Egypt
21 Estonia
22 Ethiopia
23 Finland
24 France
25 Germany
26 Greece
27 Guatemala
28 Haiti
29 Honduras
30 Hungary
31 India
32 Iraq
33 Ireland
34 Italy
35 Japan
36 Latvia
37 Liberia
38 Lithuania
39 Luxemburg
40 Mexico
41 Netherlands
42 New Zealand
43 Nicaragua
44 Norway
45 Panama
46 Paraguay
47 Persia
48 Peru
49 Poland
50 Portugal
51 Rumania
52 Salvador
53 Siam
54 Spain
55 Sweden
56 Switzerland
57 Turkey
58 U.K.
59 U. of So. Africa
60 U.S.S.R.
61 Uruguay
62 Venezuela
63 Yugoslavia

group, the professional diplomats and soldiers were and continued to be hostile to the ideal; but statesmen responsive to the pressure of public opinion sought to bring the organization of international relations into line with the remarkable developments in knowledge, industry, transportation, and communication. The Covenant of the League of Nations expressed the first attempt.

Subsequent events have demonstrated that the League failed to meet the needs of the time; otherwise World War II would not have occurred. Some individuals correctly diagnosed its deficiencies and possessed the imagination to perceive many of the essential improvements; but most politicians and the general public did not understand the issues clearly enough to demand the innovations that might have made the organization effective. The basic weakness may be implied from the name itself. The successful functioning of a league would have required the transfer of some authority from the member states to a central control body. The League of Nations was composed of sovereign states, each supposedly national in character and sufficiently satisfied with its existing territorial extent to cooperate with others in a loose international organization. In actuality the nationalism of each member proved so sensitive about sovereign independence that it rendered the League unworkable. Any adequate strengthening of the League would have impaired the doctrine of national self-determination upon which the League was founded.

The two ideals, that of federalism or confederation and that of state sovereignty, tended to pull the League in opposite directions and prevented action on major problems. Rights were not adequately balanced by duties. The Covenant conformed to the ideals of liberalism and morality, a high respect for the individual, whether person or state, and a belief in the ability of independent individuals to cooperate. It failed to take into account the fact that states as instruments of ultimate power set moral standards of their own which frequently conflict with those for persons. The interwar period produced numerous examples of actions on the part of states that by any standard were utterly immoral. In this respect few periods in history have equaled it. The Covenant was defied and the League belittled by each fresh aggression in the world.

The Covenant

The Covenant included only twenty-six clauses, most of which were relatively short. This document was expected to serve as the constitution for a world organization that would prevent society from continuing the habit of war—a habit as old as history. Brevity was justified as providing a sufficiently general statement for future interpretation and development. The Covenant permitted continued respect for national sovereignty, but it also enabled the parties to block all common action by disputes over interpretation. The clauses apportioned too much attention to political affairs and not enough to economic, social, and cultural aspects of life. Prevention rather than repression has been rightly called the real test of collective security; the Covenant reversed the order of importance. It did so from a sense of respect for state sovereignty, but likewise from ignorance on the part of its authors of the significance of nonpolitical forces in international relations. In keeping with their policy of leaving the major responsibility to the member states, the founders set up a minimal executive, thereby failing to create a permanent body of strong and varied agencies which could have acted as foci and stimulants for increasing international cooperation.

The instruments of the League were an Assembly, a Council, and a Permanent Secretariat. The Assembly consisted of representatives (not more than three) from each member state; each state had only one vote. It developed the practice of meeting once a year, when it freely discussed any and every international problem, approved the budget for the League, frequently criticized the Council, and in general developed along the lines of a parliamentary body within a state. It soon became the organ of international opinion and was used by the small states to try to curb the politics of the great powers and to press the League in the direction of international cooperation. The Council acted primarily as the organ of the great powers. It was composed of permanent members (Great Britain; France; Italy; Japan; in 1926, Germany; in 1934, the Soviet Union) and of nonpermanent members elected by the Assembly (originally four; in 1922, six; in 1926, nine; and from 1933 to 1936, ten). The Council met once a year or oftener and considered "any matter within the sphere of action of the League or affecting the peace of the world" (Article 4). Each member had one representative and one vote. The Secretariat will be discussed in connection with the League's functions. The seat of the organization was established at Geneva, Switzerland.

The Preamble of the Covenant sounded both noble and concrete:

> The High Contracting Parties, in order to promote international co-operation and to achieve international peace and security by the acceptance of obligations not to resort to war, by the prescription of open, just and honorable relations between nations, by the firm establishment of the understandings of international law as the actual rule of conduct among Governments, and by the maintenance of justice and a scrupulous respect for all treaty obligations in the dealings of organized peoples with one another, agree to this Covenant of the League of Nations.

The subsequent clauses of the Covenant, however, made sharp inroads upon these preliminary commitments.

The heart of the Covenant was contained in Articles 10 through 17. President Wilson regarded Article 10 as the most important. It read:

> The Members of the League undertake to respect and preserve as against external aggression the territorial integrity and existing political independence of all

Members of the League. In case of any such aggression or in case of any threat or danger of such aggression the Council shall advise upon the means by which this obligation shall be fulfilled.

This clause offered the nearest approach to a definition of aggression to be found in the Covenant. It initiated a long and continuing discussion of the content of an aggressive act and drew particular attention between 1923 and 1925 in the consideration of the Draft Treaty of Mutual Assistance and the Geneva Protocol, the two most noteworthy attempts to clarify and strengthen this article. The second sentence in Article 10 contained the source of the League's major weakness. The Council had no authority to act; it could not stop an aggressor; it could only "advise upon."

Article 11 stated that "Any war or threat of war, whether immediately affecting any of the Members of the League or not, is hereby declared a matter of concern to the whole League." The Council should be called in case of any emergency, and the League should "take any action that may be deemed wise and effectual to safeguard the peace of nations." Each member of the League had "the friendly right" to bring to the attention of the Assembly or of the Council any circumstance whatever affecting international relations which threatens to disturb international peace or the good understanding between nations upon which peace depends."

The stipulation was weakened by paragraph 8 of Article 15, which excluded from the jurisdiction of the League any matter which the Council regarded as "solely within the domestic jurisdiction" of a party to a dispute. For example, it could do nothing about insurrections or civil wars or the treatment of minorities in countries not subject to minorities treaties, even though these troubles might ultimately lead to international friction. The sovereignty of each state was so carefully protected that the League was restrained from doing its duty to prevent war. In these circumstances it would not intervene until war threatened or actually occurred.

In general the members agreed (Articles 12, 13, 14) to submit disputes to settlement by judicial act of the Permanent Court of International Justice, established as an adjunct to the League, or by some arbiter. By Article 15 either the Council or the Assembly could negotiate the settlement among members of disputes which were not submitted to judicial settlement or arbitration. In case the Assembly did so, its recommendation, to be effective, required the approval of the Council. The same article contained two paragraphs which aroused doubt as to the effectiveness of the League. Paragraph 6 declared:

If a report by the Council is unanimously agreed to by the members thereof other than the Representatives of one or more of the parties to the dispute, the Members of the League agree that they will not go to war with any party to the dispute which complies with the recommendations of the report.

What if the report was not adopted unanimously? In a world of sovereign states, even if united in a League of Nations, was it not to be expected that a nation determined to ignore the Council's recommendation and make trouble could find a friend or two to block the Council's action? Paragraph 7 stated that if the Council, apart from the parties to the dispute, did fail to reach agreement, "the Members of the League reserve to themselves the right to take such action as they shall consider necessary for the maintenance of right and justice." That is to say, the members apparently had a legal right to go to war and the other members might remain neutral if they pleased. In a League dependent upon cooperative action the reluctance or defection of one, particularly if a great power, would stop the action of all. Paragraph 7 was to be the subject of later attempts at improvement.

Article 16 concerning the application of sanctions had been the special brain child of the British. It read:

> 1. Should any Member of the League resort to war in disregard of its covenants under Articles 12, 13 or 15, it shall *ipso facto* be deemed to have committed an act of war against all other Members of the League, which hereby undertake immediately to subject it to the severance of all trade or financial relations, the prohibition of all intercourse between their nations and the nationals of the covenant-breaking State, and the prevention of all financial, commercial or personal intercourse between the nationals of the covenant-breaking State and the nationals of any other State, whether a Member of the League or not.
>
> 2. It shall be the duty of the Council in such case to recommend to the several governments concerned what effective military, naval or air force the Members of the League shall severally contribute to the armed forces to be used to protect the covenants of the League.
>
> 3. The Members of the League agree, further, that they will mutually support one another in the financial and economic measures which are taken under this Article, in order to minimize the loss and inconvenience resulting from the above measures, and that they will mutually support one another in resisting any special measures aimed at one of their number by the covenant-breaking State, and that they will take the necessary steps to afford passage through their territory to the forces of any of the Members of the League which are co-operating to protect the covenants of the League.

Paragraph 4 provided for the cancellation of membership in the League of any violator of the Covenant. The latter should be expelled by unanimous vote of the Council.

Except for the weakness of the word "recommend" in paragraph 2, a word which some country threatened by another might have liked to see replaced by the word "command," Article 16 seemed clear. However, in 1921, a League resolution interpreted this article as meaning that the members would not be automatically at war with the offending state; for that purpose the government of each member would have to declare war officially. This interpretation was given in deference to the power to declare war as stated in the Constitution of the United States. It deprived Article 16 of effectiveness by leaving the ultimate decision to each state.

Weakness of the League

A student of the history of the League has summarized the weakness of that body as follows:

> Unfortunately, the theoretical automatism, immediacy, and directness of the Members' obligations was more than cancelled out by the discretion granted to them on a number of vital points. Firstly, the duty to apply sanctions and render assistance did not arise until and unless the Member concerned was satisfied, according to his own lights and conscience, that aggression had in fact been committed; he was not bound by the recommendations or findings of any organ. Secondly, the League Assembly declared in 1921 that the quantity and quality of the economic pressure required in concrete cases could not be decided in advance. This left each Member Government to work out its own scheme of economic sanctions; although the Council was expected to submit a plan for joint action, no Member was under any legal obligation to accept it. Thirdly, the Assembly in 1921 also authorized the postponement of action, wholly or in part, if that was desirable in order to minimize "the losses and embarrassments which may be entailed in the case of certain Members of the League by the application of the sanctions." In this way the "sledgehammer method" of pressure contemplated in the Covenant was reduced to a dead letter and the discretion of Members became virtually complete; each of them could decide individually not only the "whether" and the "how" but also the "when" of sanctions.[1]

As for the members' participation in military sanctions, it became entirely optional.

> Had that option ever been exercised [the same writer has stated], the resulting armed forces would not have been in any sense the armed forces of the League as such. The Covenant carefully avoided any words that might have been so construed; it deliberately employed the cautious phrase "the armed forces to be used to protect the covenants of the League."

This was a League of sovereign states just emerged from the greatest and closest collective action that the world had ever seen. Nonetheless almost every member determined to return rapidly and completely to the prewar condition of international anarchy.

The one major state to object to the dominant conception of the League as an instrument for arbitration and discussion was France. She preferred the League to be strong enough to offer security against renewed German aggression. To that end the French advocated three reforms in the Covenant. Arbitration should be made compulsory. Since, however, aggression might still occur, it should be so precisely defined that the aggressor would be automatically designated. The French opposed discussion and a vote on the matter at the time of a specific instance for fear of differences of opinion and dangerous delay or even failure to act. If a vote had to be taken, the French wished the issue to be settled, not by unanimity, but by a majority. The states should know with speed and precision

[1] Andrew Martin, *Collective Security* (Paris: UNESCO, 1952), p. 143.

exactly when they had to apply sanctions. To overcome the danger arising from the slowness of economic sanctions against an aggressor, the French proposed the creation of a collective military force. Each state should keep in constant preparation, at the disposal of the League, specialized air troops and long-serving contingents equipped with weapons denied to the regular armies. The naval powers should hold naval units in readiness for the same purpose. The League itself should maintain an "organically international air force" on a permanent basis, with a commander appointed directly by the League. In the version of 1932 the French recommended this plan for the continent of Europe and proposed that the rest of the world be organized into two circles around Europe as a center, with the powers in each circle having fewer duties to perform.

The entire plan expressed the most advanced thinking on the part of a responsible government about world organization for peace. France knew that a hydra-headed Council might have great difficulty in executing the proposal, but it acted on the belief that defense against aggression entailed the acceptance of common responsibilities. Not even the lesser European states like Czechoslovakia went so far; they continued to seek a league of sovereign states that at the same time would be sufficiently powerful to protect the smaller states.

The League became primarily a European organization. By 1920, forty-eight states joined it and fifteen others subsequently; but Europeans dominated in both Council and Assembly. Except in so far as the European imperial powers spoke for them, most of Asia and almost all of Africa were not represented. Germany was excluded until 1926, Communist Russia until 1934, and the isolationists in the United States Senate prevented this country from joining—or for years even from cooperating with the League on nonpolitical, humanitarian affairs. Mr. F. P. Walters, who served in the League secretariat from 1919 to 1940, has judged the significance of the United States' absence as follows:

> The abandonment of the League by the United States was a blow whose effects can hardly be over-estimated. That country had seemed to be marked by circumstances and by character for moral and political leadership. First in power, she was also unique in her freedom from ancient feuds, from present embarrassments, and from fears of the future. She had no desire for military glory or for territorial expansion. . . .
>
> The immediate loss in the power and influence of the Council and Assembly . . . was . . . destined to show itself in a hundred ways as the years went by. The indirect effects were no less calamitous. Within each Member State the anti-League elements were encouraged. Had they not said all along that Wilson was an unpractical idealist? What aggressor would fear the economic sanctions of the League when the world's greatest markets were open to him? What League Member could dare use its fleet to close the seas to trade between such an aggressor and the United States? Again, with the United States outside the League, any dissatisfied Member could henceforth make effective use of the threat to withdraw. To leave the League was not to isolate oneself, but to follow an illus-

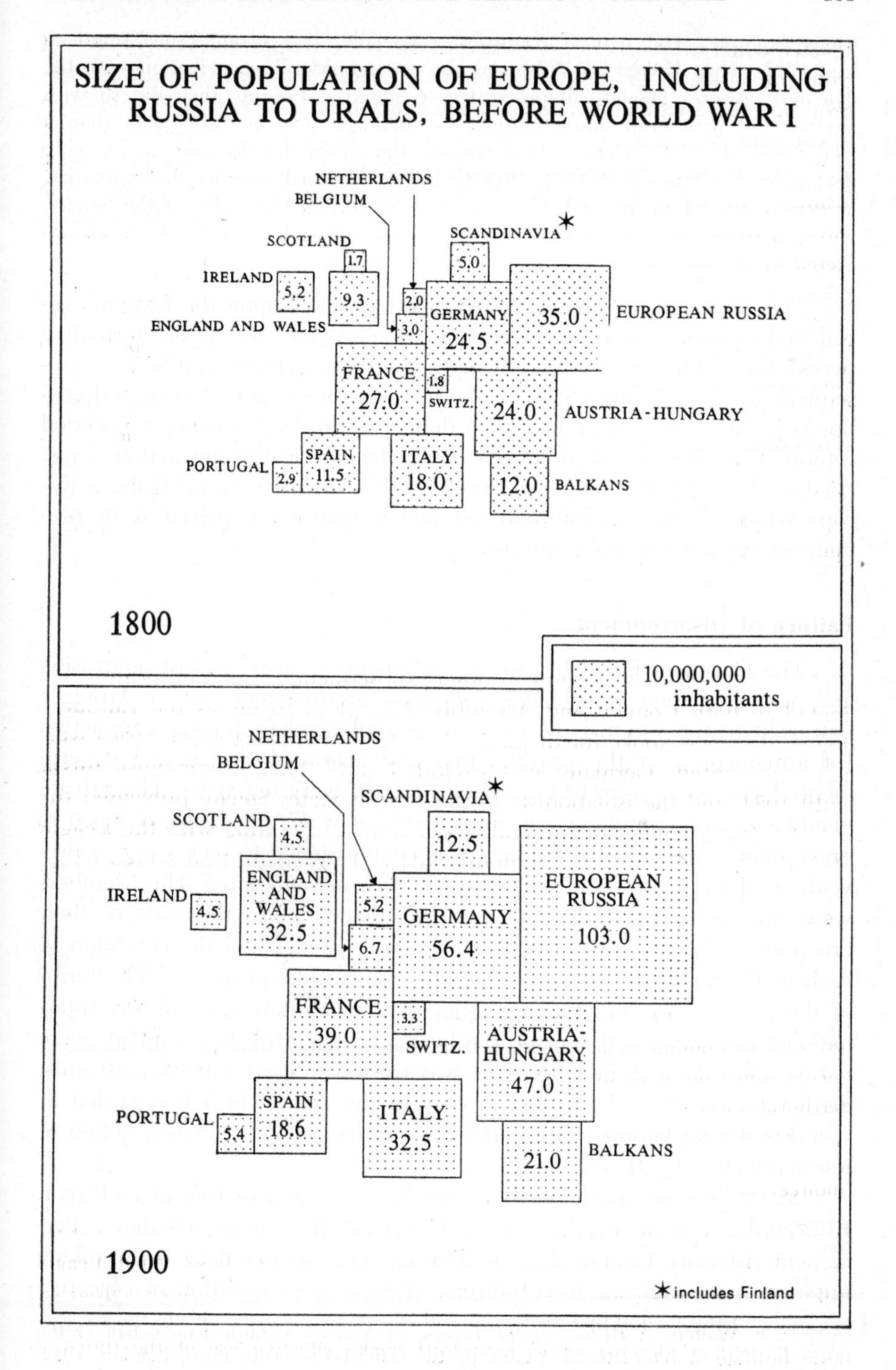
SIZE OF POPULATION OF EUROPE, INCLUDING RUSSIA TO URALS, BEFORE WORLD WAR I
NETHERLANDS
BELGIUM
SCOTLAND
1.7
SCANDINAVIA*
5.0
IRELAND
5,2
9.3
2.0
ENGLAND AND WALES
3.0
GERMANY
24.5
35.0
EUROPEAN RUSSIA
FRANCE
27.0
1.8
SWITZ.
24.0
AUSTRIA-HUNGARY
PORTUGAL
2.9
SPAIN
11.5
ITALY
18.0
12.0
BALKANS
1800
10,000,000 inhabitants
NETHERLANDS
BELGIUM
SCANDINAVIA*
SCOTLAND
4.5
12.5
ENGLAND AND WALES
32.5
IRELAND
4.5
5.2
6.7
GERMANY
56.4
EUROPEAN RUSSIA
103.0
FRANCE
39.0
3.3
SWITZ.
AUSTRIA-HUNGARY
47.0
PORTUGAL
5.4
SPAIN
18.6
ITALY
32.5
21.0
BALKANS
1900
* includes Finland

trious example. The neutral countries, especially, had counted on American leadership. They looked on Wilson as the protagonist of reconciliation with the defeated powers. Though all proceeded to join the League, they did so with anxiety, not with enthusiasm, fearing lest it might now be little more than a confederation of the victors. In Germany the desire for League membership declined, while opposition to the Treaty increased. Small wonder that militarists in Berlin, Paris, London, and Tokyo were delighted by the action of the Senate, and that many exponents of the old diplomacy rejoiced in the set-back administered to the new.[2]

The effects of the absence of the United States upon the League's social and economic work were equally discouraging, for in the formative period the United States directly opposed these activities. When in subsequent years the United States came to cooperate with the social and economic bodies, the damage had been done and time was lacking for needed reform. Europe was left in control of the League, a Europe that had just tried to destroy itself in war, a Europe filled with hatred and fears, a Europe whose decline in international power had not deprived it of preeminent capacity to make trouble.

Failure of Disarmament

The Covenant failed to provide automatic security against aggression and permitted some wars; but it called for disarmament and by Article 8 entrusted to the Council the duty to "formulate plans for such reduction [of armaments] for the consideration and action of the several governments." The plans were to be revised at least every ten years. The private manufacture of "munitions and implements of war" was declared "open to grave objections," and the Council was commissioned to seek ways of preventing "the evil effects attendant upon such manufacture." The Members were "to interchange full and frank information as to the scale of their armaments, their military, naval and air programmes and the condition of such of their industries as are adaptable to war-like purposes." The terms of the article respected the principle of national state sovereignty. International inspection and control, the heart of successful disarmament, were not mentioned. Each member state was trusted to carry out commitments. Each retained the right to disarm only to the point which it regarded as "consistent with national safety and the enforcement by common action of international obligations."

The failure of disarmament cannot be attributed to lack of endeavor. In accordance with Article 9 of the Covenant, the League created a Permanent Advisory Commission on disarmament composed of high-ranking military, naval, and air force officers. With a fine exposition of objective

[2] F. P. Walters, *A History of the League of Nations*. Published on behalf of the Royal Institute of International Affairs, by the Oxford University Press, London, 1952. I, 72-73.

arguments these members advised against disarmament. In 1921 the Council tried a Temporary Mixed Commission composed predominantly of civilians, not government appointees but persons chosen for individual merit. This body worked for five years and showed that disarmament was a political as well as a technical question. In 1925 the Council appointed a Preparatory Commission in anticipation of a general disarmament conference. The Commission needed five years to produce a Draft Disarmament Convention for submission to the general conference. The latter convened in February, 1932, with delegates from sixty of the sixty-four recognized states of the world. After two years of discussion the conference broke up. Officers, private civilians, and statesmen all found the problem of disarmament insoluble. Not merely did the conference fail to achieve its purpose; it opened the way for the rearmament of Germany.

In March, 1919, during the peace conference, Lloyd George had said to the Allies:

> The first condition of success for the League of Nations is a firm understanding between the British Empire and the United States of America and France and Italy that there will be no competitive building up of fleets and armies between them. Unless this is arrived at before the Covenant is signed, the League of Nations will be a sham and a mockery.

Lloyd George was arguing from prewar experience. The British and the Americans were determined to preserve their naval supremacy, but on the whole they pressed for the reduction of arms for moral reasons. The French emphasized the practical side. The British declared that disarmament would bring security; the French replied that security must be achieved beforehand. Neither heeded the international danger of Communist Russia as an argument against disarmament. Their eyes were riveted on Germany. France feared that disarmament would lessen her ability to protect herself against a resurgent Germany. She asserted that with her comparatively small population she could restrain Germany only if she had an army in constant readiness, and only if Germany were disarmed. After the Fascists seized power in Italy in 1922, the government of that country manifested no interest in disarmament, and in East Asia Japan was bent on conquest in peace or war. None of the great powers was inclined to execute Article 8.

The practical difficulty of finding a unit of measurement of disarmament enabled the powers to justify their continued disagreement. The success of the Washington Naval Conference of 1922 called by the United States may seem to offer an exception to the general rule; but naval armaments were simpler to compare than military. When the richest and most powerful country in the world proposed stabilization of tonnage and fire power in capital ships and aircraft carriers, the other naval powers faced the alternative of competition with that state or agreement. They chose agreement, on a ratio of 5 (United States), 5 (Great Britain), 3 (Japan),

1.67 (France), and 1.67 (Italy) with respect to capital ships, and a total tonnage in aircraft carriers of 135,000 each for the United States and Great Britain, 81,000 tons for Japan, and 60,000 tons each for France and Italy.

When in 1927 the United States advocated to the same powers the extension of the Washington treaty to cover cruisers, destroyers, and submarines, it encountered difficulties. France and Italy said that naval armaments could not be considered apart from land armaments. They claimed that for defensive purposes they needed particularly these smaller, less expensive naval vessels. Neither liked the prospect of the other's submarines in the Mediterranean, but each preferred to compete with the other rather than forego the protection of these types of craft. The gravest trouble arose between the United States and Great Britain, for the naval staff of each regarded the other country as a potential enemy and deadlocked the negotiations. The Americans apparently thought that their navy would have to operate solely from United States bases; the British assumed that their navy alone would be required to protect British commerce on all the high seas. Not until 1930 were statesmen able to approach a solution. By a treaty of that year the United States, Great Britain, and Japan extended the Washington Treaty of 1922 to cover cruisers, destroyers, and submarines, but with the stipulation that upon due notification to the others each could build additional ships to meet the competition of any nonsigning power. Italy and France, mistrustful of each other's aims, accepted only the unimportant parts of the agreement. Naval armaments showed little inclination toward quantitative or any other kind of limitation.

Land disarmament encountered fundamental conflict of opinion on every aspect. The size of the national expenditures on armaments could not be used as a yardstick because of national differences in price levels and in economic efficiency. Quantitative standards were equally rejected as far too simple; one country needed a different proportion of categories of personnel and armaments from another, for example, more trained soldiers and fewer reserves or more air power and less infantry. What constituted armaments? Should actual guns be counted, or the industrial potential for making guns? What constituted military, naval, and air personnel? Only those in uniform, or those as well in the inactive reserve or in civilian organizations where training would partly prepare them for war? Were planes and pilots in civilian airlines to be included?

The attempt made to distinguish between offensive and defensive weapons failed completely, for criteria were neither absolute nor objective. The bomber aircraft

> . . . was denounced as an aggressive weapon by countries whose population and industrial resources were concentrated in or near large cities; by the same token it was claimed as a defensive armament by States preparing to meet an attack backed by larger industrial resources than their own. The character of mobile guns and heavy tanks was (or should have been) less ambiguous. Experience since 1939 has proved that tanks are the typical and decisive weapons of

sudden aggression; and it is now being argued with some force that they should take top rank on the list of armaments to be outlawed. At the Disarmament Conference, however, by the irony of history, the abolition of tanks was strongly supported by Germany, and decisively resisted by France who, a few years later, was to suffer crushing defeat under the overwhelming weight of German armour; while the Soviet Union took a leading part in the denunciation of the weapon which is the mainstay of its present military superiority on land.[3]

It came to be recognized after years of argument that the armed strength of a country depends upon technological and industrial efficiency, the state of knowledge, the attitude of the people, the effectiveness of the government—in fact, upon the total culture, or, as the authors of the Covenant wrote without understanding the full significance of their statement, upon the "circumstances of each state." It was not merely a technical question; it was above all a political problem. Disarmament, as the French correctly said, could not be divorced from the wider political search for security. Experience showed that in a world of sovereign states, no matter how poverty-stricken the members—particularly just after a major war—disarmament was impossible.

Search for Security by Political Agreement

The search for security by political agreement did not produce much better results than the search for security by disarmament. The attempt took two lines, one within the League and one outside but associated with the League. The most far-reaching proposal originated in the League's Temporary Mixed Commission on disarmament. This Draft Treaty of Mutual Assistance (1923–1924), as it was called, included in compact form the essential power given subsequently to the United Nations:

> It proposed (a) a joint and several guarantee by all contracting parties to furnish armed assistance to any one of their number in the case of a war of aggression; (b) that the most effective form of assistance should be determined with binding force by the Council of the League; (c) that the Council should have power to select the States whose assistance was required, and determine the forces to be contributed by each of them; (d) that if necessary a Higher Command should be appointed by the Council; (e) that all States called upon to render assistance should be entitled to participate in the deliberations of the Council; (f) that regional organizations for collective defence (and no other purpose) should be permitted, and allowed immediately to go into action in the case of an armed attack, subject to the Council being at once informed of the measures taken; (g) that a plan of financial co-operation should be prepared in advance, with a view to providing funds for the victim of aggression and the States furnishing assistance.[4]

No state was to be required to provide troops for action outside its own continent, and no state which did not limit its armaments in accordance

[3] Martin, *op. cit.*, pp. 56-57. [4] *Ibid.*, p. 131.

with a general plan to be drawn by the Council would be eligible to enjoy the protection of the treaty:

Sanctions were treated as measures complementary to mutual assistance, and not as an alternative to it; and in contrast to the Covenant, the right to decide on economic sanctions was to be vested in the Council.[5]

The Draft Treaty was approved by France, Italy, and the lesser states of Eastern Europe who feared their powerful neighbors. The United States would have nothing to do with it. The Russians sharply criticized it. The British Labor government, supported actively by the Dominions and tacitly by the Latin American countries, criticized the treaty as too rigid to meet the diverse needs of the empire, and objecting in general to the increase of international commitments, delivered the fatal blow.

The second important effort (1924–1925) was likewise made within the League under the leadership of the British and French delegates and with the enthusiastic support of the smaller states. Eduard Beneš of Czechoslovakia and Nikolaos Polites of Greece played an important part in it, together with Ramsay MacDonald of the British Labor government and Édouard Herriot of France. The product of their work, known as the Geneva Protocol, endeavored to close the gap in the Covenant by making compulsory the arbitration of all disputes. Any state that rejected arbitration and went to war would be condemned as an aggressor, and all signers of the Protocol agreed to aid the attacked state and resist the aggressor. The weakness of the Protocol lay in two provisions: first, each signer retained control of his own forces and agreed to help only in so far as his geographic position and the state of his armaments would permit; and second, the entire treaty should not come into operation until a general conference had adopted a universal plan of disarmament.

Actually, the Protocol did not offer much more protection against aggression than did the Covenant. The document was unanimously recommended by the Assembly for adoption; but when the Conservatives took over the British government in November, 1924, they refused to approve it. Foreign Secretary Austen Chamberlain knew that the Protocol would not satisfy the French request for security, that the Dominions objected to such potential interference in their domestic affairs and to becoming involved in European troubles, and that to many of his party the Protocol evoked, in the words of *The New Statesman*, "the disagreeable possibility of our being called upon to coerce those with whose grievances we sympathize." Unlike France, Great Britain refused to assume any responsibility, for example, for the defense of the peace settlement in Eastern Europe. Nor did the British government and the Dominions overlook the possibility that the Protocol could involve them in a conflict with the United States. If the latter power should insist on trading with or otherwise assisting a state which

[5] *Ibid.*

under the terms of the Protocol had been declared an aggressor, the signatories might find themselves faced with a disagreeable choice.

Locarno Agreements

The sole major achievement of the great powers in the field of international political relations during the 1920's concerned a regional pact of 1925 about the Rhineland frontier. The policy behind this kind of agreement may be exemplified by the statement in March, 1925, of the British foreign secretary, Sir Austen Chamberlain:

> Since the general provisions of the Covenant cannot be stiffened with advantage, and since the "extreme cases" with which the League may have to deal will probably affect certain nations or groups of nations more nearly than others, His Majesty's Government conclude that the best way of dealing with the situation is, with the co-operation of the League, to supplement the Covenant by making special arrangements in order to meet special needs.

The initiative for such a regional pact was taken by the German foreign minister, Gustav Stresemann, who had two aims in mind: to prevent the former Allies from allying once more against Germany, and to gain for his country equality with the other powers in international relations. In October, 1925, after extensive negotiations, the interested states signed a set of agreements at Locarno, which the respective parliaments subsequently approved.

The Locarno treaties applied the terms of the Covenant and of the Geneva Protocol to a region. Whereas the integration with the Covenant might have been expected, the acceptance of the main provisions of the Protocol marked an innovation in international relations, one which was justified by the crucial significance of the Rhineland for European peace. The pact was aimed at no one. It consisted of a Treaty of Mutual Guarantee among Germany, France, Belgium, Great Britain, and Italy, and four arbitration treaties between Germany on the one hand and France, Belgium, Poland, and Czechoslovakia, respectively, on the other. By the terms of the first, Germany on the one hand and France and Belgium on the other agreed that the existing frontier between them and the demilitarized zone in the Rhineland were inviolable. They promised not to resort to war against one another. All disputes between them were to be settled by arbitration along the lines of the Geneva Protocol. The terms were placed under the guarantee, not merely of the three states directly concerned, but of Great Britain and Italy. The Council of the League should hear any complaint that the treaty was being violated; if it confirmed the complaint, the guarantors were immediately to act. If the aggression was flagrant, they should move at once without waiting for Council approval. The aggressor was automatically defined as that power which rejected arbitration, another stipulation borrowed from the Protocol. The arbitration treaties contained the standard terms and defined the machinery of execution. Those between Germany and Poland and Germany and Czechoslovakia differed from the other two with the Western states in that they did not in every case renounce the use of war. The entire set of treaties was to become effective as soon as Germany became a member of the League.

The British government hoped in theory that the Locarno precedent of regional security would in time be applied all over the world. In actuality no similar agreement was ever made, for in no other region was the problem so clear cut, the advantage of commitments by specific powers so well understood, public opinion so willing to approve, as in the matter of the Rhineland. France strove to include Eastern Europe in the agreements, for, although the statement "peace is indivisible" had not yet come into general usage, the French believed that war would arise over Germany's eastern boundary, not over her western one, and that it would then involve the Western powers as well. When, as was to be expected, Great Britain and Germany refused the French plan, France tried to assure stability in the region by signing a defensive alliance with Poland and one with Czechoslovakia; in the event of a German attack, each promised to come to the military defense of the other.

Germany Admitted to the League of Nations

The prospect of entry into the League gave Germany an opportunity to gain further advantages. In January, 1927, she obtained the abolition of the Inter-Allied Military Control Commission. Then Stresemann argued that in her disarmed condition, Germany could not assume the obligations in respect to Article 16 of the Covenant. He objected to the transit of troops across the country in the performance of League duties as likely to involve Germany in war and expose her to military action against which she was defenseless. Even the French had to acknowledge the validity of Stresemann's reasoning, and a formula was taken from the repudiated Geneva Protocol which postponed settlement to the future. It was agreed that Germany was committed "to co-operate loyally and effectively in support of the Covenant and in resistance to any act of aggression, in the degree which its geographical position and its particular situation as regards armaments allow" (Article 11). The decision was left to Germany, as Stresemann had wished. He was building the groundwork for Germany's subsequent claim to the right to rearm, so that, as he would argue, she could fulfill the obligations of the Covenant on terms of equality with all other members.

When in 1926 a large German delegation headed by Stresemann arrived in Geneva for the ceremony of the country's entry into the League, the world was edified by a quarrel among the lesser powers over membership in the Council. Poland requested a permanent seat. Belgium and China asserted that if any power other than Germany obtained a seat, they should each have one. Spain and Brazil, both nonpermanent members of the Council, demanded a permanent seat; otherwise Spain would withdraw from the League, and Brazil would veto Germany's promised place in the Council. The Assembly was hostile to the aspirations of these states; but, as the dictators remained adamant, Germany's entry had to be postponed while the member states haggled. By the September meeting of the League a compromise had been worked out, according to which Germany became the sole new permanent member of the Council. The number of nonpermanent members was increased from six to nine, and they were to sit for a three-year term, but not more than three of them might be re-elected for an indefinite number of terms. These three could become semi-permanent, a new category in Council membership. The compromise satisfied everyone except Spain and Brazil; Spain ceased to be active in the League, and Brazil resigned.

Whether participation of Germany would further peace depended upon the course of future events. The British and most of the German people were favorable to her membership, whereas France and Poland harbored grave doubts of its value. Germany was committed to the Covenant, but the League was weak. As soon as she joined the Council, the peace treaties became a matter of more importance to that body than the Covenant, for Germany was in a position to push revision. Instead of working within the League, the representatives of the great powers while at Geneva for the sessions of the Council began to meet privately and to discuss the problems of Europe among themselves. The "Locarno cabal," as it was called, tended more than ever to transform the League into a European organization exploited in the interest of the great powers. The risk had to be taken at some time of bringing Germany back into the comity of states; the question was whether the Locarno Pacts and the League were sufficiently strong to channel her revival in the direction of peace.

Germany was already maneuvering to gain an independent position between Russia and the West. In 1922 the two outcasts had suddenly signed a treaty of friendship at Rapallo, Italy. In 1926 Germany assured Russia by the Treaty of Berlin that the Locarno Pact and membership in the League did not imply any antagonism on her part, that friendly relations would continue. At the time the agreement seemed harmless; but it denoted German intention once more to play the game of power politics. Stresemann and his successors brought up before the League, in a way which indicated future national objectives, various problems of the minorities, mandates, disarmament, and other matters arising out of the peace treaties. The Allies, especially the British, had opened the road for the German maneuvers by failure to strengthen the League and curb or abolish the disastrous game of power politics. The Kellogg Pact of 1928, proposed by the United States, committed the signers to outlaw war but created no means of enforcement. Signed by everyone, this paper pledge in no sense compensated for the failure of the powers to use the prosperous and peaceful years, 1927 to 1929, to develop the League into an effective organization.

The League Handles Minor Disputes

The weakness of the League was revealed by the type of political controversies which that body attempted to resolve. The disputes had secondary importance; they can have slight interest for the student seeking the main forces at work in this period. In 1921 the League settled the quarrel between Sweden and Finland over the Aaland Islands. These islands, traditionally a part of Finland and in the possession of that country, were Swedish in population and political inclination. At the request of Great Britain, the Council took up the issue and decided that the islands must remain part of Finland but that they should not be fortified or used as a naval base. The disputants accepted the decision. In the long-continuing conflict between weak Poland and weaker Lithuania over the possession of Vilna and the surrounding territory, the League failed to achieve a solution. The city was predominantly Polish in population, the countryside Lithuanian, and the entire area had formerly belonged to Lithuania. Poland seized it and retained possession by force; the League was powerless to intervene, and the conflict continued to embitter Polish-Lithuanian relations. When the Greeks invaded Asia Minor in 1922 and with British backing tried to conquer part of Turkish territory, the lesser states in the League urged that body to take up the conflict. The great powers rejected the proposal and kept the affair in their own hands. When the Turks under the leadership of Mustafa Kemal Pasha drove the Greeks into the sea, the powers deemed the League worthy to help in the exchange of population between Greece and Turkey and the resettlement of the refugees.

The League handled the Corfu incident somewhat more effectively. In August, 1923, the Italian General Tellini, three Italian subordinates, and an interpreter, while participating in an international commission at work drawing a boundary line between Greece and Albania, were killed from ambush on Greek soil. Neither the murderers nor any witnesses were ever found. The Italian government, which had been at odds with Greece since the war over the question of the Albanian frontier, was eager to seize Albania and any other possible territory along the east coast of the Adriatic Sea. It took the opportunity to bombard and occupy the Greek island of Corfu. Greece was willing to make amends, but the Italians wanted an excuse to hold the island. The conflict immediately came to the attention of the League, and, as the Assembly was just convening, the representatives of the lesser states demanded action against the aggressor. The question arose whether the Council or the Conference of Ambassadors should deal with the situation. In the end the Conference took charge, and the Council then registered approval of the ambassadors' work. Italy had to evacuate Corfu, but she received a large indemnity. In the opinion of the angry members of the Assembly, the great powers in the Council had permitted Italy to attack a small state and to ignore the League. The Council had avoided the challenge and, by leaving the settlement to the traditional processes of diplomacy, had subjected the League to a definite setback. When almost contemporaneously Great Britain treated Egypt, a League member, in the same way that Italy had abused Greece, the affair scarcely stirred a ripple.

In the Mosul dispute, 1924–1926, between Great Britain and Iraq on one side and Turkey on the other, and in the Graeco-Bulgarian crisis in 1925 the League succeeded in settling the conflicts. The former concerned the possession of the territory around Mosul inhabited predominantly by Kurds, who disliked both Turkey and Iraq. Great Britain became involved as holder of the mandate of Iraq. When all parties accepted League arbitration, a solution depended merely upon an objective investigation and recommendation. A League commission sent to the area proposed a frontier line—which left most of the territory to Iraq—and legal protection for the minorities. None of the parties liked the decision, but they accepted it. The conflict between Greece and Bulgaria had the nature of a more serious frontier dispute than usual. Greek troops took the occasion to invade Bulgaria, whose government appealed to the League. The Council was able to manage these two little states. It stopped the fighting, ordered the withdrawal of invading troops, required Greece to pay an indemnity, and introduced neutral officers into the region to prevent future incidents.

The League and the Far East

The League never wielded significant influence in the Far East. Japan and China, although charter members, continued to oppose each other, the one as aggressor, the other as defender. At the Washington Conference of 1921–1922, the affairs of the Far Eastern world held the center of attention. The Anglo-Japanese Alliance of 1902 was to expire in 1921. Since the United States, in contrast to its isolationist policy toward Europe, had taken the initiative in blocking Japanese expansionist ambitions, Canada, for one, urged Britain not to renew the treaty. The British government, supported by Australia, favored retention of the alliance, hoping through it to restrain Japanese aggression. Japan sought by renewal to protect herself against possible attack from the Anglo-Saxon powers. Negotiators at Washington found a solution to the problem temporarily satisfactory to all parties. They replaced the former Anglo-Japanese Dual Alliance by a treaty, to last for ten years, among the United States, Great Britain, France, and Japan, in which the signers promised "to respect their rights in relation to the insular possessions and insular dominions in the region of the Pacific Ocean," and to confer with each other in case of controversy.

The United States successfully pressed Japan to recede from demands on China and to commit herself, with eight other states of Europe, North

America, and the Far East in the Nine Power Pact, "to respect the sovereignty, the independence, and the territorial and administrative integrity of China; to provide the fullest and most unembarrassed opportunity to China to develop and maintain for herself an effective and stable government." Japan further disclaimed officially any ambitions to acquire Russian territory and promised to withdraw her troops from Siberia and Northern Sakhalin. As a *quid pro quo,* in addition to the terms of naval disarmament discussed above, the United States and Great Britain promised to build no fortifications in their island possessions in the Far East, a concession which left Japan secure against attack by sea.

In China during the 1920's civil war and attacks on foreigners continued to characterize the search of the nation for a new society and government. Japan, Great Britain, and the other powers with interests in China suffered from violence, Japan in particular from economic boycott. Liberal groups grew in influence in Japan during the decade and restrained the militarists and imperialists; but Japanese troops clashed with the Chinese Nationalists in Shanghai in 1926, and in Tsinan, capital of Shantung, in 1928. Firmly entrenched in Southern Manchuria, where they were rapidly expanding their economic interests, the Japanese were bound sooner or later to strike against the military resistance of the Chinese republic. The United States endeavored by diplomacy to protect China, but by refusing to become a member of the League of Nations, it had sacrificed the opportunity to develop an institution for marshaling world opinion and world force against Japanese imperialism.

Protection of Minorities

When the Allied powers forced the lesser states of Eastern and Southeastern Europe to sign the minorities treaties, they assigned responsibility for executing the terms to the League Council. The latter was expected to guard the rights of 20 to 30 million people. Since the minorities treaties prescribed no machinery and specified no power of inspection or enforcement, the Council introduced a system which depended upon the cooperation of the states in question. Petitions from private individuals and groups could be sent directly to the League secretariat, where they were processed by a minorities section and reported to the Council. A committee of three members of the Council was set up to consider each petition and, if need should arise, report to the whole Council. From 1921 to 1929, 150 such committees were established. They manifestly depended to a considerable extent upon the exploratory work and intimate knowledge of each situation by the minorities section; nonetheless, the fact that each petition was considered by leaders of Europe carried the democratic ideal into the most sensitive social relations. Without such an institution of collective, impersonal, and continuing supervision the fate of the minorities might have been tragic. Two groups, that of the Germans in Poland and that of the

Percentage of Total Population Consisting of Main Minorities in Certain States about 1930

State	Minority	Percentage
Albania	Greeks	5.6
Austria	Jews	2.8
	Yugoslavs	1.2
Bulgaria	Romanians	1.2
	Turks	10.5
Czechoslovakia	Germans	22.5
	Hungarians	4.9
	Jews	2.4
	Ruthenians	3.9
Estonia	Germans	1.4
	Russians	8.2
Greece	Turks	1.7
	Bulgarians	1.3
	Jews	1.1
Hungary	Czechoslovaks	1.2
	Germans	5.5
	Jews	5.1
Latvia	Germans	3.3
	Jews	4.9
	Lithuanians	1.1
	Poles	2.6
	Russians	12.3
	White Russians	1.8
Poland	Germans	5.2
	Jews	8.3
	Ruthenians	12.8
	White Russians	4.6
Romania	Bulgarians	2.0
	Germans	4.2
	Gypsies	1.6
	Hungarians	8.0
	Jews	4.1
	Russians	2.3
	Ruthenians	3.3
	Turks	1.6
Yugoslavia	Albanians	2.5
	Czechoslovaks	1.3
	Germans	3.6
	Hungarians	3.4
	Romanians	1.6

SOURCE: Jacob Robinson and others, *Were the Minorities Treaties a Failure?* (New York: Institute of Jewish Affairs, 1943), Chart 2.

Hungarians in Romania and Czechoslovakia, proved particularly stubborn, for the mother countries were determined not to accept the severance of their people as final. That these minority issues caused no more trouble than they did may be attributed to Council supervision.

The contradiction implicit in the enforcement of minority protection on sovereign states by a league of sovereign states always handicapped the work. The question was constantly asked whether the protection did not augment the hostility between the peoples which the treaties were expected to alleviate. The principal task was not to secure the interests of special groups but to provide political stability and cooperation, and it may be doubted whether the Council was equipped to advance this objective. It could not anticipate and prevent trouble over minorities; it had to wait until the difficulty had arisen and had been called to its attention. It acted most effectively by negotiating a settlement in secret, bringing the two parties together, and persuading the government to take remedial steps against a recurrence.

The work was weakened by the attitude of the states concerned and by the Council's procedure. The states under minorities treaties complained about discrimination, since Italy, France, Belgium, and Denmark, all with minorities, had not signed such treaties. They strove to restrict the control of the Council. Lithuania and Turkey refused to cooperate at all, though Turkey under Mustafa Kemal Pasha treated its minorities fairly. Czechoslovakia and Latvia had good records, but kept their relations with the Council strictly within the letter of the treaty. In almost no instance were the terms enforced in municipal law, and without such routine enforcement through the ordinary courts the minorities remained outsiders, subject to exceptional treatment. In Poland and Romania, to mention two of the worst examples, the local government officials lacked the will, the understanding, and the ability to handle the minorities with justice. Nor did some of the great powers in the Council perform their duty. Italy would not; she was behaving toward her German and Slavic minorities like the worst of the offending treaty states. France was caught between two fires; wishing to protect minority rights but also needing to keep on friendly terms with her East European allies, she left the initiative to others. Japan took an active role; since the problems affected European states, except for Turkey, she could be disinterested. Great Britain and the Latin American countries did most.

The members of the Council who tried to protect the minorities were handicapped by structural difficulties in enforcement. Sometimes the government of a state succeeded in delaying the dispatch of a petition from one of its citizens to the Council for several years. The Council itself never set a maximum time limit for the reply from a minorities state about a complaint. A government might wait two or three years before answering; the correspondence could be endlessly protracted. Many petitions granted by the Council came to nothing because the state in question refused to act. The entire system depended for its effectiveness upon the prestige of the Council's democratic members. In the last analysis, the relations of the minorities with the rest of the population were decided by the extent to which each group practiced the ideals of toleration, mutual respect, and cooperation. In the turmoil of postwar Europe, in the confused conditions of the new states of Eastern Europe, classes of even the same nationality lacked harmonious relations. That the system of minorities protection worked as well as it did was a tribute to the sense of duty of a few members of the Council and of a few leaders in the minorities states.

Mandates

The most successful activity of the League concerned the administration of the former German colonies and Turkish possessions. Article 22 of the Covenant dealt with the subject and offered evidence to support the view that Europe was moving away from imperialism to a sense of humanitarian responsibility. The Covenant spoke of the mandated peoples as "not yet able to stand by themselves under the strenuous conditions of the modern world." It stated that with respect to them "there should be applied the principle that the well-being and development of such peoples form a sacred trust of civilization and that securities for the performance of this trust should be embodied in this Covenant." Imperialistic exploitation should give way to "a sacred trust of civilization." The responsibility for carrying out this work was delegated to certain "advanced nations" as "Mandatories on behalf of the League," each of which should submit an annual report to the Council about the territory in its charge. "The degree of authority, control, or administration to be exercised by the Mandatory shall, if not previously agreed upon by the Members of the League, be explicitly defined in each case by the Council." A permanent Mandates Commission was created "to receive and examine the annual reports of the Mandatories and to advise the Council on all matters relating to the observance of the mandates." Freedom of conscience and religion, "subject only to the maintenance of public order and morals," should be guaranteed; slave trade, arms and liquor traffic, and other abuses should be prohibited. The territories should not be fortified or the natives given military training "for other than police purposes and the defence of territory"; and "opportunities for the trade and commerce of other Members of the League" should be equal.

The mandates were divided into three groups according to the conditions of culture in the territories. The "A" mandates, consisting of the former Turkish possessions, were almost ready for independence and were regarded as needing some "administrative advice and assistance" by the mandatory until they could "stand alone." Of these Lebanon and Syria were entrusted to France; Iraq, Palestine, and Transjordan to Great Britain. Iraq was the only one to become a member of the League (1932). The "B" mandates, all in central Africa, needed more tutelage. Great Britain took charge of the administration of a part of Togoland, part of the Cameroons, and Tanganyika; France, of the rest of Togoland and the Cameroons; and Belgium, of Ruanda-Urundi. The Class "C" type of mandates, all with one exception in the Southwest Pacific and all notably deficient in population and cultural resources, was established at the insistence of Australia, New Zealand, and South Africa. For reasons of strategic security these states would have preferred to annex the areas in question. They were persuaded instead to accept them as mandates placed "under the laws of the Mandatory as integral portions of its territory, subject to the safeguards above mentioned in the interests of the indigenous population." In this way, the Union of South Africa received Southwest Africa; New Zealand, Australia, and Japan assumed responsibility for certain islands or parts of islands in the Pacific.

Although many members of the Permanent Mandates Commission were nationals of mandatory states, they acted in their official capacity, not in any selfish interest of their respective country, but as international civil servants. Under the chairmanship of Lord Lugard, the Commission established a reputation for fairness and efficiency. The Covenant forbade investigation of conditions in the mandated areas; the Commission's work was restricted to the *ex post facto* criticism of annual reports. These reports, however, covered every aspect of life, and the Commission, cooperating fully with the International Labor Office, was able to suggest many ways for improvement. The Security Council, to which the Commission reported, was dominated by those powers which had accepted most of the mandates, and for a number of years the advice of the Commission was received with mistrust. The Assembly, on the other hand, contained representatives of a large number of countries that had formerly been colonies and had fought for their independence. This body, under the stimulation especially of the Latin American states, supported the Commission fully, and in time all mandatories, except Japan, which fortified its islands, learned to respect the judgment of the experts. They sought its advice not merely about mandates but about their other possessions as well, and other imperial countries followed suit.

Experience with the conduct of international relations in the 1920's left no cause for optimism. The attempt by creating the League of Nations and by disarmament to eliminate prewar conditions of international anarchy led only a short way toward change. The preservation of a precarious peace in Europe during the decade depended primarily upon the temporary decline of Germany and Russia as great powers. The power system centered in Europe felt a degree of restraint from the League. The other locus of power, that in the Far East, remained close to traditional practices. The United States, while committing itself in Europe by loans and investments, held aloof from all political commitments there. In the Far East it reversed the order, striving to curb Japanese aggression but showing itself reluctant to invest much in the China it sought to save. At no time did statesmen seriously try through an effective world organization to utilize the ten-year pause to implement ideals of peace and democracy, strengthened though these were by general revulsion against war. Some statesmen were reluctant to admit that reparations could not be collected by bayonets; almost all were ignorant of the economic dislocations caused by the war; many, suspicious of the idealism inherent in the mandates and the protection of minorities, preferred unvarnished imperialism. The minds of statesmen much more than those of intellectuals proved incapable of drawing lessons from the war about how to avoid another disaster; the public lagged far behind both. Europe and the world were unprepared either to avoid or to overcome new crises such as appeared in the 1930's.

Suggestions for Further Reading

CRAIG, GORDON A., and GILBERT, FELIX, eds. *The Diplomats, 1919–1939*. Princeton, N. J.: Princeton University Press, 1953. A volume of biographical studies.

JORDAN, W. M. *Great Britain, France and the German Problem, 1918–1939.* New York: Oxford University Press, 1943. Compact and illuminating.

LENCZOWSKI, GEORGE. *The Middle East in World Affairs.* See the Readings for Chapter 2.

MARTIN, ANDREW. *Collective Security.* Paris: UNESCO, 1952. Comparison of the League of Nations and the United Nations. Brief and full of insight.

ROBINSON, JACOB, and others. *Were the Minorities Treaties a Failure?* New York: Institute of Jewish Affairs, 1943. By scholars with firsthand knowledge of the question.

WALTERS, F. P. *A History of the League of Nations.* 2 vols. New York: Oxford University Press, 1952. Fundamental. Written by a British official of the League of Nations.

Chapter 6 · International Organization and Relations—Economic and Social

EFFECT OF THE WAR ON CIVILIAN SOCIETY

The nature of modern industrialized war can be clearly perceived in the impact of the conflict on civilian society. Capital equipment and stocks had been destroyed or used without replacement. Plant and skills had been concentrated in war industries, many of which would be superfluous in peace. The international position of debtor and creditor had been profoundly changed. Consumer demand for durable and semidurable goods had been blocked and financial means saved with which to purchase such goods after the war. The normal channels of international trade and investment had been closed. The price structure was full of distortions, with some prices fixed by the government, others allowed complete freedom, and still others controlled indirectly. Rates in foreign exchange had been pegged, so that once the controls were removed no one knew what the value of a currency on the international market would be. The relation between a country's price levels and the exchange rate was artificial. Distortions had occurred in the pattern of wages and in the location of employment. Essential armaments industries, for example, drew far larger numbers of laborers and employees than they would need in peacetime. Man power which had been adjusted to war service would have to be absorbed into civilian life. The system of internal trade, payments, and investments had been radically altered, Europe's economic influence in the world being greatly diminished. The relations of social groups within a national state had been similarly transformed. The workers in almost every country had risen in prestige and power. The loss of young men and the diminution in the birth rate during the war had thrown out of order the age distribution of the population. Revolutions, especially those in Eastern Europe, had driven people into exile. In both the economy and the social organization the war had caused structural upheavals, the full implications of which would be revealed only over a period of years.

A consideration of the new map of Europe after the war will reveal why both Europe and the world would continue to emphasize the political factor in economic and social life. Politics, by the way of the military, had dominated society for four crucial years; people had become accustomed to governments' playing a much greater role than before the war. In the defeated countries prewar economic and social organization had been more profoundly affected than in the victorious nations, and the significance of political and governmental forces had become greater. As for the small nations of Eastern and Southeastern Europe, whether entirely new like Poland or essentially new like Romania by virtue of the enormous increase in size, each depended upon political leadership to create an economy and a society. Russia had withdrawn entirely from international trade and turned collectivist. Under such conditions governments could not restore the prewar guiding ideal of laissez faire.

FAILURE TO COMPREHEND POSTWAR REALITIES

Statesmen, almost all economic leaders, and the masses of the people failed to comprehend postwar realities. In spite of the effects of the war, in spite of the destruction of material and spiritual values, in spite of the increase in the number of European states and the lengthening of the European customs barriers by 12,500 miles, in spite of the isolation of Communist Russia, the Americans and Europeans tried to restore prewar standards. Millions of men were speedily demobilized and thrown on the labor market. Price controls were quickly removed, and rationing abolished. People were given economic freedom to produce what they wished and to buy what they could. For a few months production could not satisfy demand, and prices climbed. Raw materials became scarce and expensive. In Central and Eastern Europe food was lacking to such a degree that in some areas, especially the cities, famine conditions prevailed. Nonetheless the Allies disbanded their wartime economic organization at once. Late in 1918 Herbert Hoover stated the American policy as follows:

> This government will not agree to any programme that even looks like inter-Allied control of our economic resources after peace. After peace over one-half of the whole export of food supplies of the world will come from the United States and for the buyers of these supplies to sit in majority in dictation to us as to prices and distribution is wholly inconceivable. The same applies to raw materials. Our only hope of securing justice in distribution, proper appreciation abroad of the effort we make to assist foreign nations, and proper return for the service that we will perform will revolve around complete independence of commitment to joint action on our part.

European leaders reacted in about the same way. Their attitude may be seen from a report on the distribution of raw materials submitted in

1921 by the Provisional Economic and Financial Committee of the League of Nations:

(a) It would, in our opinion, be impracticable to obtain the general consent of the producing and consuming States to delegate the important functions contemplated by the scheme to an international body, and the League of Nations has no power of compelling its Members to enter into any such arrangement against their will. (b) No scheme for the international control of the distribution of raw materials could be operated without fixing prices and allocating supplies on some principle of rationing. In our opinion, this necessarily involves the international control of the whole internal economic life of the countries concerned. (c) No scheme of rationing is possible without the power of compelling the consuming countries to take up their rations and to pay for them, which is clearly impracticable under present conditions. (d) There is no criterion by which an International office could fix a reasonable ration of any raw material to be allowed to any country, except either on the basis of previous consumption (which would stereotype the existing distribution of industry), or on some arbitrary estimate of needs which would empower the International Office to dictate the lines of future industrial development of all the States of the League. (e) If all the above objections could be overcome, the mere loss to productive industry from the inevitable inefficient operation of the bureaucratic machinery of the International Office would probably be fatal to the scheme.

The problems so solemnly exorcised pertained not merely to raw materials but to other commodities as well. Fully documented at an economic conference called by the Allies at Genoa in 1922 at which nothing significant was accomplished, they persisted throughout the interwar years and were to receive constructive handling only after World War II. In the formative months of policy just after World War I, the United States, an oasis of prosperity and freedom with an intact economic organization, high productivity, low taxes, and no social security, was the only major country in the world that could afford to continue the prewar policy of laissez faire. It set the standard in policy for war-torn Europe, much of it on the verge of poverty. All states had yet to learn that the too-speedy elimination of governmental and international control of the economy after the war would eventually force the use of more governmental interference and more international action than before.

Condition of International Trade

An analysis of the extent to which the European economy was out of gear may begin with the state of international trade. In 1920 the continent imported from overseas only three fourths as much in quantity as it was to do in 1927. The imports of the western Allies and of the neutrals were almost as great as they were to be seven years later, but those of the defeated countries and those of Eastern and Southeastern Europe amounted to only 40 per cent, and in raw materials and semimanufactured products to only 25 per cent. Europe required all kinds of goods. The severe shortages in food, mainly in Central and Eastern Europe, were overcome primarily by the American Relief Administration under Herbert Hoover, which by June, 1919, delivered to Europe $1,214 million worth of food and added $201 million more during the next four years. The recipients paid for a relatively small percentage. Until the depression of 1921 reduced prices, the countries in these regions were able to afford few of the raw materials from abroad necessary to revive their industries. There followed years of severe competition for markets.

The role of international trade in the European economy may be seen by comparing the share of the continent with that of the United States.

Percentage of Total Value of World Exports

AREA	RAW MATERIALS AND SEMIMANUFACTURED GOODS			MANUFACTURED GOODS		
	1925	*1929*	*1935*	*1925*	*1929*	*1935*
Continental Europe	24	29	31	47	49	49
Great Britain	5	5	6	25	20	21
Total (Europe)	29	34	37	72	69	70
United States	20	18	15	14	18	13
Rest of World	51	48	48	14	13	17
Total (World)	100	100	100	100	100	100

SOURCE: *International Cartels* (New York: United Nations, 1947), p. 3.

The data in the accompanying table reveal the extent to which Europe and the world depended upon the export of European manufactured goods. Among these commodities steel may be even more indicative of the nature of the economy, for it is used in the manufacture of everything. In the years 1925–1929 Europe produced annually 45,882,000 metric tons of crude steel (equivalent) and exported 17,453,000, or 38 per cent. Of the total amount, 7,432,000 metric tons, or 16 per cent, were shipped to non-European countries. In the same period the United States exported each year only 5 per cent of its production. In 1929 Europe supplied 99 per cent of the steel imports of Africa, 95 per cent of those of the Middle East, 87 per cent of those of the Far East, and 73 per cent of those of Latin America, or a weighted average of 85 per cent. It can be assumed that the United States supplied the greater part of the balance.

Most of Europe's nonferrous metals had to be imported, almost all the oil she used, and all the tropical products. As for agricultural commodities, Europe—exclusive of the U.S.S.R.—was in the middle 1930's able to produce about four fifths of its consumption needs. The highly industrialized areas were most deficient. The United Kingdom imported two fifths of the caloric value of its food supply, Belgium more than one half, the Netherlands nearly two fifths, and Norway and Switzerland more than one half. Greece, Austria, and Finland had large deficits. The surplus food areas lay in Eastern and Southeastern Europe, plus Denmark and Spain. Taken as a whole, Europe lived on international trade to a far greater extent than did any other continent. The countries were all relatively small, densely populated, and unable to be self-sufficient. The channels of Europe's world trade had been equaled in number and variety by those of her intracontinental trade. For centuries she had led the world in commerce. What policies did she set after World War I for a revival of her former position?

Economic Self-sufficiency as the National Objective

Each country, the new ones and the old ones, strove to be as self-sufficient as possible. Great Britain, the traditional home of free trade, kept some wartime import duties and added a few others. Each state tried to build an industry that would supply its needs and provide it with goods to export. If, like Romania, it had no iron ore, few technicians and little capital, it nonetheless built a steel industry as a mark of economic sovereignty and as insurance in the event of war. France acquired, with Alsace Lorraine, many German steel and textile plants. Germany thereupon duplicated by new construction those lost. Other countries followed the same policy. Each wanted its own chemical industry; each endeavored to maintain the expanded industrial productive capacity from the war years; each strove to increase its national product in order to raise the national income and enable it to surmount the losses caused by the war. This uneconomical practice was supported by tariffs to bolster the home market. The general level of tariffs did not rise beyond that of 1914; but increases were placed to enable the surplus industries and the new industries to survive. High overhead costs were met by price rises, which handicapped the products on the international market.

The European states ignored the transformation in the world division of economic function which the war had brought about. They neglected to consider the fact that during the war countries had developed industries to supply their own markets and even to export, and that Europe's dominant role as the provider of industrial goods, especially basic consumer goods, was past. Europe ignored the enormous expansion overseas in agricultural production: if she wished to sell her industrial goods abroad, she would have to change her own agricultural pattern so that she could buy from these customers. No country was willing to carry through a program of economic adjustment to postwar world conditions. No government felt able to attempt to do so by itself, and none was willing to entrust the responsibility to an international organization.

THE IMPORTANCE OF INVESTMENT CAPITAL

As soon as the war closed the Europeans urgently needed investment capital. During the hostilities capital had been blown from the cannon's mouth, and the material substance of the belligerents had diminished by the amount that the war cost. Each European participant required capital resources with which to rebuild its economy. Assuming efficiency in use, the sooner the essential capital was made available, the quicker would be recovery, the more stable the society. In this respect victor and vanquished were alike, the latter being distinguished from the former primarily by the worse condition of its finances. Each had to reconvert war industry to peacetime production; each had to make repairs which had been neglected for four years; each required the replacement of worn-out machines; each had a four-year backlog of housing needs; each had to revive a transportation system and a public utilities system that had been overworked for the duration of hostilities. The new states faced these problems, and in addition all those which attended the emergence of new political and social organisms. Each people which had experienced the horrors of war expected its particular country to assure it an improved standard of living. Each state feared its neighbor, whether ally or foe, and maintained or built a large defensive force.

The calls for money were numerous and insistent. The mature countries like France and Great Britain could and did obtain foreign loans; the states of Central, Eastern, and Southeastern Europe, that urgently needed investment funds, faced the greatest difficulty in obtaining them. In most countries the governments could not balance the budget and had to increase paper money and other credit instruments in circulation. Import and, wherever possible, export duties were raised in order to obtain funds for balancing the budget and building up the national economy. Most countries, irrespective of their political role during the war or the side on which they had fought, suffered from inflation. No one of them seemed able to overcome its own financial difficulties; all of them needed foreign financial assistance. Two possible sources of capital aid existed: one, the United States and, to a much lesser extent, the neutral countries and Great Britain, which in turn was dependent upon the United States; the other, international cooperation under the auspices of the League of Nations.

International Investment Market

The war had transformed the international investment market with the rest of the economy. Prior to the war Great Britain, France, and Germany had supplied about three fourths of all long-term foreign investments. In 1913–1914 the approximate value of these investments had been as follows:

INVESTING COUNTRY	MILLIONS OF U.S. DOLLARS
United Kingdom	18,000
France	9,000
Germany	5,800
United States *	3,500
Belgium, Netherlands, Switzerland	5,500
Other countries	2,200 †
Total	44,000

* Foreign investments in the United States amounted to some $6,800 million; on balance, therefore, the United States was a debtor country.

† Rough estimate; includes the investments of Japan and Russia (e.g., in China), of Portugal (e.g., in Brazil), and of Sweden (e.g., in Russia).

These sums were invested, by continent, as follows:

	MILLIONS OF U.S. DOLLARS
Africa	4,700
Asia	6,000
Europe	12,000
North America (north of Mexico)	10,500
Latin America	8,500
Oceania	2,300
Total	44,000

SOURCE: *International Capital Movements during the Inter-War Period* (New York: United Nations, 1949), p. 2.

Of these funds the French had gone mainly into Russian government bonds. The others, particularly the British, had been used to develop new resources in Europe and overseas. The war forced heavy losses upon the holders of these foreign investments. Great Britain sold about $4,000 million of hers—about two thirds in the United States—in order to purchase supplies. The French sold only $700 million, but they lost more than $4,000 million invested in Europe, particularly through the Bolshevik Revolution in Russia. Germany was practically stripped of her investments, either because she had placed about one half of them in the wrong continent—Europe—and saw them wiped out by war and revolution, or because the Allies confiscated the rest wherever they could locate them. Sweden, Belgium, and Switzerland lost their investments in Russia. The United States, on the other hand, emerged from the war as the world's creditor. Instead of being a debtor, as in 1914, she was owed by the European allies about $10,000 million. She occupied the position of the world's leading banker, which prior to 1914 Great Britain had held.

In the nineteenth century, which ended in 1914, Great Britain had served as the center of world trade and of world finance. The one function furthered the other. The country bought food and raw materials abroad, especially overseas, processed the materials, and sold manufactured articles on the international market. With market connections all over the world, it acted as an intrepôt for goods of all sorts. Great Britain usually bought more from Europe than she sold; thus she enabled the peoples of the continent to acquire pounds sterling with which they could pay for overseas raw materials. With this foreign exchange the overseas countries were able to pay for manufactured goods and for services from Great Britain. The large British merchant marine acted as the world's main carrier, thereby earning additional profits. The British invested their savings to a large extent abroad to open up new resources. The railways, port facilities, and public utilities overseas were in great part built by British engineers using British industrial products and financed by British loans. The many industries overseas intended primarily for export, like rubber, tin, and other mining enterprises, were developed by British capital and technique, with the commodities shipped abroad in British bottoms, sold on the British market to international customers, and financed by British banks. All along the line of the economic process the British private entrepreneurs were able to earn a profit, and the world benefited by the openness and freedom of exchange of this economic organization. Britain had the connections and she knew the market, not as an economic abstraction, but as a varied assortment of individual firms, each with different problems, risks, and credit rating. She knew how to make this most unsystematic system work.

The United States was unprepared for its role as the world's greatest creditor nation. Its bankers acquired the gold but not the experience in managing world finance which the British possessed. They were to make costly mistakes from ignorance—mistakes of commission and of omission, of acting too precipitately, of failing to assume responsibility in the world economy commensurate with their financial power. The United States did not perform essential duties, described above, which Great Britain had assumed in connection with being the world's banker. This country was largely self-sufficient. Its purchases abroad were small in comparison with those of Great Britain. It put up high tariffs to prevent the inflow of goods and supplemented them by difficult customs regulations, procedures of food inspection, and other administrative obstacles. During the war it had expanded the American merchant marine and wished to maintain this service in peacetime for both American and foreign goods and passengers. When it made foreign loans, it practically blocked repayment by excluding the borrowers from earning dollars through sales and services. The difficulties arising in the change from the broad, experienced British economic leadership to the erratic financial leadership of the United States were to plague world economy during interwar years.

ECONOMIC RECOVERY AND FOREIGN LOANS

Hindsight has shown that reparations and war debts severely handicapped the economic recovery of Europe and the world. A few war-poor states were expected to pay huge sums for the war losses of another group of war-poor states. The expectation that these sums would be paid retarded the revival of foreign investment. Bankers could not rely upon the behavior of peoples according to normal economic standards as long as political forces dominated international finance in the shape of reparations and war debts. For example, France, depending upon reparations payments to cover her abnormal expenditure for reconstruction, did not bring her own finances in order. When Germany would not or could not pay, French financial stability suffered just as that of Germany did, although not on the same scale. The United States, with funds to lend abroad, tried to collect war debts from states which urgently needed new loans. This antieconomic policy with regard to both reparations and war debts proved in the end to be a failure; it was abandoned after the collection of relatively small amounts. Not until the one was stabilized for the time being by the Dawes plan and the other by agreement on the terms of payment did the international financial market become active. Inflationary movements which had reduced or destroyed savings and deprived people of the incentive to save were brought under control, currencies stabilized, and the way prepared for foreign loans. The years 1924–1925 may be taken as the general dividing point.

The European economic recovery during the latter half of the 1920's depended upon foreign loans, primarily from the United States. France reentered the capital market in her traditional form. To a much greater extent than the other capital-exporting countries she lent money to governments or put it in other foreign bonds rather than investing it in private stocks. In spite of the fact that she had lost her capital by so doing, she still preferred portfolio investments to entrepreneurial ones. She lacked the material resources, the trained man power, and the will to risk extensive participation in business enterprises abroad. She obstructed international investment by her erratic monetary policy. Until the franc was stabilized in 1927, French investors sent their money abroad to London and New York on short-term loans. They wished to keep it in stable currencies. When the value of the franc was finally fixed, it was set at a price well below that on the actual international exchange. In consequence, France began to acquire large amounts of gold which she did not need and which she did not lend abroad for productive purposes.

Great Britain tried to resume her role of banker—to lend large sums to European countries while she was paying war debts to the United States and borrowing abroad. Her resources were limited, for her people were spending more and saving less than they had formerly done. Prior to

World War I British foreign investments had sometimes exceeded the net income which the country received from interest, dividends, and profits from existing investments; by the middle of the 1920's British net capital investments abroad averaged less than two fifths of foreign income. Lacking the material basis for the revival of prewar investment policy and yet recognizing the dire need abroad for loans, British bankers began to borrow American, French, and other money on a short-term basis and to lend it for a long-term program. Experience was to show that, in spite of their valiant attempt to revive the international economy by loans, they overestimated their strength.

The United States occupied a unique position, which it had the funds and the will adequately to fill. In 1919–1920 it had exported $7,000 million, primarily to Europe. Much of the money had been lost in the inflation, but by 1924 the country was prepared to lend even more. Between that date and the world economic crisis that began in 1929 the United States annually invested abroad $1,142 million, and Great Britain $587 million, or about one half that amount. The total movement of capital from creditor to debtor country in these years amounted annually to $2,000 million.

The foreign loans went primarily to developed or semideveloped countries. The Argentine and the underdeveloped countries of Latin America received large sums, particularly from the United States. The British Dominions also benefited. The bulk of the funds, however, was invested in Europe, as the following table will reveal. To these sums should be

Long-Term Loans to Europe, 1924–1928
(Average Annual Figures)

	GERMANY	ITALY	OTHER DEVELOPED AND SEMI-DEVELOPED COUNTRIES *	UNDER-DEVELOPED COUNTRIES
From				
United States	$224	$69	$45	$62
United Kingdom	34	4	10	37
Netherlands	35	1	3	2
Switzerland	11	1	1	4

* Austria, Czechoslovakia, Estonia, Finland, Danzig, the Saar, and Spain.
SOURCE: Figures taken from *International Capital Movements*, pp. 18-26.

added the short-term loans, which to Germany equaled in size the long term ones. That country had more than $4 billion in net capital imports during the six years from 1924 to 1929. The major ex-enemy country thus received most financial aid for recovery.

The loans to Europe, used mainly to recover from the war, did not mean an absolute increase in the world's wealth. They did not open up fresh sources of income. In many instances they were devoted to the construction of public buildings and to purposes which raised the standard of living but did not increase production. Other loans, particularly those from the United States to Germany, enabled that country to pay reparations and to purchase materials abroad. The foreign exchange acquired from Germany permitted the recipient countries to pay sums on their war debts to the United States. In 1929 world trade reached an interwar peak of $36.6 billion; but the annual payments for interest and amortization on international loans totaled $2 to $2½ billion, an excessively heavy burden that revealed how thin was the margin of economic safety. Thus the circle was complete. The United States lent money with which to purchase American goods. It lent money with which to pay reparations so that the countries could pay war debts to it. It even lent money with which to pay the high rates of interest on the preceding loans. For five years at least the United States kept international trade and finance in operation by shouldering the cost of the war. It helped Europe and itself to cover up the fact that Europe in particular had not adjusted its economy to the changes caused by the war in the world economy.

A European financial system characterized by reparations, war debts, and postwar loans sought means of conserving gold. Ostensibly the countries returned to the gold standard, Great Britain making that move in 1925. Actually the gold standard of prewar days was never restored; the countries lacked the resources. A number of the lesser states adopted the gold exchange standard. Instead of holding this metal as the basis of their currency, they used the currency and securities of countries which kept the gold standard. The British pound sterling found favor for this purpose. The practice meant that much less actual gold was employed to back the credit structure of countries, that supposedly sovereign countries were appendages to the financial system of one or the other foreign country, that the risk in finance had greatly increased. The gold exchange standard made countries which acted politically as sovereign powers financially interdependent; if one erred in either political or economic policy, all suffered.

Production and Foreign Trade

The revived flow of international finance proceeded in step with the recovery of European production and international trade. By 1925 Europe's output of industrial goods had reached the level of 1913, and agriculture had almost achieved that goal. British production for export, which by 1918 had fallen to one half that of 1913, was coming back. Except in Russia and in the war zones, the physical capacity to produce had actually increased during the war, even though much of it had to be converted to peacetime use. In the next four years world production of foodstuffs and raw materials increased 11 per cent, world trade by 19 per cent, world manufactures by 26 per cent. By 1925, not scarcity of goods, but excess capacity in industry and overproduction in mining and agriculture had become the sources of danger to world economy.

During the war food shortages had been mainly caused by the mobilization of manpower into the armed forces and by lack of equipment, fertilizer, and motive power. Livestock had been slaughtered for lack of fodder, and the production of dairy articles and eggs had fallen. In France and Germany the production of milk had declined by 1918 almost to one half the prewar amount. Even in 1920 the area devoted to cereals in Europe remained 15 per cent lower than that in 1914, whereas in North America during the war it had increased by 16 per cent. By 1926 technical innovations in agriculture, mechanization, and the use of improved seeds brought production back to normal and revived the competition for markets between European grain and overseas grain. World stocks of wheat after the harvest of 1925 were 9,300,000 metric tons; after the harvest of 1929 they amounted to 21,300,000 tons. The increase of sugar output was similar. During the war European production of beet sugar had declined by two thirds, whereas the world production of cane sugar had expanded. Once the war ended both Europe and the colonial areas increased output. By 1925 the export of sugar had become unprofitable. Between 1923 and 1930 the price of raw sugar fell 75 per cent. Using the years 1923–1925 as a base of 100, the index of world stocks of agricultural products had risen by 1927 to 146, whereas the price index had fallen to 81. By the end of 1929 the respective figures were 193 and 64.

The situation was similar for minerals and manufactures. In 1926 the major steel producers of Europe could supply about 35 million metric tons, but the market called for only 26 million tons. By 1928 the zinc smelting capacity of the world was 2.3 million tons; the actual output was 1.4 million tons. The development in Germany during the war of means to extract nitrogen from the air led to the postwar expansion of that industry; each country wished to produce for itself a commodity so essential for munitions and for fertilizer. Manufacturing productive capacity in 1913 amounted to 0.4 million tons of pure nitrogen, in 1926 to 1.4 million tons, and in 1929 to 2.4 million tons. World consumption in 1926 and 1929 took 1.0 and 1.5 million tons, respectively. Examples of surplus capacity, that is, capacity unused even in prosperous years, could be multiplied from numerous lines—shipbuilding, coal mining, cement, glass, rubber, almost any commonly used commodity.

Combinations, Cartels, and Tariffs

The war had accentuated certain trends in modern industrial development which had already begun to appear before 1914. The most significant were that toward large-scale organization of production and that toward the reduction of competition. A new conception of business and its relations with government was emerging. Bernard Baruch, chairman of the

United States War Industries Board, reported as follows to the President on the lesson which American businessmen had received from the war: "Many businessmen have experienced during the war, for the first time in their careers, the tremendous advantages, both to themselves and to the general public, of combination, of cooperation and common action, with their natural competitors."

Mr. Baruch's description applied with equal accuracy to the European countries, where particularly in Germany and France such action was traditional. "In each case," stated a minority group in Great Britain in a report on industry and trade in 1929, "coordination is the major premise in the full application of scientific results to industry, both in the utilization of research, the training of management, the pooling of ideas, and the establishment of cooperative selling organizations." In 1928 Sir Alfred Mond, head of the Imperial Chemicals Industries, Limited, one of the largest companies in its line in the world, published a book entitled *Industry and Politics,* in which he condemned competition in favor of cooperation and advocated the creation of large-scale combinations within the national borders as "an essential prerequisite to the conclusion of international agreements." In this way he expected to reduce costs by eliminating the duplication of physical plant and the need to tie up money in large inventories of raw materials and finished products. Cartels, he said, provided the only means to assure an "equitable pooling of the world's supply of the required raw materials," to achieve a steady "interchange of information and invention of technical discoveries and processes," and to make certain the "equitable distribution of the products" of industry without "the wasteful cost of unnecessary and often inimical competition."

Acting on the basis of the ideas of cooperative control and concentration, business after the war demanded protective tariffs as a first line of defence. From behind this fortification it sought cartel or other agreements with its foreign competitors. Agricultural commodities, minerals, and industrial products were all represented in the movement, and, although the resulting associations in the 1920's made many mistakes and frequently failed in their objectives, they sometimes did succeed and they did not relinquish the method of insuring profit. Some agreements were reached through private channels; others needed and obtained government support. On the whole, agricultural articles faced more difficulty in achieving cooperation than did industry. Wherever the producers were numerous, as in agriculture and sometimes in mining, the expense of organizing them and the difficulties about assuring their adherence to an agreement on restricting production rendered the international agreements temporary and uncertain. A pool for tin mining (1921–1923) accomplished its purpose of disposing of surplus stocks, but a plan for rubber in the twenties failed because the agreements did not cover every producer. Since restrictions on output raised prices, other producers entered the market and wrecked the scheme.

Industry did not face quite the same handicap, for it could consolidate small firms into one or a few large corporations within a country and thereby have a firm basis for negotiation. Nonetheless the twenties marked a period of experimentation for this branch of the economy as well. Patent agreements worked more smoothly than production or marketing cartels. Industry, however, had by no means solved the problem of maintaining each member's responsibility for economic efficiency on some matters while pooling responsibility for others. A member who saw a temporary opportunity for earning a profit at the expense of his cartel commitment might find the temptation too strong to resist. Cartels had trouble in keeping the members in line; quarrels broke out, for example, among members over the relative amount of production to which each was entitled. As long as the agreements lasted, and their average life was short, they reduced production. Whether the system improved the economy was and is a debated question. The unused capacity had to be paid for, and other overhead costs had to be covered by raising the price of the articles sold. The stimulus to improved efficiency and economy had to come, not from competition, but from the leadership of the particular company.

The cartels and other economic associations tended to preserve the economic undertakings that had emerged from the war and to postpone indefinitely the time when inefficient and uneconomical enterprises would give way to those serving the world at low cost. The cartels exploited the channels of private international agreements and the means provided by economic nationalism. Business was assuming, in the international field, responsibilities of national importance. A cartel in steel or copper or chemicals, for example, gave to a few private persons power over national military strength that no government could ultimately ignore. In utilizing the tariff and other forms of government aid, business in turn became involved in politics. Relations between government and economics entered a new period.

ECONOMIC ACTIVITY OF THE LEAGUE OF NATIONS

The League of Nations attempted to lead in exploring and solving economic problems on an international scale. Its efforts amounted to little because of three factors: vague authority granted by the Covenant, together with the limitations of its administrative machinery; the exclusion of the fundamental problems of reparations and war debts from its consideration; and the aversion of the members of the League to encroachment on their sovereignty. The governments of the world preferred to try to solve their problems on a national basis.

The Covenant devoted one clause of Article 23 to the economic aspect of life. The members of the League "will make provision to secure and maintain freedom of communications and of transit and equitable treatment for the commerce of all Members of the League. In this connexion, the special necessities of the regions devastated during the war of 1914–1918 shall be borne in mind." To give meaning to this laconic clause the League established a Financial Committee and an Economic Committee, each responsible to the Council and aided by a secretariat under the expert guidance of Sir Arthur Salter. In 1922 each consisted of twelve members, appointed by the Council, not as official representatives of their countries, but as individuals. Leading members in government administration, private finance, and private economy served on these advisory bodies. The prestige of each committee was sufficiently high to accomplish some good in spite of nationalism.

The members of the League secretariat were from the start acutely conscious of the vital significance of economic problems that required international handling. They convened international conference after conference to consider these problems and to recommend remedies. That of 1927 at Geneva may be regarded as typical. The agenda was prepared by experts working over a period of months; the conference brought together economic experts and leaders from many countries. The International Chamber of Commerce, founded in 1920, cooperated closely, and all the recommendations adopted by the delegates had the ring of deep concern for the revival of international trade and finance—lower tariffs, the abolition of export and import quotas and prohibitions, the free circulation of raw materials, the general introduction of the most-favored-nation clause guaranteeing to all nations the rights, tariff rates, and concessions granted to any one nation, the prohibition of unfair trade practices like dumping—in fact, the release of trade and finance from all the shackles of postwar practice. The conference disbanded and the members went home, where the governments heeded the pleas of the well-organized and vociferous special interests and mainly ignored the experts' advice. Within two years of the greatest gathering of economic wisdom that the world had seen, there occurred the worst economic crisis in history. By contrast, a Communications and Transit Organization created under the auspices of the League by forty-four nations functioned with efficiency, for it dealt exclusively with technical problems, drawing up conventions on the passage of automobiles across state boundaries and the like.

Although the League proved a failure in dealing with major problems of international economic relations, it did solve temporarily the financial difficulties of several small states. Reparations, war debts, tariffs, overproduction, inflation, and many other economic issues affecting the major powers were beyond League influence, but Austria, Hungary, Bulgaria, Greece, Danzig, and Estonia were small enough to come under League care. All suffered from unstable budgets, inadequate gold backing for their currencies, weak governments unable to collect sufficient taxes or to reduce expenditures, the lack of foreign markets for their products, the urgent need of capital with which to build or rebuild the economy, the equally urgent need of a foreign voice to press them to do what their own best people already knew they should do. In every instance the economic disorder was expressed by inflation, and in every one the essential remedy was financial reform.

The Austrian problem came before the League first. Its solution set the precedent for others and even for the main lines of the Dawes Plan for Germany. In each country requesting assistance, the Financial Committee of the League sponsored an investigation and a program of action. An international loan guaranteed by the Allied powers was the first essential. The country in question earmarked certain taxes to service the loan, but, should occasion demand, funds could be taken from other revenues. The budget had to be balanced, expenditures sharply reduced, the currency stabilized. A foreign financial expert was installed in the country, with wide authority to supervise the finances and indirectly the entire economy. He reported to the Financial Committee and the Council, but he wielded wide powers of discretion. The League assumed the economic tutelage of these small countries for a few years until they could become sufficiently stable to resume their independence. In Austria this supervision lasted from 1922 to 1925; in the other countries it remained for shorter or longer periods. The basic forces affecting the life in every country came from outside and lay beyond its control, as they did that of the League. When the depression began in 1929, these financial protégés of the League suffered like everyone else, and, although not in as great a degree, League loans declined in value like other international bonds.

SOCIAL ACTIVITY OF THE LEAGUE OF NATIONS

The social achievements of the League were of significance mainly as harbingers of developments under the United Nations. A Health Committee was established, at first tentatively because of vigorous objection against the expense from certain members of the Assembly, notably Sir William Meyer, the principal delegate from India. Within a year or two the Health Committee proved to be so useful in combating epidemics in Eastern Europe, Russia, and elsewhere, in collecting statistics about health conditions, in instituting research on certain diseases of special social importance, that the opposition declined. The United States agreed after grave hesitation that cooperation with the Health Committee would not entangle this country in foreign political difficulties, and Soviet Russia and Germany also participated.

The Advisory Committee on Traffic in Opium and other Dangerous Drugs, set up by the first Assembly, contained both defenders of the status quo and vigorous crusaders. The obstacle to reform lay in the fact that India, the Dutch East Indies, the Malay States, and other dependencies, whether French, British, or Portuguese, used the tax on drugs as a main source of revenue, and that states like Switzerland with a large chemical industry processing drugs were equally opposed to control of the traffic. Stirred by the reformers, the Committee collected such appalling data about the spread of addiction to drugs that by the Geneva Convention of 1931 the manufacture of narcotics was actually restricted to the medical and scientific needs of the world. Two supervisory international bodies were created,

> . . . with power to consider and criticise the quantities of such drugs which each signatory State proposed to manufacture or import, and even to suspend exports to a country whose imports were exceeding the estimates it had submitted—an extraordinary innovation, since it gave to a small international body direct authority over the actions of more than sixty States, including the United States and Russia.[1]

The committee, however, was never able to control the cultivation of the poppy and to curb the traffic in opium.

The League Advisory Committee on the Traffic in Women and Children persuaded states to improve their ways in handling these evils. Merely as one of its acts it formulated a Declaration of the Rights of the Child, which fifty countries approved.

The League Committee on Intellectual Co-operation was composed of some of the greatest scholars in the world—Albert Einstein, Gilbert Murray, Madame Marja Curie, Henri Bergson, and others. It strove to fulfill three purposes: to improve the material lot of intellectuals who had suffered during the war, to develop the international contacts of teachers, artists, scientists, authors, and other intellectuals, and to further the League's work for peace. The Committee received small sums from national governments, especially the French, and from private organizations. Its share of the League budget amounted annually to about $20,000, enough to sketch what ought to be done.

The Refugee Organization was established by the League in 1921 on a temporary basis, to assist in rescuing and settling the millions of people who had fled from their country or had become displaced and homeless. The Norwegian explorer Fridtjof Nansen took charge, his first major task being that of aiding 2 million Russians who had escaped from bolshevism and were scattered over Central and Eastern Europe. After the Graeco-Turkish War came a wave of refugees from Asia Minor to Greece. The League set up a temporary organization to help with this emergency, leaving the Nansen group to struggle with the refugee problems in Eastern and Southeastern Europe. For this work the League granted the Nansen Organization between $40,000 and $60,000 a year. The great powers, including the United States, looked upon this activity with mistrust, and usually shut their doors to the immigration of these people. Nansen raised

[1] F. P. Walters, *A History of the League of Nations.* Published on behalf of the Royal Institute of International Affairs, by the Oxford University Press, London, 1952. I, 185-186.

small funds privately, but with such amounts he was able to accomplish little. His only real achievement lay in persuading states to recognize the Nansen passport, a certificate of identification issued by his organization to refugees who had lost all their papers. With this certificate the refugees were for the first time able to move to countries where they had relatives or friends willing to care for them or where there were opportunities to settle. In the main, the wealthiest culture in the history of man left most of these millions of victims to fend for themselves, to depend upon private charity, or to succumb to hunger and disease in a world economy suffering from overproduction.

International Labor Organization

The establishment of an International Labor Organization was provided for in the peace treaties. It recognized the wartime elevation in social importance of the laboring class. The interdependence of social groups had been established by the fact that the upper classes could not win the war without the cooperation of the masses. The workers were thus able to demand an improvement in their working conditions, their compensation, and in their right to organize into trade-unions. The membership of the unions increased during and just after the conflict in countries on both sides. A war fought "to make the world safe for democracy," and concluding in some countries with a socialist revolution, created an atmosphere favorable to the political rise of organized labor. People sought a better life, believing that a country able to mobilize all its resources for destruction could improve peacetime living. The demands grew for governments to provide social insurance, to expand public education, and in numerous other ways to add to a family's real income. Labor wished recognition as an integral member of industrial society. The International Labor Organization responded in its character and function to this changed environment.

Although a separate body with its own bureaucracy, the International Labor Organization associated closely with the League and received its funds from the League's budget. It was guided by an annual conference, a governing body, and a secretariat. Each member state sent to the conference four delegates, two representing the government, one the employers, and one the workers. In the governing body of twenty-four members, selected by the conference, twelve represented the governments, and six each the employers and the workers. Since each group held a stake in industrial society, each was expected to work with the others for the common good. In that common effort labor took its recognized part. The secretariat prepared the work of the directing bodies, collected data on wage scales, hours of work, sanitary conditions in places of work, systems of social security, standards of living, work of women and children, trade-union organization, extent and methods of collective bargaining, and the numerous other matters of interest to workers. It drafted model laws on these questions or model international treaties, which after approval by the governing board and the conference were submitted to the individual states for ratification. In numerous instances the recommendations became part of national legislation. The national representatives in the I.L.O. acted as the means of contact and helped by way of education and the spread of popular information to win the country to the new proposals.

The organization propagated the standards of labor conditions of Western industrial society in the less developed areas of the world. It aimed to improve living conditions everywhere, and hoped thereby to reduce the tensions that make for war. Its goal could not be achieved in the short span of time between the two wars; but it laid down effective lines of action, and it showed more positive results than any other international organization. Led in its formative years by French socialist Albert Thomas, it expressed the profound change that had occurred in the labor movement. In 1848 Karl Marx had admonished the workers of the world to unite and destroy the capitalists by revolution. Under its socialist director the I.L.O. cooperated with the capitalists and used peaceful, rational means to improve the lot of the workers. The Western labor movement renounced social revolution in favor of social evolution.

Size of the League Budget

The extent of internationalism in the interwar years may be measured by the size of the budget of the League. The entire expense of that body, including the International Labor Organization and the Permanent Court and the purchase cost of its building in Geneva, amounted annually between 1920 and 1939 to $5,400,000. Great Britain paid 11 per cent of that amount; Canada, Australia, South Africa, New Zealand, India, and Ireland together contributed 15 per cent. The Secretariat, under constant fire to reduce the budget, had to justify its request for funds annually before three groups. Delegates who sought to curb the League's activities did so by attacks on the finances. Since Sir Austen Chamberlain wanted no interference in the affairs of a sovereign state, he expressed concern in the Council over the increase in expenditure of the Health Organization: his government was asked for an additional sum of $5,000. There were many private families in the world with an annual income larger than that of the League. Equipped with such funds the League was expected, according to the Covenant, "to promote international co-operation and to achieve international peace and security." It is surprising that its work became as fruitful as it often was.

Suggestions for Further Reading

HILL, MARTIN. *The Economic and Financial Organization of the League of Nations: A Survey of Twenty-five Years' Experience.* Washington: Carnegie Endowment for International Peace, 1946. A study to provide perspective in creating the United Nations.

Industrialization and Foreign Trade. Geneva: League of Nations, 1945. One of the many valuable studies made under League auspices.

KIRK, DUDLEY L. *Europe's Population in the Interwar Years.* Geneva: League of Nations, 1946. Indispensable. Discusses population change in the social setting.

KULISCHER, EUGENE MICHEL. *Europe on the Move: War and Population Changes, 1917–1947.* New York: Columbia University Press, 1948. A book of startling facts and questionable thesis.

Preliminary Report on the World Social Situation. New York: United Nations, 1952. The first comparative study on a world basis of health, housing, education, and the like.

SVENNILSON, INGVAR. *Growth and Stagnation in the European Economy.* Geneva: United Nations, 1954. Difficult but basic.

WILSON, FRANCIS GRAHAM. *Labor in the League System.* Stanford, Calif.: Stanford University Press, 1934.

Chapter 7 · The Stable Countries of Western and Northern Europe

LACK OF CULTURAL HOMOGENEITY IN EUROPE

Europe lacked cultural homogeneity. The heartland consisted of the central and western regions that had been industrialized. Germany, France, Great Britain, to a less extent Italy, and the neighboring small states of Switzerland, Belgium, the Netherlands, Czechoslovakia, Austria, and Scandinavia provided Europe with its wealth and power. Within this group some areas emphasized industrial production; others specialized in raising and processing food for the industrial market. On the periphery of this central region lay the predominantly agricultural states of low productivity and low standard of living—Spain and Portugal and the states of Eastern and Southeastern Europe. As a United Nations report said:

> Low-income countries tend to have: high crude death rates, high infant mortality rates, high birth rates, high proportion of children in the population, high rates of infectious diseases, low ratio of doctors to population, low calorie consumption, low protein consumption, low textile consumption, low literacy rates, low primary school enrollment, low circulation of newspapers, magazines, and books, low circulation of mail, low ratio of radios and telephones to population, etc.[1]

High-income countries tend to have just the opposite.

The low-income regions of Europe lay in such close proximity to the advanced countries that they sought to attain similar standards. In their efforts the less advanced areas encountered obstacles which grew out of the lack of political experience. Europe was as divided in this respect as it was economically. The states with a high standard of living had a tradition of political liberty. The sole exception was Germany, which had developed an industrial economy in a social and political system still run by groups with the standards of caste and absolutism. In the rest of Europe

[1] *Preliminary Report on the World Social Situation* (New York: United Nations, 1952), p. 134.

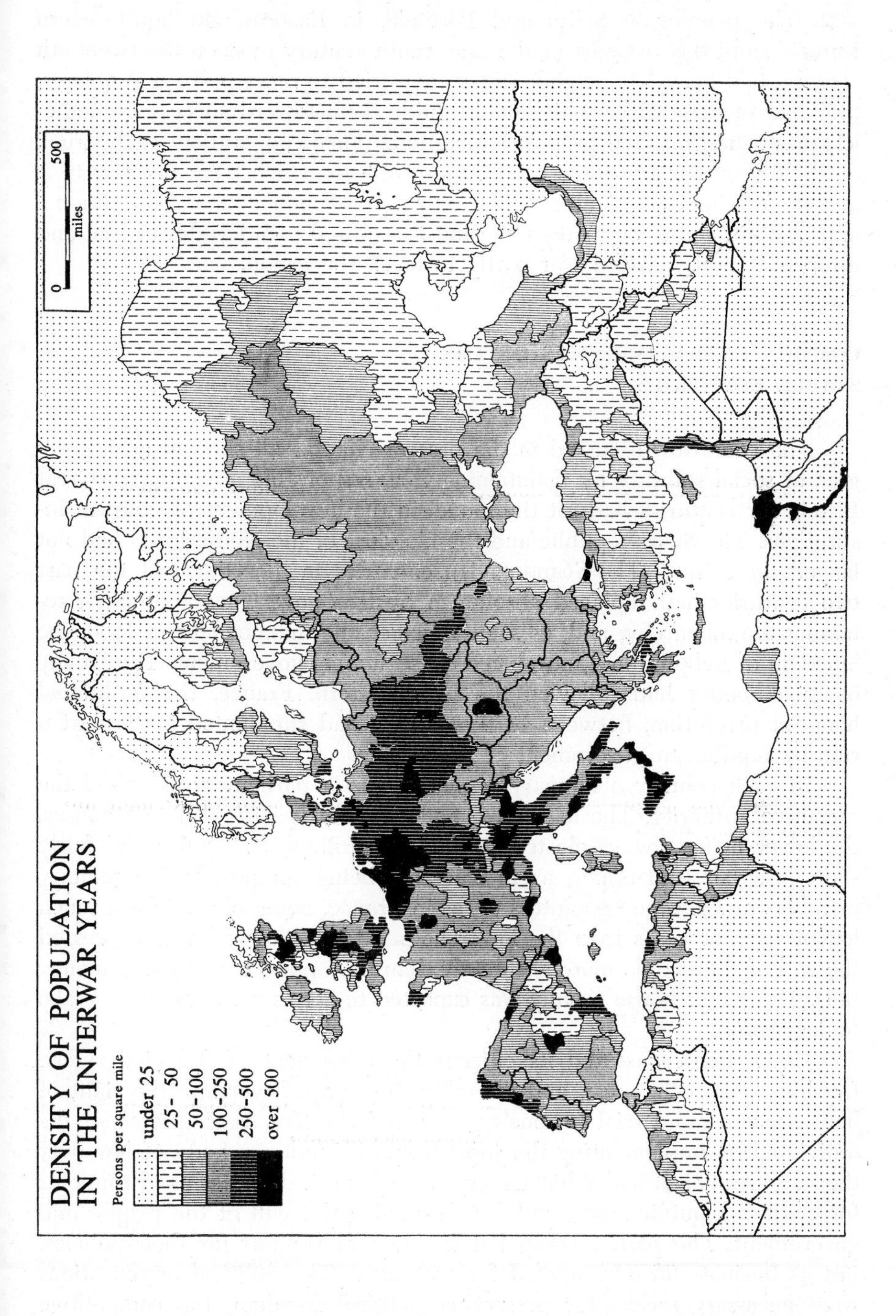
DENSITY OF POPULATION
IN THE INTERWAR YEARS
Persons per square mile
under 25
25 - 50
50-100
100-250
250-500
over 500
0
500
miles

the ways of free government and free society were to a large degree absent. The peoples in Spain and Portugal, in Eastern and Southeastern Europe, until the last part of the nineteenth century or even the twentieth century, had been left behind. When they tried to meet postwar problems, they had few traditions which could guide them toward success. Nonetheless, each state rejected proposals for international cooperation; each struck out boldly by itself to solve both those problems which were peculiar to it and those which could be handled only by common action. The national approach proved to be inadequate; but it required two decades of trial and error and another world war partly to teach the lesson.

COMMON CHARACTERISTICS OF THE STABLE COUNTRIES

The countries discussed in the present chapter all showed a high degree of social stability by maintaining free, responsible government. Great Britain for centuries had set the model in the development of political institutions. The Swiss republic and the kingdom of the Netherlands had not lagged far behind. The Scandinavian countries in the course of the past two centuries had replaced absolutism by free government, although retaining the monarchy; and, as soon as it became independent in 1830, the kingdom of Belgium had introduced constitutional government. The Duchy of Luxembourg had followed the same pattern. France, the traditional home of revolution, between 1870 and 1875 had supplanted authoritarian rule by republican government of the people.

In each country a ministry responsible to a parliament exercised the executive authority. The legislative body usually consisted of two houses, the lower being always elected by popular suffrage at regular and fairly short intervals, the upper, as in England, being composed of hereditary members or life-time appointees or, as in France, being elected for a much longer term of years than the lower house. As the lower house expressed the will of the people more accurately than the upper, it controlled money bills. The upper house usually was expected to act as a conservative brake on legislation.

Each country assured its citizens the enjoyment of full civil rights, freedom of speech, press, and assembly, freedom of worship, the right of habeas corpus and trial by one's peers, and the like. Each protected the individual by implementing the supremacy of a uniform body of law over the state. And each had achieved a system of political parties as instruments for clarifying public issues and for channeling the will of the people into government. The parties competed for popular support for their policies, just as business firms competed for customers. The political organizations were necessary means for preserving political freedom, the competitive businesses for maintaining economic freedom. Each supplemented the work of the other.

Among the stable countries were found the most important owners of colonial territory. Their habits and institutions of popular government did not prevent them from misjudging the effects of World War I upon relations with their dependencies. Each colonial people had enhanced its importance to the mother country according to the extent to which its aid had been needed in pursuing the war. Each shared in the heightened prestige which common danger had everywhere brought to the masses, whether European laborers or colonial underlings. The slogans "self-determination" and "make the world safe for democracy" were heard by non-Europeans as well. In many instances European states had placed colonial man power in military service. The colonials had learned that in combat, with proper equipment, they could equal imperialist troops. The participation of the Japanese on the side of the victorious European whites had strengthened the pride of Asiatics and stirred ambition for similar equality with white men. As new standards of social welfare received acceptance for Europeans, they did so by indirection for colonials.

War-inspired development of facilities for transportation and communication and for the cultivation of articles like rubber and the mining of ores like tin, copper, and manganese had increased the impact of Western industrialism upon outlying regions. When at the close of the war Germany was deprived of her colonies and the Ottoman Empire of its dependent peoples on grounds of moral unfitness to rule, the judgment indicated a high standard of treatment of subject peoples. Many colonials no doubt wondered whether the behavior of other imperialist powers toward dependent peoples differed essentially from that of Germans and Turks. The extent of awakening differed widely among the dependent peoples, but the trend away from imperialism was apparent. Except in so far as the Covenant in the Mandates system formulated a set of standards and objectives for colonial development, each imperialist state handled its dependent peoples according to its own national tradition and interest.

Great Britain

After the peace treaties were signed, Great Britain abolished her wartime coalition government and returned to party competition as the best means to preserve political freedom. The Conservative party ruled from 1922 to 1924, the Labor party for a short term in 1924. The Conservatives remained in power from that year until 1929, when the Labor party once more gained control.

GOVERNMENT AND POLITICS

The Liberal party, which had governed the country from 1906 to 1915, declined in the 1920's to the position of a small minor group, able occasionally to hold the balance of power, as in 1923 and 1929, between the two large parties and serving mainly as critic of the others and as propagandist for new policies. The Liberal party had last won a majority in the election of 1906. It had shared authority with Conservatives during the war, but, having retained the premiership, it suffered from the unpopularity which wartime governments frequently encounter at the peace. Personal rivalry for party leadership between Lloyd George and Herbert Asquith weakened party unity and campaigning vigor.

The main cause of decline seems to have been the public belief that the doctrines and policies of liberalism had been exhausted. The country had realized liberal ideals in democratic suffrage, free trade, the beginnings of social security, progressive taxation, the abolition of privilege, and free and compulsory education. The public associated liberalism with high-minded individuals who enjoyed a comfortable income and considerable education. The experience of war had persuaded many English that the philosophic bases of liberalism no longer held:

> It is *not* true [the English economist John Maynard Keynes wrote in 1926] that individuals possess a prescriptive "natural liberty" in their economic activities. There is *no* "compact" conferring perpetual rights on those who Have or on those who Acquire. The world is *not* so governed from above that private and social interest always coincide. It is *not* so managed here below that in practice they coincide. It is *not* a correct deduction from the Principles of Economics that enlightened self-interest always operates in the public interest. Nor is it true that self-interest generally *is* enlightened; more often individuals acting separately to promote their own ends are too ignorant or too weak to attain even these. Experience does *not* show that individuals, when they make up a social unit, are always less clear-sighted than when they act separately.[2]

Since the war had forced the government to intervene in many spheres of life, collective action, through the state if necessary, often became accepted in practice instead of individual action. Liberalism, which had believed in the greatest good of the greatest number, found that the Labor party had taken over its moral values, that Labor was implementing these values more generously and aggressively in social life than the Liberal party had done. During the 1920's the Labor party supplanted the Liberals as the major competitor to the Conservatives.

In 1918 the Laborites for the first time declared in favor of state socialism but advocated the introduction of the system gradually and peacefully, with public approval. Appealing predominantly to the workers

[2] John Maynard Keynes, *Essays in Persuasion* (London: Macmillan & Company, Ltd., 1931), p. 312.

and subject to close control by trade-unions, the Labor party during the war and in the 1920's gained the support of some of the middle class, particularly intellectuals, who, together with trade-unionists, had assumed positions of prominence. Inasmuch as the Labor party soon became a cross section of national society, it lacked unity. An aggressive bloc advocated the speedy nationalization of basic industries; the trade-unionists demanded economic policies that would improve the standard of living, but they were not inclined toward extreme political and social changes. Ex-Liberals from the middle class who joined the Labor party, persons like the eminent lawyer Lord Haldane, were equally averse to socialism. Ramsay MacDonald, elected in 1922 as leader of the party, although he had written books in favor of evolutionary socialism, turned out to be a cautious moderate, eager to convince the public of Labor's political reliability.

The Conservative party had been a prominent member of the Coalition Cabinet from 1918 to 1922, and from then until 1929 with one short interruption it governed the country. The legislation of the period in the main expressed its program. The word "conservative" indicates an inclination to maintain the status quo; but as the status quo changed with time the Conservatives made the necessary adjustments. The war had brought about such profound changes in British society and had aroused such expectations of a better life that the Conservatives had to institute reforms. The decade was characterized by experimentation in legislation, with some successful action, some hesitant measures, and some major mistakes of commission and of omission. Standards and motives were mixed. Laissez faire guided many acts; the state's sense of responsibility for the welfare of its citizens inspired others. The Conservative leader, Stanley Baldwin, respected and sympathized with labor and proposed to treat the Labor party with the consideration due His Majesty's opposition. He found his sentiments reciprocated by Ramsay MacDonald, head of the Labor party. Lloyd George, the most active leader of a divided Liberal party, had cooperated with members of both other parties, and he and his group were able to shift support from one to the other according to interest and will. The three parties differed over proposed legislation. The Labor party's goal to nationalize basic industries, banking, transportation, and public utilities, was rejected by the others. Nonetheless, judged by continental standards, the parties showed remarkable unanimity on rules of political action and considerable agreement on policies, differing mainly on timing and in degree of support for a specific policy.

The shift in party strength in the 1920's may be seen from the following table:

NUMBER ELECTED TO HOUSE OF COMMONS	*1922*	*1923*	*1924*	*1929*
Conservative party	344	257	413	260
Labor party	142	192	151	290
Liberal party	117	157	40	60

The results of the election in 1922 expressed the popular appeal of the Conservatives' promise of "tranquillity and freedom of adventures and commitments both at home and abroad." Labor increased its popular vote from 2,300,000 in 1918 to 4,200,000, and two Communists were also elected. The new Conservative government (1922–1923) under Bonar Law included almost none of the party members who had belonged to Lloyd George's Coalition Cabinet. These members considered socialism and communism the gravest danger to the country and believed that Conservative-Liberal alliance was necessary for adequate resistance. The Conservative rank and file, eager to rise to political office, objected to cooperation. Bonar Law, the party leader, feared that Lloyd George would split and destroy the Conservative party as he had the Liberal; thus he heeded the demand for pulling away from the Liberals. When Austen Chamberlain, Arthur James Balfour, and other prominent Conservatives remained loyal to Lloyd George and refused for the time to join Bonar Law's cabinet, new men of moderate ability became entrenched in party positions. The hold of these second-rate persons, of whom Neville Chamberlain was typical, persisted through the interwar years; consequently, British policy in both internal and international affairs showed timidity, complacence, and lack of imagination and courage.

In 1923 Stanley Baldwin, successor to the ailing Bonar Law as Conservative leader, carried to the country the issue of whether to introduce protective tariffs. Labor and Liberals fought the proposal as a break with the past which would benefit few and would not increase employment. The voters thoroughly repudiated protection, though they returned no one party with a majority. The Liberals, who held the balance, believed that Labor should be given a chance, and a Labor government under Ramsay MacDonald was called to power (1924). This first Labor government pursued a cautious policy of reform at home but showed more initiative in foreign affairs. It recognized the government of the Soviet Union and negotiated a commercial treaty and a settlement of existing difficulties caused by the Soviet's seizure of British-owned property in Russia. In return for this settlement the British government agreed to guarantee a loan to Russia, although the Conservatives fought the proposed treaty as furthering communism.

In October 1924, after nine months in office, the Labor government fell from power over a minor matter unconnected with foreign policy. The ensuing campaign was enlivened by the publication in the British press of a letter purported to be from Zinoviev, Soviet minister of foreign relations, containing instructions about conducting revolutionary activity in Great Britain. The Conservatives exploited the opportunity to accuse Labor of being pro-Communist, and, with public opinion already strongly in their favor, they won an overwhelming victory, mainly at the expense of the Liberal party. Labor's popular vote actually increased, from 4.2 million in 1922 to 5.5 million, but the party lost seats. The authenticity of the Zinoviev letter has never been proved; the Conservative government would not allow an investigation. Internal evidence seems to prove the document a forgery. The incident heightened the hostility of the British people to the Communist experiment but did not for long hurt the prestige of the Labor party.

When the normal five-year term of a parliament ended in 1929 and new elections were held, the Conservatives campaigned by placarding the country with a large picture of Baldwin carrying the phrase, "Safety First." The government's failure to reduce unemployment, to stimulate economic activity, and to support the League of Nations and collective security, and its general record of inactivity in all lines except that of holding down labor lost it popular support. Labor, after campaigning to persuade the country of its moderation, gained the largest number of seats of any party. The Liberals, running a candidate in almost every district, succeeded in splitting the vote in such a way that 118 Laborites (of 288) and 150 Conservatives (of 260) were elected by a minority vote. Even so, the 60 Liberal deputies who were returned would hold the balance of power and would support a government on sufferance. Under these uncertain political conditions, with MacDonald and a Labor-Liberal Coalition in charge, Great Britain entered the world economic crisis.

ECONOMIC TROUBLES FUNDAMENTAL

Britain's fundamental troubles were economic. For several decades her economic position in the world had been declining, and the war had accentuated that change. The staple industries, coal, iron and steel, engineering, shipbuilding, and textiles, remained in the 1920's steadily depressed. The nation failed to modernize equipment and methods, and stubbornly refused to apply science to technological and administrative problems. Businessmen persisted in the customary ways of marketing goods through agents in the ports, neglecting to search for new markets. Their goods, of high quality, were turned out in relatively small plants by skilled workmen at high cost. British producers hesitated to adapt types of machines, for example, to new market possibilities; instead, they stood by with their excellent products while the Germans, Americans, and others took over many of their markets.

Staple Industries

In analyzing the position of each staple industry one must recognize the fact that the British were subject to forces beyond their control, but one must note that there were many points at which they could have made essential improvements. Coal constituted the only industrial raw material of which Britain possessed large quantities. In 1913 she had mined 287

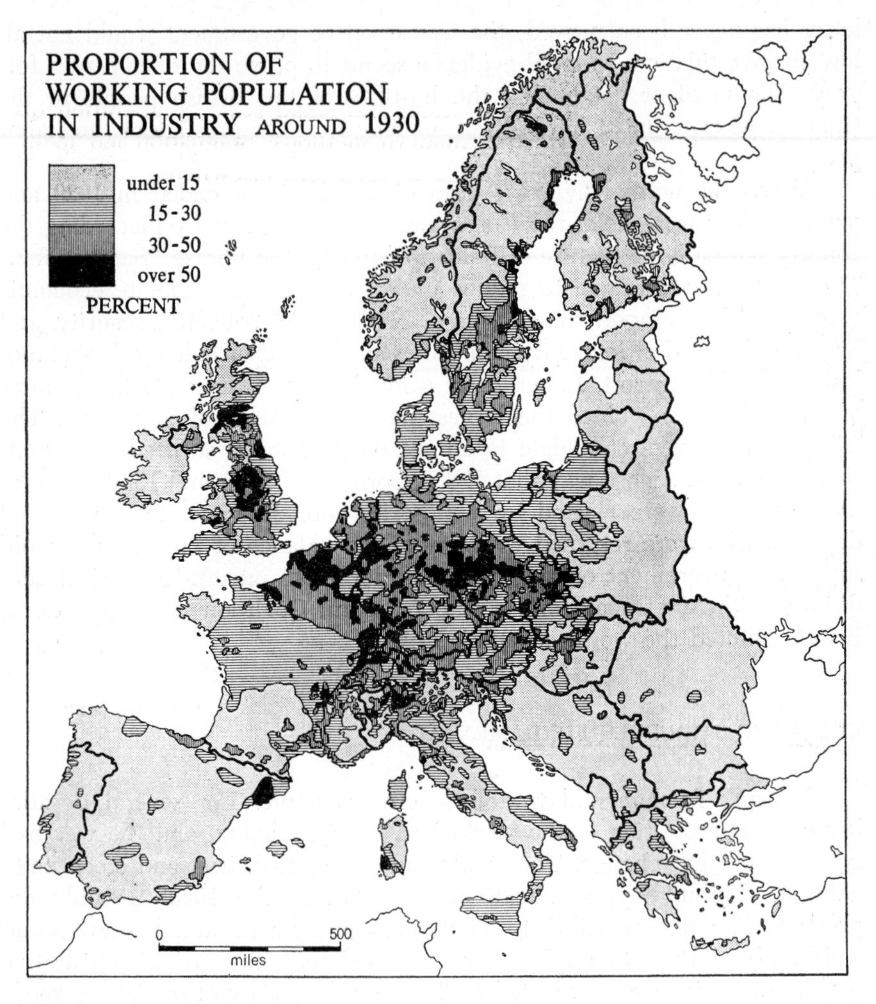

million tons, a figure not reached again. Before the war she had exported, on the average, 90 million tons, afterward 40 million. Coal consumption had declined, as furnaces improved in the utilization of the heat content and as oil and gas began to offer competition. Ships turned increasingly to oil, and less coal was transported as ballast to a distant point where a return cargo would be picked up. The decline in international trade was immediately felt in the coal industry. Foreign competitors, reparations coal from the Ruhr, and coal from Poland, which urgently needed foreign exchange, cut into British coal markets in Scandinavia. In the postwar years the international supply of coal outgrew the demand. Nonetheless, the British industry had itself in part to blame, for coal mining was technologically backward and inefficiently organized. With more than 3,000 mines, the scale of operation was small and costs excessive. The great depth of many mines and the thinness of the veins of coal added to the difficulties.

The royalties paid to the owners of the land on which the coal was mined increased costs. Low profits or frequent losses, a strong trade-union determined to maintain the high wage scale, and small scale of operation disinclined the industry to invest in modern methods. Stagnation led to unemployment and drove young people to seek jobs elsewhere.

The leaders of the miners advocated state ownership as the solution of the coal problem. The chairman and the labor representatives on a Royal Commission reported in 1919 in favor of nationalization; but the government rejected the recommendation and kept conditions as they were by subsidizing miners' wages. In 1926 another Royal Commission disapproved nationalization but advised drastic unification of the industry and state purchase of all mining royalties paid to the owners of the mining land. The government again temporized. The theory of laissez faire remained supreme at the expense of a stagnant industry.

The story was repeated in the instance of all other staple industries. Shipbuilding faced the fact that in 1921 the world had 65 million tons of shipping capacity as against 45 million tons in 1913, whereas international trade did not reach the volume of 1913 until 1929, the year in which the depression began. In the textile industry between 1913 and 1927 British production of cotton yarn declined by almost 50 per cent, while the export of cotton yarn fell by 84 per cent. The production of cotton cloth fared worse than that of yarn, but the export of it held up much better. When a country industrializes, the textile industry is usually the first to be developed. The British had been suffering before the war from the growth of textile mills elsewhere. When British exports fell off during the conflict, countries like Japan and India pushed their textile manufacture ahead. The British turned in part to the production of finer articles than before, but they could not maintain the previous volume of output. The iron and steel industry developed a productive capacity estimated in 1927 at 12 million tons; yet in 1917, at the height of the war demand, it had turned out less than 10 million tons, and in 1923 only 8½ million tons. In the engineering industries the country lost markets to the United States, Germany, and Japan. The production of agricultural machinery and textile machinery was particularly hurt. Small size of plants, obsolescent machinery, and unstandardized products prevented the industry from competing with the mass output of the United States and the rebuilt Germany. During 1925, the best year, British production in industry and mining was 14 per cent below that of 1913.

In the decade before the world economic depression Great Britain lost ground in the export trade but was still able to maintain a favorable balance of international payments. In 1921 the British shipped abroad one half as great a quantity of goods and in 1927 only 79 per cent as much as in 1913. The British were not earning enough on current account from the sale of industrial products to balance their international payments. They had to make up the deficit by performing services in shipping, insurance, banking, the tourist trade, and by using the income from foreign investments. We have already noted that they were saving less (by about three fifths) than before the war for investment. The British economy was in a far from secure position.

That the picture was not all black appeared evident from the development of new industries catering particularly to the domestic market. Rayon, electrical appliances, automobiles, and chemicals established themselves, not in the depressed areas of the north, but in the midlands and the southeast where 86 per cent of the growth in population between 1921 and 1938 was concentrated. These industries applied science and modern methods to production and earned profits in competition with foreign firms. They set an example of entrepreneurship that contradicted the charge of permanent stagnation in Britain; but they accounted in 1930 for only 12.5 per cent of British industrial output.

Mass Unemployment and Government Action

Stagnation in the staple industries brought mass unemployment. Prior to the war these industries had supplied work to 20 to 25 per cent of the total gainfully occupied population and to 50 per cent of those in industry. From 1921 on, Britain always had more than a million persons out of work. In 1922 the number rose to 2 million, or 17.7 per cent of all insured workers; in 1929 it was 1,466,000, or 12.2 per cent. For years on end men lacked jobs through no fault of their own; children grew to manhood with no assurance that they would find work. The effect upon morale was distressing.

To meet the difficulties, the coalition government and that of the Conservatives took a position somewhere between laissez faire and social welfare, but much nearer to the former than the latter. The general policy of the government, apart from the few ineffective months of Labor rule in 1924, was expressed by the Conservative leader and for a time prime minister Bonar Law. "I do have at the back of my mind a feeling that in a condition so critical as ours the real cure must come from better trade and better industry." Since extensive trouble between labor and employers in the postwar years could be anticipated, the government in 1919 passed a law setting up industrial courts which with the consent of both parties could attempt to mediate labor disputes. In accordance with a recommendation of a parliamentary committee by 1921, 73 Joint Industrial Councils, Joint District Councils, and Works Committees were created. These consisted of representatives of employers and employed and were intended to provide the workers with "a definite and enlarged share in the discussion and settlement of industrial matters." Although established in industries employing nearly 4 million workers, they did not succeed. The employers ignored them on important business decisions, and the workers lacked leaders competent to influence business policy.

Before the war Britain had introduced a comprehensive system of social insurance against accidents, sickness, old age and invalidity, and unemployment. By 1921 the system of unemployment insurance had broken down. After a man had been out of work for six months, he was placed on relief, or, as it was called, the dole, given a sum barely sufficient to keep him and his dependents alive, and usually subjected to an investigation of his total resources. Although forced to accept doles or starve, labor denounced as a humiliation the system and the means test it involved. With such an enormous backlog of unemployed, industry was easily tempted to blame high wages for its inability to compete in the market and sought to reduce this item of cost. In the conditions of postwar economic adjustment, wages and prices were frequently out of line; each side complained about the unfairness of the other, and trouble ensued.

Labor was too well organized to accept a reduction of wages and a worsening of working conditions without a fight. The war had revealed its strength, and British democracy enabled it freely to defend its position. It was encouraged by the belief that the workers had seized control in Russia and that a model society might develop. The number of trade-unionists had increased from 2½ million in 1910, to 4 million in 1914, to 6½ million in 1918, to more than 8 million in 1920. After that peak the membership declined to about 4½ million, where on the whole it remained stable. The three large unions of miners, railwaymen, and transport workers had formed a triple alliance in 1915, which enabled them from 1919 to 1926 to play the leading role in labor relations. Strikes during the period were numerous and bitter, nearly 3,000 occurring in the two years 1919–1920, with the main disturbance in mining and railways. The discontent culminated in the general strike of 1926. This strike started among the miners, who had been threatened by the owners with an extension of working hours and a reduction in pay which would have reduced their standard of living to that of poverty. It soon involved the entire Trade Union Congress. The general stoppage lasted nine days.

The government opposed the strike by two lines of action, the first being an exercise of the ultimate power of the state, the second a makeshift. The issue of the right to strike on any question had been posed in theory in 1920 during an exchange of remarks between J. H. Thomas, a trade-union leader, and Prime Minister Lloyd George. In defending strikes Thomas had "recognized that to support these men would mean a declaration of war on the government." The prime minister had replied, "Not on the government but on government, which is a much more serious thing." Concerned over the amount of social conflict, the government had passed in 1920 an Emergency Powers Act. When the General Council of the Trades Union Congress in 1926 reluctantly called a general strike, the Conservative government invoked the power under that act to discipline labor. Refusing to negotiate, it pronounced the general strike unconstitutional and workers and leaders as liable for damage. It mobilized civilian volunteers and had Peers and members of the House of Commons serving in subway stations. It ran trains, put out a newspaper, distributed food. Since the strike was generally condemned and many workers drifted back to their jobs, the Trades Union Council surrendered unconditionally. Only the miners led by some self-styled "humble disciples of Lenin" remained; after seven months they accepted terms, somewhat less favorable than those they had rejected at the time the conflict began.

The government promised to use its influence in having the strikers reinstated in their jobs and sought to revive harmony. At the same time it passed the Trade Disputes Act (1927). Strikes and peaceful picketing were permitted as before, but a general strike was made illegal and the use of intimidation in picketing was prohibited. Governmental policy toward the basic economic difficulty back of the strike provided subsidies to mines and railways with which to maintain the wage levels. The subsidy to the mines was not intended to be permanent; it was recognized that this kind of aid merely postponed the necessity of structural reform. The government, however, had no other remedy. It tried public works to relieve unemployment but on a limited scale which could not solve the total problem.

During the 1920's the British debated whether to impose protective tariffs and erect preferential trading rights within the empire to aid the country in recovering its prosperity. Conservative imperialists advocated both innovations, but the party lost the election of 1923 on that issue. Liberals and Laborites opposed the measures, and the country was not yet ready to break with tradition. Some tariffs were introduced or increased, some imperial preference was arranged; but, on the whole, trade relations remained as they had been. Trade with the empire declined as it did with the rest of the world. The United Kingdom supplied to the empire 44.3 per cent of the total imports in 1913, 38.6 per cent in 1924, and 31.3 per cent in 1929. The reverse showing was somewhat better: in 1913 the empire supplied 24.9 per cent of British imports; in 1929 the amount was 26.0 per cent. Imperial economic relations were not closer than before the war.

Restoration of Gold Standard

The sole clear-cut action of the government in the economic field consisted of restoring the gold standard. This measure, taken by Winston Churchill as chancellor of the exchequer in 1925, received the support of bankers, labor leaders, and businessmen—in fact, of almost everyone except a few economists. The act proved to be the severest blow struck at the British economy. The sponsors expected the gold standard to restore Britain's position as world banker, to sanify the monetary basis for international trade, and to revive credit and thereby the multilateral free trade of the prewar period. They overrated monetary reform as a cure for an international economy weakened by war. London lacked the money to compete with New York as a financial center. On the international exchange the pound sterling did not have its prewar value. That value in 1913 had reflected Britain's position as the world's banker, the major world's carrier and insurance agent, one of the world's leading industrial producers, and the greatest foreign investor. Great Britain was not worth in 1925 what she had been in 1913, and she owed enormous sums abroad and at home. Revaluation meant that her debts had to be repaid at prewar value by a much poorer country. Whereas France wiped out a large part of her debt by stabilizing the franc in 1926 at about one fifth its prewar value and Germany inflated her debt completely out of existence, the British made theirs larger.

Since the pound sterling was overvalued by an estimated 20 per cent, British prices were high in comparison with those of inflation countries, and British export goods were severely handicapped in international competition. It has been argued that the general strike occurred because the introduction of the gold standard in the preceding year made it necessary for owners to cut the price of coal and therefore wages so that British coal could compete abroad. As an economy of high prices Britain attracted the exports of other countries. Although in urgent need to export her own goods, she pursued a monetary policy which resulted in exactly the reverse of her intentions. Goods entered over low tariff walls; then Britain had to pay for them by working harder to produce goods too expensive to sell readily in a highly competitive market. The economy required large investment sums for renovation; nonetheless, money became expensive and scarce. By devotion to an inappropriate monetary theory Britain made recovery impossible. Not calculation, but the world economic depression of 1929–1933 forced a change of policy.

The presence of unemployed labor and unused productive capacity imposed extra burdens upon a country where taxation was already high. Unlike France and Germany, Britain had paid a considerable part of her war expenses out of current taxation. An extensive system of social insurance piled upon the debts left over from the war, expanded services to the people, and an enlarged bureaucracy called for a continuation and even an increase of heavy taxes. The income and inheritance taxes restricted the accumulation of wealth and of savings and, together with a desire to spend after wartime austerity, accounted for a diminution in funds for investment. An income tax three times that of 1914 and increases in the graduated surtax on high incomes began to reduce the real income differential for all classes of the population. The nation had to pay for the war; since the poor could pay only so much, the wealthy had to provide the rest.

British experts investigated the living conditions of the working people in the large cities during the interwar decades. Although the report was not then completed, the evidence showed that in the 1930's more than 20 per cent of the working class, even with the aid of social insurance, could not afford a diet sufficient to preserve health. The sums paid in social insurance were found to be inadequate, and the earnings of an ordinary worker when fully employed often failed to maintain more than two or three people. It was estimated that 25 per cent of working-class children belonged to families unable to afford the minimum diet recommended by the British Medical Association. The life of these working people spanned a period of hardship while the family was young, a period of comparative ease while the children added their earnings to the family budget, and closing years of grim poverty for the parents as the children left the home and the earning capacity of the old people declined. In the meantime the children had married and begun the same cycle.

EFFORTS TO IMPLEMENT DEMOCRATIC IDEALS

In contrast to the hardship stood the continued effort by Great Britain to maintain democratic ideals. The first example is that of the Education Act of 1918, a major step in cultivating talent irrespective of social background. Universal public education, which prior to the 1890's had not existed in the country, was recognized as an indispensable force in an industrial society. In a power world of modern war a nation could no longer afford to waste the ability of its people merely because some were born poor and of lowly class. The act prohibited children under the age of twelve from working and limited the employment of those under fourteen. School attendance was made compulsory to the age of fourteen; part-time day education became compulsory to the age of sixteen. Fees in public elementary schools were abolished, and increased funds were made available for scholarships in secondary schools. Nursery schools, medical inspection and treatment, and special facilities like playgrounds, holiday camps, and centers for physical training were provided. Lack of funds caused subsequent curtailment of the program; but the principle had been written into law and set a standard for future achievement.

A second example in democracy was offered by the Suffrage Act of 1928, which practically completed a century of reform. The law of 1918 had restricted the right of women to vote to those of the age of thirty and above. The discrimination was removed in 1928; the voting conditions of men and women were equalized. A few instances of plural voting remained the only limitation to complete electoral equality.

"Safety first" and caution characterized British foreign and imperial as well as internal policy. On the whole, the people were modest in their demands upon the state, either to assure them against the recurrence of war or to provide them with work. The majority left the formulation of foreign policy to a few individuals, just as it had done for centuries. Cool reserve toward the League, aversion to entangling alliance with continental powers, hostility to domination by any one power in the international relations of the continent, even if that power was the recent ally France (scarcely strong enough to play a Napoleonic role), a willingness to compete with the United States in naval armaments, the assumption that Great Britain continued to be as great a power as she had been in the previous century—these formed during the decade the main elements of British foreign policy. Like the decision in 1925 to restore the prewar value of the pound sterling, the Conservative ministers acted in international relations as though the country and the world had not changed. They were willing to accept Canadian and other Anglo-Saxon colonies as dominions in a commonwealth of constitutional equals. With respect to the rest of the empire and to other backward peoples, they considered imperial rule of subjects to be the proper relationship for an indefinite future. After long tutelage, subject peoples might be sufficiently schooled for the British government to decide whether to entrust them with self-government. Inasmuch as the British masses had been content with a slow rate of constitutional change, it was not thought unreasonable for colonial peoples to acquiesce in a long apprenticeship prior to self-rule, and the sovereign states of the world, it was thought, should be reluctant to experiment with new international institutions infringing upon British sovereignty. Britain in the 1920's had not learned that war had relegated the world of 1914 to the past and that in internal as well as in international relations new problems and new opportunities had arisen and the tempo of change accelerated.

France

FRENCH DILEMMA

After the war France sought to reconcile two conflicting objectives: to remain true to her cultural tradition and at the same time to survive as a great power in an age of industrialism. Few Frenchmen understood the serious dilemma of the country. During the interwar period a choice was not made; indeed, it was scarcely considered. In France, as in Great Britain, the ideal of returning to prewar ways and conditions continued to guide action, and insofar as changes were introduced, they were forced on leaders and people by circumstances.

The wartime loss of population hurt France more severely than the other European belligerents because of the shortage of demographic reserves. The French birth rate had been low for several generations, and in the interwar years barely maintained itself. The population was composed of fewer children and more elderly people than that of any other country. Germany recovered her war losses in population, including that caused by the cession to France of 7 million people in Alsace-Lorraine, within about a decade. In order to recoup her losses France needed the addition of the people of Alsace-Lorraine and a total immigration of 3 million from other countries, particularly Italy, Poland, and Spain.

The existence of an overage population affected French life in basic respects. It augmented the fear of Germany, for another war might bleed the nation to death. The government worked out in succession two contradictory policies for defending the country against a possible German attack. In the 1920's it favored aggressive action, a quick knockout blow delivered by a highly trained army which depended for effectiveness, not upon numbers, but upon quality of weapons, thoroughness of preparation, and speed of action. In the 1930's it reversed this policy and relied upon defense. The Maginot mentality, called from the line of fortifications built under the direction of General Maginot along France's eastern frontier, became characteristic of an overage people desirous of quiet. The matured France tended to oppose experimentation and innovation; the low birth rate indicated an absence of celebrated French *élan vital* and of entrepreneurial spirit. The French failed to develop their economy. In an age of dynamic industrialism they inclined toward a static economy and toward conservatism in social relations, education, and social services. The social groups fought over the apportionment of the limited national income. Government served little purpose other than that of obstructing change in the distribution of economic and social power among the various groups of the population. The old culture was to be shored up against innovation from within and from abroad.

ECONOMIC RECONSTRUCTION AND REVIVAL

During the 1920's France appeared to be prosperous. The war losses offered the opportunity to modernize a considerable part of industry and transportation. The fighting, which had occurred in some of the most industrialized parts of the country, had destroyed 900,000 buildings of various kinds, among them 9,300 factories; it had flooded coal mines and iron-ore mines. In addition, in the war area 6,000 bridges, 1,500 miles of railroad, and 700 miles of canal routes had been demolished in whole or part, and half the roads made unusable. In the region of battle 85 per cent of the arable land had been scourged and 94 per cent of the cattle had been lost. The magnitude of the destruction set the size of the task of reconstruction; for this purpose France had adequate facilities. The loss of the battle area early in the war had forced France to build industries in the interior, and these new plants, in production long before the fighting ceased, were ready to provide materials for postwar tasks. The acquisition of Alsace-Lorraine increased France's steel production by 30 per cent and brought her one of Europe's largest beds of iron ore. Textiles and many other consumer goods industries in these two provinces added to France's wealth an amount which one may roughly estimate to have been at least sufficient to counterbalance the losses in the devastated areas. With the return of

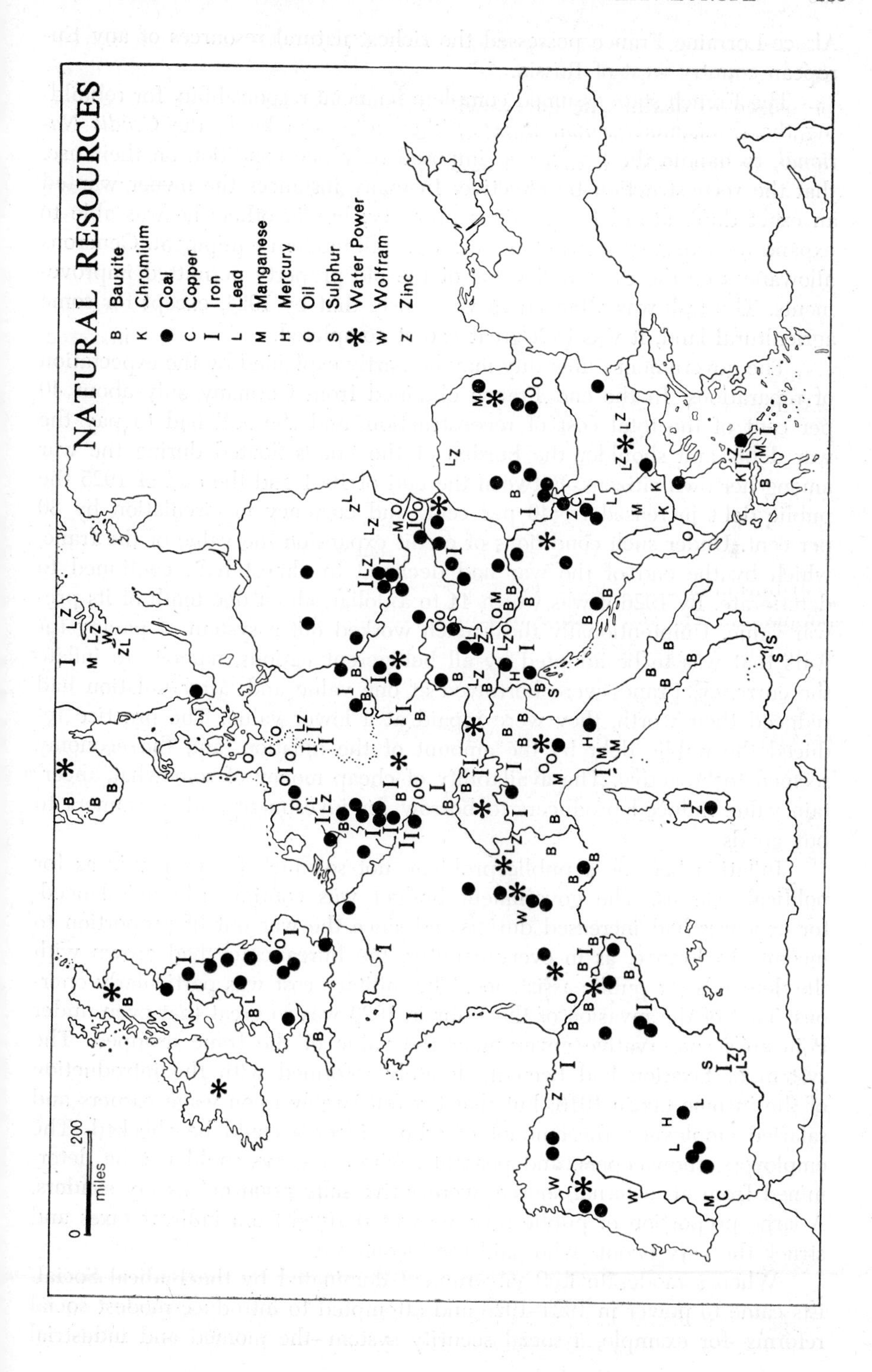
NATURAL RESOURCES
B Bauxite
K Chromium
● Coal
C Copper
I Iron
L Lead
M Manganese
H Mercury
O Oil
S Sulphur
* Water Power
W Wolfram
Z Zinc
0
200
miles

Alsace-Lorraine France possessed the richest natural resources of any European country west of Russia.

The French state assumed complete financial responsibility for rebuilding the devastated region. It established a special bank, the *Crédit National,* to handle the funds, and imposed only one condition on their use, that the reconstruction be effective. In many instances the owner wanted an exact duplicate of his previous property; but in others he was able to expand the capacity of his plant and to install modern equipment. Generous allowances on the estimated value of the old property permitted improvements. The task was attacked so vigorously that by 1924, except for some agricultural land, it was to a great extent completed.

The government's liberality may be partly explained by the expectation of reparations. In the end France obtained from Germany only about 40 per cent of the total cost of reconstruction, and she still had to pay the war debts and shoulder the burden of the bonds floated during the war among her own citizens. Between the end of 1921 and the end of 1925 the public debt increased by 40 per cent, and currency in circulation by 30 per cent. Under such conditions of credit expansion the value of the franc, which by the end of the war had declined to almost half, continued to deteriorate. By 1926 it was worth 44 to a dollar, about one tenth of its prewar value. Unintentionally the French worked out a system of paying for wars that was to be adopted by all belligerent nations, namely, to inflate the currency. Francs were borrowed at one value and, after inflation had reduced their worth, they were repaid at a lower value. The practice reduced the public debt by the amount of the inflation, and the economy seemed to be active. The availability of cheap money of somewhat uncertain value induced producers to borrow for investment and consumers to buy goods.

Inflation became a public problem, not so much for economic as for political reasons. The government budget was continuously unbalanced, for expenses had increased during and since the war out of proportion to income. In France, as in every country, the bureaucracy had grown with the demands for public assistance. The military cost was particularly onerous. That of the invasion of the Ruhr in 1923 was so great that even under Poincaré's conservative government the value of the franc dropped. The system of taxation had been moderately reformed with the introduction of the income tax in 1916; but that tax fell largely upon wage earners and salaried employees, the amount of whose income could be checked. The employers, shopkeepers, and peasants, whose income could not be determined from an external source, were universally regarded as tax evaders. A large proportion of public revenue was derived from indirect taxes and struck the very people who paid the income tax.

When a moderate Left government dominated by the Radical Socialists came to power in 1924–1926 and attempted to introduce modest social reforms—for example, a social security system—the monied and industrial powers of France, headed by the Bank of France, used their financial resources to cause a sharp decline in the value of the franc. They sold francs and bought foreign currencies; they left abroad their earnings from foreign sales. The resulting financial panic caused the fall of the reform government and the return of conservative Poincaré to power. He dropped the social reforms, increased taxes mainly upon the lower classes, and balanced the budget. The wealthy recalled their money to France; the government credit was readily restored; and the franc was stabilized at one fifth of its prewar value. By 1928 France owned more gold and foreign exchange than she had before the war.

Within its limits the French economy remained sound. Reconstruction kept everyone busy; unemployment was unknown, and foreigners were imported under international agreement to do rough labor in mines, agriculture, and various industries that Frenchmen shunned. During this decade French manufactures expanded over the level of 1912 by 40 per cent. Not merely were governmental funds available for investment; private resources were forthcoming. In 1910–1913 80 per cent of all the securities issued were bought on private account; in 1924, the amount had fallen to 50 per cent, but in 1930 it was up to 72 per cent. The French were again lending money abroad, although in small amounts. By 1929 they owned in value one half as much abroad as they had in 1914; but they were still putting a large proportion of their money in foreign government bonds and into political loans instead of tying the funds to French industrial contracts or investing them in local economic enterprises.

To judge from her balance of international trade and payments in this decade, France recovered remarkably well. Her imports of raw materials were especially heavy for a couple of years after the war. By 1925 exports equaled imports, and in 1927 reached a level of 166 (1913 = 100), while imports stood at 117. From then until the depression two years later the balance of trade continued to be favorable, and, with income from a flourishing tourist business and from foreign investments, France enjoyed a highly favorable balance of international payments. It was so advantageous that when Poincaré stabilized the franc at 20 per cent of its prewar value, he did so at a rate far below its real worth. By undervaluing her money France stole a march on the other countries, especially Great Britain. The one made her exports too cheap; the other her exports too dear. The one earned more gold and foreign exchange than was good for the world economy; the other took in too little.

Fundamental Weakness of Economy

The essential weakness of French economy becomes apparent as soon as one investigates production. The country had accepted the industrial revolution but had preserved the small enterprise. World War I marked the first significant change to mass production, and then in only a limited number of industries. In 1931, of 1,600,000 registered industrial undertakings, 64 per cent had no paid employee; of the rest, 34 per cent paid fewer than 10 employees, and 0.5 per cent employed 100 or more. Two million shops continued to exist on an artisan basis, not quite one half of them located in the rural districts. In 1926, 43 per cent of the 6 million wage earners were employed in industries with more than 100 employees, an increase of 80 per cent since 1906. The large enterprises were to be found primarily in coal, iron and steel, automobile, rubber, rayon, and chemicals. The paper, rubber, and automobile industries especially used modern techniques; others, like cotton textiles, leather, construction, and metallurgy, continued primitive.

In referring to large-scale industries the term "modern" must be used with caution. France possessed no industries comparable in size to those in the United States, and she lagged far behind Germany. In coal output per manshift (underground and surface workers) in 1937 France averaged half as much as Germany and one fifth as much as the United States. In the same year the French output in merchantable iron ore per man per year was less than half that of the United States, and in 1935–1938 the average annual consumption of steel per capita for France was 126.7 kilograms, for Germany 255.6 kilograms, and for the United States 301.5 kilograms. A country with such a low steel consumption could scarcely be using enough machines to produce on a mass scale. Advanced industrialization usually relegates the textile industry to a place of lesser importance; in France textiles continued to employ more labor than did any other industry. An advanced country tends to manufacture much of its raw material; France mined eight times as much bauxite as Germany but produced only one fourth as much finished aluminum. In France iron ore cost one third as much as in the United States and wages were low; but processing was so expensive that the cost of sheet iron in the two countries was about the same. During the first thirty years of the century French industry increased per capita consumption by probably 20 to 30 per cent. In the United States the comparable figure was 55 per cent. There had been no essential change in the use of resources and little if any over-all improvement in productivity during the past half century.

The retarded condition of French industry may be explained by those mysterious forces known as national mores. The small businesses and many or even most of the large ones continued to be owned as family enterprises. Railroads, coal mines, gas, and electricity fell outside the family-type business, but the iron and steel and machine industries conformed to the general dimensions of the small plant. The family wished to retain control of its own affairs, to supply funds for capital needs out of its own savings. It used the business to maintain the family; it did not subordinate the family to the interests of the business. It did not allow the opportunities for making more profit to entice it into expanding the business to a size beyond its control. The acquisitive spirit was curbed by the desire to live well and enjoy life. The competitive spirit was restrained by the respect for the rights of other businesses to make a profit and support other families. Combinations and cartels became standard. The large firms with relatively low costs of production raised their prices to the point where the small, inefficient businesses of high costs could profit. They helped to preserve inefficient and uneconomic enterprises at the expense of the country. France continued to apply to machine-run industry the standards of her traditional luxury economy.

The system of distribution remained less economical than that of production. Every petty employee hoped to become an independent shopkeeper. The number of retail outlets exceeded the need; the average size was too small, the turnover of durable goods too slow, the prices charged too high, the profits too great, and the sales too few. Modern methods of salesmanship were little used. The chain store and other outlets which in other countries have reduced the cost of retailing were excluded by discriminatory taxation and restrictive legislation.

Condition of Labor

In this economy the position of labor was necessarily low. The workers were poorly organized and exercised little social influence. Collective bargaining was legal and national industrial unions were organized, but a relatively small proportion of the workers belonged to them. The membership figure of 1.8 million at the beginning of 1920 meant a threefold increase since 1914; but by the end of the year it dropped to 750,000 or less, and as late as 1936 less than half a million workers, or 6.3 per cent of those in private employment, had organized. With one worker here and half a dozen there scattered all over France and with very few concentrated in moderately large industries, the obstacles to signing members, collecting dues, and forcing employers to recognize unions proved almost insurmountable. The unions were concentrated in and around Paris, in the north and in Alsace-Lorraine; elsewhere, that is, in most of the country, they scarcely existed. The railway workers had their own organization; it numbered 165,000 members and was subject to special legislation. Another 350,000 belonged to the federation of civil servants, but as these remained separate from the trade-unions proper prior to 1929, their influence on the movement did not become significant until the next decade. Collective bargaining had little import. In 1933 only 7.5 per cent of all the workers in industry and commerce had succeeded in imposing collective agreements upon their employers. These included the miners and the maritime trades, where collective bargaining had become well established. Of the 1.3 million employed in the metal industry only 1.4 per cent worked under collective bargaining, and only 2 per cent in the textile industry. Thus in labor-capital relations likewise, France had not advanced beyond the early stages of the industrial revolution.

Since an alternative was lacking, the workers interested in organization became attracted to radicalism. During and immediately after the war the movement split into two parts, the Confederation of Centralized Trade Unions (*Unitaire*) and the General Confederation of Workers. The former advocated revolution by violence and looked to the Communists in Russia for leadership. The General Confederation of Workers opposed such violence but was by tradition hostile to capital, to the state, and to cooperation with middle-class parties in forming a government; it had aimed to use the general strike in order to transform the French economy into a body of state-owned and state-managed syndicates. During and after the war the non-Communist trade-unionists turned to evolutionary tactics within the framework of bourgeois society. Their radical members tried the general strike in 1920 and 1924, with disastrous results to labor; radicalism, including communism, continued during the 1920's to lose influence. The communist unions claimed to have a quarter of a million members but manifestly had fewer, with many of those uncertain. Reformism was winning labor from revolutionary tactics. Nonetheless, the way was hard, for the bourgeoisie did not distinguish between the two factions in the unions and treated them all alike. As a group, virtually of second-class citizens, labor reacted in a class-conscious way to the class-consciousness of the employer-bourgeoisie. The land of liberty, equality, and fraternity was torn by class hatred as intense as that to be found in any Western nation.

In restricting the size of their enterprises and holding down production, the employers earned a large margin of profit on a small output and forced labor and employees to accept low wages. Prior to World War II it was estimated that the per capita average real income of all persons employed amounted to about one half that of the American worker and two thirds that of the British. In the fields of commerce, communications, transportation, and public and private service, income was less than one fifth of the American, and scarcely more than two fifths of the British. With such a wage the French urban masses could not afford to purchase more than a minimum of the goods which the economy produced; that is, an internal market for mass output at low prices was lacking, and with it the material basis for military power appropriate to a great state.

Backward Agriculture

Agriculture shared the prevailing backwardness. By the 1930's French farm output ranked lowest per acre of that of any country in Northwestern Europe. Between 1914 and 1931 the number of the working population engaged in agriculture declined by 10 per cent, a reduction caused rather by the loss of life in the war than by transfer to urban occupations. But at 35 per cent it was still, in comparison with other industrial countries, far too large. Age-old agricultural methods survived, with the state offering almost no educational program to assist the peasants. Credit facilities for agriculture had not been developed, and marketing suffered as in industry from excess of middlemen, each bent on taking a large profit. Property ownership among the peasants remained widespread, with two thirds of them owning their own land or cultivating the rented land at their own expense. Nonetheless, from one fourth to one third of the land was owned in such small plots that the proprietors became agricultural proletariat. Some large estates existed in Normandy and Brittany; but the peasants predominated, cautious, individualistic, hostile to government, averse to paying taxes, antagonistic to social insurance, ignorant of the problems of industrial insecurity and of what a modernized industry could achieve for agriculture and the country. In sum, the peasantry formed a class whose social and political views so resembled those of the bourgeoisie that the two groups were able to impose their stamp upon France and prevent the country from following the trend toward full-fledged industrialism. These were the groups that gave France her characteristic features, a relatively static society cherishing the pretentions from preindustrial days of being a great power.

GOVERNMENT AND POLITICS

Since peasantry and bourgeoisie dominated the country, the government expressed their wishes of preventing fundamental changes in the order of things. The parliament was divided into two houses, the Chamber of Deputies, elected for four years, and the Senate, whose members served for nine years. If the Chamber passed a progressive measure, the conservative Senate, composed of elder statesmen, would reject it. The executive, apart from a figurehead president, consisted of a cabinet responsible to the parliament, primarily to the Chamber. Although composed of deputies, as in Great Britain, the ministry was unable to exercise leadership. In Great Britain the two-party system assured that one party was responsible for the conduct of government while the other played the role of loyal opposition and critic. The party members in the cabinet and in the House of Commons shared a common responsibility for the execution of their program. In France no such precise division of function existed. The parties were numerous and small in size, and among the bourgeois parties only one, the Radical Socialist, had developed permanent organization. The others were loosely grouped around personalities and lacked continuity. The rigidly disciplined Communist party counted for little. The socialist party, also well organized, was larger in official membership, but in the election of 1924 it polled only 750,000 votes to the Communists' 876,000. It doomed itself to ineffectiveness by refusing to join moderate or left-center bourgeois parties in forming a government. On the far right a few royalists and an increasing number of fascists took their stand against everything to the left of them.

In the confusion of parties the difficulty of maintaining a government kept France in almost constant political crisis. Cabinets were formed and overthrown several times a year. Issues lacked clarity because of the multiple party system. A party could resoundingly proclaim its program, assured that at the time of forming a cabinet it would have to associate with other parties and need not carry out its promises. Government by bloc made the shift in the composition of cabinets an ever-continuing game. In general, the parties in the government agreed on fundamentals; but the right center bloc, in which Poincaré stood as the most important figure, inclined toward conservative policies, while the left center bloc, with leaders like Herriot, the Radical Socialist mayor of Lyons, favored a program of mild social reform. During the 1920's Poincaré was in power more often than Herriot. The election system assured the return in any circumstance of a moderate majority. The laws of 1919 and of 1927 extended the practice of proportional representation, but the complicated changes made little difference in the bourgeois composition of the Chamber of Deputies. The conservative peasantry continued to be represented out of proportion to their numbers, whereas the workers were always underrepresented.

In 1919 a spokesman for the General Confederation of French Production, an association of 2,500 employers, including the most powerful ones in coal and steel, declared that his confederation intended to press parliament in favor of bills "in the interest of general prosperity," that is, of the employers. The industrialists were well organized to achieve their purpose, for in addition to the General Confederation there existed in 1924 6,596 associations of employers with nearly 500,000 members. The peasantry lacked such efficient organizations, but it could be relied upon to join business in opposing the introduction of undesired reforms. Because of their resistance France lacked a system of social insurance until 1928, when a beginning was made partly because the people of Alsace-Lorraine insisted upon maintaining the benefits of insurance gained under German rule.

The close connection between economic interests and the members of parliament was traditional and well known. Some businesses soon learned that reparations in kind from Germany reduced their markets; they therefore took steps to prevent such competition, acting on the view that a private interest was synonymous with a national interest. Exceptions to the general policy were approved, however, wherever the state could be utilized advantageously by business. The railroads had for decades depended upon public aid; in 1921 the government saved them from bankruptcy, required them to increase their rates, and set up a Superior Railways Council composed of representatives of the railways and of the state to determine policies and try to make them self-supporting. It controlled them but refused to nationalize them. By a law of 1925 it created a National Office for Liquid Combustibles to plan the development of the oil industry. The government had found the country sadly lacking in oil during the war; it thereupon acquired an interest in Iraq oil production and worked out a system of inducements and prohibitions by which it persuaded oil companies, French and foreign, to build refineries in France. It created new banks to care for the financial needs of various parts of the economy, one for foreign commerce, one for agricultural credit, one for the artisans, and one for colonial development. By way of the peace treaties the Alsace potash mines fell to its possession, together with a fleet of boats on the Rhine and the Danube. A National Economic Council was created in 1925, composed of representatives from industry, commerce, agriculture, and labor, to advise the government on matters of policy and on legislation. The Council never achieved significance; the important groups knew how to exert their influence through other channels.

The outstanding and ever-popular act of the government to save the economy consisted of tariff protection. Since France came so close to being self-sufficient, she could use the tariff to keep up the price of both agricultural and industrial products. During the war the most-favored-nation clause had not functioned, and France did not revive it. Instead, she developed a policy of tariff reciprocity, with maximum and minimum rates fixed by law. Thus she would bargain with a particular country for tariff concessions, offering the minimum rates but threatening to apply the maximum. As the value of the franc declined, the government met increasing difficulty in raising the tariff rates quickly enough to keep out undesired competition. The officials administering the tariff were finally empowered to raise tariffs by administrative action as much as 400 per cent. At the time of the World Economic Conference in 1927 the government negotiated a commercial treaty with Germany which reintroduced the most-favored-nation clause. Some Frenchmen had learned that commercial jockeying and isolation were hurting everyone; but the treaty was opposed by business and agricultural interests and did not last long. Since high tariffs preserved inefficiency and high costs in industry and agriculture, the French nation paid the price, in low national income, poor standard of living, and reduced material power.

EDUCATION

Education shared the characteristics of the economy and society. French critics were beginning to condemn their system as urgently in need of reform, but the forces of passivity remained in control. The curriculum continued to be based on the humanities; it neglected almost entirely the social sciences and offered inadequate training in the physical and biological sciences. Young people were taught to express themselves fluently; they were acquainted with art and literature but not with economics or the functioning of government. The schools lacked playgrounds, medical care, and other services for which education in this century has assumed responsibility. Secondary education cost too much for the masses, and the universities were reserved for a small elite. Technical schools were few in number and poorly equipped. The government spent smaller sums on education than did its neighbors, and the results were evident in the absence of intellectual drive to reform the society. Leading literary and professional personalities opposed science and the social sciences as anti-humanistic; the few defenders of them found little support in the public.

ASSIMILATION OF ALSACE-LORRAINE

Recovery of Alsace-Lorraine at the end of World War I failed to be the happy ending of a sorrowful tale that France expected. The people of the provinces had the characteristics of frontiersmen between two cultures: they were neither good Frenchmen nor good Germans but a mixture. Although of necessity adaptable to changing political circumstances, they wished to preserve their own way of life. They had opposed German attempts after 1871 to assimilate them into German culture, and they were equally prepared to resist efforts after 1918 to shape them to the French pattern.

Frenchmen were surprised by the discovery. They learned that in 1910, 1,634,260 of the inhabitants spoke German, mainly a South German dialect rather than the literary High German, and that only 204,262 spoke French. When the government imposed the use of French in official business, in the elementary schools, and planned to do so eventually in the secondary schools (relegating German to the role of a foreign language), the natives protested and forced concessions to local tradition.

The French government proposed to separate church and state and to laicize schools as it had done in France during the decades before World War I. In Alsace-Lorraine the German government had retained the Concordat of 1801, the state paying the salaries of the clergy. A government of Radical Socialists headed by Herriot announced in 1924 the cessation of this practice, whereupon the native clergy of the strongly Catholic new provinces compelled postponement of the measure. Clergy had led the resistance against Germanization; now they continued to be popular leaders against the French. When the French government immediately began to shift control of the education system from the Roman Catholic Church to the state, the local clergy resisted the change; but the French here remained adamant. The schools were considered the means of transforming a somewhat untrustworthy population into loyal Frenchmen, speaking French, serving in the French army, and conforming to the French manner of life.

Economic problems added to the embarrassment. Not all Frenchmen were enthusiastic about the return of the provinces; they feared competition from the efficient textile, iron and steel, and other manufacturing industries. The natives shared some of the reluctance; they had prospered under German rule from the large market and considerable capital investments, and from the stimulation of an aggressive economy. By the terms of the peace treaty, they retained free access to the German market for five years. They anticipated with something less than pleasure the prospect of becoming at the close of the period a part of a much less progressive economic system.

The German government had permitted a large amount of local and provincial autonomy. Municipalities had raised funds for improvements on a liberal scale, and in 1911 the local diet of the two provinces had been granted substantial powers of government. The introduction of the French centralized system ended the era of responsibility and transferred all authority to Paris. The French financial policy of pinching pennies supplanted that of German liberality.

The antagonism of the Alsatians to France culminated after 1924 in a popular movement in favor of autonomy. When in 1928 the government arrested fifteen of the leaders, the people replied by electing three of them to the Chamber of Deputies. Neither side wished a showdown, however; the government finally reduced the tension by making concessions to local customs. The world economic crisis, which hit Germany far more severely than France, increased the attractiveness of the French market, and the accession of Hitler to power reduced the pro-German element to a small group. Alsace and Lorraine continued to be a border province, but by the 1930's its people were reconciled to union with France.

REVIVED POPULARITY OF CATHOLIC CHURCH

The French Republic appeared more stable than before the war. Generals who mistrusted it still led the army; but having fought victoriously for the state during four years, they had lost some of their previous disrespect for republicanism. The Catholic Church had changed more than the military. Since disestablishment, the church had gained in popularity. Although a majority of Frenchmen ignored the church except for ceremonial purposes of baptism, marriage, and burial, the people had about ceased to consider it synonymous with monarchism and conservatism, and the number of its supporters increased. The younger clergy adhered to the Republic. They and many of the newly appointed bishops interested themselves in social questions and were often condemned by conservatives as dangerously radical. Priests attempting to regain influence in workers' districts sympathized with popular demand for factory legislation, social insurance, improved housing, and the like. Many advocated creating a Catholic political party comparable to the Centrist party in Germany, with a progressive program and nation-wide appeal. They opposed nationalism, worked for peace and understanding among nations, and supported Pope Pius XI's move to place the nationalistic and monarchistic writings of

Charles Maurras and *Action Française* on the Index. Numerous new churches were built in the suburbs of Paris, some in modernistic style that expressed the new vigor of the church. Anticlericalism—the antagonism to attempts by the clergy to dominate private and public life—continued widespread, but common resistance to the German menace in World War I had somewhat blunted its edge.

Small States of Northwestern Europe

COMMON CHARACTERISTICS

The six countries under discussion in this section possessed two common characteristics—the small size of their population and the advanced state of their culture. Geography and history had been kind in placing them in the region which became industrialized. They shared in the expansion of wealth and were able to develop a large national income per capita and a high standard of living. Devoid of ambition to play an aggressive role in international politics, they set an ideal of behavior for the rest of the world.

In 1930 the states supported the following numbers of people: Belgium, 8 millions, to which the 300,000 of Luxembourg may be added; the Netherlands, 8 millions; Switzerland, 4 millions; Denmark, 3,500,000; Norway, 2,800,000; and Sweden, 6,140,000. Only two, Norway and Sweden, owned large land masses; but since a great deal of this land was useless to man except as scenery, the amount of their habitable area approximately equaled the 30,000 to 42,000 square kilometers of land mass of each of the other four. France, by contrast, had 551,000 square kilometers. The population in Belgium and the Netherlands was among the densest in the world, 265 and 244 per square kilometer, respectively; Denmark showed 84 and Switzerland 102; in the inhabitable regions Norway and Sweden showed similar figures. France had 76; Germany, 139; England and Wales, 264.

Limited resources precluded the states from playing an aggressive role in power politics. In 1926 Belgium maintained a defense force in Europe of 83,000 men, whereas among the others Sweden had the next largest with 50,000 men and Denmark the least with 14,000. The size of the figure for Belgium can be explained by her experience in World War I. She occupied the low area between Germany and France, where a modern mass army could deploy its numbers for speedy invasion; but she, like the others, recognized her inability to build an adequate defense. These states were protected against imperialistic neighbors by the refusal of any great power to allow a competitor to dominate the areas. Location at important junctions for transportation and communication made them favorite wards of the balance of power. They were able to concentrate resources upon the peaceful pursuits of life; and when the great powers were intent upon mutual destruction during World War I, with the exception of Belgium, they succeeded not merely in remaining neutral but in profiting from the sale of materials to the belligerents.

The six countries laid the bases of industrial society during the decades before World War I. Each had created a homogeneous culture, to which the economy, the social organization, and the government all contributed. Each country differed somewhat in the way in which it achieved this new society and in the degree of its success; but the results were markedly similar.

Intensive Use of Resources

The density of population was made possible by the intensive use of knowledge, man power, and capital in all branches of the economy. With the exception of Sweden (which owned large resources of rich iron ore), Belgium, and to a small extent the Netherlands (in which lay part of the coal field of West-central Europe), these countries lacked the natural resources regarded as economically most significant. They were all too small to possess the variety of materials necessary for self-sufficiency in either industry or agriculture and depended upon imports and exports to an unusual extent. They compensated for deficiencies in native material by entrepreneurial ability.

Although small, the nations acquired and applied scientific and technological knowledge as easily as did a great power, and kept in the vanguard of economic development. The harnessing of electricity provided the easy basis for all six countries—Switzerland, Sweden, and Norway by means of water power—to expand production in relatively small industries distributed widely throughout the land. Scientific progress in metallurgy, engineering, and chemistry proved to be of comparable value. A few of the nations, Belgium and Sweden especially, had some heavy industry; but most of them imported materials like pig iron and steel, sulphur, and coal and used their skilled labor to transform them into machines or other commodities of high value in proportion to the cost of material. As chemistry revolutionized the use of wood, Norway and Sweden, and to a less extent Switzerland and Belgium, took advantage of their vast forests to open up additional opportunities for wealth. Science applied to agriculture achieved similar results. The amount of capital required for their industries was relatively small, compared with that needed for heavy industries like iron and steel, and could in the main be raised within the country itself. Value was added to the raw materials by the skill of the workers. These peoples succeeded in raising their standard of living to the level of the world's highest cultures.

The magnitude of the industrial expansion may be expressed by statistics. Between 1897 and 1925 the total number of persons employed in industry in Denmark rose about 30 per cent, but the total amount of motive power increased almost tenfold. In Norway the number of workers between 1897 and 1918 doubled, and the amount of motive power grew five- or sixfold. Between 1896 and 1928 Sweden witnessed a doubling of the number of her industrial workers and an increase of more than tenfold in the amount of motive power. In Belgium the total power resources increased as follows: for steam engines, from 3,100,000 horsepower in 1913 to 5,400,000 in 1929; for electricity, from 500,000 kilowatts in 1913 to 2,500,000 in 1938. These figures indicate an enormous expansion of industrial production within the short period of thirty years or less. The handicap of the small number of industrial workers was overcome by multiplying the amount of motive power.

Before World War I the countries had been developing a mature industrial economy, and they continued the process, accentuated by the war, in the 1920's. They shifted emphasis from the production of textiles and other consumers' goods to producers' goods like machines and machine tools. They expanded the engineering, pharmaceutical, electrotechnical, and similar industries for the export market. They rationalized and mechanized industrial methods as a means of increasing production while reducing costs, and they were so efficient that once the immediate postwar depression was overcome they maintained employment at a high level while reducing hours of work and introducing labor-saving devices. In Sweden, for example, the number of industrial workers grew between 1920 and 1929 by less than 10 per cent, but the volume of industrial production increased one and one-half times and the production per man-hour by more than 40 per cent. The export industries expanded production at a much greater rate than did the industries catering to the home market. Between 1913 and 1928 the value of Swedish exports in engineering increased by 320 per cent. The country rationalized its industrial processes to an extent comparable to that in the United States and Germany and to that of the five other small states of Northwestern Europe.

The results were evident in the gross value of manufacturing per capita in 1926–1929. Expressed in dollars, they were as follows: Belgium, 240; Switzerland, 170; Sweden, 160; Netherlands, 160; Denmark, 140. No figure is available for Norway. These figures may be compared with those for the United States, 350; United Kingdom, 190; Germany, 180; France, 160; and Italy, 80. Their per capita exports were of comparable proportions. Except for Denmark, where export of industrial goods was not as large as that of agricultural products, the industrial position of these small countries was similar to that of the great powers.

In agricultural production the six countries likewise set a standard for the world. The evidence may be seen in the indices of per capita productivity in agriculture in 1930. Denmark led the continent with 354, to be followed by the Netherlands with 259, Belgium with 220, Switzerland with 194, and Sweden and Norway with 146 and 116, respectively. The figures for the last three states were small because of the difficulties of farming in their mountainous regions. The dimensions of the achievements may be judged by comparison with the figures for the other leaders: England and Wales, 319; Germany, 195; and France, 176.[3]

The farmers had accomplished these results by shifting emphasis from grain to livestock, fruits, and vegetables. They catered to the industrial, urban market, not merely in their own countries, but in neighboring Great Britain and Germany. They had begun to change when the opening of the new grain-growing areas in North and South America had in the latter part of the nineteenth century foreshadowed the doom of their traditional crops. The transformation required the spread of popular knowledge, in which the Danish folk high schools took the lead, the use of capital, and the introduction of new methods of processing and marketing the commodities; but the prospects of profit were convincing. Standardization and mechanization were applied to agriculture as to industry. A peasant's dairy resembled a rural factory, with the cows instead of the mines providing the raw materials. The countries imported coarse grain to feed the animals and profited from the sale of bacon, butter, cheese, eggs, and the like.

None of these countries was self-sufficient in food. The Netherlands was engaged in draining the Zuyder Zee, a project which would increase its land mass by 6 per cent, in order to increase its resources for capitalistic farming. During World War I the five neutrals arranged with the blockading powers to obtain some imports of food and to trade some food with the Central Powers for needed commodities. Nonetheless, their agriculture suffered from the war restrictions in the same way, although not to the same degree, as did that of the continental belligerents. The shortage of man power, of fertilizer, and of equipment was universally felt; but the war experience did not deter the countries from continuing specialized agriculture.

The extent to which the six countries depended upon international trade may be seen in all aspects of their culture. Norway and the Netherlands specialized in ocean shipping and ranked in tonnage among the half dozen leading carriers of the world. Their ships largely transported materials for other countries. Belgium and the Netherlands possessed harbors at or near the mouth of the Rhine, Rotterdam and Antwerp being especially important, which were well suited for the transit trade. Before World War II it was noted that in Rotterdam harbor, one of the major ports of the world, English ships were most numerous, German ships next, with Netherlands' ships assuming third place. Switzerland occupied an inland position of comparable nature by owning most of the Alpine passes. Figures on per capita international trade show that in 1928, excluding transit ship-

[3] "The figures are indices of the average per capita productivity of persons dependent on agriculture as related to European average equaling 100." Dudley Kirk, *Europe's Population in the Interwar Years* (Geneva: League of Nations, 1946), p. 262.

ments, the Netherlands with $244 and Belgium with $218 ranked superior to that nation of traders, the United Kingdom ($215). In 1929 Switzerland exported 52 per cent of its total industrial production, a high percentage for any country. Danish exports of butter and bacon and Swedish exports of timber, iron ore, and foodstuffs were similar bearers of international co-operation. All of these countries favored low tariffs and freedom from trade restrictions, and Belgium and the Netherlands followed these principles in their colonies. After World War I the states, in self-defense, had to protect their industries; but Belgium, for example, changed her tariff policy in favor of protectionism primarily in order to have a basis for bargaining with other countries for reduction in import duties.

HOMOGENEOUS SOCIETY

The population in each country except Belgium was economically and socially homogeneous, and during and after the war Belgium was gradually coming into line with the others. The rural population consisted of farmers rather than of traditional peasants. Industrial workers were not considered an inferior class; they shared pride of position with the financially better-situated people. Property ownership was widely distributed in each country, although less so in Belgium than in the others. Both agriculture and industry were organized in small undertakings. In agriculture the land was mainly owned by those who tilled it. Fifty-two per cent of all cultivated soil in Switzerland in 1939 was divided into farms of 12 to 37 acres, and only 7 per cent was owned in farms of 75 acres or more. The Scandinavian countries contained almost no large estates; independent peasants in Sweden and Norway owned and farmed practically all the agricultural land in holdings of 25 acres or less, and the average size of the farms in Denmark was 38 acres. Roughly similar conditions were to be found in Belgium and the Netherlands. The industrial plants were comparably small. Belgium offered the sole exception, where 6 per cent of the enterprises employed 70 per cent of the workers, and a small number of banks played a leading role in industry. Each of the other countries had a few fairly large industries. The Netherlands, for example, had the vast Philips electrotechnical company, which produced for a wide international market. The few large concerns did not affect the general social and economic pattern of the "just mean."

The wide geographic distribution of industrial plants enabled the population to remain residents of small towns. Transportation and communication were so highly developed that the countries ranked in this respect with the United Kingdom and France as leaders of Europe, evidence in itself of their wealth. Where industries were located in towns, workers commuted from the surrounding villages, and many were able in addition to own and cultivate a garden or a small farm. In some Swiss towns the factory labor force outnumbered the local residents. Many industries in these countries had found it profitable to build the factories at the source of their raw materials. The people of the towns and of the rural areas kept in close working contact; the huge urban agglomerations found in the United Kingdom were avoided and preindustrial living conditions were preserved in an age of machines and factories.

The economic system proved its social value by raising the national income and the standard of living, an achievement for which industry deserved most credit. Data are available for Sweden which show that between 1860 and 1930 manufacturing, mining, and handicrafts had increased their share in the national income by more than two and one-half times as much as agriculture, and in addition had offered a market and an example of efficiency to agriculture. The results were manifest in the size of the national income per capita. The figures for the Scandinavian countries (1929) are as follows: Denmark $282, Norway $249 and Sweden $342. These should be compared with those for the wealthy large countries of Great Britain ($426) and France ($253). That all classes participated in the increase may be seen from data about labor. In Denmark in 1930 the workers continued to take about 35 per cent of the national income as they had for two generations; however, the real average hourly earnings of the working class increased between 1914 and 1930 by 64 per cent in Denmark, 69 per cent in Norway, and 75 per cent in Sweden. Except for the workers in Belgium, where improvement was slow, the conditions of the people in the other countries kept approximate pace with those of Scandinavia. The gains supplied the economic basis for political and social democracy.

TRADE-UNIONS AND COOPERATIVES

The two main institutions which were developed to assure an equitable distribution of the national income were the trade-unions and the cooperatives. The unions were strongest in the Scandinavian countries and weakest in Belgium. Like their colleagues in the large industrial states, the workers gained most concessions from employers during and just after the war, when their aid was indispensable and employment was full. In most of the countries collective bargaining had regulated labor-employer relations from the turn of the century. In Belgium it was not won as a right until after the war, and during the 1920's it was not recognized in all industries.

Strength through organization brought the eight-hour working day and other improvements in working conditions, an integrated program of social insurance in the Scandinavian countries, and the beginnings of one in the other countries. It led to experimentation in the administration of labor relations. In Scandinavia particularly the well-organized employers agreed to the use of lockouts and strikes when a new labor contract was being negotiated; but once the contract was approved, they wished assurance that its terms would be fulfilled. They were willing to accept collective responsibility for the behavior of the individual members of their association toward labor, and they demanded in turn that the trade-unions organize to assume responsibility for the conduct of their members, a proposal which labor could not accept. Various states, not merely the Scandinavian, set up labor courts to adjudicate controversies over the interpretation of labor contracts. The courts did not prevent strikes and lockouts, especially in the years of postwar readjustment, but they greatly reduced the number, and they helped to cultivate in both parties the feeling of responsibility for the common good. In these six countries, except for a short time in Norway after the war, communism had little attraction.

The cooperative movement did not gain ascendancy over the economy in any one of the states, but it assisted farmers, workers, and the middle class to improve their economic and social situation. In each country the farmers set up both consumers' and producers' cooperatives. In Denmark 90 per cent of the farm population belonged to one big cooperative, which handled almost all the processing and marketing of farm products. The Swiss Union of Consumers' Societies in 1930 represented more than 40 per cent of the population. The agricultural cooperative in that country included practically all the peasants. In Belgium the cooperative movement was strongest among the workers; cooperatives owned and ran banks, stores, and insurance companies. In 1928 the movement there had 342 buildings for educational and recreational activity, including restaurants, libraries, theaters, and halls for lectures and concerts. Although the Swedish cooperative association numbered in 1930 only 400,000 members, it aided the entire population by combating monopolies in favor of economic competition. Before the war it had entered the margarine industry, broken a monopoly, and forced a great reduction in price. It subsequently followed the same policy with respect to flour milling, galoshes, boots, and shoes, chemicals, and other products. The cooperatives everywhere aided people to reduce costs and to compete in the international markets. Their educational and moral influence was as important as their economic and social significance. Like the trade-unions, they enabled the little man to join forces with his neighbors to the advantage of the entire society.

POLITICS AND GOVERNMENT

The economic and social changes were paralleled by the achievement of political democracy. All were monarchies except Switzerland. Constitutional government and parliamentary institutions had become thoroughly established in each country long before the twentieth century. As in Great Britain and France, they had been controlled by a small upper class until far into the latter half of the nineteenth century. Thereafter reform consisted mainly of extending the franchise, an act simplified by the widespread distribution of property holding and the general uniformity of the economy throughout the country. The necessary steps were accelerated by the experience of World War I, another example of a democratic effect of modern war upon society. Sweden had given the vote to all adult males in 1909; ten years later she included females. Norway put through similar legislation between 1898 and 1913. Denmark approved universal suffrage for men and women in 1915, the Netherlands in 1919, and Belgium at about the same time; Switzerland alone restricted the franchise to males. As a means of assuring the expression of the will of all interests, voting was done according to the system of proportional representation. It produced multiple parties and government by coalition, but the homogeneity of these stable societies prevented the deleterious effects of proportional representation revealed in large countries like France and Germany.

The party division into liberals and conservatives typical of the nineteenth century tended to give way in this century to one by class or occupation. In the Scandinavian countries five parties became usual. On the extreme right stood the conservatives, composed of bankers, big businessmen, and members of the former ruling group. Next to them were the agrarians, the representatives of the peasantry, determined to keep agriculture strong and prosperous and to oppose monopolies and heavy taxation. The liberals were a holdover from the formerly powerful group of middle-class people, the professions and other intellectuals. They had lost their numerical strength, but their knowledge preserved for them influence on legislation out of proportion to their popularity. The social democrats represented labor, and were closely affiliated with the trade-unions.

As the workers became numerically the largest group in the nation, their party in the 1920's showed prospects of leading the country. The first labor government was appointed in Denmark in 1924, in Norway in 1928. In the general election in Denmark in 1929 Socialists polled 43 per cent of the popular vote and were able from that year until World War II to govern the country in alliance with the moderate Radical party. Even before this time, however, the Socialists were learning the responsibility of administration by taking over the government of the industrial towns and cities, not merely in Denmark, but in other countries. At the far left of the party system were the numerically insignificant Communists. The parties divided in the Netherlands on the religious issue and in Belgium to some extent between the Flemings and the Walloons, the one with a Germanic cultural orientation, the other a French; but in these countries as well the general lines of party division resembled those in the other countries. After the war the Socialist party in the Netherlands nearly equaled in size the combined force of conservative Catholics and Protestants that had ruled the state for nearly half a century. In every country all parties except the Communists practiced compromise and considered the general welfare.

In the small states as well as the large, industrialism and the war increased the popular demands upon the central government. The Belgian government had the special burden of meeting the expense of restoring the area devastated in the war; but the need for improved transportation and communication, the expansion of social security, the request for public aid to business and agriculture, and many other measures in every country imposed responsibilities beyond the capacity of private individuals and the local governments to meet. Even Switzerland, where the rural cantons had for centuries opposed increasing federal power, moved along the road which every state was taking. Tax systems were revised to produce additional revenue; wherever, as in Belgium, it had not already been introduced, the progressive income tax was enacted. The sense of national unity and social responsibility strengthened by the war included respect for minority rights and growth in tolerance.

The most important example of tolerance was offered by Belgium's handling of the Flemish problem. The Flemings sought legal equality for their language with the French language used by the Walloons. During the war a small group had treacherously cooperated with the Germans and discredited the loyal Flemings, who merely wished cultural autonomy. After the war the government gradually acquiesced in the two main Flemish demands, that of transforming the University of Ghent into a Flemish-speaking institution and that of creating Flemish regiments in the army. The quarrels continued to cause political trouble, as Belgium went through the travail of accepting that cultural heterogeneity which had characterized Switzerland to a far greater extent for centuries. The effects were slowly counteracted, however, by the rapid postwar industrialization of Flanders and the increased integration of the people with the rest of the country.

KNOWLEDGE OF FOREIGN CULTURES

Since these peoples were too small in number to afford many translations and since they needed to know foreign cultures in their business, an unusually large number learned foreign languages, read foreign literature, and were true cosmopolitans. The Scandinavians pioneered in holding conferences among numerous private and public groups for the sake of settling any controversies and of making the relations of the three peoples cordial and intimate. Parliamentarians, representatives of cooperatives, teachers and professors, lawyers, and many others had special Scandinavian associations for this purpose. They set a precedent for much of the work of the Economic and Social Council and its affiliated agencies created as part of the United Nations after World War II. Building upon their tradition of craftsmanship all of the six peoples became world leaders in architecture and in the household arts, ceramics, weaving, glassmaking, silversmithing, and furniture making. They maintained the highest standards in their universities and produced some of the world's most renowned scientists (Niels Bohr in Denmark for example) and engineers. In these small states many a gifted person preferred international fame as a scholar to national renown as a political or business leader. These were prosperous, middle-class societies, averse to extreme nationalism, averse to power politics, devoted to good living, internationalism, and peace—truly civilized peoples.

During the 1920's the citizens of the small states fared better than those in the larger states. They could devote to creative activity and to social welfare the funds that Great Britain and France expended to sustain their position as great powers. The small states were able to handle problems more easily and more quickly than the large ones, partly because the lesser dimension brought problems within popular understanding and considerable control by reason. The inability to act as great powers saved the people of the small states from many complications caused to internal affairs by international relations. One thinks immediately of how much more difficulty Sweden would have faced with her industrial policy if she had had, like the British, to consider the interests of an empire, or, like the French, the prospect of a revived hostile Germany. As might have been expected, the small states recovered from the impact of the war much more effectively than France and Britain, and on the whole their society retained a higher degree of cohesion.

All the countries exhibited the qualities that led the Anglo-American T. S. Eliot to write the poems *The Waste Land* (1922) and *The Hollow Men* (1925) and the Frenchman Julien Benda to publish *The Betrayal of the Intellectuals* (1927). Eliot found postwar Europe a "dead land" of "stuffed men/ Leaning together." [3] Benda accused the intellectuals of having betrayed their mission by joining the masses in exalting "racial passions, class passions and national passions," to the destruction of human values. No country was able to recruit for the church, Protestant or Catholic, enough young men to fill vacancies. Everywhere the decade bore the marks of uncertainty about broad objectives. People seemed to live in the present and to be waiting for something to come, those in the small states because of inability to exert influence in shaping the future, those in Britain and France because of postwar lethargy. The period fared better materially than it did in the realm of the spirit. In a later chapter we shall see how material life collapsed, leaving the peoples to rely for guidance not so much upon spiritual creativeness as upon their tradition of freedom.

[3] From "The Hollow Men" in *Collected Poems 1909–1935* by T. S. Eliot. Copyright, 1936, by Harcourt, Brace and Company, Inc. By permission also of Faber and Faber Limited.

Suggestions for Further Reading

BROGAN, DENIS. *France under the Republic.* See the Readings for Chapter 1.

EARLE, EDWARD MEAD, ed. *Modern France.* Princeton, N.J.: Princeton University Press, 1951. Essays by several scholars. Useful and often revealing of social, economic, and political values.

GORIS, JAN ALBERT, ed. *Belgium.* Berkeley: University of California Press, 1945. Chapters by several scholars. Useful survey.

LAMARTINE YATES, PAUL. *Food Production in Western Europe.* New York: Longmans, Green & Company, Inc., 1940. Excellent. Places the subject in its social setting.

LANDHEER, BARTHOLOMEW, ed. *The Netherlands.* Berkeley: University of California Press, 1943. Similar to the Goris volume.

MAYER, KURT BERND. *The Population of Switzerland.* New York: Columbia University Press, 1952. Discusses many more aspects than the title indicates.

MOWAT, CHARLES L. *Britain between the Wars, 1918–1940.* London: Methuen & Co., Ltd., 1955. Judicious, full of interesting material. Indispensable.

SCOTT, FRANKLIN D. *The United States and Scandinavia.* Cambridge, Mass.: Harvard University Press, 1950. Compact, basic study.

Chapter 8 · The Unstable Countries of Central and Western Europe

OLD REGIME VERSUS NEW SOCIAL FORCES

The grouping of the four countries, Germany, Italy, Spain, and Portugal, in a single chapter needs explanation. These nations suffered from internal instability, but they were not the only ones that did so. To a greater or lesser extent all the new countries of Eastern and Southeastern Europe had yet to prove their ability to survive. Potential enemies without and animosities within made them risks for any investor. They shared, however, the common qualities of states recently formed, and their problems can be analyzed together from that standpoint. The four unstable nations of Central and Western Europe had developed beyond the historical stage of major concern about preserving political unity. Two of them in the recent past had asserted themselves as important powers in international affairs. In the postwar period the four ranged in influence from the potential status of Germany as a great power to the relative insignificance of Portugal. They varied in internal conditions from an attempt at democratic government in Germany to Fascist dictatorship in Italy and military dictatorship in Spain and Portugal. Germany supported one of the world's most efficient industrial economies; Italy lagged far behind her; Spain and Portugal lived mainly from antiquated agriculture.

In all four countries many forces of the Old Regime, such as monarchy, aristocracy, and a class-conscious bourgeoisie, continued either to be powerful in government and society or determined, as in Germany, to recover their prewar power at the first opportunity. Each country illustrates a stage in the change from the Old Regime to modern society. Germany contained strong elements of both the old and the new society; during the twenties neither side won ascendancy. Italy had a comparable social structure, full of class antagonism and without the economic resources which for a decade made internal peace in Germany possible. Spain had begun to support industry and a small active middle class and proletariat; but the army, the aristocratic landlords, and the church, together with a few like-minded industrialists, preserved conditions that resembled those of the eighteenth century. Portugal in the 1920's provided an example of extreme backwardness. The church, the army, and the noble landowners held control, and political quarrels took place mainly among the members of these groups. Whereas Spanish social relations contained the potentiality of mass violence, Portuguese society had scarcely advanced so far. The study of the four countries, especially in the 1920's, resembles a tour through previous centuries.

Italy

Italy became the first country west of Russia to experience the collapse of the old order in favor of dictatorship. Having fought on the winning side, the nation expected to emerge from the conflict a prosperous and exalted victor. Modern war tends to test all participants alike; the effects of the experience vary according to the strength of the society involved. The postwar troubles of Italy were enlarged beyond those of other West European states by the fact that historical development had left it unprepared. When none of the established political parties seemed capable of solving the multitude of postwar problems, a new party of fascism seized control by force.

ECONOMIC DEFICIENCIES

The nation struggled with the constant burden of a rapidly increasing population in a society incapable of providing sufficient employment. Between 1900 and 1915 Italy had exported a surplus of 5 million people to the United States and Latin America, where they had earned enough to send large sums home for the support of relatives. After the war these countries greatly reduced their immigration quotas. Between 1921 and 1925 less than half as many could emigrate as before, and after that period the number dropped even further. Italians now went mainly to France, which could not provide them with economic opportunities comparable to those in the new world. The population of working age (15 to 64) was increasing at the rate of 200,000 to 250,000 a year, whereas the number employed grew at the average rate of 50,000 a year and never went beyond the figure of 80,000 to 90,000. In 1931 Italy was able to provide work for 40.6 per cent of her total population, a figure to be compared with that of 51.4 per cent in France and 49.2 per cent in Germany. In 1936 the Italian figure rose to 43.2 per cent for the whole country, that in Piedmont and other northern regions being between 45 and 52.8 per cent; in Sicily, 33.9 per cent; in Apulia and Sardinia, 36 per cent. The birth rate was consistently high throughout the country, although much greater in the south and in the rural areas than in the industrial sections of the north. The normal effect of

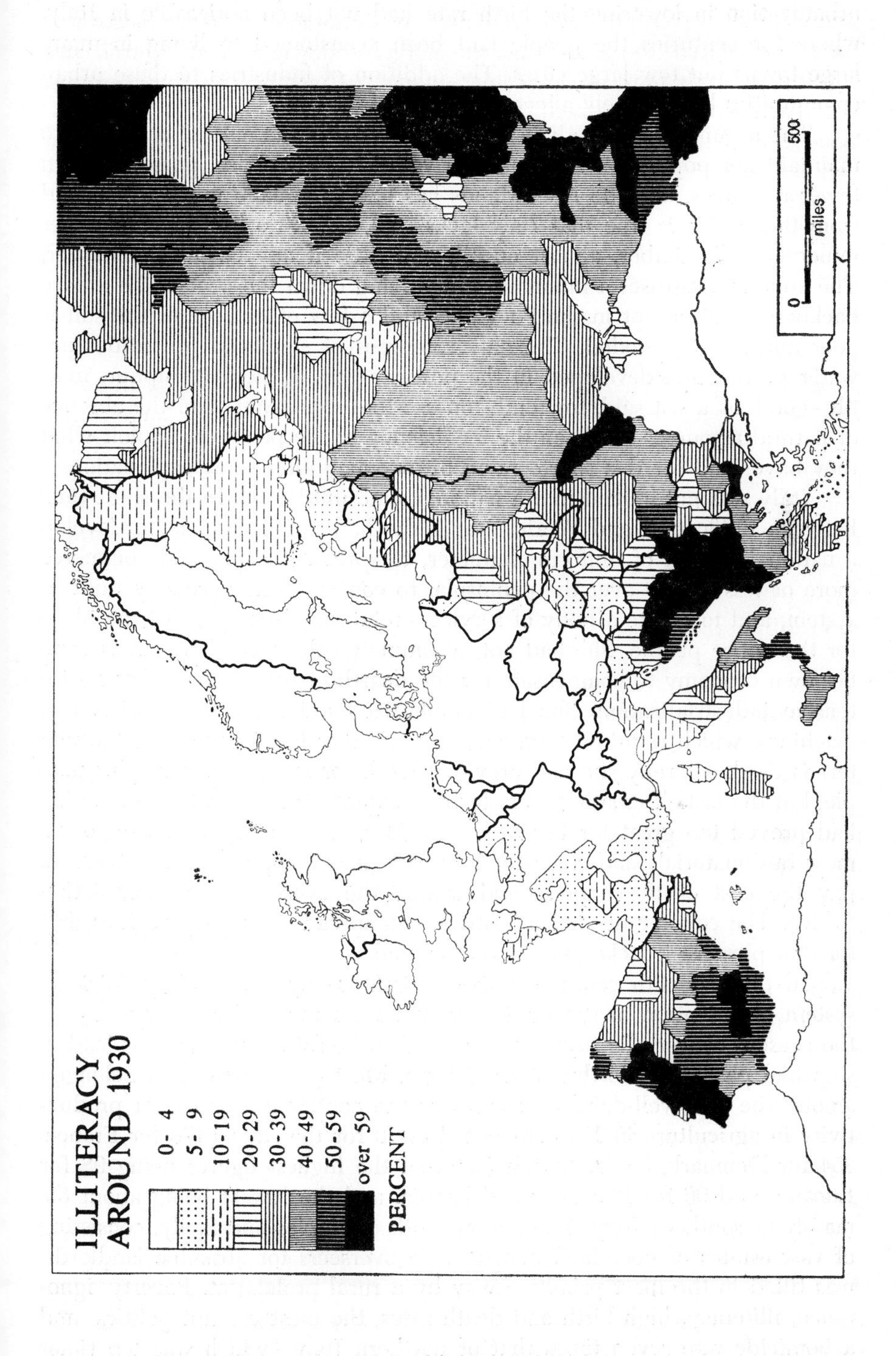
ILLITERACY
AROUND 1930
0- 4
5- 9
10-19
20-29
30-39
40-49
50-59
over 59
PERCENT
0
500
miles

urbanization in lowering the birth rate had not been noticeable in Italy, where for centuries the people had been accustomed to living in many large towns but few large cities. The addition of industries to these urban communities had scarcely affected the mores.

The argument often advanced that Italy lacks the natural resources to maintain her population has doubtful validity. Switzerland possesses even fewer resources, and the Netherlands has had to reclaim much of its land from the sea. It is true that Italy lacks coal, has little iron ore and other minerals, little timber, almost no oil, and little if any chemical fertilizer. The country possesses a mountain range lying down the center like a bare backbone, and except in the Po Valley and a few other regions the soil is poor and heavily eroded. The only resources of significant quantities are water power, first developed in the postwar period, Sicilian sulphur, marble—good, as a wit said, for tombstones. More significant than the absence of natural resources has been the inefficiency of the people to exploit what they have; and for this shortcoming history may offer some explanation.

Italy was not unified into a national state until 1860. In the short time between unification and World War I she had not been able to develop a national market of uniform character, to spread industry and commerce more or less evenly over the peninsula, to construct the necessary railroad system, and to create a body of services—retail, professional, and the like—for the entire people. She had not accumulated the capital resources from her own economy to compensate for the dearth of natural resources by intensive industrialization. She had emphasized industries like textiles and machines, which required large amounts of labor in proportion to the materials used. Thereby she had provided work for some of her surplus people, but the task of creating an industry adequate to support her population had proved too great for her to handle in so short a time. She imported most raw materials and some food; exports had to be sufficiently large to pay the cost of the imports and enable the ever-increasing population to live. The country needed industries well spread among the regions, but for that purpose it lacked investment capital.

In the sixteenth century Italian agriculture by means of an intricate system of irrigation in the Po Valley had set a model for Europe. Up to the present century Po farming continued to be fairly efficient, but leadership had passed to Northwestern Europe. Most of the peninsula belonged among the less well-developed areas of the continent. Per capita productivity in agriculture in 1930 amounted to 73 for the state (176 for France, 354 for Denmark, 50 for barren Greece), the highest figures being 98 for Lucania and 96 for Piedmont and Emilia, and the lowest being about 50, mainly in southern Italy. The region south of Naples and Sicily, consisting of vast estates of poor land managed by overseers for absentee landlords, was tilled in the most primitive way by a rural proletariat. Poverty, ignorance, illiteracy, high birth and death rates, the most corrupt politics, and a homicide rate seven times that of northern Italy (which was ten times

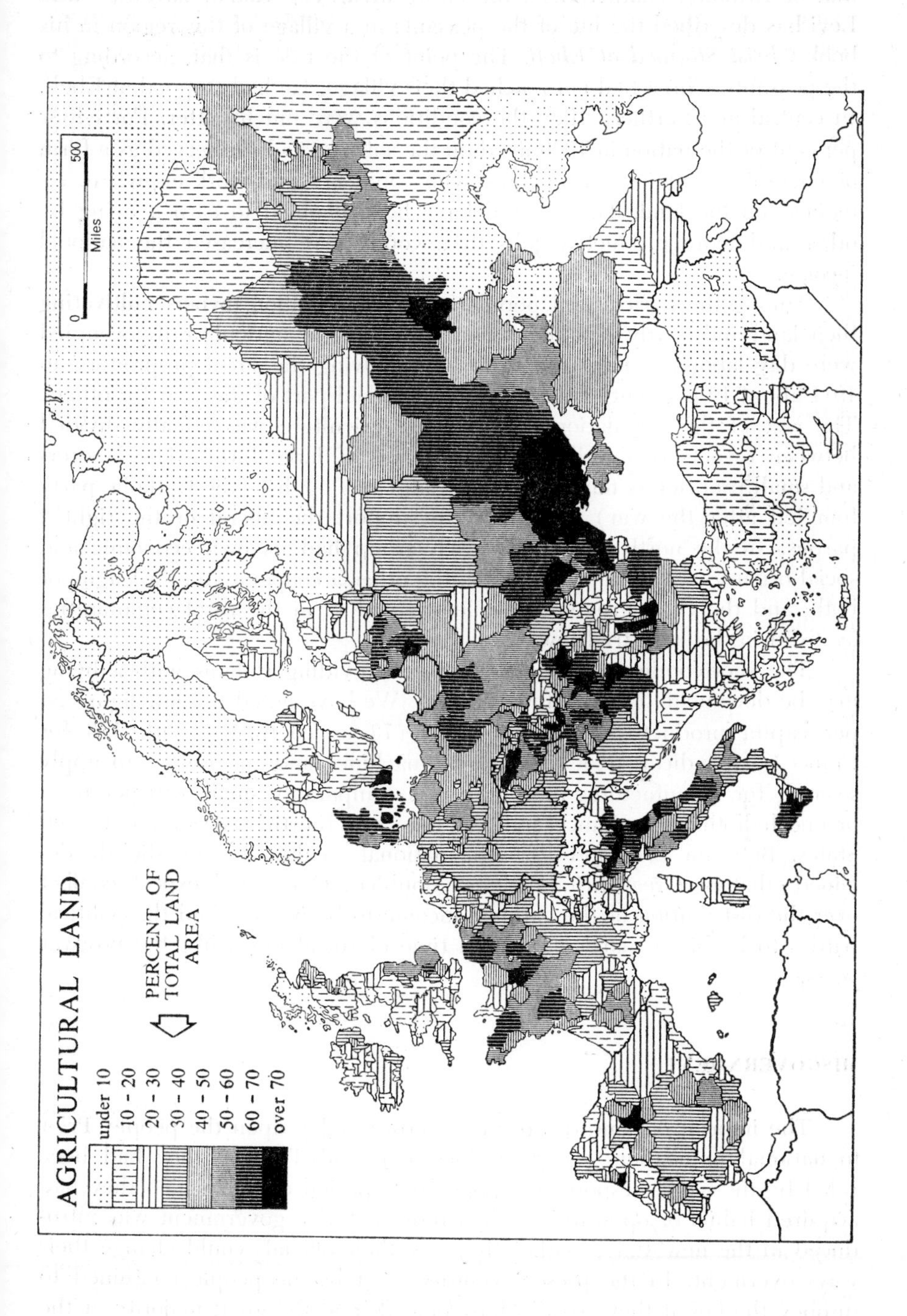
AGRICULTURAL LAND
PERCENT OF TOTAL LAND AREA
under 10
10 - 20
20 - 30
30 - 40
40 - 50
50 - 60
60 - 70
over 70
0
500
Miles

that of Britain), characterized the entire area. The Italian novelist Carlo Levi has described the life of the peasants in a village of this region in his book *Christ Stopped at Eboli.* The point of the title is that, according to the peasants, Christ had not reached their village; He had stopped at Eboli. In central and northern Italy the conditions were much better. Forty-four per cent of the nation in 1930 lived on the soil. Agriculture served as a form of unemployment insurance; those who could not find work elsewhere remained on the land. They should have been enabled to earn a living by other and more productive jobs that would have increased the national income.

Among the agricultural population were 3 million owners cultivating their land and nearly a million tenants. Half of the agriculturally occupied were day laborers, and in order to earn a living the small proprietors—in 1911 about 19 per cent of the total—also worked part of the year for others. The rest of the population occupied in agriculture was equally divided between owners of middle-sized farms and of large farms. The laborers and small proprietors tended to be socialist or Populist (the Catholic party founded after the war), the others to support the liberal or the rightist parties. In the north and center each group had its own economic and social organizations, the one a union, the other a cooperative or a league or both; and the class struggle prevailed as widely in the rural communities as it did in the industrial towns.

The shortcomings of the economy in providing Italians with a living may be documented with a few statistics. We have noted the low figure on per capita productivity in agriculture (73 as contrasted with 176 for France), an indication of the lack of machines and the failure to apply science; for manufactures the figure was comparably small, $80 per head or one half that for France and less than one fourth that for the United States. Between 1914 and 1925 the national wealth of Italy slightly declined; that of Great Britain almost doubled. One could expect conflict over the distribution of the national income to be intense, and the political battles to be bitter, particularly in a time of social upset like the postwar years.

MISGOVERNMENT

The imprint of centuries of misgovernment lay upon the people. Prior to national unification, except in Piedmont and Tuscany they had been ruled by the worst despots in Europe, an experience from which they had acquired habits of opposition. When representative government was introduced in the new Italy, neither they nor their officials could change their ways overnight. In the present century most of the people continued to disobey the law if they could. Many officials and the great majority of the elected representatives persisted in exploiting their offices for personal

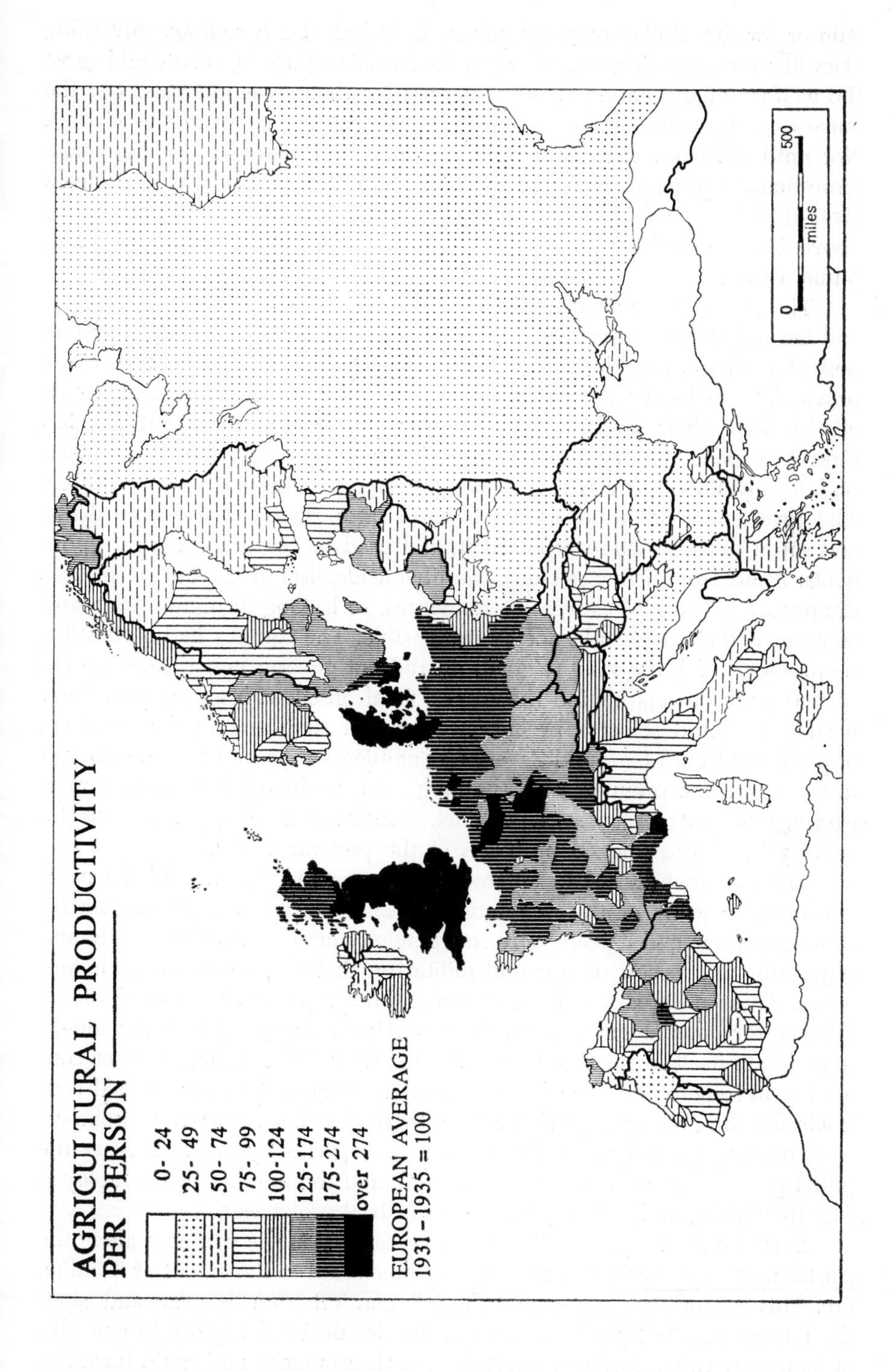
AGRICULTURAL PRODUCTIVITY
PER PERSON
0- 24
25- 49
50- 74
75- 99
100-124
125-174
175-274
over 274
EUROPEAN AVERAGE
1931 – 1935 = 100
0
500
miles

gain or for the display of petty power. Italy lacked a hereditary governing class like the English gentry or even the Prussian Junkers, who could serve the welfare of the nation while looking after their own interests. For the masses government remained something of which they were the victims. Not until 1913 did they gain universal manhood suffrage, but not much more than 50 per cent bothered to vote. The illiteracy rate was so high—in 1930–1931 it was still 22 per cent for the entire country and 40 per cent or above for the southern part—that citizens could not be informed about public issues.

The people were accustomed to government by horse-trading, bribery, and intimidation of voters by private citizens and public officials, a system perfected in the decade or so before the war by Premier Giolitti. Since provincial and local government was controlled from the capital at Rome, officials kept their position by producing the desired results at election time. In a poor country a government favor or an official position carried with it a livelihood; it was eagerly sought after, for alternatives were scarce. The government doled out contracts, tariff rates, roads, flood-control dams, and so on to those who supported it, and used its resources against opponents. Apart from a few persons, the liberal idealists of Cavour's type had disappeared. The parties were so numerous, so lacking in organization and continuity, that they could not be responsible. The country had a constitution under which the king reigned but did not govern; nonetheless, he exercised wide powers behind the scenes. Confronted with an array of loose parties, he could select a premier who would shop among the members of parliament until he found a working combination. Once this group began to fall apart, the premier, with the king's aid, could rid himself of a minister or two and reorganize the cabinet. Under this kind of government the country faced the colossal problems of the postwar world.

The fact that Italy had entered the war against the will of the overwhelming majority of the population affected postwar reactions. The returning soldiers and officers were so frequently attacked, both verbally and physically, as symbols of war and militarism that many took off their uniforms. These outbreaks did not enhance the sympathy of the professional military for popular government. The wartime armaments industry sought to maintain itself in time of peace either in its initial function or after conversion in some other line of production. How could it obtain needed contracts for the one, or capital for the other? The numerous war profiteers were prepared to fight any efforts to cut their profits by taxation. After the initial postwar boom, a recession occurred, and the number of unemployed rose to 400,000, or 10 per cent of the industrial proletariat.

Between 1919 and 1920 the extensive damage in the war area along the Austrian frontier was overcome by government aid to the extent of 8 billion lire. This expenditure augmented the inflation left from the war, and, since the budget was badly out of balance, the lira declined rapidly to one fifth of its former value. Business profited from cheap money and rapid turnover, but the salaried class and those living on fixed incomes suffered severely from inability to adjust income to rising prices. Labor protected itself somewhat by strikes, which angered the other social groups. When the government tried to levy higher taxes, the wealthy advocated that the increase be shifted to the backs of the masses. The masses replied by demanding that the rich assume a fair share of the public burden. The one strove to preserve its gains; the other sought to improve its lot.

Uncertainty and expectation of a better life to come were in the air. The war had aroused new hopes; the events in Russia stirred ambitions for radical action. When Italy did not receive at Versailles all the territory which she had expected, the nationalists cried that the country had been betrayed. Nationalism was used in the traditional way to turn attention from the solution of urgent problems at home. When the poet D'Annunzio, with a free corps, broke international law in 1919 by seizing Fiume, the nationalists shouted approval. After the wartime experience extremists continued to approve of violence as a method of political action.

CONFLICT OF POLITICAL PARTIES

In the main, four political parties competed for power, the Socialists, the Catholic Populist party, the liberals, and the Fascists. The last named won out in 1922, but to explain the victory the career of all four and the roles of the king, the police, and the military need to be sketched.

Founded on Marxism, the Socialist party had followed the typical course of the movement in Central and Western Europe. From the beginning, several decades before the war, it had had a left wing of revolutionaries and a right wing of evolutionaries, the dominant influence definitely shifting to the latter. The leadership contained many intellectuals, but by the end of the war the trade-unions had become strong in party councils. The official membership in the party, which had increased from 50,000 in 1914 to 200,000 after the war, received mass support from the 2,300,000 members of the Socialist trade-unions and from the numerous and well-established cooperatives in town and country. In 1920 the party governed one fourth of the municipalities; it was well organized and, although very weak in the south, had a following in all parts of the country. In the parliamentary election of 1919 the Socialists polled 1,880,000 votes and seated 156 deputies. Two years later they returned only 123 deputies, but their popular vote remained about the same. In 1921 the Communist wing formed its own party, which at the election of 1921 returned 15 deputies.

During the economic troubles of 1919–1921 the Socialist leadership proved to be uncertain of its goals and policies. The party was thoroughly constitutional in behavior and standards, but some members talked revolutionary language, and the extremists, who became Communists, openly advocated a bolshevist program. In 1920 the workers in many north Italian towns seized the factories and set up committees to take care of technical and commercial matters. They did not intend permanently to exclude the owners or to force nationalization; they sought to gain a voice in management and to be treated as responsible members of industrial society. Knowing that the workers lacked trained personnel to play the role of copartner, the union leaders hesitated over the next step, and the strikers gradually drifted back to work. The government mediated, to restore relations as they had been.

The Populist party arose in 1919 when the church finally lifted the ban on participation by Catholics in politics, a ban imposed at the time Italy had seized the Papal States fifty years earlier. Alarmed over the rise of socialism, which it considered an atheistic movement, the church organized a popular competitor. Led by Don Sturzo, a Sicilian priest of extraordinary ability, the party appealed, in the name of social reforms, to the little shopkeeper, peasant, and worker, but it did not attack the framework of private property. It was supported by the 1,800,000 members of the Catholic trade-unions, whose interests so often coincided with those of the Socialists that in spite of continuing hostility the two parties on many issues took the same stand. The Populists seated 100 deputies in 1919 and 108 in 1921.

The liberals had for decades represented the middle classes. Whether called by that name or referred to as conservatives, they supported the constitution and, in so far as political interests allowed, upheld the civil rights of a free people. Since they governed the country from the close of the war until the Fascists took control in 1922, their program can best be described through their actions. Their fundamental mistake lay in attempting to continue the old way. When the workers occupied the factories, the government, then under the elderly Giolitti, delayed action and finally negotiated a settlement. To help the agricultural workers it approved their seizure of unoccupied land but objected when the workers seized other uncultivated land as well. To balance the budget and stabilize the lira, the liberals introduced high taxes on the wealthy, hitting especially the war profiteers. The government advised officers to avoid personal attack by not wearing uniforms on the railway. When the Fascists began to engage in violence it did not oppose them vigorously in the name of constitutional government; rather, it temporized, negotiated, allowed them to have weapons, permitted sympathetic officials and officers to aid them, and did not protect the citizens against violations of civil rights. Up to the last minute the liberal deputies and ministers continued to horse-trade for offices and favors, turning out one ministry at a crucial moment in order to replace it with another of the same kind. The liberals offered no leadership to a nation going to pieces in a civil war. They could not agree among themselves; they would not form a united front with the other two parties, the Socialists and the Populists, devoted to freedom, nor would the others unite in a government with them or with each other.

FASCISM—DOCTRINE AND LEADERSHIP

It has happened a number of times in this century that just as conditions in a country began to improve the forces of violence seized power. An instance of such a seizure occurred in 1922. In spite of incompetence in government, Italy had begun to recover from the war; the budget was balanced, industry was reviving, and moderation had gained ascendancy among the workers. Because the Fascists saw order emerging they dared not wait longer. In October they struck for power and won. Who were these Fascists and what did they offer?

The official historian of the movement has described fascism as "demagogic, nebulous, political futurism." The motto of its leader, Benito Mussolini, was "To Believe, to Obey, to Fight." The terms "relativism" and "dynamism" are correctly applied to fascism. "We do not believe in dogmatic programmes," Mussolini has written. . . . "We permit ourselves the luxury of being aristocrats and democrats, conservatives and progressives, reactionaries and revolutionaries, legalitarians and illegalitarians, according to circumstances of time, place and environment—in a word of the history in which we are constrained to live and to act." (March 23, 1921.) "It [fascism] has often announced reforms when the announcement was politically opportune," the Fascist philosopher Giovanni Gentile has written, "but to the execution of which it, nevertheless, did not believe itself to be obliged! The true resolutions of the Duce are always those which are both formulated and carried out."

The Fascist movement was built around the principle of leadership. The Duce, that is, leader, as he was called, had to take account of the forces behind him, but he also was able to shape those forces to his will, a fact that lends his person a special significance for our understanding of the movement and its success. Born in the Romagna, Benito Mussolini grew up in an environment of revolutionary ideas and practices. He received an education, taught country school for a time, and wandered to Switzerland, where he came into contact with Marxism. During his intellectual apprenticeship he learned something at least about the important radical ideas of his time, those of anarchism, communism and socialism, and syndicalism, spiced with the superman philosophy of Nietzsche and powered with the adaptation to social philosophy of Darwin's theories about the survival of the fittest. Mussolini became a socialist, joined the party, entered politics in Italy and edited various socialist papers. He showed the traits of exalted ambition, egoism, aloofness, a feeling of great superiority over others, a scorn for human beings, erratic rebelliousness as long as he was not leader, hatred of those who opposed him, and a liking for brutality, and he displayed courage in breaking with groups who would not accept his views. He became in turn a pacifist, an ardent advocate of intervention in the war, a soldier, a war casualty, a furious opponent of socialism, and an editor of a radical newspaper in Milan subsidized by industrialists. Immediately after the war he organized a group known as Fascists (from the Italian word *fasci,* meaning groups or bands) and sought to enter politics, denouncing capitalists, employers, the church, and the Socialist party; and he added an extreme nationalism to his creed.

FASCIST SUPPORTERS

The great change in his fortune began early in 1920, when, concluding that he could not win the workers to his cause, he took up the defense of people of property against the so-called revolutionists. The war profiteers seem to have been among the first to perceive the advantage of using the Fascists against a government bent on taxing away some of their gains. Frightened by the workers' occupation of the factories, the industrialists followed the profiteers' example, and were joined by the agrarians, who were alarmed over the seizures of land, and by the merchants, who hated the competing cooperatives. Funds poured in; Mussolini's following increased in numbers to such an extent that he decided for the sake of discipline to transform it in 1921 into a regular party.

At that time the party claimed to have 320,000 members. It included a large number of students, peasants, industrial proletariat, and little people. The portrayal of the feeling of the time may be grasped from the words of Italo Balbo, then a student of twenty but a leader in the movement in Emilia:

> When I returned from the War—just like so many others—I hated politics and the politicians, who in my opinion had betrayed the hopes of the soldiers, reducing Italy to a shameful peace and to a systematic humiliation Italians who maintained the cult of the heroes. To struggle, to fight in order to return to the land of Giolitti, who made a merchandise of every ideal? No. Rather deny everything, destroy everything in order to renew everything from the foundations. Many at that time, even the most generous, tended towards communist nihilism. There was the revolutionary programme already, and apparently the most radical: fighting against the bourgeoisie and against the Socialists, equally engaged on two fronts. And, certainly, in my opinion, without Mussolini, three quarters of the youth of Italy returning from the trenches would have become Bolsheviks.[1]

The Duce directed their revolutionary fire into fascism.

The groups who supported the movement had ample opportunity to learn from the methods of action what the Fascists stood for and how they could be advantageously used. The party trained storm troopers along military lines. Arms were obtained from sympathetic members of the regular police and army; government officials permitted the use of trains and trucks; the propertied classes supplied the money; ex-army officers led the

[1] Herman Finer, *Mussolini's Italy* (New York: Henry Holt & Company, Inc., 1935), pp. 139-140.

rioters to battle against fellow Italians. Balbo has portrayed their methods as follows:

That night our storm-troops proceeded to destroy the vast headquarters of the Confederation of the Socialist Co-operatives of the province. . . . The old palace was completely destroyed. . . . We undertook this task in the same spirit with which we demolished the enemy's stores in war time. The flames from the great burning building flashed ominously into the night. The whole city was illumined by the glare. We had to strike terror into the hearts of our opponents. Fascists are not slain with impunity. . . . Scarcity of water assisted the work of the flames. The large amount of provisions with which the building was stocked rendered the fire inextinguishable. . . . I went to the chief of police and announced to him that I would burn down the houses of all the Socialists in Ravenna unless he gave us within half an hour the necessary means of transporting the Fascists elsewhere. I demanded a whole column of trucks. The police officers lost their heads, but after half an hour had passed they told us where we could find trucks already supplied with gasoline.[2]

This act began a night of arson and violence in village and town throughout the provinces of Forli and Ravenna.

Similar raids occurred all over Italy, particularly in the north and center. The Socialists did not give in as easily as Balbo reported; they fought back but, like the Catholic Populists and the liberals, who were equally attacked, they could not comprehend that people would treat one another in peacetime with such brutality. The opponents of fascism underestimated the power of the new movement and failed to unite in the face of danger. As late as the election of 1921 the Fascists seated only 35 deputies. Nonetheless, the police and the military looked with approval on these nationalists who defended property with violence and destruction. The Duke of Aosta, a royal cousin, openly sided with them, and other members of the royal family were sympathetic. When in October the liberal government asked the king to sign an order declaring a state of siege against the Fascists, the ruler delayed and refused. He, too, inclined toward them, and upon the resignation of the ministry, he called Mussolini to head the government. Thus the Duce crossed the Rubicon in a Pullman; the movement of "demogogic, nebulous, political futurism" conquered Rome by train.

The primary interest of a dictatorship is to maintain its authority. If physical force and extraordinary measures were not necessary for that purpose, there would be no dictatorship. With the king's aid Mussolini adhered to the constitution in appearance while destroying it in substance. He first assured himself of adequate physical force; he increased the size of the army by more than one third, and to overpower internal enemies he founded the Fascist militia. In 1924 he put through a new election system to obtain a docile majority in the Chamber. The party gaining the largest number of votes would receive two thirds of all the seats. In the election

[2] William Ebenstein, *Fascist Italy* (New York: American Book Company, 1939), pp. 25-26.

campaign Fascists murdered a Socialist candidate with impunity; after the election, in which with the aid of brutal intimidation and assault the Fascists polled 4½ million votes to their opponents' 3 million, some intimate colleagues of Mussolini had the Socialist deputy Matteotti assassinated. The affair aroused scandal, but Mussolini brazenly continued his ways. The opposition unintentionally assisted him by withdrawing in a body from the Chamber, leaving him free to consolidate his position in its absence. The Fascists turned against the Catholic Populist party and the liberals and treated them in the same way that they had treated Communists and Socialists. Anyone who did not support fascism was regarded as an enemy. "There is no place for anti-Fascists in Italy," Mussolini declared.

FASCIST REORGANIZATION OF GOVERNMENT AND SOCIETY

Mussolini reorganized the government to make it a docile instrument of his will and to protect himself against competitors. In 1923 the Grand Council of the Fascist party became actually the highest organ in the state (officially so in 1928–1929). It selected the candidates to run for the Chamber of Deputies; it acted as the supreme organ of the Fascist party, set its policies, and selected its officers. It had to be consulted on all matters of constitutional change, and it might be consulted by the prime minister on all other questions of national significance. Its members were above the law and received immunity from prosecution.

Because Mussolini worked through this body, he needed to control it. He did so in three ways: 1. Although certain high officials were members by virtue of their positions, Mussolini exercised the authority to appoint others for a term of three years. In case of need, he could swamp the Council with his own followers. 2. The Council met only when Mussolini as its president called it, and he alone determined the agenda. 3. The Council could act without a quorum; that is, Mussolini could call a meeting at which he alone was present and the decisions of that meeting would be legally binding.

As for parliament, through the right of the Grand Council to select the candidates, Mussolini made certain of a docile majority; even so, he wished more power. He deprived parliament of the right of initiative; he alone could propose bills. Nor were sessions of parliament necessary, for the executive obtained the authority to issue decrees with the force of law. The parliament became a façade for dictatorship, a position similar to that of the ministers. The latter were all Mussolini's appointees, removable at will. Their former responsibility to parliament was replaced by that to the prime minister and the king. The premier, Mussolini, was made responsible solely to his dependent, the king. Provincial and local government received its orders through officials appointed by the central government. The dictator directed the administration of the entire country.

The Fascists dared not preserve the independence of the courts for fear that the judges might send party murderers to prison. In 1925 parliament approved a law which turned justice over to the Fascist executive. By law the government could now dismiss civil and military officials "who do not furnish full guarantees as to their loyal fulfillment of duty or who show a lack of sympathy towards the general political direction of the government." The arbitrary will of a dictator became the law; any judge who adhered to the conception of law as objective norm was dismissed and could be tried and condemned as a criminal. The *ex post facto* principle was abolished, as also were the right of *habeas corpus,* the right of open trial, the right of trial by jury, the right to be treated as innocent until proved guilty, the principle that the punishment must fit the crime, and all other safeguards in a free society against injustice.

To supplement the labor of the purged regular courts, the Fascists established a special tribunal "for the defense of the state," which was used to convict opponents of fascism. The thirty members of the tribunal were appointed by Mussolini. The right of defense was so curtailed as to be worthless. Under this system persons were given long sentences on suspicion; others were tried and put to death within twenty-four hours; persons guilty of attempting to keep the family of an anti-Fascist from misery were condemned to imprisonment; persons were exiled to a different part of the country, a favorite being some wretched village in the south; Fascist grafters and assassins were acquitted. As far as the Fascists were concerned, the system worked. "No one respected the independence of justice," Mussolini asserted in 1924, "more than the Fascist government."

All the instruments of public enlightenment were brought under Fascist domination. Freedom of the press disappeared in 1924, after the liberal and Catholic journals dared to reveal the acts of Fascist brutality and graft and associated Mussolini with the murder of Matteotti. In 1928 the Fascists restricted the right to practice the profession of journalism to those approved by the government. Long before that time under the threat of financial ruin and of imprisonment of the editors press criticism had ceased. "In a totalitarian regime," Mussolini declared to an audience of editors in 1928, "the press is . . . a power in the service of the regime. . . . The Italian press is the freest in the world. In other countries papers serve the orders of groups of plutocrats, parties and individuals. Journalism is free just because it serves but one cause and one regime."

It was as free to serve Mussolini as were the radio, the movies, the theatre, the schools. Educational institutions were transformed into centers for inculcating fascism and for training the young people in militarism. Physical education was emphasized; drill and warfare were practiced; the boys were to fight, the girls to become the mothers of fighters. Science and social science were neglected in favor of emotional rhetoric. Independence of mind was regarded with hostility as a sign of individualism and disloyalty to the party. Because universities contained distinguished professors hostile to the regime, the government imposed upon all professors a special oath of loyalty. The professors, who in a free society are expected to develop personalities and to train leaders, were forced to produce loyal followers of a dictatorial system. They were required to equate the good of fascism with the good of Italy; they had to deny the freedom of the mind, of research, and of teaching or leave their profession to others. Many of them emigrated and enriched the staffs of universities in free nations.

FASCIST REORGANIZATION OF THE ECONOMY

A government must be judged by its accomplishments for society. The satisfaction of the industrialists and the large agrarians over the assumption of power by the Fascists presaged the nature of future economic and social policies. The government organized the various industries, agriculture, and the trade-unions into syndicates. The syndicate of iron and steel manufacturers, for example, should express the democratic will of that interest; the old free trade-unions were transformed into syndicates that should do the same for labor. In practice, the industrial and agricultural syndicates were permitted to select their own officials and to run their own affairs.

Since labor was anti-Fascist, the labor syndicates were brought under officers appointed from above by the regime for the purpose of holding the groups under control. Collective bargaining continued; it amounted to labor's acceptance of terms agreed upon by Fascist officials and the employers. Strikes and lockouts were equally forbidden, although both occasionally occurred. Hours of work were lengthened, averaging from ten to fourteen a day, with usually no pay for overtime. Wages were lowered, in some regions between 45 and 60 per cent. If the wage scale in Great Britain, the highest in Europe, in 1930 is taken as 100, that in Italy was 39, the lowest in Europe. The Labor Charter promulgated by the government set two standards for wages: in prosperous times the worker should receive enough to satisfy the "normal exigencies of life"; in bad times his wage should depend upon "the possibilities of production."

The employers of agricultural workers were permitted to restore the system, abolished just after the war, of remunerating their workers partly in kind. Whatever was grown was used for that purpose; if the worker could not eat the articles at once, he had to sell them, provided he could reach a market. Mussolini inaugurated the Battle of Wheat to make Italy self-sufficient in that product. The battle failed to raise the per acre production any higher than that in countries which waged no battle. It forced the expansion of wheat growing to land which was better suited to other purposes. Mussolini accompanied the battle by an increase in tariff and made sure thereby that breadstuffs, of which the Italians were large consumers, increased in price. The people were able to afford less food than before; the calorie content of the diet, between 2,500 and 2,700, became one of the lowest in Europe; only those of Portugal, Greece, and Albania were less. "Fortunately," Mussolini said to the Italian Senate in 1930, "the Italian people have not yet accustomed themselves to eat several times a day, and in consequence of their yet humble standard of living, they feel the suffering and privations less acutely."

The big landowners were the only persons to profit from the Battle of Wheat. This preference meant nothing new to fascism. "For Fascism," stated a loyal author, "the social problem is a question of production and not of distribution of wealth." A former Fascist minister for national education asserted that "the wealth of the few in whose hands capital is concentrated is also the wealth of the proletariat." The theory did not seem specious to party members who believed that Mussolini felt and thought and acted in harmony with the wishes of all Italy; it was specious only to persons who were, or should be (according to the Fascist party), in prison or exile.

Unemployment continued and probably grew. The government, which did not care to advertise the fact, concealed the evidence; but the patronage of pawn shops increased, the recipients of handouts from the party remained numerous, and occasionally officials spoke of the large numbers out of work. Nonetheless, the Fascists forbade emigration and encouraged an increase in the birth rate. Italy should have a large population in order to make imperial conquest both essential and possible. Prior to the Fascist revolution the government had introduced a comprehensive system of social insurance. In one of its first acts, the Fascist government, at the urging of landowners, abolished the coverage of unemployment insurance of agricultural workers. A number of other categories were likewise excluded. The few groups that remained insured received compensation for ninety days and were then left to private charity, a means by which the Fascist party, the main collector and dispenser of charity, kept a hold on the masses. The amounts of insurance disbursed varied from 6½ to 19½ cents a day, a starvation level. The government devoted insurance funds to other purposes. It provided some employment in public works. It built a few auto highways for a nation with one seventh as many cars as Britain or France, but left some regions to use stream bed for roads. Handsome public buildings were erected to glorify the Fascist state, but far less land was reclaimed from marsh or taken from large estates and distributed among the peasants than in the era of the despised liberal regime.

The Fascists determined to develop into reality Italy's claim to the status of a great power. For the purpose they encouraged a rise in the birth rate so that other states would be compelled to make room for surplus Italians. The emigrants would in time, it was hoped, become the basis for annexation of territory. The government sought to arouse pro-Fascist sympathy among Italians already settled in France, French North Africa, the

United States, South America, and elsewhere, and it displayed the vigor of fascism, as we have seen, by expanding the army and navy and by attacking Greece and extending control over tiny Albania. Fascists referred to the Mediterranean as "our sea," and they claimed the return at some future time of Nice and Savoy, Yugoslav territory, and the acquisition of Tunisia. The government could safely risk intrigue in the Danubian states, since it committed Italy to little and sustained her interest in the region. Mussolini found it advisable, however, to settle the dispute with Yugoslavia, lest it become dangerous to security, and to participate in the League of Nations. He did almost nothing by way of improving the Italian dependencies either for colonization or for production of needed materials. He and his cohorts were for the present too busy establishing dominion over Italy to seek to fulfill Fascist imperialist hopes.

The Fascist regime proved to be expensive. It received an 80 per cent reduction in Italy's war debts from the United States and an 86 per cent reduction from Great Britain, and Wall Street poured loans into the country. Whereas the liberal regime had left an almost balanced budget and a national debt of 22,000 million gold lire, which was easily managed, the Fascist government increased expenditure threefold in actual value over prewar days, and by the middle thirties had doubled the national debt. The government spent a pittance on education and social services, and channeled the funds into the bureaucracy, the police, and the military—the three pillars of dictatorship. In 1931 Great Britain allocated 10.8 per cent of her national budget to the military, France 26 per cent, and Italy 27 per cent. The Fascist party emulated the governmental bureaucracy in making away with vast sums. Taxation was increased upon foodstuffs like bread and sugar, which the masses consumed, whereas the income tax remained low and was easily avoided. The government stabilized the lira in 1927 at too high a rate, 19 to the dollar, when it was worth 25 or 26, thereby hurting the Italian economy in the same way that the British economy had been injured two years earlier by similar action. Because of this miscalculation the economic crisis hit Italy earlier than it did the rest of the world. It found a country unprepared to overcome the trial.

Far from introducing any basic improvements, the Fascists had caused economic and social conditions to deteriorate. Their dictatorial power enabled them to prevent public recognition of deterioration and to suppress what in a free society would have been the logical consequences of failure.

Germany

WEIMAR REPUBLICAN GOVERNMENT AND POLITICS

The German Republic established in 1919 received its popular name from the city of Weimar, where the constitutional convention met. The city was chosen, because of its association with Goethe and Schiller, as a symbol of the peaceful, cultural character of the new republic. Created under the most unfavorable conditions, the republic maintained itself with success until the mistakes of its leaders and the world economic crisis brought about its destruction.

The constitution was formulated by the same body that accepted the Treaty of Versailles, and it was always associated by its enemies with that document. In the constituent assembly, elected by popular suffrage, the political parties that had opposed the imperialist domination formed a majority and took responsibility for accepting both documents. Social Democrats, Democrats, and Catholic Centrists provided the main support for the republic throughout its existence, and bore the opprobrium of having accepted the Treaty of Versailles. Whenever in the Weimar Republic anyone suffered or any new burdens were imposed upon the population, all parties blamed the treaty; in addition, the nationalists condemned those who had accepted it. The members of the German Nationalist party aroused patriotic feeling and often threw the supporters of the republic on the defensive. They forced the latter to show that in spite of having opposed the Kaiser and demanded the end of the war, in spite of having signed the treaty of peace, they were loyal, patriotic Germans. That the parties of the Weimar coalition played this game of competition in nationalism as little as they did enabled the republic in the twenties to be fairly successful.

The relations between the opponents and the supporters of the republic varied according to circumstances. After the Armistice the Social Democrats in the government and the heads of the army cooperated in maintaining order. In 1919 Gustav Noske, the Socialist minister, used army personnel to suppress revolutionary acts and prevent Communist or other left-wing *putsches*. In 1923 the German People's party temporarily gave up its monarchist beliefs in order to accept responsibility for rescuing the country from the Ruhr invasion by the French and Belgians, and from the inflation. Gustav Stresemann, its leader, devoted his energy to the republic until, in 1929, he died of exhaustion. He approached the stature of a statesman more nearly than anyone else in Germany during the period and ranked among the ablest leaders in Europe. In 1925 the German Nationalist party, backbone of monarchism and reaction, agreed to cooperate with Stresemann in the government; the members found it politic to do so to obtain economic aid from the state.

The first president of the republic, Friedrich Ebert, a saddlemaker, had come up through the Social Democratic party and the trade-unions. The next president (1925), General von Hindenburg, was a monarchist and a conservative supporter of the Old Regime, who nonetheless took the oath of loyalty to the republic. In the election of 1928, during Hindenburg's first term in office, the Social Democratic party won twice as many seats in the *Reichstag* as any other party, and a member of the party became chancellor. The German Nationalist party, which stood in closest relation to the president, declined in strength from 103 seats, in 1924, to 73. Externally it looked as though the German people were slowly coming to accept the Weimar Republic, not as an imposition by the victorious Allies, but as their own creation. Underneath, however, deep animosity among the social classes intensified political antagonism. Economic instability made the middle class an uncertain political force; at one time this large and influential class voted democratic, at another Nationalist. The Weimar Republic was not so stable as it appeared.

The Weimar constitution offered a progressive framework within which to solve political problems. A popularly elected president replaced the authoritarian hereditary Kaiser. The parliament consisted of two houses, the upper representing the states, the lower the people. The lower house, or *Reichstag*, wielded much more power than its predecessor. The executive cabinet under the leadership of a chancellor was responsible to the *Reichstag* and could be overthrown by an adverse vote. The *Reichstag* was elected by a system of proportional representation intended accurately to express the people's will. The civil rights of a free country were guaranteed; judges were declared independent and responsible to the law. Germany's political duty to the world was recognized by the assertion in Article 148 that "all schools must strive to inculcate morality, civic-mindedness, and occupational skill in the spirit of the German nationality and international conciliation," and in Article 4, that "the universally recognized rules of international law are accepted as integral and obligatory parts of the law of the German Reich." These and other provisions in the Weimar constitution exemplified the best political thinking of the West.

In its economic clauses the constitution went beyond that which other peoples had accomplished. Article 151 stated that "the organization of economic life must conform to the principles of justice to the end that all may be guaranteed a decent standard of living. Within these limits the economic liberty of the individual shall be assured." Article 156 enabled "private economic enterprises suitable for socialization" to be transferred to public ownership. Article 159 safeguarded the right of trade-unions to organize; Article 161 assured a "comprehensive scheme" of social security. Article 162 declared ambitiously, "The *Reich* shall endeavor to secure international regulation of the legal status of workers to the end that the entire working class of the world may enjoy a universal minimum of social rights." Article 163 set the standard that "Every German shall, without prejudice to his personal freedom, be under the moral duty to use his intellectual and physical capacity as may be demanded by the general welfare." Article 165 provided for a set of councils representing workers, employees, and employers at factory, district, and national levels to serve "in the regulation of salaries and working conditions, as well as in the entire field of the economic development of the forces of production." The economic council for the *Reich* should advise the ministry on "drafts of politico-social and politico-economic bills of fundamental importance" and should have the power to initiate such bills. Thus the constitution offered the possibility of a full democratic life; whether the clauses would be executed depended partly upon the German people and partly upon the course of world events beyond their control.

OBSTACLES TO LIBERAL DEMOCRACY

In trying to govern themselves the Germans suffered from a historical handicap similar to that of the Italians—late unification and inexperience in popular government. Except in some of the small states like Baden, the Germans first acquired parliamentary responsibility in 1918. The ways of democracy were alien to them in the numerous nongovernmental aspects of life such as education and civic and social organizations. They did not practice social equality, free discussion under an objective chairman, election of officers in private clubs, and private initiative in civic affairs, which train people for democratic action in public life. They tended to wait for official guidance. The Social Democrats had learned something about self-government from activity in the party and in the trade-unions, as had the Center party from participation in the numerous private Catholic associations. Even in these mass parties the leaders tended to conform to the general pattern by guiding from above. Business leaders, who prior to Bismarck had been thoroughly liberal, had become attached to authoritarian ways. Big industry, particularly powerful in the German Nationalist party and the German Peoples' party, proved a danger to the republic.

Proportional representation, introduced as the most democratic means of expressing the will of the people, became actually a handicap. In each of 35 election districts a party would submit a list of candidates. Because the number of those it would seat depended upon the size of its vote, the candidates whose names were near the top of the list were most likely to win. The party leaders determined the names on the list and the order of preference, thereby exercising undue influence. In addition, the system caused the multiplication of parties, for any group or combination of groups that could muster 60,000 votes in a district, or that number from left-overs in all the districts, could return a deputy to the *Reichstag*. A multiple-party system comparable to that of France and pre-Fascist Italy plagued Germany, with similar diffusion of political responsibility. The coalition governments suffered frequent internal stalemate or disruption and failed to lead the nation. The bureaucracy from necessity often decided a question secretly, in order to carry on government at all.

The major obstacle to political democracy came from the prevalence of nationalism. The shadow of the Treaty of Versailles lay across the republic during its entire existence. The Germans and many Austrians wished the two countries to unite; yet the peace treaties prohibited the union. The disarmament clauses were enforced upon Germany; no other state disarmed. The Nationalists, including thousands of ex-army officers, agitated for rearmament in the name of international equality; the Socialists and Democrats, who disliked militarism and feared the political and social effects of rearmament within Germany, hesitated to say so for fear of being accused of supporting "the Versailles slave-system." The Socialists and Democrats wished Germany to be a member of the League of Nations; when they advocated this policy, the Nationalists accused them of selling German honor to the enemy. The German Peoples' party under Stresemann took the ambiguous position that Germany should accept the Locarno pact and join the League in order to improve her prospects for securing equality and eliminating the treaty obligations.

When Communist Russia was discussed, the Nationalists and the German Communists, although for different reasons, demanded that relations be close, and almost every party wished them to be improved. The Nationalists saw a chance for the two outcast nations to revive their power and defy the West; many political leaders in moderate parties sought to strengthen Germany's position with the ultimate objective of playing between East and West. The nation generally approved the Rapallo treaty of 1922 with Russia and its subsequent renewal. The Social Democrats mistrusted the policy most, on two counts: it might play into the hands of the German Communist party, and it would strengthen the revival of nationalism. When the most powerful nation in Europe loses a war, many of its members are likely to resent the loss as an injustice; and when the nation is not psychologically as well as physically defeated, the result may be that even the moderate groups are caught in the toils of nationalism. That happened to Germany.

Social antagonisms and the conflict of economic interests became involved in politics. To have Ebert, a trade-unionist, succeed Kaiser William II as head of Germany seemed to the ruling social groups of the former regime a humiliation. It deprived them of positions at court and their center of power for retaining the class structure. The conservatives in the German Nationalist party were compelled to acquiesce in the new system, but they turned hostile at the first opportunity. They included persons of the kind that assassinated Republican ministers like Matthias Erzberger of the Center party and Walter Rathenau of the Democratic party and that participated in the many petty revolts attempted against the republic in its early years, the most notorious being that in 1920 led by an insignificant official named Kapp. They lacked, however, the popular following necessary to become dangerous.

Much more important was the accentuated interconnection between economics and politics. The socialization clauses of the constitution were pushed by the Socialists and resisted by the industrialists in political battles. The Social Democrats prized the control of the ministry of labor, which industry longed to remove from their power. The ministry of economics carried so much authority, for example, in the handling of cartels and in the management of public and semipublic corporations, that possession of it was eagerly sought. Labor and capital quarreled over the distribution of the tax burden and imposed an excessive load upon the group least able to defend itself—the salaried middle class. The industrialists disliked the burden of the system of social insurance; the workers defended it. The big agrarians after 1924 urgently needed tariff protection and government loans and subsidies. They sought them by political action; and when they abused the financial aid, they used politics to conceal their misdeeds.

The Revolution of 1918 had overthrown a constitution and created a new type of government, but it had not changed the distribution of property ownership, and time alone could eradicate the distinctions and antagonism among social classes. The republic helped the agrarians and the big industrialists, its severest enemies, to survive and recover. It likewise aided the rise of the trade-unions and enabled the Social Democratic party to become the largest political organization and so to counterbalance the rightist groups. From the stabilization of the mark in 1923–1924 to the world economic crisis in 1929 the system of political and economic balance of power preserved the peace and enabled Germany to stage a remarkable recovery.

ECONOMIC TROUBLES—INFLATION

The country's main problem concerned whether it could support the population. The enormous population growth from 41 million in 1870 to 66 million in 1914 had depended upon an economy of exporting finished goods which the people manufactured out of raw materials partly supplied from within Germany but to a large extent provided by imports. Like Great Britain, Germany lived by international trade, and any loss in her ability to import and export caused suffering.

Until the stabilization of her monetary system she endured severe economic hardship. The course of misfortunes began with the loss of territory, population, and resources by the terms of the peace treaty. It continued with the drain from reparations payments, the failure of the government to approximate balancing the budget and to keep the monetary system in order, and it culminated in inflation.

When the mark became worthless in 1923, a revolution took place in the distribution of property and in the reaction of the public toward the government. The state, the industrialists, the agrarians, or anyone with debts benefited to the extent of being able to pay them with marks of rapidly declining value. Business organizations and individuals fled from money into goods. Banks suffered from this process, for their business consisted of handling money; but business firms and corporations accumulated all the property or other material resources they could, regardless of whether these purchases fitted into any plan. Those who were adept at playing this ruthless game became wealthy in a few months. It has been estimated that by way of inflation the economically powerful took more than 25 billion marks worth of property from the rest of the population and that 40 billion marks in debts were wiped out. When it is recalled that the state had indemnified the owners for industrial property lost in the territorial cessions, it becomes evident that a large-scale transfer of national wealth to the rich occurred.

Labor suffered from inability to force increases in wages at the rate of speed of the decline in the value of the mark. In October, 1923, at the peak of inflation, a skilled worker needed to work nine or ten hours in order to pay for a pound of margarine, and six weeks in order to afford a pair of shoes. Being organized and able to exert pressure, the workers suffered, however, much less than the middle class that lived on salaries or fixed incomes from bonds. This class, usually regarded as the stable force in society, was economically ruined and, as Stresemann said, "proletarianized." The catastrophe was permitted by a government in 1923 under Wilhelm Cuno, the director of the Hamburg-American Shipping Company. The middle class had invested its savings to a large extent in government bonds, which became worthless. Many accused the state of betraying its own citizens. Economic ruin prepared the middle class for the acceptance of nazism.

ECONOMIC REVIVAL

The successful stabilization of the mark in late 1923 and in 1924 showed the dependence of financial sanity upon political leadership. At the time Germany possessed no gold and no foreign exchange; she had just destroyed her monetary system. Yet almost overnight a government with a courageous policy succeeded in reintroducing the mark at its former value. It did so by reaching agreement with France and Belgium over the Ruhr, by cutting government expenditures to the level of income, and by promising not to exceed a fixed limit in issuing new currency. The economic forces battening on inflation prophesied their own early death and demanded that more money be put in circulation; but the government under Stresemann, acting on the advice of President Hjalmar Schacht of the *Reichsbank,* understood that to do so would renew the inflationary spiral. By an act of will it revived the confidence of the people in its money; and when the government used as backing for the new currency a general mortgage on the land and resources of the country, the people in Germany and elsewhere accepted this unorthodox, nonliquid basis. The possibility that politics might use the monetary system in one of many ways for its own advantage experienced here its first successful postwar test.

In spite of war losses and the effects of the inflation, German economic resources remained essentially sound. Agriculture had declined in productivity from lack of man power, machinery, and fertilizer during the war, and much of industry had emerged with worn machines. Nonetheless, the country had not suffered devastation from invasion like France and Belgium, and the Germans preserved the sound technological basis for revival. Once the Dawes Plan regulated the reparations question and the country regained a sound medium of exchange, the people started to work with vigor. Agriculture, especially the wheat growers on the big eastern estates, received high protection and other government aid in order to maintain itself. The election of Hindenburg as president favored the agrarians, for they knew that as a military aristocrat he belonged to their Junker tradition. A group of them made sure that he learned about their economic troubles by presenting him with a large estate in eastern Germany. Industry possessed greater power of adaptation and expansion than did agriculture. This branch of the economy gave to Germany wealth and power. With the aid of enormous loans from abroad after 1925 it proceeded toward recovery.

The most important branches of industry were those concerned with coal, iron and steel, electrotechnical equipment, chemicals, and textiles. They constituted roughly one half of the country's industry and employed one third of the industrial workers. They accounted for nearly 40 per cent of the total annual production and for nearly half of the value of national exports. Foreign loans enabled these industries, which lagged behind the United States and some other countries in competitive power, to install modern machinery and construct the newest plants to be found in Europe. The industrialists simplified products and types and introduced business machines and scientific management. They developed a system of cost accounting for checking on the expense of operation. They studied the flow of production through the plant and tried to adjust output to market demand. They stressed vocational education and the application of science to industry. By 1929 they disposed of the largest and the most efficient plant to be found in Europe. They could not develop technologically to the extent of the United States because they lacked an internal mass market and because, with labor so cheap and interest rates so high, they did not need to mechanize to a comparable extent. Nonetheless, German industry, to a greater extent than the British, was on the way to solving its economic problems. The victor country allowed its basic industry to continue to stagnate; the defeated nation applied brains and initiative in achieving an industrial revival.

Cartels and Combinations

Germany continued from prewar times to be the land of cartels and combinations for controlling competition. The experience of inflation in concentrating ownership haphazardly was in the latter half of the twenties renewed in a rational way by the organization of big trusts. The United Steel Works and the International Dye Corporation achieved most renown among these, because of their mammoth size and because of the essential role of their commodities in the economy. The Rhenish-Westphalian Coal Syndicate and the potash cartel compulsorily organized by the government some years previously were similarly important. The government itself controlled between 12 and 15 per cent of the business of the country, and in the field of industry alone, 20 per cent. Before the war the Imperial Supreme Court had declared:

> If in any branch of industry the prices of products sink too low and if the thriving operation of the industry is thereby made impossible or endangered, then the crisis which occurs is destructive not only for individuals, but also for the social economy in general, and it is therefore in the interest of the whole community that unduly low prices in a branch of industry shall not permanently exist.

The prevailing policy favored the creation of large monopolies by the formation of cartel agreements on price, distribution of market, patent exchange, pooling of research, and any one or more of numerous such matters. The trade-unions, aiming ultimately at the socialization of large monopolies, the industries themselves, and the general public approved the policy as the most efficient; and the government created by law in 1923 a system of registration of cartels and special cartel courts which should prevent abuse of the public by these private interests. The method did not work well, for trusts and huge corporations that dominated a field by themselves without belonging to cartels were not subject to its control.

Industrial rationalization and combination made German industry by the time of the world economic crisis almost as powerful as it had previously been. It contained some serious weaknesses, but its achievement was impressive. Productivity per worker increased between 1907 and 1929 by 25 per cent, mainly through a 38 per cent increase in horsepower. Industrial production as a whole was, in 1928, 2 per cent greater than in 1913 in spite of the loss of territory; but in that time the production of lignite had increased 90 per cent, electricity 312 per cent, aluminum 557 per cent, and rayon 533 per cent. The output per miner in the coal fields of the Ruhr increased from 175 tons in 1925 to 315 tons in 1929, and the production of coke grew from 32 million tons in 1913 to 40 million tons in 1929. Germany did not turn out quite so much pig iron in 1929 as in 1913, but the production of 18 million tons of raw steel in 1929 compared favorably with that of 17 million tons in the larger state of 1913.

The effects of planning purely in terms of the national state were seen in the existence of unused productive capacity. The situation of Germany resembled that of the other industrial powers. By the end of the twenties the average productive capacity was 30 to 40 per cent greater than in 1913, or even more, whereas the demand was less than 15 per cent above that of 1913. In consequence, German firms pressed for the formation of international cartels or working agreements of other kinds. The large firms, like Krupp, International Dye, General Electric, the optical instruments firms, and rayon firms, acquired plants abroad. They did so not merely for the sake of profits; Germany needed to obtain foreign exchange in order to pay for her imports. Except for coal, and to a large extent chemicals, she imported the bulk of her industrial raw materials—practically all of her wool, all of her cotton, three fourths of her iron ore, almost all her nonferrous metals, almost all her oil, and so on. The average ratio of her imports of raw materials to her exports was estimated to be one to two; that is, for every two marks worth of exports she had to pay one mark for prior imports, and in some instances the ratio was higher.

The great weakness lay in the fact that the German economy depended to a large extent upon the continued receipt of foreign loans and the continued expansion of international trade. Excess productive capacity and high interest rates, amortization charges, and reparations payments placed the economy in a potentially dangerous position, which was made worse by the need to import so much raw material. The German share of world exports had declined—from 13.1 per cent in 1913 to 9.7 in 1929—about the same decline as that for Great Britain. Germany was manufacturing more than in 1913 but was exporting less. Although by 1929 her exports were almost able to balance her imports, her international payments were balanced solely by foreign loans. She had concentrated on the production of goods for export, neglecting consumers' goods for her own people. She needed time to adjust her economy from one of the world's great creditor nations in 1914 to the world's greatest debtor nation. Any sudden stoppage in the flow of foreign loans would make her position desperate.

Standard of Living

For a few years in the latter half of the twenties the German people enjoyed the highest average standard of living in their history. The middle class suffered, but in spite of the constant presence of an average of 1,350,000 unemployed at the peak of industrial production in 1928, the workers had gained. They had developed one of the best-organized systems of trade-unions in the world. Even though it contained only about one third of the laboring population, its membership of 5,250,000 in 1928 set the standard for all workers. Through the Social Democratic party acting as their political representative and in the favorable general climate of democracy, the workers were able to impose collective bargaining, raise wages, improve working conditions, and gain a comprehensive system of social security far better than that under the empire. With rent control and free schooling, and with socialist governments in many cities using loans for the improvement of public facilities like recreation centers, the real income of the workers was by 1928 above that of 1913.

Nonetheless, real income did not reach a very high level. An American economist investigating conditions there in the late 1920's concluded that the average German worker had an economic position comparable to that of a French or Italian worker, one much below that of an English worker, and far below that of an American. The difference was evident from statistics. The national income per capita for Germany in 1928 was $231; for Great Britain in 1924, $435; for France in 1927, $218; for the United States in 1927, $652. The estimated increase in the national income since 1913 was about 12 per cent, or approximately the same as in other European industrial countries. When one considers that the country had just been defeated in a world war, the condition of the masses showed that the economy was performing well.

The improvement in real income of the workers came to a considerable extent from governmental aid in the form of social welfare. These expenditures, amounting to 40 per cent of the total cost of government, took up the slack left by the Allies' compulsory reduction of the military burden. The sphere of state activity had broadened since 1914, with the resulting increase of 65 per cent (45 per cent without reparations) at prewar prices in the cost of government. In 1928 the Germans paid 27 per cent of their national income into taxes, 9 per cent more than in 1913, a burden which ranked among the heaviest in the world. Fifty per cent of the revenue was derived from indirect taxes, which struck the workers and salaried middle class most heavily; 45 per cent came from taxes on income and property, with the amount exempted for a man, wife, and two children being $400. The tax system was regarded as uneconomical. In contrast with the empire, the central government was given the main authority to levy taxes. It then allocated to the states a certain percentage of the income, irrespective of whether the states needed the amount or not. The latter, not being directly responsible to any representative body for the tax rate and the amount of expenditures, tended to waste money which the central government urgently needed. The unsoundness of the system became evident once the economic crisis struck the country and the burden of supporting the unemployed grew. As was true of the foreign loans, the Weimar Republic would no doubt have solved this problem if it had had more time.

Spain and Portugal

CONTINUOUS TROUBLE

The two Iberian countries have in the present century undergone almost continuous internal trouble. A fundamentally preindustrial society was subjected to stresses arising from the introduction from abroad of the new social and political ideas of liberalism, socialism, communism and anarchosyndicalism, and from the beginnings of modern industry. In international affairs Portugal, except for token participation in World War I, remained passive, and Spain retired into that condition after her ignominious defeat in the Spanish-American war. Both countries faced problems that arose when an elite made up of the aristocratic owners of large estates, the few big industrialists, the army, the church, and many intellectuals, and overwhelmingly devoted to standards of the seventeenth century, faced the awakening desires of impoverished masses. Both nations have sought a solution in dictatorship.

ECONOMIC DEFICIENCIES

The basic fact in each country was the presence of surplus population. In Portugal 47 per cent of those in agriculture was excessive; in Spain as a whole the figure was 12 per cent, but in Andalusia it rose to 34 per cent and in Estremadura and Galicia-Asturia to 21 per cent. The situation existed in spite of the fact that the average density of the population in 1930 was, on a European standard, quite low—for Spain, 47 per square kilometer; for Portugal, 74 per square kilometer. About 75 per cent of the Spanish people and 80 per cent of the Portuguese lived directly or indirectly from agriculture. The countries failed to utilize the available natural and human resources and ranked among the least-developed areas of Europe.

Agriculture was affected by the fact that the mountainous areas of northern Portugal and of northern and northeastern Spain, blest with ample rainfall, were divided into small peasant properties, whereas the rest, consisting of dry plains, was owned in large estates. Neither country had undergone a reform in the distribution of land. In Portugal in 1930, 45 per cent of the agricultural population consisted of employees, mainly day laborers. In Spain 7,000 proprietors held 15 million acres of land in Estremadura, Andalusia, and La Mancha, and 10,000 families owned nearly one half of the land other than that in the mountains in the north and northwest. Ninety-eight per cent of the holdings were under ten hectares each, but they included only 36 per cent of the arable area. Four one-hundredths of one per cent of all the holdings contained about one fourth of the total agricultural area. A large proportion of the small farms was in units of less than one hectare. The independent peasant, who owned and cultivated a family-sized farm, was almost entirely absent in both countries.

The technical state of agriculture had decayed since the flourishing centuries of Moorish rule. The few estates that were managed efficiently betrayed the level to which the others had sunk. Southwest Spain, under the Moors a garden, had particularly suffered. Grain was planted where fruit and vegetables had once grown. Sheep and cattle roamed over former fields; fertile land had returned to a state of nature from neglect of irrigation ditches. Landlords had gone to the cities to live, leaving the direction of affairs in the hands of managers and rarely inspecting the condition of their estates. In the previous century burghers had invested in land but had quickly adopted the careless ways of the nobles. In Portugal the per capita productivity in agriculture in 1930 was one seventh of that in Denmark; in Spain it was about one third. European agrarian reform in landholding and in technology of the past two centuries had halted at the border.

The results of backward agriculture were seen in the size of rural incomes and the standard of living. Peasant holdings in the north of both countries had been subdivided by inheritance to the point of poverty. In the center and west of Spain in 1929 three fourths of the owners or renters had a daily income of less than twenty-five cents. In the Castilian province of Avila only 320 of 13,530 who paid a land tax earned more on an average than $1.25 daily. In Andalusia three fourths of the population of towns like Carmona, with 22,000 inhabitants, consisted of agricultural laborers and their families. These workers, hired by the day, month, or season, found employment for about one half of the year. The men earned from fifty cents to one and a half dollars a day or less. This poverty had remained unchanged from at least the eighteenth century.

Because industry was subject to the law of its own active nature and faced some competition, it did not sink into the economic coma of agriculture. Nonetheless, it had failed to take advantage of opportunities. Although Portugal possessed some minerals, including coal, iron, and wolfram, industry employed in 1930 only 19 per cent of the gainfully occupied males. Spain did better with 31 per cent; but Spain was one of the main world producers of iron ore, mercury, potash, pyrites, copper, and wolfram, and in addition it disposed of considerable deposits of coal. Spain largely exported these as raw materials. A small metallurgical industry at Bilbao constituted the main exception; but the slight significance of this branch, essential for all industrial development, may be seen from the fact that in 1935 Spain consumed 26 kilograms of steel per capita, whereas Sweden with about one fourth the population consumed 179 kilograms, or seven times as much. Spain in 1926–1929 produced only $40 worth of manufactures in gross value per capita, a figure to be compared with that for France ($160) and for Italy ($80). It exported manufactures to the extent of $3.50 per capita (France, $34; Italy, $10), whereas it imported them to the extent of $10 per capita (France, $8.30; Italy, $6.40). Figures are not available for Portugal, but one can infer that they would have been much lower than those for Spain.

High tariffs, introduced to protect the youthful enterprises, became a shield against competition and eliminated the incentive to rationalize production. The workers improved their economic conditions above those of the landless proletariat; but their income could not provide a mass market for industrial goods. Most Spaniards continued in the twentieth century to despise industry and commerce as materialistic and vulgar. Whenever they accumulated money from these occupations, they tended, not to improve and expand their enterprises, but to buy land and to live on the income from an estate. In both Spain and Portugal industry failed to attract economic leaders.

SOCIAL CONDITIONS

The extent to which a country utilizes its human resources may be judged from the birth and death rates and from the percentage of the people that it allows to remain illiterate. Since industrialism had not yet inculcated a sense of the importance of the individual, life in the Iberian Peninsula remained cheap. Births were plentiful, deaths equally so. In 1930–1931 Portugal had nearly 30 births per thousand of the population, Spain nearly 28 per thousand. Romania and Yugoslavia had more than 34 per thousand; the USSR, 45; the United Kingdom and Wales, 16 per thousand. The Iberian peoples did not assure the care necessary to keep their members alive. The death rate for Portugal and Spain, 17 per thousand, should be compared with that for the United Kingdom and Wales, 11.9 per thousand. The greatest contrast lay in the figures on infant mortality: Portugal, 143 per thousand; Spain, 117; and the United Kingdom and Wales, 63 per thousand. The two countries failed to provide those who stayed alive with the key for improving their lot. In Portugal 60 per cent remained illiterate at the age of ten; in Spain, 32 per cent; in the United Kingdom and Wales, almost no one. If the age-specific mortality in the Netherlands is taken as a standard, 46 per cent of the deaths in Portugal and 56 per cent of those in Spain in 1939 would have been excessive. Under Netherlands conditions the people would have continued to live. Not merely in an economic sense but in a demographic one, Spain and Portugal retained the characteristics of a colonial land.

A few years before World War I a French writer referred to Portugal as a nation of "five million honest barbarians and about 12,000 politicians." On the eve of World War II an English student of Spain divided the Spanish people into two groups, the upper classes—constituting about one fifth of the population, who ran the affairs of the state—and the politically indifferent peasants and workers. Numerical weakness prevented the middle class from playing its historic role of uniting these two groups in a modern society.

The Spanish government had in the previous century confiscated the ecclesiastical land, but in Portugal the church continued to be one of the largest landowners. The Spanish church had turned to investments in business of various kinds—real estate, utilities, transportation, industries, and banks—and had become one of the major capitalistic forces. The Jesuits alone were said to control in 1912 one third of the capital wealth of the country. The church monopolized and obstructed education and used political power to exclude Protestantism. It ignored the social question of poverty, joined the wealthy in fighting social reform, and condemned liberalism as sinful. Except in Navarre and the Basque country, the clergy had lost contact with the masses, and the church was regarded popularly as a symbol of reaction. Writing in 1936, Father Francisco Peiro stated that rural as well as urban dwellers turned against it. He found that among the village population of New Castile and central Spain only 5 per cent attended mass or observed the Easter obligations; in Andalusia 1 per cent of the men attended mass; in one parish in Madrid, 3½ per cent of the 80,000 parishioners attended mass, 25 per cent of the children were not baptized, and 90 per cent of the children educated in convent schools discontinued confession and attendance at mass after leaving school. Unlike the Catholic Church in France and Germany, that in Spain had ceased to be a national leader.

The Spanish army had formerly represented the nation and had been an object of popular pride. The decline, which characterized the army as much as the nation, reached its nadir in the Spanish-American war, and no improvements were in sight. In 1898 the army maintained an officer for every seven or eight soldiers, and one general for every hundred soldiers; thirty years later the proportion was little changed. The peacetime contingent of officers in 1931 equaled that in the German army at the outbreak of World War I. Services were so inadequate that 200,000 troops are said to have died in Cuba during 1896–1898 of wounds and disease. In 1936 the army possessed no modern planes and no tanks, and transportation had not been motorized. Salaries for officers and soldiers' pay were so low that graft and corruption became commonplace; soldiers had to be given long furloughs so that the state might save money. The sale of rifles and other supplies to the Moors in Spanish Morocco afforded a widely used means of supplementing one's income. Although in 1922 it was reported to have received 51 per cent of the national budget, the army wasted the funds. Strategic and tactical thinking was so deficient that the army could scarcely contend with the Riffians in Spanish Morocco. Since Spain had remained neutral and Portugal had participated to a slight degree in World War I, their armies did not benefit from the lessons to be gained from that experience. They served mainly as instruments of domination by the ruling groups within their respective countries; for that purpose they were fairly adequate.

In such conditions violence became a standard form of social relations. The workers and peasants felt angry and embittered over their poverty, and, perceiving no way of improvement, they took to the physical destruction of their enemies. By the present century they had come to regard the upper classes in the same way that their ancestors had thought of the Moors. Marxian socialist doctrines entered the country but found slight reception; they represented a stage of thinking in advance of that among most of the people, for they demanded more organization and discipline than the masses would accept. The ideas of anarchism proved most congenial—ideas of extreme individualism, of murder, bombing, and burning. A hungry village worker believed that the landlord and all his allies should be put to death; the urban worker wished the factories to be confiscated and run as self-dependent syndicates by the workers themselves. In the country the landlords employed local bosses to control the villagers. Arms were used when necessary, but economic pressure was simpler. The peasant was kept in line by the threat of nonemployment, of cancellation of a lease, of loss of the house in which he lived, of ostracism by cowed neighbors, and of expulsion from the village. Back of the local bosses stood the civil guard, a carefully picked body of police, and, whenever necessary, the army. In urban districts the employers likewise aligned with government and army. When workers tried to organize unions and to improve their lot by strikes, the employers applied the lockout, brought strikebreakers from the country, and used spies and *agents provocateurs.* If order seemed endangered, they called the military. The situation was worst in Barcelona, where all means of violence were used.

In that city labor troubles, combined with outbursts of Catalonian nationalism after the war, led to the local imposition of martial law. In 1920 General Martinez Anido was made civil governor of the province. Blocking a peaceful settlement between labor and owners, he had certain labor leaders shot on sight (21 were disposed of in 36 hours). When others were arrested, he had them shot while they were trying to escape on the way to prison; when still others after imprisonment were released, he ordered them shot as they left the prison gates. The anarcho-syndicalist workers undertook reprisals, and in sixteen months 230 persons were murdered on the streets of Barcelona. In the next two years the prime minister was shot, then a labor leader, then a cardinal—and the slaughter continued.

DICTATORSHIP

King Alfonso XIII, who had ruled Spain from 1902, referred to his people as "canaille" and aimed to exercise autocratic rule behind the façade of parliamentary government. To do so he aligned with the forces of reaction and strove behind the scenes to make parliamentary government impossible. The economic dislocations occurring in and after World War I assisted him in this endeavor; and when the army officers in 1917 organized a committee to demand an increase in salary, the elimination of royal favoritism in army appointments, and an improvement of the medical corps and the commissariat—the two branches most significant for their low standard of living—he faced the constant threat of dictatorship, not by himself, as he wished, but by the generals. When in 1921 a relatively small force of Moors under Abd-el-Krim annihilated an army under General Silvestre, with 10,000 killed and 4,000 prisoners, the deputies in parliament began to demand reform. To prevent a parliamentary commission from publishing a highly critical report, army and king combined (1923) to overthrow the government and create a military dictatorship under General Primo de Rivera.

The new dictator came from the Andalusian landowning aristocracy. Accustomed to a life of dissipation, he nonetheless for a time proved energetic in the promulgation of popular reforms. He felt some sympathy for the poor and sought to improve conditions in the industrial regions by compulsory arbitration of labor disputes. He spent money lavishly on public works—road construction, irrigation and electricity projects, and public buildings—and he encouraged industry by favors of various kinds to revive the economy. He reduced the drain of blood in Morocco by speedily conquering the native rebels and pacifying that territory. At home he repressed with comparable vigor the Catalonian nationalists, but he quarreled with the liberal intellectuals and drove many of them into exile. Unlike Mussolini, he possessed no party following of his own but remained dependent upon the old reactionary forces. Even if he had wanted to, he was unable to execute the one reform which Spain most needed—redistribution of land. Nor did Primo de Rivera comprehend that the purchasing power of the rural people had to be increased in order to maintain prosperity in the towns. In failing health, he reached the end of his usefulness within a few years; when the world depression began to affect Spain, the king dismissed him in 1930 in favor of another general. He once said that if he had known in his youth that he would become dictator, he would have studied more and dissipated less.

Portugal had undergone a revolution in 1908–1910, which began with the assassination of the king and one of his sons in 1908 and culminated in the establishment of a republic and the introduction (1911) of a new constitution. Between 1910 and 1926 the country had eight presidents, even though the constitution of 1911 fixed the term of a president at four years, and forty-three different ministries, including two dictatorships. The ultimate authority resided in the army, which, with the country's finances approaching chaos, in 1926 once more introduced a dictatorship and placed in charge of public finance a general, who is reported to have declared, "I know absolutely nothing about finances myself, except that my own are in complete disorder." Two years later the military transferred responsibility to a professor of economics, Antonio de Oliveira Salazar, who inaugurated his long term of authoritarian rule.

The four states under review in this chapter anticipated in the 1920's what most of Europe became during the 1930's, a continent of social and political conflict, of frustration and irascibility. Germany and Portugal at the time least represented the course of the future, the one because it was temporarily governed by groups whose interests lay in the direction of liberal democracy, the other because its subject masses had just begun to shake off the Old Regime. Italy set the precedent by developing a new political and social philosophy as justification and objective for dictatorship.

Spain still employed the army to carry on traditional revolutions among the elite and to crush mass revolts. Militant nationalism competed with liberal democracy and with Marxism in its several forms in Germany, but in Italy it had won by gaining the support of the middle classes. The peoples of the Iberian Peninsula had scarcely reached the social and political stage at which nationalism becomes a popular ideal.

Literature and the arts throve in precariously balanced Germany as nowhere else in Europe. The excitement of uncertainty offered extremes of experience that stimulated creative work. Italy shared in this rousing life, until Mussolini became afraid that creative freedom might suggest the value of political freedom. Spain sustained some of the finest writers and artists of its modern history, Ibanez the novelist and Gonzales the sculptor being examples; but Portugal in this aspect of life, as in others, slumbered.

At the end of the decade none of the four dissimilar states was able to overcome or change the forms of its internal instability without serious repercussion in international relations. In each of the four both internal and international conditions were due for change, and each through its weakness was acutely susceptible to an outside crisis. The situation in these states did not make European life appear secure.

Suggestions for Further Reading

BRENAN, GERALD W. *The Spanish Labyrinth: An Account of the Social and Political Background of the Civil War*. New York: The Macmillan Company, 1943. Excellent. By an intimate student of the country.

EBENSTEIN, WILLIAM. *Fascist Italy*. New York: American Book Company, 1939. Brief, compact, interesting.

HALPERIN, SAMUEL W. *Germany Tried Democracy: A Political History of the Reich from 1918 to 1933*. New York: The Thomas Y. Crowell Company, 1946. Standard and thorough.

SALVEMINI, GAETANO. *Under the Axe of Fascism*. New York: The Viking Press, Inc., 1936. A mine of information by a refugee whose insight proved to be correct.

WHEELER-BENNETT, JOHN W. *Nemesis of Power*. New York: St. Martin's Press, Inc., 1953. Basic study of the role of the military in Germany since 1919.

Chapter 9 · The Countries of Eastern and Southeastern Europe

REGION OF NEW POLITICAL ENTITIES

During and after World War I the geographic area lying between Russia and Germany underwent the greatest change of any part of Europe. In the breakup of the German, Russian, Austro-Hungarian, and Ottoman empires the tendency for the continent to be organized into small or medium-sized national states spread from Western to Eastern Europe. In the area lay thirteen states, Finland, Estonia, Latvia, Lithuania, Poland, Czechoslovakia, Austria, Hungary, Romania, Bulgaria, Yugoslavia, Albania, and Greece. In land mass the region was 72 per cent as large as that of the rest of the continent exclusive of Russia, and its population of 116 million in 1930 amounted to 55 per cent of that of the twelve states west of it.

The thirteen states either were created at the end of World War I or were so transformed that they had the characteristics of new political entities. They all had similar political backgrounds: subordination to an imperial authority in a region of backward culture. Finland, Estonia, and Latvia had belonged to Sweden or to Russia for seven centuries. They had received some privileges as separate units at times during the preceding century, but they had never been independent; in recent decades they had been subjected to Russification. The formerly independent states of Lithuania and Poland, united under one king in the fourteenth century, were partitioned by their Russian, Prussian, and Austrian neighbors in the last third of the eighteenth century. Their revival as states in 1918 terminated more than a century of foreign subjection.

Czechoslovakia was formed entirely of provinces of the Austro-Hungarian Empire, the western half having for centuries belonged to Austria, the eastern half (Slovakia and Ruthenia) since the tenth century to Hungary. Although Romania had asserted her independence of the Ottoman Empire in 1877, her acquisition at the end of World War I of the areas of Transylvania, Bucovina, Bessarabia, and the Dobruja more than doubled the size and population. Serbia, independent since 1829, Slovenia, released from Austria, and Croatia and the Banat, gained from Hungary, united to

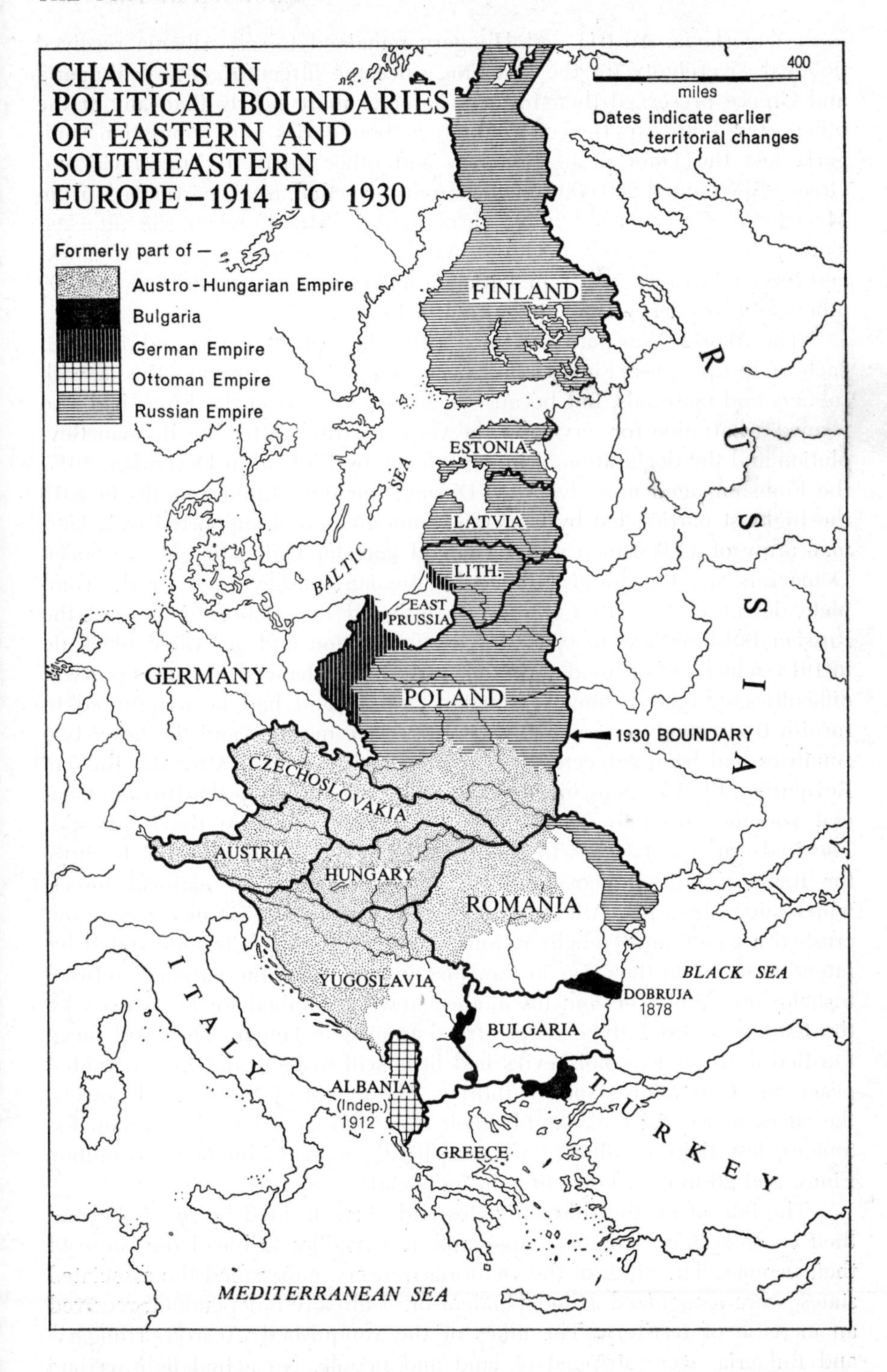
CHANGES IN POLITICAL BOUNDARIES OF EASTERN AND SOUTHEASTERN EUROPE—1914 TO 1930
0 400
miles
Dates indicate earlier territorial changes
Formerly part of —
Austro-Hungarian Empire
Bulgaria
German Empire
Ottoman Empire
Russian Empire
FINLAND
RUSSIA
ESTONIA
LATVIA
LITH.
BALTIC SEA
EAST PRUSSIA
GERMANY
POLAND
1930 BOUNDARY
CZECHOSLOVAKIA
AUSTRIA
HUNGARY
ROMANIA
YUGOSLAVIA
ITALY
BLACK SEA
DOBRUJA
1878
BULGARIA
ALBANIA
(Indep.)
1912
TURKEY
GREECE
MEDITERRANEAN SEA

form Yugoslavia. Austria and Hungary remained torsos. Albania received political sovereignty for the first time since the fifteenth century. Bulgaria and Greece preserved their former character more nearly than any of the others, but both experienced changes in boundaries and population. Bulgaria lost the Dobruja to Romania and other areas to Yugoslavia and Greece; she gained 200,000 refugees from the ceded areas, particularly from Macedonia. Greece tried imperialism in Asia Minor, when she attacked Turkey and was severely defeated. As a result, she gave up 400,000 Turks and received as refugees from Turkey a million Greeks; in addition, 200,000 others fled to Greece from Bulgaria and Russia.

The World War had extended over the entire region and involved each of the peoples. Finland had been compelled to provide Russia with soldiers and materials, but because of hatred for Russia the Finns had also formed a battalion for service in the German army. After the Russian Revolution and the declaration of independence by Finland in December, 1917, the Finns engaged in a civil war. During four devastating months in 1918 the Rightest parties, led by General Mannerheim and supported by a German army of 11,000 men under General von der Goltz, fought the Social Democrats and Communists aided by Russian Bolsheviks. After the complete defeat of the latter, the war continued for a short time until the Russian Bolsheviks were ejected. The devastation and an Allied blockade in 1918, which cut off food and other materials, enhanced Finland's postwar difficulties. Latvia, Estonia, Lithuania, and Poland had been required to furnish troops and materials to their respective masters, and the latter two countries had been subjected to a scorched-earth policy. After the Russian Revolution, the Germans invaded the Baltic region, while the Russian General Yudenich tried to organize there a campaign against the Bolsheviks. The Red army sent forces to counterattack and to reconquer the territory for Russia. The Estonians and the Latvians organized national forces, which, aided by a few Allied naval ships, drove out the German forces and crushed a Communist rebellion. Since General Yudenich frankly stated his intention to retain the areas in the Russian monarchy, the nationals refused to help him. When he and his motley crew succumbed to the Bolsheviks, the Estonians and Latvians were freed from one danger. They still faced the Red army, but as Bolsheviks had little will to fight and Lenin wanted peace, the Communists soon withdrew. The defeat of the Central Powers, the chaos in Russia, and notably their own courage enabled a million Estonians, less than 2 million Latvians, slightly more Lithuanians, 3 million Finns, and 20 million Poles to gain independence.

The fate of all the thirteen states had been decided by forces beyond their control. Representatives appeared at Versailles to plead the cause of their peoples. The allies of the victorious powers, now called the associated states, were recognized as independent or, if already independent, received an increase of territory. The allies of the vanquished, Austria, Hungary, and Bulgaria, were stripped of land and people. No actual fighting had occurred on the territory which was to become Czechoslovakia and Austria, nor did a revolution or civil war subsequently break out. Hungary was likewise spared until after the war. Then in 1919 fighting broke out between a Communist government headed by Béla Kun and Rightist forces, and the confusion was enhanced when Romanian troops pillaged the country for three months. Of the states that united to form Yugoslavia, Serbia alone had been a center of hostilities, in which she had lost one sixth of the population. The fighting in Bulgaria and Greece had not crippled either country nearly so much as did the subsequent civil conflict in Bulgaria or the war against Turkey fought by Greece. Each of these little states began its peacetime career under the shadow of war and revolution. It was born in battle and its most recent and decisive experiences were hatred, fear, and violence.

PROBLEMS OF CREATING NATION STATES

After the war each state had to achieve national unity and the material conditions for survival. Austria existed as a small German state not allowed to unite with Germany proper. Its population contained equal numbers of Social Democratic workers and conservative Catholic peasants. The conflict of these interests might prevent the voluntary cooperation essential for successful governance. The economy, which had served an empire, required adjustment to be viable in a state of 6½ million people. The Magyar rulers of a former empire were left with less than one third of the previous territory. Hungary therefore had to build an economy in an area which had lost many of its major natural resources and which lived contiguous to 2½ millions of its own nationals transformed into minorities in neighboring states. The state could not be considered unified, for an elite of big landowners and a small upper middle class dominated a mass of wretched peasants and a growing proletariat, many of whom had just supported Béla Kun. The Hungarian ruling groups needed to arouse the nationalism of their people to oppose the treaty of Trianon, while preventing the peasants and workers from using the same nationalism to demand a fair share in national life.

The rest of the thirteen states faced problems that might have awed peoples of wealth and political maturity. They all had a large ignorant peasant population, an immature and numerically small middle class, a weak and undeveloped economy, a low standard of living, a shortage of skilled leaders in all fields, and class antagonism intensified by war and lack of political experience. Each presented a heterogeneity of cultures. Albania, for example, contended with tribal organizations alongside some urban life, and Islam and Greek orthodoxy. Greece had to absorb 1¼ million refugees of economic, social, and political background different from her own. Bulgaria had to settle 200,000 refugees, mainly Macedonians, accustomed to approach all problems by violence. Yugoslavia contained 6.5 million Greek Orthodox Serbs using the Cyrillic alphabet, Roman Catholic Croats (4 million), and Slovenes (more than 1 million) using the Latin alphabet, together with followers of Islam, and some Magyars, Germans, and Romanians. The Serbs had governed their own independent state since the early part of the nineteenth century; the Croats had lived in a subject kingdom under Hungarian rule; the Slovenes, Bosnians, and Herzegovinians had been governed from Vienna, the people of the Banat from Budapest. The Serbs, Croats, and Slovenes spoke different dialects of the same language. Laws and judicial systems were as different in the several regions as were political habits and folk customs.

Similar conditions existed in Romania, Czechoslovakia, and Poland. Romania now comprised the old kingdom, Transylvania, part of the Banat, and Bessarabia, gained from Russia. Czechoslovakia consisted of peoples formerly ruled, some by Austria, some by Hungary. In her population were 3 million Sudeten Germans, 9 million Czechs and Slovaks, 745,000 Hungarians, and 460,000 Ruthenians. Poland had even greater complexity. One part of her people was accustomed to Prussian law, money, government, economy, education; another to Austrian; a third, by far the most backward, to Russian. The Polish state included a million Germans in the west, 2 million Jews, nearly 4 million Ukrainians in the southeast, a million White Russians in the east, and about 70,000 Lithuanians in the northeast. Each of these states in 1919 would have taken additional territory and peoples, irrespective of nationality or cultural background, if the Allies had permitted.

Finland and the Baltic states had a common background of Russian government, law, economy, and military and social organization, modified somewhat by German and Swedish culture. The Finns, who had profited from periods of tolerance in the preceding century, were able to develop their own national standards. In the Baltic a German aristocracy and a vigorous German burgher class in the coastal towns had supplied a counterpoise to Russian tradition. The Baltic German barons had served the Russian government loyally, but they had defended some degree of cultural autonomy for the nationalities there as well as for themselves. Count Hermann Keyserling, who was one of them, later wrote that "In 1918 the Estonians did not exist as a nation—the Estonians were merely the lower class." This assertion contained some truth, not merely with respect to Estonians but to Latvians and Lithuanians as well. They and the Finns organized independent states with a fairly homogeneous population; but, accustomed to foreign rule, they had to become integrated, self-governing nations. Differences between burgher and peasant had to be bridged, a new equalitarian, free society had to be created, and a sense of mutual responsibility and reasonable cooperation had to be aroused. Things Russian, things German, and things Swedish had gradually to be eliminated or adapted to the needs of a developing national culture.

REGION OF PEASANTS AND AGRICULTURE

The states lay predominantly and in most areas overwhelmingly in a region of peasants and agriculture, as the following figures will show. Austria, Czechoslovakia, and Greece offered exceptions, the first with only 26 per cent of the population dependent on agriculture, the second with 33 per cent, and the third with 46 per cent (1930). Except for Hungary with 51 per cent, the number rapidly increased as one traveled from north to south, reaching a peak in Albania's 80 per cent. The area has been described as an ocean of peasant villages with rare islands of cities. The conditions remained in most regions those of a preindustrial society. Vast areas of Poland and Hungary, for example, preserved the life of the eighteenth century. Albania was even more retarded. Areas of capitalistic agriculture like those to be found in parts of former Prussian Poland and among the Czechs were exceptions. The peasants were incompetent to play an active and constructive part in building the new national states. They needed leadership from other classes and public aid in adjusting agriculture and their ways of life to the new conditions of political independence and international interdependence. On the whole they continued to be neglected during the interwar period, and this neglect seriously weakened the states.

Land Reform

The sole fundamental change in the condition of the peasantry concerned the redistribution of land. The reform aimed at a social and political objective of increasing the number of landowners by dividing the large estates. Economic objectives, such as an increase in production, were entirely secondary or ignored. Nationalism called for an attempt to improve the lot of the peasant masses—the supposed backbone of the nation—by offering them the opportunity to own land. States differed, however, in the extent to which they implemented the ideal.

Finland learned from the civil war in 1918 that her land-hungry agricultural proletariat supported the Social Democrats and the Communists. The example of Russia, where the peasants were ostensibly being given land, encouraged the Finnish peasants in their radicalism. The government leaders therefore decided as early as 1918 that the large estates, even though owned by Finns, should be divided. In that year a law enabled tenants to purchase, with government loans, the plots they cultivated. In 1922 the Lex Kallio provided state aid for the purchase of two kinds of holdings, one of not more than 20 hectares of agricultural land and 20 of woodlot, and the other of not more than 2 hectares for a cottage and a vegetable plot. The first should go to peasants, the second to wage earners. The necessary land was obtained by state purchase of portions of large estates. Estates of 200 hectares or less were not affected. Those of 500 hectares could be required to give up 25 hectares; those of more than 500 hectares could be forced to turn over to the government as much as 50 per cent of their uncultivated land.

The reform proved to be successful in every respect. In 1910 only 24 per cent of the 478,222 families living on the land had been owners. By 1934, 65,000 renters had acquired land, and another 53,000 had bought the small plots. In all, 31,000 new estates had been created on land previously uncultivated, and 2 million additional acres brought under cultivation. By World War II one family in three owned land. Agricultural productivity increased; cooperatives were active and widespread. The extraordinarily high number of landowners furthered property and stabilized Finnish society. The Social Democrats approved the reform; the Communists fought it and, in spite of the proximity of Finland to Leningrad and other centers of aid, declined in numbers and became a conspiracy rather than a party.

In Estonia, Latvia, and Lithuania the big estates covered a far greater part of the area and were owned by nonnationals, the Russian church, the Russian crown, Baltic German, and Russian nobles (in Lithuania, in addition, Polish nobles), and banks run by nobles. In Estonia 1,149 estates included 58 per cent of the land; 600 Baltic German families owned nearly half the country. In Latvia the few nobles held almost half the arable land. Two German families in the Baltic provinces, the Stackelbergs and the Ungern-Sternbergs, owned 44 and 33 country seats, respectively. In Lithuania 50 per cent of the area was in large estates. One of the first pieces of business of each new regime was to transfer the land to its own nationals. Latvia never compensated the former owners; she was willing but could reach no agreement with them. Estonia and Lithuania paid some owners, but nothing to those who had fought against the new states in the wars of independence. The families who had acquiesced in the new regimes were permitted to retain between 50 and 150 hectares of their lands. The rest of the holdings was divided among the peasants, with a general standard set of creating family-sized farms.

The reform was executed without difficulty. By 1933 Estonia had formed 55,104 new holdings with an average of 43 acres each. Latvia established 80,000 new farms within half that time. Lithuania lacked enough land to satisfy the demand of the peasants, but followed the same line of attack in reducing the estates, to a size at first of 150 hectares and a few years later of 80 hectares. These laws enabled the peasants to move at once from feudal tenure (with the lords retaining milling, hunting, fishing, and other rights and exacting goods and services from their subjects), to the position of free farmers. Land reform remade these nations.

The governments aided with funds, education, and leadership, and the peasants responded with flourishing cooperatives. More land than ever before was put into cultivation; dairying and the raising of livestock were emphasized. By 1936 in Estonia the number of milk cows had increased 32 per cent and the output of milk trebled. In 1938 the three states exported 47,449 metric tons of butter, a figure not far short of that for the Netherlands and representing a larger per capita export. Since these are branches of agriculture requiring skill and capital, these "subjects" were proving their worth as free citizens.

That Poland urgently needed land reform may be evident from figures on the distribution of land ownership. Estates of more than 100 hectares constituted, in 1921, 43 per cent of the total land area, or 0.6 of the number of land holdings, and 27 per cent of that used for agricultural purposes. Of the total land in 1931, 16.6 per cent belonged to the state or its political subdivisions and to public foundations. The large private estates, although found in the west, were especially prevalent in the east of the country, where the provinces of Vilna (Marshal Jozef Pilsudski's ancestral home), Polesie, and Volhynia were controlled by a few families. According to the census of 1921, 10 million people owned plots of 5 hectares or less, an amount incapable of sustaining a peasant family. These 10 million constituted two thirds of the agricultural population, but owned only 15.3 per cent of the land. Although one hundred times as numerous as the rich landowners, they owned altogether one third as much land. Another 30 per cent of the agricultural population was landless. In sum, the distribution of land was such in 1920 that of 16 million people in agriculture almost 15 millions lived in poverty. These conditions were hardly conducive to the successful evolution of a new state.

Land reform in Poland suffered from the fact that the Polish landowning nobles, who shared the national leadership, were averse to relinquishing their land under any circumstances. But in 1920 the Polish diet (the *Sejm*) was frightened into passing the basic law on land reform by the attitude of the peasant-soldiers toward the Bolshevik invaders. Instead of fighting the invaders, the soldiers proved lax in discipline and inclined to desert. The law on land reform was intended to give them an interest in the new state and to arouse in them the will to defend it. As soon as danger to the country lessened, the social groups opposed to land reform slowed down its execution. A new law passed in 1925 set a figure of 200,000 hectares to be distributed annually, but it was disliked by Pilsudski, the most powerful person in the state and son of the landholding nobility. When in the next year he became dictator of Poland, the breakup of the large estates and the distribution of the land to the peasants soon declined. Thus Poland, together with Hungary and Albania, had the worst record of any of the states of Eastern Europe. Between 1921 and 1931 only 116,000 new agricultural holdings were established, a figure not nearly so large as the combined one for tiny Estonia and Latvia.

Since the pattern of land reform was everywhere about the same, the results of the movement in the remaining countries can be quickly summarized. In Austria, the amount of land in large estates was too small to be of any significance. The contrary was true of Hungary, which did far less about reform than Poland. As soon as the Polish defeat of the Russian Communist armies removed the danger of the westward spread of bolshevism, the Hungarian nobles dropped any ideas of distributing the land. Between 1921 and 1938 not more than 271,000 hectares were divided. In 1937 Prince Paul Esterhazy still owned his hereditary entailed estates of 80,000 hectares, and Prince George Festetics his of 30,000 hectares. Forty-three per cent of the total land area was owned by less than four tenths of 1 per cent of the landowners. In contrast, 800,000 persons, or 40 per cent, of all those people engaged in agriculture were landless workers.

Romania executed as thorough a reform as any state; the example of Communist Russia just across the frontier made the peasants restive, especially those in Bessarabia and Bucovina. Since most of the large noble landlords, Romanian by nationality, belonged to the Conservative party, the bourgeois Liberal party in power decided to accomplish two objectives in one act. In carrying through measures to divide the big estates, it created a peasant bulwark against the lures of communism and at the same time it crippled the Conservative party. By 1930, 4 million hectares of cultivatable land had been distributed to peasants with little or no property. The shortage of land was so great, however, that in that year 75 per cent of the peasants remained rural proletariat.

Czechoslovakia and Yugoslavia used land reform to destroy the economic power of landlords who belonged to other nationalities. In the Czech provinces 37 per cent of the land was held in estates of 100 hectares or more, mainly by German nobles; in the Slovak part the large properties, in the possession of Hungarian nobles, amounted to 50 per cent of the land, and in Ruthenia to 42 per cent. The Czechoslovak government pursued a policy of land reform similar to that of Estonia; within the next decade it created a balanced distribution. Yugoslavia similarly dealt with the feudal estates held by Turks, Hungarians, and Croatian nobles.

The land in Albania was controlled by a few Moslem or Christian families, who exploited their tenants as serfs and succeeded in preventing reform. In Bulgaria the amount of land in large estates was too small for reform appreciably to affect society. The government divided the few remaining "large estates" (those of more than 30 hectares) and the state-owned lands so thoroughly that by 1934 farms of more than 30 hectares of cultivated land accounted for only 2.7 per cent of the entire cultivated area. In Greece, where only 20 per cent of the land was arable, the reform was directed at the Moslem-owned lands primarily in the north. The government expropriated without compensation the land belonging to the Sultan, to foundations and other organizations, and to all individuals who did not habitually reside in Greece. It took all property above 200 hectares from all owners who farmed their land, and paid them a small amount in return. The problem of distribution grew to unmanageable proportions by the influx in 1921 and 1922 of 1,200,000 refugees from Turkey, Russia, and Bulgaria. The League of Nations enabled Greece to obtain foreign loans and technical advice for settling most of these wretched people.

Shortcomings of Agriculture

The absence of an economic, as distinct from a social, program with respect to landholding was evident from the failure in most countries to contend with the question of parcelization. The land had for centuries been divided into small strips, a system suitable to the tools and methods of primitive farming but not to modern ones. In certain areas a peasant might farm or own several of these strips, some not more than a meter wide and possibly several miles apart. The administrative difficulty of consolidating the strips into a unified farm was such that the advanced countries of Central and Western Europe had not entirely overcome it. In the Baltic countries and Czechoslovakia the inheritance laws limited parcelization, but not elsewhere.

Since population growth was the highest in Europe, farm plots became smaller and smaller. Where the big estates were divided, economic conditions often rapidly deteriorated, for peasants were unable to maintain the level of agricultural production. The peasants who took over the land lacked the knowledge to improve their ways, and the capital to purchase necessary equipment. Where their holdings were small, they did not use artificial fertilizer for fear of unintentionally helping their neighbor. The small peasant consumed a large part of his own produce and had little to sell. After he had paid the annual sum for his land and his taxes and had bought indispensable supplies, he had little or no money left for the purchase of tools, fertilizer, improved seeds or payment for the prevention of soil erosion. His fixed costs were high, for he invested a larger proportion of his capital in land, buildings, and livestock than an owner of more land did. The supply of capital for loans to peasants was so scarce and banking facilities so inadequate that interest rates ranged from 10 or 12 per cent to 45 and even more. Peasants with dwarf holdings could frequently not afford a plough or any draft animal; their condition resembled that of the poorest farmers of Japan and China.

Whenever the peasantry found a market for diversified crops and the necessary transportation facilities, it quickly adopted the ways which in the West were standard. The Czech peasant and those in western Poland had begun to grow sugar beets and other commercial crops before the war. They continued to be efficient and, like their Baltic colleagues, would in time have caught up with the West. They lacked capital and technical knowledge for modernization, and they were the victims of tax discrimination; but the contrast between their farms and those in the backward regions of their own and other countries was striking. In the succession states (those formed in whole or part from Austria-Hungary) national independence and the disruption of former markets caused some reduction in efficiency. Czechoslovakia increased her production of wheat in order to be independent of Hungary, and reduced her acreage in sugar beets. Austria turned to raising sugar beets on land better suited to stock raising and dairying, in order not to buy sugar from Czechoslovakia. The change reduced production per unit of capital and therefore cut income.

From the standpoint of productivity per capita in agriculture, the countries under review ranked among the lowest in Europe. Denmark's index figure of 354 should be compared with the highest figures for the eastern states—Austria's 134 and Czechoslovakia's 105—and with the lowest —Albania's 22, Yugoslavia's 38, and the figures of 47 to 49 for Bulgaria, Romania, and Poland. In yield per hectare of the seven crops, wheat, rye, barley, oats, maize, potatoes, and sugar beets, between 1931 and 1935, Austria (109.6) and Czechoslovakia (116.7) rank superior to France (105) but far behind Switzerland (148.4) and Denmark (177.8). The others stood well below the European average of 100, with Greece being lowest at 60.5. The difference may be largely explained by the fact that a Swiss peasant used per hectare ten times as much capital as a Romanian, four and a half times as much as an Austrian, and nearly three times as much as a Czechoslovakian. Since these figures indicate the amount of technical knowledge used and the general standard of efficiency, a marked difference in peasant income per hectare may be expected. Income in Switzerland in 1928–1929 was twice as large as that in Czechoslovakia, three times that of Poland and Austria, and ten times that in Romania.

Overpopulation

Except in three countries the system of agriculture could not adequately maintain the population directly engaged. Denmark, a country of highly developed industry and intensive agriculture, supported only 36.6 people per square kilometer of arable land, whereas the figures for selected East European countries read as follows: Hungary, 80.6; Romania, 116; Bulgaria, 119; and Yugoslavia, 157. In certain regions the pressure of population on the soil was even greater; in Bosnia and Dalmatia the number in some districts reached 300, and in Bucovina 192. If one considers as surplus population in agriculture that which could have been removed to other occupations without loss in production, Czechoslovakia and Latvia were the only two eastern states that could have used more people in this occupation: the first 5 per cent; the other, 11 per cent. In Estonia the surplus population was insignificant, but the figures for the other states show human waste: Albania, 78 per cent; Bulgaria, 53 per cent; Greece, 50 per cent; Hungary, 22 per cent; Lithuania, 27 per cent; Poland, 51 per cent; Romania, 51 per cent; and Yugoslavia, 61 per cent. The figures represent people who were underemployed, for whom work had to be found merely to keep them alive. These people faced a life of dependence and poverty. Agriculture served as a national poorhouse.

Living conditions repeat the story. Almost every society reveals some people in poverty; the distinguishing feature about these new states was the number of such people and the abjectness of their situation. The Baltic states and Czechoslovakia had least; in most sections the states compared favorably with some of the Western countries—France, for example. Where the peasants had sufficiently large holdings they ate well. As a whole, the people consumed an excessive quantity of starches and too little meat, dairy products, fruits, and vegetables. These are standard deficiencies of an underdeveloped economy at any time, for grain and potatoes are the cheapest form of nourishment and the easiest to grow and to store. In Hungary and the Balkans the peasants suffered from ailments caused by eating too much corn. In Poland a peasant from the Radomsko district described conditions in the 1930's as follows: "We eat potatoes three times a day, potatoes, of course, without any seasoning. We are crawling with lice because we cannot afford soap. The children wear appalling garments. A slice of bread is only for a big occasion. Four persons sleep on one bed. Once a week we wash our faces with soap." [1] High rates of tuberculosis and of infant mortality resulted. If the mortality rate in the Netherlands is taken as standard, the percentages of excess deaths, that is, of those who would have continued to live had they resided in the Netherlands, were as follows: Northwestern, Central, and West-Central Europe, from 23 to 25; Northern Europe, including Estonia, Latvia, and Finland, 15; Eastern Europe (Albania, Bulgaria, Greece, Lithuania, Poland, Romania, and Yugoslavia), 54. Romania had most excess deaths in this group, namely, 65.

The entire countryside lacked professional services, doctors, dentists, veterinarians, public health experts, teachers, agricultural experts. In some regions a few persons, like the public health expert in Yugoslavia, Doctor Stampar, accomplished profound results, only to be accused of bolshevism; but on the whole the services could not be afforded, even if trained personnel had been available. The illiteracy rate was declining, for the leaders recognized that a people striving to develop a national state need to read and write. In 1930 in Austria and Czechoslovakia (except for Ruthenia and some parts of Slovakia) illiteracy scarcely existed. The rate was low in Estonia (8) and highest in Greece, Romania and Yugoslavia (41 to 45 per cent), and Albania (65 to 75 per cent). Since education offers the cheapest and the most essential means for a people to raise its standard of culture, it is evident that most of this region had not advanced much beyond the initial stage in the effort to catch up with the West.

[1] George Kagan, "Agrarian Regime of Pre-War Poland," *Journal of Central European Affairs,* October, 1943, p. 251.

THE CONDITION OF INDUSTRY

The national leaders recognized that in order to build a strong state agriculture must be supplemented by industry. They particularly regarded an iron and steel work essential, for it was the basis of armaments. The importation of instruments for defense was considered both humiliating and dangerous to security. In most instances industries were chosen for development, not according to their capacity to provide work for masses of people (and raise the standard of living), but according to their political and military prestige and their ability to produce goods for export in competition with the West.

The countries varied in the extent of industrialization according to historical background. Among all the states Czechoslovakia alone possessed a balanced economy. She inherited 48 per cent of the Austrian Empire's factory capacity, including an integrated organization of coal mining, iron and steel works, and consumers' goods industries, a fact that helps to explain the stability and efficiency of her democratic government. Her neighbors, Austria, Hungary, and Poland, exemplified the different ways in which the breakup of empires and the formation of new states affected the economy. Both Austria and Hungary lost mineral resources upon which their industrial development depended. Austria had been an industrial center for the empire; now she retained parts of certain industries or the whole of others, like that for luxury goods, for which she had lost the imperial market. Much less industrialized than Austria, Hungary sought without her former natural resources to create an industry for her needs. The situation of Poland differed from that of the other states in that she inherited rich coal mines, some iron ore, some zinc and lead, some oil, an extensive iron and steel industry in Upper Silesia, and a large textile industry. Most of the zinc and lead ore, however, had been smelted in Germany, and the oil industry remained at a primitive level. She possessed the natural resources to be an industrial power, but not the industrial plant, scientific equipment, and economic organization.

Among the Balkan countries, Bulgaria and Albania contained hardly any natural resources associated with industrialization and even less technical proficiency. Albania's oil reserves were too insignificant to be counted. As for the other three states: Greece had modest quantities of some minerals; Romania possessed oil and some minerals; Yugoslavia had copper, some lead, large bauxite deposits, and extensive amounts of lignite. All were deficient in capital, technical knowledge and personnel, and in economic organization. Hence they chiefly exported the resources as raw materials.

The example of Switzerland, almost devoid of natural resources associated with modern industrialism, indicates that in last analysis the character of the people conditions the quality of accomplishment. Industries in the new states lacked an internal market, they depended almost exclusively upon government contracts, or their production costs were so high that they survived only with the aid of government subsidies and heavy import duties. The Astra works in Romania and the Kragujevac plants in Yugoslavia, both in armaments production, were two such artificially nourished industries, and several of comparable extravagance were built in other states. By way of contrast, the Baltic peoples and the Finns followed the example, not of an industrial great power, but of a processing country like Denmark. They established industries which used their native resources, primarily wood, livestock, poultry, dairy products, and other foodstuffs, and on the whole they benefited the entire nation.

The rate of industrialization in the 1920's was greater in the countries of this area than in those to the west, and their achievement in so short a time was remarkable. The succession states—Czechoslovakia, Austria, Hungary, and Romania—were not so successful as Poland, for in 1929 they still produced industrial goods of less total value than in 1914. Between 1921 and 1931 Poland increased the number of persons employed in industry and mining by 25 per cent, and between 1922 and 1928 industrial production by 55 per cent. The amount of production of these and the other states remained behind that of the advanced industrial countries. The gross value of manufacturing per capita in 1926–1929 was $350 for the United States, $190 for the United Kingdom (the highest in Europe), $110 for Czechoslovakia and Finland, $50 for Hungary, and $20 for Romania. The differences may be transformed into differences in standard of living and degree of contentedness among the population. It helps to explain why Charles University in Prague ranked as one of the best in Europe and why Helsinki supported the largest bookshop on the continent.

Foreign Trade

The economic shortcomings of the states may be seen most clearly in an analysis of their foreign trade and of their capital resources. Nationalism took toll from them all. Foreign Minister Beněs of Czechoslovakia expressed more or less common views when in 1920 he rejected any thought of a confederation or a customs union among the Danubian states:

> A political union with Austria and Hungary would mean that these countries would gain influence in our internal affairs: Austria by way of the Germans living in our State, Hungary through the Magyars in Slovakia. The unfavorable economic conditions of Austria and Hungary form an obstacle to an economic union, and the consequence of any such alliance would be that the wealth of Czechoslovakia would again pour into Austria and Hungary. It is true that they must be helped, but by the whole of Europe. . . . We must indeed work with Austria and Hungary, but instead of political and economic alliances of long duration, the solution seems to lie in a system of short-term contracts for certain different kinds of deliveries, and arrangements by which the independence and special interests of each of the three states concerned would be maintained.

In the practice of economic nationalism Czechoslovakia introduced a novel system. The ministry purchased the entire home production of sugar, sold the amount required at home at a relatively low price, and exported the rest at 20 to 25 times the domestic price, on which in addition it collected an export tax. It acted similarly with regard to other crops, selling oats, for example, to Switzerland at twelve times as much as it paid the peasant producers. The enormous profits were used to support the new government.

Other countries behaved in the same way. Food and other products were so scarce that these agricultural countries were able until far into the 1920's to impose export duties. Import tariffs were advanced to shelter the home market for the infant nationalistic industries. They failed to exclude the articles, but they greatly increased the price. The domestic producer profited; the domestic consumer suffered; and the goods were priced out of reach of the peasant. In fact, little attention was paid to the peasant consumer; nationalism did not extend to planning production for a potential domestic mass market. Statesmen aimed at building an export trade to obtain foreign exchange. The effect may be illustrated in the case of sugar. In 1928 the internal wholesale price of 100 kilograms of sugar varied from 39 Austrian shillings in Cuba to 76 in Austria, 109 in Poland, and 152 in Yugoslavia. Even so, the governments were treating their people better than Italy did, where the price was 240 shillings. When Austria, a country with a city of nearly 2 million people in a total population of 6½ million, tried free trade, she found herself swamped with imports in return for which the other countries refused Austrian manufactures. Although she still had to trade abroad to live, she introduced protective tariffs in self-defense and began the harsh process of adjusting her industry and agriculture to a small internal market. The countries were all new, all with a low standard of living, all in urgent, even desperate, need of goods, all too small and too overpopulated to be self-sufficient, all dependent on international trade and the exchange of their food and raw materials for manufactures. The economic policy of isolation and self-sufficiency accomplished the opposite of what they most needed.

Capital Resources

Each of the states urgently required capital in order to overcome the effects of the war, build factories, purchase machinery, construct houses, and attend to the multitude of other tasks associated with founding new states. The people, now independent, expected a better life than before, and requested more services from the governments, which under such demands could not balance their budgets. They depended mainly upon indirect taxes—on foodstuffs and other articles consumed by the masses—to provide revenue, partly because of the great difficulty of collecting direct taxes from peasants, partly because of the ability of the upper classes in control of the government to shift the burden. The public income was so inadequate that governments took to borrowing and printing paper money. The result was inflation, a common story for countries east and west.

These states differed from those to the west, however, in that they lacked not merely capital but often a modern banking system. Their insecurity disinclined foreign investors to risk capital in loans. At home mass poverty cut private savings to a small figure, and inflation reduced the financial resources that were available. By 1925 the Viennese banks, which had provided the funds for investment in Southeast Europe, had lost five sixths of their prewar resources. Poland used no more than 5 per cent of her national income per annum for industrial development, about one half or less of the normal rate in an industrial country, and only one fourth of that in several countries since World War II. Adequate sums were never forthcoming; but after a number of states obtained assistance from the League in balancing their budgets and stabilizing the value of their money, foreign loans became available to them. French money was particularly invested in allied Poland and Czechoslovakia, and Italian funds in Albania and to some extent in Hungary, for political as well as economic reasons. Romania curbed foreign investments in the name of nationalism until in 1928 the bourgeois Liberal party lost control of the government; the ministry of the Peasants party then opened the doors for the sake of accelerating the pace of economic development.

GOVERNMENT ACTION IN ECONOMIC AND SOCIAL LIFE

The newness of the states forced the government to assume a much greater role in the economy than was customary in the industrial nations to the west. Large tracts of forests and lake lands were located in the area, for which public ownership was customary throughout Europe. Whenever the governments took over large estates they kept possession of most of the land unsuitable for agriculture. In some countries mineral resources were also declared to be in the public domain. The governments were called upon to supply capital and leadership in numerous industries. The process was carried farthest in Poland, where public ownership by 1939 covered the entire armaments industry, 80 per cent of the chemical industry, 40 per cent of the iron and one half of the other metallurgical industries, all the commercial aviation lines, almost all of the merchant marine and the railroads, and 3 million hectares of forest. The state operated five monopolies, salt, matches, tobacco, alcohol, and a lottery; it dominated the banking and credit business, through which it wielded a strong influence over private industry. In Czechoslovakia the government participated in the ownership of the Skoda armaments works, and in Romania the oil industry was under joint public and private ownership. Paucity of private capital for investment threw an extra burden upon the one agency which through its tax power was able to accumulate large sums. The practice of at least partial government investment and ownership was to become characteristic in this century for the economy in underdeveloped countries throughout the world.

Transportation and Communication

Government initiative became immediately necessary in transportation and communication. The existing lines had been built to serve empires and transcontinental traffic. The Baltic states possessed those which the Russian government had considered worth while. Poland's lines went east and west, connecting St. Petersburg and Berlin, for example, but nothing of consequence ran north and south. Czechoslovakia inherited railroads which tied the western section to Vienna and the eastern to Budapest. Romania, Yugoslavia, and Greece all had to extend railroads, roads, and communication lines in the same way to the areas which had previously belonged to other states. In Hungary and Austria the facilities suited an empire rather than a small state, and Bulgaria was no worse off than most in the absence of roads throughout her countryside. The people within a state were unaccustomed to trading with one another. Kwiatkowski, the powerful Polish minister of industry and commerce during the interwar years, has illustrated that deficiency by the following data. In 1913 the Polish provinces—German, Russian, and Austrian—carried on with their respective imperial masters 84.5 per cent of their total foreign trade, with other countries 8.1 per cent, and among themselves 7.4 per cent. The Polish peoples in the three empires had been tied together by cultural nationalism but certainly not by economics. National facilities for transportation and communication were indispensable for changing the course of trade in favor of a national market.

The deficiencies were so great that the countries could not overcome all of them during the short period of peace. They built indispensable lines, improved roads, and developed river and canal navigation. Poland constructed a port, Gdynia, on its own land on the Baltic in order to free itself from the monopoly held by Danzig. Latvia and Estonia improved harbors. Poland connected the industrial sectors of Upper Silesia by railroad with the coastal parts. Czechoslovakia put in a line running east and west the length of the state. The other countries pursued similar policies. These achievements required capital; and although railroads usually attracted foreign investment, the countries lacked the funds to purchase rolling stock and other supplies abroad. The expenditures on railroads left little for the construction of roads. Peasants with natural transportation facilities like the Baltic Sea soon learned to diversify crops for serving foreign markets with perishable commodities. In most regions they were restricted to raising grain. Low standard of living and lack of transportation facilities were two aspects of a common condition. Poland, which possessed some industry, never had more than 50,000 civilian motor vehicles. In 1930 crude oil was still being transported from the fields to the refinery in wooden barrels drawn by oxen. An American touring the country in an automobile found that just outside Warsaw the peasants were as frightened as the livestock by the sight of a car. The Danubian states fared much better because of the Hapsburg heritage; but the Balkan countries were as backward in this respect as any part of Europe.

Except in Austria and Czechoslovakia the urban population formed a minority in each country. As commerce and industry expanded in the 1920's, the salaried employees increased in number and began to form a middle class. The industrial workers shared in the growth, but these were still mainly skilled workers, weak in influence. The industries had not developed in size to the point where they could use unskilled or semiskilled masses. The trade-unions, composed of craftsmen, were not yet subject to pressure from peasant migrants to the cities. The governments introduced the advanced social legislation recommended by the International Labor Organization but usually omitted to execute it. In Austria the workers were well organized and powerful; in Czechoslovakia they were less so but still formed an important force.

Commerce and industry lacked the social prestige that attached to them in Western countries. Both occupations in Eastern Europe had been traditionally associated with Jews and uncultured parvenus. The aristocratic ideal of a gentleman as one who did not earn his living by money making remained strong among the middle class, although in Budapest, Warsaw, and the few other cities prestige of the ideal was declining. The Baltic peasants and the traders in the coastal towns were willing to make money at any time. Greece had lived to a large extent from commerce and shipping for centuries, and Austria and Czechoslovakia possessed a bourgeois entrepreneurial class. Nonetheless, the retardation of economic development had left a social stigma upon the pursuit of business careers. Potential leaders often turned to the spectacular field of politics and away from the indispensable hard work of building a solid material basis for the new nations.

Popular Enthusiasm for Education

The enthusiasm for education which national independence aroused moved into channels which enhanced the maldistribution of talent. The sons of middle-class parents and in some countries even of peasants flocked to the universities. Estonia, which did not possess a language capable of satisfying the requirements of modern culture, devoted almost 20 per cent of her budget to education. In 1929 her University of Tartu had a teaching staff of 174 and a student body of 3,713, and the Technical Institute of Tallin served another 300 students. In Latvia 7,000 students enrolled at the University of Riga. In every other country the influx to the universities was comparable. A university degree gave an opening into free professions or into a position in the civil service. The creation of an administrative structure in each new state and the expanded demand for professional services assured educated young people a livelihood in occupations with social prestige and security of tenure far beyond those which business could offer. The new intelligentsia expected to receive leading positions in society merely because it was educated, just as in the Old Regime, where knowledge set the individual apart from the masses. In countries predominantly of ignorant peasantry, society offered few outlets for the practical use of knowledge. The universities continued to train lawyers, doctors, and teachers, but they did not guide students into careers of business, science, technology, agriculture, and others of value in building a nation.

GOVERNMENT AND POLITICS

When the states began their postwar careers, they all introduced modern constitutions, with parliamentary government, the guarantee of civil rights, an independent judiciary, and the rule of law. Parliament might consist of one house, directly elected by universal manhood—sometimes also women's—suffrage, or of two houses. If the latter, the lower house was popularly elected, the upper one might be, or it might be indirectly elected, or its members might be partly elected and partly appointed. In any circumstance, the executive power was responsible to parliament, or sometimes to parliament and an elected president of the state. Civil rights included the usual guarantees of freedom of speech, press, and assembly, of freedom of worship, and guarantees against arbitrary treatment of the citizen by the government. The state added to these traditional liberal rights others of recent acceptance: the right to work, the assurance of conditions of work and living that make for good health, the right to social security and to protection of the family, and the like. The judiciary was free from executive interference, but it usually lacked the power to pass upon the constitutionality of legislation, a limitation that prevented the courts from requiring the executive and the legislative authority to conform to the standards set in the constitution. The states had taken as models primarily the governmental structure of France, Great Britain, or the United States, the victorious liberal democracies. They soon learned that a model constitution could not assure popular government.

The difficulties of setting up new states were so overwhelming that within a decade almost every one succumbed, or threatened to succumb, to authoritarian rule. The Karolyi constitution in Hungary fell first; the Communists overthrew it in 1919, and they in turn were ejected later in the same year by a Rightist coup. The Magyar nobles and their urban allies retained power throughout the interwar years. In 1922 they changed the election law in such a way that almost all peasants were disfranchised. In order to vote, a person had to satisfy a residential and an educational requirement; the ballot was secret in a few towns, but it was open in the countryside, so that the politics of peasants with the temerity to vote could be controlled. The results proved satisfactory to the stagnant aristocratic dictatorship.

In other countries the process took somewhat longer. Marshal Pilsudski seized power in Poland in 1926 and introduced an authoritarian system which lasted to World War II. Lithuania followed suit; after two years of rule by Professor Voldemaras, President Smetona established a partially free but not fully representative government, which assured conservative rule until 1940. The free governments in the other Baltic states and Finland continued to function under difficulty until the depression and the rise of nazism. That in Czechoslovakia enjoyed the stability which an advanced culture made possible. Austria preserved her free constitution, with some modifications and under the constant menace of being overthrown by the conservative party under Monseigneur Ignaz Seipel, until after the depression and the advent of Hitler in Germany. Yugoslavia remained in an open or suppressed state of mild civil war until the king in 1928 introduced autocratic rule. In Romania the Liberal party exercised a sort of constitutional dictatorship until 1928. In 1926 it introduced an election law by which the party winning 40 per cent of the popular vote obtained 60 per cent of the seats in the parliament—a popular method, also used in Fascist Italy, of keeping a minority party in power. The economic crisis spelled the end of the constitution; in 1930 the king seized control.

Bulgaria lived first under the authoritarian Premier Stamboliski. In 1923 he and his regime were overthrown by violence, and the country was governed by bloodshed for two years. A regime described as mild in the Balkan scale of values replaced it in 1926 and lasted until the troubles caused by the world economic crisis proved to be its undoing. In 1934 the dictatorship was restored. Albania never had a free government. Greece was torn by persistent fighting between Venizelos and the republicans on the one hand and the monarch and the conservatives on the other. Arbitrary power was wielded by the side in control at the time, irrespective of the constitution. Elections were rigged in the standard manner of most of the other states. With the exception of Czechoslovakia and to some extent Estonia, Latvia, and Finland, this part of the globe did not become safe for democracy.

The peoples in the region were deficient in experience and material resources for founding states. Emerging from the chaos left by a world war, they expected to create ideal societies out of debris. In most of the countries, history had not granted the people the opportunity to learn from practice how to govern themselves. The leaders had been schooled in destruction in underground politics and conspiracy against imperial masters; the masses, in passivity and evasiveness. A political tradition ranging from persistent opposition against foreign domination to assassination of persecutors did not prepare these peoples for successful self-government. That some of them performed as well as they did is remarkable.

The Peasantry and Politics

The numerical preponderence of the peasantry affected the character of government and politics in all the states. The political passivity of this backward mass enabled public life to be dominated by the few. The society missed the stabilizing, mediating influence of a large middle class. The cleft between the peasants and the elite could not be bridged until the society became sufficiently complex to permit close working relations at graded levels from top to bottom. Czechoslovakia most nearly approached that model, and her social and political conditions were most stable. In the other countries the political parties lacked an enduring social basis. Political battles were fought in the main among factions in the small group of nobles, merchants and industrialists, intelligentsia, and officials—and, in a few states, of trade-union leaders—at the top of the society. Members of this group guided peasant parties, one of which was usually found in each country, not in the interest of the peasants but in that primarily of the urban elite. Yugoslavia was predominantly a peasant state, and the most powerful party in Croatia was called the Peasant party. Its first great leader, Stefan Radić, stemmed from the peasantry and devoted his life to its cause. As a youth he had been expelled from school because of his political opposition to Hungary. He had graduated from the *École politique* in Paris and had later run a bookshop in Zagreb. Although he inspired the peasants with his demagogic oratory, one may question how much he had in common with that class. Certainly he used the peasantry in his nationalistic fight, first against Hungary, then against the Serbs in Yugoslavia, until in 1928 he was assassinated in Parliament at Belgrade. His successor as leader of the party was Macek, a bourgeois lawyer.

The sole attempt in the 1920's to govern a country according to a peasant program occurred in Bulgaria. Stamboliski, a peasant son with all the physical strength and the appearance popularly associated with a member of that class, had received an education which included a period of study of agriculture in Germany. He became the editor of a journal published by the Agrarian party and in 1908 was elected to the *Sobranje*, or Bulgarian parliament. His opposition to the king and his denunciation of the country's entry into the world war against Russia caused his imprisonment. On his release in 1919 and after the flight of King Ferdinand, he became prime minister, signed the peace treaty of Neuilly, and until 1923 dominated the country. He favored the peasants over the townsmen, declaring that "Sofia, that Sodom, that Gomorrah, may disappear—I shall not weep for her." He persecuted the intellectuals, whom he despised, and praised the "wholesome ignorance" of the peasantry, whose common sense he valued above all education. He divided the few remaining large estates

This painting by P. Belousov on the twenty-seventh anniversary of the death of Lenin illustrates the fine line which divided "socialist realism" and propaganda in Russia. —Sovfoto.

French occupation of the Ruhr, 1923: an attempt to force payment of German reparations. —Wide World Photos.

German inflation: economic troubles increased with the expenditure of gold for reparations. —United Press Photos.

Mussolini, the Fascist ideal, leads the Blackshirts in their march on Rome, 1922. —Brown Bros. photo.

Fascist indoctrination of children in the cult of war. —Brown-Bros. photo.

Annual meetings of the League of Nations enabled statesmen to maintain personal contacts. Among the representatives shown leaving the League headquarters in Geneva in 1926 are (front row, left to right) Scialoia, Vandevelde, Luther, Briand, and Stresemann. —Brown Bros. photo.

Agreements designed for the mutual protection of countries in the Rhineland area were reached at Locarno, 1925. —Photo from The National Archives.

Contrast in living conditions between typical peasant farms in Rumania (top picture) and Czechoslovakia in the 1920's. —Photos from Doreen Warriner, *The Economics of Peasant Farming* (Oxford University Press, England), 1939, pp. 104 and 120. By permission of the author.

Unemployment: the waste of human resources in Great Britain. —Underwood & Underwood photo.

Poland transforms a marsh into the port of Gdynia. —Underwood & Underwood photo.

CHELSEA BRANCH
TENANTS' DEFENCE LEAGUE
WE DEMAND
BETTER HOUSES LOCALLY
AT
WE WANT WORK

JACQUES LIPCHITZ, *Figure*, 1926–1930. An artist's reflections on a man of the 1920's. –The Museum of Modern Art, New York; Van Gogh Purchase Fund.

and completed the work of giving the country a sound basis of peasant proprietorships. He tried to reform the legal system and to bring the execution of justice within the financial range of the people. He changed the system of taxation with the intention of distributing property more equitably than before. He aided the peasants by public works and introduced a compulsory labor service. In attempting to form a South Slav federation of peasant states, he hoped to create what has been called a Green International for the spread of his ideals about helping the peasantry.

Stamboliski's severe handling of enemies conformed to East European custom, and he has been condemned as overbearing and tactless. His peasant followers became somewhat unmanageable, as his party members, unused to power, sought quickly to fatten their purses. The end came in 1923, when the bourgeoisie and the army revolted and overthrew the government. Macedonian terrorists siding with the rebels caught Stamboliski, took him to his home, where they mutilated him, tortured him, forced him to dig his own grave, and put him to death. There followed a two-year manhunt for his supporters. Government of, by, and for peasants had lasted only three years; when the ruling groups were threatened by the masses, they temporarily buried their differences, joined forces, and suppressed the danger at the cost of dictatorship. They seemed to approve parliamentary government only as long as it sustained their authority.

Introduction of Authoritarian Rule

The political parties in the eastern tier of states tended to be numerous, weak in organization, and centered upon personalities. Wherever proportional representation was introduced, it aggravated the situation. Governments, formed by coalitions of parties, suffered from the incapacity to lead the country. Ministries rose and fell with such speed that, although many of the same individuals remained in office, continuity of policy was difficult or impossible. During the 1920's the Yugoslav cabinet changed on an average three times a year. A small country of homogeneous society like Finland, Estonia, or Latvia could in spite of this instability keep government and people in personal contact. Larger states found this intimacy impossible. In all of them leaders frequently believed that their policies were not merely the best but the only ones capable of serving the country. They reacted toward political colleagues and competitors as they had formerly done toward the foreign rulers: they grew stubborn and dogmatic, inclined to use any means, including force, to achieve their ends. They had not learned the need for rational discussion and compromise in the conduct of politics among persons of common good intentions. The problems of the new states were sufficiently vast and vital to have caused grave trouble in a country of mature political experience; these peoples were unprepared to deal with them on a democratic basis. They needed efficient governments at once; and when these were not forthcoming, especially at times of crisis the countries turned to authoritarianism.

Poland

The outstanding example was offered by Poland. When the constitution was drawn up, the majority of the convention favored the creation of a weak presidency, whereas Marshal Pilsudski wished that office to be given strong power. In the succeeding years the coalition cabinets proved incompetent to maintain a stable monetary system. The worst years occurred in 1922–1923, when the demands upon the government for funds led to severe inflation. Since the taxes supplied insufficient revenue, the budget became unbalanced. A new ministry created in 1924 with Professor Grabski in charge of finance was given emergency power, which it used to cut expenditures and restore the value of the currency. In stabilizing the zloty, Grabski made the mistake of overvaluation, which brought on severe depression. When the minister asked in 1925 for a renewal of his emergency authority, he failed to muster a majority in the *Sejm* and resigned. The next government was likewise unable to stem the demand for public expenditure, showed an unbalanced budget, and printed more money. The zloty began to fall in value and brought down the ministry. In 1926 the Peasant party leader Witos, who had been in power in the disastrous times of 1922–1923, took office with the usual coalition support. The public lacked confidence in his ability to save the zloty, and when he and his colleagues tried to eliminate the pro-Pilsudski personnel from command of the army, the marshal rebelled. In May 1926 Pilsudski overthrew the government and initiated a period of personal rule that lasted until his death nine years later.

The significance of the revolution must be understood in the light of Pilsudski's personal career and beliefs. This Polish aristocrat had devoted his life to the cause of nationalism. Born into a prosperous landed family, he early learned the fate of a patriot from the treatment of the Poles after the revolution of 1863. While a university student he turned to Marxian socialism as a means of furthering the unity and freedom of his people. The czarist government sent him to Siberia in 1887 for five years, and he returned to Poland an iron-souled conspirator against Russian rule. He entered the socialist party, waged guerrilla warfare against the Russians, was imprisoned, escaped by feigning madness, studied military history, and in the years preceding World War I organized a secret legion of Polish soldiers. During that war he worked constantly for Polish independence, which he believed more likely of achievement by cooperating with Austria and Germany than with Russia. When he refused to be a tool of these powers, he was imprisoned in Germany until the end of the conflict. Having become famous as the greatest Polish soldier of the period, he won a personal following among the army and the people that made him the most influential single figure in the country.

Pilsudski's experience in organizing diverse social forces and fighting for national independence had instilled in him the belief in leadership, in firm action, and in the use whenever necessary of extralegal means. He was convinced that in order to overcome internal dissension and to ward off foreign enemies the new state required concentrated authority. When he could not win the constitutional convention to his view he first protected the country against the Bolshevik invasion and then withdrew from public life. The attempt to remove his partisans in the army command induced him to interfere in politics by force. Most of the army and many workers and middle-class people swung to him: in a civil war lasting three days and concentrated in Warsaw, he won complete victory. The president and the cabinet resigned, the former transferring the authority to Pilsudski. "I made a kind of insurrection," the marshal subsequently wrote, "and succeeded in legalizing it at once."

After the revolution, Pilsudski refused to be either president or prime minister, but, knowing where power lay, he took over the ministry of war. He believed that for purposes of popular unity the *Sejm* should be preserved, and he caused the executive authority to be greatly strengthened, particularly in budgetary affairs. His chosen cabinet immediately overcame the financial troubles; and as the foreign bankers thought well of dictatorship under the circumstances, they granted Poland a large loan. The economy revived, and until the economic crisis struck the world Poland enjoyed its most prosperous and peaceful years. Pilsudski's rule had little similarity to that of Mussolini or Hitler; rather, it looked toward the past, to that of Louis Napoleon in France. Although it assumed at the moment only sufficient power to accomplish what Pilsudski thought necessary, time revealed that it did not escape the temptation to abuse arbitrary authority.

Succession States

The politics of the three beneficiaries of the destruction of the Hapsburg empire—Czechoslovakia, Yugoslavia, and Romania—and of the Austrian torso were complicated by the issue of centralism versus federalism. Before the war ended the leaders in exile of the first two states had reached agreement for the creation of a federal form of government, the Czechoslovakians by the Pittsburg Pact and the Yugoslavs by the Corfu Agreement. When the constitutions were being drawn, the issue immediately arose, and certain Slovak and Ruthenian leaders and almost all the Croats objected to them as violating the approved federal principles. The Czechs did not quite trust the political ability and devotion of the Slovaks and Ruthenians to the new republic, and the Serbs absolutely demanded to be the pivot for the Yugoslav state. Eagerness to make the states speedily successful enhanced the trouble, for given the condition of international uncertainty the leaders of these and of the other states felt pressed to accomplish everything at once. The situation in Czechoslovakia was largely corrected within a few years, when Slovaks joined their Czech colleagues in common political parties and in the government, and shared bureaucratic positions and authority throughout the state. Backward Ruthenia, which had been at first governed largely by Czechs, became an area where all three groups—Czechs, Slovaks and Ruthenians—cooperated.

In Yugoslavia the issue caused bitter fights between Serbs and Croats. The Croat leader, Stefan Radić, was addicted to obstructive tactics and could never formulate a constructive program for the Serbs. The latter, led by Nikola Pašić, one of the craftiest politicians of a region of guile and intrigue, was convinced that unity could be preserved solely by Serbian rule over the other peoples. Pašić had never approved federalism, and after his death in 1924 his Serb successors and the king, with occasional strategic retreats, continued the centralist policy. That the Serbs used their power to shift the greater tax burden to the other groups, that they monopolized the government positions, that they fattened on government contracts seemed to them entirely proper; the Croats (the pacific Slovenes scarcely counted) regarded these acts as humiliating. When in 1928 a Serb deputy shot Radić and several other Croat members of parliament, the Yugoslav state threatened to break up. In the emergency the king seized power and began a period of personal rule.

The problem appeared in Romania and Austria with a degree of intensity somewhere in between that in the other two states. The Liberal party, dominated by the Brătianu family, represented the old Romania and was centralist; the National Peasant party spoke for the leaders of some of the peasants in the old kingdom but especially for the new province of Transylvania, in favor of federalism. Until 1928 the Brătianus controlled the country by the use of political chicanery and force comparable to that of Pašić's Serbs. On the other hand, the relations among the parties kept within the bounds of acceptance of state unity.

Austrian political life was organized into two major parties, the Social Democratic and the Christian Socialist, and one minor party, the German Nationals. The first two were almost equally strong, and since the German Nationals normally sided with the Christian Socialists, the latter controlled the country during the period under review. The Social Democrats were revisionist Marxians, thoroughly hostile to communism, and led by men like Otto Bauer, Karl Renner, and Victor Adler, famous as thinkers and writers as well as political leaders. The party represented the trade-unions and drew its strength from Vienna and the few other industrial towns. Although many of its members were good Catholics, it was known as a body of freethinkers or atheists, and its advocacy of socializing private property enhanced its reputation among the rest of the population for radicalism. The Christian Socialist party represented the peasantry, the middle classes, and the Catholic hierarchy, and during the period a Catholic cleric, Monseigneur Seipel, acted as its leader. The Socialists favored centralized government; the Christian Socialists, strong in the provinces, advocated federalism. The party antagonism involved such basic issues of property, religion, and culture that the makings of a struggle between two ways of life were always present. Civil war did not break out mainly because of postwar exhaustion and the nearly equal strength of the two hostile groups. As the German Nationals, whose one policy was unification of Austria with Germany, favored tranquillity, the political life of the state continued on its doubtful way.

Greece

Although Greece had gained independence a century before, the people had never found political stability, nor were they to do so during the interwar period. Under the guise of a constitution the monarch and a few families with large landholdings had ruled the ignorant peasants and the townsmen with authoritarian firmness. In the years prior to World War I the urban population had increased in numbers and sought political influence. Combining with army officers discontented over the condition of the country, they had revolted in 1909 and called in Venizelos, a young lawyer from Crete, to be their political spokesman. This brilliant orator, astute thinker, and magnetic personality became the leader of the reform forces against the king and the great families. He preached a nationalistic creed of conquest of all the area around the Aegean Sea. He helped to engineer the First Balkan War in 1912 against the Ottoman Empire, by which Greece obtained Crete, Macedonia, and Epirus; and in the Second Balkan War, fought in 1913 among the former allies over the division of the spoils, Greece gained more land, this time from Bulgaria. The increase almost doubled the size of the country. At the peace conference in 1919 the Greek statesman played such a brilliant role that he gained for his country a large area in western Asia Minor. In the vicissitudes of party strife, the Liberals lost out in 1920, and King Constantine, exiled during the war, was able on the death of his ruling son to return to the throne.

In need of popularity, King Constantine and the great families now pushed the war i Asia Minor to protect the Greek acquisitions against the rejuvenated Turks under Mustapha Kemal Pasha. The disastrous defeat for the Greeks in that war and the resulting flood of more than a million refugees into Greece set the conditions for Greek political life during the next decade. Revolt against the royal government in 1922, the establishment of a republic in 1924 and of a dictatorship under General Pangalos in 1925–1926, the restoration of the republic in 1926, government under Venizelos as premier from 1928 to 1932—these events marked the continuing struggle between Liberals and the conservatives. When the Liberal party held power, especially after 1927, it introduced reforms, which the poor country needed—division of the large estates; road building; control of water resources, drainage, and irrigation projects; the settlement of the refugees with the help of foreign loans. The feeling of hostility between the two major political, social, and economic groups continued to be so intense, however, that the country could not settle down. The world depression struck it in the midst of the one short period of actual reform and relative calm during the interwar years.

Power of the Bureaucracy

In the daily life of the people the government of these thirteen states meant the bureaucracy. The intellectuals who flocked into public office were on the whole devoid of a sense of public trust. The peasantry was too ignorant and powerless to force correction of the abuses. The spoils system prevailed on a vast and effective scale. Some countries seemed to exist for the bureaucracy; the number of officials had no relation to need. In every European country the postwar bureaucracy expanded; in these new states it flourished. In 1908 Bulgaria had employed 35,920 officials; in 1934, 88,000 for an area of about the same size; and if municipal and communal officials are included, the number reached 140,000. Salaries and maintenance consumed more than two thirds of the national budget. Before the war Austria had expended 13 per cent of its taxable national income on public services, and in 1927, 31 per cent or more; Czechoslovakia, between 20 and 26 per cent. The poorer the country, the higher the percentage of officials it nourished, for the intelligentsia, increasing in number with each class graduating from the universities, succeeded in combining nationalism with the material demand for more official jobs.

The quality of the bureaucracy was highest in the northern states and in those which inherited officials trained in honesty and a degree of efficiency by former Austria. Those of former Hungary fell far below this standard, and as one entered Poland or the Balkans the public servants' corruption, laziness, arbitrariness equaled their feeling of social superiority. The lower officials received such small salaries that the temptation to graft often proved irresistible. A government contract, an inspection report, a tariff rate, a tax return, these and numerous other pieces of official business in these poor states carried the possibility of such economic advantage that officials succumbed to bribes. There were honest bureaucrats, but the concentration of politics among the few and the absence of enlightened masses opened the way to exploitation.

For similar reasons the protection of civil rights, so thoroughly guaranteed on paper, was deficient in practice. The officials mishandled peasants and workers, whose objections to such treatment could be silenced by a threatened accusation of communism and a term in prison. The Romanian officials enjoying a tasty tea while peasants waited in the anteroom, the summons of a defenseless person to the capital at his own expense in order to straighten out administrative trivia, the brutal seizure of property for taxes, the beating of private citizens—these and numerous other examples of violation of personal rights could be cited. Minorities were usually treated worse than nationals. Estonia introduced model relations with her minorities, but in Poland and Romania the officials' brutality became a world scandal, and well-governed Czechoslovakia in this respect was not entirely free from arbitrary action. Bureaucratic autocracy reflected the backwardness of these societies, and its elimination or persistence varied with the extent of improvement in living conditions.

ROLE OF THE CHURCH

The church did little or nothing toward alleviating conditions in either internal or international affairs. It had helped to preserve the culture of each people during the years of imperial submersion. It continued to bolster the basic political attitudes in the independent states. When the country consisted of largely one nationality, formerly dependent, with a common religion, as in Latvia and Estonia, the church added its social and political discipline to that of the government in transforming a subject people into a nation. Where, as in Finland, the Swedish minority—like the Finnish majority—belonged to the Lutheran religion, the church aided in bridging the difference between nationalities. In a country like Hungary, of uniform nationality but of divided religious affiliation, the fact that most Magyars were Roman Catholics and the others were either Lutheran or Calvinist affected political action only slightly; the nationalistic ardor transcended the sectarian. Austria, almost entirely German and Roman Catholic, suffered from social conflict between Social Democratic workers, supposedly antichurch but actually loyal to Roman Catholicism, and conservative aristocracy, bourgeoisie, and peasantry. The church actively sided with the latter group. In the multi-nationality states of Poland and Romania the Roman Catholic Poles mistrusted the political loyalty of all Germans, whether Lutheran or Roman Catholic, and of all Greek Orthodox White Russians and Ukrainians. Religious difference strengthened the centrifugal force of nationalism. Comparable conditions existed in Romania, where Greek Orthodox Romanians opposed Catholic or Protestant Magyars or Germans; but they had similar difficulty in relations with Greek Orthodox Ukrainians, Bulgarians, and Serbs.

In Czechoslovakia and Yugoslavia, religious differences aggravated cultural and political antagonism, less in the former state than in the latter. A larger number of Czechs belonged to the Roman Catholic Church than to a Protestant faith and had common religious affiliation with the Roman Catholic Slovaks. Slovak Catholics, however, mistrusted the Czechs as too tolerant of Protestantism and too independent of clerical influence. Greek Orthodoxy among the Ruthenians carried no more weight in state affairs than the people themselves; but in the west the German minority, Catholic or Protestant, definitely placed nationalistic antagonism to the Slavs above common religious affiliation. The South Slav state found the Roman Catholic Church to be a bulwark of Croat political aspiration, and the Greek Orthodox Church a main support of Serb demands to rule the state. Bulgaria and Greece, being almost entirely Greek Orthodox, used the church as an instrument for furthering nationalistic feeling.

In all these countries, from the Baltic to the Mediterranean, the state exercised in its financial support of the church a means of control over both state religious institutions and those of the minorities. The fact that religion formed a main ingredient of nationalism made state intimacy with a particular church a two-edged weapon. It added the emotionality of religion to the passions of nationalism, among majority and minority nationalities. Being representative of the elite, political leaders and church officials usually worked closely together and controlled the priests and pastors, who came from the docile peasantry. If in a state of homogeneous or nearly homogeneous nationality, they easily aroused the feelings of the population against foreign countries. If in a state of multi-nationalities, the leaders of each group in addition to poisoning foreign relations stirred up animosity against the others.

RELATIONS AMONG THE STATES

The thirteen states with a combined population of 116 million people inexperienced in self-government, and economically undeveloped, lay between Russia with nearly 150 million people, on the one hand, and Germany with 65 million and Italy with 41 million, on the other. During the 1920's Russia was too exhausted and too engrossed in internal difficulties to take much initiative in international affairs, but the imperialist objectives of her Communist leaders were frankly stated. Germany never willingly assented to the peace settlement in the east as she did that in the west. She planned to regain the possessions lost to Poland and Lithuania and to absorb Austria; and her staunch Nationalists still dreamed of imperialist conquest from the Baltic to the Mediterranean. It was to be expected that upon recovery of her strength she would quickly seek to change the eastern frontiers.

After the rise of Mussolini Italy sought to dominate the Danubian-Balkan states. With the acquiescence of Great Britain and France but against the will of Yugoslavia and Greece, she gained full control of supposedly independent Albania. Italian economic aid and a treaty in 1926 of "mutual support and cordial collaboration," followed in the next year by a formal military alliance, marked the steps in this process. When in 1928 the political leader, Ahmed Zogu, declared himself "King of the Albanians" with Italian approval, the Yugoslavs saw in this act a bold assertion of Italy's intention to break up their state: Yugoslavia contained an

Albanian minority. Italy intrigued with Hungary and Bulgaria and encouraged their demands for revision of the peace treaties; she attacked Greece in the Corfu incident; she took Fiume and territory along the Dalmatian coast by force. Although by far the weakest of the three sources of danger, prior to the emergence of National Socialism in Germany, Italy caused most trouble. The Western great powers interfered in this region occasionally and helped to prevent peaceful, active cooperation from developing, but their political role was of lesser significance. The thirteen states had every reason to anticipate attempts by their neighbors to destroy their independence. How did they use the few years of security granted by the weakness of Germany and Russia to prepare for future crises?

The efforts in this region to set up mutual defense amounted to almost nothing. The leaders subsequently offered a thousand alibis, the main one being the value of national sovereignty for enabling each people to live according to its own wishes and develop its own culture. Unfortunately, within two decades national sovereignty was to prove incapable of preserving national culture. Federal union might have enabled these thirteen states to impress big neighbors with the risk of attack, but few people, and those were mainly dreamers or Poles ambitious of empire, thought of such a possibility. A system had not been evolved by which peoples of diverse national culture and scattered across a continent could allow cultural autonomy while pooling their resources for protection. The states became some of the staunchest supporters of the League of Nations, but in that amorphous body as well they opposed any move which would have restricted their own independence in favor of a supernational organization endowed with real power to act.

The manner in which the new states used the decade of respite exemplifies the shortcomings of interwar nationalistic statesmanship. Each of the Baltic states and Finland and Poland had had to defend itself by war against the Russian Communists; and Bolshevik power, even though quiescent, was steadily increasing. Each Baltic state sought in every way to reassure the Russians that it had no hostile intentions and that it would not permit anyone to use its territory as a basis of attack. Latvia and Estonia guaranteed freedom of transit and extensive port facilities to the Communists. Estonia and Russia agreed on the creation of a neutral zone. Nonetheless, Russia aided an attempted *putsch* in 1924 against that small state. To counter the common danger, the states negotiated each year over defensive treaties, regional pacts, customs unions, and the like. Finland decided that she was a Scandinavian country and refused to join the Baltic states in an alliance. Lithuania was so angry at Poland for seizing Vilna that she would participate in nothing with that state and broke off not merely diplomatic but all commercial relations. In 1923 she seized Memel, then under the auspices of the League of Nations, and thereby angered Germany.

Estonia and Latvia had quarreled over their boundary line; but they worked together better than any of the others. They disliked the prospect of becoming involved in the Polish-Lithuanian dispute and equally that of siding with aggressive Poland against the Soviets. The total result of the negotiations by all these peoples living under the shadow of their great eastern enemy was a defensive alliance of 1923 between Estonia and Latvia, each with an army in 1926 of 20,000 men. The Bolsheviks signed a treaty of nonaggression and peaceful settlement of disputes with each state, using the Kellogg pact to outlaw war as the occasion for this achievement. These pacts remained in force until, during and after World War II, the Soviet Union swallowed the three Baltic states and went to war with Finland.

Nursing pretensions to be a great power, Poland behaved with superior self-confidence toward her neighbors, including Germany and the Soviet Union, quarreling with them all. The government alienated Lithuania by taking Vilna. Polish leaders at Versailles had claimed that the Lithuanians were incapable of self-government and should be ruled by Poland, and that attitude persisted. Polish imperialistic ambitions seemed to rise with the state itself. In 1920 Pilsudski proposed a federation of free states from the Baltic to the Black Sea as means of withstanding the aggression of Bolshevik Russia. He advocated assisting the nationality groups, like the Ukrainians, to separate from Russia and form independent states within this federation; but he achieved no tangible results. The behavior of his own government aroused mistrust among the prospective members. In the war with the Bolsheviks Poland gained by the treaty of Riga in 1921 part of White Russia and the Ukraine—she had seemed to aim to take all of the Ukraine—and her relations with the Soviet Union were henceforth cool at best.

Poland began life alongside Czechoslovakia by quarreling over the possession of Teschen and two neighboring bits of territory. A treaty of friendship negotiated in 1921 between the two states was never ratified. Poland's proposal to join the Little Entente came to naught, as did a Polish offer of alliance to Czechoslovakia early in 1926. The two eastern allies of France, contiguous in territory and subject to the same geopolitical dangers, never established good working relations. Poland's relations with Germany were bad from the start, for Poland had been the main beneficiary from Germany's loss of land. A tariff war after 1925 and a constant flow of recrimination over the treatment of their respective minorities expressed their mutual aversion. Poland was apparently more able to reach accord with states some distance away than with immediate neighbors. In 1921 she signed a defensive alliance with Romania against an attack from Russia, and we have already discussed her treaty with France.

During the twenties the relations of the Danubian states centered upon one source of danger, that of a revived Hungary. Czechoslovakia, Romania, and Yugoslavia as the beneficiaries of Hungary's dismemberment determined to keep that imperious state in check. The effort of Hungary to remain a kingdom with the manifest aim of restoring her former frontier and two attempts of Charles of Hapsburg to return to the Hungarian throne induced the three opposing states to join forces. In 1920–1921 they formed a defensive alliance against attack from Hungary, and they persuaded the great powers to ban the Hapsburgs from that country. The Little Entente consisted of three treaties, one between Czechoslovakia and Yugoslavia, one between Czechoslovakia and Romania, and one between Yugoslavia and Romania. These, together with the treaties of alliance between France and Czechoslovakia and France and Poland, served as the foundation of international stability in the East European area.

The relations among the Balkan states were complicated by difficulties among all the nations, but Bulgaria was a common object of mistrust by all the others. Having been on the defeated side in the war, Bulgaria had lost the Dobruja to Romania, territory in the west to Yugoslavia, and had seen Greece take coveted Macedonia and part of Thrace. The alliance between Romania and Yugoslavia, aimed at Hungary, also included similar terms with respect to Bulgaria. That they also signed a treaty of nonaggression with France did little to improve their situation in the Balkans.

The corner where Bulgaria, Yugoslavia, and Greece meet offered particularly favorable conditions for the complications of international politics. In that area Macedonian terrorists were active, some for one side, some for another. Border raids were customary; even if they had so desired, governments seemed incapable of stopping the useless slaughter. Whether these raids were actuated by patriotism or by the lust for adventure and for robbery cannot be judged. Young men went there to show their courage by learning how to kill. Occasionally the raids led to shooting between regular troops, as occurred in 1925, when General Pangalos temporarily ruled Greece as dictator. The League settled that quarrel; but during this decade nothing was done to clean out the Macedonian disturbers.

A little farther to the west, Albania, with Italian connivance, acted as the center of trouble. The drawing of a frontier between that country and Greece led to the Corfu incident already discussed. When Greece divided the large estates in the northern part of the country, Albania protested that property owned by her people had been expropriated. Greek boundary difficulties with Yugoslavia persisted. Where peoples were poor and dissatisfied, tempers short, traditional methods those of physical coercion, states found easy excuses for conflict with their neighbors. Local hatred surpassed fear of major powers farther away. The Albanian rulers preferred to become satellites of Italy rather than to harmonize their interests with Yugoslavia and Greece, who were likewise subject to Italy's imperialist thrusts.

The Little Entente pertained to Hungary (population 8,700,000) and partly to Bulgaria (population 6,000,000). Neither it nor, with the exception of the defensive alliance between Poland and Romania, any other treaty among these thirteen states concerned the potential danger from the Soviet Union or Germany.

The relations among the states of Eastern Europe were of too recent origin and too uncertain in nature for an eastern Locarno to be acceptable. From Finland to Greece political conditions had changed so rapidly after 1914 that one could not know whether they would endure. When states became independent for the first time in 700 years, when states were created that less than a century and a half earlier had lost their independence because of political incompetence, when territories changed hands several times in the course of a decade, when century-old empires were broken up, economic and social ties and unities destroyed, and an entirely new political organization created, when people devoid of political experience suddenly started a career of self-government—when such cataclysmic changes occurred, statesmen in old and established Western countries, and in Germany and Russia, might well ask how long these states would last. Uncertainty about the future policies of the Soviet Union discouraged every nation except France from agreeing to defend a state system in which the small members were physically incapable of contributing much toward protecting themselves and were unable to settle their own regional problems and to cooperate for their own defense. France looked upon them, not as constituting a regional problem of their own, but as actual or potential aid against Germany. The warning of the English historian attached to the British Foreign Office, Headlam-Morley, was unheeded.

> Has anyone attempted to realize what would happen if there were to be a new partition of Poland, or if the Czechoslovak state were to be so curtailed and dismembered that in fact it disappeared from the map of Europe? The whole of Europe would at once be in chaos. There would no longer be any principle, meaning, or sense in the territorial arrangements of the continent. Imagine, for instance, that under some improbable condition, Austria rejoined Germany; that Germany using the discontented minority in Bohemia, demanded a new frontier far over the mountains, including Carlsbad and Pilsen, and that at the same time, in alliance with Germany, the Hungarians recovered the southern slope of the Carpathians. This would be catastrophic, and, even if we neglected to intervene in time to prevent it, we should afterwards be driven to interfere, probably too late.[2]

With cultural bonds lacking and economic relations deficient in organization and to a large extent devoid of mutual advantage, these peoples built their society on the basis of national self-determination. "A state of effervescence set in," wrote Professor Ants Oras about the early days of his native Estonia, "that it is still a delight to remember." The nations were making mistakes but they were learning in the process. By the end of their first decade some were progressing at a rapid rate; the others, in spite of corruption and inefficiency, were in better condition than they had been

[2] James Headlam-Morley, *Studies in Diplomatic History* (London: Methuen & Company, Ltd., 1929), pp. 182-184.

prior to the war. All could credit their achievements primarily to their own efforts; for the great powers and, except on technical matters of finance, the League of Nations had supplied slight assistance. The important sources of danger to them lay beyond their control. Would the economy of the world continue on even keel and enable them to maintain their own weak economic systems? They lacked the resources and strength to influence the course of the business cycle and prevent depression. Would their neighbor great powers permit them to survive? In the international economic and political system these thirteen new and inexperienced nations led a precarious existence.

Suggestions for Further Reading

HERTZ, FRIEDRICH O. *The Economic Problem of the Danubian States: A Study in Economic Nationalism.* London: Victor Gollancz, Ltd., 1947. By a distinguished Austrian scholar. Excellent.

MACARTNEY, C. A. *Hungary and Her Successors.* New York: Oxford University Press, 1937. Portrays in detail the way of life of the peoples in the entire region.

MOORE, WILBERT E. *Economic Demography of Eastern and Southern Europe.* Geneva: League of Nations, 1945. Invaluable on economic conditions and population growth.

REDDAWAY, W. F. *Problems of the Baltic.* Cambridge, Mass.: Harvard University Press, 1940. Brief and useful.

ROBERTS, HENRY L. *Rumania: Political Problems of an Agrarian State.* New Haven, Conn.: Yale University Press, 1951. Thorough study of social, economic, and political conditions.

SCHMITT, BERNADOTTE E., ed. *Poland.* Berkeley: University of California Press, 1945. By several Polish and other authors. Useful survey.

SETON-WATSON, HUGH. *Eastern Europe between Two Wars, 1918–1941.* New York: The Macmillan Company, 1945. Indispensable analysis of many aspects of life on a comparative basis. The best single work on the region.

TOMASEVICH, JOSA. *Peasants, Politics and Economic Change in Yugoslavia.* Stanford, Calif.: Stanford University Press, 1955. Illuminating for a much larger area than Yugoslavia.

Chapter 10 · The U.S.S.R.

THEORETICAL FOUNDATION

The Communists who seized control of Russia in 1917 proposed to establish a society different in every respect from that of the Western or free world. The institutions and practices which they introduced have evolved into a working system, the intrinsic weakness of which in some aspects has been compensated by strength in other aspects. Although subject to change, Communist society in the U.S.S.R. has remained loyal to the fundamentals of Lenin. In the present chapter, devoted to the pre-Stalinist period, we shall emphasize the creation of instruments of political authority and the experiments made in seeking to organize society according to Communist ideals. Inasmuch as the economic structure did not receive final form until Stalin seized power toward the end of the decade, we shall discuss it in a later chapter.

Unlike democratic societies, the Communist state was built solely upon an untried theory evolved by a small number of revolutionary intellectuals. Although every Communist had to know the writings of Karl Marx and Friedrich Engels, the fathers of scientific socialism, it will suffice for our purposes to discuss the ideas of their successor, Lenin, who adapted the theories of his two predecessors to what he considered the needs of changed circumstances. His views in turn were subjected to interpretations by his successor Stalin, and those of Stalin have been modified by men who followed him in power. Nonetheless, Lenin remains the most important theorist for the Soviet state, as he is the person most responsible for the establishment of the Communist regime in Russia and for the nature of that regime. We may first consider the objectives of social and political organization which he set and then the methods which he institutionalized in order to achieve these objectives. Analysis reveals that the Communists, including Lenin, had an exceedingly vague conception of their ultimate society. They soon recognized that they could not introduce communism at once or even in the foreseeable future. Thus they were mainly concerned with holding power to enable them to work toward a social objective as yet scarcely defined. It remained for Stalin to postpone the realization of communism to an indefinite future; but the ideal continued to haunt the minds of the orthodox and to stimulate all Communists, especially in times of trouble, to renewed zeal. It has always been useful in propaganda.

The Communists were far more fluent in denouncing the kinds of society which they hated than in portraying that which they sought. Since the bourgeois capitalistic society of the West was efficient and strong, they paid particular attention to attacking it. An exposition of communist theory may begin with the following quotation from Lenin (July 4, 1920):

> The victory over capitalism requires a proper correlation between the leading, Communist, Party, the revolutionary class—the proletariat—and the masses, i.e., all the toilers and exploited. The Communist Party alone, if it is really the vanguard of the revolutionary class, if it really contains all its best representatives, if it consists of fully conscious and loyal Communists who have been educated and hardened by the experience of the persistent revolutionary struggle, if this Party has succeeded in linking itself inseparably with the whole life of its class, and through it, with the whole mass of exploited, and if it has succeeded in completely winning the confidence of this class and this mass—such a Party alone is capable of leading the proletariat in the most ruthless, decisive and final struggle against all the forces of capitalism. On the other hand, only under the leadership of such a Party can the proletariat display the full force of its revolutionary onslaught and neutralize the inevitable apathy and sometimes resistance of the small minority of the aristocracy of labour, the old trade union and co-operative leaders, etc., who have been corrupted by capitalism—only then will it be able to display its whole might, which is immeasurably greater than the proportion of the population it represents owing to the very economic structure of capitalist society. Finally, only after they have been actually emancipated from the yoke of the bourgeoisie and of the bourgeois state apparatus, only after they have obtained the opportunity of organising in their Soviets in a really free (from the exploiters) manner, can the masses, i.e., all the toilers and the exploited, for the first time in history, display all the initiative and energy of tens of millions of people who had been crushed by capitalism. Only when the Soviets have become the sole state apparatus is it possible really to secure the participation in the work of administration of the whole mass of exploited, ninety-nine hundredths of whom even under the most enlightened and free bourgeois democracy were actually debarred from taking part in the work of administration. Only in the Soviets do the masses of exploited really begin to learn, not from booklets, but from their own practical experience, the work of Socialist construction, of creating a new social discipline, a free union of free workers.

"A new epoch in world history," Lenin declared on April 15, 1919, "has begun."

The new society would include the election and recall of the officials by the people "without any bureaucratic formalities." The army and the police should be replaced by "the universal arming of the people." Although discipline and subordination would be necessary, there should be established "on a nation-wide scale a precise and scrupulous system of accounting and control, *control by the workers,* over the production and distribution of commodities." The management of industries and banks would consist merely of the "simple operations of registration, filing and checking that . . . can be easily performed by every literate person." There should be equality of compensation for all kinds of work, "so that the technicians, managers, bookkeepers, as well as *all* officials, shall receive salaries no higher than 'workmen's wages.'" "When people have become so accustomed to observing the fundamental rules of social life and when their labour is so productive that they will voluntarily work *according to their ability*," then, Lenin declared, the whole state apparatus will wither away. "From each one according to his ability and to each one according to his needs," was the summary slogan. This economic determinist believed that human nature would change with the environment, that communist society would develop *pari passu* with communist man, each the antithesis of its hostile bourgeois predecessor.

Condemnation of Bourgeois Capitalism

Lenin's vagueness about the nature of the future communist society contrasted with the concreteness of his analysis of the bourgeois order. Capitalism, he said, meant competition, class struggle, war, and brutal exploitation. "Competition among individual enterprises," he said, "makes it inevitable for the entrepreneurs either to become ruined, or to ruin others." "Competition between individual countries places before each of them the alternative of either remaining behind . . . or ruining and conquering other countries." From this analysis he drew two conclusions:

> Thousands and tens of thousands of men and women, toiling all their lives to create wealth for others, perish from starvation and constant underfeeding, prematurely die from diseases caused by the horrible conditions . . . in which they live and overwork. He who prefers death in the open struggle against those who defend and protect this horrible system, rather than the lingering death of a crushed, broken-down and submissive hag, deserves the title of hero a hundredfold.

When Lenin spoke about the leaders of trade-unions in a country like Germany, who cooperated with the capitalists and refused to join the Communists, he used phrases like "a handful of arch scoundrels," "the filthiest blackguards," "the most revolting executioners." In July, 1919, he declared:

> They [the German Social Democrats] failed to understand that voting within the limits, the institutions, the customs of bourgeois parliamentarism is *part* of the bourgeois state apparatus which must be broken and smashed from top to bottom *in order* to effect the dictatorship of the proletariat, in order to pass from bourgeois democracy to proletarian democracy.
>
> . . . . . .
>
> They failed to understand that the dictatorship of the proletariat is the rule of *one* class, which takes into its hands the *whole* apparatus of the new state,

which *vanquishes* the bourgeoisie and *neutralizes* the whole of the petty bourgeoisie, the peasantry, the lower middle class and the intelligentsia.

Lenin rarely wasted words in denouncing the bourgeoisie; he merely stated the means essential to destroy them:

> Only the violent overthrow of the bourgeoisie, the confiscation of its property, the destruction of the whole of the bourgeois state apparatus from top to bottom—parliamentary, judicial, military, bureaucratic, administrative, municipal, etc., right up to the very wholesale deportation or internment of the most dangerous and stubborn exploiters—putting them under strict surveillance in order to combat inevitable attempts to resist and to restore capitalist slavery—only such measures can ensure the real subordination of the whole class of exploiters.

Believing that the "victory over the bourgeoisie is impossible without a long, stubborn and desperate war of life and death, a war which requires perseverance, discipline, firmness, indomitableness and unity of will," Lenin demanded "the strictest discipline, truly iron discipline in our Party," together with "absolute centralization." The party must "periodically purge" the membership in order to eliminate any weakling or petty bourgeois elements. It must be organized on the principle of "democratic *centralism*."

An International Movement

Whether communism could be achieved in one country without constant attack from bourgeois-capitalist countries or whether it must pause before conquering all peoples was a question which has been debated in Communist circles at least ever since the seizure of power in Russia. Lenin expected the movement to conquer every people: "The victory of the proletarian revolution all over the world is assured," he declared in March, 1919. "The foundation of the international Soviet Republic is impending." Although he later modified this prediction, he and the other Communists formed in 1919 the Third International, or Comintern, as it came to be called, as the world organization of Communists. In it they demanded iron discipline and centralized authority:

> Every party that wishes to affiliate to the Communist International must render selflessly devoted assistance to every Soviet republic in its struggle against counter-revolutionary forces. . . . All the decisions of the congresses of the Communist International, as well as the decisions of its Executive Committee, are binding upon all parties affiliated to the Communist International.

That is to say, the British or French Communist party must defend the Communist regime in Russia and must place the commands of the Communist International above the interests and laws of its own nation-state.

Lenin laid down the policies by which he and his colleagues had gained power in Russia and by which he expected the Communists to repeat their achievement in other countries.

> . . . it is necessary, immediately, for all legal Communist Parties to form illegal organizations for the purpose of systematically carrying on illegal work, and of fully preparing for the moment when the bourgeoisie resorts to persecution. Illegal work is particularly necessary in the army, the navy and police. . . . On the other hand, it is also necessary, in all cases without exception, not to restrict oneself to illegal work, but also to carry on legal work, overcoming all obstacles that stand in the way of this, forming legal organs of the press and legal organizations under the most varied titles, which may often be changed in the event of necessity.

He argued that the struggle against the bourgeoisie must be "sanguinary and bloodless, violent and peaceful, military and economic, educational and administrative." One word of caution was required.

> To accept battle at a time when it is obviously advantageous to the enemy and not to us is a crime [Lenin wrote in 1920] and those political leaders of the revolutionary class who are unable "to tack, to manoeuvre, to compromise," in order to avoid an obviously disadvantageous battle, are good for nothing.

Dialectical Materialism

A small group striving for extreme objectives and employing radical means to achieve them needed some built-in assurance that it would win. The Communists found that stimulus in the theory of dialectical materialism. They believed that the mode of production determined the character of the entire culture. If a capitalistic system of production of material goods existed, the culture would be bourgeois capitalist—in government, the arts, social organization, religion, everything. If the communist system of production of material goods prevailed, the entire culture would be communist. The Communists could force the natural adaptation to the new environment. Capitalism, they argued, herds the masses into factories, and because of the necessity of competition, it reduces wages and working conditions to the point of common misery and accumulates the ownership of property in the hands of a few individuals. It therefore unintentionally teaches the workers, and the employees, who are likewise crushed, the principles of communism, of working together without owning any private property except a few personal items. When the Communist leaders point out this abuse the workers and employees will rebel, destroy the owners, take over control of the property, and communism will be there. By a dialectical process capitalism will have transformed itself into communism.

To the Communists it was essential that big industry be developed; for with it would come a proletariat and through this proletariat the social and political basis of communism. The peasant owned and loved private property and was a danger to communism; the proletariat, free from the shackles of private possession, would make the ideal Communist. With enough big industry, communism was inevitable. Lenin added that one should not use the theory of inevitability as an excuse not to fight for the goal; he demanded that theories be tested by facts, as he had done in 1917. The theory at that time called for the creation of a capitalistic society in Russia before communism could be introduced. Lenin jumped over the bourgeois-capitalist stage of development to that under Communistic control, and let the theory of dialectical materialism adjust itself to the new historical fact.

The theory condemns any belief in forces not subject to direct human control. Since the Communists planned speedily to change society, they eliminated belief in all supernatural power and in all influences of so slow-working a character as to lie beyond the ability of the Communists to change. Hence Lenin said, "We must combat religion." The reason he gave runs as follows: "The roots of religion today are to be found in the social oppression of the masses, in their apparently complete helplessness in face of the blind forces of capitalism." In the same way the Communists came to denounce the power of heredity to affect the character of living things. They believed in the influence of the environment as determining the nature of life, for they could subject the environment to Communist dictatorship, whereas heredity, like supernatural religion, lay outside their domination. Belief in the determining power of the mode of production allowed no place for forces which do not adjust to change in the system of property ownership and of turning out material goods.

The Leaders

The individuals who led the Communist party in Russia had a background of experience conducive to radical ideas. They were intellectuals rather than workers, many of them members of minority groups that had long been subject to persecution. The police had rarely allowed them to live in Russia but had driven them to spend most of their adult life abroad. Whenever clandestinely in Russia they had constantly risked being arrested and sent to Siberia or executed. They rarely had any family life; if married, they usually had no children, and husband and wife participated in the revolutionary activity. As exiles they had studied, written, tried to smuggle their writings into Russia, and quarreled among themselves over points of dogma. When in Russia they had kept on the move, organizing secret cells, spreading propaganda, collecting meager funds to continue the work. It was a life of frustration, of poverty, of constant danger, of uncertainty whether their colleagues were stool pigeons, of bitterness and hatred, of lack of contact with or understanding of any of the constructive forces in society. This kind of experience among intellectuals with passionate ambition to save the world from itself and in spite of itself does not entirely account for the nature of communism, but it helps to explain its radicalism.

Lenin offers no exception. He differed from his colleagues only in ability and in the courage not merely to argue in favor of his views but to act. From 1917 until his death in 1924 he was recognized as the leader, the source of ultimate authority, a position which he maintained by brilliant analysis of social and political situations and formulation of policies, by his realism in learning from mistakes, and by his stubborn defense of essentials while compromising on matters of less significance. He was an opportunist in the choice of methods, and among other things he appreciated the value to the proletariat of the cultural achievement of mankind. With respect to the necessity of communism he remained a ruthless dogmatist.

CIVIL WAR AND CHAOS

During the three years 1918 through 1920 Russia plunged into chaos as far as society could go and survive. These conditions were brought about by the disintegration of the army, the revolution, the issuance of Communist decrees, the civil war, and foreign intervention. Except for the last named, which was of significance mainly as a cause for alarm to Communist leaders, any one of the other four would have sufficed to upset a country. Occurring simultaneously in incompetent, disorganized Russia, they spelled ruin.

With the onset of revolution millions of soldiers deserted and either went home or joined the ranks of the revolutionaries in the cities. No authority existed to help them; boldness in scrounging aided the venturesome ones to survive. Most of the others were peasants, who returned home to partition landed estates. For months Russia teemed with these self-demobilized fighters, armed and carrying out the revolution wherever they went, unconsciously preparing the way for the Communists.

Lenin had expected to take over the existing organization of finance, production, and distribution and much of the government and, while developing the communist society, to use the expert knowledge and ability of the professional middle class. He knew that the Communists lacked the personnel to assume these responsibilities immediately, and he was willing to maintain a differential scale of income during a transitional period. His noted practical judgment of people and situations failed him in this instance, as in many others. The bourgeois experts refused on the whole—there were exceptions—to cooperate with a band which it regarded as ferocious and unprincipled, and the left wing of the Communists demanded immediate execution of the program. The Communist government nationalized banks, industries, commercial establishments, and land—even the small units—and the handicrafts. The systems of transportation and communication already belonged to the state; but the government now added all printing and publishing business, all theaters, large dwelling houses, and municipal services. It forbade private trade, introduced a system of rationing for the urban population, and allocated housing, fuel and light, transportation, entertainment, and newspapers. The peasants were ordered to turn over to state collecting agencies all food and raw materials above a certain amount kept for their own use. Since the Communists considered money "a testimony of the right of the exploiter to obtain social goods with a view to speculation, profit, and plundering the workers," they immediately started printing more of it. Thereby they achieved two objectives: first, they obtained easy money, which in spite of their scorn of it they desperately needed; second, by the resulting inflation they quickly destroyed the value of the monetary system and completed the pauperization of the middle class and aristocracy, already deprived of their property.

The effects surprised the Communists. The workers in the factories enjoyed the experience of running the industries themselves. They held endless soviets, or meetings, over questions of what to do and how to do it, if they did decide to do it. The index of industrial production fell as follows:

	1913	*1916*	*1917*	*1918*	*1919*	*1920*
LARGE SCALE	100.0	116.1	74.8	33.8	14.9	12.8
SMALL SCALE	100.0	88.2	78.4	73.5	49.0	44.1
TOTAL	100.0	109.4	75.7	43.4	23.1	20.4

SOURCE: *Communism in Action* (Washington, D.C.: Government Printing Office, 1946), p. 2.

Since industry offered the peasant nothing and money was worthless, he refused to supply the urban population with food. "We can do without kerosene," the peasant declared. "Let's see if he (the townsman) can do without grain."[1] The transportation system, already badly crippled during the war, collapsed. The war between townsmen and countrymen began; the latter hoarded food and the former, threatened with starvation, flocked to the country with a bag of possessions to trade for food. Fuel was so lacking that people tore down houses for wood. In the desperate effort to keep alive, two thirds of its inhabitants abandoned Petrograd.

The Communists knew that their survival depended upon the reaction of the urban workers. If these turned against them, the communist experiment was doomed. Lenin and his group strove to supply food at least to the workers, irrespective of cost. That a little freedom and responsible government would have immediately started Russia on the way to revival meant nothing to these men, for such a policy would have entailed the sacrifice of communism. This was not the last time that the Communists were willing to see millions of lives destroyed in order to introduce the only system of society which they thought would make men happy. They sent task forces in the country to seize food; when the peasants hid their supplies, the raiders applied torture or burned cottage and barn and carried off the spoils. For the time being the Communists obtained food, which they immediately used for political purposes. The city proletariat and party members received rations; persons of the upper classes were fed only

[1] Bernard Pares, *Russia* (Baltimore: Penguin Books, Inc., 1943), p. 121. Copyright, 1943, 1949 by The New American Library of World Literature.

if it was to Communist advantage to keep them alive. The control of food offered a convenient means of eliminating class enemies. That the task forces frequently took the peasants' seed grain was evident at next year's harvest, and nature aided their action by drought. Starvation spread to the countryside, where people ate weeds, bark, anything; instances of cannibalism occurred. Disease attacked the weakened bodies, and epidemics spread over the land.

The disintegration of Russian life was accentuated by the refusal of military forces to acquiesce in Communist rule. These groups were scattered around the periphery of the state, whereas the Communist party held the center and the cities. The military operated hundreds of miles apart without the facilities of transportation and communication for coordinating their activities. At Yaroslavl, not far to the north of Moscow, a group of army officers rose in July, 1918, fought courageously for a few days, and was suppressed. In the Kuban, in the far south, other officers gathered around Generals Alekseev and Kornilov, and, after the early death of these two officers, around General Deniken.

On the lower Volga another center of resistance, inspired mainly by civilians, was created; it depended upon the legion of Czech soldiers to the east in Siberia. These Czechs had deserted from the Austrian army during the war and had fought on the Russian side. They remained together after the revolution and negotiated with the Communists an agreement to permit them to return home across Siberia. The Communist government secretly instructed its officials to arrest them all as soon as they had laid down arms; but the Czechs were too well informed to fall into any such trap. They retained their strength, successfully resisted arrest, and controlled the whole trans-Siberian railway as they slowly crossed to Vladivostok. Their presence aided other centers of resistance in Siberia, at Chita, and at Omsk, where Admiral Kolchak took charge.

In the Far East at Vladivostok an assortment of Allied troops, Japanese, American, British, French, Poles, Italians, Serbs, and Czechs, spent their time less in fighting the Bolsheviks than in quarreling among themselves. In European Russia, the Allies occupied Archangel and the British and French sent troops and supplies into the south by way of the Black Sea. General Yudenich advanced on Petrograd from the Estonian frontier, the Ukrainians rebelled under Petlyura, and the Poles invaded Russia under Pilsudski. None of the forces of resistance reached impressive size; the leaders proved to be no statesmen, quarreling rather than planning a common strategy. Kolchak advanced west alone, succeeded for a time, and then was defeated and driven back. Later, Deniken attained striking distance of Moscow before he was defeated. After Wrangel took over Deniken's command, his forces were driven into the Crimea and withdrew to the Bosphorus. Yudenich reached the outskirts of Petrograd before he was defeated. And so it went. Each in turn was eliminated; and after the surrender of the central powers in November, 1918, the Allies lost heart and in 1919 withdrew from Archangel and from the south.

In explaining the survival of the Bolsheviks, Lenin recognized that the Western powers were so busy fighting one another that they could not concentrate upon destroying the Communists in Russia. He added that the vast size and the cultural backwardness of the country enabled the Communists to hold pockets of power from which they could gradually extend their conquest. The peasants' hatred of the landlords and their fear of the officer class prevented the Whites, as the forces of Deniken and the others of the former society were called, from gaining popular support. Since many peasants likewise hated the Communists, they frequently opposed the side that happened at the time to be pillaging their neighborhood. Their indifference enabled the party that finally won in the civil war to expand control over them. All of these favorable circumstances would not have meant victory for the Bolsheviks, Lenin knew, if the latter had not organized under the direction of Leon Trotsky an effective fighting force of their own.

Organization of Red Army

Trotsky had spent his life as a professional revolutionary with journalism as a means of livelihood. Although inexperienced in military affairs, his brilliance in analyzing a problem, his speed in learning, and his care in attending to details came to his aid. Resourceful and optimistic, a brilliant orator, a daring experimenter with ideas often anathema to colleagues, he inclined to be rash, domineering, and dogmatic. Assigned the duty of forming an army, he soon realized that he would need to employ the services of officers from the czarist army in training and leading the raw recruits. He speedily eradicated the Bolshevik ideas about soldiers electing their officers and holding soviets on questions of strategy and tactics. He reintroduced discipline, hierarchical organization, and chain of command. Instead of developing a nation in arms, a people's army, he obtained personnel wherever and however he could; but the backbone of the new army consisted of the industrial proletariat. Throughout the new force were stationed trustworthy Communists as political commissars, who had the authority necessary to enforce loyalty to the new government.

By November, 1918, Trotsky had accumulated an army of 23,000 former officers and military civil servants, 110,000 former noncommissioned officers from the old army, and 164,000 private soldiers. It was a heterogeneous, often antagonistic array. The officers had recently been denounced as class enemies and were still mistrusted. The political commissars were regarded by the officers as persecutors of the upper classes and as traitors to the country. The noncommissioned officers believed that they as loyal sons of the revolutionary class should be given the positions of command. The peasant soldiers often hated military service, were disobedient, and sought to go home. The uncertain future of the Bolshevik regime was reflected in the army, where a sense of loyalty was as yet absent.

The difficulties arising from the use of officers from the czarist army exemplified the complications to be met in every aspect of a social revolution. The Bolsheviks employed these officers to staff command courses for training raw young Communists to be officers. One of the trainers wrote in his report (1919) that although most of the Red officers belonged to the Communist party, they had little stability and lacked the general and the military education formerly acquired in a good school for noncommissioned officers. The young Red officers accused these czarist holdovers of being selfish and egotistical, of misusing their power, and of behaving, not in the comradely way of Communists, but in the autocratic way of the former army. The czarist officers, however, were willing to apply their expert knowledge in return for the right to exist; the young Communist officers showed enthusiasm, exalted ideals, and the expectation of an entirely new standard of behavior.

The lasting success of the Red army must be credited to the young men who, inspired by the opportunity to assist in what they thought to be the creation of a new life, spurred the less idealistic workers and peasants to defend the regime. Young Communists became the military commissars, who, according to the order creating this office in April, 1918, should "see to it that the army does not become a thing apart from the entire Soviet system and that the various military establishments do not become foci of conspiracies or instruments against workers and peasants." They should, in other words, watch over the loyalty of the officers. By 1920 their duty of supervision had become inclusive. The military commissar should be able to run the supply service; he had to be fully acquainted with the commanding personnel and with the administration of his unit; if necessary he must be able to replace the commander at a moment's notice. Young men also formed the personnel of the political departments attached to the military, with the special obligation to educate the soldiers and officers in communism and to develop Communist cells in the army. They likewise extended their responsibility to the local population among which the military was stationed. They proved equal to the task, and, aided by the incompetence of the enemy, they brought victory. By 1920 the Bolsheviks had not merely survived; they had developed the nucleus of a competent armed force.

Victory at Home, Failure Abroad

An effort to reconquer the czarist territorial possessions began immediately. The Bolsheviks failed only in Poland and in the Baltic region, where Allied forces assisted, or if needed were in a position to assist the natives in expelling the Russian Communists. The Bolsheviks recognized by treaty the independence of these states. Elsewhere the normal Communist strategy of encouraging local revolution and of sending Red troops upon request of the local party brought victory. Byelorussia succumbed as soon as the German army withdrew in 1918; it became a Soviet republic. In the Ukraine, fighting continued between local factions, forces of the former army, and Trotsky's Reds; by the middle of 1921 the Bolsheviks had largely mastered the region and made it into the Ukrainian Soviet Republic. The Transcaucasus republics, Azerbaijan, Armenia and Georgia, which tried to assert independence from Russia, fell in that order.

The fate of Georgia may be used as an example. In 1920, when the Russian Bolsheviks were suffering defeat by the Poles, they signed a treaty with Georgia recognizing her independence and promising "to refrain from any kind of interference in the internal affairs" of the new state. Within less than a year Georgian Communists rebelled; when they requested Soviet aid, it was immediately sent, and Georgia became another Soviet republic. The Bashkir, Tatar, and Kazakh Autonomous Soviet Republics and all the others in Central Asia and Siberia owed their existence to the same strategy. Successful in every encounter, the Soviet army continued its progress to the Pacific coast. When in October, 1922, Japanese troops withdrew from Vladivostok and the Maritime Province, the Bolsheviks had regained most of the czarist patrimony.

The Bolsheviks thought that labor and the peasantry in European and Asiatic countries would follow Communist leadership in rebelling against the capitalist, imperialist order and would align with Russia. These expectations soon proved illusory. The Spartacists in Germany were crushed in 1918, the Béla Kun Communist government in Hungary was destroyed in the next year, and Communist attempts to gain power in countries as diverse as Bulgaria, China, and the Dutch East Indies failed. Popular hostility or indifference to the new doctrines, Communist demand for absolute dominance, and refusal to cooperate with any other parties set handicaps that could not be overcome. By 1922 the party began to reduce emphasis upon world revolution until times were more propitious. It retained the Comintern and used it as a tool to stir up trouble anywhere possible, and it paid special attention to Asiatic countries on the Russian periphery; but it also took the first steps toward learning to conduct normal international relations. It obtained diplomatic recognition from many of the European states, and in 1925 it initiated a series of negotiations for treaties of arbitration and nonaggression, not merely with neighboring counties but with some like France and Italy, removed from its borders. It sought to convey the impression of a desire for peace and international cooperation by interesting itself in some of the activities of the League of Nations, especially disarmament, which it could exploit for propaganda in favor of communism and against bourgeois nations. Dedicated to the destruction of free government and society, it lived a dual existence as an actual social outlaw but a self-styled messiah.

RECOVERY

The end of civil war brought grave internal difficulties. The Communists had to find out what to do with the power they had acquired. They could no longer restrict their efforts to destroying bourgeois-capitalistic society; they had to introduce a working organization of their own. Russia was for them in the 1920's a laboratory in which they searched for a system that would implement their ideals. They emerged with what is now called Stalinism, a regime to be examined in another chapter. To analyze the experiments of the twenties, let us adopt the Marxist order of priority and begin with a discussion of the economy.

New Economic Policy

The country was so exhausted early in 1921 that the Kronstadt sailors, one of the earliest and most influential groups to join the Communists, rebelled against their own favored government. Peasant revolts were widespread, and famine was raging. It has been estimated that between 1914 and the end of the civil war the Russian loss in population was 28 million—2 million by flight, 10 million by deficit in what should have been the normal number of births, and 16 million by death of both military and civilian population. Of these 28 million losses, one third occurred during World War I and two thirds during the revolution and civil war.

> We are living in such conditions of impoverishment and ruin, of over-strain and exhaustion of the principal productive forces of the peasants and the workers [Lenin told the Tenth Congress of the Communist party in March, 1921] that for a time everything must be subordinated to this fundamental consideration—at all costs to increase the quantity of goods. . . . On the economic front, in our attempt to pass over to Communism, we had suffered, by the spring of 1921, a more serious defeat than any previously inflicted on us by Kolchak, Deniken, or Pilsudsky. Compulsory requisition in the villages and the direct Communist approach to the problems of reconstruction in towns—this was the policy which interfered with the growth of the productive capacity of the country and proved to be the main cause of a profound economic and political crisis which confronted us in the spring of 1921.

Lenin recognized that in order to obtain supplies people had rejected communism in practice by maintaining private trade in goods. He proposed that the country allow the capitalists sufficient freedom to reknit the economy and to teach the Communists how to build and to run an industrial system. He assured his comrades that the temporary use of capitalism would be dangerous but not fatal to communism, for, he said, "there is no question, and can be none, of sharing *power*, of renouncing the dictatorship of the proletariat over the bourgeoisie."

The New Economic Policy, the N.E.P., as it is called, introduced in 1921, permitted the revival of private trade and of privately run small-scale industry, and allowed the peasants to cultivate their little farms as they pleased. After paying a grain tax that amounted to about 50 per cent of the amount previously requisitioned, a peasant could sell any surplus in the open market. Retail merchants sprang up everywhere, saleable goods appearing like magic. Within a little more than a year private merchants conducted 75 per cent of all retail trade, state stores handled 15 per cent, and cooperatives the rest. The government retained possession of large industrial enterprises, but they restored some small shops to their owners and allowed small private enterprises to operate. In 1923 it reported that it owned only 8.5 per cent of all industry, but that this amount employed over 84 per cent of all industrial workers. The private sector of industry was restricted almost wholly to shops of one or two artisans. The government soon learned that communist society required a medium of exchange; it reintroduced money, retaining control of banking and all credit facilities. As it likewise owned the systems of transportation and communication and monopolized foreign trade, it kept "the commanding heights" of the economy, as Lenin said, in its possession.

As production and trade revived, the Communist government endeavored to channel them into collectivist institutions. The leaders expanded the state and cooperative network for wholesale and retail distribution. They imposed high taxes upon private traders, restricted their purchases, and curbed their use of the railroads. By 1928 the private retailers did only 22.5 per cent of the trade instead of the 75 per cent of five years before; in 1930 they handled only 5.6 per cent, and in 1932 private retail trade was made a criminal offense. Private industry declined in the same way. Raw materials, credit, and the use of the railroads were withheld, and taxes were far heavier than for state-owned enterprises. In 1925–1926 small industries produced 20 per cent of all manufactures; in 1930 only 5.6 per cent; within another year they had disappeared.

Agriculture proved more difficult to control because of the millions of peasants with whom the government had to deal. During this period the Communists' concern to maintain the peasants' income allowed peasants to lease land and hire machinery and workers as in capitalist society. Food production revived much more effectively than industry, but agricultural prices then dropped far below those of manufactures. Unable to afford or even to obtain industrial goods, the peasants began to withhold grain from the cities and either eat it themselves or feed it to livestock, which they could sell at a much better price. To obtain necessary food for the urban population, the Communists applied orthodox bourgeois methods of agricultural subsidies and guaranteed prices, and forced down the prices of manufactured products by reducing bank credits. Even then the government could not obtain the grain required to feed the population. By the second half of the twenties it was evident that the existing agricultural system was unsatisfactory.

Social Experimentation

The introduction of communism brought experimentation in social life and education. The rebellion against bourgeois forms included the repudiation of the bourgeois family. Women were declared emancipated and equal to men with respect to jobs and compensation, civil rights, and duties. Family ties were loosened by the practice of free love and easy divorce, and the question was debated whether children should be left with parents or reared by the state. The Communists knew that millions of parents hated the party and that young children could be won to the cause more easily without parental influence. Although deciding not to deprive the family of the custody of their children, the Communists taught the youth to report to the authorities any parental deviation from communism. The government set up a complete system of social insurance and theoretically made medical assistance and education free to everyone. With regard to the church, another institution considered bourgeois, the government seized the property, including the buildings, using most of these for what were called social purposes. For a time the Communists persecuted the priestly class, putting to death a number of the high ecclesiastical officials. They declared the profession of a person's faith to be inviolate, but they forbade the teaching of religion to anyone under eighteen years of age in groups of more than four. A loyal Communist was forbidden to practice any religion.

Social reformers have always believed that control of the schools will give the means to redeem society according to their particular panacea. The Communists were no exception, although they had no clearer idea about the pedagogical reforms necessary for their end than about any others. From the start they emphasized the vital importance of education to increase production, and they condemned distinction of race or color. Class was a different matter; the proletariat were to be preferred, for they most readily became Communists. The peasantry ranked next in prestige; since they labored with their hands and had been oppressed, they were expected to be favorable to communism. The bourgeoisie were discriminated against as dangerous enemies. Among them the intellectuals were most to be feared and were to be excluded from educational facilities, for they had read and thought, were critical, and were almost certain to disapprove of Marxism.

For setting up schools and preparing a curriculum, almost everything was lacking—buildings, supplies, and teachers. Industry was lacking to produce paper, pencils, and books; most of the teachers were anti-Communist bourgeoisie. Educational theories were as numerous as books and teachers were scarce. One Communist proposed that the school be abolished in favor of the practical education of the street, the workshop and the party. The most popular slogan for education became "freedom for the children, independence and self-government."

In the early days young people were entrusted with teaching themselves communism; children ran the schools and students the universities, and teachers and professors were kept or dismissed on their recommendation. When the Communists heard about the Project method, the Dalton plan, and other forms of progressive education in the United States, they introduced aspects of these methods in the hope that they might answer needs. The teachers were unprepared, however; in addition, American education aimed to nurture individualism, whereas Russia sought to turn out loyal Communists. The brigade system then followed. Children and university students alike, each in their proper institution, were organized into brigades, whose members studied collectively. The strong members helped the weak; written work was done by the group; reports were made by the group leader for the brigade; the group failed or passed as a unit. This system was considered proletarian in character, avoiding individualism and forming collectivist habits. The system failed, however, to train the child well in any respect except that of collectivist responsibility, and by the end of the decade the educational problem remained unsolved.

HOW TO KEEP IN POWER

Experimentation in government was more dangerous to the Communists than that in other fields, for the margin of safety was smaller. Precedent for mass action and mass appeal was lacking; but something could be learned from past mistakes, especially from the Communist experience in 1848, in the Paris Commune of 1871, and in the Russian Revolution of 1905. The Russian leaders knew that retention of political power by a small minority demanded the rise of appropriate institutions and methods. In a country in which 90 per cent of the people were peasants who cherished private ownership of land and in a world where the institution of private property prevailed, Communist government had to be dictatorial. At the same time it had to win the masses to its views, and it had to try to attract other peoples. To perform the three functions the Communist leaders developed in theory, and after 1917 introduced in practice, a system of government by monopoly party.

The easiest problem to solve was to devise an outer frame for the regime. In 1923 the Communists fixed upon the name of Union of Soviet Socialist Republics, ostensibly at that time a federation of seven republics. The Russian Socialist Federated Soviet Republic, itself a federation of states, constituted the largest and most influential member. The central government was composed of two houses, the Soviet of Nationalities, representing the several republics, and the Soviet of the Union, composed of deputies elected to represent the people as a whole without respect to nationality. The use of the federal principle permitted other states in time to be added.

Role of the Communist Party

The role of the Communist party may be understood from two statements. In 1915 Lenin declared that "masses without organization are deprived of a unified will." In 1920 he agreed with an English comrade that "by the dictatorship of the proletariat we, in essence, mean the dictatorship of the organized and class-conscious minority of the proletariat . . . only this class-conscious minority can lead the broad masses of the workers." The members of the Communist party should be the advanced guard of the movement, the leaders at all levels and in all aspects of society, winning the masses to the cause. They must serve the party at all times, in every way, at any sacrifice. They must set a model of behavior and guide the people, not by virtue of the power they wield, but by the excellence of their thought and action.

> In mobilizing the workers around productive tasks [the Communist Kaganovich stated] it is necessary to pay especially close attention to their enquiries, to their needs in regard to living conditions, their material and cultural requirements. One should not command, but lead; instead of flattery, there should be mutual criticism of one another's errors, correcting them along the way, arming one's self with new strength, new examples and new energy for the successful execution of the hardest tasks of socialist construction.

The leaders must be selected with the utmost care, on the recommendation of a stated number of other party members and after a period of probation. They remained members on sufferance; for the party must be purged from time to time of its incompetent personnel. By incompetence was meant any backsliding into petty bourgeois ideas and practices and any moral or intellectual behavior that hurt the interests of the party. The Communists formed the elite of the new society. The number of members reached its highest figure of 1½ million in 1928. A periodic check assured due representation for all major occupational and nationality groups in the state. The party took steps to obtain a continuing supply of excellent members and a loyal following outside the select group by organizing the youth from the age of eight, with the Comsomol being for the oldest, ages nineteen to twenty-three, and serving as the final testing ground prior to acceptance into the party proper.

Government

The government of the state was organized along lines similar to the Communist party. The legislative and the executive powers were united in order to give the government speed to act. The soviet had developed as the most efficient type of assembly for carrying out a revolution. Used in 1905 in Russia, it appeared again spontaneously in 1917, as soldiers and workers assembled informally in a factory, a regiment, or wherever they were, discussed problems, and selected a spokesman or leader, perhaps a committee, to represent them with other groups. These meetings did not differ in form from those developed wherever private persons have to create their own instruments of government; but the Communists claimed that they were the unique communist solution to the question of achieving democracy. Then they twisted them out of democratic shape. They imposed upon them a hierarchical or pyramidal organization to concentrate power at the top. The local units elected representatives to the district soviet, the district delegates elected representatives to the regional soviet, the regional soviets to the soviet of the republic, and the latter to the supreme soviet for the entire union. The last named selected a Central Committee as its executive body and set up ministries called commissariats, to distinguish them from similar bourgeois offices, to handle administration.

The Communist party always chose the candidates for election at each level. In the locality some nonparty members might be included on the list; but, as the elections continued up the pyramid, extraparty candidates were eliminated in favor of Communists. In the elections the peasants, considered unreliable, were given only one fifth as much voting power as the workers. In the party itself a similar procedure was followed, beginning with the cell and continuing through the grades to the executive committee, at first a body of five members, and known as the Politburo. Since the party directed the affairs of the entire union, the personnel of the Politburo acted as the most powerful members of the Central Committee and filled the most important commissariats. Thus, by its choice of candidates, by interlocking membership in all positions of power, and by its constant exercise of leadership, the Communist party dominated the government.

The phrase "democratic centralism" with which the Communists described their form of government concealed a dilemma which they have never solved. The leaders sought to allow democracy and to execute their policies with popular approval and participation; at the same time, they had to meet one emergency after the other requiring immediate action, and they had to maintain themselves in the midst of a population apathetic or hostile to their ideas and of an international state system totally inimical to them. How could they reconcile the two needs? "If a deputy of a soviet goes to a meeting and knows beforehand that all questions and decisions have been already decided by a narrow committee of the Party, he won't show much liveliness," Kaganovich declared in 1925. If the deputy was allowed to discuss, nothing was accomplished, and Lenin grew exasperated over the loss of time and energy spent on minor issues. He intensely disliked the search of the writings of Marx and Engels for arguments. At other times he recognized the value of full discussion, and he knew that many Communists opposed dictatorship or any other form of authoritarianism. Lenin enjoyed sufficient prestige to gain party support for his policies; until a year after his death the rank and file expressed their views with some freedom, and the leaders reported to the congress and subjected themselves to questions and criticism. Nonetheless, the system inclined in the opposite direction, for dictatorship supported by a monopoly party did not foster criticism.

The Cheka, or secret police, was founded December 20, 1917, almost as soon as the Bolsheviks seized power, and it was followed by the establishment of the Workers' and Peasants' Inspection to check on the effectiveness of officials in industry and agriculture, and by the Party Control Commissions to perform similar functions within the party. The Cheka expanded during the civil war, particularly after the attempt on Lenin's life and the murder of the head of the secret police in 1918, and in the course of that conflict it put to death an estimated 50,000 persons. By 1921 it had grown to a staff of 31,000 employees. Lenin criticized it for excessive ruthlessness; but he approved of its purpose, arguing that it was beneficial to the masses, since it was used against their exploiters and enemies. He legalized terror by making it a capital crime for anyone to be a member of or to participate in "an organization supporting that section of the international bourgeoisie that tries to overthrow the Communists."

Since the other two institutions were similar in purpose and organization and differed mainly in the area of responsibility, it will suffice to describe only one of them. The Party Control Commissions were intended to combat bureaucratism. They fought careerism, misuse of official power by party members, and especially the "spreading of rumors and insinuations . . . destructive of the Party's unity and authority." In 1923 they were instructed in addition to "become initiating organs in learning about, and removing the causes themselves, of anti-Party acts and diseased manifestations within the Party." They were filled with persons of the "Chekist type," according to party orders, and were a secret police to guard the purity, not merely of bureaucrats in general, but that of the purest, the members of the Communist party. They and the Cheka with their thousands of informants helped to preserve the dictatorship of the proletariat, the self-government of the masses, by destroying mutual trust among the citizens.

Nationality Problem

Since Communists expected their dogma ultimately to dominate the world, they sought to exemplify how all could live in "mutual friendship" and "real fraternal cooperation" in "a multi-national state," a "single federated state" (the words are Stalin's). The test came in the treatment of the non-Russian nationalities, of whom there were about 170, numbering in 1939, 38 millions, or 23 per cent of the population. Most of them resided in the Caucasus and in Asia, had no written language, and might be living as nomadic tribes.

Nationality Groups of a Million or More within the U.S.S.R., 1939

NATIONALITY	POPULATION	PERCENTAGE
Great Russians	99,019,929	58
Ukrainians	28,070,404	17
White Russians	5,267,431	3
Uzbeks	4,844,021	3
Tatars	4,300,336	3
Kazakhs	3,098,764	2
Hebrews	3,020,141	2
Azerbaidzhanians	2,274,805	1
Georgians	2,248,566	1
Armenians	2,151,884	1
Mordvinians	1,451,429	1
Germans	1,423,534	1
Chuvash	1,367,930	1
Tadzhiks	1,228,964	1

SOURCE: George B. Cressey, *Asia's Lands and Peoples,* p. 257. By permission of McGraw-Hill Book Co. Copyright, 1951.

As commissar for nationalities, Stalin had set the program for social, economic, and political reform, expressing himself in 1923 as follows:

> Formally, all the backward nationalities and all the tribes enjoy all the rights enjoyed by the other more advanced nationalities of our federation. But the trouble is that some nationalities have no proletarians of their own, have never passed through the stage of industrial development or even entered that stage, are frightfully backward culturally and are entirely unable to take advantage of the rights granted them by the revolution. . . . Apart from schools and languages, the Russian proletariat must take every necessary measure to establish centres of industry in the border regions, in the republics which are culturally backward.

Stalin repeatedly said that any national group had the right to secede from the Soviet Union at any time, and he was to include that stipulation in the Constitution of 1936. His meaning becomes clear from his further assertion that "besides the right of nations to self-determination there is also the right of the working class to consolidate its power, and to this latter right the right of self-determination is subordinate." He declared that "the right to self-determination cannot and must not serve as an obstacle to the exercise by the working class of its right to dictatorship." That is, the right of national self-determination and the constitutional right of secession were Communist propaganda. Far from organizing a nationality into a separate federal republic or autonomous district within a republic, the government preferred often to draw boundary lines to mix the nationalities. When national feeling could be used to further communism, it was tolerated; when not, it was crushed.

STRUGGLE OVER LENIN'S SUCCESSION

When Lenin died in 1924, a triumvirate came to power, composed of Kamenev, Zinoviev, and Stalin, three illustrious Communists, who had been prominent in the revolution and closely associated with the deceased. Lenin had dominated his colleagues by his personal ability, thus preserving unity in the party. Would a committee of three be able to do so, or would the dictatorial system require the concentration of power in the hands of one individual? The committee system was found lacking; thirst for power and the possibility of achieving power proved too great to resist. By the close of the twenties the internal conflict for control had culminated in total victory for Stalin and one-man rule.

Shortly before his death Lenin made a will in which he discussed the merits of two outstanding colleagues. He thought Trotsky the abler but criticized him for having shown "too far-reaching a self-confidence and a disposition to be too much attracted by the purely administrative side of affairs." "Comrade Stalin," he wrote, "having become General Secretary, has concentrated an enormous power in his hands; and I am not sure that he always knows how to use that power with sufficient caution." Later Lenin added as a postscript:

> Stalin is too rude, and this fault . . . becomes unbearable in the office of General Secretary. Therefore, I propose to the comrades to find a way to remove Stalin from that position and appoint to it another man . . . more patient, more loyal, more polite and more attentive to comrades, less capricious, etc.

Lenin anticipated with deep concern the fight for power that would occur between these two figures, and wished them both removed from the succession. His testament was read at a meeting of the Central Committee a few months after his death, and would most likely have led to Stalin's dismissal, had Zinoviev not interceded by recommending that in this matter the committee disregard Lenin's judgment. Zinoviev wished to preserve Stalin's power as an ally in the struggle against Trotsky, whom he feared more.

Defeat of Left and Right Wings

After Lenin's death the triumvirate was not expected to endure. The potential heirs had already begun to spar for position. Trotsky believed that communism could not be won in one country alone; he was convinced that world revolution must continue as the sole condition in which Russia could achieve communism. Stalin opposed these beliefs and carried the party with him. In 1925 Trotsky lost the position of commissar for war; then he was forbidden to speak in public, dismissed from the Politburo and the party, and, finally, in 1929 exiled from Russia. He had fought Stalin with courageous and brilliant oratory, but he had failed to act against him. Since Stalin kept the party on his side, Trotsky as an old, disciplined Communist was blocked by his own training. He reacted as all party members did when caught in the dilemma of disapproving what those in charge of the party were doing; for, as he said to Zinoviev:

> The party in the last analysis is always right, because the party is the single historic instrument given to the proletariat for the solution of its fundamental problems. I have already said that in front of one's own party nothing could be easier than to acknowledge a mistake, nothing easier than to say: all my criticisms, my statements, my warnings, my protests—the whole thing was a mere mistake. I, however, comrades, cannot say that, because I do not think it. I know that one must not be right *against* the party. One can be right only with the party, and through the party, for history has created no other road for the realization of what is right. The English have a saying: "Right or wrong—my country." With far greater historic justification we may say: right or wrong, on separate particular issues, it is my party.[2]

Trotsky allowed himself to be maneuvered into exile by a man whom he considered a "dull mediocrity."[3]

The views of Trotsky formed one extreme in the party; those of a group of whom the most prominent were Bukharin, the party theoretician, Tomsky, president of the All-Union Council of Trade Unions, and Rykov, member of the Politburo and a prominent economic administrator, constituted the other. These men advocated the continuation of the N.E.P., the co-existence of a private sector and a public sector of the economy, the preservation of a considerable degree of freedom, and a peaceful evolution of communism. They thought that eventually big capitalism in industry would absorb little capitalism and that, since big industry was already in the hands of the proletariat, the coming of socialism or communism would be only a matter of time. Bukharin wished the peasants brought into line, not by collective farms, but by cooperatives, state credit unions, and other means of increasing agricultural prosperity. In foreign affairs he proposed that the Soviet Union seek the support of non-Communist groups abroad. For advocating these views, Bukharin and Tomsky lost their positions in the Comintern, and the one his position as editor of the leading Communist paper *Pravda*, the other his presidency of the trade-unions. Rykov was temporarily not molested, but by 1929 the entire conservative group had been forced to repudiate their ideas in public.

[2] I. Deutscher, *Stalin: A Political Biography*, p. 278. Copyright 1949 by Oxford University Press, Inc.
[3] *Ibid.*, p. 248.

Victory of Stalin

Stalin, the victor in the internal struggle for power, had never been outside Russia. Born in Georgia of poor parents, he had gone to a seminary to prepare for the priesthood. He soon became a Communist and applied his talents in the underground. He rose within the party as an organizer and administrator, a shadowy figure who proved unusually successful in dodging the police. He was no theorist, and he did not follow the example of illustrious colleagues, Trotsky, Bukharin, and Lenin, in propounding a theoretical solution to all problems, within an international framework. He concentrated on matters at hand—in his early years setting up a clandestine press or robbing a train to obtain funds for the party, in his later years organizing the party. He was a person to whom one gave the plodding, onerous tasks of detailed administration. His patience in listening to the outpourings of others without committing himself, his puritanical private life, his extraordinary gift of silence, his lack of confidants, his plainness and even crudeness made him seem devoid of egotism or of any ambition other than that to serve the cause. He appeared calm, good-natured, and optimistic, not unusually dogmatic, and devoted to the memory of Lenin.

At the time of Lenin's death, Stalin (the word means steel; his family name was Djugashvili) held four positions in the state which gave him far greater power than his competitors. In addition to being a member of the Politburo, he served as commissar for nationalities, head of the Workers' and Peasants' Inspection, head of the Party Control Commissions, and executive secretary of the Communist party. In each of these four posts he was able to fill the important offices under him throughout the U.S.S.R. with personal followers. As commissar of nationalities he was responsible for administration among the 65 million people of non-Russian nationality, not quite one half of the total population of the U.S.S.R., and assured himself of their support. Through the Workers' and Peasants' Inspection he accomplished the same objective in industry and agriculture, and through the other two posts he made certain that the party itself became his instrument. When in 1924, in commemoration of Lenin's death, the membership was expanded, Stalin packed the party. By 1929, 73 per cent of the party were members who had entered since 1923; these were his choices, and in the struggle with his competitors he could muster a popular majority for his policies.

Stalin understood the value of tactics and manuevers; he waited while his opponents talked, involved themselves in difficulties over points of communist dogma, and exposed themselves to attack before the party. Trotsky lost out by criticizing Lenin, whose words had become sacred. Then came the turn of the others, each exposing himself in his own way and creating precedents for subsequent accusations and condemnations which Stalin could use. Zinoviev, for example, demanded that Trotsky surrender in thought as well as deed, a beginning of that useful device for destroying one's enemies known as "crime of conscience." Stalin sided with one group to help destroy another. He succeeded so well that in the middle of 1928 Bukharin in terror turned to his enemy Kamenev for support. "*He* will strangle us," he said to Kamenev. "He is an unprincipled intriguer who subordinates everything to his appetite for power. At any given moment he will change his theories in order to get rid of someone." "We consider Stalin's line fatal to the revolution. This line is leading us to the abyss."[4] Nonetheless, Bukharin and the other opponents feared to act. By 1930 Stalin was called the "Lenin of to-day."

During the years of conflict over the succession, Stalin drafted a new party program, which won public approval. Like all Communists, Stalin aimed to industrialize the country, to collectivize agriculture, to introduce central planning for that purpose, and to continue to encourage revolutionary action elsewhere in the world. He and his opponents differed over questions of method and of timing. He repudiated permanent revolution as demanded by Trotsky, and the war-weary people applauded. His declaration that communism could be won in the Soviet Union alone, flattered Russian national pride; and his assurance that the proletariat of other countries would support the revolution offered comfort. To the party members he asserted that world revolution would continue, that victory was near, and that the Soviet Union would assist in that final achievement. He emphasized, however, the immediate work to be done at home. His program was not one of national communism, as Stalin's Communist critics asserted; but it definitely shifted interest from arousing new revolutions in Western Europe to fulfilling the one in Russia. By this policy Stalin laid the theoretical basis for the change from Leninism to Stalinism. The story of the execution and elaboration of that policy will be told in a subsequent chapter.

Suggestions for Further Reading

BAYKOV, ALEXANDER. *Development of the Soviet Economic System.* Cambridge, Mass.: Harvard University Press, 1948. Basic work.

DEUTSCHER, ISAAC. *Stalin: A Political Biography.* New York: Oxford University Press, 1949. Admirable. One of the best biographies of the period.

FAINSOD, MERLE. *How Russia Is Ruled.* Cambridge, Mass.: Harvard University Press, 1954. Basic work.

KING, BEATRICE. *Changing Men: The Education System of the USSR.* New York: The Viking Press, Inc., 1937. Illuminating analysis by one who studied the system at firsthand.

MOORE, BARRINGTON. *Soviet Politics: The Dilemma of Soviet Power.* Cambridge, Mass.: Harvard University Press, 1950. Basic work.

PARES, BERNARD. *Russia.* New York: Mentor, 1949. Mainly about the twentieth century. A model of its kind, brief, learned, well written, critical in the best sense.

WHITE, D. FEDETOFF. *The Growth of the Red Army.* Princeton, N.J.: Princeton University Press, 1944. Basic work.

[4] *Ibid.,* p. 314.

Chapter 11 · Imperial Relations in the 1920's

DIVERSITY OF IMPERIAL RELATIONS

The subject of the present chapter poses a difficult problem of synthesis. We were able to analyze as a unit the many countries of Eastern Europe which fill the area from Finland to Greece, for they belong to a single geographic area and share many conditions in common. How can we discuss in a single chapter territories on every continent, of every possible range of natural resources, of every known level of culture, economy, and governmental and social organization, of the widest difference in relations to the mother country, and in exposure to the workings of power politics? These colonial areas belonged to relatively few countries, but the mother states followed no uniform method of administration. The British way and objective of imperial relations differed sharply from those of the French. The Dutch lay closer to the British; the Belgians developed a system peculiarly their own. The Spanish and Portuguese had little system except to leave their dependencies to stagnate. The Fascists in Italy after 1922 applied their new philosophy of rule to the colonies as well. The Soviet Union incorporated the colonial peoples within reach, subjecting them to communism, while claiming to destroy imperialism as a purely capitalistic phenomenon. Each state tended to transfer to subject peoples its own way of life.

We may attempt to achieve a measure of unity in our discussion by concentrating attention upon questions that arise from the imperialist relationship, that of ruler and ruled. The psychological effects of power upon the ruler may be illustrated by a conversation in E. M. Forster's *A Passage to India* between a young British member of the Indian Civil Service and a native.[1]

> We're not out here for the purpose of behaving pleasantly.
> What do you mean?
> What I say. We're out here to do justice and keep the peace. . . .

[1] E. M. Forster, *A Passage to India* (Everyman's Library; E. P. Dutton & Company, Inc., 1942), p. 39.

Your sentiments are those of a god. . . .

There's no point in all this. Here we are, and we're going to stop, and the country's got to put up with us, gods or no gods. . . .

We shall explore the extent to which this attitude prevailed. We shall note how and to what extent the ruling nation attempted to train the dependent natives in its own civilization, and which elements of the native peoples reacted first and in what ways. Except with regard to France—where deputies in the French parliament from Algeria and a few other colonial areas exerted a conservative influence upon legislation for France proper—the psychological effects of domination over subject peoples were not mirrored in the relations between government and people in the mother country. The responsibility of imperial defense, however, profoundly conditioned the life of the master nation, even of those countries too small to be able adequately to protect their empires. These aspects of imperialism we shall consider at the close of the chapter.

IMPACT OF WORLD WAR I ON IMPERIAL RELATIONS

The experience of World War I led to a rapid decline of traditional imperialism, and this decline has continued to the present. The dependent peoples differed in capacity and ability to profit from the change. The British dominions had been interested in the war because they understood the need for defense against German *Weltpolitik*. They were sufficiently advanced economically to be of service to Great Britain, and sufficiently advanced politically to be able to capitalize on their aid by gaining complete self-government in return. In countries like India, Burma, Indochina, and the Dutch East Indies, and in the Near and Middle East, the war stimulated the awakening of nationalism. Intellectuals usually led the action, particularly those trained in European universities and by experience in the imperial bureaucracy in their own country. European culture lost prestige by permitting a war to be fought, and dependent peoples with historic cultures began not only to appreciate their importance to the mother country but to believe in the moral superiority of their culture over the materialistic, power-minded West.

Particularly among the peoples of Asia, World War I marked a time of great national awakening. The Africans remained far behind, as we might expect of peoples who for centuries had lacked an advanced civilization of their own. The student of European history will recognize in this awakening a process similar to that through which European nations had passed during the previous two hundred years. World War I stimulated the colonial peoples just as international conflicts in the seventeenth and eighteenth centuries had affected European peoples; but since World War

I was fought mainly in Europe, the impact upon imperial relations did not equal that of World War II, a truly global war. The imperial powers at the peacemaking still sought to gain territory and they did so under the guise of mandates, even though they lost control to a greater or lesser degree over old dependencies. However, we shall see that imperial relations in the twenties and thirties, in comparison with those during the years after World War II, were relatively quiet. They witnessed the projection abroad of European civilization; they tested the attractiveness of that civilization; they challenged the sense of moral responsibility on the part of the Western nations; and they foreshadowed great changes, most of which lie ahead of us.

BRITISH IMPERIAL RELATIONS

The mandate system under the League of Nations was based so much upon the British ideals of imperial practice that the one has been called an outgrowth of the other. Ever since the loss of the American colonies, Great Britain has in theory—and, under urging, to a considerable extent in practice—sought to assist her imperial dependencies toward popular self-government and equality with the mother country. The colonies which have most easily taken this road were inhabited by Europeans: first Canada, which received dominion status in 1867; then Australia, in 1900; New Zealand, in 1907; and the Union of South Africa, in 1909, just seven years after defeat of the Boers. By the outbreak of World War I, the British dominions controlled all their internal affairs and a great part of their foreign relations. Because they had shared in the defense of the mother country and the empire during that war, they as well as India were invited in 1917 to send representatives to London to create an Imperial War Cabinet and to hold an Imperial War Conference. India was promised responsible government by successive stages. Each dominion and India sent its own official representative to the peace conference at Versailles in 1919, and each became a charter member of the League of Nations.

In 1926 the dominions and Great Britain held another in the series of imperial conferences that had begun in 1887, and agreed upon the following statement: "They [Great Britain and the dominions] are autonomous Communities within the British Empire, equal in status, in no way subordinate one to another in any aspect of their domestic or external affairs, though united by a common allegiance to the Crown and freely associated as members of the British Commonwealth of Nations." The declaration received legal sanction in 1931 by the Statute of Westminster, which by repeal of the Colonial Laws Validity Act of 1865 deprived the British parliament of the right to legislate for any other members of the Commonwealth unless requested to do so and which empowered any other Member to repeal or amend any British law applying to it.

> The British Empire [the report of the Imperial Conference of 1926 stated] is not founded upon negotiations. It depends essentially, if not formally, on positive ideals. Free institutions are its life-blood. Free co-operation is its instrument. Peace, security and progress are among its objects. . . . And though every dominion is now and must always remain the sole judge of the nature and extent of its co-operation, no common cause will, in our opinion, be thereby imperilled.

The Commonwealth had no constitution, no written obligations, at first no permanent secretariat. In the next decade it set up a small organization to facilitate the conduct of business, but it never formulated legal conditions for membership. It depended for effectiveness of operations upon the continued meeting of ministers and parliamentarians in informal conferences and upon day-to-day clearance of voluminous business among the pertinent governmental agencies. Meeting problems as they arose on a basis of mutual respect and aid, and trusting to the reasonableness of parliament in each country, the members assured success. "If it [the Commonwealth] did not exist," an eminent British scholar has written, "you could not invent it."

Ordinarily the position of each dependency within the British Empire changed in accordance with the ability to impress its readiness for self-government upon the British government. The areas settled by people of European origin who shared a common cultural heritage acquired dominion status easily. The test of British sincerity came in the mother country's relations with India, the dependencies in the Near and Middle East, and Ireland.

India

In 1917 Great Britain promised "the progressive realization of responsible government in India as an integral part of the British Empire." The difficulty of fulfilling the promise may be seen in the contradictory events of the ensuing decade. In 1919 the British government approved a new constitution for India based on the principle of dyarchy, or double rule, and subject to review after ten years. Although reserving powers—particularly over justice, police, and finance—to British appointed officials, it created a legislative assembly for matters of concern to the whole of India—for example, tariff policy—and one for each province, with authority to pass on bills pertaining to all other affairs. The British viceroy and each British governor of a province retained the right to issue decrees on any matter considered essential; but the viceroy was advised by an executive council containing a minority of Indians, and in each province the governor appointed a ministry from the members of the legislature responsible to that representative body. The viceroy and the governors benefited from the criticism of bills by the legislature, most of whose members were elected by the Indian people. The constitution was granted in the belief that "the placid, pathetic contentment of the masses is not the soil on which such

Indian nationhood will grow, and that in deliberately disturbing it, we are working for her [India's] highest good." (Montagu-Chelmsford Report on India of 1918.)

Reaction of British and Indians to the constitution was mixed. British Tory imperialists condemned the document on the ground that it surrendered British rights and responsibility to unprepared natives. Indians were rioting in many places, and in the spring of 1919 a mob in the Punjab city of Amritsar murdered a number of Europeans and threatened to wipe out the British community. Called to the rescue, the British General Reginald Dyer with native troops fired on the mob, killing about four hundred and wounding twelve hundred. The British government dismissed Dyer from the service, although many British in India and in Great Britain applauded his act, saying it had saved India from a repetition of the mutiny of 1857.

The Indian National Congress, a party predominantly Hindu, founded in 1885 to press for Indian independence, at a meeting in the same city of Amritsar a few days after the passage of the constitution, condemned the document as "inadequate, unsatisfactory, and disappointing" and demanded "full responsible government in accordance with the principle of self-determination" for the whole of British India "within a period not exceeding fifteen years." The Moslem League, the largest party representing Indians of the faith of Islam, inclined toward the same stubborn attitude. Indians of moderate liberal views, whether of Hindu or of Moslem religion, welcomed the constitution, participated in the government, and enabled it to realize to a considerable extent the hopes which the British had had of providing the people with experience in self-government. The electorate actually casting a vote increased from 29 per cent in 1920 to 43 per cent in 1926, and it continued to grow. Only ten times during the life of the constitution (1919–1935) did the viceroy use his reserved authority to promulgate as law a measure which the legislature refused to pass.

As the country ultimately responsible for the fate of India and for the security of British lives and investments there, Great Britain felt compelled to advance with caution. The National Congress party was guided by the Mahatma, Mohandas Gandhi, a Hindu educated in England, who preached nonviolent noncooperation with the British. His followers occasionally took to riots and bloodshed. After one such outbreak in 1922, when Hindus murdered twenty-one policemen, Gandhi was imprisoned, but by resorting to a hunger strike he secured his freedom. The National Congress party, approximately 4 million strong in a country with a population greater than that of Europe, claimed to represent all India. It demanded complete freedom, rejected membership in the British Commonwealth, and proposed to set up a centralized government with some concessions to cultural autonomy for the non-Hindu minorities. The largest of these groups, the Moslems, advocated independence within the Commonwealth and a federal form of government that would assure them control in the three provinces in which they formed a majority of the people. Neither party, based essentially on religion, trusted the other, and at some place in the Indian subcontinent at almost any time fighting occurred between Hindu and Moslem. Among the Hindus, caste opposed caste, each of the dozens of language groups feared encroachment upon its speech by some other. Everywhere poverty reigned, and somewhere famine stalked.

The British were certain that no party and no individual, the Mahatma included, spoke for India, and feared that grant of the National Congress's demands would precipitate civil war. They understood that, in order to learn, the Indians must be allowed to make mistakes and to govern badly; but would the people accept the degree of toleration and cooperation necessary for the most elementary government? In 1928, at a conference representing all Indian parties, the Indians attempted to draft an acceptable constitution. Their work collapsed because of the old antagonism between Hindu and Moslem. The decade of the 1920's ended with the British still preserving internal peace and maintaining the institutions of limited self-government.

Near and Middle East

British interests in the Near and Middle East concerned strategy and oil. Having agreed with Russia in 1907 on a division of Persia, later called Iran, in order to keep the Russians away from India, Great Britain immediately profited from the discovery in 1908 of oil in her part of the country. The Australian discoverer obtained a sixty-year concession and formed the Anglo-Persian Oil Company. The British navy rapidly shifted to oil as fuel, and in May, 1914, the British government purchased a controlling interest in the Anglo-Persian Oil Company. At about the same time it obtained a promise from the Sheiks of Kuwait and Bahrein to grant oil concessions only to persons "appointed from the British government." By 1919 the oil wells produced 10 million barrels a year, and output rapidly increased.

When the Soviet Revolution cost Russia her control of northern Persia, the British government endeavored, in 1919, to fill the void by subjecting the entire country to its control by treaty. The Persians successfully avoided the trap; but, in negotiating a treaty of friendship with Russia in 1921 as a counterweight to British power, they accepted the inclusion of the following stipulation:

> If a third party should attempt to carry out a policy of usurpation by means of armed intervention in Persia, or if such Power should desire to use Persian territory as a base of operations against Russia, or if a foreign Power should threaten the frontiers of Federal Russia or those of its allies, and if the Persian Government should not be able to put a stop to such menace after having been once called upon to do so by Russia, Russia shall have the right to advance her troops into the Persian interior for the purpose of carrying out the military operations necessary for its defence. Russia undertakes, however, to withdraw her troops from Persian territory as soon as the danger has been removed.

The article bore no danger to Persia at the time because of Russia's weakness, but it allowed an entry to Iran which the Communists would attempt to exploit in the future. During the postwar decade Persia extended her economic relations with Russia. By 1924 she succeeded in clearing the country of British troops, and four years later she abolished British extraterritorial privileges. During the decade, disputes with Russia and with the oil-hungry Western power remained quiescent.

Of Persia's two neighbors, Afghanistan and Iraq, the British attempted to keep the first free to serve as buffer between Russia and India. This backward, tribal country suffered from internal wars. Mistrustful of Western imperialism and believing itself capable of handling any Communist menace, its local temporary victors attempted to play off Russia against Great Britain. In consequence, Russia expanded her influence, until in 1929 a leader, Nadir Shah, able, realistic, Western in his orientation but no puppet of the British, seized power and restored a degree of order.

Iraq, as Mesopotamia came to be officially called upon receiving independence, formed part of Great Britain's spoils in the partition of the Ottoman Empire. The British placed a puppet Arab, King Faisal, over it as ruler. Immediately, in 1920, faced with a popular rebellion, they preferred to dispense with the legal status of mandate. Signing a treaty (1922) duly approved by the League of Nations, they acknowledged the country's freedom while maintaining British control. A large British personnel was brought from India and placed in all the ministries and in the provincial administration. These officials practiced the authoritarian methods of administration to which they were accustomed. Army, foreign affairs, fiscal affairs, police, health, irrigation, telegraph, public works—everything of consequence—was subordinate to a British adviser. As for the tribes, who constituted approximately one sixth of the population, the British preferred to rule indirectly through the chiefs, thereby assuring usually the loyal support of the most reactionary elements of the population. The urban dwellers, more or less acquainted with Western ideals, and eager for independence, opposed British domination and urged nationalism and reform. The British, under native pressure, signed further treaties in 1926 and in 1927, with some concessions to form but almost none to substance. When the well-known oil resources began to be exploited in 1927, imperialist Great Britain had a conclusive reason for protecting the country against the imperialist Soviet Union.

The first draft of the mandate for Palestine, drawn in 1920, included Transjordan as well. In need of a throne for a loyal Arab supporter, Abdullah, King Husein's second son, Great Britain arranged, in the final form of the mandate, for Transjordan to be a separate state. According to the treaty, Palestine would be placed "under such political, administrative and economic conditions as will secure the establishment of the Jewish national home." The mandate did not mention the Arabs by name, although they made up the vast majority of this wretchedly poor territory. Native Arabs and those in the surrounding countries absolutely opposed the creation of a Jewish state. Great Britain thus assumed responsibility for implementing the Balfour Declaration of 1917. Since Abdullah depended upon her for a large subsidy to cover the expense of his government, Great Britain assured herself of a solid expanse of friendly territory from the Iran oil fields to the Mediterranean coast. She took care to assure the friendship of the Arab rulers further south in the Arabian peninsula, particularly the ablest of all, King Ibn-Saud. Once the territories were partitioned and assigned, in the British part of the Near East, the twenties proved to be a comparatively quiet period.

In terms that would have done credit to the Conservative viceroy of India, Prime Minister Ramsay MacDonald, leader of the Socialist Labor party, enunciated in 1924 the importance of control of Egypt to Great Britain. MacDonald told the Egyptian government that

> . . . the security of the communications of the British Empire in Egypt remains a vital British interest and . . . absolute certainty that the Suez Canal will remain open in peace as well as in war for the free passage of British ships is the foundation on which the entire defensive strategy of the British Empire rests. . . . No British government . . . can divest itself wholly, even in favour of an ally, of its interest in guarding such a vital link in British communications. Such a security must be a feature of any agreement come to between our two Governments.

This strategic interest had led Great Britain in December, 1914, to abolish the nominal suzerainty of the Ottoman Empire over Egypt and to declare the country of the Nile a British protectorate.

The experience of World War I antagonized the Egyptian people, urban and rural, against their masters and fired the cause of nationalism. Native cotton growers, who lost much of their export market, blamed the British. Native grain producers had to feed those whose export trade collapsed; they also denounced the British. Conscription of peasant labor for war purposes and requisitioning of animals and supplies angered the country people. Collection of Red Cross funds among Moslems, shortage of imports, and similar effects of the war augmented the animosity of the sensitive urban population toward the British, whose domination in contrast to that of the Ottoman ruler had reality and seemed permanent. As soon as the war ended, a popular leader, Zaghlul Pasha, of peasant origin but thoroughly trained and experienced in the British-controlled bureaucracy in Egypt, agitated for independence. When the British exiled him and his aides in March, 1919, people rioted all over the country.

Under native pressure the British in 1922 terminated the protectorate in name and tried to restore it in fact by treaty. They proposed to secure the communications of the British Empire in Egypt, to defend Egypt against "all foreign aggression or interference, direct or indirect," to protect foreign interests in Egypt and minorities, to control the Sudan. Since no Egyptian government would sign such a document, the British government issued it as a unilateral declaration, and riots continued. In November, 1924, Egyptians murdered Sir Lee Stack, governor-general of the Sudan and commander in chief of the Egyptian army. The British government imposed a fine upon Egypt of £500,000, excluded all Egyptian soldiers and most Egyptian officials from the Sudan, and threatened to curtail the flow of Nile water to Egypt in favor of competitive cotton growing in the Sudan. Inasmuch as Egypt lived from the Nile, the terms showed the entire nation its dependence upon the will of the British. Nationalism flourished, and Zaghlul's party, the Wafd, gained nation-wide support for its aims to eject the British and control the Sudan. The decade closed with nothing settled and the British in possession by force.

Ireland

Possession of Ireland had for centuries been considered vital to the defense of the British Isles. In 1914 the British government had passed a law in favor of home rule but, with the approval of Irish leaders at the time, postponed execution until the end of the war. During the next four years, 250,000 Irishmen volunteered for service in the British army and fought valiantly on the western front and at Gallipoli. A much smaller number seized the occasion of Britain's involvement to rebel at Easter, 1916. Expecting aid from Germany, which never came, they attempted to establish an independent republic. The rebellion failed completely, but by shooting fifteen of the leaders and imprisoning many others, the British government assured the Sinn Fein movement, initiated in 1904, to work for independence under a republican government, of overwhelming popular support. The Irish condemned the punishment of the rebels as another act in the long history of British injustice. They could not forget that in the past three quarters of a century of British rule their population had declined by half. British troops occupied Ireland after 1916 as an enemy country.

The Irish republicans, the Sinn Feiners, took advantage of the British elections of December, 1918, which were held in Ireland as well, to return their own leaders. They won every seat except two in counties outside Ulster and ten seats in the latter, a total of seventy-three. All the representatives pledged to sit in Dublin, not in London, and on January 21, 1919, in defiance of the British, twenty-seven of them—the rest were in British jails or in hiding—gathered in the Irish capital as a sovereign parliament. Savage warfare between the Irish republicans and the British broke out immediately. In 1920 the British government under Lloyd George offered the Irish dominion status, by which certain matters—army, navy, currency, tariffs, and excise—should be handled by the imperial parliament. Since the Sinn Feiners repudiated dependence in any form, the conflict continued. By 1921 the guerrilla ferocity began to affect British relations with the Dominions and the United States. A British journal, the *Round Table*, expressed the growing conviction, "If the British Commonwealth can only be preserved by such means, it would become a negation of the principle for which it stood." On both sides leaders recognized that the chaos should not continue, and in July, 1921, signed a truce.

Negotiations for a settlement proved possible in the matter of defense, but they struck two snags, one of a formal nature, the other of substance. The parties agreed that Great Britain should provide coastal defense for five years and that the question would then be reconsidered. The British were to use four ports, one of them in Ulster, in peacetime and maintain facilities for oil storage, and in time of war they should have additional unnamed privileges. Lloyd George led the Irish negotiators to believe that in return for taking an oath of allegiance to the British crown and for becoming a member of the British Commonwealth with status like that of Canada, Ireland would be able to include the northern part of the island inhabited by Protestants. According to the agreement, Ulster, as the northern counties were called, should remain within the new Irish dominion unless within a certain brief time its local parliament voted to withdraw. The Irish negotiators expected that the British would arrange for the boundary between the southern part and Ulster to be so drawn that the Protestant north would be compelled to join the new state. They were soon disillusioned.

Ulster, consisting of nine counties, received in 1920 both its own parliament and representation in the British parliament at Westminster, terms which the Irish had rejected. Since three of the counties were definitely Catholic, Ulster agreed to transfer these to the new Irish state. In the remaining six counties the Catholics, numbering one third of the population of 1¼ million, were almost all in favor of union with Ireland. The Protestants had developed a flourishing industry, particularly in linen and shipbuilding. Labor was well organized and enjoyed high wages. The owners feared that in the event of union with Ireland the Catholic politicians of the twenty-six southern counties would impose heavy taxes on their prosperous economy in order to relieve the poverty of the south. The workers objected to the prospect of inundation by cheap, unskilled Irish labor. Ulster, repudiating any idea of leaving the protection of Great Britain for a precarious future in Ireland, immediately voted to preserve its own political identity under home rule.

In Ireland proper, fighting began again, this time on two fronts, as soon as the Dail Eireann, the Irish parliament, ratified the agreement. The first lay between the Irish who supported the treaty, and the determined Irish republicans who rejected any arrangement short of independence under a republic for the entire island. Eamon de Valera, born in the United States and thereby able to claim United States citizenship, resigned as president of the Dail to direct the rebellious forces. Arthur Griffith and Michael Collins, who had negotiated the agreement, took most responsibility in the government for suppressing the Republican army.

The war, as ruthless as that fought against the British, caused the death of Griffith from heart failure and of thirty-one-year-old Collins, an excellent organizer, by assassination. The republicans attacked a building which contained the Irish Public Record Office and in the fighting destroyed Ireland's official records extending back to the Middle Ages. They burned historic houses belonging to supporters of the treaty, among them that of Sir Horace Plunkett, which was filled with manuscripts, paintings, and other works of Irish achievement. Like so many people in so many countries in this macabre age, they placed matters of form above the preservation of their nation's culture. At last, in 1923, de Valera called off the rebellion. Its destructiveness was exceeding that of the resistance against Great Britain.

The second front, along the border of Ulster, shared the fate of the other. No Irishman willingly accepted the partition of the island, but the government acquiesced in the act, whereas the outlawed Republican army refused. When the die-hards employed the only methods they knew, the people of Ireland, as well as of Ulster, suffered, and their respective armies and police were called to the defense. Remnants of the Republican army continued to destroy life and property on both sides of the frontier, and occasionally in Great Britain proper. They represent the last effects of centuries of British misgovernment in Ireland.

After the civil war ceased in 1923, de Valera and his party abstained from political life until 1927, and the Irish Free State, under the moderate guidance of William Cosgrave, entered a period of political stability and economic recovery. The government administered justice fairly, treated the pro-English minority with tolerance, encouraged industrial growth, and assisted agriculture, particularly dairy farming. Bankers came to trust the government and to invest some funds. In imperial relations the Irish government strove, as its minister of foreign affairs said in 1926, "to uproot from the whole system of this State the British Government." As the trend in intraimperial relations lay in that direction, the Irish found the report of the Imperial Conference of 1926 and the Statute of Westminster of 1931 to their liking. By the end of the 1920's, Ireland enjoyed practically complete political independence.

The Practice of Gradualism

In the rest of the empire, covering 3,250,000 square miles and including 14 per cent of the empire's population, the British system of government was being gradually introduced.

> Every feature in a British colonial constitution [a report by the Hansard Society stated in 1953] has its counterpart in British history. Thus the Governor is in many ways like the Sovereign—not a twentieth-century monarch but one of the Tudor period. The Executive Council corresponds to the Cabinet—not, in the majority of cases, a modern British Cabinet, but one of, say, the late Stuart period.

The legislature may consist of one or two chambers and the lower house may (as in the case of the West Indian Colonies) be elected by universal franchise or in some colonies the franchise may be restricted as it was in the United Kingdom at one time. Political progress tends to be conceived in terms of removing the restrictions—limiting the veto power of the Governor, increasing the representative character of the Executive and Legislative Councils, reducing the minimum qualifications for voting, and so on.

The British followed the general policy of indirect rule, leaving the indigenous institutions and the distribution of social influence as far as possible untouched.

The practice of gradualism, associated with the name of Lord Frederick Lugard, governor in Nigeria in the early part of this century, has been criticized on two counts, apparently but not necessarily inconsistent. Its slowness prevented the natives from adjusting their way of life to the modern world. Using India as an example, an American scholar has written as follows:

Late Victorian England was unwilling to accentuate the secularizing impact of the Western World upon the whole complex of superstition, backwardness, bigotry, discrimination and medievalism which Indian religious life tended to foster. This unfinished business of history hangs over modern India, and no man can tell how much commotion and tragedy may be caused by the unavoidable pressures to which India must subject her ancient ways of life in order to acquire her full share of science, technology and economic development.

And he adds,

There is so much unfinished business in Africa that the trained and experienced observer shudders at the thought that the temper of the times may precipitate major political decisions which the continent is unprepared to make.[2]

The Western institutions that were introduced often had destructive effects on native society. Western concepts of law, for example, exposed people accustomed to tribal, customary law, and communal or mixed property ownership, to the sharp practices of moneylenders. Institutions of self-government easily fell into the hands of an elite lacking the Western sense of social responsibility. The British system compassed a profound concern for enabling the native peoples to develop themselves. It led, however, to the faults which one might expect from the attempt to apply standards of Western legality and parliamentary rule to peoples accustomed to an entirely different kind of social and political organization.

FRENCH IMPERIAL RELATIONS

The French colonial policy after World War I continued to be affected by two sets of ideals, the revolutionary tradition of liberty, equality, and

[2] Cornelis W. de Kiewiet, "African Dilemmas," *Foreign Affairs*, April, 1955, p. 450.

fraternity, and belief in the world pre-eminence of French culture. The two had merged in the first half of the nineteenth century, with the result that the colonials at that time in Réunion, Martinique, and Guadeloupe, East India, Cochin China, and Guiana had received French citizenship, and after the founding of the Third Republic elected representatives to the French parliament. The wide expansion of dependent possessions in Asia and Africa added to the Third Republic so many peoples, and of such exotic cultures, that assimilation of these natives into the body of France, adhered to in theory, became difficult in practice. Between 1875 and 1939, France did not grant a single new seat in parliament to the dependent areas, and in only one instance, that of four small communes in Senegal in 1916, was blanket citizenship bestowed. Otherwise the privilege had to be earned by conscious assimilation of French culture and official repudiation of the culture of the applicant's native people. Many of the native elite who had absorbed French ways shunned French citizenship for fear of breaking the ties with their own people without becoming accepted as full-fledged metropolitan Frenchmen. In Madagascar, for example, under the Third Republic, only two thousand natives took the risk.

Direct Rule

The French government during World War I conscripted soldiers from the dependencies for service on the western front and continued to use them to occupy the Rhineland. After peace was restored, the government proposed to develop the dependencies as an extension of France. The resources of 100 million people seemed able to assure the revival of the country as a great power. At the same time, France hesitated to assimilate the natives into French culture or to expand the budget for colonial development. Instead, she cultivated an elite in each region and largely neglected the masses. For the few she established French schools in the dependencies and brought some of the promising students to France for advanced study. The French have "instinctively allotted native culture and language no place in their educational system," a French official and expert on colonial affairs wrote in 1947. "This is true everywhere, or practically everywhere, of elementary education as well as of secondary and higher education. Consequently, French culture and language have become predominant everywhere." By these means France satisfied her own pride, practiced liberty, equality, and fraternity for all who would become French, and siphoned off the potential native leaders. She spent money for public health and other medical work in the colonies and developed essential means of transportation and communication—Frenchmen as well needed to move in and out of the territories—but she devoted small amounts to improving the economy.

Since the governmental system in metropolitan France was centralized, that in the dependencies followed the same pattern. Paris became the capital of the empire, the colonial minister ruled largely by decree through the colonial governors and set up a staff of inspectors with headquarters in Paris to tour the vast possessions. The method of direct government, as contrasted with the British and Dutch systems, required the service of many Frenchmen to fill posts from high to low in the colonial bureaucracy. Personnel in France was available, for the stagnant nature of the French economy drove many people to seek an official position wherever it might be. French bureaucrats at all levels were needed in order to destroy native institutions and habits and prepare the way for ultimate assimilation. At the beginning of World War II the French used, for example, almost 900 French officials to administer the 3,500,000 people in French Equatorial Africa, whereas the British governed the 20,000,000 in Nigeria with only 1,300 British officials.

A British official of many years' experience in Africa summarized his conclusions about the relative merits of the British and the French colonial systems in terms of the character of their officials, the persons who made the administration real:

> The Englishman by temperament feels little sympathy with the new class of schooled African; his preferences are for the "savage." The Frenchman by temperament feels little sympathy for the "savage"; his preferences are for the literate. French administration has slight interest in and gives little time to native customs and ideas and languages. The ignorance of French officials is in fact astonishing. I have met scores of French colonial officials, including men who had spent ten years or longer in the one community, but only two men amongst them all had learnt an African language. Interpreters are in universal use; a corps drawn from the famous *élite*. The interpreters, like the clerks in the District Commissioner's office, are generally foreigners in the community, by race and still more by sympathies. And as a single District Commissioner might be running a district with as many as a hundred thousand to a quarter of a million inhabitants, and as, too, the extreme centralization of all French administration keeps him closely to his files and records, the *de facto* power of the interpreters and clerks is great. The corruption is equally great. They are hated and feared by the villagers. In many towns the biggest house is the interpreter's house. Yet one of the beliefs of the French which I have heard repeated many times is that they are closer to the African than are the British. Some Frenchmen are closer to some Africans, . . . but the sympathy and the knowledge of British officers is closer to the African than that of their French colleagues as a whole.[3]

The French colonial system did not train the natives for self-government, and tended to admit fewer and fewer colonials to French citizenship. Native life in the French colonies was subject to slight change.

The three dependencies in North Africa legally occupied a special place in the French Empire, but they received about the same treatment as the colonies proper. Tunisia and Morocco ranked as protectorates and Algeria as an integral part of metropolitan France, divided into depart-

[3] Walter Russell Crocker, *On Governing Colonies* (London: George Allen & Unwin, Ltd., 1947), pp. 76-77.

ments and sending representatives to parliament. Nonetheless, the Moslems in Algeria did not possess the benefits of French citizenship any more than did the masses in the protectorates; the privilege was restricted as elsewhere to Frenchmen and the few French-trained native elite. "The Frenchman," General Louis Lyautey, the first French ruler of Morocco, had said, "has direct administration in his blood."

The French took over rule of the natives in all three territories; in Morocco they needed the help of the army until 1934, when fighting against the protectorate finally ceased. French settlers moved into the regions, acquired the best lands, developed commerce, banking, and some industry, controlled the newspapers, dominated politics, and obtained government funds for road building, irrigation, and the like to help themselves rather than the natives. The improvements in public health and the suppression of disorder enabled the population to increase much more rapidly than did opportunities for earning a living. The French settlers raised grapes and produced wine, which the Moslems did not drink; the consumption of grain by the Algerian natives decreased to three fifths of that of a half century earlier. The standard of living of the Moslem masses in 1940 did not greatly exceed that of India, one of the lowest in the world. Although the French public knew nothing about conditions in North Africa, the Arabs and Berbers were learning new standards of judgment; World War II was to stir them to action.

French Indochina felt the exciting effects of the Bolshevik Revolution in Russia and the Kuomintang movement in China. Canton, a center of revolutionary activity uniting Communists and followers of Sun Yat-sen, was so close to Hanoi in Indochina that ideas and enthusiasm easily spread. After 1918 the French found the natives much more difficult to satisfy. The intellectuals were no longer content to be imitation Frenchmen, the University of Hanoi produced radicals, and the middle class was increasing and demanding improved administration. The French introduced councils in the government but gave them merely advisory power and made certain that the French members always outnumbered natives. By 1930 an increasing number of Indochinese were dissatisfied with such constitutional window dressing; they began to preach nationalism.

The share of France at the peace conference in the grab of German and Ottoman dependencies consisted in Africa of part of Togoland and the Cameroons (the rest went to Great Britain), and in Asia of Syria and Lebanon. France treated the African mandates as she did her other possessions in that region. Syria and Lebanon caused trouble.

Syria and Lebanon

When the French moved to take possession of Syria and Lebanon they were acting on the basis of cultural interests extending back to the sixteenth century. They had claimed to be the protector of Latin Christianity in the entire Levant, had sponsored there educational and religious institutions like the Jesuit University of Beirut, and had maintained modest commercial relations with the peoples. To the disappointment of the French, they discovered that the Syrians now preferred the United States or Great Britain as a mandatory power, and really wanted independence. In order to apply the principle defined in the League Covenant that "the well-being and development of such peoples form a sacred trust of civilization" (Article 22), the French first had to drive out Emir Faisal, the Arab ruler, and conquer the people by force of arms. By way of preparing the natives for independent statehood, they applied the maxim of divide and rule. After some experimentation, by 1925 they decided on organizing the people into five separate political units, the most important being Lebanon and Syria. In each they introduced the centralized administrative system characteristic of France proper, and ruled without regard to local autonomy.

In 1926 France gave Lebanon a Western-type of constitution, with a president, a ministry, and an elected parliament but used the government as a façade for continued French control. Syria was forced to wait a little longer for her Western constitution. During a rebellion in 1926, the French troops bombarded Damascus, the capital. Two years later the French high commissioner convoked a constitutional assembly, which was dominated by a powerful National bloc in favor of independence. The constitution which the delegates approved called for the union into one independent state of Syria, Lebanon, and other areas under French mandate, plus British-controlled Transjordan and Palestine; it did not mention France. The French high commissioner found this behavior inadmissible, dissolved the constituent assembly, and promulgated in 1930 his own constitution, keeping matters as they were. He justified the action by France's obligations under the mandate of the League of Nations.

The French endeavored to help the economy by constructing roads, tunnels, bridges, and irrigation works, but the country was poor and the quality of French officialdom mediocre. In order to accomplish the work, the French resorted to forced labor, thus antagonizing all elements of the population—conservative, liberal, urban, rural, Christian, and Moslem. A few landlords controlled the wretched peasantry; because the country lacked attractive natural resources, France devoted little effort to its advance. The Moslems disliked their ruler as an infidel nation and as the disturber of customary ways. Thus whatever France did for education and the economy only created more intellectual and middle-class nationalists. This sociological fact held for all imperial relations; but France did not follow the example of Great Britain and to some extent the Netherlands of gradually creating organs of local and central self-government as outlets for the newly aroused passion.

ITALIAN IMPERIAL RELATIONS

The Italian colonies of Libya, Eritrea, and Somaliland cost the imperialist master far more than they were worth. Excessively hot and deficient in rainfall, they consisted mainly of desert. The scanty population would not have resisted Italian colonization, but in the twenties it was spared the ordeal. Instead of attempting to settle their excess population in the colonies, the Fascists proclaimed to the world their intentions to acquire better dependencies. "You see this map [a Fascist deputy stated in a speech in Rome in 1929]: it is a map of the Roman Empire. Every school must have it in its hall. Look at the Mediterranean, *Mare Nostra,* where Italians have ever been victorious. This sea has always been ours and will be ours once more." The reader may analyze the logic of the deputy's statement and note the disregard of historical and contemporary fact. To realize the ambition would have necessitated the defeat of Great Britain and France; and although Mussolini nourished this aspiration, he confined his public assertions at that time to generalities. The sole value of colonies derived from strategic situation and it pertained to the future. Libya would assure Italy a base for defense on the south shore of the Mediterranean, and Eritrea a base at the south entrance to the Red Sea. The bases still had to be built and naval strength developed to maintain connection with them. For the time being Italy's statesmen confined their efforts to bold words.

Six of the lesser European countries possessed dependent territories. Norway's consisted of a few islands with a total population of about a thousand; and Denmark, after the sale of the Danish West Indies to the United States in 1916, retained only Greenland and its 17,000 people. Spain did nothing to develop the small remnants of her former empire, all of them situated in or near Northwest and West Africa. Portugal imitated Spain in this respect in the few small areas in Southern Asia and the East Indies and in Mozambique and Angola in the southern half of Africa. The only two small states whose colonial activity deserves attention, the Netherlands and Belgium, actually ranked among the great colonial powers, the one primarily by virtue of its ownership of the East Indies, the other by its control of most of the Congo region in Africa. In 1930, 8,000,000 Netherlanders ruled over 65,000,000 colonials; 8,000,000 Belgians were responsible for the fate of 13,000,000 Africans. Each of these two countries considered retention of the empire essential to the prosperity of the nation, and each sought a way of assuring the continuance of the relationship on lines of advantage to ruler and ruled.

NETHERLANDS IMPERIAL RELATIONS

After a past of exploitation of the natives, the Dutch under the moral stimulus of liberalism changed their colonial program to one of paternalism.

In the speech from the throne of 1901 Queen Wilhelmina officially declared in favor of an "ethical policy." "As a Christian power," she said, "the Netherlands is obligated in the East Indian Archipelago to imbue the whole conduct of the Government with the consciousness that the Netherlands has a moral duty to fulfill with respect to the people of these regions." The indirect system of rule continued, but the Dutch introduced as well organs of self-government, first in the form of district and municipal councils. In 1916 they set up a central representative assembly, the People's Council. The central body began with merely advisory authority, but in the twenties it received legislative power under the veto of the Dutch governor-general, including the right previously held by the Netherlands States General to discuss the annual budget. The Dutch in 1922 ceased to apply the term colony to their possessions and introduced a new relationship, somewhat similar to that of the British Commonwealth, by which the Kingdom of the Netherlands would consist of four parts, the Netherlands, the Netherlands Indies, Surinam, and Curaçao.

The Dutch continued to develop the economic resources of the main dependencies, being responsible for the introduction into the Indies of all the major agricultural products, tea, quinine, rubber, vanilla, tobacco, and others, and for the exploitation of tin, bauxite, and oil. They expanded educational facilities and created an excellent system of care for native health. They brought natives to the Netherlands to be trained as doctors, engineers, and other professions in Dutch universities; they established a university at Bandung and spent large sums in scientific research.

Nevertheless, the Dutch antagonized the natives by remaining paternalistic. A few native leaders became important officials in the administration, and an increasing number entered the lower ranks of the bureaucracy, but the People's Council remained a body half appointed and half elected on a limited franchise. Approximately half the members were East Indian; most of the others were Dutch. The council's requests for political reforms were ignored, and natives were excluded from service in the army and navy. The relatively enlightened Dutch rule was failing to win the people to its support.

BELGIAN IMPERIAL RELATIONS

In 1947 the Belgian minister for the colonies wrote about the Congo as follows:

> . . . when we arrived in Central Africa, we found there some of the most backward tribes in the world, addicted to barbarous practices, to inter-tribal warfare, subject to devastating diseases, dying often from hunger, ruled by local and sanguinary despots, and hunted by Arab slave-dealers. They were certainly much more backward than the natives whom Caesar found in France and Belgium or Claudius and Hadrian in Great Britain nearly two thousand years ago, and these

have required two thousand years to attain the very relative standard of civilization which is ours to-day.

Within a quarter of a century, he continued,

Wars and hunger have come to an end; diseases are being fought. I do not mean to say that it will take us another two thousand years to complete our task in Africa; the means put at our disposal by modern science will allow us to achieve it in a measurable space of time. But let us not display undue haste, and let us never forget the wise French saying: . . . "Time takes its revenge for what has been done without it." [4]

The Belgian government in 1908 forced King Leopold to transfer the Congo from his personal rule to that of the state. It then set to work to undo the exploitation of natives and native resources which had enriched the king and his friends and shocked world opinion. Belgium's eclipse during World War I delayed the consistent introduction of reforms until the early nineteen-twenties, when the government set up a unique system of rule. This system has achieved impressive results.

Belgium's goal was not to prepare the colony for self-government but to develop economic resources and to improve social conditions. The Belgian parliament, which passed all legislation for the colony, left control mainly in the hands of the minister for the colonies. This official was advised by a colonial council composed, in addition to himself, of fourteen members, six appointed by parliament (three for each house) and eight appointed by the king. Most of the policy for governing the colony was laid down through ministerial decree, with discretion for implementation being largely left to the governor-general residing in the colony. He and the lesser administrators, all Belgians, were assisted by advisory councils composed almost entirely of Europeans. A colonial legislative body was not created, but responsibility for local government remained largely in the hands of tribal chiefs.

The state took a major share in economic development, for the kind of natural resources which the Congo possessed required large investments of capital. The exploitation of timber resources and of minerals such as copper and later uranium and the raising of cattle and crops like the oil palm, rubber, tea, and cinchona were considered to be most economically handled on a large scale. The construction of means of transportation and communication proved to be unusually expensive because of the expanse and inaccessibility of this tropical region. The natives lacked all resources to assist in opening up their land except that of their own labor.

The Belgian government solved the problem mainly by participating up to as much as 50 per cent in capital and control in companies formed by private individuals for investment in the region. It received in return not merely a large sum in the form of taxes but a high percentage of the

[4] *Colonial Administration by European Powers* (London: Royal Institute of International Affairs, 1947), pp. 66-67.

profit. In this way it obtained funds to found and support, from 1926 on, the National Institute for Agricultural Research in the Belgian Congo, giving to it responsibility for work on a wide variety of problems, from exploring the cause and control of sleeping sickness to spreading helpful knowledge to native farmers of fibers and foods, from doing geological research to studying the effects of urbanism. It subsidized popular elementary education but left teaching entirely to Catholic and Protestant missionaries under governmental supervision. It discouraged the immigration of Europeans except for specific tasks, and it encouraged the natives to assume responsible positions in the economy, in social work, and in the administration as fast as they would and to advance as high as they could. Wherever the natives reached the necessary level of cleanliness and other forms of personal responsibility, they were encouraged to associate as equals with the whites, no color bars being imposed. The Belgian government believed that these problems ranked as most important at the time, that the natives knew nothing about politics, and that questions relating to government should wait until the economic and social bases of a new society had been laid. "Of all the parts of Africa I have seen," a traveling American Negro woman has declared, "it is certainly in the Belgian Congo that the greatest care has been taken of the native welfare."

IMPERIAL DEFENSE

During the twenties the question of how to protect the dependencies did not arise in acute form. The colonial world shared with the states of Europe the respite afforded by the temporary eclipse of Germany and Russia, and the temporary alignment of Japan with the West made in 1921–1922 at the Washington conference. The other imperialist powers were both satiated and tired of fighting. The small states with colonial empires, the Netherlands, Belgium, Spain, and Portugal, continued to depend for security upon the mutual antagonism of the great powers and, particularly with regard to the Netherlands, upon the British navy.

World War I had made evident the need for each British dominion to assist in its own defense and to be able to rely upon aid from the entire Commonwealth. Canada had learned that its defensive interests lay with the United States as much as with Great Britain, perhaps even more, and that, ideally speaking, the Commonwealth and the United States should always cooperate. The Union of South Africa was situated so far away from the centers of power conflict that especially the Boer part of the population remained as isolationist with respect to the rest of the empire and the world as before the war. As small states, Australia and New Zealand clung to Great Britain. They most feared Japan and wished Great Britain to maintain friendship and alliance with this potential predator. Great Britain herself had learned that she needed the defensive support of the empire, that she could no longer pursue a European policy, or one anywhere, without consulting the dominions. Most of the reluctance to commit herself to any official continental responsibility, either by way of an alliance or by way of the League, stemmed from the necessity to hold together an empire of such disparate interests.

France had scarcely begun to think in this decade beyond the German menace. She expected her empire to help in her defence, but she took no steps of consequence to develop the peoples in that direction other than by prewar policy of turning native leaders into pseudo Frenchmen. She did not try to build up a spirit similar to that of the British Commonwealth. The difficulties of doing so were great because of the backwardness of the people and their alien race and culture; but she tried no other method of drawing the empire together than that of French political and cultural centralization. She quarreled from time to time with Great Britain over policies in Europe. Her main rival and object of mistrust with respect to the dependencies was Italy, and the center of their antagonism was the western half of the Mediterranean. France knew that Fascist Italy inherited the desire to acquire Tunisia. The two powers therefore quarreled over naval armaments. Each accused the other of being a potential threat, which it was, to its connections with African dependencies. As we have seen in Chapter 5, the two powers compromised on naval armaments, without any diminution of mutual mistrust.

Apart from the British dominions, the dependent peoples showed little or no concern with the issue of their own defense. Most of those in Africa and Asia were too ignorant to be aware of the problem. Others, like those in India and the states of the Near and Middle East, were so busy trying to advance their own independence that they had no thoughts left for troubles that might ultimately arise. The few dependencies in the Western Hemisphere were protected by the Monroe Doctrine and the Pan American Union. The Soviet Union was beginning to infiltrate backward countries of Asia but had not yet aroused the West's fears. The natives were much more concerned over the danger of Western imperialism than they were over that of Russian communism. The only antagonism of great powers that might affect future imperial developments was that between Japan and the United States, the one bent on acquisitions in China, the other seeking to preserve China's integrity. During the decade this potential clash remained under some diplomatic control.

In general, one may say that the twenties marked the stirring of many dependent peoples for the realization of the ideals which the League Covenant had set for the mandates, but that with the exception of Great Britain in relation to the dominions the imperialist powers did not utilize this decade of respite from war to change their colonial system. We have seen that they did not tackle with imagination and initiative Europe's own problems; they did not turn the League into an adequate instrument for handling power conflicts. In the same way they neglected to anticipate the changes that were being prepared in the minds of colonial peoples. They lacked the creative force of statesmanship.

Suggestions for Further Reading

BURT, ALFRED LEROY. *The Evolution of the British Empire and Commonwealth from the American Revolution.* Boston: D. C. Heath & Company, Inc., 1956. Judicious and interesting survey.

GORIS, JAN ALBERT, ed. *Belgium.* See the Readings for Chapter 7. Contains useful discussion of the Belgian Congo.

LANDHEER, BARTHOLOMEW, ed. *The Netherlands.* See the Readings for Chapter 7. Contains useful survey of Dutch colonial possessions.

LATOURETTE, KENNETH SCOTT. *A Short History of the Far East.* See the Readings for Chapter 1.

LENCZOWSKI, GEORGE. *The Middle East in World Affairs.* See the Readings for Chapter 2.

ROYAL INSTITUTE OF INTERNATIONAL AFFAIRS. *The Colonial Problem.* New York: Oxford University Press, 1937. Report of a British study group. Full of information.

WARRINER, DOREEN. *Land and Poverty in the Middle East.* London: Royal Institute of International Affairs, 1948. By an experienced British scholar.

ZINKIN, MAURICE. *Asia and the West.* London: Chatto & Windus, Ltd., 1951. Invaluable study of the impact of Western civilization upon the Asiatic peoples from Pakistan and India to the East Indies and Japan.

Part III

Europe in the 1930's

Chronological Preview

1928
Salazar becomes ruler of Portugal
First Five-Year Plan in U.S.S.R.

1929
Concordat and Lateran Accord with Italy
King Alexander becomes dictator of Yugoslavia

1929–1930
Acceleration of collectivization of Soviet agriculture

1929–1931
British Labor government

1929–1933
World Economic Crisis

1929–1934
Conferences on Balkan union

1930
Return of King Carol to Romania

1930–1932
Brüning government in Germany

1931
Spanish Republic established
Japan begins conquest of Manchuria
British Ministry of National Union formed
Statute of Westminster
Sept. Britain abandons the gold standard

1932
British Import Duties Law
Imperial Conference at Ottawa
De Valera becomes head of Irish Free State
Anglo-Iraq Treaty—Iraq enters League of Nations

1932–1934
Failure of the Disarmament Conference

1933
Japan and Germany resign from League of Nations
World Economic and Financial Conference at London
United States devalues the dollar
Jan. 30. Formation of National Socialist government in Germany

1934
Authoritarian government in Austria
Treaty of nonaggression between Germany and Poland

1934 (Cont.)
Rome Protocols
Soviet Union joins League of Nations

1935
Van Zeeland cabinet in Belgium
King Boris becomes dictator in Bulgaria
Beneš becomes president of Czechoslovakia
Germany begins to rearm
Soviet treaties with France and Czechoslovakia
India Act

1935–1936
Ethiopian Crisis

1936
Metaxas becomes dictator of Greece
Anglo-Egyptian Treaty
Formation of the Axis Pact
Anti-Comintern Pact between Germany and Japan
German military occupation of the Rhineland
Nazi Four-Year Plan initiated
New Soviet constitution adopted
France devalues the franc

1936–1937
Popular Front government in France

1936–1938
Governmental purges in the U.S.S.R.

1937
Neville Chamberlain becomes prime minister of Great Britain
Break between National Congress party and Moslem League
New constitution of the Irish Republic adopted

1938
France passes National Service Law
Daladier government established in France
Feb. Germany seizes Austria
Sept. Germany destroys Czechoslovakia

1939
Spring. Great Britain and France promise to defend Poland and other lesser states against aggression
Aug. Nazi-Soviet Treaty
Sept. Nazi invasion of Poland. Great Britain and France declare war on Germany

Chapter 12 · Europe in the World Economic Crisis, 1929-1933

VIOLENT IMPACT ON ALL ASPECTS OF LIFE

Between 1929 and 1933 an economic crisis struck the world with a violence unequaled by any of the six similar crises of the previous half century. As an example, the figures available for Germany reveal that in the worst of the former depressions industrial production had declined by 6 per cent; in 1929–1933 it shrank by 39 per cent. German production of pig iron in the depression of 1907 suffered a loss of 20 per cent and in that of 1921 of 39 per cent; between 1929 and 1932 it fell by 58 per cent. The approximate loss to the world from this depression has been estimated at between 149 and 176 billion gold dollars at 1928 prices—102 to 117 billion in industrial production, 1 billion in agricultural production, 31 to 35 billion in trade, and 15 to 23 billion in transport, an amount comparable to the total cost of World War I. The economic crisis, like World Wars I and II, is one of the world catastrophes of this century and forms the bridge between the two wars.

Although exerting its main force in the economic sphere, the economic depression involved all aspects of life. The impact was greatest in countries like Germany where the war had left, in addition to major problems of economic stability, angry disagreement over political organization and social relations; but to greater or lesser degree it was felt by all peoples except those in the Soviet Union, whose leaders had isolated the economy from that of the non-Communist world. These four or five years of desolation brought about the swift change from the attempted restoration in the twenties of prewar standards and practices to nationalistic totalitarianism. By accepting dictatorship, nations transferred the crisis from the economic to the social and political spheres, thereby unwittingly multiplying their troubles.

FAILURE OF POSTWAR ECONOMIC ADJUSTMENT

The crisis of 1929–1933 was more than an ordinary downswing of the business cycle. It developed from the matrix of economic problems inherited from World War I, which had remained unsolved during the preceding decade—overproduction in both industry and agriculture, inequitable redistribution of national income, inflation, international financial instability, excessive restrictions on trade, and attempts of nations economically crippled by war to live beyond their means. Since the war had left these conditions in most of the world, the economic crisis took on similar scope.

The depression began in the United States with a sudden break on the stock market. In the latter half of the twenties Americans had had so much money and optimism that they had speculated heavily in industrial shares. Economists' warning that the size of production and of profits did not justify the current price of stocks and that a collapse was imminent went unheeded. When the break came in 1929, the crisis spread immediately from the stock market to the entire economy. Prices tumbled, investment almost ceased at home, goods could not be sold, unemployment mounted, sums for foreign loans became scarce to the vanishing point, and existing foreign loans were recalled. Since the United States served as one of the two great capital markets of the world and since it produced 45 per cent of the world's industrial goods, the effects of the crisis were immediately transmitted abroad, not merely because of loss of confidence but through the collapse of international trade and finance.

All branches of the economy were affected. Farmers were desperate over the inability to market their products, while millions of people were as desperately in need of food. Industrial production was severely curtailed in the face of a vast market which lacked money. Capital was plentiful; yet its owners feared to invest it. Millions of people eager for work were forced to remain as idle as the facilities that might have employed them. Compelled to maintain workers by dole, governments entered a field of public support for which they were unprepared both financially and administratively. Heavy taxation on those who could pay curtailed private ability to accumulate capital and forced upon the state much of the responsibility for investment. Private leadership thereby lost severely in prestige, and the state became a major entrepreneur. Each country sought to maintain or expand its export trade while curbing imports, thus preventing other countries from earning foreign exchange with which to buy abroad. International loans dried up and existing loans were recalled, just when they were most urgently needed to maintain the flow of trade. Each country endeavored to isolate itself to the limit of its ability from the depression in other countries.

In a world economy of interdependence each country tried to be self-sufficient, irrespective of cost and of ability to do so. Each individual, organization, or country was uncertain about its immediate future; each took any emergency measures that seemed to promise relief. The guiding policies became those of "beggar my neighbor" and "save yourself if you can."

Agriculture

Agriculture fell as an easy victim to the crisis. The overexpansion of world production during the war had persisted, and, in spite of attempts during the succeeding decade to restrict output and stabilize prices, the situation by 1929 was so unbalanced that the crisis on the stock market immediately affected the prices of farm products. Since the agricultural market was world-wide, the organization of millions of farmers in order to curb output proved impossible. Commodities continued to pour from the soil, as farmers strove to offset the effect of falling prices upon income by expanding output. Low-cost producers flooded any open market, thereby threatening ruin to native growers. The exporting countries suffered to a much greater degree than the importing ones, because they could not protect their agriculture by tariffs. The industrial countries of Europe, being the largest market for foodstuffs and raw materials, benefited from this position and saved their farmers from the worst effects of the depression. Only when farmers produced on a large scale for export (for example, potatoes in Germany, oats in France, or wine in Italy) were they subject to the same economic exposure as the wheat or rubber growers of the colonial world. The peasants of the Balkans and of Eastern Europe, producers of surplus foodstuffs, suffered as intensely as any overseas large-scale exporters.

The agricultural exporting countries suffered doubly because the industrial states of Europe could shift some of the loss of income to the agricultural countries from which they imported materials. Industry was able to maintain prices at a higher relative level than agriculture could because of its greater facility by cooperation to adjust production to the market. It benefited from the difference in price between food and raw materials, on the one hand, and manufactured articles, on the other. Thus the agricultural exporters were compelled to give more of their wheat or rubber than they had previously given for a machine or other factory article. The terms of trade had turned strongly against them. In this way between 1930 and 1933 Great Britain was able to transfer 50 per cent of the loss in national production to the agricultural countries; Germany, 15 per cent; and France between 1930 and 1932, 36 per cent. The farmers were able to escape this disadvantage only by refusing to purchase industrial goods. Subsistence farming increased at the expense of the production of commercial crops; and wherever farm indebtedness, taxes, and other expenses requiring current money were too heavy to be met, the farmers turned to politics for relief.

The extent of the depression in agriculture may become clear from a few figures. World production from 1929 through 1933 increased slightly above the average of the preceding five years, but European importations radically declined. Between 1927–1928 and 1932–1933 the amount of wheat imported by European countries, excluding the United Kingdom, dropped by more than 50 per cent. Germany and Italy, two of the largest importers, reduced their purchases from 24 million quintals each to 1⅓ and 3 million quintals, respectively. The importation of beef and veal into the principal European importing countries, excluding the United Kingdom, dropped in 1933 to less than one third of the amount brought in five years before. For Germany the importation fell from 151,000 tons to 600 tons. The results were evident in the collapse of prices. By the end of 1929 the agricultural price index was less than two thirds, and by the end of 1932 it was less than one fourth that of the average level of 1923–1925. Between 1928 and 1932 the price of raw sugar fell from 2.46 cents to 0.93 cents per pound. During the same period that of rubber moved from 22.33 cents per pound to 3.43 cents. During 1931 the price of wheat declined below that of 1927 by 60 per cent.

Industry

Fortunately for Europe, the industrial countries by means of high tariffs were able to prevent extreme hardship to farmers. The price of wheat in exporting countries like the United States or Romania fell to about one half that in importing states like Germany or France. Farm indebtedness and family income tended to follow similar lines. The peasants in the exporting countries were forced to borrow money with which to support their existing debt burden and to meet any extra expenditures. Their income dropped to a much greater degree than that of the farmers in countries like France and Germany. With government aid the peasants in these states, considering the general severity of the crisis, came through fairly well. Their income remained about the same; in Germany, for example, the percentage of the national income going to the farmers increased between 1928 and 1933 from 7.7 to 8.7. By way of contrast, the example of Bulgaria may be offered. In that country the share of the national income going to agriculture dropped between 1929 and 1932 by 35 per cent, and similar decline held true for Poland, Hungary, Romania, and the other agricultural states of Eastern and Southeastern Europe.

As industry has increased the volume and variety of production it has rendered the economy susceptible to the business cycle to an extent unknown in the simple economies of previous ages. The greater degree of interdependence of the parts of the economy throughout the world has augmented uncertainty in the relations of those parts and has created conditions in which fear and panic may spread from one area or one branch to the entire world economy. When the stock market in the United States collapsed, the effects were immediately felt in European industry, partly by way of the abrupt withdrawal of American loans, partly by way of the curtailment of buying, partly by way of the spread to the European peoples of doubt about the stability of their own economy. Since before the depression the United States (45 per cent), Germany (11 per cent), United Kingdom (9 per cent), and France (7 per cent) accounted for the production of nearly three fourths of the world's industrial goods, the relation between them was particularly close.

In contrast to agriculture, where the volume of production was maintained, industry responded to market changes in the depression and curbed output. World industrial production declined in quantity from 1928 to 1932 by 34 per cent; during the five years 1930–1934 the total amount of decline was greater than the entire world industrial output in either 1928 or 1929. Even if the United States is excluded, the size of the decline for Europe alone remains impressive—for industrialized Europe (Germany, United Kingdom, France, Czechoslovakia, Belgium, Netherlands, Austria, Sweden, and Denmark), 30 per cent from 1929 to 1932; for industry in agricultural Europe (Poland, Italy, Hungary, Romania, and Greece), 22 per cent. The difference may be explained by the greater dependence of the former states upon the export market, where competition was most intense.

The severest reduction occurred in the branches of industry manufacturing goods the purchase of which could be postponed. Producers' goods or capital goods belong in this class, together with durable consumers' goods and housing. Existing factories, machines, refrigerators, houses, and the like could function through the depression years. Although consumers' goods continued of necessity to be produced and bought in the wealthy society of Western industrialism, the reserve of many of these was sufficiently large to permit delay in restocking. Apart from the United States, Germany suffered most and the Netherlands next. Germany, for example, turned out in 1932 only 47 per cent as great a volume of producers' goods as of consumers' goods (1925–1929 equal 100), indicating a catastrophic decline in economic activity. The impression is confirmed by the drop of 65 per cent in Germany between 1929 and 1932 in the production of crude steel. No other European state underwent so great a reduction, even though for Europe as a whole, excluding the Soviet Union and including the United Kingdom, the decline in those years amounted to 50 per cent. Since steel is used in the manufacture of all production goods, the small amount of it being turned out revealed a sick economy.

Foreign Trade

Data on the size of European exports and imports reveal the dimensions of the dislocation of markets. The figures given in the table on page 330 include both industrial and agricultural products. The year 1929 is used as a basis of 100 for comparison, and the year 1932 is chosen because it marked the lowest point in the depression. Industrial countries maintained a fairly high level of imports of foodstuffs and raw materials, and their exportation of manufactures declined. For agricultural countries, the reverse was usually true. In Italy, however, both exports and imports were kept relatively high because of the country's great dependence upon foreign trade and her lack of a reserve such as existed in Switzerland, for ex-

INDUSTRIAL COUNTRIES		*1932*
United Kingdom	Imports	88.3
	Exports	62.9
Germany	Imports	68.8
	Exports	58.8
Switzerland	Imports	97.4
	Exports	49.9
France	Imports	88.8
	Exports	58.5
Czechoslovakia	Imports	59.8
	Exports	50.0
United States	Imports	61.6
	Exports	52.2
AGRICULTURAL COUNTRIES		
Italy	Imports	72.2
	Exports	77.4
Hungary	Imports	45.4
	Exports	49.7
Yugoslavia	Imports	49.7
	Exports	72.3

SOURCE: W. S. Woytinsky, *The Social Consequences of the Economic Depression* (Geneva: International Labor Office, 1936), p. 316.

ample. Hungary merely retreated into local self-sufficiency. In view of the greater fall in price of agricultural products and raw materials than of industrial products, the industrial countries found it economical to continue the purchase of relatively large quantities of these commodities. They could pay for them with a smaller volume of industrial goods than previously. Nonetheless, the main reasons for the decline in industrial exports were the inability of countries to afford them and the policy of preserving the national market for national producers. Countries like Germany and Czechoslovakia were particularly affected, the latter even more than the former. Both had large agricultural interests, which in a crisis were able to satisfy most of the basic food needs at a reduced standard of diet; both lived to a large degree from the industrial processing of imported raw materials and export of the finished goods. The extent to which they were struck by the depression may become more vivid from figures on the export of steel products. In Germany it declined between 1929 and 1933 by 66 per cent; in Czechoslovakia, by 83 per cent.

Drop in Prices

Prices dropped with precipitate speed. By 1933 the volume of world production was down from the level of 1929 by one fourth, whereas prices in terms of gold had dropped by 53 per cent, and in the next year they sank even farther. The maximum fall in price level of certain European countries below that of 1929 varied from 50 per cent in the Netherlands (April, 1933) to 24 per cent in Czechoslovakia (January, 1934), with most industrial countries showing a drop from 30 to 40 per cent. Such extreme price changes in so short a span of time were new to the world. Man had experienced inflation at an even dizzier pace, but not deflation of these dimensions. The effects of the one upon society had been catastrophic but had been restricted to relatively few countries; those of deflation were now world-wide.

Rigidity had developed at many points in the economic structure of the industrial society and prevented speedy adjustment to a new price level on which economic revival could build. The inequality in the price fall among the different branches of the economy accentuated the uncertainty of prospects and disinclined individuals to risk steps toward overcoming the depression. Cartels and monopolies existed in some industries that enabled them to preserve prices which even at the bottom of the depression were almost twice as high as free prices. Tariff protection afforded similar advantage. As a rule, manufacturers were able to keep up their prices much better than could producers of foodstuffs and raw materials. Retailers were able to preserve the price level much more effectively than wholesalers could; indeed, the cost of living kept fairly steady, as did also the wages of organized labor, at least for those actually employed. The predepression level was for some articles and in some countries retained; but, in general, prices varied according to time, place, and circumstance.

Unemployment

The social effects of crisis were evident in two major respects, the incidence of unemployment and the decline and redistribution of national income. The former actually constituted a part of the latter, but each requires special analysis.

As a rule, unemployment was particularly heavy in parts of the economy like mining, manufacturing, and building, which were most susceptible to changes in the business cycle. These were the producers of goods which other businesses could temporarily forego.

It has been estimated that world unemployment in 1929 amounted to about 10 million persons. By 1932, that is, within three years, the figure had trebled, and if workers on short-time employment or on jobs made merely to keep them alive are added, the number would reach more than 40 million. The following figures show the percentage of the population that was unemployed in several European countries.

COUNTRY	*1929*	*1932*
Great Britain		
Wholly unemployed	8.2	17.6
Temporarily stopped	2.2	4.5
Belgium		
Wholly unemployed	1.3	19.0
Partially unemployed	3.0	20.7
Germany		
Wholly unemployed	13.1	43.7
Partially employed	7.5	22.6
Switzerland		
Wholly unemployed	1.8	9.1
Partially unemployed	1.7	12.2
Netherlands	7.1	29.5
Austria	12.3	26.1
Czechoslovakia	2.2	13.5
Sweden	10.7	22.8
Norway	15.4	30.8
Denmark	15.5	31.7
Poland	4.9	11.8

SOURCE: Woytinsky, *The Social Consequences of the Economic Depression,* p. 334.

The average amount of unemployment at that time for the countries included was about 25 per cent. The omission of France may be explained on the grounds that unemployment remained insignificant in that country until 1932, when it reached the relatively small figure of 305,000 of a total population of about 40 million. The country by far most affected was Germany, where, as figures reveal, only 33.7 per cent of the workers were regularly employed.

Unemployment affected the size and distribution of the national income. Those who were steadily employed and were so organized that they could protect their interests found that their nominal wages declined but that their real wages actually increased. They could buy more goods for a given unit of money than previously, primarily at the expense of the farmer. The trade-unions maintained their membership fairly well, in some countries like Germany declining in numbers, in others like the small countries of Northwestern Europe and Czechoslovakia and Hungary actually increasing. At all times the unions retained as members many unable to pay dues. Part-time employment and the pooling of resources by the members of a family enabled workers to exist who according to official statistics should have been starving. Millions, however, depended upon the state insurance systems; and when these systems broke under the load, as they did in most countries, the government substituted some kind of dole. The amount of the dole varied according to the country; in Great Britain it barely kept a person alive, and in Germany it was from one third to one half as much as in Great Britain. Without supplementary private aid the recipients would have starved.

The middle class was better protected against mass unemployment than the workers were because the services it performed continued to be essential; but it suffered from loss of income and some unemployment. Salaries of white-collar employees were severely cut and taxes increased. Many of this class sought as a last resort to remain independent by investing their small capital in retail trade. In Germany, for example, the retail trade in 1933 was 13 per cent lower in amount than in 1925; nonetheless, the number of persons employed in commerce had declined by less than 5 per cent, and there were one third too many shops. Similar, or even worse, conditions prevailed in Great Britain and especially France. When shopkeepers inevitably found that they could not avoid bankruptcy, they blamed their plight upon the competition of cooperatives, department stores, and new kinds of retail outlets like chain stores. Those members of the middle and upper classes who lived from investments in stocks or bonds were at the mercy of the forces at work on the undertakings. If the investments continued to pay as before, the recipients gained from the increased value of money; if they failed, partially defaulted, or reduced interest or dividend rates, the rentiers suffered. The bourgeoisie were few who could live on reserve funds. Some, particularly those in essential industries like food processing, continued to prosper even during the depression.

Financial Relations

The change in the value of money profoundly affected financial relations. The burden of debt increased by the amount of the rise in monetary worth. Shrinkage of the market and the difficulty of earning a profit multiplied the handicaps to repayment. Many farmers found it impossible to pay the interest on their debts and wherever possible borrowed additional amounts. In Hungary farm indebtedness increased 40 per cent during 1932; in Bulgaria it rose from 1930 to 1933 by 50 per cent; in Germany, by 40 per cent. Industry and commerce faced similar shortages. Money was plentiful in quantity; but the prospect of declining prices, collapsing profits, and bankruptcy did not attract investment funds, and capital was hoarded. Between 1929 and 1932 anyone with ready money might lose much of its value by investment, but he could add to its real value by holding it inactive. In 1931, instead of showing a favorable balance of investment, Germany withdrew from investments and reserves a sum equivalent to $1,250 million. Other countries suffered, not in the same proportions, but in the same way.

Closely connected with domestic financial difficulties were those of an international character. Heavy borrowers of foreign funds, like Germany and the states of Eastern and Southeastern Europe, whose prosperity during the preceding five years had depended upon the continued inflow of foreign capital, found themselves in 1929–1930 abruptly deprived of further funds and faced with the demand for repayment. They could at no time have met this demand without dire results; they were utterly unable to do so in a depression. Banks had borrowed large sums abroad on short terms of three to six months and had lent them on long terms. When the crisis struck they could not recover the money, and many were caught short of funds. The most disastrous bank failure proved to be that of the *Kredit-Anstalt* in Vienna in May, 1931, an institution closely associated with German and Balkan banks. Its closing shook public trust and threatened Europe with financial catastrophe.

When the crisis reached the stage of endangering financial stability, the governments intervened. The first piece of housecleaning concerned reparations and war debts. As early as June, 1931, President Herbert Hoover proposed a moratorium on reparations payments, which was accepted. Through the sudden rise in the value of money the economic crisis increased the burden of reparations to the point at which further attempts at payment would have meant monetary disaster. After a year of moratorium the powers agreed at the Lausanne Conference in 1932 to cancel 90 per cent of the reparations payments provided that they could reach agreement with their own creditors, that is, with the United States for the cancellation of war debts. Since the United States government refused to consider the proposal—it was an election year—the question of both war debts and reparations found a solution in default. In spite of the protests of the United States Congress, Europe, with the exception of Finland, declined to pay the United States further sums on war debts. European governments excused themselves by arguing that they no longer received an equivalent from Germany. A world depression thus was the means of settling a political problem which ever since the war had kept international and European national economic relations in a state of strain.

GOVERNMENT INTERVENTION

Within each country the government intervened to preserve the financial organization from collapse. The means employed included a moratorium on the repayment of debts, the advance of government credit at low rates of interest, official assistance to banks, and the introduction of official control over the use of gold and foreign exchange. Peasants and owners of land were enabled to avoid the foreclosure of mortgages; depositors were assured the safety of their funds; and the flight of scarce capital from national currency to a sounder and safer foreign currency was curbed. The British government left the gold standard in September, 1931, by suspending payment of the pound sterling in gold; other countries, including the United States in 1933, followed suit. France, Italy, Switzerland, Belgium, and the Netherlands pretended financial orthodoxy; but by employing the same trade practices as others, they rendered impossible the functioning of the traditional gold standard.

The main hindrance to recovery came from the effort of every country to sell the maximum amount of its commodities abroad but to buy a minimum of essentials. Each sought to accumulate sufficient foreign exchange with which to purchase essentials and to maintain its foreign credit. Declining prices made it necessary to sell more and more abroad in order to try to preserve as much as possible of one's economy. Each state tried to export in order to keep its people at work, while refusing to purchase the imports which would have enabled foreign peoples to remain at work. This procedure came to be known as the export of depression. Great Britain, for example, came into the crisis with low tariffs and a large export-import trade. She was relatively well prepared to withstand the depression because she had already partially adjusted her economy to changed international conditions. Not even she could maintain an open market. Her departure from the gold standard reduced the domestic value of her money and, by raising the price of imported goods, protected the market for domestic producers. She and other countries supplemented this type of protection in other ways. First they tried higher and higher tariffs; when foreign goods continued to enter, they licensed imports and allowed only specified amounts to come in. The quota system was preferred because it could be used to force a country to purchase an agreed amount of goods in return. Multilateral trade gave way to bilateral trade, and the government controlled foreign exchange and allowed each importer only a certain amount of a particular foreign currency with which to purchase materials.

The system violated all the principles of economics. The bureaucrat supplemented to a large extent the businessman as the expediter of international trade. Primitive barter was adopted by nations leading in the new industrial economy. A country would in some instances be compelled to purchase an article from an expensive producer rather than from a low-cost producer merely because it could sell something to the former in return. In order to conserve foreign exchange, every state sought to produce everything it could, irrespective of cost. Three-cornered trade became difficult and in numerous cases impossible. With the gold standard eliminated, nations had no medium of exchange for measuring values and reckoning up accounts. They reverted to the tedious process of comparing the value of a pair of shoes, a bushel of wheat, a pound of coffee, a liter of milk, a sewing machine. They became economic Neanderthalers in the most complicated economy in the history of the world.

In the welter of bilateralism Great Britain played a special role by virtue of her position as the world's greatest trading and banking center, as the mother country of the world's greatest empire and of the British Commonwealth. Her extensive trade and banking connections enabled her to negotiate a series of bilateral trade treaties with some of her most important markets, especially those of Scandinavia. Thus began the Sterling area. The name itself did not become used in official documents until 1940, but it had actually existed in operation for several years. The Sterling area was composed of those countries that, being closely related to Britain by trade, used the sterling exchange standard with London as their center for international banking. The British Commonwealth countries were members, as were the British colonies, altogether the largest area with a relatively free monetary exchange to be found in the world. Trade stipulations varied among its members, the most notable being that of imperial preference agreed upon at the imperial conference in Ottawa in 1932. At that time Great Britain broke with her traditional policy of multilateral trade in favor of reciprocal preferential trade within the empire. In this respect Great Britain followed France, which as early as 1892 had broken with the policy of equal opportunities for all nations to trade with her dependencies. At that time France put in practice a policy of assimilation in economic affairs by binding colonial trade to the mother country through preferential tariff rates. The world economic crisis caused her to add quota restrictions, in order to keep foreign trade from the colonies. The Belgium government, bound by the Treaty of Berlin of 1885 to maintain the Open Door in the Congo, could not change the commitment by unilateral action. The Dutch kept the existing policy, with the addition of severe quota restrictions for Japanese imports threatening ruin to native industry in the East Indies. In 1933 the Portuguese followed the French in assimilating the colonies to the mother country.

The mother countries not only imposed trade restrictions but changed from a policy of laisser faire for the development of colonial economy to one of planned aid. The construction at government expense of essential public works, roads, harbors, and the like, had proved insufficient. The economic crisis encouraged the view that dependencies needed official planning and public investment in order to introduce the commerce and industry needed to improve living conditions among natives and to utilize idle resources. In 1929 Britain passed the first Colonial Development Act, allocating £1 million a year for investment in the empire. Little was accomplished, however, before World War II. France made similar plans, in 1934, and other colonial powers augmented their expenditures for capital developments. In the thirties the percentage of total imports and exports enjoyed by trade between the mother country and the dependencies rose appreciably. That imperial preference caused the increase may be doubted, for countries like the Netherlands and Belgium that had not changed trade policies shared in the gain about as much as did Great Britain and France.

Empires and commonwealths of nations were being cultivated while the bonds of multilateral trade and the gold standard among all nations broke apart. The Europeans were awaking to the opportunities and the responsibility for modernization of the dependencies just when native peoples responded to the ideals of nationalism and dreamed about the speediest means for achieving a form of life comparable to that of the West.

FAILURE OF THE LEAGUE OF NATIONS

Since the economic crisis crippled the entire world, one might have expected that the League of Nations would take an active part in overcoming the effects. It had not grown to a stature equal to so great a task; the League served as scarcely more than a spectator. The Covenant had not given it definite responsibility in economic affairs. The convention for the abolition of import and export prohibitions and restrictions negotiated at the world economic conference in 1927 proved an early victim of the crisis; it was buried in 1930. A tariff truce proposed in 1930 found no acceptance. The next year saw the failure of an idea submitted by bankers on the League Finance Committee to create an International Mortgage Credit Company. Plans were numerous, but the will to act was absent.

Final proof of the League's inadequacy came when the World Economic and Financial Conference convened in London in the summer of 1933. An agenda had been prepared by a committee of leading economists, and the conference was attended by distinguished political leaders from the participating countries. When discussion began of a program looking toward cooperation in trade and finance, it became evident that no statesman would recede from nationalistic economic policies. Two leading nations, Great Britain and the United States, had left the gold standard, and Germany adhered to it only in name. The restoration of that standard and hence the stabilization of foreign exchange rates became thereby impracticable. The United States had in 1930 introduced the highest tariff in its history, an example that Great Britain and every other power followed. Quotas and all the other means for throttling the international exchange of goods had been created. Prospects for restoring the flow of trade did not exist. Germany's recent turn to National Socialism showed the extent to which ultranationalism was on the march.

The economic officials of the League had opposed the convocation of the conference as futile, and results confirmed their prediction. The last days of the meeting were devoted to the offer by statesmen of alibis for failure; and since President Roosevelt had attracted world attention during the conference by refusing to consider as yet the stabilization of monetary exchange rates, the United States received most of the blame. The great powers, who as the possessors of almost three fourths of the world's industrial productive capacity might have cooperated to lead the world out of depression, set the worst example.

SOCIAL AND POLITICAL IMPACT OF THE CRISIS

The effects of depression appeared in the condition of both physical and mental health. Since the situation was similar in all countries, a summary of the statements by the Prussian minister of social welfare may be used as representative. Dietary habits changed to fit the reduced income. People ate more bread and potatoes, rye rather than wheat, and margarine instead of butter; they were rarely able to afford the protective foods, meat and dairy products, and except for the cheapest, like cabbage, they often found vegetables beyond their reach. The Prussian minister reported that after the autumn of 1931 the health of school children in large parts of the country had deteriorated. He found especially prevalent the diseases resulting from lack of food during the period of growth (diseases like anemia, scrofula, caries of the teeth, and nervous conditions), which rapidly led to fatigue and inattention. He found diseases caused by uncleanliness, such as impetigo. The public health agencies reduced the staff of doctors and dentists and the number of hospital beds available. School baths closed; school kitchens were suspended. A reporter to the Health Organization of the League described the psychological state observed among the unemployed and members of their families in Great Britain, Germany, and the United States as one of anxiety, fear, bitterness, loss of self-confidence, and despair.

In most countries the economy reached the bottom of the depression in 1932. Thereafter, natural powers of economic revival set in. Inventories had sunk so low that essential goods had to be manufactured; thus a few people were able to return to work. As these few acquired money to spend, they created a demand for additional goods. The recovery occurred so slowly, however, that society was scarcely aware of it. Until the onset of World War II the European peoples lived under the shadow of the depression. Many of them drew conclusions about political action necessary to overcome an economic crisis. By an ironic twist of fate they perpetuated the characteristics of crisis in the instruments of government and politics, of social relations and culture, after the worst phase of the economic crisis had passed. They increasingly succumbed to the wild words of political extremists. Anger, bitterness, and hatred spread within nations and among nations, as each group or each nation threw the blame for its troubles upon someone else. Countries with a long tradition of responsible government, like Great Britain and Switzerland, behaved reasonably; others, like Germany and Japan, threw themselves into the arms of advocates of violence. The unemployed in Germany sought salvation in the private armies of the Communists or the National Socialists.

Is it then to be wondered at [declared the German Chancellor Heinrich Brüning, a right-wing Catholic, in a speech on May 28, 1932 about the youth] if in the hearts and minds of these millions of adolescents there grows up a political extremism which can conceive of an improvement only in the collapse and destruction of all that now exists and if instinctively they should regard this as their last hope.

In Japan militarists utilized the unrest to seize control, and, correctly gauging the strength of the League of Nations, in September, 1931, launched the conquest of Manchuria and the rest of China. During the same year the German government, in a country that was worse than bankrupt, announced an intention to build a second pocket battleship of 10,000 tons. The nations defeated in the last war or disappointed with the results blamed others for their hardships and demanded revision of treaties. When in 1931 Germany and Austria sought to alleviate Austria's misery and at the same time to strengthen both countries by a customs union, the powers, led by France and Czechoslovakia, blocked the project on grounds of treaty rights and security. The inextricable confusion of politics, economics, social issues, cultural ideals, and religion, helped any violent group to enhance its power. The instruments of totalitarianism were being forged. The delicate fabric of postwar society and of postwar international relations was threatened with chaos.

The movement for disarmament, which had dragged out a frustrated existence since World War I, fell an early victim to the exacerbation of international relations. The greatest disarmament conference in history met in February, 1932, and did not adjourn until June, 1934. It was convened to consider the report of a distinguished preparatory commission which had devoted five years to analyzing the problems and to drafting recommendations. The conference was preceded by a world-wide campaign of churches, trade-unions, youth organizations, ex-service associations, teachers, and numerous other national and international bodies in favor of disarmament and peace. Leaders like Robert Cecil and Philip Noel-Baker of Great Britain, Edouard Herriot and Henry de Jouvenel of France, and Antonio Scialoia of Italy took the initiative in the campaign. The disarmament conference had slight chance of success at most, but the accentuation of emotional tension during the depression made any concessions—any show of patience—seem weakness. War, or the threat of war, was spreading. In 1930 Mussolini had declared to his Blackshirts, "Words are very fine things; but rifles, machine-guns, warships, aeroplanes, and cannon are still finer things. They are finer, Blackshirts, because right unaccompanied by might is an empty word. . . ." In that year Polish and German feelings became heated over Danzig and the minorities question. In 1931 the Chaco dispute in South America exploded into actual hostilities, and, four days before the Disarmament Conference assembled, the Japanese extended their Manchurian war to Shanghai.

The Disarmament Conference immediately chose to ignore the five years' work of its preparatory commission. The French sought once more to associate disarmament with strengthening the League's power to act. Sir John Simon for Great Britain advocated "qualitative" disarmament, that is, the prohibition of weapons of aggression. President Herbert Hoover of the United States offered his idea of a quantitative reduction all around of about one third of existing armaments. The Italians demanded naval equality with France. The German governments of Heinrich Brüning, Franz von Papen, and Adolf Hitler all strove simply to abrogate the restrictions laid upon the rearmament of their country in the treaty of Versailles. By the end of the first phase of the conference in 1932 the members had agreed to ban chemical and bacteriological warfare, a point substantially accepted at the time of the Geneva Protocol.

On all other matters the members remained at odds; and when Ramsay MacDonald submitted to the reconvened conference in 1933 an extensive proposal incorporating all the previous ideas which seemed to have some chance of acceptance, his efforts met no better fate. By that time Hitler had come to power in Germany with the intention to rearm. Since without international security France would not agree to the German proposals for rearmament and since Great Britain would not guarantee aid to France against Germany, the negotiations took the worst of all possible turns. Germany withdrew from the conference, announced her resignation from the League of Nations, and declared her intention to rebuild her armed forces. Italy threatened to resign from the League. Great Britain did not object to Germany's expanding her army, which could be used against France, but disliked the plan to reconstruct an air force, which could be turned against Great Britain. France felt more isolated than ever, fearing that any change in the existing relations of naval and military strength would be to her disadvantage and, possibly, peril. A contemporary writer remarked that "all hope of disarmament had vanished, that of limitation of armaments had grown tarnished and faded, and the fear of general rearmament and its possible ghastly results had become a threat and a nightmare before the mind of the world." The conference adjourned, knowing that it had completely failed.

In the field of economics and of power politics internationalism gave way to nationalism. The old international economy revolving around Great Britain was replaced by the competitive anarchy of nations aspiring to autarchy. The ideals of the League of Nations were fading before the revival of imperialism, not aimed at the colonial world, but at other European nations. Although unable to pay their debts and too poor to maintain an adequate standard of living for their peoples, the European states found sufficient funds with which to increase armaments. In this upside-down world, production of arms became the main means by which totalitarian nations supplied their people with work and revived their economy. It frightened the Soviet Union, the implacable enemy of all other states, into seeking limited cooperation with free countries and into joining the League of Nations. Politics and economics worked henceforth hand in hand to bring about the third catastrophe of the century, World War II.

Suggestions for Further Reading

BASCH, ANTONIN. *The Danube Basin and the German Economic Sphere.* New York: Columbia University Press, 1943. Impact of the crisis on one region.

CONDLIFFE, J. B. *The Reconstruction of World Trade.* New York: W. W. Norton & Company, Inc., 1940. The most useful survey of the crisis and the efforts at recovery.

WALTERS, F. P. *A History of the League of Nations.* See the Readings for Chapter 5. Indispensable for understanding the relation between the economic crisis and international affairs.

WOYTINSKY, W. S. *The Social Consequences of the Economic Depression.* Geneva: International Labor Organization, 1936. Invaluable. The only study of its kind. Detailed and interesting.

Chapter 13 · The Free Countries of Western and Northern Europe

Since the national governments were much stronger and much closer to the citizens than any international organization, they bore the immediate responsibility for aiding their peoples to recover from depression. The 1930's became the culmination of more than a century of nationalistic growth. That it ended disastrously was the logical conclusion of an illogical movement to solve by national means problems which were mainly international or transnational in character. The countries that preserved free government on the whole recognized the ultimate necessity to restore international cooperation and considered their national efforts a part of this inclusive action. The totalitarian states drew from the crisis the moral that they should become self-dependent by conquering territory and peoples. The free states took emergency measures, which in time they praised as evidence of astute planning according to new and forward-looking principles; the totalitarians turned their emergency action into preparation for war.

Great Britain

FROM LABOR GOVERNMENT TO NATIONAL COALITION

At the outbreak of the economic crisis a Labor ministry under the premiership of Ramsay MacDonald governed Great Britain. Labor had come to power in 1929 as a minority government, with 290 members in the House of Commons to 260 for the Conservatives and 60 for the Liberals. The cabinet was largely composed of representatives of the right and center of the party, most of them averse to trying to introduce socialism. Since the fate of the government depended upon the vote of the Liberals, Labor had an alibi for not attempting thorough reform. When MacDonald offered his cautious program to the House of Commons, Winston Churchill offered "cordial cooperation in the government's self-imposed task of carrying out the Conservatives' policy and making the world easier, if not safer, for capitalism."

The Laborites put through three laws, none of which can be said to have done much against unemployment and the depression. They eased government payments to the unemployed; they reduced hours of work in the coal mines from eight to seven and a half, conciliated the owners by permitting them to organize the market according to area and to set up a system of output quotas, and they laid out a plan for housing and slum-clearance. They acquiesced in the House of Lords' rejection of an education bill which by raising to fifteen the age for leaving school would have taken young people off the streets for an additional year. For a country with more than a million unemployed when the government took office in June, 1929, and 1,700,000 in the following May, this was not an impressive record.

Chancellor of the Exchequer Philip Snowden's budget of 1930 confirmed the impression of capitalistic orthodoxy. He rejected deficit financing and any departure from the gold standard. With revenue declining because of the depression and government expenditures increasing to keep alive the unemployed, he proposed further deflation, reduction of expenditures, heavy increases in taxation, and maintenance of the sinking fund with which to repay the public debt. By this policy the government made money more difficult than ever to obtain, provided no leadership in stimulating capital investment, and increased unemployment. By the end of the year there were 2 million out of work, and the number continued to rise. MacDonald, who knew little about economics, never consulted the Labor economists or those, like John Maynard Keynes, whose thinking rose above party consideration; and the vitriolic Snowden overestimated his own ability as an economist. In consequence, the Labor cabinet followed the orthodox laissez faire of big business and civil service as a policy for weathering the depression.

The government fell in August, 1931, over the state of finances. It became evident in the summer of that year that Snowden's budget would leave a deficit of nearly £180 million. The Bank of England was hurt by the failure in May of the Austrian bank, the *Kredit Anstalt,* to which it had lent considerable sums. In June one of the largest German banks failed, and at the same time it became known that Great Britain had been financing long-term investments abroad, especially in Germany, by money borrowed on short term. British capital began to flee from the pound sterling into French francs and into dollars to such an extent that by September 20, 1931, British gold holdings fell to £130 million. When French and American bankers refused further loans to Great Britain unless the government cut unemployment pay by 10 per cent, MacDonald asked for the resignation of his cabinet members, and, to the surprise of his colleagues, formed a national coalition government composed of three of his Labor colleagues (among them Snowden), the Conservatives, and the Liberals.

Snowden offered an emergency budget in September of a typical deflationary character. It provided for increased taxes, a 10 per cent cut in unemployment benefits and a reduction of 10 to 20 per cent in the salaries of public officials. The budget failed to revive international confidence, and on September 21 the British government suspended gold exports. "We firmly believe," Chancellor of the Exchequer Snowden had said in the previous month, "that if sterling collapses . . . you will have chaos and ruin in this country. You will have unemployment rising not merely to five million but to ten million." Now the pound sterling had collapsed, but ruin did not follow.

From the crisis of September, 1931, to the outbreak of World War II the national government continued in power. In the elections of 1931 it won 554 seats, among which 471 were for Conservatives, of a total of 615. Labor returned only 56 members, and almost all its leaders were defeated. When elections were held in 1935 the results were less one-sided; but the national government preserved a majority of 247. During the decade Britain faced no constitutional crises, no threat of fascism within the country, no growth of communism. The abdication of King Edward VIII in 1936, forced by his intended marriage to an American divorcée, caused little more than a ripple. The good upper-class ministers, serving until 1935 under the figurehead MacDonald and from then until 1937 under the common-sensed and even-tempered Stanley Baldwin, represented the traditional leadership of the country. They had full authority, if they had wished to use it, to guide the nation out of the depression.

The most influential member with respect to internal affairs was Snowden's successor as chancellor of the exchequer, Neville Chamberlain, who in 1937 became prime minister. The son of Joseph and younger brother of Austen, Neville Chamberlain had remained in business until he was middle-aged. He had shown ministerial caliber as soon as he entered politics and had already proved himself an efficient public administrator. Rather unimaginative and in his social relations extremely reserved, he possessed the fine qualities of the British upper middle class. In his leisure he enjoyed string quartets, salmon fishing, and wild flowers. He had such intellectual honesty that he is described as having purred with satisfaction over the intellectual brilliance of an attack on one of his own budgets by the Laborite, Stafford Cripps. Although helped by the good fortune of Britain's enforced abandonment of the gold standard and the fact that he came to power at the bottom of the depression, he had a general if rather nebulous plan for restoring the country's economic vigor.

ECONOMIC PROGRAM

"The two main pillars of the policy," Chamberlain stated in 1936, "have been the introduction of the tariff and the establisment of cheap money." The tariff had come as a Conservative victory, but a lowering of the discount rate had been forced upon the government by circumstances. Both, but especially the tariff, were used to introduce measures of business reorganization and new relations between business and government which were, so Chamberlain said, "of a really revolutionary character." They only postponed the time when Great Britain would be forced to face the essential problem of how to increase the efficiency of production and distribution in order to cease living on capital reserves.

In February, 1932, after brief debate, Parliament passed the Import Duties Bill, thus destroying a tradition of eighty years of free trade. Up to this time a few moderate duties had been levied, particularly those after World War I on certain goods like chemicals and opticals for which Germany had had a practical monopoly. From 1932 forward a flat import duty of 10 per cent ad valorem was imposed on everything except some raw materials like cotton, wool, and wood and a few foodstuffs—wheat, meat and fish. A statutory Import Duties Advisory Committee was created with power to recommend to the Treasury an increase or reduction in tariffs. Within a very short time it succeeded in raising duties on a large number of articles, including iron and steel, to 33⅓ per cent. Finding that these relatively low duties did not stop the import of goods, the government initiated a complicated system of bilateral agreements and quotas with countries upon whose economy it was able to exert pressure. The procedure was intended to insure the sale of British goods abroad, particularly coal, in return for preferential treatment in the British market. With countries like Argentina, Denmark, Sweden, Norway, the Baltic countries, and Iceland, Britain made treaties providing for the reciprocal sale of commodities in certain amounts. She imposed similar agreements upon her colonies, and at the conference of the Dominions at Ottawa in 1932 she and the Dominions abolished the most-favored-nation clause and granted each other preferential treatment. The system did not extend nearly so far as its advocates had hoped, for Dominion industrialists disliked British competition, and British agriculturalists feared Dominion rivals. Nonetheless, its acceptance and the practice of bilateralism marked the end for many years of that multilateral trade which had made Britain rich.

The institution of cheap money emerged from the enforced devaluation of the pound sterling. To its surprise the government discovered that this act did not cause disaster; in fact, until the other countries, especially the United States in 1933 and France in 1936, followed suit, devaluation proved beneficial. The cheaper pound stimulated the export of British goods by making them cheaper than those from other countries which had not devalued their money, and it reduced imports by making them more expensive. More important because of long-term influence was the lowering of the interest rate. The bank rate was reduced to 2 per cent; the government was able in 1932 to convert a £2 billion war loan from 5 per cent interest to 3½ per cent. The average rate of mortgage loans fell from 6 to 4½ per cent, to the great advantage of home construction. Within the next nine years Britain built 2,400,000 houses, three fourths of them by private individuals, thus accounting directly and indirectly for from one third to one half of increased employment.

"Self-government in Industry"

The government had granted tariff protection on the assumption that industry would use the opportunity to overcome its backwardness in organization and technology. The iron and steel industry offered an example of what happened. In 1934 the government raised the tariff on iron and steel to 50 per cent ad valorem and sanctioned the establishment of the Iron and Steel Federation, a "comprehensive organisation capable of exercising a powerful influence on the conduct of the industry" and of negotiating with foreign competitors "on equal terms." The new system was called one of "self-government in industry." The Federation was guided by an executive committee selected by the members organized in branches (Pig Iron Producers, Sheet Makers, and so on). Each branch held its own conference, where representatives to the general conference were selected. The executive committee negotiated for the Federation with trade-unions, the government, and foreign interests on matters concerning the members. The conference of each branch in turn assumed a similar responsibility of guiding its member corporations and trade associations. The Federation, as the London *Economist* said, amounted to "an orderly organisation of industries, each ruled feudally from above by the business firms already established in it, linked in associations and confederations and, at the top, meeting on terms of sovereign equality such other Estates of the Realm as the Bank of England and the government." [1]

The industry introduced a few improvements and built at Corby a new integrated iron and steel plant, the most modern in Europe. Pig-iron production increased from 6,600,000 tons in 1928 to 10,890,000 tons in 1939, and raw-steel production from 8,315,000 to 13,400,000 tons. Soon, however, interest in investing funds for rationalizing production receded in favor of profit. When World War II began, Great Britain had much the same technical equipment and plant in iron and steel that she had had prior to reform. The main change had taken place in price and profit. Under the monopolistic system of self-government the high-cost, out-of-date producers earned a substantial profit (more than 10 per cent in 1937) on their capital,

[1] Quoted in Robert A. Brady, *Crisis in Britain* (Berkeley: University of California Press, 1950), p. 195.

and the most efficient producers earned as much as 74 per cent. Prices of iron and steel rose on an average 30 to 40 per cent. British industrialists had to pay from 50 per cent to 200 per cent more for iron and steel bought from their own Federation than their foreign competitors had to expend for American material of identical quality. They protested vigorously against such prices. Lord William Nuffield, the biggest British manufacturer of motor cars, in 1937 called the steel industry "a perfect ramp, an absolute ramp . . . big cigars and nothing to do." He blamed the steel manufacturers for his inability to produce a cheaper motor car. "They are overcharging us." "Self-government in industry" proved to be profitable to those governing themselves, but not to other industries forced to use their products and not to unemployed labor looking for jobs.

The government chose remedies for other industries according to circumstances. It bought and dismantled the inefficient cotton, wool, and shipbuilding plants and concentrated production in the rest of them. It saved the more productive plants from bankruptcy and renewed their ability to compete in the foreign market, not to the prewar extent—for much of the market had been lost to other nations—but enough to make them economically sound. Since ocean shipping was likewise subject to expanding foreign competition, the government followed the cutthroat example of other states in subsidizing its own carriers, and aided in the construction of the "Queen Mary" and other luxury ocean liners catering to an already overbuilt passenger service. By 1936 one half of the ships lying idle in the depression had been restored to action. The coal industry used the law of 1930 to set up district marketing boards, fix prices, and restrict production; but the owners refused to improve efficiency and set prices at a height sufficient to remunerate the submarginal producers. As the industry remained sick, the government in 1938 passed a law nationalizing coal royalties. By eliminating the owners of the land under which coal was found, it prepared the way for essential reforms, which the outbreak of war temporarily halted.

Market Regulation in Agriculture

As agriculture became particularly hard hit by the flood of foreign food and other materials pouring in during the depression, the government introduced measures for its protection. During several decades, British agriculture had adjusted to the successful competition of cheaper production abroad, in Canada, the United States, the Argentine, and some of the European countries by emphasizing the output of foods for which it had the advantage of a naturally sheltered market, especially milk, eggs, fruits, and vegetables, and to some extent meat. As labor became scarce and expensive, agriculture had reduced the amount of plowed land in favor of grasses; and as it expanded the numbers of cattle and of poultry, it imported large quantities of fodder from countries of extensive agriculture.

Productive efficiency increased with the use of fertilizers and machinery and modern methods of farming. The quantum of gross output rose from (1908 = 100) 104 in 1930–1931 to 122 in 1936–1937; but net output increased much less.

Since natural adjustment was unable to save agriculture, the government in 1933 passed the basic Agricultural Marketing Act and varied the form of aid according to the particular situation of each product. In some situations the branch of agriculture benefited by tariffs and import quotas; in some, wheat for example, tariffs were imposed and a minimum price was also guaranteed; in some, like dairying and potato growing, where trouble arose, not from foreign competition, but from excessive output, marketing boards were set up to fix minimum prices, allot production quantities, and restrict the entry of new producers into the field. Special excise taxes, like a milling tax, were levied to obtain funds for the purpose of paying the subsidies. These examples by no means exhaust the list of methods which the government employed; but it may suffice to indicate that the Conservatives were extending the power of the state into the economy far beyond anything that had happened for a century or more.

Economic Recovery

By means of modern statistics the relative effectiveness of the policies pursued by the National government may be measured with considerable accuracy. The results were not particularly impressive. The average number of unemployed per year in 1931–1933 was 2,785,000, or the equivalent of one worker in every five. After that date conditions improved, but until 1939 the number was always larger than it had been prior to 1930. Approximately 20 per cent of these had lacked employment for at least twelve months. In spite of the increase in the average number of insured workers employed per annum from 10,036,000 in 1931–1933 to 12,239,000 in 1937–1939, the economy proved able to provide work for only two thirds of the net increase in the insurable population. That is to say, one third of those reaching the age of work were doomed to idleness.

What was the explanation? Great Britain depended upon world trade to a greater extent than any major country. Yet her own share in that trade continued in the thirties to decline. In 1929 she was responsible for 11 per cent of the world's exports, in 1937 for only 10 per cent. In 1929 she had had a favorable balance of payments on current account of £103 million, but she had a deficit in every year of the 1930's except one. By 1937 the deficit reached £56 million. Britain's export trade, upon which for decades she had mainly depended to keep the population at work, no longer provided leadership. By good fortune, not of her own making in the least, the terms of trade during this period were usually in her favor; otherwise her population would have suffered more than it did. Imports ceased under the impact of economic crisis to grow at a faster rate than production. The ratio of imports to national income declined from 25 per cent in 1929 to 16 per cent in 1938, but it was still higher than the country could afford. Exports were insufficient to pay for even this small amount of imports. The policy of bilateralism, quota, and imperial preference may have been justified by the emergency. It did augment sales to the empire and to those countries with which Britain made bilateral agreements. On the other hand, her basic economic problem was like that of every other nation—how to increase the volume of world trade; and her policy was antithetic to the achievement of this objective.

Since British foreign trade continued to decline, one might have expected the government to create jobs and increase purchasing power by encouraging industry for home consumption. During and after the world economic crisis the economist Keynes advocated that the government utilize resources in man power and materials by putting money into public works and home industry. The productive plant might thereby have been modernized, technology brought up to date, equipment renewed. All the work of renovation upon which Britain has embarked since World War II could have been accomplished in the thirties, and full employment and a high standard of living achieved. The National government did not think in such terms. It believed in starting at the top, helping those who already had wealth to make more; then, in time, some of the increase would trickle down to the lower classes. The Conservatives did not consider the economy as a whole; they could not comprehend one simple fact which recent economic theory had propounded, that to increase national wealth one must put resources, human and material, to work and enable the masses to purchase the objects produced. As one British economist said, they endeavored "to maintain the *status quo* even at the sacrifice of the greater wealth which might be secured by readjustment." The Conservatives, however, were satisfied, and claimed credit for having saved the economy from bankruptcy and for having achieved its reconstruction.

Criticism should not detract from the fact of slow economic improvement. The national income of the United Kingdom increased between 1928–1930 and 1937–1938 by 19 per cent in terms of 1924 prices. Inequality in the distribution of the national income had been declining since the severe increases in taxes during World War I. In 1938 there were fewer wealthy persons (those with incomes of over £5,000 in 1914 and £7,500 in the late thirties) in the country, and they received much less of the national income (2 per cent instead of 8.5 per cent in 1914). Just before World War I 170,000 persons (less than 1 per cent of those aged twenty-five and above) had owned two thirds of the national wealth, and 16 million people had owned 8.5 per cent. By 1936, 1 per cent of the population still owned 55.7 per cent of the national wealth, and 19 million owned 4.2 per cent. In between were the rest who possessed relatively small amounts of property. The highest income class had manifestly been declining in numbers, but the lowest group had also been losing out in the effort to obtain a larger portion of the national income. The share of the national income from rents, interest, and profits appears to have increased slightly in the thirties at the expense of that from salaries and wages. The prestige of the upper classes remained strong, but labor's power was rapidly growing and the state under both Conservatives and Labor was assuming more responsibility than ever before for the welfare of the entire people.

Labor Relations

Relations between management and labor definitely improved during this decade. After the failure of the general strike in 1926, both groups gradually accepted the slogan of "Peace in Industry," and in the late twenties they held conferences on common problems. Labor retained the use of the strike but ceased to depend upon this ultimate weapon as much as it had previously done. During the depression and the thirties it seldom went on strike. The economy had suffered an annual average loss of 16,100,000 working days in industrial disputes between 1910 and 1914, and only 10 per cent as many between 1934 and 1938. The change was in keeping with labor's growth in power and in political and social maturity. Labor organizations had on the whole tended to increase in size and in the diversity of occupations contained within one union. Alongside the specialized craft unions there developed the general unions with wide interests and large membership. The industrial union, of the type of the Congress of Industrial Organizations in the United States, never gained a firm hold. The Trade Union Congress became in the twenties a well-organized body, with an influential Council and, in Walter Citrine, an able and enterprising secretary.

After the debacle of the second Labor government the trade-unions and the Labor party came into closer working relations than they had had while MacDonald was head of the party. Both unions and party needed to assess their objectives; both therefore sought the assistance of intellectuals in working out their theory. In consequence, the Fabian Society, which had been allowed to decay, once more became active, and many intellectuals of the middle class were attracted by opportunities to serve the Labor party and the trade-unions. This intellectual and moral rebirth prepared labor for its role after World War II. In addition, labor approved the policy of the National government in encouraging the concentration of ownership and closer cooperation between the government and business. The replacement of competition by regulation opened a possibility for labor to participate in the future in the control of the large monopolistic, state-regulated businesses. Hence labor began to emphasize not merely the fight for an ever higher share of income but increased efficiency and prosperity in industry as the essential basis for the development of its own power. Industrial self-government was an old slogan dear to socialists, for it could apply not only to owners and managers but to employees and workers. After Chamberlain in 1934 restored the cuts made three years before in payments to the unemployed, the workers were content to go along, recuperate from the crisis, and bide their time. As nazism got under way in Germany, British problems ceased to be mainly economic; rearmament put the unemployed to work. Labor and capital faced the common threat of renewed war.

France

MAGINOT MENTALITY

When World War II began to test the strength of nations, France was in a worse condition than at any time since the previous war. Her industrial and agricultural production was far below that of 1929–1930, and her people were divided to the point of latent civil war. France could show neither the unified confidence in freedom of the British nor the will to totalitarianism of the Germans and Italians. She avoided the example of the Spanish internal war and preserved parliamentary government, but with frequent use of rule by decree and by physical force. The nation and its component social parts kept on the defensive in every respect; the Maginot mentality, as it has been called, prevailed.

An analysis of French life in the 1930's may begin with the economy, not because the economic was the most important aspect, but because it fixed the material basis for the political and social difficulties. Since the economy failed to expand and provide an improved life for the people, the social groups increasingly used political power in dividing the limited national income.

The world economic crisis affected France somewhat later than it did other countries and lasted longer. At the beginning the country was protected by high tariffs, a monetary unit recently devalued, and an economy more self-sufficient than that of any major state of Europe. Agriculture felt the inroads of the crisis first, for the tariffs proved insufficient to exclude foodstuffs from abroad. The French government quickly added a quota system to higher tariffs, regulating thereby not merely the price at which goods would be imported but also the amount. Agriculture had already concentrated on the growth of wheat, grapes, and beets, which were well protected by tariffs, to the neglect of the production of vegetables and other commodities, which could have found a ready market at home. The other crops had been easier and simpler to grow, as they required little or no improvement in techniques, in the use of fertilizer and new implements. The French farmer had no inducement to change as long as he could continue to make money behind a protective wall; and since the agricultural population was unusually large (30 per cent of the total) and the election law favored the rural voters at the expense of the urban, the peasant could preserve the system. With wheat at 150 per cent above the world price, French agriculture remained a backward and expensive means of supplying food for a nation.

Industry followed a similar policy. Using 1913 as a base of 100, the index of industrial production rose to 140 in 1930, fell to 94 in 1935, and rose to 101 in 1937; that is, industry in the late 1930's produced about the same amount that it had before World War I and had dropped 39 points below its achievement of 1930. The French had never been inclined to risk savings in their own industry, and in this decade the amount of investment failed to maintain the existing plant. Most of the investing had to be done by the state. In 1910–1913 private sources had supplied 80 per cent of the total funds for security issues; in 1924, 50 per cent; in 1930, 72 per cent; and in 1936–1938, only 10 per cent. In consequence, the average age of machine tools in France in 1938 was about twenty-five years, as compared with seven to nine years in Great Britain and five to seven years in the United States. The French worker in that year had an average of 7,500 horsepower of mechanical energy at his disposal, the British worker 20,000, the American worker 33,500. A few of the new industries (automobile, paper, rubber, radio) had recent tools, but the textile, metallurgical—in fact practically all other industries—were technically far out of date.

Industry failed to specialize and to provide the spread of branches necessary for a modern economy; it lacked concentration of key lines; and it mistrusted modern methods. It preferred security in backwardness behind high tariff walls and expended its vigor in a successful fight against the stimulus of competition. The economy became so inelastic that in contrast to other countries the armament race initiated in the late thirties failed to arouse it to life. Instead, rearmament meant fewer goods for the consumer, a lowered standard of living, and inflation. The French had a closed and rigid economy in which prices were no longer in contact with world prices. Exports were falling, and investments abroad were being withdrawn for current consumption. France was caught in a vicious circle; inefficiency, needing protection, encouraged more inefficiency, which entailed more protection. By 1938 national income was less than it had been a decade before, less by far than that in Great Britain, and the nation was living partly on capital.

During the decade under review France continued to make fundamental mistakes in financial policy. Her system of taxation remained as inequitable and poorly enforced as ever. The workers and the employees paid income taxes, which the farmers and especially the businessmen were in whole or in large part able to avoid. To escape from taxes was considered legitimate by these classes. The indirect taxes, falling proportionately most heavily on the poor, continued high, but they and the direct taxes together were unable to supply sufficient funds to balance the budget. With the burden of maintaining the unemployed, not very numerous at any time, of paying subsidies, and of meeting the payroll of a large bureaucracy, the government during the decade was constantly in need of loans.

The government sought to maintain the franc on the gold standard after Great Britain, the United States, and many other countries had devalued their currencies. France had in the preceding decade reduced the value of her monetary unit by 80 per cent, and the government feared the effects of a new devaluation upon public confidence. The all-powerful industrial and financial interests in control of the Bank of France opposed any further reduction and forced their will upon any hesitant ministry. Consequently, the franc became overvalued in the world market. French exports, already excessively expensive because of the high costs of production behind the tariff barriers, became still higher in comparative price and had great difficulty in competing on the world market. The amount of France's balance of international payments declined sharply as her share in world exports fell from 6 per cent in 1929 to 3.66 per cent in 1937. After the dollar was devalued in 1933, it was believed that the franc would be forced off the gold standard. Frenchmen and others began to flee from the franc into stronger currencies, and France lost gold at a rapid rate. Political troubles associated with the Popular Front government (1936) accelerated the movement of gold.

The French economic leaders and politicians tried to meet the crisis by the method that in Germany had caused Brüning's fall and that had brought severe trouble to Great Britain—namely, deflation. They introduced measures to reduce government expenditures, prices, salaries, and wages. The most vigorous assertion of this policy occurred during Pierre Laval's ministry in 1935, when 549 decrees were issued in a period of six months to lower these items. The worst hit were the peasants; they were required to cut the price of their products, but they found that the prices of articles they had to buy were well sustained by cartel and other agreements and did not fall to a comparable extent. Everyone lacked currency, and, as purchases declined, unemployment rose. The number of fully unemployed reached a peak in 1936 of 600,000, and those partially employed increased to a million. The government sent several hundred thousand foreign workers and their families back home to Italy, Poland, Spain, and elsewhere; but the cost to the state of maintaining the unemployed was still high. Industrial activity did not revive until in September, 1936, the government reduced the value of the franc by 30 per cent and brought it into line with that of other currencies.

POPULAR FRONT GOVERNMENT

The change in monetary policy was an unintended by-product of the one concerted effort at reform of French life, that of the Popular Front government in 1936–1937. For the first time in French history the Socialist party agreed to participate in government and to align with the bourgeois Radical Socialists to that end. The Communist party, the third member of the Popular Front, united with the others in the election campaign of 1936 but refused to participate in the cabinet. In the elections the Popular Front polled 56 per cent of the vote; the Radical Socialists, 14 per cent; the Socialists and Communists, 40 per cent; and 2 per cent were scattered. The Popular Front seated 63 per cent of the deputies. In opposition were the moderate center parties, which lost 15 per cent of their previous vote, and the authoritarian Republican Federation, which increased its vote by 28 per cent. France seemed to be divided between a leftist majority and a sizable rightest minority. Events were soon to show that the accuracy of this distinction was exaggerated, but in the meantime the Popular Front government existed.

Three main factors explain the willingness of the French majority to entrust its fate to a leftist government. The first, although not necessarily the most important, was the failure of the deflationists to revive the economy. Even the peasants turned against a government which after passing a minimum price law for wheat lacked the courage to enforce it. The second and the third were closely connected: the Nazi accession to power in 1933 made the potential threat of French fascist movements too real to be tolerated further. What if French fascism should develop as nazism had across the border, or as totalitarianism had in many small states; what if its leaders should emulate Franco in Spain?

The French fascist organizations, mainly concentrated in Paris, were noisier and more of a nuisance than an actual power. Their attack, verbal and physical, upon the Chamber of Deputies and the government, the Socialists and Communists, gave them notoriety beyond that justified by their actual strength. They were divided into a number of groups: the royalist *Camelots du Roi* associated with Charles Maurras and the *Action Française;* the *Solidarité Française,* maintained by the funds of the perfume manufacturer René Coty; the *Francistes,* who tried to appear like Hitler's storm troopers; and, most important, the *Croix de Feu,* bourgeois in memship and led by the aristocrat Colonel de la Rocque. The *Croix de Feu* had begun as an organization of war heroes with decorations for courage in action. In time it added front-line soldiers and then the sons of heroes, in an effort to increase membership. Following its initial function of defending legislation in favor of war veterans, it had turned to politics and proposed a fascist program. The leader indulged in turgid oratory unleavened by political acumen. Since the depression caused nothing like the amount of unemployment that it did in Germany, the fascist groups lacked the mass recruits which the Nazis gained. Nonetheless, in those years one could not predict what might happen.

The fascist exploitation of the Stavisky scandal of 1934 particularly alarmed the moderate and leftist parties. Serge Stavisky, the son of a Russian-Jewish dentist, lived on graft, seemingly immune from police and courts. In his most recent shady deal he had issued millions of francs' worth of bonds against the security of the pawn shop in the little town of Bayonne. The fraud was discovered and eventually involved seventeen members of the Chamber of Deputies, one of them a current cabinet minister, Prime Minister Chautemps' brother-in-law, who was responsible for prosecuting persons like Stavisky. That the minister had not initiated suit reflected on the honesty of Camille Chautemps himself, especially when the latter refused to allow a parliamentary enquiry. Stavisky's suicide fed the excitement; the fascists denounced the government in the press, rioted with the cry, "Down with the Thieves," and tried to attack the Chamber of Deputies. The Communists added to the turmoil by attacking the fascists while singing the International. The police did not lose control; the use of the army never became necessary; but the events vividly recalled similar ones in Italy and Germany.

To counter the danger, on February 12, 1934, the socialist and Communist workers organized a general strike, which to their own surprise as well as that of others they executed successfully. The Communists manifestly had orders from Moscow to help prevent a repetition in France of the fate of Germany. Heartened by this achievement, the two wings of the labor movement in the next two years amalgamated. The General Confederation of Workers absorbed the Communist organization, but for the time being preserved the leadership to a large extent in the hands of non-Communists. When, similarly alarmed, the left wing of the bourgeois Radical Socialist party, largely composed of commercial interests attracted by the prospect of large-scale state aid, won control over the predominantly rural right wing in 1935, that party voted to participate in a Popular Front, and on July 14, 1935, 600,000 men and women of these parties massed on the site of the old Bastille, sang alternately the Marseillaise and the International, and took the following oath: "We solemnly swear to remain united in order to disarm and dissolve the fascist leagues, to defend and develop democratic liberties, to provide bread for the workers, employment for youth, and peace to the world."

Reform Program

The Popular Front offered a program that was intended to be broad in appeal but that did not cut very deep. It promised laws against fascist organizations; by requiring publicity about ownership, it proposed to make the press more responsible for unbiased news; it would reduce hours of work without a reduction of wages; it would raise agricultural return to the peasants without raising prices to the consumers by, so it intimated, curbing the profits of the middleman; it would abolish speculation in wheat by creating a central Wheat Board; it would reform the stock market, the tax system, the Bank of France; it would strengthen military defense and also the League of Nations. The program marked no sharp departure from the Radical Socialists' previous promises. Its cautious nature indicated the intention of Léon Blum, the Socialist prime minister of the Popular Front government, with Communist approval, to preserve the coalition.

The modesty of the program may be gathered from a comparison with reforms which were advocated by groups as different as Right-wing Gaston Doumergue and his followers, on the one hand, and certain Socialist economists and lawyers, on the other. Doumergue proposed to strengthen the authority of the executive at the expense of the Chamber of Deputies. It was realized that the Stavisky scandal involved the government primarily because the prime minister lacked authority. Doumergue therefore hoped to deprive the individual deputies of the right to propose specific expenditures in the budget. He and his friends attributed the excessive delay in passing the budget and the excessive size of the budget to the exercise of this right, for each deputy strove to earmark funds for interests in his own constituency.

The plan affected too many political interests to win acceptance. The socialist intellectuals in their project of 1934 sought to transform the structure of the economy by nationalizing the credit system and transferring to public ownership the key industries, armaments, mining, power, and transportation. In the other branches of the economy private ownership was to continue but be subject to a Superior Economic Council with extensive power. The planned economy was to be guided primarily by the credit policies of a nationalized Bank of France. Parliamentary institutions of free government were thereby to be relieved of the detrimental effects of the pressure of special interests. In its economic and social terms the program resembled that advocated by the British Labor government after World War II. Although approving it in theory, Blum refused to try to implement it. This was the Socialists' first time in power and they had shy colleagues. The Communists opposed these and any other fundamental reforms that were not of Communist origin; all the Radical Socialists disapproved socialism and at least half of them were very fearful of this unusual coalition.

Labor and Capital

When the Popular Front came to power in the summer of 1936, the workers everywhere in France were enthusiastic. Sit-down strikers occupied plants, sang the national anthem, the International, and popular songs, polished the machinery, and were joyous and hopeful. The General Confederation of Workers grew overnight from a small organization of possibly 1½ million petty officials, small tradesmen, and a sprinkling of real industrial workers to a body of 5 million, overwhelmingly worker in composition. The Cardinal Archbishop of Paris called for a new basis in relations between labor and management, the employers were temporarily cowed, and the government was able quickly to push through parliament, even through the rock-ribbed conservative Senate, a program of reforms.

The most important innovations affected the relations between labor and capital. The government passed a law establishing the forty-hour week with the pay formerly received for forty-eight hours of work, and a paid holiday. It introduced collective bargaining, set up government machinery for mediation of labor disputes, and created the system of selecting the most representative groups of labor and management in each industry and in each district concerned as those whose collective agreement would be binding for all the others. At the same time the government had to settle the actual strikes then in progress. In an agreement named Matignon, from the building in which it was negotiated, management accepted the appointment of shop stewards to represent labor in a particular plant and a pay increase of from 7 to 15 per cent, with the assurance that abnormally low wages would be subsequently corrected. By these reforms France received social legislation which had existed in most countries for twenty years or longer and had already been won and lost in Italy and Germany. Industrial unionism became the predominant type, and the unions within the General Confederation rather than those belonging to the far smaller Catholic Trade Union Association became almost everywhere the representative body for collective bargaining.

Almost immediately the new relations ran into trouble. The General Confederation of Workers was unprepared to handle the administration of a sudden quadrupling of membership. It lacked trained personnel to lead the unions and to educate the workers to the responsibilities of unionism; it could scarcely do more than receive membership dues. When Popular Front miracles ceased, the union members got out of hand. The workers would not always respect the terms of agreements with management which their leaders made for them, and always the Communists fought the socialist members and tried to gain control of the unions. Except for this difficulty, the internal problems could have been solved with time and experience. Management, however, seemed determined from the outset to destroy the whole program as soon as possible. The employers' organization expanded to include small business, hitherto almost entirely ignored. A new manager was appointed for this association who should exert full pressure in government and public. A new propaganda department was created to war against labor, and centralized authority was vested in the association for negotiating with labor.

Conflicts arose between the two social classes on almost every point. Both sides recognized that the shop steward as the spokesman for labor in the plant held the key position. If the steward were protected, labor would be able to assert its rights at the place of initial grievance; if he could be dismissed at will, management would have blocked the effective functioning of the trades union. The law did not protect the shop stewards, and the Senate saw to it that no new law to that effect was passed. Deprived of any legal assistance, the trade-unions tried to defend their stewards by strikes, which proved ineffective. When the unions sought to control the hiring and firing of workers or at least to require employers to use the state labor exchanges in employing personnel, the employers refused and blocked the proposal. They wanted no state interference in these questions. They likewise successfully opposed compulsory arbitration of labor disputes, which the unions advocated; and they endeavored to break the position of the General Confederation of Workers as the sole representative group for labor in negotiations with management.

Both sides opposed the closed shop, the General Confederation maintaining that it was a Communist device for seizing control. Both sides found themselves deeply involved in state affairs. They participated in committees for collective bargaining and arbitration, and in some thirty or more boards and on the National Economic Council, concerned with numerous kinds of social and economic problems. The employers had long since learned the economic importance of control of the government, the latest example being that of the Popular Front social legislation. Labor, however, failed to understand the change in its position. It continued to discuss socialism, syndicalism, revolutionary tactics, and "direct action," and almost entirely ignored the fact that the success of its program depended upon practical politics and influence upon the government. Instead of negotiating a solution of their problems between themselves, both labor and management refused to compromise and by default passed the responsibility for deciding issues to the government. The experience of Popular Front aggravated class conflict.

Economic Reforms

The economic reforms caused less controversy than did reform of social relations. For the peasants the Blum government created a Wheat Board to stop the wide fluctuations in price and assure the growers a just return by fixing the price each year. The Board was composed of representatives of producers, consumers, and the state in an effort to assure fairness to all interests. It monopolized the purchase of wheat and then sold the grain to the mills. In order to have the data for fixing the annual price, it required extensive information from the agriculturalists about the acreage sown, the crop harvested, and so on. The plan worked; the price of wheat, and of other agricultural products, went up 40 to 50 per cent, and the growers received a better return than they had had for years. The nationalization of railroads carried through by the government amounted to little more than transfer of official title, as the state had long ago had to control and finance this branch of transportation. Nationalization of war industries was popular, for the munitions makers were not trusted to work for peace. It involved the state's assuming ownership and responsibility, not merely for separate industries, but for those parts of corporations, like the tank section of the Renault automobile works, that manufactured articles for war. The results proved to be a severe decrease in the production of tanks, planes, and the like just at the time when France needed to keep pace with the rearmament of Germany.

The reform of the Bank of France failed to achieve as much as had been expected. Founded in 1801 by Napoleon, the Bank had practically determined the credit policy of the country ever since. It had been hostile to governments left of center and to tinkering with the gold standard or to any deviation from the most orthodox finance. The board of regents had become almost hereditary in some fifty families, for the charter enabled the 200 largest stockholders of 40,000 to elect the fifteen members and three advisers of the board. The government appointed the governor and two vice-governors of the bank, but to be eligible for the office these had to own at least 100 shares of stock. The board members usually supplied these stocks to the appointees, who came and went, and were able to control their views. During the discussion of the proposed reform it was revealed that either directly or indirectly twelve regents were directors of 95 corporations, including private banks, insurance companies, railroads, shipping concerns, metallurgical and chemical industries, mines, and public utilities. Fifteen men, without obligation to account for their actions to a public representative body, decided the course of the economy of 40 million Frenchmen.

The Blum government pushed through a law by which it hoped to break or at least to diminish the power of the Bank. The main terms consisted of changing the personnel of the board in order to represent the varied interests of the country. The new board was composed of a governor, two vice-governors, three advisers, and twenty councilors chosen for a period of three years. Each stockholder, regardless of the amount of his holdings, could cast only one vote. Of the members of the board, the stockholders elected the three advisers and two councilors; the government chose twelve of the members and designated the governor and the vice-governors, and a number of other members were selected from groups opposed to high finance. On the new board were representatives of consumers, artisans, labor, industry, and agriculture. Léon Jouhaux, the head of the General Confederation of Workers, participated, together with the representative of heavy industry; the state controlled a majority of the votes. The Bank was expected henceforth to serve national interests as seen, not by fifteen economic Bourbons, but by representatives of all elements of the population. The significance of the reform was diminished, however, by the failure of the Blum ministry to nationalize or control the five or six big private banks and, much more, by the reformers' neglect to stabilize their political power. The character of future economic policy, this time of the Bank, would depend upon the policies of those in charge of the government.

Blum had counted on the shortening of hours of work, an increase in wages, a program of public works, and aid to agriculture to revive the economy. By September, 1936, he realized that. contrary to his public assurance, he would be forced to devalue the franc. The flight of gold from Popular Front France, with her social experiments and unbalanced budget, reached the danger point and had to be stopped. The devaluation by 30 per cent turned out to be beneficial, as it had in Great Britain. Exports increased, and by the time France started seriously on rearmaments she had recovered from unemployment and needed more man power.

The country, which had never suffered heavily from unemployment, was much more the victim of contradictory and confused policies. Blum's forty-hour week and other reforms had increased hourly wages by about 60 per cent within a year, thus heightening the cost of production. In such turbulent times incentives to invest remained dormant; and when production revived, after devaluation, the economy found itself severely handicapped by the forty-hour week, the absence of foreign workers, and the deficiencies in French population growth. Between 1929 and 1937 French industry lost 21 per cent of its man power to other branches of the economy, particularly agriculture. On the eve of World War II France was less industrial and more agricultural than it had been in the previous decade.

From almost every point of view the Blum experiment had been a failure. The sole beneficiaries had been the industrialists, the opponents of the Popular Front. The workers had seen their gains in wages disappear with devaluation and rising prices and were left with the sole advantage of a shorter work week. The farmers had held a balance between rising prices and rising costs. The middle class, living on fixed incomes, salaries, pensions, rents, and interest, had been the sufferers.

SOCIAL CONFLICT CONTINUES

In 1937 the bankers and the conservative Senate forced the resignation of the Popular Front government. Although Blum returned as premier for a short time in 1938, the forces of the right were once more on the march. Many Frenchmen preferred Hitler to Blum, and blamed the Popular Front for all the country's ills. The endeavor of labor to preserve its benefits incurred the wrath of the upper classes, and, while most of labor was fighting to keep down communism within its midst, the rest of the population tended to denounce the entire proletariat as sold out to Russia.

When the Radical Socialist Édouard Daladier formed a government in 1938, he immediately put through a National Service law, approved as well by the Socialists, which should enable the government to meet emergencies. The Munich crisis had just occurred, and anything might happen. The law authorized the government to mobilize the labor force in the event of war or of external tension. In executing the law the government should constantly consult the most representative organizations of labor and management, a stipulation intended to preserve harmony in behalf of national defense. In November, 1938, Minister Paul Reynaud issued decrees with the force of law in the effort to stimulate production and strengthen France in the face of Hitler's threat. Management demanded the abolition of the forty-hour week before it would seriously try to increase production, and Daladier and Reynaud acceded. They technically retained the short work-week, but, contrary to trade-union agreements, they authorized compensation for overtime work to be set at 10 per cent of the wage. If a worker refused to work overtime for national defense, he was declared to have violated his labor contract and would have difficulty in finding future employment. Anyone who sought to persuade others not to work overtime was liable to fine and imprisonment.

Labor condemned the decrees as a violation of its rights. It hoped to negotiate a peaceful solution with the government, but when the latter ignored the hint, the General Confederation half-heartedly tried a general strike. The government then seized the opportunity to discipline labor. It invoked the National Service Act, used the police, and broke the strike, a failure in any case, by physical force. Then it excluded the General Confederation of Workers from responsible positions in the national life. Jouhaux was dismissed as a member of the general council of the Bank of France, and two secretaries of the railway men federation were eliminated from the administration of the National Railway Company. The General Confederation replied by withdrawing members from other government boards and councils; and, apart from necessary cooperation on technical bodies like arbitration boards and unemployment committees, government and labor from the close of 1938 to the outbreak of World War II remained hostile. Management used the opportunity of the general strike to dismiss hundreds of thousands of workers, and the Chamber of Deputies sided with the employers.

The unions were so severely weakened from internal conflicts caused by the Communists and from mass withdrawals from the unions that they could not defend the interests of the workers. The unions had made their mistake in calling the general strike, for, as René Belin, assistant secretary of the General Confederation, said afterward, "It is impossible to appeal to the law and to violate it at the same time . . . impossible to play simultaneously the so-called reformist and the so-called revolutionary strategist without the risk of losing on both grounds." [2] The government and industry made an equally grave mistake by exploiting their power to try to crush labor. As one of the speakers for the civil servants federation declared, "wherever there are humiliated or defeated Frenchmen, France herself is in danger of being defeated." [3]

[2] Henry W. Ehrmann, *French Labor from Popular Front to Liberation* (New York: Oxford University Press, 1947), p. 121.

[3] *Ibid.*

Small States of Northwestern Europe

HOW TO RECOVER FROM ECONOMIC CRISIS

The six small states, Norway, Sweden, Denmark, the Netherlands, Belgium, and Switzerland, overcame the economic crisis with varying degrees of effectiveness. Sweden, Norway, and Switzerland fared best, whereas the others recovered after considerable hardship. Since all greatly depended upon international trade, they understood that they could not revive by their efforts alone. Although compelled by circumstances to adopt practices of autarchy, they constantly strove to free the exchange of goods. Some of the countries improved the welfare of their people while recovering from the depression, and all introduced social reforms. Common suffering stimulated a feeling of social interdependence and a desire for social improvement similar to that aroused by World War I. On the whole, these states, particularly the Scandinavian, set an example to the rest of Europe of how to deal with an economic crisis. Their purpose was not to benefit the few in the vague hope that the effects would gradually reach the rest of the population but to offer direct and immediate assistance to the entire society.

The institutions and habits of free government had become too thoroughly imbedded among these peoples for the new panaceas of totalitarianism and communism to win many followers. The most notorious exception was offered by the fascist Rexists in Belgium, who suddenly emerged in 1935 and faded into insignificance again four years later. Prior to World War II the peoples had no political or constitutional problems. Their difficulties lay in the economic field and, for Belgium, also in the relations between the Flemings and the Walloons.

International Trade

Since each of the six countries depended for prosperity so heavily upon international trade, a discussion of achievements in this field will indicate the limits of their effective activity in other areas. The difference in the showing of the countries will then need to be explained, and for that purpose differences in economic policy must be considered. The following table gives the course of the imports and exports of each.

Course of Imports and Exports—1938 as Percentage of 1928 in New Gold Dollars

COUNTRY	IMPORTS	EXPORTS
Sweden	67	65
Denmark	48	48
Norway	63	63
Netherlands	43	42
Belgium-Luxembourg	51	50
Switzerland	42	45

Apart from the size of the decline the most striking points to be noted about these figures are (1) the ability of each country to balance the value of its imports and exports, and (2) the much better showing of Sweden and Norway than that of the others and the relatively poor showing of Switzerland and the Netherlands. Data on the "movement of manufacturing and the quantum of trade in manufactured articles between 1926–29 and 1936–38" confirm these conclusions.

Movement of Manufacturing Between 1936–1938 as Percentage of 1926–1929

COUNTRY	MANUFACTURING	TRADE IN MANUFACTURED ARTICLES (QUANTUM) IMPORTS	EXPORTS
Sweden	166	165	134
Denmark	147	112	132
Norway	143	153	117
Netherlands	118	99	88
Belgium	90	111	104
Switzerland	(75)	96	98

SOURCE: *Industrialization and Foreign Trade* (Geneva: League of Nations, 1945), p. 95. The figure on manufacturing for Switzerland is uncertain.

The Scandinavian countries were able greatly to increase both the output of manufactures and, especially Sweden and Norway, the size of their foreign trade in these lines. The Netherlands showed a rise in output but not in foreign trade, whereas the reverse was true for Belgium. Switzerland suffered a loss in every respect.

The difference between the rate and extent of recovery of the Scandinavian countries on the one hand and of the Netherlands, Belgium, and Switzerland on the other may be explained by the economic policy adopted and by the speed with which it was introduced. Since the Scandinavians found one of their most important markets in Great Britain and used the pound sterling as the medium of their international payments, they could not afford to allow their price scale to rise above that of the British. They immediately followed Britain in leaving the gold standard and aligned the value of their currencies with that of the British pound. The resulting ability to compete in price on the international market enabled Scandinavia to prevent the excessive rise in unemployment. Denmark suffered most among the three because she was most dependent upon agricultural exports. Even she, however, had an advantage over the Netherlands, Belgium, and Switzerland. Like France, these latter three countries defied the lead taken by Great Britain and the United States; they refused to align the value of their currencies with that of others until 1935 (Belgium) and 1936 (the Netherlands and Switzerland). Devaluation alone does not explain the difference in the rate of recovery, but the policy with respect to it determined whether or not a country imposed an unnecessary handicap upon its other efforts at revival.

Monetary Policy

The effects of the hard-money policy may be illustrated by the Netherlands and Belgium. In them, as in Switzerland, the matter of policy became an issue between the banker-capitalists, to whom the existing value of money was sacred, and the entrepreneurs, who sought cheap money and easy credit to revive business activity.

The government of the Netherlands tried to straddle the issue. It maintained the value of money, and at the same time it sought to lower costs to the level necessary for the economy to compete in price in the international market. For the latter purpose it reduced government expenditures by cutting salaries, social welfare payments (to unemployed, for example), and other items in the budget. Since agricultural products were especially difficult to market abroad and sank in price, the government paid subsidies to farmers and enabled them to charge a higher price in the national than in the foreign market. It bought up surplus agricultural products like meat and gave them to the poor, sold them at a loss, or destroyed them. It encouraged the transfer of land from the raising of vegetables, since it had lost almost the entire market in Germany for these products, to that of wheat. In doing so, it reduced the expenditure of foreign exchange; but since wheat growing requires much less labor than market gardening, it swelled unemployment at a time when the Netherlands already had 400,000 unemployed, five times the world average. The government reduced unemployment by the initiation of public works, such as improvement of roads and railroads, the electrification of the principal railway lines, the draining of polders, and the construction of canals, especially the continued draining of the Zuider Zee; but the outlay augmented the size of the public budget. To cover the increased expense, the government needed more taxes or loans, although the public lacked income to be taxed. The incomes of those assessed for the income tax fell 30 per cent in four years.

When deflation had been thoroughly tried and the population reduced to such extremes that, in 1935, 294,000 votes were cast for a National Socialist party and 127,000 for the Communists, the government finally sided with the entrepreneurs and devalued the currency. Within a year export trade and business in general began to revive; and, although unemployment remained about as high as before, it was restricted to the number of new persons which the steady growth of population added each year to the labor market. In the election of 1937 the National Socialist vote fell to 171,000. The Netherlands seemed on the way back to normal.

In Belgium the law permitted banks to use deposits for investments in industry, and a few large banks dominated the entire economy. In such conditions the government left to private initiative the responsibility for combating the economic crisis. Under a policy of laissez faire and deflation, unemployment increased from 42,000 in 1932 to 355,000 in 1935, the index of national production at the end of 1934 was 30 per cent below that of 1929, and in 1935 the Socialist Bank of Labor and the Flemish farmers' cooperative bank, the *Baerenbond,* failed. Bank deposits were being withdrawn and capital was fleeing the country. As early as September, 1934, the government had begun to reorganize the banking business by giving to a semiofficial credit institution the authority to take over the frozen assets of banks in difficulty. In the elections of 1935 to the Chamber of Deputies, a new man in politics, Paul von Zeeland, vice-president of the National Bank, advocated an unorthodox program of economic recovery. Winning an overwhelming victory, he organized a government of national union and introduced reforms which would enable private enterprise once again to function. Among the essential measures were the following: commercial banks had to choose between serving as deposit and as investment banks, so that depositors' money would be on instant call. Almost all kinds of financial operations were brought under central control. Loans from the Central Bank and state aid were used to assure the solvency of credit institutions, and the currency was devalued. These measures, especially the last named, immediately restored confidence, and recovery began. Von Zeeland's ministry was supported for two years, a long time in the history of Belgian governments, for he had brought the nation out of threatened bankruptcy.

Economic Recovery and Reform

At an early date the Scandinavian governments initiated a policy for overcoming the depression. Sweden and Denmark were controlled during most or all of the thirties by governments in which the Socialists played the major part. The most prominent political figures in those two countries were the Socialist party leaders Thorvald Stauning (Denmark) and

Per Albin Hansson (Sweden). The Socialist party likewise exercised a powerful influence in Norway, especially after its large vote in the election of 1933. Two years later it became the dominant force in the government. To these parties the gold standard did not inspire awe, and when in Sweden the Social Democrats campaigned in the election of 1932 on an economic program for overcoming the depression, the population, not merely workers but many of the middle class as well, gave them a large vote. They and the Farmers party of peasants formed the government which set the example for other countries.

The program of reform and recovery was formulated by Swedish economists and other social scientists who ranked among the ablest in the Western world. One of them, Wigforss, assuming in the new government the key position of minister of finance, administered the policies. He declared that the state should stabilize the economy. In time of depression it should initiate measures to put people back to work and use public funds to the extent necessary for that purpose. Instead of trying to balance the budget in time of depression, the Swedes unbalanced it; they financed recovery by incurring deficits. Wigforss hoped to revive spending and investment on the theory that money was an instrument to be used in whatever way seemed needed to keep the economy functioning. He believed that deflation made money and credit scarce, that it reduced incentives to invest, and that, by depriving people of jobs, it sacrificed the purpose of an economy to maintaining the value of the monetary unit. Government should help private enterprise to recover from a depression; it should also restrain excesses in times of booms. It should spend money in depressions and pay back loans in times of prosperity.

The program maintained the wage scale and, except where economic activity would clearly not be hurt, it did not increase taxes. The government provided work for the unemployed, not at charity rates, but at regular wages; it lent money to business on easy terms or subsidized economic activity with borrowed funds. For example, in 1931–1932 the predecessor to the Socialist government had used on capital account 73 million kroner obtained by loan and 22 million gained from taxes. The Socialist ministry in 1933–1934 spent 269 million obtained by loans and only 7 million out of taxation. Loan expenditure had in 1929 amounted to less than 5 per cent of total expenditure; in 1933–1934 it was 27 to 29 per cent. The standard practice in public finance had been for the government to borrow money only for productive projects which would repay the loans and to support the unemployed out of tax proceeds. The Socialist-Farmer government borrowed money to use in any effective way for restoring economic life, and it succeeded.

General recovery began in the late summer of 1933, as soon as the new economic program was initiated. Not even agricultural prices suffered. Unemployment, which had risen from an average of 46,500 in 1931 to 164,100 in 1933, dropped to 114,860 in 1934, to 61,600 in 1935, and to

35,344 in 1936. The results caused Bertil Ohlin, a Swede recognized as one of the world's most distinguished economists, to conclude in 1935 that "intelligent and sound public finance does not require the Budget to be balanced each year, but only over a number of years, including both good and bad business conditions."

The Swedes liked the results, and in the elections of 1936 gave the government parties more than 60 per cent of the votes, an increase of nearly 5 per cent. The Conservative leader, Professor Baggë, whose party declined by 5 per cent to only 17.5 per cent of the vote in 1936, gloomily predicted that the government, supported by workers and farmers, could hardly be removed. Sweden, he said, was a totalitarian state, since the government parties alone ruled. He saw as the only difference between Sweden and Germany the fact that in Sweden criticism of the government could be openly expressed.

Of the other two Scandinavian countries, Norway suffered much less than Denmark. Her fishing industry, especially whaling, and her ocean shipping continued to earn foreign exchange to pay for the surplus of imported manufactures and of foods. The people hardest hit were the Danes, whose imports prior to the depression equaled nearly 50 per cent of the national income, a figure about twice as high as that of Great Britain, and whose exports amounted to 40 per cent of the total national output. Agriculture was particularly vulnerable because it was both highly capitalized and dependent on exports, which between 1930 and 1932 fell by 25 per cent.

Agriculture

The Danish effort to aid this branch of the economy assumed forms which in severity of control were equaled or surpassed only by those of Switzerland. In addition to the usual rise in tariffs, the restriction of imports on a quota basis, differentiated prices (a high one for home consumption, a low one for exports, and the like), Denmark introduced policies which may be exemplified by the scheme to aid one of her principal products, bacon. The export of bacon depended almost exclusively upon the British market. When Britain introduced protection and placed bacon on the quota system, Denmark curtailed output in a way which has been described as follows:

> The scheme is based on the issue of pig-cards, the number issued corresponding to the number of bacon pigs required for the ensuing period. To obtain the market price, each pig has to be accompanied by one of these cards. Any pigs which the farmer produces over and above the number of cards he has, he is perfectly free to sell, but he can only obtain a low price for them, something under half as much as the carded pigs fetch. This wide difference of price has been sufficient to produce the desired effect. The farmers only produce 2 percent more pigs than they have cards, and the total pig population has been reduced

from 5 million to 3 million. A pig census is carried out every six weeks in order to know exactly how many pigs are coming on to the market. The conditions for the allocation of cards among farmers are highly complicated and have been constantly amended. . . . Usually a general quota of cards has been established for a year at a time, but the details are only known three months or even only one month ahead. The scheme is administered from an office in Copenhagen with three hundred employees and a file for every pig farmer in the country. It is financed by a levy of 15.9½d. per pig slaughtered.[4]

The farmers argued over the allocation of cards, but they approved the system, for it succeeded between 1932 and 1938 in more than doubling the price of pigs.

In Switzerland agriculture was so regulated by policies laid down by the Federal government that it offered "the first example of a democratic country developing a planned system run by corporative institutions, not unlike those of Germany and Italy." [5] Landlocked Switzerland was determined to preserve her agriculture, among other reasons, as insurance for food in the event of war. She had introduced high tariffs, which had raised prices, and had turned agriculture away from grain growing to dairying and the raising of livestock. Farms were small and farm population dense. Fodder was scarce, and, since winters were severe, livestock required winter housing, a factor which increased costs. To make agriculture economic under such handicaps, the government planned production, but endeavored to preserve the appearance of a free economy by allocating responsibility for execution mainly to producers' associations. The nature of the system has been sufficiently indicated with reference to Denmark and does not require analysis. It helped Switzerland to maintain a nation of 4 million people, many of whom in a world of free trade would have emigrated.

The sole exception with respect to agricultural policy among the six states was offered by Belgium. The government interfered here less than in any other country in Europe. It spent little money in the form of direct agricultural subsidies and relied upon the indirect effects of industrial revival. Marketing schemes and compulsory restriction of output were avoided; producers' debts were not reduced by decree or law, and agriculture did not, as in the Netherlands, go on the dole. The peasants were relatively content. Many of them drew several incomes, with the father working the little farm, the sons employed in industry, and the daughters earning money as domestic servants. Their income and their standard of living were low, their farming methods mainly those of a self-sufficient peasant family. The depression did not greatly affect them. When one adds that "the Belgians are a nation of stubborn individuals who dislike cooperation, loathe State interference, and will undertake nothing which might give away information to the tax collector," [6] one may understand

[4] Lamartine Yates, P., *Food Production in Western Europe* (New York: Longmans, Green & Company, Inc., 1940), pp. 93-94.
[5] *Ibid.*, p. 406. [6] *Ibid.*, p. 240.

why the relation of the state to agriculture differed so markedly from that in the other countries.

Belgium alone among the six states did not utilize the opportunity of economic change in the 1930's to improve the living conditions of the workers. Although membership in the trade-unions grew, nominal wages remained low. Just before World War II a law set the minimum wage at 13½ cents an hour. Compulsory sickness insurance did not exist; unemployment support was left to workers' funds supplemented by the state, and payments amounted to two thirds of the person's wages, or to three fourths if he had a large family. In 1939 a payment amounted to about 60 cents a day, and did not apply to agricultural workers or to domestic servants. Three fifths of the taxes were obtained from levies on consumption, mainly paid by the poor. The first national consideration of social problems occurred in 1939, when a proposed annual Conference of Labor was called, composed of representatives of labor, employers, and the government to consider recommendations to the state about wage increases, government subsidies, and other measures to maintain the real value of wages. Like that of the peasants, the standard of living of the workers was low but apparently adequate to meet their modest expectations. The few big banks had set economic policy for so long that innovations in the distribution of the national income had been avoided, and the economic reforms of van Zeeland's New Deal did not change the situation. Nonetheless, some industrialists disliked these reforms so intensely that they subsidized the fascist movement of the Rexists and gave it an artificial existence.

The depression accentuated the drive of the Flemings for cultural autonomy. The Belgian economy provided fewer opportunities than ever for making Flemings and Walloons aware of their interdependence. The Flemish extremists, or Nationalists, as they were called, continued to agitate with success. They had 10 members in the Belgian parliament in 1929, 8 in 1932, 16 in 1936, and 17 in 1939. By the middle of the decade the Flemings had gained their cultural demands. Linguistic equality with French was extended to civil, commercial, and military courts. The army was divided into Flemish and French speaking regiments; officers were required to know the language of their men, and both languages were used in the military academy in Brussels. The University of Ghent and certain technical schools became Flemish, and further steps were taken to equalize the two languages in primary and secondary schools. With these achievements behind them, the Nationalists turned to political and constitutional demands. Many called for Flemish autonomy within a federalized state; others asked separation from Belgium and annexation to the Netherlands, an aspiration which in spite of linguistic kinship the Netherlands did not share. A few became fascist. None of these nationalist groups gained much support. Their political strength was diminished by the achievement of cultural equality. Their heyday came with World War II, when many of them acted as Nazi stooges. In the meantime Belgium ran little danger from within of disruption as a state.

IMPROVEMENT IN SOCIAL RELATIONS

In the Scandinavian countries the conditions of all groups in the population continued to improve during the thirties. Economic crises are frequently times in which management exploits the existence of mass unemployment to weaken the trade-unions. These countries proved that it was of mutual advantage for both employers and labor to be strong. The employers' associations were tightly organized on a national basis, and during the decade the trade-unions doubled their membership. The industrial workers were almost completely organized and, except in Norway, a large percentage of the white-collar employees as well. The presence of a powerful labor party in the government furthered the cause of trade-unionism and augmented the high morale of the workers; the fact that the Socialist parties were so strong indicates the decline in Scandinavia of old-style labor-management hostility still to be found in France and elsewhere. The development of employers' associations, trade-unions, cooperatives, farmers' associations, and other bodies enabled these nations to achieve a condition of social checks and balances. Instead of fighting a class war, the members of these pluralistic societies supplemented each others' activity by stimulation and competition.

The advantages were evident in many lines. The number of work days lost in strikes greatly decreased. In each country the system of social insurance was fully developed and was used to improve the real income of the working groups. Real wages were raised, more in Norway and Sweden than in Denmark, and the workers had enough confidence in the economy to accept labor-saving technological improvements. Government continued to aid in mediating conflicts between management and labor; in Denmark legislation put through by a labor government in important cases required the acceptance of recommendations by mediation boards. Public funds assisted society wherever it seemed useful to do so, as the outlay of the Swedish government in millions of kroner before and after the depression—that is, before and after the Socialists and the Farmers party took over the government—will show. The proportions were roughly similar for the other two countries.

YEAR	SOCIAL DEPARTMENT	COMMUNICATIONS	EDUCATION	AGRICULTURE	DEFENSE
1929–1930	107	63	143	29	133
1933–1934	121	85	146	47	103
1937–1938	288	119	197	74	174

SOURCE: Margaret Cole., ed., *Democratic Sweden* (New York: Greystone Corporation, Publishers, 1939), p. 73.

Such items as old age pensions and other forms of social insurance account for the large increase in the social department. The improvement in communications meant opening the countryside and increasing the opportunities for the farmers to participate in the life of the nation. The size of the expenditure on education showed awareness of the importance of maintaining intelligent action on the part of the citizens in politics, and in assuring high productivity and a high standard of living. Similar insight applied to the big rise in the outlay for agriculture. All these peoples intensely disliked military activity. They were inclined to be pacifist and strove to keep out of the way of power politics; they did not see how with their small size they could possibly defend themselves. The menace of nazism accounts for a reluctant increase in expenditures for defense. All in all, the budget indicated that the people wished the government to expand its role, and were willing to pay the price.

The improved sense of social responsibility was manifest on the part of private associations and political parties. In Norway the trade-unions introduced what was called the "solidaristic" wage policy. The well-paid unions desisted from pressing for higher wages, which their bargaining strength would have enabled them to obtain, so that the poorly paid workers could be aided in securing adequate increases. They were all thinking in terms of a national wage program. In Denmark the social services were administered mainly by welfare committees of local authorities, which in 1933 received the power to decide on the size and nature of payments. Central planning and settling of standards were thus combined with local responsibility for execution. In 1938 the Federation of Labor and the Employers' Association in Denmark agreed to tie wages to the index of the cost of living on a national scale.

Each country furthered adult education, and in Denmark in 1930–1933 the penal code was brought into conformity with the ideals of social responsibility. Although dangerous and incorrigible criminals were to be imprisoned for indefinite terms, an offender was no longer to be treated exclusively as a willful criminal and punished for his offense. His or her mentality, environment, and motives were to be considered, and the punishment to be educational in purpose. In 1936 the Danes added lay judges to the bench in courts of first and second instance, who should see that the layman's point of view was represented not merely in the jury but on the bench.

The private citizen in these countries by way of his membership in many organizations was so integrated with governmental activities—on social service boards, housing committees, labor-relations boards, committees for guiding the state-owned radio, agricultural commodity boards, and numerous others—that the masses as well as the moneyed bourgeoisie considered these to be their states, their governments. These were democratic societies, living in proximity to Communist Russia and Nazi Germany, not to mention Fascist Italy, Spain of the civil war, and France of embittered class relations. These smaller nations possessed the reasonable stability which the rest of the continent might have had.

The free countries under review, however different in size and in international significance, shared the desire to live in peace. Those that had fought in World War I still felt tired from the effort, and they and the former neutrals alike wished if at all possible to avoid another such ordeal. They gave precedence to internal affairs over international in this period, seeking to recover fully from the economic depression and to improve the living standards of their people. The British economy was unprepared for war, and the French economy, society, and government alike showed confusion and distress. Both countries, with the lesser imperial states, Belgium and the Netherlands, hesitantly planned to develop their imperial economies, but their programs would require decades to complete. They, as well as Switzerland and the Scandinavian nations, hoped to escape participation in power politics; but so long as their neighbors were Nazi Germany, Fascist Italy, and Communist Russia, they could do so only at the expense of security. All the states discussed in this chapter watched with fascination the rise of nazism and the grouping of authoritarian powers for aggression. Yet they found difficulty in believing what they saw and refused until too late to take countermeasures. Great Britain and France especially continued to live according to the system of international relations of the preceding decade.

Suggestions for Further Reading

The Readings at the end of Chapter 7 are useful for this period as well. The following titles pertaining to the 1930's may be consulted in addition.

ABRAMS, MARK ALEXANDER. *The Condition of the British People, 1911–1945.* London: Victor Gollancz, Ltd., 1946. Compact analysis of social conditions.

EHRMANN, HENRY W. *French Labor from Popular Front to Liberation.* New York: Oxford University Press, 1947. The best study of any continental labor movement during the decade. Highly revealing for the character of French life.

GIRAUD, A. *(Pertinax). The Grave-Diggers of France.* New York: Doubleday & Company, Inc., 1944. A French journalist attempts to account for the collapse of France in 1940. A gripping story.

KAHN, ALFRED E. *Great Britain in the World Economy.* New York: Columbia University Press, 1946. Strong on the economic aspects.

Chapter 14 · The Authoritarian Countries of Central and Western Europe

UNSTABLE INTERNAL CONDITIONS

In the events of the thirties we find new reasons for having grouped, and for continuing to group, Germany, Italy, Spain, and Portugal together as countries of unstable internal conditions. The reader may reflect on what measures might have preserved the Weimar Republic from Nazism. Certainly one could argue that a different economic policy on the part of the Brüning government and a constructive program supported by the great powers, including the United States, for overcoming the world depression would have prevented the victory of Hitler. Such measures were not taken, and Germany followed Italy in turning to a totalitarian state system. She sought to unite a divided society by force of dictatorship and guided the nation by the social and political philosophy of extreme nationalism. The animosity among the Spanish social groups exploded in revolution, first in one of Republicans against the monarchy, then in one of the church, the nobles, most of the capitalistic bourgeoisie, and the army against the republic. Spain produced a weak imitation of fascism in the Falangist movement, but the authority that survived the civil war lay, as of old, in the army. In Portugal, the dictatorship introduced by the army took the mildest form of that to be found in any country and avoided civil war. Even though diverse as to dictatorial systems, economic conditions, degrees of material and spiritual power, all four countries strove to maintain internal order by recourse to authoritarian rule. The reader will find a logical consistency in studying these countries as examples of a common movement opposed to liberal democracy.

Germany

ATTEMPTS TO OVERCOME THE DEPRESSION

The means which Germany used to meet the economic crisis revealed the fundamental weakness in her political, social, and moral heritage. She

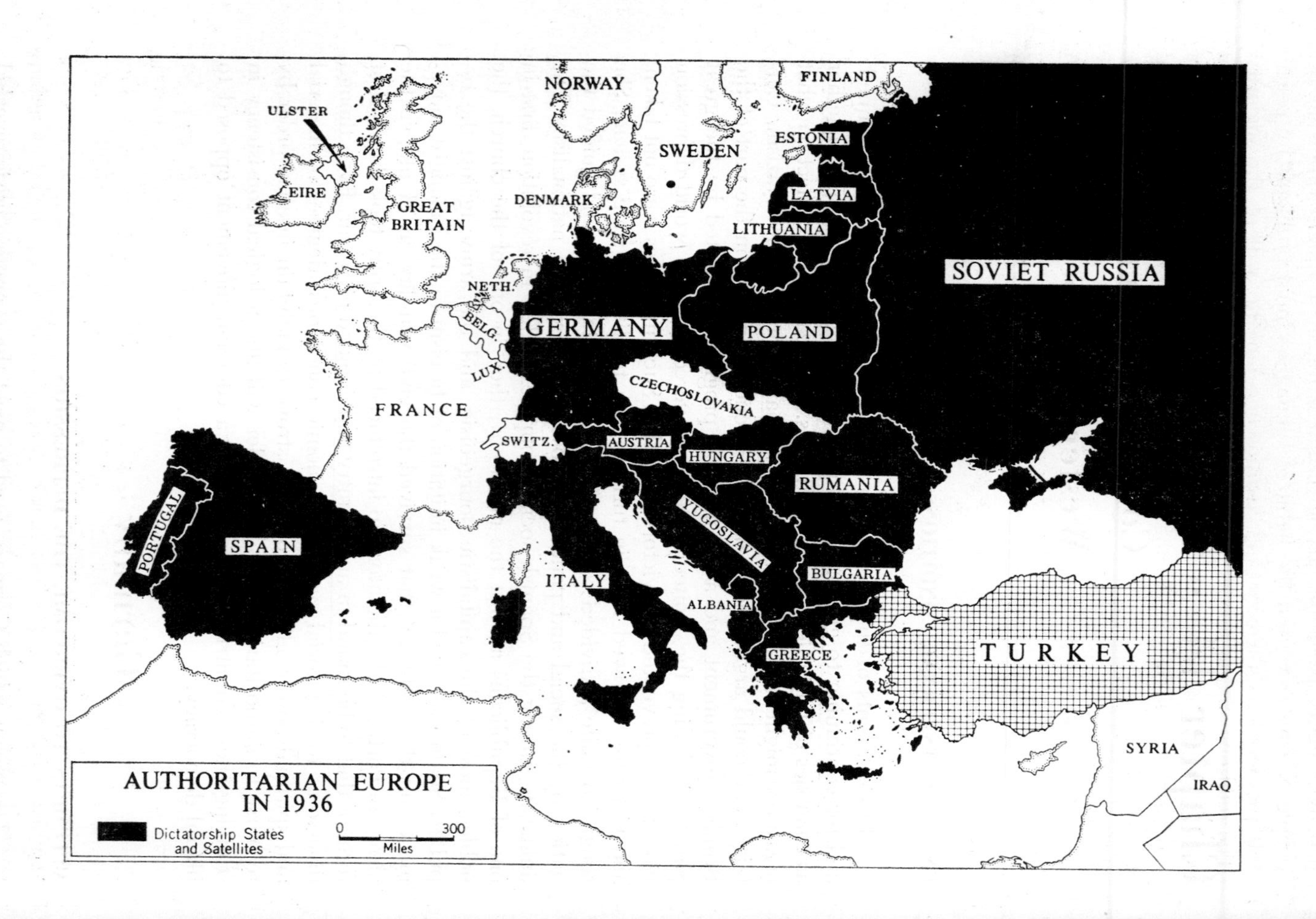
AUTHORITARIAN EUROPE
IN 1936
Dictatorship States
and Satellites
0
300
Miles
ULSTER
EIRE
GREAT
BRITAIN
NORWAY
SWEDEN
DENMARK
FINLAND
ESTONIA
LATVIA
LITHUANIA
SOVIET RUSSIA
NETH.
BELG.
LUX.
GERMANY
POLAND
CZECHOSLOVAKIA
FRANCE
SWITZ.
AUSTRIA
HUNGARY
RUMANIA
PORTUGAL
SPAIN
YUGOSLAVIA
ITALY
BULGARIA
ALBANIA
GREECE
TURKEY
SYRIA
IRAQ

had lived under parliamentary government for such a short time that her people had not acquired the habit of solving national problems by peaceful, reasonable agreement and acquiescence in the will of the majority. The relations among her social classes remained embittered from the recent loss of dominant power by the upper classes, from the economic ruin of the middle class during the inflation, and from the inability of millions of people, particularly the young generation, to find work. This immature and divided society was forced by the depression to wrestle with all the basic issues of government and of social and economic organization. A country like Great Britain with a sound, stable tradition weathered the storm; Germany, loaded with the extra burden of defeat in World War I and a national sense of having been unjustly treated at Versailles, succumbed to dictatorship.

Brüning Government Fails

From 1930 to 1932 Germany was governed by a coalition of moderate parties under the chancellorship of the leader of the Catholic Center party, Heinrich Brüning. This prorepublican, constitutional group took measures which it thought in the interest of orderly government and society. Brüning's government, it was widely believed, offered the last hope for putting people back to work before they turned in despair to revolutionary action. Fearful of another runaway inflation, the government introduced and adhered to an economic policy of deflation, scarce money, and reduction of prices. Economists urged the government in 1931 to reverse the program and introduce one of public works, low interest rates, and expanding credits. One economist prophesied that if the present policy continued the government and the republic would fall. Brüning kept his faith that he could increase foreign trade by reducing the price level, and he refused to change. The results, under which regular employment was provided for only one third of the working population, proved disastrous.

Economic conditions immediately affected politics. In the *Reichstag* elections in September, 1930, 30 million Germans cast ballots. The National Socialist vote increased from 810,000 in 1928 to 6,409,600, and Nazi representation in the *Reichstag* jumped from 12 to 107. The Communist gain was also spectacular, from 3,265,000 in 1928 to 4,592,000, with an increase in the number of deputies in the *Reichstag* from 54 to 77. These two parties polled more than one third of the votes. The right-wing Nationalists lost 2 million votes and returned only 41 deputies, and the middle parties loyal to the republic were similarly hard hit. The Catholic Center party held its following, and the Social Democrats remained strong. Nonetheless, it was evident that the young people were turning Nazi or Communist, that the middle-class parties with democratic or liberal programs were losing to nazism, that the conservative Nationalist party was weakening in favor of the Nazis, and that the Social Democratic party retained the devotion mainly of the employed older men of the trade-unions. The Center party alone was confident of preserving its position.

The two elections held in 1932, one in July, the other in November, proved catastrophic to the republic. In July the Nazis polled 13,745,000 votes and seated 230 deputies, more than doubling the size of their support in 1930 and becoming the largest party in Germany. The Social Democrats received just under 8 million votes, the Communists increased to 5¼ million, and the Center retained 4½ million. The Nazis continued to win votes from the middle-class parties, which they now reduced to relative insignificance; they had since 1928 taken 1½ million votes from the Nationalist party, and they had captured the support of most of the 6 million new voters since 1928. In the November elections the Nazis lost 2 million votes, while the Communists polled nearly 6 million, returning a hundred deputies to the *Reichstag*. The increase in the Communist vote came from those who, disappointed in the Nazis and the Social Democrats, preferred revolutionary action. Except for the Center party, the Weimar Republic had almost no supporters left. Although for different reasons, the Nazis, the Communists, and the Nationalists alike wished to destroy it completely, and the Social Democrats hoped to transform it by evolutionary democratic action into a socialist state. Of a total of about 30 million votes, 25 millions opposed the Brüning government.

From Papen to Hitler

Unable to form a working majority, Brüning governed by emergency decrees issued under the authority of Article 48 of the constitution. He fell from power in 1932 through the intrigues primarily of General Kurt von Schleicher, an officer with a zest for politics behind the scenes, whose influence lay in his control of the army. Von Schleicher disapproved of Brüning's effort to ban the paramilitary formation of the Nazis, advocating instead the inclusion of the Nazi party in a new government, which would thereby be based upon a parliamentary majority. General von Schleicher in his planning had the support of industrialists, who complained about low prices, and especially the aid of big landowners in eastern Germany, who denounced as agrarian bolshevism the government's proposal to colonize the many insolvent large estates with peasants. These gentlemen had access to senile President von Hindenburg, (born 1847), who was surrounded by conservatives of similar views. When von Schleicher declared that the army had no confidence in the chancellor, Hindenburg in June, 1932, replaced Brüning by the general's choice, the Catholic Franz von Papen, and a cabinet of the extreme right. Called the Cabinet of Barons, it had almost no popular following and depended entirely upon Hindenburg and the army.

Once von Papen attained power he began subtly to compete with von Schleicher for the favor of President von Hindenburg. An elegant man of the world with a superficial, irresponsible mind, he proposed, like von Schleicher, to solve the parliamentary stalemate by bringing the Nazis into the government. He differed with the general over the kind of program to be adopted. Von Papen wished to restore the authoritarian regime of the prerevolutionary period, or even go farther and transform the Reichstag into an advisory body; the reintroduction of monarchy would provide the copestone.

Since von Papen proved unable to gain the support of a parliamentary majority, Hindenburg dismissed the cabinet and in December, 1932 appointed von Schleicher as chancellor. The latter sought to play "the impartial trustee of the interests of all in an emergency"; but in doing so he antagonized the same interests that had pulled wires against Brüning—big industry, which opposed his conciliatory policy toward labor, and the big Junkers, who hated him for advocating the reduction of agricultural protection and for his plans of breaking up estates in favor of peasant holdings. Nor was von Schleicher able to win the confidence of the Social Democrats and the trade-unions, the Center party, and the Nazis. By January, 1933, he had failed to organize a government based on a parliamentary majority—extending from the Social Democrats to the Nationalists and the Nazis—which could replace the minority of von Papen.

At this point von Papen concluded an agreement with Hitler for the formation of a Nazi-Nationalist government, expecting thereby to gain the support of a majority of the deputies. Hitler was to be chancellor, but von Papen reserved for himself the post of vice-chancellor and minister-president of Prussia, and the right to be present when the chancellor reported to the president of the republic. Von Papen was to place his Nationalist colleagues in the key ministerial posts, and to give to the Nazi Wilhelm Frick the *Reich* Ministry of the Interior, which did not control the police of the states, and to the Nazi Göring a ministry without portfolio and the Prussian ministry of the interior. The latter post carried with it the control of the Prussian police, but by virtue of his power as minister-president of Prussia von Papen expected to keep tight reins on Göring. In this way von Papen and the Nationalists thought that Hitler would be their prisoner. They aimed to exploit Nazi popularity in order to keep the gentlemen of the imperial regime in power. Some of the most distinguished industrialists and bankers, many Junkers, and many of the highest military approved the plan and persuaded von Hindenburg to accept it. On January 30, 1933, the new government came to power. Six months later a more surprised group than these distinguished epigones of Imperial Germany could not have been found.

As long as free elections were held the Nazis failed to attract a majority of the votes. In July, 1932, they had polled 37 per cent, in November, 33 per cent; in March, 1933, after they had the governmental machinery at their disposal and a fairly free run for coercing voters, they obtained only 44 per cent of the vote. They were given power by a clique of reactionaries just when their decline seemed to have begun. Nonetheless, they enjoyed a far greater popularity than any other single party; although the Social Democrats and the Catholic Centrists remained as loyal as ever to Weimar ideals in that first election under Nazi rule, a large percentage of Germans turned to nazism.

NATIONAL SOCIALISM AND HITLER

The Nazi party won popularity, not by its official program, but by relatively simple proposals and by its method of action. The German people did not know how to use freedom. They considered defeat in World War I to have come unjustly, and they hated the treaty of Versailles. They were overwhelmed by the inflation, another devastating blow to their confidence in the justice and reasonableness of fate and of man. World economic crisis completed their conversion to belief in the power of irrational forces and the inability of man to govern himself in freedom. When Hitler denounced the treaty of Versailles he was certain of a popular issue; but his condemnation of parliamentary government did not prove appealing until the parties under the Weimar Republic failed to overcome unemployment. When he demanded sole power for one individual supported by one party (himself as Führer, or leader, and his organized following of Nazis), he found response among a people unaccustomed to selfgovernment, confused and frustrated by the nature of politics, and demanding action at a quicker pace than free government set.

The Germans sought a scapegoat for their troubles, and Hitler found several for them: the "slavery of the treaty of Versailles," the Jews, the Communists. He preached to them that these enemies were in their midst; the Social Democrats and the democrats who had accepted the treaty of Versailles were as readily available for vengeance as were the German Jews and the German Communists. Since the Communists offered the greatest current menace to Germany and indulged in violence as ardently as the Nazis, he used them as whipping post. By constant denunciation of the Communist menace, he conditioned the Germans to accept any action, no matter how illegal and how brutal, to eradicate the plague. He smeared everything and everyone he hated and feared with the accusation of Jewish communism or procommunism—for example, socialism, capitalism, freedom of speech, freedom of press and assembly, liberalism, internationalism, pacificism, and modern art. He demanded that all these be destroyed, the nation purified, the race once more restored to the primal vigor of its Nordic blood. Instinct, he asserted, should guide the people to feel and act in unity; the instinct of blood would enable the Führer to know what the nation wished and what was best for all. Western freedom was a Communist, Jewish, capitalistic curse; German freedom to follow Hitler, a blessing for Germans and for the world. The entire program could be summed up in two phrases, Mein Führer and Heil Hitler! Once assured of the acceptance of unquestioned obedience, the Führer aimed to guide an unwitting people into imperial conquest. He reorganized government and society in the way most effective for waging war.

The Führer was born April 20, 1889, in Austria, in a little town on the German frontier. As son of an irascible petty official, he knew poverty and bitter disappointment. His wish to become an artist was frustrated by penury and lack of talent; he educated himself by casual reading of newspapers, cheap pamphlets, and popular historical fiction, through which he gained ideas of anti-Semitism, anti-Christianity, racialism, and Nietzsche's superman. The experience of war, of being a soldier at the front, of living exclusively in male company, and of fighting and killing under orders gave him a lifetime ideal of social and political organization. Unemployed after the war, he joined one of the many radical reform clubs that sprang up among ex-soldiers; this he transformed during the twenties into the National Socialist party. He proved to be a voluble and persuasive orator, a master at dominating other persons, and a courageous leader. When he and his group, assisted by no less a person than General Eric Ludendorff, attempted a revolution in Munich in 1923, they failed dismally and Hitler landed in prison. There he wrote the Nazi Bible, *Mein Kampf*, the frankest and the completest statement of nationalism ever written by a nationalist in the process of implementing his own ideas.

By this time Hitler had manifested the dominant characteristics of his personality. He believed that providence functioned through him and sanctioned his use of any means to achieve his ends. He lacked a feeling of pity and mercy and enjoyed the suffering of his enemies. His gift for simplifying issues, his keen sense of timing, and his thorough opportunism in the choice of means and occasion for accomplishing his objective were as brilliant as his ability to sway people in a vast audience, in a diplomatic conference, or in negotiation among rival factions of his own party. Once he had decided an issue, he had the will to act. He was charming to high and low when he wished to be, intimidating when he chose to be. He had no friends, he never let down his guard.

Hitler read nothing for the sake of culture. Notwithstanding his devotion to Wagner's operas, he had never advanced in aesthetic taste beyond the sentimental genre work of decadent romanticism. He hated the upper bourgeoisie and its culture, which he had never achieved, and he despised intellectuals. A biographer has written:

> To read Hitler's table talk at his headquarters in 1941–1942 is to feel continual astonishment at the lack of magnanimity and wisdom in his conversation, the main qualities of which were cunning and brutality, a cocksure ignorance and an ineradicable vulgarity. Yet this vulgarity of mind, like the insignificance of his appearance, the badly fitting raincoat and the lock of hair plastered over his forehead, was perfectly compatible with brilliant political gifts.[1]

[1] Alan Bullock, *Hitler: A Study in Tyranny* (New York: Harper & Brothers, 1952), p. 372.

This was the person whom Admiral Karl Dönitz, when commander in chief of the German navy, avoided as much as possible in order "to disengage myself," as he said at the Nürnberg trials after the war, "from his power of suggestion." This was the person of whom Göring, possibly the boldest of the other Nazis, once said, "I often make up my mind to say something to him, but then when I come face to face with him my heart sinks into my boots."

National Socialist Government

When Hitler became chancellor on January 30, 1933, his greatest asset lay in the strength (1) of the party organized in such a way as to parallel that of the state throughout the country and (2) of the party paramilitary troops known as the Brown Shirts. The young unemployed, particularly from the middle class, had joined this private army and had received a uniform, maintenance, and a purpose in life. Led by ruthless ex-soldiers, they fought the battles against the Communists, Social Democrats, and the defenders of the Weimar Republic in the streets, in taverns, or wherever the two sides might meet. Murder had become fairly common. Once in power, the Nazis went to work with the assurance that the apparatus of the state would not block them. Göring paid no attention to von Papen: he rooted opponents out of the Prussian police and filled it with Nazi stalwarts. He purged the bureaucracy in the same way. On the night of February 27, 1933, the Nazis set fire to the *Reichstag* building and threw the blame on the Communists. The event served its purpose, for on the next day Hitler persuaded the president to sign a decree suspending all civil liberties guaranteed by the constitution. The attacks on the Social Democrats, their leaders, their press, their buildings, their rallies, expanded into battles, in which the Brown Shirts were aided by Göring's Nazified Prussian police. On March 3 Göring told an audience in Frankfurt: "Fellow Germans, my measures will not be crippled by any judicial thinking. My measures will not be crippled by any bureaucracy. Here I don't have to worry about Justice, my mission is only to destroy and exterminate, nothing more."

Hitler had hoped that the elections in March, 1933, would return a majority of Nazi deputies. When the voters failed him, he jailed most of the Communist deputies and a dozen Social Democratic deputies and terrorized the other Communists into staying away from the *Reichstag*. On March 24 he put through the *Reichstag* the so-called Enabling Law (Law for Removing the Distress of People and *Reich*). It permitted the cabinet to make laws without *Reichstag* approval; it allowed the laws to deviate from the constitution insofar as they did not affect the position of the *Reichstag* and the *Reichsrat;* and the cabinet could make foreign treaties without the consent of the *Reichstag*. The Enabling Act was to run for four years. It did not abolish the constitution; it put that document in cold storage.

The parties in the *Reichstag* were so overwhelmed by the course of events that in a lopsided vote they approved the death warrant of the Weimar Republic. The Center party joined the majority, relying on Hitler's equivocal promise that the number of cases in which the law would be used was "a limited one." In a few months the Nazis "coordinated" the state governments, the trade-unions, and the political parties. The states were forced to accept Nazi governments, Nazi police, and their own Enabling Act. The bureaucracies were purged and filled with Nazis, and over each state Hitler appointed a governor with powers in his state like Hitler's own over the *Reich*. All self-government ceased, as the pattern was extended to the localities. The entire apparatus of government was thereby transformed into one of extreme centralization.

The once powerful trade-unions were similarly treated. Nazi police and Storm Troopers raided and looted union headquarters, beat up and threw into concentration camps many union leaders. The trade-union organization was replaced by a Nazi-controlled Labor Front. Collective bargaining and strikes were outlawed; Labor Trustees were appointed under government control to settle the conditions of work. In May the buildings and newspaper offices of the Social Democratic party were occupied and party funds confiscated. In June and July all parties, including the Nationalist party with members in Hitler's cabinet, were abolished, and the Nazi party was officially given a political monopoly. The powerful veterans' organization, or *Stahlhelm*, held out until the end of 1933, when it was incorporated into the Nazi Storm Troopers. Similar fate befell the schools and universities, the press, radio, and movies as instruments of propaganda, and, with less effectiveness, the church. The Nazis demanded that everything be placed under the authority of the Führer. The many jobs now opened to loyal Nazis were considered just rewards for devotion to the Fatherland by way of the party; and for those who opposed the new regime numerous concentration camps were built.

Hitler and the Army

The acquiescence of the army made possible the Nazi seizure of authority. General Werner von Blomberg accepted the post of minister of defense in Hitler's cabinet in the expectation on his part and on that of numerous other generals that they could control the Nazis while utilizing the latter to rearm Germany. Hitler was acutely aware of his debt to the army, and as long as his authority was insecure he cultivated its support almost to the point of fawning. His opinion of army officers was that of the ex-corporal, one of envy, hate, and scorn, but he played for time until he could gain ascendancy over the army comparable to that over the government. He intended to remilitarize Germany, and he needed the technical knowledge of the officers corps.

When Ernst Röhm, the Nazi head of the Storm Troopers, grew impatient and endeavored to develop the Brown Shirts into the national army, absorb the *Reichswehr,* and acquire the highest military positions for himself and his entourage, Hitler opposed his aims and assured the army that no such change would occur. Röhm, a brutal, corrupt, disorderly person, did not dare to use his two to three million Storm Troopers in a revolution against his own Führer; but his persistence in the demands gave two of his arch enemies and competitors for power, Göring and one of the latter's subordinates, Heinrich Himmler, an opportunity to eliminate him. They trumped up a charge of a plot against the Führer and induced the latter on June 30, 1934, to strike. The army was kept out of this internal fight among the Nazis; it preserved the purity of its political objectivity, as it was called. When Nazi party forces murdered Röhm and his leading associates, the army heads and President von Hindenburg congratulated Hitler on having crushed treason.

The army's potential rival had been reduced to insignificance, but the military had also received a severe blow. During this "night of the long knives" the Nazis also assassinated General von Schleicher and General von Bredow, and several of von Papen's close associates among the Catholic political leaders. The army disapproved the shooting of two of its most important officers as an affront to the uniform of a general and a dangerous precedent; but Hitler's assurance to von Hindenburg that the matter would be investigated, a promise never carried out, calmed the generals into inactivity. Shortly after the purge, Hitler declared to Hermann Rauschning:

> They underestimate me because I have risen from below from the lower depths; because I haven't had an education, because I haven't the "manners" that their sparrow brains think right! . . . I have spoiled their plans. They thought I would not dare; they thought I was afraid. They saw me already wriggling in their net. They thought I was their tool. And behind my back they laughed at me and said I had no power now, that I had lost my party. I saw through all that long ago. I've given them a cuff on the ear that they'll long remember. What I have lost in the trial of the S.A. [Storm Troopers] I shall regain by the verdict on these feudal gamblers and professional card-sharpers, the Schleichers and company. . . . I stand here stronger than ever before. Forward, Messrs. Papen and Hugenberg [Nationalist leader and one of Hitler's cabinet members]! I am ready for the next round.[2]

In General Werner von Blomberg Hitler found an aid who kept the army in line. When President von Hindenburg died on August 2, 1934, the Führer merged the office of president with that of chancellor, and he and Blomberg were ready with an oath of unconditional obedience to Hitler for the army to take. Henceforth any officer however opposed to Hitler felt bound by this oath; his honor might be and often was at stake in executing Hitler's commands, but his honor was also engaged by the oath.

The active creation of the new armed force of Germany began imme-

[2] Hermann Rauschning, *The Voice of Destruction* (New York: G. P. Putnam's Sons, 1940), pp. 172-173.

diately after the purge. Himmler was rewarded for his share in the suppression of the supposed rebellion by being permitted to establish his *Schutzstaffel,* or S.S. troops, hitherto a part of the Storm Troopers, as a body directly responsible to Göring. Under Himmler's direction the S.S. soon became an efficient organization upon which Hitler could depend. It ultimately rivaled the regular army. When in 1936 Himmler was placed in charge of all the German police as well, Hitler was secure against any internal enemy. The introduction of military conscription in 1935, contrary to the advice of the generals, who feared the reaction of France and the British, opened the way to incorporating the Nazi young people into this institution. Whether they served as privates or as lower officers, they increased the popular strength of the regime.

One further move remained for Hitler, that of gaining complete authority over the high command. He achieved this goal in 1938, when Minister of Defense von Blomberg became involved in a personal scandal and resigned. Hitler personally took over his position, as well as that of the new supreme command of the combined armed forces, appointing the servile General Wilhelm Keitel as chief of the latter. At the same time, Göring and Himmler, who had attended to the publicity leading to Blomberg's fall, transmitted to Hitler evidence accusing the commander in chief of the army, General von Fritsch, of sex crimes. The general denied the evidence, but Hitler believed the accuser, a convicted blackmailer, and dismissed the commander in chief. In this instance the army forced a military trial, but when von Fritsch was proved innocent, Hitler refused to restore him to his former position. In von Fritsch's stead he appointed General Heinrich von Brauchitsch, another weakling. Göring was promoted to the rank of field marshal, and Himmler and his right-hand man Reinhard Heydrich, who had worked up the case against von Fritsch, increased their power. Von Fritsch grasped the fact that the attack on him as commander in chief dishonored the entire army, but his fellow generals, who did not demand his reinstatement, let the case close with Hitler in complete control.

National Socialist Economics—Schacht

The Führer had no knowledge of, and no interest in, economics. When he laid down political objectives he expected the economy to produce the necessary resources, and he listened to no arguments and accepted no excuses. The Nazi program had denounced capitalism and promised the economic revival of the middle class, and the party name included the word "socialist." Hitler, however, was no socialist. Big bankers and industrialists had helped to finance the party during lean years before 1933; Hitler expected them to provide the economic means for the execution of his political program, in the same way that he depended upon the *Reichswehr* to supply the military technicians for rearming Germany. He had no intention of allowing the economy to run itself; the economic leaders were to learn, as the generals had learned, that they could not use the Führer to suppress the workers and save private property. The individual Nazis bent upon quick fortunes had considerable opportunity to enrich themselves from the confiscated property of Jews, of the Social Democratic party, of the liberal, democratic, Socialist, and Communist press, and of many who were thrown into concentration camps. A great deal of wealth changed hands quickly, often in the form of bribes and other types of corruption; since the party started businesses of its own, like publishing and making patriotic decorations, an enterprising party member could forge ahead.

Hjalmar Schacht became the main person responsible up to 1938 for economic policy. He had won a reputation in the twenties as an astute, bold president of the *Reichsbank* who used government funds and credit for economic purposes irrespective of the taboos of orthodox economic theory. During the first years of its regime the Nazi government substituted an inflationary for a deflationary policy, greatly expanding public works, the volume of credit, and other means to abolish unemployment. The speed with which they succeeded impressed the Germans more than any other single action of the Nazis and won the support of a majority of the population. The way the program worked has been illustrated by a German economist hostile to the Nazis as follows:

> For example, an iron merchant was indebted to the bank to the extent of 100,000 marks and owned a large stock of iron girders. Under the new policy a builder was allotted a big state contract and received state-accepted bills in payment. He discounted these bills—for, say, 100,000 marks—at the bank and, with the amount placed to his credit, paid the iron merchant, whose girders he had bought. What happened? The bank's liquidity was restored; for the iron merchant's debit account of 100,000 marks vanished and the bank received instead a bill for 100,000 marks eligible for discount at the Reichsbank and hence immediately convertible into cash. Simultaneously the iron merchant's stock was reduced, and new building took place, giving employment to previously unemployed workers. The upshot was a fall in unemployment and stocks, and improved liquidity for the banks. In 1937 unemployment fell below one million and then vanished completely.[3]

A change in fiscal program seemed to work miracles.

When Germany initiated rearmament in 1935, the economy immediately set about providing the necessary resources. The country entered a period of gearing itself for either peace or war, a condition of opportunism ideally suited to a totalitarian state. An industrial economy was placed completely at the service of a dictator.

The main economic policies came from the central government. The country strove for self-sufficiency. Industry was guided by direct or indirect means to produce the materials for rearmament. Since Hitler de-

[3] Walter Eucken, *This Unsuccessful Age* (New York: Oxford University Press, 1952), pp. 59-60.

manded speed, the government used credit, subsidies, public ownership, guaranteed markets, and terror to achieve results. Labor policy embraced assurance of work and, by propaganda at least, paid vacations and pleasure trips (though relatively few workers actually got them) under the auspices of an organization known as "Strength through Joy." Strikes were forbidden and labor leaders appointed by the government. As employment increased, man power became scarce. The government curtailed production of consumers' goods and kept both the wage and salary scale and the standard of living down to that of 1932, a low level but an assured one. Since the government acted as the main consumer and sought ever more products, it could direct production into desired channels. The manufacture of capital goods, iron and steel, machines and machine tools, electrical goods and related lines received every assistance. Raw materials within Germany were especially developed. The low-grade iron ore and the small amount of oil were exploited by existing companies or newly created companies liberally supplied with public funds. The aluminum industry was greatly enlarged in central Germany to take care of airplane production; plants were built to extract oil from lignite and to manufacture synthetic rubber. Electric power resources were increased to meet the expanded requirements. The armaments industry boomed.

The new regime retained existing management and stressed its respect for private property. It nonetheless subjected management to official guidance and curtailed the power of the owners almost to the point of being receivers of fixed income from shares. It utilized a system of differential taxes in order to encourage certain industries and discourage others. Except in industries which it wished to expand, it siphoned off savings by the compulsory purchase of bonds, and everywhere it controlled investments. The economic organization was modified to assure close cooperation of government and industry. The cartel tradition was used to institute a system of syndicates in the various lines of the economy. For example, iron and steel formed a syndicate under a board of government officials and managers of the main corporations in the business. Frequently the officials were merely managers on loan to the state. The government in consultation with the syndicate board determined the amount of iron and steel to be produced and left to the board the responsibility for output. The latter allocated production quotas to members down the line, and the big companies with contacts and productive volume received the contracts. The little companies complained constantly that the system of subcontracting from large competitors was destroying their independence, but the Nazis found it most convenient to work with big companies.

Agricultural control followed the same principle but was somewhat different in organization. The farms were given production quotas, and the farmers had to live up to them under threat of loss of their land. Marketing boards were created, agricultural credit was supplied, though not in sufficient amounts, and the use of improved seeds and breeds and of chemical fertilizers was pushed. Within a few years, 1933 to 1936, Germany increased the amount of foodstuffs produced from 75 per cent to 81 per cent of consumption.

In every aspect of production and consumption, in every phase of foreign trade, the government steered the economy into planned channels while preserving some of the realities of private property. The economy was much more difficult to control from the top than was an institution like the army; but insofar as it was possible, Hitler's officials brought it under control. Schacht had set the system (except in agriculture, which never received as much attention as industry); when he retired in 1938, Göring took nominal charge. By that time the economy was going at high speed. Freedom had been sacrificed, but the people were content.

Hitler expected to breed a race of the future. Some Germans, but not all, were worthy to belong to it, and some foreigners were considered of the elect. The Nazis would provide the elite, irrespective of nationality or present race, although most of them would be German. Hitler believed in a crude Darwinism—that the fittest survived; and his criterion for fitness was almost exclusively one of physical prowess. "Only force rules. Force is the first law," he said. These were the standards for Nazi education, for the law courts, for everything. These were the ultimate cause of the Nazis' conflict with the Catholic and a large part of the Protestant churches (the rest of the Protestants accepted nazism and reconciled it with Christianity). Hitler knew that "force" was an inclusive term. At the Nürnberg trials Albert Speer, the ablest of the Nazi war ministers, said:

> Hitler's dictatorship . . . made complete use of all technical means for the domination of its own country.
>
> Through technical devices like the radio and the loudspeaker, eighty million people were deprived of independent thought. It was thereby possible to subject them to the will of one man. . . .
>
> Earlier dictators needed highly qualified assistants, even at the lowest level, men who could think and act independently. The totalitarian system in the period of modern technical development can dispense with them; the means of communication alone made it possible to mechanize the lower leadership. As a result of this there arises the new type of the uncritical recipient of orders. . . . Another result was the far-reaching supervision of the citizens of the State and the maintenance of a high degree of secrecy for criminal acts.
>
> The nightmare of many a man that one day nations could be dominated by technical means was all but realized in Hitler's totalitarian system.

Minister Speer exaggerated, even if he had included in his list Himmler's efficient card-index secret police. There had to be a powerful inclination among the Germans to believe Hitler. The shortcomings of their historical development were revealing themselves in the behavior of these people. The Führer's will was supreme.

Italy

FASCISM FAILS TO OVERCOME THE DEPRESSION

Italy was the only Western country which faced the world economic crisis with government and society already under a dictatorship. Since fascism claimed to have the solution to all troubles, the Italians might have expected the government to surmount depression. The efficiency of the Fascist organization, the devotion of its elite officials to the nation, and the supreme wisdom of Mussolini long extolled by propaganda should have come to Italy's aid. The system failed in every respect; the depression began earlier in Italy than elsewhere and continued until 1936 without abatement.

In spite of his socialist background, Mussolini understood little about economics. Having stabilized the lira in 1927 at much too high a value, he stubbornly persisted until 1936 in maintaining the level and in keeping the gold standard. Unlike other states, Italy went into the depression after two years of self-imposed economic suffering, the direct effects of which have been summarized as follows:

> The Act of December, 1927, had pledged the Bank of Italy to keep its gold reserve at 40 percent of the paper currency and at the same time to prevent the lira from falling below the level at which it had been stabilized. Therefore the Bank had to redeem with gold all the lire which were being sent out of the country as far as the excess of imports over exports were to be paid for. Thus gold reserves which had shrunk from 12.1 billion lire in December, 1927, to 10.3 billions by December, 1929, fell to 7.3 billions by December, 1933. But in order to keep its gold reserve at the required 40 percent level, the Bank had to destroy a large proportion of the paper lire as it redeemed them; and note circulation, which amounted to 18.7 billion lire in December, 1927, had contracted six years later to 13.3 billion. As a result, wholesale prices kept on dropping from the index number of 691 in August, 1926, until they reached 299 by December, 1933. The Parliamentary Committee on the estimated budget for the fiscal year 1932–33 traced 34 percent of this price drop to the revaluation of the lira, that is, to Mussolini's own monetary policy, and 66 percent to the world depression.[4]

As money became scarce and as the value of the lira rose on the international money market, the typical results followed. Italy faced great difficulty in competing abroad with her exports and had to curtail imports. In 1928 she imported 21,920 million lire worth of goods and exported only 67 per cent as much. In 1933 she could import only 7,432 million lire worth of goods and exported 80 per cent as much. In 1937 she had almost doubled the amount of imports but exported only enough to cover 75 per cent of

[4] Quoted in Frances Keene, ed., *Neither Liberty nor Bread* (New York: Harper & Brothers, 1940), p. 213.

the cost. Throughout the decade she was never able to balance her international trade. Since the population continued to grow (41,176,671 in 1931, 45,536,000 in 1943), it was to be expected that fewer people would find work. By 1932 one half of the industrial labor force was wholly or partially unemployed. Industrial production, which dropped to a lower point than that of backward Romania, was slow in recovering.

To meet the economic crisis Mussolini had recourse to the well-known Fascist methods of squeezing the poor and bailing out the bankrupt rich. Whenever an industry, bank, or other economic enterprise faced closure, the government bought the stock or made loans or granted subsidies according to need. By 1933 it was so involved in business that it created the Institute for Industrial Reconstruction to serve as trustee for these multifarious interests. Actually the work consisted mainly of providing state funds while leaving private management in complete charge. According to Mussolini, by 1934 three fourths of the Italian economic system, both industrial and agricultural, existed solely by means of government support.

When Alcide de Gasperi took over the government after World War II he found that the state controlled 60 per cent of the metallurgical industry, 100 per cent of passenger shipping, 75 per cent of the telephone system, 90 per cent of the shipyards, 35 per cent of the electric power, and 87 per cent of all savings. To obtain funds for this aid, Mussolini took measures along several lines. Between 1927 and 1934 he reduced wages of industrial workers by one half, and of agricultural workers by much more, although retail prices declined by only 25 per cent. He continued to rely upon indirect taxes, mainly paid by the masses, which grew heavier with the decline in prices, and he allowed the price of wheat, the main article in the nation's diet, to rise by 1936 300 per cent above that on the world market.

The explanation for the extraordinary cost of wheat may be found in the "Battle of Wheat," to which we have referred in an earlier chapter. Inaugurated to make the country self-sufficient in bread, the battle did increase acreage and productivity, and it came very close to meeting Italy's need, but at the expense of the rest of agriculture and of the living standard of the people. The only area where acreage could be expanded was on huge estates in the south with their poverty-stricken peasantry. This region was suited by climate and soil to fruit and vegetable growing, but these branches of agriculture were neglected. Exports of olive oil, oranges, and lemons fell sharply or ceased, while rising in Spain. Since work in wheat is largely seasonal, the south's peasantry found less employment than ever. As tariffs protected wheat and raised the price, farmers elsewhere turned grazing land under the plow. Except for hogs, the number of livestock declined, while the price of meat soared. The population was compelled by high prices to change its dietary habits. Though in 1921–1925 the per capita consumption of wheat each year had been 458 pounds, in 1931–1936 it was 407 pounds; that of meat was in proportion even less. The people returned to the consumption of potatoes, rice, and especially maize; with the last-named came the revival of pellagra. "We are probably moving toward a period of humanity resting on a lower standard of living," Mussolini stated in May, 1934. "Humanity is capable of asceticism such as we perhaps have no conception of."

Beginning in 1935, Italy went through a decade of continuous war, first through her conquest of Abyssinia, then through her intervention in the Spanish civil war, and finally by participation in World War II. In a sense the Fascist economy had always been organized on a war basis, but in the middle of the 1930's Mussolini accentuated the policy. "Italy need no longer buy abroad," he declared in 1935. "She is freed from any bondage to foreigners, and consequently free in her foreign politics." "In these days, too," wrote the exiled former minister Nitti in Paris in 1938, "the Italian papers are full of the most absurd news. There is a shortage of milk and wool, but they announce that they are already producing artificial wool from milk. There is a textile shortage, but they announce that they are producing textiles from all sorts of possible and impossible things, including genets!" [5]

That the Duce's assertion was untrue did not lessen his attempt to deceive himself, the Italian people, and foreign nations into believing that it was true. He clamped rigid control on transactions in foreign exchange to prevent wholesale exodus of gold, and he curtailed imports. In 1937 he created a National Autarchy Commission to direct the economy toward the goal which Italy had supposedly reached two years earlier; and at great cost he began to develop industries using substitute or marginal materials. To cover the expense he could scarcely levy more taxes, for the Italians already paid 30 per cent of their aggregate private income to the state. He therefore imposed a capital levy of 15 per cent, then a compulsory loan, and after 1936 he borrowed. Money became cheaper, prices rose, wages were held down; unemployment declined. Insofar as it was paid for at all, the war economy was also maintained at the expense of the poor.

Mussolini never attempted to execute the economic reforms which the country needed. He mastered the technique of occasional spectacular innovations which could be exploited for purpose of propaganda. He boasted of draining the Pontine marshes, conveniently located near Rome where the work could be well advertised. The results were an addition of 65,000 hectares of land, enough for about 19,000 people, at the cost of one third of the total fund for this kind of enterprise. The land of the Pontine marshes was allocated fairly to small proprietors; in other reclamation projects it went to large landowners, with Fascist officials receiving compensation on the side.

In almost every state of Europe except Hungary, Spain, and Portugal, and to a less extent Poland, World War I had brought the breakup of large estates in favor of peasant holdings. In Italy fascism continued to

[5] *Ibid.*, p. 219.

protect 3.4 per cent of all the agricultural proprietors in their possession of 68.3 per cent of the agricultural land. The Duce favored concentration of land ownership as a means of controlling the peasantry, for a disobedient share tenant could be more easily coerced than a peasant proprietor. The number of the small holders actually declined. Below these were the 7½ million families of agricultural laborers, who remained unable to raise their standard of living—unable to afford the goods which the surplus capacity of Italian industry could have produced. Mussolini left the south, where conditions were worst, in the same state in which he found it.

Of all the great powers Italy was the most exposed to economic hardship in the event of an international conflict; yet the Duce preferred war. He did not even enable Italy to maintain her intellectual position of pre-Fascist days. The number of students in technical schools greatly declined; the number of patents taken out diminished between 1924 and 1937 by nearly two thirds. Fascism had become a means of protecting the wealthy upper classes and the new Fascist elite.

CHAMBER OF FASCES AND CORPORATIONS

The change from old to Fascist Italy continued in governmental organization, particularly in the gradual replacement of the former parliament by the Chamber of Fasces and Corporations. The first important step was taken by two laws of 1928 which transformed the system of elections. The terms deserve some analysis, even though one should always keep in mind Mussolini's statement of the next year: "Let no one cherish the illusion that a pile of ballot papers will jeopardize the future development of the regime, which tomorrow will be more totalitarian than it was yesterday."

By the terms of these laws, elections were to occur in three stages. In the first, the syndicates or legally recognized associations of employers and employees and cultural and patriotic organizations were to nominate 1,000 persons. From these lists the Grand Council of Fascism should select 400 candidates whose names should appear on the ballot. The electorate would then vote "yes" or "no" for this list. Males alone were entitled to vote; they had to be twenty-one years of age and to pay a certain minimum of direct taxes or be a member of a legally recognized association. The system eliminated all public initiative, all public participation except that of voting for or against a list provided by Fascist-dominated or completely Fascist organizations. At elections "yes" ballots were printed in the colors of the Italian flag, and "no" ballots were left white. Elections were overwhelmingly favorable to the Fascists, or officials doctored the vote.

In March, 1938, the Chamber of Deputies, having obediently voted its own death warrant, was replaced by the Chamber of Fasces and Corporations. The membership of the new Chamber was to be identical with that of the National Council of the Fascist party and of the National Council of Corporations, and henceforth there were to be no elections. Since the members of the Grand Council of the Fascist party were appointed by Mussolini on the recommendation of the secretary general of the Fascist party, and those of the National Council of Corporations were appointed by royal decree on the recommendation of Mussolini, it is clear that parliament had ceased to represent anyone except the Duce.

The National Council of Corporations, created in 1930, was intended to supplement that of the Fascist party by organizing employers and employees along Fascist lines. In 1926 Mussolini had transformed the associations of these two economic groups into syndicates; each should have its syndicate in one of thirteen categories of work, for example, agriculture, industry, banking, and inland transport. It was expected that the two groups in each category would cooperate for the national good. The National Council of Corporations should include representatives of both employer and employee syndicates in a national economic advisory body. Still, the corporations were not established until 1934.

The economy was distributed among twenty-two of them, with employers, employees, and a new member, a Fascist bureaucrat from the Ministry of Corporations, participating in each one. From these corporations the members of the National Council were chosen to represent the public, as Fascist theorists said, in its working, natural activity. The corporations were subjected completely to the control of the Minister of Corporations, at the time Mussolini himself. He either presided over their meetings or selected the official to substitute for him; he had the power to pass on the selection of each member of the corporation board, and indeed he had to approve everything of any significance that the corporations did. Although they merely approved decisions already reached at the political level, Mussolini used them for advice, for feeling out the play of interest groups, and for gathering statistics and controlling production. The last-named functions became particularly useful after the introduction in 1936 of autarchy.

Theoretically, the employers' syndicate and the employees' syndicate in a corporation were equal; actually, the former dominated. The employers sat in these syndicates in person, and the big employers were able to impose their will on the lesser ones. In the workers' syndicates the executives were, except at the lowest level, not elected but appointed from above. The party and its instrument, the government bureaucracy, controlled these persons, and as the Fascists settled down to a comfortable relationship with big business and big agriculture, the spokesmen of the wealthy were those whose advice was heard. Mussolini remained the deciding figure, and the first interest of the regime was how to keep in power. Within this limit the Fascists, like the Nazis, favored the economic leaders, and the latter found fascism a great source of reassurance and comfort. That between 1934 and 1937 five thousand lesser industries became bankrupt hardly concerned them. Both the economic magnates and the Fascists wanted no strikes, no insurrections, no questioning of authority; both believed in the right of the few to command and the duty of the many to obey; both practiced concentrating power and leadership in one man with a hierarchical chain of command; both liked tariff protection, government economic aid to business when necessary, and a war economy; both approved the corporative state by which they controlled, each in his proper sphere, the entire society.

The Fascist government had succeeded in crushing all overt resistance. Between 1926 and 1936 underground activity all but ceased. Mussolini once said, "What is the State? The police." He spent ten times as much on the police as his predecessors had done and four times as much as France, a state of far larger land mass. The results were, to him, satisfactory. Many critics were permitted or forced to leave the country; if one of these abroad became too persistent, like Carlo Rosselli with his program for harmonizing freedom and socialism, he could easily be assassinated. Internal enemies were not placed in concentration camps; they were exiled to remote villages in the south or placed on a desolate island. Mussolini kept the masses ignorant and in poverty by low expenditures on education and social services, while he poured funds into the military. Like the Nazis, however, he was never able to suppress the church, the sole organization left to criticize and oppose him.

RELATIONS WITH THE CATHOLIC CHURCH

Mussolini's relations with the Catholic Church had run from warm to cold. The church's fear of communism inclined it toward supporting both fascism and nazism. The Catholic Populist party had acquiesced in the ascendancy of fascism and had dissolved itself. In 1926 the Duce and Pope Pius XI began secret negotiations for a settlement of old disputes between church and state. The negotiations culminated in a Concordat and the Lateran Treaty of 1929, from which the Duce derived more popular prestige than from any other single act of his career. By the Lateran Treaty the pope ceased to be the prisoner of the Vatican. When the Italian state had occupied Rome in 1870, the pope had refused to approve the transfer of sovereignty over that city from the papacy to the new Italian kingdom. In addition to other reasons, he had feared that the Italian state might try to exploit the papacy for its own interests, or at least that the rest of the world might suspect such national interference in the affairs of the head of the church. He had remained within the limits of the few acres of Vatican ground and would not set foot on Italian soil. By the Lateran Treaty he finally accepted the fact of Rome's belonging to Italy; in return he was assured sovereignty over the tiny Vatican state.

The Concordat covered more difficult matters—education, marriage, church property, the appointment of ecclesiastics—all the problems of relations between church and state. Mussolini accepted the Catholic religion as "the sole religion of the state"; he allowed the church full freedom to teach and to acquire property, and he agreed that church marriages were legally binding and that no additional civil ceremony by the state was necessary. The state law on marriage was to conform to canon law, and church courts were given exclusive power of decision on questions of dissolving marriage ties. Protestantism and Judaism and other religions were labeled "admitted cults," and were placed in a subordinate position. Marriage of their adherents was civil, and official permission had to be obtained before the members of these religions could open a place of worship. The Catholic Church and Mussolini seemed to be in full harmony; the Italians were enthusiastic over the agreements.

Almost immediately trouble between the two powers began. The laymen's organization, the Catholic Action, had in a sense taken the place of the Populist party as the center of church activity in public life. It had grown steadily in public appeal, particularly in its organization of the Catholic youth. After two years of polemics, Mussolini dissolved the Catholic youth and university organizations on grounds that the Catholic Action was interfering in politics. He wanted no centers of potential resistance to his own Fascist youth organizations and took this opportunity to strike, not merely at these Catholic associations, but at the sponsoring Catholic Action as well. When the pope in reply denounced these "pagan" aims of the Fascists and fought back, Mussolini suddenly dropped the attack on the Catholic Action and agreed to a compromise whereby its youth work continued but was subject to severe restrictions. He had hoped that the attractiveness of these youth organizations would diminish in favor of his own, but the contrary occurred. Pope Pius XI seems never to have trusted the Fascist regime again. He supported it when the Fascists fought for General Franco and the church in Spain; but he condemned the unchristian character of nazism, its crude racialism, particularly in the most notorious form of anti-Semitism. Although he disapproved of belonging to any religion except the Catholic, he regarded a Catholic of Jewish ancestry as the equal of any other. By the end of the 1930's fascism and the church were once more in open or latent antagonism.

By the time of the Ethiopian war the Italian people became increasingly aware that the Fascist revolution had introduced no fundamental reforms. In contrast with Nazi Germany, and to a certain extent with the Soviet Union, it had not changed the social structure, redistributed the national income, or invigorated the economy and the army. Graduates of professional schools who in the twenties had found positions in the Fascist bureaucracy were in the next decade left unemployed. In Germany individuals of this type joined the Nazi party, but in Italy they were becoming ripe for communism. As the threat of World War II cast its shadow ahead, Italy was weaker in every respect than she had been when the Fascists seized power, and the Duce himself was ill and aging. He often expressed hatred for "this second-rate Italian race," which he said had been made flabby by art. It deserved, he said, a "beating, beating." He wished to have written on his tombstone the statement, "Here lies one of the most intelligent human beings who ever lived," and he saw "surprising analogies between [his] own fate and that of Christ." In this mood he led Italy into partnership with Hitler for world conquest.

Spain and Portugal

Considering the similarity in the internal conditions of the two Iberian countries around 1930, one might not have expected the course of history of the two nations in the next decade to be so different. After the death of the dictator Primo de Rivera, Spain overthrew the monarchy and set up a republic. The forces of the Old Regime refused to accept the new government and its efforts at social and economic reform. Led by the army, they engaged Spain in one of the bloodiest civil wars in history. When in 1939 organized hostilities ceased, Spain lay exhausted at the feet of another dictator, General Franco. In Portugal the army in 1928 placed the country under the rule of a civilian professor of economics and supported him loyally while he brought the country back to order.

SALAZAR IN PORTUGAL

Professor Antonio Salazar was installed by the Portuguese army as minister with complete power over finance. He acted from the beginning as the supreme power in the government, setting the policies and overseeing the administration in all lines. He and his supporters claimed that the regime was neither dictatorial nor totalitarian; they called it authoritarian.

Salazar remained close to the common people from whom he sprang. His father was a village innkeeper, his mother a peasant. He grew up in the school of want, but with the help of the church he received an education and in time entered an academic career.

> A Professor he was [a writer stated in 1936, after Salazar had become famous], and a Professor he remains. He works at the affairs of State with the same rigorous method and the same objectivity that he brought to the preparation of his lectures, of his books, and of his studies. He does nothing without careful consideration. He will not be hurried or disturbed; he shields himself from the importunate. Being at heart a shy man, he appears as little as possible in public. Deliberately he has earned the reputation of being inaccessible. He does not cultivate popularity; he mistrusts it. Finally, he is fiercely independent, and withdraws the moment he perceives that anyone is seeking to override his

judgment, to influence him, or to enlist his support. These are the characteristics of the intellectual.[6]

He spent his leisure on his farm at the village where he was born, traveling like any ordinary citizen. He lived frugally on a state salary of £550 a year, and he was as scrupulously honest about his personal finances as he was about those of the state. He is a profound Catholic.

Salazar sought to transform the government in harmony with the principles of the encyclicals of Popes Leo XIII and Pius XI. He intensely disliked political parties as factional, disruptive, and inclined toward selfishness. After abolishing them, he organized in 1930 the National Union, not a party, but an association of men of good will which supported his work, and he cooperated closely with the religious organization, the Catholic Action. In 1933 he introduced a new constitution based on spiritual principles, particularly as formulated in the Papal Encyclical of 1931 *Quadragesimo Anno*. The people were brought into employers' guilds and workers' syndicates, which were united under public direction into corporations. The noneconomic activities, the church, education, the arts, and so on were similarly organized. A National Assembly was formed of the leaders of all these corporations. The government controlled the actions of these bodies entirely, but it also promulgated laws without any regard to their existence. Censorship and other restrictions were exercised by the executive at any time. The only safeguard which the citizen had against arbitrary rule lay in the conscience and judgment of Salazar.

As authoritarian regimes go, Salazar's permitted a remarkable degree of personal freedom. Of the two institutions which were its main support, the church and the army, the former took its important place in national life secure against persecution and relatively free from the ambition, so characteristic of the Spanish prelates, to dominate the state. Mutual interest and common ideals united church and government. Both feared communism, neither liked totalitarianism, racialism, and the current extreme forms of nationalism and stateism. At Christmas, 1937, the Cardinal Patriarch of Lisbon condemned these creeds for opposing divine law. Communism, he said, denied God; totalitarianism absorbed Him. He called the cult of race or nation "a return to paganism." Salazar agreed with these views; and although he kept the church separate from the state, he sought to improve its role in society as educator and moral guide of the people.

Salazar followed a similar line of independence toward the army. He kept it small—38,000 for the home country and the colonies, with an additional 100,000 available for mobilization; but, fearing that after the outbreak of the civil war in Spain some Spanish faction might attack Portugal, he sought within the limited resources of Portuguese industry to bring the army up to date. He tolerated no army interference in state affairs and

[6] Michael Derrick, *The Portugal of Salazar* (London: Sands & Company, Ltd.–Paladin Press, 1938), pp. 53-54.

forced the army to live on the same economical basis as the other branches of the government service. He supplemented its force by developing in 1936 a Portuguese Legion of 60,000 men and a compulsory youth organization, intended, not for his personal aggrandizement, but for the defense of the country.

Salazar achieved most for Portugal by his economic and, to a less extent, his social policy. He balanced the budget within one year, the first time it had been balanced since 1914 and the third time since 1854; and he continued to keep it balanced until in 1938–1939 excessive expenditures for defense became necessary. He consolidated the floating debt, quadrupled the gold reserves of the Bank of Portugal, reduced the national debt, and made the currency one of the strongest in the international economy. He kept indirect taxes as the main source of revenue but distributed the tax burden more equitably than it had been, and honestly collected the taxes. He cut down public expenditure by stopping graft and abolishing sinecure jobs, and he utilized the surplus revenue for urgently needed economic reforms. He accomplished these financial improvements during the world economic depression.

For the economy Salazar brought about the reorganization of the sardine and the port-wine industries to enable the participants in each to cooperate, improve their techniques, protect their labels against adulterated products, and maintain their international markets. He increased the growing of wheat by the same means that were used in Great Britain, and within a year Portugal, instead of importing, was actually exporting the grain. He found a road system in the condition of a hundred years ago, and by 1939 he had built 700 miles of new roads and reconstructed more than 3,000 miles of old roads. Thereby he began to open the provinces to new activity. In 1928 omnibuses were almost entirely lacking; within a decade there were 2,000. Between 1926 and 1938 the number of telephones increased from less than 5,000 to 36,000. Ports were improved, and electrification, railroad, and drainage systems expanded. The number of schools was increased but remained far too few. Village institutes were created all over the country as educational and social centers to bring the peasants into touch with modern life. That illiteracy continued to be high, that wages were very low (sometimes 25 cents a day) and poverty extensive can be understood, for he had been at work only since 1928. Foreigners who visited Portugal in this decade concluded that Salazar was popular and trusted; he had imparted to his people the hope for a better life.

SPANISH REPUBLIC

In Spain, after the unexpected death of Primo de Rivera, King Alfonso XIII strove for fifteen months to preserve his throne. When local elections held in 1931 revealed that every provincial capital except four voted overwhelmingly republican—the rural vote scarcely counted, since it was dominated by local bosses under the thumb of the landlords—the king turned to the army to keep him in power. Since neither the army nor the Civil Guard would move in his favor, he departed for Paris with his family, saying that he had done so to save his country from bloodshed. The Republicans took charge of the government, and two months later held elections for a constitutional assembly, which returned an overwhelmingly Republican vote. The Left Republican group won 150 seats; the Right Republicans, just over 100; the Socialists, 115; the anti-Republicans, among these only 19 being staunch Monarchists, won about 50 seats. In the towns the vote was almost completely Republican.

Social and Political Conflict

The Spanish people were divided into two irreconcilable groups and a numerically small lower middle class. On the one extreme stood the traditional elite, the army, the church, and the big landowners, with the few industrialists tending to side with them. These interests were not entirely harmonious; but, fearful of losing their political predominance, their property, their social position, and, for the church, the religious monopoly, they were compelled to cooperate. Having little mass support, they withheld their attempt to destroy the government until the latter showed weakness. On the other extreme was a mass of angry peasants and workers, more or less organized around radical ideals.

When the republic started its career, the industrial proletariat and shopworkers, in so far as they were organized at all, supported the Socialist party, which emphasized the need for centralized government. It was strongest in Castile, but within a short time its popularity spread widely and agricultural workers soon accounted for nearly one half its strength. The masses of the rural proletariat, however, adhered to the doctrines of anarchosyndicalism, which likewise prevailed among the urban workers in Catalonia. These groups favored federalism amounting to provincial autonomy; in fact, anarchism could scarcely be said to tolerate any kind of organization. The Socialists and the Anarchosyndicalists hated each other as well as their masters and cooperated if at all only with the greatest difficulty. These urban and rural masses demanded speedy reform of landholding and improvement in living and working conditions.

Between the two extremes stood the politically active lower middle class, a small group, predominantly of small retailers, which had led and failed in every revolution for a century. The intellectuals, teachers, journalists, and some of the professional groups aligned with this class to support republican ideals. They were divided into two main political parties, the Left Republican, which stood for the kind of reforms one associates with English liberalism of the nineteenth century, and the Right Republicans, who were hostile to monarchy, army, and church and devoted to the ideal of liberalism but who became alarmed over the actuality of reform. The former included many intellectuals and had its headquarters in the Ateneo, a famous literary and political club in Madrid. It furnished the drive behind the Republican reform movement. Both liberal parties lacked numerical strength to maintain themselves against mass parties on the one hand and powerful vested interests on the other, unless they could develop leaders of extraordinary political ability. Since the survival of the republic depended upon them, the chances of Spain's pursuing a course of steady progress were slight.

Republican Mistakes

The Constitutional Assembly wrote and obtained the national approval within a few months of a constitution that followed the tradition of all free Western countries. The document need not concern us, for it solved no problems. A conflict of views arose immediately over the question of agrarian reform. The Republicans wished to break up the large estates into individual peasant holdings; the Socialists demanded that the estates be transformed into collective farms. After months of wrangling, in July and September, 1932, the parties passed statutes creating an Institute of Agrarian Reform of twenty-one members with regional committees. It was to select the estates for expropriation and to decide on the disposal of the land. The grandees lost their estates entirely; other estates of more than 56 acres were liable to expropriation. The owners were to be compensated on the basis of evaluation in the tax returns, and since nearly all had for years sent in false returns, they stood to lose from one third to one half of the value of their property. The laws did nothing about helping the numerous peasants in the north, who had far too little land, or to regulate the uncertain and very high rents in Castile. Where the law did apply, that is, to the regions of the big estates, the quarrel continued over the form in which to dispose of the land—whether to individual peasant families or to collectives. Therefore, except when the peasants took the land and worked it without legal title, not much was accomplished. Republicans and Socialists wasted their opportunity to win the active support of the rural people.

A similar lack of political sense appeared in the treatment of the church. The juridical commission of the constituent assembly recommended the separation of church and state but allowed the church to become a special corporation, to keep its own schools, and on certain conditions to teach religion in state schools. Church marriages were legally binding, and ecclesiastical functions could occur in public if the participants took an oath of allegiance to the republic. Most Catholics would have accepted these conditions, for there were many laymen and priests who disapproved of the church's social and political policies and favored reform in the relations of the church to society and the state. To the majority in the Assembly, however, the proposals were much too mild. The members recalled that the Church had been and remained the strongest support of king and dictator, and that in pulpit and press it had denounced the Republican candidates in the recent elections as "sold to Moscow gold." They knew that the Cardinal Primate had in a pastoral sermon denounced the republic two weeks after its establishment. Hence the majority now made the church an association subject to ordinary laws; it abolished state financial aid to the church, ordered the dissolution of all convents and the nationalization of their property, and closed all religious schools except seminaries.

These extreme terms alienated numerous Catholics friendly to the republic and blocked possible reform of the church from within. Henceforth the church was solidly hostile to the new regime. When one group under Azaña proposed to soften these terms, the Republicans split among themselves. As a by-product of the dispute, the educational system was undermined, for the church conducted one half of the secondary schools and about as many of the primary ones. These would be forced to close at a time when the government lacked resources for replacement.

The coming of the world economic crisis just when the republic was established enhanced the government's difficulties. Foreign trade dropped, unemployment increased, and persons were afraid to invest their funds because of the disorder; the banks withheld credits in order to bring down the republic. Catalonia demanded autonomy; and it had to be given to her. The Basques claimed similar rights, and other requests for loose federalism were expected. Strikes and riots grew in numbers and intensity of feeling as living conditions deteriorated. The republic was failing to preserve the support of the masses. The Anarchists took the lead in resort to violence, and the Socialists followed suit. The government used the extraordinary power granted it by the Law for the Defence of the Republic of 1931 in order to fight force with force. It filled the prisons and appointed 50 per cent more police than Primo de Rivera had employed, but it could not preserve its authority and, in September, 1933, resigned. A deputy of the Center called it the Republic of "mud, blood and tears."

Monarchist Reaction

The failure of the Spanish republic may be called an act of fate. The middle class lacked the numbers, intelligence, and experience to correct the abuses of centuries. The Right was adamant against change; the peasants and workers were equally determined to achieve immediate reform. Neither Right nor Left respected the constitution or had any intention of maintaining it. Since the weak middle class was divided, some fearing revolution more than the Right, and all opposing revolutionary socialism and anarchism, liberalism had slight chance of succeeding.

The caliber of the bourgeois leaders did not rise much beyond the general level. Niceto Zamora, the president of the republic from 1931 until 1936, was a highly respected Andalusian lawyer and landowner, but a florid orator of commonplaces. Manuel Azaña, the premier during the two first years of reform and the successor of Zamora as president, came nearest to being a statesman. His church education as a poor orphan had converted him into an anticlerical. After a mediocre career as writer he had turned to politics and served under the republic first as minister of war and then as prime minister. He was the leading man in the Cortes, where his willingness to act inspired fear among enemies. Nonetheless, he found the antagonisms of the parties too much for him to reconcile. Particularly after he became president, he refused to permit the Socialist leader, Largo Caballero, to assume power. By this uncompromising attitude he prevented the Socialists and Republicans from uniting in defense of the Republic at the time of its gravest danger.

In November, 1933, new elections were held, in which the pro-Republican parties fought each other, while the Rightist ones combined. The Left Republicans were almost obliterated, the Socialist party was reduced by half, and the Rightist coalition moved up from 42 seats to 207. From this time until the eve of the civil war in 1936 the pro-Monarchists and the Right Republicans controlled the government. During that period they nullified all reforms. The Right was on the aggressive, and the big agrarians furnished ample funds for party organization and propaganda. Gil Robles, the Rightist leader, son-in-law of one of Spain's wealthiest men, had learned in Germany and Austria the methods of totalitarian politics. He introduced these into Spain and organized the Falangist party. When late in 1933 the Anarchists, the Catalonian autonomists, and others revolted, the new Rightist government, using for the first time in centuries the Foreign Legion and the Moors against Spaniards within Spain, crushed them all. Atrocities occurred on both sides, and Minister Gil Robles denounced the Republicans as assassins, thieves, and criminals.

While the Rightists were planning the return of prerepublican order, the population, especially in the country districts, became ever more wretched. A million or more agricultural workers were unemployed; the landlords were punishing the peasants by cutting wages and fixing rents to suit themselves. A few Catholic clerics became deeply concerned over the behavior of the landlords and asked Gil Robles to intervene. The latter refused. When a Catholic minister introduced a mild piece of legislation to help the peasant owners of ploughing mules or oxen but no land, the bill was thrown out. The landlords penalized these Republican team-owners by letting much of the land lie fallow. When the minister invoked canon law in favor of his proposal, a Monarchist deputy declared: "If you try to take away our land with your encyclicals, we shall become schismatics." In the towns conditions of unemployment, scarcity, and high prices continued. Spain had not seen so much misery for years.

Civil War and Nationalist Victory

When elections were conducted in February, 1936, the Leftist parties held together and won a majority of the seats. The Right was bitterly disappointed and speeded up preparations for its own rebellion. A weak moderate government took office; but Left Republicans and the Socialists would not cooperate, President Azaña would not permit Largo Caballero to take over the government for fear of socialism, and the Socialist party was divided between a right and a left wing. The Socialists sought in vain an understanding with the Anarchosyndicalists. Although faced with full evidence about the impending Rightist rebellion, the Leftist parties continued divided. In the spring and early summer of 1936 the country was in chaos, and in the middle of the year the Monarchists struck.

In ability to wage war the two sides were evenly matched. The advantage in trained troops lay with the rebels, or as they came to be called, the Nationalists. They had the Civil Guard, the Foreign Legion, a division of Moors from Spanish Morocco, almost all of the infantry and artillery officers, a number of regiments of reliable soldiers recruited in the north, the Carlist levies which had been drilled for some time, and the assurance of German and Italian military aid. The Republicans could display no such organized force, only a small and badly equipped air force and the Republican Assault Guards. They immediately took their cause to the people, and, turning arms over to workers and peasants, they created a militia, poorly trained, at first uncertain in battle, but devoted to the cause. The government lost all authority in the first months to the Workers' Committees, which appeared spontaneously and prepared the Republican population for conducting the war. They organized and armed the militia, terrorized or destroyed the enemy in their midst, and administered the estates, factories, and businesses which the owners had abandoned or had been forced to relinquish. At the beginning the Republicans held Madrid, the eastern coast, La Mancha, New Castile, and Estremadura. The north was divided, with the Republicans holding Guipuzcoa, Biscay, and Santander, and the Nationalists the rest. Since the rebellion had started by moving Moorish troops from Spanish Morocco, the Nationalists' stronghold lay in the western half of the country. The Republicans possessed most of the industrial resources and the government administrative machinery, but they were insufficiently supplied with food.

The Republican side was greatly aided by the Soviet Union. Military supplies came in together with some skilled man power. An International Brigade under Communist auspices was formed of persons from many countries, not all of them Communists or even Communist sympathizers, and this Brigade defeated the initial Nationalist attack on Madrid. The Republican side suffered severely from latent or open civil war within its own ranks. Largo Caballero formed a Peoples' Front government soon after the outbreak of war and maintained it until May of next year. He was

followed by the Socialist Manuel Prieto, who lasted until April of 1938. From that time on the Communists were the main power, with the non-Communist Juan Negrin serving as premier. None of them was able to prevent the Anarchists, the Socialists, and the Communists, each in their own way, from exploiting the opportunity of civil war to seek to gain absolute control. The Communists had the smallest following, but, because Stalin channeled arms through them, they grew in power. Although never able to break the hold of the Socialists and the Anarchists over the two big trade-union organizations, they won the support of those who gambled on the winner and of those who took seriously their Popular Front slogans. Many industrialists, businessmen, intellectuals, bureaucrats, people of the middle class primarily, joined them as the safest and most promising refuge. Ruthless, thoroughly opportunistic, and always active, the Communists during the last two years carried the brunt of the war. In spite of unpopularity they became supreme on the home front in army and government, but they gained victory over their hostile Republican competitors at the cost of Republican defeat.

On the Nationalist side, the organization of the war was somewhat simpler than on that of its heterogeneous opponents. The Nationalist officers of the old army used Moorish troops and borrowed Italian divisions while they gained time to drill new recruits for an army of Spaniards. The generals needed no program except victory. They turned the weak Falangists and the Carlists of the North against the Republican sympathizers in the civilian population, and prevented the Spanish imitators of totalitarianism from acquiring the significance of their models in Italy or Germany. Rivalry among the generals resolved itself when the two ablest, Sanjurjo and Mola, were killed, leaving the typical militarist General Franco as supreme commander. He had initiated the rebellion by leading the Moors into the Spanish peninsula. He had the good fortune for his side to become a pawn in the international ambitions of Hitler and Mussolini. The former furnished arms, planes, and military experts, and used the occasion to try out some of the new tactics developed by his army, like that in which the town of Guernica was destroyed by dive-bombers. The Italians provided several divisions of troops and many supplies. In spite of the exasperation felt by the Germans and Italians at Franco's failure to take advantage of many opportunities to defeat the Republicans, the Nationalists finally developed a good army of Spaniards, and in March, 1939, emerged the victor.

The London *Times* reported in 1940 that some observers estimated the losses from murders and executions during the civil war to have been 800,000 or more, and the purely military losses to have reached only 400,000. The figures indicate the nature of the war. Terror and atrocities were commonplace. The Republican government officially disapproved of the private excesses and tried to channel the elimination of enemies through official agencies. The Nationalist government never bothered about legality. When war ceased the Nationalists began the systematic extinction of Republicans, men, women and children, and two and a half years later they were still killing.

The country lay prostrate. Half the population was on the verge of starvation. Industry lacked raw materials and agriculture lacked workers. The railroads had lost two thirds of their locomotives and a large percentage of their wagons. The transportation system almost ceased to exist. The police and the black market run by the Falange flourished. The middle class was almost ruined. The Nationalists filled the government with supporters; the landlords, the army, and the church were once more dominant; the night clubs were crowded. Spain had to be rebuilt, and for that task General Franco surrounded himself with men like the director of fine arts in the ministry of education, the Marques de Lozoya, who in 1938 blamed the misfortunes of Spain on "the stupid desire of the governments to teach the Spaniards to read."

The four authoritarian regimes shared in common many ideals of governmental and social organization—the necessity for dictatorial government, a monopoly party, a powerful army and police force, censorship in all forms, obedience of the masses, and subordination of the economy to political ends. They differed in the extent of execution. Nazi Germany implemented the ideals with ruthless efficiency and in half a decade became the most powerful state in Europe. Italian fascism could not conceal signs of failure to realize its early promises. Spain lay exhausted from class hatreds and bloodletting, dominated by a general and his supporters, who were loyal to the Old Regime rather than to the modern totalitarianism they imitated. In Portugal class and ideological antagonism had not reached the point of intensity which forced the dictator to preserve order by organized or threatened acts of violence. The evaluation of similarities and differences in internal structure of the four countries provides the basis for anticipating the extent to which the dictators would pursue power politics. This subject will be analyzed in a later chapter, but one can easily infer that Salazar will appreciate the inability of his weak country to enter international politics. Franco, barely victorious in spite of foreign help and ruling over a devastated land, will regretfully remain a spectator. Mussolini, always prodigal of boasts and promises, will fearfully join the wolfpack, allied to Hitler, who will force Europe into war. The internal policies of a country in this period of history reflected international aims. The German historian Leopold von Ranke wrote in 1836 that the state is "obliged to organize all its internal resources for the purpose of self-preservation. This is the supreme law of the state." In the period of the interwar dictators, the reverse was true: totalitarian powers in a position to do so organized internal resources for the purpose of aggrandizement abroad.

Suggestions for Further Reading

The Readings for Chapter 8 are useful for this decade. The following additional titles may be consulted with benefit.

BULLOCK, ALAN LOUIS CHARLES. *Hitler: A Study in Tyranny*. New York: Harper & Brothers, 1953. The best biography of Hitler. Throws much light on the entire history of the decade.

KEENE, FRANCES, ed. *Neither Liberty nor Bread: The Meaning and Tragedy of Fascism*. New York: Harper & Brothers, 1940. Conditions in Fascist Italy.

MANUEL, FRANK E. *The Politics of Modern Spain*. New York: McGraw-Hill Book Company, Inc., 1938. Treats much more than politics.

NEUMANN, FRANZ L. *Behemoth: The Structure and Practice of National Socialism, 1933–1944*. New York: Oxford University Press, 1944. Difficult but profound and worth while.

Chapter 15 · The Countries of Eastern and Southeastern Europe

By the time World War II began, all of the states of Eastern and Southeastern Europe except Czechoslovakia and Finland had succumbed to authoritarianism. The world economic crisis struck this region so severely that seven states were added to the four that had already given up democratic rule. The collapse of free institutions must be explained, not by the desire to imitate Mussolini and Hitler, but by weakness within the societies themselves; and the degree of authoritarianism varied according to the conditions in each state. The Baltic countries, where economic difficulties were added to political tension, fared less badly than those in which the economic crisis found both political and social tension. Czechoslovakia and Finland likewise experienced the threat of authoritarianism from within but mustered sufficient moral reserve to remain free.

THE BALTIC STATES AND FINLAND

The four small countries bordering on the Baltic Sea, Finland, Estonia, Latvia, and Lithuania, were predominantly peasant and agricultural and possessed a sound social structure. In them, economic crisis had primarily economic effects. Government by strong executive, already introduced in Latvia and Lithuania in 1926, functioned adequately during the depression and was imitated in 1934 by Estonia. All three states continued to believe in the democratic ideal and sought a constitution which would combine representative government with a strong executive. By the outbreak of World War II Estonia had gone farthest in that direction in the constitution of 1938, but none had found a solution. Finland alone retained its original constitution.

Economic Reforms

Since the countries were dependent upon the export of foodstuffs and industrial raw materials, like wood, for funds to pay for imports and to amortize loans, they suffered from the collapse of international trade. Finland, for example, accustomed to selling about one third of its total production abroad, found that the market had suddenly disappeared. Between 1928 and 1932 Estonia's imports and exports fell in value by 60 to 70 per cent. The four countries were accustomed to keep monetary reserves in pounds sterling, and when Great Britain devalued her currency they lost heavily in foreign exchange. Although Finland and Estonia soon devalued their own money, they went through several bad years. Finland, which had never before needed to collect unemployment statistics, found in February, 1932, that about 12.4 per cent of her population was unemployed, three fourths of it in the rural areas. Foreign debts were not so large that they required repudiation, however, and the peasants were able for a time to live on their own resources.

In addition to taking the usual steps to overcome the depression, the governments initiated long-range plans for economic reform by cooperation of public and private interests to aid both industry and agriculture. From the standpoint of the international division of labor the plans were uneconomic, but they enabled the nations to survive. The governments proposed to make the countries as self-sufficient as possible. They helped to develop industries (1) which would satisfy the requirements of the local market and enable them to dispense with industrial imports and (2) which would increase national income by processing raw materials hitherto exported. They initiated the transfer of some agriculture from the production of exports to that of foodstuffs which had hitherto been imported. The policy amounted in these small countries to an economic revolution.

An expansion of industrial production got under way early in the depression. Each country found the financial means for purchasing capital goods abroad necessary for that purpose. The most inclusive action was taken by Estonia, which in 1936 introduced government control over investments. She devoted not more than 3 per cent of the budget to subsidize new industries, selecting ones almost exclusively which would use Estonian raw materials, especially those heretofore commercially neglected. A factory for using the phosphate deposits near Tallin, another at Kehra for the manufacture of sulphate of cellulose, others for using milk to manufacture penholders, buttons, and combs, and plants to extract oil from the extensive deposits of oil shale along the northern coast indicate some of the results of governmental and private cooperation. In Finland mining and woodworking were expanded, and the other two states likewise utilized their natural resources. The indices on industrial output for three of the countries, using the figures of 1925–1929 as a base, were as follows:

	FINLAND	LATVIA	ESTONIA
1929	109.4	146.3	106.9
1932	91.1	120.6	81.4
1933	104.8	163.7	85.2
1938	166.1	254.0	143.5

SOURCE: *Industrialization and Foreign Trade* (Geneva: League of Nations, 1945), pp. 141, 143. Comparable figures for Lithuania are not available.

The figures reveal the small size of the decline in the depression, the speed of recovery, and the rapidity of expansion of output far beyond that of the best years in the preceding decade. They show why unemployment did not last; by 1937 Estonia was actually short of summer labor and imported workers from Poland.

Although agriculture mainly supplied the funds for accelerating industrial growth, the governments did not show partiality. They protected agriculture by tariffs, commodity boards for stabilizing prices, and market agreements, and assisted the peasants in adapting production to existing needs and to improving methods of production and distribution. The number of peasant farms continued to increase during the decade. Wheat growing was encouraged in order to reduce imports and save foreign exchange for the purchase, among other items, of industrial machinery. The use of artificial fertilizers increased; better seeds were introduced; livestock breeds improved, and the numbers raised decreased. In 1924–1928 Finland produced only 60 per cent of its food at home; in 1934–1935 it grew 81 per cent. That the peasants' economy revived may be judged from the fact that in Estonia the net farm income per acre of agricultural land doubled between the crisis and 1939 and at the latter date was 10 per cent higher than it had been prior to the depression.

The economic policies enabled the countries to restore international trade. The following figures indicate the success, but they also reveal the decline in value of the articles in trade. The sums are in millions of dollars as devalued in 1933.

	IMPORTS		EXPORTS	
	1928	*1938*	*1928*	*1938*
Finland	342	183	267	181
Latvia	101	44	85	44
Lithuania	49	38	44	40
Estonia	60	29	58	28

SOURCE: *Europe's Trade* (Geneva: League of Nations, 1941), pp. 38-39.

The success in reorienting industry and agriculture toward the national market is shown in the sharp decline in imports. The figures are even more striking when it is recalled that a considerable item in the imports was that of machinery for the new industrial plants. The other point of special interest was the ability in 1938 to balance imports and exports. By the end of the thirties these countries were once again in a condition of prosperity, and there appeared to be no economic reason why they should not continue to improve their standard of living.

Political Conflict

When the depression struck, critics in each country feared that special interests would prevent the parliaments from remedial action. They first found a scapegoat in the few Communists but soon turned against the social democrats and the liberals who had supported free government.

> We demand [a Pietist pastor declared, July 7, 1930, to the Finnish government on behalf of a delegation of 12,000 farmers] vigorously, unconditionally and with no room for compromise, the expulsion of Communism in this country from every public field to that subterranean darkness where crime dwells and which is the field of labour of the criminal authorities. . . . We demand the due punishment of treason, in all of its forms, even in its preparatory stages. . . . We demand the cessation of petty party calculations in Parliament and the creation of combinations and laws which will constantly ensure the existence of strong and lasting Governments in this country. . . . We are ready to fade again into obscurity, each to his labours, but only on the day we see our demands on the road to real fulfillment and only until we are once more needed.[1]

The gentle pastor spoke for the farmers, the vast majority of the powerful Lutheran pastors, ex-service men, and a considerable number of the military. The leadership actually lay in the hands of a farmer named Kosola of the Lapuan region, from which the name of the movement was derived. He shared the publicity with General Wallenius, who had until recently served as chief of staff of the army and who had a strong taste for fascist politics.

In the emergency, Pehr Svinhufvud, one of the elder statesmen, formed a ministry of National Union and handled the political crisis in a manner which saved Finland from dictatorship. First, he proposed anti-Communist legislation, including the authority to issue emergency decrees. When the Social Democrats blocked these bills as a potential threat against themselves as well, the government appealed to the country. In the election campaign the Lapuans used terror of all kinds against their opponents, Communists, socialists, and others. The government tolerated these excesses, for as the premier said later, "political unrest had been so intense that strong measures by the government would have resulted in bloodshed and civil war." In the election the government gained, by a majority of one, sufficient votes to pass the legislation against the Communists. With the party outlawed and the government taking effective measures against the depression, the country calmed down.

When two years later the Lapuans proposed to rebel against Svinhufvud's government and introduce fascism, the old premier appealed successfully for obedience to the law. The masses of the population, who had supported the strong-armed critics in 1930, turned away from them. The Civil Guard of 100,000 men refused to follow the lead of General Wallenius, and the rebellion collapsed without a shot being fired. Once more the government treated the participants with the greatest leniency. The combination of firmness toward the Communists, effectiveness in meeting the economic crisis, gentleness toward the Lapuan hotheads, and popular appeal

[1] J. Hampden Jackson, *Finland* (New York: The Macmillan Company, 1938), pp. 148-149.

for support of free government enabled the prime minister and his aids to bring Finland through the storm relatively unscathed.

Estonia was not so fortunate. The fascist movement started a little later and reached its peak in 1933 and 1934. About the same social groups supported it as in Finland and in the other two countries, but the leader of the V.A.P.S., or Liberators, as they were called (V.A.P.S. are the initials in the native language of the name League of Soldiers of the War of Liberation) was an emotional young lawyer named Sirk, in his early twenties, who after the failure of an attempt to overthrow the government in 1934 fled the country and committed suicide. The leader of the conservative Agrarian league, Konstantin Päts, who became prime minister in 1933, proved to be a worthy opponent of the fascists. A cool opportunist, he established a mild authoritarian regime in order to forestall an extreme one. Since the issue of constitutional reform had been under hot discussion for several years without final decision, Päts in 1934 blocked the threat of civil war by imposing reforms which in substance gave him ultimate power. Then he took four years to work out a new constitution, which was accepted in 1938 by an overwhelming vote.

The constitution established two houses, the lower house to be composed of representatives of the people as consumers, the upper of representatives of the people as producers. The lower chamber should be elected on a constituency basis, one member from each district, whereas the members of the second chamber should represent professional associations, trade-unions, local governments, and cultural councils, an idea borrowed from fascism. By means of the first chamber Päts hoped to introduce the stabilizing influence of second thought. He intensely disliked political parties, and the ban of 1934 on them continued.

Because the two chambers could merely check the authority temporarily of the president and of the prime minister and cabinet appointed by him, the constitution has been called a façade for continued one-man rule. The criticism is too severe; the constitution afforded opportunities for each side, the legislative and the executive, to assert its influence. In times of stress the latter would be able to dominate; in peaceful and prosperous times the legislative power could expand. Like his colleagues, Karlis Ulmanis, the authoritarian ruler of Latvia, and Antanas Smetona, who performed the same function in Lithuania, Päts had no wish to become dictator. He hoped and expected that his people would learn the ways of self-government. The three countries were not given time to work out this problem before international events overwhelmed them.

In spite of political and constitutional troubles, the social solidarity of each of the four nations was not shaken. Finland set a standard for the others. By preserving a free constitution, she enabled the social forces to improve their mutual relations. By 1937 the Social Democrats were the strongest party in parliament and members of a coalition government. The Social Democratic trade-unionists had in 1930 set up their own labor organization after breaking with the Communists; and the government in the thirties made the system of social insurance as complete and efficient and as democratic as that in the neighboring Scandinavian countries. The People's Pension Act, which came into force in 1939, was the crowning achievement; it placed everyone under an old age and disability plan on a contributory basis. The Childrens' Welfare Act of 1936 revealed more fully the extent of the public's expectation of state guidance. That act required the communes properly to care for the children; they should provide nurseries, kindergartens, and summer homes, and family allowances were paid for about one sixth of all children under sixteen years of age. This social assistance helps to explain why the Finnish people were so united when attacked in 1939 by the Soviet Union.

Nor were the peoples in the other states lacking in this respect. Authoritarian rule did not offend the large majority of the population. The 67 per cent in Estonia and similar numbers in the other states which lived from agriculture did not object to the loss of some political and intellectual freedom. They were faring well economically; so were the urban businessmen. The governments undercut the complaints of workers about the lack of free unions by such measures as the eight-hour day, a week's vacation with pay, representation on boards of arbitration, and a rising standard of living. Housing remained scarce, and workers in small industries were inadequately protected against exploitation, but these problems were relatively small. More unfortunate was the disregard, even the rebuff, of the knowledge of academic personnel, for these countries could scarcely afford to waste intelligence. All in all, however, these were vigorous, optimistic nations, making good in their internal economic and social affairs and showing promise of emulating the Scandinavians in the development of free political institutions. The major trouble which they faced came from their geographic position in the path of big predatory powers.

POLAND

In 1926 Poland had come under the rule of Jozef Pilsudski, assisted by the leaders of the Polish Legion. From then until his death in 1935 the marshal ultimately decided all matters. After that date authority was retained by the clique of colonels which had established itself around the national hero; but since no one of them either had the prestige or displayed the ability to assume his position, power shifted uneasily from person to person until Hitler conquered Poland. During the period these few individuals bore the responsibility for the country's progress.

Pilsudski and Parliamentary Government

Although preserving the rudiments of the constitution, Pilsudski amended that document to strengthen the executive at the expense of parliament. During his years of control he permitted the latter to convene to debate and criticize and to pass laws, but the government could issue decrees when the legislature was not in session, and the president of the republic, the distinguished scientist Professor Ignacy Mościcki, a disciple of the marshal, could dissolve parliament and hold new elections. Pilsudski himself took the office of prime minister and minister of war according to need. His real power lay in the army, of which he continued to be inspector general. He induced the aristocratic large landowners to return to political life and aligned himself with them, the wealthy bourgeoisie, and the army as an elite for dominating the state. He placed personal henchmen in the important offices in all branches of government, irrespective of whether they had any technical understanding of the work. He soon alienated the Social Democrats, many of whom had supported his seizure of power, and drove them into opposition.

The insignificance of parliament under the amended constitution quickly became apparent from the marshal's arbitrary behavior. The government promulgated a decree restricting freedom of the press. When parliament repealed it, the government adjourned that body and reissued the decree. In the elections of 1928, fought over the issue of whether one was for or against Pilsudski, the government organized a new Non-Party Bloc to give it popular support. Composed of persons from all groups in the population, peasants, workers, industrialists, aristocrats, landlords, Jews, anti-Semites, and clergy, it had one common interest, that of keeping Pilsudski in power. Dominated by the latter's assistants known as the "colonels," the Bloc polled about 3 million votes and seated 122 of 444 deputies. Nonetheless, it was the largest party; with the opposition hopelessly divided, it dominated the new legislature.

By 1930, when new elections were held, the depression was beginning and the opposition parties were critical and active. Pilsudski therefore took no chances. He turned the police against the opposition and put eighteen of the latter's most prominent men in prison, among them Wincenty Witos, the peasant leader and former premier, who later escaped and fled to Czechoslovakia, and Liebermann, president of the executive committee of the Socialist party. These persons were treated like ordinary criminals, beaten and insulted in prison at Brest Litovsk irrespective of age or the position which they had held. Under this manifestation of terror as an adjunct to constitutionalism the voters returned a large majority for the Bloc. Henceforth the opposition, although not reduced to silence, was cautious in its criticism, and the majority supported arbitrary government under a constitution.

After 1930 the government faced the unrest caused by the economic crisis. Pilsudski was growing old, his health was poor, he might not live much longer. Coercion on an expanded scale was employed in keeping down popular criticism, but the Pilsudski clique decided that the system needed permanent legal form. Taking advantage of the temporary absence of the opposition, it slipped through parliament in 1935 the "theses" of a new constitution and then declared these to be the bases for a new form of government. This document abolished the division of power among the three branches of government and made the president "the one and indivisible authority of the state." Cabinet, courts, and parliament were subordinate to him. "The responsibility before God and history for the destinies of the State rests on him," and he nominated his own successor. The lower house and the senate were granted the right to discuss and vote and to control the budget, but the president was given large powers to legislate by decree. Elections were managed by reserving to certain privileged economic, social, and other organizations the right to nominate candidates. It was expected that political parties would thereby become superfluous and that politicians would be replaced in parliament by expert representatives of corporative bodies. With this form of government the colonels planned to preserve their authority after the death of their leader.

The constitution lasted until the new partition of Poland, but it failed to accomplish its purpose. The president lacked the prestige and stature of Pilsudski and could not always control his subordinates. In the elections the government picked the candidates, and the voters remained apathetic. The first election under the new constitution brought out only 46 per cent of the voters as against 75 per cent in 1930. The opposition parties boycotted the election, maintaining that the constitution had been illegally adopted and that the election law made it impossible for the public to express its views. After having dissolved the nonparty Bloc with the constitutional reforms in 1935, the colonels found that they needed a similar organization to supply a political following. In 1936 the president and Marshal Edward Smigly-Ryd'z, who considered themselves the most important of Pilsudski's heirs, gave their blessing to the formation of a new bloc known as the Camp of National Unity fashioned somewhat after totalitarian parties. The other parties were not banned, however, and on the eve of the supreme military test in World War II Polish fascists, anti-Semites, liberals, and socialists of many shades continued to quarrel over the best way to serve the nation.

Inadequate Economic Policy

Political disunity was accompanied by the severe hardships of the depression, which the authoritarian government was unable to overcome. The colonels executed a deflationary policy with a thoroughness for which they were otherwise not noted. They reduced the circulation of money per capita to the equivalent of less than $8 in 1935, an amount one seventh of that for Great Britain and less than that for Romania. The people lacked money to spend; the economy slowed down for want of capital. Investment declined between 1928 and 1932 by 67 per cent. Industrial production dropped 36 per cent from 1928, wholesale prices by 47 per cent, and the cost of living by 42 per cent. The government income from taxes, monopolies, and duties declined by 40 per cent, and the budget was constantly unbalanced. The fall in foreign trade, because of decline in quantity and price, was catastrophic—75 per cent in imports and 62 per cent in exports. The reserves in gold and foreign exchange in the Bank of Poland were reduced between 1927 and 1935 by two thirds, and a similar percentage of foreign credits was withdrawn. By 1936 at least half of the workers in industries and mines employing twenty or more persons were still unemployed or partially employed, not to mention those in small factories and in agriculture. The workers in jobs were receiving an average of 12 cents an hour; and, since prices of farm products dropped between 1929 and 1935 far below those for industrial goods, the peasants were probably in a worse condition.

Poland was a country of cartels and state monopolies, and the depression greatly accentuated this development. As numerous private banks proved unable to stand the strain, the government took them over and quickly became the supreme source of credit throughout the state. Monopoly political power seemed to encourage the growth of monopoly economic power. Bankers, industrialists, and government all favored cartels, and practically every important industry in the country except textiles organized a monopoly. Opportunities to exploit political power for private gain were numerous and attractive.

In 1936 the government approved a four-year plan with emphasis upon the development of a vast industrial region in central Poland between Warsaw, Krakow, and Lwow. Electric power, gas, heavy and light industry, and transportation were to make this the economic heart of the country. The state should assume the initiative, but private interests should cooperate. Realizing that imports of machinery and other materials would be heavy for some years in order to accomplish this objective, the government introduced the entire system of exchange control, quotas, and state planning of foreign trade. It sought funds mainly from agriculture and coal mining and supervised domestic as well as foreign commerce. It fixed the price of agricultural products in order to squeeze additional funds out of that sector of the economy for investment in industrial projects.

The economic program in the brief span of time before World War II proved useful to industry but not to agriculture. Unemployment was not overcome by 1939; indeed, it may be questioned whether the existing birth rate would have permitted it ever to be ended. Industrial production took a decided upturn, being in 1938 42 per cent above the average for both 1925–1929 and 1935. Agricultural indebtedness was reduced with the aid of the government, which set up a National Land Bank for that purpose. Unfortunately, the sums provided were small, and, in spite of the moratorium on land debts and the scaling down of the size of debts and of interest rates, the financial condition of agriculture was scarcely improved. The rate of creating separate farms for the peasants declined. In 1929 the peasants, composing 64 per cent of the population, had consumed only 47 per cent of the national real income; ten years later its situation was much worse. Agriculture on the eve of World War II produced one half of the nation's goods, but governmental spending aided industry, not agriculture.

Stanislaw Poniatowski, the liberalminded minister of agriculture in the late thirties, was fully aware of the peasants' troubles:

> Agricultural and industrial prices can be compared regardless of the year which is taken as the basis of our calculations. A farmer sells various products. In order to estimate the market value of all the commodities produced by a farmer, one ought to consider those products in the proportion in which the farmer actually sells them on the market. With regard to Polish peasants we can accept it as being 1 quintal of wheat, 2 quintals of rye, 50 kgs. of hogs, 40 kgs. of cattle and 10 kgs. of butter. We deal here with a certain group of products chosen on the basis of studies made by the Institute [Government Institute of Agricultural Research] in Pulava on the income of small agricultural holdings.
>
> The purchasing power of that group should always be the same, if there is to be an equilibrium between agricultural and industrial prices. Now, such a group of products in Poland, sold by a farmer, brought 143 zlotys in 1935; in Great Britain, 192; in Czechoslovakia, 258; in France, 209; in Germany, 346. But what could a farmer buy for it?
>
> In Poland he could buy 150 kgs. of sugar, in Great Britain 409 kgs., in Czechoslovakia 208 kgs., in France 245 kgs., in Germany 258 kgs. Or he could buy in Poland 372 liters of petroleum, in Great Britain 576 l., in Czechoslovakia 853 l., in France 378 l., in Germany 492 l. Or in terms of iron he could buy in Poland 620 kgs., in Great Britain 778 kgs., in Czechoslovakia 981 kgs., in Germany 1,470 kgs.[2]

The explanation for high prices of industrial articles lay in the hold which cartels exercised over production. Industry compensated for its inability to compete abroad by imposing excessive prices at home. The cartel law of 1933 provided means for prohibiting such practices, but it was enforced by the group that benefited from its violation. As usual in Poland, a fine law was nullified by failure in execution.

A progovernment deputy in parliament, in reporting on the official investment plan in the second half of the thirties, denounced the cartels and state monopolies as an encouragement to industrial inefficiency. He declared that the practice of cartelization warped the psychology of the nation. A businessman with initiative found himself caught between a government concession and a cartel. The spur of economic competition was blunted, as small-scale industry suffered from the difficulty of obtaining credit. Like the peasant, the little businessman faced the almost insurmountable obstacle of the colonels' preference for monopoly. The cost to the nation may be suggested by the size of the return on the state's 11 billion zlotys of investment in business enterprises. The state budget for 1937–1938 estimated that these would produce 81,300,000 zlotys in revenue

[2] Simon Segal, *The New Poland and the Jews* (New York: Lantern Press, Inc.–A. L. Furman, Prop., 1938), pp. 116-117.

for the government. If they had yielded a profit merely of the standard 5 per cent, that sum would have been 650 million zlotys a year. In actuality they yielded only 0.74 per cent, in spite of the fact that they paid no state or local taxes. Someone derived a handsome income from inefficiency.

The difference between reality and façade may be seen in every aspect of the economy. Real wages rose in the thirties, but the figures applied only to industrial workers in employment, and omitted the 50 per cent who were not employed. The wages of agricultural workers in 1937–1938 were still about one half of the figure for 1928–1929. Although one third of the sums advanced by foreign capital was redeemed between 1929 and 1935, the transactions were made at bargain prices and the creditors received nothing like the full sum lent. The zloty continued theoretically to be based on gold after 1936; the catch lay in the government's control of all dealings in foreign exchange. On paper the country had one of the most inclusive systems of social insurance in the world; in actuality it was not enforced. The same distinction existed with respect to hours of labor and conditions of work. The bureaucracy became ossified as the new elite settled into comfortable positions. The government employed its centralized political authority to keep the economy under control, and the colonels eliminated persons, like Minister of Agriculture Poniatowski, who wished to improve the lot of the masses.

Toward the end of the period the dissension among the people augmented. Unemployment in the academic professions inclined the middle-class youth toward fascism and anti-Semitism. The peasant movement turned from conservatism to radicalism. The government clique hurled accusations of communism, but Communist party leaders had fled to Moscow, where they lost their lives in the purge of 1937–1938. In 1938 the Polish Communist party was so weak that Stalin ordered its dissolution. The angry peasants knew almost nothing about communism but intensely disliked the sound of what they heard and were eager for the execution of land reforms and other measures of economic and social aid. In August, 1937, they refused to bring produce to market, and the workers in some large towns allied with them. The government dispatched police into the villages and broke the resistance. It claimed that only forty-two were killed in the action, but observers asserted that the number was larger. In 1938 municipal elections were held in fifty-two cities without the usual official coercion. The results were devastating for the government—639 seats for the opposition to 383 for those in power.

The Socialists gained most. Anti-Semitism flourished as an outlet for embittered feelings. Municipal governments passed orders against ritual slaughtering of livestock. Universities, professions, bar, trade-unions—almost every organization physically segregated the Jews from Polish life. The ultranationalists and the fascists took the lead, and the Cardinal Primate Hlond in 1936 gave the movement his blessing. "A Jewish question exists [the Cardinal declared] and there will be one so long as the Jews remain Jews. It is an actual fact that the Jews fight against the Catholic Church, they are free-thinkers, and constitute the vanguard of atheism, bolshevism and revolution. The Jewish influence upon morals is fatal." Whether anyone noted his conditioning statement that "Not all the Jews are, however, like that," may be questioned, since he called for an economic boycott of that people.[3] Colonel Josef Beck, the Polish foreign minister, proposed at Geneva that the Jews be removed en masse from Poland to other parts of the world. When Hitler struck Poland, the colonels were still setting one faction in Polish life against another. Controlling the army, the police, and the bureaucracy, they thought themselves safely in command of the country, and they acted on the assumption that should outside danger arise the Polish people would forget their quarrels, their discontent, their misery, and rally to the defense.

Visitors to Poland during the two decades of independence assert that underneath the play of authoritarian politics and economics was the deep current of Polish individualism and belief in freedom and democratic government. The people had shown on many occasions their wish for an improvement of their conditions even to the point of radical change. They wanted neither communism nor fascism; they mistrusted both the Soviet Union and Germany and wished to align with the democratic nations of the West. Again, as in the twenties, they found no leaders to articulate and carry through these ideals. The cleft between the ignorant masses devoid of political understanding and the political elite was too great for the latter to speak for anyone other than themselves. The weak middle class was unable to bridge the two extremes.

CZECHOSLOVAKIA AND AUSTRIA

A comparison of the history of Czechoslovakia and Austria in the thirties will show how differently two states of somewhat similar social structure and similar industrial advance may react to the experience of a severe depression. Both states had a balanced society of middle class, workers, and peasants; both supported about the same occupational distribution of the population. In one fundamental respect Austria had a potential advantage over her northern neighbor: she possessed a solidly German population, whereas Czechoslovakia included several large and compact minority groups. Nonetheless, Austria succumbed to dictatorship in 1933–1934, leaving Czechoslovakia the distinction of being the sole state in the Danubian and Balkan region that preserved free government.

Czechoslovak Economic Recovery

Between the years 1919 and 1939, 60 per cent of Czechoslovakia's total industrial production had to be marketed abroad. Many major industries

[3] *Ibid.*, pp. 79-80.

relied almost entirely upon export trade; among these were furniture, glass, and china (each dependent to the extent of 90 per cent of output) and beer, sugar, textiles, and agricultural machinery (each dependent to the extent of between 70 and 75 per cent). When international trade collapsed, Czechoslovakia experienced by 1932 a drop in the value of her exports and imports alike in the national currency of 71 per cent. From 1929 to 1934 her national income declined by 38 per cent. In 1933, 738,300 or 25 per cent of the total number of workers were unemployed, and in 1937, 409,000 remained in that condition. The index of her industrial production, using 1929 as a base, declined to 60 in 1933 and slowly revived to 70 in 1936 and 96 in 1937. The crisis brought the collapse of the industry in metallurgy, textiles, and food processing in Slovakia which had been built in the years of Hungarian rule for the Hungarian market. The denunciation of the Czechoslovakian-Hungarian trade treaty in 1930 closed down an already precarious business and left many Slovaks with an economic grievance against the government. The industry in the Sudetenland also suffered severely, as it catered particularly to the export trade. Its condition stimulated the nationalistic hostility of the Sudeten Germans, who owned or worked in these industries, against the Czech state.

Czechoslovakia enjoyed one major advantage over the countries to the southeast: she depended much less than they did upon the export of agricultural products. Under leadership with initiative, industry could be much more quickly adapted to changing market conditions than could agriculture, and the Czechoslovaks set to work immediately to revive the economy.

To assist agriculture, the state took the lead and imposed strict control over imports of agricultural materials. In 1934 it created a grain monopoly and applied similar principles to other commodities like milk, cattle, and animal products. The grain monopoly was run as a semipublic corporation with shares subscribed by the agricultural cooperatives to the extent of 40 per cent, the consumers' cooperatives to the extent of 20 per cent, the Association of Flour Millers (20 per cent), and representatives of private traders (20 per cent). The chairman of the company was named by the government. By these means the government assured the farmers a fixed price at a profitable level, at the expense of countries, especially in the southeast, which had heretofore provided much of the imported food.

Agricultural imports in 1933–1934 amounted to only 30 per cent in value of the precrisis level. Since the country was already practically self-sufficient in staples, it could protect itself against imports more easily than, for example, Austria, and it encouraged agriculture to adapt itself even more fully to the internal market. Under state guidance the farmers increased the production of grain, fodder crops, and root crops but reduced the cultivation of hops and of sugar beets on the ground that they were too vulnerable to competition. The application of artificial fertilizers increased, a considerable item in imports because the country was able to supply very little. Aid therefore to agriculture did not consist of the usual moratorium on debts, direct subsidies, and protective tariffs alone; it also took the form of constructive guidance toward new or expanded home markets, toward emphasis upon new crops, and toward improvement of methods of production.

Industrialists criticized the policy of protecting home agriculture as being insufficient to achieve its purpose and as hurting their own international competitive position by raising the cost of living. The government took the view that it was responsible for maintaining a national economy, that both agriculture and industry must prosper. It aided industry in the most important of all respects, the encouragement of rationalization in industrial and business methods and the search for markets in a period hostile to imports. With its aid the industrialists used large amounts of capital to adjust the nature of their commodities to the international market. They learned to specialize for markets which showed some prospect of permanency, and they stressed both cheapness and quality. Finding from experience that large combines were most able to compete abroad, they consolidated heavy industry into six main companies and formed selling organizations in fields like the glass industry. Machinery and whole lines of production were scrapped with considerable frequency in order to keep abreast of the market, a capital-consuming procedure but one essential to an export industry.

Guided by adventurous spirits, Czechoslovak industry began to recover. Between 1934, when the state devalued its currency (it did so again in 1936 with the new wave of devaluation), and 1938 heavy industry, chemicals, and cement lines showed most improvement. They were able to sell not merely war materials but other goods as well. Coal mining, the manufacture of paper and cellulose, and of leather goods and machine tools, and sugar refining took an upturn, with new industries, electrical equipment, automobiles, scientific instruments and cameras, and rubber also increasing. One extraordinary entrepreneur, Bata, continued to develop large-scale shoe production and to make his factories at Zlín into one of the greatest economic achievements of the Western world. The businessmen succeeded in expanding their markets in the countries of Northwestern Europe and elsewhere. In a period of cautious recovery from the economic crisis, they reoriented a considerable amount of their trade from exchange-controlled countries to those with free exchange. If the production of textiles, porcelain, and glass in the Sudetenland had been able to exhibit a similar degree of revival, the country would have recovered by 1938 the level of manufacturing which it had attained prior to the crisis.

Stable Government in Czechoslovakia

The government remained stable throughout the decade. During the worst years of the economic crisis a coalition of Agrarians and Social Democrats held office, and the presence of the latter assured fair treatment to the workers. The wage scale was low, in order to enable industry to compete abroad; and social insurance, although inclusive, did not involve sums comparable to those in neighboring Austria. Nonetheless, labor did not engage in violence. The Communist party won almost one half of the labor vote; but in these years it did not attempt extreme action. The Agrarian party served as the most important stabilizing force in the political life, the Socialist party next. The Agrarians represented peasants and the middle class in industry, commerce, and banking, particularly among the Czechs but also among the Slovaks and some Ruthenians. The Slovak Milan Hodža, for example, served with Czechs as one of the prominent leaders. The government settled its quarrel with the Vatican over relations between church and state by an agreement in 1928, and, notwithstanding the fact that the people were largely Catholic, they resisted clerical influence on politics.

When the beloved Tomaš Masaryk retired from the presidency in 1935 at the age of 85, he recommended as his successor the man who had stood close to him and came nearest to personifying his ideals, Eduard Beneš. "Four times I have been elected President of the Republic," he said to his people. "This fact may give me the right to ask you . . . always to remember that states can be maintained only by respecting those ideals which brought them into being." Justice, he continued, must be "equal for all citizens regardless of race and religion." Beneš filled the presidential position as worthily as any man could. When Masaryk died two years later he was mourned by the entire free Western world.

In spite of the stability of government and society, the economic crisis did aggravate internal antagonism. Backward Ruthenia had in 1927 been placed on equal legal basis with Bohemia and other provinces and was well administered by the Czechs. The Ruthenians, however, were divided into three groups, autonomists, those wishing to join the Ukraine, and Communists. Although hurt economically by the separation from Hungary, the region would in time have become fully integrated with Czechoslovak economic and political life, if World War II had not decreed otherwise.

Much more serious was the discontent in Slovakia expressed by the Slovak Peoples' party. In 1935 the party gained 22 seats of 300 in the parliament, and was led by Catholic priests in an area of backward Catholic peasants. The party stirred up antagonism against the godless Czechs and their wicked republic. It was hostile to democracy, socialism, and the Jews, and demanded provincial autonomy. When Professor Tuka, a party leader, asserted in 1928 that the Czechoslovakian union had become null and void, he was tried for treason and condemned to fourteen years' imprisonment. In 1933, however, Father Andrej Hlinka, the most important leader of the party, stated at a political rally in Nitra, "There are no Czechoslovaks. We wish only to be Slovaks." The economic crisis drove many peasants and workers into this party as well as into that of the Communists. As in Ruthenia, these problems would have been solved in time, if Nazi Germany had not transformed the Sudeten Germans into a Trojan horse.

Sudeten Issue

The last four years of Czechoslovak independence before World War II were dominated by the Sudeten issue. The gravity of the conflict between nationalities was enhanced by the fact that the state had built in the mountains of the Sudetenland fortifications against Germany modeled after those of the Maginot line in France. After Hitler came to authority in Germany the 3½ million Sudeten Germans almost entirely followed his lead and organized themselves into a compact party along Nazi lines. All classes and all occupations joined in the enthusiasm over prospects of vengeance on the Czechs and annexation to Germany. Only a few persons, primarily Social Democrats, under their leader Wenzel Jaksch, and Communists, withstood the nationalistic urge. The Nazi leader among the Sudetens, Konrad Henlein, a hitherto insignificant figure in the German gymnastic organization, managed the party as Hitler's tool.

The Czechs had treated the German minority remarkably well, if one compares their attitude to the contempt with which the Germans regarded the Czechs. They had divided German estates among German as well as Czech peasants; they had passed and implemented most lenient laws about German schools, press, and other cultural matters. They had aided German business and had granted fair representation in parliament and taken spokesmen of German parties into the cabinet. Nonetheless, the Germans complained about the settlement of Czech peasants and businesses in territory hitherto solidly or predominantly German and exaggerated each minor incident of friction.

When, during the economic depression, the Germans were unable to revive the prosperity of the German-owned industries, they blamed the Czechs; and, as Nazi funds poured in from Germany to enhance their wrath, the Sudetens became violent. "A Socialist schoolmistress in a small German town which I visited in the summer of 1938," writes an English student of the country, "who tried to prevent her pupils from kicking little Jews in the classroom, was shown by them the lamp-post on which she would be hanged when He should come. Social Democrat Party meetings were attended by Henleinist photographers who announced that everyone whose face appeared on their photographs would be put in a concentration camp or suffer a worse fate." [4] Henlein increased the demands for privileges from the Czech state, came out openly for nazism in Sudetenland, and ordered the government to adopt a foreign policy dictated from Berlin. Rapidly preparing the country of Masaryk to become a small part of Hitler's empire, the Sudetenlanders rejoiced at the prospect of losing their liberty.

[4] Hugh Seton-Watson, *Eastern Europe between the Wars, 1918–1941* (New York: Cambridge University Press, 1945), p. 282.

Economic Hardship in Austria

Austria was particularly vulnerable to the economic crisis because it had not yet adjusted the economic organization, which had served an empire, to the needs of a small state. The following statistics on the level of production in the heavy industries and in engineering fields tell the sad story:

	1913	*1929*	*1933*	*1935*
Pig iron	100	76	15	32
Steel	100	71	25	41
Iron ore	100	93	13	38
Engineering	100	69	22	32

SOURCE: Julius Braunthal, *The Tragedy of Austria* (London: Victor Gollanz, Ltd., 1948), p. 129.

Prior to the depression the country had had 10 to 20 per cent of the workers unemployed; in February, 1933, more than two thirds were idle, and that figure is regarded as too low to be accurate. The slowness with which the economy recovered may be seen from the fact that in 1937 employment was still 33 per cent below that of 1929. Imports and exports declined by 1932 to 35 per cent of their value in 1929, and were late in revival. One fourth of Austria's food and most of the industrial raw materials had to be imported, and manufactured goods exported.

Such dependence upon foreign trade would alone have exposed the credit system to unusual danger in a crisis; since the Austrian banks continued the practice from imperial times of serving the Balkan countries, they were caught by the blockage of funds in those highly vulnerable economies. Funds borrowed abroad by Austrian banks as traditional intermediaries for the Balkan market became frozen; loans to Austrian industries could not be repaid. Every bank including the strongest and biggest of them all, the *Kredit Anstalt,* broke down. The government had to intervene and guarantee funds to them in order to prevent destruction of the country's credit system. The wonder is that the entire economy did not collapse.

Austrian business leadership did not display initiative at all comparable to that of the Czechs. The attempt to maintain a sound currency failed, and in 1932–1933 Austria devalued the currency. Water power was partly developed, but oil was neglected. Under the republic about 20,000 tons were annually extracted; after Hitler took hold, output increased to a million tons a year. Agriculture fared no better. The use of artificial fertilizer increased, as did the production of wheat and sugar beets, but at a high price to the consumer. In comparison with that of a country like Switzerland, agriculture remained inefficient. A Swiss peasant obtained per hectare 3½ times as much in value as an Austrian. Some efforts were made to help agriculture and industry recover from the depression, by high tariffs, quotas, and so on, and to stimulate production for the home market of 6½ million people; but on the whole, throughout the thirties, the Austrian economy remained sick.

A key to understanding this policy may be found in a comparison of the percentages of the total budget expended around 1937 by the Czechoslovakian and the Austrian governments in certain fields. The Czechs devoted most funds to improving the economy and were sparing in all other

	ECONOMIC EXPENDITURE	EDUCATION	PUBLIC WELFARE	ADMINISTRATION
	%	%	%	%
Czechoslovakia	16.0	8.5	10.2	12.9
Austria	9.9	14.0	19.8	18.7

SOURCE: *Economic Development in Southeastern Europe*, p. 164. By kind permission of the publishers, Political & Economic Planning. London, 1945.

respects. The Austrians put most funds into the education of persons for whom they had no jobs and especially into public welfare and administration, neither of which created new wealth. The state finally sought salvation in civil war and dictatorship.

Authoritarian Rule in Austria

When the economic crisis occurred, hostility among the social classes was already acute. The Social Democrats controlled Vienna, where they had separated church and state, laicized education, put up model housing for workers, and made possible nonchurch marriages. About 250,000 persons had left the church up to 1934, the crowning evidence to Catholics of the godlessness of Socialist Vienna. Ignoring the fact that the overwhelming mass of the Social Democrats remained loyal Catholics, the Christian Socialist party under the leadership of Monseigneur Seipel hoped to destroy the republic and introduce an authoritarian state run according to Catholic principles, with Marxism of all varieties banned. The political priests and the big businessmen and bankers, who guided the party following of loyally Catholic peasants, used the depression as an opportunity for stimulating social hostility.

Since the two parties were equal in voting power, with one strong in Vienna and among the workers and the other concentrated in the provinces among the peasants, the only way to change the system seemed to be by force. Each side had a private army, the *Schutzbund* for the republic, the *Heimwehr* under Prince Stahremberg for the Christian Socialists. The outcome ultimately depended upon control of the police and the army, and on July 15, 1927, to the surprise of both parties, the Vienna police fired on striking workers and killed a number of them. The incident revealed that in the party struggle the Socialist government of that city no longer could rely upon the support or the neutrality of its own police.

Monseigneur Seipel died in 1932, but his successor continued the policy of undermining the republic. As premier and head of the Christian Socialist party, Engelbert Dollfuss in early 1933 took his cue from the Hitlerites in Germany and paralleled violations of the German constitution with those of the Austrian. Acting under an emergency clause, he issued decrees which closed parliament, introduced censorship of the press, abolished trial by jury and the right of habeas corpus, suppressed workers' associations, established concentration camps, and endowed Austria with other fascist institutions. After almost a year of undermining the opposition, Dollfuss, on February 11, 1934, ordered the dissolution of all political parties and trade-unions, and, knowing that this decree meant civil war, he seized the leaders. The workers rebelled, but in a four-day battle, mainly in Vienna, the government won. The official figures listed 239 dead and 718 wounded; no one knows the actual number. Nine Socialists were hanged and others would have been if the British and French governments had not protested. Between March, 1933, and the end of 1934, Dollfuss arrested on mere suspicion 38,132 persons and searched 106,319 houses. He introduced a new constitution with a preamble which stated: "In the name of God from whom all right proceeds, this Constitution is issued for the Austrian people for its Christian, German, Federal State on a corporative basis."

The constitution of 1934 was based on the papal encyclical *Quadragesimo Anno* of 1931. It was praised by Catholic conservatives as the model of Christian government. The encyclical read in part as follows:

> . . . the demand and supply of labor divides men on the labor market into two classes, as into two camps, and the bargaining between these parties transforms this labor market into an arena where the two armies are engaged in combat. To this grave disorder which is leading society to ruin a remedy must evidently be applied as speedily as possible. But there cannot be question of any perfect cure, except this opposition be done away with, and well-ordered members of the social body come into being anew, vocational groups namely, binding men together not according to the position they occupy in the labor market, but according to the diverse functions which they exercise in society. For as nature induces those who dwell in close proximity to unite into municipalities, so those who practice the same trade or profession, economic or otherwise, combine into vocational groups. These groups, in a true sense autonomous, are considered by man to be, if not essential to civil society, at least its natural and spontaneous development.

The encyclical further discussed the fear felt by some that "the new syndical and corporative institution possesses an exclusively bureaucratic and political character," and that "it risks serving particular political aims rather than contributing to the initiation of a better social order."

> We believe [the encyclical continued] that to attain this last named lofty purpose for the true and permanent advantage of the commonwealth, there is

need before and above all else of the blessing of God, and, in the second place, of the cooperation of all men of good will. . . .

It is scarcely worth while to analyze the constitution. It substituted for the democratic parliament a body composed of representatives of seven corporations, agriculture and forestry, industry and mining, trades, commerce and transport, finance and credit, liberal professions, and public services and railways. The Diet mainly had advisory power; its members were appointed by the government in which the chancellor was supreme. The majority of the members were noblemen, priests, big landowners, state officials, and industrialists. Among these "men of good will" no workers were admitted. The clerico-fascist government abolished the municipal housing program which Socialist Vienna had made world-famous. It restored to the Hapsburgs the crown property, which the republic had confiscated for the benefit of disabled soldiers. It stopped strikes and drove underground the evolutionary, peaceful Socialist party, as well as the handful of revolutionary Communists. It created a new monopoly party, the Fatherland's Front, actually Stahremberg's fighting troops under a new guise. It completed the destruction of Austrian social unity.

This weakened Austria became the bone of contention between its own clerico-fascists and the German Nazis. The latter sent huge sums of money into the state for subversive purposes and found a response among the middle class. In 1934 the Nazis assassinated Dollfuss, and although the assassins were hanged and the coup failed, the Nazi movement scarcely received a setback. Kurt von Schuschnigg took over Dollfuss's position, and continued his policies. He tried to defend Austria against nazism, and until the venture into Ethiopia reduced Mussolini's international prestige, he could rely upon Italy to oppose Germany. He even made overtures to the Austrian Social Democrats for cooperation against the menace, but the Socialists had no confidence in a regime which a few years before had shot their members and destroyed their organization. The model constitution did not save Austria from easy Nazi seizure.

THE AGRICULTURAL STATES OF SOUTHEAST EUROPE

In the predominantly agricultural states of Hungary, Romania, Yugoslavia, Albania, Bulgaria, and Greece, the economic crisis accentuated the conflict among members of the upper classes for power. Except for some industrial development, which increased the wealth of a few persons, nothing constructive was accomplished for the people or the state. By the end of the thirties conditions were almost uniformly as bad as, or even worse than, they had been; the ruling elite had staved off thorough national reform during another decade by everywhere supporting authoritarian government.

Failure to Overcome Economic Crisis

Since these nations primarily depended upon agricultural exports for wealth, their incomes dropped with agonizing speed. By 1934 Greece had 73 per cent as much national income as in 1929; Bulgaria, 61 per cent; Hungary, 60 per cent; Romania, 49 per cent; and Yugoslavia, only 46 per cent. The decline may be understood by considering the drop in prices of agricultural exports. According to a League of Nations report of 1932, wholesale prices of raw materials and foodstuffs had fallen since 1928 by 40 per cent, increasing the burden of fixed charges on the producers by 70 per cent. Bulgaria, for example, tried to maintain her income by increasing exports. The result was that in 1930 she sent abroad 80 per cent more in weight than before and received 3 per cent less money for the total; in 1931, she exported 40 per cent more by weight and earned 4 per cent less money. That animal products, wheat, timber, and similar materials would meet with difficulty abroad may be deduced from the increase in production by both European importing and exporting countries; the former expanded the raising of wheat from 1,000 million bushels in 1927 to 1,358 million in 1933, whereas the latter produced 2,524 million in 1928 and 2,653 million in 1931. In value the foreign trade of the Balkan countries sank in 1932 to the following percentage of the figure for 1929:

	EXPORTS	IMPORTS
Greece	65.7	59.1
Hungary	32.3	30.9
Yugoslavia	38.5	27.1
Romania	48.9	39.2
Bulgaria	39.0	27.0

SOURCE: Antonín Basch, *The Danube Basin and the German Economic Sphere,* p. 92. Copyright 1943, Columbia University Press, New York.

The fact that each country had an export surplus does not alleviate the severity of the reduction in both exports and imports. From the diminished income in foreign exchange the states were expected to service a foreign debt of the following dimensions in 1931–1932:

	TOTAL PER CAPITA OF POPULATION (IN GOLD FRANCS)	TOTAL AS PER CENT OF EXPORTS IN 1931
Bulgaria	118	16
Greece	378	49
Hungary	432	48
Romania	292	28
Yugoslavia	235	29

By way of comparison the figures for Austria, Czechoslovakia, and Poland may be added:

Austria	361	22
Czechoslovakia	138	5
Poland	139	24

SOURCE: Basch, *The Danube Basin and the German Economic Sphere*, p. 92.

These countries, except Czechoslovakia, were actually insolvent.

The depression accelerated the fundamental economic change which had started after the war. The slump in agricultural prices coupled with the cessation of foreign loans, the drop in agricultural wages, the continued existence of a large percentage of the population either un- or underemployed were conditions which led to an attempt to reduce the importance of agriculture, to turn its attention toward the internal market, and to stimulate industrialization. Out of despair, autarchy became the objective.

The first step toward recovery was to declare a partial or total moratorium on foreign debts; this was done in 1931–1932. Simultaneously, these countries introduced the gamut of protective devices for agriculture and industry—grain monopolies, quotas, and the like. They reduced the peasants' debts, a move of particular advantage to owners of middle-sized and large holdings. They sought to produce those industrial articles which they had hitherto purchased abroad, and to that end the governments played a leading part. Political, economic, and social conditions were so uncertain that private investors required a high rate of return to compensate them for the risks involved, and capital was scarce. The state, which was expected to provide the investment funds, forced the peasantry as usual to carry most of the burden by heavy taxes and high prices for manufactured goods. Since the ruling group in each country was composed in large part or exclusively of those most concerned with banking and industry, the governments encouraged the formation of cartels and monopolies. Big enterprises were considered most economical in the use of capital. In Romania King Carol became personally involved in the new industries, and the government granted them preferential taxes, special transportation rates, direct subsidies, enormous tariffs, quotas on competitive imports, assured markets, and other forms of aid. Heavy industry of a hothouse variety was stimulated to a flourishing growth; but textiles, behind a protective wall, showed most quantitative gain in catering to the national market. Entrepreneurs, some state officials, and ministers in the cabinet in each country during this decade quickly acquired fortunes. Romania was reputedly most corrupt, but each country produced persons whose public morals showed low standards.

In their public finance the governments tried to live like those of modern states, but they relied upon antiquated means of raising and administering revenue. The cost of administration and collection of taxes in Hungary consumed nearly 20 per cent of the yield, a figure to be compared with that of 5.4 per cent for Germany. In or about 1937 between 21 and 30 per cent of the budget was used for central and local administration. Greece made the only exception, with 14 per cent, a figure that may be set against that of 13 per cent for Czechoslovakia. Expenditures on public welfare amounted to between 4 and 8 per cent. Far too much money was spent on maintaining an excessively large and inefficient bureaucracy that did little for the people. The example of the special aviation tax in Romania, which produced revenue but scarcely any aircraft, could be duplicated in each country.

Students of this region of Europe agree on the poor living conditions of the people. "The situation in Yugoslavia in the postwar period," a foreign scholar has written, "cannot be painted in colors too dark." [5] "The Greek prewar [World War II] economy was unsound and inadequate," another has stated. ". . . Prewar governments made gestures. They divided the land; they put into effect irrigation and drainage projects; they set up an agricultural bank to loan money to peasants. But these were only a drop in the bucket. Lacking an over-all program they failed." [6] In Hungary, some estates used modern agricultural methods; the peasants did not. Industrialization increased the volume of production from 1913 to 1939 by two thirds but did not improve the real wages of the workers. The position of the agricultural workers, the mass of the population, was not improved at all. Bulgaria was no better off. In Romania the peasantry was losing land and wherever possible was doing seasonal work in urban industry, the first stage in becoming an urban proletariat. This class was unable to construct durable houses and was beginning to wear cheap factory-made clothes. The standard of living was so low that many families suffered from undernourishment. That a modest program of social security like the one introduced in the thirties in Hungary could help people in such conditions bespoke, at most, good intentions.

Authoritarian Government

The politics of the decade are the story of conflict primarily among the exploiters, with a rare interlude when they united to block some genuine effort to help the people. Sometimes the exploitation occurred as a result of ignorance about how to use power. Usually it was considered the natural order of things. Always the elite feared the changes which political awakening of the masses might bring.

Hungary. Within the span of a decade Hungary moved from a gov-

[5] Robert J. Kerner, ed., *Jugoslavia* (Berkeley: University of California Press, 1949), p. 166.

[6] L. S. Stavrianos, *Greece: American Dilemma and Opportunity* (Chicago: Henry Regnery Company, 1952), p. 27.

ernment directed by aristocrats of the old order to one increasingly modeled after the totalitarian regimes of Italy and Germany. Count Istvan Bethlen, who had dominated the affairs of state in the twenties, resigned in 1931, leaving the responsibility for dealing with the crisis to other hands. He regarded the aristocrats and the big landowners as "the really politically-trained class destined to lead the nation." The count was succeeded by another aristocrat, an honest, puritanical one, Count Gyula Karolyi, who continued in office until 1933. Then the lower nobility took office under the premiership of General Gyula Gömbös. The general strove to compensate for his German origin by being more Hungarian than the Hungarians. A person of tremendous vigor and strong imagination, he orated in bombastic fascist language, advocated reforms from time to time, visited Italy and Germany in his extensive travels, and did almost nothing for the country. He followed the lead of Mussolini and Hitler in creating a fascist movement native to Hungary, but he opposed the spread of Nazi propaganda in the country.

The depression stimulated in Hungary as elsewhere the formation of fascist groups. For some years they were small and fought each other as well as the other parties. Anti-Semitism became popular as the Hungarians in the interwar years advanced far enough economically and socially to regard business as a respectable occupation. Jews were rarely admitted to the professions, but they were entrenched in the economy. Since the depression augmented unemployment, the temptation to attack these half million loyal Hungarians became irresistible. The government curbed the Social Democrats to discreet utterance and continued the aristocrats' policy of preventing socialism from spreading to the peasantry; but it was tolerant toward the extreme patriots.

The decline of Gömbös' power in 1936 brought no important change in government policy. His two immediate successors courted Hitler and encouraged totalitarianism. When the brilliant economist Imredy, who was pro-German, talked vigorously about land reform, the aristocrats eliminated him by showing that he had had a Jewish grandmother. During his premiership the two strongest totalitarian groups united to form the Arrow Cross party. Led by Szálasi, a fanatical major, and supported by a member of the Festetics family, owner of 40,000 acres of land, the party agitated against the Jews and for land reform. It took subsidies from the German Nazis, indulged in extremist promises, demanded the reannexation of the territory lost to the succession states, and denounced the government. Szálasi was imprisoned in 1938, but the movement was tolerated and inadvertently aided when the government proposed to restrict the number of Jews in commerce and the professions to 20 per cent. Questions of freedom of speech, press, and assembly were argued back and forth, while the totalitarians increased their following. In the elections of May, 1939, the government received the usual majority, but the totalitarians won 43 seats, of which 28 belonged to the Arrow Cross party. The opposition vote of the

Social Democrats and Tibor Eckhardt's Independent Small Landowners' party declined, the latter to insignificance.

Although faced with a Nazi-fascist menace inside Hungary and without, the parties favoring freedom and parliamentary government, in addition to being intrinsically weak, failed to cooperate. About the only sign of reasonable public life in prewar Hungary was provided by a group of young intellectuals calling itself the March Front in memory of the revolution of March, 1848; this group began to study and write about the conditions in the Hungarian villages and to advocate social reforms. They accomplished nothing, however, against the angry, vituperative forces that were turned loose under the auspices of reactionary aristocrats and landowners. Hungary entered World War II unreformed, unregenerate, divided in spirit, frustrated, and surrounded by danger from supposed friends and real enemies.

Romania. The politics of Romania during the thirties were dominated by the personality of King Carol II. Forced during his father's lifetime because of a morganatic marriage to renounce his rights to the throne, Carol had gone into exile to await the day when he could recover the crown. That moment arrived in June, 1930, when with the acquiescence of the National Peasant party then in control of the government he flew to Bucharest to be immediately accepted as king. He admired Mussolini to the point of imitation, and in the next ten years used terror and the standard Balkan methods of intrigue and corruption to consolidate power in his own hands. He succeeded in disrupting all the major parties, driving the leaders to prison, to exile within Romania or abroad, or to subservience. In doing so he used fascist clichés, spoke about the corporative state, and exalted the "younger generation"; but he had no technical knowledge of economics or of society and regarded himself as the model for all classes and occupations. When he ultimately acquired personal power, he began dimly to perceive that it might be used for a social purpose.

As the first step on the way to absolute authority Carol disrupted the strongest political parties, the National Peasants and the Liberal. He and Premier Maniu, the revered head of the National Peasant party, lacked all personal or political affinity. Schooled in the hard but honest Transylvanian politics of the former kingdom of Hungary, Maniu upheld high moral ideals in political and in private life, and when Carol, against his promise, brought back his mistress, Madame Lupescu, the straight-laced premier resigned. The king's men spread the rumor that Maniu was a prude, and they intrigued with the others in the party against the leader. First Carol put in Professor Jorga as premier, an elderly, conceited scholar, the author of a vast number of historical volumes, and amateur politician. The professor conducted an election in which corruption and brutality surpassed even Romanian standards.

After a year Jorga was replaced by Vaida-Voevod, another National Peasant leader. The king had aroused enduring hostility between Vaida and Maniu; and when in 1934 Vaida formed a new party, the Romanian Front, and attracted a good many of Maniu's young men to it, the royal objective had been reached. There were now two weak parties in place of a single strong one; the leader of the old group was out of power and temporarily isolated, and the head of the other depended upon the king. The once strong Liberal party split in the same way as the National Peasants. Jealousy among leaders gave Carol an opening, and the assassination of the able, honest head, Ion Duca, in 1933, by native fascists removed the last obtacle to manipulating the party. The king then put his own stooge Tatarescu into the position of prime minister and through him ruled the country.

Duca was murdered by members of the Iron Guard, a terrorist organization whose history is intertwined with that of the king. The organization arose among students or ex-students at the University of Jassy (Laşi), the capital of Moldavia, where after World War I a number of young men had earned extra money by acting as strike breakers, Jew-baiters, *agents provocateurs,* and general toughs. The police aided them, and the political party in power employed them to break up meetings of democratic opponents. When the prefect of police in Jassy tried to stop this rowdy conduct, a young student of mixed German and Ukrainian origin named Cornelin Zelea-Codreanu murdered him and upon acquittal became the hero of the extreme nationalists.

Codreanu organized the young terrorists into the League of the Archangel Michael, later called the Iron Guard. When Carol returned to the throne, he and his politicians together with many industrialists supplied the group with funds. The Guard became nation-wide in its propaganda, its organization, and its bloody acts, and the king planned to turn its energy into channels of his own choosing. Anti-Semitism did not affect his relations with them, even though Madame Lupescu was a Jewess. The Iron Guard prospered as the economic depression grew worse. Its appeals for agrarian reform, "one man, one acre," its denunciation of Jews, officials, and politicians attracted not merely middle-class persons but peasants. It expanded to such size that Codreanu and his cohorts grew ambitious to emancipate the movement from political control by others, to become the monopoly party and possessor of power.

The turn of fortune came in 1937. Elections to parliament were to be held, and Maniu outwitted himself. In an effort to protect his followers from governmental oppression in the elections, he temporarily allied with Codreanu. Thereby he confused his own supporters, who as proponents of decent government did not know what line to take. In the elections both government and National Peasants lost votes. The Iron Guard polled only 16 per cent of the ballots, but the king became afraid of his own creation and called on an elderly poet, Octavian Goga, leader of the anti-Semitic National Christian party, to form a government. Goga lasted a few weeks, long enough to have Jews persecuted throughout the country.

Economic life ceased under these circumstances; and King Carol used the opportunity to introduce personal rule under a new fascist constitution. The Patriarch of the National Church became prime minister; Codreanu and aides were arrested and some time later he and thirteen other prominent guard members were "shot while trying to escape."

In December, 1938, Carol created a monopoly party, the Front of National Rebirth. He dominated a reliable army and police force, well equipped to suppress insurrections. He had the intellectuals of the capital at his feet, and he and his industrialist and banker friends controlled all of the economy that was worth controlling. He had reached his life's goal, preaching a crusade against corruption amidst the most corrupt of regimes and exalting the younger generation as he kept old men in power.

Carol was surrounded by sycophants and intriguers, whose advice was untrustworthy. He had learned that reforms were needed everywhere, but even if he had known which to apply he lacked the character to execute them. He turned to such measures as sending a "sanitary train" through the country and compelling the peasants to take a bath. He maintained order by force, while he made romantic, bombastic speeches. He did nothing to prepare Romania for the test of World War II.

Yugoslavia. The politics of Yugoslavia during the years under review were in the main not directly concerned with economics. The depression enhanced the discontent of peasants, workers, and middle class; but, except for members of the middle class in Belgrade and Zagreb with political pull, these groups lacked the power to do other than acquiesce in their bad conditions. The most important political issue continued to be that of unifying Serbs, Croats, and Slovenes into a nation; in this respect the dictatorial regime set up by King Alexander in January, 1929, and continued by his cousin and successor, the Regent Prince Paul, fared no better than the parliamentary system.

King Alexander had been brought up at court in St. Petersburg, where he had absorbed the ideals of autocracy. He condemned both communism and liberal democracy as manifestations of anarchy, and determined to create Yugoslav national feeling by coercion. For this purpose between 1929 and 1931 he introduced an authoritarian constitution, a new organization of provincial government, and a new election law. They formed the framework for his program of action.

The system of government established by the royal dictator included unified control at the center and a considerable degree of provincial and local self-government. The constitution placed the ultimate authority in the monarch, with the two houses of parliament being docile adjuncts to the executive. The laws were actually formulated in the ministerial council subordinate to the ruler, and strict censorship, curtailment of personal liberties, and heavy penalties against acts which furthered provincial autonomy were approved. The thirty-three administrative provinces were consolidated into nine provinces under appointed prefects with conscious disregard of historic associations. The king then brought thousands of new persons into these units of government for the purpose of breaking provincial loyalty in favor of service to a unified Yugoslavia.

The provincial administrations included both national and regional officials, to be assisted by elected bodies of extensive legal competence. Below that level the local government remained about as it had been, fairly representative of, and responsible to, the people in the localities. The system did undermine provincial patriotism everywhere except in Croatia; and by permitting local and provincial elections to be held in the main without coercion, it kept alive the practices of responsible government at the grass roots while destroying it at the center.

The constitution permitted the survival of political parties, but the election law, borrowed from Fascist Italy, introduced the practice by which the party receiving 40 per cent of the votes was entitled to two thirds of the seats in the parliament. With these institutions the king expected Serbs, Croats, Slovenes, and minorities to learn to work together. The constitution lasted until the Germans occupied the country in World War II. Its history showed that the troubles dividing the peoples could not be overcome by dictatorship or other purely institutional means.

The king was assassinated in France in 1934 by a Macedonian terrorist. The act had been plotted by the Macedonian secret society I.M.R.O. (Internal Macedonian Revolutionary Organization) and by Ante Pavelic, a Croatian living in exile, with the aid of the Hungarian and Italian governments. Since the heir to the throne was a minor, Prince Paul, the ex-king's cousin, became regent and ruled until Hitler conquered the country. The prince had no taste for politics, no liking for his own people, no desire for responsibility. He loved to collect art and was most at home in refined society of Western capitals. He wished peace among the quarreling peoples of his state, but he did not know how to achieve this goal. In 1935 he appointed Milan Stojadinovic, a banker with English connections, as premier, and in the main turned over to him the conduct of internal affairs. Far from attempting to reach agreement with the Croats, the banker-politician continued the old methods of coercion, of relying upon the Serbs to hold the state together. His sole innovation amounted to the addition of fascist oratory and fascist techniques of government.

The Croats continued to resist the central government. During the dictatorship the Peasant party fell under the control of the wealthy, conservative (if not reactionary) business and professional people of the towns, the peasants being pushed down to the position of mass followers. Macek, the successor to the Radićs as leader, sought to defend their interests and kept his contacts with the villages, but power in the party lay elsewhere. The peasants still wanted Yugoslavia to succeed as a state, with reforms beneficial to themselves; the Croat bourgeoisie demanded autonomy. Belonging to the same class that was ruling in Belgrade, they could display their own examples of new-made wealth, and they adhered to the same principles and practices of government, provided they were in charge.

The Slovenes fared much better than the Croats under the dictatorship. They were better educated than the other groups in the state, the peasants were better situated economically, and the pressure of population was less. Stojadinovic appointed Monseigneur Korošec, head of the Slovene Clerical party, to his cabinet as minister of interior. Korošec began to fill the ministries with his fellow nationals and to obtain for Slovenia privileges little short of legal autonomy. The Catholic church worked closely with the population and assisted the general intellectual and economic development. The people, though advocating autonomy, were much more satisfied than the Croats or the liberal elements among the Serbs.

The political events between 1937 and 1939 revealed the demands upon statesmanship necessary to bring Serbs, Croats, and Slovenes into harmony, and the failure of the leaders to live up to needs. In 1937 the government negotiated a generous concordat with the papacy, in the hope of winning favor with the Catholic Croats. The Orthodox Serbs grew angry, while Macek mistrusted the government far too much to consider the concordat an inducement to cooperation. From this affair came an agreement between the Croat Peasant party and liberal and democratic parties among the Serbs to work together for the establishment of a democratic government and for the solution of the Croat question. The Serbs were as enthusiastic as the Croats about the possibility of replacing the dictatorial government, and when Macek went to Belgrade in August, 1938, to confer with the Serb opposition leaders, he was welcomed by a crowd of 50,000 people, most of whom were Serb peasants who had come for that purpose. Macek described to the audience the terroristic treatment of his people and asked, "Can you expect men who have suffered like this to fight for the State that oppresses them?" The Serbs cried in response, "No, and we wouldn't either." [7]

The government was alarmed by such harmony. Prince Paul dismissed the heavy-handed Stojadinovic in favor of a less outstandingly compromised figure, Cvetkovic, mayor of Nis, and initiated negotiations with the Croats. In return for the grant of considerable autonomy to Croatia, Macek deserted his Serb allies and entered the cabinet; but disagreement immediately revived. The Croat extremists demanded more territory and more rights for their autonomous region; the Croats peasants wished beneficial reforms which would enable them to govern Croatia for the improvement of their lot. Hotheads made violent speeches against the Serbs and occasionally murdered a Serb official. The Serbs reciprocated. The last attempt before World War II to reconcile the peoples of this state proved a complete failure.

Bulgaria. Within the framework of the existing economy, the diffi-

[7] Seton-Watson, *op. cit.*, p. 236.

culties of nationally homogeneous Bulgaria were mainly political, and party battles were fought with as much ferocity as in any of the Balkan states with populations of mixed nationality. At the beginning of the decade the country was still subject to terrorist domination by the Macedonian society I.M.R.O. Directed from headquarters in the Southwest Petrich department, the members openly shot citizens in the streets of Sofia, stirred up attacks in Greece and Yugoslavia, murdered a deputy in parliament who demanded the eight-hour day in all industries, and in general set their own laws. The king and the government supported the gang, as their counterparts did the Iron Guard in Romania, for these murderers were considered "brave patriots." When their behavior became too repulsive and the existing government proved incapable of coping with the economic crisis, the people in the election of 1931 returned the oppositional parties to power by a large majority. As the new government proved to be no more effective in handling the I.M.R.O. than its predecessors, a group of intellectuals and army officers led by Colonel Velchev revolted in 1934 and established a new dictatorial rule.

The government members were not fascist; they introduced no totalitarian institutions; they were honest patriots determined to clean up the state. They reduced the peasant debt and reorganized the nation's credit system. They abolished trade-unions in favor of nonpolitical associations in accordance with corporative ideals. They proposed to strengthen technical and scientific education, and they encouraged physicians to leave the comforts of urban centers and move into rural communities. They created state monopolies for alcohol, tobacco, and salt, which, however, soon became the objects of traditional graft. Their greatest achievement was that of destroying the I.M.R.O., which succumbed quickly to the use of force. Ordinary citizens could for the first time in sixteen years go about their business in peace.

Unhappy about the loss of authority, King Boris stirred up conflict among the reformers and in 1935 dismissed the government. Next he charged Colonel Velchev with plotting to overthrow the monarchy and had him imprisoned for life. Then, aided by army and police, he ruled as dictator. He banned party strife and prohibited the I.M.R.O. from reviving. In the parliamentary election of 1938, the first in seven years, he required candidates to stand, not as representatives of political parties, but as nonpolitical individuals. Opposition candidates met every possible obstruction of terror and bribery. When one third of the deputies elected were opponents of the government, the king first unseated the Communists and then the group formerly associated with Colonel Velchev. The remainder proved to be docile, and the outbreak of the war found King Boris still dictator. That to some he was "the best Democrat in the Balkans" and to others "a monster of cruelty and perfidy" may indicate the limits of the unity and happiness of his people.

Albania. The pattern of Albanian history in the thirties conforms so nearly to that of the other Balkan states that a separate analysis is not necessary. King Zog ruled arbitrarily. Like other tribesmen, he shot his enemies; but he also introduced a veneer of Western culture. The gravest danger to him, as to the other Balkan rulers, came from outside in the play of international power politics.

Greece. The Greeks were considered with the Serbs as most interested in politics of all Balkan peoples; nevertheless, they succumbed to dictatorship. The issue of republicanism versus monarchism in Greece concerned in the main whether one group of politicians and generals or another should hold power. By 1930 neither showed much interest in reforms which would help the masses. In the thirties almost every year someone led a rebellion. In June, 1935, the promonarchist government exerted sufficient pressure to win a large majority in the parliamentary elections and quickly restored the monarchy. King George II insisted upon an amnesty for all political prisoners and men in exile. He hoped that under his rule the Greeks would forget their old habits and work in political harmony. The parliamentary elections of January, 1936, caused disillusionment: 142 for the republicans, 143 for the monarchists, and 15 for the Communists. The first two groups despised each other and the Communists, but under a parliamentary system the Communists held the balance of power. By coincidence, important leaders in each of the two parties died in 1936, leaving General Joannes Metaxas as the outstanding figure. The general bore party quarrels until August, 1936, when with the king's approval he established a dictatorship which he maintained until his death in 1941.

Metaxas had no special popular appeal. He had been a competent officer, and he continued to be most interested in improving the army, the roads on which the army could march, and the means of communication which it could use. He surrounded himself with certain mediocre persons prone to violence, who shared some of his own devotion to what he understood to be the common good. He allowed himself to be portrayed as a new savior of Greece, who would revive her ancient greatness, but he remained personally modest. His reforms covered many aspects of Greek life—compulsory arbitration to stop strikes, the eight-hour day in industry, a minimum wage for workers, health insurance and health service, and a program of house construction. He reduced the peasants' debts by about one third and spent large sums on defense, roads, and communications. He banned politics from the army and introduced rigorous censorship of the press. In order to abate the national passion for controversy he permitted Sophocles' *Antigone* to be performed only with severe cuts and forbade the secondary schools to teach the Darwinian theory or to read Pericles' *Funeral Oration.*

Metaxas thought that the introduction of a youth organization, a fascist salute and censorship placed him abreast of the times. The results proved otherwise. The circulation of the guided press dropped by 40 per cent, as people refused to read the dull pages. Most teachers continued to repudiate the regime, and labor remained hostile. The laws to introduce minimum wages and other reforms were not executed, as the employers ignored them and threatened to accuse any worker as Communist if he caused trouble. The new system of medical services failed because the government did not provide funds to pay the doctors or to purchase supplies. The workers found that the program of public works caused inflation and a rise in the cost of living. Spies and informers were everywhere; members of the youth organization were encouraged to betray their parents. The rule of law ceased, as political prisoners included not merely Communists but liberals and democrats, and sometimes royalists who disapproved of the extreme measures. An American correspondent estimated in 1942 that at least 80 per cent of the population hated the dictatorship; but the army stood loyally by the king, and the king by Metaxas.

The small states in Eastern Europe could control the course of their own careers to a much lesser extent than could the big countries on either side of them. Even with the most modern and popular form of government, the most efficient economy, and a balanced, well-integrated society, in their exposed geographic position they would have been unable to overcome the dangerous handicaps of small size. Poland could have done most, for she had 30 million people; but she was no more capable of defending herself than were the others. In the twenties, these states had profited from the exhaustion of Russia and Germany, and were temporarily able to pose as sovereign states. In the thirties their margin of security faded with the revived might and imperialistic ambition of their neighbors. Their fate was to be decided by the international relations of the great powers.

Suggestions for Further Reading

The Readings for Chapter 9 should be used for this decade as well. The following titles may also be consulted.

BASCH, ANTONIN. *The Danube Basin and the German Economic Sphere.* See the Readings for Chapter 12. Essential for understanding how Nazi Germany gained control over most of Southeastern Europe before World War II.

GESHKOFF, THEODORE I. *Balkan Union.* New York: Columbia University Press, 1940. Story of the failure of the Balkan countries to help solve their own problems by union.

WISKEMANN, ELISABETH. *Czechs and Germans.* New York: Oxford University Press, 1938. Objective analysis of the Sudeten problem.

Chapter 16 · The U.S.S.R.

STALIN'S ECONOMIC PROGRAM

During the first years of Stalin's rule the Soviet economy, social structure, and government underwent drastic transformation. The greatest took place in the economy, where Stalin had had least experience. He understood power and its uses in politics, and he apparently believed that with the exercise of all the force at his disposal he could execute any policy. His program for the economy entailed the adaptation to its needs of other aspects of Soviet life, until by the close of the thirties the Stalinist system was consolidated. By that time Stalin had dropped much of the original Marxian program and had introduced many forms of capitalism which would serve his own version of communism. Throughout the decade he continued to be the source of all activity; every measure was in the last analysis judged by whether it would support or undermine his dictatorship. The execution of the entire program seemed to depend upon his being able to compel the people to do what he thought was good for them.

Industrialization and the collectivization of agriculture had from the beginning been the Communist objectives; the New Economic Policy (N.E.P.) had signified merely a retreat. By 1926 plans for extensive expansion of industry were under way, and in 1928 the first plan for a five-year period of industrialization was inaugurated, calling for large capital investment. Abruptly in 1929 Stalin demanded an amount for that purpose five times as much as the commissar for finance had proposed, and in June, 1930, he declared, "We are on the eve of our transformation from an agrarian into an industrial country." Simultaneously he began to collectivize agriculture completely. Writing in *Pravda* in November, 1929, he saw new bonds being thereby created between town and country:

"They [the new forms of bonds] signify, first, that besides the old forms of the bond between town and country, whereby industry chiefly satisfied the *personal* requirements of the peasantry (calico, footwear, cloth, etc.), we now need new forms of the bond, whereby industry will satisfy the *productive* requirements of peasant farming (agricultural machinery, tractors, improved seed, fertilizer, etc.)." These would enable agriculture to be reconstructed "on a new technical basis." The expansion of industry (iron and steel, chemical and machinery, he especially mentioned) would create new towns and expand old ones and multiply the demand for food and raw materials. If the old methods of tillage and the old system of ownership in individual peasant farms were used, agriculture could not produce the required amounts.

Hence, the danger of a rift between town and country, between industry and agriculture. Hence, the necessity for increasing, whipping up the tempo of development of agriculture to that of our industry. And so, in order to avoid the danger of a rift, we must begin thoroughly to re-equip agriculture on the basis of modern technique. But in order to re-equip it we must gradually [the next month he was to say speedily] amalgamate the scattered peasant farms into large farms, into collective farms; we must build up agriculture on the basis of collective labor, we must enlarge the collective farms, we must develop the old and new state farms, we must systematically employ the contract system on a mass scale in all the principal branches of agriculture, we must develop the system of machine and tractor stations which help the peasantry to assimilate the new technique and to collectivize labor—in a word, we must gradually transfer the small peasant farms to the basis of large-scale collective production.

The style is characteristically wooden, and scarcely in keeping with the enthusiasm expressed in this materialist's conclusion:

We are advancing full steam ahead, along the path of industrialization—to socialism, leaving behind the age-long "Russian" backwardness. We are becoming a country of metal, a country of automobiles, a country of tractors. And when we have put the U.S.S.R. on an automobile, and the muzhik [peasant] on a tractor, let the esteemed capitalists who boast so loudly of their "civilization," try to overtake us! We shall see which countries may then be "classified" as backward and which as advanced.

Stalin believed that the N.E.P. had carried the Soviet Union toward socialism as far as it could and that henceforth it would constitute a danger. He demanded of the economy superhuman achievements. Two examples will suffice. In 1928 the country had only 20,200 engineers in industry, whereas the Five-Year Plan called for an additional 25,200. In 1928 the Russian output of pig iron amounted to only 3½ million tons; Stalin demanded that in 1932 the output should reach 17 million tons, and he denounced skeptics as "wreckers" and "right-wing opportunists," accusations that dried up comment among persons inclined to keep alive.

The Soviet planned economy used a span of five years as the duration period for each program, with the expectation of shortening this term. The first Five-Year Plan was introduced in 1928, the second in 1933, and the third in 1938. The Politburo issued the directives and gave the final approval; but the plan itself was laid out by the State Economic Planning Commission, called Gosplan, assisted by planning officials at each level of the entire economic hierarchy—a long, detailed process. The plan covered all aspects of the economy. It stated where a new factory should be built, how large it should be, how many workers it should employ, what its costs should be, what prices it should set—all the details connected with running each enterprise.

Since each sector of the economy was state-owned, the personnel were actually state officials and received directives from above. Industry, for example, was organized in hierarchical form. At the bottom was the individual enterprise; those in the same branch of production (iron, machine tools, and so on) were united into a state trust, those into a Glavsk, those into an All-Union People's Commissariat. For certain industries largely situated or catering to the market in one republic (light industry, building materials, textiles, and so on) the latter would have its own commissariat, and a few industries like the Magnitogorsk Metal Works in the Urals were so big that they operated alone as trusts. Although modified in detail from time to time as experience revealed need, the system remained fixed.

The collectivist economy engendered problems peculiar to the fact of state ownership, and enhanced by the possibility and in many instances the certainty that in this country of dogma and dictatorship an economic mistake would be considered treason. In order to escape this danger, the officials in charge of drawing up the plans set minimal norms which they thought almost anyone could achieve. Even so, persons were inclined to shun responsible managerial positions as too full of risk; far too many factors essential for success lay beyond the reach of the person designated as responsible. The uncertainty was enhanced by the government's emphasis upon heavy industry to the neglect of other branches and by the demand for speed. Plant, equipment, and labor were forced to turn out goods immediately without regard for the future. That machinery might be abused and labor exhausted did not matter to administrators in Moscow commanded to produce at once. Under such conditions economic hitches were bound to arise, and each person sought to avoid the blame by insisting upon a written order for every act.

Strength and Weakness

A few illustrations will convey the manner of functioning of the Stalinist economy. Victor Kravchenko occupied a number of medium-high positions in the economy before he sought asylum in the United States (1944) while on a mission to this country. In his memoirs he tells about the order in 1939 to build a steel pipe mill at Stalinsk in Siberia. Placed in charge of the operation, Kravchenko, to the horror of the commissar of ferrous metals, insisted upon inspecting the site. The project had been approved by "the Commissariat, the State Planning Commission (Gosplan), the Metallurgical Project Institute, the War Commissariat, the Central Committee of the Party and the Politburo." The funds had been allocated; the blue prints worked on for months. "Are you in your right mind?" asked the commissar.[1]

[1] Victor Kravchenko, *I Chose Freedom: The Personal and Political Life of a Soviet Official*, 1946, p. 324. By permission of Charles Scribner's Sons and Gerald Dickler.

Kravchenko was finally allowed to inspect the place, and condemned it as completely unsuited. The site was "a huge naked stretch of muddy river front a considerable distance from town, without electric or gas lines, without railroad tracks or a trolley line, without so much as a negotiable road." [2] He discovered that the terrain chosen would not support a heavy metallurgical plant. He gathered evidence and fought for weeks against the decision. A way to save face for everyone was found by exchanging the site for one 160 miles away. Then came the problems of construction.

> From the outset [Kravchenko has written] our efforts were snarled in red tape and blocked by bureaucratic stupidity. I had to accumulate materials and tools and arrange for their transport and storage. Thousands of skilled and unskilled workers had to be mobilized, then provided with homes and elementary care. Under normal conditions such problems would not involve insurmountable difficulties. Under our Soviet system every step required formal decisions by endless bureaus, each of them jealous of its rights and in mortal dread of taking initiative. Repeatedly petty difficulties tied us into knots which no one dared untie without instructions from Moscow. We lived and labored in a jungle of questionnaires, paper forms and reports in seven copies.

His frustrations about housing, transportation, everything may be illustrated by his story about bricks:

> We were in critical need of brick. . . . Hundreds of prisoners marched from their distant camps to toil fourteen hours a day to meet construction demands for this material by various Kemerovo [the name of the town where the plant was being built] administrations. At the same time, however, two large and well-equipped brickyards stood idle. They happened to belong to another commissariat which was "conserving" them for some mythical future purposes. I begged and threatened and sent emissaries to Moscow in an attempt to unfreeze these yards, but bureaucracy triumphed over common sense. The brickyards remained dead throughout the period of my stay in the city.[3]

Reports like those of Kravchenko, which could be multiplied many times by those of other eyewitnesses, must be balanced by others showing accomplishments. The American John Scott, who worked in the Soviet Union during this period, has described his experience as follows: "In Magnitogorsk I was precipitated into a battle. I was deployed on the iron and steel front. Tens of thousands of people were enduring the most intense hardships in order to build blast furnaces, and many of them did it willingly, with boundless enthusiasm, which infected me from the day of my arrival." And he concluded, "I would wager that Russia's battle of ferrous metallurgy alone involved more casualties than the battle of the Marne." [4] Alexander Barmine, like Kravchenko a high economic official before he escaped abroad in 1937, has written a story which further explains why things were completed. Coke furnaces for Kuznetsk were ordered from a

[2] *Ibid.*, p. 325. [3] *Ibid.*, p. 328.
[4] John Scott, *Behind the Urals* (Boston: Houghton Mifflin Company, 1942), p. 9.

French company and delivery in nine months was asked. The director of the French company protested.

> But I've just come back from Kuznetsk. . . . The place is a trackless desert. What is the point of taking delivery of stuff which you can't possibly use until the district has been opened up? And that won't happen for two years at least!
>
> . . . . .
>
> Actually Stalin's ruthless determination had thrown into Kuznetsk gangs composed of old Bolsheviks, Young Communists, workers' shock brigades, engineers fired by enthusiasm or terrified by threats, convicts condemned to forced labor, and expropriated kulaks. These men lived in huts and ate black bread and stale cabbage. But the factory was ready in a year.[5]

Problem of Incentives

The Communists soon learned that to increase production they had to find a substitute appropriate to communism for the free market as a means of creating individual incentives and as a test of efficiency of operation. The state could decide how much to produce, for what purpose, where, and by whom; but it could not depend solely upon enthusiasm on the one hand and coercion on the other to develop the new complex economy. The Communists placed secret agents all through the economy; but they also built into institutions a considerable number of means which have proved to be indispensable in every advanced economy, whether Communist or bourgeois capitalistic. The most important of these were personal responsibility, personal advantage, competition, price, and profit. Each deserves some discussion.

It has been historically true that the character of the government at the top is imparted to the heads of agencies down the line. Thus, a feudal king ruled over feudal lords; an absolute monarch allowed his nobles to be little absolute monarchs in their respective districts; representative government is practiced at the national, state, and local levels. In the Communist organization, Stalin found it necessary to loosen his personal reins somewhat in order to expand production. The tendency under a dictatorship to refer all decisions to the top was slowing down achievement. As dictator he began to increase the authority and the responsibility, not of everyone below him, for such an act would have been too dangerous to him, but of economic officials in particular. The planners and bureaucratic administrators remained under control; the managers in charge of the actual day-to-day production were given some power of decision. They could not bargain for supplies, decide on output, set prices, and determine investments or the size of plant. They were permitted, however, to borrow money from the state bank for certain purposes of aiding production approved by the bureaucracy. They could retain a sum out of profits to reinvest under higher

[5] Alexander Barmine, *One Who Survived* (New York: G. P. Putnam's Sons, 1945), p. 178.

approval in the plant. They were allowed to keep a further sum out of profits with which to reward subordinates, especially workers, for increasing production, to aid in training programs, and to improve creches, clubs, dining rooms, and other recreational and social facilities.

Of particular importance was the fact that in the thirties by often uniting in their persons the power of economic official and that of party official, the managers overcame some of the mistrust and jealousy previously shown between the holders of the two offices. They were able to keep in line their employees and workers, who might have appealed to the party representative against the manager. The other source of conflict, that between the managers and the government officials, was of much less importance. The officials in the three organizations—the government strictly speaking, the party, and the economic administration—frequently settled their affairs on a private basis by local cooperation and mutual assistance, and the managers of various lines of production made deals among themselves outside channels as the only way to accomplish the goals set by the Five-Year Plan. Extralegal arrangements could be dangerous; but they enabled individuals successful in their use to gain a reputation for achievement and to rise in the hierarchy.

In the drive for increased production personal ambition was appealed to in the Soviet Union as in a free capitalistic country, and rewards were somewhat the same—power, fame, a sense of public service—and difference in material compensation according to achievement and position. The old communist idea of equal compensation for everyone irrespective of the type of work was soon denounced as "petty-bourgeois capitalistic." In this country of scarcity, housing, servants, rations, an automobile, and other items were furnished according to one's position as stimulants to effort. Competition entered the economy not in the capitalistic sense of bidding for labor, materials, and market by way of price, but in that defined by the English Socialists Sidney and Beatrice Webb as the use of "the sporting instinct to augment the wealth of the nation." Factories vied with each other in output. Accelerated utilization of men and machines was encouraged by propaganda, prizes, and the like. The winner in a prominent contest might achieve All-Union fame. The competition might also wear out the machines by overuse and exhaust the personnel, causing the factory to produce below normal or not at all the next year; but in the meantime production had been, to use a favorite Soviet word, maximized.

Price, Profit, and Investment

We have already noted that the Communists soon learned about the advantage of money as a medium of exchange. With the Five-Year Plans they likewise restored the concepts of price and profit in terms of money. They discovered that communism did not preclude the necessity of some one's earning more than he spent and of using the price scale as a means for gauging whether or not an enterprise was making a profit. They incorporated the profit motive into the planned economy in the following way. They fixed the prices of articles and the costs of production; thereby every enterprise was set a standard by which to judge the efficiency of its work, and the government could raise these standards from year to year according to plan. A further question, however, was, How could one force an enterprise to improve upon the official standard set for it and thereby show in practice what the others could and should be doing? The answer was found in the offer of incentives to the enterprise to turn out goods at a cost below that set by the government. It was forbidden to lower the quality of the article, and the wage scale was set; it therefore had to reduce costs and increase profits by improving the efficiency of production, by utilizing to the fullest extent possible the machines, materials, and personnel available. The managers were allowed to keep a percentage of the extra profit gained and to divide it among the employees and workers. With these profits left as a reward at its disposal the industry could improve the housing of its workers, introduce facilities for rest and recreation, pay for vacation trips, and grant bonuses.

The government obtained the funds for payment of administrative expenses and for capital investment primarily from two sources. Sixty per cent came from the turnover tax, levied on each item of consumption and to a much less extent upon goods of heavy industry at the point of production. Another 10 per cent derived from a tax on profits, and the remaining 30 per cent from various sources, such as enterprises directly managed by the state outside the economic administration. The turnover tax had first importance not merely because of the amount of revenue it produced but because it gave the government an efficient means for guiding the distribution of goods. If a commodity were scarce and the government wished to restrict sales, it could ration the article, but by increasing the turnover tax it could price the article out of the mass market. The Politburo was able to raise or lower the standard of living by way of this tax and force the people to supply a greater or a lesser amount of its income for capital investment.

ROLE OF WORKERS AND TRADE-UNIONS

Since the revolution had introduced the dictatorship of the proletariat, the workers might have expected to gain all their wishes and become the dominant class. Within a short time they discovered that they, with every other class, suffered from the destruction caused by the revolution and civil war, and within a decade they learned the dictatorship of the proletariat meant that of the Communist party.

The revolutionary government had introduced the standard labor reforms of Western industrial society with some additions—the eight-hour day, protection of women and children, annual holiday, and social security in abundance. Then it had had no funds and no agencies for implementing them, and the workers, growing hungry on the diet of civil war, had left the cities in masses and returned to their relatives in the villages. The NEP had brought them back, with others, and made the role of trade-unions a real issue. Workers and employees were organized into unions; but since the proletariat now ruled and capitalists were all destroyed and class conflict had ended or would soon end, were trade-unions necessary?

The question received many answers. Trotsky had advocated the subjection of labor to military discipline. Lenin had declared that

> with respect to socialized factories, trade-unions have therefore the absolute duty to defend the interests of the workers. As far as possible they must help to raise the workers' material living conditions. To achieve this, the unions have to correct systematically errors and exaggerations committed by organs of economic administration and resulting from bureaucratic distortion in the State apparatus.

The All-Russian Congress of Trade Unions meeting in 1918 had declared that trade-unions should be "fully developed" and become "organs of the socialist state." The Congress expected "all people employed in any industry" to do their duty toward the state by becoming trade-unionists. It wished the unions to be the essential organs of the state for industry and also to be in a position to defend the interests of the workers. The congress of the next year soft-pedaled the latter point and strongly emphasized the former. ". . . the Trade Unions ought in the end actually to concentrate in their hand all the administration of the entire national economy," it declared.

During the next decade the unions learned that difficulties over pay and conditions of work could arise when industry was owned by the state and was directed by the dictatorship of the proletariat, and that strikes were still useful. In December, 1928, Mikhail Tomsky, in his last speech as head of the trade-unions, was still arguing like a trade-unionist in any bourgeois-capitalist society. He wanted freedom of discussion and negotiation between labor and management, irrespective of whether management was communistic.

Stalin destroyed all traditional trade-union ideas. He had the party congress reject "with determination such 'freedom' of criticism which the right elements demand in order to defend their anti-Leninist political line." Together with everything else, labor was subjected to intense discipline, and trade-unions became a major instrument, not for protecting the interests of the workers, but for driving them to increased industrialization. Under the system of Five-Year Plans Stalin would not tolerate the uncertainty of negotiating with trade-unions over working conditions, wage scales, and the total amount of the payroll. These matters were settled in the plans themselves. The trade-unions helped to draw up the plans, but the Politburo had the decisive voice. Strikes were not legally forbidden, but workers found them too dangerous for use. The local unions could negotiate with management about minor matters of local interpretation of the plan—classification of jobs, plant inequalities, incentive rates, and setting daily quotas of production. In the main, unions were allotted new duties. They administered social insurance, handled recreational activity, organized lectures on Soviet policy, attended to safety and hygiene inspection, looked after social welfare, and participated in election campaigns. They were expected to maintain discipline among the workers by combatting idleness and absenteeism, organizing "socialist competition," and speeding up work.

When, as inducements to increased output, the government introduced the piece wage instead of the time wage and varied wages according to the quality of the work, the trade-unions propagandized for the new measures and joined the government in condemning wage equalization as "counterrevolutionary." "Socialist emulation," an elegant term for competition among workers over size of output, became the official slogan and Stakhanovism, named after the miner Stakhanov, who set the highest record for coal production in one day, was popularized to arouse trade-unionists to greater productivity. "On par with the propaganda of ideas, which should influence the mind of the toiling masses, and with repressive measures, used against deliberate idlers, drones, and disorganizers," said the Sixteenth Congress of the Communist party in 1929, "emulation is the most powerful means toward raising productivity of labor."

The definition of the categories "deliberate idlers, drones, and disorganizers" was as diverse as Stalin's array of "repressive measures." By 1938 the government, preparing for possible outbreak of international war, began to restrict freedom of movement of workers, set severe penalties against idling and absenteeism, lengthened the hours of work, and used social insurance as means of forcing the workers to stay on the job. For violation of the laws the workers were subject to loss of employment, a severe penalty in a country where the state was the sole employer, or to "correctional labor," the Communist term for imprisonment.

COLLECTIVIZATION OF AGRICULTURE

The greatest difficulty which the Communists had to meet concerned agriculture, upon which in 1926, 82 per cent of the population depended for a living. Theoretically nationalized during the revolution but immediately divided among the peasants in individual holdings, the land during the twenties had produced insufficient food to meet requirements. With population growing rapidly and moving to the towns to implement the Five-Year Plan, the government sought a way to augment the food supply and at the same time to bring industry and agriculture into social and political harmony. Collective ownership and the prospect of communism in industry could survive only if agriculture were similarly reformed. The individual peasant holdings, Lenin had said, were strongholds of bourgeois capitalism which had to be liquidated. The production of steel or cloth, items of uniform size and quality made by a machine, could be collectivized; the workers were disciplined by the machine process and could be controlled. Growing things seemed to require individual attention; thus the imposition of communism on the farms would be more difficult. The Marxians had always studied industrial economy and had been vague about agriculture. Peasant agriculture could be forcibly destroyed, but what should take its place?

Experience in the twenties had shown that the poor and middle peasants with small holdings produced least grain for the market, that the kulaks did almost twice as well, and that the few state and collective farms marketed almost one-half of their grain. In 1929 Stalin inaugurated a campaign of speedy collectivization. He enticed the small and middle peasants into collective farms with promises of generous state aid in seed, machinery, and technical advice but demanded the elimination of the kulak as "a sworn enemy of the collective farm movement." In the villages Stalin stirred up civil war by inciting the poor peasants against the kulaks, and he sent party shock troops, among them 25,000 reliable industrial workers, into the countryside to lead the campaign.

The speed-up of collectivization began early in 1930. On February 20, 1930, there were 59,400 collective farms with 4,400,000 families. Six weeks later the official report gave the number as 110,200 with 14,300,000, or 55 per cent of all peasant families. The term "kulak" was stretched to include anyone rich or poor who was unwilling to join a collective farm. A few peasants liked the idea, but many acquiesced under threat of force and in despair immediately began to slaughter their livestock. Many refused, and men, women and children were liquidated by machine-gun fire. Even Stalin became alarmed over the rebellious reaction of the peasants. He feared that in addition to slaughtering their livestock they would refuse to sow the spring crop and starve Communists as well as themselves. In March 2, 1930, he issued a statement, "Dizzy with Success," blaming "our enemies" for the "distortions" of orders, and allowed the peasants to withdraw from the collective farms.

After Stalin's speech accusing others for something he had done but permitting the peasants to leave, the number of collective farms dropped to 82,300 with 5,800,000 households. The retreat did not mean the relinquishment of the objective. The government slowed the tempo and applied somewhat subtler means. It placed emphasis upon preferential taxation, gave aid in the form of machinery, seeds, and credit, and increased the burdens on the individual peasants outside the collectives. In 1936 the 245,700 collective farms included almost 90 per cent of the peasant families and practically all the land they cultivated. As early as March, 1931, the

Congress of the Soviets had declared, "by that policy [collectivization] we have conquered hunger."

The impact of the revolution in agriculture from above (the expression used by the Communists) may be estimated in material terms, in numbers of human lives, and in an incident from the life of Stalin himself. During the period of coercion the peasants killed one half of the horses (18 million of 34 million), 45 per cent of the cattle, and two thirds of all sheep and goats. They left large areas untilled, and in 1931–1933 famine settled over the land, including the rich agricultural region of the Ukraine. Stalin had said that the tractor must replace the horse, but the country possessed only 7,000 tractors, and with great exertion in 1929 obtained 30,000 more, few for so vast a country. Five million kulak families were deported to Siberia and the Far North, of whom probably one fourth died. By the middle of 1935 the Soviet Union had only 20,100,000 peasant households; in 1929 it had had 25,800,000.

Stalin's own position was shaken. He became tense, and apparently for the only time in his career he almost lost his nerve. One evening in November, 1932, at a small party where several members of the Politburo were gathered, Stalin's wife denounced the effects of the terror upon the country. When Stalin turned abusively against her she committed suicide. It was at this time that Stalin offered his resignation to the members of the Politburo. After an embarrassed silence one of Stalin's faithful supporters, Molotov, said, "Stop it, stop it. You have got the party's confidence." Stalin remained.

The victory of collectivization came at the cost of concessions to the peasantry. The communist ideal of "factories in the field" was not realized; agriculture was not organized like industry, and the peasants did not become the equivalent in agriculture of factory workers. The occupations were too dissimilar for the agricultural workers to acquire common status and common character. As the state-owned farm, employing hired labor, had not succeeded, the government in the thirties emphasized the artel, or cooperative type of kolkhoz (the Russian term for collective farm). The number of peasant families in one varied, but about 75 was average and they worked about 1,000 sown acres. According to the Model Statute of 1935 a peasant transferred to the kolkhoz ownership of items like seeds, working livestock, ploughs, and other major implements and farm buildings; he retained the possession of a cow, two calves, a pig or two with sucklings, a maximum of ten sheep or goats, small implements, rabbits, bees, and the like, and a house and small outbuildings, and he was permitted to cultivate individually about two acres of land or less.

The peasant was required to work so many days a year on the kolkhoz—the number varied from thirty to several hundred—and a system of weighting the kind and the efficiency of the work done was set up. In some lines, like pure manual labor, a day's work counted as the equivalent of only one half a day on a common scale of measurement, whereas running a tractor during the same length of time would equal two days' work. At the end of the year the number of such workdays was counted, and the individual received a proportionate share of the profits of the kolkhoz. Thereby the factory system of differential wages was applied to agriculture. In the time not required for work on the collective farm the peasant could cultivate his own small plot. This piece of ground became so attractive that the peasant tended to expand it at the expense of the collective land and to devote to it most of his attention. The government had to watch carefully to protect the common land and to obtain its share of the peasant's time.

The difference in working conditions on the kolkhoz and on one's own plot was considerable. The kolkhoz depended upon the implements of the Farm Tractor Stations established in the countryside with the necessary machines for serving a number of collective farms. The peasants then did the rest of the work. They were organized in brigades, each with a leader, and assigned a special task or a particular piece of land as their responsibility for from one to three years. Like factory workers, the brigades were stirred to compete and were paid bonuses for special achievements. Major decisions for a collective farm were made by the government in the All-Union economic plan—how much acreage to plant and in what crops, what minimum amounts to produce, how much of each crop to deliver to the state at what prices, how much taxes to pay, how much of the crops to keep for the farm and sell on the free market. Not much was left to the peasant members except to carry out orders, and the Tractor Stations were used for the additional purpose of checking on loyalty and efficiency. When the peasant came to his tiny plot of land, his cow, his bees, his hand tools, he felt once more like a peasant, and he lavished care upon them. On the produce from this endeavor he paid a stiff tax and turned over a fixed amount in kind to the state; but he was allowed to sell the rest in the local free market, where prices were several times as high as those set on the goods he delivered to the government.

One student of the subject has argued that the private plots were tolerated because the collective farms did not provide enough food for the townspeople. The big farms produced cotton, grain, sugar, flax, and similar raw materials, but the peasant plots supplied much of the fruit, vegetables, poultry, dairy products, and the other items requiring intensive care. In 1938 these private plots amounted to less than one per cent of the total cultivated area, but they produced a quantity of food out of all proportion to their surface expanse. The Communists profited from putting to work in agriculture a precarious remnant of private enterprise. They were thereby able to reduce the compensation to the peasant for work on the kolkhoz and in doing so press him to satisfy personal needs from the small plot. In fixing the amount which the peasant had to produce on his plot and which he and the other peasants had to provide from the kolkhoz, the government achieved two important objectives: first, it set a standard of performance for each, just as in industry, and prevented the economy from degenerating into an exchange of alibis; and, second, it made food deliveries independent of the actual crop yield each year and assured the supply of enough food for the urban population. At any time the government could further curb the peasant's income by raising the price of the goods he bought, increasing his taxes, and lowering the price of the articles he had to sell. It could dangle profit incentives before his nose to induce him to extra work and nonetheless be sure that he would not become a small capitalist.

The Communists continued to have difficulty with the peasantry after agriculture had by the middle of the thirties received a somewhat stable organization. Shortage of trained personnel retarded essential education of the peasants and improvement of agricultural methods. According to Communist slogans, the collective farm was democratically run, in that all peasants discussed policies, decided issues, and elected the farm officials. Communist democracy, however, also meant the dictatorship of the working class and was considered consistent with the statement that "where there is no Bolshevik leadership, there is no *kolkhoz* democracy, since *kolkhoz* democracy in its essence is a method of Bolshevik leadership in the *kolkhozy*." In practice the chairman of the collective farm and the other officials were usually not elected but appointed from above. The party disapproved this method from time to time, but, as Stalin said in 1933, "If we do not hold the leadership in one or more *kolkhozy*, that means that anti-Soviet elements will lead them." The chairmen tended to decide all important questions without consulting his managing board and the general assembly of the peasants.

The Communists were caught in a dilemma: If they permitted the peasants to choose the farm officials, they might soon face the breakdown of the collective farms; if they chose officials from outside, the peasants might not be cooperative and production would decline. The high percentage of turnover of chairmen each year—as late as 1947 only 28 per cent of them had been in their position for more than three years—indicated the difficulty in obtaining the service of persons who could make the system efficient. Instead of criticizing collectivism, the Communists blamed the incompetence of personnel and kept trying new individuals in the job. The whole program—mechanizing agriculture in large farms when machinery, oil, and gasoline and electric power were insufficient, collectivizing agriculture when the peasants were eager for private property, increasing output at a speed appropriate to industry when technical personnel were lacking to train and guide the peasants in modern methods—has been described by a student of the subject as "a piece of prodigious insanity." [6]

[6] I. Deutscher, *Stalin: A Political Biography* (New York: Oxford University Press, 1949), p. 326.

The peasants apparently thought so too. In industry the Communists were able to produce quick results, for the machine-process enabled goods to be produced in mass quantities as soon as one had machines and a few technicians. In agriculture, production depended upon nature, and technical knowledge would have had to be decentralized and diffused almost as widely as the peasants themselves. A factory worker could be quickly trained to run a machine which some expert had built; a peasant had to know how to use not one but a number of machines, to choose suitable fertilizers, to select the best seed and breeds, and to apply this knowledge.

A discussion of the economic organization under communism should include the subject of forced labor. The secret police was the largest employer in the country, particularly after the wholesale imprisonment of kulaks. The government acquired an annual crop of persons suspected of opposition to the regime and condemned these enemies in secret to help build the economy. The exact number of forced laborers is unknown; it has been estimated variously from 6 million to 18 million. The prisoners were found all over the Soviet Union, working on construction, in factories, in forests, at any place where masses were needed. Sometimes they were well treated, sometimes harshly. Most were kept in concentration camps, but some of those exiled in Siberia or elsewhere were permitted to live there in freedom. John D. Littlepage, an American mining engineer, has stated about his experience in the Soviet Union from 1928 to 1937:

> As a matter of fact, there is not a great deal of difference so far as I could observe, between the treatment accorded to those in free exile and those who are presumably entirely free. From the American viewpoint, all Soviet citizens are treated very much like prisoners on parole, especially since the old Tsarist passport system was revived in 1932. Every citizen must have a passport and register it with the police at regular intervals; he must show his "documents" whenever he turns around. He has to get special permission to travel from one part of the country to another, and register with the police wherever he goes.[7]

DIMENSIONS OF THE ECONOMIC ACHIEVEMENT

In considering the economic achievement of the Soviet Union before World War II, one must keep in mind the fact that the country had lagged at least a half century behind Western industrial countries and that it started with an economy ruined by war and revolution. Comparison with the United States of the years immediately after the Civil War would be more appropriate than with contemporary America. Of the decades between the two world wars that of the thirties alone witnessed a deliberate, planned economic revival on a large scale. If one takes into account the short time, the lack of technical facilities and of skilled man power, the

[7] John D. Littlepage, *In Search of Soviet Gold* (New York: Harcourt, Brace & Company, Inc., 1938), pp. 140-141.

Soviet achievement becomes remarkable. As great, however, was the waste of human life and materials.

The results of the effort in the thirties may best be summarized with the aid of statistics. The national income of the Soviet Union grew between 1928 and 1937 at the average rate of 6.5 to 7 per cent a year, and industrial production increased at the average rate of nearly 16 per cent a year. The rate of net investment was 12 to 15 per cent; that of the United States was 6 to 11 per cent. In 1923–1928 agriculture received almost 60 per cent of the total investment, whereas in the period 1933–1938 it received 19 per cent, industry 40 per cent, and transportation about 16 per cent. The figures for the United States (1933–1938) were—industry 25.5 per cent, agriculture 7 per cent, and transportation 17.3 per cent. The fixed capital in 1938 among various branches of Soviet industry had increased above that of 1928 by the following amounts (the figures are far too large, but they give fairly accurate proportions):

	PER CENT
All large scale industry	565
Producers' goods industries	758
Consumers' goods industries	295
Chemicals industry	1003
Ferrous metallurgy	772
Nonferrous metallurgy	1903
Metalworking industries	796
Food industries	398
Textile and apparel industries	197

SOURCE: Norman M. Kaplan, "Capital Formation and Allocation," in Abram Bergson, ed., *Soviet Economic Growth* (Evanston, Ill.: Row, Peterson & Company, 1953), note on pp. 83-84.

From these figures three points should be noted: first, the emphasis placed upon large-scale industry; second, the even greater concentration of effort upon heavy industry, including the chemicals industry; and third, the relatively slight attention paid to the production of consumers' goods.

The Soviet Union thus reversed the normal course of industrial development in a free economy; it built the producers' goods first and let the consumers suffer. It could do so since it was a dictatorship. In comparison with industry, agriculture played a small part; but it received almost three times the investment capital given agriculture in the United States, whereas industry obtained only about 15 per cent more. The high percentages in both industry and agriculture offer evidence of the backwardness of the Soviet economy.

In terms of output and of increased productivity the results in industry were equally impressive. A comparison of the average annual rates of increase of output of selected commodities in the U.S.S.R. and the United States in percentages gives the following figures:

	COAL	PIG IRON	STEEL	ROLLED STEEL	CRUDE PETRO-LEUM	CEMENT	COPPER	ELECTRIC POWER
U.S.S.R. 1932–1937	14.6	18.7	24.5	25.3	5.9	9.4	16.7	21.9
U.S.A. 1922–1929	7.9	6.6	6.8	6.5	8.7	5.5	11.2	9.4

SOURCE: Bergson, *Soviet Economic Growth*, p. 76.

That the two dates used are not identical does not matter, since we are concerned with prewar capabilities and the United States production was higher in the twenties than in the early thirties. Apart from crude petroleum, production in the Soviet Union was growing at a rate from one and one-half to almost four times that in the United States. Economists have explained the increase in the national production on primarily two grounds: first, the shift of 25 million workers from agriculture with its low output to industry with high output; and second, the borrowing of technological knowledge from advanced industrial countries. Since this borrowing on a large scale could occur only once, the rate of growth would, the economists argue, in time have to slow down.

If labor productivity is used as a gauge of efficiency, the Soviet Union worker ranked in 1938 far behind his counterpart in the United States. An American scholar has estimated that in over-all terms a Soviet industrial worker was by the outbreak of World War II about 40 per cent as productive as an American worker. Being relatively rich in man power and short of capital, the Soviet Union utilized men instead of adding and constantly improving machines. It had not yet acquired a tradition of skilled craftsmanship in engineering. The test came, not so much in labor productivity, for there the use of more labor and less capital might have been the most economical policy, but in actual production. Was its production increasing? Again the answer is affirmative. If one uses the year 1927–1928 as a base of 100, the index of industrial production rose to 172 in 1932, to 371 in 1937, and to 430 in 1940. In 1940 the country produced 166 million tons of coal and lignite (the figures in 1938 for Germany, including lignite, were 142 million tons; for the United States, 358 million tons), 48.3 billion kilowatt-hours of electricity (in 1938 Germany had 48 billion and the United States 113.8 billion), and 18.3 million tons of crude steel (in 1938 Germany had 19.6 million tons and the United States 28.8 million). In considering the figures one should remember that since many of the Soviet industries were new any production meant a vast increase in the percentage of output. Even so, the Soviets were expanding their industries at a rate which in World War II was to help them withstand the attack of Germany, the greatest industrial power in Europe.

Agriculture

That agriculture would not fare as well as industry may be inferred from the fact already noted that it received less than one half as much capital for investment. By the end of the thirties the country still had less draught power in agriculture than in 1928. The peasants' slaughter of horses had not been compensated by the addition of tractors. The traditional method of increasing output in Russia had been to till more land, and the Communists continued that policy. They sought to make each region as self-sufficient in food as possible, and, as industry expanded into new areas, the cultivation of bulk foods like potatoes, grain, and vegetables was also introduced there even on marginal land. The strain on the inadequate system of transportation was thus reduced, but cost of production grew while yield declined.

Notwithstanding her enormous size, the Soviet Union did not have much more land under cultivation than the United States (373 million acres as compared with 342 million); when differences in quality are allowed for, it possessed only 70 per cent as much standard land as the United States, with no soil like that in Illinois or Iowa. Its valuable agricultural land amounted in 1940 to only one eighth of the total surface; much of the rest was desert, semiarid, or frozen tundra. The increase in acreage meant expensive cultivation of land of lower quality. The expansion of agricultural output therefore depended mainly upon improving the methods of utilizing present acreage, and the collectivization of the peasants did not in this decade achieve the expected results. Average crop yields per acre showed small increase. Wheat, for example, produced about 12 bushels to the acre, a sum to be compared with that of 13.8 for the United States and 40 for Denmark and the Netherlands.

The output of animal products in 1940 remained below that of 1928, whereas that of grain had increased between 1928 and 1938 from 73.1 million tons to 85 million tons (14 per cent) and potatoes from 42.5 million tons to 60 million (30 per cent). When one recalls the magnitude of the increase in industrial production, one must conclude that the radical revolution in agriculture had not produced results at all commensurate with the effort. In 1940 agriculture remained both a social and an economic problem. If Stalin had been religious, he might have quoted Czar Alexander I, who said, "The peasants, our loyal people, will be recompensed by God."

Population Changes

The economic transformation in the decade before World War II was associated with changes in the size of the population and in its occupational and geographic distribution. Russians seemed on the march. The population grew from 147 million in 1926 to 170,500,000 in 1939. In 1926, 18 per cent of the labor force was engaged in nonagricultural occupations and 82 per cent in agriculture. In 1939 the former figure had risen to 33.4 per cent, and the latter had declined to 53 per cent. The urban population grew by 112 per cent, from 26.3 million in 1926 to 55.9 million in 1939. In 1926 only 17.9 per cent of the people lived in urban centers, fewer than had lived in towns of 2,500 or less in the United States in 1860. By 1939, the percentage had reached 32.8, less than that for the United States in 1890. About 23 million people, or one eighth of the population, moved during these years from rural to urban centers, a mass migration with few if any parallels. Most of the urban increase occurred in the European area of the U.S.S.R.; but 6.5 million went to cities in Siberia and about a million to those in the Transcaucasus and Dagestan, Kazakhstan, and Central Asia. Most of the loss of rural population occurred in the European part.

The heartland of the Soviet Union lay in a triangle with irregular sides drawn between Leningrad, Odessa, and Irkutsh. This area contained most of the cities, the population, the agricultural land, the natural resources, and the system of transportation. Within it were five relatively small concentrations of industry and people: Leningrad; the Moscow-Iaroslavl-Gorkii triangle; the eastern Ukraine; the Urals; and Omsk, Novosibirsk and Kemerovo Oblasts in Western Siberia. Transportation consisted mainly of a shuttle among these regions. They were far apart, however, for distances are continental in the Soviet Union, and the demands of developing transportation facilities were so great as to require a high rate of investment.

The changes in the economy introduced by the Five-Year Plans made transportation more important than ever before. Forty per cent of the grain was marketed in 1938, compared with 26 per cent prior to the revolution; and, with machine cultivation, agriculture depended upon bulky commodities like implements, oil, and fuel, and needed artificial fertilizer. The townspeople required food and raw materials to be brought to them, and the natural resources like coal, mostly located far from the place of use, had to be transported often a thousand miles to their destination. Since coal was burned as fuel in transportation, for these long hauls one third or more of the load was consumed in shipping. River transport increased, but it was limited by two factors: the rivers froze in winter, and most of them flowed in the wrong direction for commercial advantage. The Soviet Union had to depend largely upon railroads, and a major problem became that of reducing the requirements. One way was to make a region as self-sufficient as possible; another, to reduce passenger traffic to a minimum; and a third was exemplified by the Kuzbas, Karaganda, Magnitogorsk combination, where steel mills were built at each terminal, and coal was hauled a thousand miles one way to iron ore, and iron ore the other way to coal. Although the transportation system did not keep pace with all needs, it served industrial expansion and the shift in population.

A Swedish room. Scandinavians have mastered the art of living inexpensively and in good taste. —Design by Carl Malmsten. Photo courtesy of The American-Swedish News Exchange, Inc.

In England, housing developments were designed for families of low income. —Wide World Photos.

During the Paris strikes, this lifesaver on the Seine bore the sign: "The crew is on strike. Refrain from throwing yourself in the water." —Wide World Photos.

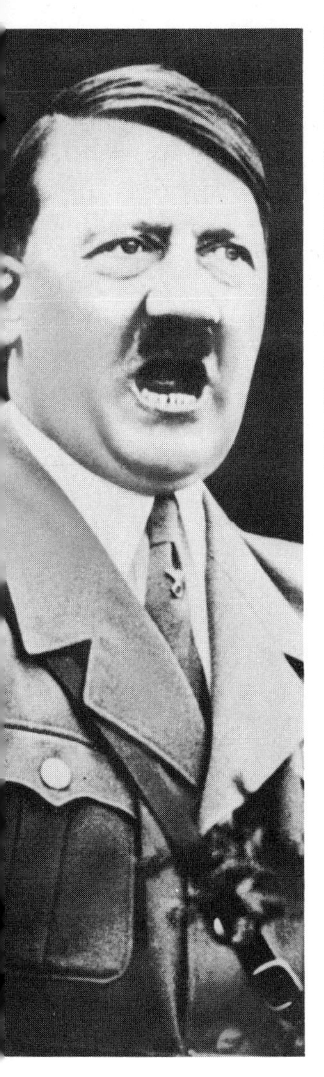

Adolf Hitler: Germany's answer to improvements in living. His hatred fed anti-Semitism. —Brown Bros. photo.

An everyday occurrence: an optician's shop in this German town has been smeared with a swastika and the word *Jude* (Jew). —Brown Bros. photo.

Italian boys of school age, elaborately equipped for their training in gas warfare. —Underwood & Underwood photo.

Abyssinian warriors in the Italo-Ethiopian War, simply equipped and garbed. —Photo from The National Archives.

Christmas in the Soviet Union, 1937. The poster behind a display counter laden with ornaments portrays Stalin as a kind Santa Claus. –Sovfoto.

Premier Joannes Metaxas of Greece, King Alexander of Yugoslavia, Marshal Josef Pilsudski of Poland: three strong men from small countries upon whom the times imposed crucial roles. —Wide World Photos.

Primitive means of transportation and grain milling continue in Greece even in the middle of the twentieth century. —Photo by Peter Buckley.

Mussolini, Hitler, and Chamberlain (Schmidt, third from left, is an interpreter) agree at Munich to the partition of Czechoslovakia, 1938. Daladier, who was also present, is not shown. —Brown Bros. photo.

How to impress a Communist civilian. Field Marshal Keitel and Minister of Foreign Affairs Ribbentrop welcome Soviet Foreign Minister Molotov in Berlin, November, 1940. —U.S. Army photo.

PABLO PICASSO, mural painted in memory of the destruction of *Guernica*, 1937.
—Collection, the artist; courtesy The Museum of Modern Art, New York.

GOVERNMENT UNDER STALIN

During the economic transformation the government remained essentially unchanged. Stalin exercised more authority than any of his predecessors, and the Politburo was now filled with his henchmen, tough, ruthless, practical administrators, unintellectual, entirely reared in the Soviet Union and ignorant of the rest of the world, a different type from the revolutionaries of the world who had worked with Lenin. Stalin tightened control over the Communist party by postponing party congresses (one was held in 1934, the next in 1939, although they were supposed to convene every three years), and by selecting leaders down the line, not by election, but by co-optation and appointment from above. He changed the communist theory on one essential point: he postponed the time when the state would "wither away" until the whole world had become Communist, that is, until the Greek calends. He and his followers stressed the "vocation of leadership." "He who wants to lead a movement and at the same time keep in touch with the vast masses," Stalin said in 1930, "must wage a fight on two fronts—against those who lag behind and against those who rush on ahead. Our Party is strong and invincible because, while leading the movement, it knows how to maintain and multiply its contacts with the vast masses of the workers and peasants."

In these words Stalin described his approach fairly well. When "the vast masses," for example, the peasantry, opposed his policy, he ruled by dictatorship, and the country suffered from the usual evils associated with the excessive concentration of authority in the hands of a few persons—aversion to making decisions by anyone under them, reference of important and unimportant matters to the top, and bottlenecks and delay. Matters which reached the attention of these few men were despatched; many others tended to be postponed and buried under red tape.

Constitution of 1936

The introduction of the constitution of 1936 did not change the system of government in any important respect. Called by the Communists the "Stalin constitution" and also "the most democratic in the world," it was drafted by a commission headed by Stalin and including Nikolai Bukharin, Karl Radek, and Grigori Sokolnikov and their future prosecutor in the great trials of 1936–1938, Andrei Vishinsky. On a superficial reading the document seemed to live up to its official reputation—a free, popular, responsible government of two houses, the Council of the Union and the Council of Nationalities, and a Council of Peoples' Commissars; all the rights of the individual which any citizen could wish, and so on.

Three articles, however, revealed the source of power. Article 4 stated:

> The economic basis of the U.S.S.R. is formed by the socialist system of economy and the socialist ownership of implements and means of production, which have been firmly established as a result of the liquidation of the capitalistic system of economy, the abolition of private ownership of implements and means of production, and the destruction of the exploitation of man by man.

By this and other articles along the same line the constitution sanctioned the destruction of economic freedom and of all classes in society except the workers and the peasants. Articles 125 and 126 might have been almost disarming in their consideration for personal freedom. The former stated:

> In accordance with the interests of the toilers and in the object of strengthening the socialist system, the citizens of the U.S.S.R. are guaranteed by law: (a) freedom of speech, (b) freedom of the press, (c) freedom of assemblies and meetings, (d) freedom of street processions and demonstrations. These rights of citizens are secured by placing at the disposal of toilers and their organizations printing presses, supplies of paper, public buildings, streets, means of communication, and other material conditions necessary for their exercise.

The skeptical reader may wish to know whether these freedoms would have been permitted if their exercise was *not* "in accordance with the interests of the toilers and in the object of strengthening the socialist system." Article 126 supplied the answer. It read:

> In accordance with the interests of the toilers and with the object of the development of the organized self-expression and political activity of the popular masses, there is ensured to the citizens of the U.S.S.R. the right of union into public organizations, professional unions, cooperative organizations, organizations of youth, sport and defense organizations, cultural, technical and scientific societies, and the most active and conscious citizens from the ranks of the working class and other strata of toilers are united in the All-Union Communist Party (Bolsheviks) which is the vanguard of the toilers in their struggle for the strengthening and development of the socialist order and represents the directing kernel of all organizations of toilers, both public and State.

The first part of the article can be eliminated from consideration; the last part contained the gist of the entire constitution. The Communist party remained in power. As long as it did so the Politburo ruled the Soviet Union and Stalin dominated the Politburo.

In November, 1936, Stalin reported on the constitution to the Eighth Congress of the Soviets. ". . . we now have a new, socialist economy," he said, "which knows neither crises nor unemployment, which knows neither poverty nor ruin, and which provides our citizens with every opportunity to lead a prosperous and cultured life." The proletariat had become "an entirely new class," the soviet peasantry "is an entirely new peasantry." The intelligentsia are "people who have come from . . . the working population." We have not yet reached communism, he said, but we have achieved socialism. "I must admit," he stated, "that the draft of the new constitution does preserve the regime of the dictatorship of the working class, just as it also preserves unchanged the present leading position of the Communist Party of the U.S.S.R." He regarded this retention not as a "flaw" but as a "merit." "A party is a part of a class, its most advanced part," he added; and since there were only two classes left, the workers and the peasants, and they cooperated in harmony, "there is ground only for one party, the Communist Party." "Democracy in capitalist countries, where there are antagonistic classes, is, in the last analysis, democracy for the strong, democracy for the propertied minority. In the U.S.S.R., on the contrary, democracy is democracy for the working people, i.e., democracy for all." So he concluded that "the Constitution of the U.S.S.R. is the only thoroughly democratic constitution in the world."

That is to say, the Communists wiped out the aristocracy and the middle class, they forced the peasantry into collective farms, they set up a dictatorship of the Politburo under one man, and they destroyed all political life except that channeled through the Communist party; and when Stalin needed to bolster his regime, he called forth a propaganda constitution and called it the model of democracy. He rejected a proposal to allow the Praesidium, or Executive Committee of the Supreme Soviet, to issue provisional acts of legislation, for, he said with piety, "Such a situation runs counter to the principle that laws should be stable. And we need stability of laws now more than ever." He likewise insisted that one man should not be elevated by popular election to the presidency of the U.S.S.R.; the presidency was exercised by the Praesidium of the Supreme Soviet, a collegiate body. And he approved of an election law which replaced the open voting, indirect elections, and preference to the workers over the peasants by the secret ballot, direct elections, and equality for all, including former kulaks, White Guards (of the czarist regime), and priests. Did it matter who voted or how? There was only one candidate, picked by the Communist party on orders from above. "It is a distinctive feature of our revolution," Stalin declared in 1935, "that it brought the people not only freedom, but also material benefits and the possibility of a prosperous and cultured life. That is why life has become joyous in our country."

Purges of 1936–1938

While introducing the constitution, Stalin was involved in a gigantic man hunt. Among the "prosperous," "cultured," and "joyous" workers and peasants in the Soviet Union there remained some discontent. Stalin was being criticized in his own entourage for the ruthless collectivization of the peasantry and the furious haste of the Five-Year Plans. Communist leaders disliked the autocracy, the suppression of freedom of discussion, the atmosphere of tension and fear. In Leningrad the Communist governor, Sergei Kirov, was assassinated in December, 1934, by a young party member who belonged to a small group hostile to oppression. Fearing that he had allowed too much freedom, Stalin began a purge, not merely of actual, but of potential sources of opposition. He had already, a few months previously, issued a decree that made the entire family responsible for the treason of any one of its members and that threatened any member with heavy penalties who did not report a disloyal relative to the authorities. He mistrusted his own bodyguard, had forty of them tried, two executed, and the others given penal sentences. He determined to destroy not merely his opponents but the environment that had created them. Leningrad was thoroughly combed. In the spring of 1935 tens of thousands of its residents were exiled to northern Siberia, and numerous people from other cities were put in prison and concentration camps. Political prisoners henceforth were given especially harsh treatment.

In 1936 the purges began again and lasted into 1938. The indicted were all accused of planning to kill Stalin, of being British, German, Japanese, or other spies, of aiming to destroy the Soviet regime and to restore capitalism. They were said to have engaged in these activities for years. They were tried, some in public, some in secret, some not at all, depending on the propaganda value to be derived from them. Some of them confessed in public to everything demanded; some refused. The evidence brought out in public against them was either too unreal to be believed or was proved by foreigners to be false. Why would persons closely associated with Stalin not have murdered him long ago, if they had planned to do so during all those years?

The purges reached a crescendo in 1937 with the involvement of the army, which had been hostile to Stalin's abuse of the peasantry, his bloodletting, his methods of rule, and planned to overthrow him. Stalin's secret police uncovered the plot, struck in time, and the army leaders went the way of the civilian opponents. Vishinsky, who served as prosecuting attorney at these trials, concluded his denunciation of each defendant with the cry, "Shoot the mad dog." And Trotsky in exile wrote, "Stalin is like a man who wants to quench his thirst with salted water."

> Among the men in the dock at these trials were all the members of Lenin's Politbureau, except Stalin himself and Trotsky, who, however, though absent, was the chief defendant. Among them, moreover, were one ex-Premier, several vice-Premiers, two ex-chiefs of the Communist International, the chief of the trade unions (Tomsky, who committed suicide before the trial), the chief of the General Staff, the chief political Commissar of the Army, the Supreme Commanders of all important military districts, nearly all Soviet ambassadors in Europe and Asia, and, last but not least, the two chiefs of the political police.[8]

Involved with these were all the persons who might in any way be considered their followers, persons of whom they had spoken a favorable word. "Having destroyed the first team of potential leaders of an alternative government, he [Stalin] could not spare the second, the third, the fourth, and the nth team." [9] The number of the victims ran into the hun-

[8] Deutscher, *op. cit.*, p. 372. [9] *Ibid.*, p. 380.

dreds of thousands. Bloodletting of this kind was the Communist substitute for the competition of political parties.

Armed Forces

The Communists continued to expand the armed forces, to improve the technical equipment, and to raise the intellectual level of the personnel. The Five-Year Plans had as a main objective the production of military materials, and as a by-product came an increasing premilitary acquaintance with machinery. Improvement in education was equally valuable for the services. The army had not attempted to expand its numbers until in the thirties it had sufficient personnel trained in the new weapons supplied by industry to manage the recruits. By that time illiteracy in the forces had almost disappeared, draftees had received some experience in schools and clubs in marksmanship, athletics, parachuting, and the like, and officers with advanced military training were numerous. By 1940 one company of soldiers, for example, planned its day of rest as follows: 28 men participated in a ski tournament; others went to a circus, others to a patriotic film; one half of the company visited the city museums; and a few remained in the barracks to read and discuss together the newspapers. The social composition of the army had changed. In 1927, 20 per cent of the soldiers were workers; in 1937, 43 per cent; and three fourths of the officers were former workers and peasants. With these changes came a great improvement in the material well-being of the soldiers, in living quarters, food, and services.

The constitution of 1936 imposed upon each citizen the duty to defend the country, and when the law on universal military service was introduced in 1939 the government stressed an ideal which it had been propagandizing for several years. "The defense of the fatherland," stated the law, "is the sacred duty of every citizen of the U.S.S.R." Stalin's new line should be contrasted with the original Communist internationalism. As late as 1930 a political primer for soldiers referred to the army as "the army of the international proletariat, the fighting vanguard of the world's socialist revolution."

Military improvement was accompanied by tightening political control over the army as a potential danger. Communist party cells permeated the forces to assure obedience to the regime. Political commissars were appointed, who in crises like that of the purge jointly controlled the army with the military commanders, and in political matters ranked superior to the latter. They helped to educate the entire personnel, officers as well as privates, in communism. The party cells, the political commissars, and the 250,000 secret police enabled Stalin to forestall the coup d'état of the generals in 1937 and save his head. He began to choose military officers and political commissars on grounds of devotion not merely to communism but to him.

Although the purge hurt the fighting efficiency of the army, in some respects it assisted in making a new force. The impact was identical with that upon the bureaucracy. For a time the army was torn by mistrust, until Stalin noted the danger of disruption and declared that there would be no more great purges. He filled the thousands of vacant positions in army and bureaucracy by young men, who, although immature and inexperienced, were enthusiastic and loyal to Stalin. Reared under communism, they belonged to the new technical intelligentsia that knew no alternative system of life and were content with nonpolitical assignments, including that of political commissar in the army. They did not question principles; they took orders. Within a remarkably short time the country settled down to its daily tasks. By 1940 the army was subjected to strict discipline and taught to regard any lessening of authority as bourgeois-capitalistic. Stalin was creating a professional force, with safeguards against military professionals imagining that communism might not be the best form of society for developing a strong defensive body.

Non-Russian Nationalities

The Five-Year Plans and the collectivization of agriculture affected the non-Russian nationalities in the same way that they did the Russians; but since they were lesser peoples in number and much more backward they suffered from certain extra handicaps. Russians tended to occupy the important positions and to act as colonists in spreading the Communist civilization. The nationalities were given industries, particularly for providing local consumers' goods, but they were mainly used, just as under the czars, to supply raw materials, cotton, sugar, oil seeds, and the like in agriculture, and minerals in industry. Their national leaders were members of the Communist party subject to orders from Moscow. Their representatives in the Soviet of Nationalities, all picked by the Communist party, followed the central line. The nationalities received schools and were allowed to develop their own languages, but the Communists gained a twofold advantage from this cultural encouragement: they broke the control of the old intelligentsia and they prepared the masses for reading communist propaganda. They forced the Cyrillic alphabet upon the peoples, partly in order to facilitate the teaching of Russian as the common language of the Soviet Union. Anyone with ambition in any line had to learn that language. The party might bring to Moscow a long-bearded Kazak or Caucasian tribal bard to sing folk songs and praise Stalin to the accompaniment of a harp; but the nationality languages and culture remained local and secondary.

EDUCATIONAL POLICY AND ACHIEVEMENTS

The economic revolution executed by Stalin entailed the adjustment of educational policy. Since under the Five-Year Plans concrete objectives had to be achieved, experimentation with curriculum, methods of instruction, and school administration was replaced by emphasis upon discipline and learning a definite body of knowledge. The initiative of pupils and students was restricted to minor matters, and the authority of the teacher and of the school administrator, like that of Stalin, was enlarged. Pupils and students were held responsible for learning, not as members of a brigade, but as individuals, and examinations were reintroduced to test factual knowledge. History and geography were restored to the curriculum; but, to assure a communist interpretation of these and all other subjects, each school for a time was subject to a political head and an educational head, the one to check the political reliability of the other and of his staff. As was true of the factory managers, the two positions usually merged, and teachers were relieved somewhat from pupils' spying and were made responsible for the pupils' visiting theaters, museums, and the like for further education. Each school organized a management board composed of a methods master, a psychologist, and a cultural supervisor, which cooperated with the Parents' Council. Instead of spying on each other, the school and the community were ordered to join forces.

The educational system proposed to include all groups in the population and to be so integrated that a pupil or student could move easily from one school to another. As Article 121 of the constitution of 1936 stated:

> Citizens of the U.S.S.R. have the right to education. This right is ensured by universal, compulsory elementary education; by education, including higher education, being free of charge; by the system of state stipends for the overwhelming majority of students in the universities and colleges; by instruction in schools being conducted in the native languages, and by the organization in the factories, state farms, machine and tractor stations and collective farms of free, vocational, technical, and agronomic training for the working people.

The kindergarten cared for children of working mothers. The primary school was common to all; but diversification began with the secondary school and continued into higher education. Great stress was placed upon scientific and technical education and upon training in association with each aspect of the economy. The Commissariat of Transport, that of Agriculture, and so forth took over some of the tasks of the Commissariat of Education, leaving the latter to manage only the teachers' training colleges and the arts' faculties. A factory would thus have attached to it a school. Vocational education was so popular that the government found it necessary to balance the program by more work in the liberal arts. Professional schools and research centers grew in number of institutions, teachers, and students, with the military taking a prominent part in the advance; and everywhere adult education strove to spread the ability to read and write.

The quality of instruction was often poor; the restrictions imposed by communist dogma upon knowledge were severe; the equipment was often inadequate almost to the point of nonexistence; the forced isolation of scholars from the rest of the world was a serious drawback. Nonetheless, a deep concern about improving education was evident. As an American study states, "It appears . . . that in proportion to the national income the Russian people are supporting education several times as generously as the people of the United States."[10] The explanation may be the same as that for the greater proportion of the national income devoted to investment in industry and agriculture than in this country: the Soviet Union had much farther to go to catch up with the West.

The achievement has been extraordinary both in the increase in numbers attending school and in the social spread of educational opportunities. Before World War I Russia had between 8 and 9 million pupils in elementary and secondary schools; in 1939, more than 47 million. In 1914 there had been 81 universities and institutes with 24,700 students; in 1941 there were 782 with 564,573 students. In 1935 students from worker families in the institutions of higher education accounted for 45 per cent of the total, and in 1938, for 40 per cent; those of peasant background, for 16 per cent and 21.6 per cent, respectively. Certainly no other European society could have approached the number from these social classes. A growing tendency toward a new social stratification was already evident, however, in the percentage of the students from families of employees and intelligentsia, 36.2 per cent in 1935 and 42.3 per cent three years later. The superior cultural opportunities of those who in a capitalistic society would be called the middle class were beginning to have effect: the children had more incentive to go to institutions of higher learning than those of peasants and workers, and better preparation. Since the Communist leaders in the middle thirties ceased to discriminate against young people of bourgeois background and permitted them equal opportunities with the sons and daughters of the toilers, education began to assume the characteristics of social stability that Stalin proposed to inculcate throughout the state that refused to "wither away."

LIFE IN THE SOVIET UNION

What was it like on the eve of World War II to live in the Soviet Union? Generalizations are difficult to make because of the diversity of conditions. Certain points seem fairly established facts. Society was beginning to differentiate into what one would ordinarily call classes. Incomes were about as varied in size as under any capitalistic system. Except for the few elite, the standard of living was, to Westerners, appallingly low. The economy turned out machines but bothered with consumers' goods only to the extent essential to keep the population alive and quiet. The

[10] *Communism in Action* (Washington, D. C.: Government Printing Office, 1946), p. 113.

quality and number of retail stores were in keeping with the indifference to individual needs for physical comfort. The standards for food, clothing, and housing remained bad. A worker had to put in twice as much labor in 1937 as he had in 1928 in order to buy the same amount of food; his real wages had fallen by half. If that condition had existed in a capitalistic society, a Communist would have declared that the workers were ripe for revolution. Medical care was free, and the number of physicians had increased since 1914 five and a half times, but neither that number nor the hospitals approached Western standards of adequacy. The people had no way of gauging how much the Communists were exploiting them to build a power economy and maintain a dictatorship. Laws were becoming standardized; a judiciary was functioning and administrative tribunals were developing a sort of common law of their own. Some kind and some degree of regularity are necessary for the functioning of any society, including that of communism. No one could know, however, when the next purge would occur or whether he or she might suddenly be seized for an unknown reason and disappear into a camp for correctional labor.

Concentrating its energy upon the creation of a communist society, the Soviet Union continued to regard the rest of the world as hostile. It kept its people in isolation from foreign influences as completely as possible, rarely allowing an alien to travel at large in the country and filling its citizens with distorted propaganda about the achievements of communism and the weakness and degeneracy of capitalistic society. Foreign trade remained a state monopoly. Foreign relations were restricted to professional diplomatic channels. Foreign newspaper correspondents lacked freedom of movement; their despatches were subjected to official censorship. The Soviet government was too busy with its own first Five-Year Plan to exploit the world economic depression for spreading communism. Thereafter at an early date, unlike the British and French governments and those of the small free states, it became concerned about the predatory intentions of Hitler's Germany, of Italy, and of Japan and began on a limited scale to participate in international relations. Since Stalin drew no distinction in the basic attitude toward the Soviet Union of the three aggressors mentioned on the one hand and the free nations on the other, he believed that any or all non-Communist countries would destroy the Soviet Union. For the time being, just before World War II, he most feared Germany, but the reader may anticipate that the lack of discrimination will lead him into mistakes in judgment. In spite of his awareness of a crisis, Stalin failed as completely as Neville Chamberlain to secure peace by international action. We shall follow the story of his failure in a subsequent chapter.

Had communism changed the Russian people? Again, no simple answer is possible, but stories by the English life-long student of Russia, Sir Bernard Pares, who was permitted to travel in the Soviet Union, may offer an impression.

In Kiev, still as always a beautiful city on its lovely site, in the late summer of 1936, I saw a march past of all the wards in turn. They swung past with splendid vigour, squads of men or of women—one squad of women had in the middle of it a fine old man with a long beard who looked very pleased with his company. There were flowers and dancing everywhere; each ward was preceded by a dancing band of girl skirmishers in the picturesque Ukrainian costume, sometimes singing the charming Ukrainian folk songs. At one point various forms of recreation and amusement were represented: the fishermen carrying long fishing rods with coloured paper fish hooked to them, the chess players carrying enormous cardboard knights, bishops and castles. Interspersed between the detachments came curious and fanciful constructions, sometimes very ingenious; an effigy of Trotsky with long nose and black eyes and curls made an excellent Mephistopheles. It was a family feast of old and young, and we all exchanged our comments as each new surprise went past. With the usual courtesy to guests there was a chair set for me, and when I wanted to let a lady have it, I was genially told, "that I had to submit to the will of the majority." At one time a torrent of rain came down, but the marchers swung past with all the more vigour and enjoyment. And so it was with the onlookers. After several hours of it, I asked a neighbouring policeman whether I couldn't go away: "No," he said very nicely, "you must stay and enjoy it." And enjoy it they certainly did, for in spite of more downpours of rain, from my room in my hotel I could hear them singing and dancing on the square outside till two in the morning. The one thing that fell below the level of all the rest was the exhausting reiteration of the portraits of Stalin and the other "big noises" of Communism. There must have been about forty of Stalin alone: one ten feet high, of the face alone. I noticed a sympathetic cheer when there came past a single portrait of Lenin.[11]

Sir Bernard writes again:

The Russians have a wonderful physique. . . . What they can stand is surprising: the soldiers used to tell me they couldn't go through more than *four* nights running without any sleep; and a Scottish surgeon, landed in Russia in the last war, said: "I don't think there can be a wound from which the Russian can't recover: you cut off his leg without anaesthetics, and he says: 'Thank you, Sir!' " There is a fine Russian word for a fine Russian quality—VYNOSLIVOST, lasting a thing out, and it applies not only to the man but to the nation, not only to the body but the mind.[12]

Perhaps such a people can "last out" communism.

Suggestions for Further Reading

The Readings for Chapter 10 should be used for this period as well. The following titles may be consulted in addition.

BELOFF, MAX. *The Foreign Policy of Soviet Russia, 1929–1941.* 2 vols. New York: Oxford University Press, 1947, 1949. Basic study.

[11] Bernard Pares, *Russia* (Baltimore: Penguin Books, Inc. Copyright, 1943, 1949, by The New American Library of World Literature, Inc.), pp. 212-213.
[12] *Ibid.*, pp. 10-11.

HODGMAN, DONALD R. *Soviet Industrial Production, 1928–1951.* Cambridge, Mass.: Harvard University Press, 1954. Thorough economic analysis.

KOESTLER, ARTHUR. *Darkness at Noon.* New York: Signet Books, 1955. A novel based on the story of the trials of 1936–1938. One of the most illuminating books on communist mentality.

KRAVCHENKO, VICTOR. *I Chose Freedom: The Personal and Political Life of a Soviet Official.* New York: Garden City Books, 1947. Justly famous memoirs of one who fled to freedom.

KULSKI, W. W. *The Soviet Regime: Communism in Practice.* Syracuse, N.Y.: Syracuse University Press, 1954.

TIMASHEFF, NICOLAS S. *The Great Retreat: The Growth and Decline of Communism in Russia.* New York: E. P. Dutton & Company, Inc., 1946. An evaluation of all aspects of Soviet life.

The map of Soviet resources, industry, and transportation in Chapter 26 also should be consulted.

Chapter 17 · The Failure of Diplomacy

NEW INTERNATIONAL SETTING

Within the span of a decade Europe moved from the most severe economic crisis in history to a second world war. Europe made a few unsuccessful attempts to overcome the depression by regional agreements and to adjust to the entry of totalitarian states into international relations, to the emergence of the Soviet Union as a world power, and to the decay of the League of Nations. Liberal and democratic, Socialist, Nazi, Fascist, and Communist states with their varying conceptions of international relations suddenly were in competition. Mistakes in understanding and evaluating policies were made, as no one in a position of authority possessed the imagination to compensate for lack of experience with the new kinds of rivals. The totalitarian states, including the U.S.S.R., underestimated the strength of the free countries; the liberal-democratic leaders were unable to conceive of the determination of totalitarian regimes to use physical power in foreign relations. Fear of war and the devotion of their nations to peace kept the leaders of free peoples from taking the creative and bold measures in international affairs which might have deterred predators. National feeling and the ideal of state sovereignty persisted so strongly that both leaders and peoples in free countries hesitated to set up adequate international barriers against the new aggressive forces. Within a period of five years, 1933 to 1938, Germany under National Socialism changed from a position of the greatest victim of world depression to that of undertaking the conquest of Europe and the world.

The global setting was such as to leave the European states to arrange their own affairs. The conquest of Manchuria and the attack on China involved Japan from 1931 until the outbreak of World War II, so that the European colonial powers were fairly secure against Japanese aggression toward their Asiatic dependencies. They restricted their defense of China mainly to diplomatic protests over Japan's violation of the League Covenant and other international agreements. Although aware of the severe loss of prestige on the part of the League of Nations in this affair, they were able to console themselves by the fact that the League essentially pertained to Europe; China and Japan were far away. The colonial dependencies of the European states were still relatively quiet. Except for India, where riots occurred in demand for self-rule and the British took some extraordinary measures, colonial unrest had not yet affected a large number of the population. The relations between the imperialist powers and subject peoples were conducted within the framework of the respective empire, whether British, French, Dutch, Belgian, Spanish, Portuguese, or Italian. The intensive effort of colonials to transform imperial relations into international relations was to come after World War II. Nor did communism loom as an immediate threat to the European states. Stalin sought in this decade to cooperate with the League of Nations; he ordered the Communists to support popular front governments in European states where they were set up. The crushing of the Chinese Communists by Chiang Kai-shek in 1927–1928 quieted temporarily Communist forces in Asia. The sporadic fighting between Japanese and Russian troops along the Manchurian frontier did not prevent the Soviet Union from focusing attention upon the rising totalitarian threat in Europe.

Of the other states, those of Latin America played no significant role in international politics. The British Dominions held aloof from European affairs and strengthened Great Britain in her policy of peace. The United States government tried to win the support of Britain and France in 1931 for strong diplomatic action against Japanese aggression in Manchuria, was rebuffed especially by the British, and became even more isolationist than it had been.

United States Isolation

The American public, encouraged by isolationist congressmen, looked upon Europe as a den of international iniquity, whose intentions were to draw the United States into its evil game. The nations that had borrowed money from the United States during and after World War I had, except for Finland, just repudiated their debts. The continent teemed with dictators of obnoxious creeds, and governments close to bankruptcy were once again wasting money on vast programs of armaments.

In 1934–1935 a Senate committee chaired by Senator Gerald Nye disclosed the large profits made by the American armaments industry during 1914–1917 and the intimate connection between economic interests in this country and the Allied war effort. It concluded that by means of these material bonds the Allies had drawn this country into war. Congress between 1935 and 1937 passed stringent legislation, with the intent to prevent involvement in another war. Laws prohibited, in the event of war between foreign states or of foreign "civil strife," the export from the country of arms, ammunition, or other implements of war "to any port of such belligerent state, or to any neutral port for transhipment to, or for the use of, a belligerent country." Loans or credits by an American national were likewise prohibited. The President was given authority to define whether a state of war existed, and at his discretion he could for a period of two years forbid the export of other materials to belligerent powers. The United States showed itself isolationist just at a time when Hitler, Mussolini, and the Japanese militarists were violating at home and abroad (and Stalin and many authoritarian rulers of lesser significance were violating at home) all the ideals for which the United States stood. Free nations abroad were rapidly losing their power superiority in the world and were certain, if war came, to need American aid in protecting the common Western heritage.

The neutrality laws also came at a time when because of the depression the productive capacity of the United States, although surpassing that of any other country, remained to a large extent unused. Mass unemployment continued, and purchasing power was low. A vigorous rearmament program would have initiated a boom, but the Congress sacrificed economic advantage in an effort to keep the country free from the horrors of another war. It thought that when protected by oceans a great power could ignore the course of events in the dangerous areas of Europe and Asia and live in isolation. The efforts of President Franklin D. Roosevelt to warn against the predatory forces had no appreciable public effect before the outbreak of World War II. The United States took almost no part in the thirties in the direction of the international affairs of Europe.

Small Countries of Northern and Northwestern Europe

The small countries of Northwestern, Eastern, and Southeastern Europe depended in varying degrees upon the big powers to help them recover from the economic crisis. Those of Northern Europe—Switzerland, Belgium, the Netherlands, the Scandinavian countries, the Baltic countries, and Finland—were advantageously situated geographically as well as culturally to fend for themselves. The test of international action came in the case of the other states, from Poland south, whose need for aid was greatest. The states in each area endeavored to about an equal extent to cooperate among themselves, and with similar results. Their experience in international affairs offers insight into the difference in methods and objectives of free and totalitarian states in international relations.

The states of the northwest and the north were situated near the largest markets of Europe, Great Britain, and Germany. They traded with these countries, but very little among themselves. The Baltic states, Estonia, Latvia, and Lithuania, negotiated from time to time over ways of cooperating, but neither the economic and customs union of 1927 between Estonia and Latvia nor a similar one of all three countries in 1934 was put into force. The Scandinavian countries and Finland granted one another some preferential trade treatment, and in 1930 at Olso the Scandinavian states, Belgium, the Netherlands, and Luxembourg drafted a convention and a protocol over economic relations, which three years later Finland also accepted. The signers agreed to notify one another prior to intended tariff changes, to cooperate on economic matters, and to reduce trade barriers, and their representatives met annually until the war. Belgium, the Netherlands, and Luxembourg drew up a convention at Ouchy in 1932 for reduction of tariffs among themselves and for the ultimate establishment of a customs union. The great powers objected to both the Oslo and the Ouchy agreements as violations of the most-favored-nation clause, and prevented the former from ever accomplishing much and the latter from being implemented at all. The record of attempts to cooperate was not impressive.

During the thirties important changes occurred in the trade relations of the countries around the Baltic with Great Britain and with Germany. Germany's share in providing goods for each of these states declined, whereas Great Britain's rose. As an importer from these countries, Germany lost ground in three countries and showed modest gains in the other four; Great Britain took a much larger amount of goods. Norway and Sweden were most favorably situated in that they did not depend on either market so much as did the other countries. The British in 1933–1934 negotiated a series of bilateral trade treaties with the northern states, by which each assured the other of a definite market for certain products, mainly foodstuffs and timber materials against British coal and textiles and other manufactures. The British proved to be hard bargainers, but they did enable the countries to earn foreign exchange which could be spent elsewhere. Except for Lithuania, the states kept a large amount of their exchange in pounds sterling and became members of the sterling area, to which Portugal, the British dominions, and the British colonies also belonged. London served as the trading and banking center, but the British government never endeavored to use its economic power to dominate the member states.

Poland pursued the same commercial policy as the Baltic countries in greatly decreasing her trade with Germany and increasing it with Britain. She made a successful effort to expand trade with other continents, from which she needed raw materials.

Small Countries of Southeastern Europe

Of all the European countries the Danubian and Balkan states faced the bleakest economic prospect. They lived remote from important markets, had high costs of transportation and undeveloped market facilities, heavy foreign debts, and, except for Czechoslovakia, mediocre or poor leadership. First of all came the problem of foreign debts. Having taken the initiative in obtaining and supervising the use of foreign loans to several of these states, the League of Nations sponsored a conference at Stresa in 1932 to consider the economic and financial difficulties of the area. The delegates carefully analyzed the troubles and recommended direct settlement of financial questions between debtors and creditors, scarcely an original or a helpful piece of advice.

Intimately connected with the fate of foreign debts was the question of finding foreign markets for surplus agricultural products. The agrarian states, Bulgaria, Hungary, Poland, Latvia, Estonia, Yugoslavia, Romania, and Czechoslovakia, considered this matter in a conference at Warsaw in 1930 and elsewhere during the next years, and proposed, among other measures, that the food-importing countries of Western Europe grant them in the emergency a preferential tariff rate. Romanian grain, for example, would be permitted to enter France at a lower duty than the grain from overseas. The members of the agrarian bloc, however, never acted in concert. Czechoslovakia did not agree with the plan; and when some Western states refused to waive the most-favored-nation clause in their commercial treaties and others remained lukewarm, the idea collapsed.

At about the same time France proposed in the Tardieu Plan that Austria, Czechoslovakia, Hungary, Yugoslavia, and Romania—that is, the Danubian states, grant each other a preferential tariff reduction of 10 per cent, abolish exchange restrictions and import and export prohibitions among themselves, and possibly introduce a common currency. Germany and Italy sabotaged the project as a threat to the expansion of their economic interests in the region. The proposed members likewise failed to cooperate; they thought the market too small; some of them feared the revival of the Austro-Hungarian Empire; they disliked the idea of becoming dependent on neighbors, whom they did not trust. When one considers that trade among these states amounted to only one fourth to one third of their total trade, one realizes that the Tardieu Plan showed little promise of meeting Danubia's needs. After three years of conferences not a single crucial Danubian or Balkan economic problem had been solved.

In 1933, as a counter to Hitler's assumption of power in Germany, the members of the Little Entente—Czechoslovakia, Romania, and Yugoslavia—signed an agreement for consolidating their relations. They set up a permanent commission of foreign ministers, with secretariat and a council for coordinating the economic interests of the three members. A long-range plan for economic adjustment was drawn.

The basic difficulty lay in the difference in the economic needs of Czechoslovakia, on the one hand, and Romania and Yugoslavia, on the other. Czechoslovakia sought to export manufactures but, since she was almost self-sufficient in food, did not need to import the agricultural products by which Romania and Yugoslavia could have paid for her industrial goods. Czechoslovakia had as well to keep an eye on other markets, like the Scandinavian countries, where she faced the same problem. Romania had oil to export, and Yugoslavia had some minerals; but, as they could sell these in other markets and obtain urgently needed foreign exchange, they preferred not to trade them to Czechoslovakia for industrial articles. Diligent efforts on the part of all three states resulted in increasing their mutual trade, already very small, by only 3 per cent. Nor were they any more successful in bringing neighboring small states into the Little Entente organization.

The policies of all these Danubian and Balkan countries continued to be based mainly on post-World War I fears and rivalries. They failed to reorientate their thinking and actions to the complete change taking place in their international position. For instance, the Little Entente still aimed its alliance at Hungary and did not adjust its foreign relations to counter the vital menace from Italy, Germany, and the U.S.S.R.

A number of leaders in the Balkan states used the occasion of the Universal Peace Congress held in Athens in October, 1929, to call for the creation of a Balkan entente. A conference held each year brought together unofficial delegates from the participating states to discuss agenda that covered political, economic, social, and cultural subjects. Responsible leaders hoped that out of the discussion of common problems a formal and official Balkan Union might ultimately emerge. The Greek delegation submitted to the conference in 1930 the draft of a constitution based largely upon the organic laws of several international organizations. Nationalism immediately intervened. The Bulgarians balked at any move until the minorities problem was settled, that is, until they received back territory lost to their neighbors at the end of World War I. Political rapprochement and Balkan Union never materialized.

In nonpolitical lines, the Balkan conferences proved to be unexpectedly successful. They founded a Balkan Chamber of Commerce and Industry, a Balkan Medical Union, and a Balkan Agricultural Chamber, and drafted a project for a customs union. In view of Bulgaria's stubbornness, Greece, Turkey, Romania, and Yugoslavia signed a treaty of mutual guarantee of their frontiers and went ahead with economic and cultural cooperation, some aspects of which Bulgaria supported. Their economic council set up a permanent marine commission; it put through a convention facilitating air communication, and a postal, telegraphic, and telephone union. The National Banks of Issue consulted together on ways to aid commercial and financial cooperation.

These novel forms of international relations promised a profound change from the usual Balkan methods of wars, revolutions, and assassinations. But they required time if they were to improve political relations, and time was not granted them. The Balkan conference did not prepare the participants for the imminent ordeal by fire. Like the Little Entente, the Stresa Conference, and the Warsaw Conference, it solved none of the essential problems.

Failure of the Balkans to recover enabled Germany to expand her influence in the area. The German Finance Minister Hjalmar Schacht worked out a foreign trade policy which was applied generally but which especially affected the small agricultural states of Southeastern Europe. When in 1936 the Nazi government initiated a Four-Year Plan to prepare the country for war, execution of the trade program was accelerated. Göring, who administered the plan, declared to a group of industrialists that the purpose was not necessarily to produce economically but to produce, not to acquire abroad cheaply but to add to the country's supply of materials. Debts were to be increased to the limit of creditors' tolerance, for, unlike raw materials, money could not be built into cannons. Germany's reputation as a reliable creditor was used to reduce foreign states to economic dependence, not as debtors, but as creditors. Once the relationship was established, Germany planned to force her creditors to concentrate on the production of commodities which she particularly needed. By offering higher prices for the commodities than her competitors did, she steadily raised the price level in the selling country above the level of world prices, thus encouraging dependence on the German market. The agricultural countries of Southeastern Europe at first welcomed the program as a means of disposing of surplus foodstuffs and other materials to a large market within easy distance. In time they came to see that they were contributing to the creation of a regional economy dominated by Germany.

Germany argued that the policy was economically sound in that it benefited all parties. Under the Weimar Republic the statement would have been correct. The Nazi government twisted the initial market relation of independent states into one between a great power and satellites. Germany pressed the southeastern states to grow fodder, oil seeds, fiber plants, and other crops which she needed, and she negotiated commercial treaties for acquisition of the entire harvest for several years in advance. She sent in return not merely aspirin and cameras, as has been charged, but machinery and other articles and technicians to help in production. As the table indicates, the direction of the foreign trade of the small states shifted.

COUNTRY	EXPORTS TO GERMANY AS A PERCENTAGE OF TOTAL EXPORTS		IMPORTS FROM GERMANY AS A PERCENTAGE OF TOTAL IMPORTS	
	1927	*1937*	*1927*	*1937*
Bulgaria	23.0	43.1	21.0	54.8
Greece	21.3	31.0	7.4	27.1
Hungary	13.3	24.1	17.8	26.2
Romania	18.6	19.2	22.3	28.9
Yugoslavia	10.6	21.7	12.3	32.4
Austria	18.4	14.9	16.9	16.3
Czechoslovakia	24.1	15.0	20.9	15.5

SOURCE: Antonin Basch, *The Danube Basin and the German Economic Sphere* (New York: Columbia University Press, 1943), p. 194.

The low figures for Austria are explained in part by a tariff war, fought to undermine Austrian independence. Romania tried to keep a world market for her oil, with diminishing success as Nazi influence over her agriculture increased. Czechoslovakia alone kept economically independent. After

Germany absorbed Austria and Czechoslovakia, her share of the trade of the other states became overwhelming; she was gaining complete ascendance over these states without war. The contrast between her policy toward them and that of Britain toward the Baltic countries will become increasingly evident as we proceed.

The fundamental developments in European international relations in the thirties were the resurgence of German imperialism under the Nazis and the expansionist activity of Fascist Italy. The policies of France, Great Britain, and the Soviet Union came in response to the behavior of the two totalitarian states. France took the defensive, endeavoring to maintain her system of alliances from the previous decade and to bolster it by a treaty with the Soviet Union. Great Britain strengthened her ties with the Dominions and introduced into the British Commonwealth the system of preferential tariffs which she opposed on the continent. Her policy toward the continental powers may be roughly summarized in the phrase appeasement of Germany and Italy and in a statement of 1931 by Minister Arthur Henderson of the Labor party, ". . . we shall examine all these proposals with the sympathy they deserve." The governments of both France and Great Britain lost the initiative in international affairs and slid from defeat to disaster. The Soviet Union, confronting a new menace in Europe and Japan in the Far East, emerged from isolation and sought international assistance.

SOVIET UNION ABANDONS ISOLATION

Two major factors conditioned Soviet foreign policy, namely, communist dogma and the rules of power politics imposed upon every state that entered into international relations. The Soviet Union had been able to keep aloof from this dangerous game of power politics both because of the exhaustion of the major powers after World War I and because of the strong belief of free peoples in the right of national self-determination. When Japan seized Manchuria in 1931, attacked China, and threatened Eastern Siberia, and when Nazi Germany denounced communism and discussed the seizure of Soviet territory, the Soviet Union reacted by employing, according to circumstances, both the conspiratorial techniques of communism and traditional diplomacy. The manifesto of the sixth World Congress of the Communist International in September, 1928 (this was the year of the Kellogg Peace Pact), may be used to exemplify the conspiratorial method. It read in part as follows:

> Despite all the contradictions and antagonisms which exist between the capitalist powers, and despite their deep and growing mutual hatred, they are preparing with Great Britain at their head for a war against the Soviet Union. . . .
>
> The Communist International appeals to all toilers, and in particular to the industrial workers, to take up the struggle for every inch of ground that has been

won, to fight against the offensive of capitalism, to fight against the ruthless exploitation of capitalism, to fight against the enslavement of the proletariat, to fight against the policy of the imperialists and against imperialist war. . . . The Communist International appeals to all honest proletarians to form a wall of iron around the Soviet Union against which imperialism is raising the sword of war.

When some "bourgeois" states appeared more dangerous than others, the Soviets decided that their earlier, simple classification of other countries needed to be modified. They thought it advisable to look for bourgeois allies against bourgeois enemies; therefore, temporarily softening the revolutionary line of policy, they stressed the Soviet Union's wish for friendship with all the world.

Our orientation in the past and our orientation at the present time [Stalin stated to the Seventeenth Party Congress in 1934] is towards the U.S.S.R., and towards the U.S.S.R. alone. And if the interests of the U.S.S.R. demand rapprochement with one country or another which is not interested in disturbing peace, we take this step without hesitation.

. . . Those who want peace and seek business relations with us will always have our support. But those who try to attack our country will receive a crushing repulse to teach them not to poke their pig snouts into our Soviet garden.

Stalin warned the bourgeois powers about the results of another world war. "As you see," he said in the same report, "things are heading towards a new imperialist war as a way out of the present situation. . . .

As is well known [he continued] during the first imperialist war the intention was to destroy one of the Great Powers, viz. Germany, and to profit at her expense. And what was the upshot of this? They did not destroy Germany; but they sowed such a hatred for the victors in Germany, and created such a rich soil for revenge, that they have not been able to clear up the revolting mess they made even to this day, and will not, perhaps, be able to do so for quite some time. But they did get the smash-up of capitalism in Russia, the victory of the proletarian revolution in Russia, and—of course—the Soviet Union. What guarantee is there that the second imperialist war will produce "better" results for them than the first? Would it not be more correct to assume that the opposite will be the case?

In the event of a war against the Soviet Union Stalin left no doubt about the role of one part of the population.

It would be the most dangerous war ["for the bourgeoisie"], not only because the peoples of the U.S.S.R. would fight to the very death to preserve the gains of the revolution; it would be the most dangerous war for the bourgeoisie for the added reason that it would be waged not only at the front, but also behind the enemy's lines. The bourgeoisie need have no doubt that the numerous friends of the working class of the U.S.S.R. in Europe and in Asia will do their best to strike a blow in the rear at their oppressors who start a criminal war against the fatherland of the working class of all countries.

One wonders why Stalin did not encourage the bellicose forces as the surest and quickest means for making the world communist. He might not have survived the victory; but in a dictatorship of the proletariat the individual was not supposed to count for much.

Stalin's speech contained by direct assertion or by implication all the essentials of his foreign policy. The Soviet Union would continue to be the fatherland of all workers in all countries; it would remain the center of conspiratorial action to destroy the bourgeois-capitalistic enemies; it would hold these forces somewhat in abeyance in order to find supporters among the bourgeois states against other states at the time more inimical to the Soviet Union than the rest; in the event of war or whenever it saw fit, it would stir up the revolutionary workers behind enemy lines, using French or German or British Communists against their respective governments; it would attempt to live in peace with the Nazi, fascist, or any other system. All were bourgeois-capitalistic and all bad; but one could under necessity work with them. And always "Our orientation in the past and our orientation at the present time is towards the U.S.S.R."

In reorienting the foreign policy Stalin acted on a broad front. In the late twenties and early thirties his government signed treaties of nonaggression with neighbors, in Asia as well as Europe—China, Finland, the Baltic states, Poland, Czechoslovakia, Romania, and Turkey. The Soviet Union thereby received assurance that none of these states would attack her or allow other countries to launch an attack from their territories. Stalin made a reciprocal promise, but the countries which tolerated the presence of a Communist party continued to have trouble with this fifth column. The Soviet Union and France, in fear of Germany, endeavored to introduce an East European Locarno. The Soviet Union, Finland, the Baltic states, Poland, Czechoslovakia, and Germany were to be members, and the agreement was to be supplemented by a treaty of alliance between France and the Soviet Union. France proposed a similar pact for the southeastern states. The entire project failed because of the opposition of Germany and Poland.

That Nazi Germany would dislike a treaty stabilizing the frontiers of the region where it intended to expand can be readily understood. The Polish reaction is more difficult to explain. Pilsudski had never approved the Western Locarno system; he declared that it created two kinds of frontiers, those in the West, which were secure, and those in the East, which were left without guarantee. "Every good Pole spits with disgust at the name" (Locarno), he said. Colonel Beck, the Polish foreign minister after 1932, opposed regional pacts and upheld the superior advantage of bilateral agreements. "History teaches us," Colonel Beck explained to the French minister Pierre Laval in January, 1935, "(1) that the greatest catastrophe of which our nation has ever been victim has been the result of concerted action by these two Powers [Germany and Russia], and (2) that in this desperate situation there was not to be found any Power in the

World to bring us assistance. . . . Another conclusion which imposes itself is that the policy of Warsaw should never be dependent upon Moscow or Berlin." [1] Beck hoped to keep on good terms with both states without allowing either an opportunity to interfere in Poland. He renewed in 1934 the nonaggression treaty with the Soviet Union and at the same time signed a similar one with Germany. He feared the Soviets much more than he did the Nazis, arguing that the Austrian Hitler was interested in expanding Germany toward the southeast, not, as the Prussians had done, toward Poland.

The failure of the negotiations for an Eastern Locarno was offset by the Soviet Union's success in becoming a member of the League of Nations (1934) and in signing in the next year treaties of alliance with France and with Czechoslovakia. The value of these three events for purposes other than propaganda proved to be not very great. They mainly served for a time to cloak the difficulties inherent in working with a Communist power.

The Communist International had at its first congress condemned the League of Nations as "the Holy Alliance of the bourgeoisie for the suppression of the proletarian revolution," and in 1928 it had asserted that "The League of Nations, the product of Versailles, the most shameless robber treaty of the last decade, cloaks the war-like work of its members by working out projects for disarmament." In 1930 Stalin denounced France, the country which later took the leading part in helping the Soviet Union to become a member of the League, as "the most aggressive and militaristic country, among all aggressive and militaristic countries of the world." Some of the small states with strong religious feelings like Eire and Portugal objected to permitting the Soviet Union to become a member of the League; but the big powers and most of the others wished to bring that state into the working organization of the comity of nations. An invitation to membership was extended and accepted. Upon adherence to the Covenant, the Soviet Union made only one reservation, namely, that all disputes involving the U.S.S.R. which had arisen prior to entry into the League should not be subject to the stipulations about arbitration or judicial settlement. Although the entire system of Communist government and society violated the spirit of the Covenant, for the time being Stalin found it useful to cooperate with the League.

The Soviet alliances with France and Czechoslovakia were defensive. Article II of the French treaty read as follows:

> In the event of France or the U.S.S.R., in the circumstances specified in Article 15, paragraph 7, of the League of Nations Covenant, being the object, in spite of the genuinely peaceful intentions of both countries, of an unprovoked attack on the part of a European state, the U.S.S.R. and, reciprocally, France, shall immediately give each other aid and assistance.

[1] Gordon A. Craig and Felix Gilbert, eds., *The Diplomats, 1919–1939* (Princeton, N.J.: Princeton University Press, 1953), p. 599.

The Soviet-Czechoslovakian treaty contained an identical clause, except for the additional statement that if attacked each would aid the other only if France did. Although nominally aimed at no one, the alliances predicated Germany as the enemy. The French government seems to have been lukewarm about the treaty, and none of the states took steps to supplement its agreement by arrangements for joint military action. The Polish and Romanian governments refused to consider the passage of Soviet troops through their territories to the defense of Czechoslovakia. They feared that the Communist military forces might remain, turning their countries into Soviet satellites. While making the treaties Stalin was feeling out the Nazi government toward an agreement, and through the Comintern in 1935 he also ordered the Communist parties in other countries to cooperate with bourgeois governments in a Popular Front aginst nazism and fascism. The Soviet bow had several strings.

TOTALITARIAN DIPLOMACY

In comparison with the Soviet Union the totalitarian governments had both advantages and disadvantages in the conduct of international relations. Being nonnational, the communist ideology gained for the Soviet Union some followers behind the lines of so-called friends and of enemies. The nationalistic ideals of the Nazis and, to a less extent, those of the Fascists restricted the opportunity for obtaining aid abroad mainly to Germans and Italians who had emigrated, of whom few accepted the new gospel. The communist ideology antagonized the bourgeoisie and middle class and most of the workers elsewhere; the totalitarian ideas found admirers among the upper classes in other countries. The Communists' claim to being international offset somewhat the rigidity of their class antagonism; the nationalism of the Nazis and Fascists angered all other nationalities and created actual or potential enemies everywhere. Both doctrines lacked export value; in other countries both undoubtedly alienated far more people than they attracted.

ITALIAN EXPANSION—ETHIOPIA

Of the two dictators, Mussolini first upset international relations. He wished to achieve glory somehow, somewhere. He aspired to transform the Mediterranean into an Italian lake by taking the islands and North Africa, to conquer Ethiopia, where an Italian army had been disgracefully defeated in 1896, and to extend Italian influence into the Danubia and the Balkans. In 1926, by agreement to help Zog maintain himself as ruler of Albania, he had tied that little state economically and politically to Italy. In March, 1933, he proposed to France, Great Britain, and Germany a four-power pact for governing Europe. The small and new states were completely hostile to this plan, which would have relegated them to an inferior position. They and the Soviet Union persuaded France to amend the pact into a statement of vague generalities. In March, 1934, Mussolini signed the Rome Protocols with Hungary and Austria, by way of expanding his power in the Danube region. He had inherited Italy's antagonism to any state on the other side of the Adriatic, and hoped by these new agreements to strengthen his position against Yugoslavia. He likewise mistrusted Germany and intended to keep Austria independent. After encouraging Dollfuss and Prince Stahremberg in their seizure of power in Austria, he made the agreements with Austria and Hungary for mutual economic advantage. Hungary urgently needed markets for her grain, Austria and Italy for their manufactures.

The Rome Protocols arranged for a preferential exchange chiefly on that basis, but the benefits proved less than expected. Italy soon became involved in the Ethiopian adventure, was boycotted by the powers, and needed all the materials she could obtain. Hungary and Austria refused to join the boycott and poured their surplus into the country without receiving anything of consequence in return. Italy felt the economic pinch of the war so acutely that by 1937, far from sending manufactures in return, she could not pay on her debts to these states. The countries had failed to adjust their economies to each other's needs, and could only shift from emergency to crisis. In the meantime, in July, 1934, the Nazis had murdered Dollfuss and attempted to seize Austria. The Austrian police and army remained in control and, backed to the limit by Mussolini, suppressed the putsch. In October the Duce participated in the murder of his enemy, King Alexander of Yugoslavia, and of Foreign Minister Jean Barthou of France. In 1935 he began the war against Ethiopia and showed the world how one member of the League of Nations could conquer another member.

Mussolini chose the opportunity of a clash on the border between Ethiopia and Italian Somaliland to attack the African state. Emperor Haile Selassie of Ethiopia immediately appealed the case to the League of Nations. The Council of the League, led by Great Britain and France, tried to hedge, to negotiate, to compromise. In September, 1935, the Assembly debated the issue. The small states were deeply affected, for, as Alfred Nemours of Haiti declared, "Great or small, strong or weak, near or far, white or coloured, let us never forget that one day we may be somebody's Ethiopia." In Great Britain a peace poll taken in June showed an overwhelming majority in favor of executing the Covenant. The results had startled the complacent Conservatives in the cabinet and driven them against their will into action. When Mussolini continued to defy the League, the Council under British initiative declared Italy an aggressor and, in accordance with Article 16, called for the imposition of sanctions against the offending power. The Assembly concurred.

The execution of Article 16 proved from the beginning to be difficult.

Statesmen had during the decade and a half of the League's existence avoided all serious discussion of how to apply sanctions. The Japanese attack on Manchuria in 1931 had led to no practical action, and the new crisis found the League as unprepared as ever. The members never thought of breaking off diplomatic relations with Italy or of preventing private intercourse with Italians. They did impose against Italy economic and financial sanctions of four kinds: an embargo on the shipment of arms, the prohibition of loans and of extension of credit, an interdict on imports from the offending country and of exports to it of many manufactured goods and raw materials needed to carry on war. They did not ban the export of food to Italy; and, although they discussed the proposal many times, they never prohibited the export of coal, steel, and especially oil—all indispensable to Italy for winning the war. The argument offered was that Italy would continue to obtain these materials from non-League states like the United States as well as from League members, and that the other sanctions would suffice anyway. The Soviet Union, Romania, Venezuela, Great Britain, each a League member, continued to sell oil to Italy, without which, according to reports of experts, Italy would have had to cease the war.

No one suggested that the simplest way to defeat Italy was for Great Britain to close the Suez Canal to Italian traffic. That act might have brought on war against Great Britain, whose suffering would have been out of all proportion to its responsibility under the Covenant. Switzerland, Austria, and Hungary never agreed to apply sanctions. As the Swiss government said, the loss of trade with Italy would throw a few thousand Swiss out of employment and anger its Italian-speaking citizens. Austria and Hungary, tied to Italy by the Rome Protocols, remained loyal to the aggressor.

The League effort to stop Italy ended in total defeat. From the start the British and French governments had tacitly agreed that the League action should not be pushed to the point of Italy's declaring war on other powers, that is, on either Britain or France. The French minister Laval immediately informed the Duce of this position, thereby enabling Mussolini to bluff his way to victory. The two powers continued to seek a compromise with Italy, and this line of action culminated in the Hoare-Laval agreement of late 1935. Laval was already showing signs of the pro-Fascist leanings which led to his execution as a traitor by the postwar French state. Sir Samuel Hoare, after vigorously taking the lead against Italy in the League, suddenly succumbed to pressure from influential persons in the Foreign Office and in British high society and agreed to Laval's proposal. Italy and Ethiopia were to exchange pieces of territory, whereby the former received 60,000 square miles and the latter 3,000 and an outlet to the sea. Italy was to be given the whole southern half of Ethiopia to exploit and to own in everything but name.

The outcry among League members and in the British public against this offer was so great that the agreement had to be repudiated and Hoare dropped from the British cabinet. Nonetheless, the signing of that agreement aroused mistrust among the League members and caused delay in applying further sanctions. The League Council itself violated a clause of Article 16 by refusing Ethiopia's appeal for financial aid, and the whole program was scuttled by two acts. One was a speech by Chancellor of the Exchequer Neville Chamberlain, who declared that the continuation of sanctions would be "the very midsummer of madness" and called for a reduction in the functions of the League to accord with its real power. The other was Hitler's military occupation of the Rhineland. The Western powers feared Germany more than they did Italy. Hoping to align Mussolini against Hitler, the British and the French canceled sanctions and allowed the independence of a League member to be destroyed. Emperor Haile Selassie went into exile.

The failure to stop the aggression against Ethiopia terminated the significance of the League. Henceforth the great powers paid that organization lip-service only, the Scandinavian states openly renounced sanctions, and the small powers looked elsewhere for protection. Yet Germany, not Italy, gained most from the Ethiopian conflict. Italy acquired a country which not even a Fascist geographer could make into an actual or a potential land of wealth. Hitler for his part seized the opportunity to execute the momentous first steps in his drive for European domination. Henceforth the international relations of the continent revolved about the actions of this one man.

GERMAN EXPANSION UNDER HITLER

Göring told the court trying the Nazi war criminals at Nürnberg in 1945 that "foreign policy on the one hand, and the leadership of the Armed Forces on the other, enlisted the Führer's greatest interest and were his main activity." Hitler was unacquainted with foreign countries at first hand; he knew neither foreign languages nor the culture of other peoples. His knowledge of foreign policies and of diplomatic conduct had been gathered from superficial reading. Mistrusting professional diplomats just as he did professional army officers, he set his own standards and objectives. The international situation in Europe favored his policy, because popular aversion to war, weakness of leadership, and disintegration of the European state system through nationalism had left a power vacuum which he might fill. He proved to be amazingly astute at negotiation, at exploiting the weakness of others, and at combining the most exalted propaganda for peace with the most daring and ruthless acts of aggression. He stated his objectives in public on many occasions, but people abroad and many in Germany failed to understand him. He planned to destroy the treaty of Versailles, to complete the work of German national unification by taking all the areas where Germans lived (and they were scattered from the Baltic to the Black Sea), and to acquire "living space" in Eastern Europe. As success proved so easy, by 1937 he was ready to extend the range of his action.

Hitler began his career in international affairs by measures which pleased the German people. In the same year in which he became chancellor he withdrew Germany from membership in the League, accompanying this act by a speech intended to neutralize the adverse effect abroad:

> Former German governments entered the League of Nations, in the hope and confidence that in the League they would find a forum for a just settlement of the interests of peoples, above all for a sincere reconciliation with their former foes. But this presupposes the recognition of the ultimate restoration of the German people to equality of rights. . . . To be written down as a member of such an institution possessing no such equality of rights is, for an honour-loving nation of sixty-five million folk and for a government which loves honour no less, an intolerable humiliation!
>
> No war can become humanity's permanent state; no peace can be the perpetuation of war. One day Conquerors and Conquered must find their way back into the community of mutual understanding and confidence. For a decade and a half the German people has hoped and waited for the time when at last the end of the war should also become the end of hate and enmity. But the aim of the Treaty of Versailles seems not to be to give peace to humanity at last, but rather to keep humanity in a state of everlasting hatred.

The statement exemplifies Hitler's propaganda method. He always blamed other countries for forcing him to act as he did; he always accompanied aggression by statements of hope for the future and a warning of his next offensive deed.

In 1934 Hitler attempted to gain Austria by an internal coup but momentarily failed. The next year, however, for the sake of nationalism the Saarlanders, although almost entirely Catholic, voted overwhelmingly to give up their international position under the League and return to a Germany ruled by anti-Catholic, pagan Nazis.

In 1935 Hitler openly declared that Germany was rearming; he introduced conscription and set as his goal an army of 550,000 men. He regretted the decision, he said, but Germany had to be able to protect herself against enemies. He used as a pretext the action by France four days earlier in doubling the term of military service in the army and reducing the age limit. He did not mention the fact that France had made this move because she was entering a period of decline in the number of recruits resulting from the fall in the birthrate during World War I. Hitler rightly judged that the British, French, and Italians would restrict their protest against this violation of the treaty of Versailles to words. He denounced collective security as "unrealistic," a view shared by Neville Chamberlain and many other, if not most, statesmen of the decade, and offered instead nonaggression agreements with all Germany's neighbors except Lithuania.

In the same year, 1935, Hitler persuaded the British government to sign a treaty approving Germany's right to build a navy up to 35 per cent of Britain's naval strength and submarines up to 100 per cent of the submarine power of the British Commonwealth. The treaty was negotiated without prior consultation by the British government with any other state. By it the British government, hoping to limit Germany's naval rearmament, which it considered inevitable, violated the treaty of Versailles a few weeks after having jointly with France and Italy condemned Germany's unilateral violation of the same treaty.

Formation of the Axis

The Ethiopian war and Italy's conflict with the League offered Hitler the opportunity in 1936 to move fast on several fronts. Mussolini had up to now mistrusted Hitler as a rival in power and glory, and Hitler had failed to win his cooperation. The difficulties with Britain and France forced the Duce to seek support in Germany, the enemy of the League, the opponent of collective security, and a colleague in totalitarianism. The Axis Pact between these two powers was achieved in October, 1936; henceforth Mussolini was tied to a state greater than his own and far more ably and daringly led. He quickly became the first Nazi foreign victim.

Taking advantage of Mussolini's lack of freedom to act in Europe, Hitler forced upon Austria in July, 1936, a treaty which, seeming to assure Austria's continued independence, contained the means for further German control. Austria promised to "maintain a foreign policy based always on the principle that Austria acknowledges herself to be a German State," a clause which could justify Germany's demanding that Austria follow the Nazi foreign policy. By secret terms Austria agreed to stop the press war against Germany, free the Austrian Nazi prisoners involved in the murder of Dollfuss and other affairs, and resume normal economic relations and tourist traffic between the two countries; that is, Austria agreed to permit the country to be filled with Nazi agents. Lastly, the Austrian government had to take crypto-Nazis like Glaise-Horstenau and Artur von Seyss-Inquart into the cabinet, where they would be in a position to prepare Austria for absorption into Germany.

Military Occupation of Rhineland

The most important and the most dangerous move by Germany, the military occupation of the neutralized Rhineland and the denunciation of the Locarno pact, occurred in the same year as a by-product of the Ethiopian crisis. Hitler acted against the advice of his generals to wait for adequate military preparations. Certain that the British and French governments would do nothing but protest, on March 7 he sent German troops into the Rhineland. He justified the action on grounds of self-protection against the Franco-Russian alliance, which the French Chamber had just ratified. In place of the Locarno agreement, he offered to France and Belgium nonaggression treaties to endure twenty-five years; to Great Britain, a treaty against aggression from the air; and to France a new demilitarized zone treating both France and Germany alike. The whole arrangement should be guaranteed by Great Britain, Italy, and, if she wished, the Netherlands. To her Eastern neighbors Germany also offered nonaggression treaties; and now that she was in a position of equality with other states, Germany, Hitler said, was prepared to discuss the question of the disposal of the former German colonies, re-entry into the League, and the reform of that body. As the French ambassador in Berlin said, "Hitler struck his adversary in the face, and as he did so declared: 'I bring you proposals for peace.' "

"The forty-eight hours after the march into the Rhineland," Hitler later admitted, "were the most nerve-racking in my life. If the French had then marched into the Rhineland we would have had to withdraw with our tails between our legs, for the military resources at our disposal would have been wholly inadequate for even a moderate resistance." The occupation of the Rhineland not merely violated the treaty of Versailles; in the Locarno treaty it was specifically designated as a *casus belli.* Yet Hitler's prediction was correct: the Locarno powers and the League Council met, discussed, denounced, and acquiesced. Britain had already made the naval treaty with Germany. Why should she oppose this new act? France would have had to mobilize her entire army to resist, and she did not wish to do so. The Popular Front government in power at the time was so unpopular among French rightist circles that many Frenchmen were saying, "Better Hitler than Blum."

By inaction at this moment France allowed her entire military and diplomatic superiority in Europe to go by default. She faced a rearmed Germany divided from her by no demilitarized zone and with a far larger and more populous territory and a much more efficient industry. Her system of alliances with small powers on Germany's eastern frontier no longer looked impressive. Henceforth France's resources could not meet the demands of her diplomatic commitments. As for the British, Hitler, in October, declared to the Italian foreign minister that they were governed by "incompetents."

Anti-Comintern Pact

The Führer used anticommunism as part of his line of agitation. He admired Stalin and borrowed many ideas and methods from the Communists, and he had no objection to treaties with them. In the first years of his rule, however, he needed to destroy the Communist competitor within Germany, and he found diatribes against communism useful in winning support at home and abroad. "Perhaps the time is coming more quickly than we think," he said in a speech in November, 1936, "when the rest of

Europe will no longer regard with resentment the founding of a National Socialist German Reich, but will rejoice that this dam was raised against the Bolshevik flood."

The line proved useful in reaching an agreement with Japan. In November 1936, the two powers signed the Anti-Comintern Pact, directed, according to the open clauses, against the "world-conspiracy" of communism, but without mentioning the Soviet Union. In secret clauses, the two agreed to sign no political agreements with the Soviet Union and in the event of an unprovoked attack or threat by the latter against either of them to "take no measures which would tend to ease the situation of the U.S.S.R." Other states signed the Anti-Comintern Pact in time, among them Italy; the German-Japanese relations were to develop into an alliance and partnership in war.

Hitler Woos Poland

Hitler set out to win the favor not merely of Italy but of Poland. Whereas Mussolini reluctantly acquiesced in the Axis Pact, the Polish foreign minister, Colonel Beck, turned for a time toward Germany, and in 1934 signed a treaty of nonaggression with that state. Hitler planned to weaken Poland's alliance with France and to assure good relations with a potential opponent while taking the aggressive elsewhere. That the German people disliked the treaty did not matter; they and the rest of the world misread its intent. Hitler played on Beck's vanity and mistrust of the Soviet Union. When France negotiated an alliance with the Soviet Union, the Führer found Beck angry at the French ally and ready to assert Poland's independence by inclining toward Germany. The latter's withdrawal from the League conformed to Beck's own views about that organization, and in the same year that he signed the nonaggression pact with Germany, Beck notified the League of Poland's cancellation of the minorities treaty.

This unilateral breach of an international legal commitment set a precedent for Hitler to cite when he subsequently tore to shreds the Treaty of Versailles, which happened to be the treaty basis for Poland's existence. Göring was sent in the next year to woo the Poles, "almost suggesting an anti-Russian alliance and a joint attack on Russia." He let it be understood "that the Ukraine would become a Polish sphere of influence and North-western Russia would be Germany's." He did not say how Germany would be able to reach northwestern Russia, unless through Poland. The Poles were too wary to take the bait, but Beck later came to Berlin and found "a far-reaching agreement of views."

In the next year the Nazi agitation in Danzig for a return to the Reich disturbed the Poles, and, upon the German remilitarization of the Rhineland, Colonel Beck offered to the French to live up to treaty obligations and enter a war against Germany. The French preferred peace, and Hitler sent Göring again to Poland with the message that "Germany was completely reconciled to her present territorial status. Germany would not attack Poland and had no intention of seizing the Polish Corridor." Germany, he said, needed a strong Poland to offset Soviet aggression. And Hitler told the Polish ambassador that "Danzig is bound up with Poland." The Führer climaxed this display of cordiality by signing a treaty with Poland to end the quarrels over the treatment of their respective minorities. The Polish nation and the Polish state, he said in a speech in January, 1937, "have become realities." Lulled by Germany, Poland prevented the emergence of any new diplomatic obstacle to Germany's plans for eastern conquest.

Intervention in Spain

In Spain affairs were developing admirably for Germany. The outbreak of civil war enabled Hitler to expand his range of action. General Franco seemed a likely candidate to emulate the totalitarian dictators and might align with his colleagues in Germany and Italy to checkmate France. Hitler sent large supplies and a good many military technicians to Franco, among which were the material and personnel for an air force, to test new tactics of warfare. In return, Germany received iron ore, mercury, and other raw materials needed for the Four-Year Plan. That Mussolini participated actively on Franco's side was similarly advantageous. Having won a glorious victory in Ethiopia, the Duce hoped for good fishing in Spain. Just what fish and how many he expected to catch were questions never answered, but the Balaeric Isles might change hands, economic concessions in Spain might be acquired, military and naval bases established, France restrained, and one more move taken to transform the Mediterranean into an Italian sea.

Mussolini miscalculated on all points. The Spanish nationalists refused to become an Italian satellite. They gave Mussolini nothing except thanks and general promises of cooperation. They, too, accepted the Italian aid in troops and supplies while privately laughing at the fighting inefficiency of many of the troops. The Duce found himself more dependent on Germany than he had been during the Ethiopian crisis. As his aggression in Spain continued to antagonize Great Britain and France, the possibility of playing between these two powers and Germany was destroyed. In late 1937 he had to acquiesce in Austria's loss of independence to Germany; his dependence was just beginning.

The blessings from the Spanish civil war for Hitler were so manifold that they affected his relations with Great Britain and France. These two powers and the Soviet Union had insisted on setting up international machinery for enforcing nonintervention in Spain. No one entirely abided by the program—least of all Germany, Italy, and the Soviet Union. International cooperation once more proved a fiasco, and the prolonged failure became a source of embarrassment and loss of prestige to both Britain and France. The French people were so divided in their sympathies toward the two sides in Spain (the rightists for Franco; the socialists, Communists, and some bourgeois groups for the Republicans) that French activity in foreign relations was blocked. The longer the Civil War lasted, the more disunited the French people became, and Germany saw to it that the war endured.

On November 5, 1937, Hitler disclosed his plans to a small group in the Reich Chancellery. The war minister, Field-Marshal von Blomberg, the commander in chief of the army, Colonel-General Werner von Fritsch, the commander in chief of the navy, Admiral Erich Raeder, the commander in chief of the air force, Göring, and the foreign minister, Konstantin von Neurath, attended the meeting. The Führer spoke without interruption for four hours. The course of events was proving so favorable to his policies that he felt expansive and exalted as he sketched the line of future action. According to the minutes taken by Colonel Hossbach, he said that Germany required living space to supply her growing population with food and raw materials. "There had never been spaces without a master," he declared, "and there were none today; the attacker always comes up against a possessor. The question for Germany ran: where could she achieve the greatest gain at the lowest cost." Since Russia, Great Britain, and France all hated Germany, the latter could achieve her ambitions solely by force. She would reach the peak of her military power in 1943–1945; her equipment would then be new, whereas that of her enemies would remain out of date. "It was while the rest of the world was preparing its defences that we were obliged to take the offensive. . . . One thing only was certain, that we could not wait longer. If he was still living, it was his unalterable resolve to solve Germany's problem of space at the latest by 1943–1945."

First of all, Hitler intended to overrun Austria and Czechoslovakia and secure Germany's flank on the east and south. He did not beleive that either France or Great Britain would defend Czechoslovakia and thought that, anyway, Germany's western defenses were sufficient to restrain them. He expected Italy to remain neutral, and he planned the conquest to occur so swiftly that Poland and the Soviet Union would not interfere. He envisaged two other possibilities, one of internal strife in France, the other of a Mediterranean war between Italy and the Western powers; in either development his first objective remained the same, the seizure of Austria and Czechoslovakia. Blomberg, Fritsch, and Neurath, who expressed doubts about the wisdom of his judgment, were shortly replaced by more pliable figures; Göring and Raeder remained silent. When the student of these years considers the question of the causes of World War II, he need go no farther than Adolf Hitler. The sole remaining point of interest is the way in which he brought about the conflict.

German Seizure of Austria

The seizure of Austria came with the speed which Hitler liked to display. The Austrian Nazis planned a coup d'état in the spring of 1938; and when Chancellor Schuschnigg discovered the fact he became so concerned over German-Austrian relations that he agreed to a conference with Hitler at Berchtesgaden, in Bavaria. As soon as the chancellor arrived, February 12, 1938, he was submitted to an outburst of fury from Hitler which lasted two hours.

The whole history of Austria [Hitler shouted] is just one uninterrupted act of high treason. . . . Listen. You don't really think that you can move a single stone in Austria without my hearing about it the very next day, do you? You don't seriously believe that you can stop me, or even delay me for half an hour, do you? . . . After the army, my S.A. and the Austrian Legion [Austrian Nazis who had fled to Germany and were organized there into a fighting force] would move in, and nobody can stop their just revenge—not even I. Do you want to make another Spain of Austria?

No power would aid Austria, he declared; and he demanded that Schuschnigg legalize Austrian Nazi activity, appoint the Nazi Seyss-Inquart as minister of interior with control of the police, reinstate all Nazi officials who had been dismissed, systematically exchange officers between the German and the Austrian armies, and assimilate the Austrian economy to that of Germany, appointing a Nazi nominee as minister of finance.

Schuschnigg acquiesced under the menace of German military action, but once back in Austria, his courage revived. He proposed to hold a plebiscite on March 13 over whether the Austrians wished the country to remain independent. When Hitler learned of this attempt to block his plans, in fury he immediately started the army toward the frontier, instructed the Austrian Nazis concerning their part in the assault, and rushed Prince Philip of Hesse to Rome to reassure the Duce. He demanded substitution for this plebiscite of one of his own formulation to be held in three weeks.

By the time Schuschnigg agreed, Hitler had raised the price to include the replacement of Schuschnigg by Seyss-Inquart and the appointment of a list of other stooges as ministers. The Austrian president, Miklas, accepted Schuschnigg's resignation but refused to appoint Inquart as his successor—down that road lay the death of Austria. Göring thereupon telephoned Seyss-Inquart (it was 5:30 P.M.):

Look here, you go immediately together with Lieutenant-General Muff [the German military attaché] and tell the Federal President that, if the conditions which are known to you are not accepted immediately, the troops already stationed at the frontier will move in tonight along the whole line, and Austria will cease to exist.

The president refused to accept the demands within the two hours granted him, but Göring had a way out.

If Schuschnigg had resigned, Seyss-Inquart should still consider himself officially a minister and should execute Göring's orders in the name of the Austrian government. Göring then dictated a telegram for Seyss-Inquart to send to Berlin asking for military aid "to support it [the Austrian government] in its task and to help to prevent bloodshed." At the last minute, Miklas capitulated, but the German troops were already on the way into Austria. On March 12 the occupation was complete; and when on the next day Austria became a province of the Reich, Hitler, weeping with emotion, remarked, "Yes, a good political action saves blood." On that same night the Nazis arrested in Vienna alone 76,000 persons. When the annexation was approved by plebiscite in an almost unanimous vote, directed, supervised, and counted by the Nazis, Hitler said, "For me this is the proudest hour of my life."

The other powers had foreseen the latest violation of the treaty system of post-World War I. The French and the British governments had only verbal protests ready; in addition to their aversion to war, they were disarmed by Hitler's appeal to the right of national self-determination. Italy alone caused Hitler worry; but Mussolini had involved himself too deeply in Spain and was too much at odds with Great Britain and France to risk alienating Germany. When Prince Philip of Hesse arrived with a personal message of reassurance from Hitler, Mussolini was "very friendly" and sent his regards to the Führer. The latter was overjoyed and replied, "I will never forget him for this. . . . As soon as the Austrian affair is settled, I shall be ready to go with him, through thick and thin, no matter what happens." He kept his promise longer than he kept that given by Göring at the same time to the Czechoslovakian minister in Berlin. "I give you my word of honour," Göring said, "that Czechoslovakia has nothing to fear from the Reich."

German Destruction of Czechoslovakia

The destruction of Czechoslovakia ranks as Hitler's masterpiece. For this act the Führer inveigled his enemies, Great Britain and France, into preparing the victim and into cooperating in the promulgation and the execution of the sentence of death. He involved his reluctant partner, Italy, into helping without any other reward than a note of thanks. He destroyed the Little Entente while enjoying the cooperation of two future victims, Poland and Hungary, in tearing the present victim to pieces. He blocked the Soviet Union from intervention and forced France and Russia to renege on their alliances with Czechoslovakia. After the first partition of Czechoslovakia he completely ignored the French and British guarantee of the independence of the remnant state Czechia. The League of Nations had been established to prevent such aggression, and the interest of France, Great Britain, Italy, the Soviet Union, and every other state in Europe lay in the preservation of Czechoslovakia. One man ruling one country defied them all, and his success in doing so nipped in the bud a plot among his own military and civilian leaders to eliminate him as ruler. He not only won, he humiliated his enemies, although at the time they remained unaware of the fact.

The strategic importance of Czechoslovakia to Germany may be seen from the map. The country extends far into Central Europe, offering easy range for attack by land and air on the industrial areas of eastern and southern Germany and of Austria. Rich coal deposits, large industrial facilities including the famous Skoda armaments works, and fertile soil made the region one of the wealthiest of Europe, and the acquisition of its industrious population would increase German man power. To Hitler, however, these economic and demographic advantages meant little. The former Austrian petty bourgeois had been brought up to hate and despise all Slavs, particularly the Czechs, as "subhuman." The fact that 3¼ million Sudeten Germans lived in a Czech state was in his eyes an insult to the German race. He readily believed the lies reported by his intriguing colleagues, Ribbentrop, Goebbels, Himmler and others, about atrocities committed by the Czechs against the Germans.

The Nazi government had immediately after 1933 begun to subsidize the pro-Nazi Henlein party among the Sudeten Germans, for it planned to use this minority as the means to destroy the Czechoslovak state. As soon as Austria was occupied, Hitler called Henlein to Berlin and instructed him continuously to stir up trouble which German propaganda could employ to accuse the Czech government of persecution. He would then demand concessions which the Czech government could not accept. The Nazis in Germany would assist by speeches denouncing the Czechs as barbarians. A diplomatic campaign would be conducted to divert the sympathy of the other powers, especially Great Britain and France, from Czechoslovakia and to prevent them from assisting that state against a German offensive. The main arguments would be the right of national self-determination to justify the annexation of the Sudetenland by Germany, and the inhuman conduct of the Czechs to vindicate Germany's destruction of the Slav part of the state.

The propaganda campaign was already bearing fruit in April, 1938, when the British and French governments assured the Reich that they were pressing the Czechs to come to terms with the Sudeten Germans. Thereupon Hitler inquired of his general staff the number of divisions ready on the Czech border, receiving the satisfying answer of twelve. He was, however, still unprepared for an invasion, when on May 20 the Czech government suddenly became alarmed and ordered partial mobilization. To Hitler's surprise, the British and French governments immediately warned the Reich against the danger of a general war, and France and the Soviet Union promised Czechoslovakia to abide by their alliance. Hitler was seething with anger, as he assured the foreign powers, including Czechoslovakia, that he harbored no aggressive aims toward the country. Within ten days he issued the following secret instructions: "It is my unalterable decision to smash Czechoslovakia by military action in the near future," and he set October 1, 1938, as the deadline.

Through the summer the conflict between the Sudeten Germans and the Czech government continued, with Germany making sure that she held the center of international attention. In August the British government intervened in the internal affairs of Czechoslovakia without any invitation (although Prime Minister Neville Chamberlain claimed that the Czechs had invited him) by sending Lord Walter Runciman on a mission to explore what could be done about settling the dispute. Runciman paid special consideration to the Sudetens, stayed briefly with wealthy ex-Austrian aristocrats who disliked the Czech government, and prepared the way for subsequent British policy of selling out completely to the Nazis. In the meantime Hitler's own generals with two exceptions opposed his policy. They argued that the seizure of Czechoslovakia would cause a European war, which Germany could not win. Hitler cursed the generals to their faces and accepted the resignation of the chief of staff, General Beck.

In the crucial month of September events occurred thick and fast. Toward the end of the Runciman mission the Czech government greatly embarrassed the Sudeten Germans by suddenly accepting their demands, thus forcing them to improvise additional ones. Some German civilians and a few generals led by Beck plotted the deposition of Hitler, and other generals tried once more to dissuade Hitler from the attack. The London *Times* on September 7 in an editorial suggested that Czechoslovakia cede the Sudetenland to Germany. On September 12, to a wildly cheering audience at the Nazi party rally in Nürnberg, Hitler denounced the Czechs as an "irreconcilable enemy," accused Beneš of playing a "tactical game," and shouted, "The Germans in Czechoslovakia are neither defenceless nor are they deserted, and people should take notice of that fact." The speech brought an uprising in the Sudetenland, the Czech government imposed martial law, and the Sudeten leaders countered by crying, "We want to return to the Reich." Henlein and his cohorts fled to Germany, leaving a relatively quiet situation, but the German press screamed about a Czech "reign of terror." The crisis was developing as Hitler had anticipated.

Suddenly, on September 13, Neville Chamberlain proposed a personal interview with Hitler. He had consulted his colleague Daladier, whose cabinet was so divided over policy that the French premier left it to Chamberlain to settle the Czech affair as best he could. Hitler was surprised at Chamberlain's request, but he made the elderly British premier fly to Berchtesgaden for the interview. There on September 15 the Führer acted out his rage before Chamberlain. "He would face any war, even the risk of a world war, for this" (the annexation of the Sudeten Germans to the Reich), Hitler told the prime minister. "Here the limit had been reached where the rest of the world might do what it liked, he would not yield one single step. . . . He did not wish that any doubts should arise as to his absolute determination not to tolerate any longer that a small, second-rate country should treat the mighty thousand-year-old German Reich as something inferior." As the Führer continued to roar out these grievances, Chamberlain in turn grew angry and demanded, "If the Führer is determined to settle this matter by force without waiting even for a discussion between ourselves to take place, what did he let me come here for? I have wasted my time." This blunt assertion cooled the Führer somewhat, and they began to discuss terms. "Well," Hitler said, "if the British government were prepared to accept the idea of secession in principle, and to say so, there might be a chance then to have a talk." With that concession, if one may call it such, Chamberlain flew back to London for more consultation.

Hitler did not wish a peaceful solution. He was eager to destroy Czechoslovakia by war, and he did not believe that the French and the British would fight. In the conference at Berchtesgaden and in the subsequent conferences at Godesberg and at Munich he strove either to prevent agreement on any terms or to sign one which would leave him free subsequently to obliterate the Czech state. He continued the propaganda attacks on Czechoslovakia as before; he organized a Sudeten German Free Corps and prepared five armies for the invasion. He stirred up the Slovak Peoples party to demand autonomy for the Slovaks; and he encouraged the Polish and Hungarian governments to claim Czech territory which they coveted. He was afraid that the Czech government might agree to cede the Sudetenland and deprive him of a war. When he met Chamberlain at Godesberg on September 22 he found that his fears were justified; the Czechs had given in. What should he do?

Hitler appears not to have hesitated. In the face of the opposition of his generals, in the face of the opposition of France, Great Britain, and the Soviet Union, he replied, "I'm exceedingly sorry, but after the events of the last few days this solution is no longer any use." He now demanded not merely that the Sudetenland be ceded but that it be occupied at once by the German army prior to any plebiscite, and he set September 30 as a deadline for acceptance. Chamberlain showed Hitler his indignation at the way he had been treated, but he refused to abandon hope of saving the peace.

After discussion with the French and Czech governments, the British decided that Hitler's terms were too humiliating to be accepted. The Czech government reacted in the same way, and the British promised support should France and Czechoslovakia become involved in war. As a final effort, on September 26, Chamberlain sent Sir Horace Wilson to Berlin to appeal to the Führer. Sir Horace found the latter adamant, regardless of consequences. In a speech to a mass meeting that evening, Hitler declared:

> This Czech State began with a single lie, and the father of this lie was named Benes. . . . There is no such thing as a Czechoslovak nation, but only Czechs and Slovaks, and the Slovaks do not wish to have anything to do with the Czechs. . . .
>
> Now two men stand arrayed one against the other; there is Herr Benes, and here am I. We are two men of a different make-up. In the great struggle of the peoples, while Herr Benes was sneaking about through the world, I as a decent German soldier did my duty. And now today I stand over against this man as a

soldier of my people. . . . With regard to the problem of the Sudeten Germans, my patience is now at an end. I have made Herr Benes an offer which is nothing but the execution of what he himself has promised. The decision now lies in his hands: Peace or War. . . . Now let Herr Benes make his choice.

When Sir Horace saw Hitler after the speech and remarked that Great Britain would support France if the latter aided the Czechs and that a general war could hardly be avoided, Hitler in a state of frenzy replied, "That means that if France chooses to attack Germany, England feels it her duty to attack Germany also. I can only take note of this communication. . . . If France and England strike, let them do so. It is a matter of complete indifference to me. I am prepared for every eventuality. It is Tuesday today, and by next Monday we shall all be at war." Several times he shouted, "I will smash the Czechs."

The speech did not rule out Hitler's hesitation to risk a war. Ribbentrop and Himmler urged him to persevere, but Göring, von Neurath, the generals, and Admiral Raeder advised caution; and, although Hitler was not aware of the existence of the plot against him, Beck, Schacht, and others were renewing preparations with the use of the army division stationed at Potsdam to destroy him. The Führer reflected on Sir Horace Wilson's assertion that Great Britain and France would fight, and he was disturbed by the almost complete silence with which the people watched a mechanized division on September 27 roll through Berlin. When the Duce proposed a conference of himself, Hitler, Chamberlain, and Daladier, the Führer acquiesced.

Munich Agreement

The conference was held at Munich on September 29. Czechoslovakia was barred from attendance, and the Soviet Union was likewise excluded. Hitler would not have the former; no one wanted the latter. The Führer demanded and secured that agreement be reached by October 1. The British and the French accepted Hitler's terms, which a few days earlier they had rejected. On October 1 German troops marched into the Sudetenland. The plebiscite was never held, and the new frontier followed strategic more than nationality lines. It left 250,000 Germans in Czechoslovakia and incorporated 800,000 Czechs in the Reich. The Germans occupied without a shot the Czech system of fortifications, which, being built in the same way as the Maginot Line in France, gave them information about the latter. Beneš went into exile; the Czechs canceled the treaty with the Soviet Union; Poland seized Teschen, and a month later Ribbentrop and Ciano, Mussolini's foreign minister, dictated a new boundary between Czechoslovakia and Hungary.

The explanation for Hitler's victory at Munich is simple: the British and the French sacrificed everything, particularly another state, in order to preserve peace. In France Foreign Minister Georges Bonnet had worked closely with the Nazi government, both through official channels and behind the back of his colleagues. He had supported its demands and ordered the Czechs to give in. Prime Minister Daladier understood the import for France of the sacrifice of an ally, and feared that on his return from Munich he might be lynched. Actually the French were relieved over the preservation of peace; the French Chamber debated the Munich agreement only six hours, and supported the government by a vote of 543 to 75. In Great Britain Neville Chamberlain declared to an enthusiastic crowd gathered at the airport to welcome him back from Munich, "I believe it is peace in our time."

Chamberlain set most store by Hitler's agreement with him to negotiate over difficulties as they arose in the future; for, as a colleague said, Chamberlain regarded Hitler as a member if not of the Corporation of Birmingham at least of the Corporation of Manchester, and he thought that he knew how to manage the Führer. The British prime minister represented the desire to preserve peace held by the vast mass of the British people and the peoples of the Dominions. The government assured the public that it would accelerate rearmament and that the new Czechoslovak state was more secure than the old had ever been, for Great Britain and France had both verbally guaranteed its frontiers. The House of Commons voted 366 to 144 to approve the government's Munich action. Few Britishers, among them Alfred Duff Cooper and Winston Churchill, foresaw the tragic results of the policy of appeasement.

The two Slavic states, the Soviet Union and Czechoslovakia herself, were compelled to take a passive role. Russia said she was willing to honor the alliance with Czechoslovakia and fight; but according to the terms of the alliance she would do so only if France went to war, and France gave the Soviet Union no opportunity. The question of how the Soviet Union could reach its ally with troops still remained unsettled, for both Poland and Romania denied it transit rights. The Czechoslovaks were equally uncertain about whether they wished Soviet aid: the remedy might be worse than the disease. The Czechoslovakian government decided to leave its fate in the hands of Western powers. The state was too small to defend itself alone, and its existence ultimately depended upon world opinion. On October 1, 1938, the day on which the German troops crossed the frontier, the Cardinal-Primate of Bohemia ordered the following prayer to be read in all the Catholic churches and the identical prayer, with the substitution of "John Huss" for "St. Wenceslas," was offered in the Protestant churches:

> The land of St. Wenceslas has just been invaded by foreign armies and the thousand-year-old frontier has been violated. This sacrifice has been imposed on the nation of St. Wenceslas by our ally, France, and our friend, Britain. The Primate of the Ancient Kingdom of Bohemia is praying to God Almighty that the peace efforts prompting this terrible sacrifice will be crowned with success, and,

should they not, he is praying to the Almighty to forgive all those who impose this injustice upon the people of Czechoslovakia.[2]

When Chamberlain had driven through the streets of Munich after making the agreement with Hitler, he had been given an ovation. The German people shared the universal repugnance to war. The Führer reacted otherwise. "That fellow Chamberlain," he declared to S.S. companions, "has spoiled my entry into Prague." He set to work to destroy the remnant state, with the Slovaks and a German minority this time playing the part recently taken by the Sudeten Germans. On March 13 he called Father Tiso and Durcansky, the Slovak National party leaders, to Berlin and ordered them under threat of military occupation by the Germans and the Hungarians to secede from the Czech state. The Slovak parliament passed the necessary resolution on the next day. Simultaneously, Hitler settled the fate of the Czech portion. Throwing up violent propaganda about Czech atrocities toward the Germany minority, the Nazis on March 14 commanded President Hacha and his foreign minister to Berlin.

The crucial interview began at one o'clock in the morning with a demand by Hitler that Czechia sign a treaty making it a German protectorate. If the Czechs signed, their territory would be given autonomy and some national freedom; if they refused, the German army would march in and the state would be "trodden underfoot." Hitler then retired, and left Göring and Ribbentrop to attend to details. Hacha protested vehemently: "If I sign that document I shall be forever cursed by my people." The two Germans chased him around the table and forced a pen in his hand; Göring asserted that Prague would be immediately bombed to rubble if he did not sign at once. The ordeal lasted until 4:30 A.M. Hacha fainted three times, but this event had also been foreseen, and Hitler's personal physician was present to revive him. The exhausted president finally consulted his cabinet by telephone, and signed the treaty. "Our people will curse us," the Czech foreign minister said as the two left the Chancellery, "and yet we have saved their existence. We have preserved them from a horrible massacre."

The story given to the world was that President Hacha had requested the interview and had "confidently placed the fate of the Czech people in the hands of the Führer." Hitler exclaimed to his secretaries, "Children, this is the greatest day of my life. I shall go down to history as the greatest German." Within two hours the German troops began to occupy the Czech territory, and on March 15, 1939, Hitler was on the way to Prague. Back in London, Prime Minister Chamberlain informed the House of Commons that Great Britain would not have to honor its guarantee of Czechoslovakia's independence, because the country had broken up from within. In Rome the angry Mussolini received another telegram of thanks from Hitler for Italy's loyal support. "The Italians will laugh at me," the Duce

[2] John W. Wheeler-Bennett, *Munich: Prologue to Tragedy* (New York: Duell, Sloan & Pearce, Inc., 1948), p. 196.

said to Ciano; "every time Hitler occupies a country he sends me a message."

Soon after closing the story of Czechia and Slovakia Hitler set the date, which he kept, for smashing Poland at September 1, 1939. The negotiations which led to war concentrated on the competition between Great Britain and France, on the one hand, and Germany, on the other, for the cooperation of the Soviet Union. The relation of Poland to these two parties carried subsidiary significance, as did also that of Italy to Germany. The reader should keep in mind that during all these months Nazi propaganda about Polish atrocities and threats of war alternated with protestations of peaceful intentions and accusations that the other countries were determined to start a war.

The import of the Nazi destruction of Czechoslovakia in March, 1939, gradually became clear to Chamberlain, particularly when his own Conservative party threatened to rebel against his leadership. Then his anger at Hitler became as great as his trust had been, and from that time he never wavered in his determination to resist. Knowing that Poland stood next on the list, he declared in the House of Commons on March 31 that if that country were attacked Great Britain would lend it full support. Similarly disillusioned, the French government followed suit. Later the two powers extended their promise to apply to Greece and Romania, in which the Axis had shown interest, and to the Netherlands, Denmark, and Switzerland.

The British statement marked a revolution in policy suddenly forced upon an unprepared nation by events beyond its control. In 1925 Sir Austen Chamberlain, Neville's brother, had privately said that "for the Polish corridor, no British government ever will or ever can risk the bones of a British grenadier." Just before the Munich crisis, Neville Chamberlain had declared in a broadcast speech, "How horrible, fantastic, incredible it is that we should be digging trenches and trying on gas-masks here, because of a quarrel in a far-away country between people of whom we know nothing." The guarantee of the integrity of Poland revealed the failure of British postwar foreign policy. Great Britain had helped to sabotage the League, her dominions were opposed to becoming involved in European affairs, and, except for weak and vacillating France, she had no ally.

COMPETITION FOR STALIN'S SUPPORT

The British and French governments thought of strengthening their position by negotiations with the Soviet Union. In March Stalin proposed a conference of Britain, France, and the U.S.S.R. with Poland, Romania, and Turkey to find means of stopping aggression. Negotiations continued in a rather desultory way throughout the spring and summer. "I must confess to the most profound distrust of Russia," Neville Chamberlain wrote in his diary March 26, 1939. "I have no belief whatever in her ability to maintain an effective offensive, even if she wanted to. And I distrust her motives, which seem to me to have little connection with our ideas of liberty, and to be concerned only with getting everyone else by the ears." [3] Stalin suspected that the British and French were seeking to turn Nazi and Japanese aggression against the Soviet Union. His conditions for alliance were unacceptable to Britain and France, and theirs to him. The negotiations finally reached an impasse because of the policy of Poland.

Poland's Dilemma

The Polish government thought that its state could continue independent solely by keeping free of either German or Soviet entanglements. Hitler proposed to solve the Polish problem by regaining Danzig, acquiring a corridor across the Polish corridor, and enticing Poland into an aggressive war against the Soviet Union. When he offered these terms to Colonel Beck late in 1938 and again in March, 1939, the latter absolutely refused them. Beck, understanding what Poland's fate as a German satellite would be, replied that Poland would meet force with force. During the negotiations between the Western powers and the Soviet Union Colonel Beck likewise repelled any suggestion that the Soviet Union should use Poland as a base for military action against Germany.

The completely negative attitude taken by the Poles toward the Soviet Union may be seen in the remarks of the Polish ambassador to Soviet Foreign Minister Molotov, in May, 1939.

> We could not accept a one-sided Soviet guarantee. Nor could we accept a mutual guarantee, because in the event of a conflict with Germany our forces would be completely engaged, and so we would not be in any position to give help to the Soviets. Also we could not accept collective negotiations, and made our adoption of a definite attitude conditional on the result of the Anglo-Franco-Soviet negotiations. We rejected all discussion of matters affecting us other than by the bilateral method. . . . I indicated our favorable attitude to the Anglo-Franco-Soviet negotiations, and once more emphasized our entire loyalty in relation to the Soviets. In the event of conflict we by no means rejected specified forms of Soviet aid, but considered it premature to determine them definitely. We considered it premature to open bilateral negotiations with the Soviets before the Anglo-Franco-Soviet negotiations had achieved a result.[4]

The Poles were determined to keep the Soviet Union out of Poland; they might accept military or other supplies, preferably at the border, but no troops.

The predatory character of communism precluded any cooperation

[3] Keith Feiling, *Life of Neville Chamberlain* (New York: Saint Martin's Press, Inc., 1947), p. 403.

[4] Gordon A. Craig and Felix Gilbert, *The Diplomats 1919–1939* (Princeton, N. J.: Princeton University Press, 1953), p. 609.

between these two states, and the same reaction was true of the Baltic and the other border states. An alliance between Great Britain, France, the Soviet Union, and the small states of Eastern Europe seems to have been possible solely if the small states were sacrificed to communism. The British and the French found no way in which to defend these states against Germany without the aid of the Soviet Union; but the price of Soviet aid would be the loss of their independence, not to Germany, but to the Soviet Union. As the Polish general, Smigly-Rydz, said, "With the Germans we risk losing our liberty; with the Russians, our souls." That fact, clear to the Poles, vaguely felt by the British and French, underlay the failure of the negotiations between the Western powers and the Soviet Union.

Hitler's Plans

When Hitler learned about the British and French guarantee to Poland, he shouted to a private audience, "I'll cook them a stew that they'll choke on." The "stew" was immediately prepared. In the previous November Göring had demanded a rise in armaments production from an index level of 100 to that of 300. The size of the army was constantly growing. In March, 1939, Hitler delivered an ultimatum to Lithuania and received back Memelland. In April he was pleased when Mussolini, prey to fear, jealousy, and ambition, seized Albania, because that act enhanced Italy's need for German aid. On May 22 the two powers signed the Pact of Steel, as the Nazis called it, one of the most frankly aggressive treaties in history. The next day Hitler called together the senior officers in the army, navy, and air force, and informed them of his plans. War, he said, was inevitable.

> Danzig is not the object of our activities. It is a question of expanding our living-space in the east, of securing our food-supplies and of settling the Baltic problem. . . . There is no question of sparing Poland and we are left with the decision: To attack Poland at the first suitable opportunity.
>
> We cannot expect a repetition of the Czech affair. There will be war. Our task is to isolate Poland. The success of this isolation will be decisive. . . . There must be no simultaneous conflict with the Western Powers.
>
> If it is not certain that a German-Polish conflict will not lead to war in the west, the fight must be primarily against England and France.
>
> . . . The idea that we can get off cheaply is dangerous; there is no such possibility. We must burn our boats. It is no longer a question of right and wrong, but of life or death for eighty million human beings.

The occupation of the Netherlands and Belgium would be necessary in order to protect the Ruhr, and he planned to take the French Channel ports, instead of Paris, immediately. Then Germany would possess bases from which the air force and the navy could conquer Great Britain by blockade. He scarcely mentioned France, a country in his opinion too weak to be worthy of much consideration.

The program was rather comprehensive—the seizure of Poland, the

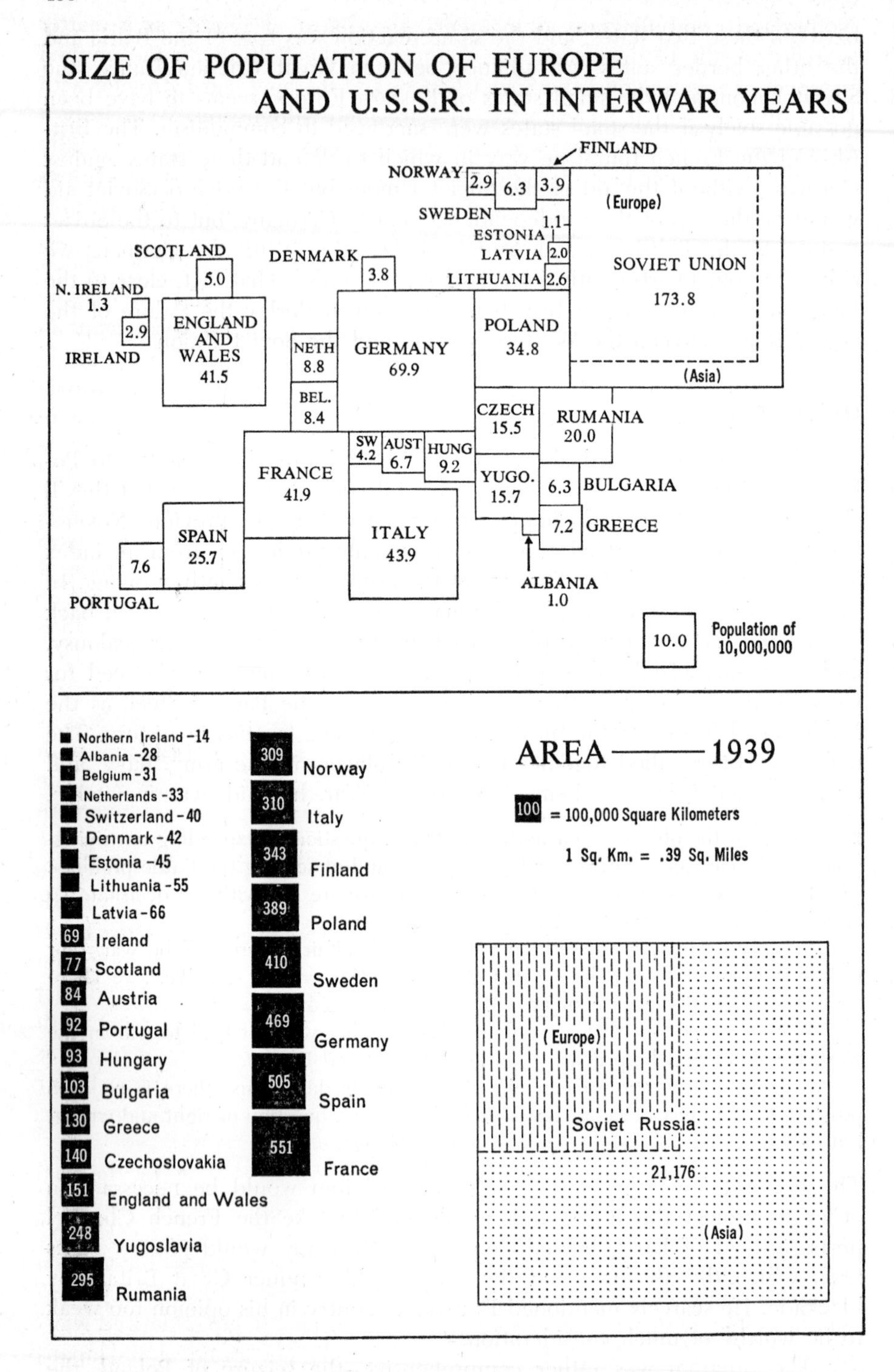
SIZE OF POPULATION OF EUROPE AND U.S.S.R. IN INTERWAR YEARS
FINLAND
NORWAY 2.9
6.3
3.9
(Europe)
SWEDEN
1.1
ESTONIA
LATVIA 2.0
SOVIET UNION
173.8
LITHUANIA 2.6
SCOTLAND
DENMARK
5.0
3.8
N. IRELAND
1.3
2.9
IRELAND
ENGLAND AND WALES
41.5
NETH 8.8
GERMANY 69.9
POLAND 34.8
(Asia)
BEL. 8.4
CZECH 15.5
RUMANIA 20.0
SW 4.2
AUST 6.7
HUNG 9.2
FRANCE 41.9
YUGO. 15.7
6.3 BULGARIA
7.2 GREECE
SPAIN 25.7
ITALY 43.9
7.6
PORTUGAL
ALBANIA 1.0
10.0 Population of 10,000,000
Northern Ireland -14
Albania -28
Belgium -31
Netherlands -33
Switzerland -40
Denmark -42
Estonia -45
Lithuania -55
Latvia -66
69 Ireland
77 Scotland
84 Austria
92 Portugal
93 Hungary
103 Bulgaria
130 Greece
140 Czechoslovakia
151 England and Wales
248 Yugoslavia
295 Rumania
309 Norway
310 Italy
343 Finland
389 Poland
410 Sweden
469 Germany
505 Spain
551 France
AREA —— 1939
100 = 100,000 Square Kilometers
1 Sq. Km. = .39 Sq. Miles
(Europe)
Soviet Russia
21,176
(Asia)

Netherlands, and Belgium as incidents, the defeat of France as a matter scarcely worthy of discussion, the conquest of the Baltic with the implied prospect of a war against the Soviet Union, and the long, hard struggle with Great Britain, which he expected to starve into submission. With Italy a dependent ally, Austria and Czechoslovakia already absorbed, the friendly dictator Franco in Spain, and the Balkan states easily disposed of, Hitler's goal was the conquest of most of Europe and the domination of the rest. He still hoped, however, that he could take Poland without a general war, and he sought to accomplish that end by an agreement with the Soviet Union. He was willing to sign one on almost any terms, for in any case he expected subsequently to attack his proposed partner. A little delay in gaining part of Poland or the Baltic states or whatever else the Soviet Union would demand did not matter, since these areas as well as much of Russia would in time be conquered. What he wanted was an agreement prior to the deadline of September set for the attack on Poland. With any treaty he could prevent the Soviet Union from aligning with Great Britain and France against him, and he did not expect these two powers alone to risk a war over Poland. He ordered the Polish campaign to be executed with such speed that no one could interfere before it was over. The shock of surprise would keep Europe inactive.

Nazi-Soviet Agreement, 1939

In the Soviet Union Stalin had recently replaced the Jew Litvinov as foreign minister by Molotov, in a move interpreted as easing relations with Germany. Almost immediately each government felt out the other. The Soviets saw definite advantages to be gained from an understanding with Germany. Since they suspected the British and French of repeating the appeasement policy of the Austrian and Czech crises, they could block any attempt to turn Nazi attentions against them by reaching prior understanding with Germany themselves. Although under no illusions about the trustworthiness of the Nazis, they might expand their territory and strengthen their defense along the Baltic by treaty with Germany. They feared that they would derive nothing but German enmity from an agreement with Great Britain and France, whereas a treaty with Germany might turn this power's aggression toward the West and away from the East. When Hitler began in August to press the Communists for a settlement and proved entirely agreeable on terms, Stalin acquiesced.

Foreign Minister Joachim von Ribbentrop flew to Moscow for the final negotiations on August 23-24. He assured the Soviets that "the German-Japanese friendship was in no wise directed against the Soviet Union." Quite the contrary, it enabled Germany "to make an effective contribution to an adjustment of the differences between the Soviet Union and Japan." Stalin replied with a variation on a Hitlerian speech. "If Japan desired war," he said, "it could have it. The Soviet Union was not afraid of it [Japan] and was prepared for it. If Japan desired peace—so much the better!" He refused to take the initiative; he left that to Germany. Ribbentrop said that "England was weak and wanted to let others fight for its presumptuous claim to world domination." Stalin "eagerly concurred." "If England dominates the world in spite of this," he said, "this was due to the stupidity of the other countries that always let themselves be bluffed." A little later in the conference, however, Stalin "further expressed the opinion that England, despite its weakness, would wage war craftily and stubbornly."

On the Anti-Comintern Pact, Ribbentrop said that it was "basically directed not against the Soviet Union but against the Western Democracies." Stalin replied that it "had in fact frightened principally the City of London and the small British merchants." And Ribbentrop quoted the Berlin humorists, who were saying that "Stalin will yet join the Anti-Comintern Pact." Ribbentrop knew that the German people "felt instinctively that between Germany and the Soviet Union no natural conflicts of interests existed," and Stalin "readily believed this." They ended with toasts, one of Stalin's being, "I know how much the German nation loves its Führer; I should therefore like to drink to his health." [5]

The agreement consisted of two parts, a public one guaranteeing nonaggression toward each other, and a secret one dividing the territorial spoils. The Soviet Union gained Finland, Latvia, and Estonia as within her sphere of influence. Vilna was to return to Lithuania. Poland was to be divided between the two powers approximately along the lines of the Narew, Vistula, and San rivers. The Soviet Union asserted a special interest in Bessarabia, and Germany declared its "complete political disinterestedness" in Southeastern Europe.

Italy was kept more or less informed of Hitler's moves, and grew increasingly alarmed. After Ciano visited Germany during the middle of August, he confided to his diary, "I return to Rome completely disgusted with the Germans, with their leader, and with their way of doing things. They have betrayed us and lied to us. Now they are dragging us into an adventure which we do not want and which may compromise the régime and the country as a whole." The Duce was torn between approval and doubt. He wanted spoils in Croatia, Dalmatia, and elsewhere; he felt honor bound to Hitler; he hoped the democracies would not fight; he was afraid of Hitler's rage. "He believes that a denunciation of the Pact of Steel might induce Hitler to abandon the Polish question in order to square accounts with Italy," Ciano wrote. "This makes him nervous and disturbed." [6] The Duce knew that Italy could not fight a major war, and at the last moment he politely informed Hitler that Italy would remain neutral. The Führer did not greatly mind; he had a better thing in the Soviet agreement.

[5] *Nazi-Soviet Relations 1939–1941* (Washington, D.C.: U.S. Department of State, 1948), pp. 72-75.

[6] Alan L. C. Bullock, *Hitler: A Study in Tyranny* (New York: Harper and Brothers, 1953), pp. 479, 490-491.

The attack on Poland began on schedule. The British and French governments declared war on September 3, but were unable to help Poland. Within two weeks the German mobile armored troops and the air corps cut the Polish army to shreds. Foreign Minister Beck and Marshal Smigly-Rydz fled the country. They had overestimated Poland's strength and misunderstood Hitler. They had helped to destroy the only means of security against both Germany and the Soviet Union which small states had, the League of Nations and collective security. They, the leaders of Poland, had made a mistake. It looked for a time as though the Soviet Union had also made one. The destruction of "this ridiculous state" (Hitler's expression) proceeded so fast that the Soviet leaders were shocked and had to speed preparations for occupying their share of Poland. The Nazis, still needing Soviet cooperation, showed their friendship by agreeing to the Soviet request to exchange a part of Poland for the inclusion of Lithuania in the Soviet sphere of influence. Stalin immediately forced treaties of mutual assistance on the three Baltic states and sent Soviet troops to protect them, as he said, against aggression. For Germany everything went according to schedule.

After the annexation of Austria one of the older German diplomats remarked that Bismarck would have consolidated his position over a period of years before attempting something else. Foreign Minister Ribbentrop replied, "Then you have no conception of the dynamics of National Socialism."

Suggestions for Further Reading

The Readings for Chapter 5 should be used for this decade. The following titles may be consulted in addition.

BELOFF, MAX. *The Foreign Policy of Soviet Russia, 1929–1941.* See the Readings for Chapter 16. Basic work.

BULLOCK, A. L. C. *Hitler.* See the Readings for Chapter 14. Indispensable for the story of German diplomacy. It throws much light on the personalities and the diplomacy of other countries.

HOFER, WALTHER. *War Premeditated, 1939.* Toronto: Longmans, Green & Company, Ltd., 1956. The best survey of the origins of World War II. By a Swiss scholar.

LANGER, WILLIAM L., and S. EVERETT GLEASON. *The Challenge to Isolation, 1937–1940.* New York: Harper & Brothers, 1952.

———, and ———. *The Undeclared War, 1940–1941.* New York: Harper & Brothers, 1953. Although these two volumes by Langer and Gleason pertain primarily to the foreign policy of the United States, they discuss in detail the policies of foreign powers as well.

Chapter 18 · Imperial Relations in the 1930's

ECONOMIC CRISIS AND IMPERIAL RELATIONS

The world economic crisis affected all empires, and World War II drew all colonies into the global holocaust. Between these two catastrophes lay a decade of European experience with empire during which some dependencies played a passive role or temporarily drew closer than before to the mother country, while others strove for political freedom. Most colonies increased their need for economic aid from the imperialist power; in a few colonies the need diminished. In some instances the dependency drew closer politically to the mother country because of fear of a predatory power; in others it tried to play a new power against the old. In most colonial areas the natives followed the European lead. One may argue that World War II grew from acts of imperialism such as Japan's seizure of Manchuria in 1931 and Italy's conquest of Ethiopia in 1936. Neither of these two crises, however, brought general war.

Such a global conflict came when Hitler threatened the European balance of power by aggression in Europe itself. The possession of colonial territories committed European states to the defense of their dependencies, quickly transforming a limited war into a global one. Imperialism connected Europe's conflict with Far Eastern aggression, and the United States, the most active power in trying to protect China, also became involved. This chapter will supplement that on international relations by discussing the imperial ties from the economic crisis to the outbreak of World War II. Much of this development had secondary importance for the outbreak of the war, but it is significant in explaining the war's global nature and in providing background for understanding the impact of the war upon imperial relations.

The effects of world depression placed non-European regions at an economic disadvantage. Areas of subsistence economy hardly felt the impact of crisis, except when natives employed elsewhere returned home to find food and shelter. Areas integrated into international economy and producing almost entirely food and raw materials found that the price of these articles dropped far more than prices of industrial goods. Terms of trade changed radically in favor of the industrial states. Europe could therefore shift part of the effects of the crisis from its own people to the colonials. Fluctuations in the price of colonial products reduced the already low income; ability to pay for imported industrial goods declined sharply.

Colonial leaders concluded that their territories must industrialize in order to withstand the effects of another such crisis. To do so they needed Western investment capital, but they did not trust the guidance of Western industrial nations which had been unable to prevent crisis. Since capital for industrialization was unavailable, the colonies faced unemployment, large debts, and lack of market. By raising more of its own food, Europe reduced the need for colonial products, importing less in proportion to population than it had before. The colonials tried to stabilize their economy by local legislation or by international agreements to regulate output, but the limits to self-help were narrow. In the latter half of the thirties the League of Nations called a conference to consider the question of bringing producer and consumer of raw materials together. Its efforts failed completely. Dependent areas that normally needed immigrants with European skills in some instances actually lost population; people found it easier to live in the home country on a dole than in the colony.

FORMATION OF IMPERIAL BLOCS

Each mother country except civil-war Spain proposed to compensate for losses in the international market by seeking to organize its empire into a more or less closed economic system. France went farthest in this direction. The government held a conference of colonial representatives in Paris in December, 1934, to plan the broad lines of development. The dependencies were to emphasize the production of such food and raw materials as France had hitherto imported from foreign countries, and were to obtain in France the manufactured articles they needed. The mother country would provide funds and technical aid. Forty million Frenchmen would be supplemented by 60 million colonials, all working under French guidance.

The theory never became fact. The vast size of the colonies and the thin spread of the population, resulting in an acute shortage of labor, prevented France from rapidly developing her dependencies. Lacking sufficient investment capital for all purposes, she concentrated on enterprises of direct interest to the mother country and to Frenchmen resident in the colonies. The government encouraged the raising of necessary crops by paying bounties and spent considerable sums on the construction of means of transportation and the development of modern sections of cities like Casablanca and Dakar. France had introduced imperial tariff preference in the last decade of the preceding century. The tariff law of 1928 strengthened this bond, and during the depression France supplemented tariff unity by subjecting foreign imports into France and the colonies to quota control.

Portugal under Salazar followed the French example; for the first time she began to send out colonists, to protect native labor from exploitation in the mines of the Union of South Africa, and to invest funds in constructing means of transportation and in producing materials for the Portuguese economy. In the Congo, Belgium advanced toward the same objective by dominating the carefully planned investment in the colony, but because of the terms of the international treaty of 1885 guaranteeing the "open door," she could not prevent foreign competition in imports.

In each of the three countries mentioned, the government during the decade increased its initiative in colonial economic affairs. The Netherlands did likewise. The Netherlands officials in the East Indies, for example, under guidance from the home country, reacted to the economic crisis by measures similar to those which European states took in their own internal affairs and by others which were possible only in a colonial region. They restricted production of tin, copra, sugar, and minerals, for which the market had dropped. They stimulated the growth of food in order to make the islands self-sufficient. To take care of the rapidly increasing population, they helped the natives of densely settled Java to put into cultivation family-sized farms in the outlying islands; and they directed the establishment of small industries for local consumption goods. From 1934 on they curtailed the importation of Japanese goods, and they encouraged the sale of materials to the United States and to Europe.

Unlike France, the Netherlands lacked sufficient size to absorb much of her colonial production. Her main aid to her dependent territories lay in the advancement of capital, notoriously a weak means for impressing one's importance upon a subject people, and in providing officials, whose places the natives would soon desire to occupy. The Dutch encouraged popular and advanced education among the natives and improved health and medical facilities. They trained native leaders, whom they employed in the bureaucracy and whom they helped to progress in the economy and in the intellectual life at a faster pace and to a greater extent than the French, Portuguese, or Belgians were doing for their dependent peoples.

The British imperial response to the economic crisis was necessarily far-reaching. Britain held about one fourth of the population and land of the world, a figure approximately equal to that pertaining to continental Europe and its overseas possessions. When, after a decade of indecision, Great Britain in 1931 introduced protective tariffs, except on basic foods and many industrial raw materials such as wheat, livestock, meat, cotton, and wool, she laid the basis for a program of imperial preference.

The ideal of a self-sufficient empire centering in Great Britain had long interested British Conservatives and was shared, in a modified version, by many in the dominions. At the Imperial Economic Conference in Ottawa in 1932 negotiations to realize this ideal led to hard bargaining among the members of the Commonwealth. Each dominion wished to expand its market for meat, wheat, and other foodstuffs in Great Britain while protecting its own infant industry behind high tariffs against British industrial competition. The British government dared not expose its own agriculture, which it was encouraging, to unlimited overseas competition. Each dominion and Great Britain herself desired not to offend foreign customers, particularly the United States, by preferring members of the Commonwealth too advantageously. Each sought a formula for abolishing the most-favored-nation clause in intra-imperial trade while demanding that other nations abide by this clause.

The Ottawa conference found only a makeshift compromise among all the points of dispute except with regard to the most-favored-nation condition. The members stated that imperial relations differed from others, although no one by that time saw just how, so that the empire had a duty to lift the most-favored-nation clause. Of the other issues the most important was resolved in that Great Britain added wheat, meat, and some minerals to the list of articles protected against importation from foreign countries but free to imperial imports. In return, the dominions lowered the tariff on some British industrial goods and raised it on those from other countries. The British government referred the terms of the Ottawa agreement to the Crown colonies and either received their approval or, as for Ceylon, imposed imperial preference by fiat. The dominions and colonies traded relatively little among themselves; the heart of the Ottawa arrangement consisted of the agreement between each imperial member and Great Britain.

The special importance of imperialism in accounting for a shift in trade relations may be indicated in two ways. Most of the overseas territories depended upon the mother country for capital. Loans or direct investments, normally more easily obtained in the mother country than elsewhere, depended upon the purchase of industrial goods and the employment of technical personnel from the lending state. Australia, practically independent and culturally advanced, as well as Portuguese Guinea, poor and backward, were both subject to this general rule. In territories like Portuguese Guinea or the French possessions and in all the British Crown colonies the power of the imperial state covered major transactions. The basic investments, those in means of transportation and communication, and in education, public health, and the like, had to be supplied by the government. The crown agents in the British Crown colonies, for example, included among their responsibilities the following:

1. The purchase, shipment, insurance and, where necessary, inspection of public stores of all kinds.

2. The detailed design of bridges, public buildings and engineering structures of all kinds, the preparation of specifications for, and the examination and approval of, detailed designs of locomotives, rolling stock, cranes, etc.

3. The negotiation of contracts for the execution of large public works, and the preparation of designs, and general advice relating to such works whether

Percentages

EXPORTING COUNTRY	YEAR	EXPORTS TO						
		EUROPE	U.S.A.	CANADA	LATIN AMERICAN REPUBLICS	OVERSEAS STERLING AREA	DEPENDENT OVERSEAS TERRITORIES	OTHER OVERSEAS COUNTRIES
United Kingdom	1928	32	6	5	10	34	4	8
	1938	32	4	5	8	38	3	8
Germany	1928	70	7	–	7	4	2	5
	1938	65	3	–	12	6	2	10
France	1928	63	6	1	5	2	18	5
	1938	54	6	1	5	3	27	3
Italy	1928	57	11	–	12	5	4	10
	1938	49	8	–	8	4	7	24
Belgium-Luxemburg	1928	70	8	1	7	5	4	5
	1938	69	7	1	6	5	5	4
Netherlands	1928	74	4	1	3	6	10	2
	1938	69	3	1	4	5	12	3
Spain	1928	70	10	1	13	–	5	1
	1938	74	8	1	4	1	7	1
Portugal	1928	70	7	–	9	–	12	2
	1938	69	6	–	6	–	15	2

Percentages

IMPORTING COUNTRY	YEAR	IMPORTS FROM						
		EUROPE	U.S.A.	CANADA	LATIN AMERICAN REPUBLICS	OVERSEAS STERLING AREA	DEPENDENT OVERSEAS TERRITORIES	OTHER OVERSEAS COUNTRIES
United Kingdom	1928	39	17	5	12	17	2	6
	1938	31	13	9	8	26	4	6
Germany	1928	47	14	3	12	11	5	4
	1938	50	7	1	15	9	7	8
France	1928	43	12	1	10	11	14	7
	1938	34	12	1	7	10	27	7
Italy	1928	47	18	4	13	10	2	5
	1938	60	12	–	7	8	6	7
Belgium-Luxemburg	1928	65	10	3	10	6	4	1
	1938	55	11	2	8	9	9	2
Netherlands	1928	61	10	2	12	5	7	2
	1938	59	11	1	8	5	10	3
Spain	1928	49	17	2	11	5	7	7
	1938	66	9	–	5	3	5	5
Portugal	1928	74	11	–	7	–	8	–
	1938	64	12	–	3	4	14	3

SOURCE: Ingvar Svennilson, *Growth and Stagnation in the European Economy* (Geneva: United Nations, 1954), pp. 176-177.

carried out by contract or departmentally, consulting engineers being employed in special cases.

4. The negotiation, issue and management of loans, including management of sinking fund and payment of interest, and repayment of loans; the investment of surplus balances, reserve and depreciation funds, and the like.[1]

The agent directed business to the mother country.

Particularly in the thirties, officials of every imperialist power, as well as private individuals, were subject to currency restrictions. The collapse of the international system of monetary exchange in favor of regulated national currencies meant that all would need approval of the home government before borrowing funds in a foreign state. Under these conditions membership in a large empire became an advantage, a fact recognized at Ottawa when the representatives of the British Commonwealth passed a resolution in favor of common monetary standards. They accepted the pound sterling as the basis of exchange stability and monetary value. The British Empire became the largest area of free monetary exchange in the world. So great did the prestige of the London money market remain that its managed currency, recently devalued and pegged at a new price, was accepted as standard by one fourth of the people of the world. Even non-imperial countries like Sweden, with close commercial ties to Great Britain, accepted the pound sterling as standard.

Whether the formation of imperial economic blocs, particularly those of the British and of the French, proved advantageous has been a question argued on both sides. Trade data, as in the preceding table, which give percentages of the total world trade for each country, indicate some advantage that it had. By way of comparison, data for Germany, a country without dependencies, are included. They show that Germany found markets in the free overseas areas other than the United States. Critics of the system of blocs have replied that the economy of French colonies suffered from forced concentration upon the market for raw materials in France, that it would have benefited from freedom to trade in natural markets elsewhere and from freedom to develop local industries.

Undoubtedly these objections are valid; yet it is equally true that France provided many colonials an assured market at high prices for commodities which could not have been sold abroad. For the British, or the sterling bloc, imperial trade increased; but so did the trade of Great Britain, the dominions, and the crown colonies with countries outside the imperial group. In 1938, Great Britain and Canada, with the strong approval of Australia, concluded treaties with the United States in which both sides conceded reductions in tariff rates. Imperial preference could not withstand the attractiveness of the American market.

[1] Royal Institute of International Affairs, *The Colonial Problem* (New York: Oxford University Press, 1937), pp. 297-298.

Nonetheless, on the part of Great Britain, a shift in quantity of trade took place. The European continent, where Britain had bought meat, butter, bacon, and the like and had sold coal and machinery and other manufactures, lost to the empire. The total amount of British foreign trade did not increase. Imperial preference meant that the leading free countries of Europe were setting an example of exclusiveness. It encouraged have-not nations like Italy, whose colonies were few and poor, and Japan and Germany to demand empires of their own. The attempt of nations with democratic institutions to draw their dependent peoples close together on a basis of actual or promised equality aroused authoritarian nations to practice the imperialist methods of the past.

IMPERIAL POLITICAL RELATIONS

Not economics, but politics and government vitally affected imperial relations. Issues of power such as stirred the pride and passions of awakening nationalism among the colonials came to the fore. Events of the thirties continued in the direction of those of the preceding decade and at an accelerated pace.

British Commonwealth

The British Commonwealth settled questions of power with a minimum of effort. In 1931 each dominion parliament and the British Parliament approved the terms of certain conventions and of the Statute of Westminster, whereby all imperial limitations upon dominion legislative authority were abolished. The dominions were not required to implement this power immediately, but they could do so at any time. They accepted the principle of a single indivisible crown for all members and declared that any change in royal titles or succession to the throne required the approval of each parliament. The Union of South Africa and the Irish Free State brought the agreements into effect at once. Canada, Australia, New Zealand, and Newfoundland, free from mistrust of Great Britain felt by peoples in the other two states, preferred for reasons of domestic policy or of defense to postpone the date of severance. New Zealand waited until 1947 to act. Newfoundland, small, poor, and severely affected by the world depression, renounced her dominion status and after World War II became a Canadian province. Except for the Irish Free State, the history of the negotiations over the Statute of Westminster will interest the student of constitutional and legal subtleties but will add nothing to our search for major lines of development. The members of the Commonwealth enjoyed high standards of living and affected Europe primarily as adjuncts to the British defense system.

Irish Free State

Relations between Great Britain and the Irish Free State changed when in 1932, as a result of the economic depression, Eamon de Valera supplanted the moderate William Cosgrave as head of the Irish government. De Valera at once began to exploit the new freedom under the Statute of Westminster to achieve his declared intention of making Ireland a republic. He sought to abolish the oath to the crown, to maintain only external association with the Commonwealth, and to absorb the province of Ulster. Since a majority of the Irish people opposed these extremes and, except for the fanatical remnant of the Irish Republican army, absolutely objected to further war with Britain or Ulster, de Valera had to proceed cautiously. First he pushed through the Dail a law abolishing the oath of allegiance to the British crown. Then he withheld payments to Great Britain for land which between 1870 and 1909 the British government had acquired and sold to Irish tenants. He deprived the position of governor-general of all prestige and authority, although he did not at that time eliminate it. He abolished appeals from the Free State to the Judicial Committee of the Privy Council in London, an act recognized by the Judicial Committee in 1935 as legal under the Statute of Westminster. He enacted a bill taking from the Irish the status of British citizens; henceforth they were Irish citizens only.

In 1937 de Valera promulgated a new constitution and obtained its acceptance in an election by a small majority of the voters. It established a republic with a popularly elected president and a parliament of two houses. The constitution maintained relations with the Commonwealth by the devious route of empowering the government to use "any organ, instrument, or method of procedure used or adapted for the like purpose by the members of any group or league of nations with which the state is or becomes associated for the purpose of international cooperation in matters of common concern."

Refusal to pay the land annuities brought on tariff war between Great Britain and Ireland. The British government, to obtain funds to cover the land payments, imposed tariffs on Irish exports to the British market. Irish retaliation proved costly. The Irish economy lacked capital to pursue agricultural and industrial development. The civil war had caused devastation; being predominantly dependent on agriculture and lacking almost all other natural resources, the Irish Free State was a home of poverty. Great Britain provided a market for Ireland's surplus food. When de Valera engaged his little state in a tariff war with her indispensable customer, he severely retarded the economic revival of his people.

Finally, in 1938 de Valera found Prime Minister Chamberlain in an appeasing frame of mind. By the terms of agreement Ireland was to pay a lump sum to liquidate the annuity obligation, and Irish food once more entered Britain, with only small restrictions. Britain also abandoned the right to use certain ports for naval defense. In view of European stresses Chamberlain considered it more useful to have a friendly Ireland than to hold the treaty ports by force. Winston Churchill and other defense-minded British denounced the relinquishment of the ports, but Parliament supported the cabinet. De Valera failed in respect to Ulster, which refused to consider joining the Irish Free State. When World War II began, Ireland, or Eire as it was called under the new constitution, was a sovereign state that needed Great Britain as a market for her products and for her supply of industrial goods, and depended for security upon British naval and air power.

India

The history of India in the thirties illustrates the difficulty of adapting Western institutions to the cultures of the East. The effort had to be made, but the mistakes in the process brought much suffering to the natives. In denouncing the British government for proposing to release its hold over India in favor of dominion status, Winston Churchill, the astute prophet of disaster on many subjects during this period of rapid change, stated in the House of Commons (December, 1931):

> There are mobs of neighbours . . . who, when held and dominated by these [communal] passions will tear each other to pieces, men, women and children, with their fingers. Not for a hundred years have the relations between Moslems and Hindus been so poisoned as they have been since England was deemed to be losing her grip and was believed to be ready to quit the scene if told to go.

In 1940 Indian unity survived solely because of British control.

In 1930 a British Parliamentary Commission under the chairmanship of the Liberal Sir John Simon submitted a report in two volumes on the revision of Indian government. The most thorough analysis ever made, it led, after extensive discussion in Parliament, to the passage in 1935 of the Government of India Act. Through this law Britain transformed India into a federation, with certain powers reserved for the central government, others for the provincial governments. The British governor-general retained responsibility for defense and foreign affairs, and he and the British governor in each province were empowered to act on their own initiative in emergencies such as the preservation of internal peace and of the legitimate interests of minorities. Otherwise the duties of government were to devolve upon Indian legislatures, one for each province and one for the entire country, and upon ministers responsible to the legislature. The constitution enabled native government progressively to assume authority upon evidence of competence—a procedure which each dominion had followed—and so within a short time, as the British hoped, to become a fully self-governing community.

That India failed to follow the path toward dominion status opened by the India Act must be attributed mainly to the ambitions of the National Congress party. The organization of the party was such that it enabled an oligarchy to rule within a seeming democracy, an Indian version of authoritarianism. In each town, municipal ward, and village the party members elected delegates to a central body. The central congress met annually and elected an All-India Congress Committee of several hundred members, which then chose an executive committee of a dozen or so. The membership of the committee continued about the same year after year, and over it ruled the Mahatma Gandhi, who, as Jawaharlal Nehru, then a younger member of the executive committee, said, held the position of "permanent super-president."

The leaders of the National Congress rejected the constitution of 1935, mainly on the grounds that it did not create a centralized government and that it did not make India independent. Gandhi ordered "civil disobedience" to the new system until the vestiges of British authority were abolished. His mass following substituted rioting for passive resistance, and local conflicts broke out between Hindus and Moslems and among different Hindu groups. In the first election under the new constitution the National Congress party won less than one half of the seats in all the provinces; but it claimed to represent the country and expressed its monopolistic aim by breaking with the Moslem League. It declared that all religions, races, and languages should be represented through the Congress party alone.

When Gandhi in 1937 at last recognized that the British would not give in at once to his demand, he allowed members of the party to assume ministerial posts. The party executive committee picked the ministers, thus alarming Mohammed Ali Jinnah, the head of the Moslem League. In the autumn of 1937 Jinnah denounced the Congress party as an exclusive agency for Hinduism and blamed it for stirring up civil war. Under its rule, he said, Moslems could "expect neither justice nor fair play." He labeled it fascist, and Moslems increasingly advocated a transfer of population along religious lines and the partition of India. Congress leaders continued to demand political unity of the entire peninsula. Nehru and others looked forward with satisfaction to the impeding war in Europe, which would engross Great Britain's full strength and enable the National Congress party to supplant British rule in India.

Far East—Japanese Aggression

Imperialism in the Far East during the thirties appeared primarily in the aggression of Japan. As European powers and the United States attempted to thwart Japanese expansion, they inadvertently encouraged international interdependence. This aspect of Europe's role in the world must now be analyzed.

The world economic depression destroyed the market for many of Japan's exports. In contrast to the preceding decade of experiments with liberalism, the government of Japan in the thirties fell into the hands of chauvinists. The commanders of Japan's Kwantung army in China, becoming more imperialistic than the government, in 1931 exploited one of the innumerable petty conflicts between Chinese and the Japanese forces to seize Manchuria and declared it an independent state. They sought to develop it economically as a replacement for Japan's lost markets. China refused to recognize the conquest and appealed to the League of Nations. The League sent a commission under Lord Lytton to the Far East, which, after thorough investigation, condemned Japan as the aggressor and recommended the preservation of Chinese, Japanese, and Russian interests in Manchuria and the restoration of a largely autonomous Manchuria under Chinese sovereignty.

When the League approved the report, Japan resigned from the organization (1933) and, spurred by popular Chinese boycott of her goods, exerted diplomatic and military pressure to force China under her protection. The foreign office in Tokyo declared in 1934 that the Japanese "consider it only natural that to keep peace and order in the East of Asia we must even act alone on our own responsibility. . . . There is no country but China which is in a position to share with Japan the responsibility of peace in East Asia." Japan proposed to form mixed corporations dominated by the Japanese to develop China's resources.

When the Chinese government still refused to cooperate, Japan sent her armies into the country in 1937 to enforce what it called "co-prosperity." Simultaneously she sought to arrange by diplomacy similar cooperation with the Dutch East Indies. At a conference requested by her at Batavia in 1934, her representatives endeavored to rouse the natives against the Netherlands while suggesting joint Dutch-Japanese exploitation of the islands. A rebuff caused delay in executing the plans; but when Germany invaded the Netherlands in May, 1940, Japan immediately proposed another conference in Batavia. Six months after this one ended in Dutch refusal of sweeping economic and political demands, Japan expanded World War II to the Far East.

Protection of China mainly depended upon the United States. But this country employed diplomacy, not the sort of weapon that Japanese imperialists respected. At the time of the Manchurian crisis (1931), Secretary of State Stimson, unable to associate the United States officially with the League of Nations, laid down the policy known as the Stimson Doctrine. It read in part as follows: The United States government "cannot admit the legality of any situation *de facto* nor does it intend to recognize any treaty or agreement entered into between those governments [Chinese and Japanese], or agents thereof, which may impair the treaty rights of the United States or its citizens in China." He demanded preservation of the "open door" and of the sovereignty, independence, and territorial and administrative integrity of China. The declaration placed the United States directly at odds with Japan's intentions, and as President Roosevelt continued to uphold the policy and Japan to defy it, the two countries became increasingly hostile.

Great Britain and France, who had relatively small interests in China, after 1933 were too engrossed in the Nazi-Fascist menace to initiate action in the Far East. France found that her subjects in Indochina, after minor rebellions in 1930, quieted down as the threat of Japanese aggression made French rule seem mild. The Netherlands faced less trouble with the natives of the East Indies for the same reason. The Dutch continued in the main efficiently to rule through white officials but associated native leaders in advisory councils, some members of which were elected, others appointed.

The most serious antagonism involved Japan and the Soviet Union, competitors for power in the Far East. Mistrusting Japan, the Soviet Union forced the development of her two Far Eastern territories, increasing the population to 3 million by 1939, building heavy industry at the new city of Komsomolsk (founded in 1932), and improving transportation. Prior to Japan's seizure of Manchuria the Soviet Union had had strained relations with China over the Chinese Eastern Railway and other matters. Japan inherited China's antagonism toward Russia, and throughout the next decade the two opponents shifted from uneasy settlement of certain issues to local war over others. At the end of 1932 they concluded a trade agreement, and in 1935 the Soviet Union sold to Japan her interest in the Chinese Eastern Railway. But each year their troops fought pitched battles along the Manchurian border, and the Japanese gained strategic advantage by pressing into Inner Mongolia.

When in 1935 the Japanese Kwantung army endeavored to penetrate Outer Mongolia, Stalin warned that an attack on the state would be considered an aggression against the Soviet Union. Each antagonist sought outside diplomatic assistance. The Soviet Union entered the League of Nations just after Japan and Germany resigned, a move on the part of the Soviets which seemed doubly astute after the negotiation in 1936 of the Anti-Comintern pact between Japan and Germany.

The spread of the Sino-Japanese war in 1937 led the Soviet Union to sign a nonaggression treaty with China and to join the West in criticizing Japan. The Russo-German agreement of 1939 alarmed Japan by seeming to preclude the possibility of checking the Soviet Union through a Japanese-German treaty. As Japan saw trouble with the United States loom ever larger and as the Soviet Union watched Germany's expansion with deep concern, each state decided to reduce the number of its opponents. In 1941 Japan and the U.S.S.R. negotiated a nonaggression treaty, by which the two powers promised to respect each other's territorial integrity and to remain neutral in the event of attack by a third party.

Imperialism involved the Far East more deeply than other regions of the world in international relations. It directly affected the interests of six major powers, China and Japan in the region itself, France and Great Britain in Europe, the Soviet Union stretching into both continents, and the United States. Imperialism had contributed to the outbreak of World War I and was to cause future trouble; but in the interwar years no other non-European area of the globe approached the Far East in international significance.

Near and Middle East

In the Near and Middle East, British influence, supposedly dominant at the end of World War I, continued to decline; and French rule in Syria survived mainly by superior physical power. The states, whether supposedly independent like Persia, or mandates like Iraq, Syria, Lebanon, and Transjordan, lived in various stages of defiance of the Western powers. Palestine, a British mandate, poisoned relations between Great Britain and the Arabs. Only the states of the Arabian peninsula enjoyed the proceeds of oil wells; others were sunk in poverty.

Iran, which regarded Great Britain as her main adversary, sought to eliminate British influence without having to receive Russian Communists. She channeled trade with Russia through a government agency and used the police effectively to suppress native Communists. Succeeding in reducing British influence, she abolished the right of the British to try their subjects in Iran in British courts and forced the Imperial Airways Company to obtain permission for its planes to fly over the country to India. By precipitating a crisis in 1932 over the share of profits from the Anglo-Iranian Oil Company, she obtained a considerable increase in royalties, limited the concession to sixty years, and assured the gradual employment by the company of Iranian personnel. After Hitler came to power, Iran cultivated cordial relations with Germany, by 1939 employed 2,000 German experts, and directed 41 per cent of her foreign trade to that country. Nazi racial propaganda spread effectively; the Iranian ruler considered Germany the best protection against Russian communism. Except for her oil interests, Great Britain appeared weakened, and even the oil interests were being confined by American expansion. Iran claimed possession of the Bahrein Islands, a title which Britain disputed. The discovery of oil on the islands profited the Americans, who, in spite of a pledge of the local sheiks not to grant oil concessions without British consent, turned over to American interests exclusive rights.

The decline of British influence in Iraq reached a level of relative stability in 1932 in the Anglo-Iraq treaty and the admission of Iraq to the League of Nations. The treaty contained infringements upon the country's sovereignty, and expressed the simple fact of relative power. Since similar terms were included in a subsequent treaty of 1936 between Britain and Egypt, and proposed treaties between France and Syria, and France and Lebanon, of the same year, an analysis of them will reveal the strategy of control used by both powers in this area on the eve of World War II.

In foreign policy Britain and Iraq agreed on "full and frank consultation" and promised not to undertake a policy "which is inconsistent with the alliance or might create difficulties for the other party." Britain promised to defend Iraq in the event of war, and Iraq would furnish to her ally "on Iraq territory all facilities and assistance . . . including the use of railways, rivers, ports, aerodromes and means of communication." Iraq leased to Great Britain air bases near Basra and west of the Euphrates, and permitted her to maintain forces in these places. For five years Britain could keep forces at other points and at all times transport her troops across the country. Britain retained the right to provide all military instructors and all arms equipment to Iraq. And British forces in Iraq were exempt from local jurisdiction and taxation. As soon as the treaty was signed, the Iraq government began to campaign for revision in favor of greater independence. American oil interests penetrated this British preserve, acquiring nearly 24 per cent of the shares in the Iraq Petroleum Company's concessions. The Iraq government at the time of the European war remained faithful to the alliance; but in 1939 a mob in Mosul murdered the British consul, and Nazi and Fascist propaganda was spreading.

Transjordan, a state lacking resources to support herself economically, militarily, or administratively, remained on the British dole. Lebanon, containing a large number of Christians, held to France with some degree of loyalty, but Syria proved troublesome. Under the constitution granted by the French in 1930, Syria elected a parliament in which extreme nationalists held one fourth of the seats and placed several influential members in the cabinet. The government, strengthened by developments in Iraq, demanded the end of the mandate. When Léon Blum assumed power in France as head of a Popular Front government, he negotiated in 1936 a treaty with each of the mandates similar to the Anglo-Iraq treaty. After he fell from power, the succeeding French governments refused to ratify the agreements, and in 1939, in the face of intense hostility on the part of the natives, France used her army to restore direct rule. As war approached in Europe she esteemed the military value of her Near East dependencies so little that in 1939 she negotiated a treaty of mutual assistance with Turkey, whereby she permitted Turkey to acquire the Sanjak of Alexandretta, a territory of mixed Turkish, Arab, and Kurdish population that was claimed by the Turks but had been a part of Syria.

Palestine

At the time of the Armistice in 1918 Palestine contained 55,000 Jews and over a half million Arabs, a ratio of one to ten. By 1932 the ratio had risen to one Hebrew to four Arabs, and in 1940 the ratio was one to two. The total population of Palestine had increased from 752,000 in 1922 to a million and a half in 1940. Persecution by Nazi Germany and to a less extent by peoples in other countries drove thousands of Jews to seek refuge in the barren land of their Biblical forefathers. In accordance with the terms of the mandate, a Jewish Agency had been established to act as official spokesman for world Jewry and to cooperate with the mandatory. The Agency screened candidates for immigration, collected funds for aid in settlement, and brought pressure to bear on governments, particularly of Great Britain and the United States, in support of Jewish interest in Palestine. In the mandate itself the Jews had efficiently organized an elected assembly and a general council as instruments of self-government among themselves and had set up social and economic organizations such as trade-unions, cooperatives, collective settlements, and the like. More than three fourths of the Jews earned their living in towns and cities; those in agriculture cultivated crops like citrus fruit, which required capital investment and which were aimed mainly at the export market. Without continuing financial subsidies from wealthy coreligionists abroad, the Jewish settlement in Palestine could not have developed.

The Arabs of the mandated territory lacked any organization of comparable efficiency and had no support from abroad. They had as governmental organ a Supreme Moslem Council, whose president was the grand mufti of Jerusalem, and a number of political parties. They divided into two groups, one led by the grand mufti that fought Jewish settlement in favor of the retention of Palestine as an Arab state, the other willing to compromise with the British and accept some Jews. The Arabs, wretchedly poor, lived mainly in rural areas; 75 per cent of their children did not attend schools; hospitals, modern schools, and other institutions to be found in the Jewish communities were lacking. Racial, religious, economic, and social differences kept the two peoples apart; as more Jews fled to Palestine from Nazi torture, the Arabs, squeezed out of their ancestral land, became bitter toward the peaceful invaders.

Great Britain tried to resolve the conflict between two cultures by the use of normal political procedures. Although the mandatory power, she did nothing to help the Arabs to attain Jewish standards. At one time she restricted Jewish immigration to appease the Arabs; at another she opened the borders to appease the Jews. Solicitude for the Jews led her to respect the promise of the mandate agreement that Palestine should become a Jewish home. Concern to retain the friendship of Arabs in states with oil indispensable to her economy and her navy counseled caution.

In 1938–1939 the Nazis and the Fascists began an intensive campaign of anti-Semitism among the Arabs. They blamed Great Britain for supporting the Jews. The British reacted in 1939 by virtually surrendering to Arab demands for curbing Jewish immigration, a repudiation of the Balfour Declaration of 1917. The Jews were likewise eager to prevent the Nazis and Fascists from winning the Arab world to their side, but they thought they needed a refuge in Palestine from persecution. At the outbreak of war in Europe Arabs in neighboring countries were supporting materially as well as spiritually the demands of the Arabs in Palestine, the grand mufti and other leaders were in exile denouncing the Jews and Great Britain, and the mandatory anticipated future Arab rebellions similar to one of 1937, which was suppressed by force. After twenty years of life as a mandate, Palestine was less "able to stand alone" than it had been before Great Britain had agreed to apply "the principle that the well-being and development of such peoples form a sacred trust of civilization" (League Covenant, Article 22).

The discovery of the Middle East as a major oil-bearing area attracted the attention of the United States. The American government entered into diplomatic relations with Arab states. By insisting upon respect for the principle of the "open door," it helped American oil interests—to the satisfaction of the Arabs—to compete with British. Although unable to gain a share in Iran, between 1927 and 1940, American oil companies acquired nearly a fourth interest in the concessions in Iraq and Qatar, half interest in the Kumayt Oil Company, and exclusive rights in Saudi Arabia and the Bahrein Islands. The Americans offered much more favorable terms than the British, and their government, unlike the British, had no political or strategic reasons for interfering in the internal affairs of these countries. The American Jews furnished much of the money to sustain the immigrants in Palestine, but the United States Department of State restricted its action to expressions of "the keenest sympathy" for the development of Palestine as a Jewish national home. American missionary schools, particularly the universities in Beirut and Cairo, trained many young Arabs in the professions, winning friends throughout the Near and Middle East. The importance of oil in this region for the American economy did not become fully appreciated until after World War II.

Egypt continued in the thirties to be the battleground between the Wafd party, which overwhelmingly won elections under the constitution of 1923, the king, and the British. Both the Wafd party and the king wished to rule; both suffered from subordination to British control. In the face of economic depression, the king in 1930 replaced the constitution by an authoritarian government. For five years Egypt lived in peace. When Mussolini invaded Ethiopia in 1935–1936, the Egyptians learned that British protection offered some advantages. British treatment of Africans was far preferable to Italian, and Egypt wished to avoid the risk of conquest by Fascists. Sobered by Mussolini's aggression, the king and the Wafd agreed in 1935 to restore the constitution of 1923, much to the disapproval of the British, who feared a recurrence of trouble.

In 1936 the Egyptian and the British governments reached agreement on a treaty. Britain promised to defend Egypt and could use Egyptian communication facilities in wartime. Britain was to maintain a garrison of 10,000 men and 400 pilots in the Suez Canal zone, but would evacuate her troops from the rest of Egypt. She was to keep the naval base at Alexandria for eight more years. The Egyptian army and police were henceforth to be directed, not by British, but by natives; a British military mission was to advise the Egyptian army, and Egyptian officers could be trained abroad only in Britain. Egyptians were permitted to settle in the Sudan and Egyptian troops to return to that region. Egypt was to become a member of the League of Nations. As a sovereign state she should be free to try, in her own courts, foreigners resident in Egypt, and Britain agreed to help her obtain permission of other powers to abolish capitulations. The treaty was to run indefinitely. Within a year capitulations were dropped, and Egypt entered the League. Finding itself deprived for the time being of its main appeal, hatred of Great Britain, the Wafd lost the election of 1938, and for the next four years the king and a ministry of moderates governed the country. Anglo-Egyptian relations improved.

Africa

Whereas in the Near and Middle East, including Egypt, imperialism was entering its last phase, that of preserving strategic interests for the defense of the last stage of imperialism elsewhere, the continent of Africa continued to be exploited almost entirely for Europeans. It has been estimated that between 1884 and 1939 the amount invested there did not greatly exceed the total gold reserve of the British Empire and France before World War II. Africa exported $700 millions' worth of products annually, an amount about equal to the value of Belgium-Luxembourg's exports in 1938, and much less than that for France. The policies of the imperial powers and their citizens remained about the same as they had been.

The white settlers of Kenya expressed the crudest aspect of the European policy in 1923 as follows:

> It has been shown that the black race possesses initiative but lacks constructive powers, characteristics which justify Lugard's judgment that for the native African "the era of complete independence is not yet visible on the horizon of time." The controlling powers may, therefore, aim at advancing the black race as far along the road of progress as its capacity allows, without misgivings that the success of their endeavours will lead to a demand for their withdrawal, entailing loss of prestige and trade. The development of British territories in Africa opens up a vista of commercial expansion so endless that calculated description is difficult.

At the other extreme one might cite the request by the first National Congress of British West Africa, meeting in Accra in 1920, for the introduction of instruments of self-government. The memorial gave the record of such persons as the late Hon. Sir Samuel Lewis, Knight, C.M.Q., an acting Chief Justice, the late Mr. J. Renner Maxwell of Oxford University, Chief Magistrate of the Gambia, and many others, all native Africans, as evidence that their people were ready for this momentous step.

Neither statement contained more than a partial truth. From the Mediterranean coast to the Cape of Good Hope the people on the whole acquiesced in white rule. The exceptions consisted of the 80,000 pastoral

Arabs in the Cyrenaica, whom General Rodolfo Graziani in 1932 drove into the desert to make way for Italian settlers, and the free state of Ethiopia, which resisted Italian attack in 1935–1936 until her spears succumbed to modern weapons. Otherwise blacks and browns took advantage of educational facilities offered by the whites and as town dwellers and wage earners acquired some acquaintance with capitalistic methods of production. A few heard of socialism and communism. Some learned about the ideals of British, French, and Belgian culture by being told of its superiority over the racial theories of nazism and fascism. The large urban Arab population in Tunisia contrasted its centralized government, dominated by the French, with constitutional self-government in Egypt. It likewise noted that the Tunisian native population had doubled under French rule, and that next door in Libya the native population had halved since Italy seized control.

For the African peoples the decade before the second world war brought more economic developments, even though primarily for Europeans, more cultural facilities in the form of schools and hospitals, more opportunities to become acquainted with Western ways of life, more destruction of traditional African organization than ever before—and more danger, from Fascists and Nazis, from the Boers of South Africa, and the English settlers in Kenya. In Spanish colonies and in some other isolated areas society remained largely as it had been for centuries. In most of Africa forces among the peoples were stirring, without as yet knowing how to move or what direction to take. World War II speeded up their education and turned their attention to politics, the key to independent life in culture as well as government.

COLONIAL DEFENSE

Defense of the dependencies seemed hardly more difficult in the thirties than it had in the previous decade, except in the Far Eastern area. The European imperial powers concentrated attention upon Nazi Germany and, to a much less extent, Fascist Italy. Japan, the sole predator to fear in the colonial world, caused no such alarm as Germany's announced intentions of aggression in Europe. The Netherlands and France were unable to protect their possessions in the Orient, and Great Britain, though developing Singapore as a major naval base, left Japanese aggression to the United States. Concentration on Europe became easier because of the belief that the Soviet Union also feared Germany. Stalin was thought to understand that Germany lay between London and Paris and Moscow, and that he should not alienate potential allies by spreading communism in their dependencies. The Soviets committed themselves to neither side. They defended their interests in the Far East against Japanese aggression, and in the Near and Middle East, potential area of conflict, they created no international crisis. In this region petty rulers could safely try to wrest political freedom from the British and French. Africa lay beyond the center of attention. The Nazis demanded the eventual return of the former German colonies there and elsewhere, but they realized that they had to regain these colonies by action in Europe. Italy's ambition to take all of North Africa caused concern only to the extent of Italy's European military and naval strength; Britain and France believed themselves competent to restrain this third-rate power.

The mother countries took few measures to put the dependencies in shape either to defend themselves or to help defeat Germany. France had enlisted natives for decades for both purposes, but she rated the colonials as subsidiary to her own forces and to the value of the Maginot line. The ideal of a French Union of 100 million people had not yet affected the basic conceptions of French defense. At the last moment before Japan's attack the Netherlands futilely endeavored to organize an East Indian army. Belgium's empire and that of Spain and most of Portugal's lay in Africa, their front line of defense the Franco-German border. Great Britain, the power accustomed to global strategy, had encouraged the dominions to develop armed forces of their own. Of these the Union of South Africa, far away and half-populated by Boers, many of them sympathetic to nazism, as yet needed small defenses. Canada could always rely upon protection by the United States. New Zealand, Australia, and India caused most concern, for they were situated remote from Europe and within reach of Japan. The naval base of Singapore, with a sizable portion of the British navy and the resources of the Eastern dominions, was expected to withstand an Oriental aggressor. The British always reckoned on the strategic interest of the United States in preventing Japan's conquest of the East.

On the eve of World War II the course of imperial relations seemed set for the immediate future. Japan would remain entangled in Eastern China. The British possessions would continue to gain freedom little by little from the mother country. The peoples of the Near and Middle East, caught between fear of Soviet aggression by infiltration and the urgency of the Western states to assure the steady flow of oil, would in time gain independence. Africa from the Mediterranean to the Cape of Good Hope showed few signs of political and social maturity. Means of modernizing the economy had scarcely begun to penetrate most of Asia and Africa; the industrial powers had thought little about the problem and had not considered the effects of industrialism upon native peoples. Indeed, they had not thought much about the impact of industrialism upon their own civilization. At the outset of World War II they had advanced in their thinking about imperial relations little beyond the point reached by 1920. Colonial peoples seemed willing to advance slowly toward the ultimate goal portrayed by the League Covenant. World War II shocked imperialists and dependents into realization that both had changed more profoundly than either had thought. The interwar period may be described as calm before storm.

Suggestions for Further Reading

The Readings for Chapter 11 should be used for this decade as well.

Part IV

Europe since 1939

Chronological Preview

1939
Sept. German conquest of Poland

1939–1940
Winter war of Soviet Union against Finland

1940
April. German seizure of Denmark and Norway
May-June. German conquest of the Netherlands, Belgium, and France
June 11. Italy enters the war
Aug.-Sept. Battle of Britain
Sept. Tripartite Pact between Germany, Italy, and Japan

1940–1941
Sept.-May. German occupation of, or conquest of, the Balkans

1941
March. Lend-Lease Law passed
April. Soviet-Japanese treaty of neutrality
June 22. Germany attacks the Soviet Union
Aug. Atlantic Charter promulgated
Dec. German troops in the suburbs of Moscow
Dec. 7. Japan attacks United States at Pearl Harbor

1942–1943
Allied conquest of North Africa and Southern Italy

1943
Jan. German troops surrender at Stalingrad
Sept. Allied-Italian armistice

1944
Formation of the Arab League
June. Allied invasion of Normandy
July 20. German attempt to assassinate Hitler

1945
Feb. Yalta Conference
April-June. Drafting of United Nations Charter at San Francisco
April. Death of Mussolini and of Hitler
May 8. Unconditional surrender by Germany
July-Aug. Potsdam Conference
Aug. 6, 9. United States drops atomic bombs on Japan
Sept. 2. End of war with Japan

1945–1948
Communists gain power in Romania, Bulgaria, Czechoslovakia, Hungary, and Poland

1945–1951
Labor government in Great Britain

1946
Acceptance of constitution of Fourth French Republic
United Nations Atomic Energy Commission established
May-Sept. United States break with Soviet policy toward Germany

1946–1947
Peace treaties made with Italy, Bulgaria, Romania, Hungary, and Finland

1946–1949
Civil war in Greece

1947
Initiation of the Monnet Plan in France
March. Truman Doctrine promulgated

1947–1948
Establishment of Commonwealths of India and Pakistan

1948
Independent state of Israel created
Arab-Jewish war
Tito-Stalin controversy

1948–1950
Marshall Plan (European Recovery Program)

1949
NATO established
U.S.S.R. explodes its first atomic bomb

1950
Colombo Plan introduced
Italy passes basic law on land reform
Nov. General Assembly of UN passes Uniting for Peace Resolution

1950–1953
Korean War

1951
Conservative government takes office in Great Britain
Peace treaty with Japan

1952
Coal and Steel Community established

1953
Balkan Pact between Yugoslavia, Greece, and Turkey

1953 (cont.)
Khrushchev becomes secretary of the Communist Party in U.S.S.R.
Mar. Death of Stalin

1954
France defeated in Indochina and agrees to partition
War begins in Algeria
Southeast Asia Treaty Organization created
Colonel Nasser becomes head of Egyptian government
Western European Union approved

1954–1955
French agreements with Tunisia and Morocco

1955
Bandung Conference
Bagdad Pact signed
Soviet treaty with Austria
Fall of Malenkov and rise of Khrushchev

1956
Khrushchev attacks Stalin
Riots in Poland; Gomulka returns to power

1956–1957
Suez Crisis
Oct.-Jan. Revolt in Hungary

1957
West Germany rearms
Ghana becomes a Commonwealth

Chapter 19 · World War II, 1939-1941

On May 21, 1940, French Prime Minister Paul Reynaud declared: "The truth is that our classic conception of the conduct of war has come up against a new conception." He drew this conclusion during the height of the Battle of France, when his country, Great Britain, Belgium, and the Netherlands experienced the Nazi blitzkrieg.

DIFFERENCE IN STRATEGY

French and British Plans

The British and French general staffs planned for a war which would start where World War I had ended. They anticipated one fought from trenches, where again the defensive would be superior to the offensive. In 1929 the French began to construct, along the German border as far as Belgium, a modernized trench called the Maginot Line, an underground fortress in which the smaller French army could hold back German man power without the bloodletting of 1914–1918. The completion of the line in the thirties represented security to the French nation and disinclined the responsible authorities from studying the implications of industry for strategy. Some of the junior officers complained in print of lack of initiative in the use of tank and airplane, but the generals ignored their proposals. In Great Britain the small Expeditionary Force was well trained and equipped for service on the continent, and the air force was being shaped along offensive lines. The field manuals used for training the cavalry even in the late thirties, however, applied to armored car regiments the principles of operations used for horse cavalry and advised fox hunting as a means of training officers in speed of decision and action. Neither the British nor the French army had developed offensive strategy and striking power; thus neither had prepared to counter the Nazi type of warfare.

Nazi Plans

Under Hitler the Germans rebuilt their army around the heavily armored tank, the airplane, motorized transport, and mobile artillery. They stressed quality rather than quantity and planned to strike with speed. The general staff evolved tactics of "deep infiltration." Mobile armored units probed for weak spots and drove through without regard for defense of flanks or maintenance of communications with the forces that followed. They expected to surprise and disorganize the enemy by breaking through to the latter's rear. The Germans employed the air force for reconnaissance but mainly as a flexible artillery subordinate to the infantry and as a means for bombing enemy troops, transportation facilities, forts, supply depots, and other targets. The German army had restored superior power to the offensive. It had tested the blitzkrieg in the Spanish civil war and with devastating success in the Polish campaign, without alarming French and British authorities; and it was to continue successful until the vast distances of the Russian plain proved to be too great for German resources to overcome.

Being always on the offensive during the first part of the war, the Germans were able to employ psychological warfare. "Who says I'm going to start a war like those fools in 1914?" Hitler demanded. He struck either before the delivery of the declaration of war or simultaneously. "What is war but cunning, deception, delusion, attack and surprise?" he asked. "There is a broadened strategy, a war with intellectual weapons. Why should I demoralize him [the enemy] by military means, if I can do so better and more cheaply in other ways." "Mental confusion, contradiction of feeling, indecisiveness, panic: these are our weapons. . . ." He expected to exploit the fundamental differences in ideology among the groups in each state in order to gain allies among the fascist sympathizers.

The war was fought by the totalitarian powers with all the ruthlessness at their disposal, arousing in opponents the determination to endure until complete victory could be achieved. Diplomatic negotiation was excluded except as a means of psychological warfare. The Nazis as aggressors set the standards of total warfare. They fully understood the risk they were taking; when Great Britain declared war on Germany at the inception of the Polish campaign in 1939, Göring remarked, "If we lose this war, then God help us." Every opponent of Nazi Germany could well have made the same remark.

After completing the Polish war Hitler immediately ordered an attack on the Western states of the Netherlands, Belgium, and France, setting the date of November 12. His generals, appalled by his low regard for the French army, respectfully delayed the opening of the campaign until the next year. Hitler's mistrust of generals grew with the resistance to his commands, and on one occasion (November 5, 1939) he heaped every insult which his imagination could muster upon their representative, Commander in Chief General Walther von Brauchitsch. A few days later, on November 8, the Gestapo without his knowledge arranged to have a bomb exploded in the Bürgerbräu Keller in Munich just a few minutes after Hitler had left the building. When the Führer, who had not been forewarned of the plan, learned about the explosion, he excitedly exclaimed, "The fact that I left the Bürgerbräu earlier than usual is a corroboration of Providence's intention to allow me to reach my goal." On November 23, calling together the generals and admirals for a lecture on plans and prospects, he spoke as follows:

> Everything is determined by the fact that the moment is favorable now: in six months it may not be so any more. As the last factor I must in all modesty name my own person: irreplaceable. . . . I am convinced of my powers of intellect and decision. . . . I shall attack France and England at the most favourable and quickest moment. Breach of the neutrality of Belgium and Holland is meaningless. No one will question that when we have won.
>
> . . . Every hope of compromise is childish: Victory or defeat! The question is not the fate of National Socialist Germany, but who is to dominate Europe in the future. . . . No one has ever achieved what I have achieved. . . . I am setting this work on a gamble. I have to choose between victory and destruction. I choose victory. . . .
>
> . . . I shall shrink from nothing and shall destroy everyone who is opposed to me. . . . In the last years I have experienced many examples of intuition.

The generals, trained in the coldly rational school of German military science, were rapidly learning to obey a civilian guided by intuition. Within another six months they were to be his subordinates in fact and theory.

Soviet Union Attacks Finland

While Hitler was stalled in the "phony war" in the west, his partner in aggression conducted a winter war against Finland. Stalin expected this little country to follow the example of the Baltic states by acquiescing in his demands for territory and for military and naval bases. He justified his action on the grounds that Leningrad and the Murmansk railway needed to be protected by the addition of territory. Finland was willing to negotiate an agreement with the Soviet Union which would offer every assurance of peaceful relations, but she would not accede to the latter's territorial claims. The Soviet Union began war on November 29, 1939, and found the Finns in the defense of their existence stubborn and efficient fighters. The Soviet army stalled on the Karelian Isthmus for weeks. Early in February of 1940, however, Stalin threw twenty-seven divisions against the three of his opponent and compelled the little country to sue for peace.

The Communists set somewhat stiffer terms than those offered prior to the war but did not attempt to destroy national independence. The Soviet Union had been expelled from the League of Nations on December 14 for having attacked Finland, and Stalin did not wholly trust Germany. Should Britain and France carry out their threat and send troops and supplies to aid Finland, Stalin might be forced to rely on Nazi Germany beyond the point of safety. Thus in the treaty of peace of March 12, 1940, Finland remained independent but ceded to the Soviet Union the entire

TERRITORIAL ADDITIONS
IN RUSSIA'S WESTERN BORDER (1939-1940)

Karelian Isthmus, including the town of Viipuri, territory to the north and west of Lake Ladoga, and islands in the Gulf of Finland. She had to lease the peninsula of Hangö to the Soviets for thirty years, to permit transit rights across the country to Norway and to Sweden, and to demilitarize her northern coast. A country of 180 million people had defeated one of 3½ million. This victory, Molotov declared, added "another glorious page to their [the Red army and the Red fleet] history"; it had shown, he said, that "the springs of valour, self-sacrifice and heroism among our people are inexhaustible."

GERMAN AGGRESSION

Against Norway

Fear that the British and French might aid Finland in the war against the Soviet Union aroused Hitler's interest in Norway. Admiral Erich Raeder urged the seizure of Norway and Denmark as vantage points for the use of the navy, and late in January, 1940, Hitler set April 9 as the date for invasion. Almost simultaneously the British cabinet decided to begin mining the Norwegian waters on April 8; and if the Germans opposed the action, British and French troops were to occupy the Norwegian ports. Each side was therefore bent on violating neutrality. When even before this date a British destroyer stopped a German prison ship, the "Altmark," in Norwegian territorial waters on February 17, to rescue British prisoners, the British were guilty of breaking neutrality, but so were the Germans by being within these waters and so were the Norwegians by allowing them to be there.

The stakes in the Norwegian venture were high. The Nazis depended upon Swedish iron ore to supply the steel industry. They expected the Swedish mines to provide during 1940 11½ million tons of a total of 15 million tons of crude ore. This was shipped partly by way of the Baltic and partly along the coast of Norway, the latter route being vital in winter when the Baltic was frozen. The Germans set three aims in occupying Norway: to keep the ore route open; to protect the Baltic as a German-controlled inland sea; and to provide naval and air bases for attacking Great Britain, particularly for destroying British ocean commerce. The British stake in Norway was roughly the reverse of these three objectives. The question was which side would act first.

Since the German general staff would not assume responsibility for the campaign against Norway, Hitler entrusted its planning and execution under his own constant supervision to General Nikolaus von Falkenhorst. Success depended upon secrecy and speed. Troops concealed in merchant vessels, coal barges, and ore boats were shipped to Norwegian harbors in time to join airborne troops in seizing the ports. The army moved into Denmark almost without opposition and occupied all ports and air fields. The German navy took landing troops into the harbor of Oslo; although it lost some ships to the harbor defenses, it captured the capital without much difficulty. A few traitors, led by the Norwegian Nazi Major Vidkun Quisling, assisted the invaders, but their part in the campaign was insignificant. Neither the Danes nor the Norwegians had prepared for an attack; they had remained neutral during World War I and had since continued the same policy. After the first World War, they—especially the Norwegians—had taken underfed German children and restored them to health. The Nazis sought out these recipients of Norwegian kindness and applied their special knowledge in conquering the country.

The British landed troops at various Norwegian ports to resist the Nazis, but the latter, in control of the air, held off the British navy. Within six weeks the campaign ended. Germany held the Norwegian coastline, from which to launch air and naval attacks against the British Isles. The Norwegian king and government escaped to Great Britain; those of Denmark had had no time to do so. The British had been, as Mr. Churchill said, "completely outwitted" and defeated on their own element, the sea. In London on May 10 Chamberlain's cabinet was replaced by one under the leadership of Winston Churchill, and Britain became aroused to the gravity of the war.

Against Western Europe

Churchill assumed office on the day when Hitler invaded the Netherlands, Belgium, and France. On May 15 the Dutch army surrendered; on the night of May 27-28 the Belgian army surrendered; by June 4 the British Expeditionary Force had been ejected from the continent; on June 14 the Germans occupied Paris; on June 22, the French signed a German-dictated armistice at the same spot in the same railway coach in which the Germans had been forced to accept the armistice of 1918. Stalin and the Western nations were shocked at the ease of German victory; the German generals looked on amazed, while the Führer danced for joy and for the first time in his life went sightseeing in Paris.

Hitler chose a plan of campaign which caught the Allied troops off guard. Instead of concentrating his force for an attack across the coastal

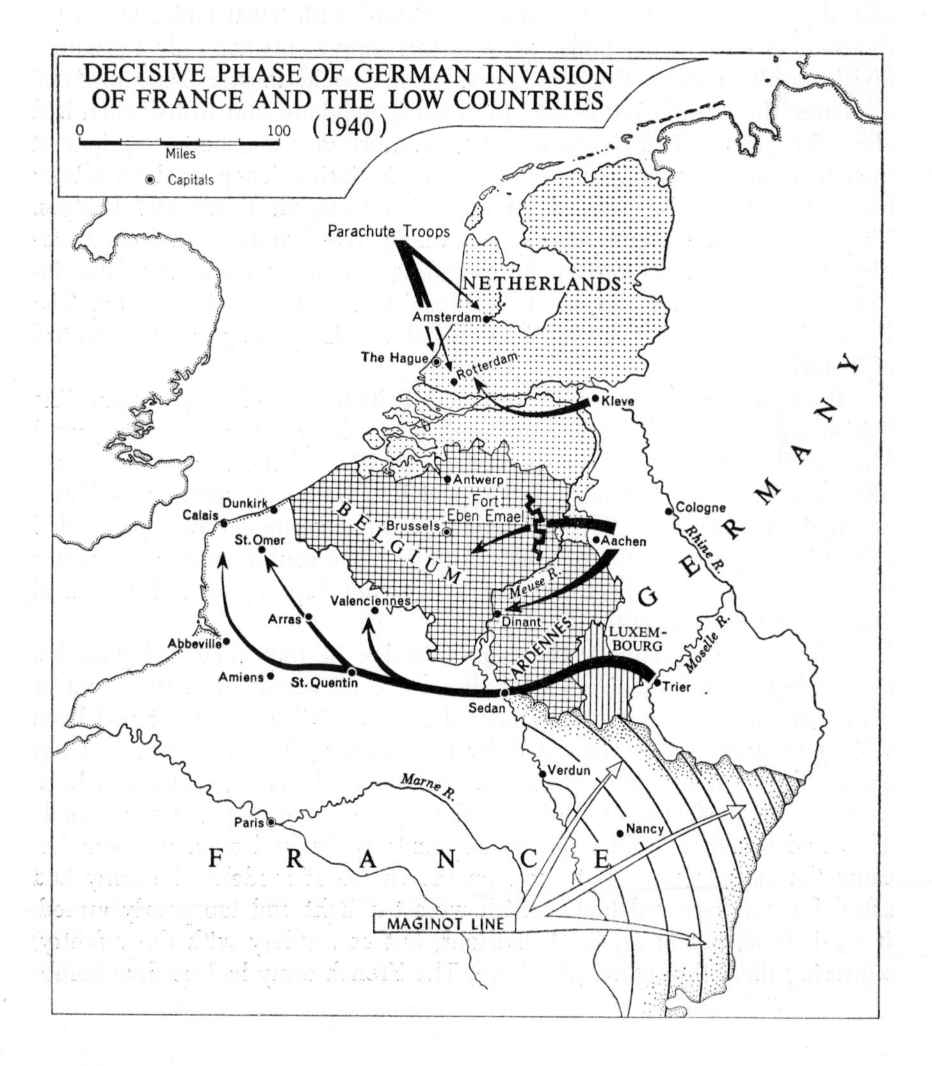

plain as the Germans had done in 1914, on a proposal by General Fritz von Mannstein he sent the main body of forty-four divisions, including five armored divisions supported by motorized infantry, through the forested hills of the Ardennes, and he used a lesser force to overrun the Netherlands and Belgium and enter coastal France. The French, assisted by the small British Expeditionary Force, arranged their troops in expectation of a repetition of the attack of 1914. The German armored and motorized drive through the Ardennes went so fast that Hitler himself became alarmed. The advance continued, however, and by May 20 the German army reached the coast at Abbeville, to trap the main French force and the entire British army in a pocket. The 26 French divisions locked in the Maginot Line became practically useless.

The Germans had 150 infantry divisions and their opponents 106, plus the 26 in the Maginot Line; but the main German superiority lay in tanks and airplanes. They had 10 armored divisions with 3,000 tanks, at least a thousand of them heavy tanks, whereas their opponents had only 4 armored divisions, all of them French. The Germans could muster 3,000 to 4,000 airplanes, the French 700 to 800; the Dutch, Belgians, and British each had about 200 planes. The Germans possessed more men and better equipment than their enemies, and showed far more initiative. They used parachute troops to capture Netherlands and Belgian forts, air bases, and bridges. They terrified the population by screaming dive bombers; and they employed psychological warfare in spreading rumors, telephoning false instructions, and other devices to confuse and bewilder the enemy. The French high command did not know what was happening and lost control of its forces.

Back of the chaos lay French and British lack of preparation. The British government had not introduced compulsory military training until May, 1939, and then did not speed the execution of the law. It had voted increased funds for the navy and especially for the air force after Hitler rearmed in 1935, but Neville Chamberlain's government had proceeded slowly in carrying out the program. Although the country was much better prepared than it had been in 1914, it had not kept up with the tactical changes introduced by the Germans.

The French had made the same mistake: in 1938 they had passed a law setting up an organization for the use of all resources in the event of war, without ever having implemented it. The civil government had been willing to grant funds requested by the military, but the latter had not chosen the right weapons. Both military and civil bureaucracies had been dilatory and perfectionist, and had played the game of passing the buck. They had failed to build sufficient airplanes, tanks, and other weapons because the experts could not agree on the choice of models. The army had asked for and received tanks which were too light and too poorly armed. It used these, not in armored divisions, but as artillery with the infantry, scattering them throughout the force. The French army had no dive bombers. French industry, which should have supplied the armaments, was so outmoded in some factories that shells were still being handmade. The industrialists were more concerned with fighting French labor than with preparing for a German attack, and often the supplies remained lost in warehouses. The army bureaucracy functioned inefficiently and was supervised by a government fully as incompetent. French experts had expected a leisurely war of at least three years' duration; they encountered a blitzkrieg.

When the fall of France became certain, Mussolini entered the conflict (June 11). Hitler cordially welcomed this display of Axis solidarity but did not allow it to affect the terms of the armistice. He was determined to control France as a satellite and to bring her back into the war on his side. He had conquered the army and occupied the land, but he also wished to keep the French fleet and the colonies, which were still beyond his reach, from joining the British. He understood that the French held these cards in the diplomatic game and that Great Britain would take bold steps to prevent his acquiring the French fleet. Mussolini, after having fought France for a week, wished to acquire the French Empire in North Africa, Nice, Corsica, and French Somaliland, an outlet to the Atlantic in French Morocco, Malta, and control over Egypt. Hitler vetoed such claims completely and imposed an armistice which left France a national government but which placed three fifths of the country (down to the Loire River with strips extending to Switzerland and along the coast to Spain) under German occupation; it left the French colonies undisturbed during the war. The armistice stipulated that, apart from the vessels needed to safeguard the French Empire, the French fleet should be assembled and disarmed in specified ports under the control of Germany or Italy. The German government declared that it did not intend to use the fleet "during the war or for its own purposes, . . . excepting for the units necessary for surveillance of the coasts and for sweeping of mines."

The article of the armistice concerning the fleet was so loosely worded that neither the British nor the United States governments, both deeply concerned not to permit Germany to gain this enormous increase in force at sea, expected the terms to prevent Germany from using the French fleet. The French government assured the others secretly that it would never permit the fleet to fall under German control; but the British and the Americans did not trust the government established in Vichy after defeat. It was headed by Marshal Pétain, eighty-four years of age, a pessimist and an authoritarian by nature, who the British thought had been too ready to surrender. When he set up a totalitarian government after the fascist model and included in his cabinet Pierre Laval and other persons willing to collaborate with the Nazis and Fascists, the British and the Americans watched the disposal of the French fleet with the closest care. No other issue was to continue to arouse so much trouble. In less than two weeks after the armistice the British seized all French war vessels in British ports and in Alexandria, and attempted to capture those at Mers-el-Kebir in Algeria. When the French resisted this last attempt the British sank or captured all but one ship, the battle cruiser "Strasbourg," which escaped to Toulon under cover of night.

Against Great Britain

From the military debacle in northeastern France the British had recovered more than 300,000 of their troops, together with a few of the French. They had been able to do so by a mistake in tactics which Hitler had made; instead of permitting his armored forces coming from the southwest to advance immediately and capture the cornered Allied troops, he had held them back for two days, with the thought of first conquering the rest of France. The British used the respite to withdraw by sea. Mustering all available naval and civilian boats, they picked the troops off the beaches of Dunkirk and carried them to safety, while the British air force fought off the German planes. Prime Minister Churchill declared in the House of Commons on June 18 that the government would continue the fight irrespective of odds, "so that if the British Empire and its Commonwealth last for a thousand years, men will still say: 'This was their finest hour.' "

Hitler was accustomed to remarking, "Our enemies are little worms; I saw them at Munich." After the conquest of France he could not understand why Great Britain, being defeated, did not sue for peace. He was apparently willing to offer her favorable terms, for, as he said to his commander in chief, the disintegration of the British empire would benefit, not Germany, but Japan, the United States, and others. He had a naval program underway, but he was too impatient to wait for its completion and he was confident that he could win without it. He failed to comprehend that he lacked both necessary naval and air power and the natural resources for global war. His shortage of oil was already hampering the attack on Great Britain. Romania served as his main source of supply, apart from the fuel which he could extract from coal. By imposing a blockade, he expected to starve Britain into making peace, but he had not prepared sufficient planes or U-boats for the task. At the beginning of the war Germany had 57 submarines, of which 17 had been lost by July, 1940. The force available for duty in the Atlantic at that time had declined to about half a dozen, and Germany needed at least 300 to make the blockade effective. The air force had been developed to support the infantry, not to do strategic bombing of a country like Great Britain or to war on ocean shipping.

As the British would not make peace, Hitler was forced to continue the war against them, even though he recognized the difficulties involved. "The invasion of Britain is an exceptionally daring undertaking," he said to Admiral Raeder on July 21, "because even if the way is short this is not just a river crossing, but the crossing of a sea which is dominated by the enemy. . . . The prerequisites are complete mastery of the air, the operational use of powerful artillery in Dover Strait, and protection by minefields. The time of the year is an important factor too. . . . If it is not certain that preparations can be completed by the beginning of September, other plans must be considered." Göring was confident that his air force could gain mastery of the air and enable the invasion to succeed, but Hitler hesitated for several weeks in the hope that the British would acknowledge defeat.

Since the mass air attacks did not begin until August 12, the British had had precious time to prepare. The Germans were far superior in number of planes and pilots, having 3,242 combat planes on August 10 to Britain's 1,350, and the British had no reserve in pilots. The Germans, however, had not kept up with the British in a number of essential branches of science. The British development of radar and of the radio telephone, which the Germans lacked, plus the excellence of the Spitfire and Hurricane models of fighter planes, enabled the few British pilots to parry the attack. Between August 8 and 26 the Germans lost 602 aircraft; the British, 259. In the air battle of September 15 Göring lost 34 of 123 bombers, in spite of their being protected by 679 fighter planes. He erred in strategy, first, by bombing London instead of destroying the air fields and, second, by keeping his planes in close formation, where the speedy British fighters could attack them with ease. In September it became evident that Germany had not gained sufficient control of the air for invasion. The British air force had even bombed Berlin and had destroyed a large proportion of the boats which the Germans had collected to transport troops across the Channel. Hitler did not officially cancel the Battle of Britain; he indefinitely postponed it. A few hundred pilots had saved Great Britain.

The German–Italian–Japanese Alliance

The Nazi victory over France and the seeming doom of Great Britain helped to bring to power in July, 1940, the expansionist military group in Japan. Led by the Konoye-Matsuoka cabinet, the imperialists, eager to share the spoils, revived discussions for a formal treaty, which during the previous two years Hitler had unsuccessfully endeavored to negotiate. The Nazis sought the alliance as a means of warning Great Britain to come to terms and the United States to remain neutral. Mussolini approved the proposal for its propaganda value. The Japanese army and navy cliques and Foreign Secretary Matsuoka harbored extensive ambitions. Four of the ministers, Prince Konoye, General Tojo, Admiral Yoshida, and Matsuoka, held a conference on the subject in anticipation of negotiations with Germany, from the record of which the following statement of their aims is quoted:

> Japan and the two countries of Germany and Italy will mutually coöperate in order not to allow the United States to interfere in regions other than the Western Hemisphere and the United States possessions, and also in order to safe-

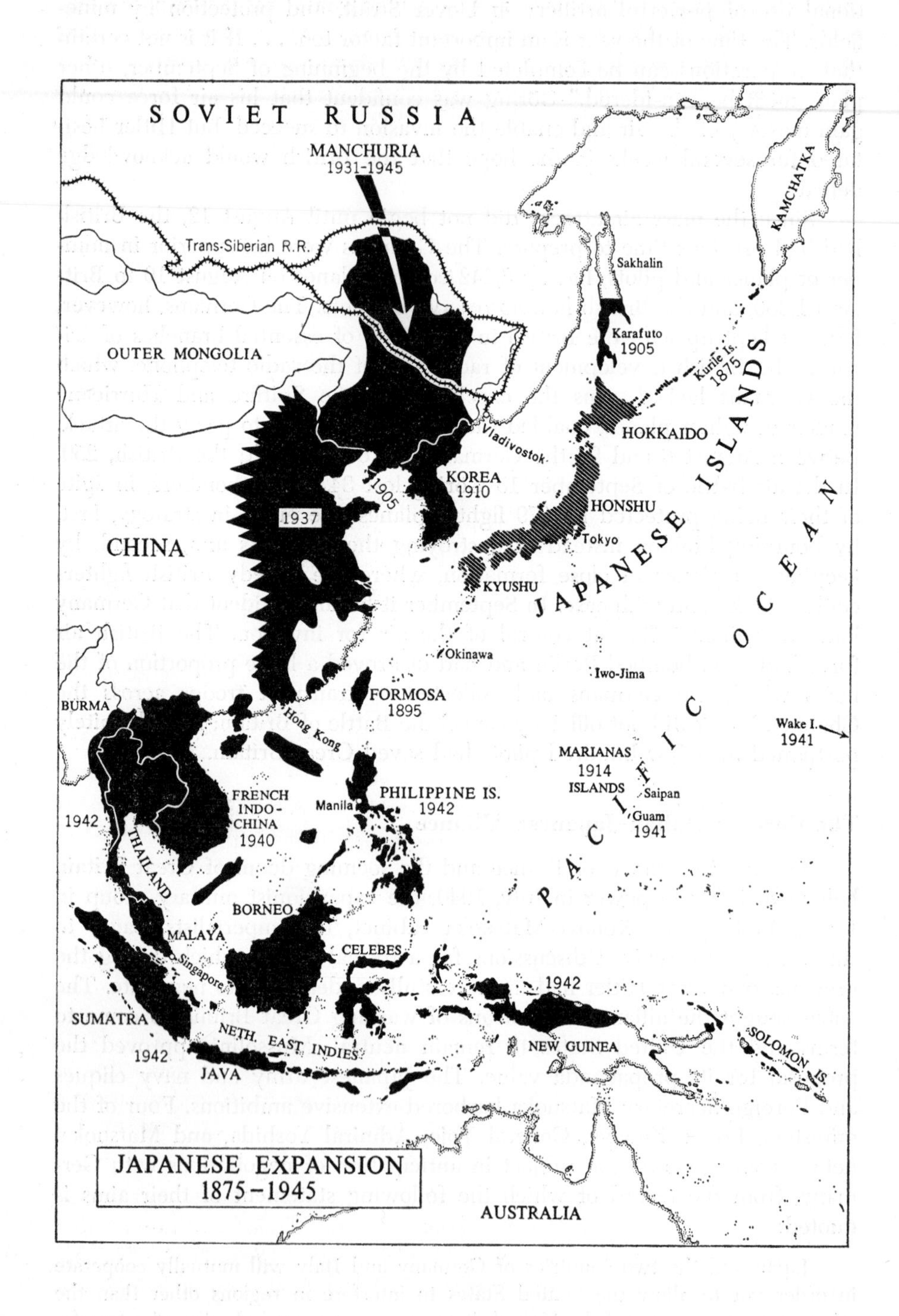
SOVIET RUSSIA
MANCHURIA
1931-1945
Trans-Siberian R.R.
OUTER MONGOLIA
KAMCHATKA
Sakhalin
Karafuto
1905
Kurile Is.
1875
HOKKAIDO
Vladivostok
KOREA
1910
1905
1937
CHINA
HONSHU
Tokyo
KYUSHU
JAPANESE ISLANDS
PACIFIC OCEAN
Okinawa
Iwo-Jima
FORMOSA
1895
BURMA
Hong Kong
Wake I.
1941
MARIANAS
1914
ISLANDS
Saipan
Guam
1941
FRENCH
INDO-
CHINA
1940
Manila
PHILIPPINE IS.
1942
1942
THAILAND
BORNEO
MALAYA
Singapore
CELEBES
1942
SUMATRA
NETH. EAST INDIES
NEW GUINEA
SOLOMON IS.
1942
JAVA
AUSTRALIA
JAPANESE EXPANSION
1875–1945

guard the political and economic interests of both contracting parties in this connection. Further, in the event of either contracting party entering upon a state of war with the United States, the other contracting party will assist that party by all possible means. Japan and the two countries of Germany and Italy will closely coöperate with respect to the action to be taken in regard to Central and South America.

The Japanese hoped to use German and Italian influence in bringing the China Incident, Japan's ten years of undeclared war with China, to a close, and they envisaged "Japan's Sphere of Living for the construction of a Greater East Asia New Order" as including "the former German Islands under mandate, French Indo-China and Pacific Islands, Thailand, British Malaya, British Borneo, Dutch East Indies, Burma, Australia, New Zealand, India, etc., with Japan, Manchuria and China as the backbone." They agreed to continue the China Incident and to push the other imperialist action "within limits short of war"; but they added:

If, however, domestic and foreign conditions take a decidedly favorable turn, or if it is deemed that, irrespective of whether our preparations are complete or not, the development of the internal situation permits of no further delay, Japan will resort to armed force.

The Japanese totalitarians did not quite dare to tell the Nazis, themselves accustomed to global thinking, about all the items; but to their agreeable surprise they encountered no difficulty from either the Germans or the Italians about approving the general area of their aims or about the other terms of a treaty.

The severest critics of the proposed alliance were found within the ranks of the Japanese cabinet and court, where great fear was expressed that a pact with Germany and Italy would bring about war with the United States. The critics expressed concern over Japan's lack of preparation, her shortage of oil, steel, and other materials which she imported from the United States. General Tojo countered by declaring:

It is the United States that is encouraging the Chungking Government or anti-Japanese movement at the present time. Should a solid coalition come to exist between Japan, Germany and Italy, it will become the most effectual expedient to restrain the United States. The more effectually we restrain the United States, the more possibly and quickly we shall be able to dispose of the Sino-Japanese conflict. On the other hand, if we can bring about a *rapprochement* between the Soviet Union and our country as a result of the Tripartite coalition and through the good offices of Germany and Italy, especially Germany, we shall be able to spur the quick ending of the Sino-Japanese conflict.

Matsuoka argued that nothing could be gained by friendliness toward the United States. He advocated a "determined attitude," and his military and naval supporters declared that "there is nothing to worry about." The opposition was overcome, and on September 27, 1940, the Tripartite Pact was signed.

The treaty clearly expressed the intention of the signers to reorganize the globe. The three governments considered it "the pre-requisite of a lasting peace that every nation in the world shall receive the space to which it is entitled. They have, therefore, decided to stand by and coöperate with one another in their efforts in Greater East Asia and the regions of Europe respectively." They proposed "to establish and maintain a new order of things, calculated to promote the mutual prosperity and welfare of the peoples concerned," and they were ready to cooperate with other nations for that purpose. Germany and Italy recognized Japan's "leadership" in the establishment of a new order in Greater East Asia, and Japan that of Germany and Italy in Europe. Article 3 read: "Germany, Italy and Japan agree to coöperate in their efforts on aforesaid lines. They further undertake to assist one another with all political, economic and military means if one of the three Contracting Powers is attacked by a Power at present not involved in the European War or in the Chinese-Japanese conflict." Since none of the signatories at the time sought trouble with the Soviet Union, they stated in Article 5 that "the above agreement affects in no way the political status existing at present between each of the three Contracting Parties and Soviet Russia." That is to say, they would assist one another with all means if one of them were attacked, but they did not explicitly define the word "cooperation" in achieving the "new order." Would "cooperation" include military action, or merely economic and political? Not trusting one another very far, the three powers left the answer to circumstances.

The reader may let his fancy play on the possible significance which predatory totalitarian governments in justifying their own aggressive action might give to the word "attack" when referring to the action of another power. Hitler expertly performed such semantic tricks, and the Japanese imperialists made apt pupils. Ribbentrop defended the treaty by the following remarks: "This pact is not directed against any other people. It is aimed exclusively against those warmongers and irresponsible elements in the rest of the world who, contrary to the real interests of all nations, strive to prolong and extend the present conflict." The Nazi foreign minister assumed that Germany's conquests were in "the real interests of all nations"; he then accused any state hostile to these conquests of being a "warmonger." His colleague in Japan surpassed him in hypocrisy. He denounced as warmongers "the countries which attempt to obstruct, directly or indirectly [the reader should always scrutinize with care the meaning of the word "indirectly" when used in a political statement], our construction of a New Order in Great East Asia, and even those who resort to all sorts of stratagems in order to block the path of Japan's advance toward the fulfillment of her great historic mission—that of establishing world peace." The traditional meaning of words was being destroyed by these peace lovers, together with the freedom of peoples, their own included. The negotiation of the pact has been explained as a reply to the British-United States agreement transferring fifty American destroyers to Great Britain. A more accurate explanation may be a common lust for conquest.

Hitler's Failure in Spain and Vichy France

The success in negotiating the Tripartite Pact was offset by failure with Spain and Vichy France. In the summer of 1940 Hitler urged Spain to enter the war. The Spanish asked for French Morocco, territory in Algeria and around Rio de Oro and Spanish Guinea, and extensive economic aid in grain and oil; in return they would enter the war at some uncertain date. In a personal conference on October 23 Hitler attempted to overwhelm General Franco with his charm and greatness. The Spanish dictator countered with embarrassing questions about Germany's ability to furnish military and economic aid to Spain and suggested that, even if Germany conquered the British Isles, she would still have to fight the British government and fleet in Canada, where they would be supported by the United States. Hitler struggled with Franco for nine hours, nearly lost his temper, and later told Mussolini that rather than go through that ordeal again "he would prefer to have three or four teeth taken out."

How much Franco's cautious attitude was caused by British and American control over oil and grain shipments to Spain cannot be stated; that these two states could provide or withhold indispensable products showed the Spanish that Hitler had not yet won the war. Nor could Franco be enthusiastic over the offer of Nazi troops to help seize Gibraltar: the troops might stay in Spain and she become another Italy.

Marshal Pétain, whom Hitler saw on the next day, appeared to be more amenable. He accepted the principle of collaboration and agreed that France had an interest in British defeat. He listened to Hitler's assurance that France would be compensated from British territory in Africa for present colonial areas which would be taken from her. When Hitler left, momentarily satisfied, the marshal remarked to a friend, "It will take six months to discuss this programme and another six months to forget it." In December the marshal privately stated French policy to be as follows: "The situation of our country requires the maintenance of a careful equilibrium between collaboration with Germany (inevitable in the economic sphere) and what the British and Americans propose." Regarding Laval as too pro-German, he took the risk in December of dismissing him as foreign secretary and persuaded the Nazis to acquiesce in the decision. Hitler's plans to gain Spanish and French participation completely miscarried.

Italy and the Mediterranean

From the conference with Pétain Hitler traveled to Italy, where Mussolini announced that he had just invaded Greece. Earlier in the summer the Führer had advised Italy not to disturb the peace of the Balkans; to go ahead was the Duce's way of showing independence. Mussolini mistrusted Hitler's negotiations with Spain and France, for he wished Italy to obtain the French Empire in North Africa, and he was disturbed over Hitler's project for creating a vast German colony in Central Africa. He therefore spread the war in a direction advantageous to Italian interests, namely, to Greece, and left his ally to adjust to the accomplished fact.

Hitler accepted the move with good grace, but he rightly anticipated trouble. The Greeks defeated the Italians in every battle and by December were pursuing them into Albania. On the night of November 11 the British fleet under Admiral Andrew Cunningham attacked the Italian fleet at its base at Taranto and hit three battleships. Early in February, 1941, the British fleet bombarded Genoa, and the British aircraft carrier H.M.S. "Illustrious," which the Germans had already claimed to have sunk, sailed through the Mediterranean from Gibraltar to Alexandria. In North Africa in the autumn and winter General Archibald Wavell, with at most two British divisions, drove the Italians under Marshal Rodolfo Graziani back from the Egyptian border and in two months' time captured 130,000 Italian troops, 400 tanks, 1,290 guns, and much transport. The British casualties were 500 killed, 1,373 wounded, and 55 missing. The Duce could conquer neither Greece nor Egypt and had to be rescued by the Germans. Relegated to the position of junior partner, he cried in anguish, "I am sick and tired of being rung for."

GERMAN-SOVIET CONFLICT OF INTEREST

In December, 1939, Stalin cabled Hitler, "The friendship of the peoples of Germany and the Soviet Union, cemented by blood, has every reason to be lasting and firm." Nonetheless, almost as soon as the treaty of that year was signed, differences between the two governments arose. Hitler disliked the Soviet attack on Finland, even though he recognized that country as belonging within the Soviet sphere of influence. Germany acquired food and raw materials, especially nickel, from Finland, and the Nazis knew that a main reason for the Soviet war lay in Finland's close economic and cultural relations with the *Reich*. Hitler felt sufficiently concerned in September, 1940, to station German troops in the country. When during the Battle of France Stalin annexed the three Baltic states, the speed and the method of action disturbed the Führer, who, however, took no counteraction.

Soviet Occupation of the Baltic

The Communist treatment of Estonia may be taken as typical. The Soviet government sent an ultimatum demanding the creation of a new government "able and willing to secure the honest application of the Soviet-

Estonian Mutual Assistance Pact." It demanded the immediate right for Soviet troops "to be stationed in sufficient numbers in the most important centres of Estonia." It accused the government of having failed to break its alliance with Latvia, with having enlarged the alliance to include Lithuania, and with having tried to bring in Finland. It demanded acceptance inside of 8½ hours under threat of invasion. Without waiting for negotiations, the Soviet government sent in troops accompanied by Andrei Zhdanov, a member of the Politburo, to complete the work. Zhdanov brought by special trains some of the Russian minority from the southeastern corner of the state in order to organize on June 21 "the spontaneous uprising of the working people"; the Estonian workers would not cooperate.

On the same day Zhdanov set up a puppet government; about two weeks later he held a "free" election for a new parliament. When the Estonians did not understand the communist meaning of freedom and put up candidates in opposition to the Communists, Zhdanov declared that these were trying to "deceive the people," and he blocked the move. The Communists counted the ballots and settled on the favorable figure of 84.1 per cent. Within a few weeks the Estonian people "freely" gave up their independence and asked for membership in the U.S.S.R. The absorption of the three Baltic states marked another act in the Soviet imperialistic expansion by way of the army.

The difference of interest in the Balkans between Germany and the Soviet Union was much greater than that in the Baltic region. When Stalin seized the Baltic states he also compelled Romania to relinquish both Bessarabia and Bucovina. Although Germany had agreed to Bessarabia's being in the Soviet sphere of influence, Hitler feared to have Soviet troops within a hundred miles of the Romanian oilwells at Ploeşti. He had disavowed political interest in Romania; but heavy economic interests there nonetheless involved Germany in politics. The *Reich* government had negotiated a treaty with Romania in September, 1939, bringing the economy within the German system. It had likewise forced the country as well as the other Balkan states to grant the German minorities the role of a state within a state; the minorities became members of the Greater German Folk Community under Nazi leaders. When the loss of Bessarabia and Bucovina brought forth demands by Bulgaria and Hungary for Romanian territory, Hitler had to intervene. Bulgaria easily regained the Dobruja, but Hungary's claim to Transylvania caused trouble. The Führer wished to keep the good will of both Hungary and Romania. At Vienna, on August 30, he divided the territory between them, a solution satisfactory to neither. Within two months Romania was deprived of one third of her territory and 3 million Romanian and 2 million non-Romanian subjects. Under these circumstances King Carol abdicated, leaving the field to a new prime minister, General Ion Antonescu, a Hitler stooge. In September Romania joined the Axis, and to the alarm of the Soviet Union, German troops occupied the country. When the U.S.S.R. protested, Germany replied with assurance that the occupation was temporary and directed against Great Britain.

Nazi-Soviet Negotiations Fail

During the Battle of Britain Churchill predicted to his friend Jan Christian Smuts, "If Hitler fails to beat us here he will probably recoil eastwards. Indeed, he may do this even without trying invasion." The surmise proved to be correct.

> In the event that invasion [of Great Britain] does not take place [Hitler said on July 31, 1940] our efforts must be directed to the elimination of all factors that let England hope for a change in the situation. . . . Britain's hope lies in Russia and the United States. If Russia drops out of the picture, America, too, is lost for Britain, because the elimination of Russia would greatly increase Japan's power in the Far East. . . . Decision: Russia's destruction must therefore be made part of this struggle. . . . The sooner Russia is crushed the better. The attack will achieve its purpose only if the Russian State can be shattered to its roots with one blow. . . . If we start in May 1941 we will have five months in which to finish the job.

He ordered the general staff to prepare an attack.

Before embarking on this venture Hitler once again sought a satisfactory agreement with his eastern neighbor, and for that purpose on November 12-13, 1940, Molotov came to Berlin. The negotiations, which failed completely, interest us only as revealing the ambitions and the quality of thinking of the participants.

Hitler opened the discussion by proposing that the Soviet Union associate itself with the Tripartite powers in a division of the British Empire. "After the conquest of England the British Empire," he said, "would be apportioned as a gigantic world-wide estate in bankruptcy of forty million square kilometres. In this bankrupt estate there would be for Russia access to the ice-free and really open ocean. . . . All the countries which could possibly be interested in the bankrupt estate would have to stop all controversies among themselves and concern themselves exclusively with the partition of the British Empire." The United States, Hitler added, must be kept out.

After the Führer outlined the vast proposal, Ribbentrop took over the detailed negotiations and "wondered whether Russia would not also turn to the south for her natural outlet to the sea." "Which sea?" Molotov asked, and Ribbentrop mentioned the Persian Gulf and the Arabian Sea. As to the Black Sea Straits, he said, a new convention should assure "certain special privileges to Russia," including "freer access to the Mediterranean."

Later in the day, Hitler joined the conversations, and pointed his remarks by saying that they should "prevent this war from becoming the father of a new war." Molotov did not object to participating in the Tripartite Pact, "but the aim and the significance of the Pact must first be more closely defined. What was the meaning of the New Order in Europe and in Asia, and what role would the U.S.S.R. be given in it? . . . Moreover, there were issues to be clarified regarding Russia's Balkan and Black Sea interests with respect to Bulgaria and Romania and Turkey." Hitler's interpreter was amazed. "The questions hailed down upon Hitler," he wrote in his memoirs. "No foreign visitor had ever spoken to him in this way in my presence." The conversations were interrupted at that point by the threat of a British air-raid.

On the next day the negotiations were again held in an air-raid shelter. Hitler and Ribbentrop resumed the subject of partitioning the British empire. This time the Soviet Union was urged to expand in the direction of the Indian Ocean. Hitler was pushing it a little to the east of the oil resources of Iraq and Iran; he needed these for himself. Molotov, though cool and reserved, insisted that "all these great issues of tomorrow could not be separated from the issues of today and the fulfillment of existing agreements. The things that were started must first be completed before they proceeded to new tasks."

Molotov wanted to know what Germany was doing in Finland; he said the German guarantee of Romanian territory was "aimed against the interests of Soviet Russia, if one might express oneself so bluntly." What would Germany say if Russia gave a similar guarantee to Bulgaria? As a parting shot, Molotov declared that not only Bulgaria and Turkey "but the fate of Romania and Hungary was also of interest to the Soviet Union and could not be immaterial to her under any circumstances. It would further interest the Soviet Union to learn what the Axis contemplated with regard to Yugoslavia and Greece, and likewise what Germany intended with regard to Poland. . . . The Soviet Government was also interested in the question of Swedish neutrality . . . and the question of the passages out of the Baltic Sea. The Soviet Government believed that discussions must be held concerning this question similar to those now being conducted concerning the Danubian Commission" (for the regulation of navigation on the Danube, to which the Soviet Union insisted on being a party). Ribbentrop complained of being "queried too closely"; and, trying again to shift the discussion to global issues, he repeated his frequent assertion that Great Britain was defeated and powerless. "If that is so," Molotov asked, "why are we in this shelter and whose are these bombs which fall?"

The reader, who now knows Hitler's intention to seize territory in European Russia for German colonization, may wonder what might have happened if the Soviet leaders had accepted Hitler's proposal. The Soviet Union would have been involved in war with Great Britain and the British empire; the defense against Germany would have had to be reduced; and the Nazis might have seen the collapse of their British enemy while being in a position to attack the Soviet Union, weakened by its military endeavors in Southern Asia. Apparently the Communists as well as Hitler knew *Mein Kampf*.

Two weeks after the conversations in Berlin, Stalin replied by agreeing to the German proposals on condition that (1) German troops be withdrawn from Finland, (2) Germany agree to a mutual assistance pact between the Soviet Union and Bulgaria and to long-term lease by the Soviet Union of a base for land and sea forces within range of the Bosporus and the Dardanelles, (3) "the area south of Batum and Baku in the general direction of the Persian Gulf [be] recognized as the center of the aspirations of the Soviet Union," and (4) Japan renounce "her rights to concessions for coal and oil in Northern Sakhalin." Stalin appeared to be testing the sincerity of the German protestations of friendship. Hitler had said to Molotov that Germany's aspirations, apart from those in Europe, lay in Central Africa and Italy's in Northern and Northeastern Africa. If the Nazis accepted the Soviet terms, Germany might possibly be trusted and the Soviet gains be worth the risk. If that was the Soviet strategy, it failed; the Nazis never answered the Soviet proposal.

Nazi Conquest of the Balkans

In preparation for the attack on the Soviet Union Hitler turned his attention to the Balkans. In November, 1940, he induced Hungary and Romania to join the Tripartite Pact, and in the next year he pressed Bulgaria and Yugoslavia to follow suit. On the last day of February, 1941, German troops crossed the border into Bulgaria, which on March 1 signed the Tripartite Pact. The advance alarmed the Greek government, which had endeavored to prevent Germany from assisting Italy in the local war. The Greeks, reluctant to invoke the defensive alliance with Great Britain for fear that the Germans would use this aid as an excuse to attack, finally asked for help, and on March 7 British and Imperial forces began to land. Hitler countered by requesting Yugoslavia to join the Tripartite Pact. On March 25 the Yugoslav government signed, but was immediately overthrown by officers willing to work with Germany but not to such an extent. Hitler thereupon ordered immediate preparations, so the official order stated, "to destroy Yugoslavia militarily and as a national unit, without waiting for any possible declarations of loyalty from the new government." That the U.S.S.R. signed a nonaggression treaty with Yugoslavia a few days before the Nazi invasion did not affect the decision.

The military campaign was as brief as usual. Hitler sent 28 divisions into action; 24 of them had been intended for the attack on the Soviet Union, and among these came one third of all the mobile divisions. Ordering the Balkan satellites to participate, he began the war on April 6, 1941, against both Yugoslavia and Greece. For three days the Nazi air corps methodically and unopposed bombed Belgrade from housetop level in "Operation Punishment" (the Nazis appellation), killing over 17,000 people. The Nazi mobile force shattered the Yugoslav army in eleven days and forced its surrender. The defeat of Greece quickly followed, and on April 27 the

Germans hoisted the swastika over the Acropolis. The British staged another Dunkirk. They evacuated 43,000 of 57,600 soldiers and lost all heavy equipment.

The British were not safe in the island of Crete, which they had occupied during the preceding year. They had failed to fortify the island, and when on May 20 the Nazis attacked with airborne troops towed in gliders and followed by seaborne troops, neither the ground force on the island nor the navy, devoid of air protection, was able to withstand the invasion. In one of the most daring and best planned and executed acts of the war, the Nazis drove the British and Imperial defenders out of Crete. In this Dunkirk the British saved only one half of their troops.

Almost simultaneously the Germans sent an armored division under General Erwin Rommel to North Africa to help the Italians. In a spectacular campaign the Nazis sped across Cyrenaica and in two weeks' time reached the Egyptian frontier (April 12). They stalled in front of well-fortified Tobruk. With a little more help they could have conquered Egypt and the Suez Canal and gone on to the Middle East. Syria was under the control of French officials loyal to the Vichy regime. In May the pro-Nazi Rashid Ali, premier of Iraq, led a revolt against the British garrison and appealed for German aid. Fortunately for the anxious British, Hitler failed to support the offensive.

In September, 1940, at the time of the failure of the German plan to invade Great Britain, Admiral Raeder urged the Führer to consider the strategic importance of the Mediterranean and the Near and Middle East:

> The British have always considered the Mediterranean the pivot of their world empire. . . . While the air and submarine war is being fought out between Germany and Britain, Italy, surrounded by British power, is fast becoming the main target of attack. Britain always attempts to strangle the weaker enemy. The Italians have not yet realised the danger when they refuse our help. Germany, however, must wage war against Great Britain with all the means at her disposal and without delay, before the United States is able to intervene effectively. For this reason the Mediterranean question must be cleared up during the winter months.

Admiral Raeder stated that Britain "with the help of 'de Gaulle France,' and possibly also of the U.S.A., wants to make North-West Africa a center of resistance and to set up air bases for attack against Italy." He urged the seizure of Gibraltar, Dakar, the Canary Islands, and cooperation with Vichy France in forestalling an enemy attack against the French possessions in North Africa. Once these places were secure, he argued, Germany and Italy could capture the Suez Canal, Palestine, and Syria. "If we reach that point," he said, "Turkey will be in our power. The Russian problem will then appear in a different light. Fundamentally Russia is afraid of Germany. It is doubtful whether an advance against Russia in the north will then be necessary."

Hitler rejected the proposal as a "very lengthy operation" that "would involve very great difficulty." After being rebuffed by Franco and Pétain on entering the war, he turned his back on the Mediterranean in disgust. "That operation," he replied to the persisent Raeder, "is contemplated for the autumn of 1941, *after* the completion of Barbarossa" (conquest of Russia). He took no action when British forces seized Syria, restored order in Iraq, and continued to use Middle Eastern oil. On June 18, 1941, he signed a neutrality treaty with Turkey. Hitler aimed at bigger game to the east by the direct approach.

The spring of 1941 became notable not merely for Hitler's conquest of the Balkans and preparation against the Soviet Union but for political action by the United States and Japan. In both enterprises Germany suffered a severe reverse.

UNITED STATES AND JAPAN TAKE PRECAUTIONS

The United States had passed legislation during the thirties against all types of activity that, according to Congress, had drawn the country into World War I. American citizens were prohibited from traveling on belligerent ships, which might be sunk. A system of licenses controlled munitions makers. Congress prohibited loans to belligerent governments and forbade American merchant ships to arm or to enter danger zones in time of war. Propagandists were required to register. When the war began in earnest in Western Europe, these preventives soon gave way before the needs of American security. President Roosevelt and most of his advisers recognized this fact before the people did and endeavored to enlighten the public. They had the help of a nation-wide organization led by William Allen White, a Kansas publisher, called the Committee to Defend America by Aiding the Allies.

In persuading the public, the Nazi-Soviet Pact, the fall of France, and the threat to Britain proved far more effective than speeches. Beginning in the summer of 1940 the government initiated a series of measures which within the year brought about the collapse of the American policy of neutrality and began undeclared naval conflict with Germany. Private corporations bought all kinds of munitions and rushed them to Britain. Airplanes were manufactured and flown across the sea in armadas by American and British pilots. In September, 1940, the United States exchanged fifty destroyers for the long-term use of strategic bases in British possessions in the Western Atlantic. At the end of the year President Roosevelt spoke of the United States as the "arsenal of democracy" for the defense of Britain and for any other people defending itself against an aggressor.

In March, 1941, Congress passed the Lend-Lease Act, whereby nations seeking to purchase supplies in this country no longer were required to pay cash; for their aid Congress voted credits of $7 billion. Two months later the President declared an unlimited national emergency, and by summer American forces were keeping sea lanes open as far as Iceland and were jointly establishing bases on the island with Great Britain and Canada. Further measures followed in rapid succession. They enabled a country like Britain, which was running out of foreign exchange and exhausting its productive resources, to look to the future with confidence. Churchill subsequently called the Lend-Lease law "the most unsordid act in history." This judgment should be balanced by President Roosevelt's own, "We have made no pretense about our self-interest in this aid. Great Britain understands it—and so does Nazi Germany."

At about the same time the Japanese Foreign Minister Matsuoka visited Berlin (September, 1940) and Moscow (April, 1941). In the former capital he was urged to attack the British possession of Singapore. He was told that this was a unique moment in history for the Tripartite powers to defeat Great Britain. Ribbentrop, with his usual tact, asked Matsuoka for maps of that British base "so that the Fuehrer, who must certainly be considered the greatest expert of modern times on military matters, could advise Japan as to the best method for the attack on Singapore." The Japanese foreign minister listened attentively but made no promises. In Moscow he was received with comparable warmth. Stalin said to him, "We are both Asiatics," and Matsuoka, a member of an illustrious feudal family, called himself a "moral communist" and told Stalin that the war in China was directed, not at the Chinese, but at Anglo-Saxon liberalism seeking to destroy Japan's "moral communism." After hard bargaining, the two leaders signed a treaty that assured each of the neutrality of the other in war with a third power. Japan was thereby safe against Soviet attack if and when she went to war with Great Britain or the United States; the Soviet Union, if Germany struck her, was secure against Japanese attack. The treaty was adhered to until the closing days of the war, when the Soviet Union agreed to join in the last campaign against Japan.

GERMAN ATTACK ON THE SOVIET UNION

As the spring of 1941 advanced, signs of the impending assault on the Soviet Union increased in such number that the British and the American governments warned Moscow about Nazi plans. Stalin suspected these powers of trying to bring to pass the event about which they were warning him. Almost to the end Germany continued to receive large shipments of food and raw materials and to send manufactures to Russia. Early in May Stalin took from inflexible Molotov responsibility for foreign relations, and sought in every way to restore cordial political relations with Germany. Apparently duped by the Nazis' and his own propaganda, he refused to believe that Hitler would attack. On June 22, the anniversary of the Nazi armistice with France, the German invasion of the U.S.S.R. began.

Like Colonel Beck of Poland, the French politicians, and many other individuals, Stalin had made a mistake. His subtlety in hunting with the Nazis while watching them overrun most of Europe proved to have resulted from illusion. In self-imposed Marxian blinders he had failed to distinguish between the international policies of Nazi Germany and those of liberal-democratic countries. He had thought them all alike and had been happy to watch them tear each other to pieces. Now it was his turn to be the Nazi victim, and he faced the ordeal almost alone. Poland was destroyed, France was destroyed, the Balkan states lost—all those with whom he might have joined in resistance to Hitler were gone from the combat. His subsequent alibi, that he had joined the Nazis temporarily in order to gain time for further military preparation, is not in harmony with the fact that the Nazis caught his armies only half mobilized and in other respects far from ready for war. Stalin had miscalculated.

Hitler had Mussolini called out of bed in the middle of the night to receive the news of the extension of the conflict. "I do not disturb even my servants at night," the Duce grumbled to Ciano, "but the Germans make me jump out of bed at any hour without the least consideration." He and the other little satellites loyally followed suit in declaring war. As Hitler said to his Italian ally, the treaty with the Communists had often been "very irksome to me," and he was "happy now to be delivered from this torment."

Hitler had set the outbreak of the war for May 15, but the Balkan campaign and bad weather delayed the invasion for a month. He expected that the Soviet Union would be conquered in two or three months, that severe defeat would lead to popular rebellion against Stalin's regime. "We have only to kick in the door," he said to General Alfred Jodl, "and the whole rotten structure will come crashing down." He had reason for speed, for on the day of the invasion, June 22, Churchill broadcast to the world this message:

> We are resolved to destroy Hitler and every vestige of the Nazi regime. . . . Any man or State who fights against Nazidom will have our aid. Any man or State who marches with Hitler is our foe. . . . It follows therefore that we shall give whatever help we can to Russia and the Russian people.

Within the limits of his ability as executive of a nonbelligerent state, President Roosevelt supported this view by offering Lend-Lease aid to the Soviet Union. Hitler had vowed never to be caught in a war on two fronts; by his own action he was now involved in such a war. He had prided himself on fighting only as a last resort; since Munich he had had to fight for every gain. He had become increasingly overbearing in diplomacy and dependent upon brute force for success. The war against the Soviet Union proved to be his supreme diplomatic and military blunder.

Hitler planned the strategy for the invasion of the Soviet Union against the advice of his generals. He called for simultaneous attacks aimed in the direction of Leningrad, Moscow, and Stalingrad by way of Kiev and the

Donets basin. The generals advocated concentrating the main blow against Moscow as the center of Russian resistance. They followed the traditional German military theory of destroying the enemy's armed forces before turning to the conquest of territory and economic resources. Hitler demanded that political, economic, and military objectives be simultaneously pursued. He planned to employ ever-greater pincer movements; the German mobile forces—tanks, mobile artillery, motorized troops, and airplanes—were continuously to surround the defenders, cutting them off from retreat and forcing them to surrender. He believed that 150 divisions could compass the goals in the vast Russian plain; his generals persisted in skepticism, and the disagreement between them and the Führer caused confusion.

German Success in Russia

The invaders gained such success that by October 3 Hitler declared to the world that "the enemy in the East has been struck down and will never rise again." He ordered forty infantry regiments to be disbanded and the personnel returned to industry, and he began to plan further attacks on the British Isles and the Middle East. General von Runstedt took Kiev late in September, the Germans claiming 665,000 prisoners, and the army continued on toward the Black Sea. In the center, on August 7, General von Bock captured Smolensk, while in the north General von Leeb in October put Leningrad under siege. Hundreds of thousands of Soviet forces were captured or destroyed; yet the Germans always found more ahead. They had underestimated Soviet strength, which they thought to be 200 divisions. They were now able to identify 360 divisions and learned that the main strength lay in front of Moscow. By December, German advanced troops penetrated the suburbs of Moscow, but there they stalled.

Stalin knew that both he and the Soviet Union were defending their lives. During the second half of 1941 he appears to have been in private deeply worried about the outcome, but in public he remained calm, determined, and confident. He told the people on July 3 that the enemy "is out to restore the rule of the landlords, to restore Tsarism . . . to germanize [the peoples of the Soviet Union], to turn them into the slaves of German princes and barons." He called upon the people to "scorch the earth" in case they had to retreat. "In occupied regions," he ordered, "conditions must be made unbearable for the enemy and all his accomplices." As the German army continued to roll ahead, he ordered evacuation of industries and of workers and their families from western Russia to the Volga, the Urals, and Siberia. Within the short time which the Nazi advance allowed, he rescued in this way 1,360 plants and factories and millions of people. Seventy-five per cent of the war industries were located in and around Leningrad, Moscow, and Kharkov; enough of these facilities was saved to revive Soviet war production.

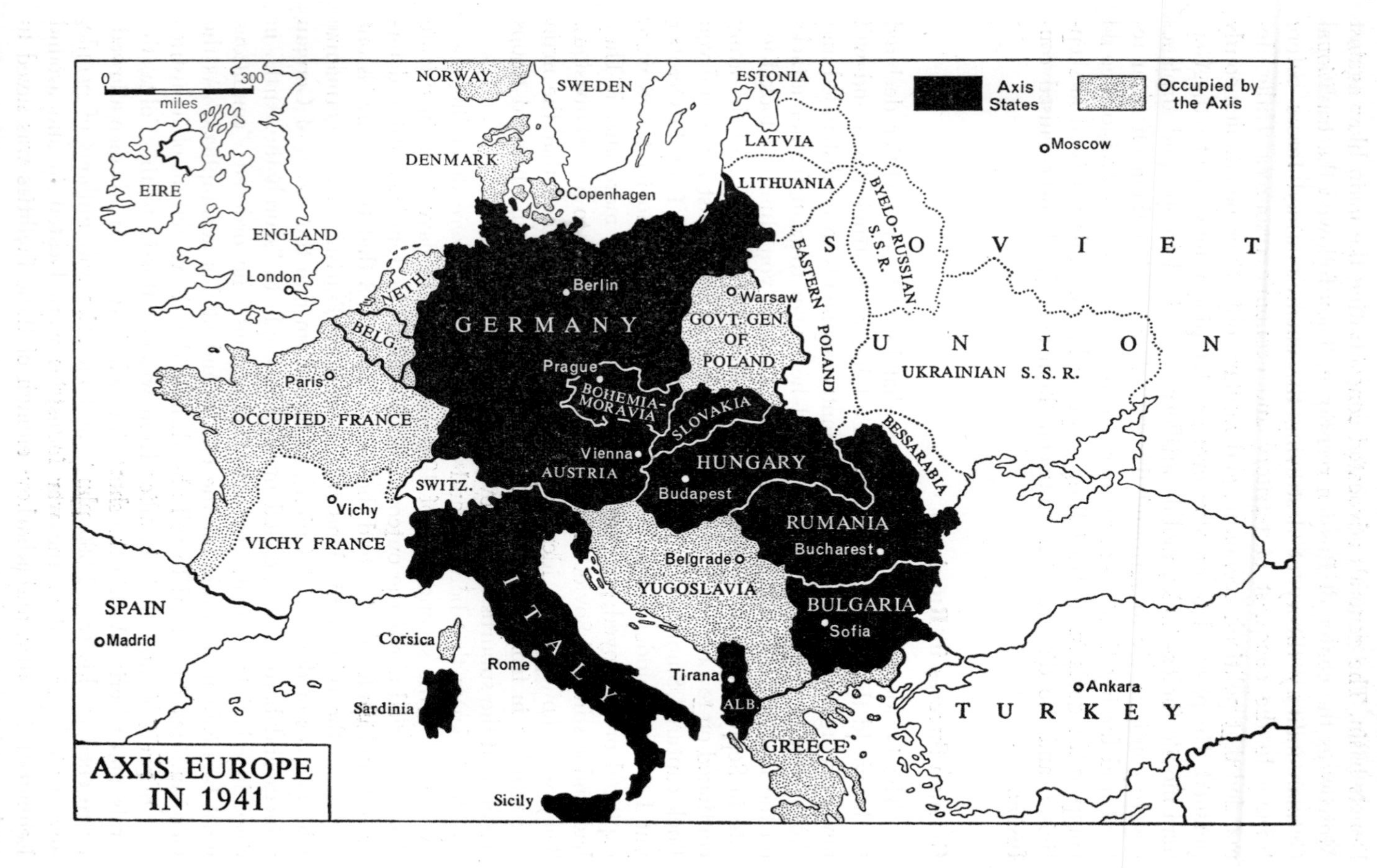

AXIS EUROPE IN 1941

Nonetheless, the size of the Soviet loss was enormous. "On the territory that had been occupied by the Germans in November 1941," according to the director of the Soviet State Planning Commission, "lived about 40 per cent. of the whole Soviet population. About 65 per cent. of the whole pre-war output of coal had come from there, 68 per cent. of all pig iron, 58 per cent. of all steel, 60 per cent. of aluminum . . . , 38 per cent. of the grain, 84 per cent. of sugar . . . , 41 per cent. of all railway lines of U.S.S.R." During these months the Soviet industrial output declined by more than one half, the output of steel by more than two thirds, of ball bearings by more than 95 per cent. Stalin transferred the government to the east, but he remained in the capital. He was trading space for time, as a country the size of the Soviet Union could do.

Germany Stalled by Resistance and Winter

Stalled by the Soviet armies and the Russian winter, Hitler established headquarters in eastern Germany and from there directed the campaign. General von Halder has written about his activity as follows:

> Hitler's belief in his own infallibility and in the omnipotence of his will increased; so did his nervous irritability. His interference in the direction of the Army, even in small matters, increased too, and tense debates about strategic and even tactical questions, which were purely the responsibility of the C.-in-C., Army, became more and more frequent. Spoiled by the quick successes of the previous campaigns, he expected operations to be carried through in a space of time that completely ignored the conditions of terrain and roads in the East.

After the war General von Runstedt gave an example. During the campaign of 1941 Hitler ordered him to take the coast of the Black Sea and Rostov and advance to the Volga and the Caucasus. "We laughed aloud when we received these orders," Runstedt said, "for winter had already come and we were almost seven hundred kilometers from these cities."

When rain and snow struck the armies, whose tanks and trucks were already suffering from overuse, Hitler commanded continuation of the advance. Expecting the forces to winter in the cities which they captured, he had provided no warm clothing for the troops and had not prepared the machines for use in subzero weather. The speed of his military progress had not sufficed to overcome the handicap of space. The losses in the battles against the countries previously conquered had been trivial; now Germany began to pay the blood tax. By the end of February, 1942, the German forces suffered 210,572 killed, 747,761 wounded, and 47,303 missing. Frostbite alone had caused at least 112,627 casualties. Accepting such losses, Hitler refused to allow the troops to retreat and dismissed a number of the ablest generals who disagreed with his orders. The winter hardship exalted his spirit. In a speech on January 30, 1942, to his people he expressed his "unbounded confidence, confidence in myself, so that nothing, whatever it may be, can throw me out of the saddle, so that nothing can shake me."

UNITED STATES BECOMES INVOLVED IN THE WAR

During the momentous events on the European continent in 1941, Hitler had continued to attack Great Britain from the air and on the sea. Although he expected the United States to enter the war at some time, he sought to avoid any direct move which would lead to hostility. His policy on submarine warfare in particular suffered; he wished to sink ships supplying Britain but without angering the United States to the point of action. Thus in March, 1941, he extended the combat area in the North Atlantic as far west as the line running south from Greenland, but he still did not stress the construction of submarines. Up to the time of Pearl Harbor Germany had increased her submarine fleet from 57 to 249 but had sunk only 10 million tons of shipping. The battle fleet was used with similar caution. Not daring to risk an engagement with the British, the fleet remained in harbor protected by planes and shore batteries, except when single ships ventured out as raiders.

Hitler knew that Churchill was straining to bring the United States into the war, and he was aware of the growing intimacy not merely of British and American leaders but of the peoples. The Lend-Lease Act was followed by, among others, the assumption in July of the defence of Iceland by the United States, the declaration in September that United States merchant vessels would be armed and ordered to shoot submarines on sight, and the declaration late in October that the United States would deliver goods into the harbors of friends. Hitler appears not to have been greatly concerned. Ignorant of the United States, he estimated its strength according to his prejudices. To him it was a weak power, made so rotten by the mixture of races that it could not sustain a war. At a conference with Mussolini on August 25, the Führer, according to the Italian report,

> gave a detailed account of the Jewish clique which surrounds Roosevelt and exploits the American people. He stated that he could not, for anything in the world, live in a country like the U.S.A., whose conceptions of life are inspired by the most grasping commercialism and which does not love any of the loftiest expressions of the human spirit such as music.

Atlantic Charter

In August, 1941, shortly before Hitler conferred with Mussolini, Churchill and Roosevelt met off the coast of Newfoundland to discuss the progress of the war. As a by-product they formulated the ideals for which the free world stood. This was the Atlantic Charter, the essential portions of which read as follows:

> First, their countries seek no aggrandizement, territorial or other; Second, they desire to see no territorial changes that do not accord with the freely expressed wishes of the peoples concerned; Third, they respect the right of all

peoples to choose the form of government under which they will live; and they wish to see sovereign rights and self-government restored to those who have been forcibly deprived of them; Fourth, they will endeavor, with due respect to their existing obligations, to further the enjoyment by all States, great or small, victor or vanquished, of access, on equal terms, to the trade and to the raw materials of the world which are needed for their economic prosperity; Fifth, they desire to bring about the fullest collaboration between all nations in the economic field with the object of securing, for all, improved labor standards, economic advancement and social security; Sixth, after the final destruction of the Nazi tyranny, they hope to see established a peace which will afford to all nations the means of dwelling in safety within their own boundaries, and which will afford assurance that all the men in all the lands may live out their lives in freedom from fear and want; Seventh, such a peace should enable all men to traverse the high seas and oceans without hindrance; Eighth, they believe that all the nations of the world, for realistic as well as spiritual reasons, must come to the abandonment of the use of force. Since no future peace can be maintained if land, sea and air armaments continue to be employed by nations which threaten, or may threaten, aggression outside of their frontiers, they believe, pending the establishment of a wider and permanent system of general security, that the disarmament of such nations is essential. They will likewise aid and encourage all other practicable measures which will lighten for peace-loving peoples the crushing burden of armaments.

A short time later President Roosevelt added to the Charter two other ideals which had been overlooked—freedom of religion and freedom of information.

The statement should be contrasted with the dictators' conception of the New Order laid down in the Tripartite Pact. During the latter half of 1941 Hitler began to emphasize the solidarity of Europe as revealed in the war against bolshevism. Late in November he called his stooges to Berlin to renew the Anti-Comintern Pact. Italy, Spain, Hungary, Romania, Slovakia, Croatia, Bulgaria, Finland, and Denmark were represented. "The Germans were the masters of the house," Ciano wrote in his diary, "and they made us all feel it, even though they were especially polite to us." What this New Order could mean may be inferred from Göring's reaction at this conference to the report of an impending famine in Greece.

We cannot worry unduly about the hunger of the Greeks [he declared to Ciano]. It is a misfortune which will strike many other peoples besides them. In the camps for Russian prisoners they have begun to eat each other. This year between twenty and thirty million persons will die of hunger in Russia. Perhaps it is well that it should be so, for certain nations must be decimated. But even if it were not, nothing can be done about it. It is obvious that if humanity is condemned to die of hunger, the last to die will be our two peoples.

Japan Attacks the United States

The next act in the expansion of the war showed that Hitler had lost the initiative in international affairs. He had been torn between the desire to prevent the United States from becoming a belligerent and the fear that the United States and Japan might reach agreement behind his back, leaving Germany to bear the full force of American hostility. Since the United States would not go to war of its own accord, the initiative remained with the authoritarian militarists in control of Japan. These leaders had already used the opportunity of France's defeat to occupy French Indochina; and they were planning expansion southward. The United States opposed their moves, demanding withdrawal from China, respect for the integrity of all Far Eastern states, the Open Door for trade in China and elsewhere, and the withdrawal of Japan from the Tripartite Pact. During 1941 the United States, joined by Britain, extended its economic embargo against Japan, depriving her of vital oil and iron.

The American government assisted China with credit and military supplies, just as it aided Great Britain against Germany and Italy. As the American attitude stiffened, the imperialist groups in Japan gained in authority over their opponents. In October, the thoroughgoing chauvinist, General Tojo, became prime minister, and final negotiations between Japan and the United States began. Since neither side would recede from its position, on December 7, with no preliminary declaration of war, the Japanese suddenly struck the United States fleet at Pearl Harbor in Hawaii. They informed Hitler and Mussolini at the same time, surprising them as much as the United States. Although the Tripartite Pact called for mutual aid only in the event of attack by another power, Hitler immediately declared war on the United States and Mussolini reluctantly followed suit. In November the Führer had assured the Japanese that he would do so. He was exalted by the thought of a war between continents and by his power to affect the lives of added millions of people. "I can only be grateful to Providence," he said, "that it entrusted me with the leadership in this historic struggle which, for the next five hundred or a thousand years, will be described as decisive, not only for the history of Germany but for the whole of Europe and indeed the whole world."

Suggestions for Further Reading

BULLOCK, A. L. C. *Hitler*. See the Readings for Chapter 14. Essential, for Hitler directed strategy and tactics.

BUSH, VANNEVER. *Modern Arms and Free Men*. New York: Simon & Schuster, Inc., 1949. Indispensable for understanding the relation between science and modern war.

DEUTSCHER, ISAAC. *Stalin*. See the Readings for Chapter 10.

Food, Famine and Relief, 1940–1946. Geneva: League of Nations, 1946. Brief and illuminating.

FULLER, J. F. C. *The Second World War, 1939–1945*. New York: Duell, Sloan & Pearce, Inc., 1949. By a distinguished British military historian. Covers more than Europe.

KULISCHER, EUGENE MICHEL. *Europe on the Move: War and Population Changes, 1917–1947*. See the Readings for Chapter 6. Demographic evidence of human suffering. An appalling story.

LATOURETTE, K. S. *A Short History of the Far East.* See the Readings for Chapter 1.

LENCZOWSKI, GEORGE. *The Middle East in World Affairs.* See the Readings for Chapter 2.

MC NEILL, WILLIAM HARDY. *America, Britain and Russia: Their Coöperation and Conflict, 1941–1946*. New York: Oxford University Press, 1953. Invaluable. Judicious and thorough analysis of a complicated story.

WILMOT, CHESTER. *The Struggle for Europe*. New York: Harper & Brothers, 1952. Excellent military history with insight into the workings of diplomacy as well.

Chapter 20 · World War II, 1941-1945

Great Britain had avoided the appearance of wishing the United States to enter the war, but once Japan had forced the issue the nation felt the relief which Churchill expressed in his memoirs as follows:

> So we had won after all! Yes, after Dunkirk; after the fall of France; after the horrible episode of Oran; after the threat of invasion, when, apart from the Air and the Navy, we were an almost unarmed people; after the deadly struggle of the U-boat war—the first Battle of the Atlantic, gained by a hand's-breadth; after seventeen months of lonely fighting and nineteen months of my responsibility in dire distress. . . . Once again in our long Island history we should emerge, however mauled or mutilated, safe and victorious.[1]

War between Great Britain and Japan was immediately declared, and the British and the American leaders began the intimate cooperation which culminated in victory.

COOPERATION AMONG THE ALLIES

Even before Pearl Harbor Stalin had asked the British and the Americans to start a second front against Germany in the West. After the expansion of the war he reiterated this urgent request. At the same time he made certain that Japan would not attack the Soviet Union, thereby avoiding a war on two fronts against his own country and revealing the actual lack of cooperation between the Axis powers. Able to concentrate his forces against the Nazis, Stalin fought the war under the most favorable international conditions for him.

Cooperation between the free and capitalistic Great Britain and the United States, on the one hand, and the Communist Soviet Union, on the other, proved difficult to achieve. The sole bond of union was the war against Germany.

Stalin endeavored to adjust Communist policies to the exigencies of alliance by toning down Communist revolutionary propaganda and em-

[1] Winston Churchill, *The Second World War* (Am. ed.; Boston: Houghton Mifflin Company, 1950), III, 606-607.

phasizing Soviet patriotism and ideals of democracy, a word capable of varied interpretations. In a speech of July, 1941, he declared:

> In this war of liberation we shall not be alone. In this great war we shall have loyal allies in the peoples of Europe and America, including the German people who are enslaved by the Hitlerite despots.

In September he accepted the Atlantic Charter, and in November he stated in a speech:

> To cover up their reactionary, blackguard essence, the Hitlerites are branding the Anglo-American internal regime as a plutocratic regime. But in England and the United States there are elementary democratic liberties, there are trade unions of workers and employees, there are labor parties, there is a parliament, whereas the Hitler regime has abolished all these institutions in Germany.

In the same speech he seemed to renounce the ambition to conquer other peoples. "We have not and cannot have such war aims," he said, "as the seizure of foreign territories, the subjugation of foreign peoples." That free peoples could not trust this assurance was evident from Finland's entering the war on Germany's side against the Soviet Union and from Stalin's demand that his new allies recognize the Soviet acquisition of the Baltic States and of the eastern part of Poland. Since defeat of Hitler outweighed all other considerations at the time, the free world had to accept Stalin's words at their face value, assisting the Soviet Union with all possible means to overcome the common enemy.

The British and the American governments early agreed to a fundamental strategy for conducting the war. The two heads of state recognized that Germany was a more dangerous enemy than Japan and must be defeated first. Situated between the European allies, Germany was likewise more subject to immediate and concentrated attack. A few American admirals and generals, especially General MacArthur, as well as some British, objected to this order of priority, for it placed naval commanders and the generals stationed in the Far East in a position of secondary importance. Roosevelt and Churchill adhered to the decision, however, and Stalin placed the full weight of his influence behind their plan.

Allied Strategy

In executing the strategy, the British and the American governments followed different conceptions of the relation between political and military factors. Both countries traditionally excluded the military from political decisions, regarding the defense forces as technicians for carrying out policies set by civilian political leaders. In Great Britain the government bore responsibility for the fate of a widespread empire, and, since the country possessed limited material resources for waging war, Churchill advocated a combination of political and military strategy for achieving victory. He believed that the empire could be most effectively defended and the fortress of the Central Powers defeated by striking at various places on the perimeter, compelling the Axis to divide its forces and to expend them in relatively small defensive operations. He kept political objectives always in view, foreseeing that the course of military strategy would profoundly affect the international political situation at the end of the war.

The Americans thought in much simpler terms. President Roosevelt was conscious of his own limitations as a military and naval strategist and deferred to the judgment of experts. His generals and admirals, backed by the vast resources of the United States, hoped to exclude all politics from consideration by concentrating upon the most direct way to defeat the enemy. The acceptance of this approach meant that the nonpolitical American generals actually influenced political decisions more than their British colleagues. By pushing through strategic decisions without consideration of political implications they played directly into the hands of the Soviet Union. Their mistrust of Churchill's subtler conception of the relation between military strategy and international politics coincided in part with the thinking of the President, who disliked imperialism and aimed to use his influence to emancipate the colonial possessions of the European states and to start them on the road to self-government. Churchill resisted this aim with the assertion that Britain was not fighting in order to "liquidate" the British empire. He kept a closer control over military strategy than Roosevelt, but, since Britain was the lesser of the two powers, his advice did not carry the necessary weight to be accepted.

By January 1, 1942, twenty-six states had entered the war on the Allied side; but the United States, Great Britain, and the Soviet Union bore the brunt of the fighting. Anticipating a long conflict, they created machinery for policy making or for administration on both a national and an international scale. That the cooperation should be far closer between the two free countries than between these and the Soviet Union was to be expected. Nonetheless, considering the basic difference between the free peoples and the Communists, the extent of their acknowledged interdependence and mutual aid was considerable.

When, a few weeks after Pearl Harbor, Roosevelt and Churchill held in Washington their first war conference, General Marshall, chairman of the United States Joint Chiefs of Staff, declared to his British and American colleagues that

> the most important consideration is the question of unity of command. . . . We cannot manage by cooperation. Human frailties are such that there would be emphatic unwillingness to place portions of troops under another service. . . . I favor one man being in control, but operating under a controlled directive from here. We had to come to this in the first World War, but it was not until 1918 that it was accomplished and much valuable time, blood, and treasure had been needlessly sacrificed.

Marshall's proposal, referring only to the free countries, not to the Soviet Union, won approval. Henceforth one man was given supreme command over all the forces in each theater of war. As a necessary corollary the two Allies created a Combined Chiefs of Staff Committee to sit in Washington, whence it directed on a global basis at first logistics and within a few months strategy as well.

Economic Cooperation

Economic cooperation became a more complicated and more difficult problem than that of military aid. During the first half of 1942 the two governments established five joint boards, the Combined Munitions Assignment Board, the Combined Raw Materials Board, the Combined Shipping Adjustment Board, the Combined Production and Resources Board, and the Combined Food Board. They were intended to cover all essential economic aspects of the war.

The Food Board worked without difficulty, for the United States had a sufficient surplus to fill the essential needs of the other two countries. The Combined Production and Resources Board never achieved its set objective; neither government would, in fact, permit the complete integration of its economy with that of the other, and neither economy admitted of speedy integration with the other; their technical methods were too diverse. For example, in such a simple matter as the pitch of screw threads they used different standards, which prevented machine parts from being interchangeable. It was quicker for each country to utilize its own productive resources irrespective of ultimate economy of materials and man power. Great Britain as the lesser productive power kept postwar prospects in mind. She refused to give up the manufacture of tanks in favor of the more economical American production, fearing to jeopardize the peacetime revival of her automobile industry. This board therefore operated mainly as a statistical center, which pointed out bottlenecks and waste in production and which particularly helped the British to hold their own against the vast American economy.

The Combined Shipping Board never functioned effectively, largely because of the disparity in power of the two Allies. Since losses in ships were enormous, the British agreed to devote their shipyards primarily to repair, leaving to the Americans the construction of new ships. The Americans utilized the emergency to build up a huge merchant fleet, which could ultimately supplant the British as a peacetime carrier. The British protested against this exploitation and pointed out that they had surplus seamen, whereas the United States lacked trained personnel. Churchill eventually arranged for the wartime loan of American ships, thus preventing his country from having to depend upon the United States to bring in food and other materials.

The Munitions Assignment Board became the center for a struggle over the allocation of limited supplies not merely between British and Americans but between branches of the armed services. Decisions had repeatedly to be referred to Roosevelt; otherwise the British would have been slighted. Every general, every admiral, very fighter, every trainer desperately seeking supplies, claimed priority. The British stressed the short-term needs, the Americans the long-term needs. Since the United States was the major producer, Roosevelt tried to be fair to everyone, on many occasions improvising distribution according to urgency. No one was satisfied and complaints were continuous; but the system, or lack of it, proved ultimately effective.

Of the five the Combined Raw Materials Board functioned most efficiently and smoothly. Its responsibility could have aroused as much argument as that of the Munitions Board; but in this instance the British were able to maintain a rough equality with the United States by providing from the empire about as many raw materials in as great quantity as the Americans provided. Balance of power made for mutual consideration, and the American representative on the board, William Batt, and his British counterpart, Sir Clive Baillieu, were both cooperative and persuasive in their relations with bureaucratic colleagues. They concentrated on the allocation of only the materials, like copper and rubber, which were in very short supply, and they sought means to increase production and to economize use.

Examples of bickering and selfishness in the joint conduct of war were remarkably few and inconsequential in comparison with the magnitude of the achievement. The enormous difficulty in each capital of developing new bureaucratic agencies and of adjusting old ones for the conduct of the war—the War Production Board in the United States and the Ministry of Production in Great Britain, to offer two examples—and of gearing these into the war effort with the greatest possible speed, and the labor of coordinating with even greater speed the action of two vast armies, navies, and air fleets were bound to rasp nerves and to cause friction. In spite of everything, the two governments introduced, as General Marshall has written, "the most complete unification of military effort ever achieved by two allied nations." Not the least of the reasons for success was the close personal harmony between General Marshall and his British colleague, General Sir John Dill, chief of the Imperial General Staff, and especially between the two chiefs of state, Roosevelt and Churchill.

Two Separate Wars in Europe

The Western governments and the Soviet Union coordinated their efforts so little that two separate wars were fought in Europe, one on the Russian front, one on the western. The nature of this "strange alliance," so called by the American General John Dean, stationed in Moscow during the war, may be inferred from the reason why in 1942 Stalin concluded a twenty-year treaty of alliance with Great Britain: he wanted to be certain that Britain would not make a separate peace with Germany and turn the full Nazi force against the Communists! Stalin was unwilling to share data on production or to pool resources with his allies. He was amazed to receive Lend-Lease materials for no other reason than the pursuit of common war. As soon as he overcame his surprise, he demanded larger and speedier deliveries than before. When the Allies opened the route by way of the Persian Gulf and Iran, Soviet officials received the supplies at or near the Soviet border, to prevent British and Americans from entering the country. The personnel of the agencies which the Soviet Union established in London and Washington were never permitted to associate outside official channels with their Allied colleagues. The Soviet army avoided military cooperation even more carefully. Allied troops in the Soviet Union might learn too much or set a bad example to the Russian people; and the same fears prevented the despatch of Soviet forces abroad.

The western Allies were eager to have air bases in western Russia in 1944 which they could use for introducing a shuttlecock system of bombing Germany and her satellites. Militarily speaking, the Soviets would have benefited greatly from the plan, but they suspected Allied motives. When they consented to American use of three bases in the Ukraine, they failed to protect them against Nazi air attack and would not permit Americans to bring in necessary means for defending the fields. After the Russians allowed the Germans in one raid to destroy forty-three American bombers on the ground without bringing down a single German plane, the project became a source of friction; the bases were henceforth used by Allied planes for emergency landings and repairs. Nonetheless, the Soviet economy became crucially dependent upon that of the western Allies, and Stalin received a fair share of the common resources. Churchill and particularly Roosevelt hoped to relax the tension between the free and communist worlds and to build a foundation for postwar cooperation.

Lend-Lease

Soon after Pearl Harbor the Allies called themselves the United Nations and formally agreed to fight until the Axis powers were defeated. The Lend-Lease arrangement became the material expression of their interdependence. In a report to Congress of June, 1942, President Roosevelt formulated the ideal of Lend-Lease as follows:

> The real costs of the war cannot be measured, nor compared, nor paid for in money. They must and are being met in blood and toil. But the financial costs of the war can and should be met in a way which will serve the needs of lasting peace and mutual economic well-being.
>
> All the United Nations are seeking maximum conversion to war production, in the light of their special resources. If each country devotes roughly the same fraction of its national production to the war, then the financial burden of war is distributed equally among the United Nations in accordance with their ability to pay.

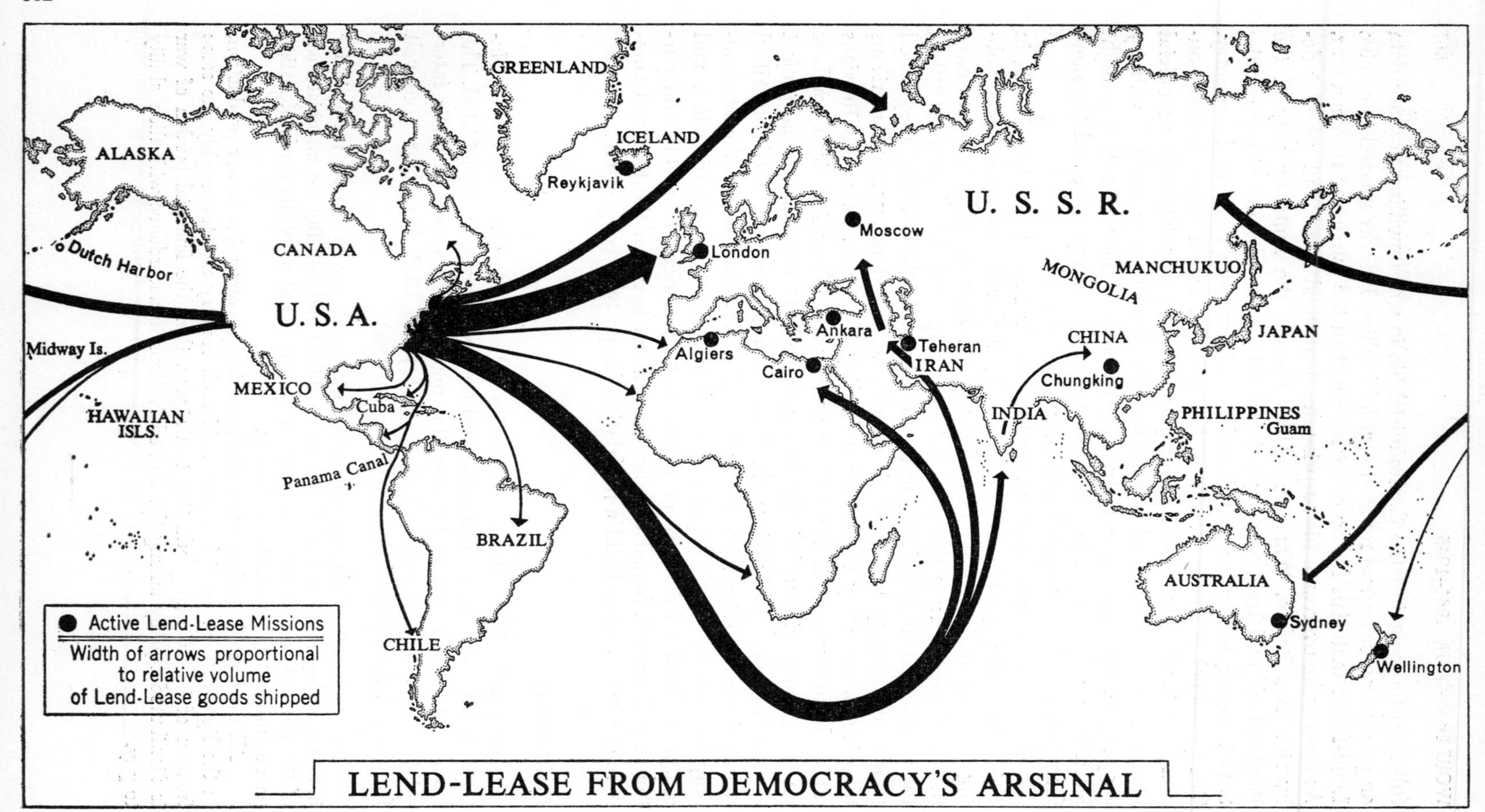

LEND-LEASE FROM DEMOCRACY'S ARSENAL

The United Nations signed agreements among themselves in 1942 calling for mutual aid to the fullest possible extent. Thus Great Britain would supply housing for American troops in that country; Canada would contribute nickel; Australia would provide food to troops stationed there; and so on. The possibilities for utilizing local services and economizing on scarce transportation were vast.

One clause of the standard Allied agreement read as follows:

> . . . as large a portion as possible of the articles and services which each Government may authorize to be provided to the other shall be in the form of reciprocal aid so that the need of each Government for the currency of the other may be reduced to a minimum.

Roosevelt and the other heads of state were seeking a means of preventing the accumulation of huge war debts which would dislocate postwar international finance. Lend-Lease in this version of mutual aid was the means chosen. The only possible exception was the Soviet Union, where devotion to a dogma ran counter to the interests of the country. Stalin had almost no goods to exchange and from mistrust of bourgeois powers refused to offer services. According to the terms of the Lend-Lease agreement of November, 1941, the Soviet Union was expected to pay for the materials which it received.

The efficiency of the administrative system was proved by the results of national production and international distribution. At the start of hostilities the United States had just completed plans for economic mobilization in war time. These were immediately executed, under an initial basic decision to expand the productive capacity for steel by 10 million tons. President Roosevelt set goals for 1942, calling for the production of 60,000 planes, 45,000 tanks, 20,000 antiaircraft guns, and 8 million tons of shipping. The objectives were not reached, except for shipping, mainly because experience revealed the need of lesser quantities of these materials and greater output of others. Nonetheless, nearly 48,000 planes were turned out, with 25,000 tanks and 14,400 antiaircraft guns, an impressive record for an unprepared nation in the first year of war.

Almost two years were required for the United Nations economies, primarily those of the United States, Great Britain, and the Soviet Union, to adjust to war needs and to learn what each should do for the others. The British produced a bare minimum of consumers' goods and concentrated on turning out munitions and, in an attempt to earn their way at least in part, exports. They expanded agricultural output in caloric value and in proteins 70 per cent beyond the prewar level and reduced food imports by half. They sacrificed much of prewar economic independence in favor of associating their economy with that of the United States and, to a lesser extent, that of the British dominions. In consequence, Great Britain transformed many of her machine and machine-tool industries into producers of munitions, and depended upon the United States for machinery with which to replace worn-out tools. By the middle of 1943 Great Britain had reached the limit of her productive capacity. One example may suffice. In 1941 only 31.7 per cent of Lend-Lease aid to Great Britain consisted of munitions, but in 1942 the figure rose to 53.6 per cent and in the next year to 70.3 per cent. The British had increasingly to rely upon the United States and the dominions.

The situation of the Soviet Union resembled in some respects that of Great Britain. Having lost productive resources in industry and agriculture to the German invaders, the Soviet Union depended upon immediate British and especially United States aid in armaments and food. Since the Soviet soldier was accustomed to the barest minimum of equipment and services and the civilian population was disciplined to a simple life, the government was able to concentrate upon the production of essential articles. By shifting several million workers out of occupied Russia and mobilizing women, Stalin during 1943 nearly supplied the army with necessary guns, tanks, artillery, and munitions, items which should be produced as near the front as possible in order to reduce the pressure on transportation. By 1945 the Soviet Union increased the output of armaments 500 to 600 per cent, averaging an annual production between 1943 and 1945 of 30,000 tanks and fighting vehicles and almost 40,000 planes and 120,000 artillery guns. In 1914–1917 Russia had turned out less than 4,000 artillery guns each year. The Soviets provided nearly 450,000 machine guns annually, compared with about 9,000 under the Romanoffs. They depended, however, upon Lend-Lease for supplies of food, trucks, and other motor vehicles and machinery. More than 400,000 American, British, and Canadian trucks gave the Red army mobility. It drew likewise upon the West for shoes and boots, much of the clothing and canned food, for 850,000 miles of field telephone wire, and 275,000 field telephones. These helped to make the economic recovery possible, but most credit for that remarkable achievement must be given the Soviet people.

HITLER FAILS TO PREPARE FOR LONG WAR

The outcome of the war proved that the Nazis had not prepared the German economy and that of the conquered areas for the long conflict. Hitler felt so confident of speedy victory that from the outbreak of war in 1939 to February, 1942, he permitted the economy to operate in a leisurely fashion, to manufacture many consumers' goods, and to use scarce materials for nonessential purposes. Whereas in 1939 Germany produced more munitions than Great Britain, in 1941 and 1942 Britain greatly excelled in output of tanks, munitions, and aircraft, and the British were working much harder than the Germans.

The Nazis had grown accustomed to graft, and party and bureaucracy contained many corrupt and inefficient loyal Nazis who could not easily be dismissed. Hitler, Göring, and other prominent figures set an example of plundering which lesser figures followed. When in April, 1942, Mussolini and Ciano conferred with Hitler in a former palace of the Bishop of Salzburg, they found it furnished for the occasion with loot from France. Such practices weakened the moral stamina needed for vigorous exploitation of the economy for war.

Since he had the resources of most of the continent at his disposal, Hitler did not believe it necessary to change fundamentals. He was fortunate in appointing in February, 1942, as minister of arms and munitions the architect Albert Speer, an honest and efficient person; but not until a year later did he give Speer power over the entire economy. In the meantime Speer increased output by mobilizing idle industrial capacity and improving the utilization of materials and man power. He secured the appointment of a tough Nazi Gauleiter, Fritz Sauckel, as plenipotentiary-general for man power to increase the labor supply. Speer could not, however, compensate for Hitler's failure during the preceding few years to expand the production capacity in iron and steel. By 1942 materials could not be spared for the construction of new plants; they had to be used to meet the increasing demand for munitions. Through conquest Germany had added nearly 50 per cent to her output of crude steel, but by 1943 her annual production of 34,644,000 tons was less than one fifth of that of her opponents.

Hitler's solution of most problems consisted of personally assuming more power. Military reverses in Russia in 1941 and the addition of the United States to the list of opponents offered the occasion for his taking over the direct operating command of all the armies. He actually destroyed the general staff by depriving it of over-all responsibility. He confined its duties to the eastern front and transferred those for the western front to another military body. He himself provided the sole unity for all the forces, and henceforth he tended to ignore expert advice in favor of his own intuition. Speer later stated:

> Hitler's decision to assume command of the Army was the most unfortunate decision of the war, because in consequence the Army was left without a Commander in Chief. A C.-in-C. is expected to defend the interests of his service and to have close contact with his troops; he must make endless specific rulings on matters of detail. Hitler had not the time for this and no expert knowledge.

In April, 1942, the Reichstag passed a law to the following effect:

> The Führer must have all the rights demanded by him to achieve victory. Therefore—without being bound by existing legal regulations— . . . the Führer must be in a position to force, with all the means at his disposal, every German, if necessary, . . . to fulfill his duties. In case of violation of these duties the Führer is entitled, regardless of rights, to mete out punishment and remove the offender from his post, rank and position without introducing prescribed procedures.

He was subject to no restraint. He continued the policy of divide and rule among his subordinates, and took the logical step of expanding the *Waffen*-SS under Himmler into a competitor to the army. The power of the forces led by regular army officers, whom he mistrusted, was checked by the new military organization devoted to him personally. Any commander of the *Waffen*-SS, just as any in Göring's air force, could appeal to his respective chief, Himmler or Göring, over the heads of the field commanders. The arrangement caused confusion at the front but gave a sense of security to Hitler and the other Nazi leaders.

Except for these innovations, Hitler did not adjust the German strategy to the exigencies of global war. He continued to concentrate on the Russian front, with some additional notice paid to the Battle of the Atlantic. After a visit to Hitler's eastern headquarters in March, 1942, Goebbels wrote: "His [Hitler's] aims are the Caucasus, Leningrad and Moscow. . . . Possibly this may mean a hundred years' war in the east, but that need not worry us." Hitler apparently was incapable of planning strategy on a global scale and of preparing the economy and the morale of the nation for the kind of war which his country faced.

COURSE OF THE WAR, 1941–1943

By the summer of 1943 the Allies had won victories over the Axis powers and had taken the initiative in all four major theaters of war, the Central and Southwest Pacific, Southern Russia, North Africa and Italy, and the Atlantic. The first theater, although lying outside Europe, deserves attention because there the defeat of Japan was prepared. Achievements in the other three regions made probable the defeat of Nazi Germany.

The Pacific

The war in the Pacific and Far East assumed a different character from that centering in Europe. Japanese attack by airplanes at Pearl Harbor crippled the United States fleet. A comparable defeat of the British fleet based on Singapore came soon after. The capture of almost all islands in the North Pacific seemed to assure Japan of the means of defending the homeland against a revived American navy. Behind the shelter the Japanese army, transported in vessels of all kinds and sizes and requiring few supplies except armaments, infiltrated country after country in Southeast Asia. It reached the border of India, took the Philippine Islands and the East Indies, and bombed points in India, Northern Australia, and the Aleutian Islands. Within six months Japan had replaced the Western powers as the ruler of the entire region and was making headway in China. India and Australia expected to be invaded at any moment, and some Indians would even have welcomed the Japanese.

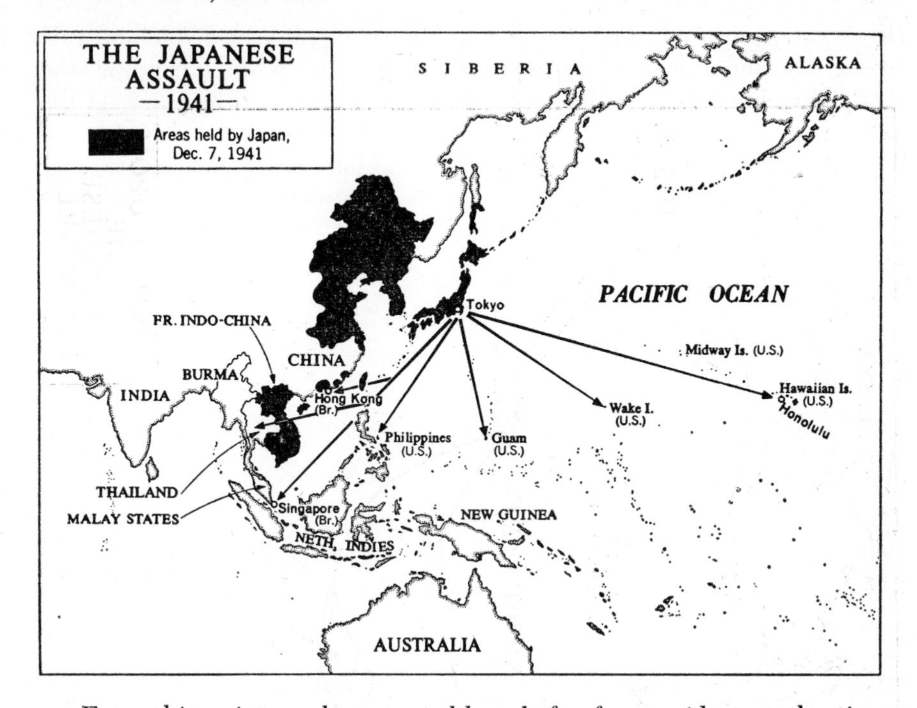

From this point on, however, although far from evident at the time, the superiority of the Allies began to tell. The United States assumed most responsibility for the war in the region, and in May and June, 1942, severely defeated the Japanese navy in the Battle of the Coral Sea and the Battle of Midway. American forces in the summer gained a foothold on Guadalcanal as the initial act in reconquering the islands in the Southwest Pacific by amphibious assault, while airplanes operating from carriers began to bomb Japan proper. The end of 1944 found the Americans dominant on islands within bombing range of Tokyo and engaged in reconquering the Philippines. American planes were operating in China against Japanese troops, Manchurian industrial and rail centers, and Japan itself; and American supplies in small quantities were reaching Chinese troops by way of India. A war in which Japan's success had at first been due to naval superiority had rapidly become one in which the American navy, with its air arm, swept the seas, while American land forces and the few Australian troops that were active in the Southwest Pacific tackled the Japanese in jungle fighting. The West seemed certain victor, but no one could predict when the surrender of Japan would come.

Russia

In Europe the fighting adhered to orthodox lines. Hitler directed the campaign for 1942 toward the Volga and Stalingrad; and when the armies advanced with greater speed than he had anticipated, he extended his objective to include the Caucasus oil fields. His existing supply of oil did not

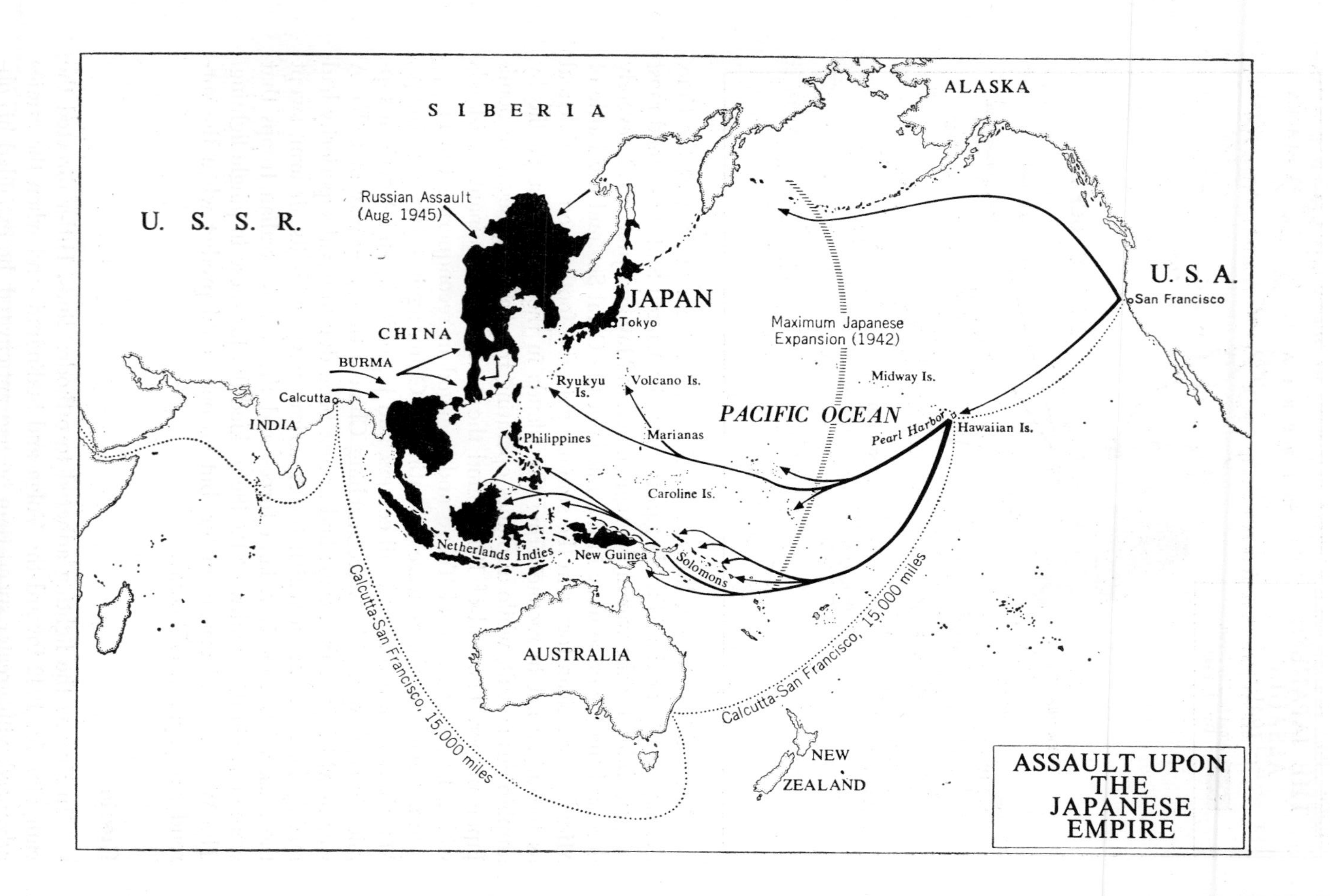
ASSAULT UPON THE JAPANESE EMPIRE
ALASKA
S I B E R I A
U. S. S. R.
Russian Assault (Aug. 1945)
U. S. A.
San Francisco
JAPAN
Tokyo
CHINA
BURMA
Calcutta
INDIA
Maximum Japanese Expansion (1942)
Midway Is.
Ryukyu Is.
Volcano Is.
PACIFIC OCEAN
Pearl Harbor
Hawaiian Is.
Philippines
Marianas
Caroline Is.
Netherlands Indies
New Guinea
Solomons
Calcutta-San Francisco, 15,000 miles
Calcutta-San Francisco, 15,000 miles
AUSTRALIA
NEW ZEALAND

suffice. The Romanian field was declining in output; in 1937 it had produced 8.7 million tons, in 1941 only 5.5 million tons, and Romania kept for her own use one half of that amount. Synthetic plants were turning out 4 million tons of oil in 1941 and increased the yield to 6 million by 1943. The demand, however, was growing. Fuel shortage severely crippled the air force in 1941, and in December Admiral Raeder reported that in view of the oil shortage the navy's requirements had been cut by 50 per cent. Romanian exports to Germany and to Italy, he said, had ceased entirely. In June, 1942, Hitler declared to the commanding officers of his Army Group South, "If I do not get the oil of Maikop and Grozny, then I must end this war."

Eager for oil and for speedy victory, Hitler repeated the mistake of the preceding year in overextending his forces. Whereas he could have captured Stalingrad easily in the summer, he chose to withdraw the Fourth Panzer Army to aid the campaign toward the Caucasus oil fields. General Franz Halder, chief of the army general staff, tried to warn him against exposing the northern flank of the army, but Hitler refused to listen.

> When a statement was read to him [Halder subsequently related] which showed that Stalin would still be able to muster another one to one and a quarter million men in the region north of Stalingrad (besides half a million more in the Caucasus), and which proved that the Russian output of first-line tanks amounted to twelve hundred a month, Hitler flew at the man who was reading with clenched fists and foam in the corners of his mouth, and forbade him to read such idiotic twaddle.

In September, 1942, Hitler dismissed Halder and appointed Kurt Zeitzler as chief of staff; but he could not change the facts. The Soviets stopped the German advance before it reached the oil fields, and in November three Russian army groups attacked the German line north and south of Stalingrad and encircled twenty-two German divisions between the Volga and the Don Rivers. Irrespective of cold, hunger, disease, and shortage of supplies, Hitler refused to permit commanding General von Paulus to retreat from Stalingrad; when on the last day of January, 1943, von Paulus was forced to surrender, the Führer demanded to know why instead of surrendering the commanding officers had not shot themselves. In that one battle Germany lost 300,000 men and an amount of armor and vehicles equal to six months' production, of artillery equal to three to four months' production, and of small arms and mortars equal to two months' production. Stalingrad marked the turning point of the war on the eastern front.

Hitler's treatment of German commanders should be contrasted with that by Stalin of Soviet generals. The Soviet dictator shared the Communist's traditional mistrust of army leaders. Shortly before the war he had purged the army of thousands of officers, and he still feared that the generals might follow the example of Napoleon and take the occasion of war to overthrow the regime. He wanted to prevent any competition from arising in the shape of a popular general, and he sought to maintain a strict curb upon military action. During the first year of the war he divided the forces into relatively small armies and directed the action of each from Moscow. When he perceived the resulting confusion, toward the end of 1942 he changed methods and permitted the creation of large army fronts under unified command. He was able then to keep in daily contact with fewer generals; he heeded their expert advice and arbitrated their differences. He identified himself with the officers and in March, 1943, assumed the title of Marshal of the Soviet Union. Thus at the time that the Nazi dictator's relations with his commanders were becoming embittered, the Communist dictator was improving the position of his generals.

North Africa and Italy

The campaign in North Africa and Italy was inspired by Churchill and undertaken only when President Roosevelt supported it. The American generals in Washington advocated the direct invasion of France and disagreed with Churchill's claim that the Allies were as yet unprepared for it. The American naval commanders and General MacArthur insisted on priority for the war against Japan. Churchill argued as follows:

> The paramount task before us is, first, to conquer the African shores of the Mediterranean and set up there the naval and air installations which are necessary to open an effective passage through it for military traffic; and, secondly, using the bases on the African shore, to strike at the underbelly of the Axis in effective strength and in the shortest time.

Only then, he said, after German forces were scattered, should the Allies cross the Channel into France for the final phase of the war.

Once the plan for invading North Africa was accepted, Roosevelt personally had to order Admiral King to divert enough ships from operations elsewhere in order to make the invasion possible. The attack agreed to in July, 1942, did not begin until November; the American opponents fought a delaying action against it, and the task of preparation proved to be greater than anticipated. In the end the campaign inflicted upon the Axis a defeat second in severity only to that of Stalingrad and proved to be valuable as training for the subsequent invasion of the Normandy coast. In it the commander in chief, General Dwight Eisenhower, received his first experience in the conduct of troops in the field and in the fine art of molding troops and officers of several nations into a unified army.

Fighting in North Africa between Axis troops and British forces had been under way since the outbreak of war. In May and June, 1942, General Rommel advanced rapidly to the Egyptian frontier, capturing Tobruk with 33,000 men, and seemingly headed for the easy conquest of Egypt, the Suez Canal, and beyond. Fortunately for the Allies, Hitler did not support Rommel with men and materials, and the Axis advance was stopped at El

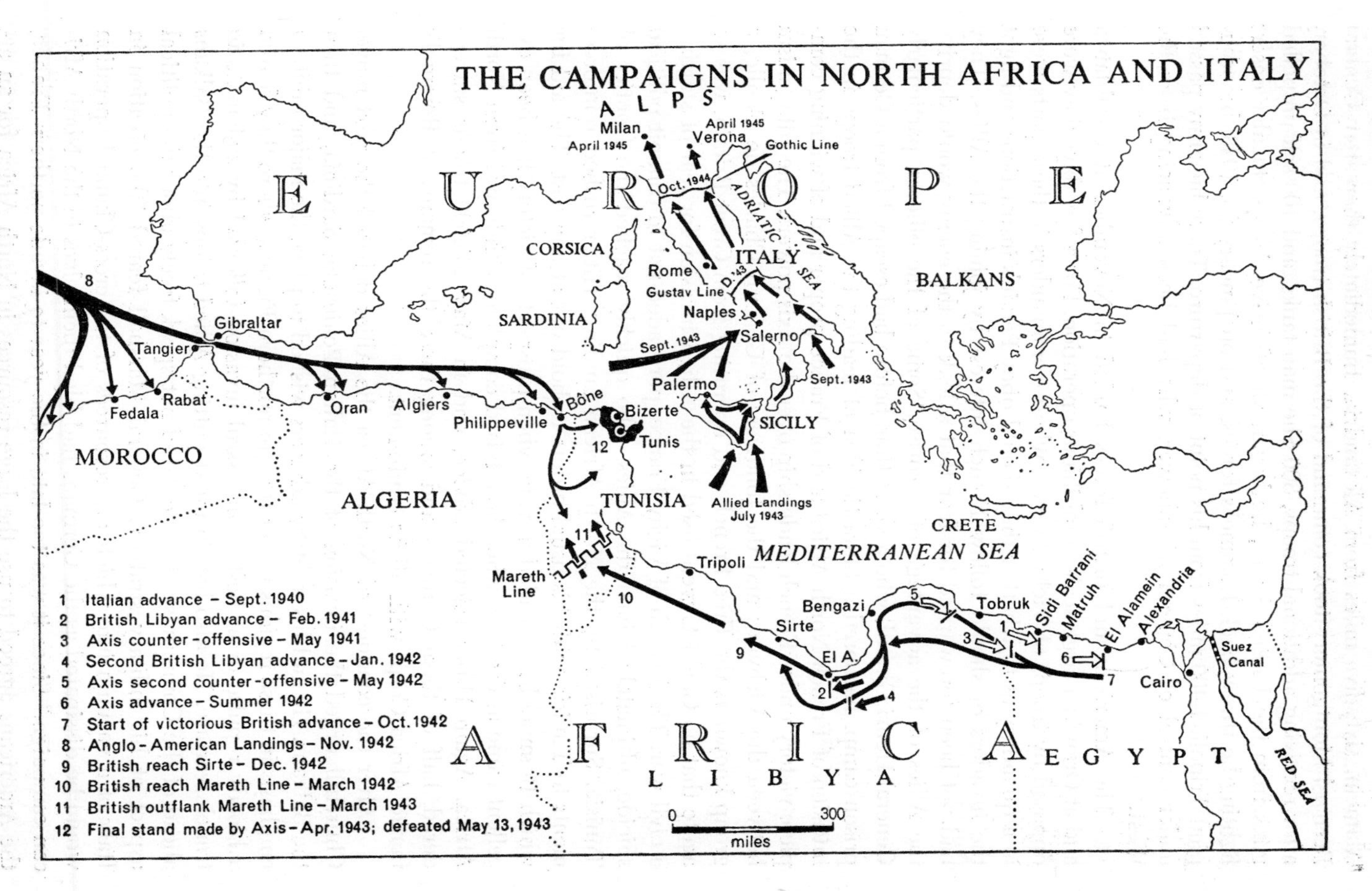

THE CAMPAIGNS IN NORTH AFRICA AND ITALY

Alamein, sixty-five miles from Alexandria. Immediately thereafter General Bernard Montgomery took command of the British troops, and in October, after receiving additional troops, 300 Sherman tanks, and 100 self-propelled guns from the United States, he began an offensive. In spectacular desert fighting he threw back Rommel's forces, and on January 23, 1943, he occupied Tripoli, 1,400 miles from his point of departure. There his army passed under control of General Eisenhower, who had been advancing from the West.

The American and British forces landed in November at Casablanca and at Oran in a large-scale amphibious operation. For a few days they were opposed by troops of Vichy France, whose commanders in these ports were in a quandary as to whether they should obey Pétain's instructions and fight the invaders or should follow French interest by joining the Allies. They had not been forewarned for fear that a leak to the enemy would deprive the Allies of the advantage of surprise. Some of the officers, particularly General Henri Giraud, who a short time before had escaped from a German prison camp, harbored a fantastic idea of leading the Allied troops in the invasion of French North Africa and of France proper and of winning complete victory under French leadership over the Axis powers. The antagonism between the Vichyites and the followers of General Charles de Gaulle, a group known as the Free French and operating from Great Britain, was so acute that no Gaullists were used in the Allied invasion for fear of starting a civil war. The French of Vichy France, persuaded not to commit political suicide, ultimately joined the Allies, who quickly reached the frontier of Tunisia. Surprised by the North African landing, Hitler rushed reinforcements to Tunisia with his usual orders to hold out at any cost. The aid for which Rommel had pleaded in vain when prospects of victory had been excellent came at the time when he advised complete withdrawal from North Africa. Again Hitler rejected advice, and in May 250,000 troops surrendered, half of them Germans and among these the remains of Rommel's famed Africa Corps with all its equipment.

After the conquest of North Africa the Allies debated the next move. Churchill urged the invasion of the Italian Peninsula, Sardinia, and then the Balkans. He and his military advisers wished to place the major military emphasis in these regions rather than in northern France, where they feared a bloody repulse or at best a successful invasion followed by stalemate in trench warfare. He also had in mind putting Allied troops into the Balkans ahead of the Communists, but he dared not speak freely about the political aspect of his military strategy. General Marshall feared "the creation in Italy of a vacuum into which the resources of the cross-Channel operation would be dissipated as the Germans had bled themselves in the North African campaign." Since it was too late in the year to invade northern France, the Americans agreed to use the large resources in North Africa for an attack on Sicily. This conquest, begun in July, was quickly concluded, and the

Americans grudgingly agreed to use the assembled troops during the subsequent months for an attack on the Italian mainland.

Collapse of Italy

Hitler tried to arouse Mussolini to action, but he found him a sick old man, silent, and longing for repose. The Italian nation had equally tired of the war and was eager to be released from German dictation. Italy had neither the material resources nor the will to fight farther, and Germany had not been able to provide the supplies she had promised. The Axis powers had not conquered Malta, whose strategic significance for driving Britain from the Mediterranean Hitler had not grasped. Now that North Africa and Sicily were lost and the Italians foresaw that their peninsula would become a battleground, their anger turned against the Duce and his German master. Late in July, during the Allied attack on Sicily, the Fascist Grand Council repudiated the Duce, the king placing Marshal Badoglio in charge of a non-Fascist government.

Hitler knew that this government, while feigning loyalty to the Axis, was secretly negotiating with the Allies for surrender. He augmented the forces in Italy, and when the Allied-Italian armistice became public on September 8, he struck. He rescued Mussolini from prison and set up a Fascist republican government as a façade for German domination. When in September the Allies landed troops at Salerno, much farther south than Churchill had wished, Hitler moved the front line of defense from north of Rome down to meet them and compelled the Allies to fight for every foot of the area. Italy was officially out of the war, the king and the Badoglio cabinet had escaped to the Allies, and the Italian people repudiated their German masters.

Hitler maintained his front line south of Rome until June, 1944; he replaced the Italian troops in the Balkans with his own forces; and he showed his other satellites that they could not escape from his grasp by surrendering to the Allies. More than counterbalancing these defensive achievements were the facts that from south Italian bases Allied planes could bomb the oil fields of Romania and the aircraft factories of south Germany and Austria and that Eisenhower's eleven divisions forced Hitler to retain twice that many divisions in Italy, when, as General Jodl said, "the Eastern Front . . . was begging for reserves more urgently than ever."

War on the Seas

The entry of the United States into the war opened the western waters of the Atlantic to U-boats, and the Germans found easy targets. American coastal shipping and that in the Gulf of Mexico became objects of devastating raids. In May, 1942, 95 per cent of all the losses occurred in waters supposed to be guarded by the United States Navy. In June, 1942, General

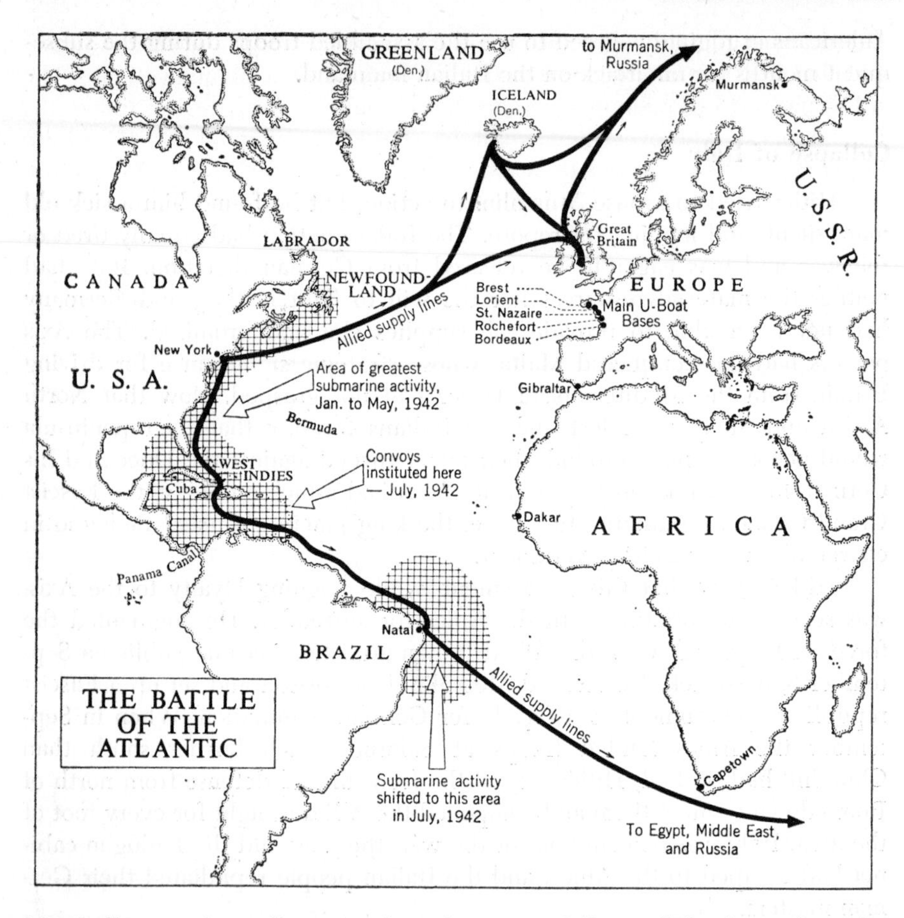

Marshall wrote his colleague Admiral King as follows: "The losses by submarines off our Atlantic seaboard and in the Caribbean now threaten our entire war effort." In that month the Nazis sank ships at the rate of one every four hours, for a total of 825,310 tons, the highest figure reached, and no relief was in sight. They accomplished feats like these in the first six months of 1942 at a loss of only 21 submarines. During that year they sank more than 6 million tons of shipping, and not until autumn did the rate of new construction by the British and Americans begin to exceed the rate of sinking. The submarines attacked suddenly in packs, often for several successive days, and struck vessels in convoy as well as those traveling alone. They were so effective along the route to Murmansk that for months they stopped all traffic. Hitler was at last aroused to the value of the submarine and in February, 1943, he replaced Admiral Raeder by Admiral Karl Doenitz, a submarine expert, and accelerated the construction of underwater vessels.

Not until the British-American conference at Casablanca in January, 1943, did the Combined Chiefs of Staff recommend that "the defeat of the

U-boat must remain a first charge on the resources of the United Nations" and that first priority be given to the "security of sea communications." The Allies began to provide more escort carriers and more patrols to follow the U-boat packs wherever they might be. Most important of all, they built long-range aircraft, based them on Newfoundland, Iceland, and Northern Ireland, as well as on Great Britain and the American continent, and equipped them with new radar apparatus for detecting the presence of submarines.

The Germans lacked this radar equipment and were alarmed when in April the rate of sinkings of Allied ships began to decline. During the last part of May, in an attack against a trans-Atlantic convoy, the Germans lost four submarines and did not sink a single ship. Doenitz reported to Hitler that he urgently needed "an efficient radar interception set . . . which will show the frequency used by the radar-equipped planes and will warn the U-boats of impending attack." He was forced for a time to withdraw the U-boats from the North Atlantic. When in September the Nazis reappeared in that area with improved submarines equipped with a new acoustically-guided torpedo, the Allies were prepared. The new German radar was no more effective in detecting the approach of an airplane than the old, and the new torpedo was soon countered. In November, 1943, Doenitz wrote in his diary, "The enemy knows all our secrets and we know none of his."

NAZI MISTAKES

At the end of the war General Halder, whom Hitler deposed in 1942 as chief of staff of the German army, wrote as follows:

> Towards the end of 1943 at the latest it had become unmistakably clear that the war had been lost. . . . Would it not have been possible even so to beat off the invasion and thus provide the basis for a tolerable peace? Had the "Fortress Germany" no hope of consuming the enemy's strength on its walls? No. Let us once and for all have done with these fairy tales. Against a landing fleet such as the enemy could muster, under cover of a complete and undisputed air superiority, Germany had no means of defence. . . .
>
> By the sacrifice of German blood and at the cost of exposing the homeland to the enemy Air Forces, the war could still be kept going for a little longer. But were the results to be gained by such a course worth the sacrifice?

Nothwithstanding the reverses of the preceding year and a half Hitler felt confident about his ultimate victory. Early in 1943 he gave Speer complete authority over production for both military and civilian use, except in the one field of Göring's special interest, that of aircraft. By reorganizing inefficient plants, reducing civilian production, introducing methods of mass production with the use of the assembly line and other modern techniques, and placing experts in industrial management in charge, Speer saved time, labor, and materials. As the year 1943 closed, he had increased the rate of output of armaments by 150 per cent over that of February, 1942. "In general," the United States Strategic Bombing Survey concluded after its postwar investigation, "despite the retreats and consequent losses in the latter part of 1943, the German army was better equipped with weapons at the beginning of 1944 than at the start of the Russian War." The severest shortage was in steel; as the war spread to the Mediterranean and then to the Western front and as the Soviet economy recovered, Hitler was to learn that his resources did not satisfy the constantly growing demand. Industrial weakness ultimately proved to be a major cause for Germany's defeat.

Nazi Deficiencies in Science and Technology

Hitler's expectation of a short war and his relative indifference to science led to fatal delay in preparing for the kind of conflict actually fought. To the evidence provided by the construction of submarines should be added that of the development of rockets and of airplanes. As early as 1939 General von Brauchitsch submitted plans for long-range rockets, but the Führer did not become interested until the end of 1942. At that time the experts successfully launched a rocket at the experimental ground near the Baltic, and Hitler recognized the possibility of using rockets to destroy Great Britain. The British secret service, aided by the Polish underground, learned about the work, and in August, 1943, the Royal Air Force bombed the experiment station at Peenemünde out of operation for some time. When the Germans built launching platforms along the Channel coast, the British airforce struck most of them before they were used; and mistakes in construction of the rockets further delayed the Nazi program. Conflicts over control of the work among Nazi chieftains accentuated the troubles, and by March, 1944, the Germans were producing only 2,000 rockets a month.

Use against England was further delayed for several months in the expectation of employing the rockets to counter the Allied invasion across the Channel. By that time the Germans had developed the more efficient silent rocket, the V–2. A pilotless plane like the V–1, it had 1,000 kilograms of explosives in its warhead and was capable of covering 200 miles at a much greater velocity than the V–1. Neither rocket could be accurately guided; both were used for indiscriminate bombing of towns and cities. Neither was sufficiently perfected to influence the course of the war. The V–2, for example, caused less than 3,000 casualties in England and injured only 6,500. The rockets were mainly significant for the future.

Failure of German Air Force

The German air force similarly failed. Göring kept production and use of planes exclusively under his control. Becoming lazy and boastful, he did not maintain the quality or the quantity of planes necessary to counter Allied attacks. The British and the Americans, who had developed bigger and faster planes with superior radar equipment and bombing sights, bombed German transportation centers, industries—especially for the production of ball bearings, airplanes, and synthetic oil—and began the mass destruction of key cities.

The Allied bombing of Hamburg in the last week of July, 1943, may be described as an example. That city was raided eight times, and a total of 7,500 tons of bombs was dropped. According to the report of the United States Bombing Survey made after the war, 55 to 60 per cent of the city was destroyed, three fourths of the devastation being caused by fire. From 60,000 to 100,000 persons were killed, 300,000 dwellings destroyed, and 750,000 people left homeless. People were roasted or they drowned when seeking escape in the canals.

> As the many fires broke through the roofs of buildings [the Bombing Survey stated] there rose a column of heated air more than two and a half miles high and one and a half miles in diameter, as measured by aircraft flying over Hamburg. This column was turbulent and was fed at its base by inrushing cooler ground-surface air. One and one and a half miles from the fire this draft increased the wind velocity from eleven to thirty-three miles per hour. At the edge of the area the velocities must have been appreciably greater, as trees three feet in diameter were uprooted. In a short time the temperature reached the ignition point for all combustibles and the entire area was ablaze. In such fires complete burn-out occurred; that is, no trace of combustible material remained and only after two days were the areas cool enough to approach.

The Allies justified the mass bombing of cities on the grounds that, as the Archbishop of York said, it would "shorten the war and may save thousands of lives." The Nazis had gloried in their indiscriminate bombing of civilians in England and elsewhere; now they received a dose of their own medicine. The Allies expected that area bombing would destroy German civilian morale; but the Nazis' belief that it would not succeed in doing so proved to be correct. As the United States Bombing Survey concluded:

> Under ruthless Nazi control they [the German people] showed surprising resistance to the terror and hardships of repeated air attack, to the destruction of their homes and belongings, and to the conditions under which they were reduced to live. Their morale, their belief in ultimate victory or satisfactory compromise, and their confidence in their leaders declined, but they continued to work efficiently as long as the physical means of production remained. The power of a police state over its people cannot be under-estimated.

The Nazis were confident of preventing the raids from crippling the war effort; not until the spring of 1943 did Hitler agree to shift emphasis from the production of offensive bombing planes to that of defensive fighters. In addition, he ignored the urgent advice of the air force general staff from 1940 on, to develop jet planes. When late in 1942 he became interested in jets he succumbed to the personal influence of Willi Messerschmitt and gave priority to a jet fighter that proved a failure.

By the end of 1943 Germany produced only one fifth as many planes as Great Britain and the United States. When early in 1944 the latter had ready long-range bombers, well protected by long-range fighter planes and their own armor, and sent them over Germany by day or by night, the Nazi air force could not compete. In March, 1944, Speer was made responsible for the production of aircraft, and he increased output. He lacked time and materials, however, to produce new models equal to those of the Allies. The Führer cursed Göring and the air force, but he took to his air raid shelter and never voluntarily visited a single bombed city to show his sympathy for the suffering of the German people.

Nazi Mistreatment of Subject Peoples

At the peak of their conquests the Nazis dominated 270 million people and economically could have been self-sufficient. They might have exploited the hostility of the Poles and of a large minority of the Ukrainians and other Soviet citizens against the Communists. They might have won support among the Vichy French against the British. Instead of doing so, they aroused such hatred among the subject peoples that they had to employ 2 million troops, direly needed elsewhere for fighting, merely to hold the population under control.

The degree of maltreatment differed from country to country. The Scandinavians and the Dutch, members of the "Nordic" race, fared best; the French and the Belgians were less well treated as being of inferior blood. All of these were looted systematically by government officials and businessmen, who followed the armies and seized stocks, bonds, raw materials, machines, transport equipment, historic archives, libraries, works of art—indeed, anything to which anyone took a fancy. They sometimes paid for the loot with national currency demanded from the local government; they sometimes claimed it as property of Jews or of traitors or of opponents to Germany. "It used to be called plundering," Göring said in August, 1942, to the commissioners of the occupied areas. "But today things have become more genteel. In spite of that, I intend to plunder and to do it thoroughly." Hitler had still more inclusive plans for these and other countries. "All the rubbish of small States still existing in Europe," he declared, "must be liquidated as fast as possible. The aim of our struggle must be to create a unified Europe: the Germans alone can really organize Europe."

The Nazis revealed the nature of their rule most clearly in Eastern Europe among the Slavic peoples. Himmler and Göring were made responsible for administration, with *Reich* Minister of Justice Thierack occasionally participating. Hitler usually excluded the regular army from this work and depended upon the S.S. The words of the Nazi leaders themselves convey the nature of the objectives. After a dinner at the *Reich* Chancellery on October 2, 1940, Hitler spoke as follows:

> The Poles in direct contrast to our German workmen, are especially born for hard labour. . . . The Government-General [Poland] should be used by us merely as a source of unskilled labour . . . the Polish landlords must . . . be exterminated. . . . There should be one master only for the Poles—the Germans. . . . Therefore all representatives of the Polish intelligentsia are to be exterminated. . . . The Poles will also benefit from this, as we look after their health and see to it that they do not starve, but they must never be raised to a higher level, for then they will become anarchists and communists. It will therefore be proper for the Poles to remain Roman Catholics: Polish priests will receive food from us and will, for that very reason, direct their little sheep along the path we favour. . . . If any priest acts differently, we shall make short work of him. The task of the priest is to keep the Poles quiet, stupid and dull-witted.

As for the Czechs, Hitler planned to absorb one half of them into the German race. "The other half of the Czechs," he said, "must be deprived of their power, eliminated and shipped out of the country by all sorts of methods." He ordered the intellectuals to be handled with particular ruthlessness. Germany should extend her control to the Urals. "*We must never permit anybody but the Germans*," he declared, "*to carry arms*."

Himmler executed the Führer's order by instructing (October 4, 1943) his S.S. men in the following way:

> One basic principle must be the absolute rule for the S.S. men: we must be honest, decent, loyal and comradely to members of our own blood and nobody else. What happens to a Russian and a Czech does not interest me in the slightest. What the nations can offer in the way of good blood of our type we will take, if necessary, by kidnapping their children and raising them here with us. Whether nations live in prosperity or starve to death interests me only in so far as we need them as slaves for our *Kultur:* otherwise it is of no interest to me. Whether ten thousand Russian females fall down from exhaustion while digging an anti-tank ditch interests me only in so far as the anti-tank ditch for Germany is finished. We shall never be rough and heartless when it is not necessary, that is clear. We Germans, who are the only people in the world who have a decent attitude toward animals, will also assume a decent attitude toward these human animals. But it is a crime against our own blood to worry about them and give them ideals, thus causing our sons and grandsons to have a more difficult time with them. . . . Most of *you* know what it means when a hundred corpses are lying side by side, or five hundred or one thousand. To have stuck it out, and at the same time—apart from exceptions caused by human weakness—to have remained decent fellows, that is what has made us hard. . . .
>
> If the peace is a final one, we shall be able to tackle our great work of the future. We shall colonize. We shall indoctrinate our boys with the laws of the S.S. . . . It must be a matter of course that the most copious breeding should be from this racial *elite* of the Germanic people. In twenty to thirty years we must really be able to present the whole of Europe with its leading class. . . .

The Nazi government inaugurated a program of exploitation of foreign workers, experimentation on prisoners and extermination of Jews and of others whom it regarded as undesirable. The number of slave laborers increased by the end of 1944 to about 5 million, of whom Fritz Sauckel said, "Not even two hundred thousand came voluntarily." Men, women and children were included. The treatment which they received differed according to circumstances. Those used on farms suffered less than those in industrial areas, who often met the fate of epidemics, hunger, wretched housing, and brutal treatment. Göring's Economic Staff East in May, 1941, planned the starvation or the flight to Siberia of "tens of millions" of Russians in the industrial areas, for the agricultural products were to be used by the invaders on the spot or shipped west.

The Jews wherever caught were usually put to death. Additional concentration camps and extermination facilities were built for this purpose. Medical and other scientific experiments were conducted upon them before final destruction. "This will not be a boring guard duty," Himmler said in April, 1941, to his S.S. men. In August, 1944, one of his assistants reported that about four million Jews had been exterminated. Himmler was dissatisfied with the figure; he thought it was above six million. Rudolf Hoess, commandant of the Auschwitz Camp in Poland, made the following affidavit after the war at the Nürnberg trials: "I estimate that at least two and a half million victims were executed and exterminated at Auschwitz by gassing and burning and that at least another half million succumbed to starvation and disease. . . ." In Russia Commandant Hoess's colleagues introduced mobile gas vans. These methods, Himmler stated, "will be the best indoctrination on inferior beings and the subhuman race." When the Soviets and the Western powers finally conquered Germany, they found the dozens of concentration camps full of human skeletons. "The Germans alone," the Führer had said, "can really organize Europe."

Resistance Movements against the Germans

Acts ranging from economic exploitation to brutality aroused spontaneous opposition to the Germans among all conquered peoples. In non-Communist countries hatred of the oppressor obliterated class and occupational lines, age distinctions, and party differences. In the Ukraine, where many peasants and townsmen had at first welcomed the Germans as liberators from communism, sabotage against the Germans was the order of the day. In countries accustomed to freedom, Communists, already trained in underground activity, for the time being played a major role in support of national resistance.

French resistance centered around the Maquis, clandestine groups spontaneously organized. A biology professor led one such group, for instance, in Haute-Savoie in eastern France. He maintained headquarters in a town under the nose of the Germans or their Vichy allies in order to communicate with other parts of the country. His troops in the mountains, many barefoot in the snow, asked for guns rather than shoes. Peasants hung meat in open barns and automobile owners left keys in their cars to provide for the Maquis. Parish priests made excellent messengers; factory owners and workmen, forced to produce for the victors, replied with sabotage; women and children refused to speak to German occupation forces and helped with supplies for the guerrillas. From Great Britain or other Allied bases airplanes by night dropped arms and equipment at appointed spots in France. The few collaborators with the Germans were marked for punishment. The thousands who resisted actively were, however, outnumbered by millions who as opportunists helped the Germans when they had to, aided the resistance movement when they dared. The activists everywhere cherished the ideal of a renewed national life once the war was over.

How much the resistance movement contributed to liberation in each country is difficult to estimate. Much depended upon the character of the people, the tightness of the German grip, the possibilities offered by the terrain—compare the flats of little Denmark with the mountains of Greece or France or the wide spaces of Poland or the Soviet Union—and the amount of Allied military aid. The Maquis of eastern France, for example, recovered this area from the Germans in anticipation of the arrival of Allied armies. In Yugoslavia, a country of stout-hearted resistance, the victories of the Soviet army reinforced the achievements of a successful national uprising against German occupation. Every country, including Germany and Italy, had some share in the popular resistance to Nazi control of Europe.

ALLIED MILITARY SUCCESS, 1943–1945

In Russia

By 1943 military events in the two European areas of conflict began directly to affect each other. Strategic planning remained separate, for the Communists still refused to share; but the fact that the forces on east and west engaged a common enemy made possible some coordination of blows. The Soviet armies, victorious at Stalingrad, recaptured Rostov and then Kharkov in February; but when they lost the latter city to the Nazis in the next month, Stalin blamed the defeat on the failure of the Allies to pin down German troops by a vigorous campaign in the west. In mid-July, 1943, the Nazis attacked Kursk with half of their entire armored force, only to be severely defeated. When Mussolini was overthrown on July 25, Hitler for lack of mobile reserves had to transfer a half dozen of his ablest divisions from Russia to bolster the Italian front. On August 3 the Soviets began an offensive lasting until the thaw in the following April bogged the forces in mud. During that time the Soviets pressed the attack so closely that the Nazis could not prepare a defensive position.

Hitler disapproved such a position anyway; once the generals knew one existed, he said, they would immediately wish to retreat to it. He insisted upon holding the Crimea in order to prevent Turkey from joining his opponents and to keep sufficient space between the Red air force and the Romanian oil fields. He refused to evacuate the Baltic states for fear that Soviet naval strength in the Baltic might stop the transport of the indispensable Swedish iron ore to Germany and might stop use of that inland sea for submarine training.

During 1943 the Soviets kept the initiative but had to recoup their losses by resting between offensives. By the beginning of 1944 they possessed sufficient supplies and man power for a continuous series of attacks. In January, 1944, they reached the Pripet Marshes; in February, 1944, they drove the Nazis back from Leningrad. In March they began a large-scale offensive in the south, reached the Prut River and in places crossed the 1940 Romanian boundary. In April and May they regained the Crimea and reconquered almost all prewar territory of the Soviet Union. By March, 1944, Hitler was forced to defend a longer front than that from Leningrad to Rostov, which eight months earlier he had failed to maintain, and he had no reserves.

In January, 1944, the British and Americans landed two divisions on the beachhead at Anzio just south of Rome, forcing Hitler to use all the reserves he had in Italy. In the last days of that month he transferred four of the best divisions from the western to the eastern front.

> The Allies [wrote Brigadier Williams, chief intelligence officer to General Montgomery at the time] benefit by the interdependence of their assaults. A break-through towards Lwow affects a division at Lisieux (10th S.S.); the supply line of the divisions moving back into the Galatz Gap is bombed from Foggia. The Russian advances were made possible by the Allied bombing of Germany, by Lend-Lease, by the containing actions in the Mediterranean and by the imminence of invasion in the West. Two-thirds of the German Air Force and 100 German divisions were kept preoccupied. Thus was the Red Army given opportunity. They grasped it with both hands. . . . So, in their doughty turn, the Russians make OVERLORD more possible.

Allied Invasion of Normandy

On June 6, 1944, the Allies began the invasion of Normandy, an operation known as Overlord. This invasion marked the culmination of strategic plans initiated soon after the outbreak of the war.

Since Overlord was prepared in southern England, the choice of the area for invasion was limited to the 300-mile coastline from Flushing to Cherbourg which could be covered by fighter planes based on England. The entire coast contained good landing beaches and harbors; but the eastern part, the Pas de Calais from Dunkirk to the mouth of the Somme, was eliminated as too well covered by German air power. The planners argued in favor of the stretch between Caen and the Cotentin Peninsula as follows:

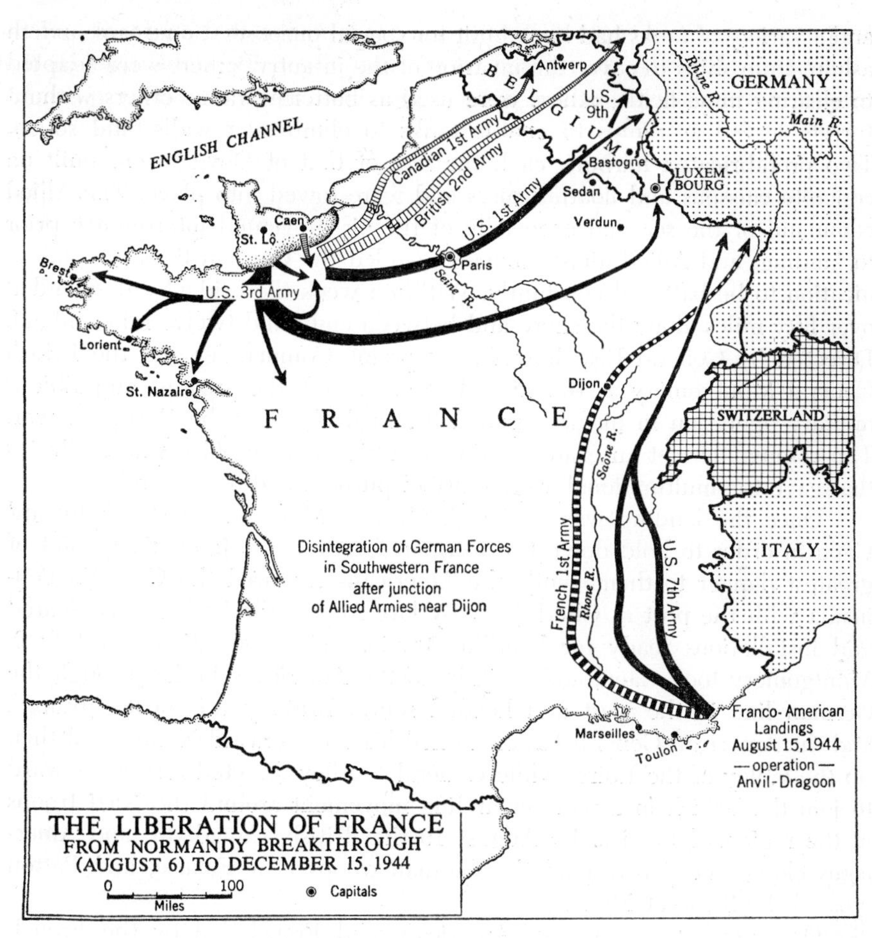

From *Crusade in Europe* by Dwight D. Eisenhower; adapted from maps originally drawn by Rafael Palacios. Copyright 1948 by Doubleday & Company, Inc.

The Caen sector is weakly held; the defences are relatively light and the beaches are of high capacity and sheltered from the prevailing winds. Inland the terrain is suitable for airfield development and for the consolidation of the initial bridgehead; and much of it is unfavourable for counter-attacks by panzer divisions. Maximum enemy air opposition can only be brought to bear at the expense of the air defence screen covering the approaches to Germany; and the limited number of enemy airfields within range of the Caen area facilitates the local neutralization of the German fighter force. The sector suffers from the disadvantage that considerable efforts will be required to provide adequate air support for our assault forces and some time must elapse before the capture of a major port.

Five British, Canadian, and American divisions were landed from the sea and three others were dropped from the air. Landing craft which had been developed for operations in the Southwest Pacific were employed, and a variety of tanks had been built for special purposes. Some tanks swam ashore from ships to cover the invasion of the infantry; others were adapted to clearing mine fields; others were used as battering rams; others without turrets served as ramps to enable tanks to climb over walls, and so on. Two prefabricated harbors, each the size of that of Dover, were built on concrete caissons and floating piers and were towed into place. The Allied command of the sea and especially of the air prevented interference prior to landing, and Allied air supremacy enabled the German lines of communication to be battered constantly. Within a week the bridgehead extended over fifty miles along the shore and between eight and twelve miles inland. Directed by General Eisenhower as Supreme Commander and the British General Montgomery as the second in command, the greatest amphibious military operation in history opened the final phase of the European war. The commander set an example of cooperation among officers and privates that gave the multinational army unity of purpose and high morale.

Once the landing was achieved, General Montgomery struck toward Caen in order to hold down the German forces at the immediate point of greatest danger to them, while the Americans captured the Cotentin Peninsula with the port at Cherbourg. By late August the harbor was cleared and installations ready for handling traffic. In the meantime, on July 9, Montgomery took Caen, and on July 25 the Americans broke through the German line in the west and headed south. Brittany was next captured, and the American General Patton turned his army toward Nantes and then up the valley of the Loire, while General Bradley directed forces eastward to join the British in a wide encircling movement around the Nazi troops in the region of Falaise. By August 19 the British, Canadians, and Americans closed the gap around the German troops near Falaise, and Patton crossed the Seine at Mantes.

On August 25 a force of Americans and French led by the French General Jean Leclerc entered Paris, where the French Resistance movement had already revolted. Contrary to Hitler's orders to destroy the city, the Nazi troops in Paris surrendered. In the south, American and Free French forces from Italy landed between Cannes and Toulon on August 15, without difficulty, captured Toulon and Marseilles, from which the Germans had withdrawn, opened these ports to Allied supplies, and headed north to join Patton's troops on September 11 northwest of Dijon. By September the battle of Normandy was over; the enemy had lost half a million men (210,000 as prisoners), and a vast amount of supplies. Of 2,300 tanks and assault guns used in Normandy the Germans brought back across the Seine about a hundred. The Allies were rapidly approaching the German frontier and the Siegfried defenses; they captured Antwerp in September and by the end of November had that port in working order for bringing in supplies. Spread from the Channel to the frontier of Switzerland, the Allied forces were poised for the final attack on Germany.

Hitler and his generals had expected the Allies to invade the continent, and Karl von Rundstedt, one of the ablest of the generals, had been placed in command of the defenses. Old and tired, he had intended to withstand the assault in a way in keeping with German military tradition, to fortify the main ports and to build up a large mobile reserve for containing the invasion after it had been made. When Hitler sent General Rommel to inspect the defenses, the latter advocated an entirely different plan. The invading forces, he declared, must be destroyed on the water or on the beaches. If they were allowed to establish a beachhead, he argued, their superiority in supplies and especially in air power would enable them to expand their forces and be victorious. Hitler approved Rommel's proposal, and in the first months of 1944 the Germans dispatched troops and civilian labor to build defenses along the south coast of the Channel—concrete shelters, mine fields, underwater obstacles, gun emplacements—all the means that Rommel's imaginative mind could devise. Happily for the Allies, the time was too short for the western part to be as heavily fortified as the eastern.

The Germans were surprised at the actual time and place of the invasion. Himmler's victory over Admiral Canaris crippled the entire intelligence system in the months prior to the attack. His personnel, new to the work, were unable to winnow the truth about the invasion from the falsehoods which the British spread abroad.

Allied Air Supremacy

The prediction made by General Rommel in regard to the value of air power proved accurate. On June 1, 1944, the Allies had more than 5,000 planes flying from Great Britain, whereas the Germans were able to muster 1,789 machines for day fighting, and only 119 on the Channel front. On June 12 Rommel reported the results to Hitler's headquarters as follows:

> The enemy has complete command of the air over the battle zone and up to about 100 kilometres behind the front and cuts off by day almost all traffic on roads or by-ways or in open country. Manoeuvre by our troops on the field of battle in daylight is thus almost entirely prevented, while the enemy can operate freely. . . . Neither our flak nor the Luftwaffe seem capable of putting a stop to this crippling and destructive operation of the enemy's aircraft. The troops protect themselves as well as they can with the means available, but ammunition is scarce and can be supplied only under the most difficult conditions.

When on July 1, von Rundstedt told General von Keitel to "make peace, you fools," he was replaced by General Günther von Kluge. On July 22, the latter advised Hitler to the same effect.

> My discussion yesterday with the commanders in the Caen sector has afforded regrettable evidence that, in face of the enemy's complete command of the air, there is no possibility of our finding a strategy which will counter-balance its truly annihilating effect, unless we give up the field of battle.

Whole armoured formations, allotted to the counter-attack, were caught in bomb-carpets of the greatest intensity, so that they could be extricated from the torn-up ground only by prolonged effort and in some cases only by dragging them out. The result was that they arrived too late. The psychological effect of such a mass of bombs coming down with all the power of elemental nature upon the fighting troops, especially the infantry, is a factor which has to be given particularly serious consideration. It is immaterial whether such a bomb-carpet catches good troops or bad, they are more or less annihilated. If this occurs frequently, then the power of endurance of the forces is put to the highest test; indeed it becomes dormant and dies.

German Plots against Hitler

The prospect of early defeat aroused the many Germans who recognized that Hitler and the Nazis would destroy the country. These dissident elements included representatives of the bureaucracy, the army, the Catholic and Protestant churches, the business world, and labor. They ranged in political affiliation from monarchists and reactionaries to conservatives, liberals, democrats, socialists, and Communists. General Beck, the former chief of staff, acted as one important leader, with Karl Goerdeler, former mayor of Leipzig and prominent official under the Weimar Republic and the Nazi government, Ambassador Ulrich von Hassell, Admiral Canaris, head of the Counter-Espionage to 1944, and Leuschner and Leber, former Social Democratic and trade-union leaders. Military defeat, often the result of Hitler's mistakes in strategy and interference in day-to-day tactics, led increasing numbers of army officers, including Rommel, to recognize by the time of the Allied success in Normandy that the Führer must be eliminated.

The almost constant plotting against Nazi rule, which had begun as early as 1934 without accomplishing anything, came to a head in July 1944, as the participants saw that any possibility of a negotiated peace would soon be destroyed by the collapse of the country. They sought to overthrow the Nazis, form a government representing all non-Nazi groups, and maintain the military resistance while treating for peace with the enemy on better terms than unconditional surrender.

The execution of a revolution during the continuation of a war was a desperate venture. For ten years these highly-placed plotters, many of them willing to sacrifice their own lives in the act, had been unable to achieve the first essential, namely, the assassination of Hitler. On July 20 Colonel von Stauffenberg, as courageous an opponent of Hitler as could have been found in any country, tried to achieve this objective, but likewise failed. In his official capacity he was able to attend Hitler's small military conferences, and at the one on that date he introduced a time bomb by means of a brief case. The bomb exploded, wounding but not killing the intended victim. The Nazis retained control of the situation, arrested the plotters, put the leaders to death by slow hanging and made films of these actions with which to edify the Führer. Himmler issued orders for all members of the families of anyone connected with the plot to be exterminated, men, women and children; German blood must be purged, he said, of such diseased parts.

Defeat of Germany

Late in June, 1944, the Soviet armies began an offensive which continued practically without interruption until the end of the year. They first attacked in the center and north, quickly taking the key cities of Minsk, Pinsk, and Grodno, and threatening East Prussia. After the few remaining German reserves were thrown into the battle in this area, the Soviets concentrated in the southern sector, and in late August Romania surrendered to them. In September Bulgaria was occupied and Finland asked for peace. In October the British occupied Athens and the Soviets invaded Yugoslavia and connected their action with that of the local insurgents under Tito. Early in November the Soviets attacked the Nazis along the line of the Danube in Hungary, and by December they besieged Budapest. Superior in man power and equipment, they rolled back the German forces with speed that frightened the German generals but left Hitler confident of the outcome.

The Führer, stated General Heinz Guderian after the war, "had a special picture of the world, and every fact had to fit into that fancied picture." Hitler blamed reverses on the generals and the German people and shouted at one of the few officers sufficiently courageous to criticize him, "There's no need for you to try to teach me. I've been commanding the German Army in the field for five years, and during that time I've had more practical experience than any 'gentleman' of the General Staff could ever hope to have." His strategy became the reverse of that of the earlier part of the war; instead of depending on mobility, it consisted of holding fast to whatever positions the army occupied. As his health failed under the stress, he depended on drugs administered by the quack Doctor Morell. His delusions grew with his self-pity, but he did not lose control of the army and the government until these crashed about his head. He increased the power of Himmler, the *Waffen*-S.S., and Goebbels, and the nation kept fighting because of fear of Allied retribution for Nazi misdeeds and because of fear of bolshevism.

The disclosure in the autumn of 1944 of the American Morgenthau Plan to destroy Germany's industry and restrict the economy to agriculture was particularly useful in determining the Germans to persevere. When in October Hitler ordered a levee en masse of the entire nation, it was accepted. When in December he ordered a counterattack in the west in order to recapture Antwerp, split the Allied forces, and push the northern part into the sea, the generals considered it futile but obeyed his command.

The Nazis began on December 16 their offensive in the west, called

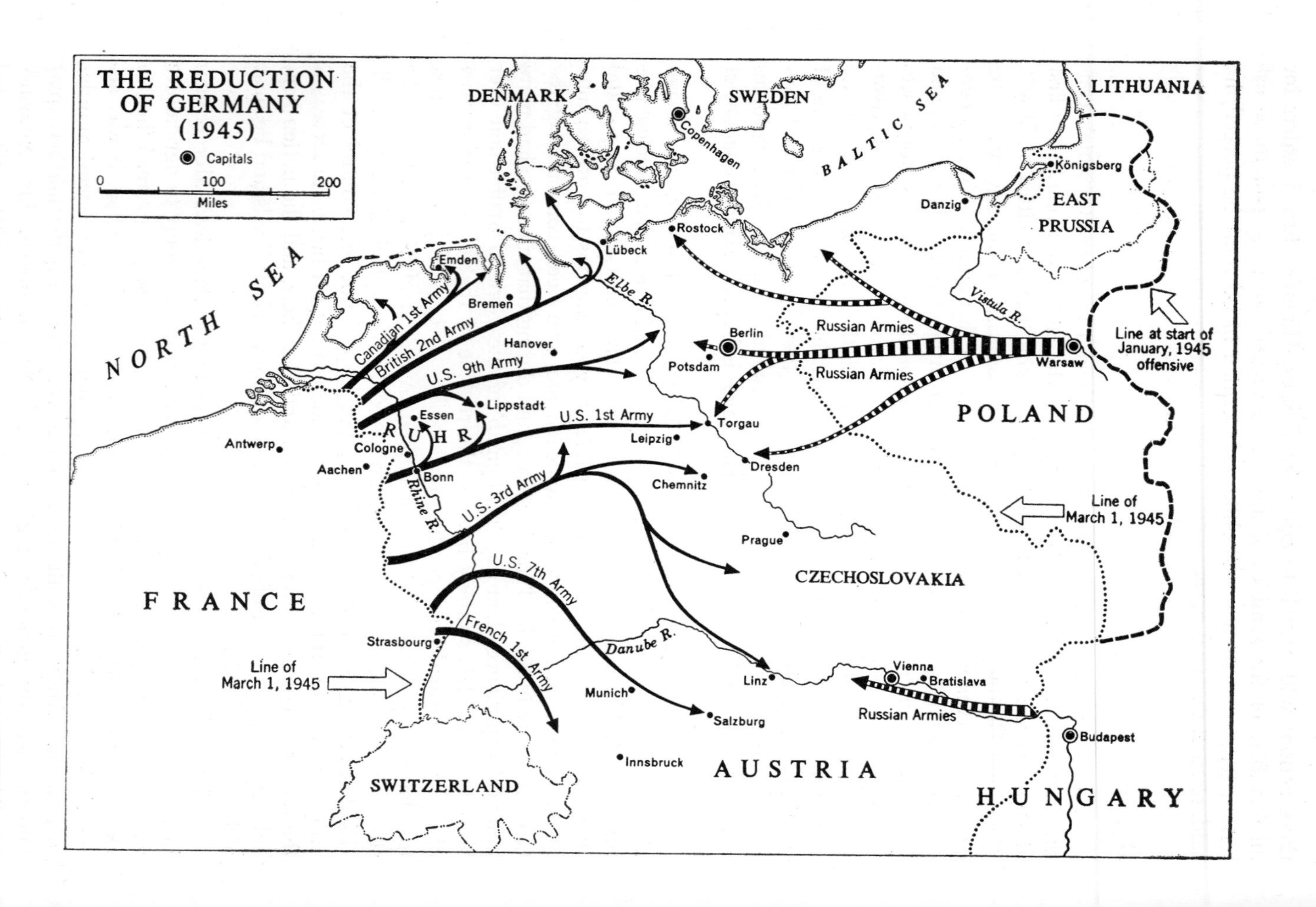
THE REDUCTION OF GERMANY (1945)
Capitals
0
100
200
Miles
DENMARK
SWEDEN
Copenhagen
BALTIC SEA
LITHUANIA
Königsberg
EAST PRUSSIA
Danzig
Rostock
Lübeck
Elbe R.
Vistula R.
Line at start of January, 1945 offensive
Russian Armies
Russian Armies
Berlin
Potsdam
Warsaw
POLAND
Torgau
Dresden
Leipzig
Chemnitz
Prague
Line of March 1, 1945
CZECHOSLOVAKIA
NORTH SEA
Emden
Bremen
Hanover
Canadian 1st Army
British 2nd Army
U.S. 9th Army
Lippstadt
Essen
RUHR
U.S. 1st Army
Antwerp
Cologne
Aachen
Bonn
Rhine R.
U.S. 3rd Army
U.S. 7th Army
French 1st Army
FRANCE
Strasbourg
Line of March 1, 1945
Danube R.
Munich
Linz
Salzburg
Vienna
Bratislava
Russian Armies
Budapest
Innsbruck
AUSTRIA
SWITZERLAND
HUNGARY

by the Allies the Battle of the Bulge. They broke the thinly held Allied line in the Ardennes but could not capture Antwerp. In less than a month they retreated with the loss of 120,000 men, 600 tanks and assault guns, and more than 1,600 planes. The Allied losses, smaller than those of the Germans, could be replaced; the Germans lacked the necessary resources, and Hitler insisted upon retaining hold of conquered areas. While the defense of Germany was collapsing, he kept 10 divisions in Yugoslavia, 17 in Scandinavia, 30 in the Baltic States, 24 in Italy, and 28 in Budapest and a remnant of Hungary. He engaged 76 divisions on the western front while in the east he had only 75 divisions to restrain 180 Soviet divisions.

The Allies now swept into Germany, crossed the Rhine, took the Ruhr, and cut the country into pieces. The Soviet troops in the meantime moved on Berlin, and the two armies, the Soviet from the east, the Allied from the west, met at the Elbe River. In Italy the Nazi generals negotiated a surrender. Finally recognizing that his forces could not prevent defeat, Hitler ordered the application of a scorched-earth policy in Germany. "If the war is to be lost," he said to Speer on March 19, "the nation also will perish . . . those who remain after the battle are of little value; for the good have fallen." Speer sabotaged the orders, for he thought the Führer had become mad, and the latter was too isolated in the ruins of Berlin to be able to force the execution.

On April 29 the Führer learned that Mussolini had been caught by Italian partisans in northern Italy on the preceding day and hanged. On April 30 Hitler committed suicide and his body was burned in the garden of the *Reich* Chancellery. A few Nazi leaders, among them Goebbels, who had remained faithful, and Himmler, who first tried to save himself by negotiating with the Allies, followed his example; most of the others were captured. On May 8 the German armed forces unconditionally surrendered; the war in Europe was ended.

Defeat of Japan

The war continued in the Far East, where the Japanese authorities were divided on whether to ask for peace. Their veiled efforts in the late spring and summer to negotiate an armistice were mistrusted. After the collapse of Germany the Soviet Union on August 8 declared war on Japan. It had agreed to do so at a conference held with the British and the Americans at Yalta in February, 1945, for then and later the Western powers greatly overestimated the strength of Japan and the probable duration of the war and sought Soviet aid. The United States had until then insisted on conducting the eastern war alone as much as possible and on its own terms. In August, 1944, the Americans captured the last of the Mariana Islands; in March, 1945, they seized Iwo Jima, and in late June Okinawa; and in July they regained the Philippines. Chinese troops with American aid were by that time pushing back the Japanese on the mainland, and

American bombers steadily raided Japan. Supreme in the air and on the sea, the United States forces were ready for the final siege of Japan proper. On August 6 President Truman announced the dropping of an atomic bomb on Hiroshima. On August 9 the Americans used the second bomb, this time on the naval and industrial city of Nagasaki. The Japanese government accelerated its suit for peace, and on September 2, 1945, the war ended.

A portrayal of the destruction caused by the two bombs may fittingly close the story of the most devastating conflict in history. The effects were investigated by United States officials, from whose reports the following description is taken. Of Hiroshima's approximately 320,000 inhabitants at the time, 78,150 were killed and 14,000 missing, and another 90,000 probably injured, making a total casualty list of about 180,000. In Nagasaki about 80,000 of 260,000 inhabitants were killed or injured. Father Siemens, a Catholic priest in Hiroshima, portrayed the effects as follows:

> Where the city stood, there is a gigantic burned-out scar. . . . More and more of the injured come to us. The least injured drag the more seriously wounded. There are wounded soldiers, and mothers carrying burned children in their arms. . . . Frightfully burned people beckon to us. Along the way there are many dead and dying. On the Misasi Bridge, which leads into the inner city, we are met by a long procession of soldiers who have suffered burns. They drag themselves along with the help of staves or are carried by their less severely injured comrades.

The effects of radiation were portrayed in the United States Bombing Survey as follows:

> Bloody diarrhoea followed, and the victims expired, some within two or three days after the onset and the majority within a week. Autopsies showed remarkable changes in the blood picture—almost complete absence of white blood cells, and deterioration of bone marrow. Mucous membranes of the throat, lungs, stomach and intestines showed acute inflammation. . . . Of women in various stages of pregnancy who were within 3,000 feet of ground zero, all known cases have had miscarriages. Even up to 6,500 feet they have had miscarriages or premature infants who died shortly after birth. In the group between 6,500 feet and 10,000 feet, about one-third have given birth to apparently normal children. Two months after the explosion, the city's total incidence of miscarriages, abortions and premature births was 27 per cent, as compared with a normal rate of 6 per cent.

Suggestions for Further Reading

See the Readings for Chapter 19.

Chapter 21 · The Postwar Settlement

World War II, like its predecessor, left a legacy of international problems that determined the sequence of events in the history of postwar Europe. Whereas the world economic crisis of the thirties brought increased activity to internal affairs within each country, war made international relations decisive alike for external and internal affairs.

The settlement after World War I differed from that after World War II in two main respects. During the former war the Allies did little to shape the League of Nations; the victors of World War II, on the other hand, drafted the constitution of the United Nations before the war closed. We shall therefore begin the discussion of the second postwar settlement by analyzing the objectives and structure of the new international organization. The Allies of World War II proposed to negotiate a more enduring peace than that of Versailles by using the deliberate process of diplomacy rather than a special peace conference. They left preparation for a peace settlement until after victory. Postwar international affairs were thus handled in two ways, contradictory or supplementary according to the point of view. Through the organization of the United Nations the Allied governments attempted to preserve peace and improve society by cooperation. Within and outside it individual members continued to pursue power politics to attain what each regarded as a basis for security. Subsequent conflict arose primarily between free nations of the West, on the one hand, and the Communist states led by the Soviet Union, on the other. It will be necessary for us to follow both lines of development and to note their interaction.

The United Nations and Its Affiliated Agencies

World War II turned the thoughts of people in free and in Communist countries alike toward finding means of preventing another such disaster. The need became increasingly urgent because the development of the atomic bomb, guided missiles, and less publicized weapons threatened the total destruction of humanity.

ALLIED PLANS FOR A UNITED NATIONS

American and British political leaders, pressed by a large and determined segment of public opinion, took the initiative in planning to replace the League of Nations, but Stalin likewise approved. All sought to utilize the impetus of wartime cooperation to found the organization. On October 30, 1943, the three governments, the American, British, and Soviet, and, at the insistence of the Americans, the Chinese, publicly supported five essential points: that an international organization was necessary; that membership should be open to all "peace-loving states"; that it should be composed of equal sovereign states; that future war was to be outlawed "except for the purposes envisaged in this declaration and after joint consultation"; and that armaments were to be regulated by a general agreement. These principles were all followed in creating the United Nations.

The three governments (China did not count, and France did not yet have a free representative government) held varying conceptions of organization. Speaking, not for his cabinet, but for himself, Churchill favored a world organization with three regional councils, one for the Pacific, one for the Americas, and one for Europe. Each nation, he proposed, should divide its armed forces into two sections, one for traditional use and one for immediate use by the regional council against any aggressor. In 1943 he envisaged the creation of a United States of Europe, composed of the major powers of that continent including Great Britain and having as members regional federations of the smaller states, for example, the Scandinavian states, the Danubian states, and the Balkan states. He likewise favored some kind of common citizenship for Great Britain and the United States, the retention of the wartime Combined Chiefs of Staff Committee, and the creation of institutional means for a concerted foreign policy.

Churchill's line of thinking in favor of this program ran as follows: He doubted that an international organization could by itself prevent war; he believed strongly that the balance of power was an abiding necessity as a supplement to a United Nations, and he was seeking ways of restoring it; he feared that the United States might withdraw into isolation as in 1919–1920, leaving Britain to face the Soviet Union, and he knew that his country was much too weak to counterbalance the Communist state alone. He also understood that Britain would be subject to most unpleasant pressures if left without support in a world dominated by the United States and the Soviet Union. Mistrusting the Communists, he sought to rebuild the strength of non-Soviet Europe and to align his country closely with both Europe and the United States.

Churchill soon gave up his ideas in favor of the American plans, not because he lost confidence in them, but because he knew that they could not be realized. He learned that the Soviet Union would oppose the establishment of a United States of Europe as weakening its own position of power, and he was forced to acknowledge that a politically united Europe able to preserve a balance between the United States and the Soviet Union appeared premature. His ideas are significant only as evidence of his anticipation of the lines of future developments. He refused to agree with those Americans who condemned regional organizations as instruments for reintroducing spheres of influence, the principle of the balance of power, and the practice of power politics and who feared that they would restrict American trade. He consoled himself for his defeat by the fact that the United States was relinquishing its traditional isolation in favor of active leadership in world affairs. He placed his country's trust in the United States as the power best able to defend the West against Soviet aggression.

Stalin evolved a conception of an international organization which suited Soviet purposes. He proposed in November, 1944, that the organization be used for about the same purpose that Clemenceau had set in 1919 for the League of Nations: it should prevent German aggression. Stalin thought of it as an indefinite extension of the wartime alliance. He held the opinion, which he expressed many times thereafter, that peace depended upon agreement of these three powers, that the lesser states would accept their decisions. He apparently found it more in harmony with his dictatorial experience to negotiate in secret with heads of two other states than to discuss international problems in an assembly of delegates from many sovereign political bodies.

THE UNITED NATIONS

The United Nations Charter was written in two conferences. The first one, attended by officials from the United States, Great Britain, the Soviet Union and, in the final stages, China, was held at Dumbarton Oaks in Washington in August and September, 1944, to compose a preliminary draft. The second one, at which delegates from fifty-one governments met in San Francisco, April 25 to June 26, 1945, revised that draft into the final document. For purposes of explaining the nature of the United Nations, the work of the two conferences can be considered together.

The basic structure developed for the League of Nations appeared suitable for its successor. The Security Council of the United Nations is composed of permanent representatives from the great powers, the United States, Great Britain, the Soviet Union, France, and China, and of one representative elected for a two-year term by the general assembly from each of six other powers. The custom soon began of selecting the six nonpermanent members in such a way as to provide equitable geographic distribution. Thus, delegates from the Near East, Europe, Latin America, and the Far East have usually been chosen, together with one from among the Soviet Union's satellites. The General Assembly consists of not more than five delegates from each member state, but the delegates have only one vote among them. The large number was allowed so that a state could have sufficient personnel to represent it on several of the important committees. The equality of vote among all the member states was included out of respect for the principle of state sovereignty.

The practice in the Assembly introduced some curious problems of democracy, which show how far removed the United Nations is from being a world government. It was found that when the membership consisted of sixty states the system of representation in the Assembly would enable states containing only 5.5 per cent of the total population of the sixty members to cast a majority vote (31 to 29), that it would permit states containing 11 per cent of the population to cast a two-thirds majority vote (40 to 20). Since most actions in the Assembly require a two-thirds majority, twenty-one small states containing only 2.3 per cent of the population could block any measure advocated by all the others. At the other extreme is the fact that China, India, and the Soviet Union include about one half of the population of the member states, and each of them is given one vote. The distribution of voting power would indicate that the organization depends for its effectiveness not so much upon legal authority as upon the ability to arouse and guide public opinion. This view is further supported by the fact that one half of the Charter is devoted to the establishment of a Social and Economic Council and a Trusteeship system, and that the United Nations is the head of a group of affiliated international organizations devoted to a wide variety of purposes, food and agriculture, health, education and science, civil aeronautics, labor, and so forth. The inclusion of these social and economic functions marks a distinct advantage over the League.

Security Council

The Security Council is given major legal responsibility for the preservation of peace. It was made small so that it could act with speed, and it functions continuously. By Article 25 "the Members of the United Nations agree to accept and carry out the decisions of the Security Council in accordance with the present Charter." The stipulation was based on the view that the great powers were most likely to cause an international war, that working harmony among them in the Security Council would do most to stabilize peace, and that the lesser states inclined to break the peace were most susceptible to great-power restraint. One of the major issues in drafting the Charter arose over whether the great powers would be able to carry on power politics among themselves while using the Security Council as an instrument for domination over the lesser states, or whether they would be subject to the same standards of action as all the others. The Soviet Union sought to provide the Security Council with the former character; the other great powers and especially the smaller nations objected. The Soviet leaders argued bluntly that peace depended upon agreement among the United States, Great Britain, and the Soviet Union, and were reluctant to grant equal status to France and China, not to speak of any lesser states. The others refused to permit the Security Council to continue the role of the wartime alliance without fixed responsibility to the entire organization, and the Soviet Union seemed to acquiesce.

The two powers that did most to limit the authority of the United Nations were the United States and the Soviet Union. Each was geographically removed from Europe, where most crises had occurred which made an international organization indispensable. The United States government feared the isolationist sentiment of the nation, whereas the Soviet government refused to subject itself without strict safeguards to an organization composed overwhelmingly of capitalist states. Two issues were of particular importance, one concerning the right of veto, the other concerning the system for the enforcement of collective security.

At the insistence of the United States and the Soviet Union, each of the five permanent members of the Security Council was given authority to veto the action of that body. The discussion concerned the extent of the veto: did the right apply to all matters, or could and should questions of substance be distinguished from those of procedure, and the veto apply in the former case but not in the latter? The original plan of the United States apparently called for absolute veto power on everything. By the time of the conference at Dumbarton Oaks this country had advanced to the position accepted by the British and the Soviets at Yalta and formulated as follows:

> Decisions of the Security Council on procedural matters shall be made by an affirmative vote of seven members. Decisions of the Security Council on all other matters shall be made by an affirmative vote of seven members including the concurring votes of the permanent members; provided that, in decisions [concerning peaceful settlement] . . . , a party to a dispute should abstain from voting.

The formula seems clear until one begins to explore the meaning of "procedural matters" and of "all other matters." The United States government tried to distinguish between them. "All other matters," it proposed, should include such questions as admission and suspension of members of the United Nations, regulation of armaments, and threats to, and breaches of, peace. "Procedural matters" could be those of a quasijudicial character "for example, whether an international dispute was likely to threaten peace if long continued, whether the Council should call on the nations concerned to settle a dispute themselves or should pursue peaceable procedures suggested by the Council, whether a dispute should be referred to the International Court of Justice, or whether a regional association of nations should be asked to try to settle a quarrel." If a permanent member of the Security Council were involved in one of these quasijudicial issues, the United States government contended, its delegate on the Council should not vote.

At San Francisco the delegates of the lesser states found the distinction in the Yalta formula so unclear that they submitted a list of twenty-three questions to the conference. Could a decision to investigate be vetoed, they asked? Was the question whether or not a matter was procedural subject to veto? And so on. The Soviet delegate declared in effect that anything and everything was subject to veto. Harry Hopkins, then in Moscow, persuaded Stalin to accept the American distinction; but that in itself was confused. The best that could be achieved at San Francisco was to write the Yalta formula into the Charter as Article 27, and to leave to the future the clarification of its meaning.

The Soviet Union has persisted in its inclusive interpretation, and during the first seven years of the United Nations it exercised the veto more than fifty times on questions of substance and of procedure alike. It argued that the distinction does not exist, that questions of procedure may easily and quickly become questions of substance. Its acceptance of the clause pertaining to abstention from voting if an issue involves the USSR was held to refer solely to the period of investigation; if enforcement was to follow, it reserved the right of veto—a solemn piece of diplomatic cant.

Procedure for Collective Security

The procedure for the collective maintenance of security became greatly elaborated in the Charter as compared with the Covenant. Both established an International Court of Justice, but whereas the League could act in times of "external aggression," "war or threat of war," or "rupture," the Security Council, given more flexible authority, emphasized the prevention of international difficulties. Under the Charter the states in a dispute are first of all enjoined to solve their own international difficulties "by negotiation, enquiry, mediation, conciliation, arbitration, judicial settlement, resort to regional agencies or arrangements, or other peaceful means of their own choice" (Article 33). This action followed from their agreement in Article 2 to "settle their international disputes by peaceful means" and to "refrain . . . from the threat or use of force against the territorial integrity or political independence of any State." If, however, a dispute should arise, the Security Council was given a wide variety of powers to achieve settlement by negotiation, arbitration, and other peaceful procedures.

The Charter does not limit its scope to acts of aggression or attempt, like the League, to define aggression. It outlaws private war, that is, war not empowered by the United Nations, and calls any state an aggressor that threatens to use or uses force against the territorial integrity and political independence of any state, as (Article 2) well as one that refuses to accept the decision of the Security Council. It empowers the Security Council to act in the event of "any threat to the peace, breach of the peace, or act of aggression" (Article 39). If states do not settle their difficulties by peaceful procedures, the Security Council may decide first what non-military measures to apply "to give effect to its decisions" (Article 41), like the "complete or partial interruption of economic relations and of . . . communication, and the severance of diplomatic relations" (Article 41). If these do not suffice, "it may take such action by air, sea, or land forces as may be necessary to maintain or restore international peace and security" (Article 42). These statements sound like an expanded version of those contained in the Covenant. The crux of the matter lies in whether the Charter empowers a more effective method of enforcement than the Covenant; the answer has proved to be that it does not.

The procedure for implementing the Security Councils' decision for preventing war contains numerous loopholes. In the first place, at the request of both the United States and the Soviet Union, as well as of other states, "matters which are essentially within the domestic jurisdiction of any States" (Article 2, paragraph 7) are excluded from the jurisdiction of the United Nations. The meaning of the clause has been debated; but the result has been that local Communist uprisings, however well known to have been sponsored by Moscow, are at the demand of the Soviet Union not subject to the consideration of the United Nations. They are a new kind of hybrid breach of peace which may be called a "domestic" affair or an "international" affair, depending upon whether or not one is a Commuist. If the revolt succeeds, as in Czechoslovakia in 1948, the Communists have recourse to Article 2, paragraph 7, to exclude United Nations intervention; if it fails and they see a possibility of arousing international animosity, as in the matter of Greece, they may try to bring the case before that body.

Once the Security Council has decided to take military action against an aggressor, the member states are expected by Article 43 to place the necessary forces at its disposal. Instead of depending upon the voluntary action of each state, as under the Covenant, with no one in charge, the Charter requires that the Security Council itself be the responsible head of these forces. The Soviet Union had desired the establishment of a United Nations air force ready on the instant to attack an aggressor. The other great powers, especially the United States, objected on grounds of sovereignty.

Out of the discussion came a compromise that rapidly degenerated into nothing. The forces were to be placed at the disposal of the Security Council by a "special agreement" with each state about "the numbers and types of forces, their degree of readiness and general location, and the nature of the facilities and assistance to be provided" (Article 43). These agreements were never made. Nor was Article 45 executed, by which, "in order to enable the United Nations to take urgent military measures," each member should "hold immediately available national air-force contingents for combined international enforcement action." The plans for these agreements and the creation of these forces were to be drawn by a "Military

Staff Committee" subject to the Security Council. The powers could never agree on the terms for creating this staff.

The mistrust of both Communist and free governments blocked action. The two had barely cooperated during the war; they were unable to cooperate in the quadripartite government of Germany and Austria. They could scarcely have been expected suddenly to harmonize their views under the United Nations. Agreement on the selection of a Secretary-General of the United Nations as head of the Secretariat could be reached by picking one from a small state like Norway or Sweden; but military personnel chosen from such a state would be inexperienced in handling mass troops and the latest weapons. The great powers were primarily, if not solely, capable of affording that training.

Nor did Articles 48, 49, and 50 improve upon the terms of the Covenant. They call for action by all or any of the members to execute the decisions of the Security Council by the use of economic, military, or other means. They do not take into account the differential in the extent to which the various states might be affected, or solve the problem that brought about the failure of sanctions against Italy in 1936. If states are confronted with "special economic problems arising from the carrying out of those [enforcement] measures" they should have "the right to consult the Security Council with regard to a solution of those problems." This "right" cannot reassure a state in the direct line of action. And when in Article 51 a state is granted "the inherent right of individual or collective self-defence if an armed attack occurs against" it, the door is open for arguments over the meaning of "self-defense."

The Charter encourages the establishment and use of regional organizations for "the pacific settlement of local disputes," but it states that these organizations must keep the Security Council informed of their activities "undertaken or in contemplation" at all times for this purpose and that they must receive authorization from the Security Council for their "enforcement action" (Articles 52, 53, 54). The United States and the Latin American countries objected to the subordination of their regional Pan-American Union to the Security Council, for they foresaw the interference of the Soviet Union in their affairs by the application of the veto. They finally decided to accept the articles, however, since the right of self-defence gave them freedom from control.

The Soviet Union similarly criticized the articles as allowing interference by the Security Council in its relations with the Soviet satellites. It demanded and obtained exclusion from the jurisdiction of the Security Council of measures by regional organizations "directed against renewal of aggressive policy" on the part of the ex-enemy states of World War II. Since Germany's international relations remained the major international problem in Europe, if not in the world, the inclusion of this clause greatly reduced the authority of the United Nations.

General Assembly

In contrast to the terms of the Covenant, the Charter differentiates between the functions of the Security Council and the General Assembly in preserving the peace. Under the Covenant, as under the Charter, the larger body controls the budget, and the Council has to report its actions to the Assembly. When the four great powers drafted the Charter at Dumbarton Oaks, they reduced the authority of the General Assembly in peacemaking beyond the point which the smaller states would accept. At San Francisco the latter expanded and strengthened this responsibility and opened the way to future increase in its functions. They successfully avoided becoming the objects of power politics of the great states by way of the Security Council. Even so, the action of the General Assembly in the all-important area of maintaining the peace was restricted. It can "discuss," "recommend," and "call attention to"; but "while the Security Council is exercising in respect of any dispute or situation the functions assigned to it in the present Charter, the General Assembly shall not make any recommendation with regard to that dispute or situation unless the Security Council so requests" (Article 12, paragraph 1). It is given no explicit authority to implement its recommendations; it depends for effectiveness upon arousing public opinion and upon marshaling the many smaller states against disapproved action. As the Security Council has been stalled by the veto, the General Assembly has sought to accomplish some of the Council's functions and has grown in political significance. The achievement of the United Nations should be gauged not merely by the political failures of the Security Council but by the success of the General Assembly.

Economic and Social Council

A basic weakness of the League had been the slight attention paid to social and economic problems. At San Francisco the states agreed that the United Nations should strive "to achieve international co-operation in solving international problems of an economic, social, cultural, or humanitarian character, and in promoting and encouraging respect for human rights and for fundamental freedoms for all without distinction as to race, sex, language, or religion" (Article I, paragraph 3). The lesser states insisted on including an extensive section in the Charter on "International Economic and Social Co-operation," and the great powers acquiesced. An Economic and Social Council was created directly responsible to the General Assembly. It consists of eighteen members elected by the General Assembly for a term of three years, and no privilege is allotted to the great powers. Their prestige and ability to serve the common good alone have entitled them to recurring election. The body of eighteen acts under the following instructions (Article 55):

With a view to the creation of conditions of stability and well-being which are necessary for peaceful and friendly relations among nations based on respect for the principle of equal rights and self-determination of peoples, the United Nations shall promote:

(a) higher standards of living, full employment, and conditions of economic and social progress and development;

(b) solutions of international economic, social, health, and related problems; and international cultural and educational co-operation; and

(c) universal respect for, and observance of, human rights and fundamental freedoms for all without distinction as to race, sex, language, or religion.

In Article 56 the member states pledge themselves "to take joint and separate action in cooperation with the Organization" to fulfill these purposes.

The program of objectives had a precedent in a few official international bodies, like the International Labor Organization, and in many private or semipublic associations in educational, health, and civic lines. Its acceptance was made possible by the achievements of modern industrialism, which set a social and economic standard for the underdeveloped peoples of the world. The fact that Article 55 could be included in the Charter as any other than a noble ideal, the fact that it was phrased in concrete terms each of which could be implemented in institutions, paid tribute to the unique ability of this Western industrial society to make into reality the ideals about which men of philosophy and religion have dreamed for several thousand years. A "higher standard of living" is something which a member of industrial society, whether employer or worker, understands and struggles to obtain. A society which had seen and fought the Nazi degradation of human beings on grounds of race knew something about the realistic value of "universal respect for, and observance of, human rights." A society which was rapidly learning about the methods of communism appreciated the meaning of "fundamental freedoms for all" and understood that these freedoms had to be defended.

The Economic and Social Council is divided into nine permanent commissions, each composed of from fifteen to eighteen members, usually of expert knowledge. They cover the following fields of interest: (1) Economic, Employment, and Development, (2) Human Rights, with subcommissions on Freedom of Information and the Press and on the Prevention of Discrimination and Protection of Minority Groups, (3) Narcotic Drugs, (4) Transport and Communications, (5) Fiscal, (6) Statistical, (7) Social, (8) Status of Women, and (9) Population. Their work is supplemented by three regional commissions, one for Europe, one for Latin America, and one for Asia and the Far East. Attached to the Council are a number of special organizations like the Permanent Central Opium Board, the United Nations International Children's Emergency Fund, and the International Refugee Organization, which execute programs approved by the Economic and Social Council.

The twelve commissions make studies and reports and submit recommendations for action by the Economic and Social Council and through it by the General Assembly, and in turn by the member states. The purpose of some of the commissions is clear from the title; that of Narcotic Drugs could refer only to the prevention of abuse, and that of the Status of Women refers to such problems as the elimination of the white-slave traffic and the improvement of the legal rights of women to inheritance and to political and social equality. The Statistical work offers for the first time in history the prospect of comparable data about all countries. "Fiscal" may puzzle the reader until one recalls the enormous variety of systems of public finance in the world and the great need for comparative studies to assist those countries with inefficient, or no system of, taxation and public expenditure.

The problems of opening up most areas of the world by facilities for Transportation and Communication are so vast and so varied that the inclusion of this subject may be readily justified. In a continent like Europe itself the smooth connection of a system in one country with that in another has been the object of study and constructive action for almost a century, but much remains to be done.

On Population the data are still so inadequate that we are uncertain about the size of the population in most countries, and we know even less about fertility rates, death rates, age distribution, and the many other questions which must be regarded as fundamental to economic and social improvement. The Population Commission strives to obtain these data, to use them, and to recommend policies and legislation.

The Social Commission deals with such matters as housing standards and accommodations, health, education, working conditions, income and welfare, and food and nutrition. Under its direction, for the first time in the history of man, in 1952, a report on the World Social Situation was published, making possible a preliminary comparison of standards of living.

The Economic, Employment, and Development Commission has been particularly active in obtaining and analyzing data and recommending policies and programs in the whole range of production and trade, with a view to the recovery of international economic cooperation and to the assistance of all states to improve the efficiency of their economic systems. When one compares economic situations as diverse as those of the United States, Italy, India, Libya, and Afghanistan, the usefulness of the work of this commission in assisting them ultimately to achieve parity becomes evident.

The Human Rights Commission continues, in an official international capacity, the humanitarian achievements of the past two centuries or more. It seeks to abolish slavery, to prevent racial persecution, to eradicate caste distinctions, to further religious freedom, and to assure the equality of treatment of human beings just because they are human beings.

Trusteeship Council

The San Francisco Conference wrote into the Charter an extensive chapter regarding "non-self-governing territories." This successor to the Covenant's provision about mandates was named the Trusteeship system. Roosevelt had hoped that all dependent territories would be transferred to it. Churchill and the governments of those states with colonial empires, France, Belgium, the Netherlands being the main ones, opposed, and the American president acknowledged that the administrative problems of turning hundreds of millions of peoples over to the new United Nations would be difficult if not insurmountable. He soon accepted the restriction of the system to the former mandates, to ex-enemy dependencies, and to any territories which an imperial nation might wish to place under the responsibility of the United Nations. For administering dependent peoples the Charter establishes standards which by implication should serve the imperial powers; and when one recalls how numerous the colonial peoples were at the end of World War II, the section of the Charter devoted to this question does not seem too extensive. These standards were incorporated in Article 73, which reads as follows:

> Members of the United Nations which have or assume responsibilities for the administration of territories whose peoples have not yet attained a full measure of self-government recognize the principle that the interests of the inhabitants of these territories are paramount, and accept as a sacred trust the obligation to promote to the utmost, within the system of international peace and security established by the present Charter, the well-being of the inhabitants of these territories, and, to this end:
>
> (a) to ensure, with due respect for the culture of the peoples concerned, their political, economic, social, and educational advancement, their just treatment, and their protection against abuses;
>
> (b) to develop self-government, to take due account of the political aspirations of the peoples, and to assist them in the progressive development of their free political institutions, according to the particular circumstances of each territory and its peoples and their varying stages of advancement;
>
> (c) to further international peace and security;
>
> (d) to promote constructive measures of development, to encourage research, and to co-operate with one another and, when and where appropriate, with specialized international bodies with a view to the practical achievements of the social, economic, and scientific purposes set forth in this Article. . . .

The origin of these ideals can be traced back to the great religions of the world, and to documents like the Bill of Rights, the American Declaration of Independence and the French Declaration of the Rights of Man. The implementation of the Trusteeship system has been equally based upon centuries of experience in the development of administrative machinery for free peoples. The state assuming the Trusteeship signs an agreement with the United Nations in accordance with which it is to act. The United Nations created a Trusteeship Council to direct all the work. This Council is composed of the members administering trust territories, the permanent members of the Security Council, and "as many other members elected for three-year terms by the General Assembly as may be necessary to ensure that the total number of members of the Trusteeship Council is equally divided between those Members of the United Nations which administer trust territories and those which do not" (Article 86, paragraph 1.c). This may be regarded as an adaptation of the principle of checks and balances.

Each member of the Trusteeship Council is instructed to "designate one specially qualified person to represent it therein" (Article 86, paragraph 2). The vote is decided by a majority of those present and voting (Article 89). The trustees are required to furnish full information about their actions and the conditions in the territories, and, in contrast to the rights of its predecessor under the League, the Trusteeship Council is given full power of inspection in the territories themselves. The only exception was made at the request of the United States. The American Navy and Air Force wished to maintain possession of Japanese islands in the Pacific, and won the government to their imperialist view. Since the United States had been the staunch supporter of the ideal of trusteeship, face was saved by placing certain trust territories in the special category of "strategic areas." The Security Council became responsible for supervising their administration, and the Trusteeship Council was relegated to a minor role.

Affiliated Organizations

The United Nations is surrounded and supported by many more specialized international organizations than the League had been. World War II had taught people the necessity for institutionalized international cooperation. These agencies range in character from official or semiofficial to purely private. Some, like the International Labor Organization, are affiliated with the United Nations through the Economic and Social Council; others, like the International Rotary Club, maintain their independence. All of them reflect the fact that international relations have come to include the relations not merely among governments but among peoples organized in their private capacities. The elaborate society of industrialism, with its numerous occupations and its facilities for individuals of all countries to pursue common interests, has made possible a range of international relations different from those of absolute monarchs or other forms of undemocratic governments.

The affiliated organizations which have so far been created may be divided into three groups according to function. The first group handles problems of transportation and communication and consists of the Universal Postal Union, the International Telecommunications Union, and the International Civil Aviation Organization. In connection with these, although serving a wider clientele, may be listed the World Meteorological

Organization; everyone is interested in the weather. The Postal Union and Telecommunication Union had their origins in the third quarter of the nineteenth century and had steadily grown in importance with the expansion of the subject of their concern. Such questions as categories of mail, postal weights, limits to dimensions, and rates to be charged, had to receive international answers; the Postal Union takes the initiative in making the necessary agreements. Telecommunications became especially the object of international negotiation after the development of the radio. Agreement has to be reached on frequency allocation for maritime, aeronautical broadcasting, and other purposes in order to avoid a Babel of voices in the air.

The Civil Aviation Organization deals with technical matters for increased safety, with multilateral agreements on commercial air rights to use bases in foreign countries, and with the establishment of adequate facilities for international air systems.

> A wholly unworkable situation would arise [one official has explained] if each nation were to fix its own rules in total disregard of those in force in neighboring countries, and if every airplane pilot had to familiarize himself with a different set of rules for each country and change his operating procedure at every frontier.

A plan for an International Maritime Consultative Organization has likewise been drafted, but so far it has not been ratified.

The second group consists of two economic organizations, the International Monetary Fund, founded to ease difficulties of foreign exchange, and the International Bank for Reconstruction and Development, which grew out of an international conference at Bretton Woods, New Hampshire, in 1944. These will be considered later in connection with postwar economic revival.

From the viewpoint of mass influence the third group, composed of social organizations, is by far the most significant. These are the International Labor Organization, the World Health Organization, the Food and Agriculture Organization, and the United Nations Educational, Scientific and Cultural Organization. Each of them had interwar predecessors, the I.L.O. being actually the continuation of the organization founded at the end of World War I. If one were to enumerate those areas of social life, basic to all peoples, one would probably agree on labor, health, food, and knowledge. One would then conclude that these four bodies cover the most elemental common problems of mankind and that international organizations devoted to them should stir popular interest and arouse popular participation. In these, international relations are brought to the level of peoples, of individuals and of professions trained to serve human welfare. Public officials and private citizens can cooperate as delegates of a country in conferences of these associations; here the functions become democratically managed and the citizen made aware of the fact of universal brotherhood.

The organization of each body resembles that of the United Nations in that each has a general assembly composed of delegates from each member in equal numbers and an executive board. The delegates to the assembly are chosen by the governments concerned from the bureaucracy or from private life because of their professional competence and standing. The executive board selected by the assembly is therefore also composed not of politicians but of experts. The constitution of the I.L.O., for example, states that the government of a country should choose two representatives from its bureaucracy, one from employers' associations and one from labor unions. Each international organization has a secretariat of experts, and each utilizes the service for shorter or longer time of many private individuals, and draws together and supplements the work of existing national organizations.

The four bodies have, each in its respective area, the common objectives of international peace and improvement in the material and spiritual condition of peoples. The I.L.O. continues to work for the rise in the status of labor with respect to such issues as the right to organize and to bargain collectively, increase in pay and in living standards, and better factory legislation and vocational guidance, and to transmit these gains of Western industrial workers to labor in the underdeveloped regions of Asia, Africa, Latin America, and elsewhere. The W.H.O. takes as the point of its departure the simple fact that a disease germ does not respect national boundaries and should be subjected to international control. The agency defines health as "a state of complete physical, mental and social well-being" and declares that "the enjoyment of the highest attainable standard of health is one of the fundamental rights of every human being without distinction of race, religion, political belief, economic or social condition," that "the health of all peoples is fundamental to the attainment of peace and security." The organization assumes among others the following functions:

To act as the directing and co-ordinating authority on international health work;

To assist governments, upon request, in strengthening health services;

To furnish appropriate technical assistance and, in emergencies, necessary aid upon the request or acceptance of governments;

To establish and maintain such administrative and technical services as may be required, including epidemiological and statistical services;

To stimulate and advance work to eradicate epidemic, endemic, and other diseases;

To propose conventions, agreements, and regulations, and make recommendations with respect to international health matters and to perform such duties as may be assigned thereby to the Organization and are consistent with its objectives;

To promote and conduct research in the field of health.

After becoming acquainted with this list of duties the reader scarcely needs to be told in detail about those of F.A.O. and UNESCO. His imagination can depict the possibilities of these international bodies achieving in their respective fields what W.H.O. proposes to accomplish for world health. All of them prepare model legislation and seek through their national members to gain acceptance of it by the member governments. The international models become the law of each land, enforceable in the local courts; international and national standards become identical.

". . . Since war begins in the minds of men," the UNESCO constitution declares, "it is in the minds of men that the defenses of peace must be constructed." W.H.O. adds that men must be healthy, F.A.O. that they must be adequately nourished, I.L.O. that they must enjoy good working conditions and a high standard of living. Then for the first time in history democracy would be possible for everyone. Supported by the popular action of the many specialized organizations, the United Nations might achieve its objectives.

From Peacemaking to the Cold War

INTERNAL AND INTERNATIONAL ASPECTS

Peacemaking was made unusually difficult by the fact that it involved not merely traditional problems of international relations but a conflict of views about the internal organization of states. Nazi or fascist totalitarianism, liberal democracy and communism, each had supporters among most peoples, and each group was actually or potentially hostile to the other. The confusion of international and civil conflict had two basic effects. In the first place, victors could not be clearly distinguished from vanquished. Divided between the fascist Vichy regime under Marshal Pétain and the Resistance movement, France could scarcely be called a victor nation. Germany and Italy contained nationals who rejected totalitarianism as completely as any free state, but who until the Allies defeated Hitler and Mussolini had been unable to liberate their countries. The same conditions existed in scale in the other enemy states, Austria, Hungary, Romania, Bulgaria, and Finland. In the second place, the close of the war between Allies and Axis powers brought into the open the mistrust and hostility between freedom-loving peoples and Communists led by the Soviet Union. Austria endured a decade of military occupation by the four major powers because of the antagonism. Finland retained her freedom. Hungary, Romania, and Bulgaria moved swiftly from freedom to native Communist rule supported by the Soviet army. Nor did Czechoslovakia and Poland, nominally on the side of the victors, fare differently. Local communism grew in prominence as the fascists withdrew and the U.S.S.R. advanced. Within a few years the Communists controlled both countries. Only in Belgium, the Netherlands, Denmark, Norway, all freed by Western forces, and Finland did both fascists and Communists prove so few and weak that prewar regimes recovered power, allowing peacemaking to be restricted to traditional functions.

The conclusion of peace, like the conduct of the war, was the work of a few individuals. During hostilities Stalin, Churchill, and Roosevelt had made themselves responsible for planning the peace. After Roosevelt's death in April, 1945, Harry Truman and Secretary of State James Byrnes took over for the United States. In Great Britain, as a result of the election victory of the Labor party in July, 1945, Churchill left office in favor of Clement Attlee as prime minister and Ernest Bevin as foreign secretary. The problems facing these men were so complex and so urgent that public opinion had neither the training nor the time to understand them and could do little other than acquiesce in the decisions of the leaders. The lesser states, however vitally concerned, were scarcely in a more influential position than the general public of the free great powers. They saw, as did everyone else, that they were too weak to maintain themselves against powerful aggressors. France, a nation still torn by internal dissension, concentrated in the peace negotiations upon forcing her way back among the great states.

Of the countries whose leaders were responsible for the future of Europe, two, the Soviet Union and the United States, were peripheral to that continent; the third, Great Britain, claimed to be so. Stalin directed a country with a political and social system alien to the Western tradition. Truman had unexpectedly become President of a former European colony recently grown to a great power and separated from Europe by an ocean. Attlee presided over the government of an island whose interests were divided between the continent and the rest of the world. What success would the leaders of these powers have in reviving a continent which had guided the course of the world for five centuries?

The war left seemingly insurmountable difficulties. Peacemaking involved not merely international relations of the traditional kind like drawing frontiers, or those of recent origin like disarmament and reparations; it concerned as well the transformation of a totalitarian into a free, peaceful, democratic society. It meant seeking to convert Europe from the traditional practice of war, which had almost destroyed her, to that of international cooperation. To prevent a recurrence of aggression the victors had to try to eliminate totalitarians from positions of influence in the defeated countries and to replace them with the most trustworthy persons to be found. They had to encourage the acceptance of ideals and the introduction of institutions which might assist the revival of society suffering both physical and moral exhaustion.

During the war, Roosevelt, Churchill, and Stalin had glossed over possible differences of policy and conflicts of interest by restricting their statements about the future to the general principles contained in the Atlantic Charter and the United Nations Declaration. Roosevelt's carefully studied demand for "unconditional surrender" of Germany, approved by Churchill and his war cabinet and advanced in January, 1943, at Casablanca, fitted into this political strategy of postponement. It reassured Stalin of Allied loyalty at a time when the West still could not create a Western front. That it might harden German national resistance was apparently not realized at the time.

The President and his advisers believed that the three powers might develop habits of cooperation and mutual trust which would continue in time of peace. Military strategy was to be divorced from political strategy; approval of general ideas was to precede later realization; negotiation with the enemy during the conflict was to be denied, both because the opponents were criminals and because the Allies might be diverted from complete destruction of the enemy by disagreement over what to do with them after the fascists were defeated. In consequence, the Allies did not face the gravest of all problems of peacemaking, whether free governments and a Communist regime could reconcile their fundamental difference to cooperate in negotiating a postwar settlement. Roosevelt, Churchill, and Stalin from time to time asseverated in public their mutual confidence and admiration, but differences in basic values remained unbridged.

American and British Objectives

The historian from his vantage point can see in discussions among the three powers during the war the potential conflict of policies and interests which subsequently came to light. The American position allowed most room for negotiation and a new approach to peacemaking because of the absence of vested interests in European affairs. Roosevelt wished to stabilize the conditions for peace so that the United States could withdraw its troops from Europe. He thought that American public opinion would demand return to isolation, and he planned to guide the country into internationalism, at least to the extent of active membership in a United Nations. American naval leaders urged retention of island bases in both Atlantic and Pacific oceans, and they won this point. While acquiring dependencies, Roosevelt advocated the breakup of other empires, like those of the British, the French, and the Dutch, and the transformation of the parts as soon as possible into independent states. President Roosevelt had hoped that he could keep Churchill and Stalin working in harmony, but at the time of his death he had begun to share Churchill's mistrust of the Communists. The British prime minister aimed at close cooperation with the United States, but he defended imperialism and he approved the creation of spheres of political influence and expected to see the principle of balance of power function in the future. He sought to revive Western Europe, particularly France, as a counterweight to both the Soviet Union and the United States.

Soviet Objectives

Stalin allowed almost no room for negotiation and compromise with other powers. As ruler of Russia, like the czars he desired to obtain seaports open all the year and to realize the dreams of the Pan-Slavists to take all Slavic peoples under Russian protection. As leader of an invaded country, much of it devastated, he determined to secure safeguards against a resurgence of German imperialism and to squeeze out of the Axis all reparations possible. He hoped to realize these aims by furthering Communist imperialism and then living in isolation from the rest of the world. He continued above all to be successor to Lenin, that is, at war with all free, capitalistic countries. Possession by the United States of the A–bomb alarmed him because of the threat it implied to Communist power. (It did not alarm a free country like Britain.) Before the war actually ended or the existence of the A–bomb was known, the U.S.S.R. leaders publicly expressed mistrust of the West, and in February, 1946, Stalin declared in a speech that "the capitalist system of world economy conceals in itself the elements of general crisis and military clashes." The Allies lost their wartime status of friends to become again the enemies of Soviet security.

Stalin demanded early in the war recognition of Soviet rule of the territories gained with Nazi aid, that is, the Baltic states, the eastern part of Poland, and Bessarabia. As Soviet arms pushed westward, he determined to hold the small states of Eastern and Southeastern Europe as a Soviet sphere of influence. Military control at the close of hostilities became the basis for political influence, a principle which Stalin found the West also following when he tried to participate actively in the peace settlement with respect to Italy, the Mediterranean, and Japan. The British and the Americans hoped to exclude him from influence in these regions, just as he expected to bar them from his sphere in Eastern Europe.

Instead of calling a conference to draft the peace treaties, the Allies allowed a "cooling-off" period, in which the foreign secretaries would negotiate the terms of individual treaties. The time necessary for this work varied according to the country concerned, the treaties with Italy, Bulgaria, Romania, Hungary, and Finland being completed by February, 1947, that with Japan by the end of 1951, and that with Austria needing until the middle of 1955. Agreement on a treaty with Germany has never been reached. The Soviet Union declared the absorption of Latvia, Estonia, and Lithuania an accomplished fact. For all treaties peace negotiations were unilateral; the Allies decided upon the terms and the defeated state acquiesced in them. In conformity with his dictatorial habits, Stalin demanded that the big three exercise the power of decision, but the American government supported by the British insisted that before final action the lesser states that had participated in the war be consulted. Against Stalin's wish, France was permitted to share as an equal in the negotiations over Germany and Austria. In general, the degree of influence in drafting the terms depended upon military realities, although the suggestions of states that had had little or no part in military events in an area were respectfully heard.

PEACE WITH ITALY

Since Italy had been the first enemy country to surrender, she was the object of the first peace negotiations. The U.S.S.R. participated in the discussions, but, not being one of the military occupants of the country, she lacked the military power materially to affect the outcome, nor did she try to do so. The treaty expressed the views of Britain and the United States.

The armistice terms of 1943 were severe, authorizing the Allied commander in chief to cancel any laws, to demand reparation payments and funds to cover the cost of occupation as he saw fit, to arrest Fascist war criminals, to exclude all Fascists from office, and to dissolve Fascist organizations. He ruled the country. In the course of the same year, under British and American pressure, Italy entered the war against Germany on the Allied side. Although Italy contributed little to ultimate victory, she claimed to be a Fascist captive which had thrown off totalitarian shackles and become a free nation. She expected corresponding treatment in the peace settlement and was severely disappointed at being handled as an ex-enemy.

The Allied states were to decide which of the former treaties between them and Italy should be retained. Italy was required to restore or compensate for the loss of property which belonged to nationals of the United Nations. She was deprived of colonies and of any right to mandates. She agreed to eliminate fascism in all forms and to accept an article which read: "Italy shall take all measures necessary to secure to all persons under Italian jurisdiction, without distinction as to race, sex, language or religion, the enjoyment of human rights and of the fundamental freedoms, including freedom of expression, of press and publication, of religious worship, of political opinion and of public meeting." Military and naval forces were curtailed to the point where they would suffice solely for local action on the frontier and the preservation of internal order. She was forbidden to make atomic weapons, guided missiles, and certain other war articles and had to demilitarize a strip of 20 kilometers on the French and Yugoslav frontiers. She was required to cede small districts to France, territory around Trieste to Yugoslavia, and some Adriatic islands to Yugoslavia and Albania, respectively. The main territorial losses consisted of the spoils from her aggressive wars of the past half century, the Dodecanese Islands (to Greece), Albania, and Ethiopia (both restored to independence), and the colonies in Africa. For the time being, Italy was reduced to a country of local interests, of so little weight in international relations that the British and the Americans agreed to terminate military occupation by the end of 1947.

That peacemaking with Italy involved far more than the elimination of fascism may be seen from four issues that arose. The first concerned the form of government. The Italian Communists were instructed from Moscow to cooperate with the democratic parties, and hence initially caused little difficulty. They joined the parties of center and left in seeking to throw out the monarchy and to establish a republic. The American government approved publicly of this popular demand; Churchill angrily opposed it in the name of the preservation of order. A year before the close of the European war Italy became a republic. The second issue, that of reparations, needs some general explanation that will likewise pertain to other defeated countries.

As a result of failure after World War I, exacting of reparations had become unpopular. During World War II a demand for reparations revived for two main reasons. First, the heinous crimes of the Nazis against Jews and other peoples and the less numerous crimes of German allies called for material atonement. In addition, the devastation of the Soviet Union caused Stalin to attempt through reparations to gain a multiple objective. He determined to recoup losses and speedily revive the power of his country so that no capitalist country would dare to attack. He expected to weaken the former enemies of the U.S.S.R. by seizing their capital resources and by requiring deliveries for years to come out of current production. The Germans, Italians, and others were to be made to work for the Soviet Union. The Soviet government was to share in control of the economy, an ideal situation for infiltration, for ousting Allied colleagues, and for sovietization. The standard of living of the defeated would be lowered to that of the Russians. If the masses should rebel against such treatment, local Communists could direct popular anger against the upper classes and the capitalist system and impose dictatorship of the proletariat. Since Stalin considered fascism as the last stage of a declining capitalism, he thought collection of reparations might speed final collapse. He considered all private property ill gotten, and since the interests of the Soviet Union, the sole Communist state, held priority over those of any non-Communist society, he felt justified in taking what he wanted.

The Soviet Union and the states of Eastern and Southeastern Europe, which the U.S.S.R. aimed to dominate, had undoubtedly suffered most from war. Communists knew that in comparison Britain, France, and the small states had undergone relatively little damage; that the United States had profited. France supported the Soviet state in demanding reparations. Britain, the United States, and the lesser Allies recognized the danger of impoverishing the enemy countries to benefit the Soviet Union. As occupying powers, they saw Germany and Italy urgently needing food, fuel, and other materials to revive the economy and to keep the people alive, and they were already supplying these items. If Germany and Italy had to pay reparations, they would do so at the expense of the United States and Britain. The Soviet leaders ignored this argument. They may privately have asked, Why not? If Britain and the United States paid, so much the better: they as capitalist powers and potential enemies would be weakened. In public the Communists reiterated demand for compensation, and the reparations question plagued the making of each treaty.

In the final negotiations for the Italian peace treaty (1946), the U.S.S.R. asked reparations of at least $100 million, and Albania, Yugoslavia, Greece, and Ethiopia requested a sum which would have increased the total burden to $600 million. Since the United States alone between the end of hostilities and the middle of 1946 had spent nearly a billion dollars to bolster the Italian economy, the British and United States governments tried to block reparations. In the end they obtained Soviet agreement to a compromise on $360 million, of which $100 million would go to the U.S.S.R., $125 million to Yugoslavia, $105 million to Greece, $25 million to Ethiopia, and $5 million to Albania, and payments were to last only seven years. After two years Italy was to pay a certain amount out of current production, with the recipients required to provide necessary raw material on commercial terms.

The third problem, involving the disposition of Trieste and the surrounding area, was not finally settled for another decade. Yugoslavia, ruled by the Communist Tito and with the Soviet Union supporting his claim, sought to gain the entire Trieste region. France, the United States, and Britain favored a partition of the territory along lines of nationality. Because of the intermingling of the Slavic and Italian peoples over the centuries, the powers could not agree on a valid frontier. In general, at the time (1946) the Western states favored internationalization of the port of Trieste under the administrative supervision of the United Nations Security Council. After months of negotiation the four powers accepted a frontier line. Trieste itself was to be self-governing under the auspices of the Security Council, with a governor appointed by that body. Unfortunately, the four powers could not agree on the choice of a governor, the Soviets sponsoring one favorable to communism, the others advocating one with Western standards. The city existed under the protection of occupying British and American troops until 1955, when Tito, having broken with the Soviet Union, reached direct agreement with Italy. Trieste became once more an Italian port.

The fourth issue, that of the disposal of the Italian colonies, Libya, Eritrea, and Italian Somaliland, encountered similar Allied disagreement. The Soviet Union sought to gain a foothold in the Mediterranean and in Africa by becoming the United Nations trustee for Tripolitania. The Western powers absolutely opposed this expansion. Italy as a recent ally in the war against Nazi Germany wished to be made trustee of her former colonies, a relationship which the natives, especially those of Libya, opposed. The four powers referred the question to the Assembly of the United Nations, where debate brought out expressions of numerous interests. The Latin states of South America supported Italy, Egypt wanted Libya in whole or part, the Arab states defended the right to independence of Moslem peoples, the United States maintained its right to the big air base near

Tripoli, and France showed concern that independence would encourage the nationalists in her own North African territories to seek independence.

Finally, in 1950, the Assembly worked out an acceptable solution. Libya was to become independent by 1952; Italian Somaliland was to be made an Italian trusteeship in preparation for independence ten years hence; and Eritrea was federated with Ethiopia. The decisions affected the lives of only a few million people, but they exposed the difficulties of settling international problems in a world torn by nationalism, imperialism, and conflict between free nations on the one hand and Communist states on the other.

Being subject, not to Soviet, but to Anglo-American military conquest and occupation, Italy was able within a short time (January 1, 1947) to recover control of its own internal, and to a great extent its own international, affairs. In contrast, Germany and Austria were conquered and occupied by both Anglo-American and Soviet troops, whereupon they became and remained objects of disagreement.

FAILURE TO MAKE PEACE WITH GERMANY

The treatment of Germany caused the deepest concern. How could that powerful state be prevented from again resorting to war? The means used after World War I to hold Germany in check had palpably failed. The British, American, French, and Soviet governments agreed on the necessity to punish war criminals and to eradicate nazism. The French wished to dismember Germany, the other three governments, after initial hesitation, had rejected the proposal as impracticable. A plan sponsored by the United States Secretary of the Treasury Morgenthau took a different line, namely to destroy Germany as an industrial power and reduce her to an agrarian economy. Approved for a short time in 1944 by Roosevelt and Churchill, the plan was condemned by other members of Roosevelt's cabinet, Secretary of War Stimson declaring to the President: "It would be just such a crime as the Germans themselves hoped to perpetrate upon their victims—it would be a crime against civilization itself." When Roosevelt became aware that execution would force the starvation or emigration of millions of German people, he repudiated the plan, and Churchill followed suit. At the Yalta Conference Stalin, however, submitted a proposal on reparations which would have deprived Germany of 80 per cent of the capital equipment of her heavy industry. He would thereby have penalized Germany about as heavily as Morgenthau proposed to do. In the months before and immediately after the end of the war most of the thinking about the treatment of Germany was punitive, restrictive, and negative and did not face the question of how to bring the difficult state back into international comity.

Under the terms of the armistice the victors assumed complete authority over the country, its government, its economy, the determination of its frontiers, and its military resources. Since they had previously been able to agree on almost nothing with respect to the future of Germany they quarreled over the use of the power they now wielded.

Boundaries

The first problem concerned the settlement of boundaries. The three powers had agreed that Germany should be deprived of the Nazi acquisitions. At the Teheran Conference in November, 1943, Stalin had won British and American approval for the Soviet Union's annexation of part of East

Prussia and of the ice-free port of Königsberg. At Yalta in February, 1945, they had approved Poland's claim to be compensated out of German territory for the cession of her eastern part to the Soviet Union. Without waiting for British and American reaction, Stalin arbitrarily assigned to Poland the German territory up to the Oder and to the western branch of the Neisse

River, and at the Potsdam Conference in July and August, 1945, he confronted the Allies with this *fait accompli.* He understood that this transfer of territory would probably so embitter German-Polish relations that the new Poland would have to depend indefinitely upon support by the Soviet Union. The enlargement of Poland therefore meant an expansion of Soviet power, a fact which the British in particular clearly grasped.

Allied bitterness against the Germans was still so great that the British and the Americans approved the compulsory removal of the German population from Eastern Europe to Germany. It was evident that the area given to Poland, almost solidly inhabited by Germans, would be the scene of mass expulsion. Germans were already fleeing into the part of their country occupied by the Western powers. Since the Poles and the Soviet Union gained the land on which food had formerly been grown for these people, the United States and Great Britain faced the disagreeable prospect of having to sustain them.

When neither side would give way on the issue of the Polish-German boundary, Secretary of State Byrnes found a formula. The area assigned to Poland by the Soviet Union should remain in Polish control pending a final settlement in a peace treaty with Germany. After this verbal compromise was reached, in fact if not in so many words granting the Soviet Union its demand, the other territorial problems caused little difficulty. France did not seek this time to separate the Rhineland from Germany but strove to safeguard herself against the revival of German power in other ways. She asked for and received the right to incorporate the Saar, rich in coal, in the French economy, but she agreed to the political internationalization of the area. Minor boundary rectifications between Germany and Belgium, the Netherlands, Denmark, and Austria completed the marking of Germany's new frontier.

Cession of territory to other states did not wholly conclude Allied remaking of the German map. The victors had to find a means of controlling the rest of the country. Prior to the end of the war the British, American, and Soviet governments had rejected as too complicated a suggestion that quadripartite control be introduced (France being the fourth power) throughout Germany, with a representative of each power expected to cooperate at each level of government. The British and the Americans anticipated that this organization would cause such quarrels among the powers that control over the country would be destroyed, thus facilitating the spread of communism. Early in 1945 the three governments therefore divided the country into zones, one for each of the three victors and a fourth carved from the American and British zones for France. Berlin was similarly divided into four sectors, but was to remain the capital of a unified Germany.

The British and American armies could have captured Berlin and much of the region marked for the Soviet zone of occupation ahead of the Soviet forces. Churchill wished them to do so, for he deeply mistrusted the Communists, and he proposed to hold these areas as a gauge of Soviet good behavior. General Eisenhower refused to advance beyond the line of zonal demarcation agreed upon by the heads of government.

Commensurate with her effort in the war the U.S.S.R. received the largest zone, one extending well into the west and containing the industrial regions of Upper Silesia and Saxony and a high percentage of Germany's agricultural land. The United States and Great Britain quarreled over the allocation of the western zones, for both wished to occupy the important industrial region of northwest Germany and the ports. The United States finally accepted the largely agrarian and much less populous southwest Germany, and it and Great Britain gave to France as her zone the southern part of Württemberg and Baden and a stretch of territory in the Rhineland along the French frontier.

The four powers set up an elaborate system of quadripartite boards in Berlin in lieu of a central German government; but since each member was sovereign in its zone and sector and subject to no inspection and no control by the others, the result was a speedy division of the country. Cooperation between officials of free governments and of a Communist government proved to be impossible.

The powers agreed on the principle of demilitarization and de-Nazification, and they were able to cooperate at the Nürnberg trials of the leading war criminals, among whom were Göring, von Ribbentrop, generals, and admirals. When their representatives began to execute the policy of de-Nazification, however, they struck differences of definition as to who was a Nazi. The Communists accused the Western powers of coddling ex-Nazis merely because they were capitalists; the Western powers accused the Communists of abusing the accusation of nazism in order to confiscate private property, destroy the middle class, and pave the way for communism. The Soviet officials acted in their zone toward the Germans, the overwhelming majority of whom rejected communism, by reference to standards of communism; the Western powers in their zones followed the practices of free, capitalistic society.

De-Nazification was attempted on a mass scale in all zones, but in the West the setting of a standard of nazism proved to be too complicated for administration. The Communists simply treated the Nazis in the way that best served the cause of communism. Thus, ex-Nazis willing to follow the new masters were welcomed, with few exceptions, irrespective of their record. Former victims of Nazi persecution who opposed communism were treated as enemies and once again made to suffer. The Western powers destroyed the remnants of the German army and stopped the manufacture of all military objects. They loyally carried out the agreement to deprive Germany of an air force, civilian or military, and a navy, and to prevent her from carrying on research in atomic energy, guided missiles, or in similar lines of use in war. The Soviets accused the Western powers of not carrying out these terms, while they built up a new German Communist army in their zone and violated all the other provisions for demilitarization.

Reparations

The question of reparations involved the standard of living which should be permitted the German people. Stalin proposed at Yalta to set German reparations at $20 billion with one half going to the Soviet Union. He asked for part to be taken from existing capital stock within two years to the extent of 80 per cent of what Germany possessed. The rest should be paid from current production over a period of ten years, and all heavy industry as well as all secondary industry which could be used to produce war goods was to be internationalized, that is, put under the control of the three powers. Stalin wanted to take away an amount which would reduce the German standard of living to approximately the low level of the East European states.

The Western powers refused to agree to any fixed sum before investigation by technicians at the end of the war. Their aversion to the payment of reparations from current production held true in the treatment of Germany as in that of Italy, and they hoped to avoid participation by the Soviets in the control of industries in the Western zones. They foresaw that if Soviet claims were allowed, the Germans in the Western zones would become international paupers, dependent upon British and especially American aid.

When the reparations question was considered at the Potsdam Conference, the British and American representatives (the French had refused to attend because their country was not yet granted equality with the other three powers) proposed terms which in lieu of better the Soviets had to accept. Each power was to remove capital stock from its own zone in payment of reparations. Since the British and the Americans realized that the loss in their respective zones would sooner or later have to be replaced at their expense in order to keep the German economy functioning, this stipulation affected only the Soviets and the French. The British and the Americans agreed to transfer to the Soviet Union 15 per cent of the capital plant in their areas regarded as surplus and an additional 10 per cent in return for food and coal from the Russian zone. The latter clause owed its origin to the great concern of the British, who administered a region dependent upon imports of food and raw material from the area under Soviet occupation.

The catch in the stipulation lay in the definition of surplus capital equipment. The responsibility for deciding what factories and what machines and rolling stock were not necessary for peacetime economy was left to the Allied Control Council, where each power had a veto. Since selection would take time and the Communists needed equipment at once, the powers agreed to "advance reparations"; but one fundamental restriction was included, which read as follows:

> Payment of reparations should leave enough resources to enable the German people to subsist without external assistance. In working out the economic balance of Germany, the necessary means must be provided to pay for imports approved by the Control Council in Germany.
>
> The proceeds of exports from current production and stocks shall be available in the first place for payments for such imports.

By way of further clarification it was agreed that the German standard of living should not rise above the average for continental Europe; the inference was that it should not be permitted to fall below that level. As one last item, the powers approved the Soviet claim to German assets in the countries, except Czechoslovakia, occupied by Soviet forces. The source for reparations to the Soviet Union was thereby confined mainly to the Soviet zone, which the Communists would have exploited without a reparations agreement. When one recalls that they acquired domination directly of the Soviet zone and indirectly of the area occupied by Poland, their failure to obtain extensive reparations from Western Germany was less of a reverse than it seemed to be.

Stalin remarked in August, 1944, to the Polish statesman Mikolajczyk that "communism fitted Germany as a saddle fitted a cow." The statement has been interpreted as implying a lack of interest in extending Communist rule over Germany; but this view underestimates Stalin's ambition and his tactical sense. First he sought to weaken anti-Communist Germany. In the Soviet zone he imposed a Communist regime at once. In the Western zones where almost the entire industrial proletariat opposed communism, he had slight opportunity to undermine the government and society by infiltration and had to employ other means. Through the Soviet official on the Quadripartite Commission he obstructed all attempts by the occupying Western powers to aid German recovery. Thereby he hoped to keep Germany weak and perhaps produce such despair as to drive the Western Germans to communism. He called upon world opinion to support his efforts to punish and restrain the unregenerate Nazi Germans, and he denounced "the capitalistic conspiracy" of the Western powers to revive the German menace to the Soviet Union. From time to time he also appealed to the Germans by accusing the Western powers of treating them with inhumanity.

Split among the Allies

Lack of clarity on the part of the Western powers in the long-range policy toward Germany permitted Soviet obstruction to succeed for several years. France was likewise eager to keep Germany weak, but she did not wish to drive the country to communism, and she lacked the prestige to exert major influence upon policy. The British Labor government, in power since the British elections of July, 1945, wanted to introduce socialism into Germany by way of its zone of occupation and to raise the standard of living of the workers. The government followed Churchill's program of building up Germany and France and the smaller western countries as a counterbalance to the great increase in power of the Soviet Union, and it recognized that a democratic Germany with a sound economy was essential for the recovery of Western Europe. It lacked the resources to subsidize the Germans and soon objected to their being prevented from helping themselves. As after World War I, Great Britain was first to understand the dependence of her own welfare upon that of the German people.

The United States policy evolved similarly at a slower pace and from somewhat different motives. The initial American policy as expressed in the Joint Chiefs of Staff's directive was mainly punitive. The commander in charge of the American military government, General Lucius Clay, thought it a shocking document because of "its failure to grasp the realities of the financial and economic conditions which confronted us." It "contemplated the Carthaginian peace which dominated our operations in Germany during the early months of occupation." He thought that the directive from the Potsdam Conference to develop an economy that would enable Germany to be self-sustaining was "a policy change of major import." Faced with confused instructions from Washington, General Clay chose to lift from the backs of the American taxpayers the burden of maintaining the German people.

The four powers agreed that one essential way to prevent Germany from again becoming a menace to peace lay in breaking up Prussia and in decentralizing governmental authority to the separate states. Economic unity had to be preserved, for the industrial society required a single customs frontier, a common currency, a unified system of transportation and communication, a national system of taxation, and freedom of movement of goods and people within its borders. The banking system was to be decentralized; that is, no national bank allowed. On United States insistence an attempt was made to destroy the big cartels and introduce competition as an essential means for forcing business to serve the interests of the people instead of dictating to them and supporting authoritarianism in government. The British Labor government preferred a German central government sufficiently strong to nationalize the basic industries and large credit institutions. It believed that socialism would change Germany into a democracy and permanently destroy the will to war. Its program was scarcely considered. The Soviet Union rejected all endeavors to achieve German unity. She refused to abide by the Potsdam Agreement on handling Germany as an economic unit; she blocked every effort to stabilize German currency, to revive production, to start the flow of goods throughout Germany, to do anything toward economic recovery. When General Clay decided to revive the German economy, the Communists accused him of violating the Potsdam Agreement, which they had consistently flouted, and of being a bourgeois-capitalistic warmonger.

In May, 1946, General Clay announced that except for "advance reparations" the United States would deliver no more German surplus capital equipment from its zone to the Soviets until the latter agreed to administer the country as an economic unit and to submit an accounting of the reparations they had already taken from their zone. The general argued that the German people had to be permitted to support themselves. He pointed to the costly drain on the American economy, and he might have added the British, in order to provide the Germans with food and fuel. He condemned the system as an indirect way of forcing the United States to pay German reparations to the Soviet Union. Ruhr miners were living in bitter cold on top of coal mines which they were unable to exploit because of weakness from hunger. The whole of Europe needed coal, which had to be imported at high cost from the United States. General Clay proposed to enable the Germans once more to work. He declared that the amount of surplus capital stock for reparations could be estimated only after a thorough inventory had been taken in all four zones, and he added that the economy of the various parts of the country was interdependent. The Soviets had a few months before rejected an American proposal for a four-power treaty to insure the complete disarmament of Germany for twenty-five years with the possibility of renewal. They liked General Clay's statement even less.

Creation of West German and East German Republics

In September, 1946, Secretary of State Byrnes declared in a speech: "The German people throughout Germany, under proper safeguards, should now be given the primary responsibility for the running of their own affairs. All that the Allied governments can and should do is to lay down the rules under which German democracy can govern itself." Although willing to continue negotiations with the Soviet Union for a German peace treaty, the United States and Great Britain united their zones. The French as well as the Soviets at first protested; but in the course of 1948 the French agreed to join their zone with the English and American zones, and in the next year the Germans in the Trizonia set up their own government. The Western Allies reformed the German currency, and for the first time since the war the Germans enjoyed a medium of exchange other than the American cigarette.

The Belgian, Netherlands, and Luxembourg governments participated in the negotiations leading to the creation of the West German Republic (formally the Federal Republic of Germany), and they and the three Western occupying powers at French insistence agreed that the Ruhr should be placed under international control and that they should encourage "the closest integration, on a mutually beneficial basis, of the German people under a democratic federal state within the framework of a European association." Germany was subjected to an occupation statute giving the three powers the right "to resume the exercise of their full powers in an emergency threatening security," and the new German constitution had to receive prior Allied approval. The Soviet Union countered by establishing a "German Democratic Republic" in its zone and once more demanding "the restoration of the unity of Germany as a democratic, peace-loving state." The prospect of negotiating a treaty over Germany no longer existed.

FAILURE TO MAKE PEACE WITH AUSTRIA

Peacemaking with Austria might have been expected to be simple and brief. In 1943 at Moscow the United States, Great Britain, and the Soviet Union, and a short time later the French Committee of National Liberation in Algiers agreed

> that Austria, the first free country to fall a victim to Hitlerite aggression, shall be liberated from German domination. . . . They declare that they wish to see reestablished a free and independent Austria . . . and thereby to open the way for the Austrian people themselves . . . to find that political and economic security which is the only basis for lasting peace.

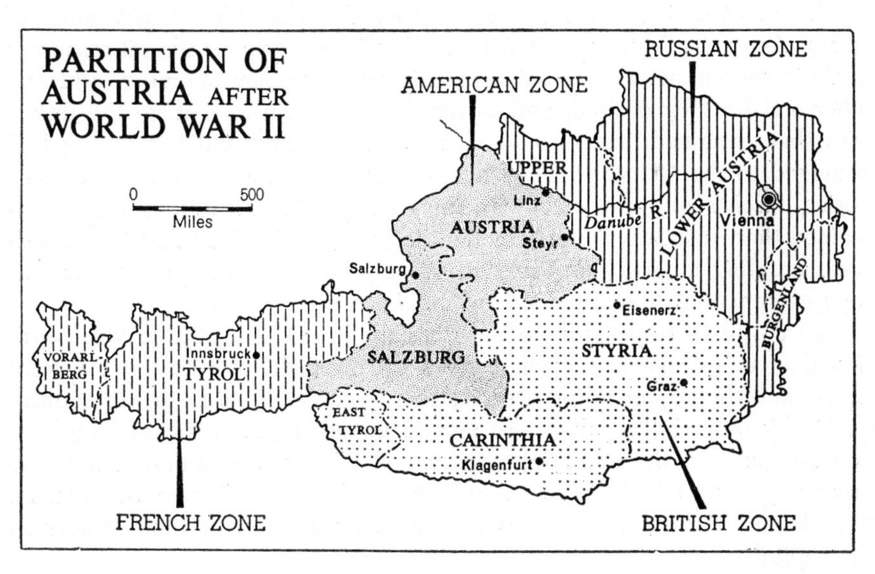

It would seem that Austria would have been immediately restored to the territorial boundaries of 1937 and permitted to set up a democratic government. The only condition imposed might have been that of excluding Nazis and other totalitarian forces from participation in the government, and the Austrians might have been trusted to take these measures themselves.

Two events changed prospects. The first was the fact that Austria was liberated by Soviet troops coming from one direction and by Anglo-American forces coming from another. Nothing was more difficult than to secure the removal of Communist troops once in occupation. The second occurred when in the free elections of November, 1945, for setting up a permanent government the Austrian Communist party polled 5 per cent of a heavy vote. In the provisional government formed by all parties in April 1945 the Communists had received three cabinet posts, including the crucial ones of the Interior, with its police power, and Education, with its possibility for propaganda. After the November elections the Communists received one seat in the cabinet, the Ministry of Electrification and Energy Control. The Soviet Union turned against such a people and such a government and began to make trouble. It supported a claim made by Communist Tito's Yugoslavia for $150 million reparations and for a portion of the Austrian provinces of Carinthia and Styria. That these demands violated the Moscow Agreement did not trouble the Soviet government any more than did the fact that as early as 1920 the people in the territory sought by Yugoslavia had proved overwhelmingly to be German-speaking Austrians. Rebuffed in regard to these two demands, the Soviets asserted a right to ownership of the "German assets" in Austria, and when the other powers rejected this claim as preposterous, the Communists seized those assets in the region of their military control.

The fact that the four powers had divided the country into zones of occupation as in Germany enabled the Russians to exploit the oil resources in their zone as well as to seize machinery, Danubian shipping, and any other articles they desired, and to run for their own advantage the industries that remained. They could claim that anything and everything had belonged to the Germans. They accused the Austrian government of harboring fascists and protecting enemies of the Soviet Union; they complained that Austria was not "democratic"; they maintained that the British were building an Austrian army to use against the Soviet Union. It was soon evident that they intended to remain in occupation.

In only two respects were the Russians in a less favorable legal position than in Germany: they had given up the right to veto any Austrian legislation, thereby enabling the Austrian government to keep the country politically unified. They had also agreed in writing to connection by land and air between the non-Soviet zones and Vienna, a stipulation that the army negotiators had failed to include in Germany. Hence the British, French, and Americans were assured of connection with their sectors in the capital.

PEACEMAKING IN EASTERN AND SOUTHEASTERN EUROPE

During the war the Soviet government had asserted to the British and the Americans that it regarded Eastern and Southeastern Europe as its sphere of influence. Its argument of needing protection against another German attack did not diminish the significance of the fact that the Soviet Union would expand its influence to an extent which the czarist regime had never achieved. Churchill was aware of the double implication of Soviet policy and had sought to counter it, first, by extending Anglo-American military activity to the Balkans in order to control some of that area by arms at the end of the war and, second, by arranging a partition of influence in the peninsula.

The American president and military leaders prevented military occupation, and Roosevelt had disapproved an agreement between Churchill and Stalin in May, 1944, delimiting zones of activity in the Balkans, with Greece and Yugoslavia being in the British zone and Bulgaria and Romania in the Soviet. By October of the same year Soviet troops had advanced so far that the British had to add Hungary to the Soviet sphere and accept equality of influence in Yugoslavia. The sole wartime assurance which the Soviet government gave about its postwar activity in this large region was to the effect that it would not interfere in the internal affairs of the countries concerned. In December, 1943, Stalin signed a Treaty of Friendship, Mutual Assistance, and Postwar Collaboration with the Czechoslovakian government in exile, assuring mutual "non-intervention in the internal affairs of the other State." "Communism does not fit the Poles," Stalin said to Mikolajczyk in October, 1944. "They are too individualistic, too nationalistic. . . . Poland will be a capitalist state."

Yalta Agreement

At Yalta Stalin joined Churchill and Roosevelt in issuing a Declaration on Liberated Europe which seemed to clinch the Western policy:

> The establishment of order in Europe and the re-building of national economic life must be achieved by processes which will enable the liberated peoples to destroy the last vestiges of Nazism and Fascism and to create democratic institutions of their own choice. . . .
>
> To foster the conditions in which the liberated peoples may exercise these rights, the three governments will jointly assist the people in any European liberated state or former Axis satellite state in Europe where in their judgment conditions require (a) to establish conditions of internal peace; (b) to carry out emergency measures for the relief of distressed peoples; (c) to form interim governmental authorities broadly representative of all the democratic elements in the population and pledged to the earliest possible establishment through free elections of governments responsive to the will of the people; and (d) to facilitate where necessary the holding of such elections. . . .
>
> When, in the opinion of the three governments, conditions . . . make such action necessary, they will immediately consult together on the measures necessary to discharge the joint responsibilities set forth in this declaration.

In the course of 1944 the Nazi military forces in the Balkan and Danubian regions began a fighting retreat. As the Soviet armies approached

Romania's frontier in August, the Romanian government under King Michael rebelled against the Nazis. Cooperating with the Soviet army, the Romanians helped to push the Germans through the Carpathians and to capture the whole of Transylvania. Promises and cooperative action did not save the country from communism, however; the Soviet army brought back Moscow-trained Romanian Communists. Between December, 1944, and February, 1945, in a series of internal crises the Communists forced the government to hand over the Ministry of the Interior and Police to one of their stalwarts. They next compelled the king under threat of violence to appoint a ministry dominated by Communists.

In Bulgaria the people had for generations been pro-Russian, to such an extent that the country, although a Nazi satellite, had not declared war on the Soviet Union. As the Soviet army reached the frontier, Stalin legalized the invasion of Bulgaria by declaring war. The Bulgarian government immediately sued for an armistice, and at the same time the Communist party led a rebellion against the government and installed a popular front ministry in which the Communists were prominent but not supreme. The new Bulgarian government joined the war against the Nazis.

As the Red army advanced into Hungary, Admiral Horthy and the government attempted to surrender but were seized beforehand by the Nazis. A part of the Hungarian army followed Horthy's orders, joined the Soviets, and set up a provisional government. The compulsory introduction of a Communist regime into that country occurred later.

In the north, Finland came to terms with the Soviets at about the same time; but she was in a more advantageous position than the others in that she had not been overrun and occupied by Soviet armies. Her government was able to remain in power and present a united national front to the Soviet victor.

Soviet Dictation of Peace Terms

The negotiation of peace treaties with the defeated Nazi satellites showed Soviet determination to dominate these countries in one way or another in the face of Western endeavor to save as much of a free way of life there as possible. Secretary of State Byrnes recognized in 1945 that the Soviet Union had special security interests in the Eastern and Southeastern region; he had in mind not the relation of master and dependent but that of the good neighbor. Since the fact of military occupation was against them, the Western powers were able at most to include in the treaties a few face-saving clauses, which, except with respect to Finland, the Soviet Union soon ignored.

The terms of the armistice with each state, negotiated by the Soviet Union, introduced the new era. In each country a tripartite Allied Control Commission was set up, but its instructions were so loosely worded that the Soviet commander acted much as he pleased. Since the terms for each defeated state except Finland were identical, those for Romania may be used as an example. The amount of reparations was fixed by the Soviets, and a clause was included which placed the fate of the entire economy in Soviet hands.

> The Rumanian Government must make regular payments in Rumanian currency required by the Allied (Soviet) High Command for the fulfillment of its functions and will in case of need ensure the use on Rumanian territory of industrial and transportation enterprises, means of communication, power stations, enterprises and installations of public utility, stores of fuel, fuel oil, food and other materials, services in accordance with instructions issued by the Allied (Soviet) High Command.

The Soviet commander was entitled to exercise full censorship and to arrest persons accused of war crimes, and the Romanian government was required to carry out the "instructions and orders of the Allied (Soviet) High Command issued by them for the purpose of securing the execution of these armistice terms." Similar terms had been written into the Italian armistice; in Italy the British and the Americans used their power to influence the character of the government and society in a free sense, whereas the Soviet Union employed its authority to introduce communism.

When the peace treaties were negotiated in 1945 and 1946, the Soviet Union consolidated and even increased its gains. The Communist state, although accustomed to denouncing the imperialism of all capitalistic societies, was the only great or small power that demanded and obtained extensive territorial additions—from Finland, the province of Petsamo with its rich nickel mines and warm-water port, a large region on the Soviet frontier farther south, and the province of Karelia; from Romania, the areas of Bessarabia and Northern Bucovina; from Czechoslovakia, sub-Carpathian Ukraine. The other territorial changes introduced in these three treaties were with one exception minor. The exception was the return of Northern Transylvania to Romania; at the time, the Romanian government was dominated by Communists, whereas Hungary was still supporting a bourgeois-capitalistic regime. Czechoslovakia received a small area around Bratislava from Hungary; Bulgaria regained South Dobruja from Romania, but she had to cede some territory to Yugoslavia, and, because of British and American pressure, she had to restore western Thrace to Greece and lose her port on the Aegean Sea. These were mainly time-honored areas of trouble, where the inhabitants had long been shuttlecocks.

The Soviet Union imposed upon these little states a relatively heavy burden of reparations and other economic demands. As in the treatment of Italy, Germany, and Austria, the Western victors did not ask for reparations; but the country with the largest land mass of any in the world claimed a total of $800 million in reparations from three of the smaller countries of the world and an additional $125 million for its new satellites and $45 million for Greece, which it hoped would become a satellite. The

Western powers protested in vain against the size of this burden. For eight years, according to the treaties, the economies of the conquered countries were to produce goods for the Soviet Union, a stipulation which afforded Russia unending opportunity to bring the economy into the Soviet orbit of production and trade. When one recalls British and American approval at Potsdam of the Soviet claim to all German assets in these countries—and what had the Nazi lords or their stooges not seized for themselves?—the means of economic control were fairly complete.

The Soviet Union had agreed in the armistice to respect the property rights of members of the United Nations; but when the time came to implement this promise, for example in the case of the Romanian oil resources, she made difficulties. The foreign former owners were legally entitled to compensation for the oil wells, but the Soviet Union needed the oil and got it as reparations payment; and the Romanian Communist government denounced the claimants as bourgeois imperialists and successfully stalled a settlement. The British and the Americans insisted upon the inclusion of the most-favored-nation clause in an attempt to keep open economic channels with the West; but this was a paper victory. They further requested that the Danube River be internationalized as it had been, except for the Nazi period, after World War I, and some of it as far back as 1856. The Soviet negotiator Molotov fought this claim as imperialistic. When at Western insistence a special conference was held on the problem, the Soviet delegate and the Communist representatives from the Danubian states blocked every effort to keep the river free and open.

The technique of interpreting treaty terms in a pro-Communist sense extended to all clauses. Each treaty included a guarantee of human rights identical with that in the Italian treaty; the new governments cited it to justify the condemnation as fascists of all opponents of Communism. In the Romanian and the Finnish treaties a further clause forbade any organization hostile to the Soviet Union or to any of the United Nations. Since all organizations of which the West would approve could be considered hostile to the Soviet Union, the latter had a right to almost limitless interference. The treaties called for sharp reduction in the military, but these clauses were ignored in favor of pro-Communist military forces. The Soviet Union retained her right to keep troops, with no particular number indicated, in Romania and Hungary in order to protect her lines of communications into Austria. The Western states suspected that the Soviets refused to make a treaty about Austria in order to justify the retention of troops in the two satellites.

The Western powers soon learned that written and oral agreements did not prevent the Communists from gaining absolute control in the defeated states. Stalin acknowledged at Potsdam that "a freely elected government in any of these countries would be anti-Soviet, and that we cannot allow." Nonetheless, he needed Western approval of the peace treaties, for one thing, in order to abolish the Allied Control Commissions, and he wished the new governments to receive diplomatic recognition. He therefore acquiesced in the holding in November, 1945, of elections in Austria and Hungary, where the Communists received a small minority of the votes, and in Bulgaria and Yugoslavia, where they or they and their political allies won a large majority. Mistrustful of the outcome in Romania, he stalled the elections for another year, when carefully controlled balloting gave the Communists a large majority. The Communists tolerated a few non-Communist members in the government of Romania and Bulgaria, and permitted a bourgeois ministry to function in Hungary until Great Britain and the United States recognized these governments and signed the peace treaties. Then the Communists during the next two years eliminated all opposition. That story will be told in a subsequent chapter.

Soviet Treatment of Three Small Allies

Whereas the former Nazi satellites received relatively uniform treatment from the Soviet Union, each of the three states on the winning side in the Soviet sphere of influence, Yugoslavia, Czechoslovakia, and Poland, was handled in a somewhat different way. Yugoslavia achieved the distinction of being the sole state able to prevent the Soviets from gaining domination. Czechoslovakia sought in every way to cooperate with the Soviet Union, whereas Poland mistrusted her. Both fell under Communist dictatorship.

Yugoslavia was fortunate in two respects. She was situated advantageously to receive certain Western war supplies, and she was farthest removed geographically from the Soviet area of operation. She sustained guerrilla action against the Nazi conquerors throughout the war. During the first years the British and Americans supported Colonel Mihajlović; but in late 1943 and early 1944 the British decided that this member of the regular Yugoslav army was less effective in fighting the Nazis than the partisan group led by the Communist Tito. Mihajlović was accused of indirectly working occasionally with the Nazis against the Titoists; he tried both to conserve Yugoslav social and political ideals and to defeat nazism. Churchill had grave doubts about the political reliability of the Moscow-trained Tito, but he respected the efficiency of the latter in organizing resistance. As the Nazi forces were driven from the country and the Soviet armies approached the Yugoslav frontier, Tito grew cooler toward the British. At the same time he maintained an extraordinary degree of independence toward the Soviet Union. He gained from her the assurance that his government would "continue to function in those districts of Yugoslavia where Red Army units were operating," and, even more remarkable, he received a Soviet promise to withdraw the Red troops from the country "on the completion of their operational tasks."

Czechoslovakia

The case of Czechoslovakia illustrates the tragic results of trusting Communists. President Beneš and his government in London concluded from prewar experience that Czechoslovakia had far more to fear from the Germans than from the Russians, even though the latter were Communist. They believed that the country could not depend upon the support of France and Great Britain against Germany, and that its salvation lay in close alliance with the Soviet Union. In December, 1943, Beneš journeyed to Moscow, found Stalin affable and understanding, and signed a treaty of friendship, of mutual respect of each other's territory, and of alliance against Germany or of countries allied with Germany. They promised to conclude no alliance against each other, and they agreed to "develop their economic relations upon the broadest possible scale and to afford each other all possible economic assistance after the war." Beneš believed that the treaty would contribute to East-West understanding, a condition he regarded as indispensable both for maintaining peace after the Nazis were overcome and for preserving the independence of his country.

Within less than a year Beneš began to doubt the honorable intentions of his ally. As the Red army entered Czechoslovakia the few Communists in the Carpatho-Ukrainian region agitated for annexation to the Soviet Union, an objective which they achieved. Then the Red army seized industrial plants, raw materials, and anything valuable as war booty and shipped them to the Soviet Union. Beneš protested to Moscow that this action resembled that of the Nazis seven years before. Molotov promised that the Soviet Union "would think of a new formula" on this question, and the looting somewhat diminished. Filled with concern, the Czech president went to Moscow in March, 1945. Stalin repeated that "we will never interfere in the internal affairs of our allies"; he merely left matters in the hands of the Moscow-trained Czechoslovak Communist leaders.

Beneš negotiated with these men, Gottwald, Slansky, and others, for reorganization of the government in preparation for return to the homeland. The Czech Communists demanded that the new cabinet be formed in Moscow, that the Communist party program be accepted, and that the premiership and all the key positions of power be given to them and their fellow travelers. Beneš knew that, with the Soviet army in occupation in Czechoslovakia, he faced the alternative of either accepting this cabinet with all the implied risk or breaking with the Soviet Union and causing grave trouble between East and West. In the latter development Czechoslovakia would be lost; by keeping on with the U.S.S.R., he hoped to be able to diminish Communist influence in the government and restore the balance. When the American and the Red troops that had rescued Czechoslovakia withdrew in December, 1945, the Communist party was already so powerful that with Soviet military forces just across the border the country was safely within the Red orbit.

Poland

The sole difference between the fate of Czechoslovakia and that of Poland was that the latter country had lost out to communism at an earlier date. Inasmuch as the immediate occasion for the British declaration of war against Germany had been the Nazi attack on Poland, the British felt a special obligation to restore Polish independence, a sentiment which her Western allies and, to judge from his utterances, Stalin shared. Which set of Poles, however, would be accepted as the government of the liberated country—that of the London government in exile, or that of the Polish Communists in Moscow? Throughout the war relations between the government in exile and the Soviet Union remained strained.

The source of friction between the Poles and Moscow lay in the Nazi-Soviet pact of 1939, whereby the Soviet Union acquired possession of Eastern Poland. Stalin determined not to relinquish that area, even after the Nazis forced him to enter the war on the side of Poland and the Western powers. The British government brought the Soviets and the Polish government in exile together sufficiently to secure an agreement between them in July, 1941, which read in part as follows: "The government of the U.S.S.R. recognizes the Soviet-German treaties of 1939 as to territorial changes in Poland as having lost their validity." The Poles argued henceforth that the Soviet Union had accepted the prewar Polish boundary; the Soviet government denied this interpretation. Almost all Poles refused to give in, and some influential men expressed the ambition for their country to become the political, cultural, and military leader of a vast East European federation.

The Polish question caused more trouble between the Soviet Union, on the one hand, and Great Britain and the United States, on the other, than any other single issue. Roosevelt took no initiative, but Churchill's government tried to bring the Poles and the Soviets to accept the Curzon line as the boundary. This line, worked out after World War I by an international commission under Lord Curzon, would have given the Soviet Union most of the White Russian and Ukrainian population in prewar Poland. Stalin would have had to relinquish some area gained in the Nazi treaty, but he was willing to compromise and to support the Poles in acquiring compensatory territory from Germany. The Polish government in exile refused to consider the offer, and when in 1944 the leader of the group, Mikolajczyk, seemed inclined to come to terms with Stalin, his colleagues dropped him in favor of an adamant nationalist. Churchill publicly expressed his disgust with the Poles, but he could not persuade them to compromise.

In the spring of 1943 the Nazis reported that they had found at Katyn in Poland the graves of several thousand Polish army officers slaughtered, they said, by the Russians. When the Polish government seemed to accept the story by asking for an international investigation, the Soviet government denounced it for spreading Nazi propaganda, and broke off relations.

Subsequent research has shown it to be fairly certain that the Communists were guilty of this atrocity as one way of eliminating a considerable number of troublesome Polish patriots of military skill. Stalin took the occasion to set up a competitor to the London government in the form of a Committee of National Liberation in Moscow dominated by Polish Communists. As the Soviet armies drove the Nazis out of Poland, they met the forces of the pro-London Polish Home Army, which they forcibly incorporated. As the Red troops neared Warsaw, the last remaining independent Polish force in the capital in August 1, 1944, rebelled against the Nazi army and tried to take the city before the Communists arrived. Anticipating the outcome, the Soviet armies halted outside Warsaw for a month and a half and watched Nazis and anti-Communist Poles kill each other, and Stalin would not permit the British and Americans to assist the Poles from the air. By that time world opinion had become so critical of Soviet stalling that Stalin once more started the armies slowly toward Warsaw. On October 3 the Polish insurgent remnant was forced to surrender to the Nazis amid a city in ruins. When this last military support in Poland of the government in exile was destroyed, the Soviet armies proceeded to drive the Nazis out of the country. In December, 1944, Stalin formally recognized his own Committee of National Liberation as the provisional government in Poland.

Convinced of the necessity to preserve the anti-Axis alliance until the defeat of Germany and Japan, the British and American governments were unable to oppose Stalin's unilateral action except by words. At the Yalta conference in February, 1945, they persuaded Stalin to accept a formula which more or less saved their faces. The Polish provisional government was to be more broadly based than at present and "free and unfettered elections" were to be held "as soon as possible on the basis of universal suffrage and secret ballot," with "all democratic and Anti-Nazi parties" having "the right to take part and to put forward candidates." Both Roosevelt and Churchill knew that the Soviets could interpret this agreement to suit their purposes, but the terms were the best they could obtain. The broadening of representation in the government stalled until in May, 1945, Harry Hopkins, assistant to President Truman, went to Moscow. In the course of negotiations over a number of issues, Hopkins persuaded Stalin to agree to a list of names of Poles from the London government who would be acceptable in the provisional government. In June the Polish ministry was accordingly reorganized.

The Communists kept control of fourteen of twenty-one cabinet posts, including all those valuable for dominating internal affairs. On July 5 Great Britain and the United States formally recognized this new Provisional Polish Government of National Unity. At Yalta Stalin had declared with intense emotion that the Soviet Union needed an independent, strong, and democratic Poland to act as a bulwark against the Germans. He had now won his battle, military and diplomatic, on every count; he had retained the area of Eastern Poland acquired by agreement with the Nazis and he had a Polish government under Communist control. In his last conference with Hopkins in 1945 Stalin said that "even though the Russians were a simple people, the West often made the mistake of regarding them as fools."

Having acquired the sphere of influence in the region where the Soviet Union faced the Central and Western European powers and a possibly resurgent Germany, Stalin was less interested in pushing his advantage on the periphery. He did not attempt to force communism upon Finland. He required that country to work for Russia on reparations and brought it into considerable dependence upon the Soviet market. He turned over to the local Communist party the German assets which the Soviet Union had gained and he made clear to the Finns that they should pursue a foreign policy friendly to their large neighbor. He apparently recognized, however, that the sovietization of Finland would strain relations with Great Britain and the United States, and all the Scandinavian states, and he seems to have thought that in contrast to Poland, for example, the gain did not outweigh the international disadvantages.

The same calculation prevailed regarding Iran, far to the south. Soviet forces had occupied the northern part of that country during the war, British the southern part, each on the treaty understanding of 1942 that it would leave once the war ended. Soviet troops remained, however, stirred up local agitation for a separatist movement under Communist leadership, and barred Iranian troops from entry. When the Western powers protested, Stalin stressed the possible danger from the south to the Baku oil field; but Iran's appeal to the United Nations forced him to retreat. By the end of 1946 Iran was free of foreign troops and once more under the jurisdiction of her own government.

Stalin did not press his demands upon Turkey at the end of the war for the right to maintain Soviet garrisons in the Straits region and to regain the former Russian provinces of Kars and Ardahan acquired by Turkey after World War I. The claim with respect to the Straits seemed especially dangerous to the British, and they and the Americans encouraged Turkey to be adamant. Stalin backed down.

The problem of Greece was more complicated than that of the other peripheral countries, but again Stalin decided against making a test of strength. During the war he had recognized the country as belonging to the British sphere of action, and he more or less respected his word. He permitted the bourgeois Greek government, supported first by the British and then by the Americans, in several years of intense civil war to defeat the powerful Communist guerrillas and to regain control of the country.

PEACEMAKING WITH JAPAN

In the Far East the United States excluded all powers, including the Soviet Union, from influence on Japan during occupation and from other than token participation in the formulation of peace terms. It asserted the same right of political dominance by virtue of military conquest that the U.S.S.R. applied in Eastern Europe. The Soviet Union imposed a Communist dictatorship guided from Moscow upon her dependencies, whereas the United States tried to prepare the Japanese for free government and society and participation in the defense of free peoples against communism. From the Soviet standpoint American policy appeared as another example of imperialism, directed at the exploitation of Japan and the encirclement of the Soviet Union. The United States intended its own program to assist the Japanese people in achieving a free, democratic way of life and in aligning themselves with other free nations against imperialism.

The United States government placed General Douglas MacArthur in command of the forces of occupation in Japan and acquiesced in his assumption of almost complete authority to formulate American policy. With little but token help from twelve other nations, among them the Soviet Union, General MacArthur ruled the occupied country for five years. He required the Japanese Emperor to report to him in his headquarters palace. Assisted by a large staff of Americans, he induced the Japanese to change profoundly their government, economy, religion, and society. Emperor worship was abolished; land was distributed to peasants; the right of a few to charge fishermen for use of choice fishing areas was canceled; militarism was eliminated; the government became responsible to the people; the large combines that had dominated the economy were broken up. Through these and many other reforms, General MacArthur created institutional bases on which Japan could develop along Western lines. By 1951 the United States government, concluding that it could safely negotiate peace, appointed John Foster Dulles to arrange a settlement.

Mr. Dulles aimed at four primary objectives: (1) to transfer to Japan responsibility for the conduct of Japanese affairs while taking precautions against a revival of imperialism; (2) to assure other countries in the Far East of protection against a resurgence of Japanese militarism; (3) to include Japan in the defense system in the Far East against the Soviet Union and against the Communists who since 1949 had seized control of China; (4) to commit the United States to sufficient action in the region to accomplish the aims without alarming the United States Senate over entangling alliance. A skilled international lawyer, Mr. Dulles negotiated a treaty that was accepted by his country, Japan, and forty-seven other states and was denounced by Communist governments.

Japan received back her sovereignty and agreed "to give the United Nations every assistance in any action it takes in accordance with the Charter, and to refrain from giving assistance to any State against which the United Nations may take preventive or enforcement action." General MacArthur's constitution for Japan had included a clause forbidding any rearmament. The Dulles treaty, by contrast, stipulated that Japan "as a sovereign nation possesses the inherent right of individual or collective self-defense referred to in Article 51 of the Charter of the United Nations and that Japan may voluntarily enter into collective security arrangements." To make doubly sure, the treaty contained another clause to the effect that "nothing in this provision shall, however, prevent the stationing or retention of foreign armed forces in Japanese territory under or in consequence of any bilateral or multilateral agreements which have been or may be made between one or more of the Allied Powers, on the one hand, and Japan on the other."

The United States then made a security treaty with Japan whereby American troops of occupation were to protect Japan. The United States retained possession of the Ryukyu Islands, including Okinawa, where it developed naval and air bases, with the understanding that it should become the United Nations trustee for these territories. It also signed security pacts with the Philippine Islands, Australia, and New Zealand, adopting in each the language of the Monroe Doctrine, to which the Senate was accustomed. It agreed that "an armed attack in the Pacific area on any of the parties would be dangerous to its own peace and safety" and that such "parties" should develop "their individual and collective capacity to resist armed attack." The governments of the countries involved understood the reality of American interest behind this devious language and considered the terms trustworthy. The peace treaty with Japan, the four security treaties, and retention by the United States of the Ryukyus created an "offshore island chain" (Dulles) against the Communists, to which President Truman added another link by assuming responsibility for the defense of Formosa, refuge of the Nationalist government of China driven from the mainland, against attempts at seizure by Communist China.

In the Far East, partly by means of superior power, partly by negotiation with free and equal governments, the United States built a line of defense against Communist power. The defense might be compared with that which the Soviet Union by coercion of small nations created in Eastern Europe against the Western powers. The United States, Britain, and the other free countries sought to cooperate with the Soviet Union, but not at the risk of permitting an increase of Soviet influence in areas under their control. The Soviet Union apparently wished to cooperate with her Western allies, provided she could dominate her small European neighbors. The two sides found their policies incompatible and chose the reality of power relations to the uncertainty of harmony with nations opposed to their ways of life. Since neither party would make more than nominal concessions to the other in the negotiations, it is difficult to see how the outcome could have been changed, except possibly by war among the victors. Neither wanted extreme action, and stalemate resulted. The United Nations, which "determined . . . to save succeeding generations from the scourge of war, . . . and to unite our strength to maintain international peace and security," was by general consent excluded from the negotiations.

Suggestions for Further Reading

DEUTSCHER, ISAAC. *Stalin.* See the Readings for Chapter 10.

GREEN, JAMES F. *The United Nations and Human Rights.* Washington, D.C.: The Brookings Institution, 1956.

LIE, TRYGVE. *In the Cause of Peace: Seven Years with the United Nations.* New York: The Macmillan Company, 1954.

MC NEILL, W. H. *America, Britain and Russia.* See the Readings for Chapter 19. Indispensable.

MARTIN, ANDREW. *Collective Security.* See the Readings for Chapter 5.

OPIE, REDVERS, and others. *The Search for Peace Settlements.* Washington, D.C.: The Brookings Institution, 1951.

PENROSE, ERNEST F. *Economic Planning for the Peace.* Princeton, N.J.: Princeton University Press, 1953.

Chapter 22 · The Cold War

WHY THE COLD WAR

Settlement of postwar problems would have taxed the good will of powers determined to cooperate. Global disorganization offered so many opportunities for aggrandizement that large states, conscious of their superior strength, would have had to repudiate the practices of centuries in order to abide by the principles of the United Nations. The Soviet Union was open to the suspicion of planning to impose communism upon as much of the world as it could. To Communists the wartime allies of the U.S.S.R. appeared as enemy capitalists, and communism prepared to take over as imperialists where nazism and fascism had left off. Each side had been accustomed to conceiving of the other as willing to use physical coercion, propaganda, and intrigue against other peoples as occasion permitted. The United States, the only other substantial world power, dared not allow its rival to upset the balance of power. That the U.S.S.R., not content with traditional political alliances, forced the communist system upon subject peoples enhanced the alarm. When the United States finally took the lead of the free world in curbing Communist aggression, the ensuing conflict, called the "Cold War," quickly assumed global dimensions. Most of the states of Asia and Africa sought to remain neutral while benefiting from Western defense against communism, but to some extent they also became involved.

The Soviet Union touched off the conflict by exploiting the confusion, in some areas amounting to chaos, which the war had left in Europe. It profited from the aversion of free nations, particularly that of the United States, to maintain a large armed force and from the desire of the American people to withdraw from European affairs. In May, 1945, the United States had an army of 3,500,000 men in Europe, with 149 air groups of planes and an extensive system of supplies. The Western allies added a half million men to this strength. Within ten months the American force in Europe had diminished to 400,000 men, and the Air Force had disintegrated. By July, 1946, the United States had available only 90 bombers and 460 fighter planes for emergency flight to Europe. By 1947 the British had reduced their army from 4,700,000 men to 1,247,000, and held only 30,000 in the crucial area of Germany. The French kept about an equal number in Germany, and the French minister of national defense belonged to the Communist party. The Soviet Union had preserved and continued to develop her fighting strength. In 1947 she had 500,000 combat troops in Central Europe, more than twice as many in reserve, and within easy range the rest of the millions of the Soviet military force. During the years after 1945 the only obstacle to Soviet expansion into Central and Western Europe lay in her fear of a war in which the United States alone would possess the atomic bomb. The Communists believed that they would in time be victorious over capitalist society without the expense of open fighting; they preferred the arts of subversion.

Weakness of Postwar Europe

The Communist prospects of expansion were aided by the failure of the Western powers to anticipate the dimensions of Europe's postwar economic needs. In August, 1945, the United States abruptly stopped Lend-Lease. The law required it to do so; but the effects upon the economy of Great Britain, for example, were alarming. The cessation of a flow of assistance which amounted to $31 billion, offset by a reverse Lend-Lease from Great Britain to the United States of $5 billion, without any preparations for change to a suitable peacetime system of continued aid, meant endangering the stability of the British economy. The United States transferred responsibility for aid to the Export-Import Bank, but gave it neither funds nor authority to meet international needs. The Anglo-American Combined Boards were rapidly dismantled, and the international responsibility for economic recovery was vested in the United Nations Relief and Rehabilitation Administration, founded in 1943, and in the International Monetary Fund and the International Bank of Reconstruction and Development.

UNRRA functioned until the middle of 1947, handling resources amounting in value to $4 billion. Sixty-five per cent of the total came from the United States, 15 per cent from Great Britain, and 3½ per cent from Canada. Since the recipients of UNRRA aid were those considered to be in greatest want, China, Italy, and the countries of Eastern and Southeastern Europe benefited most. Enemy states, except Germany and Japan, were made eligible, as well as the Allies, and peoples under Soviet occupation were assisted. When the Communist determination to hold these states became evident, the United States government ceased subsidizing peoples who were being exploited and dominated by the Soviet Union, and the agency was abolished. It had scarcely touched basic postwar economic problems.

Failure to Anticipate Postwar Needs

The two financial agencies established at Bretton Woods were planned on the basis of needs and problems experienced in the interwar years rather than those foreseen for the post-World War II period. The International Monetary Fund (I.M.F.) was to help to prevent competition in currency devaluation by making the currencies which a country lacked available on loan. The Bank endeavored to assist in the long-term restoration of a multilateral trading community. It was to offer loans on its own behalf for sound investments, but its main purpose was to encourage the revival of private loans. The I.M.F. managed in theory a fund of $3.4 billion; in actuality it disposed of less than one fourth that amount. The Bank had an authorized capital of $10 billion but was allocated far smaller sums. By June, 1949, the transactions of the former amounted to $725,500,000; of the latter, $720,000,000. In comparison with Europe's need the sums were insignificant. The war-torn continent was left with an economic vacuum as great as the military void; the disintegration of the West's military power was paralleled by the dissolution of economic defense against subversion. Under the leadership of the rich and secure United States, economic thinking failed to grasp postwar realities almost as badly as it had after World War I. The menace of communism first dramatized the gravity of conditions.

Wartime damage to the economy of non-Communist Europe had been less than expected, for speedy repairs had maintained industrial plants in working order. Consumers' goods industries had been in part neglected, but some lines of textiles, for example, had increased output. Steel-making capacity had not grown, coal production had declined, and electricity-generating plants had not expanded sufficiently to satisfy postwar demand. The greatest damage and neglect of repair occurred in housing and transportation. In other lines productive capital had actually enlarged, and population had increased. By the end of 1947 both production and the size of the working population reached prewar levels, with variations in conditions according to country and according to the branch of economy. Agriculture had suffered more severely than industry. Losses in livestock, especially draft animals, had been heavy. Nonetheless, the general level of nutrition not merely of Germany but of most of Europe during the war had been surprisingly high. The areas of greatest want were in Eastern and Southeastern Europe; France's malnutrition resulted as much from poor distribution as from general shortage of food. Great Britain's nutritional standard had actually improved during the war. The restoration of the prewar quantity of production, however, was insufficient; Europe had to increase output and to revive and improve international trade.

At the end of the war Europe immediately needed capital to restore transportation and housing, to revive agriculture with the use of machinery and other means, to introduce the technological improvements of the United States and of a few neutrals, and to pay for essential imports. To a much greater extent than any other continent Europe's processing economy depended upon overseas imports and exports. One half of its imports before World War II had consisted of food for human beings and fodder for livestock, with most of the rest raw materials; it had to export finished products in order to pay for these essential materials. Before the war it had run a deficit on trade with the dollar area (the United States, Canada, and other countries of North and South America primarily using the dollar in their foreign transactions) of $2 billion. It had been able to meet this deficit by the income from foreign investments, from the earnings from shipping, insurance, and other services, and from the sale of primarily consumers' goods to Southeast Asia, which in turn paid for them in dollars acquired from the sale of tin, rubber, rice, and other products to the United States. After the war these sources of income either greatly diminished or disappeared. Investments abroad had been largely liquidated to pay for the war. Heavy losses in ocean shipping occurred, while the United States and other overseas countries were building up a large merchant marine and expanding other international services. At the close of the war Southeast Asia, in a revolutionary turmoil, did not resume its former role in international economy. The native peoples demanded better living conditions, although the market for their products declined. Less tin, for example, was used with the introduction of the electrolytic process in the making of tin plate and the substitution of aluminum; the war shortage of natural rubber had forced the development of substitutes; and the indigenous peoples were eating more of their grain and shipping less abroad. Thus they earned fewer dollars than before; wishing rapidly to industrialize, they spent their dollars for American capital machinery rather than for European consumers' goods.

As Eastern Europe fell under Communist domination, the industrial states lost another source of food and raw materials and an outlet for manufactured goods. The dollar area enjoyed the unique distinction of having surplus food, surplus raw materials, a large capacity for producing machinery needed for capital investment, replacement and improvement, and surplus capital. The whole world was forced to turn to this region, and, as the United States hastened the rise in prices by abolishing wartime controls in 1947, Europeans had to offer more manufactured commodities in exchange than before the war. For several decades Europe had been undergoing a structural change in its market relations; World War II accentuated and accelerated the transformation. This small continent had to contend with long-range adjustments at the same time that it recovered from the most exhausting war in history. To perform the double task it urgently required investment capital; otherwise its economy would be unable to support the dense population. The postwar crisis, because it came at a time when the people were exhausted, discouraged, and anxious about whether the continent had a future, brought conditions well suited to the spread of communism. The answer to the question whether Central and Western Europe could revive and remain free could not be given by Europe alone; the United States as well was involved in any solution.

UNITED STATES ASSUMES FREE WORLD LEADERSHIP

As the United States became aware of Europe's plight and of the resumption of hostility by the Soviet Union, it reluctantly assumed international leadership in resisting Communist aggression. The execution of this responsibility involved it not merely in world economic affairs but in world politics, and not merely in relations with individual nations but in the work of the United Nations. It began with negotiation of the General Agreement on Tariffs and Trade (G.A.T.T.), and continued with the Marshall Plan, the Truman Doctrine, and attempts at regional organization.

World War II disorganized Europe's trade, and therefore world trade, more thoroughly than had World War I. Acting from experience, almost all countries of the world continued quota restrictions, government control of foreign exchange, and protective tariffs. In Europe particularly, war needs had reinforced the trend in the direction of central planning, and governments preserved the instruments of economic control in order to overcome the disorder left by the conflict. The United States, bursting with productive capacity, wealth, and vigor, stood practically alone in pressing for the restoration of multilateral trade. The government in 1945 published its *Proposals for the Expansion of World Trade and Employment,* which in 1947 served as the basis for discussion at conferences in Geneva and in Havana.

At Geneva twenty-three nations representing 70 per cent of world trade created G.A.T.T., by which they accepted the American policy in substance but subjected it to conditions allowing them to continue existing restrictions until they felt safe gradually to remove them. The participating states signed 123 bilateral agreements of a mutually interdependent character for reducing tariffs. When the nations met at Havana to establish a permanent International Trade Organization, they drafted a charter full of loopholes to permit trade restrictions. The United States refused in the end to accept the document, and ITO died; G.A.T.T., although temporary in the beginning, persisted. At its annual conferences the signers negotiated further reduction of obstacles to trade without commiting themselves to restore complete freedom of market relations. The United States itself has not consistently adhered to its own policy; it has also retained high tariffs on many commodities and has protected a number by quotas. G.A.T.T., cautious and tentative in procedure, should be placed with imperial preference and regional economic agreements, particularly in Europe, as an effort to find ways appropriate under present conditions to restore the multilateral trade relations of the nineteenth century.

The United States suffered a second reverse to its postwar economic program when in the latter part of 1945 and in 1946 it considered negotiations for loans to Great Britain and the Soviet Union. For each country the United States set conditions which would have reintroduced a system of free international economic relations. The U.S.S.R. refused to accept the terms, and negotiations for a loan never actually started. The British fearfully agreed to restore free convertibility of the pound sterling within a certain date but refused to relinquish imperial preference. They sought a much larger loan than that of $3,750 million which they received, and they were disappointed in being required to pay interest, even though at the low rate of 2 per cent. Within a year the terms proved to be unworkable. Yet debate on the loan marked the turn in the United States from isolationism to acceptance of leadership in the defense of the free world.

In the education of the United States in international affairs the United Nations, located within our borders, has taken a major part. The Soviet Union boycotted almost all economic and social work of the United Nations and its affiliated agencies. It participated finally in the World Health Organization, and it allowed a few satellites to join UNESCO; but, accustomed to interpreting all activity in political terms, it forbade further co-operation with free nations. In the Security Council, usually outvoted by an overwhelming majority, the Soviet Union vetoed measures it disliked. The most striking instance was that of membership in the United Nations. Up to 1954 nine applications for membership had been accepted, and fifteen had fallen victim to the conflict between the Communists and the free world. At first the United States and its friends were willing to accept all applicants, whereas the Soviet Union objected. Later the free nations receded from this stand, as they saw how the Soviet satellites, asking for admission—Albania, Bulgaria, Hungary, Romania, and the Mongolian Peoples' Republic—violated the principles of the charter. The free nations supported the applications of non-Communist states, like Eire, Finland, Italy, Austria, Jordan, Japan, and Portugal, but the Soviet Union vetoed their being accepted. The Soviets were then willing to compromise by admitting all; but the others refused in this way to seem to condone the satellites' abuse of freedom. In 1956 the two sides finally agreed to admit almost every state except Communist China, and since that date most applicants have had no difficulty in being accepted.

Impasse over Disarmament—Control of Atomic Energy

The discussion of disarmament, including that of the control of atomic energy, early reached an impasse. Having learned from the experience of the League, the United Nations Charter placed security before disarmament. Countries were entitled to arm themselves for safety under the United Nations; then they were expected to accept the international reductions of arms. The Soviet Union revived the futile League position of putting disarmament first, and at the same time sought to preserve its own military supremacy by proposing that each state reduce armaments by a common percentage. In that way the ratio of postwar Soviet superiority over others would persist. More revealing was the divergence of policy toward the control of atomic energy. The making of the atom bomb had been so ominous for the future that the United States, the homeland of private enterprise and the defender of national sovereignty, took the lead in advocating the complete internationalization of everything having to do with atomic energy. The United Nations Assembly in 1946 created an Atomic Energy Commission with instructions to report on means to control this source of potential devastation. The American, British, Canadian, French, and other members of the free world appointed to that commission agreed upon a plan which departed as radically in its content from tradition as atomic fission had from old-fashioned physics. The first chairman of the commission, Bernard Baruch, said in 1946:

> We are here to make a choice between the quick and the dead. . . . Behind the black portent of the atomic age lies a hope which, seized upon with faith, can work our salvation. If we fail, then we have damned every man to be the slave of fear. Let us not deceive ourselves: We must elect World Peace or World Destruction.

According to the plan of the free world development of atomic energy from mining the ore to utilizing the energy was to be under strong international control. An International Control Agency would be established with exclusive power to operate dangerous atomic facilities but with authority to license governments or individuals to operate nondangerous ones. It should have the power of inspection in any country in any plant at any time. All atomic weapons were to be prohibited, and atomic energy would be employed exclusively for the betterment of mankind.

The Soviet Union condemned the plan as a violation of national sovereignty. It offered the alternative proposal to outlaw the use of all atomic weapons and to destroy all existing ones, and seized the opportunity to denounce the United States, the sole possessor of the atomic bomb at the time, as an imperialist menace to the survival of mankind. At first it rejected all forms of international control; then it saw fit to accept control in words but not in fact. The International Control Commission should "make recommendations to the Security Council on measures for prevention and suppression with regard to violators of the conventions on the prohibition of atomic weapons and on the control of atomic energy." If one recalls that on the Council the Soviet government wielded an absolute veto, one can understand why the other states were skeptical of the efficacy of this internationalism.

The Soviets imposed other restrictions as well upon the Control Commission and claimed the right to carry on their own research and develop their own program without limitation. The Soviet policy applied to disarmament and to all other aspects of the work of the United Nations. The Communists feared to allow institutions or organizations with bourgeois-capitalist personnel, no matter how international, to enter their country, mingle with their people, learn about their conditions.

In 1949 the Soviet government announced the successful explosion of its first atomic bomb. At the Geneva conference in 1955, the heads of the United States, the Soviet Union, Great Britain, France, and other states once more discussed the issue. Although they conceded minor points, they remained deadlocked over the essential question of international control. The race in atomic armaments has continued. The main hope for peace lay in the mutual awareness that, as Einstein later said, if a third world war occurred the fourth would be fought with rocks.

Truman Doctrine

By 1947 the Communists had seized control by force in Bulgaria, Romania, and Poland, in violation of the Yalta Agreement; they seemed about to wage a successful, partly civil, partly international, war in Greece and were threatening Turkey. When the British Labor government abruptly declared its inability to defend and support the Greek government any longer, in March President Truman went before the Congress to ask for aid to both Greece and Turkey. In doing so he formulated a new doctrine in international relations that bears his name. "I believe," he said, "that it must be the policy of the United States to support free peoples who are resisting attempted subjugation by armed minorities or by outside pressures." He affirmed American faith in the United Nations and explained that this unilateral action was in response to an emergency. The American government, like all free governments, had been perplexed over how to prevent national Communist party members from destroying free government and society in their country in favor of direction by Moscow. Adapting the ideal of the Monroe Doctrine, the President pledged economic as well as military aid to peoples in danger. He recognized that "totalitarian [Communist in this case] regimes imposed upon free peoples, by direct or indirect aggression, undermine the foundations of international peace and hence the security of the United States." Congress approved his request, and the United States assumed the active defense of Greece and Turkey.

Marshall Plan (European Recovery Program)

Open breach between the United States and the free European countries, on the one hand, and the Soviet Union and its satellites, on the other, occurred over the question of American economic aid to European recovery. The position of the European countries may be seen from a few figures concerning the states later participating in the Organization for European Economic Cooperation (Austria, Belgium-Luxembourg, Denmark, France, Greece, Ireland, Iceland, Italy, the Netherlands, Norway, the United Kingdom, Sweden, Trieste, Turkey, and the West German Republic). The per capita production in 1948–1949 of Great Britain, France, and Benelux amounted to only $640 (in current dollar prices) against $1,770 for the United States. The United States' national income made up 40 per cent of that of the entire world. Europe's population had increased since the war, primarily from the influx of refugees from Eastern Europe, but per capita production, in comparison with the prewar figure, had fallen. Its per capita consumption had also declined from $470 in 1938 to $410 in 1948–1949; that of the United States at the latter date was $1,360. The region was investing a much higher percentage of its gross national product (20 as compared with 12 in 1938), evidence of strenuous effort to revive by its own efforts; but its export deficit had increased from $2 billion in 1938 to $5 billion ten years later. This sum indicated inability to pay for vital imports. Of this deficit with the outside world in 1948, that with the United States accounted for 64 per cent, and Europe was able to cover only 15 per cent of it by exports to this country.

By 1947 the United States government recognized that free Europe was almost bankrupt and that some greater assistance than the makeshift efforts since the war was essential.

> Europe's dollar resources are running low [the claimants for American aid declared]. If the flow of goods from the American continent to Europe should cease, the results would be calamitous. . . . Life in Europe will become increasingly unstable and uncertain; industries will grind to a gradual halt for lack of materials and fuel, and the food supply of Europe will diminish and begin to disappear.

The decisive shock came from the speedy loss of confidence in the pound sterling. The British government conformed to the agreement with the United States by introducing in the summer of 1947 free convertibility of pounds into other currencies. In consequence, the many countries with holdings in the British currency immediately seized the opportunity to buy dollars. Within a few weeks Great Britain was threatened with the loss of all its gold and foreign exchange, and in order to stave off disaster had again to prohibit free convertibility.

Even though the free European nations possessed skills comparable to those of the United States and Canada, on the whole their economy during the interwar years had not progressed. It needed to be re-equipped and expanded. Since Europe, together with the United States, accounted for two thirds of the world's production, the restoration of its economy to a position of world leadership would assure powerful allies for freedom in the struggle against communism all over the globe. The amount of production per capita ($400) and of the gross capital formation (the high figure of 32 per cent, twice that of the United States) in the Soviet Union in 1948–1949 should have sufficed to arouse the American government and people to the danger of allowing Europe to continue to stagnate. At the time (1947) the United States was using at home all the goods and materials, except a few agricultural articles, that it could produce. That it went to the rescue of Europe and laid out a program of continuing aid stands unique in history. A victor country, the most powerful state in the world, sought, not the destruction or the subordination of supposed economic rivals, but the actual recovery of a free society everywhere; and it was willing to donate billions of dollars to achieve that objective. The program was formulated in a speech at Harvard University on June 5, 1947, by Secretary of State Marshall, chief of staff of the United States defense forces in the recent war. Such is the nature of modern democracy and modern industrialism that a general advocated the grant of aid to both Allies and ex-enemy peoples! The Clemenceau tradition of vengeance and repression by force was supplanted by a policy of cooperation.

In explaining the program Secretary Marshall said:

> Our policy is directed not against any country or doctrine but against hunger, poverty, desperation, and chaos. Its purpose should be the revival of a working economy in the world so as to permit the emergence of political and social conditions in which free institutions can exist.

He defined the part which the United States should play and the role which the European countries should assume:

> . . . there must be some agreement among the countries of Europe as to the requirements of the situation and the part those countries themselves will take in order to give proper effect to whatever action might be undertaken by this Government. . . . The role of this country should consist of friendly aid in the drafting of a European program and of later support of such a program so far as it may be practical for us to do so. The program should be a joint one, agreed to by a number of, if not all, European nations. . . . Any government [he declared] that is willing to assist in the task of recovery will find full cooperation, I am sure, on the part of the United States Government.

In a press interview Marshall specifically mentioned the Soviet Union as eligible for aid, provided she met the conditions.

The European governments immediately responded to the invitation. A general conference was set for Paris early in 1948, which was attended by the Soviet Union and its satellites, as well as by the countries of most of the rest of Europe. For a short time it looked as though Communist states would participate in the new venture, and the Polish and Czechoslovakian governments expressed warm approval of it. At Paris, however, Molotov suddenly denounced the Marshall plan as furthering the "deterioration in the situation of the working class," as capitalist imperialism, as an intrusion in the domestic affairs of sovereign European nations. The Communist leaders feared the economic recovery of Europe. They had encouraged after the war the formation of popular front governments in France and Italy, the two countries most vulnerable to communism, in the expectation of successful infiltration and domination. Once the Marshall plan was announced, they faced a dilemma: if they supported it, the nations would recover and reject communism; if they opposed it, the national Communist parties would lose supporters. Moscow decided that the latter way constituted the lesser evil. Communist resistance might keep the plan from succeeding and prevent the United States from becoming further involved in Europe, and Europe from becoming strong once more. The Communists were excluded from the governments in France and Italy; the party clung to purity of dogma.

E.C.A. and O.E.E.C.

The free governments soon created the necessary machinery for implementing the Marshall plan, and funds began to flow. On the American end the government first advanced emergency money to Italy, France, and Austria, the three states in most economic danger, and in 1948 Congress created the Economic Cooperation Administration (E.C.A.) for handling what was called the European Recovery Program (E.R.P.). In the same year the European states established the Organization of European Economic Cooperation (O.E.E.C.) as their counterpart for negotiating with the E.C.A. The European agency, in which each member was equally represented, drew up a plan of needs; and, since the United States contributed a fixed amount, the member states found it necessary to negotiate among themselves on priorities and indeed on the allocation of investment funds among themselves. In this way the United States sought to further one of its main objectives, the economic and political integration of Europe. After drafting the plan for the use of American funds for the year, the O.E.E.C. negotiated with the E.C.A., which approved or disapproved the proposals. American money was then put at the disposal of the governments, which used it for the specified purposes and sold the foreign articles to their own nationals. The funds, if we may use France as an example, acquired by the sale would be in francs; they would be held by the French government as the counterpart of dollars, hence the name "counterpart funds"; and their use by the French government was subject to American approval.

The United States and the O.E.E.C. members understood that Europe had to increase production or it would never recover from dependence on American financial aid. Once emergency needs were satisfied, the money went into investment. Although in proportion to the size of the budgets of the participating countries the amounts available were not great, they spelled the difference for most of the members between being able to invest and stagnating. "For every dollar of our aid to Europe," the American administrator of the E.R.P., Paul Hoffman, told Congress, "Europe puts six dollars into capital formation." In a few instances, especially in France, the counterpart funds helped to balance the budget and to fight inflation; in the main, they went for improving industrial equipment, creating new power resources, and the like.

Technological and Administrative Aid

Material aid was accompanied by American technical and administrative know-how. Business men, technicians, labor leaders, experts from all aspects of the economy and frequently of governmental administration came to this country to learn American methods, or Americans went abroad as advisers. Although any other could be used, the British experience will be discussed as an example. In 1948 Sir Stafford Cripps of the British Labor government and Paul Hoffman, head of E.C.A., created an Anglo-American Council on Productivity composed of representatives of management and labor in both countries. The Council strove to promote "economic well-being by a free exchange of knowledge in the realm of industrial organization, method, and technique, and thereby to assist British industry to raise the level of its productivity." The Council sent teams of about sixteen members each and composed of an equal number of persons from technical, supervisory, and workshop levels. These examined industries as varied as cotton spinning, pressed metal, packaging, freight handling, Diesel locomotive, and engineering. The experience revealed to the British that the best of their industries equaled the best in the United States, but that the country lagged in general behind the United States in productivity. Among the explanations which the various British teams gave, and they all agreed on fundamental points, were the following:

The Education for Management Team wrote:

> Practically every Productivity Team which has visited the U.S. is agreed that productivity per man-year is higher than in Britain. They attribute this mainly to two factors. First, there is a climate of opinion which regards maximum effort by *every* individual as the primary guarantee not only of material standards but of the way of life of a free society. Second, there is a quality in management, inspired by this climate of opinion, and stimulated by the American system of higher education in general and, in particular, by that part of it which is devoted to administrative studies. American business employs graduates because it believes that higher education helps business. Strict adherence to promotion by merit avoids the danger that graduates will become a privileged class. . . . American experience has shown that productivity and education for management are closely related.

The Cotton Spinning Team wrote that the high productivity came from "the realization that the high standard of living apparent on every hand in America and eventual security of employment depend on producing more at a lower cost rather than less at a higher cost." Labor as well as management was found to be "productivity conscious" and to accept technological improvements and other means to increase production and lower costs.

Operation Overlord. American assault troops join Allied forces in penetrating the Continent from the beachhead at Normandy, June 6, 1944. —U.S. Army photo.

Destruction: members of an American infantry unit work at removing debris from the streets of St. Sauveur, France, June 9, 1944. –U.S. Army photo.

PLANS FOR PEACE:
(top picture) The Yalta Conference, February, 1945. Seated left to right are Prime Minister Churchill, President Roosevelt, and Premier Stalin. –Underwood & Underwood photo.

(bottom picture) The Potsdam Conference, August, 1945. Seated left to right are Prime Minister Clement Attlee (who succeeded Churchill at the end of the conference), President Truman, and Premier Stalin. –Brown Bros. photo.

THE EUROPEAN RECOVERY PROGRAM IN ACTION:

(top picture) A postwar housing development is provided for workers in Valdagno, Italy. Rents are low, and tenants can eventually own their own units. —Wide World Photos.

(bottom picture) An electric power station in the heart of the Pas de Calais mining area of France is shown in its final stages of construction. —Wide World Photos.

The need for change: families in Transjordan encamped, for the protection of their flocks, throughout the valleys of the Moab mountains during the winter grazing months. —Wide World Photos.

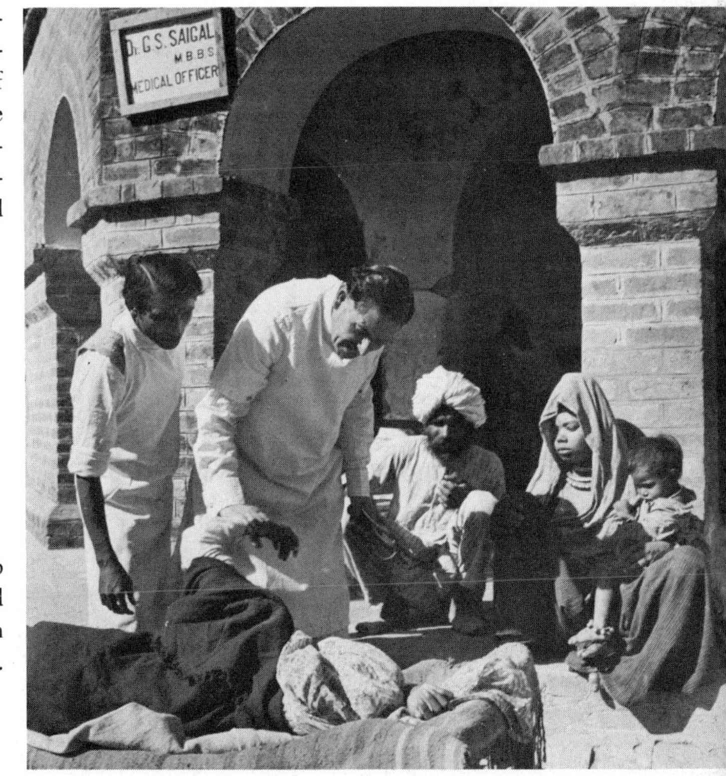

Fight against malaria: two UN agencies, WHO and UNICEF, combine strength in India to combat disease. —United Nations photo.

The means for cooperation: the Japanese delegation to the United Nations is shown in discussion prior to a meeting of the General Assembly, September, 1957. —United Nations photo.

The United Nations Emergency Force, designed to stop fighting in the Middle East, on patrol in Port Said, December, 1956. —United Nations photo.

November, 1956: the Hungarian nation failed in a rebellion against Soviet domination, and thousands of its people fled for their lives by any open route. Photo shows refugees crossing the canal which forms the border between Hungary and Austria. —Wide World Photos.

March, 1957: the Duchess of Kent reads a message from Queen Elizabeth which welcomes Ghana as an independent state into the Commonwealth of Nations. —Wide World Photos.

In architecture the emergence of a modern style is advanced by technological development. The structure shown is Le Corbusier's Savoye House, Poissey-sur-Seine, 1929–1930. –Photo by Lucien Hervé.

The Welding Team expressed a view unanimously held:

In the U.S., cartels, monopolies, and price rings, after due trial, were outlawed, so that real and sharp competition developed between firms, and this, to a large extent, prevented any major rises in prices. The unions obtained a high wage level. Since selling prices could not be raised, the manufacturers' only recourse was to organize their factories to the highest possible degree of efficiency.

The teams marked how willing the Americans were to make technical information available to anyone interested, including competitors, and argued that everyone benefited therefrom. As one company manager said, the practice kept one's own staff alert.

During the life of E.R.P., from 1948 to July, 1950, the United States contributed $12 billion to the members of O.E.E.C., a large sum in international financial transactions, a small sum in comparison with the size of the budgets of the countries involved. The American hope for European union failed to be realized. The O.E.E.C. set up expert committees on key commodities like iron, steel, and oil, to rationalize investment on a European basis, and the advice of these experts had some influence. On the whole the pattern of investment remained national, in part because of the inordinate difficulty of changing a mature industrial structure. Within the national framework the rate of investment of national savings was more rapid than that of the decline of foreign aid. Europe's real per capita gross investment, measured at constant prices, rose by more than 10 per cent above that of 1938, and the increase in net investment probably reached 40 per cent—a remarkable achievement.

Effects of E.R.P.

The effects of E.R.P. upon production and trade were proportionately impressive.

After World War I it took seven years to regain the prewar level of production in Western Europe. At the end of 1951 industrial production was 41 percent above prewar, 64 percent above 1947, and well beyond the target originally set for 1952. Agricultural production was 9 percent above prewar and 24 percent above 1947. Gross national product—the sum total of Western Europe's production of goods and services—had risen 25 percent in real terms in less than four years and was 15 percent above prewar. The transportation system had been rehabilitated. Electrical output had doubled over prewar. Steel production has doubled since 1947 (and is one-fifth above prewar), giving a total production last year of 60,000,000 tons as compared with 35,000,000 produced by Russia and her satellites. Refined petroleum products have quadrupled over prewar.[1]

Coal production still fell behind prewar achievement, and the cost of coal imported from the United States remained the largest drain on Europe's dollar supply.

[1] John H. Williams, "The End of the Marshall Plan," *Foreign Affairs*, July, 1952, p. 594.

Depending on the country, per capita consumption also showed little or no improvement over the prewar condition. The people, particularly by way of heavy taxation, were saving funds for investment. The flow of trade, both among the members of O.E.E.C. and with the rest of the world, greatly increased, and the member states removed the quantitative controls on imports from between 50 and 90 per cent of their products. The amount of removal depended on the country, with France and Austria showing least. The revival of multilateral trade among the members was assisted by the creation in 1950 of a European Payments Union (E.P.U.), which functioned like a bank clearinghouse. Since some member countries would have deficits and some credits with the Union, the United States supplied a reserve of dollars which could be used to balance accounts. The board of the E.P.U., on which each O.E.E.C. member and representatives of a few other states sat, took one further step by a frank annual criticism of the economic policies of the participating states. Thus Europeans slowly began to consider the impact of national policies upon the entire continent.

The American funds achieved one of their main purposes in stopping the growth of communism in Western Europe, especially in the states of gravest danger, France and Italy. They likewise enabled the Europeans to increase imports and exports. But the recipients still were unable to balance their payments, particularly with the United States. They lacked time in which to adjust their economic structure to that of the world. When in 1949 Great Britain once more faced grave trade and financial difficulties, the Labor government, much against its will, devalued the currency. Other countries followed suit, and trade at once revived. More influential for the economic future was the shock which the Western world received from the political and military aggression of communism.

COMMUNIST AGGRESSION IN EUROPE AND ASIA

The Communist advance may have been a riposte to the European Recovery Program; it may have occurred at this time from pure opportunism. In 1948 the Communists staged a coup d'état in Czechoslovakia, eradicating the vestiges of free government and society and introducing a dictatorship. In the next year the Chinese Reds gained control of China and drove the Nationalist remnant under Chiang Kai-shek to the island of Formosa. In the same year the Soviet Union tried, by blocking all ground transportation between Berlin and the West German Republic, to prevent the formation of the West German Republic, to force the three Western powers out of Berlin, and to starve the natives in the three free sectors of the city into submission to communism. In 1950 the Communist government in North Korea invaded the free southern half of Korea, from which United States troops had recently withdrawn. It used Soviet Union supplies and military advisers in doing so and a short time later received active assistance in the war from the Chinese Red government. Communists were likewise leading civil wars, begun during World War II, in various states in Southeast Asia; in Western Europe, they were staging strikes against Marshall aid wherever they were able, especially in France and Italy. Moscow seemed intent upon aggression.

The free world replied by measures to restrain the Communists effectively but with minimum outlay. Some action had to be military and defensive; other measures laid the constructive basis for economic, social, and political betterment, so that the people would reject communism of their own accord. Certain steps were taken by the United Nations; others came about bilaterally, and still others by regional agreement. In Czechoslovakia the free world found no means to resist. This case was appealed to the Security Council, where the Soviet Union vetoed consideration of it, declaring that the change concerned Czechoslovakia alone. The Red blockade of Berlin was overcome. The entire episode need never have occurred if the United States War Department had followed the urgent warning of the State Department against trusting the Communists at the time of the first negotiations over Berlin. The army had not insisted upon naming specific road and railroad connections through the Soviet zone. It had believed that the Soviet Union would allow ingress and egress as a self-evident right. The three Western powers met the difficulty by flying supplies into Berlin for a year. They kept the Germans and their own personnel in the free sectors of the city alive and hopeful. When the Russians withdrew the blockade in the spring of 1950, planes were transporting 13,000 tons of food, fuel, and other supplies a day, 60 per cent more than had formerly been hauled by land and water and three times as much as the essential minimum. The action was a severe defeat for the Communists. It demonstrated the power and resources of the West, and it provided free Berliners with more food and better food than the Germans in the Soviet zone received.

Korean War

The Korean war entered into European history primarily by bringing the United Nations into action to stop aggression. The Ethiopian invasion by Italy in the middle thirties had tested the effectiveness of the League of Nations; Korea now presented the United Nations with a similar crisis. The two occupying powers in Korea, the Soviet Union and the United States, had in the closing weeks of World War II tentatively fixed the dividing line of their zones at 38° north latitude. The Soviet Union introduced a Communist regime in her zone; the Americans tolerated an authoritarian government under President Syngman Rhee which retained private property and strove to develop a free society. Neither power would agree to unite Korea for fear that the government in the other's zone would obtain control. In 1947 the United States appealed the case to the United Nations, which appointed a commission to go to Korea to arrange for a free election. The Soviet Union boycotted the action, thus stalling the commission in Korea.

When in June, 1950, the North Korean Communists began a large-scale attack on South Korea, the United Nations commission, being on hand, confirmed the fact of aggression and recommended mediation. Urged by the United States, the Security Council immediately took up the question; and, since the Soviet Union was temporarily absent from the sessions in protest against the refusal of the other members to replace Nationalist China as a member by Communist China, the Security Council was able to pass resolutions recommending member states to aid in resisting the attack and creating a United Nations Unified Command under the direction of the United States. About forty nations offered to assist in the application of sanctions. By February, 1951, the United States had put in 250,000 troops; thirteen other nations, 26,000; and still other nations furnished supplies and services. The rest of the troops were South Koreans. Almost immediately after the Security Council had initiated resistance, the Soviet Union returned to the Council to block any further action. The initiative then passed to the General Assembly.

As the United Nations force gained in strength and drove back the North Koreans, the question arose whether to continue fighting north of 38° latitude. When with the acquiescence of the majority of the General Assembly the United Nations forces took this action, in November, 1950, the Chinese Communists, concerned for the security of their main industrial area, that of Manchuria, entered the war. At the proposal of the United States, the General Assembly on November 3, 1950, resolved by a vote of fifty-two to five that

> . . . if the Security Council, because of lack of unanimity of the permanent members, fails to exercise its primary responsibility for the maintenance of international peace and security in any case where there appears to be a threat to the peace, breach of the peace, or act of aggression, the General Assembly shall consider the matter immediately with a view to making appropriate recommendations to Members for collective measures, including in the case of a breach of the peace or act of aggression the use of armed force when necessary, to maintain or restore international peace and security.

It established a Peace Observation Commission of fourteen members

> which could observe and report on the situation in any area where there exists international tension the continuance of which is likely to endanger the maintenance of international peace and security.

The assistance of member states in supporting recommendations of the Security Council or the General Assembly was made voluntary, but the Uniting for Peace Resolution, as it was called, recommended that each member keep armed forces immediately available for implementing the recommendations of the Security Council or the General Assembly.

The General Assembly has no power of compulsion such as the Council legally enjoys under the Charter. The Resolution did not advance beyond the voluntary system established under the League. The difference between action now and that under the League lay in the climate of opinion. After World War II the majority of nations was willing to participate in stopping aggression. The General Assembly still depended mainly on negotiation and the pressure of world opinion to achieve its purpose; where fighting was necessary it could accomplish little or nothing without the active participation of one or more major powers. The Korean emergency met all these conditions. The General Assembly formally condemned Red China as an aggressor; it encouraged the member states to participate in the United Nations Force engaged in Korea; it placed military direction in the hands of the United States; and it either collectively or by way of individual members, especially India, negotiated between the fighting parties. Its efforts brought a truce in 1953, by which the 38th parallel remained roughly the dividing line between Communist and free Korea. The aggressors had failed of their objective. The United Nations as the successful defender of the victim of attack emerged with heightened prestige.

Aid to Underdeveloped Countries

The Korean crisis revealed the growing importance of two aspects of postwar international relations—the role of the underdeveloped areas of the world and the intimate relation between defense and economics. The E.R.P. had been intended for Europe and had assisted other parts of the world only insofar as they were associated with European countries as colonies or as members of a commonwealth. The United Nations through the Economic and Social Council and the affiliated agencies had initiated a modest program of technical assistance to the underdeveloped members, and each country, depending on its ability, had initiated a similar one. In 1949 the United States government announced its ambitious Point Four Plan. "Fourth," President Truman declared in a speech proposing the program, "we must embark on a bold new program for making the benefits of our scientific advances and industrial progress available for the improvement and growth of underdeveloped areas." By these efforts the Western countries, in cooperation with the United Nations, sought to prevent further losses to communism.

The relationship between the advanced and the underdeveloped countries became more complicated by the Korean crisis. The sudden need for armaments accentuated the demand for food and raw materials and sent up prices. The European states found themselves seriously crippled in their competitive position with respect to the United States, and confronted rising deficits in their balance of international payments. The sharp increase in rearmaments forced upon them by Communist aggression in Korea and elsewhere in Asia added inflation to their other financial troubles. Europe was unable to turn out sufficient consumers' goods to satisfy demand at a time when armaments expansion augmented the amount of money available for spending. The United States once more accepted the responsibility for aid, and this time it extended its program to other continents. In 1952 the government set up the Mutual Security Administration as the successor to the E.R.P., and gave it a budget of more than $9 billion for the first year. Its purpose, assistance in carrying the burden of rearmament as well as in promoting economic revival, expressed the accentuation of the cold war that the Korean crisis had initiated. The complications arising from the necessity for Europe, scarcely recovered from one war, to rearm can best be explained in connection with the story of regional organizations—the North Atlantic Treaty Organization, the Coal and Steel Community, the Western European Union.

FORMATION OF NATO

NATO was created in 1949 because of lack of confidence on the part of the Atlantic states that the United Nations could protect them against Soviet imperialism. The list of members shows that the phrase "North Atlantic" was capable of expansion. The United States and Canada belonged, as did Great Britain, France, Belgium, the Netherlands, Luxembourg, Portugal, Denmark, Norway, and Iceland; but Italy likewise became a founding member, and in 1952 Greece and Turkey were admitted. The new treaty reaffirmed the faith of the participants "in the purposes and principles of the Charter . . . and their desire to live in peace with all peoples and all governments" (Preamble).

The parties agreed in Article 5 that "an armed attack against one or more of them in Europe or North America shall be considered an attack against them all" and that "if such an armed attack occurs, each of them, in exercise of the right of individual or collective self-defense recognized by Article 51 of the Charter of the United Nations, will assist the Party or Parties so attacked by taking forthwith, individually and in concert with the other Parties, such action as it deems necessary, including the use of armed force, to restore and maintain the security of the North Atlantic area." The parties to NATO agreed to provide "separately and jointly," "continuous and effective self-help and mutual aid," and to "maintain and develop their individual and collective capacity to resist armed attack" (Article 3). They likewise agreed to "consult together whenever, in the opinion of any of them, the territorial integrity, political independence or security of any of the Parties is threatened" (Article 4), a function that the United Nations had been intended to perform.

To implement these clauses the treaty established a council on which each member should be represented. It should "be able to meet promptly at any time," and should "set up such subsidiary bodies as may be necessary; in particular . . . a defense committee which shall recommend measures for the implementation of Articles 3 and 5" (Article 9).

NATO has been described as an organization attempting to meet federal responsibilities by means of a Continental Congress. A United States representative to its council has written that

> except for the command functions vested in the military, no individual or agency of N.A.T.O. up to the Council itself has any delegated power of authority. N.A.T.O. is therefore not an administrative organ except in a very limited sense. It is rather a mechanism for formulating combined international plans; for obtaining agreement among the Treaty partners in support of these plans; and so far to only a limited extent for stimulating national action to carry out the agreed plans. . . . These have developed more in response to the pressure of events than according to plan or blueprint.[2]

That is to say, the initiative in strengthening NATO has lain with the Soviet Union: the more this power has tried to spread its influence and to weaken the Western states, the tighter NATO has grown.

> Unlike more conventional alliances [the *Economist* wrote early in 1955] Nato's strength no longer rests on the kind of national decisions that can be easily reversed under strong domestic pressures or after changes of government. Today, the eggs of the member countries are not merely all in the same basket; they are in the same omelette. For any member now to break away would be a formidable task of disentanglement, and extremely costly for it in terms of alternative defence arrangements, unless it chose to run the risks of lonely neutrality.[3]

The structure of NATO has expanded to enable the Council to carry out responsibilities. That Council is composed of the ministers of foreign affairs, defense, and finance of each of the member states. These policy makers meet regularly two or three times a year. Their deputies remain in permanent session in Paris and are served by a permanent secretariat and by various planning boards of experts—on ocean shipping, European surface transportation, and oil—and by a military committee. Under the last-named, three regional commands have been established, one for the Mediterranean, one for the North Atlantic, and, the most important, one for Europe. The last-named, known as SHAPE (Supreme Headquarters Allied Powers Europe) has headquarters in Paris; General Eisenhower served as it first commander. The organization recognized at once the necessity for integrating the land, air, and naval forces of the members into a defensive power under unified command. It set to work to achieve the hitherto impossible, to create a whole out of fourteen parts that were divided by language, customs, and traditions and by economic, social, and political particularities, and that were accustomed to competing among themselves, in arms, in business—in almost every way. It required a person

[2] Charles M. Spofford, "N.A.T.O.'s Growing Pains," *Foreign Affairs,* October, 1952, p. 96.

[3] *The Economist* (London), February 5, 1955, p. 437.

of General Eisenhower's prestige and faith in team work to give this motley crew momentum.

Within two years NATO built up Atlantic defenses to the point at which a Soviet attack would be exceedingly costly, and its strength has grown. By the beginning of 1953 NATO had at its disposal about sixty divisions and more than 5,000 tactical airplanes. Two years later NATO conducted combined maneuvers and began to train reserves. SHAPE was directly responsible for maintaining and training certain forces, and it developed a "common infrastructure"—operational airfields (165 by the end of 1955), thousands of miles of communication (roads, railroads, telephone, and telegraph), port facilities, 3,800 miles of common pipelines for fuel, stockpiles of ammunition, fuel, food, weapons and supplies of all sorts, barracks and depots, and a fully developed system of radar stations. Almost a billion dollars was allocated for a three-year period of expansion of these basic facilities. These "infrastructures" were built under NATO's direction on contracts by any firm in any of the NATO countries submitting the most acceptable bid. "Today," the *Economist* wrote, "a pilot of one country may fly a plane built by a second country, financed by a third, using as his base an airfield constructed on the territory of a fourth by a firm from a fifth, drawing his fuel from a Nato pipeline." [4]

NATO has suffered from political differences among its members and from the problem of economic resources to support the enormous defense budget it entails. Britain removed to Cyprus, Egypt, and elsewhere, and France to North Africa, troops marked for the protection of Europe, in an attempt to maintain some of their colonial areas. Since the United States possesses two thirds of NATO's total resources, it has covered a large proportion of the cost. Article 2 of the treaty called for the encouragement of "economic collaboration between any or all" of the members, and circumstances have led to a much greater degree of cooperation than might have been expected.

More unprecedented than the common military planning and in many respects more far reaching has been the annual review of NATO by its Council. This review is

> a year-long process by which the fourteen governments first assess the nature of the external threat; then, on purely military grounds, agree on what is required in terms of forces and equipment; then analyze together how these requirements can best be met, or how far they must be scaled down owing to other economic and political pressures on national budgets; and calculate the contribution of each country in terms of men, money and material. Although only the "force goals" become the subject of binding Council decisions, from the time a pound, franc or guilder is first tentatively budgeted for the defense of the NATO area, it becomes the concern not of one country but of fourteen. By the time an annual review is completed and the Council is setting the goals for the next year, inefficiencies and

[4] *Ibid.*

inadequacies in national planning, production and training, if not cured, have at least been thoroughly exposed.[5]

How, the Danish minister of finance asked, could the United States expect Denmark to shoulder a large defense burden when the American market was barred to one of Denmark's best dollar-earning exports, blue cheese? Under the burden of NATO European leaders cried "Trade not Aid," and many, including Americans, stated that military cooperation must be supplemented by common organs of economic and political collaboration.

The decision in 1954 to arm NATO forces with atomic weapons enhanced the interdependence of members and posed new problems. The United States could afford atomic weapons. What about Greece or Norway; in fact, what about Britain? Atomic arms gave the American colossus such superiority that it had to counteract the suspicion of other nations. Any independent action on its part was feared or might be feared as a move to dominate. Experts in every member country argued the question whether atomic weapons rendered obsolete the existing type of army in favor of a small technical force. Many government officials asserted that, as their countries could contribute little to defense by atomic weapons, present defense budgets should be vigorously cut. A great deal of the military man power, they said, should be returned to the economy, where it was urgently needed. The best method of combating communism, they declared, lay in raising the standard of living and helping underdeveloped peoples. Although NATO was solidly built into the life of member states, it could be no stronger than the will of each participant to cooperate. It had either to draw the members more and more closely together or to risk ineffectiveness.

The geographic area covered by NATO extended from the North Cape to the Black Sea. The inclusion of Turkey and Greece, although at first opposed by some North European states as an overexpansion of responsibility, was particularly urged by the United States. It placed Western striking power closer to the Soviet oil fields at Baku than the Nazi forces had ever been. When in 1953 Yugoslavia indirectly affiliated with NATO by allying with Greece and Turkey for common defense and in the next year settled her quarrel with Italy over Trieste, the West potentially had access in wartime to the inner Balkan and Danubian areas. The United States negotiated an agreement for the construction and use of air bases in Spain, and these bases added to those built across North Africa during and since World War II assured defensive power in depth. The Soviet Union occupies a central position, from which she can strike at a point of her choosing, but she and her satellites must defend a long frontier. NATO has acquired the advantage formerly possessed by Great Britain of being able to counter from one or more of many bases without the enemy's knowing which will be used. The great gap in the recovery of Western defensive

[5] *Ibid.*

strength lay in the disarmament of Germany, and at the insistence of the United States this problem was soon attacked.

REORGANIZATION OF EUROPE

The question of how to preserve peace affected the European states not merely as members of the United Nations or of the NATO community but as those of a region. In working out a plan for bringing the West German Republic into NATO and reviving German military strength to help offset the Soviet bloc, the West endeavored to prevent Germany from aggression and, at the same time, to preserve Europe's independence of action in a world dominated by competition between the United States and the U.S.S.R. In 1948 France, Britain, Belgium, Luxembourg, and the Netherlands signed the Brussels Pact, a fifty-year alliance. Since the alliance did not seem adequate to new needs, two further lines of advance were proposed. One called for federating free Europe, including Germany, under a supranational government. Although the ideal appeared unrealizable, leaders from free states organized in 1949 a Council of Europe, with headquarters at Strasbourg, where each year they could debate questions of European unity, though without power of decision. The urgency to break down Franco-German hostility led European states to consider restrictions upon national sovereignty. The five free states that had suffered intensely from German aggression and that lay in a compact group—the Netherlands, Belgium, Luxembourg, France, and Italy—employed a functional approach. They created with the West German Republic a defense union and a coal and steel community, and followed with agreements for a customs union and an atomic energy community along the same lines.

Western European Union

In October, 1950, French Prime Minister Pleven proposed the formation of a European army, and the French parliament immediately approved the idea. The plan envisaged a European Assembly, to which a European Minister of Defense would be responsible. The minister was to execute the directives of a Council of Ministers from the participating countries. The Assembly would vote a common budget, and the army would be a common force composed of battalions or brigades of national troops. The participating countries which already had armies were to retain control of troops not incorporated in the new European army and in time of need could ask permission to release forces for a particular national use. In acknowledging the necessity to gain the defensive assistance of Germany against the Soviet Union, the French sought one main objective, to subject their hereditary enemy to the control of European organization.

A defense treaty was actually drawn up and signed in 1952 by six states, France, Italy, Germany, and the members of Benelux; but successive French governments dared not submit it to parliament for fear of rejection. When Premier Pierre Mendès-France finally did so in the summer of 1954, the Chamber of Deputies voted against ratification by a large majority. Fear of Germany aligned many deputies with the hundred Communists in the chamber, who followed Moscow's line of bitter hostility, and with other deputies, for whom the treaty did not advance far enough toward European union. Mendès-France immediately proposed a different set of conditions for rearming Germany, and a conference of the six most interested states and Great Britain and the United States in September, 1954, negotiated a new treaty, which was accepted and executed.

French approval of Western European Union (W.E.U.), as the new plan was called, was made possible by two major concessions, one by Great Britain, the other by the West German Republic. The British government agreed to maintain on the continent its present military force of four divisions and the Tactical Air Force for the rest of the century. The commitment contradicted Britain's policy of undertaking nothing of this kind in which the United States did not participate. The German government submitted to inequalities in the matter of rearming. It promised not to manufacture atomic, bacteriological, and chemical weapons; it acquiesced in restrictions on its output of heavy armaments; and it accepted an upper limit of twelve divisions on the size of its army.

The W.E.U. created an agency for the inspection and control of armaments production on the part of all its members except Great Britain, and named an Italian vice-admiral as its first director. The West German Republic became a sovereign power freed from Allied control and a member of NATO. Most important of all was W.E.U.'s connection with NATO.

> It [W.E.U.] has no separate command structure. The procedure for changing the limits on forces is inseparable from the process by which Nato decides on force goals. Inspection of troops, or armaments under the direct command of Shape, is a task for Shape, not for the W.E.U. agency, and all German troops are to be under direct Shape control. The effective safeguard against any irredentist ventures on the part of a rearmed Germany is not the W.E.U. agency but the logistic powers now given to Shape, the power to stop the flow of jet fuel through the Nato pipelines, and to cut off ammunition and other supplies.[6]

In the preamble of the treaty the members resolved "to promote the unity and to encourage the progressive integration of Europe," and the treaty looked toward both closer cultural relations and cooperation in the distribution of responsibility for the manufacture of armaments. France and Germany have for the first time in history (how often is the phrase employed in this book!) joined in a common defensive agency; NATO was strengthened, not merely by the settlement of Franco-German hostility and the addition of German military power, but by the gain in geographic

[6] *Ibid.*, May 14, 1955, p. 548.

depth for employing its forces in resisting future Soviet attack; the West German Republic renounced the policy of the 1920's of playing a nationalistic game between East and West and aligned her fortunes with the free states against the Soviet Union. The imponderables of this treaty outweigh by far the anticipated addition of a mere twelve divisions to NATO's military force. Within a decade Soviet foreign policy achieved what the Communists most feared, the union of the Western states, ex-enemy and ally, into a military alliance to make sure that the United Nations preserved the peace.

The French government accepted the Western European Union subject to agreement over the Saar. This little area bears importance not merely from its material wealth but from its ability to embitter Franco-German relations. The negotiations over its disposal reveal the reluctance, especially of the French, to arrive at mutual trust. By nationality and historical tradition the population of the Saar is German. France had in 1919 acquired control of the economy and persuaded the Allies to internationalize the Saar government. In 1935 the Saarlanders had voted by plebiscite to return to Germany. After World War II France once more controlled its economy, incorporated the area into the French customs union and monetary system, and in practice determined its foreign relations. French industry needed the rich coal resources to reduce dependence upon the Ruhr. With Saar coal and steel works, France possessed 32 per cent of the resources of the Coal and Steel Community (see page 659) and Germany 45 per cent; without them French percentage would drop to 24 and the German rise to 53. France obtained one third of her coal imports and one sixth of her coke imports from the Saar, she sold agricultural products to it, and derived foreign exchange from Saar sales abroad.

The Saar steel works obtained 90 to 100 per cent of their iron ore from Lorraine. On its side, Germany did not absolutely need Saar coal. The territory appeared suited to international organization of the coal and iron and steel resources of Northeastern France, Belgium, Luxembourg, and West Germany; but in October, 1955, the Saarlanders voted by a large majority to return to Germany. France saw from the vote that she could not hope to retain the Saar or to internationalize it, and by the end of 1956, France and Germany reached agreement.

The Saar was to become an eleventh state in the West German Republic but would remain a part of the French economic system for three more years, and it or the rest of Germany was to provide France with 90 million tons of coal by the end of 1980. Germany agreed to the canalization of the Moselle river from Thionville to Coblenz, although the provision was contested by German economic interests from fear of the stimulating effect upon French competition. The French and German governments settled these and other details in a spirit of European cooperation. The Saar issue shrank in significance as the political leaders sought to unify free Europe.

Coal and Steel Community

A proposal for a European coal and steel community paralleled that for defense. The Frenchman Jean Monnet, experienced both as businessman and as high governmental official, in 1950 persuaded the French Minister Robert Schuman to advance the idea, and the governments of the Benelux countries, West Germany, and Italy accepted. A constitution drafted and approved by the six member states came into force in August, 1952. The Coal and Steel Community (C.S.C.) serves a political as well as an economic purpose, to make the countries interdependent, to accustom them to working together, to pave the way for federation. Various proposals for customs union among the European states made since the war had either failed completely, or, as evidenced in the one for Benelux, had shown at most a modest success. The C.S.C. aimed at a functional approach to European unity. It was believed that once the economic interests of the states became intertwined, common social and cultural interests might follow, and all of these would press for a political framework for the new community. The C.S.C., with NATO, came to be justly regarded as the most original and constructive of the postwar regional organizations. Its constitution, more novel than that of NATO, deserves analysis as the first successful attempt to establish a government over states by agreement rather than by war.

The federal-type constitution of the C.S.C., like that of the United States, defines the powers vested in the central body and leaves the remaining power to member states. A court passes on the constitutionality of the acts of the central authority; it has judged a considerable number of cases. The equivalent of legislation, called decisions or recommendations, passed by the C.S.C. is administered by officials of the member states and enforced by state courts. In this way a body of community law is gradually emerging. The executive power of the community is vested in a nine-man board, eight members of which are chosen from the citizens of the six states by the governments, the ninth by the other members. Members serve for six years and are selected on the basis of their "general competence" (Article 9) and not more than two from any one state. The executive board, called the High Authority, elects its own president and vice-president from among its members.

The High Authority is responsible to two representative bodies, somewhat as an American cabinet, somewhat as a British one. The first, called the Assembly, is composed of delegates selected once a year for an annual session by the parliaments of the several states from among their own members. The great difference in size of population and in wealth of the states is expressed in the number of delegates each is allowed. Germany, France, and Italy have eighteen each; Belgium and the Netherlands, ten each; and Luxembourg, four. The High Authority must report on its work to the Assembly, which has full power of interrogation, discussion and criticism. By a two-thirds vote it may overturn the High Authority and force the selection of a new board, a power similar to that in England of the House of Commons over the cabinet but more difficult to exercise because of the requirement of more than a simple majority vote. The other body, called the Council, consists of one member from the government of each state. It may meet on the request of a state or of the High Authority; it sets the salaries, allowances, and pensions of the personnel of the C.S.C.; and it serves to harmonize "the action of the High Authority and that of the governments" (Article 26). Another body, the Consultative Committee, attached to the High Authority, includes from 30 to 51 "producers, workers and consumers and dealers in equal numbers" (Article 18) appointed by the Council. The latter selects the producers and workers from "representative organizations" (Article 18). On some issues the High Authority is required to consult this Committee; on many others it may do so.

The constitution thus provides for participation in various capacities of the people of each state through their representatives (the Assembly), the governments (the Council), and the producers, workers, consumers, and dealers in the products; it assures the legality of the action by means of the Court; and it entrusts executive power to a board, the High Authority. Since this is an organization of economic governance requiring special competence, the High Authority is given a wide range of responsibility somewhat comparable to that of a governmental cabinet but also similar to that of an executive board of a corporation. It possesses authority directly over the coal and steel industries in each state, but it must work harmoniously with the government of each member.

The statement of responsibility of the C.S.C. may be considered a model of enlightenment and fairness. The organization is to "contribute to economic expansion, the development of employment and the improvement of the standard of living in the participating countries through the institution, in harmony with the general economy of the member States, of a common market" (Article 2). It is instructed to

> (a) see that the common market is regularly supplied, taking account of the needs of third countries; (b) assure to all consumers in comparable positions within the common market equal access to the sources of production; (c) seek the establishment of the lowest prices which are possible . . . ; (d) see that conditions are maintained which will encourage enterprises to expand and improve their ability to produce and to promote a policy of rational development of natural resources . . . ; (e) promote the improvement of the living and working conditions of the labor force in each of the industries under its jurisdiction so as to make possible the equalization of such conditions in an upward direction; (f) further the development of international trade and see that equitable limits are observed in prices charged on external markets; (g) promote the regular expansion and modernization of production as well as the improvement of its quality [Article 3].

The achievement of these objectives would bring about great improvement both in the economy and in the standard of living. It could transform Europe's economy and social relations.

The C.S.C. proposes to reach its goal by a program of prohibitions and by one of constructive action. It abolished and prohibited the following within the community:

> (a) import and export duties, or charges with an equivalent effect, and quantitative restrictions on the movement of coal and steel; (b) measures or practices discriminating among producers, among buyers or among consumers . . . ; (c) subsidies or state assistance, or special charges imposed by the state, in any form whatsoever; (d) restrictive practices tending towards the division of markets or the exploitation of the consumer [Article 4].

Thereby the C.S.C. establishes a free market for its products, and outlaws cartels and other instruments for restraint upon free competition. Its positive responsibility equals the negative in significance. It is instructed to

> enlighten and facilitate the action of the interested parties by collecting information, organizing consultations and defining general objectives; place financial means at the disposal of enterprises for their investments and participate in the expenses of re-adaptation; assure the establishment, the maintenance and the observance of normal conditions of competition and take direct action with respect to production and the operation of the market only when circumstances make it absolutely necessary; publish the justifications for its action and take the necessary measures to ensure observance of the rules set forth in the present Treaty: . . . [Article 5].

Its influence lies in the performance of services, informational and advisory, in its power to borrow money and assist businesses in their investments, and in providing the public with information by which to judge whether the C.S.C. is acting with wisdom and fairness. These are standard sources of prestige and authority with any government. If a business in any member country violates the constitution, it becomes subject to a fine; if a country defies the C.S.C. it may be expelled and subjected to economic boycott and discrimination. Needless to say, if conditions should reach the stage at which such drastic action would be necessary, the Community's existence would be gravely endangered. Essential for success are expansion of production, lowering of costs, and improvement of wages and standard of living.

Achievements of C.S.C.

The C.S.C. has been directed in accordance with both idealism and common sense. It has shown skeptics that a supragovernmental organization can drive toward the achievement of its goals. Progress has been slow on some crucial issues, but the High Authority has maintained its power with firmness and tact and has shown in practice the need for further integration of European countries. The simplest task consisted of abolishing tariffs, quotas, and currency restrictions and creating a common market among the six participants. In four years' time intracommunity trade in steel more than doubled, and that in coal increased 26 per cent. Steel prices have remained stable in a period of erratic demand, and coal productivity has gradually improved. High-cost steel producers in Italy and high-cost coal mines in Belgium have been subsidized by the community out of funds collected from the other businesses in order to improve efficiency and lower costs; if or when they fail, they may be closed down for good, as has been done in Belgium.

The High Authority contracted a loan of $100 million from the United States government, which it used partly to build houses for workers and partly for investment in more efficient production. It sought to overcome one of the greatest postwar handicaps to the mobility of labor, the lack of housing. The quality of its housing development set a standard for private enterprise to follow. According to the C.S.C. constitution, labor receives the right to move freely anywhere within the community. It has done so only to a small extent because of complications arising out of the existence of six systems of social security and similar matters. The High Authority's concern about housing offers, as in so many other lines, a harbinger of the solution of all these problems.

The most difficult issue met has been that of introducing a competitive economy in coal and steel. The Europeans have accustomed themselves over decades to fixing prices by national and international cartels. Behind this protection, less in Germany than elsewhere, they have kept alive high-cost producers at the expense of the general standard of living. They have preferred low productivity at high cost in an assured noncompetitive market to high productivity at low cost in a competitive market. The constitution of C.S.C. specifically prohibits any such price fixing or market allocation except with the approval of the High Authority as a special or an emergency matter. The articles were easier to write than to enforce.

Two examples of procedure may be offered. When steel consumers complained of high prices, the High Authority employed five Dutch firms of chartered accountants to examine the books of the Community's steel firms. The latter protested against this supranational policing, but they acquiesced and began obeying the rules on making the prices which they officially published agree with those which they actually asked. The second one concerns the existence of coal cartels. The French, the Belgians, and the Germans each had for coal a powerful sales cartel, which the public, including the trade-unions, supported. The High Authority attacked the issue cautiously. It set a maximum price on coal, forcing the Ruhr syndicate to lower its price and pleasing consumers everywhere. Then it negotiated an agreement with the German cartel to split the organization into six sales agencies. This agreement was a compromise, for each agency retained a special area for sales, even though the others could also sell there. A decided advantage of having the C.S.C. appeared in the conflict between the demand of the German coal producers for an increase in price and the urgent request of the German minister of economy that this request not be granted. Political pressure by economic interests for material gain seemed to be less effective in a supranational organization than in a single country.

The nationalization of the French coal mines caused some special problems, but the terms of the constitution are sufficiently flexible to apply to state-owned mines as well. For example, subsidies and other political economic privileges are forbidden, and the mines must compete in cost and price with those elsewhere, whether publicly or privately owned. As long as there is a common market, and collusion is ruled out, competition can obtain between public and private industries.

The Community has shown that planning for its special commodities entails consideration of the development of oil, electricity, and atomic energy as well as national financial policies, fiscal programs, and the like. A clear example of this extension of the Community's interests has been offered by transportation. Transport costs being one of the major factors in price, the C.S.C. constitution stipulates that discrimination based on country of origin or destination be prohibited. This article strikes against the traditional practice of charging one set of rates for national articles and another set for those from abroad, and of charging international traffic as if it began at the frontier. The entire system of profits of a country's transportation lines depended on this discrimination. Nonetheless, when the High Authority requested that it be abolished, the member governments agreed. Obstacles to equal transportation continue in other respects, for each state has its own rate system, administration, and ways of doing things, which as yet make comparable price conditions impossible. That a transportation Community will be formed seems to be a question merely of time.

Great Britain remained aloof from the C.S.C. until late in 1954. Although a major coal and steel producer, the British argued that their economic connections lay overseas rather than with Europe. They hesitated to throw in their lot with a European organization economically, militarily, or politically. This policy rested upon several hundred years of tradition. At the same time, the British came to the view that they should encourage the effort at integration. Just as they agreed to join the W.E.U. in a limited sense, so they reached an understanding with the Coal and Steel Community. The British did not join the Community; the two created a permanent board composed of four members from Great Britain (two from the government, one from the British Coal Board, and one from the British Steel Board) and four from the High Authority. These meet to discuss questions of common interest: the supply situation, the conditions of trade, policies of investment and price, technical developments, health and welfare questions, and any others concerned with coal and steel.

> Although the explicit obligation on both sides is only to consult, the treaty makes it quite clear that consultation on trade matters should lead to some real reduction on trade barriers; that the rule is to consult before, rather than after, any new restrictions are imposed, and that the object of consultation is co-ordinated action.[7]

Such cooperation may help to protect the interests of third parties like the Scandinavian countries, who have usually suffered from high prices of steel and coal.

In 1957 the governments of the six countries in W.E.U. and C.S.C. were ready to establish two further communities, one for a customs union, the other for the cooperative development of atomic energy. They found Britain and other European states receptive to the idea of close affiliation with the agencies, and the United States entirely sympathetic. The six had learned the value of united effort in enhancing their material prosperity and in enabling them to assume a significant role in the economic development of the outlying regions of the world. Failure by Britain and France to discipline the Egyptian government in the Suez crisis of late 1956 (to be discussed later) shocked Britain and France into recognizing that neither they nor any other state, except possibly the United States and the Soviet Union, could successfully execute an independent foreign policy. Atomic energy and new armaments compelled Europe to seek common means for affording modern arms, if it was not to depend on the United States for them. The six governments, all members of NATO, decided to pool resources. The practical reason for creating the new unions may be deduced from the discussion.

At a NATO Council meeting in December, 1956, the members agreed that each government should inform the others about "any development which significantly affects the alliance," that the secretary-general had "the right and duty" to put on the agenda any problem that "may threaten the solidarity and effectiveness of the alliance," and that there should be an annual review of political consultation as there already was of military achievement. The obligation had existed on paper before; henceforth it would be real. A further stimulus to the European members to pool their activity came when Secretary Dulles warned the Council that the United States had treaty obligations toward thirty other nations and that it must reserve the right to act on urgent matters without previously consulting NATO. European members feared that the United States, possessed of the wealth and knowledge needed to expand atomic power and to produce atomic weapons, might come to dominate NATO and to use it, not for the common good, but for American interests. To reduce the disproportionate American power, they have extended the organization of the six nations

[7] *Ibid.*, December 11, 1954, p. 890.

in close association with Britain and others in an atomic energy union. The proposal of a "coordinated and integrated" program of arms production outlined by the United States Secretary of Defense Charles Wilson would then mean cooperation of the United States and a European group of comparable power.

SOVIET COUNTERMOVEMENTS

The establishment of NATO and the several European functional organizations indicated the failure of a primary objective of Soviet foreign policy, that of keeping the West disunited. Revival of Western Europe, especially of the West German Republic, and the actively anti-Soviet foreign policy of the United States caused Stalin and his successors deep concern. They regarded the defensive action of the non-Communist states led by the United States as threats to peace by capitalistic imperialists. They feared NATO, SEATO, United States pacts with Far Eastern states, in fact, any pact between any free nations, as attempts to encircle the Soviet Union and its allies. They regarded Communist seizure of China, of half of Indo-china, of Northern Korea, of the European satellites, all with the active aid of the Soviet Union, not as aggression, but as the expression of the will of the masses, interpreted, of course, by Communists. In his last statement of communist theses, in 1952, Stalin reiterated the lines of dogma of thirty years or more before. The Soviet "peace fight," he said, could undermine "bellicose governments"; it might develop into "a movement for the overthrow of capitalism"; it would make war among the capitalist countries more likely than between the Communist and the capitalist countries; it would isolate the United States. Indeed, he wrote, "To think that Germany, Britain, France, Italy and Japan . . . will not try to smash U.S. domination and force their way to independent development is to believe in miracles." He continued to live in a world of his own conceiving.

The Soviets sought by propaganda to prevent the organization of Western resources. Knowing that the United States was the strongest opponent to their ambitions, they tried by a campaign of vituperation to divide it from other powers. Stalin concerned himself especially over the future of Germany; he knew from experience the might of that nation and wished above all either to transform the Germans into another satellite or to neutralize them and keep them unarmed.

For this end the Soviet government simultaneously pursued several lines of policy. It opposed any international organization of which it was not the center. It wished a European collective system excluding the United States and based on bilateral treaties which would leave the other countries weaker in comparison and exposed to superior Soviet strength. It played up French fear of Germany and proposed to strengthen the alliance between the Soviet Union and France and to make one between Poland

and France, just as before World War II. It blocked all efforts by the Western states to unify the two parts of Germany except on its terms. When the Western powers called for free elections under international supervision throughout Germany in order to form a unified constitutional government, the Soviets countered with a proposal for free elections in theory but not in fact. They wanted a joint government composed of members of the East German republic and of the West German state in the expectation that the East German Communists would be able to prepare the way for a coup d'état as in Czechoslovakia. The Western powers and the members of the West German government refused to trust this loaded argument.

After Stalin's death early in 1953 his successors began to liquidate some of his mistakes in foreign policy and to try what has been called a "soft line." "The North-Atlantic Bloc," Stalin's successor Malenkov declared, "is now torn asunder by internal struggle and contradictions; if the [international] tension is relaxed, the Bloc may end in complete disruption." The Soviet leaders instructed the Chinese and North Koreans to accept a truce in Korea and ordered the native party in Indochina to agree with France on a division of the country. Speaking once more in favor of peaceful coexistence, they accepted the recommendations of the overwhelming majority of the United Nations to permit almost all other nations to join that body; they did not insist on the inclusion of Red China. They proposed to increase trade with non-Communist countries and to help underdeveloped states with capital, machinery, and technical knowledge. By one line of action they attempted to improve relations with Western countries; by the other they tried to gain support of Asian and African countries against the West, to tie them economically to the Soviet Union, and to infiltrate them with Communists. They reestablished diplomatic and cultural relations with Tito, assured Turkey that they had no ambition to acquire any of her territory, and in 1955 accepted a peace treaty with Austria. These acts seemed to support the Western view that negotiation from strength is the condition for dealing successfully with the Soviet Union. The ratification of the W.E.U., for example, compelled the Soviets to try new tactics to prevent the execution of the agreement.

The Soviet peace treaty with Austria may have been intended to set an example to the Germans. It provides for the withdrawal of all occupying powers and the neutralization of Austria. If the West Germans would follow suit, repudiate W.E.U., and declare for neutrality between East and West, the treaty terms seem to argue, they will be able to restore the unity of the Fatherland. Austria has received back from the Soviets or been able to buy back, at a stiff price, the confiscated property; the Germans could infer that they might be similarly treated. Austrian prisoners of war were to be returned from the Soviet Union; so might the Germans. At the same time the Soviet government in 1955 lined up its satellites in an East European version of NATO. The action merely afforded an occasion for publicity of something which had long become a reality.

In October, 1956, the Hungarian nation rebelled against the Communist regime, demanding emancipation from the Soviet Union. Threatened with expulsion, Moscow did not wait for a local Communist to request aid. Soviet troops with tanks crushed the uprising and maintained a Red government in power. The action occurred just when Israel, Britain, and France invaded Egypt to seize the Suez Canal, an event that distracted attention from Soviet aggression. In the United Nations the Soviet delegate violently denounced the attack on Egypt and supported the United Nations decision to intervene, request the invading powers to leave, and to organize and dispatch an international military force to assure peaceful evacuation of the invading forces. When the General Assembly (the Council could do nothing because of the certainty of a Soviet veto) condemned by an overwhelming vote the Soviet aggression against Hungary and asked the right to send a mission to investigate and report on events in Hungary, the Soviet Union and her Hungarian supporters condemned the resolution as a violation of Hungarian sovereignty, and refused to allow a commission to enter the country.

In the meantime the United Nations had succeeded in bringing the fight in the Middle East to a stop. The contrast between the behavior of free nations and Communist states stimulated the Belgian statesman Paul-Henri Spaak, just appointed secretary-general of NATO, to write:

> Communism . . . is a new form of civilization trying to impose itself from the top, and its fundamental principles are diametrically opposed to those from which the moral, political, economic, and social evolution of both Europe and America has proceeded and on which it today is based. Our civilization is shaped to the measure of man. Its chief characteristic is respect for the human person. From that, all the rest stems. Communism, on the other hand, denies and ignores man, takes no interest in him as an individual, and certainly does not respect him.
>
> With such different points of departure, no purpose common to the two systems can be found. One of the two must triumph over the other, and if it is to be ours we [the nations of the West] must stick together.

The further import of Spaak's remarks will become evident in the discussion of relations with extra-European countries.

When in 1907 the British Admiralty was offered the Wrights' patents on the airplane, the First Lord replied, "I regret to have to tell you after the careful consideration of my Board, that the Admiralty while thanking you for so kindly bringing the proposals to their notice, are of opinion that they would not be of any practical value to the Naval Service." [8] A half-century later the possible use of the combination of airplane and atomic bomb led Air Marshal Sir John Slessor to conclude, "We have in fact reached the practical ultimate instrument of mutual destruction. We have at last ar-

[8] Quoted in John Slessor, "Air Power and World Strategy," *Foreign Affairs*, October, 1954, p. 43.

rived at the point when war—in the sense of total world war as we have known it in our generation—has abolished itself as a practical instrument of policy."[9] Neither Moscow nor Washington–London–Paris could survive an atomic attack, and both sides are aware of the fact. Wars in the Central European region where, as the major object of competition in the cold war, the stakes are too high, dare not be fought. Wars in which Communists use "the tactics of the termite"[10] continue to be waged in outlying areas. We shall next turn our attention to Europe's relations with overseas areas.

Suggestions for Further Reading

BELL, PHILIP W. *The Sterling Area in the Postwar World.* New York: Oxford University Press, 1956. An analysis of the internal workings of the area.

BIÖRKLUND, ELIS. *International Atomic Policy during a Decade.* New York: D. Van Nostrand Company, Inc., 1956. Brief, careful study by a Swedish admiral.

ELLIS, HOWARD S. *The Economics of Freedom: The Progress and Future of Aid to Europe.* New York: Harper & Brothers, 1950. Essential for understanding the Marshall Plan.

HAINES, C. GROVE, ed. *European Integration.* Baltimore: Johns Hopkins Press, 1957. Lectures at a conference in 1956 by European and American experts.

MASON, HENRY L. *The European Coal and Steel Community.* The Hague: N. V. Nijhoff, 1955.

REITZEL, WILLIAM, and others. *United States Foreign Policy, 1945–1955.* Washington, D.C.: The Brookings Institution, 1956.

ROBERTS, HENRY L. *Russia and America: Dangers and Prospects.* New York: Harper & Brothers, 1956. Summary of the discussion by a group at the Council of Foreign Relations in New York.

[9] *Ibid.,* p. 43.
[10] *Ibid.,* p. 46.

Chapter 23 · From Empire to United Nations

IMPERIALISM IN RAPID RETREAT

At the opening of the century European imperialism reached a new peak. By mid-century in the free world it was everywhere in retreat. "One is, indeed, almost inclined at times to wonder whether a situation in which certain Powers exercise jurisdiction over weaker or less developed peoples overseas is likely to have any measure of permanence in the modern world," Lord Hailey, the British authority on colonies, stated in 1947. "There was a time, and not a distant time, when that relationship seemed normal. Modern world opinion seems directed to giving it a certain air of abnormality." [1] World War II accelerated the speed of change both in Europe and the colonial areas, including the spread of European mores and ideals among colonial peoples. Since 1945 Europe's international role has moved from that of ruler to that of partner to assist underdeveloped peoples to build their own culture. The history of the relation between mother country and colony has varied according to the policy of the former and the condition of the latter; but almost everywhere one or more of the ideals of independence, equality, trusteeship, and international aid have been practiced. Colonial policy has become increasingly dynamic.

World War II directly involved not merely Europe but large parts of Asia and Africa, as well as the other continents. The dependent peoples either participated in or witnessed fighting in their own areas. Their life was interrupted by the presence of British, French, American, and other troops. In the Far East Japan's military achievements aroused the hope of independence among other yellow and brown peoples. Propaganda spread everywhere, principally through the high standard of living revealed by Western troops stationed among colonial peoples. The defeat of the Netherlands, Belgium, France, and Italy weakened the prestige of these countries. Egypt, India, and lesser members of the British Empire learned that Great Britain depended upon them for many materials needed to conduct

[1] Royal Institute of International Affairs, *Colonial Administration by European Powers* (London: The Institute, 1947), p. 90.

the war, becoming their debtor. The fratricidal conflict among the white peoples shocked many colonials into a sense of actual or potential cultural superiority over a destructive civilization. The war spun the wheel; after the imperialist powers finally defeated the totalitarians, they learned that the dependent peoples would not be content with the prewar status.

The United Nations recognized the fact of changed relationship by drafting in the Charter more explicit standards for the administration of trust territories than the Covenant had contained. Since the new international organization was directed primarily at furthering peace and security, it reversed the clause in the Covenant on colonial disarmament and allowed the trustees to "make use of volunteer forces, facilities, and assistance from the trust territory in carrying out the obligations towards the Security Council undertaken in this regard by the administering authority, as well as for local defence and the maintenance of law and order within the trust territory" (Article 84). The trust peoples thereby became integral parts of the present world with responsibility to assume the burdens necessary to help maintain "international peace and security." In order to raise them to this level the United Nations declared (Article 76) the "basic objectives" of the trusteeship system to be as follows:

(b) to promote the political, economic, social, and educational advancement of the inhabitants of the trust territories, and their progressive development towards self-government or independence . . . ;

(c) to encourage respect for human rights and for fundamental freedoms for all without distinction as to race, sex, language, or religion, and to encourage recognition of the interdependence of the peoples of the world; and

(d) to ensure equal treatment in social, economic, and commercial matters for all Members of the United Nations and their nationals, and also equal treatment for the latter in the administration of justice. . . .

The implementation of these terms implied ultimate achievement of independence and transformation of the way of life of the trust peoples. The United Nations, that is, Asiatic, African, and Latin American as well as European and North American peoples, supported the spread of social and political ideals that had guided the West to eminence. Since the large majority of the United Nations consisted of non-European states, many of them former dependencies, the United Nations became a center where the majority would try to extend the authority of the Trusteeship Council to nontrust dependencies.

In the postwar years the policies of the imperialist powers toward their dependencies have been put to severe test. The British have shown most ability peacefully to change by agreement. The Belgians have made some adjustments. The Dutch and especially the French have been obstinate in their defense of the status quo. The Spanish dependent peoples, except to some extent those in Morocco, have remained undisturbed and backward; and those under Portuguese rule, although roused by Portuguese economic improvements, have seemed to be similarly passive. Relations with Asiatic peoples have undergone much greater transformation than those with the Africans, a difference to be explained by the long tradition of civilization of the former peoples, their years of experience in government, either as independent states prior to imperialism or as dependencies, and the training in administration which some Western powers afforded to a native elite. The peoples of Africa came under Western control at a low stage of culture and have had fewer opportunities to absorb Western ways; but they are rapidly adopting Western ways and progressing toward freedom.

BRITISH POLICY

The British Commonwealth fought sturdily in World War II. Canada supplied a British Commonwealth Air Training program for pilots from Great Britain and the dominions, and Canadian troops participated in the European theater of war. Australia and New Zealand furnished forces, not merely in their own regions but in Southern Asia and in the Near and Middle East, that is, in Egypt, Greece, and Crete, and in North Africa. Indian troops participated in campaigns against the Japanese and against the Italians in Africa and in the Middle East, and South Africans shared with them in the conquest of Ethiopia and neighboring Italian possessions. Thousands of Irishmen showed disapproval of their government's neutrality by joining the British army. What opposition there was to the British concentrated in three areas, the Union of South Africa, where the Boers openly favored Germany and the doctrines of nazism; French Canada, where the people did not want to fight for Great Britain, France, or anyone else; and India. Each dominion and India furnished goods and services for Great Britain in such amounts that by the end of the war they often were Britain's creditors, as were Egypt and many of the Crown Colonies. Recognizing the rise in stature of her dominions, Great Britain in 1947 dropped the official designation of "dominion" as implying a former inferior status and referred to them as members of the Commonwealth. She proposed to increase the number of these "members" in Asia, Africa, and America. At the same time (1948), she acquiesced in the right of Eire to withdraw from the Commonwealth and of Burma to become independent without ever having joined.

INDIA BECOMES INDEPENDENT

Upon the outbreak of war Indian opinion divided over the policy to be followed. The Moslems on the whole supported Great Britain, stressing, however, that they wished to be assured of the right to decide their own constitutional future, that is, that the British would not turn them over

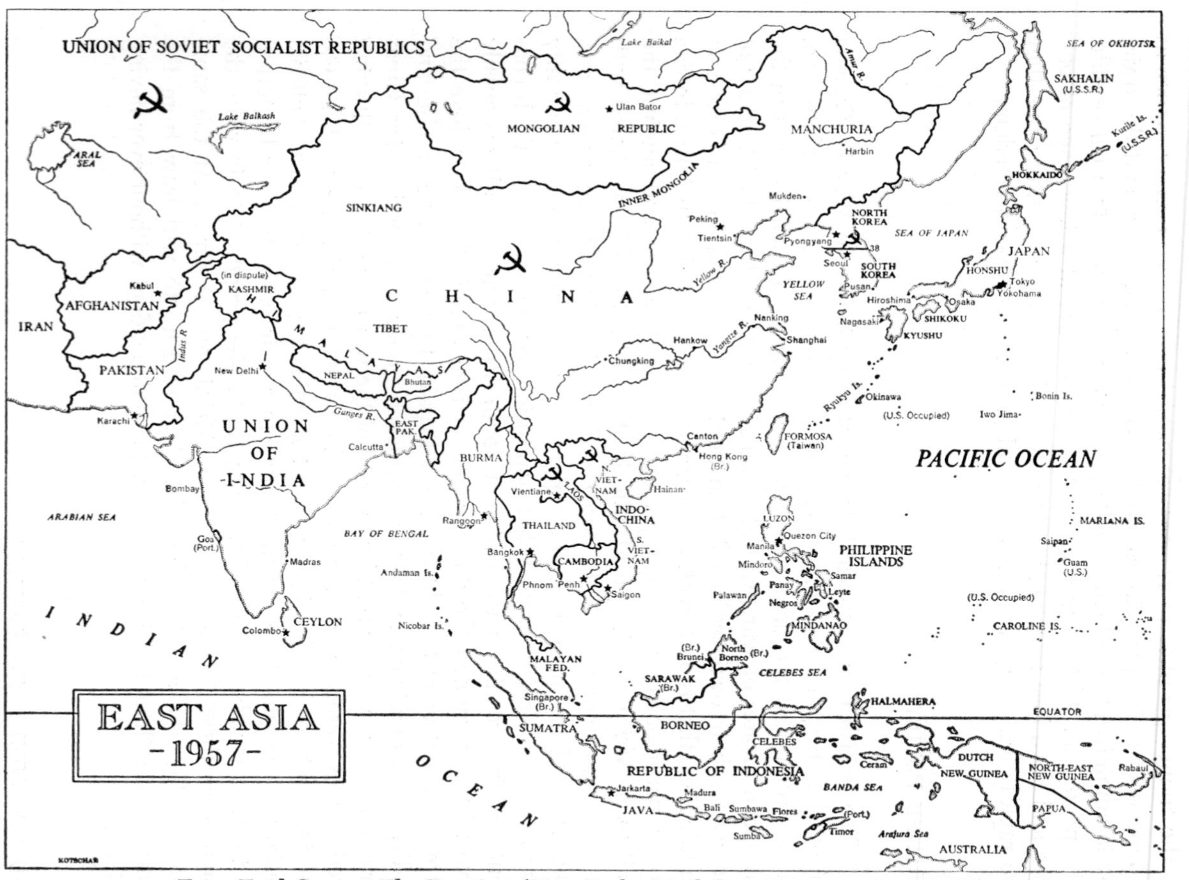

From Fred Greene, *The Far East* (New York: Rinehart & Company, Inc., 1957).

to Hindu rule. The National Congress party leaders greeted the outbreak of war with satisfaction as offering them the opportunity to force Britain to grant India independence. They immediately denounced Great Britain for involving the country in a war against its will and ordered the ministers who belonged to the party to resign their governmental positions. Thereupon the Constitution of 1935 collapsed, and the British governors had to resume authority. When war spread to the Far East, Mahatma Gandhi declared that the presence of the British in India exposed his country to Japanese aggression. He asked that the British withdraw and "leave India in God's hands." If the Japanese came to conquer, he said, passive resistance would soon overcome them and after a period of anarchy "a true India" would be born, united and free.

Interpreting these words as an incentive to riot, Gandhi's followers in 1942 initiated a mass movement of noncooperation in which they destroyed railways, telegraph lines, and police headquarters, and killed several thousand people. If the British and loyal Indian police had not been present, the peace-loving Hindus would have precipitated anarchy before Japanese arrival. The British put Gandhi and other leaders in jail, outlawed the Congress, and preserved order until after the war. They sent Sir Stafford Cripps, eminent leader of the British Labor party, to India in March, 1942, to try to negotiate a constitutional settlement between Hindus and Moslems that would protect racial and religious minorities. He accomplished nothing. The Moslem League had already (in 1940) decided upon partition of the country into a Hindu and a Moslem state, and the National Congress would accept nothing less than independence and unity under its own rule.

After the war the British Labor party strove for months to persuade Hindus and Moslems to agree on a constitution. It sent three of its most important cabinet members to India in March, 1946, to find a solution. The mission knew from the Indian general election of the preceding year that the Congress held a majority in eight provinces and was the second largest party in the other three provinces. In these three, the Moslem League was able to win enough support from minor parties to form a government. It also knew that the Moslem population was concentrated in the eastern and in the western parts of India, divided by hundreds of miles of Hindu territory. The Moslem League claimed the whole of Bengal, where, according to figures of 1941, 33 million of 60.3 million were Moslem, and of the Punjab, where 16.2 million of 28.4 million were Moslem. And there were 20 million Moslems scattered in the predominantly Hindu parts of the country.

The mission proposed the following solution. A central government organized on a basis of equality between provinces with a Hindu majority and those with a Moslem majority, should control foreign affairs, communications, defense, fundamental rights, and finances necessary to support these functions. The provinces should exercise the remaining powers of government. Between them and the central government there should be created a legislature and an executive to handle common affairs for the predominantly Moslem provinces and another for the Hindu provinces. In this way the mission tried to insure the people of each religion against abuse of power by the other while preserving Indian unity on common functions of government. Both the Congress and the League at first accepted the plan. When the Congress party revealed its intention to make essential changes, the League withdrew acceptance.

Despairing of ever bringing the two sides together, the British Labor government declared in February, 1947, that it would "take the necessary steps to effect the transfer of power into responsible Indian hands by a date not later than June 1948." The Congress had been asking for a fixed date of departure; now it had one just as the country was drifting into anarchy. Lord Louis Mountbatten, arriving as viceroy in March, 1947, persuaded leaders of the two parties to negotiate a solution. Under his dispassionate prodding, Gandhi and Mohammed Ali Jinnah, head of the Moslem League, finally agreed on partition into two states, the Moslem Pakistan, or "Land of the Pure," and Hindu India.

Plundering, religious war, and the flight of desperate people toward the state of their religion followed. From 10 to 20 million refugees left home in terror; hundreds of thousands died underway. In January, 1948, a Hindu fanatic assassinated Gandhi for approving peace with the Moslems. India and Pakistan began a bitter quarrel that has continued over possession of Kashmir, a province of 4 million people predominantly Moslem but occupied by India. Both India and Pakistan asked to remain within the Commonwealth, for both recognized the value of continuing British connections. The experience in government, the advantages in education and in economic life that for years the British had increasingly made possible enabled the states to inaugurate rule that has proved viable.

At about the same time Burma became an independent state, with Britain reserving certain bases for use in defense, and Ceylon became a commonwealth. In the Malay Peninsula the British strove to bring Malays and Chinese residents into political cooperation, with a view to transforming the area into a dominion, but communist forces delayed completion until 1957. The British West Indies have been developing a federation with common governmental institutions that make them ready for membership in the Commonwealth. East Africa and in Central Africa the Rhodesias and Nyasaland have aimed at the same objective. The states in British West Africa, Nigeria and the Gold Coast in the lead, have set up native government, and in 1957 the Gold Coast became the independent Commonwealth of Ghana. The British Commonwealth of Nations has become an organization of whites, blacks, browns, and yellows. It has members, or will soon have members, in every continent. A tribute to the attractive power of Western ideals as exemplified by the British and to the desire and the ability of the British to spread these ideals to other peoples, it has been the most effective single force for cultural cooperation that the world has seen.

BRITISH ECONOMIC AID

Great Britain has taken special care to assure the development of common material interests. She has remained for the Commonwealth and the colonies the financial center, the most important carrier of goods, the heart of the insurance business, and the greatest purchaser of raw materials and supplier of manufactured goods. She became the first power to practice on a large scale the kind of colonial investment which led after the Second World War to the introduction of the program of financial and technical aid to underdeveloped countries by the United Nations, of the Point Four program by the United States, and of similar forms of assistance by other countries. In 1940 Parliament passed an act authorizing the use of £5 million a year for ten years in loans and grants to execute "schemes for any purpose likely to promote the development of the Resources of any Colony or the welfare of its people." An additional £500,000 a year over the same period was voted for research. By this act the British government extended its responsibility to supply public funds for raising the level of productivity in the colonies. It supplanted a policy of laissez faire by one of official planning, and the step was taken by a Conservative government. It served as a precedent for governments of underdeveloped countries like India after the war to use the power of public finance to collect sufficient funds for urgent capital investment and to plan and execute a program of economic development which neither private capital nor private economic leadership was able to do.

In 1945 the British government greatly enlarged the amount for investment, and it has added further sums since that date. It created a Colonial Economic and Development Council to advise the Colonial Secretary. "Its duty," a British official with long experience has written, "is to consider the problems of each colony as a whole, to point out the fundamental needs and suggest how best to meet them, and to advise upon the relative priorities for development schemes." It should study "the possibilities of large-scale development and the requirements of the entire region of which the colony is a part." [2]

The government formed a Colonial Corporation and an Overseas Food Corporation with wide authority and considerable capital for investment, and assisted the colonial governments in obtaining further funds on the private market. Surveys of resources have been conducted; research in every field—medical, agricultural, social, economic—has begun; facilities for transportation and communication have expanded, factories have been

[2] Britannicus, "Economic Planning in the British Colonies," *Foreign Affairs*, October, 1948, p. 61.

built to process local materials, and schools and hospitals have been constructed. The government has striven to introduce economic measures for increasing the wealth and the knowledge of a colony to the point at which native private enterprise can assume responsibility.

Eire succeeded in preserving neutrality during the war, although she suffered from shortage of imports. Unable to obtain feedstuffs from abroad, the government had to reduce the number of livestock and poultry, and in order to assure a supply of food, the people plowed up pastures and planted crops, particularly wheat. They lacked fertilizers, lime to reduce the acidity of the soil, and machinery, and total agricultural production did not reach the prewar level until 1949. After the war the government took steps to improve all branches of the economy. It began a ten-year project to drain and make available for agriculture 4½ million acres of land, one fourth of the total area of the country. It subsidized the production of limestone to counteract soil acidity. It helped rural electrification and the cooperative movement, encouraging the establishment of industries to process agricultural products and to provide consumers' goods. Through the Marshall Plan, Eire received capital for these investments, and by agreements lasting four to five years with Great Britain she assured a market for commodities like livestock and meat, eggs, butter, and bacon. Public revenue is mainly derived from direct taxes, assuring an equitable distribution of the cost of government. Since Eire maintains almost no defense forces, public expenditure is concentrated on overcoming centuries of poverty. Evidence of success may be seen in the fact that before World War II Eire had less than 4,000 tractors; in 1951 she was using 16,000.

Eire in 1948 withdrew from the Commonwealth; but the act by which the British parliament recognized the severance contained the assurance that Great Britain and the colonies would not treat Eire as a foreign country and her citizens as aliens. The country still suffers most from lack of investment capital. In consequence many of its young people emigrate and contribute their creative energy to other lands.

NEAR AND MIDDLE EAST

In World War I the peoples of the Near and Middle East fought for independence from the Ottoman Empire. During World War II they preserved neutrality. Most of them favored the Axis powers, but, apart from some initial hostility on the part of Iran, a brief rebellion in Iraq in 1941, and minor obstruction by Egypt, Western Asia considered the war a matter of no direct concern to the area. The leaders recognized the difference between Nazi-Fascist and British-French methods of rule. They were aware of the fact that, for example, instead of levying tribute, the British often paid subsidies, and that Great Britain and the United States diverted production and shipping from military effort in order by way of a Middle East

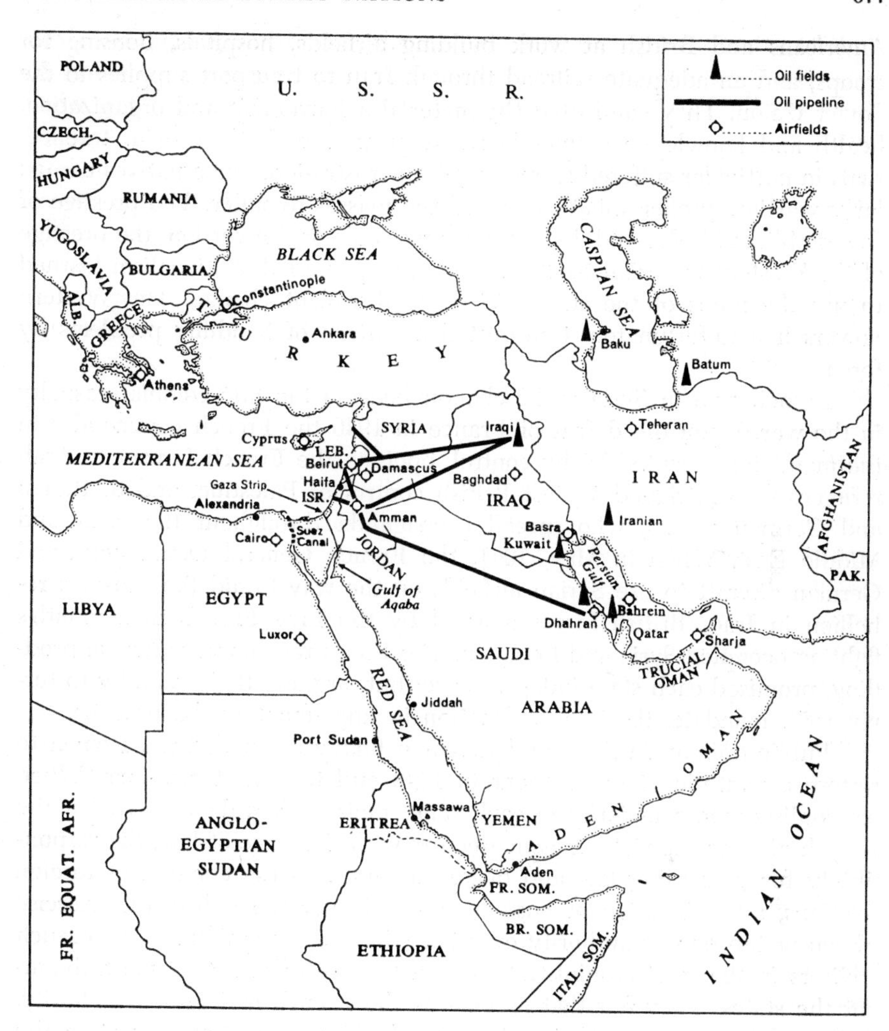

From William A. Williams, *America and the Middle East: Open Door Imperialism or Enlightened Leadership?* (New York: Rinehart & Company, Inc., 1958).

supply center at Cairo to try to satisfy local needs for consumers' goods. They saw that by selling materials, especially oil, and services to the Allies, they were rapidly developing into a creditor area, to the extent of £600 million to Great Britain at the close of hostilities. Nonetheless, rulers and peoples were hostile to Britain and France as the dominant imperialist powers in the region. They approved Nazi racial doctrines in respect to Jews.

The region could not avoid wartime social dislocation. Allied embassy staffs were enlarged to carry on propaganda; the Soviet Union profited from the respectability of its wartime alignment to establish or augment its representation in the area for the same purpose. Natives watched the

Americans and British at work building airfields, hospitals, housing for troops, and an adequate railroad through Iran to transport supplies to the Soviet Union. They contrasted the material achievement and organization, health and knowledge among Western peoples with their own. Intellectuals in particular suffered from a sense of frustration. Some natives earned large wartime profits; inflation caused the masses to suffer. The prestige of the established order and, by a curious psychological inversion, the prestige of the Western imperialist influence were undermined. Nationalism learned to use the mobs of the streets to demand violent change. The Western powers had unfortunately transmitted a pattern of handling problems by force.

French rule in Syria and Lebanon became the first colonial casualty in the war. Upon the defeat of France in 1940 the French commander in the mandates accepted Vichy control, opening the French Levant to Arab refugees who intrigued against British control of Palestine, and to Italian and German agents, who spread propaganda throughout the Near and Middle East. When in May, 1941, the French General Dentz permitted German aircraft to use Syrian airfields on the way to aid the pro-Axis rebellion in Iraq, British forces assisted by the Free French in a month's fighting occupied Syria and Lebanon. The Free French, under British prodding, promised each state independence; but, arguing their inability to terminate a mandate, they delayed action in implementing the promise.

Public opinion in Syria and Lebanon finally compelled the French to restore constitutional government in 1943 and to permit elections. When nationalists won a majority in each state, their leaders demanded that the French give up the right to issue decrees with the force of law, the responsibility for preserving law and order, defense and the conduct of foreign relations, administration of customs, control over the police, the exercise of censorship and of authority over the tribes, the appointment of French advisers in the local administration, and the use of secret agents throughout the states. They felt that as long as the French maintained authority, Syria and Lebanon would remain dependencies, no matter how often the French assured them of their freedom.

When the native governments in 1943 and 1944 dropped official connection with France, the de Gaullists or Free French first arrested the leaders. Then, under pressure of a general strike and British disapproval, they retreated, demanding only safeguards for French cultural institutions and for French economic rights, and control of Syrian and Lebanese armies, and of air and naval bases. When negotiations were about to open in May, 1945, the French landed reinforcements at Beirut. Strikes and riots immediately began. Each side knew that the moment of final decision had come, and Prime Minister Winston Churchill tipped the scales by intervening in favor of Syria and Lebanon. France acknowledged defeat, and the two former mandates asserted their independence, declared war on Germany, and became charter members of the United Nations. Henceforth, apart from Soviet influence in Northern Iran, Great Britain survived as the sole imperialist power in the Near and Middle East. The story of British decline is more complicated than that of France, for in one way or another all the states of the region, their internal affairs and their foreign relations, were affected.

Instability has characterized government and society in every country of the Near East. Apart from Iran and Egypt, the countries were products of the recent partition of the Ottoman Empire; none had secure boundaries, and plans were aired for union of two or more states. Mass poverty and ignorance enabled small groups at the top to control politics. The greater the ignorance and the more feudal the society, as in the Arabian Peninsula, the tighter the concentration of authority. Popular knowledge about oil royalties aroused desire for a faster pace of social change to improve living conditions. In most states reactionary tribes survived in the rural areas, under a landowning elite, whereas the towns and cities sustained a mixture of religious leaders, intellectuals, and students, a middle class devoted to business and to the professions, a small body of workers, and a mass mob. Election laws gave undue political representation to the moderate or conservative landowners, who effectively blocked the reform basic to all others, the breakup of large estates in favor of peasant family holdings. Government shifted precariously, sometimes resting in the hands of conservative landlords, sometimes in those of sincere reformers, sometimes in those of demagogues dependent upon an inflamed urban mob.

When the reformers assumed power, they had to compete with the demagogues, intent upon arousing nationalism and willing to allow free rein to Communists, who disguised their intentions under the cloak of nationalism. The conservatives and the reformers saw the value to their country of cooperation with Great Britain, on a diminishing scale; but the nationalists turned the general frustration of the masses into hatred of all foreign participation, good or bad, and of all those willing to work with foreigners. The army held the ultimate authority in emergencies, although its officers lacked experience in politics, in social and economic affairs, and in international relations, and although it failed to introduce constructive reforms. One group of officers, therefore, replaced another only to continue failure; or frequently a student assassinated the head of government, whereupon a new dictator had to be found. The international relations of the Near and Middle East reflected the internal instability of each state. As long as the society suffered from the ambition to be modern without the means to become so, the region would suffer from irresponsible promises of nationalists and, to a less extent, of Communists disguised as nationalists, and/or of the authoritarian power of army officers.

Iran and Iraq

During the war the Soviet Union controlled the five northern provinces of Iran, Great Britain the rest, and the United States brought in 30,000 noncombatant troops to move supplies from the Persian Gulf to the Soviet border. Both Russia and Britain carried on propaganda; the American troops kept aloof from politics. In time the Soviet Union demanded an oil concession in the northern provinces, did not obtain it, and started riots and rebellions by the Iranian Communist party and other supporters. Setting up an independent Azerbaidzhan Republic after the war, she tried to force the Iranian government into a position of actual dependence in the north and potential dependence elsewhere. Under pressure from the United Nations, she finally withdrew Soviet troops from the northern provinces, permitting the restoration of national unity. In 1947 the Iranian parliament refused to ratify a proposed agreement with the Soviets, and the latter began a program of intimidation, border raids, Communist revolts, and assassination by the Iranian party, all of which has continued to the present.

Afraid of Great Britain as well, the Iranian government sought aid from the United States. Since American encouragement brought little tangible help, Iranian hopes of large-scale economic reform, planned by American experts, died a-borning. In the winter of 1950–1951 a small party, called the National Front, under Dr. Mossadegh, in order to obtain funds, clamored for nationalization of the British-owned oil industry. An Islam fanatic shot the premier, who opposed the proposal, and the parliament was stampeded into adopting a nationalization law. From March, 1951, until August, 1953, Dr. Mossadegh ruled the country as head of a mob of socialists, Communists, religious fanatics, extreme nationalists, students, and a few merchants. The oil wells ceased to flow, the refinery at Abadan run by the British shut down, British banks and other properties in Iran were seized, life was unsafe.

The government soon exhausted its funds and could not pay officials. Dr. Mossadegh needed ever more power and aroused ever more mass hysteria to conceal the fact that he was ruining the country. When in August, 1953, the Shah fled, certain army units defied the dictator in restoring order. The United States granted an emergency loan and helped to negotiate a settlement of the oil controversy. The oil properties remained nationalized, but the extracting, refining, and marketing of oil were transferred to an international consortium of British, French, Dutch, and American companies. Iranian payments on account for the nationalized property were all but wiped out by the claims demanded by Iran from the former British owners. Iranian representatives were to sit on the board of directors of the consortium; profits were to be divided equally between Iran and the company. Oil immediately began to flow, and the army-controlled government, after uncovering a widespread Communist plot in 1954 among officers to seize control, transferred authority to a moderate civilian government.

In comparison Iraq has had much less trouble with imperialism. The oil corporation was already international in ownership and had paid the country a much higher percentage of profits than had the Anglo-Iranian Company. The Iraqi royal family owed its position to British support after World War I. Neither the king nor Iraqi leaders discounted the Soviet menace; they had learned a lesson from the experience of their neighbor to the east. The Iraqi government wished to reduce or abolish entirely Great Britain's rights under the treaty of 1930. At the same time it needed some guarantee of support in the event of attack by the Soviet Union. The Bagdad Pact of 1955, to be discussed below, achieved both objectives. Internally the threat of civil war was controlled, primarily by one remarkable individual, Nuri es-Said, former officer in Kemal Atatürk's army, a wise man with a devoted following of able moderates and conservatives, who inclined toward Great Britain. Aware that the country would benefit from increased production rather than from the redistribution of existing resources by the partition of large estates, he initiated a program of reforms. Reclamation and irrigation should make more land available for agriculture. Industries should be introduced; transportation, health facilities, and the like should be expanded. He has received support in these plans from the two influential groups, officials and army officers, and the masses are beginning to anticipate improvement in their way of life.

Problem of Palestine

The postwar history of Transjordan, Syria, and Lebanon, in the Fertile Crescent, and of Saudi Arabia and the other states of the Arabian Peninsula and, to a considerable extent, of Egypt, must consider primarily the problem of Palestine or Israel. Since the creation of this new state has affected all other states in the area and the great powers outside, the story of Israel will be discussed from a broad point of view.

Allied troops in Palestine kept Arab-Jewish hostility from violence until 1943. By that time the pressure of refugee Jews seeking a haven from Nazi and Communist Europe, and from Arab and other countries, became intense. In 1942 the Zionist organization asked that the mandate of Palestine become a Jewish state, to which Jews could migrate in unlimited numbers and create their own army. Jewish extremists in Palestine, the Irgun and the Stern Gangs, initiated terrorism against Arabs and British trying to prevent the illegal entry of Jewish refugees. Since the British continued the policy set in 1939 of cultivating the support of the Arab world, Zionists everywhere turned from Great Britain to awaken the interest of the United States in their aspirations.

Opposed by Jews, Arabs, and the United States, the British government after the war submitted the Palestine issue to the United Nations. The General Assembly appointed a commission of eleven states, with the Swedish delegate as chairman, to investigate and recommend a solution. A majority advised that Palestine be partitioned into a Jewish state and an Arab state and that Jerusalem be internationalized. The minority favored a federation of an Arab state and a Jewish state, each autonomous. In November, 1947, the General Assembly accepted the majority proposal, and noted Great Britain's decision to relinquish the mandate by August, 1948. The Arab nations voted solidly against the resolution, regarding it as evidence of Western intervention in their affairs. Great Britain refused to approve the partition; the United States, seeing that it could not work, proposed that Palestine be placed temporarily under UN trusteeship. The Soviet Union now insisted upon execution of the UN resolution.

As soon as Great Britain withdrew from Palestine (May, 1948), the Arab states of Egypt, Syria, Lebanon, Transjordan, and Iraq attacked Palestine, only to be defeated. The UN Security Council sent Count Folke Bernadotte of Sweden to mediate. Jewish terrorists assassinated him; Ralph Bunche of the United States took his place, succeeding after intensive negotiation in arranging a truce. The Jews defied the UN by refusing to give up their conquests. They increased the size of the state by one fifth and refused to readmit about a million Arab refugees who had fled before Jewish arms. The new state of Israel now permitted unrestricted immigration, receiving Jews driven in reprisal from the Arab states, as well as those from other parts of the world. Since most of these were penniless, and many from Arabia had no special skill or knowledge to contribute, Israel lived from funds supplied by the American government and especially by American Jews. It cost $3,000 to settle an immigrant, but within less than three years a half million persons found haven in Israel, and more were waiting to come.

The Arab-Jewish war of 1948 poisoned the relations of the entire region. Egypt refused to accept the Arab refugees and left 240,000 in misery in the Gaza strip; these refugees hoped to strike at the Jews. Transjordan, with disapproval from other Arab states and from the United Nations, annexed Arab Palestine, also caring for 400,000 Arab refugees from the rest of Palestine. King Abdullah of Transjordan more than tripled the number of his subjects, and henceforth the government had to deal with a new element in the population. Transjordan had loyally served British interests in return for a subsidy. The new population, embittered and passionate, and hating both Great Britain and Israel, quickly began to dominate political life. As the British subsidy increased in size, native antagonists to ties with Great Britain determined to eliminate British officers from the Arab Legion, a small, efficient force organized to protect Transjordan and the pro-British government there. As an expression of aversion to Israel, Lebanon accepted 128,000 refugees from Palestine; Syria accepted 80,000. Ibn-Saud, a loyal friend of Great Britain and the United States, denounced Israel; and Iraq, becoming anti-British, had more reason to renounce the treaty of 1930. The Arabs now judged foreign powers by a single yardstick, the attitude toward Israel.

The conflict with Israel soon disclosed the lack of common interests among the Arab states and their inability to work together. Ibn-Saud and the Hashemite family ruling Transjordan and Iraq were enemies from World War I, when each was striving to found a state and include as much territory as possible. Egypt, the largest in population and the most renowned in culture, mistrusted Iraq as a possible competitor. When from time to time plans were proposed for the incorporation of Transjordan into Iraq, or for the creation of a federation of the two states, Syria and Lebanon, Egypt fomented opposition to the project. Syria leaned toward Egypt, a state farther away than Iraq and so supposedly less dangerous to Syrian independence and an ally in case of Israeli aggression. Lebanon contained a large Christian population that feared union with any Arab state; she particularly mistrusted the project for a Greater Syria to include both Lebanon and Transjordan. Iran, as a non-Arab country, shared with Iraq deep fear of the imperialism of the Soviet Union. Others felt secure enough to use Soviet support, whenever available, against Great Britain and against Israel. As a means of furthering her influence in the region, Great Britain had aided in forming the Arab League (1944) of the seven Arab states, modeled in organization after the British Commonwealth. The fiasco of the Arabs in the war against the Jews in 1948 disclosed the inability of League members to cooperate. Egypt, paying 42 per cent of the League's budget, exerted most influence over the group and turned it to use in her conflict with Great Britain.

Egypt stayed neutral in World War II; she sympathized with Germany but was occupied by Allied troops. Communism spread widely among students and trade-unionists but could not compete in strength with Egyptian nationalism. The country suffered from inflation, unbalanced agricultural production, and a redistribution of wealth when recent immigrants from the Levant made fortunes in Allied war contracts. The Egyptian leaders determined to revise the treaty of 1936 with Great Britain to eliminate British occupation troops and to gain control of the Sudan. They expected Egyptian pressure to increase British war weariness and bring retreat. Observing that the American navy kept more tonnage in the Mediterranean than the British and that the United States was assuming protection of Greece and Turkey against the Communists, the Egyptians hoped to play one power against the other. They also took their case against continued British occupation to the United Nations. The Security Council failed to act on the complaint, as neither Egypt nor Britain could muster a majority vote; but Britain withdrew her forces to the Canal zone. When the Jews crushed the Egyptian army in 1948 and threatened to invade the country, Great Britain warned the Jews away and saved Egypt from further humiliation.

In 1946, when confidence in the peaceful intentions of the Soviet Union still prevailed, Great Britain was willing to evacuate the Suez Canal. By 1950, when she saw Communist aggression in Greece, Eastern Europe, China, and intrigues in the Near and Middle East, she realized that Western freedom required the defense of the Suez area. Egypt held a strategic position between Europe and the Orient and was unique in possessing harbors, airports, factories, technical facilities, and food to support a defensive force. The retention of Egypt as a military and naval base to supplement NATO seemed necessary, and the outbreak of the Korean war confirmed the view. In 1951 the Egyptian parliament unilaterally abrogated the treaty of 1936, requested the British to withdraw all troops, and declared a union of Egypt and the Sudan. The British government, supported by the United States, refused. Riots and mob attacks on British troops and property followed, and in July, 1952, a group of young army officers seized control, deposed the king, and promised reforms and emancipation from imperialism.

The new regime abolished political parties, suppressed communism, and instituted a few spectacular reforms such as road building. In 1953 it reached agreement with Great Britain to the effect that Anglo-Egyptian occupation in the Sudan should cease after three years (1956) and that the Sudan Constituent Assembly should decide whether to join Egypt or keep the country independent. According to an agreement of the next year, Great Britain was to evacuate her troops, but British civilian technicians under Egyptian sovereignty would continue to service the Suez Canal, and Britain preserved the right to reenter Egypt "in the event of an armed attack by an outside power on Egypt or any country which at the date of signature of the present agreement [is] a party to the treaty of joint defense between Arab League states [Egypt, Syria, Lebanon, Saudi Arabia, Yemen, Jordan, Iraq, Libya] or on Turkey." Freedom of navigation of the Suez Canal was reaffirmed, and the Canal was recognized as "an integral part of Egypt." The treaty was to run for seven years. Both treaties were made possible by compromise.

Cooperation of the Near East and the West broke down over three issues. The first issue concerned the Bagdad Pact. In 1955 Turkey, Iraq, Iran, Pakistan, and Great Britain negotiated a mutual assistance agreement. The United States, although encouraging the creation of the pact, did not join, and its refusal led to attack on the agreement from within and without. The governments signing the treaty promised to cooperate for security and defense and not to interfere in one another's internal affairs; they set up a permanent ministerial council to execute the terms. Britain abrogated the treaty of 1936 with Iraq and agreed to withdraw her troops from the country. She promised to aid Iraq with military resources and upon request to come to its assistance against an aggressor. Since Great Britain and Turkey belonged to NATO, the Bagdad treaty formed a link in the Western defense system. The Egyptian government, headed since early 1954 by Colonel Gamal Abdul Nasser, strove to prevent Iraq from joining the Bagdad group, for the agreement hurt Egypt's aspirations to leadership of the Arab world and seemed to diminish Egypt's chance to gain further concessions from Western powers. Nasser prevented Jordan (as Transjordan called itself after 1949) from joining the pact; but Nuri es-Said of Iraq, who understood the Soviet danger better than Colonel Nasser, refused to withdraw. Egypt now built a military alliance with Syria and Saudi Arabia, putting the common forces under Egyptian command.

Unending border raids and propaganda warfare between the Arab states and Israel created the second source of trouble. Since the Arabs were no match for Israeli forces, they feared acts of aggression which the United Nations could not stop and the United States might condone. Opponents of the Bagdad Pact held that the pact diverted attention from this supreme danger.

Suez Crisis

Relations with the great powers, particularly Egypt's relations, brought out a third source of friction. Israel had been obtaining arms from the United States and elsewhere, and with these in self-defense she raided neighboring countries. In 1955 Egypt began to emphasize military preparedness. Finding the United States reluctant to sell him arms, Colonel Nasser purchased military equipment from Czechoslovakia by mortgaging the Egyptian cotton crop for several years into the future. Simultaneously he sought in the West a loan to construct a dam across the Upper Nile at Aswan in order to diminish the pressure of Egypt's rapidly increasing population by adding greatly to the supply of irrigable land. The negotiations seemed almost concluded when the United States government suddenly refused a loan, indicating doubt of Egypt's credit and her ability to build the dam. Colonel Nasser interpreted the rejection as a national insult and as head of the military junta bitterly denounced the West, seized the Suez Canal, and threatened to turn for military and economic aid to the Soviet Union.

In the latter part of 1956 Israel took advantage of the confusion to attack Egypt. She excused her action on three counts: Egypt's support of Arab raids from Gaza into Israel, Egypt's refusal to permit Israeli ships or other ships bound for Israel to use the Suez Canal, and Egypt's blockage of the Straits of Aqaba to Israeli commerce. Great Britain and France, angry at Egypt for, among other acts, having seized the Suez Canal, joined Israel in military and naval action. The United Nations, supported by the United States and the Soviet Union, hastened to condemn the three nations as aggressors; with moral force it secured the withdrawal of British and French forces and the retreat of Israel. Egypt sank ships to block the Suez Canal, seized all British, French, Jewish, and other foreign-owned property (the British alone was worth £400 million), and expelled the nationals of the attacking countries from Egyptian soil.

The Suez attack evoked the gravest crisis since the Korean war. After World War II European industry had turned to the use of oil as fuel. By 1955, for example, Great Britain produced 14 per cent of its total energy from oil, France 20 per cent, Sweden 44 per cent, and Denmark 37 per cent. The stoppage of the shipment of oil through the Suez Canal and through pipelines across Syria and Lebanon deprived Europe of three fourths of its supply. Since the countries used oil in their largest and most modern industrial plants, the loss of this fuel over a period of months or the uncertainty of continuing delivery endangered the European economy. The United States and Latin America agreed to furnish oil temporarily, but the United States also imported oil from the region. The expulsion of nationals of the attacking countries deprived Egypt of most of her managerial class and opened a prospect of economic chaos. Jordan was already dropping her British connections; she now broke them completely on the dubious promise of Egypt, Syria, and Saudi Arabia to replace the British subsidy. Great Britain's prestige in the entire Arab world was destroyed, and the Bagdad Pact temporarily deprived of significance.

The oil-producing Arab states depend upon the flow of oil to provide money to run their states. Closing the canal and pipelines enhanced the possibilities of social troubles and Communist interference. France failed to stop Egyptian support of rebellion in Algeria by eliminating Nasser. The prestige of the Soviet Union in the area grew, for the Arabs believe that the threat of Russian intervention, not the action of the UN and the United States, stopped the aggressors. In Syria a group of army officers in control is working closely with Communists and with the U.S.S.R. Israel feared extinction as a result of her act and at the same time hesitated to withdraw from the Gaza strip without assurance of protection against Egyptian raids and from the heights commanding the Gulf of Aqaba without guarantee that Egypt would permit free passage to an Israeli port. France and Great Britain did not forewarn the United States of their attack; hence relations of the Western powers have suffered. The United States found itself forced into temporary cooperation with the Soviet Union against its NATO allies.

Under pressure of the realities of international interdependence the Suez crisis has gradually eased. The United Nations organized a small military force to prevent further fighting by policing the disputed area. All parties found that they were suffering from the conflict and that a solution to it must be found. Iraq and Saudi Arabia, eager to revive the flow of oil through the canal, worked together with the United States to persuade Colonel Nasser toward agreement. Not even the rulers of Egypt relished the prospect of enhanced Communist influence in the Near and Middle East, and they and the leaders in other Arab states recognized the need to maintain political and economic order.

Although no final settlement has been reached, the main lines of ultimate agreement seem to have been set. Egypt has kept possession of the Suez Canal but has assured maintenance of the canal and right of passage to ships of every state except Israel, with which she claims to be still at war. Egypt has begun negotiations with Great Britain over the settlement of economic disputes, and Great Britain and France have agreed to pay tolls to Egypt for use of the waterway. Israel has been able to keep the Straits of Aqaba open for her commerce, but she has withdrawn from the Gaza strip. The Arab states persist in their refusal to accept the existence of Israel, but this common bond is offset by their differences. When in 1957 Nasser and his Syrian allies tried to overthrow the king of Jordan in favor of their own henchmen, they failed, and the rulers of Iraq, Saudi Arabia, and Lebanon came to the protection of the threatened state.

Extremes of poverty and wealth exist in each country of the Near and Middle East. The intellectuals tend to anger and frustration and to be susceptible to communism, and the masses are ignorant and especially in the towns are easily aroused to violent action. The governments have usually been dominated by venturesome army officers or medieval rulers, all equally ignorant of how to introduce reforms. Two countries, Iraq and Iran, have broken with this tradition and are setting an example for the others. Using oil royalties, they have begun a large-scale program of economic and social improvement, road construction, water conservation, irrigation, school building, and the like. Lebanon would follow suit, were it not for lack of resources. The rulers of Saudi Arabia and of the small states of the Arabian peninsula are just beginning to be aware of their social responsibility. Egypt and Syria are both so nationalistic in respect to the West that they neglect their own people. Trouble may be expected to continue in the entire region.

The withdrawal of Great Britain from the Near and Middle East explains the sudden increase in importance of the island of Cyprus. Acquired at the Congress of Berlin (1878), Cyprus remained in 1954 the sole point of defense of British interests in the region. A Greek majority of the population was then demanding union with Greece, and a number of Cypriotes aided by Greeks from the home country resisted the British by guerrilla warfare. Greece officially claimed possession of the island; Turkey as resolutely opposed it. She feared for the safety of the Turkish minority on the island and objected for strategic reasons to Greek possession of so large a land mass near the Turkish mainland. (The Greek-owned Dodecanese islands, even closer to Turkey, had been neutralized.) While developing Cyprus into an air and naval base, the British have striven to suppress the Greek insurgents and to keep peace between local Greeks and Turks, and they have not succeeded. The British government has put forward no imaginative solution to the complicated problem. In consequence, Greece and Turkey have become alienated from each other to such an extent that the Balkan Pact of 1953 between the two and Yugoslavia has lost much of its strength, and Greece is at odds with Great Britain and much less interested in NATO than before. Even a feeble echo of imperialism has proved capable of upsetting European harmony.

DUTCH FAILURE, BELGIAN SUCCESS

The Netherlands refused to acquiesce peacefully in the loss of the Dutch East Indies. Queen Wilhelmina had promised the East Indian people equality of status under the crown with the Netherlands proper, but at the end of the war native leaders demanded freedom. Aided by the Japanese army of occupation, they set up an Indonesian government and declared the country a free republic. The Dutch possessed no army at the time and depended upon British and Australians to take over the islands from the Japanese. Since troops were scarce, the Allies used the Japanese for some months to assist in maintaining order. The delay enabled the natives to organize defense; the Japanese preferred to contribute military supplies to them rather than surrender materials to the Allies. Thus the Indonesians were prepared to resist by force the attempts of the Netherlands to restore control. The stakes in the ensuing controversy were high. One sixth of Dutch wealth was invested in Indonesia, and 15 per cent of the national income came from there. Indonesian acceptance of the status quo in property rights would preserve Dutch dominance over the economy. The question of political sovereignty was also involved, including the crucial one of responsibility for foreign affairs and defense.

The fighting proved costly to the Dutch, both in money and in prestige. At one time they were officially rebuked by the United Nations for attacking the Indonesians; and in the end their effort to retain the area proved futile. The Dutch preserved a large share of their economic holdings but lost all political control, and they failed to reach agreement with the Indonesian government over the possession of the Dutch part of New Guinea and over certain technicalities of legal ties with the Netherlands. The British had withdrawn from their far larger dependencies (India, Burma, and others) in Southern Asia to preserve the friendship and economic and political cooperation of the native peoples. Trying the opposite policy, the Dutch lost the territories and forfeited the good will and trust of the new nation.

The Belgian policy toward the Congo has satisfied the postwar desires of both Belgians and natives. Economic and social improvement has gone steadily forward; whites and blacks have received equal legal rights. Both are eligible for any position for which they qualify and both may form trade-unions. Neither has received the privilege of voting. Few natives study in Belgium proper, whereas the French have brought a thousand from West Africa alone to France for their education. Ten times as many Congo children go to elementary schools as is the case with the natives in French West Africa, a fact which led a former governor-general of the Congo to declare in 1955:

> I sincerely believe that in 30 years' time we shall have in the Congo at least as many university graduates, at least as many high school graduates, and infinitely fewer illiterates than do our French neighbors in West Africa, even though the first university in the Congo opened its doors only last year.[3]

[3] Pierre Ryckmans, "Belgium Colonialism," *Foreign Affairs,* October, 1955, p. 101.

In 1950 Belgium initiated a ten-year plan for economic development which called for the expenditure of over $1½ billion. Five years later the Congo had forty hydroelectric plants in operation, three more under construction, and three more being planned. She exported annually products valued at $3 billion, including more than one half of the free world's supply of uranium, and she had built new industries ranging from chemicals to the construction of river tugs. Outside investments amounted to $2 billion, of which Belgium supplied 75 per cent. Experimental stations for agriculture are maintained throughout the country to help native farmers and the operators of large-scale plantations.

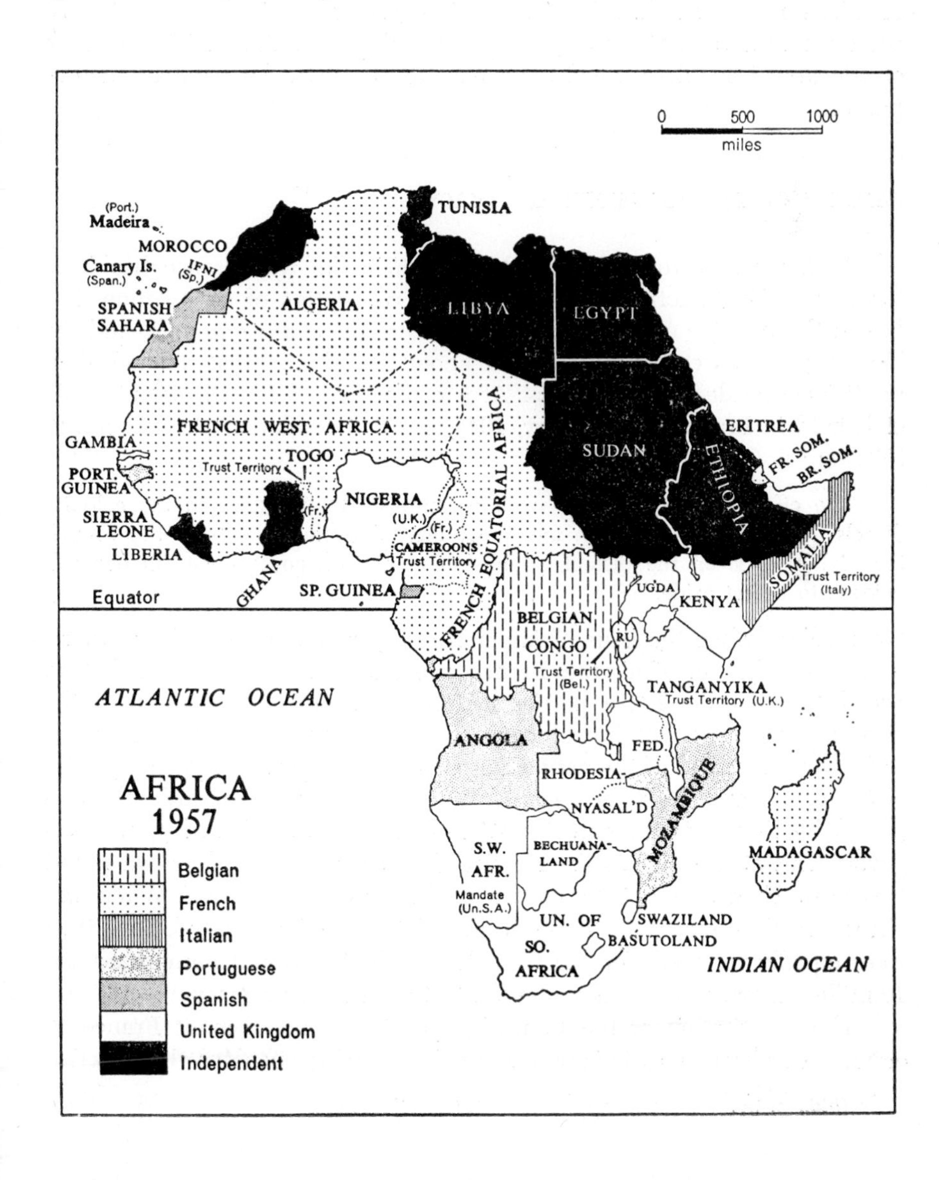

The natives are being increasingly attracted to the towns, where in contrast to French North Africa they receive adequate housing facilities and are trained to practice sanitation and to use savings banks. Political dominance by white Europeans has been prevented and racial amity preserved. "By promoting such [economic and social] progress" the former Belgian governor-general of the Congo wrote, "we are forging the weapons with which the natives will conquer their political freedom, if we do not have the wisdom to grant it gracefully when the time is ripe." [4] After the war the first move in that direction was taken by creating advisory councils at all levels of government. Conscious of the need for advice, the black members requested that Belgian officials participate in these bodies. At the same time the natives organized political parties, and in 1956 a group of educated Congolese called for a plan to be drawn for political emancipation.

FAILURE OF FRENCH IMPERIAL POLICY

In her policy toward dependencies since the war France has been forced steadily to retreat from the former conception of assimilation. She lacked the prestige or the resources to restore the *status quo ante*, and the French people were so ill-informed about the empire that a handful of politicians decided crucial issues. At a conference of French colonial officials held in Brazzaville, January, 1944, the first resolution passed read as follows:

> The effect of the civilizing work accomplished by France in the colonies dispels any idea of autonomy, any possibility of evolution outside the French imperial bloc. Even the distant establishment of "self-government" in our colonies is to be set aside.

Nonetheless, when the issue of imperial organization arose at the constitutional assembly in 1946, the French representatives were divided. The Socialists and other leftist parties mainly advocated federation, with the right of voluntary withdrawal from the union, and the development of self-government and of the native culture within each territory. The parties of the center and the right opposed the proposal, and were ardently supported by French in the colonies, who denounced the idea of native self-government at any time. Like Herriot, they argued that federalism might transform France into "the colony of her former colonies." When the French leaders faced the implications of the ideal of assimilation, they were equally repelled, for the 60 million colonials would outnumber the 40 million Frenchmen to threaten white European supremacy.

The constitution of the Fourth Republic did not commit France to either federalism or assimilation, but left the door open for the practice

[4] *Ibid.*, p. 96.

of both. It set up a French Union of Metropolitan France, overseas departments (which were to be governed as parts of the former), overseas territories (which consisted of the tropical colonies), and the Associated States (Morocco, Tunisia, and French Indochina), which France held as protectorates. The union was defined as a group of "nations and peoples which pool or co-ordinate their resources and their efforts in order to develop their respective civilizations." In view of French precedents the phrase "in order to develop their respective civilizations" would most likely be used to justify the continued spread of French culture to the natives. The constitution then created a Union façade composed of (1) the office of president of the French Union, an additional title bestowed upon the president of the Republic; (2) a High Council of States composed of representatives of France and the Associated States and resembling an occasional conference of diplomats, some of whom were subordinate to others; (3) an Assembly of the French Union composed of an equal number of members from metropolitan France and from the overseas areas. The Council and the Assembly were assigned only advisory power.

The actual authority to legislate for the Union remained in the hands of the French parliament, in which sat deputies from the overseas departments and a few from the overseas territories. In the territories and in the Associated States representative assemblies were created, as a manifest of federalism, but their purely advisory function assured the continued exercise of centralized control by the French colonial administrators and back of them the French parliament. An electoral law preserved the equal voting strength of the small number of Frenchmen and of the mass of natives in each dependency in the elections to the local assembly and in those, wherever held, to the French parliament. The native peoples were declared citizens of France and of the French Union, but the distribution of political rights indicated two classes of citizens, the French and the native elite constituting the first class and all the rest of the population the second class. As the French statesman Bidault, at the time president of the French Provisional Government, declared, the French Union was "an institution whose like cannot be found anywhere else in the world." The considerable increase in 1951 in the number of natives with a vote constituted no basic change. The French continued to rule.

Since assimilation was considered impossible and federalism was contrary to French traditions and potentially dangerous, the French government fell prey to overriding events. France had collapsed in May, 1940; within a year the Free French government recognized the independence of the mandates Syria and Lebanon. After the war it tried to retain control over military and foreign affairs of these two states and to preserve French cultural and economic interests, but by 1946 it conceded defeat by withdrawing its troops. In the East the close of World War II opened the French fight to regain Indochina. As in Burma and the Dutch East Indies, the Japanese conquerors in Indochina had encouraged independence, and

Communists had infiltrated the nationalist movement and became prominent leaders. In this jungle war the French expended blood and money which they could scarcely afford. Premier Mendès-France, in office for a few months in 1954, acknowledged the victory of the Communist forces in North Viet Nam, in an effort to hold within the French union the southern part of Indochina and the neighboring states of Laos and Cambodia. Since 1954–1955 France has suffered severe reverses in trade with these latter states and has had to transfer to them authority amounting to virtual independence. In Madagascar a postwar revolt was crushed; but conflicts began in Tunisia and Morocco and, in 1954, in Algeria. In North Africa France has undergone the most severe test of her imperial policy in recent history.

CRISIS IN NORTH AFRICA

The location on the other side of the Mediterranean from France imparted to the North African dependencies a strategic and a prestige value out of all proportion to that of any of the other territories. Geographically speaking, they seemed to be an extension of France proper. They were one of the areas, Great Britain being the other, from which Allied forces had rescued France from Nazi conquest. The British had granted independence to Ireland, which was even more important, strategically, to that country; but France at the close of the war had no thought of releasing her hold over any of the North African territories. On the contrary, Frenchmen continued to settle there, and the million Frenchmen in Algeria, the more than 400,000 in Morocco, and the 250,000 in Tunisia acted, with some exceptions, as staunch advocates of doing little or nothing for the natives and of preserving in power at all costs the reactionary local rulers. Coalition government in France enabled the elected representatives of the French in North Africa by horsetrading to wield undue influence on policy.

Colonial officials and army leaders, frequently used in high administrative positions in these areas, agreed with the representatives' views about the natives, and in all three regions turned almost all French economic aid away from the natives and to the advantage of the local Frenchmen, the so-called *colons*. In Tunisia and Morocco the group gradually transformed the protectorate into a system of direct French rule. When the natives rebelled, a well-disposed minister in the government in Paris would promise reforms; the coalition government of which he was a member would repudiate his promise, or would drop him entirely; the reforms would never be forthcoming; and direct rule would continue. In 1947, for example, Algeria received a new statute granting some autonomy; the sections pertaining to the *colons* were executed, those respecting the 8 million natives were ignored, and French officials continued to rig elections and pick the natives to be elected as representatives in the various local advisory bodies as well as in Paris.

Native reform leaders appeared first in Tunisia and Morocco and then in Algeria. Some looked toward Cairo and favored revival by way of Islam in association with Arab states. Others preferred close ties with France in matters of the economy, defense, and foreign relations but asked for the introduction of independent rule in all internal affairs. A few were Communists. In Tunisia the French had allowed native trade-unions to be formed, which became the organized mass basis for the nationalist movement. In Algeria the trade-unions never gained the strength of those in Tunisia; the movement split into two factions, and Communists gained control of the larger part and exploited it for their purposes. Morocco was prohibited from organizing a native trade-union; the French wished to avoid a repetition of the experience in Tunisia.

When the postwar rebellions occurred in North Africa, the French used tanks and planes as well as infantry, arresting natives en masse and committing illegal and brutal acts against the accused. The *colons* formed vigilantes to meet terror with terror. In Morocco the French High Commissioner, General Guillaume, organized the reactionary natives to replace the reform-minded sultan by an elderly weakling, and *colons* with the aid of the French police sought to terrorize into silence French officials and other *colons* who favored compromise. They assassinated one of the most prominent and reasonable Frenchmen in Morocco, and their counterparts acted similarly in the other two territories. As the rebellion spread, more Frenchmen were called into military service in North Africa, and these registered their protest against such action by occasional mutinies.

In 1954 Mendès-France became premier of France long enough to inaugurate negotiations for a satisfactory compromise with the Neo-Destour party, the most responsible group, in Tunisia. Although he was quickly overthrown by a combination of French parties pressed by representatives of the *colons,* his successor reached sufficient agreement with the native leaders to stop the war. Tunisia kept the French franc as her currency and belongs to a customs union with France. French economic interests in Tunisia are protected. Responsibility for defense and foreign relations remains with France; Frenchmen are to receive various privileges with respect to schools and justice. In all other respects Tunisia has gained the right of self-government. In Morocco a year later the French likewise retreated, restored the former sultan, and negotiated an agreement giving the native government greater power than Tunisia received. It could create a Moroccan army and foreign service, terms which France soon granted to Tunisia as well. In each instance the native leaders regarded the treaty as a milestone on the way to independence and have since then curtailed France's remaining authority. Spain has exceeded France's generosity by voluntarily relinquishing her part of Morocco, and the international city of Tangier has returned to its former owner, Morocco.

Fighting has continued in Algeria. The use of over 400,000 French troops, man power badly needed in the economy at home, and the expenditure of $1,400 million a year have not sufficed to subdue the natives. Week after week the Arab guerrillas attack French civilians and troops, burn houses, bomb theaters and restaurants, cut down fruit trees, and interrupt services by strikes. French troops and police try in vain to round up the rebels, and on occasion they and frequently the angry French civilians reciprocate with the kind of ruthless methods used by the natives.

The war is poisoning France's relations with Tunisia and Morocco and may jeopardize the exploitation of rich mineral resources recently discovered in the Sahara. Both Tunisia and Morocco are aware of their need for French investment funds and for the continued services of French technical and administrative personnel. Habib Bourguiba, president of the newly created Tunisian Republic, ranks as a statesman with Nehru and Smuts, persons devoted to their countries but also aware of the value of international understanding. Bourguiba advocates the independence of Algeria and the formation of a North African bloc that would then cooperate closely with France, Spain, and Italy. In the Algerian war Tunisia and Morocco side with their neighbor, and to their regret the longer the war lasts, the worse become their relations with France. The French are continuing to prospect for minerals in the Sahara, but war makes impossible exploitation of oil and other resources, and, if Tunisia and Morocco become hostile to her, how will France transport minerals to the Mediterranean coast?

In Algeria the French government faces the dilemma of granting independence or at least federal status to a territory which at present forms an integral part of metropolitan France or of bestowing first-class citizenship upon 9 million natives. If it accepts the latter policy it will have to elevate the natives to something like the French living standard, at an annual cost to the mother country of an estimated billion dollars for untold years. Shocked by the sudden discovery of dire poverty in this supposed model of governance, the French public has begun to question whether the gain is worth the price; but the government, whether headed by a Socialist or otherwise, has not changed policy. Its main purpose in attacking Egypt was to stop that country's aid to the Algerian rebels; and since the attack failed, France faces greater opposition than ever in Algeria.

COLOR PROBLEM IN AFRICA

Relations between European imperialist and Asiatic or African dependent peoples have everywhere been deeply affected by differences of color. The yellow and brown peoples of Asia possess sufficient cultural background, economic resources, and political experience to achieve political independence and to govern themselves. The Africans south of the

Sahara have needed white leadership and foreign investment capital in order to rise out of stagnation and poverty; the white settlers have required the aid of black labor in developing the country. The establishment of mutual respect and cooperation and the ability to adjust to changes in achievement and aspirations of both blacks and whites have been the cardinal standards for success in this interdependent society. The major responsibility for transforming the African cultures with a minimum of spiritual and institutional upheaval has lain with the Europeans.

More than 90 per cent of the Europeans south of the Sahara live in the Union of South Africa (2½ million as against more than 10 million blacks and those of mixed black and white blood), the two Rhodesias (200,000 versus 4 million blacks), and Kenya (30,000 versus 5,250,000 blacks). French settlers have been moving into French West Africa at such an increasing rate that in 1950 Dakar, the town made important by World War II, had a population of more than 30,000 Europeans and 250,000 Africans, and Abidjan, capital of the Ivory Coast, numbered 10,000 Europeans and 100,000 Africans, and both cities were rapidly growing. Race relations have shown considerable variation. The French in West Africa, in marked contrast to their failure in North Africa, have introduced the Africans to a market economy, to some participation in government, to education for the professions, and to the amenities of urban life without setting up a color bar. The Africans have responded to the increase in opportunities and have been content.

In South Africa the descendants of the Boers, or Afrikanders, in full control of the government since 1948, have accentuated racial separation and practice of white supremacy already begun long before World War II. The white English-speaking minority has disapproved of the action not so much in kind as in degree. *Apartheid,* the Afrikaans word to designate this policy, has been implemented by, among others, the following laws: First, a Bantu Authorities Act, which sought to re-establish the authority of the tribal chiefs, and which the reform-minded natives considered a reactionary measure; second, a complex set of pass laws which control the movement of natives outside the reserves, the special areas of eroded soil retained by the Bantus; third, the Group Areas Act, which enables the white government to expropriate the property of any individual or group where the act applies; fourth, the Separate Amenities Act, the legalization of Jim Crow practices; fifth, the Bantu Education Act, which severely curtails the opportunities for natives to receive an education; sixth, the Native Labor Act, which once more deprives the African trade-unions of legal recognition, makes native strikes illegal, and sets up complicated machinery controlled by the government for fixing wages and working conditions without consulting the native workers' leaders; and seventh, an anti-Communist law, which defines a Communist as one who "aims at the encouragement of feelings of hostility between the European and the non-European races" or who "aims at bringing about any political, industrial, social or economic change . . . by the promotion of disturbance or disorder . . . or by the threat of such acts." In order to have its way the Afrikander-dominated government has doubled the size of the Senate and packed the Supreme Court.

As from 4 to 5 million Bantus live outside the reserves and provide indispensable cheap labor for the white-owned mines and industries and for acting as servants in the homes, the Afrikanders have confronted a dilemma. The logical conclusion of *apartheid* would be complete geographic separation of blacks and whites, and this conclusion the whites cannot afford. The introduction of a modern economy brought about improvement in the skill of the native workers, increased their economic responsibility and raised their hopes and demands. Although the Afrikanders have so far been able to suppress riots by force, the prospect of private citizens' going armed has led government supporters to question the wisdom of the program. "Africa will always remain the continent of the non-White," Dr. G. P. Scholtz wrote in 1954 (the foreign editor of *Die Transvaler,* an Afrikaans newspaper of whose board of directors Mr. Strÿdam, prime minister since 1954 and a dogmatic, thoroughgoing believer in *apartheid,* is chairman), "and all Whites living there will have to reckon with this immutable fact," and he warned against the Afrikander conviction that native blacks would always remain uncivilized. A few pastors of the Dutch Reformed Church, the religious body to which the Afrikanders belong, have opposed *apartheid;* but the church officially has supported the government. It states that it "accepts the unity of the human race, which is not annulled by its diversity. At the same time it accepts the natural diversity of the human race, which is not annulled by its unity."

The South African government has refused to cooperate in any of the social or economic activities of the United Nations, and, being the object of condemnation for its racial policy by the UN majority, it has preserved only token participation in the organization. Isolated at home in Africa and abroad, defending their position by physical force, the Afrikanders, most of whom are unaware of the world's moral repudiation of their treatment of the blacks, have continued to expand their program. From suppression of the blacks they have advanced to suppression of criticism among whites in their own country, and leaders are at present campaigning to persuade the predominantly agricultural people to take over the industrial, commercial, and financial power from the native Englishmen.

Immediately to the north, in the Central African Federation, a strong group of English-speaking whites advocated *apartheid,* but their aims have been successfully opposed by other Rhodesian English, by the British government, and by British and American capital invested there in copper mining. The Kenya English have likewise favored *apartheid* in a somewhat milder form, and have had to be saved from the rebellion of the native Kikuyus, or Mau-Maus, by British military forces. Once that rebellion, which lasted several years, was defeated, the British government introduced political reforms and initiated economic and social changes to lead the natives toward self-government and a modern life. The example set by Nigeria, the Gold Coast, and several other areas in establishing a successful state and society managed by blacks has stirred all of native Africa.

THE COLONIAL MIND

The bearers of Western ideals and mores to dependent peoples have represented many occupations—the missionary, the government official, the merchant and industrialist, the skilled worker, the army officer, and the private soldier. The native reform leaders have usually been educated in Western schools, and in Asia and Africa have transmitted Western ideas to their people. Since the intellectuals have come from and returned to a society with little or no middle class, they have suffered, as the middleman between two cultures, from lack of experience, of understanding, and of assistance. As a distinguished Indian political leader wrote in 1955:

> Perhaps more alarming than the magnitude and complexity of the socio-economic problems of the region [Asia] is the spiritual and cultural condition of the Asian intelligentsia. Often the inheritor of an ancient and noble cultural and spiritual tradition, the Asian intellectual is left, as a result of many centuries of erosion and stagnation, with a legacy which is largely fatalism, passivity and the acceptance of authority. . . . There is a tendency to be a good slave or a good slave-driver. He also finds his recent historical background repellent and uninspiring. The combination of an old civilization in decay and the débris of foreign rule provides a poor foundation on which to build.[5]

"Asia suffers from chronic negatives," Dr. Charles Malik of Lebanon has written. Both observations could be applied in the main to Africa as well.

The intellectuals have found both democracy and communism attractive, the one for its devotion to freedom, the other for its ruthless will to immediate results. The introduction of political responsibility and the necessity to appeal to the masses for support in elections have compelled them to seek contacts with their people and to assume responsibility for political action. They have thereby gained in self-confidence and maturity and have begun the process, endless in any society, of learning to distinguish between socially valuable and socially dangerous ideas. Wherever a native middle class has arisen and an exchange economy has begun to penetrate the agricultural population, the people have rapidly and efficiently responded to the challenge. Wherever the native has been treated as an inferior and denied opportunity to exercise his ability, he has tended to meet coercion with violence.

At the mid-century mark, relations between Western states and the former or present dependencies were characterized by profound change.

[5] M. R. Masani, "The Mind of Asia," *Foreign Affairs*, July, 1955, p. 553.

The Western ideal of nationalism, while spreading rapidly, was at the same time meeting obstacles. In an earlier period it might have been possible slowly to amalgamate two or more cultures into a new national society. In this age it seems difficult to do so. Each of the Asiatic and the African states contains a number of cultures, which the groups, loyal to the political union, wish to preserve. The ideals of the United Nations have been spreading in both theory and practice. In Asia the frontiers of the present states have been fairly well set by history; in Africa many were arbitrarily fixed by the imperialist powers, often unaware that they were splitting tribal territory. In this continent the existing political units lack the resources necessary to develop a modern economy adequate for the population. Hence it has been proposed to change present frontier lines or federate several territories.

ECONOMIC AND INTELLECTUAL AID

Lacking the capital and technical personnel for improving their economy, their government, and their social standards, the native peoples, once independence is acquired, have sought aid from the United Nations and, with much mistrust, from countries of the West. Since the problems are not peculiar to any one country or territory, assistance from the West has often been of regional significance. The United Nations technicians have done much, and the empire builders themselves, particularly in Africa, have organized many joint conferences since World War II on matters of common concern. In 1950, for example, representatives of the governments of Belgium, France, Portugal, the Union of South Africa, Southern Rhodesia, and Great Britain founded a Commission for Technical Co-operation for Africa South of the Sahara. This commission has worked with the United Nations and has held conferences at various places in the region. Its range of interest may be seen from the nature of the four technical information offices which by 1951 operated under its direction; the bureau on tsetse and trypanosomiasis at Leopoldville in the Belgian Congo, the bureau on soil conservation and utilization at Paris, France; the bureau of epizootic diseases at Nairobi, Kenya; and the Inter-Africa Labor Institute.

In 1950 Great Britain and its former dependencies, Pakistan, India, Ceylon, Australia, New Zealand, and Canada worked out the Colombo plan, named after the meeting place, for the coordinated development of the economy of Southern and Southeast Asia. The group has continued its activities for obtaining investment funds and deciding upon the projects like flood control and the construction of hydroelectric plants which appeared to be most urgent.

The role of the European states and of the other Western industrial countries in these colonial areas has changed from one of imperial ruler to one of providing capital, technical aid, and often leadership in the development of the native human and material resources. Countries as diverse in economy as Norway and Germany have initiated plans for participating in this new global action. Europeans have realized that the development of backward areas offers an opportunity to expand their economy comparable to that of the industrialization of Europe in the previous century, with benefits to both peoples.

Now that many former dependencies have acquired freedom, colonial defense has to be redefined. The new states usually shun close ties with former imperial masters; they fear attempts to reassert the old relationship. India and others in Asia and Africa have chosen to remain neutral in the cold war between the Soviet Union and Western states. Only when the Communist threat became acute were the governments willing, as evidenced in the Bagdad Pact, to align with former imperialist powers.

THE QUESTION OF DEFENSE

Asia has undergone profound change in commitments for defense. The United States has become increasingly involved in the security of the Far East and Southeast Asia since making treaties with Japan, the Philippine Islands, Australia, New Zealand, and Taiwan. Steps in the endeavor to contain the Communist menace include a defensive alliance between the United States and South Korea and American economic assistance (including military supplies and technicians to South Viet Nam). In 1954 a Southeast Asia Treaty Organization (SEATO), modeled after NATO, was formed by the United States, the Philippine Islands, Australia, New Zealand, Pakistan, Thailand, France, and Great Britain. And the United States has encouraged Japan to rearm in the new capacity of ally.

When the Suez crisis spelled the end of British influence for protecting the Near and Middle East, the United States had to recognize the existence of extensive interests in Western as well as in Eastern Asia. Concern for the safety of the Jews, on the one hand, and the desire to assure conditions in which Arab peoples could improve their way of life in freedom, on the other, led the United States to try to reconcile the hostility of the opponents.

> The Near Eastern area [the Department of State had written to the Congress in presenting the Mutual Security Program for 1952] is important to the security of the United States and of the free world. It lies athwart the principal lines of sea and air communication in the eastern Hemisphere. It is a land bridge between Asia and Africa, Soviet control of which would expose the African continent. It is a source of prime strategic material, oil, the continuing supply of which is essential to friendly nations in Europe and Asia.

Heavy American investments in oil production in the region and missionary work in education and humanitarian services of long standing supplemented political interest.

Deeply concerned over the rapid expansion of Soviet influence in Egypt and Syria, the threatened bankruptcy of Jordan, and the utter confusion of political relations in the area, President Eisenhower at the beginning of 1957 offered to the states military aid in defending themselves and the prospect of economic help. "The world has so shrunk," he said, "that all free nations are our neighbors. Without coöperative neighbors, the United States cannot maintain its own security and welfare." He invited the rulers of Saudi Arabia, Iraq, and Lebanon to Washington for conference, and thereby checkmated Egypt's influence. The United States government granted economic aid to the menaced Jordan, and agreed to join the Military Committee of the Bagdad Pact. By sending the Mediterranean fleet to the Near East it expressed determination to prevent Communist aggression. The United States under President Eisenhower is extending its protection and leadership to one more vital area of the world.

Soviet Union Takes an Active Interest

The strategy of the Soviet Union toward underdeveloped peoples in Asia, Africa, and elsewhere after Stalin's death added the weapon of economic to that of political infiltration. Exploiting the fear of Western states, the Soviet rulers forswore publicly any intention of interfering in the internal affairs of other countries and issued a new kind of challenge. "Some people think," Premier Bulganin declared in 1955, "that capitalism is better than socialism. We are convinced that the opposite is the case. This argument cannot be settled by force, through war. Let everyone prove in peaceful economic competition that he is right." When in February, 1955, Secretary of State Dulles declared that any Communist aggression in the SEATO area would be stopped by the United States using "new and powerful weapons of precision [the tactical atomic weapons] which can utterly destroy military targets without endangering unrelated civilian centers," and threatened "massive retaliation," "measured retaliation," and "graduated deterrence," Bulganin and Khrushchev countered at the end of the year with a tour of India, Burma, and Afghanistan.

Everywhere the Soviet leaders denounced the West and offered economic aid. They agreed to exchange industrial plants for Burmese rice, that no one else would buy. They proposed to establish a technical institute at Rangoon and to build an aluminum plant and hydroelectric works in South India. In comparison with Western states, however, they have done little. At the middle of 1957 the Soviet Union had extended credits of only $1,500 million spread over a period of five years. Of this amount all but 10 to 20 per cent was devoted to the sale of arms. In the past five years Great Britain granted or loaned nearly three times as much, and since the war the United States foreign aid has been thirty-six times as much.

The Soviet government replied to the Eisenhower doctrine with a six-point program for settling Near and Middle Eastern questions. The first called for the exclusive use of "peaceful means, on the basis of the method of negotiation." The second proposed "noninterference in the internal affairs of the countries," respect for their sovereignty and independence. Coming at the time of Soviet suppression of the revolution in Hungary, these requests did not inspire confidence among Western peoples. Acceptance of the third and fourth was made impossible by lack of belief that the Soviet Union would abide by the terms of the previous points. The third asked for "refusal to undertake any attempts to draw these countries into military alignments with the participation of the great powers." The fourth proposed "the liquidation of foreign bases and the withdrawal of foreign troops" from these areas. The Soviet government argued in favor of these two points that they were pacific in intent and that the Bagdad Pact and the retention of bases by Western powers in the area constituted a potential threat to the security of the Soviet Union. It warned the Near and Middle Eastern countries not to allow their lands to be used by the United States "as bridgeheads in preparation for an atomic war," for, it argued, "blows struck by some weapons are answered by blows struck by the same weapons."

The Western governments countered by citing the long history of Soviet destruction of the freedom of weak neighbors and declared that Western military support of the states in the region was essential to offset the Soviet advantage of geographic contiguity. For the same reason they could not accept the Soviet fifth point, "joint refusal to supply arms to countries of the Near and Middle East." How could the free West be certain that the Soviet Union would not smuggle arms across the border to its fellow Communists? The sixth Soviet proposal seemed to epitomize the ideals of the United Nations. It read, "Assistance in the economic development of countries of the Near and Middle East, without putting forward any political, military or other conditions incompatible with the dignity and sovereignty of these countries." Interpreting the promise by Soviet behavior toward the countries of Eastern Europe, the Western governments trusted the proposer on this point no more than they did on the others. Since the Soviet leaders were similarly afraid of the Eisenhower doctrine, the two sides once more reached deadlock.

Of the states in the Near and Middle East, Egypt and Syria alone proved susceptible alike to the prospect of Soviet economic aid and the reality of acquiring Soviet arms and the service of Communist technicians. The military rulers of these two countries were confident that they could utilize Soviet support against the West without suffering the fate of Hungary, China, and other formerly free states.

"We value trade least for economic reasons," Khrushchev said to visiting United States senators, "and most for political purposes as a means of promoting better relations between our countries." An American economist after studying the evidence has explained the universal application of the statement as follows:

The political values are clearly uppermost. The economic effects are decidedly marginal. By expanding trade, they [the Soviets] may even improve the position of their own consumers by obtaining rice for a product such as cement [Burma]. By exporting capital, they may slow down their own rate of expansion a little or even delay the rate at which their growth is reflected in the standard of living, but neither of these will clearly appear to their citizens as a calculated and explicit burden. For various reasons, they can easily send more technicians abroad than can we under our present procedures. Furthermore, their programs often have more appeal than ours, even if they may be less sensible in terms of the allocation of resources. They may do the more conspicuous or symbolic project, such as paving the streets in Kabul, or the more impressive, such as building a steel mill in India. And always there is the steady beat of propaganda asserting that Soviet programs are disinterested without strings, while Western programs are militaristic, imperialistic and set about with conditions.[6]

Nehru Speaks for Neutralism

Not only did many of the peoples of Asia and Africa wish to remain neutral in the cold war; they mistrusted military defense as a means of combating communism and suspected American intentions. India, Burma, Indonesia, and others refused to join SEATO. Africa, where many peoples were distant from Communist powers, took little interest in these questions. The United States retained rights to air bases in Morocco and at other points in North Africa, as Great Britain did in Libya; but, except for Egypt, the African states also sought to keep free of international complications. The governments of states in Asia and Africa alike endeavored to keep on good terms with both Communist and free Western powers and to mediate between the two sides. Those in Asia kept a line open to Peiping during the Korean war. In the Suez crisis all condemned Franco-British-Israel aggression and advocated moderation among the parties, including Egypt. In the United Nations the states have pursued a policy which their leading spokesman, Nehru, while visiting the United States at the close of 1956, expressed as follows:

Countries dominated by other countries should cease to be dominated. . . . I am quite sure that as we stand today all these pacts and military alliances are completely out of place. They are even unnecessary for the people who have them. . . . The idea of the "cold war" is the very negation of the idea that the United Nations stands for. . . . The presence of foreign forces in other countries is not normal. It is not wanted by the people.

The system of military bases placed about the world

is unnecessary, is only an irritant; is evil and wickedness. . . . We can't go on much longer with the preservation of a system based on fears and hates. . . . We must work for solutions based on cooperation. We believe, therefore, in non-

[6] Willard L. Thorp, "American Policy and Soviet Economic Offensive," *Foreign Affairs*, January, 1957, p. 279.

aggression and non-interference by one country in the affairs of another, and the growth of tolerance between them and the capacity for peaceful co-existence.

In expressing the ideals of many Asian-African peoples, although not all of them (one recalls the military tradition of Islam), Nehru stated a policy that fitted urgent needs. The countries must transform backward societies into modern nations. If burdened with the necessity of defense, they would spend their small amounts of capital funds on nonproductive armaments; the life of the masses would easily become so intolerable as to invite revolt and communism. To the colored populations of these two continents foreign relations involve more than political and military power; the peoples wish above all to achieve racial and cultural equality with the rest of the world. They support the United Nations in order to curb power policies and to have a center of international social and economic work. They have held conferences among themselves, the largest being at Bandung in 1955, where white representatives were excluded, to discuss their achievements and aspirations. The leaders hope that their peoples will not repeat the mistakes of Western nationalism and materialism during the past century, that they will raise the standard of living while preserving the native spiritual heritage.

From a study of international and imperial relations during the past half century, one may draw the following conclusions: (1) One-time colonial relations will continue to change into international relations. The Suez crisis, the civil war in Algeria, and the conflicts in Poland and Hungary, to mention a few examples, all indicate that the demand of dependent peoples to be free will not abate. (2) The cost of armaments in an atomic age has become so onerous that the responsibility for military defense is being shifted to the two superpowers, the United States and the Soviet Union. The allies of the United States are protesting against the cost. Great Britain, for example, estimated at the close of 1956 that she could save £700 million for civilian use by cutting imperial defense and confining her obligations to those within NATO. The rebellion of Poles and Magyars indicates that peoples in the Soviet bloc object to low living standards caused by concentration upon heavy industry and armaments. (3) A world war in an atomic age will destroy mankind, and no one has yet devised a preventive against the possibility that a little colonial war may become a holocaust. (4) For keeping the initiative in international affairs the Soviet planned conduct of foreign relations has proved superior to the American custom of devising a policy after a crisis has arisen. The United States has shown a few signs, the Truman Doctrine and its extension, the Eisenhower Doctrine, the Marshall plan, and other programs, of learning to lay down policies in anticipation. But the refusal of Congress, for example, to commit this country to support an economic program abroad over a period of years indicates that the United States continues foreign political practices of a preindustrial, preatomic society. (5) The methods and objectives of international relations in a world of independent states of all sizes, degrees of power, standards of living, kinds of culture have scarcely begun to be clarified. For this work the United Nations and its affiliated agencies offer the most widely accepted guides. (6) The cold war between free nations and Communist nations will persist, but the free world does not lack ability to protect itself. The monolithic strength of the Soviet world can be shaken by the need of human beings for peace and freedom.

Suggestions for Further Reading

BELOFF, MAX. *Soviet Policy in the Far East, 1944–1951.* New York: Oxford University Press, 1953.

BURT, A. L. *The Evolution of the British Empire and Commonwealth.* See the Readings for Chapter 11.

CRAGG, KENNETH. *The Call of the Minaret.* New York: Oxford University Press, 1956. Excellent statement of the new objectives in Islamic society.

HODGKIN, THOMAS. *Nationalism in Colonial Africa.* London: Frederick Muller, Ltd., 1956. Excellent brief analysis of this crucial problem.

DE KIEWEIT, C. W. *The Anatomy of South African Misery.* New York: Oxford University Press, 1957. Brief analysis by an authority.

KING, JOHN KERRY. *Southeast Asia in Perspective.* New York: The Macmillan Company, 1956. Covers the last fifteen years.

LAQUEUR, WALTER. *Communism and Nationalism in the Middle East.* New York: Frederick A. Praeger, Inc., 1956.

LATOURETTE, K. S. *A Short History of the Far East.* See the Readings for Chapter 1.

LENCZOWSKI, GEORGE. *The Middle East in World Affairs.* See the Readings for Chapter 2.

Preliminary Report on the World Social Situation. See the Readings for Chapter 6.

SADY, EMIL J. *The United Nations and Dependent Peoples.* Washington, D.C.: The Brookings Institution, 1956. Brief analysis of the colonial problem and of what the United Nations has done on this crucial issue.

SCHWADRON, BENJAMIN. *The Middle East, Oil and the Great Powers.* New York: Frederick A. Praeger, Inc., 1955.

STILLMAN, CALVIN W., ed. *Africa in the Modern World.* Chicago: University of Chicago Press, 1955. A symposium.

ZINKIN, MAURICE. *Asia and the West.* See the Readings for Chapter 11.

Chapter 24 · The Free Countries of Europe

After World War II the role of nationalism declined with the general awareness that recovery of non-Communist Europe required the use of international as well as national means. The basic problems left over from an international war were international in character; these have already been discussed. The present and succeeding chapters will be devoted to the complementary efforts at recovery which each state made. The nature and extent of their difficulties depended upon prewar as well as war conditions. The former totalitarian countries had to face most problems, the nations of democratic government and stable society fewest. France stood somewhere in between, and the two countries preserving an authoritarian regime submerged their troubles by force.

GREAT BRITAIN

Great Britain emerged from World War II high in morale but financially about as close to bankruptcy as a nation can be. The crucial problems lay, not, as in continental countries, in political or social relations and governmental form, but in economics. Although the two main parties, Labor with a socialist theoretical background and the Conservative devoted to capitalism, appeared to be far apart in their programs for solving Britain's difficulties, the degree of their difference was much less than the party names would imply. The experience of past years culminating in World War II had taught British parties and classes mutual understanding and respect.

LABOR PARTY IN POWER

The first evidence of trust came between the time of Germany's surrender and that of Japan's suit for peace. In July, 1945, the nation held a general election to replace the wartime Parliament. The Conservatives returned only 197 members, the Labor party 393, among whom were 35 former miners, 66 former railway workers, and 21 women. The British had carried out by way of an election what many foreigners called a social revolution. The phrase scarcely applied; numerous people who had formerly voted Conservative now supported Labor, which did not intend a revolution even by parliamentary means. The people were registering disapproval of the stagnation and unemployment of interwar years. "Never again, it was felt, should the nation be exposed to the uncontrolled forces of markets if they worked to the detriment of the economic future of the country. It was hoped that Labor would ensure not merely full employment and social security, but also a consciously planned and accelerated development of the nation's resources." [1] This aim was to be achieved without recourse to authoritarianism. The people trusted Labor rather than the Conservatives under Churchill to make the most effective use in time of peace of the nation's resources.

The Program of Nationalization

The Labor party contained advocates of two different policies for British economic recovery. The smaller group, led by Aneurin Bevan, upheld free, responsible government as much as any Britisher, but it clung to the standard version of socialism and regarded nationalization of property as the answer to all economic and social problems. The great majority of the party, under the guidance of the thoroughly middle-class Major Clement Attlee and heads of the trade-unions, wanted to nationalize only the parts of the economy of basic significance to the entire nation. Private owners could retain the rest, but the state's power of taxation would be employed to transfer income from the wealthy to the poor and introduce that social justice of which capitalism seemed incapable. Both the minority and the majority agreed that this transfer should take the form of social security, public housing, free and equal opportunities for education, a national health service, and other additions to real income. The workers should not be treated as second-class citizens, as in many continental countries, but should be enabled to participate fully in national life, supplying leaders, sharing in decisions in the economy as well as in government and other branches of life, and enjoying the comforts of modern civilization. For the first time in history a Labor government had a sufficient majority to execute its program. Since the socialist minority within the party was busy with responsibilities of national administration, it did not cause much trouble over nationalization until toward the close of Labor's six-year tenure of office.

The Labor government quickly initiated action to nationalize the coal industry, the gas and electricity systems, and the railways, and, apart from

[1] Thomas Balogh, "British Party Programs: The Miracle and the Mirage," *Foreign Affairs,* April, 1955, p. 458.

local delivery, the motor trucks. It set up a Raw Cotton Exchange with exclusive authority to import and sell raw cotton; it established a Colonial Development Corporation to carry out major capital enterprises in the colonies and an Overseas Food Corporation to raise food on a large scale in the colonial regions. It assumed control over the Bank of England and increased the power of that bank over the large joint-stock banks. It continued most of the wartime powers of physical control over the economy, especially those pertaining to the approval of investment, the rationing of food and a few other basic consumers' items, the licensing of businesses to receive raw materials, the regulation of the flow of imports, and the monopoly of foreign exchange. Toward the end of its period in office it passed the vigorously disputed act nationalizing the iron and steel industry, but it enabled the public to decide this issue by postponing execution of the law until after the forthcoming national election.

The program did not in the main mark a radical break with the past. Many Conservatives acknowledged that government alone could reorganize the coal industry and supply the investment funds needed for improving it. Public utilities had in the main already belonged to local public bodies, and nationalization amounted to the exchange of one kind of public ownership for another for the sake of improved efficiency and economy. The existing method of generation and distribution of electricity and gas was considered too small and too expensive. A national system of interconnected stations and standardized service would assure flexibility in meeting the fluctuations in demand during the day and the seasons and could provide power to new industries in new regions. The state alone, it was argued, possessed the capital and the authority to introduce improvements. Railroads had for years been subject to government regulation and were not far removed from public ownership.

The nationalization of motor transport aroused severe criticism as impracticable and as curbing this cheap form of transportation in favor of the railroads. Motor trucks were numerous and, like tramp steamers, required flexible handling and private initiative, the opponents argued, which government management would destroy. Nonetheless, the act was passed.

The government struck severe resistance only when it proposed to nationalize the iron and steel industry. By English standards this branch of the economy had proved efficient and did not lack investment funds and competent management. Opponents accused the Labor government of seeking to nationalize steel, not for any practical reason, but merely for the dogmatic one of placing all basic industries, coal, gas, electricity, transportation, and iron and steel, under public ownership.

Nationalization of the Bank of England won general acceptance as an act transferring power over that powerful institution from a few persons to a self-governing society. The Labor government regarded the official control of money and credit as indispensable for assuring full employment.

This general view was reinforced by bitter memories of Bank of England policy during the great depression in the 1920's and 30's, when industrial well-being was sacrificed to financial interests, capital expenditure restricted by high rates of interest, and the misery of prolonged unemployment suffered by millions of men and women for nearly two decades. The Labour Party determined that never again should the Government and the people be at the mercy of a Bank of England intent on deflation at all costs. The financial crisis of 1931 was also remembered as an indication of the ease with which financiers can create a state of insecurity and bring about a political crisis [throwing the Labor government at that time out of office] by manipulating the instruments they control.[2]

Management of Nationalized Industries

If iron and steel are included, the state-owned sector amounted to one fifth of the total economy, and one person in every four was employed by the state. The manner in which these enterprises were run affected the entire economy by way, to offer one example, of the cost of production. To manage them the Labor government erected the public corporation, a new type of business organization, with the appropriate minister in the cabinet having greater responsibility than he had previously had over the British Broadcasting Company or any other state-owned business. The minister received authority after consulting the board of directors of the corporation to give "directions of a general character as to the exercise and performance by the corporation of their functions in relation to matters which appear to him to affect the national interest." He was required to appoint members of a small governing board who had experience and ability to qualify them for the work.

Membership on a typical board has been described as follows:

. . . a leading member of the industry, usually a high executive of wide experience and established reputation; an outstanding ex-trade union official; a top-flight former civil servant; a leading financial expert; an eminent engineer or scientist; perhaps a leading business-man from another industry; possibly a lawyer, or a retired air marshal or Army general who showed conspicuous organizing ability or leadership in the war.[3]

The members received a salary set by the minister and higher than those paid to civil servants but lower than those paid in private enterprise. The government approved all loans made for capital investment and required each corporation to maintain a reserve fund. The corporation set its own price policy, but usually the price had to be one that would meet expenditures.

The public corporation has had to deal with problems which are different from those of private business. It early created facilities for at-

[2] William A. Robson, ed., *Problems of Nationalized Industry* (New York: Oxford University Press, 1952), p. 285. By permission also of George Allen & Unwin Ltd.
[3] *Ibid.*, pp. 260-261.

tending to public complaints; but it soon learned that many persons sent their grievances to members of Parliament. Herbert Morrison of the Labor ministry protested against the abuse of the latter practice.

> If these men [the members of the governing boards] are to live a life which is really a Civil Service life, and are liable to be abused across the floor of the House and subjected to questions attacking them and their commercial ability we shall not get the men to serve on these commercial undertakings, and we shall not get the best out of those who are there.

The main duties of Parliament lay in deciding basic policy and in reviewing execution. In order that Parliament might perform these tasks it had to be kept informed about the corporations. An objective standard of measurement of efficiency, as well as more publicity than for private business, was sought.

In some respects the problem is similar to that of parliamentary control over a ministry with a large budget; at no time has an adequate solution been found. The difficulty in part arose because, whether privately or publicly owned, a monopoly has to fix prices and profits by some means other than competition. This question lacks a definitive answer, but experts have affirmed that prices should be kept close to costs, and they have added three words of caution.

> First, the break-even or surplus which is achieved must not be the result of exploitation. Trade unions should have an equal, but not more than an equal, bargaining power with other interested parties [for example, the consumers]. Second, it must not conceal social costs, such as the destruction of amenities or a high accident rate, which do not enter into the account. Third and most important, it must not result from a high margin on a small output . . . the prime measure of efficiency may be defined as breaking even, or slightly more than even, *at the greatest possible aggregate of production.*[4]

The corporations should not necessarily charge uniform prices, for, as Professor W. Arthur Lewis remarked, "Uniformity of charges where there is no uniformity of cost is the refuge of the lazy mind." [5]

Public ownership meant that the relations between labor and management had to be reconsidered. Parliament wrote into the statutes safeguards for the health and welfare of the workers, for the negotiation of terms of work, and the establishment of joint committees to settle problems; but it did not stop with terms standard for any labor agreement. It added that management should draw upon the practical knowledge and experience of the workers in every possible way to increase the efficiency of the corporation. Labor was thereby pressed to change its defensive and negative attitude taken toward private industry in favor of a display of "constructive leadership, understanding and cooperation with the management." [6] To that end the trade-unions would need to improve the quality of their own officials and to develop a new type of expert for use in these enterprises.

[4] *Ibid.*, p. 336. [5] *Ibid.*, p. 337. [6] *Ibid.*, p. 343.

The social transformation connected with the rise of the public corporation created new opportunities for labor, but also new responsibilities. The same general statement applied to Parliament, the public, and management. The public corporation expressed a novel relationship among the social, economic, and political groups of Great Britain. There seems to be general agreement that the experiment has proved satisfactory for labor, management, and the public, and that some of the success of British economic recovery since the war can be attributed to the cooperation between labor and management achieved by this body.

The absence of dogmatic socialism may be seen from the efforts of the British Labor government to improve the efficiency of private enterprise. To that end, among other measures, it subsidized industrial research, created development councils for industry and commerce, set up a commission against private monopolies, granted sums for research to the British Institute of Management, and cooperated with United States industry in the exchange of technical and scientific information. It used public financial power to encourage investment, and it kept prices and wages fairly stable. It retained the wartime tax rates, which were far heavier than those in the United States, and it employed taxation as a means to increase labor's share of the national income. Thus four fifths of the population, with income of less than £500 a year, consumed 63 per cent of the goods and services in 1938 and 73 per cent in 1949. Eighteen per cent of the population, in the intermediate income brackets, consumed 30 per cent before the war and only 23 per cent in 1949. The 2 per cent with the largest incomes consumed 6.3 per cent before the war and 3.3 per cent in 1949.

The standard of living recovered from the impact of the war to a point less high in 1950 than in 1939 but nonetheless above most of Europe. The man power of the rapidly demobilized army geared smoothly into the economy and was fully employed. Strikes occurred to a far less extent than in the first years after World War I, a saving in production power directly attributed to the confidence labor felt in having its own party in charge of the government. Public health, improved during the war by the high nutritive value of the food rations, continued excellent. The broad system of social insurance underwent some reforms and extensions, and a National Health Service came into effect for the entire nation which provided free medical, dental, and ophthalmic service, including the cost of hospitals, medicines, eyeglasses, new teeth, and similar items. Private medical and dental practice was not abolished, but the number of persons using it declined to a small proportion of the population. Public funds for education were expanded; for example, between 1938 and 1950 grants to the universities increased elevenfold, and the growth has continued. The share of the national income which the government commanded has greatly increased since prewar days, but this fact did not destroy the habit of private saving. In 1948–1949 real savings had increased over the amount of 1938 by 2½ times.

Weakness in International Economy

The Labor government's attack upon the "'five giants on the road of reconstruction,' Want, Disease, Ignorance, Squalor and Idleness" (Sir William Beveridge) kept the British masses hopeful and assured social peace, but it proved insufficient to overcome the economic difficulties accumulated over two generations and gravely accentuated by World War II. In 1938 Great Britain had balanced its international payments by income from foreign investments. In 1945 it owed abroad £3,500 million, and its foreign investments were less than £3,000 million. It has been estimated that between 1939 and 1944 the direct costs of the war to Britain amounted to almost £14,000 million at 1938 prices. The country met the expense in the following way: 40 per cent by increased output, 25 per cent by cutting down private and normal government expenditure, and 35 per cent by drawing on domestic and foreign capital. By way of comparison one might note that the United States increased output sufficiently to bear the cost of the war. The British reduced expenditures on consumers' goods; far more important for the future, they slashed private investment at home.

When the war ended the country was victorious, but it had become an international debtor with an economy, except for agriculture, which was not equipped to compete with that, for example, of the United States. By the end of 1945 the British merchant marine had diminished by 30 per cent from its prewar size, and commodity exports had declined since 1938 by 58 per cent. Certain unattractive industries, like coal mining, textiles, and agriculture, were undermanned; the usual war-caused dislocations in industry were everywhere in evidence; machine tools, in contrast to Germany, had increased but slightly in number. Britain owed the United States, the Dominions, the colonies, and Latin America; she lacked the means to pay; her market relations had been disrupted, while the economies of the United States, Canada, India, and elsewhere expanded their production and their exports; and her productive plant needed vast investment sums for modernization. The amount of money and credit in circulation from the war was out of all proportion to the quantity of goods available for purchase, and the urgently needed investments in industry, in housing, and in transportation augmented the threat of inflation.

Under Labor's guidance the country progressed technically and expanded its economy at a faster pace than in any other period in this century. Nonetheless, the difficulty of obtaining sufficient foreign exchange to maintain trade recurred every two years, and Britain was dependent on E.R.P. funds to balance her international payments, a sign that the nation was still living on a precarious margin. Critics maintained that she was attempting to do too much. She should not pay the war debts to India, Egypt, and other countries traditionally dependent upon her, for, the critics argued, the money had all been spent for a common cause. Britain should not carry the burden of armaments and of occupation costs in various areas of the world; instead, she should withdraw in favor of the United States in more spots than Greece. She should not support the extensive program at home of social security, public medicine, and the like; she should, the critics said, devote these sums to improving production. The Bevanites of the Labor left criticized their Labor colleagues for not going farther toward socialization.

The severest criticism attacked the retention of wartime controls, when the country seemed to need freedom. Labor set targets for various industries and tried to guide the economy into achieving them; first, by control over the nationalized sector; second, through fiscal policies, like the payment of subsidies; and, third and most irksome, through actual physical controls—price fixing, rationing, allocation of raw material, licensing of building, and guidance of capital investments.

The complications and confusion that resulted became evident during a heavy snow that struck the country in February, 1947, and left a coating of ice which stopped all transportation. Coal and other supplies were everywhere short, as no reserves had been accumulated; with the continuation of the cold weather British economic life almost halted.

CONSERVATIVE PARTY IN POWER

The Labor government could not be blamed for this exceptional freeze; but when Sir Stafford Cripps, secretary of the exchequer, imposed in the next year a program of extreme austerity upon the nation in order to meet another foreign exchange crisis and unexpectedly devalued the pound in an attempt to reduce imports and increase exports, the popularity of the government began to decline. In the election of 1950 Labor barely retained a majority. The next year the Conservatives forced it into a new election, from which the Conservatives returned with a small majority. Labor had found that nationalization did not in itself solve problems, and the party had no new program to offer. The quarrel between the Bevanites and the moderates became so acrimonious that marginal voters transferred support to the Conservatives. When a new parliament was elected in 1955, the voters, facing practically the same choice as before, again returned a Conservative majority.

The Conservative government retained the program of social welfare and government ownership and restored only the iron and steel industry to private ownership. True to its election promise, it reduced the physical control exercised by the government over the economy. Rationing of the consumer soon ended, and restraints on the commodity markets and on imports were lightened. The free market once more became in most respects the final judge of what should be produced and of where capital funds should be invested.

To the surprise of Labor and the satisfaction of the Conservatives, the results justified the change in policy. British production and consumption increased, full employment persisted, the construction of houses expanded rapidly, personal savings in two years' time multiplied ninefold; both imports and exports grew; and the balance of payments changed from a large deficit to a large surplus, which rendered further American E.R.P. contributions unnecessary. Aided by a favorable turn in the terms of trade, the Conservatives were able several times to reduce taxes and to encourage the accumulation of funds for private investment. Every social group benefited materially except the lowest paid of the working class; but the restoration of freedom of choice in the purchase of consumers' goods went far to compensate for this discrimination. Critics maintained that the nation still failed to invest sufficient funds to insure continued increase in output and to restore the country's position in international trade. They placed Great Britain's economic revival, however, with that in the West German Republic as a remarkable achievement.

Although Great Britain recovered her economic independence, this term must be understood in the sense applied to any small industrial country of limited natural resources. Imports and exports continued to provide the basis of life, a fact that may be clearly seen in the results from agriculture. The war experience had once more stressed the necessity of raising as much food as possible to safeguard the nation against starvation by blockade and to conserve transport space in favor of materials urgently required for fighting. Hence the British imported tractors and other implements, expanded the production of fertilizers, put land into cultivation formerly left as meadow or as waste, and increased technical and scientific services for agriculture. Coarse grain, wheat, potato, and dairy production received encouragement as the bulk goods most essential and most easily grown at home, whereas meat could be readily imported. Government subsidies helped to guide food production and to keep down the price of food, a system that the Labor cabinet maintained in full and the Conservatives in substantial part. By 1952 production of six cereal crops, raw sugar, and potatoes increased over the prewar average 50 to 60 per cent, and the further application of science was expected to improve this record; nonetheless, the country remained dependent for about one half its food upon imports. It continued to purchase raw materials from all over the world and to sell its manufactures in return. Interdependence with others resembled that of continental Europe.

INTERNATIONAL POLICY

The development of modern instruments of war culminating in the atomic bomb heightened British awareness of dependence upon other nations. Soviet aggression in Eastern Europe and in Iran, Greece, Berlin, and Korea caused the Labor government to approve the stationing of American troops in the island, to help organize NATO, to double the defense budget, and to support British research on atomic energy. The British sought new means to implement their traditional policy of preventing one power, this time the Soviet Union, from dominating Europe; and the majority of Labor and the entire Conservative party and the small Liberal party supported a common foreign and defense policy. Labor stressed the need for constant effort to negotiate a peaceful settlement with the Soviet Union; but, apart from the pro-Soviet and anti-United States Bevanites, the party adhered to a nonpartisan foreign policy. The British did so after mature consideration of the menace of atomic war to them as an island people.

> It is in the power of the enemy [R. T. Paget stated in the House of Commons in March, 1954] to obliterate our ports [by means of atomic bombs]. . . . It would not matter much how many people would be killed because it would only mean that there would be fewer left to starve. Not only would we be unable to carry on a war, but we should be in a geographical situation in which it would be impossible to reactivate. Doubtless the war would be continued from Canada to eventual victory, but it is not a war which would concern us as a political entity.

The British developed a system of defense against air attack with atomic bombs which used the most advanced scientific and technological knowledge. They recognized that one or more bombs might penetrate their defense screen, but in the words of the Defense Ministry *White Paper* of 1955, they concluded as follows:

> In the last resort, most of us must feel that determination to face the threat of physical destruction—even on the immense scale which must now be foreseen—is manifestly preferable to an attitude of subservience to militant communism, with the national and individual humiliation that this would invariably bring. Moreover, such a show of weakness or hesitation to use all the means of defense at our disposal would not reduce the risk. All history proves the contrary.

Particularly after World War II did the British debate whether they had committed themselves to international duties beyond their resources. India and Egypt gained independence, and protection of Greece was transferred to the United States; but Malaya, Cyprus, West Germany, NATO, to mention the most important, required maintenance of large British forces and augmented costs in money and man power at a time of stringency at home.

The Suez Canal crisis late in 1956 disclosed with startling clarity the extent of the decline in British power. The Conservative party adhered to the imperialist tradition, which since the time of Disraeli had been one of its distinguishing characteristics. Sir Anthony Eden, who in 1955 succeeded the aged Sir Winston Churchill as prime minister, was responsible for the decision to reoccupy the Suez Canal area. When world opinion demanded the withdrawal of British and French forces, the Suez attack collapsed, and Sir Anthony soon found it advisable to resign (January, 1957). He was succeeded by Harold MacMillan, a Conservative businessman, who had been chancellor of the exchequer in the Eden cabinet. The Labor party unanimously denounced the invasion and demanded a general election. Some members of the Conservative party disapproved the move against Suez; many objected strongly to abrupt withdrawal. Almost all remained loyal to the ministry.

Mr. MacMillan weathered the Labor attack, but the cost of the British blunder had to be paid. Britain was hurt economically from it so severely that she became unable to meet the interest on the debt to the United States and Canada. The government asked a loan from the United States and withdrew some of its deposit with the International Monetary Fund. Costs of production at home increased. Industry turned to the United States for help in replacing the oil of the Middle East. Foreign markets and investments in the Near and Middle East suffered, as did British morale. The British nation has become aware that it can no longer act in the grand manner of the previous century. It must compare anew resources and commitments and define for itself a role in international affairs commensurate with its strength.

FRANCE

Hostile Ideological Groups

The close of the war left the French people divided into hostile ideological groups, in somewhat different proportions from those of the previous decade. The center parties, typified by the Radical Socialists, became popularly associated with the collapse of the country in 1940, and for several years subsequent to defeat of the Nazis they were unable to recover their former following. The conservatives, tarred by their support of the totalitarian Vichy regime of Marshal Pétain, underwent a postwar purge. The official figures state that 10,000 were illegally or irregularly executed, 38,000 imprisoned, and 40,000 sentenced to "national indignity." The heroes of the underground and the guerrilla fighting against the Nazis were the Communists, the young Catholics, and many Socialists, a trio of such contrary programs that their cooperation could not long survive. They shared popularity with General de Gaulle, the wartime exile who had become a symbol of national resurgence. De Gaulle's name sufficed to gain a national following for ideals which were thought to differ from those of all the other parties. From this motley array the force to revive France from disaster was expected to come.

The Communist party had first gained mass support in 1936 at the time of the Popular Front government. As soon as the Soviet Union became involved in the war, the party was able to serve the interest of both France and the Communist mother country by fighting the common enemy. Being organized for clandestine activity and being courageous and ruthless, it now won the admiration and devotion, temporary or permanent, of many Frenchmen. It had a program of reform which concealed the objectives of communism under the guise of national revival. Many intellectuals, always influential in France, believed that the party offered the best hope for building a new nation. The rigid organization of the party after the Soviet model failed to arouse fear in a country of free institutions; many members and followers did not expect that, should there be a Communist victory, the Soviet form of government and society would be introduced.

The official membership of the party jumped from 45,000 in 1934 to 333,000 in 1937, to about 400,000 in 1944, to more than 900,000 in 1946. Then it began to drop, by 1952 to less than 600,000. Since the war the party, with about 26 per cent of the vote, has consistently outranked its competitors in popular following. Its strength has been concentrated in urban industrial centers of the north and northeast, in the ports, and in the most backward agricultural regions south of the Loire; but, unlike other parties, it has polled a notable number of votes in all districts of the country. Although its support by both agricultural workers and small peasant landowners has not enabled it to gain any footing in the main agricultural organizations, it has succeeded in winning from the socialists control of the General Confederation of Labor. The trade-unions have supplied its main fighting force and the mass basis of its power.

Of the other parties those that existed before the war have remained about as they were. Novelty has been provided by the founding of the Catholic Popular Republican Movement (known from its French initials as M.R.P.) and the de Gaullist Rally of the French People (known as R.P.F.). The former expressed the tradition of progressive Catholicism, concerned with applying the ideals of Christianity in social life. The catastrophe of the war encouraged Catholic leaders to organize a popular movement—they refused to call it a party—which would appeal to all elements of the population and win them to support a reformed republic. Founded in 1944, the M.R.P. received the approval of the Catholic hierarchy, and in 1946 it polled about 25 per cent of the popular vote, almost as much as the Communists. It initially attracted the conservatives, who since the Vichy debacle sought to attach themselves to a party with a clean record capable of covering up their shabby past. The youthful core of the party, however, proved to be so bent on actual reform in accordance with progressive Christianity that most conservatives transferred their vote to de Gaulle's R.P.F. The M.R.P. continued after 1946–1947 with less than one half its peak support, but these voters have remained loyal and given the party stability. Its strength lies geographically in two regions, the northwest and the departments along the German frontier; but its appeal to people from all classes and its devotion to Catholicism have given it a national point of view and influence. It has had members in all the postwar governments, and its leaders, especially Bidault and Schuman, have left a deep imprint upon French policy.

General de Gaulle's R.P.F. strove to unite all Frenchmen around a great man with a program of national reform. Many distinguished French intellectuals joined the general in the belief that thorough reform could come only by reducing the legislative in favor of the executive power of government. They planned a modified version of a corporative state, in which labor and capital would cooperate, labor would be raised in social and economic status, productivity increased, and the curse of political stalemate overcome. The R.P.F. suffered from two major handicaps, namely, the temperamental and politically erratic character of its leader, who seemed more interested in old style revival of French international prestige than in internal reform, and the increasing influence of conservatives, who followed the general as a last hope of protection against communism, socialism, or even a mild threat to change the status quo. The strength of the de Gaullist group depended upon the intensity of the Communist danger; as that declined, the general lost support to moderate parties.

The Fourth Republic

At the end of the war a Frenchman declared, "Defeat did not kill the Third Republic, it merely drew attention to the fact that it was dead." In 1948 another declared, "The Fourth Republic is dead—it has been succeeded by the Third." In between lay the attempt of the Communists and the socialists to obtain national approval of a constitutional draft which would have concentrated political power in a single chamber, the type of government that Communists striving for power everywhere advocate. They expected to dominate the ministries responsible to the chamber, by way of that influence to destroy piecemeal the other parties, and in the end to have a chamber with a semblance of popular representation which was in fact subservient to the Communist cabinet. The French people rejected the draft by popular vote, and the new draft, which was accepted reluctantly and with one third of the electors failing to vote, practically reestablished the prewar form of government. At the beginning of the Third Republic, Jules Ferry, one of its prominent political leaders, had declared, "What France needs is a weak government." He had the experience with Louis Napoleon in mind. After World War II the French apparently felt the same way.

The survival of the Fourth Republic as an image of the Third came about primarily through the action of the socialists, who accomplished far more than other groups in curbing the Communist menace. One of the main postwar reforms consisted of the nationalization of certain sectors of the economy. The government confiscated some industries, like the Renault automobile works, because the owners had collaborated with the Nazis. It acquired others in order to try to improve the use of them for the public good—coal, gas, electricity, the airlines and other transportation that had not already been nationalized, the Bank of France and the four largest deposit banks, and 34 of 300 insurance companies.

From 1944 to 1947 France was governed by a popular front initiated by de Gaulle as president, in which Communists received, not the desired ministries of foreign affairs, interior, and the armed forces, but those concerned with the economy, the ministry of industrial production, the ministry of reconstruction, the ministry of labor, and that of armaments. The Communist leader, Thorez, became minister with the special duty of supervising the recruitment and promotion of the civil service.

The Communists immediately began to transform these posts into party strongholds. The law for the nationalization of the coal mines, for example, called for the establishment of a board of directors in which one third of the members would represent the state, one third labor, and one third the consumers. The minister of industrial production, responsible for the execution of the law, appointed to the board of a total of eighteen members, fourteen Communist labor leaders, declaring that labor could represent both the state and the consumers. He pursued the same tactics on regional boards. Since the departments of France where coal is mined already contained numerous municipalities run by Communists, the party dominated the politics and the economy of these regions; and the non-Communist prefects and subprefects were unable to combat its influence.

In 1947, however, the Communist ministers lost their positions and did not dare at the time to start a revolution. The new minister of the interior, Jules Moch, in control of the police, and the new minister of industrial production, Robert Lacoste, both socialists, set about destroying the Communist empire. They were aided by the socialist, Léon Jouhaux, one of the secretaries of the General Confederation of Labor, who broke with the Communists late in 1947 and set up a new union. The General Confederation, which had had 6 million members, lost 1 million to Jouhaux's new *Force Ouvrière,* another million to the Christian unions; and, since 2 million dropped all union affiliation, the confederation was left with only 2 million members, a decline of two thirds.

Of the three men, the minister of industrial production had the simplest task. He interpreted the law as it was meant to be and removed Communists from the National Coal Company. The most difficult assignment came to Jules Moch. Refusing to trust any Communist, he first purged and reorganized the police force and the security troops, and then set up an entirely new motorized organization of 122,000 men, half police and half military, which should enable the civil authorities anywhere to crush an incipient rebellion without declaring martial law. This force was placed at important points throughout France and was available on a moment's notice. France was divided into eight districts in addition to Paris, and a police inspector-general was given charge of each. The results were soon evident. The government had barely been able to withstand a large-scale Communist-led strike in November and December, 1947. A year later it was prepared for the strikes against E.R.P. aid. Its efficiency in preventing outbreaks, plus the unpopularity of the strikes among labor itself, including many Communist followers, deprived the party of its strength as a revolutionary menace.

ECONOMIC REVIVAL

France imposed upon the weak government of the Fourth Republic heavy economic responsibilities which its predecessor had not faced. These were of four kinds: first, reconstruction of the damage caused by the war; second, administration of the nationalized sector of the economy; third, the execution of a plan for economic modernization; and fourth, the establishment of a stable system of public finance. The four problems, necessarily interconnected, will be discussed in order.

The French economy, which by the end of the thirties had not recovered from the effects of the world depression, was severely crippled by the war. If 1938 is taken as a base of 100, French total industrial production declined in 1941 to 65 and in 1944 to 40; agricultural production suffered similarly but not to the same extent. The Nazis caused the fall by retaining French soldiers as prisoners of war and by drafting a million and a half Frenchmen for labor in Germany. They enabled France to obtain few raw materials, reduced greatly her imports, and compelled her to maintain exports while shifting the destination of these to Germany, Belgium, and the Netherlands. The French peasants, able to reserve food for themselves, ate as well as usual, but townsmen suffered from hunger. Rationing failed to be effective, for its success would have assured that more food would be shipped to the Nazis. The French played the black market, and prices soared. The military action of liberation damaged or destroyed many more buildings than in World War I. By September, 1944, 1 per cent of the railroad tracks was in condition for use; two fifths of the railroad cars and one third of the locomotives were intact. One half of the trucks and automobiles and one half of the merchant fleet had disappeared. Ports, telegraph and telephone lines, and bridges were heavily damaged. Much arable land had been broken up or mined; the rest had suffered from lack of fertilizer. The Nazis had extracted 850 billion francs from the French in occupation costs, clearing credits, and the like, and the amount of money in circulation had expanded from 170 billion francs in 1938 to 881 billion at the end of 1944.

The French government by a law of 1946 assumed responsibility for repairing war damage, and by the end of 1949 it had expended 667 billion francs for that purpose. Its action has been severely criticized as unnecessarily generous and lacking in economic advantage to France. It permitted individuals to restore economic enterprises irrespective of whether they were efficient or well located. Many owners received excessive compensation, for the average age of the dwelling houses of France was fifty years and that of industrial equipment about twenty-five years. The financial burden upon the state contributed to unbalanced budgets and inflation.

The program of nationalization, which attempted to create something new, received the full support of all groups in the resistance movement. General de Gaulle believed in maintaining free enterprise, but he declared:

> Tomorrow it will be the role of the state itself to ensure the development of the great sources of energy, coal, electricity, and petrol, and also of the principal means of transport by rail, sea, or air, and of the financial media on which all the rest depends. It is the role of the state to raise metallurgical production to the necessary level. It is the role of the state to make use of the country's credits, to direct the national savings toward the vast investments which such developments demand, and to prevent groupings of private interests from running counter to the general interest.

He asserted that the government alone possessed sufficient power and financial resources quickly to revive and modernize the basic sectors of the economy. The French economy should be freed from existing domination by an oligarchy in finance and industry which had encroached on the sovereign power of the state.

The results of public ownership have not met expectations. The problems may be illustrated by the organization of the coal industry. The central body, called the Coal Mines of France, supervises the execution of the program of production and controls and coordinates the work in the coalfields. Under it nine coal mining corporations, one for each major coal area, are responsible for producing, processing, and selling the coal, and the governing board of each of these and that of the Coal Mines of France maintain continuous liaison. Difficulty has arisen from the fact that these corporations are administered by boards composed of an equal number of representatives of the state, labor, and the consumer—a device which labor circles originated.

> It is hopeless [an English critic has written] to expect unity of purpose, energetic administration, and a coherent policy to emerge from an assemblage of diverse and conflicting interests representing the worker, the consumer and the taxpayer. Frustration and deadlock, log-rolling, and jockeying for position are much more likely to result from the juxtaposition of discordant elements. And this, according to most accounts, is what is happening. The money power has been replaced by party politics, rather than by a solicitude for the common good.[7]

That this condition has arisen, not because of nationalization, but because of the use of a bad administrative principle can be seen from the example of Great Britain, where the ablest persons, irrespective of occupational background, are selected and made responsible for efficiency. Moreover,

[7] *Ibid.*, p. 263.

France has not solved the problem of according these public corporations the necessary degree of financial autonomy; they are too dependent with respect to wages, selling prices, and credits upon the government, and through it upon politics.

The Monnet Plan

Nationalization set the stage for a plan to modernize the French economy. Worked out by a general commission under the direction of Jean Monnet, the plan expressed the constructive thinking of representatives of all branches of the economy. It received cabinet approval in 1947, and with time and experience it has undergone modifications and become a part of French life. The plan called for large expansion and rationalization of the production of coal, oil, steel, electric power, and cement and machines and fertilizer for agriculture, and for the improvement of the system of transportation. It was believed that progress in these basic industries would set an example and stimulate activity in other lines of the economy. Later a few other industries—chemicals, pulp, and artificial textiles—received aid as well, but the major investments continued to concentrate on basic products. The spirit of enterprise of an optimistic, energetic economy built on science and fed with investment funds would rouse France, it was hoped, from its moral and political stagnation and enable the nation once more to become a world leader.

The Monnet Plan proposed as quickly as possible to expand national and colonial production of raw materials in an effort to reduce the need for imports. At the same time it intended to increase the amount of industrial exports in order to pay for the imports and reduce or eliminate France's unfavorable balance of payments. Since the country had suffered severe losses in its holdings of foreign exchange during the war, the government regarded the expansion of exports as an essential means to keep the value of the franc stable. It therefore tried, by stimulating agricultural output, to make France an exporter of food, an item which postwar Europe badly needed. It likewise expected to have a surplus of coal, another article in short supply, for export, and it set about establishing industries for processing raw materials, like bauxite, which it possessed in quantity and had formerly shipped abroad. Like other countries, France learned that flexibility in use gives oil an advantage over other fuels, and she expended large sums in creating an industry for processing the imported raw product. The funds invested under the Monnet Plan in the first three years amounted to 7,000 billion francs, one third of which was supplied by the United States in the form of counterpart funds, and most of the rest by the French government.

In following the program France has constructed modern steel mills, oil refineries, and aluminum and chemical works, and she has increased the supply of electric power, particularly hydroelectric, several hundredfold.

Some of her small industries, with American prodding, began to improve in productivity, and interest in modernizing the economy spread. The economy, however, was run mainly by trade associations, which fixed prices sufficiently high to enable inefficient members to earn a profit. In consequence, the number of those employed in industry between 1938 and 1951 increased less in France, and in Italy, than in any other country. The number in trade and services actually rose to the point at which more retail stores could add nothing to the economy. Expansion, not of distribution facilities but of production, was urgently needed. As the French statesman Paul Reynaud said in 1953, "France's position in the world is one of perpetual retreat. Since 1929, American production has doubled. In Great Britain and Western Germany it has increased by over 50 per cent. Our production has increased by only 8 per cent." Agriculture showed a worse record. Too many peasants are like the sugar-beet growers, who have turned land to that crop in order to sell alcohol to the government at a price fixed high above market value. The taxpayers shouldered the burden; the country is full of unsalable alcohol; it imports food which should have been raised on the land devoted to sugar beets.

The condition of French finance was worse than that of industry. Unlike Belgium, the government failed to call in the excess banknotes which the Nazis had forced into circulation. The Fourth Republic kept war inflation and has ever since had to contend with a resulting price level above that on the world market. Workers and employees demanded a modern program of social security, and a government fearful of the attractiveness of communism acquiesced. Reconstruction and the Monnet Plan absorbed huge sums, and rearmament proved to be expensive. The rebellion against French rule in Indochina required funds equal in amount to those advanced to France by the United States, and war in Algeria has increased the financial imbalance.

An antiquated tax system based on the indirect tax has not supplied the government with funds to balance the budget. The over-all tax burden is about as heavy as it is in Great Britain or elsewhere; but workers and employees bear the main load, whereas retailers, small industrialists, and peasants almost entirely escape the income tax. Agriculture accounts for 35 per cent of the active population, but it pays one twentieth of the direct taxes, an amount equal to about 1 per cent of the budget. Heavy indirect taxes mean a further shift of the burden for supporting the state to the low-paid masses.

The government tried to keep down prices by combining some price control with a free market. It did not succeed, and the economy failed to produce enough goods to restrain price increases. The population, fully employed, sought more consumers' goods than industry was producing; the demand forced up prices and accentuated the trend toward inflation already set by an unbalanced budget. The French government depended mainly upon mild inflation to keep supply related to effective demand, for with wages lagging far behind high prices, the masses could not afford many goods. Taxes skimmed off the surplus buying power, and they provided sums for implementing the Monnet Plan. Financial aid from the United States between 1948 and January 1, 1952, amounted to nearly $4 billion, most of it in the form of gifts, and more has been added since then.

Economic Expansion

By 1953 France began to see some of the transforming effects of the Monnet Plan. During the next four years large capital investments led to an industrial output double that of 1939. In 1957 the rate of industrial improvement as seen in production per employee was twice that of the United States. The country is enjoying a housing boom; it is gaining an international reputation for excellence in airplane manufacture, in electronics, and in many other engineering lines; and it is building industrial plants for foreign customers. Agriculture has not fared so well as industry, for peasants less easily adapt themselves to technological change than industrialists. Yet they began to use motorized machinery and other modern means to increase production. Although still hampered by the universal practice of price agreements among all lines of business and by the preference of labor for Communist-dominated unions, France is assuming a place among the progressive economies of the world.

In contrast to the industrial boom French finance continues to be unstable. The nation has been buying abroad far more than it sells, an indication of economic strength in that 60 per cent of the imports consists of fuels—coal and oil—but nonetheless a threat to the stability of the franc. As so often happened after World War I, France had in 1957 to curb imports by devaluing the franc. The government curtailed expenditures, social insurance being the main victim, in the endeavor to balance the budget and to stop inflation. After its experience the French public lacks confidence in the effectiveness of these measures.

POLITICAL STALEMATE

The explanation of this condition lies in the failure of postwar politics to keep pace with economic advance. After a popular front government to 1947, the middle parties, of which the Radical Socialists were the most important, held the balance of power. Until 1951 the Socialists wielded some influence; then the Third Force, or middle parties, found allies for constituting a ministry among the conservative right. When in 1954 the Radical Socialist Mendès-France became prime minister, with a program of vigorous internal reform, he was unable to advance it because of the pressure of foreign affairs—settling relations with Germany, liquidating the war in Indochina, and negotiating a solution of problems in North Africa.

As soon as he showed signs of accelerating the modernization of the French economy, he was overthrown. Apart from the powerful Communist party, France has been divided between conservatives and various shades of reformers. The interests vested in the status quo control more than one half of the votes in the Chamber of Deputies and block reform. Two thirds of the departments of France cling to the ways of the nineteenth century, are hostile to government, persist in ideological controversies like that over the relation of church and state, are ignorant of economics, and are unaware of the extent and serious effects of economic backwardness and weak government. The dynamic and modernized France of the big cities and large industries of the Monnet Plan has brought forward people eager to align France with the progressive countries of the West, but it also inclined many to follow parties determined to execute reforms in a hurry—the Communists or the de Gaullists.

A static France kept extreme parties out of power, but she has failed to cut the ground from under these parties by a program of social justice. Many French industrialists, who used American funds to increase their profits but disregarded American requests that they share these profits with labor, have contributed to backwardness. They approved of socialists fighting Communists to protect freedom, but they believed that socialists who were concerned with increased pay and a higher standard of living for the workers were a menace comparable to that of the extreme left. The conservative French included the critics of the Catholic priests who were seeking to win laborers back to the church by working with them and sharing their life. These conservatives correctly suspected that the priests would soon side with the workers against the employees in a demand for better pay, improved living conditions, and other advantages found in progressive free societies. The group, the largest in France, is the one whose outlook on political and social issues Monnet, Mendès-France, and others have endeavored to transform. After the elections of 1956 a coalition of moderate parties formed a government first under the premiership of the socialist Guy Mollet and in 1957 under that of Bourgès-Maunoury, a Radical Socialist, but it has not accelerated the rate of change.

Internal policy has been affected by international affairs and imperial relations, each acting in a different way. France accepted NATO, the Western European Union, and the Coal and Steel Community for reasons of self-protection. From these organizations and from the United Nations and its affiliated agencies she received stimulation from abroad in numerous lines challenging her to compete. To sustain her responsibilities she needed to improve the economy. A common market with the German steel industry, for example, meant that French steel producers must modernize their plants. In an agency like UNESCO, where she felt herself supreme, France slowly discovered that many other peoples had reached a comparable cultural eminence. The endeavor to retain the empire cost money and lives and retarded the progress at home. Loss of Indochina, Tunisia, Morocco, and the mandates of Syria and Lebanon did not prevent the government from continuing to coerce Algeria into acceptance of the French Union, a status which to the natives connotes French rule. The socialist Mollet and his successor in 1957 have used force to this end, so far without success.

The Suez debacle did not divide the French people as it did the British. Their severest crisis in morale had occurred during the war when Germany so easily crushed France. Since that low point the nation has recovered somewhat in spirit, and the failure of the world to approve the Franco-British attack on Egypt in 1956 appeared to the French merely a reflection on the good judgment of other states. The Soviet suppression of the Hungarian rebellion of 1956–1957 disillusioned many French Communists, especially the intellectuals but also numerous workers. Party membership shrank, leaving the hard core of dogmatic Marxists in splendid isolation.

In parliament the persistent opposition of the 150 Communist deputies, together with that of the 40 followers of Poujade, who are against taxes and most governmental programs, is able to block any measure on which all the other parties do not agree. The proposals for a European customs union and an atomic energy community of six nations received sufficient support to be approved, but the Algerian problem has found no solution. Although French politicians and public are recognizing the futility of the Algerian war, no government so far has been willing to risk its political life by proposing to offer Algeria status similar to that of Tunisia and Morocco. By preventing its leaders from taking the initiative with constructive measures, the French political system is threatening to ruin the republic. Will the economic revival awaken the French people to the need of creative governmental leadership, or will the dead weight of present politics slow down the rate of economic and social advance? The future of both France and European unity depends upon the answer.

THE SMALL COUNTRIES OF NORTHWESTERN EUROPE

The postwar history of the small countries of Northwestern Europe, Switzerland, Belgium, the Netherlands, Denmark, Sweden, and Norway, to which Eire, Luxembourg, and Finland may be added, records the efforts to overcome the effects of World War II by the peaceful, reasonable means to which these democratic peoples had become accustomed. Insofar as international conditions beyond their control have permitted, they have succeeded.

Extent of Involvement in World War II

The war involved each country in a different way and degree. Switzerland, Sweden, and Eire succeeded in remaining neutral, at the cost of greatly strengthening their defense. The peoples of these states favored the cause of freedom; however, the two continental states maintained their military nonparticipation only by trading with Nazi Germany. Swedish iron ore and timber, Swedish and Swiss machinery, ball bearings, and other manufactures proved more useful to the Nazis on a trade basis than by military coercion. From 1940 to 1943 the Swedes permitted the Nazis to move troops across their country to replace those in Norway, to send supplies by rail to Norway and a fully equipped division to Finland. The Swedes also shipped as many goods as they could to Great Britain. The Swiss gained the right to import essential food and other supplies across Nazi-occupied territory in return for their economic aid to Germany. Both neutral countries at the same time built defenses which commanded respect. At the end of the war they had a well-developed, intact system for production and distribution and considerable foreign exchange, and they had paid no blood tax.

Among the belligerents Belgium fared best. The Nazis exploited Belgian industry where it was without moving it to Germany, and in the final days of the war they withdrew too speedily to have time for demolition. The Belgian government in exile continued to earn large sums from the sale to the Allies of war supplies, copper, uranium ore, and the like, from the Belgian Congo, and, after the recapture of the country, from charges to the Allies for the use of Belgian harbor facilities. In contrast, the Netherlands was both severely exploited by the Nazis during the war, with starvation not unknown, and devastated in large sections where the Nazis fought a last stand. One tenth of the area was flooded, and by this and other action 30 per cent of the country's wealth was ruined. Denmark's wartime fate compared favorably with that of Belgium, whereas Norway, a center of military and naval operations, suffered to an extent comparable to that of the Netherlands. At the same time, the Nazis had expanded the production in lines of urgent concern to them, dairying in Denmark, electric power in Norway, and branches of the engineering industries everywhere.

Finland's postwar history has been conditioned by the fact that the country had become involved in the war by being attacked by the Soviet Union. Since the latter was victorious, Finland was forced to cede territory, and to pay to the Soviet Union the heaviest reparations in proportion to size of national income which history records. The reparations imposed upon Germany after 1918 had not exceeded 4 per cent of the national income; those demanded of Finland amounted to 17 per cent of the nation's income in the first year and 15 per cent in the next. Reparations were to continue until September, 1952, and if the goods were not delivered on time the Finns were to pay a fine amounting to almost 80 per cent at compound interest. In Karelia the country lost a rich agricultural area which supported 12 per cent of its population; and as these half-million people chose to emigrate to other parts of Finland rather than to live under Soviet rule, the country had to find new homes for them. One person in nearly every eight was a refugee, usually without any resources and in need of food, shelter, and livelihood.

Stable Conditions

The people in each of these countries preserved the morale for overcoming their difficulties. No fundamental changes proved necessary. The Norwegian and the Netherlands governments and royal houses had fled abroad from the Nazi invaders; the Danish had remained at home. All had retained the devotion of the people. Leopold III, the Belgian ruler, alone lost his throne; he had aroused popular suspicion of being authoritarian and pro-Nazi. After 1936 governmental instability had caused him to take a greater role in the decision of affairs than was customary under a constitutional monarchy, and he had advocated a policy of armed neutrality. This action had benefited the Nazis, who preferred their future victims to remain isolated rather than to prepare for war in coalition. When the Germans invaded the country, the king quickly recognized the hopelessness of defense; without consulting the government, then in exile, he ordered the army to surrender. He chose to remain with his people, but in subsequent years he and his associates gave the impression of too close contact with certain Nazis, and he showed what appeared to be indifference to popular suffering by remarrying. After the war the nation divided about equally between those who favored his return to the throne and those who opposed it. The question cut across class, language, and religious lines; but the Catholics and the Flemish supported him in largest numbers, and the prorepublican socialist workers were conspicuous in the opposition. Leopold was forced to abdicate, but the monarchy continued to be accepted, and the controversy created no serious breach among the people.

The war experience accelerated the trend in each country toward supplanting class or other antagonism by social solidarity. In the Scandinavian states the Socialist party continued to control government, either alone or in coalition. The Finnish Socialist party fought native communism as vigorously as any bourgeois organization and shared in the government. Its Dutch counterpart did likewise, and in that eminently middle-class country the socialist leader served for several years as prime minister. In Belgium the Labor party changed its name at the end of the war to Socialist party and stressed a reform program which would appeal to all progressives irrespective of class. In 1943 Switzerland, the land where, according to a popular witticism, people might be noisy in church but whispered in a bank, chose the only Socialist in its body of federal councilors as its minister of finance. Upon retirement in 1951 because of age, he was succeeded by another Socialist. Party politics flourished as vigorously in these countries as elsewhere; but governments rose above partisanship and represented the nation.

For all of these countries except Belgium and Finland the most abrupt change of policy concerned the question of defense. Belgium had traditionally supported a defense system, as had Finland; but the latter's army was reduced to 30,000 by the terms of the treaty with the Soviet Union. The other small nations, except possibly Sweden, had been fatalistic about protecting themselves by arms and had followed a policy of pacifism and neutrality. They now thought, as they perceived Soviet imperialism becoming the successor to Nazi aggression, that they should at least be strong enough to deter a potential invader.

The people, fully represented in the government, accepted the introduction of compulsory military training, the abrupt shift of emphasis from a program of taxation for direct social welfare to one of taxation for defense, and the extension of the power of government over the individual which awareness of danger necessitated. Military expenditures became the largest single item in the national budget, increasing between 50 and 300 per cent over the prewar figure, and precious man power for economic welfare was sacrificed to the need for military training. The fact that Norway, Denmark, the Netherlands, and Belgium joined NATO, whereas Sweden and Switzerland have remained neutral and alone, has not affected the dimensions of the change. Switzerland has developed an efficient army of at least 400,000 men, which she can mobilize on a moment's notice. Her entire able man power up to the age of 60 is subject to defense refresher courses each year, and she has built fortifications and storage vaults inside the mountains. Sweden has expanded the defense industry, and created a scientific barrier of radar, a small but up-to-date air force, and all the accessories that are needed to make her army efficient. The other countries have followed the same pattern.

Common action and common suffering during the war brought social groups in each country closer together than before. The Scandinavians had already been noted for social solidarity. As Per Albin Hansson, the Swedish Socialist leader, remarked in 1946, "We [the Socialists] have had so many victories that we are in a difficult position. A people with political liberty, full employment and social security has lost its dreams." The menace of Soviet domination forced the classes together in Finland; and the Swiss, although not comparably endangered, had also learned the survival value of social cooperation.

The greatest postwar social gains appeared in Belgium and the Netherlands. In the former country mutual aid against the Nazi oppressors led representatives of employers and workers at the end of the war to sign an agreement in which they recognized that

> . . . the smooth running of undertakings, to which the general prosperity of the country is closely linked, requires their loyal cooperation.
>
> They desire to establish relationships between employers and workers based on mutual respect and reciprocal recognition of their rights and duties. The workers respect the legitimate authority of the heads of undertakings and pledge their honour to do their work conscientiously. The employers respect the dignity

of the workers and pledge their honour to treat them justly. They undertake to create no obstacle, either directly or indirectly, to their freedom of association or to the development of their organizations.

They united in asking the government for legislation to further "social progress, based on the economic advance of a world at peace and on a fair distribution of the income resulting from increased production."

The Belgian government heeded the advice and continued to call representatives of the two groups together for consultation. In 1948 it passed the Organization of the Economy Act, setting up a National Economic Council, professional councils for each large branch of industry, and works councils in all factories and businesses with a minimum of fifty workers. Through these means employers and workers gained institutional machinery for settling differences and agreeing on common policies and for influencing the government. They had learned that increased production offers a better means of raising the standard of living than class conflict. The Netherlands achieved a similar objective by formally recognizing as an advisory body of representatives of labor and management the Foundation of Labor, originally a clandestine wartime organization to fight the Nazis. The government has convened it frequently for discussion of the whole gamut of national economic problems and followed its advice.

In all these small states governmental responsibility for national welfare has expanded. The Swedish king drew the standard old-age pension to show his solidarity with the people. In 1946, Sweden passed a law introducing compulsory health insurance and, after a decade's delay, put it into execution. Belgium for the first time introduced a comprehensive system of social security, and Switzerland accepted old-age pensions. Each government purposed to distribute the national income on an equitable basis. In 1955 Belgium recognized the need of the salaried middle class and the small shopkeepers in setting up a special ministry of the middle class. Switzerland continued to pay special subsidies to the peasantry and to help it in other ways—by road improvement, education, and recreation—in order to preserve it as a class. The Norwegian government advanced funds to the fishermen, enabling them to purchase their own boats instead of having to pay high rental, and helping them to improve methods and facilities for curing and storing fish. Under Socialist influence this government has gone farthest in making permanent a wartime right of the state, not as yet used, to interfere in the economy at any time and impose a national plan.

Belgium began to resuscitate the old industrial region of the south inhabited by the Walloons. This area suffered from out-of-date industrial equipment, the exhaustion of coal mines and mounting cost of mining in general, inadequate transportation, and accompanying low wages and bad housing. The government measures for reviving the region—over-all planning and advance of funds for capital investment—exemplify on a large scale what Norway has initiated in her barren north. This region of sparse population living in poverty has grown in strategic significance. The government has begun the extensive construction of transportation facilities; it has harnessed water power for electricity, and built there Norway's first steel mill. The mill, at Mo i Rana and government-owned, is run by electricity generated in the region, uses local iron ore, and is situated on the coast for easy transportation. In 1955 it produced 170,000 tons of steel and is to be expanded to supply the half million tons that the country uses. An aluminum plant utilizing the cheap electric power in the same region is also under way. One could add similar examples of public initiative in the other countries, but the outstanding achievement has been that of Finland in settling the citizens from the regions lost to the Soviet Union.

The refugees came from three areas, 9,000 from Petsamo and Salla in the far north, 9,000 from Porkkala on the southwest coast, and more than 400,000 from Karelia. The government has compensated each person for loss of property and has as far as possible enabled him in the new home to continue his former occupation. Land was made available from estates owned by the state, the church, municipalities, and wealthy individuals. These owners in turn were compensated for their losses. The refugees consisted of three main occupational groups, farmers, fishermen, and townspeople. Of these, the farmers have been successfully resettled. The government advanced to them funds for rude housing and for implements and food until they could raise their first crops. It began to construct roads into former wilderness, strung electric power lines, and furnished power machines to aid in clearing the forested areas for cultivation. It built schools and supplied school buses. Government officials were appointed to assist the settlers in every possible way, and the settlers have responded with a remarkable revival of Finnish agriculture.

The plan to resettle the fishermen went awry because the shore regions were inhabited by Swedes of Finnish citizenship. The Swedes objected to having their cultural communities swamped by incoming Finns, and the latter have not been permanently placed. The townspeople soon found work but lacked housing. Government subsidies have begun to overcome this shortage. The Soviet demand for reparations has, an ironic fact, provided work for everyone. The achievement of this little country in finding new homes and work for one eighth of its people offers heroic evidence of the value to civilization of these small free nations.

International Economic Relations

Labor leaders in these countries understood that the dependence of the nation's welfare upon international trade limited the safe rise of wage rates. The working population in most of the states was fully employed, Belgium being the main exception; foreign labor was imported into Sweden and Switzerland, and for certain tasks even into Belgium. The relative amount of workers' earnings has increased over prewar years, whereas the income of the middle class has tended to drop. Reparation of war damage, the neglect of investment during hostilities, and increased competition from countries like the United States and Canada have been met by the investment of an unusually large percentage ot national income. Norway had in 1938 invested 25 per cent, in 1947, 34 per cent, and in 1951, 30 per cent of its gross national product. In the other countries postwar rates were not quite so high, but in 1951 Sweden invested 25 per cent and the Netherlands 20 per cent, figures that should be compared with the United Kingdom's 13 per cent. These data imply a spartan regime; even so, the standard of living remained high, and, with full employment resulting from this rate of investment, the demand for both producers' and consumers' goods required public control to avert inflation.

In curbing the inflationary threat Belgium fared best for a time. As soon as the government returned to the country it exchanged the Nazi-expanded currency for new money at a reduced rate. In consequence of this financial action prices became low and products could compete in the world market. The fact that the country produced iron and steel and machinery, commodities most in demand in the immediate postwar years for construction, assisted recovery. Belgium quickly re-established freedom of trade for imports and exports and returned to prewar economic policies.

The other states were unable to follow suit and continued from time to time to need import quotas. The demand for foreign goods exceeded the ability to earn the foreign exchange by exports to pay for them; when an excess threatened to upset financial stability, the governments curtailed imports. A combination of control of the rate charged for loans and emphasis on a corporation tax and a turnover tax afforded the governments the means speedily to reduce the amount of money available for consumers' purchases.

Switzerland depended more upon the change in the discount rate, in the use of subsidies, and in the imposition of import controls. Traditionally the authority to levy direct taxes rested with the members of the Federation and not with the central government. The increase in military expenditures and in the use of subsidies to agriculture and other interests made the question of how to raise the necessary funds the most important political issue in postwar Switzerland. Some parties, among which were the Socialists, sought to empower the central government to levy direct taxes; the majority of the voters opposed this plan and acquiesced only in temporary grant of direct taxes to the federal government. The question has crucial significance, for the answer will decide whether Switzerland remains a loosely knit confederation or whether it follows the example of all other industrial states and strengthens the powers of the central government.

The European Recovery Program proved to be of great aid to the Netherlands, Norway, and Denmark, less to Sweden and Belgium. Switzerland did not participate in it at all, and the others were able to dispense with aid more quickly than were France or Italy. Denmark and the Netherlands especially suffered from the decline in the ability of the West German Republic and of Great Britain to purchase their food exports, and Great Britain drove hard bargains which reduced profits. Each of the countries traded with those of Eastern Europe, although the percentage of their total trade, except that of Finland because of reparations, was not very high.

Certain Swedish political leaders and economists at the end of the war anticipated a slump in the Western countries and sought to cushion it by a large-scale trade agreement with the Soviet Union. The slump failed to develop, and the Soviet Union proved unable to supply the promised foodstuffs, oil, and minerals. The Danes and the Swiss have sold limited amounts of machinery and other manufactures to the Communists in return for raw materials; but the Danes, after joining NATO, preferred to sacrifice the trade agreement rather than to violate the NATO treaty by building contraband oil tankers for the Soviet Union.

Finland has continued to trade more with Great Britain than with the Soviet Union, in spite of the fact that the reparations obligation forced her to build from the ground up new industries, machinery and shipbuilding, and the like, oriented toward the Soviet market. The Finnish economy has not become dependent upon that of the Soviet Union. The Communists have reduced the reparations burden, but they have collected the equivalent of nearly $1 billion from Finland.

In general, the greater the dependence of a country upon agricultural exports, the harder it has been struck by the dislocation of markets. Thus Denmark and the Netherlands have faced more obstacles than the others. The latter has been injured by the decline in the value of investments in Indonesia and in trade with this former dependency. The percentage of the population engaged in agriculture in all the countries has continued to fall, as people have moved to urban industries. Machines have taken their places on the farms; for example, Sweden used in 1955 more than five times as many tractors as before the war. Each country has endeavored to be as self-sufficient in food production as possible, but has sought an economic solution to providing work for its growing population (the Netherlands has an exceptionally high rate of growth) in industrial and trade expansion.

These small countries, except Switzerland, and to some extent Sweden, have sought in international cooperation a larger basis for defense and for economic development than each individually possesses. In 1949 Sweden proposed a defensive alliance to her Scandinavian colleagues, but they refused and joined NATO. The Swedes then preferred to remain neutral and well armed, depending like Switzerland upon their own efficient arms and ultimately upon the balance of power to preserve their freedom from the Soviet Union.

The three Scandinavian countries and Iceland organized a Nordic Council in 1952, composed of an equal number of representatives from each of three parliaments, with a smaller number from Iceland, and ministers from the governments. The conferences have been unofficial and informal, but they have accelerated the previous program of joint action. The airlines had already reached agreement for full cooperation, irrespective of country, and the use of common textbooks has been approved. On recommendation of the Nordic Council the parliaments have passed legislation to create a unified labor market. Measures toward making the four states a common market for commodities as well as labor and capital are under serious discussion.

Belgium, the Netherlands, and Luxembourg have negotiated a customs union, which has been partially put into execution. Differences in tax systems, price levels, and mutual fear among competitive branches of the economy have prevented the full implementation of the union. These three countries have promoted European or Western Union for both defensive and economic purposes. In spite of Germany's mistreatment of them in the war, they all believe that without a strong and prosperous Germany free Europe is weak. They have become aware of their dependence upon international cooperation.

When we speak of the Western tradition, we refer primarily to the achievement of the countries discussed in the present chapter. The tradition has been transmitted and improved by peoples in other continents, and the continued adoption of it by still more peoples will form one of the basic processes in world history of succeeding generations. Our discussion has made apparent that in some respects, having to do with the economy, the social distribution of the national income, the equalization of opportunity, and the democratization of culture, the United States, Canada, Australia, and New Zealand have outrun their European teachers. The vestige of class structure from the Old Regime and the practice of power politics have retarded the evolution of Great Britain and France. In overcoming these handicaps the small states have done much better. The countries to be discussed in the next chapter have undergone during this century crises compared to that of England in the seventeenth century and France in the revolutionary and Napoleonic period. The reader will have learned from the discussion that contemporaneity does not mean similarity, that one of the most prolific sources of international and internal conflict is to be found in the difference in interests and lack of mutual understanding among groups living at the same time but in different stages of historical development.

Suggestions for Further Reading

COLE, G. D. H. *The Postwar Condition of Britain.* New York: Frederick A. Praeger, Inc., 1957. Social and economic survey of the last two decades.

Economic Survey of Europe since the War. New York: United Nations, 1953. Based on the excellent annual reports by the European Economic Commission of the United Nations.

ELLIS, H. S. *The Economics of Freedom.* See the Readings for Chapter 22. Indispensable for the crucial years covered.

LUETHY, HERMANN. *France against Herself.* London: Meridian Books, Ltd., 1957. Brilliant and profound analysis by a Swiss journalist.

SCOTT, F. D. *The United States and Scandinavia.* See the Readings for Chapter 7.

SMITH, HOWARD K. *The State of Europe.* New York: Alfred A. Knopf, Inc., 1949.

WILLIAMS, PHILIP. *Politics in Postwar France.* New York: Longmans, Green & Company, Inc., 1954.

Chapter 25 · The Authoritarian Countries, Past or Present

THE COMMON FACTOR

If one were writing primarily political history, it would no doubt be inappropriate to group Germany, Austria, Italy, Greece, Spain, and Portugal in a single chapter. Since this book endeavors instead to analyze all aspects of European life, it is logical to make the grouping and to start with a crucial fact common to all of the countries. Each of them either remains under an authoritarian regime (Spain and Portugal) such as it had in prewar years or has only recently been relieved from such domination by an outside force. The reader will analyze in the chapter the questions of how peoples freed from dictators have reacted to liberty and what measures the two surviving authoritarian rulers have taken to preserve their power. He may further ask whether industrialism has had any effect on the reaction. In view of the struggle with fascist authoritarian systems and in view of the troubles of the future with Communist dictatorial regimes, no subject is of more significance.

WEST GERMANY AND AUSTRIA

The internal history of West Germany and Austria since the war has been conditioned by quadripartite military occupation. The problems of both states have been roughly similar; the difference in outcome has resulted from the fact that Germany has remained a potential great power, whereas Austria lacks sufficient territory and resources to arouse the fear of anyone.

Military Government in West Germany

German society in the three Western zones emerged from the war in grave danger of disintegration. Within a span of thirty years the German people had lived under the empire, the Weimar Republic, the Nazi dictatorship; they had been through two world wars and two revolutions (that of 1918–1919 and that of 1933); and they had experienced many kinds of economies—international free trade before 1914, the war economy of 1914–1918, an attempt to introduce socialism after 1918, inflation, depression, Nazi totalitarian economics, and again a war economy. After these vicissitudes they trusted neither themselves nor anyone and had lost the feeling of security. Averse to politics and long excluded from governmental responsibility, the German masses did not know how to prevent a repetition of the national disaster of nazism. In this condition of uncertainty the surviving leaders of the Weimar Republic filled the void. West German government, education, trade-unions, the economy, and the church were guided predominantly by representatives of an older generation. They alone knew how a free society under responsible government was organized and how it was supposed to function, and they understood the reforms needed to align German society and culture once more with that of Western peoples.

From the end of the war until 1948 the three Western zones were ruled by an Allied military government, which sought to secure the world against a renewal of German aggression and at the same time to assist the German people in becoming a free, self-governing, peaceful society. Theoretically, the two objectives did not clash; but the effort to achieve both simultaneously evoked accusations of inconsistency. Military government scarcely qualified as a teacher of freedom, yet some oversight of the ex-enemy had to be maintained. Actually, military government was mainly executed by civilians in uniform. As a substitute for native government, it had to enter all aspects of life and increasingly to relax discipline in favor of civilian rule. Although it made many mistakes, it operated with consideration for the German people.

The Americans, and to a less extent the British, had planned to purge ex-Nazis from all positions of influence. Execution caused confusion and injustice, because the victors sought to identify a Nazi on an objective, statistical basis and ignored the vast difference in motives for his having affiliated with the Nazi party or its organizations. The system failed to distinguish adequately between a hardened party veteran and an idealist who had joined the party and had later become disillusioned and had at the risk of his life resisted the regime. The program of denazification achieved little more than a state of exasperation. Military government soon learned that almost everyone able to run a business or to administer a government agency had been a member of some Nazi association. For the sake of efficiency denazification was quietly buried. The French never believed in or practiced it.

The trial of the twelve Nazi leaders, Göring, von Ribbentrop, and others as war criminals at Nürnberg, and of many lesser figures at other places, seemed to many Germans an example of injustice, in that international law was formulated *ex post facto,* they declared, to condemn the accused. After the sentence of death or imprisonment was imposed at Nürnberg upon the major war criminals and some lesser figures, the trials shared the fate of denazification.

The Allies did not agree on the handling of cartels. The United States demanded the breakup of these monopolies, arguing that cartels had supported the Nazis and that as opponents of free competition they were an obstacle to free, responsible government. The British Labor government did not object to cartels, in that it thought them easier to socialize than a number of competing firms. The French government paid slight attention to the issue. Some German businessmen supported the American view; most of them as well as Social Democrats and trade-unions opposed the program on practical and theoretical grounds and considered it an unwarranted intrusion into domestic affairs.

The three Western occupying powers introduced a program to reeducate the Germans away from nazism toward democracy. They sought to acquaint the people with democratic ways in formal education, in trade-union management, in the conduct of civic organizations, in youth movements—in every aspect of life. To that end they arranged for the visit of Germans to other countries and of American, British, and French civilian advisers in various fields to Germany, and for the exchange of books, periodicals, films, and music. They used the military and civilian personnel stationed in Germany to cultivate good relations with the local people and to initiate them into new sports, Parent-Teachers Associations, and many other kinds of activities. They did not intend to impose a program upon the Germans but to help them to help themselves. In spite of obvious limitations to the achievement of so bold an objective, the program proved attractive and fairly successful. Many Germans welcomed it; others denounced it as an affront to their culture.

The ill effects of Allied rule in Germany must be attributed, not to military administration, but to official policy. During the three years from 1945 to 1948, while the British and the American governments waited for the Soviet Union and France to approve the unification of the four zones, the German economy was allowed to go to pieces. The Russians and the French, unchecked, took reparations from their respective zones. The four Allies had agreed at Potsdam to dismantle approximately 1,800 German industrial plants formerly used for war production and to distribute these as reparations, to prohibit production of many objects, and to curtail that of others. The output of crude steel was limited to 4.6 million tons. The Allies proposed in this way to deprive Germany of the means to make war. They overlooked the fact that the people lived by participating in international economy, that one third of the buildings in towns of more than 100,000 inhabitants had been destroyed and an additional 45 per cent damaged, that the economy had to be revived, and that to survive the Germans needed not merely the existing but an expanded productive capacity. Under the conditions left by Allied disagreement the German economy ceased to function. The monetary system based upon the vast Nazi wartime inflation broke down completely and gave way to primitive barter. Goods went into hiding and black market operations flourished. Germans became unemployed by the millions. For three years Germany lived in chaos.

When the three Western powers broke with this policy and unified their zones into the West German Republic, they allowed the economy to revive. They had already reduced the number of plants to be dismantled and greatly increased the amount of crude steel which the Germans could produce. Within a short time dismantling ceased altogether, the limit was removed from steel production, restrictions on output of other materials were eased, and the Germans reacquired control of their economy. When in 1948 the Western Allies aided the Germans to sanify their monetary system, the people threw themselves passionately into work.

Revival of West Germany

The West German government introduced a policy of freedom from state control as the most effective way to restore the economy and as the foundation for self-government. The leading economic theorists cited against the reassertion of state planning the lesson of nazism, arguing that creative ability in all its richness could be aroused only by encouragement of individual initiative. The problems of German reconstruction loomed as too vast and complicated for state direction. Forty-seven per cent of Germany's territory had been lost to the Soviet Union and to Poland. Whereas prewar Germany had raised 80 per cent of its own food, the West German Republic could provide about 50 per cent. The rest had to be imported and paid for by the sale of goods abroad. The economy had previously been characterized by regional specialization; now the East German production of precision and optical instruments (60 per cent of the total), of electrical machinery and appliances (60 per cent of the total), of soft coal and potash (more than 50 per cent of the total), of woolen cloth and knitted goods (60 per cent of the total) was lost, as well as the reciprocal market for West German steel, cotton textiles, and numerous other articles. About 10 million Germans either fled to the Western zones from the East or were expelled by the governments of the East European states. Stripped of all possessions before leaving, these expellees brought only their work potential. The West Germans had to find the capital resources to provide them with employment, food, clothes, and shelter, articles in which the West Germans themselves were already so short that they depended upon charity from the Americans and the British. The entire productive plant needed to be renovated and modernized. Every aspect of the economy required investment capital. It was estimated in 1950 that before the war every employed person maintained one nonproducer; after 1945 every two employed individuals had to support three nonproducers.

The West Germans gained an advantage from their own desperate situation. Four and a half million persons in the German *Reich* had lost their lives during the war, and of the population in West Germany 2 million had been left crippled. The division of the country proved in one sense a benefit to the western half. Refugee man power from the East increased production at a time when other countries were short of labor. Its presence meant competition for jobs, which in turn tended to reduce costs of production by holding down the wage scale. The western half of Germany inherited more than its proportionate share of machines and machine tools; after digging these out of the ruins, it found them in better condition than anticipated. Foreign funds and materials were furnished by Britain and America in order to enable the economy to regain its place in the world. More capital flowed into West Germany than left it in payment of reparations and occupation costs, and, as soon as production revived, Germany found ready markets. The country had traditionally supplied iron and steel, coal, and machines and machine tools, the articles most in demand throughout the world. The loss of former markets in Eastern and Southeastern Europe was counterbalanced by gains among free countries, especially in Europe. Germany had recovered from the inflation of 1922–1923 by an act of will; she did so again.

The financial policy was set by the Bank of German States (organized along the lines of the American Federal Reserve system and largely independent of the government) and the ministries of economics and of finance. All three agencies were directed by courageous advocates of economic freedom from the state. The tax program was adjusted to stimulate accumulation and investment of private capital. The income-tax rate was reduced in the higher brackets; depreciation allowances were greatly accelerated on new business assets to replace those lost during the recent war; considerable amounts of profits reinvested in a business were made tax-exempt, and taxes were not levied on earnings from exports. Since the public was too poor to invest in stocks and bonds, businesses either borrowed from banks or plowed profits back into the enterprise. In 1952 it was estimated that 40 per cent of total fixed investment resulted from this latter method, a process that provided capital but did not create a wide social basis for capitalism by distributing ownership of stocks among the masses.

The West German economy has been praised as a "wonder economy" because of the magnitude and rapidity of recovery. Machinery and methods were modernized, new plants built on ruins, and productivity improved. By 1957 industrial productive capacity far exeeded that of Hitler's entire *Reich,* ranking fourth after the economy of the United States, the Soviet Union, and Great Britain. Foreign trade had climbed to third place. Production of coal lagged, but steel output (24 million tons) was outstripping that of Great Britain. In the first years the wage scale did not keep pace with profits, and the salaried and laboring classes paid for economic revival. At the end of 1956 real wages of industrial workers were one-fourth higher than in 1949, consumers' goods were flowing from the factories, and housing had been constructed for 14 million people, one half of those in need of it. The Germans were saving money again, economic prospects seemed bright, everyone had work, and the government was preventing prices and wages from spiraling upward. Having become accustomed since 1914 to living in a condition of constant insecurity, the West Germans confidently planned for the future.

The West German Republic has won its way toward recovery under a written constitution similar to that of its Weimar predecessor. The occupation powers insisted upon decentralization of authority as another preventive to the recurrence of aggression. In the main, however, the policy did not prove feasible, for a modern industrial society demands a uniform and unified handling of all major problems. The chancellor received more authority than he had had under the Weimar constitution; in order to assure some stability of rule and to prevent the sudden rise and fall of cabinets, the makers of the constitution stipulated that the *Bundestag* could not overthrow the chancellor merely by an adverse vote of confidence; it must also agree on a replacement. And Article 65 gave him the power to determine policies and made him responsible for execution.

The constitution alone could not have achieved the stability of West German government; it merely set up institutions within which, after the turmoil of nazism and war, the people's desire for quiet, orderly rule could be effective. A modified version of proportional representation did not cause the usual eruption of a multitude of parties. Politics has concentrated in the competition of three major parties: the Social Democratic, predominantly supported by workers but also appealing to some intellectuals and middle-class persons; the Christian Democratic party, composed of members of all classes and occupations but predominantly a middle and right-wing group with a moderate program appealing to both Catholics and Protestants; and the Free Democratic party, Protestant, conservative, an advocate of free enterprise, supported by big business, as nationalistic as one dared be after the Nazi disaster. The Christian Democrats have consistently controlled the government, with the somewhat reluctant cooperation of the Free Democrats, and the Christian Democrat Konrad Adenauer has occupied the post of chancellor. This former mayor of Cologne, a Catholic dismissed by the Nazis, came to express quiet moderation and firm defense of German interests. He upheld the ideals that the majority of the German people have accepted; he aimed to overcome nationalism and integrate the country into a unified Europe and a unified society of free Western nations.

Economic and Social Democracy

Unlike the socialists in other free countries of Europe since the war, the German Social Democrats have consistently formed the opposition, and the Communists, repelled and fought by all other parties, have had an insignificant following. The Germans learned too much about dictatorship from the Nazis and too much about communism from their war with the Soviet Union to nurse any illusions about extreme Marxism as a solution to their problems. The Free Democratic party has attracted many ex-Nazis, and attempts have been made (without much success) to organize a political party of the refugees and expellees. Danger of a resurgence of nationalism may lurk in the lack of a tradition of social and economic stability; but, as the people have had work and the prospect of a new life, they have supported freedom and responsible government.

The working classes have evolved a program of reform different from that of orthodox socialism. Charging to the bourgeois parties the violent ups and downs of German history since 1914, they have argued that a marked rise in the workers' social, economic, and political status is essential to prevent the occurrence of similar catastrophes. The leaders of the Social Democratic party believe that nationalization of the major means of production and distribution offers the only solution, whereas the heads of the Confederation of German Trade Unions and of the Catholic trade-unions have lost confidence in this panacea. Experience with nazism and the example of Communist Russia taught them that state control or ownership of the means of production did not necessarily increase the influence of the workers. The wrong persons might seize hold of the government. Nor did they strive primarily for economic reforms. As Viktor Agartz of the General Confederation of German Workers stated, they sought to change "the social and political structure of the German people" by participating in the direction of the industries and other businesses in which they were employed and creating a new pluralistic society. They applied the name codetermination to this plan, which as summarized by Clark Kerr, proposed the following administration:

1. A Federal Economic Council, composed of representatives from all industries and professions, to advise the government on all bills and draft ordinances in the economic field and to act as a permanent survey and planning commission. Half the members of each industry group were to be nominated by trade unions and half by employers' associations or, in public services, by the competent central authorities.

2. State Economic Councils were to be established, on the same principle, to function in all areas of state government jurisdiction.

3. Economic Chambers, covering all industries and trades, were to promote "self-administration" in the economy. These bodies, with equal labor and management representation, were envisioned essentially as bipartisan supervisory councils, empowered to determine trade practices, issue various business licenses, patrol

stock exchange transactions, and the like. In line with established German tradition, quasi-governmental enforcement power was to be granted these private chambers.

4. On the supervisory boards of large enterprises, one-half of all members were to be nonstockholding labor representatives elected by the employees from a union slate. Labor managers, acceptable to the workers, were to be members of each managerial board. Bipartisan economic committees were to be established to deal with all economic plant problems.

5. A uniform works council law was to secure codetermination rights, on the plant level, in social and personnel matters. As envisioned in the proposal, union influence at this level would have been strengthened through the institutionalization of works council and union co-ordination. The election of councilors, the development of strategy, and the daily procedures would all have taken place under watchful trade union eyes.[1]

The program was built upon theories and practices of previous decades. Under the Weimar Republic a Federal Economic Council and worker representation without a vote on supervisory councils had existed but had been powerless. The Catholic social philosophy expressed by Pope Leo XIII and his successors had stressed the equality of human beings and the cooperation and mutual consideration of workers and management. Socialism had pioneered in raising the status of workers and spreading the ideal of joint ownership. It differed from this plan in that it traditionally demanded state ownership, whereas according to the ideal of codetermination ownership and control of a few basic industries like coal and steel and chemicals should reside in unions, cooperatives, and municipalities, as well as the central government, and not in the latter alone. It retained some features of capitalism in that, apart from the few basic industries, ownership and control were mainly to be left in the hands of stockholders. It drew on syndicalism "both in the method of procurement (in part the political strike) and in the emphasis on functional (as against parliamentary) control, on worker participation at the plant level and on distrust of central government." And it emphasized "self-administration by capital and labor in areas which are sometimes considered in the public domain."[2] It marked a new kind of attempt to solve the social problem of labor in industrial society and the political problem of assuring the full and equal participation of all classes in the conduct of their affairs. The name "joint economic pluralism" has been applied to the movement;[3] a more descriptive one might be that of social democracy, without the orthodox socialism, as a supplement to political democracy.

The main part of the program described under points 4 and 5 above was introduced in the coal and steel industries in the British zone during the period of military government, and in 1951 the West German govern-

[1] Clark Kerr, "The Trade Union Movement and the Redistribution of Power in Postwar Germany," *Quarterly Journal of Economics*, November, 1954, pp. 552-553. Reprinted by permission of Harvard University Press, Cambridge, Mass.

[2] *Ibid.*, p. 553. [3] *Ibid.*, p. 554.

ment legally continued its existence. A few other industries voluntarily accepted the system, but most have resisted doing so. When the trade-unions in 1952 sought a law extending the provisions to the rest of industry they succeeded only in obtaining one so weak that its passage amounted to a severe defeat. The experiment has given the workers an interest in making a business succeed, and it has to some extent reduced the traditional antagonism between labor and management. It has not prevented strikes over fundamental issues of wage scale and the like, and it has not established a basis for social and political democracy by practicing these ideals at the plant level. Its importance rests with future development as one of a number of serious attempts in Europe at nonrevolutionary social reform.

West German Rearmament

The restoration of sovereignty to the West German Republic and membership in the Western European Union and in NATO in 1955 brought up the question of German rearmament. The United States insisted that German forces be added to those of the other states in the defense of the West, and NATO set as a goal the formation of twelve German divisions, with 1,300 aircraft and a light naval force. The German people have been as reluctant as the French to rearm Germany, and the parliament carefully considered ways and means to prevent recurrence of the authority of the military over civilian government that helped to destroy the Weimar Republic. The Social Democratic party resisted rearmament with all the means at its disposal, and many industrialists as well as others preferred the creation of a European arms pool rather than the shouldering by Germany alone of the burden of German arms production. As the industrialists had more than enough orders for civilian goods, they regarded military production as a possible obstacle to German economic resurgence.

The nature of modern warfare itself impressed upon the planners the necessity for discarding authoritarian conceptions of the relation among ranks. Count Wolf Baudissin, official in the German Defense Ministry concerned with planning the new armed force, has written:

> The range, speed and complication of military operations in the age of motor and radio, and the variety and complexity of weapons and equipment have left their mark on the military social structure. The tactical and technical specialist has taken his place as an equal in importance alongside the tactical leader. . . . The superior . . . has to rely on the cooperation of his subordinates in thinking and acting just as much as they rely on him for leadership. These new social conditions in motorized and armored units, in the air arm, and in submarines produced attitudes and codes during the war which come far closer to the concept of a free community based on mutual partnership than to the traditional picture of patriarchal authority over "minors." [4]

[4] Wolf Baudisson, "The New German Army," *Foreign Affairs,* October, 1955, p. 6.

The description may be compared to that of codetermination in labor-management relations. The prospect of using atomic arms and guided missiles further complicated and delayed German rearmament; but by 1957 a small force was in operation.

German Unity and International Policy

Since the war almost all Germans have favored some kind of European unity, and approval of membership in the Coal and Steel Community, the Western European Union, NATO, and other international organizations came quickly. The people have differed over the strategy for reunifying Germany. One group has held that the Soviet Union will permit the East German Republic to join the Western Republic only if the West Germans remain neutral in the cold war. This group wishes to preserve cultural and economic ties with the West but refuses to adhere to political and military pacts. The Social Democratic party has not demanded neutralism but always asks for one more attempt to reach agreement with the Soviet Union over reunification before deciding between East and West. The General Confederation of German Trade-Unions has taken no official position, but a large part of the members favor aligning the country definitely with the West. The Free Democratic party contains leaders willing to take the East German state as it is into a unified country in the belief that after unification the Communist infiltration into and seizure of power in the West German part can easily be prevented. Other Free Democrats agree with Adenauer and his party that the risk should not be taken. They argue that the Soviet Union will not permit reunification except on terms which would open prospects of winning all Germany to communism, and that the sole course toward unifying the two parts is to align with and strengthen the forces of the West and leave to the future the choice of means and the occasion for pressing the Soviet Union to acquiesce.

Somewhat the same division of opinion has held with respect to the Saar. France's attempt to absorb or to internationalize the area has been most denounced by the same groups that favor reunification with East Germany at almost any risk. Adenauer and his followers prevented the controversy over the Saar from destroying Western cooperation. The rejection by the Saar people in a popular vote of proposed international status for their country and the return of the area to West Germany have strengthened the belief among Germans that free elections in East Germany would show the same results. Trade between the Communist and the free republic has greatly declined, and each state has been building economic interests to replace those lost to it in the partition of the country. The steady stream of refugees from Communist tyranny and the constant threats to the freedom of Berlin have kept West Germans aroused to the plight of their fellow nationals. This continued disunity makes Germany the center of one of the gravest threats to world peace.

Austria Regains Freedom

After ten years of obstruction the Soviet Union in 1955 unexpectedly agreed to a treaty ending four-power occupation of Austria and restoring Austrian sovereignty. The price which the Communists demanded was steep—$150 million for the return to Austria of the former German properties taken by the Russians after the war, 10 million tons of oil delivered over a period of ten years, and $2 million for the Danubian Steamship Company. The Austrians believed that these economic burdens were far outweighed by the advantage of regaining freedom.

Relief from occupation had specific meaning. Foreign military courts with the right to seize and try any Austrian would be abolished. The Russian practice of arresting, sentencing, and deporting an Austrian citizen, all in secrecy, would cease. Censorship of the mails, telephones, telegraphs, and films by the Russians—a practice long since stopped in the British, French, and American zones—would end, and the broadcasting stations run by the four powers would return to Austrian ownership. More than 300 German properties, including the Zistersdorf oil field, seized by the Soviets, would be transferred to Austrian ownership and become part of the national wealth. The Soviet practice of withholding from the Austrian state taxes on these would cease, as well as with the habit of importing goods illegally from the satellite countries and selling them in the Austrian market. The country would be free from the burden of paying occupation costs to the Russians, the British, and the French—the Americans had not collected these sums since 1947; and the withdrawal of military and civilian personnel would release several thousand dwelling units to a people in great need of housing.

"Above all," an English student of the country observed a year before the Soviet Union accepted the treaty, "the occupation is hated because it draws into its net the weak, the unprincipled, and the adventurous to serve the various espionage and counter-espionage agencies of the occupying Powers. . . ." [5] The Austrians were jubilant over the departure of the four elephants from the rowboat, to use the phrase of the Austrian president Karl Renner, and they considered the future with optimism.

The foundation of the state's economy and the character of its political life have changed since prewar years, when Austria was regarded as a torso. The Nazis built up heavy industry and hydroelectric plants and expanded the production of oil. Timber resources are greater than those found anywhere in Europe except Sweden and Finland. Agriculture, which had before the war occupied 33 per cent of the population, now engages 22 per cent, and by the use of improved methods provides more food for the rest of the population. American funds have enabled the Austrians to balance their international payments while importing large quantities of food, raw materials, and machinery.

[5] *World Today*, April, 1954, p. 158.

The presence of the hated Soviet forces kept an object lesson constantly before the eyes of the Socialist workers, and taught them as well as the conservative People's party, composed of Catholic bourgeoisie, middle classes, and peasantry, the necessity of coalition government. The two parties that had engaged in civil war in the thirties learned from the experience of Nazi rule that continued political hostility might lead to repetition of that tragic fate, this time with the Communists taking the role of the Nazis. The coalition government found a counterpart in the willingness of trade-unions and management to cease their eternal fighting and to arrive at wage agreements by private negotiations. Wages and prices have kept close together, and both were held low in order to enable Austrian exports to compete in the international market.

The government has come into control of a large part of the economy by taking possession of the Nazi-owned property and that restored by the Soviet Union. Although the two parties in the government disagree on policies with respect to private property, the Socialists recognize that the many small industrial plants and farm holdings owned by the state should be returned to private ownership. The ultimate disposal of heavy industries, oil wells, and big banks has remained an open question. Both sides have understood that as an industrial nation Austria must import and export. Since her former important eastern and southeastern markets are lost to communism, she must cultivate trade with the West and overseas. She has achieved almost full employment, restored the Vienna theater and opera house and other cultural centers, and revived a flourishing tourist trade. Independent, neutral, disarmed Austria has adjusted to the realities of depending upon international prosperity and peace and of living next to dangerous neighbors.

ITALY

Politics and Government

The majority of the Italian people after the war wished to be democratic. Italy had produced fewer collaborators with the Nazis than had France, and the Italians had endured fascism and Nazi domination so long that most were disillusioned about totalitarianism and dictatorship. As soon as the events of war offered an opportunity, in contrast to the Germans they had rebelled and put their leader to death. Their popular revolt against the Nazi army in Northern Italy in the last fourteen months of the war has been called by foreign observers "one of the greatest feats ever achieved by a people in arms." On April 25, 1945, Italian partisans took Milan from the Germans and followed up this deed by capturing single-handedly most of the other North Italian cities. The partisan movement operated so efficiently that it was able to paralyze Nazi military action at almost any point. It took over the factories intact and prevented their destruction, and it placed them under the management of workers' committees. Liberation committees composed of representatives of six democratic parties assumed charge of local government and purged the Fascists. When the Allied armies occupied the region, they discharged these committees, reinstated in the name of efficiency many Fascist managers of factories and government officials, and tried to preserve the monarchy and the government of General Badoglio. For months the British, acting on the desire to maintain social and political order, blocked the change to a democratic regime. In 1946, however, the popular parties overthrew the monarchy and introduced a republic with a popular-front government. As in France, the Communists, the Socialists, and the Catholic Christian Democrats, the three largest parties, joined forces. Their rule lasted a year; in May, 1947, the Christian Democrats reformed the cabinet, omitting the left parties, but continued to seek the support of the Socialists outside the Communist bloc. The Catholic party has since then remained dominant.

In the election of 1946 the Socialist party won 21 per cent of the popular vote, thus surpassing the Communists. In January, 1947, however, Saragat, the Socialist leader, split with Nenni, his left-wing Socialist rival, before assuring the victory of the party in the struggle with the Communists, and in consequence aided the latter to become the popular party of the working classes. Nenni's group has preserved its Socialist name, but its organization has fallen under Communist control. Saragat's party has feared to align with either the Christian Democrats or the leftist parties. Traditional Western socialism like that in Germany or Great Britain has shown less strength in Italy than in France.

The Communist party revived toward the close of the war with the return of its leader Palmiro Togliatti from Moscow. Like Thorez in France, Togliatti brought orders to work for the creation of a popular front, tactics regarded in Moscow as best adapted to win support among a people overwhelmingly Catholic. Togliatti played the part of a moderate liberal, devoted to progress within the framework of the democratic constitution, and seeking victory by way of the ballot box. He endeavored to reassure the Catholics and the Socialists by advocating reforms which have long since been introduced into advanced countries. The Communists soon dominated the General Confederation of Labor, which, as in France, served as their fighting force; but their following has declined. They held the post of mayor in all major cities in North Italy after the war, and, together with the left-wing Socialists, a majority in the city councils. The Communist party attracted young intellectuals from the middle classes who, equipped with university degrees, found few opportunities for employment. It was followed by peasants as well as urban workers, and, as in France, it enjoyed the support of many who were non-Communists but who think that the Communist menace is useful or even necessary to force the government to improve conditions.

The party line troubled members who believe in direct action by violence, but the leaders remained moderate. In the election of 1953 the Communists obtained the vote of 44 per cent of the young people between the ages of 21 and 25, thus increasing their popular vote by 1,400,000 more than they received in the election of 1948. Between 1946 and 1953 they lost 900,000 votes in the north and center of Italy, and gained a million votes in the south. In 1955, although still in control of 54 per cent of the labor vote, they lost out in some crucial elections for shop stewards in the factories. The official downgrading of Stalin by Moscow and the Soviet attack on Hungary in 1956 severely hurt the party. The percentage of its vote in an election in one large industrial plant dropped from 60 to 26. Workers and intellectuals throughout Italy are repudiating communism in such numbers that they threaten the movement there.

The Christian Democratic party, like the M.R.P. in France, began as a political vehicle of Catholic-inspired social reform, democratic in ideals and equally hostile to fascism and to communism. Its founding revived the ideals of a similar party formed just after World War I by the Catholic statesman Don Sturzo, and it belongs in the tradition of the Catholic political party of Germany and elsewhere in the modern parliamentary period. As a party affiliated with a religion, it has attracted followers from left, right, and center. Thus it has been an organization within which the representatives of these various shades of political opinion have fought for control. The immediate postwar years of enthusiasm and idealism enabled the reformers to dominate, but with the passage of time the conservative wing has gained in strength.

The dominant personality in Italian politics between 1946 and 1953, the prime minister De Gasperi, belonged to the party. He was able to keep both it and Italian governmental policy in the "middle of the road." The party organized a powerful Catholic trade-union rival to the Communist-dominated General Confederation of Labor, and introduced agrarian and other reforms. At the same time it sought to strengthen the bourgeois economy, thereby receiving the support of most of the conservative forces, including many monarchists and ex-Fascists. Its main instrument of political agitation has been the Catholic Action, an organization of conservative tendencies interested predominantly in strengthening the influence of the Catholic Church.

> This party has never been able to make up its mind whether its central planks should be that of defending the interests of the small group of wealthy industrialists and landowners who control practically all the levers of power in Italy, or that of pressing a programme of economic reform which would raise the deplorably low standard of both living and productivity; if this were done, it might transform what is in effect a highly authoritarian state, where the average man is a subject rather than a citizen, into something more truly resembling an Anglo-Saxon or Scandinavian democracy.[6]

[6] *Economist* (London), July 10, 1954, p. 123.

In consequence, the Christian Democratic government has not put through sufficient reforms to destroy Communist popularity. Since De Gasperi's retirement from public life in 1953 the party has continued to execute moderate social reforms.

The relative strength of the Communist party and its Socialist ally, on the one hand, and of the Christian Democrats, on the other, may be judged from the outcome of two national elections of members of the Italian Chamber, that of 1948 and that of 1953. Three months before the earlier election the Communists were considered by Western observers to have an even chance of winning a majority. The non-Communist Italians and the Western powers, particularly the United States, roused themselves to counteraction. The center and right parties, split into 300 political groups, combined their efforts; the press, 82 per cent anti-Communist, took up the battle; the Catholic Church abandoned its tradition of political neutrality, and the Catholic Action carried voters to the polls in anything on wheels, from an automobile to a wheelbarrow. American private citizens of Italian and non-Italian origin poured personal propaganda into the country; and the United States government assisted with public statements against communism and with food, money, and goods under the Marshall Plan. The Western powers publicly supported the return of Trieste to Italy. When a Communist mayor, able and respected and a loyal Catholic, died during the campaign, the Church refused him Christian burial. In the election the Christian Democrats and their allies won 63 per cent of the total vote, the Communist bloc 31 per cent.

Five years later, when the danger of Communist victory had lessened, the center and right-wing parties did not cooperate or campaign so effectively. De Gasperi had forced through a new election law in 1952, whereby any party or coalition of parties winning a majority of the votes would be given 65 per cent of the seats in the Chamber. The Christian Democrats failed to gain that majority by 57,000 votes, or a small fraction of 1 per cent, an outcome that has been explained in part by the unpopularity of the election law, and by disillusionment with the government because of its mediocre record of reform. The greater security from communism which the people felt was seen in the fact that both the Monarchist vote and that for a revived Fascist party, although still small, more than doubled. Since then the Christian Democrats have continued along the middle road, seeking support from groups to left or right according to circumstances.

Economic Revival

Italy has needed fundamental changes in her economic and social organization in order to provide the population with work. She has had from 1½ to 2 million unemployed ever since the close of the war, and a much larger number of underemployed. Her birth rate has continued to be so high that 400,000 to 500,000 persons are added to the population each year, and 250,000 to 300,000 workers. The war loss in man power has been overcome. The destruction of economic resources during the war accentuated the poverty of a country of few natural resources. One fifth of Italy's total equipment (buildings, roads, machines, livestock, railways, and the like) was destroyed; farm land deteriorated for want of fertilizer and equipment; foreign trade almost ceased toward the close of the war; 80 per cent of the merchant fleet was lost; inflation was repressed by government action, but prices grew out of line with each other. The Italian state inherited from the Fascists the public ownership of huge industrial, banking, and shipping resources; but after the experience with fascism, aversion to public direction of the economy inclined the new leaders to introduce a free economy as rapidly as possible. They retained the state economic holdings and kept some price control of essentials like rent and food, and they did not dare to open the national market to free imports; but they sought to restore private ownership and a free internal market as the most effective stimulant to recovery of the country.

Unlike France, the government set the value of the lira as early as 1947 and stopped inflation. It aimed to establish a sound financial basis so that prices would be stable and individuals could calculate for the future with confidence. The government endeavored to keep its budget not too far out of balance, first by reducing expenditures and second by improving the efficiency of the tax system. The first part of this program entailed hardships for the people, for the state had more resources for capital investment and the general overhaul of the economy than had private investors.

It has been argued that in a country like Italy, with a working force greater than actual need, the government should direct the development of economic resources able to utilize this man power. Italy failed to do so. After an initial expenditure for restoring war damage, the government not merely reduced the amount of state investment but did not spend all that appropriated for the purpose. Nor did it use state-owned enterprises as instruments for remaking the economy. It expanded investments in the steel industry and the production of natural gas, it subsidized the private building of houses, and after 1952 it increased investments in shipbuilding and in the production of tractors; but it has no Monnet Plan. Nor has it reformed the tax system sufficiently to further redistribution of the national income, as in Great Britain. Although assessment and collection of the income tax have somewhat improved, the main part of the revenue is still derived from indirect taxes, especially the turnover tax (a kind of sales tax), which hits the masses heavily and spares the rich.

Marshall Plan aid and the continued flow of United States funds have been essential in reviving the Italian economy and preserving the country from communism. Through the year 1948 Italy received from abroad, mainly from the United States, nearly $2,500 million in gifts and credit and payment for services, three fourths of it being gifts. These amounts have been accompanied by the exchange of technical advice in the effort to rationalize the economy and accustom the population to strive for high productivity. The results have been spotty, for Italy, like France, was ridden with cartels and associations for fixing prices. As in France, however, a growing number of industrialists has begun to approve the principle of raising productivity and tried to increase output, lower costs and prices, reduce the number of models, share profits with the workers, and thereby create a mass market within Italy for Italian products.

This educational work, plus the appeal of counterpart funds for executing the program, has been strengthened by two internal factors. The high interest rates, between 8 and 12 per cent, forced businesses to be economical in the use of capital funds. Many of them introduced modern methods and equipment in order to lower costs and reduce the amount of capital needed. The second factor amounted to making a blessing out of a handicap. At the end of the war the government required industries to keep workers on their payroll, even though the services were not needed. This form of compulsory poor relief by private business slowed down economic recovery; but when American funds and know-how became available, managers used them to turn an item of expense into a means of profit by occupying this surplus labor.

The economy has received a boost in the discovery of large amounts of natural gas in northern Italy between Milan and Genoa. The country has always been deficient in fuel, and the necessity to import coal has raised costs of industrial production and severely handicapped exports. Coal, for example, has been three times as expensive to an Italian as to his English competitor. The expansion of hydroelectric resources has in recent decades reduced the amount of coal needed, but the uncertainty of the flow of water has rendered it necessary to supplement the supply of hydroelectricity by that from steam plants burning coal. The discovery of natural gas resources, primarily made since World War II, has opened the prospect of a new era. Although the resources do not compare in quantity with those of the United States or Canada, for Europe they are large. In May, 1952, a power plant using gas as fuel was inaugurated; it supplies 500 million kilowatt-hours of electricity, a landmark in Italian history. A pipeline for natural gas was installed to supply Turin, and a network begun for the entire peninsula. Italy may be able within a short time to reduce her imports of coal by four fifths and to export natural gas to Switzerland and France. The steel, chemical, engineering, and other industries have already begun to take advantage of this cheap fuel and to rationalize their production. Since Italy has volcanic resources which are being harnessed for power and also has good prospects of discovering oil in considerable quantities, the people of this rocky peninsula, poor in everything except man power, dream of a new era.

Land Reform

The change in social standards which industrialism has brought in Western countries finally induced the Italian government after World War II seriously to plan the division of large estates. These lie in parts of the north and center, and particularly in the south. Extensive, uneconomical agriculture, unemployment, poverty, and social coercion of the masses of peasant laborers by the few landlords and their officials still characterized these regions. The government passed the first important law in 1950, applying it to areas of the south and planning for long-term transfer of property to peasant ownership, provision of state aid and technical guidance to the new proprietors, and construction of roads, railways, schools, irrigation works where possible, water works, and other facilities.

Twenty million acres of land were to be purchased by the peasants in small plots, the new proprietors to pay about $30 a year for thirty years for the land, and the state to start them on their career with free seeds and fertilizer and with technical assistance if necessary in clearing and preparing the soil for cultivation. Tractors were introduced into the region for the first time, and seeing these machines clean off the shrubs and turn up the good soil at such depths has made the peasants believe that land reform has come to stay. At strategic places the government has established state farms equipped with machinery and run by technicians; these farms have set an example for the peasants and provided them with equipment at a low expense. Within two years' time both industrial and agricultural production in the south began to improve. Both the Communists and the landlords fought the program, each group for a different reason, but the work has gone slowly forward. In 1956 the government planned to provide more funds for agriculture for a longer period than before and to create local industries.

The reconstruction of the south is expected to take one or more decades. When completed, it is thought, the uneven geographic distribution of income will be overcome and southern Italy will produce her share of national goods. Young people of the south will find employment at home and will no longer migrate north or seek positions in the civil service. In the meantime, private consumption has greatly increased, but the national income continues to be inequitably distributed among the social groups.

In most countries the agricultural population has profited from an increased market; in Italy it has barely maintained the income that it received before the war. Industry had by 1951 raised its net income to about 40 per cent above the prewar figure. The employed industrial workers organized in trade-unions have gained most; their real wages were in 1951 30 per cent above the prewar figure. They have effectively used trade-union strength to improve their lot, but they are relatively few in number, and they have not aided the unorganized labor, the unemployed, the civil servants, and other salaried employees, whose share of the national income has dropped.

Employed and organized industrial labor has succeeded in tying its wage scale to a cost of living index; the others have not. Many of the former group have supported communism in order to enhance the fear of organized labor and gain concessions; many of the latter have done so out of despair.

International Economic Relations

Italy has since the war persistently advocated the abolition of quotas, high tariffs, exchange control, and similar devices. Her imports have consisted almost entirely of food products, raw materials, and semifinished goods; her exports, to a slightly less extent, of finished and semifinished goods. Like Great Britain and unlike France, she requires these imports because of her own shortage of natural resources, and she has to export processed goods in order to pay for them. The nature of her exports helps to explain why she has supported free trade. She sells abroad predominantly luxury goods, especially textiles and art objects, and foods like fruits, vegetables, wine, cheese, and olive oil, which an importing country short of funds may easily forgo.

The Italian government has been unable to practice its own ideal for fear that other countries would flood its market with manufactured goods. It has retained restrictions on many items, but it has steadily pressed for European union in all possible forms. The country has profited from the international rearmament program that began with the Korean war, when the engineering industry suddenly found a foreign market for its articles. The creation of the Coal and Steel Community opened up the prospect of wider markets, lower costs, and the stimulation of competition for the improvement of industry. Nonetheless, the country has lacked capital resources with which to support a program of thorough structural change in the economy. It has remained dependent on foreign aid to balance its international payments for maintaining the present conditions. At such a pace, the accumulation of capital resources remains slow.

The government has been aware of this handicap, and in 1954, Vanoni, the minister of the budget, proposed a ten-year plan for economic development. The promising aspect of the plan lay in the fact that the government considered Italy's man power, not as a handicap to be exported to any country admitting immigrants, but as a national resource to be used for augumenting production. The document was submitted to the O.E.E.C., whose cooperation was necessary for success. Italy hoped within the ten-year period to reduce the number employed in agriculture, to put the unemployed to work by expanding the industrial plant, the public utilities, and the means of communication, by developing a housing program, and by improving agricultural efficiency, particularly in the south. These were well-known ideals. The novel part consisted of the government's detailed proposal for balancing Italy's international accounts and obtaining funds for investment, not from foreign countries as gifts, but from internal savings. To do so, Italy would need to increase her exports by 60 per cent above the level of 1954 and her imports by 43 per cent, and to be able to compete in the international market, particularly in iron and steel and in engineering and chemical products. The achievement of such a rate of expansion necessarily would depend upon the willingness of other countries to import Italian products, and this willingness upon the general expansion of the world economy.

Having suffered from fascism with its rabid nationalism, its autarchic ideals, its disregard in practice of the welfare of the people, Italy seems to be moving rapidly in the opposite direction. She has advanced faster toward accepting the fact of her interdependence with the rest of the world than has France. She is attempting reforms of internal conditions based upon the ideal of increased productivity, with all its social and cultural effects, and reforms of international relations based upon the establishment of new organizations requiring intimate cooperation among nations. The decisive conflict is being fought within the Christian Democratic party between the forces defending vested interests in mass poverty and elite superiority and those working for a new Italy in a new world.

SPAIN, PORTUGAL, AND GREECE

At the outbreak of World War II these three countries were ruled by dictators—General Franco in Spain, Professor Salazar in Portugal, and General Metaxas in Greece. The Iberian states had remained technically neutral, whereas Greece had been invaded by both Italy and Germany. Franco had been pro-Axis as long as his dictator-colleagues appeared to be winning. Since he governed a country wrecked by civil war, he had hesitated openly to join Hitler and Mussolini. Salazar assisted the Allies by providing such indispensable materials as wolfram and by permitting them to use the Azores and the Cape Verde Islands for air and naval purposes. Both dictators survived the period of conflict with their authority and their countries intact.

In contrast, Greece had undergone devastation comparable to that of Poland. Systematic looting by the Nazis had caused starvation and had driven the people to desperate resistance. The native Communists had been active in organizing the partisans, and at the close of the war they controlled a country-wide movement of Communists, non-Communists, and anti-Communists called the National Liberation Front (referred to by the initials E.A.M., representing the Greek words for the name) and an armed force called the People's Army of Liberation (E.L.A.S.). At that time the Communists would have established their own dictatorship, but the British debarked troops in Greece to assist native forces, known from the Greek initials of their equally patriotic name as E.D.E.S., in combating the E.L.A.S.

Neutrality enabled Franco and Salazar to preserve their rule; participation in the war opened Greece to the play of international forces. The Soviet Union actively supported the Greek Communists with arms; Great Britain and, from early 1947 on, the United States assisted the anti-Communist forces with aid of all kinds and sought to introduce reforms for stabilizing free, responsible government. All three countries may be considered underdeveloped; and, since all lie in Southern Europe, they have certain common geographic conditions. The basic forces affecting the postwar career of each have differed so markedly that each country must receive separate treatment.

Spain under Franco

General Franco has in the postwar years practiced caution amounting almost to inaction, partly from his own temperament, partly from deference to the conservative forces that support his regime. He has catered to the army to the extent that Spanish technical and financial resources will allow. He has assured the Catholic Church complete control of religious and educational life. The landlords and the industrialists likewise owe the retention of their favored economic and social position to his regime. Between 1936 and 1952 the cost of living increased 600 per cent, whereas wages rose by only 50 per cent. Strikes were forbidden, and the army and an efficient police force have protected property rights against angry workers. Data covering one half of Spain have shown that, in 1950, 96 per cent of the farms consisted of less than 12 acres and that less than 1 per cent of the proprietors owned 35 per cent of the land. The main sources of potential danger to the continuance of conservative rule have been labor and a desire among the ruling groups for United States economic and military aid.

Labor has been organized into syndicates under the absolute domination of the state. Since the fixing of wages and conditions of work and the administration of the welfare and social security projects are government-controlled and strikes are crushed by the police, the workers have sparse means of improving their lot. Franco's Minister of Labor Giron boasted that he has executed almost the entire social program of the socialists during the republic, including social security, security from dismissal from work, free medical care, two months' extra pay as a bonus, and family allowances. Unemployment benefits, however, have not been included in the system of social security, and the entire program has lacked an adequate base, namely, a living wage. In 1951 an agricultural worker received 12 pesetas a day, enough to buy two glasses of orange juice in a country that raises oranges. The poverty of the workers has been so striking that members of the Catholic hierarchy have publicly criticized the employers and the regime and several bishops have begun to train their priests in economics and social service and to plan ways for helping the poor. Some clergy have attempted to maintain or to win back the devotion of the workers for the church, and for that purpose have braved the wrath of employers.

United States Economic Aid to Spain

Franco's policy has encouraged economic conservatism in a country which has urgently needed to awaken the spirit of enterprise. The dictator has steadily since the war sought to overcome the role of international pariah inherited from the Spanish civil war and his intimacy with Mussolini and Hitler, not merely for the sake of prestige but in order to obtain United States economic assistance. Since Spain could supply valuable bases for Western defense against the Soviet Union and her satellites, he proposed to exchange cooperation in defense for extensive aid in the economic development of the country as a whole, and on terms of equality. With the assistance of American Catholic politicians and American defense leaders, he first received small sums of money during the second Truman administration. The Communist attack in Korea raised the desirability of Spanish bases, and after long negotiation the United States and Spain in September, 1953, signed an agreement for the joint development of air and naval bases in Spain. Franco and his supporters did not receive the amount of aid for general use in the economy that they wished; but they sought to strengthen the economy by assuring the use of Spanish materials and labor in constructing the bases. In order to attract foreign capital to invest in Spain they have increased from the old basic figure of 25 per cent to a maximum figure of 49 per cent the amount of stock foreigners may own in a corporation.

The American action has brought a creative force into the country for the first time since Franco came to power. The full effects will not be visible for years, and prospects have caused Spaniards considerable concern. The Catholic Church disliked the presence of Protestant soldiers and civilians at the new bases in the country, with the inevitable mixed marriages and other complications. Many Spaniards feared that the standard of living made visible by the Americans would arouse ambitions in the lower classes. Almost all correctly anticipated a heavy increase in the demand for Spanish goods, cement for example, that would result in inflation. Spanish industry was for the most part incompetent to supply both quantity and quality of goods for constructing the bases, and many firms had expected to purchase the machinery in Germany and resell it to the United States authority. When the latter rejected this plan, Spanish industry received its first shock. Instead of being allowed to vegetate as usual, the owners and managers had to show some enterprise. Spanish firms were at first slow in bidding for construction contracts in the belief that it was not courteous to press their case. That the work is being executed for the army, navy, and air force, Spanish as well as American, has placed the interest of Franco and his most important supporters behind the agreement. The American influence on Spain should be interesting to watch.

Portugal under Salazar

Portugal, like Spain, has retained the broad but incomplete organization of a corporative state. She has gone farther than her neighbor in reducing illiteracy, and she has introduced some social security. At that point, however, the resemblance ceases, for Portugal under Salazar has stimulated the economy to action, whereas Franco has not.

Wartime neutrality brought both profit and loss to Portugal—profit from the sale of wolfram, tin, manganese, and a few similar articles; loss from inability to import food, fuel, and machinery and to sell abroad wine, canned fish, and other luxuries. The government has continued to balance its budget, to maintain an international balance of payments, and to enjoy a large reserve of gold and foreign exchange, not by the good fortune of wartime boom, but by steady economy. Salazar has developed the study of economics and statistics at the universities, and has trained personnel to assist him in administration. When after the war he saw that the private citizens with adequate funds were often deficient in entrepreneurial zeal, he modified his devotion to private enterprise. In 1953 he introduced a Six-Year Plan of economic construction. "We must ensure," he declared, "that the train of national resources takes a certain course and meets certain requirements." Since the population was increasing at a rapid rate, the government assumed responsibility for providing future means of employment.

The plan concerned all major aspects of the economy, but with different degrees of emphasis. Because Portugal has almost no oil and small resources in coal, she needed hydroelectric generating stations. The rivers, which had flooded and eroded the land, were to be curbed for production. Salazar allocated one third of the funds, exclusive of those for the colonies, for constructing power stations and distribution lines and gave attention to all parts of the country. Cheap power was expected to encourage the construction of a wide range of industries well placed throughout Portugal. He provided for transportation and communication almost as large a share of investment funds as for power, although he neglected country road building in favor of improvement of railroads, ports, airports, merchant marine, and the like.

Salazar cut agricultural investment to a small amount with promise of future attention. The southern half of the country continued to be held in large estates, and the peasant holdings in the north were acknowledged to be too small. Salazar has spoken about "the extreme irregularity with which land is distributed over our country," and has added, "It is more than doubtful whether, despite our respect and even our love for private landed property, the phenomenon can continue indefinitely without some legal orientation or corrective process for the more serious evils." When the Six-Year Plan went into effect he expressed the hope that its successor would deal with the agricultural problem.

Industry received somewhat more funds than agriculture. The sale of many of Portugal's standard exports, such as anchovies, port wine, and nuts, largely depends upon prosperity in the purchasing countries. Their market has suffered severely in time of war just when the export of wolfram and the like has boomed. To try to make the economy less subject to these ups and downs of the international market has been one of the aims in the allocation of funds for industrial investment. Other commodities should also be produced and the needs of the home consumer supplied. Hence the plan aimed to expand the state oil refinery, to construct modest iron and steel works, to increase the output of cellulose and fertilizer, and to turn out tin plate. These were considered essential either for conserving foreign exchange or for processing native raw materials. The state has stimulated private industry, for example, that dealing with cork, to improve its methods; but investors have persisted in waiting for official lead before committing their own funds. By 1954 the government had either directly or indirectly become the owner of so much industry and other property that it financed one sixth of its budget from profits. Since Salazar is determined that industry shall provide a larger proportion of the national income than before the war, the conclusion of state investment is nowhere in sight.

Portugal has close commercial relations with the countries of the West, the United States, Great Britain, and the West German Republic being the most important. She has cultivated her African empire and made it a source of large revenue for both Portuguese and the African natives. Salazar's regime is training engineers and scientists and other experts and enjoys the support of the nation. Its weakness arises from the inherent deficiency of authoritarianism. The arbitrary hand in politics has affected other fields. Intellectual and artistic life has ceased to be creative. In the following statement Salazar himself has recognized the authoritarian dilemma:

> Two things are certainly required: to ensure that light coming from all quarters is focused on all problems; to fight the tendency towards deification of power and the stagnation of existing situations. . . . But if we are solely concerned with finding the best solution for the nation's problems, how can we think it wise to waste time listening to voices which, owing to political passion or dogma, will disparage all those solutions? I confess I do not know how to resolve the difficulty.

Franco would not have understood the problem. Portugal has been lifting herself by her own bootstraps slowly but steadily; Spain has waited, and the government has held down its people by force. Both Salazar and Franco have reached the age for thinking about a successor. Which country will have less trouble in finding one?

Greece—Civil War and United States Aid

When the Nazi military forces withdrew from Greece in 1944, the E.A.M. and its troops known as E.L.A.S., took control and drove the small right-wing E.D.E.S. into the sea. The latter returned solely because of British military assistance, which proved so effective that in February, 1945, the E.A.M. signed the Varkiza Agreement promising to dissolve and to turn its arms over to the Greek government. The British assisted the Greek monarchists and reactionaries to regain power, on the supposition that these alone could restore order to the country.

Instead of fulfilling the British expectation, the monarchists placed their followers—thousands of them guilty of collaboration with the Nazis—in the army, the bureaucracy, and the police force. These turned indiscriminately against liberals, socialists, republicans, and Communists and soon restored the worst features of Greek misgovernment. They exploited the economy as before, they shot opponents arbitrarily, they punished villages ruthlessly that dared to vote against the monarchists, and they introduced such terrorist methods that they drove the masses into the arms of the Communists. In 1946 civil war resumed and Communist-led bands could be found throughout the country. The British, who had helped to bring about this state of affairs, announced early in 1947 that they could no longer afford to defend Greece against communism, and on moment's notice the United States inherited that role. For the first time a new influence for freedom and a democratic way of life entered Greece with sufficient prestige and material resources to initiate wholesale reform.

The Americans and the few trustworthy idealistic Greeks sought to replace traditional exploitation for the advantage of private interests by respect for public welfare. Material rehabilitation offered the least difficulty. What measures could one take, however, to prevent a repetition of the fate of UNRRA in Greece? This international agency knew that the funds which it poured into the country immediately fell into the hands of the rich and influential, who shipped them abroad for safekeeping. When the United States Mission of Aid arrived in Greece in 1947 it discovered tons of textiles donated by Americans to the Greek people were rotting in warehouses because the Greek government feared that distribution would lower the price of textiles and adversely affect the powerful textile interests. The mission further learned that, although 75 per cent of the Greek children suffered from malnutrition, the quantities of food supplied from the United States and elsewhere were going by way of the black market to the rich. They soon learned that the efficiency of the army was undermined by favoritism and politics, that the big merchants and industrialists used politicians to protect their interests, that the masses paid most of the taxes, and that governmental administration was incompetent.

Greek Revival

The American mission advanced with its program simultaneously on several fronts. First, it brought in military supplies and advisers to revamp the Greek army and enable it to defeat the Communist-led rebellion. That objective was reached during 1949. In the process the army became an efficient fighting force, and when General Alexander Papagos was appointed commander in chief in 1949–1951 he suppressed the corrupting practice of favoritism and kept the army out of politics. Second, the Americans brought experts with equipment for repairing the physical damage of war and for improving production. Means of transportation and communication, harbor works, flood control, hydroelectrical plants, the usual deficiencies in an underdeveloped economy, were subjected to investigation, and initial steps were taken toward making them adequate. Surveys of the country's natural resources led to plans for increasing the amount of land under agriculture, for constructing plants to process the native minerals—bauxite, nickel, and magnesium—for expanding the output of chemical fertilizers, and for many other agricultural and industrial changes. The Americans advocated an increase in educational facilities and persuaded Greek peasants in Macedonia to try contour ploughing. The latter alone increased output between 30 and 80 per cent. The military and the material aspects of the reform program appeared to be well initiated.

The incompetence of the government and the instability of political life caused most trouble, for these involved more psychological factors than had military and economic reforms. In the latter two types of reform results could be checked against an objective standard. In the former, intangibles predominated. In 1952, Varvaressos, the nation's ablest economist and a former governor of the Bank of Greece, surveyed the civil service at the request of the government, and concluded that it contained far too many persons, far too many incompetent, untrained members; that its members placed party and private interests too often above national interest; that excessive red tape caused delay and inefficiency and exasperated the public; and that the pay scale was utterly inadequate. "I am completely convinced [he concluded] that no actual improvement of the economic situation of the country will possibly occur in the future unless this basic problem of deficient functioning of the state machine is duly faced."

Government needed to be decentralized and local units permitted some responsibility. With 95 per cent of taxes going to the central government, every question had to be referred to Athens for decision. In the Northern provinces, acquired in 1912, local officials complained, "We had more and better local government under the Turks." Tax revenue from particular sources were by law allocated to so many special budgets that the central government never knew exactly how much money was paid in taxes or what all the taxes were. Worst of all was the custom of trading financial favors for political support.

As the United States contributed in one form or another almost $2 billion to Greece between 1944 and 1952, and has continued since then to help support the military outlay, it reached agreement in 1948 with the government for setting up an advisory American staff. Military, financial, and civil affairs experts in construction, industry and transportation, food and agriculture, health, and labor and man power worked with the Greeks to introduce modern standards into the government of the country. Pressed by the Americans, the Greek government passed a law to replace proportional representation by the majority system. The effects became evident in the election of 1952, when the Greek Rally, headed as a nonparty movement by General Papagos and composed of groups of the right and center, won 239 seats to the opponent's 61. For the first time in decades it seemed possible to form, not a coalition government doomed to fall apart in a few months, but an actually responsible ministry. The new cabinet contained vigorous personalities who began to introduce needed reforms. The currency was devalued by one half in 1953 in order to stimulate exports; the discount rate was cut as an inducement to private investment; steps were taken toward an equitable distribution of the tax burden; and the program of industrialization was advanced. Greece thus could place her first foreign loan since 1920, and inasmuch as the United States and NATO have assumed nearly one half of the financial burden of rearmament, the country almost balanced its international payments.

The outstanding cause of uncertainty lies in the Cyprus issue. The Greek people demand the return of the island to Greece, and the government has been forced by popular pressure to support the claim. Relations, especially with Britain and Turkey, have deteriorated. The conflict has not as yet affected the economy, but in a country where economic growth and political stability are so interdependent no one can be certain of the outcome. In most other respects Greece has supported the new reform program and has inspired belief in her will to maintain responsible government in a free and prosperous society.

Postwar experience of the six nations just discussed reveals that Germany, Austria, and Italy learned from dictatorial experience to appreciate freedom in government and society, and to a greater extent than the victor states expected. In the economic sector of national life they have encouraged private initiative under conditions of stress which seemed to call for state planning. Greece, exploited by foreign conquerors far worse than by native dictators, did not draw the lesson of self-government and economic liberty with comparable conviction. Spain and Portugal have lacked an opportunity to do so. Countries with a well-developed industrial system have had the means, under proper leadership, to supply the material basis for a free society. Germany had most facilities for the change, Austria fewer, and Italy has ranked a poor third. In all three countries the leaders buttressed political and social freedom with economic freedom. The other three nations have suffered from deficiencies. Greece has benefited from

American aid, and American influence has been essential politically as well as economically in keeping her stable. In the Iberian peninsula industrialism has only begun to overcome general backwardness.

Only Greece has as yet conducted foreign relations in a way out of harmony with free government and progressive society. She has continued to poison relations with other states and threaten continuity of government by riots for the sake of Cyprus. West Germany, with far greater provocation, has refused so far to be drawn into the dangers of power politics in order to reunite her lost territories. Italy and Austria have on the whole remained quiet in international affairs, and Spain and Portugal lack the resources to play the game. In each of the six countries the need for intellectual freedom has been as acutely felt as the need for food and shelter.

Two decades of fascism taught Europe the significance, for all aspects of a society, of the character and policy of government. Liberal democracy, which after World War I won appreciation in theory, has become widely accepted as desirable practice. Except for vestiges in Spain and Portugal, fascist rule has passed. Prior to World War II Communist dictatorship was restricted to the Soviet Union; since the conflict it has assumed the aggressive in defiance of Western ideals. In the next chapter we shall discuss the reaction of this Marxian form of authoritarianism to postwar conditions and shall see that it also was affected by the natural desire of man for freedom.

Suggestions for Further Reading

Economic Survey of Europe since the War. See the Readings for Chapter 24. Fundamental for the years under review.

ELLIS, H. S. *The Economics of Freedom.* See the Readings for Chapter 22. Excellent.

KOGAN, NORMAN. *Italy and the Allies.* Cambridge, Mass.: Harvard University Press, 1956. From Mussolini's fall to 1956.

MATTHEWS, HERBERT L. *The Yoke and the Arrow.* New York: George Braziller, Inc., 1957. Contemporary Spain, by a veteran observer.

SMITH, H. K. *The State of Europe.* See the Readings for Chapter 24.

SWEET-ESCOTT, BICKHAM. *Greece: A Political and Economic Survey, 1939–1953.* New York: Oxford University Press, 1954.

WALLICH, HENRY C. *Mainsprings of the German Revival.* New Haven, Conn.: Yale University Press, 1955. Basic analysis of West Germany's economic recovery.

Chapter 26 · The Soviet Bloc

THE SOVIET UNION

The Soviet Union in the postwar period strove toward two main objectives. First, she resumed the line of communist development which the war had interrupted. Second, she had to bring the new satellite states within the communist system and transfer the direction of their interests from West to East. The process in each case conformed to a pattern and lacked the rich variety of experience characteristic of free nations.

Return to Orthodox Communism

As soon as the war was successfully concluded, Stalin and his cohorts began to restore their version of orthodox communist doctrine to dominance. During the conflict they had appealed to the nationalist feelings of the numerous peoples of the U.S.S.R. as a source of morale in fighting the invaders. This bourgeois sentiment was now suppressed, for it might have led to placing nationalism above communism as an object of loyalty. The change in policy involved a change in officials in the various constituent republics: those who had encouraged the cultivation of national literature and the study of national history and had shown a modest degree of independence of Moscow gave way to men of opposite beliefs. Stalin set an example by encouraging the use of the Russian language as the common tongue throughout the Soviet Union. The war had likewise brought a resurgence of religious interest among young people as well as old. The Communists were ordered to oppose this backsliding into bourgeois habits, and the Society for the Diffusion of Scientific and Political Knowledge, an atheistic organization to which the intellectual elite belonged, received large sums for propaganda.

Military victory redounded to the glory of the U.S.S.R., but for the communist system the nature of the victory created special problems. The rulers immediately spread the fable among their subjects that the Western powers had contributed little to the outcome, that the Soviet Union had been the source of victory. Stalin and others were convinced that in the war communism had proved its durability and its superiority to all other forms of society. At the same time they made certain that the popularity of the generals did not survive the war. They wanted no competitors for power among ambitious officers. They therefore sent figures like Marshal Zhukov to the provinces and closed all publicity to them. They had to keep the defense forces powerful, but they strengthened party control by activating the party cells in the ranks and by careful selection and advancement of loyal Communists as officers. Knowing that the Soviet military advance had enabled millions of Soviet soldiers to see life in bourgeois capitalist countries, they initiated a thorough campaign of re-education among their troops to persuade them that Soviet culture surpassed all others. The devout spread the legend that Stalin was the ultimate cause of all Soviet achievement in war as in peace.

Postwar Economic and Social Adjustment

The governmental organization functioned during the war as usual and required no important structural adjustments to the condition of peace. The government had always been shaped for the "inevitable" conflict with capitalism, and the fact that war had occurred confirmed the leaders' belief in the correctness of their views. The economy required different handling. The leaders were convinced that their prewar economic program had enabled the Soviet Union to withstand the ordeal, and they intended to continue that program; but they had problems of adjustment to meet which a great war would have left in any economy, no matter how thoroughly controlled.

The first problem concerned demography. Exact figures on Soviet loss of population during the war are unknown. The government claimed in 1938 to have a population of 170,467,000 persons and at the beginning of 1950 one of over 200,000,000. During the war the Soviet Union acquired territory inhabited before the war by 25 million people. It is estimated that if the war had not occurred, the U.S.S.R. plus its added areas would have had a population of 225,000,000 people. The loss from the war is therefore placed at 25 to 28 million, of which 7 million (the figure is Stalin's) were military losses, 5 million were civilian losses, 6 million constituted the deficit in births, 3 million migrated; the other 4 to 7 million cannot be traced. The population is increasing at a rate of probably 3 million a year, with an estimated death rate of 13 per thousand and birth rate of 28 per thousand. These figures are less than before the war (for example, the birth rate was 40 per thousand in 1930) and seem to indicate that the Soviet Union is traveling the same demographic road as free industrial countries. As she becomes urban and industrial, the death and birth rate fall. The birth rate was sufficiently high, however, to enable the country speedily to recoup war losses, and by the beginning of 1950 labor and employees amounted to more than 35 million persons, 15 per cent more than in 1940.

During the war control of labor had been so strict that the government could transfer persons to any place at will. In many areas it introduced martial law, and it speeded up the education, especially the technical training, of youth. As the men were mobilized into the armed services, women took their places, accounting by 1942 for 52 per cent of all workers and employees (38 per cent in 1940). They were aided by refugees from the regions conquered by the Germans and by a wave of migrants from the farms. After the war millions of returned soldiers often lacked workbooks by which their movements could be controlled; they had never been employed and required training for jobs; and they were inclined to roam in search of a position where they could find housing. In spite of its huge bureaucratic and police apparatus the government needed several years to re-establish prewar control of the working force. The country still suffered from a shortage of skilled technicians and professional personnel of all kinds, and it sought to meet the demand by a greatly augmented program of education.

At the close of the war the Soviet Union was turning out only 67 per cent as much pig iron as in 1940, 79 per cent as much steel, 90 per cent as much coal, and 66 per cent as much petroleum. Production had reached these figures because the government had transferred to the east more than a million carloads of equipment from the invaded regions, and it soon had 1,300 of these uprooted industrial plants in operation behind the Volga and the Urals. Knowing that these resources would not suffice, it expanded industrial facilities in the eastern, non-invaded areas during the war several fold and shifted the necessary number of workers and other personnel to fill the demand. Large-scale industry, which in 1946 had still not reached the prewar level, had by 1950 surpassed it. The indices of large-scale industrial growth have been estimated to be 100 in 1928, 430 in 1940, 304 in 1946, and 646 in 1950. The government never relaxed the effort to expand heavy industry and power resources, and concentrated as previously on the production of coal and iron, steel, oil, electricity, aluminum, and copper, and particularly on metallurgical equipment.

Together with the creation of vast new industries east of the Volga and the Urals went the discovery and exploitation of new resources of coal, oil, and minerals. The declining output of the Baku oilfields was more than compensated by discoveries in the "second Baku," a large region 1,000 kilometers in expanse in the eastern part of European Russia along the Urals and crossing those mountains, as well as in other parts of Soviet Asia. In January, 1955, Khrushchev, the first secretary of the Central Committee of the Communist Party, declared:

> Developing Lenin's teachings, Stalin emphasized that it would be suicidal to retard the rate of development of heavy industry as this would undermine the whole of our industry, including light industry. . . . This only correct line . . . is being steadily followed now and will be firmly followed in the future.

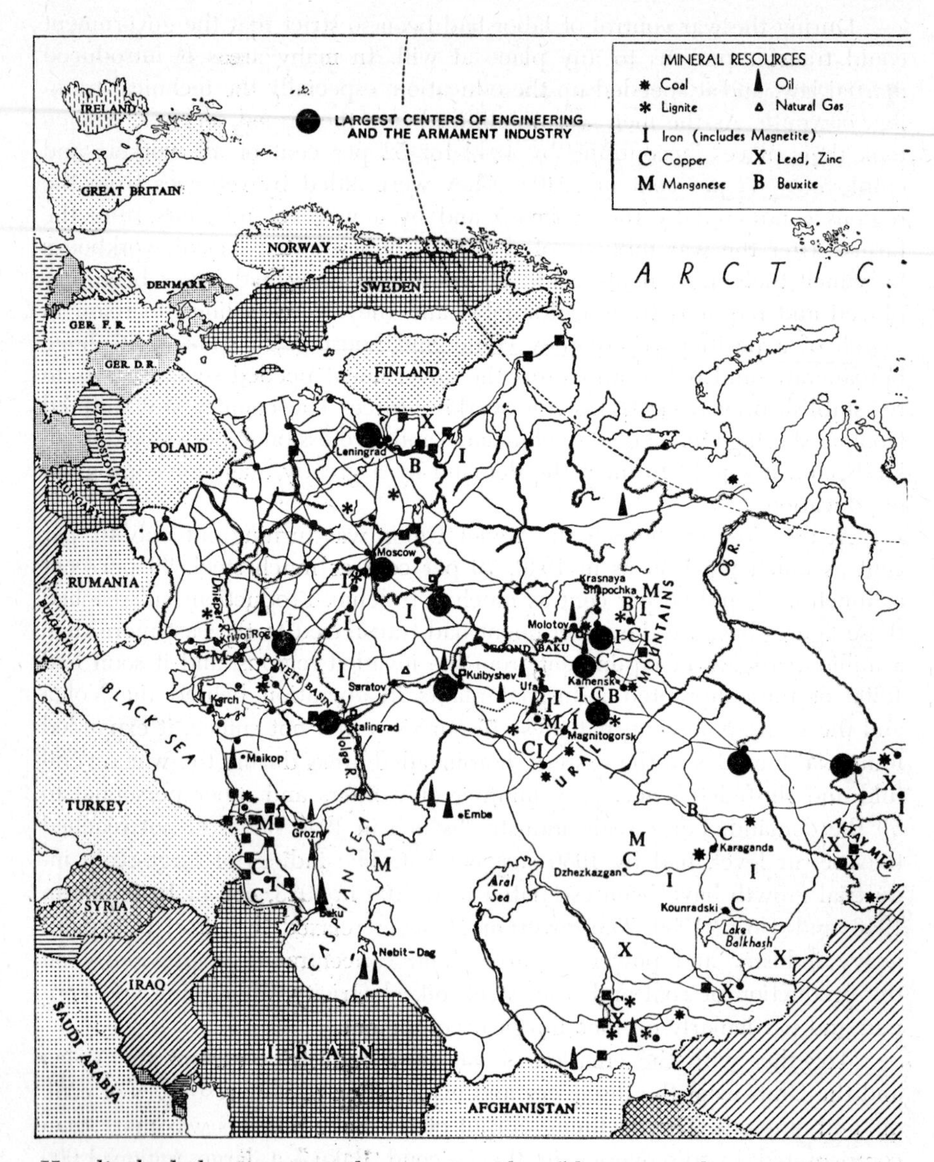

Resources and Industry of the U.S.S.R. From American Geographical Society of New York, *Focus,* Vol. V, No. 6 (February, 1955).

He clinched the argument by warning that "the imperialist states are engaged in frenzied preparations for war."

Concentration upon heavy industry required continued slighting of the production of consumers' goods. The war effort had exacted a reduction in the output of industrial consumers' goods per capita from 194 in 1940 (1928 = 100) to 84 in 1946. By 1945 the production of cotton cloth had fallen to 40 per cent of that of 1940, woolen cloth to 46 per cent, leather

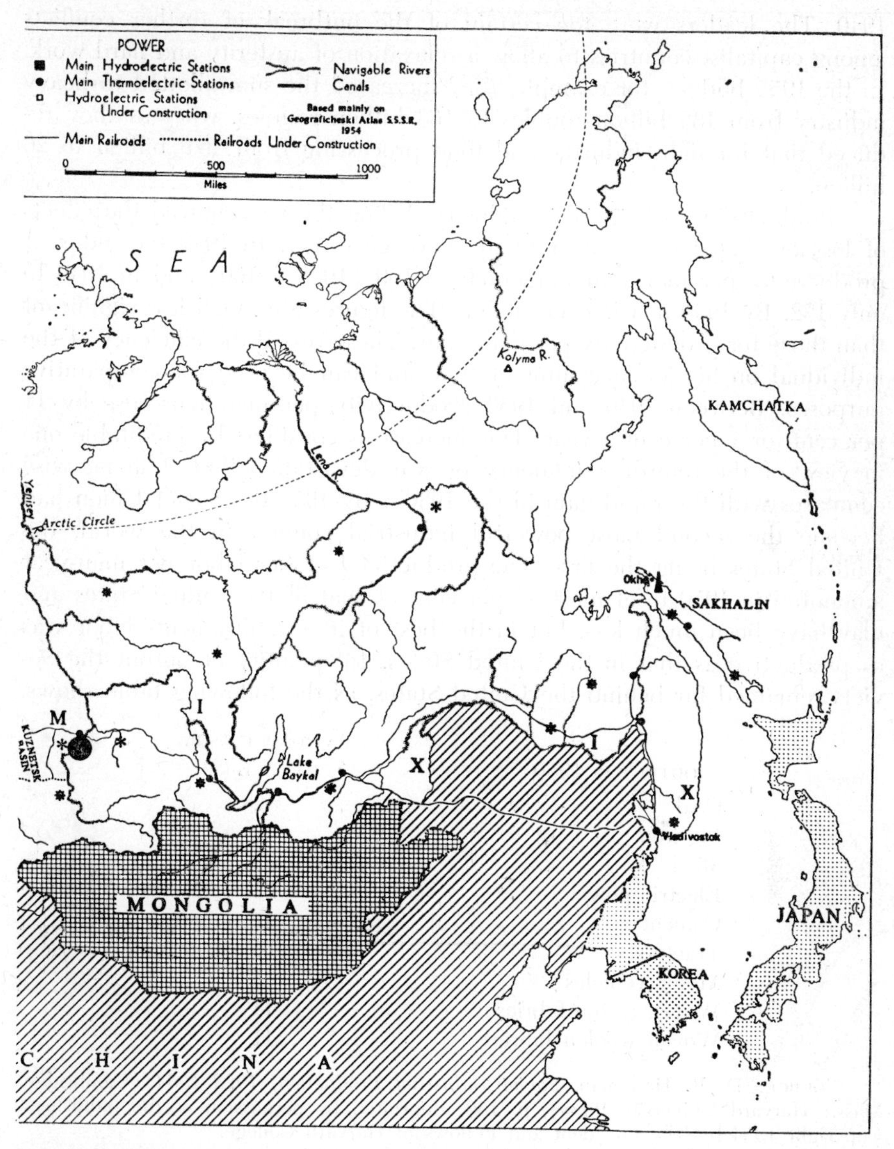

shoes to 26 per cent, and hosiery to 17 per cent. Housing suffered the wartime destruction of 1.2 million of some 2.6 million urban dwelling units in the invaded areas and 3.5 million of 12 million rural houses. Repairs were neglected, and new construction was not attempted. The Soviet peoples were accustomed to a low standard of living and took the hardships in stride. Once the war ended, the rulers made no effort to improve the situation beyond the barest necessities. By 1951 wartime losses were made good in urban centers and almost so in rural communities, and the index figure for the output of industrial consumers' goods had risen to that of

1940. The leaders were too certain of the outbreak of further conflicts among capitalist countries to allow a relaxation of austerity and hard work. In the 1955 budget, for example, they increased the sum allotted to heavy industry from 133 billion roubles to 163 billion roubles, whereas they reduced that for light industry and food processing from 36.6 billion to 26 billion.

Productivity in large-scale industry during the war showed the effects of loss of skilled man power to the defence forces. In 1940 the index of productivity per man-year amounted to 169 (1928 = 100) and in 1946 to only 132. By 1950 it had risen to 201. The figures are much less significant than those for productivity per man-hour. These reveal the efficiency of the individual on his job in a unit of time and can be used for comparative purposes. Between 1940 and 1950 productivity per man-hour rose by 11 per cent, or 1 per cent a year. This increase is considered a creditable one in view of the retarding influence of war devastation, but it in no wise compares with the rapid gain in the 1930's. By 1950 the Soviet Union had become the second most powerful industrial country in the world, the United States being the first. The productivity of her labor per man-year amounted in 1950 to at most 47 per cent of that of the United States and may have been much less, but in the best of its establishments labor was as productive as that in the United States. In quantity of output the Soviets remained far behind the United States, as the following table shows.

OUTPUT IN 1950	RATIO OF U.S.S.R. TO U.S.A. (%)
Coal	52
Pig iron	32
Steel	31
Electric power	23
Cement	27
Tractors	17
Motor vehicles	5
Woven cotton fabrics	44
Woven woolen fabrics	41

SOURCE: D. R. Hodgman, *Soviet Industrial Production, 1928–1954* (Cambridge, Mass.: Harvard University Press), p. 130. Reprinted by permission of the publishers. Copyright 1954 by The President and Fellows of Harvard College.

Five years later the United States continued to produce almost twice as much as the Soviet Union and all her satellites. Possibly of equal significance is the fact that the Soviet Union is definitely catching up in quantity of production of basic industrial articles with the whole of free Europe. There is prospect that within two decades the Soviet Union will far surpass in productivity the rest of Europe and will catch up with the United States, particularly in lines to which it gives priority.

Finance followed the course of controlled inflation during the war for the same reason that it did elsewhere. Everyone was at work earning an income and eager to spend money, and the amount of consumers' goods available for purchase had diminished. In order to induce the peasants especially to increase crops and bring more to the market, the government had raised prices on the open market and had been unable to eliminate a vigorous black market. A new class of traders sprang up who lived from buying in one market and selling in another. Many such traders became adept at supplying the peasant with urban products he desired. When the war ended the Soviet government eradicated the expanded currency. It waited until 1947, when with the revival of production of consumers' goods it could offer something for sale; then it confiscated about nine tenths of the currency in private hands, mainly those of peasants.

Agriculture Remains a Problem

The gravest impact of the war was felt in agriculture, that part of the economy which had always caused the Communists most difficulty. The region conquered by the Nazis accounted for 40 per cent of the entire area sown in crops, and a much higher percentage of some industrial crops like flax and sugar beets. During the war large tracts of land ceased to be cultivated; the already short supply of draft animals became much shorter; tractors had to be transferred to the military without replacement; and the males of working age went into the army and left the farms to be cultivated largely by women. The decline in farm output amounted almost to a collapse. Even in the uninvaded areas farm production fell in percentage more than three times as far as it did during 1914–1918. In order to obtain food the government allowed the peasants to increase the amount of time spent on the individual plots. The situation after the conflict called for vigorous reform. The government chose to continue its policy of investing small sums in agriculture in proportion to those in heavy industry, but it expanded the output of tractors as the first essential for revival. By 1950 agricultural production had reached approximately the level of 1937, perhaps a little more, but the achievement was regarded as unsatisfactory. In 1949 the government announced a three-year plan to increase the number of livestock. Since a large percentage of cows and other animals was owned by the peasants on their privately tilled plots of land, the reform seems mainly to have resulted in the transfer of ownership of these from individual peasants to collective farms.

In 1950 Khrushchev, in charge of the agricultural program under Stalin, proposed to increase production by reducing the number of farms and increasing the size of each. Within two years the number decreased from 250,000 to less than 100,000. The scattered peasant villages were to be destroyed and the rural population resettled in agro-towns. In this way efficiency in the use of machinery was expected to increase; the personnel of the tractor stations, all of them loyal Communists, could watch over and direct the peasants and further their development into a rural proletariat.

The peasants' inclination toward private ownership could be lessened by eliminating the tillage of individual plots of land. It was expected that production would then expand.

The plan seemed excellent on paper; but it did not work. The proposal to establish agro-towns aroused so much hostility among the peasants, who loved their huts and who saw no materials forthcoming to build new towns, that the government soon relegated it to the limbo of discussion, as it also did that of eliminating individual plots. The number of livestock showed little improvement and food output did not keep pace with demand. By 1953 the Soviet Union was buying food abroad from capitalists. The urban population wished a better diet, including meat, vegetables and fruits, and dairy products, than that which the peasant consumed; but the country, which still devoted 70 per cent of its cultivated land to the raising of grains, was short of bread. Agriculture failed to meet the demand placed upon it by an expanding industrial-urban society.

Stalin's method of handling the peasantry had been to lower the price of compulsory food deliveries to the state, raise taxes, and use coercion. Since this treatment had not been effective, Stalin's successors came forth with a number of new plans. In 1953 they sought by higher prices to stimulate the raising of livestock and vegetables. Financial exactions on the peasants' plots were reduced if the farmers performed the required number of days of work on the collective farms. More machinery and fertilizer were to be provided, the tractor stations to be reorganized with a permanent instead of a seasonal personnel, building material for winter shelters for livestock was to be forthcoming, the acreage of fodder crops was to be expanded—these were all improvements on existing conditions.

More grain for bread and more fodder for animals were urgently needed. In 1954 the government brought forward a plan to sow in grain 32 million acres of virgin soil within two years. From this land it expected to obtain 600 to 700 million bushels of grain, an amount not far less than the total grain crop of the United States (one billion bushels). Later in the year it raised the amount of new land to be cultivated within three years to 70 million acres. This was all semiarid, submarginal land, on which large irrigation projects and planting of shelter belts were to supplement nature. Foreign experts on Soviet agriculture labeled such measures a confession of defeat and recalled the proposal for the mass raising of rabbits to compensate for the loss of livestock in the early years of collectivized agriculture.

Struggle over Succession to Stalin

When Stalin died suddenly in March, 1953, he had recently reaffirmed his devotion to communist dogma. According to all indications he proposed to embark upon another wholesale purge, comparable to that of 1936–1938. In this type of government a law of succession would be at best a risk, for all the disappointed candidates might plot against the heir apparent, who in turn might try to accelerate the speed of his accession to power. Stalin's death caught the aspirants for his seat no better and no worse prepared than they would have been at any other time. When the Central Committee announced his death to the public, it added in the communiqué an admonition to maintain "the steel-like unity and monolithic unity of the ranks of the Party . . . to guard the unity of the Party as the apple of the eye . . . to educate all Communists and working people in high political vigilance, intolerance and firmness in the struggle against internal and external enemies." The Central Committee, the Council of Ministers, and the Praesidium of the Supreme Soviet announced that "the most important task of the Party and the Government is to ensure uninterrupted and correct leadership of the entire life of the country which demands the greatest unity of leadership and the prevention of any kind of disorder and panic." This regime had existed for more than three decades, and Stalin had ruled during most of that time; yet on his death, the leaders of the state showed deepest concern about preserving "steel-like unity" and preventing "any kind of disorder and panic."

The three main instruments of power in the Soviet Union were the Communist party, the secret police, and the army; and the heads of these agencies enjoyed the most advantageous positions from which to advance to the top. Stalin had disposed of most of the old Bolsheviks who might have claimed the mantle of Lenin; thereby he was leaving the field to younger men. Maneuvering among the aspirants for Stalin's position has continued; no one person as yet has been able to achieve Stalin's preeminence, and no one has acquired power to become the ultimate interpreter of dogma.

The first person to try, Malenkov, held the dual position of chairman of the Council of Ministers of the U.S.S.R. and secretary of the Central Committee of the Communist Party. The latter position had been the main means of Stalin's dominance and offered the most likely foothold for repetition of success. Malenkov, however, was compelled to share authority with Beria, the head of the secret police, Bulganin, the political head of the army, not himself a professional soldier, Molotov, and a few others. Within a week Malenkov lost his position as secretary of the party to Khrushchev. Next came Beria, whose secret police held a threat over any aspirant. By a sudden massing of military force his colleagues pulled him down, tried him quickly, put him to death, and purged the bureaucracy throughout the Soviet Union of his supporters. General Zhukov was brought back from obscurity and associated with the governing committee to help hold the army in line.

In February, 1955, Malenkov was forced to resign as premier and was replaced by Bulganin. He fared better than Beria. Instead of being tried and shot, he was permitted in public to confess his incompetence and to assume a position of minor importance. The position of secretary of the party still carried most power, and Khrushchev as its occupant came to the fore. The shift indicated no change in policy. Malenkov spoke of easing the burdens of the Soviet peoples by providing a few more consumers' goods. In international affairs he appeared to advocate a policy of peaceful coexistence. He never broke with the orthodox program of emphasis on heavy industry and of mistrust of all capitalist countries. Khrushchev as his successor merely canceled the slight concession to light industry and re-emphasized the orthodox line in internal affairs; he increased the defense budget and coupled threats and defiance toward the non-Communist world with an expressed desire for peace. Both men had been trained in the rough experience of the Stalinist regime, and both were thorough Communists.

Bureaucracy and the Army

The passing of Stalin enabled two institutions to grow in significance, the bureaucracy and the army. The elaboration of the functions of government and administration in all aspects of life necessarily entailed an increasing dependence upon the service of trained officials. A new class structure steadily emerged. Party leaders, business managers, bureaucrats in high positions, writers, scientists, and professional personnel have become a new upper class, whose sons and daughters receive advantages enabling them to maintain a favored position in society. Differentials in income have become normal. A person with money is able to own his home and a summer place in the country. The school system is arranged to permit children mainly of this upper class to attend the university, whereas others are trained for lesser jobs.

In 1946 a film entitled "The Great Life" appeared, in which several ordinary manual workers performed great deeds and were promoted to positions of command. The Central Committee of the Communist Party soon condemned it for encouraging reaction and ignorance. The producer and the author should have shown that not "technically illiterate workers" but only modern persons of culture and professional training were promoted. The Soviet Union, it said, had developed its own intelligentsia. Lenin's proletariat of manual workers was relegated to the bottom of society, with the peasants. The collectivist state required a new body of civil and administrative law. Trained personnel became essential. Neither Malenkov nor Khrushchev revived Stalin's technique of periodic purges; it had grown too expensive when demotion would serve as well. Soviet society shows signs of replacing revolutionary violence at home by some degree of social maturity.

The enhanced position of the army was indicated by the appointment of popular Marshal Zhukov as defense minister and by an increase in the military budget. At a conference in 1955 with Soviet novelists and other writers concerned with military subjects, army spokesmen asked for changes in the treatment of military events. They criticized Stalin's official version of the history of World War II as inaccurate and likely to lead to a repetition of mistakes. According to the official account, Stalin had been responsible for the grand strategy, a "Leader of Genius," and the Soviet retreat in the first part of the war had been a planned "Kutusov"-like maneuver to entrap the enemy in depth. The army spokesmen wished this fable corrected, the mistakes in strategy at the beginning of the war made clear, and the generals given their share of glory. The enemy should not appear always as fools, the Communists as wise heroes. Objective, accurate studies should be made in which the Soviets would have much to learn from bourgeois-capitalistic enemies. The army sought freedom of inquiry and honest writing, not propaganda. It wished biographies of Soviet military leaders and their czarist predecessors, and claimed the right for military persons to publish memoirs. These requests ran contrary to communist dogma and Soviet practice in every respect. If granted, other groups would desire similar freedom, and the Soviet people would come into direct contact with bourgeois capitalist society abroad and begin to make comparisons. The army might rise in popularity and stature to the point where its prestige could compete with that of the party.

The regime faced the dilemma of accuracy versus propaganda, freedom versus control, in technology and science, in business organization, in administrative practices, and other lines. Could a state that sought to be the most powerful in the world exclude its people from learning by direct contact about the achievements of other nations? The ruling group since Stalin's death appeared willing to relax the dictatorship sufficiently to allow some freedom at home and some contacts with the outside world, and yet it retained the power at any time to restore rigid control.

ACQUISITION OF A SOVIET EMPIRE

The greatest new achievement of the Soviet Union since the defeat of Nazi Germany has been the acquisition of a European empire. The little Baltic countries were incorporated into the Union. The other states, Poland, East Germany, Czechoslovakia, Hungary, Romania, Albania, and Bulgaria, retained their identity but became satellites. Yugoslavia started as a satellite but succeeded in escaping the fate of the others by reasserting her independence. We know almost nothing about the impact of the expansion of power upon the internal conditions of the Soviet Union; we have some data on the transformation of life in the subject states. Nearly 82 million people are involved, on whom Stalin pressed the communist organization of life in about five years.

Planned Seizure of Control

The Soviet leaders and native Communists trained in Moscow drew plans for the conquest. The one which the Czech Communist Gottwald laid out in 1945 was followed to the letter in Czechoslovakia, and similar plans in each of the other countries. It contained these instructions: First, the victorious Soviet army should assist; second, the bourgeoisie could be broken by being condemned as traitors and collaborators; their property, together with that of the Germans and Hungarians, and one recalls how much the Nazis especially had seized, would be taken and collectivized; third, a new National Front government composed of representatives of various parties but dominated by the Communists would be formed; fourth, the police, particularly the secret police, and the army would be brought under Communist authority; fifth, popular organizations, like the trade-unions, would become Communist instruments; last, the National Front government would be replaced by Communist rule.

The Communists expected to take over an operating state and so avoid the civil war and chaos of 1917–1920 in Russia. The party members who returned from Moscow with the Red armies into their native countries had benefited from experience in the conduct of affairs which Lenin and his associates had lacked. As the Hungarian Communist Rakosi remarked to the American minister in Hungary, he and his associates had worked in the Soviet Union, and, in contrast to the Communists who had remained in Hungary, were acquainted with practical government. With the Soviet army supporting them and a mass of Soviet advisers constantly at their side, they confidently faced the future.

The conditions in the countries of Eastern and Southeastern Europe favored the Communist drive for authority. The failure of previous regimes to provide a good life and to prevent Nazi conquest inclined the population in great part to look for a better system of government and society. The popularity of the Soviet Union as their rescuer made people react favorably toward its ideals and institutions, which they interpreted in terms of Western socialism. Since they had not been protected against nazism by the Western powers, they thought that they must insure themselves against a future German attack by drawing closer to the Soviet Union, even to the point of adjustments in political and social organization. The peasants associated communism with traditional land reform. The workers were either pro-Communist or pro-socialist; if the latter, they easily fell under Communist control of their trade-unions. In Czechoslovakia, for example, the trade-unions fought for communism. In Romania the Communist printers' union determined what should be published, and boycotted the publication of statements contrary to party interests. At the end of the war local government everywhere fell into a state of confusion, and the Communists arbitrarily took over the functions. In the popular-front governments the Communists demanded and obtained the key posts for the exercise of power, the ministry of interior, which controlled the police, usually the ministry of war, the ministry of education and propaganda, and often several of the economic ministries. They speedily transformed these into reliable

Communist instruments and used them for the piecemeal destruction of non-Communist colleagues.

After the Nazi period property relations were in as much confusion as everything else; since socialist ideas were popular, the Communists temporarily favored private property or the legal, peaceful introduction of socialism. Once they gained authority with the aid of these popular policies, they switched to a different line. They were masters of the use of two-edged slogans: the public interpreted their words in a democratic or socialistic sense, the Communists in a communist sense. In the Slavic countries they played up pan-Slav feeling. In Romania and Hungary they relied upon Soviet military force. In Bulgaria and Czechoslovakia they could count on a large pro-Soviet sentiment. In Poland they encountered national hostility to Russia, but the aid of the Red army in occupation assured them success. By one means or another they won absolute power in each state.

Government in Satellite States

The realities of government in the satellites were brought into line with those in the Soviet Union. The local politburo, usually dominated by the first secretary of the party, acquired the same position as its predecessor in the mother state. Where a constitution of the period of popular-front government was retained, it served as a temporary façade. For example, in the Czechoslovakian constitution drafted in 1946 private property was guaranteed, unless future laws were passed to the contrary. The constitution stated that "the institution of marriage and of the family and motherhood are under the protection of the State." When Ludvik Frejka was tried in November, 1952, his son, twenty years old, wrote the following letter to the judge: "I demand the most severe punishment—a capital sentence for my father. . . . [he] was my greatest and most wicked enemy. . . . I request you to submit this letter to my father and also if possible to allow me to tell him this personally." The father was accused of economic crimes, not of any crimes pertaining to the family; but the Communists broke up families for the furtherance of their cause. In the case of the Frejka family, soon after the execution of his father, the son, educated in England, committed suicide. The constitution also stated: "The judicial power is exercised by independent courts. . . . The judges are independent in the discharge of their office, being bound solely by the legal order of the people's democracy." The minister of national security explained in 1952 that "the question as to who is guilty and who is innocent will in the end be decided by the Party with the help of the National Security organs." [1] Revoi, the Hungarian minister of people's culture, stated in 1949: "The organism of our state should get closer to the Soviet-type of the dictatorship of the proletariat."

[1] Peter Zenkl, "On 'Human Rights' in Czechoslovakia," *Journal of Central European Affairs,* October, 1954, pp. 264 ff.

The police system which the Communists introduced contained units unknown to free society. We are acquainted with the titles national security police, secret police, frontier guards, prison guards, and people's militia, but not with many of their functions in these satellite countries. The prison guards in Czechoslovakia, for example, also include labor camp troops, and transport troops for guarding prisoners in transit and persons deported from their home to another community. The frontier guards prevent persons from escaping to free countries. They receive extra pay and rewards in cash or other forms for capturing or killing those who attempt to flee, the more important the individual the higher being the reward. The national security police act, not as ordinary guardians of the peace, but as a highly mobile reserve to use in major disturbances. The people's militia serve the ordinary purposes of maintaining order, but they have formations which betray their communist character—harvest militia, collective farm guards, railway troops—and they are paralleled by factory militia. Communism as in the Soviet Union had to coerce people into accepting its system. Slave labor camps have grown in size as kulaks, bourgeoisie, and other enemies of communism were rounded up by the police and incarcerated. Evidence submitted to a United Nations committee showed that by November, 1952, the numbers in these camps were approximately the following and may have been greater: Poland, 180,000; Bulgaria, 80,000; Romania, 175,000; Hungary, 150,000; and Czechoslovakia, 195,000. The satellites were unable as yet to compare with their master in quantity, but the quality of brutality, starvation, and disease in the camps had already reached the Soviet level.

The satellite leaders had to imitate whatever happened in the Soviet Union. Absolute obedience was difficult on three counts. First, the stakes of power were so high in these formative years that intrigue was rampant; an official might be destroyed for no other reason than that someone else sought his position and was tougher than the incumbent; second, since the satellites were expected to produce for the Soviet Union, failure exposed the technically responsible persons, irrespective of whether or not they were at fault, to the accusation of sabotaging communism, of being disloyal to Moscow, and of treason. Third, some native Communists wished to follow a national line, to preserve a degree of independence of Moscow, to go a little more slowly and not to destroy so much in the act of achieving Communist rule. After the successful defiance of Moscow by Tito, such leaders became targets of special attention and were everywhere liquidated. Many distinguished Communists, like Kostov in Bulgaria, Rajk in Hungary, Clementis and Slansky in Czechoslovakia, had been put to death by the end of 1952, and they were followed by many more. Each purge of leaders was justified as necessary to strengthen the fraternal alliance with the Soviet Union. After hanging Kostov, the Bulgarian Communist party telegraphed Stalin as follows:

Only thanks to your wise and timely instruction, highly esteemed comrade Stalin, we managed to uncover the cowardly hidden enemies of our Republic, to unmask the agents of the imperialist Powers and to cleanse ourselves of them. Only your deeply penetrating eye could see in time the criminal spy gang of Kostov!

Stalin insisted upon introducing more control of each satellite through the local armies. The way was prepared for the creation of a common defense force. The adaptation to the Soviet model occurred with greatest speed in Poland and Bulgaria, where organization and equipment are Russian. Military academies were reshaped to Soviet pattern, with new emphasis on military political training. Promotion to a senior rank depended upon knowledge of Russian and training in Soviet military schools. The commanding posts were given to Soviet officers or had Soviet officers attached to them. Members of the forces swore an oath of allegiance not merely to their own state but to the Soviet Union, and they wore Soviet uniforms and insignia. The process did not advance so far in the other satellites, but was well under way. The establishment of a central command under General Koniev in 1954 as a counter to the formation of the Western European Union served as a public statement of an accomplished fact. That the former enemy states, Bulgaria, Romania, Hungary, and East Germany, are restricted by treaty or other international agreement from developing a large army has not affected Communists' action. Ten years after the close of World War II the satellites were in a position to muster a force of well over a million men for use by the Communist dictators.

Soviet Economic Control of Satellite States

During the first two years after the war the Soviet forces seized materials from occupied countries, friend and foe alike. Both officially and unofficially, officers, soldiers, and civilians took all they could. The Soviet government gained what it wanted under the guise of reparations and occupation costs. The American minister in Budapest has described the Soviet exploitation of Hungary during the first two years of occupation as follows:

In a note to the Soviet government in July 1946, the American Embassy at Moscow pointed out that half of current manufacturing output in Hungary, then operating at an estimated one-third of prewar capacity, was absorbed by Soviet requirements. In certain industries, including coal, iron and machine production, as much as 80 to 90 percent was absorbed. Up to June 30 of the preceding year the Soviet forces had taken out of Hungary 4,000,000 tons of wheat, rye, barley and corn; the total prewar production of these grains was something over 7,000,000 tons. Of the foodstuffs available for the urban population in the second half of 1945, the Soviet Army had appropriated nearly all the meat, one-sixth of the wheat and rye, one-quarter of legumes, nearly three-quarters of the lard, a tenth of the vegetable oil, and a fifth of the milk and dairy products. The note added that extensive requisitioning of food was going on as late as April 1946.

It likewise noted that of the total war damage to Hungarian industry estimated at $345,000,000, more than $124,000,000 was a result of Soviet removals. . . .

American representatives at the [Paris Peace] Conference pointed out in October 1946 that in the year since the Armistice the national income of Hungary had dropped to half the prewar level of $1 billion. (It was estimated at only $620,000,000 for the fiscal year ending July 1947.) The total proportion of the national income then being absorbed by the costs of Soviet occupation, requisitions and reparations was about 35 percent.[2]

The exploitation of East Germany was conducted with greater thoroughness; that of Czechoslovakia was least remunerative because the opportunities ceased with the termination of Soviet military occupation on January 1, 1946. The fate of the other economies lay somewhere in between.

Since the British and the United States governments had agreed at Potsdam to the transfer of "German and Italian assets" in the enemy countries, Bulgaria, Romania, and Hungary, to the Soviet Union, the latter gained a permanent basis for controlling the economies and for shaping them to Soviet advantage. The term "German and Italian assets" was sufficiently flexible to cover almost anything the Soviets wished; the loot acquired by one imperialist power was now retained by another. In addition, Moscow included property of Nazi collaborators and Fascists. The seizure of these properties ruined the economic foundation for middle-class existence. The Soviet government devised the system of establishing mixed companies in the satellites on the basis of equal participation. Oil, gas, civil aviation, transportation, mining of all minerals, coal, heavy industry, the machine industries, and insurance and banking had been the main lines of German or Italian interest; they became the object of new cooperation between the Soviet government and the national government in question.

These companies were free from all taxes, duties, and fees, and they used their foreign exchange as they wished. They could easily earn a profit, for, in addition to the privileges just mentioned, they obtained from the state government numerous special advantages. They set up a board of directors composed of an equal number of Soviet and local representatives, but all decisions rested with the general manager, who had to be a Soviet citizen. They enjoyed complete extra-territoriality, and could and did plan economic expansion both within a country and across national lines. As they had every advantage in earning a profit, they disposed of funds for investment; and, backed by the Soviet government, they expanded their economic empire in cartel fashion.

[2] H. F. Arthur Schoenfeld, "Soviet Imperialism in Hungary," *Foreign Affairs*, April, 1948, pp. 556-557.

As the utilization of the products increased, so did the economic influence of the Soviet Union. Operating concessions, contracts for technical aid, and agency agreements provided the Soviet government with means for expansion; and the Soviet acquisition of banking and insurance companies brought with it not merely a foothold in many other businesses but a means of influencing the credit and investment policies of each country. The economic power was exerted less directly in Poland and Czechoslovakia, but agreements were soon signed for technical aid and credit with the former and credit for raw materials with the latter.

Vishinsky described the nature of the Soviet government as follows:

> Soviet state administration is an indissoluble unit of administrative and economic government, a differentiation in principle of the Soviet state machinery from that of the bourgeois state. Extended to all sides of the economic and social life of the people, Soviet state administration is one of organizational creativeness.

A student of these relations has observed:

> In effect, since Soviet shareholders in joint companies are branches of the economic government of the Soviet state and Soviet nationals in positions of control in joint companies are likewise representatives of the respective economic ministries of the Soviet government, Soviet participation in the administration and management of satellite economic resources amounts to participation in the government of the country. With the balance of control heavily tilted in favor of the Soviet interests, joint companies represent extraterritorial enclaves subject to the overriding decision of Soviet authorities.[3]

When the Soviet Union and the satellites established the Council of Mutual Economic Assistance in January, 1949, as the counter to the European Recovery Program, they recognized in public an established fact.

Economic Adjustments to Soviet Pattern

Through their subordinates in the local government Moscow began particularly after 1948 to accelerate the transformation of the economy in each satellite. The mixed companies enabled the Soviet Union to collectivize industry and agriculture and adapt them to over-all Communist plans. They received

> the decisive stimulation and assistance for the clarification of our future development [the Hungarian Communist minister Revoi wrote in 1949] from the Communist (Bolshevik) Party of the Soviet Union, from the teachings of Comrade Stalin. The two sessions of the Cominform, the first in the fall of 1947, the second in the summer of 1948, were of fundamental help for us. The first taught us that a People's Democracy couldn't halt at any but the final stage of its destruction of the capitalistic elements, and the second showed us that the

[3] Kazimierz Graybowski, "Foreign Investment and Political Control in Eastern Europe," *Journal of Central European Affairs*, April, 1953, p. 24.

Socialistic transformation couldn't be limited to the towns, but had to be extended to the rural districts and that as regards the fundamental questions of the transformation into Socialism, the Soviet Union is our model and that the way of the People's Democracies differs only in certain external forms, and not in essence, from the way of the Soviet Union.[4]

In the Soviet Union the young were taught to say, "I want to be like Stalin." The satellites shared this ideal.

Notwithstanding the relative scarcity of mineral resources in the subject countries, the Communists insisted upon adherence to the Marxian formula, the creation or expansion as the case might be of heavy industry. Bulgaria alone seems to have been spared; the absence of all materials for heavy industry apparently convinced the Communists that this peasant state should continue in agriculture. Everywhere else five-year plans were introduced and rates of investment in heavy industry and the power resources essential for it were increased to or above the Soviet level. The Upper Silesian region comprising resources in Poland, Czechoslovakia, and East Germany was organized as the leading industrial unit of the western frontier of communism. Labor was forced off farms into factories.

Economic Results

The effects of the program may be seen in two forms, first, an expansion in output of basic industries, and, second, an increasing interdependence of the members of the Soviet bloc. Evidence in regard to production may be obtained from the following table. The figures on electric power are in billion kilowatt hours, those on the other articles are in metric tons.

COUNTRY	ELECTRIC POWER		STEEL		PIG-IRON		COAL		OIL	
	1938	*1955*	*1938*	*1955*	*1938*	*1955*	*1937*	*1955*	*1938*	*1955*
Soviet Union	36	170	18	45	14.5	33	127	391.0	28	70.7
Poland	4.0	17.7	1.5	4.3	0.89	3.1	36	94.5		
Czecho-slovakia	4.1	15	1.9	4.5	1.3	3.0	35	63.9		
East Germany	16.6	29.2		2.5	0.24	1.5		201.4		
Hungary	1	5.4	.6	1.6	.3	.8	9	22.3	0.4	1.6
Romania		4.3	.3	.8	.1	.6		6.2	6.61	10.6
Bulgaria	0.2	2.1					2	10.3		

Source: Based on data by Harry Schwartz. Reprinted by permission of *The New York Times*.

[4] *Foreign Affairs*, October, 1949, p. 147.

The data are significant for the disparity between the economic strength of the Soviet Union, on the one hand, and each of the satellites, on the other, and for the acceleration of production in each country.

The growth of economic interdependence was expressed in regional specialization. Thus, Romanian gas was used to develop new branches of the chemical industry in both Romania and Hungary; Hungarian bauxite is transformed into aluminum in Czechoslovakia. The latter state, which formerly enjoyed a fairly balanced economy, has had to neglect agriculture and consumers' goods industries and import much of its food, particularly grain, from other satellites and from the Soviet Union. The three states around the Silesian coal beds were assigned a special duty to produce capital goods, not merely for the other satellites and the Soviet Union, but for North Korea, Red China, and other favored countries. The trade of the satellites, which formerly concentrated upon the free countries of the world, within a few years became Communist-oriented, especially toward the Soviet Union. Without the coercion of a dictatorship exercised in Moscow, no such radical shift in production and distribution would have occurred.

The collectivization of industrial and commercial property became easy by confiscation of German assets. Poland and Czechoslovakia in particular acquired large resources over which the Communist governments could immediately dispose. In the former parts of Germany and in the Sudetenland they gained title to property without antagonizing any of their own people and had enough positions to offer in the administration of these businesses to attract many individuals to communism. In agriculture, however, they encountered difficulty. Except in Poland and Hungary the land belonged mainly to peasants. The rural population everywhere wished private property, assisted by cooperatives. The peasants expected the government to parcel out the land seized from the Germans and to create a strong independent, landowning rural society. Once in power, the Communists pressed the campaign for collectivization. Czechoslovak agriculture had ranked high in world efficiency; it now became collectivized. Estonian agriculture had been outstanding in animal raising and mixed farming, lines which in the Soviet Union had suffered severely; the Estonian farms were amalgamated into large kolkhozes. Much of the land seized from the Germans was organized into state farms, which, being favored with the assurance of machinery, fertilizer, and the like, and managed by experts, were expected to offer a model for the rest of agriculture. The transfer of the Soviet system to the satellites produced corresponding results.

The peasants disliked collectivization so intensely that they lost interest in working beyond the minimum. When they did produce, the government paid a low price for the compulsory deliveries. When the peasants acquired a little money, they could find few or no consumers' goods for which to spend it. As in the Soviet Union, the peasants were forced to supply the state by way of taxes and low prices for agricultural products with the sums needed for investment in heavy industry. They had to struggle with regimentation and to increase production without adequate equipment and technical knowledge. Shortages ensued in countries which had formerly exported food. The Soviet Union had to make up the deficit from its own inadequate stock. The governments from time to time relieved the pressure for collectivization in order to increase production but applied it again after the crisis. Since the vast majority of the peoples of the subject area was peasant, the Communists had trouble. Arrests for rural "sabotage" continued. The Communists faced the same dilemma that their colleagues did in the Soviet Union: how to bring the peasants to support the burden of industrialization while receiving little in return.

The standard of living in the satellite states declined to an extent which cannot be measured, but some evidence may be offered. Zapotocky, the Communist premier of Czechoslovakia, told the National Assembly in 1949 to forget

> any fond illusions that a rise in the standard of living may be regarded as a necessary corollary or, even, ought to precede the successful implementation of the [Five-Year] Plan. The exact opposite is the truth: in order to make it possible that our material and cultural level might be raised, it will first be necessary to fulfill the Plan . . . so that we might henceforth live better, more contentedly and more joyfully.

The Hungarian Rakosi condemned strikes as a luxury which Communist countries could not afford.

Peasant resistance to Communist rule might have been expected; but the workers developed a similar lack of enthusiasm. When the Czechoslovak government in 1953 reformed the currency in such a way that the workers' savings were confiscated, riots broke out in various industrial centers. In Pilsen the workers paraded, shouting slogans like "We refuse to accept this barefaced robbery!" "Down with the Government!" "Give us free elections!" They threw pictures of Stalin and of local Communists out of the window. The army forces sent to suppress them joined the rebels, and not until the Security Police arrived with armored cars did the disturbance cease. In East Germany similar revolts took place on June 17 of that year, not merely in East Berlin but in other cities and towns. Workers and others fought government troops with rocks and bare fists, and were not overcome until Soviet armored troops arrived. These were apparently spontaneous outbursts of hatred caused by the wretchedness of life, amounting in East Germany in particular to actual hunger. Living conditions became so bad in 1953 at about the time of Stalin's death that the Communist governments everywhere promised an increase in the output of consumers' goods, a relaxation of collectivization in agriculture, and a slowing down of the construction of heavy industry. As soon as the crisis had passed, however, they ignored the promises; and as in the Soviet Union at the same time they maintained the rigid Communist program.

Cultural Relations

Satellite cultural relations were directed away from the West toward the East. Where French or English was formerly popular, Russian became the regional language, and a knowledge of it was indispensable for anyone of ambition. Russian publications were disseminated in quantities. Societies for Friendship with the U.S.S.R. to stimulate the exchange of persons and materials were founded in all cities and towns and were used not merely for cultural propaganda but for the spread of communism and the exertion of Soviet political influence. In Poland in 1952, for example, 250,000 lectures alone were delivered on Soviet achievements in culture, art, and science. In the same year in Hungary the Friendship Society organized ninety-six "Major Exhibitions" visited by 2,690,000 persons. The statistics read like the gigantic ones of the Five-Year plans. The propaganda was often dull, and one wonders how the Germans reacted to the following assertion by an East German stooge: "Thanks to the use made of Soviet experience it has been possible to raise the scientific level of the German Universities." The Communists expect to consolidate cultural relations by mass action. As the Czechoslovak minister of culture said to the Tenth Congress of the Czechoslovak Communist Party, "the cultivation of fashion, of female beauty and outward appearance, is a serious affair."

YUGOSLAVIA DEFIES THE SOVIET UNION

In one country alone Soviet imperialism met defeat, not by the Western powers' bolstering up local resistance, as in Greece, but by action of the national Communist party. This distinction fell to Yugoslavia, where national tradition, wartime achievement, and the personality of the Communist leader enabled the local party to defy Moscow.

The Yugoslav people had traditionally revered Russia as the Slavic mother protector. Knowing little or nothing about the character of communism, they retained their admiration after the Bolshevik Revolution. Peasants and intellectuals in particular, the one constituting the vast majority of the people, the other the popular leadership, looked to the Soviet Union for salvation, first against their local dictators in the interwar period and then against the Nazi conquerors. When the war began they took to guerrilla fighting efficiently and courageously and developed an army of 150,000 partisans. Although woefully short of arms, the partisans held down ten German divisions in the country and withstood seven full-scale offensives. At the close of the war they controlled the country as popular heroes and met the Soviet army in Belgrade on equal terms. They were Communist-led, but they included large numbers from democratic political groups and formed a National Front that shaded imperceptibly from communism into non-Marxian parties.

The leader, Joseph Broz, later called Tito, was a Croat trained in Moscow and named by Stalin before the war as head of the Yugoslav Communist party. The English Brigadier Maclean, assigned to the Partisan headquarters, found Tito already not quite of the Communist type. "From the first," the brigadier has written, "I was struck by his readiness to discuss any question on its merits, to take a decision there and then. He seemed perfectly sure of himself; he was a principal, not a subordinate. To find such assurance, such independence in a Communist was for me a new and astonishing experience." The brigadier admired his "surprisingly broad outlook," his "courage, realism, ruthless determination and singleness of purpose, resourcefulness, adaptability and plain common sense." He learned that Tito was sensitive to any slight on Yugoslav national honor, and that he and his fellow countrymen considered the victory over the Nazis and Italians to be their victory. When the Nazis began in September, 1944, to withdraw from Yugoslavia, Tito flew to Moscow for the purpose, so the brigadier reports him as saying, of "giving the Red Army his permission to enter Yugoslavia." [5]

The Tito-Stalin Controversy

Discord arose between Tito and Moscow as soon as the two countries entered into direct relations. The Yugoslav Communists criticized the misbehavior of Soviet troops in their country. They sought to federate with Bulgaria, and they and Communists in other states talked of forming an East European federation to lie between Germany and the Soviet Union. When Stalin condemned the plan, Tito suspected the Soviet Union of imperialist ambitions which a federation would thwart. When the Yugoslavs learned that Moscow was spying upon them, they in turn set spies upon the spies. They objected to the enormous salaries which they had to pay Soviet experts assigned to their country, and mistrusted these as agents sent to supplant Tito and his group by Moscow stooges. Tito had retained the National Front as a means whereby the Communists, in complete control of it, could guide the nation with least friction; Stalin denounced him for not giving the Communist party the monopolistic political role which dogma required. Tito had pushed collectivization of industry and agriculture at a more rapid speed than the satellite governments; but Moscow condemned him for retaining bourgeois capitalism, particularly in allowing most of the peasants to keep their land.

In 1948 Stalin expressed his wrath in a public statement. Tito's worst sin was that of violating the first communist commandment of absolute obedience, but Stalin soon embellished the point by damning him as a traitor, an English spy, a friend of the Fascists, a "third-rate Belgrade tsar." To Moscow's great astonishment Tito and his cohorts refused to ac-

[5] Fitzroy Maclean, "Tito: A Study," *Foreign Affairs*, January, 1950, pp. 239, 240-241, 242.

knowledge their sins; they refused to appear for trial, condemnation, and hanging. They were surprised and distressed, but they returned the fire. They claimed that they were more orthodox Communist than the Russians; and, studying the conditions in the Soviet Union and the relations between it and the satellites, they moved to the offensive. They denounced the Soviet Union for both its internal and its international policies. Tito's close associate Djilas enumerated the Soviet Union's main errors as follows:

> . . . introduction of unequal relations and exploitation of other socialist countries; un-Marxist treatment of the role of the leader which often takes the shape of even vulgar, historical falsifications and idolatries similar to those in absolute monarchies; differences in pay which are greater than in bourgeois bureaucracies themselves, ranging from 400 to 15,000 rubles; ideological promotion of Great Russian nationalism and under-estimation and subordination of the role, culture and history of other peoples; a policy of division of spheres of influence with the capitalist states; monopolization of the interpretation of Marxist ideology and tactics of the international working class movement; introduction of lying and slandering methods into the working class movement; . . . under-estimation of the role of consciousness—especially the consciousness of the masses —in the struggle for a new society; tendencies toward actual liquidation of socialist democracy and transforming it into a mere form; rendering impossible a struggle of opinions and putting brakes on the initiative of the masses, that is, the basic productive forces, and by that very fact productive forces in general.[6]

Tito elaborated upon the errors by denouncing the centralized bureaucratic strangehold upon the workers. The position of the latter, he asserted, "is not very different from the role of the workers in capitalist countries." [7] ". . . though . . . the factories are state property," his colleague Todorovic stated in a speech, "yet, if the workers play no part in the management of those factories, if nobody ever asks the workers what is to be done with the surplus of their labour, if the surplus labour is decided on and a good part of it seized by the bureaucratic caste for themselves, and for the maintenance of various services which ensure the privileged, ruling position of that caste, if this is all the case, and it certainly is today in the U.S.S.R., in what then substantially does the position of the Soviet worker differ from the position of the capitalist worker?" [8] And Djilas concluded that "it is the U.S.S.R. which strives to protect itself and shut itself away from the capitalist world." "What do these men hide," he asked, "and what do they fear? They hide their own social order and their own shape, which are monstrous even in comparison with bourgeois democracy." [9] These were Communists speaking about Communists. Attack had opened their eyes to the evils of the system in the Soviet Union. Would Tito and his group practice in their country what they had learned from this experience?

[6] Ygael Gluckstein, *Stalin's Satellites in Europe* (London: George Allen & Unwin, Ltd., 1952), p. 268.

[7] *Ibid.*, p. 271. [8] *Ibid.* [9] *Ibid.*, p. 272.

Relaxation of Communism in Yugoslavia

At first the Yugoslavs strove to be more orthodox than the Soviet leaders. They stepped up the rate of collectivization of agriculture, and they continued to lay ambitious plans for developing heavy industry. After two years they slowed down the latter for lack of capital; and, facing a stubborn, uncooperative peasantry determined to have private ownership of land, they allowed the peasants freely to revert to private ownership and the use of voluntary cooperatives to which they had long been accustomed. They abolished the compulsory sale of farm produce to the state at low prices and reintroduced the open market. They attempted to avoid centralization of authority and bureaucratism by transferring considerable responsibility to local governments. They placed the management of industries in the hands of committees of workers, a system that has been effective in progressive regions and failed in backward ones. They restored material incentives for production, including consumers' goods, instead of relying on coercion. They debated pro and con over the role of the Communist party.

In late 1953 and early 1954 Tito's close associate Djilas published a series of articles in which he criticized the Communist practices in the country, asked for more freedom and self-initiative, and intimated that a socialist competitor to the dominant party should be developed. He was tried and condemned for his views. The Titoists are in a quandary, especially over the role of the party. They wish it to lead, not to dictate and become an instrument of the bureaucracy, as in the Soviet Union. As Tito said in 1954, "Today we shall not command this or that competent institution, we shall not tell them that they must do this and that, but we must suggest it to them in various ways. And everyone—professor, teacher, official and anyone else—must know that that is the attitude of the Communists, and the Communists mean something in this country, their importance has not ceased. And if anyone afterwards goes against that, it will mean that he is against the correct development of socialism in our country." The party remains the supreme power, and socialism the objective; but Tito also perceived the need for some freedom.

In 1950 Yugoslavia suffered a severe drought and in the winter a shortage of food. The American agricultural attaché in Belgrade had noted the signs of the forthcoming shortage long before the national officials had discovered them. When the crisis struck, the United States government speedily delivered 525,000 tons of foodstuffs, with no political strings attached. The Yugoslav Communists, trained to regard all capitalist powers as implacable enemies, were impressed with the difference between this act of humanitarian generosity and the hostile imperialism of the Soviet Union. The United States and other Western countries have continued to donate or to lend funds to Yugoslavia for economic development and for rearmament, again without attempting to dictate the form of government and society which must be established. The results have continued to favor the relaxation of communism in favor of some ideal as yet of uncertain outline. One well-informed observer concluded in June, 1954, as follows:

> The present regime is probably more ruthless than that of twenty years ago, but it is also more impartial . . . it is not totalitarian. The citizen's private life is his own, and intellectual and cultural life, where they do not touch politics—in the traditional sense of the word—are surprisingly free. . . . It is perfectly possible for persons who are not Communists to hold the jobs for which they are qualified, and to perform tasks of responsibility. Such people feel that this is better service to their country than sterile opposition.[10]

Yugoslavia knows little about democracy and could scarcely stand the test of comparison with a free Western society. It has moved a long way, however, from Stalinism.

The fact that the Soviet Union could be successfully defied by a Communist state created in the world the new force of opposition to communism known as Titoism. It was especially dangerous because, like orthodox communism, it bored from within, and it held out some hope for the ultimate emancipation of the satellites. In 1955 the Soviet government acknowledged that it had erred in ostracizing Tito's Yugoslavia. The Soviet leaders journeyed to Belgrade and sought to persuade Tito to return to the Communist fold. Tito remained cool and alert to the tactic of entrapping him and continued to place his regime somewhere between Soviet communism and Western democracy—just where he did not know.

KHRUSHCHEV ATTACKS STALIN

A great shock came to the Soviet Union in 1956. At the Twentieth Party Congress in Moscow, Party Secretary Khrushchev attacked Stalin and slightly relaxed dictatorial controls. In a supposedly closed session he denounced Stalin for having substituted for "party democracy" and "collective party leadership" and "revolutionary legality" the practice of acting without consulting the Central Committee of the party, the ministers, or any other official bodies. Khrushchev cited as evidence the arbitrary condemnation to long prison terms or to death of loyal party comrades whom Stalin mistrusted. He said that "during the last years" Stalin had "acquired an absolutely insufferable character." "Sickly suspicious," Stalin "choked a person morally and physically. A situation was created where one could not express one's own will." Stalin's henchmen obtained confessions of uncommitted crimes in only one way, "because of application of physical methods of pressuring him [the victim], tortures, bringing him to a state of unconsciousness, deprivation of his judgment, taking away of his human dignity."

[10] *Economist* (London), June 26, 1954, p. 1064.

Khrushchev accused Stalin of having ignored warnings of Hitler's intention to attack and of having blundered in trying to direct the Soviet defense. Stalin, he said, later demanded complete credit for victory, as he had done for all peacetime achievements. Stalin revised the official biography by expanding the adulation in it. After the war he became "even more capricious, irritable and brutal." One never knew whom he would liquidate next. "It is not excluded that had Stalin remained at the helm for another several months Comrades Molotov and Mikoyan would probably have not delivered any speeches at this Congress." "The cult of the individual," Khrushchev went on, "has caused the employment of faulty principles in party work and in economic activity; it brought about rude violation of internal party and Soviet democracy, sterile administration, deviations of all sorts, covering up the shortcomings and varnishing of reality. Our nation gave birth to many flatterers and specialists in false optimism and deceit." Khrushchev called for the restoration of "the Leninist principles of Soviet socialist democracy. . . . Long live the victorious banner of our party—Leninism!" His words were given an ovation.

The speech denouncing Stalin as a sadist became widely known. It "angered" Stalinists, but it also gave rise to doubts about the courage of the men around Stalin. Why had the new rulers, most of them former officials, permitted such outrages to occur? Was a system where such excesses were possible a valid one? Khrushchev and his colleagues lacked Stalin's prestige, and the fact that the system had allowed one man to commit crimes of such magnitude led Russians to ask whether a little freedom might not strengthen the country. Scientists, writers, and other intellectuals had since Stalin's death been asking for freedom from political control in their lines of work. They now did so more boldly. Students in the universities put embarrassing questions; they wanted professors to explain why institutions and conditions were as they were. They founded a magazine entitled "Heresy," and a young Communist was made cynically to remark in a novel: "What a man thinks and feels should not interest anybody; it is only important that he should say what is required." The Soviet Union as a growing society needed intelligent and enterprising leaders in science, industry, party, army, and all other fields. Would it dare permit conditions of freedom essential to the development of them? Once a measure of freedom was allowed, Khrushchev and his colleagues became alarmed and moved to replace Stalin on his pedestal, but in 1957 they condemned Molotov and others as die-hard Stalinists and dismissed them from office. The struggle over Stalin's power has not yet ended. The competition for control of the government has opened the prospect, even though slight, of a change in policy in the direction of Titoism.

The people of the Soviet Union have been subject to Communist discipline for almost forty years and know little of any other way of life. In the satellites the anti-Stalinist speech hurt the prestige of local Communist dictators and aroused national opposition to Soviet domination. Some of the most notorious Stalinists had been removed after the death of Stalin, and a modicum of freedom allowed. In most of the satellites the existing government retained control, but in two, Poland and Hungary, the Khrushchev speech evoked demand for further liberty. Intellectuals seized the opportunity to draft a popular program, calling for the withdrawal of Soviet military, economic, and political control and the right for each country to advance toward Communism in its own way. Workers, angry over the low standard of living and harsh conditions of employment, and peasants hostile to collectivized farms and embittered by lack of consumers' goods, immediately supplied mass basis for a national revolt.

Revolt in Poland

In Poland the national army supported the rebels, Stalinists in the government lost control, and Gomulka, a Polish Tito, became head of the state. Except for Stalinist die-hards, all parties and groups, including the Catholic Church, supported him and approved his program. He allowed religious freedom and a limited amount of intellectual liberty. He emphasized the use of cooperatives among free peasants instead of compulsory collective farms. He promised democracy in the factories and a shift of emphasis from the production of capital goods to that of consumers' goods. He hoped to revive the Polish economy by these means and to raise the standard of living. He negotiated an agreement with the Soviet Union, enabling Poland to regain a large degree of economic independence, and, most important, he formalized in a treaty the exact status of Soviet troops stationed in Poland. Henceforth Poland was to be relatively free to conduct her own affairs, though subject to the need to depend upon Soviet economic and especially military aid. The Poles dared not lose their partnership with the U.S.S.R. for fear of Germany. In return they were willing to accept a national or Polish version of communism, which they expected would enable extensive relations with free countries to develop.

Revolt in Hungary

The Hungarian rebellion took a different course, possibly because the people did not suffer in the same way from fear of Germany. Unlike the Poles, the Magyars had no reason for retaining Soviet military and political support. Their rebellion quickly moved both against the internal organization of communism and against the Soviet alliance. When the full force of Hungarian demands became evident, the Soviet Union intervened with arms. From late October, 1956, to January, 1957, the Hungarian people fought native Communist police and Soviet troops. Workers and peasants, intellectuals and students, Catholic and Protestant churches, the supposedly Communist Magyar army, all defended the country with every available means, including the general strike. A few Soviet soldiers joined them, but not enough. The tanks and guns of an imperialist power crushed a small nation, and a pro-Soviet government led by János Kádár reigned over ruins. This century has seen many examples of heroism; none equals on a national scale that of Hungary in 1956–1957.

The Soviet government was reluctant to attack Hungary with arms. It favored the Polish solution, for it understood that forceful suppression of rebellion would be condemned abroad and would destroy the carefully built up picture of the Soviet Union as the foe of imperialism and friend of subject peoples. Faced with the need to choose, the Moscow leaders preferred actual Communist control over Hungary to respect for their own propaganda. If Hungary had gained freedom, they would have had to expect defection of other subject peoples and disintegration of the security system built since World War II. They sought to deflect the opprobrium of the world from themselves by accusing Western countries, particularly the United States, of having stimulated the revolt. The truth was so evident, however, that Nehru of India, a neutral in the cold war and reluctant to condemn, denounced Soviet suppression of the Magyar uprising as a violation of the Charter of the United Nations.

Soviet policies toward Poland and Hungary must be understood in relation to expansion of communism in Asia. The leader of Communist China, Mao Tse-tung, had been a Titoist before Tito. In 1940 he had declared that China should have an independent "national form," and he insisted upon equality of China with the Soviet Union. Stalin never accepted this interpretation; but his successors extended the new line of collective leadership in the Soviet Union to relations with other Communist countries. They relinquished possession of Port Arthur and of vital industries in Manchuria to Red China and declared, in the words of Khrushchev (1955), that "the principal feature of our epoch is the emergence of socialism from the confines of one country and its transformation into a world system." The Soviet Union as *primus inter pares* should not dominate but cooperate with other Communist countries and use her industrial resources and technical knowledge to help them to develop. The policy applied prior to 1956 more to the Asiatic states than to the European. Since the Soviet Union actually lacked the resources which Red China, North Korea, and Red Indochina needed, she required the European satellites to furnish as much as they could. Thereby she expected to turn their market relations from the West to the Asiatic countries. The defiance by Poland and the rebellion of Hungary upset this program, for Poland would henceforth use more of her products at home, and both Poland and Hungary would need large amounts of Soviet aid to restore their economies.

The Chinese premier, Chou En-lai, was brought to Europe at the beginning of 1957 to mediate between the Soviet Union and the satellites. After a series of conferences in Moscow, Warsaw, and Budapest, he and the Communist leaders from each state denounced the Hungarian revolution and approved Soviet action in crushing it. Pledging devotion to the common cause, they accepted the leadership of the Soviet Union and asserted the right of each national state to achieve communism in a national way. At the same time they defined the limits to national action that would be tolerated and condemned Tito for pursuing an independent foreign policy of neutrality, for criticizing Soviet leadership, and for encouraging defiance of Moscow among the satellites.

In September, 1955, Khrushchev declared that those who expect the Soviet Union to abandon the communism of Marx, Engels, and Lenin must "wait until a shrimp learns to whistle." The Soviet Union had become a stable power, possessing an economy expected soon to rival that of the United States, a strong middle class of intellectuals, officials, and technicians, and the largest army in the world, rapidly becoming equipped with atomic weapons. She had failed in agriculture to produce sufficient food and industrial materials, and she had not succeeded in reconciling communism with incentives to individual initiative. The "international centralism" of Stalin was being transformed into "socialist internationalism," as more states became Communist. One might anticipate a time when the interests of these states, especially of the two colossi, the Soviet Union and Red China, would not coincide. Communism finds its widest appeal among peoples of the lowest standard of living, recently emancipated from imperialist control or still struggling to free themselves, and inexperienced in countering the methods of Communist infiltration. These are peoples accustomed to hardship and domination, who are searching for a short cut to material prosperity. For some groups among them, particularly intellectuals, the post-Stalin line of "socialist internationalism" seemed persuasive; Soviet suppression of the Hungarian rebellion caused them to reconsider.

Suggestions for Further Reading

The Readings for Chapters 10 and 16 may be consulted for this chapter in addition to the following:

ALTON, THAD PAUL. *Polish Postwar Economy.* New York: Columbia University Press, 1955.

DALLIN, DAVID J. *The Changing World of Soviet Russia.* New Haven, Conn.: Yale University Press, 1956.

KERETZ, STEPHEN D., ed., *The Fate of East Central Europe.* Notre Dame, Ind.: University of Notre Dame Press, 1956.

KULSKI, W. W. *The Soviet Régime. Communism in Practice.* See the Readings for Chapter 16.

LASKY, MELVIN J., ed. *The Hungarian Revolution.* New York: Frederick A. Praeger, Inc., 1957. Accounts by participants and observers, with an introductory analysis.

MILOSZ, CZESLAW. *The Captive Mind.* New York: Vintage Books, Inc., 1955. Tries to explain why persons became Communists and why some later broke away from the movement.

SCHWARTZ, HARRY. *Russia's Soviet Economy.* Rev. ed. New York: Prentice-Hall, Inc., 1954.

SETON-WATSON, HUGH. *The East European Revolution.* 3rd ed., rev. New York: Frederick A. Praeger, Inc., 1956.

WOLFF, ROBERT LEE. *The Balkans in Our Time.* Cambridge, Mass.: Harvard University Press, 1956. Basic for the period since 1939.

Part V

The Cultural Expression

Chapter 27 · Art, Literature, and Music

Like all other periods of history, the first half of the twentieth century must be judged by the extent to which it furthered the life of the spirit. Although the appearance of genius cannot be explained and should be esteemed unique, it is worth inquiring whether the political, economic, and social organization and activity which have been described inspired creative achievement in literature, art, and music, or whether they imposed obstacles. More light can thereby be thrown upon the character of the entire culture than in any other way; for aesthetic creators, being highly sensitive to personal experience, are endowed with the ability to individualize the attributes of the age and to focus general attention upon them.

DECLINE OF TRADITIONAL CLASS INFLUENCE

Aesthetic creativity followed the culture as a whole in tending to outgrow the class divisions of the eighteenth and nineteenth centuries and in becoming all-inclusively middle class. The expectation cherished by some Marxians of a proletarian art, literature, and music failed to materialize. Opportunities were available for gifted sons and daughters of even the working class to acquire a middle-class education, including that in the field of their aesthetic interest, and, since the media of communication were so numerous and all-pervasive, young people of all groups were subjected to much the same experience. The French painter Roger de la Fresnaye and the Russian composer Igor Stravinsky had an aristocratic background; the writers André Gide (French) and Thomas Mann (German) came from the upper bourgeoisie; Pablo Picasso (Spanish artist) and Béla Bartók (Hungarian composer) were sons of lower officials; Emil Nolde (German painter) was a peasant's son, and Ignazio Silone (Italian author), although the son of a landowner, grew up among peasants; Chaim Soutine (Lithuanian painter) came out of an East European ghetto; Jean Giono's (French writer) father made shoes in a small provincial town. Although the middle class produced the vast majority of the aesthetic creators, the arts, letters, and music proved to have no social barriers. In free societies the use of motifs from the lives of the poor as social protest against the lot of the proletariat occurred in the creative work of all classes. For example, the well-educated Käthe Kollwitz, brought up in bourgeois comfort, proved to be a moving exponent of proletarian life. In fact, she, like Picasso in many of his paintings and Silone in his writings, portrayed misery and sorrow, not as class traits, but as human experience.

Diversity in Expression

The aesthetic creators of the first half of the twentieth century showed wide diversity in expression. Romanticism, realism, and naturalism of the nineteenth century maintained their popular appeal, and many new movements appeared and flourished. The isms of the twentieth century are almost too numerous to list. One might include the symbolism of the late nineteenth century as a curtain raiser and continue with cubism, expressionism, dadaism, and surrealism. Phrases like "the new realism" or "the new classicism" and words prefixed by "neo" were coined to identify still other manifestations or phases of old and new movements. The most original individuals like Thomas Mann and Gide in literature, Picasso and Henri Matisse in art, and Stravinsky and Bartók in music found inspiration in many sources and set standards of excellence for the age.

In actual terms of quantity of output the aesthetic forms of the preceding century, romanticism, realism, and naturalism, continued to dominate the field. Work in these styles catered to traditional taste and had a steady, uncritical market. There is evidence, however, that the continued supply of work in these forms was declining in popularity. Each Italian town, for example, possessed a theater which had for years served as the aesthetic center of the community. In the present century the standard repertory of romantic plays and operas failed to attract an audience. The theaters frequently remained closed. The bored audience was first recaptured when movies began to invade the precincts of culture. A similar transfer of popular devotion to movies and such forms of cheap entertainment took place everywhere. The mechanized reproduction at low cost of cultural objects such as plays, music, and publications interested a mass audience, which had been at best on the periphery of nineteenth century culture. People with discriminating and venturesome taste united into small groups willing to follow creative individuals known to them in the exciting quest of new expressions.

CHANGE IN MILIEU AND EXPERIENCE —INDUSTRIALISM

The aesthetic culture of the nineteenth century was so different from that of the twentieth that an explanation must be sought in the changed milieu and experience of creative persons. It lies in the nature of aesthetic activity for the individual to try to be original in his expression and to that effect to be critical of tradition; but for a break of the dimensions of the one under discussion there had to occur a revolution in the social experience of the artist. Romanticism, realism, and especially naturalism proved inadequate to this new experience. Romanticism had often degenerated into superficial emotionality, and realism and naturalism, in spite of their intention to portray life as it was, omitted far too much which had become important. Science and technology, urbanism, imperialism, and power politics were expanding the meaning of reality beyond the customary limits.

By the turn of the century science and technology could produce quickly and abundantly objects that seemed little short of the miraculous. The artist, accustomed to portraying life in a photographic way or to dreaming about the afternoon of a faun, found himself surpassed in concreteness, inventiveness, and resourcefulness of spirit. The electric light bulb, the motion picture, the telephone, the automobile, and the airplane were symbolic of the emerging supremacy of science. The imagination of the technician appeared to be outstripping that of the professional aesthete. The new objects, fabricated by human beings, were not natural; they were creations in the same sense as a poem. They set a precedent for the artist. The French poet and critic Guillaume Apollinaire formulated conclusions as follows:

> Poetry and creation are one and the same thing; he alone must be called poet who invents and creates, as much as it is given to man to create. . . . One can be a poet in all fields: all that is needed is to be adventurous, to be after discoveries.

Apollinaire believed that by producing marvels the scientist had challenged the artist:

> The wonders impose on us the duty of not letting imagination and poetic subtleties lag behind those of the artisans who improve the machine. Already scientific terminology is in deep discord with that of the poets. This is an unbearable state of affairs.[1]

The writer or artist, he said, should not be merely an interpreter of life but a creator. The task of interpreter should be assumed by the reader or observer, "who," in the formulation of a contemporary critic,

> loses his passive task of absorbing and feeling the message of the artist and assumes the more creative role of relating the sensations of the artist to his own experiences and his own faculties of imagination and association. Thus the flexibility of the visions of the artist are set to a perpetual motion of interpretations, which may in themselves be a form of creative activity.[2]

When regarded from this point of view, life became once more aesthetically fresh and exciting.

[1] Anna Balakian, "Apollinaire and the Modern Mind," *Yale French Studies*, No. 4, p. 83.

[2] *Ibid.*, p. 87.

The Machine

The modern machine exerted such a profound influence upon society that it affected the aesthetic aspect of life in major proportions. The evidence is as multifarious as the functions of the machine, but a selection may suffice to indicate the variety. By means of the phonograph, the two Hungarian composers, Béla Bartók and Zoltán Kodály, and musicians of other nationalities as well, were able to collect folk songs on a vast scale. By the middle of the century more than 16,000 Hungarian folk songs had been recorded, and Romanian, Slavic, Turkish, English—indeed those of every European and many non-European peoples—were in the process of being made available to the public. Bartók wrote of the relation of the music of his region to his own compositions as follows:

> This whole study of folk-music was of capital importance in enabling me to free myself from the tyranny, which I had up to then accepted, of the major and minor modal systems. In fact, the largest and most valuable part of this treasure-house of collected folk melodies was based on the old liturgical modes, on the archaic Greek mode, or on one more primitive still (the so-called pentatonic). In addition, all this music abounded in rhythmic devices and the most free and varied changes of measure, demanding now a strict *tempo giusto* and now *rubato* treatment. It thus became clear that in this early Hungarian music, there were scales which, though no longer used, had lost none of their vital force. By reviving them, one might create new harmonic combinations. By using the diatonic scale, I was able to free myself from the fixed "major-minor" convention: and the final result has been that, to-day, one may employ freely and in isolation all the sounds of the dodecaphonic chromatic system.

As one of Bartók's biographers has stated:

> It was these Magyar elements which, almost to the exclusion of other folk-music gathered in other countries, formed the setting in which Bartók's inspiration most often took fire.[3]

One might add the names of the English composer Vaughan Williams, the French composer Darius Milhaud, and others to the list of those exploiting the inspiration of the folk music made easily available by the phonograph.

New Materials and Opportunities

The extent to which the machine contributed directly to the character of twentieth-century music would be impossible to judge. The composers of this music all came from an essentially agrarian environment and undoubtedly were seeking some original means to convey their feelings to the public. Nonetheless, we know from the biography of Stravinsky that the sounds, the rhythms, the tempo of machinery offered inescapable sensations that might inspire a composer to try new combinations of sounds.

[3] Serge Moreux, *Béla-Bartók* (London: Harvill Press, 1941), pp. 60-61.

The dissonance and cacophony, the quality of beat, the strange tone found their places in many attempts to express by way of music the experience of the machine. Prior to the industrial revolution the composer had not known about such sounds; once big-scale machinery, the motor car, telephone, and other modern inventions became universal, he could scarcely escape them. If he were at all responsive to the life around him, his music would reveal the effect.

Industrialism has supplied novel materials in all fields and has thereby stirred the creative imagination to envisage ways in which they can appropriately be used. Even though much of the work continues to be done by skilled craftsmen, modern machinery and science have enabled many musical instruments, especially the winds and the percussions, to be made with precision rarely known in an earlier age. The invention of new instruments has been unusual in this period; but improvement in many of the standard ones has enabled composers to try tones and tonal combinations on a scale unknown to Beethoven or Berlioz. Similarly, in the field of the arts, the painter has had new colors developed by expert scientists and produced in quantity; he has received synthetic materials on which to paint or new paints which will adhere to new surfaces like metals; and he has adopted methods of applying color other than with a brush. The sculptor no longer needs to work in natural stone, or wood, or a few metals. He now has at his disposal the range of metals which industry has developed. He can pour stone into molds or form it with his hands; he learns from the engineer to use the blowtorch and the electric welder or other technical methods for shaping materials. Sculpture has become flexible; no longer does the sculptor work exclusively in the round or in relief; he has widened the range of expressions of spatial relations and has sought the forms suggested by the material. An artist in a metallic age like ours would scarcely be content to use iron or bronze in the same way that Cellini did. His aesthetic sense may possibly not be so keen; but he has far better technical facilities for handling material. Hence the sculpture of the Englishman Henry Moore, of the Russian Naum Gabo, of the Spaniard Julio Gonzalez, of the Swiss Alberto Giacometti meets our expectation of what a creative individual in this age would do.

Architecture offers a striking example of the impact of the machine process. Since industry provided structural steel, reinforced concrete, and glass and tile in vast quantities, the architect could put up a building of an entirely different shape from that dictated by traditional styles. He needed no flying buttresses; height was not restricted by the weight of the material; he did not have to adapt himself exclusively to the character of wood, brick, or stone. With the new materials the architect could realize the new purposes which industrialism set. He stretched a building over a vast area as a factory or shot it into the air for offices, and in both he gave it the appearance of lightness and strength. He inclosed its surfaces with glass at no sacrifice of endurance, and he embellished its appearance with a choice from the many kinds, colors, and textures of brick and tile. He explored the possibility of all these materials both structurally and aesthetically, and he used as his guide into the modernist style the concept of functionalism. During the years of experimentation beauty was considered a secondary aspect which would emerge of itself in the process of the artist's being true to the nature of the materials and of using them simply and economically to achieve the purpose. If steel were needed it should not be concealed by wood or stone but should be honestly exposed as a structural element with its own particular beauty. As it has matured, modern style has assumed a place in the history of architecture with the classical and the Gothic. It has taken hold wherever industrialism has become established, for it may be regarded as a logical way of using the materials which industry has provided. The Frenchman Charles Éduard Le Corbusier, the German Ludwig Miës van der Rohe, and the Bauhaus group in Germany led by Walter Gropius are merely a few of the prominent architects of the modern style to be found in all European industrial countries.

If one observes in a factory or in a home equipped with industrial products the wide range of colors, textures, and forms, one will understand the inspiration and encouragement behind a great deal of modern art. What is strange is not the artist's use or adaptation of the aesthetic qualities about a refrigerator or an automobile but the inclination of the public to reject the aesthetics of the painting while accepting those of the automobile. Applied or industrial art has advanced with fine art; both are creative, both are aesthetic. Each has learned from the other, a fact easily confirmed by comparing a cubist painting with an advertisement, or a Raoul Dufy painting with a textile design. Michelangelo used colors and materials available in the Renaissance; the twentieth-century artist lives in an environment of sense data provided by an industrialism unknown to his illustrious predecessor. Being a person more sensitive to the world about him than his inartistic contemporaries, the artist has incorporated the results of these stimuli into his work and has pioneered in revealing to our society the unusual aesthetic qualities of this environment.

The mechanical reproduction of cultural objects has made it possible for creators and public readily to become acquainted with the historical achievements of mankind in these fields. One may compare the relative scarcity of such material available to Goethe with the amount found everywhere in this century. Historical scholarship has opened to the artist or writer or composer the works of his predecessors in almost any period and has enabled him to receive inspiration for themes, methods, forms, and standards from any preferred master. One can find a precedent for almost any aesthetic act. One can mix the forms of several periods and come forth with a pastiche, which may even pass as original. Eclecticism may lead to actual creativeness. Stravinsky's union of motifs from oriental music, folk music, and music by various classical composers into a modern composition is akin to Picasso's study of African sculpture and T. S. Eliot's use of phrases, plots, meters, and figures from the past. The predilection for Greek plots (Gide, Jean Cocteau), for Biblical stories (Thomas Mann), and for tales set in the Middle Ages (Sigrid Undset) indicates the mass extension of the horizon of both creator and public. The allusions to other literatures found in modern poetry or plays, in paintings or sculpture or in music are accepted as legitimate because of the historical knowledge which we possess. When Paul Hindemith advocated that composers return to Bach, or Eliot encouraged the study of seventeenth-century literature, or Picasso named Velasquez among the sources of his inspiration, we realize that each intended to keep his work in the line of historical tradition and maintain its standards, and be original as well. Where an artist may have a world museum at his disposal in photographic reproductions, he runs the danger of becoming imitative or eclectic, but he has wonderful resources for encouraging him to the highest humanistic endeavor, that of individual creativeness inspired by and measured against the multiplicity of kinds of art or writing or composition that the world has produced. The demands put upon the audience to appreciate the works of our aesthetic colleagues have grown in proportion to the increasing complexity of our industrial and historical culture.

Transportation and Communication

To the sources of inspiration from past and present which books and photographs have made possible should be added those gained by means of modern transportation and communication. Within a few hours or days an individual can move from Paris to Tahiti, from an industrialized society to the primitive culture of an African tribe. Gide sought relief from French life by going to the Arabic world of North Africa or to the Congo. The German sculptor Ernst Barlach found on a short trip to Russia the peasant forms, gestures, and expressions which crystallized his artistic longings. Milhaud profited from an extensive visit to Brazil to incorporate native themes into his compositions. Nolde was one of many whose journey around the world enriched his art with subjects, palette, and manner of treatment. A person could live history by travel—a primitive society, a feudal society, an early modern one, a Buddhist culture, an Islamic culture, an atheistic culture; the diversity of aesthetic experience was too vast for an individual to absorb. We speak with justice of a growing international economy and polity, but modern transportation and communication facilities have not existed long enough to enable an international aesthetics to emerge. The creative individuals have been taking the initiative in this work by adopting from the various cultures those motifs of value to them, but they have not yet emancipated themselves from cultural provincialism, and their public lags much farther behind.

Modern transportation and communication have exerted a powerful influence especially in connection with imperialism. From 1900 to 1950 the colonial world enriched European art, literature, and music; in the aesthetic fields, the reverse movement, from Europe to the underdeveloped cultures, was almost nonexistent. Europeans studied the exotic music, the strange rhythms, the use of percussions, the tonal value of the single instrument, the means of expressing the feelings and experience of peoples with cultures utterly different from their own. They discovered in the art of a people a concentrated plastic rendition of emotions, uninhibited, elemental, an essential part of social and religious ceremonies. They found in these peoples a basis for judging the industrial, urban, intellectual society of Europe, and they incorporated particularly in literature the results of their comparisons. Anthropology became a storehouse for figures of speech and references used in poetry (see T. S. Eliot's *The Waste Land*), and travel accounts acquired the prestige of one of the most popular forms of literary composition. The artist, writer, or composer owed a debt to these primitive or underdeveloped cultures—Picasso in the "Women of Avignon," Gide in his books on the Congo, Milhaud and Stravinsky in their use of percussion instruments.

New Environment—Space and Time

Industrialism developed in the factory and the urban community an environment which could be called new. During this century the majority of people in most of Central and Western Europe came to live in these centers, and the rest depended upon them for market and personal services. To creative personalities the modern age seemed a man-made civilization, where man shaped nature to his urban, rational needs. Space became precious; spatial relations in a city or in a factory were calculated with exactitude. The artist lived in a society with a practical sense for the arrangement of parts in an area. He developed the same sense into a dominant motif in his painting, his sculpture, his architectural plan for a house, his ideas for interior decoration. The frame of a painting, the two dimensions of the canvas or board on which the colors were spread, the empty or negative spaces in painting or sculpture, the layout of rooms in a structure, the placing of the words on the printed page, the appreciation of these and of other aspects of spatial arrangement marked the reorientation of the aesthetic spirit.

The same conditions made the artist acutely aware of the importance of time, for where space is so cherished time will also be. Since agglomerations of people in large numbers in cities, factories, and office buildings had to live by the clock or succumb to chaos, the sense of time, of speed, pervaded the mind of individuals. Not merely the physical existence of the automobile and the train conveyed this fact; the spiritual presence of it became embedded in the subconscious. Speed and action acquired conceptual reality exclusive of human connotation. The literary expression of pure action came into style; architecture sought to impart to the plans of a factory or a house a sense of inner mobility. The spatial arrangement should be one of flow and easy transition and multiple use. Guiding phrases like "dynamic symmetry" came into popularity. Aesthetics, like economics, accepted the reign of space-time.

AGE OF TRANSITION

With millions of people living in close contact, the awareness of social problems opened a wide area of stimulation to creative personalities and led them to use these subjects in their work. Although the culture was dominated by the middle class, society contained the aristocracy, the handicraftsmen, and the peasantry from the Old Regime and the proletariat, salaried employees, and the bourgeois elite of industrialism. Since the transition from the Old Regime to industrialism continued during this half century at a pace greatly accelerated beyond that of the nineteenth century, the aesthetes were able to observe examples of numerous lines of social change.

The literature, especially the novel, assumed a major role as the medium for portraying these transformations. John Galsworthy, Thomas and Heinrich Mann, Roger du Gard, Marcel Proust, to mention a few authors, wrote primarily about the upper classes, but the workers and the peasants served as the focus of attention of many others, the Italian Silone being particularly effective. Class conflict and the battle of the "isms," liberalism, democracy, socialism, communism, syndicalism, anarchism, were waged in literature, as authors struggled to clarify by writing their own thoughts as well as the thoughts of their readers. Controversies were acute and issues vital; although many authors were able to ignore them, numerous others could not, and stage, fiction, and poetry resounded with arguments.

Music by its nature did not lend itself readily to social discussion, but occasionally in ballet, vocal music, opera, song, or chorus the composer attempted to express his social feelings. Art responded to a greater extent than music but by virtue of its nature less than literature. The painters and sculptors interested in these questions were limited by their medium to portraying a symbol of poverty or misery or of affluence and power and to interpreting these according to their beliefs. Picasso's women at the ironing board, George Grosz's pictures of army officers, Barlach's sculpture of peasants, Utrillo's street scenes of prosperous middle-class districts may be cited as examples of a continuing awareness among artists that they lived in a period of social transition. The diversity of social types and social experience during this period was conducive to rich aesthetic creativeness.

The advantage to the creative person of living in an age of social transition arises out of the manifold and vivid light which was thrown upon the character of man. The aesthete was able to observe the individual in situations as antithetic as poverty and wealth, factory and salon, agriculture and industry, primitivism and civilization, war and peace, uprootedness and steadfastness, hatred and love, and the many stages and combinations of these. Quantitatively speaking at least, an age of such varied cultural situations so immediately accessible to the sensitive observer had never previously existed. The creative individual sought means of expressing the experience in this complex, sometimes chaotic world, and the degree of his originality in the selection of forms and motifs has varied with that of his insight.

The most original music of this period interpreted the experience of industrialism, war, and revolution so profoundly that the listener immediately recalls the response of a composer in a comparable period, Beethoven. Exquisite tenderness of melody and purity of instrumental tone are combined with a rush of phrases, an abruptness of transitions, a violence of climax as if the composer were stretching the elements of music to the limit in order to express the results of his experience. A wild, cacophonous world of war and revolution and industry, a gentle world of delicate love, a world of extremes—these had to be put into music, and Bartók, Milhaud, Stravinsky, and others have succeeded in the effort. One should listen to Bartók's *Suite for Strings, Percussions and Celesta* of 1936, and relate its content to the experience of the composer. The music has the genuine qualities of our age, and in addition it shares the character of great music in expressing something which abides in man of all ages. It has deepened our knowledge of the human being.

The artist likewise has sought new means to portray the wealth of his experience with man. Often finding it impossible to indicate real characteristics by way of physical likeness, he has, for example, exaggerated or concentrated upon the essential aspects of a figure, or he has isolated a quality and expressed it in an impersonal way. Like the composer, he has used the resources of his medium, painting or sculpture, to reveal the violent contrasts, the dynamic movement, the bursts of revelation, the pattern of mechanized action, and the sheer, often quickly passing beauty of this society. When Oskar Kokoschka painted a portrait, he could not be content with a Sunday likeness: he knew both the figure and himself too well. When Georgio de Chirico interpreted man, he stripped off physiology and revealed the nonpersonal spirit. When Salvador Dali did so, he made him an object of aesthetic exquisiteness which, however, was neurotic. When Georges Braque observed his friends, he reduced them to geometry in color. These experiences were all true, all evident to a sensitive aesthete; they were all legitimate subjects for an art attempting honestly and sincerely to respond to the stimuli of the period.

Since the public was more accustomed to the language of words than it was to that of art or music, literature offered the most widespread form of revealing the new knowledge of man. That it had many parallels with the other media may be seen from one example, the affinity of artists to self-portraiture or to using oneself as a model, and of writers to autobiography, memoirs, and letters, whether actual or fictional. In a time of cultural change, the individual has had to find his own path, establish his own standards, and cultivate his own kind of personality. The interest turned inward as the person struggled with isms and confronted the contrast between urban and rural culture, the proletariat and the peasant, the mechanized life and the life of nature, the role of reason and of the subconscious. Everyone at every stage in life acquired fascination. The stories of youth became especially meaningful: what happened to the young person as he grew into society? The slice-of-life novel attempted to apply to writing a favorite standard in architecture and engineering, the functional. The writer sought to portray how people acted in a total way at a given time. To the account in time and the portrayal in cross section was added that in psychological depth, the stream-of-consciousness story, the concentration, like that of a Kokoschka portrait, upon the inner world. Writers followed the tradition of the preceding century in using the novel as the main vehicle of their reactions, and with the enormous choice of subjects of popular significance in this period they covered the range of man's experience. They served as the educators of adults about the character of the culture.

Concern with the Emotions

The half century showed a powerful concern with the emotions, the subconscious, the irrational forces which could be comprehended, if at all, solely by intuition. For reasons which are far from clear, the turn to this emphasis had occurred among pioneers like Vincent van Gogh in the latter part of the nineteenth century, when the subject also began to receive scientific analysis in the writings of Sigmund Freud. It may be that individual creators of intense emotional life aroused the interest by following the bent of their own personality. It may be that romanticism no longer satisfied the need for standards and ideals and that individuals dug into life and discovered the reservoir of the subconscious. In any event the aesthetes and even a great part of the public learned by experience that the change from a predominantly agrarian culture to one industrial, urban, and scientific stirred up strange emotional forces calling for a conception of man more profound than that of their immediate tradition. Freud, in emphasizing the importance of sex in the conduct of man, opened a vast subject for creative persons to exploit in their works. The libido assumed a major role, and the Oedipus complex, the inferiority complex, the oral and the anal types of personality, and all the rest of the terminology filled the pages of literature and lay concealed behind the technical façade of art and even music. Those who rejected the Freudian theses were equally impressed with the driving power of the subconscious and gave to their figures, whether human or not, the mystical, inexplicable qualities of one subject to controls beyond his understanding and his will.

Thus, contemporaneously with the remarkable achievements of the rational faculties, of planning and calculation in science, technology, business, urbanism, social science, and other aspects of the life of industrialism, the strength of irrationality grew in social significance. The one formed the obverse side of the other, and as these were transitional years in which the uncertainties of the present were everywhere visible, and the shape of the future industrial society and the assurance of its realization unclear, the persons gifted with creative imagination stressed the power of the subconscious forces at the expense of those under man's control. Their preference was enhanced by the nature of their occupation, for, since as observers and critics they did not participate actively and directly in building the new industrial culture, they lacked the steadying, balancing effect of practical constructive action.

Impact of War

In contrast to the creative urge of science and industry, the political forces of the half century seemed determined to prove that irrationality did dominate life. An international, civil, or colonial war has been fought somewhere in almost every year of the twentieth century. When it did not actually break out, it existed as a threat. The Boer War, the Boxer Rebellion, the Balkan Wars, World War I, and the accompanying revolutions—the list can be continued through the civil troubles in Russia, the Spanish Civil War, World War II, and the constant fighting, especially in Asia and Africa, since 1945. Death, the ultimate cause of insecurity, has stalked the world. The flowing of blood, the destruction of men, women, and children, of plants and animals and inanimate things, have been our physical and our spiritual companions.

That artists, writers, and composers in our age should be fascinated by the subjects of death and destruction is as natural as that they should associate these with the sway of the emotions and the irrational. They searched for means to convey the character of these holocausts to the public, and they found the conventional forms of photographic realism trivial. How should one portray the young soldier about to go into battle, the horse with stiff upturned legs and bloated body, the mother and children cowering from a buzz-bomb? How should one describe the battle of Verdun? What form and what content should one give to music when one lived under the menace of destruction? Each creative individual sought his own solution, and the aesthetic answers have differed as widely as the experience. One tried the story form, another the diary, another a religious poem, another an apocalyptic version, another the figure of a young girl cold and tense, another cacophony and the roar of drums, another the symbol of a domineering bull.

Picasso's mural commemorating the destruction by bombs of the little Spanish town of Guernica offered one of the most effective expressions.

The concentration upon cold white and gray heightens the inhuman effect; no other colors are included lest they distract attention from the action. The use of dehumanized symbols like the electric light bulb, the brutal, indifferent bull, and the screaming horse, the distorted human beings at various stages of destruction—these and other symbols in the painting were conceived by Picasso to convey his reaction to war. His predecessors Goya and Delacroix had used quite other figures; Picasso drew his means from the full artistic development of this century.

What Picasso did in painting, Ernst Jünger, Albert Camus, and others have accomplished in literature, and Bartók and Milhaud in music. War did not lend itself to pretty colors and sentimental words; a war fought with mechanical means over bitterly hostile dogmas, a war just as war, a killing and a being killed, demanded its own integrity of treatment. As an example of one style of writing which this experience evoked, let us quote Ernst Jünger as translated by J. P. Stern:

> The firing on the horizon in front of us was flaring up more and more densely, its light reflected high in the clouds as a blood-red flashing. It formed a long dancing chain and at last melted into one glowing wall. What meaning in all this had the effect of a single battery? The reports of its shells were lost without a trace in a fabulous tumult, in a thousand poisonous hisses of trajectories intertwining above our heads into a narrow-meshed net, and in a glowing surf which surrounded us, like Greek fire, as a contiguous element. But our faces were turned West, and motionless we stared into this fiery wall. We were no longer afraid, for this spectacle was so great that no human feeling can come up to it. We were waiting, for there was no doubt that this prodigious waste of material must be followed up by the deployment of men. And then I saw next to me Officer-Cadet W., a very young man, bend down and grasp a bottle of wine, which a party of carriers had brought up for him the night before and which was to be saved for tomorrow's hot hours of noon. I saw him lift it to his lips, drink it at one deep draught and laugh as he threw it over the parapet. And I understood the meaning of this act: he foresaw that tomorrow he would no longer be able to drink it. Yet there was in this simple action so rash a daring and so self-evident a superiority that suddenly I had a feeling of great release—I would have liked to embrace him, and suddenly I had become quite gay.[4]

FIVE AESTHETIC MOVEMENTS

In the theoretical formulations which aesthetic creators gave to the experience of this half century, five movements stand out, cubism, expressionism, dadaism, surrealism, and existentialism. Dadaism lasted a short time but revealed the social pathology among creative individuals. The other four movements have influenced spiritual life to an enduring degree. The supporters of all five have manifested certain common characteristics.

[4] J. P. Stern, *Ernst Jünger: A Writer of Our Time* (New Haven: Yale University Press, 1953), pp. 23-24.

They have searched for forms and symbols which would appropriately reveal the actuality of this culture of transition. They have recognized the existence of spiritual or supersensuous reality as well as the more easily experienced physical aspects and have utilized intuition and instinct as well as intelligence to apprehend this part of life. They have searched for the essence of things, the purest forms in phenomena, and to that end they have sacrificed the details that would ease the public's understanding of their work. They have been deeply concerned with questions of metaphysics and religion, of ultimate values and goals. To express the results of the search into these problems by way of their particular medium (art, literature, or music), they have crossed forms, coined new words, and brought into widespread usage other media that had not been regarded in the earlier periods as proper; they have experimented with sounds, colors, instruments, materials. In fact, they have thrown conventions overboard and have followed the one standard of employing the means, words, colors, materials, necessary to portray their conception of the reality of this culture.

Cubism

Well under way in the first decade of the century, cubism rejected the ephemeral impression and subjective symbolism in favor of the enduring qualities of nature. Cezanne had in the previous century advised artists to "see the cylinder, the sphere and the cone, all in good perspective." And the cubists subsequently found in Plato's *Philebus* a justification of their views.

SOCRATES: What I am saying is not indeed directly obvious. I must therefore try to make it clear. I will try to speak of the beauty of shapes, and I do not mean, as most people would think, the shapes of living figures, or their imitations in paintings, but I mean straight lines and curves and shapes made from them, flat or solid, by the lathe, ruler and square, if you see what I mean. These are not beautiful for any particular reason or purpose, as other things are, but are always by their very nature beautiful, and give pleasure of their own quite free from the itch of desire; and colors of this kind are beautiful, too, and give a similar pleasure.

One can feel cubism in the blocked, sharply divided phraseology and precisely related sounds of some modern music. Listen to Bartók's music of the 1920's, for instance, or Arnold Schönberg's use of the twelve-tone scale. Apollinaire was one of many writers who applied the cubist methods in literature. With respect to his first book of verse (1913), a critic has in terms equally applicable to painting commented as follows:

In *Alcools* . . . we find instances of the same mixture of perspectives and sensations. Just as the technologist formed a new world of realities with existing matter, Apollinaire believed that words could make and unmake a universe. He attempted to use his "five senses and a few more" to string side by side images often logically disconnected, demanding of the reader leaps and bounds of the imagination to keep pace with his self-characterized "oblong" vision. His dislocations of temporal and spatial perspective defy ordinary reality but are of this earth in their tactility, colors and scents.[5]

The method which the cubist artists employed has been described as follows, and one should note the musical analogy:

> The more severely the common things of everyday life, glasses, bottles, pipes, fruits, and fruitstands, are analysed from different aspects and at different angles, whole and in section, the less recognizable do they become, mutiliated and cut short as they are in a new creative effort of achievement. Thus understood, Cubism may be conceived as a fugue on a familiar theme. And as in music the air that serves as the leitmotif is not interposed save in a varied and elusive form, so that one hears only a few notes of it from time to time; so in these pictorial fugues the subject is suggested by a line; is lost; and then again imaged forth, colour and above all the interplay of line being the sole preoccupation.[6]

When Braque or Picasso portrayed a mandolin or when Jacques Lipchitz carved a human figure in cubist manner each was paying respects to the aesthetic effects of modern science, of the precise mathematical shape of machines and factories, of the geometric pattern of a city. Plato could formulate the theory of cubism as an imaginative act, but our culture has come to live in cubism. The artists and writers were the first to draw our attention to the universal significance of mathematics in our age, to reveal by way of it the aesthetic values of this new culture, and to enrich our appreciation of outer appearance and inner meaning and their interrelationship. In this emerging industrial society cubism has become an integral part of our spiritual as well as of our physical life.

Expressionism

Although expressionism had forerunners in the art of van Gogh, Eduard Munch, and others, the movement became widespread simultaneously with cubism. It extended more widely than cubism in wishing to know, not merely the geometric manifestations, but the essence of life. As Franz Marc, one of its adherents, said in 1912, "Nature is everywhere, in us and outside us," and "we are seeking and painting this spiritual side of ours in nature . . . because we see this side, just as formerly people suddenly "saw" violet shadows and the atmosphere over all things." [7] Vision, intuition, and ecstasy were the means of gaining the necessary insight, and the qualities of the grotesque, the horrible, and the beautiful were pressed to extremes. The expressionists strove to comprehend "inner experience," to grasp its "eternal significance." Instead of reproducing something passively

[5] Balakian, *loc. cit.*, p. 86.

[6] E. H. Ramsden, *An Introduction to Modern Art* (New York: Oxford University Press, 1949), pp. 7-8.

[7] *Ibid.*, p. 14.

received in the mind, they sought contact with the elemental and tried to create. They were, as one of them said, in a condition of constant excitement:

> A house is no longer merely a subject for an artist, consisting of stone, ugly or beautiful; it has to be looked at until its true form has been recognized, until it is liberated from the muffled restraint of a false reality, until everything that is latent within it is expressed.[8]

The "link with eternity" of each person or object must be sought.

> The artist now demanded images which were not accidental but essential and absolutely valid; he insisted not so much upon an adherence to formal principles of external accuracy as upon an imaginative re-creation, an "ex-pression," of the commonly concealed core of any given thing or experience. Not the artist's impression of a stable world, but the intensity of his intuitive emotional grasp was now to be the source of his work. The reality which he was to represent was not to be a mere copy, a literal transcription of casual living, but a vision different from it in shape and more intensely spiritual in quality.[9]

In order to realize this ideal, expressionism tended toward the use of abstraction, exaggeration, rhapsody, and ecstasy. The expressionist

> tries to absorb into himself the eternal element in Man and to give expression to this cosmic consciousness. Even national ties are regarded as narrowing, for the Expressionist sees Man only as a creature of God, imprisoned in a hampering and mistaken reality.[10]

What did expressionism mean in concrete terms of literature, art, and music? How was it related to society? A few illustrations may clarify the necessarily vague sentences of the general definition. One should listen to Stravinsky's *Rites of Spring* or Arthur Honegger's oratorio *King David* to see how well the descriptive terms of expressionism fit. Or one may turn to literature. In writing about Dostoevski's novel, *The Idiot,* the German novelist Hermann Hesse stated (1920):

> The future is uncertain, but the path which is here indicated is clear. It involves a spiritual re-orientation. It means that we must think "magically," that we must welcome the chaos that is to come. We must return to the realms of disorder, of the unconscious, of formless existence, of brute life, and far beyond brute life to the beginning of all things. But we do it, not in order to remain there, but to re-orientate ourselves, to rediscover the forgotten instincts and possibilities of development at the very roots of our existence, in order to be able to bring about a new creation, valuation and distribution of life. No programme can show us the way, no revolution can throw open the gates. But each individual must travel there unaccompanied. Each of us must for one hour of his life stand,

[8] Richard Samuel and H. Hinton Thomas, *Expressionism in German Life, Literature and the Theatre* (1910–1924) (Philadelphia: Dufour Editions, 1939), p. 11.

[9] Victor Lange, *Modern German Literature,* 1870–1940 (Ithaca, N.Y.: Cornell University Press, 1945), pp. 74-75.

[10] Samual and Thomas, *op. cit.,* p. 12.

like Myshkin, at that parting of the ways where old truths end and new truths appear.

In his novel, *The Way of Sacrifice,* Fritz von Unruh portrayed the reactions of soldiers at the battle of Verdun. He has one of them speak as follows:

Captain, are we unworthy of struggling for understanding before we go into the Beyond? Are we to remain slaves for ever and ever? Does not the soul march forward through the centuries? Are we to be ruled by skeletons? Do you think that those young men in the lines are dying in vain? That their splendid spirit is sacrificed to territorial gains? Don't you feel that we are striving towards a sacred community, to the solemn brotherhood of the spirit and of the nation? What do we care about fortresses and territories? And if the world becomes rotten, let it perish. Let the body again become the temple of the soul. If Verdun were a pledge of this I should be ready to fight on to the last drop of blood. For I feel the approach of a race of giants! To-day everybody feels as I do! As yet there is still silence, but soon the torrent will burst its banks! You may laugh, Captain, but the Day of Judgment is approaching! O nations of the earth, if our purpose is not the light of your spirit then all our powder is spent in vain!"

The theater was changed to expressionist standards. A production by Gordon Craig has been described as follows:

The spotlight fell into the scanty scenery while pouring a sharp bright beam of light on the face of the speaker. Black velvet curtains that absorbed the light enclosed the bare stage. The objects on the stage lay like white streaks, before which the actors stood without make-up in their timeless costumes, like chalk ghosts. Like a remonstrating solitary figure or one in impassioned despair, the actor stepped with primitive, abrupt gesture into the midst of the spectators.[11]

When Rouault painted the figures of clowns he imparted to them the characteristics of his pictures of Christ. They were expressionist portrayals of life's indivisible union of sadness and humor, the necessity to amuse irrespective of one's own feelings, the heightening of the sense of each extreme by the presence of the other. The clown with the sorrowful face and the slack exhausted body, the Christ with the immobile head, the large quiescent eyes, and the body like a useless weight—these interpret to the viewer the artist's conception of the world. Religion is manifest in all forms of life, the clown as well as the Christ; the supernatural is revealed by way of a physical presence. The individual must intuitively feel himself into the mood and spirit of the artist and derive from the picture a moral, a mystical experience, and an aesthetic satisfaction. The role of life has become inordinately complex in the eternal order of things, and art is used to convey a message and set a cultural objective. Like expressionist music and literature, it offers the response of imaginative, creative individuals to experience too profound for rational understanding. The wonder about death in war, the doubts about the purpose of organized slaughter, the

[11] *Ibid.*, pp. 121-122, 100, 66.

questioning of the relative values of man in a culture of rural nature and in a culture of machines and streets: these and numerous other problems beset individuals throughout the period and evoked the highly subjective answers to enduring, fundamental questions of existence which we associate with expressionism. The movement reached its fullest development between 1910 and 1924 and was found in every country. Its influence continued after that terminal date and made it, like cubism, one of the most fruitful achievements of the modern spirit.

Dadaism

Dadaism reflected an extreme reaction among creative individuals to the destruction of World War I. Although in a sense on the lunatic fringe of expressionism, it was so nihilistic that it merits at least special mention. The world had gone mad, the Dadaists believed, and the arts should purge civilization of the entire rotten wreckage and open the way to a new society. The origin of the name Dada is disputed; the usual one given is that an adherent slipped a paper knife at random in a dictionary and fixed on the word "Dada." The date of this event was February 8, 1916, the place Zurich, Switzerland, the locale the Cabaret Voltaire, the personnel largely refugees from the war.

The manner in which the votaries to Dada expressed their revulsion against existing society may be seen from the following description.

> On the stage of the cabaret [in Zurich] keys were jangled till the audience protested and went crazy. Serner instead of reciting his poems placed a bunch of flowers at the feet of a dressmaker's mannequin. Some marionettes and some masks of Sophie Täuber-Arp, curious objects in painted cardboard, recited the poems of Arp. Huelsenbeck screamed his verses louder and louder while Tzara followed the same crescendo on a kettle drum. For hours on end they went through gymnastic exercises which they called *noir cacadou.* Tzara invented chemical and static poems. Static poems were made by rearranging chairs upon which posters, each with a word, had been placed. For these performances Janco designed paper costumes of every color, put together with pins and above all spontaneous. Perishable, purposely ugly and absurd, these materials, chosen by the hazard of the eye and mind symbolized in showy rags the perpetual revolt, the despair which refuses to let itself despair.[12]

Soon after the war ended the movement succumbed to its own negation. It was born of agony and died with the recovery of society. It remains one of those strange aberrant phenomena of which this half century of cataclysms has so many examples.

[12] Georges Hugnet, "Dada and Surrealism," *Bulletin of the Museum of Modern Art,* IV (November-December, 1936), p. 4.

Surrealism

Surrealism, the heir to all three movements, remains a powerful cultural force to the present day, and, since the conditions of society continue to be favorable, it shows every prospect of characterizing much of future aesthetic creativeness. It used cubist shapes and dadaist methods, and in its antirationalistic search for reality above physical appearance or superrealism it was one with expressionism. Whereas the latter seemed to explode out of the repressed elemental energy of its practitioners, surrealism has had from the beginning an experimental, calculated, intentional quality, a kind of rational use of irrationality. It deliberately concentrated upon means of releasing the imagination from the control of surface reality; it set out to open the regions of the marvelous. It took the new theory of relativity as a scientific basis for discarding belief in the uniformity of natural behavior, and it had space-time doing tricks with objects—a straight line that curved back upon itself, "two clocks traveling concurrently but with different speeds," which "would, when simultaneously observed, mark different times and nevertheless both be correct." [13]

The surrealists lived in the psychoanalytic world of Freud and took their images largely from it, arranging them according to the guidance of the subconscious. They rebelled against existing bourgeois culture, its wars, machinery, contented middle class and miserable poor, its drabness and monotony, and they expected by the release and cultivation of the unused and dormant powers of the imagination to create a new world. Surrealism was not to be an aesthetic creed but a guide to cultural transformation of society, with art and literature as the most imaginative forms of human activity leading the way. It sought man's liberation.

> It aims to take man out of himself; it proposes automatism in order to draw out of man the necessary light for his total emancipation. . . . Man is surrounded by invisible forces—they must be captured. To plumb the mystery of man too many roads have been neglected. . . . With Surrealism all poetic and pictorial manifestations are situated on the level of life and life on the level of dreams. In the night in which we live, in the carefully preserved obscurity which prevents man from rebelling, a beam from a lighthouse sweeps in a circular path over the human and extra-human horizon: it is the light of Surrealism.[14]

To achieve these effects the surrealists employed "the bizarre and the anti-artistic, accident and dream, automatic writing and delirium, critical interpretation and hallucinatory symbols, paintings and ordinary objects, poetry and everyday life." [15] Being no longer tied to the physical relations of things, they made "dumbfounding juxtapositions" [16] of things. They could use an electric light to represent a girl. "Beautiful as the chance encounter of a sewing machine and an umbrella on a dissecting table," one

[13] Georges Lemaitre, *From Cubism to Surrealism in French Literature* (Cambridge, Mass.: Harvard University Press, 1941), p. 183.

[14] Hugnet, *loc. cit.*, p. 32. [15] *Ibid.*, p. 26. [16] *Ibid.*, p. 25.

wrote. Should their paintings be characterized as literary, their poetry as art? They mixed and blended the forms too much for a definite answer to be given, but they enormously enriched the domain of creative imagination. They made the simplest things complicated and fascinating; they were "infinitely disquieting."

If one is inclined to consider a painting by Dali, a poem by Paul Eluard, a collage by Picasso, a statue by Giacometti a fraud and a hoax, how can one account for the practice of surrealism by artists and writers in every country? How especially can one explain the fact that the refugees from Hitler and other totalitarians in the 1930's found in surrealism the means for visually expressing their experience? Which was more surrealistic, the Nazis who hounded people to death because of race or the painter Dali, who entitled one of his pictures "Average atmospherocephalic bureaucrat in the act of milking a cranial harp"? "The wonderful thing about the fantastic," declared André Breton, the theorist of surrealism, himself a physician specializing in nervous and mental diseases, "is that there is no longer the fantastic: there is only the real." [17] In an age of nazism, fascism, and communism, politics also suffered from "nervous and mental diseases." The surrealists portrayed, not the whole of reality, for there continued to be reasonable people and reasonable action; but they revealed to society the pathological state of millions of its members.

Existentialism

Toward the end of the 1930's the movement called existentialism began to attract attention. It has grown in strength and may be called the dominant postwar profession of belief in Europe. Although it originated in German philosophy, its leading exponent is the French writer of plays, novels, philosophic treatises, and political tracts, Jean-Paul Sartre, a veteran of World War II, who in 1947 described the setting for this belief as follows:

> . . . the very fate of our works was bound up with that of France in peril; . . . our public was made up of men like ourselves who awaited war and death. Of their war, of their death, we had to write. . . . We learned to take Evil seriously; it was not our fault, nor was it our merit, if we happened to live in an era when torture was a daily occurrence. . . . We knew that the destruction of the human in man that torture brings about, was a Black Mass being celebrated everywhere in Paris while we ate, while we slept, while we loved; we heard whole streets echo with the shrieks of the tortured ones, and we understood that Evil, the fruit of a free and sovereign will, is absolute as Good is. A day may come when a happy generation, looking back serenely, will see in our suffering and our shame one of the paths that led to its Peace. But we were not on the side

[17] Armand Hook, "The Surrealist Novel," *Yale French Studies,* No. 8, p. 17.

of completed history; we were so *situated* that every minute actually lived appeared to us as something irreducible.[18]

Existentialism was postulated on two interdependent beliefs; first, that man does not exist in and for himself alone, that he is related in a multitude of ways with other objects and beings; and second, that he develops himself within his unique situation. He acknowledges the fact of his existence in a total situation, and he is endowed with the free will and the moral attributes necessary to create something worthy out of his condition. The existentialists upheld an ideal of active rebuilding of the individual and society in a period characterized by destruction from international and civil war and by the astounding achievements of industrialism and science in improving the lot of man. Living in ultimate danger, these existentialists appreciated the need for cool and realistic heroism, for austerity, for optimism and the will to create; otherwise, society would collapse by default. "Zola's books are written in the past," Sartre stated, "my characters have a future. Each of my characters, after having done anything whatever, may still do anything whatever . . . I never calculate whether the action accomplished is logically inserted in the sequence of other acts, but I take the situation, and a liberty chained in situation. . . . The gain I make is that of unpredictability." [19] Literature was showing that one could and should "change the social condition of man and the conception he entertains of himself." [20] In his plays Sartre expressed an austere moral "in keeping with the severity of French life; their moral and metaphysical topics reflect the preoccupation of a nation which must, at one and the same time, reconstruct and recreate, and which is searching for new principles." [21] The existentialists necessarily accepted the existence of the subconscious, the irrational, the obscure forces which loomed so large in expressionism and surrealism; but they went further in advocating action guided by heroic, constructive man in freedom.

Existentialism has proved to be one of the most promising philosophical developments from the experience of World War II. Creative individuals in the aesthetic fields have not sought a solution to problems in the superreal world of dreams; they have based their works on belief in man's ability to make something out of this world existence. They have endeavored to understand political, economic, and social realities, and to couple this understanding with an awareness of the difference in human value of ideals. They have recognized the need to strive toward the realization of those ideals most conducive to the furtherance of man's development. By these means they have brought aesthetes into a closer, more practical relationship with society than in this century they have hitherto had. The cubists developed no particular political and social beliefs. They

[18] Henri Peyre, "Existentialism—A Literature of Despair?" *Yale French Studies*, No. 1, p. 30.

[19] *Ibid.*, p. 24. [20] *Ibid.*, p. 27. [21] *Ibid.*, p. 26.

tended to be radical in a general way, and some hoped to help reform society; but the movement remained aesthetic. The expressionists went in any direction that appealed to the particular individual. They were pacifists, socialists, democrats, communists, anarchists, indifferentists, or any combination of these. A good many followed their emotions ultimately into the camp of the totalitarians, especially in Germany. The Dadaist nihilism may be ignored. The surrealists in their ambition to renew man and society had various affinities, but many of them associated with, or actually became, Communists.

The leading existentialists went through the hard school of World War II and soberly learned to cherish the condition of freedom. "The freedom to write presupposes the freedom of the citizen," Sartre declared in 1947. "One does not write for slaves. The art of prose-writing is bound up with the only regime in which prose retains a meaning: democracy. . . . Writing is a certain fashion of wanting freedom."[22] He denounced communism as "incompatible in France with the free and honest plying of the writer's trade." At the same time he rejected capitalism as an instrument of oppression, and, he declared, "The chances of the survival of literature are bound up with the advent of a Socialist Europe. . . . It is our duty, as writers, to help this new Europe, *through* our writings, to be born."[23] Other existentialists kept the framework of liberal democracy or maintained belief in some free philosophy without precise political affiliation. Irrespective of party, they aimed to be both idealistic and practical in helping to solve the colossal difficulties of a war-torn, ism-torn society.

The relation of literature, art, and music to society in totalitarian countries can be briefly analyzed. Whether it be in the Soviet Union, Nazi Germany, Fascist Italy, or in any of the minor authoritarian regimes, anyone gifted with aesthetic creativeness was compelled to become a propagandist for the state. Mussolini's Italy imposed fewest restrictions, the Soviet Union probably the most. In all of them the destruction of political freedom entailed that of cultural freedom.

TOTALITARIAN CULTURE—GERMANY

Hitler joined politics and culture as follows:

> Our cultural leaders should realize, that this type of authority [his own] can be a true blessing for the cultural development of our people only when it is rooted in the blood of our people. . . . They should realize at the same time that the building of human society is conceivable only when personal liberty, that is, unrestrained license, is limited for the sake of greater unity. They should realize that in the cultural sphere too a general standard must be found which will allow the creations of the individual to be filled with a great idea, which will take from these creations the unrestrained arbitrariness of purely private

[22] *Ibid.*, p. 29. [23] *Ibid.*, p. 31.

conception and which will give to them the impulse of a common *Weltanschauung*. . . .

A Christian age can have only Christian art, a National Socialist age only National Socialist art. Just as the National Socialist State will select the tasks to be performed in the cultural field and has done so already, so it will also watch over their realization.

Translated into detailed realities, these vague statements acquire the character of rigid orthodoxy and terror. "When I hear the word culture," a Nazi remarked, "I draw my revolver." The Nazis banned and often burned books of hostile writers. "The fire of the pyres which flared up in the German lands in May, 1933," one ecstatic Nazi wrote, "is to us the sign and the symbol of an inflexible will to purity, to all that is genuine and noble, real, and true."

The unofficial Nazis began to make the life of unpopular creators a nightmare. In the little town of Güstrow in North Germany the sculptor Barlach, a quiet retiring unpolitical individual whose art did not conform to Nazi standards, was persecuted by fellow townsmen. They called him a Jew, which, he said, unfortunately he was not; they posted insults on his door; they threw stones at his windows; they spied upon him; they opened his mail and tapped his telephone; they frightened away prospective purchasers of his art.

The Nazi government forced all writers, artists, composers—in fact, anyone whose work might influence the public—to join Nazi-controlled state organizations, and it banned those in disfavor from exhibiting, publishing, or even producing anything and kept others in a state of continuing uncertainty. It drove into exile most of the best ones, the Mann brothers, the painter Max Beckmann, the composer Hindemith, who enriched the life of the countries to which they fled. Others like Nolde and Barlach it forced into what has been called domestic exile, a living death within Germany. It confiscated the works of contemporary artists and exposed them to ridicule in public shows as "degenerate art." It sold some of the pieces to eager purchasers from free countries for money which it used for rearmament. It made German art, music, and letters a drab, monotonous affair of portraits of Nazis, all alike, paintings of towheaded little girls ideally fit to bear Nordic-type children, heroic monuments, colossal buildings, military marches, and light operas. Overnight Germany became a cultural desert. Not even writers like Ernst Jünger and Ernst von Salomon, who by adoring violence and nationalism had encouraged nazism, could bear the regime; they both refused to join the movement, and within a short time Jünger was writing in veiled defense of freedom.

Under the Nazis, insecurity rendered sincere creative work impossible. The artist was forced constantly to keep Hitler's personal taste in mind. His inspiration was killed; he maintained silence, not necessarily from cowardice, but from the sheer inability to concentrate his thoughts or to force them along official lines. A policeman or a spy is not an inducement to productivity anywhere. "This regime of bandits and murderers," Bartók called the Nazis, and he joined his German, Austrian, and many other colleagues in exile.

SOVIET CULTURE

In the Soviet Union creative individuals had begun to flee the country during the revolution. The Communists demanded that they transfer their devotion from aesthetic work to communism. The standards set by the leadership in the Communist party have remained the same throughout the history of the regime. Since the death of Stalin in 1953 there has been some public discussion of loosening control, but the party line continues to be what the Central Committee of the All-Union Communist Party set in 1946.

> The task of Soviet literature [it declared] is to aid the state to educate the youth correctly and to meet their demands, to rear a new generation strong and vigorous, believing in their cause, fearing no obstacles and ready to overcome all obstacles.
>
> Consequently any preaching of ideological neutrality, of political neutrality, of "art for art's sake" is alien to Soviet literature and harmful to the interests of the Soviet people and the Soviet state.

Every author, in his creative writing, had to follow the party line, and if he failed he was denounced in such terms as the following:

> The thoroughly putrid and corrupt socio-political and literary physiognomy of Zoshchenko [Zhdanov, a member of the Politburo, declared in 1946, in speaking to the First All-Russian Union Congress of Soviet Writers about one of the most popular Russian writers at the time] was not formed in the most recent period. . . . If Zoshchenko does not like Soviet ways, what is your command: to adjust ourselves to Zoshchenko? It is not for us to reform our tastes. It is not for us to reform our life and our social order according to Zoshchenko. Let him reform. But he does not want to reform. Let him get out of Soviet literature. In Soviet literature there can be no place for putrid, empty, vulgar, and ideologically indifferent works.

The one standard set was that of "socialist realism," a standard which restricted literature and all other forms of aesthetic creativeness to the repetition of stereotypes. The plot in the novel, for example, had to be about a young man struggling to be a good Stakhanovite. He overcomes the indifference, laziness, or criminal capitalistic behavior of his superiors; he marries a heroic young woman of comparable energy; they bear many little Stalins; and they are devoted to the Communist regime. In art one had to do paintings which encouraged work for communism. As a subject a fine athletic type of worker, male or female, was especially favored. After one turned out a story or a painting like this, one was compelled to begin over again. This linoleum-factory procedure soon palled upon original minds, and the government had severely to rebuke the writers for not being creative. A few heads rolled, and the cycle was renewed.

Although the Soviet Union had in Dmitri Shostakovich, Sergei Prokofiev, and Aram Khachaturian some of the ablest contemporary composers, the government has repeatedly condemned them for failure to produce music in the manner of socialist realism. In 1948 they and others of lesser note were forced publicly to acknowledge their errors and to reform. Shostakovich's confession read in part as follows:

> When we look back on the road over which our art has travelled, it is entirely clear to us that every time the Party has corrected the mistakes of this or that artist, pointed to deviations in his creative work, or condemned severely certain tendencies in Soviet art, it has always benefited all Soviet art as well as the work of individual artists.

He had been so criticized in 1936 and thought that he had overcome "the vicious traits to which *Pravda* had pointed: the complexity of musical language, the complexity of musical thinking, the anti-esthetic tendency, and so on." Instead, he acknowledged that he had again "swerved to the side of formalism" and had spoken "in a language incomprehensible to the people." "I shall," he promised, "labor still more stubbornly on the musical incarnation of models of heroic Soviet people."

The mistake of the composers, writers, and artists from the Soviet point of view lay in the inclination to devote themselves to their own subjects, to become interested in what the Communists denounced as the "formal" aspects of music and art rather than in the use of their medium for the spread of communism. These artists sought to live in the Soviet Union as persons in their fields did in free countries. The international character of creative work was so decided—the drive, irrespective of country or type of regime, to express things in music, art, or literature in the same general way so powerful—that the Communists, like the Nazis, were forced not merely to isolate their own artists from those abroad but to whip them back into line. In his long speech of 1946 Zhdanov warned particularly against the enticements of bourgeois culture. He declared:

> However outwardly beautiful the form that clothes the creative work of the fashionable contemporary bourgeois West-European and American writers, and also film and theatrical producers, still they can neither redeem nor lift up their bourgeois culture. That culture is putrid and baneful in its moral foundations. It has been put at the service of private capitalist property, at the service of the egoistic and selfish interests of the highest stratum of bourgeois society. The entire host of bourgeois writers, of film and theatrical producers, is striving to divert the attention of the advanced strata of society from acute questions of the political and social struggle and to shift attention into the channel of vulgar and

ideologically empty literature and art, crowded with gangsters, chorus girls, praise of adultery, and the affairs of adventurers and rogues of every kind.[24]

The successors to Stalin have slightly relaxed the control and allowed some free discussion and some contact with persons in the free world; but as late as 1956 young Soviet writers had never heard of Freud.

Since Europe has suffered so much from the blight of dictatorial rule during this half century, one marvels that the spirit has continued to be aesthetically creative. An explanation may possibly be found in the stimulating experience of this period of cultural change. Individuals, who in a quiet time would never have thought of rising above the commonplace, were stirred to self-expression by the novel events in their lives. The person able to remain securely in a groove was rare. Industrialism, war, revolution, and the accompanying social changes stirred everyone to thought about those basic questions of life which are the enduring subjects of music, art, and literature. In seeking answers the individual turned to sharing his thoughts and feelings with others. The result has been and continues to be one of the most creative periods in history. The subjects treated and the forms used have broadened to include everything and anything. The creative person has thereby often lost contact with much of the public; but he has found, as one would expect, some persons who understand his aesthetic expression of their common experience. In spite of the Nazis and the Communists and the other destroyers of freedom and creativeness, in spite of the devastating effects of wars and revolutions, the period may be compared with that of romanticism and of the baroque in the originality and range of its aesthetic achievement.

Suggestions for Further Reading

BARR, ALFRED H., ed. *Masters of Modern Art.* New York: Museum of Modern Art, 1954. Excellent illustrations. Useful brief text.

COUNTS, GEORGE S., and NUCIA LODGE. *The Country of the Blind: The Soviet System of Mind Control.* Boston: Houghton Mifflin Company, 1949. Translation of Soviet statements with introductory remarks by the editors. Revealing.

"Existentialism." *Yale French Studies,* No. 1. New Haven, Conn.: Yale University Press, 1948. Essays by several scholars. Emphasis on Sartre.

LEMAITRE, GEORGES. *From Cubism to Surrealism in French Literature.* Cambridge, Mass.: Harvard University Press, 1941. Full of insight. The best book with which to start.

MOREUX, SERGE. *Béla Bartók.* London: Harvill Press, Ltd., 1953. The most interesting biography of this composer.

MOTHERWELL, ROBERT, ed. *The Dada Painters and Poets: An Anthology.* New York: Wittenborn, Schultz, Inc., 1951.

[24] George S. Counts and Nucia Lodge, *The Country of the Blind* (Boston: Houghton Mifflin Company, 1949), pp. 81-82, 84-85, 173-175, 95.

PENROSE, ROLAND. *Portrait of Picasso*. New York: Museum of Modern Art, 1957. Photographic biography with brief, excellent text.

SAMUEL, RICHARD, and R. HINTON THOMAS. *Expressionism in German Life, Literature and the Theatre, 1910–1924*. Philadelphia: Dufour Editions, 1939. Invaluable for understanding this century.

SLONIMSKY, NICHOLAS. *Music since 1900*. 3rd. ed. New York: Coleman-Ross Company, Inc., 1949. Useful survey.

STERN, J. P. *Ernst Jünger*. New Haven, Conn.: Yale University Press, 1953. Brief and brilliant. Shows the relation between literature and war in a famous example.

Chapter 28 · Knowledge

TWO EUROPES

Considered from the viewpoint of the character and social role of knowledge, Europe in this century must be divided into two parts, one in which the conditions of the Old Regime persisted and the other in which those of an industrial society were developing. The distinction was not merely geographical; it was cultural as well, for both sets of conditions existed often in the same country, and the differences among many countries were those of degree rather than of kind.

Knowledge under the Old Regime served largely political and religious purposes and, except for decoration and prestige, might be otherwise socially useless. In the professional field knowledge mainly belonged to lawyers, officials, and clerics and was acquired by a small proportion of the population. By contrast, in an industrial society, knowledge has become manifold in its uses and widespread in its social appeal. To the traditional humanistic subjects of study it has added and emphasized the natural sciences, the technical and professional studies, and the social sciences as disciplines which the new society needed. Germany may be regarded as the most industrialized state in Europe and therefore as the one with the closest working relation between knowledge and society; Spain, Portugal, and Poland may be taken as representative of the Old Regime and of the role of knowledge in such a society. Germany, however, included vestiges of the Old Regime and hence of an earlier conception of knowledge, and each of the other states could show a few individuals with a conception of knowledge belonging to the industrial society.

The difference in point of view toward knowledge resulted from the fact that in certain countries modern industrialism had transformed the social structure to a great extent, whereas in others it had scarcely obtained a foothold. One thinks of Great Britain with its many Nobel Prize winners in science, and Greece with scarcely an efficient chemistry laboratory in the entire state. Nationalism acted as a stimulus for acquiring practical knowledge, but wherever industrialism was backward the population could not afford trained services and the vast majority of the society was either indifferent to them or unable politically to exert the influence necessary to assure their use. In Poland and Romania, to choose two examples, intellectuals tended to be footlose, to feel themselves superior to the common run of mankind, to be verbose and socially irresponsible; but some, particularly in the natural sciences and the social sciences, undertook studies of the living conditions of the peasantry, of nutrition, housing, landholding, and comparable problems, with a view to improving the lot of this numerous class. Since their countries remained backward politically and economically, these reformers were isolated and uninfluential, mere harbingers of possible changes to come.

Only a Germany or a Sweden with an advanced material culture could recognize the social advantages of knowledge and supply extensive support for its activities. Size of territory or population did not necessarily affect the attitude toward knowledge. In countries like Switzerland and the small states of Northern Europe, persons of ability often chose a career of scholarship as offering far more attraction than one in politics or business. Presented with a choice of becoming president or prime minister of a state of 4 to 10 million people or of acquiring international prestige in physics or history or economics, many persons preferred the latter. In large countries like Great Britain, France, and Germany the preference often lay in the other direction, but the choice of personnel was so much greater that these nations were able to produce individuals of distinction in all fields.

SCIENCE

Even though the humanities have remained essential, the role played by knowledge in industrial society may best be illustrated by the physical and social sciences. These have grown up under industrialism and may be called its major intellectual achievement. As physical science began to transform society, problems were created for which answers had to be sought by the elaboration of the social sciences. The process of transformation, well under way in the nineteenth century, did not involve all aspects of life until the present century, when the ideal of scientific humanism became a potent reality.

Fundamental to science has been the love of research for its own sake, the right of the explorer to follow his own intellectual interests without consideration of practical application of his findings or material reward. The individual scientist working in isolation with one or two assistants was both in the previous century and earlier, the creator of new knowledge. And thinking is still an individual act; thus scientific discoveries of major importance are associated with brilliant individuals.

To supplement and speed up the achievements of single individuals the dimensions of scientific research have in this century profoundly changed. A revolution in the organization of research has taken place. The universities, some of which have been the centers of research for well over a century, have greatly expanded their facilities. As the value of science in industry and agriculture has won increasing recognition, business organizations and the government have established laboratories for research, which in size and scientific significance often equal or surpass these in the universities. All have learned to cooperate closely; but business and governmental laboratories, although far from ignoring basic theoretical explorations, have tended to work on specific practical problems. They can soon tell from application whether a new formula will succeed, whether it is simple and economical. They locate on-the-job problems that require further research, and turn their scientists in pursuit of a solution.

The combination of theory and practice has characterized the relation between science and technology in the history of the West, but not until the present century has it received extensive application in business to lay the foundation for the entirely new society of industrialism. The single research genius with his more or less accidental discoveries has become an increasingly rare phenomenon. The body of scientific knowledge in any one field has grown to such dimensions that individuals have had to become specialists. Once they are so specialized, the direction of research has been left to the few with the necessary knowledge, imagination, and administrative skill. Equipment and materials have in many fields become so expensive that only the large corporations or governments are able to afford them and to pay the necessary scientific personnel. Scientific research has come to be guided by a plan of action.

The demands on the government in scientific work have grown with the increasing complexity of society and the public expectation of state aid for improving the conditions of living. The idea that government should do little beyond preserving the peace has been supplanted by the view that public action is required wherever it may benefit society. Governments have become major research organizations, setting up bureaux of standards to test inventions, turning out scientific information of value to businessmen unable to maintain large research units of their own, experimenting with seeds, plants, and animals for the benefit of the agriculturalists, exploring the area of diseases of plants, animals, and human beings for the purpose of finding preventives or remedies, and assuming responsibility for public health. And there is no limit to be seen to these increasing scientific duties of the state.

War and Science

The effect of World War I upon science during this century is disputed. Some assert that this terrible conflict stopped all basic research and forced scientists into the immediate tasks presented by war. The result was, so the argument runs, that a great deal of time and energy was lost and considerable money expended in the exploitation of existing scientific capital for destruction, without a corresponding advance in basic, or theoretical knowledge. The example of the airplane was used to substantiate the argument. Since this machine was essential for the successful conduct of the war, one would have expected every effort during the conflict to improve its efficiency. If the rate of speed of which it was capable is taken as a standard, the airplane showed almost no wartime improvement. Between 1909 and 1913 the winning speed in the Gordon-Bennett race increased from 45 miles per hour to 123 miles per hour. When the races were resumed after the war in 1919, the winning speed was merely 124 miles per hour; that is, the machine in this crucial respect remained about the same as that of 1913. Once the rush of production of the war years was over and scientists could plan and execute a long-range program of research with sufficient staff, they quickly increased the speed of the plane, to 164 miles per hour in 1921, 195 miles per hour in 1923, and 328 miles per hour in 1928. The airplane was well on the way to achieve its present ability to move faster than sound.

Critics of the argument acknowledged that the war was not conducive to fundamental research and that it did waste vast resources of money, material, and intelligence; but they added that it nonetheless afforded to scientists the unique opportunity to test in action the validity of their ideas, that it enabled them to develop instruments and methods which in ordinary times they would have lacked for years. When theories could not stand the pressure of war requirements they were quickly discarded; thinking about the relation of theory to practice was greatly accelerated, even if along restricted lines, and the ground was cleared of disproved hypothesis and outmoded instruments and methods. Once the war was past, the basic scientific research could be greatly accelerated. The outstanding example was the invention by the German chemist Fritz Haber during the first years of World War I of a method for extracting nitrogen from the air, an achievement of prime significance for further research, even though it meant the addition merely of technological, not of basic, knowledge. Haber's further development of chlorine as a gas to be used in warfare and of a gas mask against it may be considered on a lower scientific level, perhaps indicating an abuse of the scientist's ability.

It is difficult to draw hard and fast conclusions about the complicated relation of science and World War I. In fields like chemistry and physics, where extensive theoretical research must precede practical application, the relation may not have been fruitful. In areas like medicine, surgery, and public health, research went forward rapidly in tending sick and wounded. Doctors found it indispensable to develop new techniques of surgery, new methods of treatment, and new means of combating disease in their day-to-day work. Dietary research was similarly advanced. Psychiatry as a science first became recognized during World War I, when studies of mental ailments, indiscriminately called shell shock, systematically began to be made. On the other hand, with some notable exceptions, the major improvements in medical science have come, not from medical men, but from chemists, bacteriologists, and physiologists, whose work was not furthered by the war.

The story of science in World War II is similar to that in the preceding war, except that science gained far more attention and contributed far more toward the outcome. By the 1940's it was widely recognized, at least in theory, that the strength of a country in peace or war depended upon the extent and quality of its scientific knowledge and its technical ability to apply that knowledge. The mobilization of skilled personnel, which had scarcely begun during World War I, was immediately and vigorously executed as soon as World War II began. A roster was drawn up, research work was organized on a national and an inter-Allied basis, and research projects were screened by a central agency and allocated to the most suitable personnel in universities, industries, or other private organizations. The government often built new laboratories, equipping them with staff drawn from the entire country.

The part which individual genius and group cooperation, pure research, and practical application have played in the development of a science may be seen in the field of physics. When in 1951 an American expert in this science reviewed the "principal groups of ideas that form the core" of his subject, he named Albert Einstein's theory of relativity, Max Planck's theory of quantum mechanics, and the idea of the atomic particle developed by a number of scientists, among whom Lord Ernest Rutherford was most prominent. Each one of these ideas had a long background of scientific thought, and each influenced not merely its own but many other fields of science.[1]

Achievement in Physics

In Einstein's achievement two conclusions were particularly significant. One was the dependence of mass on velocity. Einstein revealed that the mass must increase as a particle was set in motion, and that the energy of a particle consisted of an energy of rest and one of motion. The second and probably more important conclusion was the equivalence of mass and energy, which upset the accepted view of nineteenth-century physics that energy and mass are two different entities; it showed that they are different aspects of the same thing. Each can be transformed into the other with only the sum remaining constant.

> This equivalence [an American physicist has written] has been accepted by physicists for years, but its really striking demonstration came about through the release of nuclear energy. When an atom of uranium divides into two parts, the two parts together are not so heavy as the one from which they originally came. Mass is not conserved. The vanishing mass has been transformed into energy

[1] W. V. Houston, and others, "Description of the Physical World," in *The Scientists Look at Our World* (Philadelphia: University of Pennsylvania Press, 1952), p. 8.

which is available to be used in a variety of ways. The development of atomic bombs and of other methods of using nuclear energy is the ultimate application of this law, which comes from Einstein's theory of relativity.[2]

The theoretical basis for quantum mechanics was laid in 1900 by Planck, who regarded radiation as given forth in units of energy which he called *quanta*. Subsequent research showed the usefulness of this idea. Both light and electrons, for example, were found apparently to be sometimes particles and sometimes waves, not two distinct things, but two different ways of looking at the same thing. Working with this theory, Niels Bohr introduced the principle of discontinuity in physics. He explained the Newtonian principle of continuity as derived from the study of bodies of a size comparable to that of man. When small particles like electrons were investigated, Bohr learned that they did not conform to a law derived from studying large bodies, that change was in them discontinuous. Heisenberg added the principle of indeterminism. He

pointed out that as a matter of experimental fact, if one tries to measure the position of an electron by any known means, the act of measurement will so interfere with the electron's motion as to invalidate any previous knowledge of its velocity. He showed that it is impossible ever to find out, at the same time, both the position and the momentum of a particle with unlimited accuracy. Certainly one of the characteristic properties of a particle is that it be somewhere and that it move from one place to another by passing through a series of intermediate points. But Heisenberg's analysis indicated that such a statement has really very little significance, since it is never possible to know where a particle is at the same time that one knows how rapidly it is moving.

In spite of these uncertainties, quantum mechanics

has provided a theoretical understanding of the properties of molecules, of the nature of the light emitted by atomic systems, and has permitted a beginning of a detailed understanding of the physical properties of solids, in terms of the electrons and atomic nuclei of which they are composed,[3]

and it has aided in the research in nuclear physics.

The idea of the atomic particle is associated with the subdivision of the atom into electrons and protons, neutrons, positive electrons, neutrinos, various kinds of mesotrons, and a possibly unlimited variety of things referred to as particles. Studies of these have introduced

a kind of nuclear chemistry. Different kinds of nuclei can be combined to give still others. Some reactions take place easily, some with difficulty. Some give off energy, while energy must be added to others to make them go. A general survey of the nuclei shows that those of the lighter elements will combine with a release of energy. The remaining mass is less than the mass originally present in the constituent particles. The heavy elements will not combine in this way, for the mass of the combined nucleus will be greater than of the constituents; and this extra mass must be provided in the form of energy. A corollary, however,

[2] *Ibid.*, p. 12. [3] *Ibid.*, pp. 20-21.

is that heavy elements should tend to break up into lighter ones, and many of them do. Radium, polonium, and others decay radio-actively, and many others break up when appropriately stimulated. As everyone knows nowadays, uranium 235 breaks up into two approximately equal fragments when it is set off by collision with a slow neutron. This reaction has become famous, not only because of the amount of energy released, but because the reaction itself produces enough neutrons to stimulate fission in other atoms, and the process goes into a chain reaction.[4]

This is the scientific basis for the release of atomic energy and the making of the atomic bomb.

The history of the work on nuclear fission must be carried back at least to 1896, when the Frenchman Becquerel discovered radioactivity. The main steps from that beginning to the final success have been described by a historian of science as follows:

The radioactivity of the heavy elements was recognized to be a case of spontaneous atomic change by Rutherford and Soddy in 1902, and the first case of an artificial atomic transmutation was discovered by Rutherford in 1919, when he bombarded nitrogen with alpha particles and produced fast moving protons. From 1921 to 1924 Rutherford and Chadwick produced protons from all the elements up to calcium by alpha-ray bombardment, except in the cases of the stable elements, helium, carbon, and oxygen, which had atomic weights that were multiples of four. Blackett in 1925 showed that heavier elements were produced by this process, oxygen as well as hydrogen nuclei being formed when nitrogen was bombarded by alpha particles.

Besides alpha particles, the bombardment of atoms with other particles was investigated. In 1932 Cockcroft and Walton accelerated protons to high energies and bombarded lithium with them, producing two helium nuclei. In the following year Lawrence and Livingston developed the cyclotron for speeding up charged particles, and with it studied the effects produced by bombardments with heavy hydrogen nuclei, or deutrons, consisting of a proton and a neutron. After the discovery of the neutron in 1932, the effect of neutron bombardment was studied, notably by Fermi, then at Rome. He found that neutrons slowed down by transit through substances containing much hydrogen, such as paraffin wax or water, were particularly effective in bringing about nuclear reactions. Upon bombarding uranium with neutrons, Fermi obtained in 1934 another radioactive element which he presumed to be heavier than uranium. This work was taken up by Hahn at Berlin who by 1937 had claimed the preparation of several transuranic elements with atomic numbers ranging from 93 to 96. However, the Joliot-Curies at Paris in 1938 pointed out that the radioactive characteristics of the substances produced by bombarding uranium with neutrons resembled those of much lighter radioactive elements, notably radio-lanthanum. Examining the matter afresh, Hahn and Meitner in 1939 found that lanthanum and other elements of moderate atomic weight, were produced by the bombardment of uranium, indicating that the uranium nucleus had split into two. The high packing fraction of uranium suggested that much energy would be produced through the loss of mass when the uranium nucleus split into lighter fragments,

[4] *Ibid.*, pp. 16-17.

whilst the high ratio of the mass number to the nuclear charge of uranium pointed to the probable release of several neutrons during the process. Joliot-Curie in 1939 showed that neutrons were given out by disintegrating uranium, so that the fission of one uranium nucleus would bring about the break-up of others in the vicinity under suitable circumstances. Such circumstances could be controlled, as in the atomic pile, or uncontrolled, as in the atomic bomb. Fermi, now at Chicago, set up the first atomic pile in 1942, and others in America by 1945 had produced the bomb.[5]

Nuclear Research—World War II

The successful culmination of the long period of research occurred in the three centers, Chicago, Oak Ridge, Tennessee, and Los Alamos, New Mexico, where scientists from many countries, some of them refugees from nazism and fascism, came together in cooperative enterprise. Nuclear fission had a legitimate, purely scientific background; but it was evoked by political need in war. The achievement by this group of scientists has been used by Vannevar Bush, director of the scientific research for the war effort in the United States, as an example of the efficiency of democracy:

> The atomic-energy program during the war was to the *n*th degree the sort of collaborative program that was impossible at that speed outside democracy. It was not merely a matter of new physics and its incidental application—very far from it. True, some of the finest theory and experiment in the physics of the atom was involved, calling for ingenuity and resourcefulness, mathematics of a higher order, and judgment such as can be exercised only by men who are utter masters of their craft, and all this was performed magnificently by the physicists of this country [including refugees from Germany, Italy, Austria, and Hungary], England, and Canada, in close interchange and at unprecedented speed as the program of application proceeded. But then came the heaviest part of the job. It involved new, dangerous, and complex chemistry, the most refined sort of chemical engineering, industrial organization that tied together effectively the performance of ten thousand firms which supplied parts, built new and unheard-of devices, constructed and operated enormous plants where the whole affair functioned as an interlocked unit. It involved the joint action of diverse groups, theorists, engineers, instrumentalists, designers, in the production of fissionable materials and in the construction of the bomb itself. It involved management that reached a new order of functioning to bring all these elements together in an intense race against time, where nerves were bound to be frayed and patience short. It involved collaboration between military and civilian organizations, with their widely different approaches to organizational rules and systems. It required integration of new elements into the strange structure of government and competition with other programs of highest priority in the maelstrom of war.[6]

[5] Stephen S. Mason, *Main Currents of Scientific Thought: A History of the Sciences*, pp. 455-456. Reprinted by permission of Abelard-Schuman Limited. Copyright, 1956.

[6] Vannevar Bush, *Modern Arms and Free Men* (New York: Simon & Schuster, Inc., 1949), pp. 86-87.

The result was, as a British statesman has said, that "in four years our scientists have solved a problem that in peace might have taken twenty-five to fifty years."

Although the three main ideas, Einstein's theory of relativity, Planck's theory of quantum mechanics, and the theory of the atomic particle, pertain primarily to physics, they and the research connected with them have all influenced profoundly other fields of science and of thought. Nuclear fission is already opening up new research in physiology, geology, biology, chemistry, agriculture, and all the other fields of science. In addition, it is revolutionizing the generation of power and the character of technology to far greater extent than did the introduction of the steam engine and the use of coal and iron. Discoveries in other fields, like that of penicillin and the sulfa drugs, could be added to the list of nodal results of research; but discoveries in physics have dominated public attention. The physicists have done more than any other scientists to change our conception of the universe and to shock us into appreciating the impact of science on society. Their work belongs to this century not merely in point of time but in point of cultural setting. Without the precision instruments which industrialism has made possible, the research necessary to confirm, develop, and apply their ideas could not have been executed.

The indirect effects of war upon science have been twofold. War has enhanced its prestige and more or less acquainted millions of men with its workings, and war has augumented the appreciation of the value of science in the economy. The soldier respected his gun, a machine made by other machines, as the means of preserving his life. He often learned something about a motor car and a radio, and he could use this knowledge subsequently in private life. Wherever he turned, especially in World War II, he found science and engineering vital to the outcome.

In the same way industry began through the demands of war to adjust its methods and organization to the realities of science. Production of the huge quantities of armaments and other materials for war brought about changes in small and in big industry:

> Hundreds of shops in which high-speed tool-steel was little more than a name [a historian of mechanical engineering has written about the effects of World War I] began to use it regularly. Many automatic machines, and especially millers and grinders, crept into small and obscure engineering works and came to be regarded as essential elements of equipment. The use of jigs for machining or drilling objects of awkward shape, and of gauges for the production of interchangeable parts, spread to an enormous extent under the stress of military necessity.[7]

In a similar way World War II brought the general adoption by industry of many advanced discoveries in science and technology made during the preceding two decades of peace.

[7] Edward Cressy, *A Hundred Years of Mechanical Engineering* (New York: The Macmillan Company, 1937), p. 212.

Of particular significance among these was the use of tungsten carbide in the manufacture of cutting tools. Introduced in 1926, it and its subsequently developed variants enabled cutting speed to be increased six- or sevenfold, to the great gain in industrial potential. Automatic machines like the lathe and the die caster and the photoelectric cell for grading, testing, and measuring objects also furthered mass production. In many industrial lines the owners found it advisable to amalgamate small firms into one large company, which for the first time could afford the funds for integrating scientific research into the business. The combination of war and science was guiding industry in the direction of big-scale enterprise which would further the utilization of science for both war and peace.

Out of the experience of World War II came a method in the application of science which has been entitled "operational research." Although employed by business in peacetime, especially in the United States and Germany,

it arose independently in the war out of immediate ends and developed so rapidly and so effectively that by the end of the war it was considered a necessary adjunct to every aspect of military affairs. At the beginning of the war new and essentially scientific devices, such as radar, were being prepared by the research departments of the services. To hand these over directly to service personnel in the field just would not do. Prejudice against new gadgets and unfamiliarity with their handling was combined often enough with practical unsuitability of the apparatus, which had been designed by people of great scientific competence but with little knowledge of the physical and human factors that occurred under service conditions. To remedy this state of affairs, some of the actual scientists who had been concerned with the development were sent out to stations to supervise the use of the new apparatus. What might have been a mere servicing job grew into something much more important. For the first time immediate, personal liaison was effected between the scientists and the soldier, and the mutual education that grew out of it made the acceptance of further developments far easier.

But it did more than this. The scientists in the field began to study the practical performance of their devices, and this study took on an increasingly quantitative and statistical aspect. From this study they began to deduce what were the real requirements of the devices as distinct from what they had been imagined to be by the military staffs, and this led at once to new directions in development. But the reciprocal process was also at work. Scientists began to see what the operational possibilities which they either knew or could devise were likely to be, and they began to influence operations in relation to these possibilities. As a very distinguished soldier said at the end of the war, 'At the beginning tactics determined weapons; at the end of the war weapons determined tactics.'[8]

[8] J. D. Bernal, *The Freedom of Necessity* (London: Routledge & Kegan Paul, 1949), pp. 295-296.

GOVERNMENT AID TO RESEARCH

The experience of war emphasized the necessity for a country to cultivate the sciences in order to remain a sovereign power. Germany's strength lay not merely in her territorial and demographic size but above all in the use of science in technology and the great preponderance of, or even near monopoly in, certain industrial lines dependent on science. German research, which had been famous for a century, received new aids with the establishment in 1911 of the Kaiser Wilhelm Society for the Furtherance of Knowledge. The society began with two hundred private sponsoring members providing the endowment. Its general aim had been stated in the previous year by the distinguished theologian, Adolf von Harnack, who was later its president (from 1911 until his death in 1930). "Armed defense and science," he declared, "are the two strong pillars to support the greatness of Germany, the care of which must never cease or stand still." The society was organized into three sections, biology and medicine, physics and chemistry, and the humanities. It built research institutes for able scholars according to need and supplied the funds for equipment and staff. Some institutes were located in Berlin, others at various places in Germany wherever an outstanding individual was found to direct the research.

Among the personnel of the society were to be found some of the most brilliant scientists of the world, Planck the physicist, Einstein, Haber the chemist. The scholars did pure research and worked closely with industry and the government in solving practical problems. Their achievements were so valuable to the country that in spite of Germany's poor economic condition after her defeat in World War I, the scientists continued to receive full financial support. By 1930 the society had 700 financial sponsors, including businessmen, central and local governments, and trade-unions. Since German military power was gone, every effort was made to maintain Germany's scientific superiority. Although the sponsors did not spend much larger amounts on science than did the other free countries of Europe —possibly half again as much as Great Britain—they were better organized to exploit scientific discoveries.

Great Britain, supposedly a well-industrialized state, discovered to her dismay in World War I that she lacked, for example, an optical-goods industry, that she was far behind in the chemical and pharmaceutical industries, and that she was deficient in many lines of the machine-tool industry. Even so, exclusive of Germany, she was much better equipped than any other European country. The British government soon aided the training of experts, especially in optics and chemistry, and took the opportunity of the war and the defeat of the enemy to seize German patents and start its own competitive industries. In 1914 the British government organized the Medical Research Council. In 1917 it formed the Department of Scientific and Industrial Research, and a few years later it set up other research councils, all devoted mainly to the aid of industry, agriculture, and medicine. Nonetheless, the British continued to be slow in financial support of scientific research. Just prior to the outbreak of World War II, almost two decades after the need for large-scale financial assistance had become apparent, the British government, industries, and universities were spending between £5,700,000 and £8,700,000 a year on research, the United States about £47,000,000, that is, from one tenth to two tenths of 1 per cent of their national income, as against, in the United States, between two tenths and five tenths of 1 per cent. Great Britain was responsible for almost all the scientific research for her empire of 500,000,000 people; yet she was devoting less than one fifth as much for research as the United States for its 150,000,000 inhabitants.

In France the situation was even worse. The government did not create a department of scientific research for fifteen years after World War I, and French industry spent very small sums for such activity. The enormous loss of students during the war—80 per cent of those enrolled at the École Normale at the outbreak of the war and 90 per cent of those at the École Polytecnique were killed—deprived the country of almost a generation of scientists, and many professors fell behind in their scientific work and even rejected such discoveries as quantum physics. When after the war the French nation revived politically and economically, its businessmen preferred to buy rights to use foreign patents rather than to support research in their own country. This condition lasted until the arrival of the Nazis to power in Germany. In that year the French government created a Council of Scientific Research, arguing that "disinterested researches in pure science are the source of all progress in human affairs" and that "apart from motives of idealism and prestige it is of practical importance to discover those capable of scientific research." In 1935 a national fund for scientific research was established, and the Popular Front government appointed Madame Irene Curie-Joliot as undersecretary of state for scientific research, built laboratories for the Joliot-Curies' research in nuclear fission, and granted a large number of scholarships. At the end of the 1930's, however, France was still spending on scientific research probably less than one half the small amount put forth by the British.

World War II marked the turning point in the appreciation of science. France could not participate during the war because of her defeat and occupation by the Germans; but, except for Germany, where Hitler held science in low esteem, the other countries went to work with realities in mind. Between 1936–1937 and 1950–1951 the British government increased the funds for military research and development sixty-sevenfold, those for industrial research tenfold, those in medicine ninefold, and those in agriculture eightfold. Government expenditure on the universities, centers of the most fundamental scientific research, increased nearly sixfold. During the war the Nazis seized scientific equipment in conquered countries and transferred it to Germany. They had less interest in foreign scientists, since they considered their own to be superior. After the Allied victory, both the Soviet Union and the free countries of the West gained control of German scientists and scientific secrets as fast as they could, each side in competition with the other. Each kept German scientists and used them in research. The Soviet Union has retained those of value to her whom she was able to capture; the Western countries have allowed their captives to return home. Experts on nuclear fission and rockets and guided missiles were at a premium, but those in numerous other lines of science were also sought.

Higher Education

The increased role of science and of other branches of knowledge in national power brought up the question of finding and training an increased personnel. European higher education continued in this century to be organized for the elite. Of the great powers, Germany trained the largest number, but, in spite of her intellectual leadership, she retained the practice from her preindustrial period of excluding the peasantry and the workers almost entirely from the universities. The following table may indicate the extent to which the countries enabled the intellectual ability of their young people in all fields of knowledge to be cultivated.

COUNTRY	NUMBER OF STUDENTS (FULL-TIME)	ESTIMATED NUMBER OF YOUNG MEN AND WOMEN AGED 19-21 AS NEARLY AS POSSIBLE AT THE SAME TIME	PERCENTAGE
England and Wales	40,465 (1936)	2,100,000	1.9
Scotland	10,064 (1936)	260,000	3.8
Germany	116,154 (1932)	3,000,000	3.9
Germany	67,082 (1936)	3,000,000	2.2
France	82,655 (1932)	1,900,000	4.3
U.S.S.R.	524,800 (1936)	10,000,000	5.2
U.S.A.	989,757 (1932)	6,600,000	15.0

SOURCE: J. D. Bernal, *The Social Function of Science* (New York: The Macmillan Company, 1939, p. 198).

The percentage of students among those between the ages of nineteen and twenty-one was especially low for England and Wales and especially high for the United States. Continental countries neglected higher education for their young to an extent out of keeping with the current need for knowledge. The industrial countries, large and small, produced many Nobel prize winners in the sciences. They evolved the fundamental theories and in that respect were ahead of the United States; but, except to a considerable extent in Germany, they lacked the second-, third-, and fourth-line personnel for enabling science to permeate their society. Although in this area the United States was strong, World War II revealed deficiencies in scientific personnel in this country as well as in every continental state.

SCIENCE AND SOCIAL AND POLITICAL LIFE

It has been asserted that "science by itself is neither good nor evil and that the effect of science upon humanity depends wholly on the way in which we make use of the power given to us." [9] The airplane and atomic energy are cited as examples of the destructive as well as the constructive potential of this branch of knowledge. Although the statement is in many respects true, one may argue that scientific discoveries have to a degree shaped political and economic organizations to their needs. The evidence may be gathered from any branch of the subject. Electricity is a force in nature, but it was brought into the service of society by science. Efficient utilization of it requires regional and international organization of supply and distribution. Science has begun here to adjust political society to its own demands.

Chemistry permeates our lives to such an extent that this may be called a chemical age. Many foods, clothes, drugs, building materials, and so on, derive from a few basic substances like coal tar, salts, petroleum, and wood, and are structurally interrelated. The chemical industry has patterned its organization after that of its materials.

Two students of the subject have written:

> The complexity of chemical processes, combining possibilities of infinite variations in some directions with the necessity of meticulously exact uniformity in many specific processes, the exceptional importance of joint products and by-products, the large scale of production required to get the most economical results, and the extremely specialized character of plant equipment, all tend to impede competitive adjustments. These factors practically rule out even a passable approach to pure competition in these industries.[10]

The amalgamation of small firms into a few giant ones in each country, primarily in the 1920's—Imperial Chemicals Industries Limited (1926) in Great Britain, I. G. Farben Industries (1925) in Germany, Établissements Kuhlmann in France, Montecatini in Italy—the negotiation of numerous cartel agreements among them and with their American colleagues indicated the tendency of science to lead business organization in the direction of bigness. And it did not stop at the national frontier, for chemistry did not respect national sovereignty. An official of the American firm of

[9] Bart Bok, "Freedom of Science," in *Freedom and Culture* (Paris: UNESCO, 1951), pp. 249-250.

[10] George W. Stocking and Myron W. Watkins, *Cartels in Action* (New York: Twentieth Century Fund, 1946), p. 377, note 26.

E. I. du Pont de Nemours and Company has reported a conversation with Sir Harry McGowan of Imperial Chemicals Industries as follows:

> Sir Harry . . . went on to give me a general picture of what he and Sir Alfred Mond [also of Imperial Chemicals] had in mind in the matter in international agreements. . . . Sir Harry explained that the formation of I.C.I. is only the first step in a comprehensive scheme which he has in mind to rationalize chemical manufacture of the world.

Sir Harry's vision has not been fully realized; but chemical structure, business structure, as nearly as the human factor would permit, were becoming similar.

Science has rendered it increasingly difficult for the small state, no matter how intelligent the population, to maintain its sovereignty. The multiplicity of scientific interests in an age of specialization has necessitated the use of large resources in population, materials, and money, which the small state does not possess. A country like Denmark could produce a Niels Bohr, one of the greatest physicists of this century; but to develop atomic energy has lain beyond its power. In the chemical industry, to choose another example, it could specialize only in certain lines which were parts of an inclusive industry covering several countries or which were subsidiary to a big chemical industry in a big country. Even if it were to train research experts in all branches of chemistry or physics or almost any other science, it would have to place most of them in positions abroad.

Basic research in any field is done by the individuals with the keenest minds, irrespective of race, color, creed, or nationality. A Dutch-American astronomer specializing in the research on the Milky Way System has recorded the main developments in his field during the first half of this century as follows:

> During the first fifteen years of our century, the principal advancements in our knowledge of the structure and motions of the Milky Way were made by the Hollander, Kapteyn, the British, Eddington, the German, Schwarzschild, and the Americans, Pickering, Schlesinger, Campbell and Seares. Methods were developed for the wholesale measurement of stellar brightnesses, spectra, motions and distances, and the first evidence was forthcoming to show that stellar motions were not distributed in a purely random fashion. The period between 1915 and 1920 was that of the American, Shapley, who succeeded in showing that our sun was located far from the center of the system. In the decade that followed, the Swedish astronomer, Lindblad, the Hollander, Oort, the Swedish-American astronomer, Strömberg, and the Canadian, Plaskett, changed our whole outlook upon the motion of stars in our Milky Way System. In 1930 the Swiss-American, Trumpler, building in part upon the earlier work of the German, Wolf, the American, Barnard, and the Swedish astronomer, Schalen, gave proof of the existence of a layer of obscuring matter close to the central plane of our Milky Way System; his results were confirmed and extended by the work of the American trio, Stebbens, Huffer, and Whitford, and by a host of other investigators. Subsequently attention was focused upon the study of the dynamics and evolu-

tion of our Milky Way System, with important contributions by the Indian astronomer, Chandrasekhar, working in America, the Soviet astronomer, Ambarzumian, the American astronomer, Baade, who was born and educated in Germany, and many other astronomers from all over the world.

The story of the astronomers has its counterpart in every field of scientific research.[11]

UN and Research

Many, if not all, of the affiliated agencies of the United Nations, agencies like the World Health Organization, the Food and Agriculture Organization, and the United Nations Educational and Scientific Organization are based upon the fact of the international nature of their problems. For the first time in history an adequate institutional structure has begun to develop which expresses the international character of the subject. The agencies bring together information about the scientific personnel and knowledge of each member country and make it available to every people. They conduct research on their own initiative and execute projects sponsored by member states. They serve as clearing centers, sources of stimulation to activity by individual persons and states, and initiators and executors of projects of an international character.

The value of the organizations in meeting or encouraging others to meet hitherto neglected problems may be clarified by a few examples. For centuries locusts have eaten crops and destroyed lives in Eastern Africa and Southern Asia, but, as long as respect for political sovereignty limited the attack on the pest, nothing was accomplished. When the international agencies affiliated with the United Nations took over the task, they emulated the locust in ignoring political boundaries, and with the aid of science and technology they have begun to eradicate this menace. We have likewise learned that bacteria are devoid of any sense of distinction among class, race, creed, color, or nationality, and that they must be handled on an international basis. Scientific research on typhus or cancer done in India or Ceylon is as significant for us as for the Indians. As Arthur H. Compton of the United States has declared, "scientists are prototypes of world citizens," a fact, adds the astronomer Bok, "brought about by the natural one-worldness of their field." [12] That they are aware of this interest is manifest in the system of international exchange of scientists and students. According to a recent tabulation by UNESCO, nearly 20,000 individual fellowships are available for international exchange, and even though not all of these are intended for scientists, one may assume that a large percentage is used for that purpose. The number is small in comparison with need; but it indicates that Western science has begun to expand to the entire world.

[11] Bok, *loc. cit.*, pp. 252-253.
[12] *Ibid.*, p. 258.

The free world of the West has extended the use of the scientific method to numerous other aspects of life. To test ideas by facts, to request evidence for an assertion, to ask why a thing is as it is and how it works may be regarded as part of our normal behavior. Although we have wandered from that standard, particularly in politics, we may be called essentially science-minded, in the same way that the medieval man may be considered to have been religion-minded. Science, as George Sarton has said, is "revolutionary and heterodox." It is exploratory and experimental, inventive and dynamic. It is revolutionary, not in the sense of seeking to destroy something, but in the sense of wishing to replace that which is by something better.

Modern industrialism may be described as the form of society which has most completely adopted the scientific method in all phases of life, economic (the modern corporation with its research institute), political (the modern state with parliamentary government and competitive political parties), and social (the equality of opportunity irrespective of social position, the numerous private organizations for private and civic purposes, the emphasis upon education). It has sought to follow the example of science in encouraging creative action, whether in the form of business entrepreneurism, of civic initiative by private citizens, of competition among political aspirants, or in many other lines. It has applied the experimental method in the fact-finding and trial-and-error procedure of policy making in business and government. And wherever science has affected the whole way of life, and produced not merely one-sided experts but all-round personalities, it has cultivated the love of freedom.

In recent decades scientists have discovered sources of power which if misused could destroy science and society. They have seen the communistic and the totalitarian enemies of freedom employ all the available knowledge of science for purposes of dictatorial power over the world. They have themselves produced the ingredients of chemical warfare, of germ warfare, and of mass destruction by guided missiles and atomic bombs. Aware of the danger to the survival of mankind when these inventions fall into the hands of fanatics and madmen or ignoramuses, they have begun to discuss the responsibility of the scientist for the results of his own research. The traditional view that the scientist is exclusively a scientist and that for the sake of scientific objectivity he must wash his hands of the use to which his discoveries are put no longer seems to be convincing; for what if the scientist provided the means by which he himself could be destroyed? Should he work on the development of the atomic bomb? If he did, should he seek to exercise control over its use? If he decided in the affirmative, how could he remain a scientist and at the same time enter the field of politics and influence the public about the use of his inventions? At present many suggestions are offered, but no solution appears to have been found. Public enlightenment by the scientists and faith in the good sense of a democracy seem to be the most promising long-run

YVES TANGUY, *Mama, Papa Is Wounded!*, 1927.
A conscious art which employed the symbols of the unconscious, Surrealism rebelled against society and experimented in realms of the marvellous. —The Museum of Modern Art, New York; Purchase Fund.

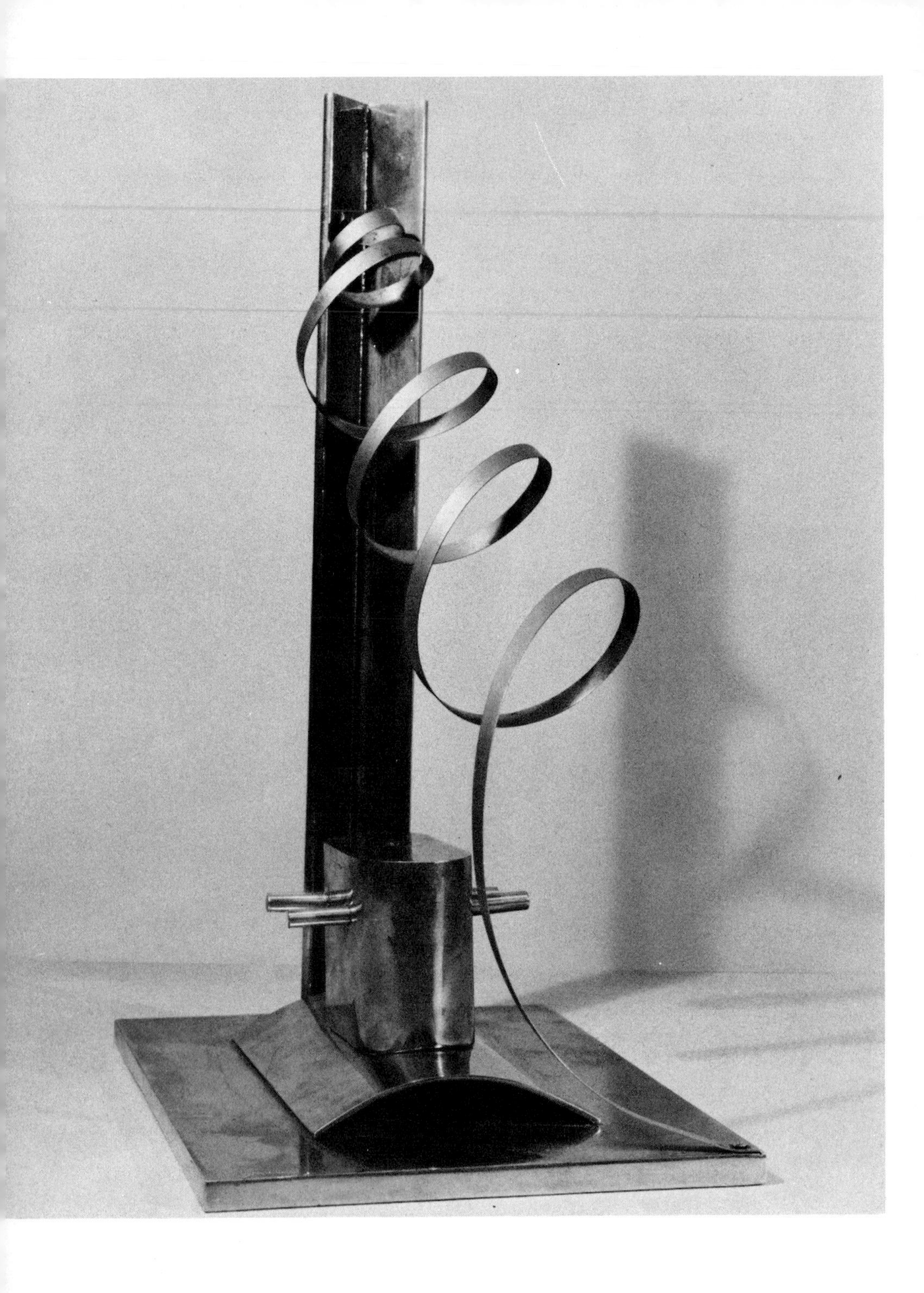

LASZLO MOHOLY-NAGY, *Nickel Construction*, 1921.
Those principles of modern design introduced at the Bauhaus in Germany are evidenced here in a reflection of the enduring geometric qualities of nature. —Gift of Mrs. Sibyl Moholy-Nagy to The Museum of Modern Art, New York.

UMBERTO BOCCIONI, *Unique Forms of Continuity in Space*, 1913.
Futurism: the artistic expression of pure action. —The Museum of Modern Art, New York; acquired through the Lillie P. Bliss Bequest.

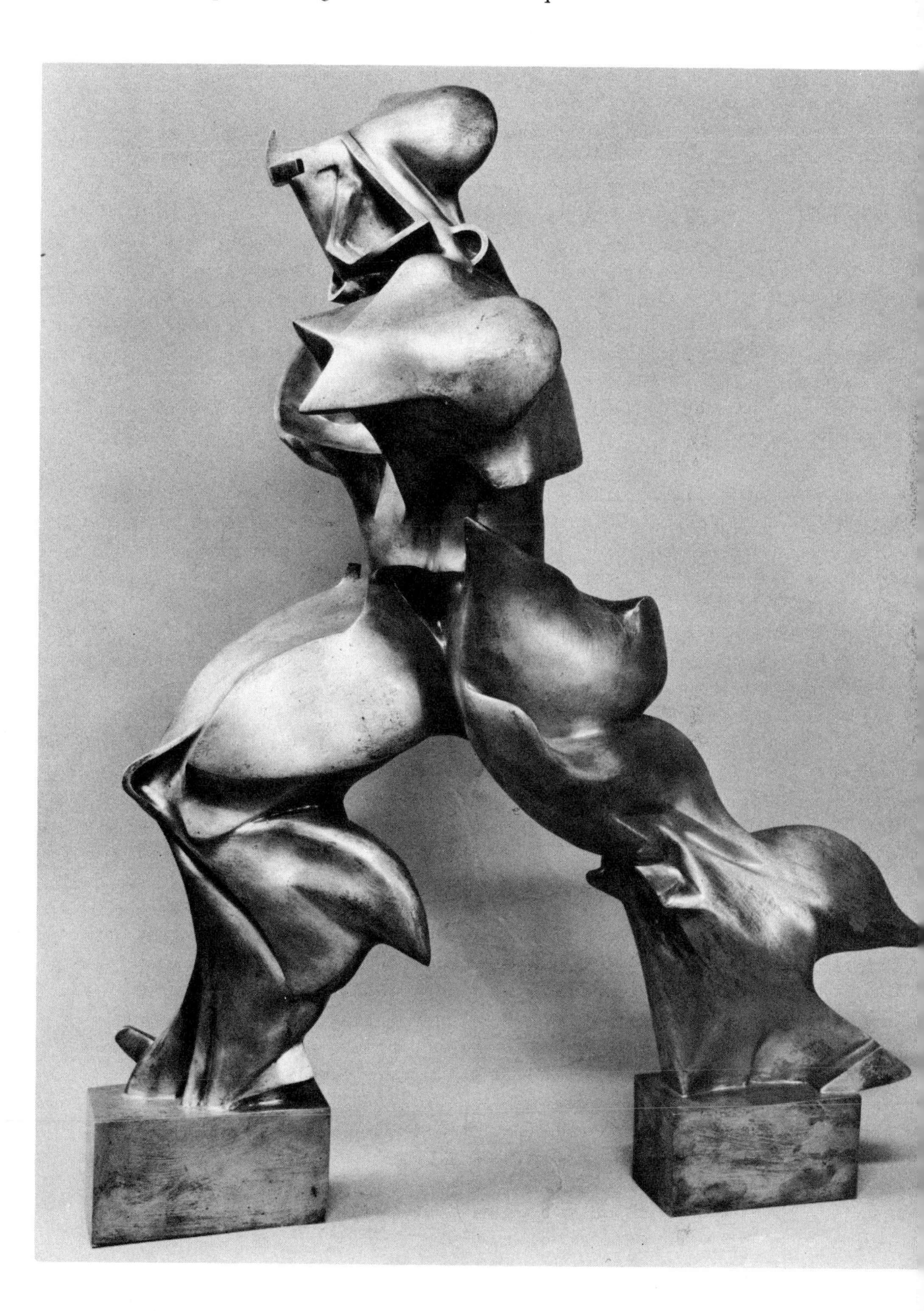

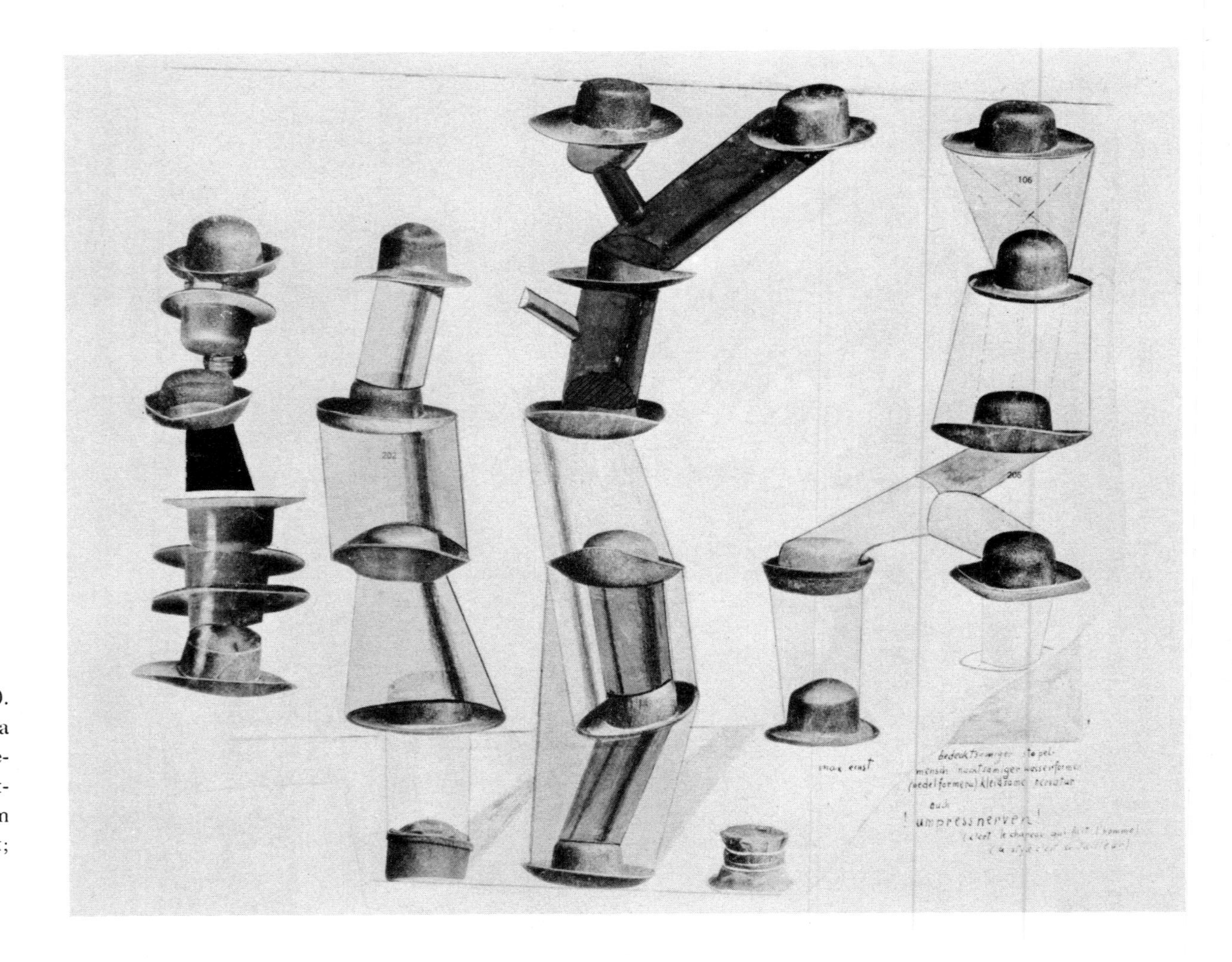

MAX ERNST,
The Hat Makes the Man, 1920.
Dadaism: reflections on a world gone mad, ". . . the despair which refuses to let itself despair." —The Museum of Modern Art, New York; Purchase Fund.

MARC CHAGALL,
Birthday, 1915.
A more personal extension of surrealistic thinking; an art again concerned with particular human emotions. —The Museum of Modern Art, New York; acquired through the Lillie P. Bliss Bequest.

CHAIM SOUTINE, *The Woman in Red,* 1922.
Reality refracted: the artist's expression of his perceptions. —Collection, Dr. and Mrs. Harry Bakwin. By permission of Dr. and Mrs. Bakwin.

HENRI MATISSE, *Piano Lesson*, 1916 or 1917.
Expressionism, enriched through the artist's concentration on form and design.
—The Museum of Modern Art, New York; Mrs. Simon Guggenheim Fund.

PABLO PICASSO, *Three Musicians,* 1921.
Cubism: at one with the age of industry. Its shapes are those of the city, the machine. —The Museum of Modern Art, New York; Mrs. Simon Guggenheim Fund.

means; but the questions whether scientific knowledge has outrun the understanding of the citizen and whether the scientist can do anything to prevent his achievements from being abused to destroy mankind remain unanswered.

PSYCHOANALYSIS AND FREUD

The problem has become acute because the growing strength of the rational forces in this century exemplified in the sciences and technology has been accompanied by the expansion of powerful irrational elements. The transformation of society involved in the spread of industrialism has created uncertainty and insecurity among individuals of all nations. The speed of change enabled many persons to rise in society and to prosper, but it also undermined the security flowing from accepted habits and customs. It exposed the less competent members of society to the vicissitudes of the business cycle, to the rigors of urban living, to frequent change of jobs, to the fickleness of fashions in consumption. Through the emphasis upon material progress and upon advertising to stimulate consumers' appetites, it seemed to place a premium upon personal dissatisfaction. Added to these forces came the play of power politics, culminating in wars and revolutions, the most startling and all-inclusive manifestations of irrationality which society could offer. Communism and totalitarianism made irrational dogmas the basis for social, economic, and political systems which their adherents have tried to impose by coercion upon the entire world. That psychology should become one of the most popular subjects of study in this period exemplifies the attempt of knowledge to keep pace with social needs. The outburst of irrationality has called forth an intellectual means for subjecting this force to scientific control.

The most famous name in the history of recent psychology is that of the Viennese Sigmund Freud. Trained as a physician, Freud found the prevailing materialistic psychology of the last part of the nineteenth century inadequate to explain the mental phenomena with which he as physician had to deal. He began to explore the role of the subconscious as revealed in dreams and concluded from his research that the sex drive was fundamental in motivating human behavior. From this work he developed the new subject of psychoanalysis. Other scientists investigated the area of comparative psychology and established clinics to attack the numerous mental ailments of this industrial war-ridden age. Terms like the libido, inferiority complex, inhibition have moved from psychology into popular usage. Society has gradually added the psychological or the psychiatric point of view to its ways of looking at things. Further research has revealed Freud's overemphasis on biological forces, especially on the role of sex, and has shown the importance of personality structure as a whole and of the social environment in affecting the spiritual and intellectual life. The study of human motivation by way of psychology has enriched every major subject concerned with man.

HISTORICAL POINT OF VIEW

Comparable in popularity as a manner of judging events has been the general acceptance of the historical point of view. Science alone has not succumbed to this treatment, for a scientific formula, a law, a technical invention can be effectively used without any knowledge of its past. In the field of the humanities and the social sciences, in the active work of politics and government, the historical approach has been almost dominant. The German Oswald Spengler in *The Decline of the West* and the Englishman Arnold Toynbee in *A Study of History* have attempted to synthesize all human history. Society in this age of transition has sought to learn from its past the stage at which it has arrived. It has used history to help preserve its cultural heritage.

Confronted with so much experience, historians have varied widely in their interests. Some have concentrated on politics, others on economic aspects of society, others on the history of ideas. The dominant professional thinking has accepted historical relativity, that is, that each age should be judged by its own standards and that the course of past events was inevitable. This approach resulted in so-called objective history and was intended to prevent the abuse of historical knowledge for ulterior purposes. That such abuse has nonetheless occurred is evident from the work of historians in all countries; that of the Germans may be used as an example. At the one extreme, leading German historians before World War I used their subject for political purposes; for example, they concluded, on the basis of studies of earlier periods, that their country would inevitably take over the world position of Great Britain, inherit her empire, and become the dominant world power. At the other extreme, German historians tended to make their subject a branch of aesthetics—one should enjoy the study of Rome for its own sake, just as one would a painting.

Critics have condemned the "objective" approach to history as socially irresponsible, arguing that each age has certain questions on which it needs light from past experience and that the historian should choose subjects for study which will offer this illumination. For example, since ours is an age of cultural transition or crisis, the historian should be interested in similar periods in the past, the transition from the Roman Empire to the Middle Ages. Since ours is a period of wars, the historian should study the conditions of society during past wars. It is difficult, however, to supply historical background from cultures overwhelmingly agrarian and commercial for one predominantly industrial. A society trained by theory and experience in social science wishes historical writing to deal with what seem to it the realities of life. The present tendency therefore appears to be to reject relativity in favor of a rapprochement between history and the social sciences. The historian studies the present in order to choose for research those aspects of the past which can provide perspective upon our industrial age.

SOCIAL SCIENCE

Industrialism and war have affected the social sciences in this century at least as much as they have affected physical science. The complex society of this age, in its effort to learn how to deal with its many novel problems, has greatly elaborated the traditional social disciplines. As the importance of politics in the economy has grown since 1900, economics has increasingly become political economy. The science of the state, as the Germans called it, has become political science. Sociology has shifted emphasis from a historical, theoretical, and classificational approach to the study of current social groups. Anthropology has moved from concentration upon primitive peoples or those in underdeveloped cultures to the inclusion of all peoples. Demography, because it provides essential data about population, has become basic to all other social sciences. Each subject has assumed responsibility for intellectual guidance in a greatly expanded area of activity; each has become functional in its approach to problems; each has attempted to live up to its designation as a social science by applying scientific method to social issues.

The study of politics in modern Europe has usually meant an analysis of the role of the state, a description of governmental organization, and an ethical consideration of state functions. With the emergence of parliamentary government after the French Revolution, other aspects of political life came into view—the nature and role of the political party, the behavior of the citizen in politics, the relation between the legislative branch and the executive and judicial branches of government, the conduct and significance of elections—in fact all those aspects which concern, not the legal and theoretical aspects of the state, but popular participation in government. The change should not be overemphasized, however, for except in Great Britain, France, and a few small states, parliamentary government had a retarded growth. In most countries political life continues to be studied as a science of the state. Germany, for instance, did not begin to develop a modern political science until the Weimar Republic, and there and elsewhere the dictatorial regimes cast a blight upon the subject. Even in the free countries where the experience of war aroused among the public demands for public assistance in improving conditions of life, the study of the aspects of politics that might be called democratic has not expanded so much as in the United States; the legalistic tradition of government has persisted.

In the field of economics changes stimulated by industrialism were accelerated by the necessities of war. Laissez faire, which concentrated upon natural laws as applied to economics in relation to the individual, has been supplanted by concepts and theories which stress the mutual role of the individual and the social group. As industry grew big it required data of an over-all character about the economy. It needed to know the size of the market, the amount of raw materials available, the level of income, the distribution of income among various kinds of purchasers, and so on. When the nations went to war, they needed similar, often identical, kinds of information: how large was the output of this or that material; what was the size of the national income; how much could and would the public pay in taxes; how much could the nation produce; how much money was required in circulation? These and other questions could be answered only with the aid of reliable statistics about the economy of the society as a whole. Ideas which stressed this requirement came to the fore. The use of the concept of national income opened up the entire field of social and economic planning and placed responsibility upon big business and upon government for formulating and executing effective policies.

Industrialism meant not merely the emergence of capitalists and managers but of laborers as well, and labor economics took its place alongside the subjects of price and market. Trade-unions participated in the demand for over-all social consideration of economics; they wished to know whether labor was receiving its fair share of the national income. Welfare economics became a respectable subject; taxation began to be considered as one aspect of public finance, the other being public expenditure.

As the activity of government spread with the demands of war and of industrial society for public leadership, the public budget acquired general significance. People wished to know how much of the national income was going to the government, how the burden was distributed, and who received the benefits. Bigness brought the threat of monopolies, which had to be controlled or prevented in the public interest. Booms and depressions had to be avoided and some means of maintaining economic equilibrium worked out. The kind of economics associated with the name of the Englishman John Maynard Keynes after World War I became popular in theory and practice. Reduced to the simplest terms, it stressed the necessity not merely to save money but to invest money in order to keep the economy alive and moving. The significant common denominator of Keynes's thought may be called a concern about the economy, not as an accumulation of separate individuals, but as an interdependent, functioning whole. This large and complicated economy was seen to require both freedom of action and over-all guidance, both social and political thinking in order to assure cooperation with all other parts of society.

The change from a conception of economics as run by natural laws to one of economics as subject to guidance by human knowledge has taken place throughout this century at degrees that varied with country, class, or group. A number of distinguished liberals in Great Britain published in

1928 an extensive report on the economy, in which they criticized British economic leaders for indifference to knowledge.

The lack of scientific management of industries, as industries, [they wrote] goes right through our economic system. An immense amount of time, of thought and ability is devoted to increasing the efficiency of the individual concern—very little to the rationalisation of industry. It is not only questions of structure, organisation, and marketing where rationalisation is required. It is also the whole question of technical development and the exchange of information—largely developed in the United States, but hardly begun here, except under the direction of the Ministry of Munitions during the war. There are questions of standard costing systems, and of adequate statistics. . . . There is the whole question of standardisation and simplication of types, where far-reaching economies are certainly possible in many industries.

Why has not more been done? There are, of course, technical difficulties. Although it is in some cases easy to see broadly on what lines reforms should proceed, it is always difficult to work out a practical detailed scheme. But the main difficulties are personal—jealousy and mistrust among people at the top of various concerns, vested interests of all kinds, the carrying on of things as they are, apathy and lack of imagination to realise the importance of reform. Clearly, this is a matter for industry itself.

The increasing need for reform makes necessary the introduction into industry of men with the training and education which fits them to wrestle successfully with its problems. The prejudice against University men in business is giving way to a growing recognition of their value. In the United States there are far more University graduates turned out every year per thousand of the population than in this country, and they are eagerly taken into industry. The principal administrative positions in most industries, both in Germany and America, are filled by University men, and there is no doubt that a University education, whatever its merits or defects in other directions, does give a wider outlook and a power of understanding the bigger problems. The present tendency towards the creation of large industrial units is a particular reason for industry to select administrators with the broadest and most highly educated outlook. The excellent work done by University Appointments Boards has already done a good deal to accelerate the flow of University men into business appointments. But there are still far too many obstacles. The improvement and extension of the educational devices for bringing the best brains of all classes to the Universities must be followed up by express arrangements for an avenue from the Universities into the higher walks of business, such as has long existed, to the great advantage of the State, into the Civil Service. This is particularly important in the case of Public Concerns, railways, banks, insurance offices, and the great industrial Trusts of the present day. But all large businesses of diffused ownership should do their utmost to replace the bad system of hereditary and family influence in the higher direction by employing the best brains and abilities of the country thrown up from all classes by the educational system.[13]

[13] *Britain's Industrial Future, being the Report of the Liberal Industrial Inquiry* (London: Ernest Benn, Ltd., 1928), pp. 129-131.

As the report indicated, economic knowledge was far more respected and used in the United States and Germany than in Great Britain. Countries like Sweden and Switzerland had likewise introduced methods of business rationalization, as the growing use of business machines revealed. France, Italy, and Belgium lagged behind, and the rest of Europe had in this respect scarcely accomplished anything. The introduction of the new economics into practical life did not make much headway until the world economic crisis drove leaders to bold, almost desperate action. In the thirties governments in most free countries tried Keynesian economic policies, and when the gargantuan demands of World War II struck the countries, traditional economic theories were forced to give way to political economy —government control, utilization of intelligence, allocation of brains, and whatever else would help in winning the war. The respect for knowledge gained during that ordeal seems to have continued in time of peace.

Sociology has achieved stature as an academic discipline only in this century. The brilliant theoretical work of men like Auguste Comte and Herbert Spencer of the preceding century has been followed by the spread of the subject over the multitude of social problems that an industrial economy, urban life, and the creation of a unified society in the new states after World War I have produced. The trend has been to allow general theory to care for itself while case studies were made—of adjustment to the factory or to the urban environment, of juvenile delinquency, of the formation of gangs, of the rise of racial and national attitudes, of the social factor in crime, of the conditions of successful and unsuccessful marriage, of the relations between the peasantry and other classes, of the social effects of different conditions of land distribution, and so on. The purpose of these studies may have originally been intellectual curiosity, but as the investigators recognized the need for improvement of conditions they turned their attention toward solving problems. Like the economists, they became functional in their desire to assist people in helping themselves. They cooperated with social workers and psychologists, both disciplines as novel as their own, in taking on many of the moral responsibilities which in previous centuries the church had assumed. They made social welfare an object of intellectual discipline. Nonetheless, they were few in number and did not enjoy the intellectual prestige of their colleagues in economics and political science. By the time of World War II, in spite of some fundamental work in countries of such diverse conditions as Poland and Romania, on the one hand, and Great Britain and France, on the other, the subject had not yet made much headway in Europe.

Although anthropology occupies a position about on par with that of sociology, the conditions of twentieth-century life have brought it growing prestige. As underdeveloped peoples through imperialism and industrialism have raised their demands and become factors in world affairs, the Western powers have had to find advice on how to handle them by other means than physical force. The anthropologist, from his training in analyzing the culture of primitive peoples, has been able to give some of the needed advice. He has also become interested in analyzing the strength and weakness of forces in advanced cultures. Modern wars, modern industrialism, and nationalism have revealed the interdependence of all aspects of a culture. A religious split as in Nazi Germany or an antihuman ideal as in communism or nazism may seriously weaken a country. After a century of resistance to foreign domination a people like the Poles had to be taught to work together. The anthropologist has been best prepared for investigating the total culture, and he has contributed that indispensable concept of culture to the study of society. By means of it we have a framework for studying a society from all its aspects; we are able to emerge with some sense of its unifying ideals and institutions. The concept has supplied a means of dealing with the interrelations of all the social sciences, and, one should add, the humanities and the sciences as they exist in a given society. The anthropological study of advanced cultures, however, has scarcely progressed beyond the initial stages.

In the main the social sciences have up to the present been developed within the limits of a nation. When a British political scientist studied the party system of France, for example, he did so from the national point of view, with only a superficial attempt to compare the system with that in his own country. World War I diminished this provincialism to some extent, in that it stimulated the comparative study of primitive cultures by the anthropologists and the comparative analysis of economic systems, and especially in that it set up a few international organizations whose research kept pace with their international ideals. The International Labor Office and the Economic and Financial Sections of the League of Nations, for example, turned out fundamental reports on international conditions. The International Health Organization, the Council for Intellectual Cooperation, and the International Agricultural Organization likewise did admirable work. The global character of World War II and the cold war with communism have pressed home the lesson of the need for international knowledge, and the organization of the United Nations and its many affiliates has provided facilities for conducting the research.

Never before in the history of man has there been such large-scaled mustering of intelligence on world problems. It is seen that unemployment, dietary deficiencies, uneconomical exploitation of natural resources, financial ignorance, and a thousand other social problems affect not merely the people of one country but those of many or even of all countries. Famine in an area may enable communism to spread and endanger all free peoples. Low standards of living deprive industrial exporting countries of markets. Government inefficiency means waste of human as well as physical resources which could be used to improve the life of all peoples. The international agencies collect and analyze such data and enable us for the first time to be informed about conditions throughout the globe. No private agency, university, or single scholar can compete with the resources of these organizations for conducting research. We live at the beginning of global social science.

INTERNATIONAL EXCHANGE OF KNOWLEDGE

The transnational, global dimensions of knowledge have introduced means for making the results available in a practical way. During World War II the United States and Great Britain began to exchange information of value to each other about science, technology, business organization, labor relations—any and every subject on which the one had something worth while to contribute to the other. After fighting ceased, the interchange continued and expanded to include France and other countries. This work meant a revolution in business ethics which had begun in the United States. It stressed the increase of production at lower costs, and to that end it practiced the lesson of modern industrialism—that the old idea of guarding trade and production secrets was uneconomical. It believed that the machine should be utilized, that to that end information should be given out freely (subject to patent and certain other controls, of course), and that thereby both producer and consumer would benefit.

The continental countries, in the main adhering to the old standards, hesitantly began to apply the new criterion. Since the Marshall Plan furthered the exchange of such data and the United Nations and its affiliates took up the practice, the new standard seemed well on the way toward victory, at least among free peoples. It was learned by experience that experts sent abroad on a mission of aid normally functioned best when organized as a team. On problems of technology a few engineers, workers, and managers might act as such a team, especially if sent from one advanced country to another. They would learn together and might improve their mutual relations upon their return. They would come to regard the industry, not as a place of combat, but as one of mutual interest.

In sending observers from an advanced country to an underdeveloped one, from Great Britain to Afghanistan, for example, it proved advisable to organize a team of scientists and social scientists. The geologist could survey the natural resources; the political scientist could analyze the condition of government; the anthropologist could advise on customs which must be considered in remaking the country; the sociologist could explore the effects of proposed reforms upon village life with a view to avoiding unnecessary trouble. This is the pattern of research which is now emerging —cooperative, transnational, respectful of cultures, equalitarian in attitude, moral in its effort to help a people in a practical way to help itself. It marks the beginning of global science, humanities, and social science.

The essential characteristic of the society of industrialism has been succinctly stated by the British philosopher A. N. Whitehead as follows:

The foundation of all understanding of sociological theory—that is to say, of all understanding of human life—is that no static maintenance of perfection is possible. This axiom is rooted in the nature of things. Advance or Decadence are the only choices offered to mankind. The pure conservative is fighting against the essence of the universe. This doctrine requires justification. It is implicitly denied in the learned tradition derived from ancient thought.

The doctrine is founded upon three metaphysical principles. One principle is that the very essence of real actuality—that is, of the completely real—is *process*. Thus each actual thing is only to be understood in terms of its becoming and perishing. There is no halt in which the actuality is just its static self, accidentally played upon by qualifications derived from the shift of circumstances. The converse is the truth.[14]

In no other period of history has free society placed comparable emphasis upon the practice of *process*. Whether applied in the sciences, the social sciences, technology, or government, the experimental method, the method of process, has been accepted as standard. In the search for new knowledge it employs the orderly procedure from the known to the unknown by way of the combination of theory and practice. The biological sciences have explored genetics, the process of growth and decay, the utilization of this knowledge in the improvement of crops and animals. The chemists have shown the interrelationship of the parts of matter and have explored the ways of building new and useful chemical combinations which are basic in every branch of science. The social scientist has stressed the value of objective investigation for the solution of social problems. Government has found the standard of rational process far superior in efficiency to that of arbitrary change by physical coercion. In order to conserve time and fuel and reduce costs, industry has introduced the system of continuous flow by the use of the conveyor belt and other means of technical and business rationalization. Rejecting rigid, compulsive behavior, industrial society has accepted the ideal of open-mindedness about change and of improvement by popular action for the lot of man. It has recognized that our civilization is built upon knowledge. As a visit to a school, a representative assembly, an industrial plant will show, it has become the society of process.

TOTALITARIAN KNOWLEDGE—GERMANY

In striking contrast, the totalitarian and communist societies have refused to accept process as a general ideal and have forced knowledge into a position of subordination to a rigid cultural dogma. They have presumed to judge knowledge exclusively on the basis of its value to political power. Hitler declared in *Mein Kampf:*

[14] Alfred North Whitehead, *Adventures of Ideas* (New York: The Macmillan Company, 1933), pp. 353-354.

> The State must throw the whole weight of its educational machinery not into pumping its children full of knowledge, but into producing absolutely healthy bodies. The development of mental capacity is only of secondary importance. Our first aim must be the development of character, especially of will-power, and a readiness to take responsibility; scientific training follows far behind.

The Communists condemned freedom of knowledge as part of capitalistic, bourgeois, wicked, or, to use a favorite communist adjective, "putrid" imperialistic attempt to destroy communism. What were the effects of these value judgments upon the state of knowledge under the two regimes?

When the Nazis gained control of Germany in 1933, some university teachers were enthusiastic, many disapproved in silence and tried to survive the storm by general acquiescence, and many were dismissed. The Nazis introduced a new basis for knowledge, which may be summarized in two quotations. Professor Ernst Krieck, trained in education and appointed by the Nazis as rector of the University of Frankfurt am Main, asserted in 1933:

> Blood and soil, as fundamental forces of life, are, however, the symbols of the national-political point of view and of the heroic style of life. By them the ground is prepared for a new form of education. . . . What does blood mean to us? We cannot rest satisfied with the teachings of physics, chemistry, or medicine. . . . In blood lurks our ancestral inheritance, in blood is embodied the race, from blood arise the character and destiny of man; blood is to man the hidden undercurrent, the symbol of the current of life from which man can arise and ascend to the regions of light, of spirit, and of knowledge.

In 1936 the lawyer Frank, one of Hitler's *Reich* ministers, said the following:

> The ideas of Adolf Hitler contain the final truths of every possible scientific knowledge. . . . National-Socialism provided the only remaining possibility of working scientifically in Germany. . . . We believe that every scientific work (whose purpose is after all to serve the investigation of truth) must coincide in its results with the starting point of National-Socialism. The programme of the National-Socialist Party has consequently become the only basis for all scientific investigation. . . . The true Front spirit [that of the soldier at the front] is more important than scientific discussion.

Guided by blood and by the writings of Hitler, the Nazi scholars set to work to lead the world in research. Johannes Stark and Philipp Lenard, two Nobel prize winners who had become Nazis, distinguished between "two main types of mental attitude among workers in the field of physics." "The pragmatic spirit, from which have sprung the creations of successful discoveries both past and present, is directed towards reality, its aim is to ascertain the laws governing already known phenomena and to discover new phenomena and bodies as yet unknown." This was the the new German physicist. He contrasted, Stark wrote, with "the physicist of the dogmatic school," and as examples he used Einstein, Schrödinger, Heisenberg,

Sommerfeld—in fact, most of the famous physicists of Germany. The non-Germans were not worthy of mention.

When Sommerfeld at the University of Munich retired just before World War II, his successor was a good Nazi named Müller, who rejected modern physics. Competent professors were forced to attend long sessions at which they argued with their Nazi colleagues over the validity of the theory of relativity and had to draw up compromise resolutions which would satisfy the Nazis without outraging scientific truth.

> A basic conflict existed between the national-socialist view that there was a privileged race, and privileged persons within that race who had a superior understanding given by intuition, and the ethos of modern science which has always held that the majority of men are equal and equivalent observers of nature, viewing the same things and arriving at the same conclusions, given the apparatus and adequate training. The postulate that all observers in the universe were equivalent and symmetrical was basic to Einstein's theory of relativity, which was especially condemned by Stark and others.[15]

Since a nonpolitical subject like physics was twisted to the Nazi shape, one can imagine what happened to biology, history, and the social sciences.

Decline of Universities

Suffering from the low prestige of knowledge, the universities declined in number of students and in the quality of instruction. They lost students to the army, the Nazi party, and to approved practical occupations. The reduction was most marked in theoretical physics. In the winter term of 1932–1933 there were 12,951 students taking mathematics with natural science; by the same term of 1936–1937 the number had declined to 4,616. In engineering the drop was from 14,477 to 7,649 in that time, relatively much less than that in the theoretical field. The character of the teaching staff may be judged from a secret report of 1943 by the director of the Reich Research Council, a position comparable to that of the head of the National Defence Research Council in the United States held by President Conant of Harvard. The director was defending himself against the accusation of incompetence, and in doing so he called attention to the

> early lack of recognition by the Nazi Party of the universities, when scientists were obviously regarded as liberal, reactionary, Jewish, or Freemason—in any case, anti-Nazi. This belief was partly justified, [he continued] and led to a purification which lasted until 1937. . . . Nearly 40% of all professors were dismissed, which led to a serious lack of personnel. This could only be repaired slowly; only a limited number of Nazi lecturers and assistants were available to fill the vacancies, and they did not always satisfy the scientific requirements.

When the standard of autonomous objectivity was abandoned, the pursuit of knowledge lost its independence of action. Teachers and re-

[15] Mason, *op. cit.*, p. 474.

searchers learned that recognition and even personal security depended, not upon the originality and scholarly value of their work, but upon the zeal of their devotion to nazism and the efficiency of their cultivation of Nazi leaders. Since the Nazis possessed no specialized knowledge of their own, they could not judge the quality of the research as such, even if they had wished to do so. Being most intent upon maintaining and expanding their own power, they quickly began to compete with one another for control of research work, to build up rival organizations, and to appoint to the highest positions intellectual mediocrities and charlatans with little beyond their loyalty to nazism. Himmler's secret police spied on all and furnished that potentate with gossip and other comparable information of use in undermining research staffs responsible to other ministers.

German Research in World War II

At the beginning of World War II, Nazi Germany set up a Reich Research Council under the direction of S. S. Brigade Commander Ministerial Director Professor Doctor Rudolph Mentzel, a person of second-rate achievement in chemistry but of first-rate ability in maneuvering his way up the Nazi hierarchy. His scientist colleagues called him "the culture sergeant" and joked about his one and only lecture on chemistry. He had never realized, Mentzel had said at that time, how much more difficult it was to deliver a scientific lecture than to speak on politics. He held this position throughout the war in spite of accusations of incompetence and complaints against him to Göring, Himmler, and others; and he enjoyed the ample company of other research directors of similar ability. The Nazis scarcely knew the difference between, on the one hand, a Heisenberg in physics and, on the other, an Erich Schumann, professor of military physics, whose few writings concerned the vibrations of piano strings. Schumann directed the army research in nuclear fission until he gave it up as futile. In 1939 the really competent physicists, of whom Germany had many, had the same knowledge about the subject that the British and the Americans had, but they were prevented by the Nazi administration from working on the project with full facilities until the beginning of 1944, when it was too late. Himmler's research organization reported in August, 1944, that the *Reich* Research Council under Mentzel was supporting almost no projects of importance for the conduct of the war. Seventy per cent of them, it said, pertained to forestry and agriculture, only 3 per cent to physics.

Himmler attempted to gain control of the research on guided missiles done at Peenemünde. On the basis of local gossip picked up by his agents he arrested the main experts and threw them into jail. After some months the general in charge of the work succeeded in gaining their release; but Himmler's interference, initial Nazi indifference, and an Allied air raid prevented the research center from producing weapons in quantities sufficient to affect the course of the war profoundly. Himmler, who had graduated from an agricultural college, maintained an active interest in research. In March, 1944, he wrote his research director from field headquarters as follows:

> In future weather researches, which we expect to carry out after the war by systematic organization of an immense number of single observations, I request you to take note of the following:
>
> The roots, or onions, of the meadow saffron are located at depths that vary from year to year. The deeper they are, the more severe the winter will be; the nearer they are to the surface, the milder the winter.
>
> This fact was called to my attention by the Führer.

Himmler likewise planned to use Heisenberg in cooperation with other scientists to test the Nazi theory that the inner core of all planets and stars consists of ordinary ice. Need one go further in explaining why the Nazi regime failed?

SOVIET KNOWLEDGE

In theory the Communists have profoundly respected science. They speak of their system of society as the only scientific one in world history, and they claim that dialectical materialism as the product of scientific thinking offers the sole means of transforming all branches of knowledge into sciences. In their eagerness for big-scale industrialization they have endeavored to harness science to production in every field, and they have required heavy sacrifices in all other aspects of life in order to achieve this goal. Soon after acquiring power in Russia they transformed the existing Academy of Science, a creation of the eighteenth century, into the leading agency in the country for all lines of knowledge. The academy not merely set policies and furnished advice; it has become an operating agency for research and has established numerous institutes for that purpose. In the past decade or more it has led in the creation of new industries based upon research and actually operates many industrial plants. In addition, it has exercised an indirect influence over research in the universities and the industrial laboratories. The Communist belief in bigness and centralization of planning and administration finds in this academy its intellectual expression.

The Communist leaders have expanded the facilities for higher education to supply professional personnel. According to Vavilov, the former president of the Academy of Sciences, the student body reached prewar size by the late 1920's, namely, some 112,000 persons in 91 universities and colleges. By 1941 the figures, he said, were 667,000 enrolled in about 800 institutions. Before the revolution, according to Vavilov, Russia maintained one scholarly journal in the physical sciences with a circulation of about 200, whereas in 1948 she supported five with a circulation of about 5,000.

The number of professional personnel, according to a study by Demitri Shimkin of the Russian Research Center at Harvard, has rapidly increased

both in absolute numbers and in relation to total non-agricultural employment. In 1952 the number of persons employed in professional positions who were graduates of higher educational institutions in industry, agriculture, and health totaled 860,000 as compared with 358,000 in 1937.

In 1952 there were, Shimkin estimates, about 475,000 engineers and natural scientists "in manufacturing, construction, transportation, and communications, plus some 145,000 in agriculture," and "about 240,000 physicians, dentists and pharmacists." In addition, there were in 1950, 80,000 professors and instructors in higher institutions. Shimkin states that the number of full-time students in colleges and universities by 1952 reached nearly a million, of whom in 1950, 21,000 were working for advanced degrees; and, he adds, in 1950 there were 880 institutions of higher education. Since the figures do not include the personnel in the military institutions, which play an important part in Soviet higher education and research, Shimkin concludes that they understate the rapid growth of Soviet professional man power.[16] Between 1950 and 1955 the number of engineers graduating from higher institutions increased from 28,000 to 63,000; if scientists are included, the latter figure was 120,000. The number was rapidly rising, for by 1957 there were 30 million pupils in primary and secondary schools, and nearly 2 million in institutions of higher education.

The figures may be compared with those for certain free industrial countries. Belgium in 1948 had about 20,000 students in institutions of higher education, an increase of 60 per cent in 25 years. Sweden had about 16,000. In Great Britain the number grew from 50,000 in 1938–1939 to 82,500 in 1948. In France, at the end of 1947, 21,000 students attended technical colleges, but only 400 were enrolled at the leading École Polytecnique. The total college and university enrollment reached nearly 142,000. In Great Britain, in 1949–1950, the universities awarded 14,000 degrees in science and technology; the United States, 110,000 degrees. The number of students in pure and applied science in Great Britain had more than doubled since the war, and the number was continuing to rise.

Since the European countries cannot compete in land mass and in size of population with the Soviet Union, the figures should be supplemented by those for the United States. A report in 1953 of the National Manpower Council provided the following data. The United States had about 5 million professional and related workers, among whom were 700,000 scientists and engineers. Of these only 160,000 were engaged in research and developmental work and only about 15,000 in basic research. In 1950 the country produced about 7,700 Ph.D's, half of them in natural

[16] Demitri Shimkin, "Scientific Personnel in the U.S.S.R.," *Science,* CXVI (November 7, 1952), 512-513.

science. It had fewer than 20,000 physicists, however, and only 4,000 of these possessed Ph.D. degrees. By 1955 it was graduating 23,000 engineers each year to the Soviet Union's 63,000. The Manpower Council deplored the small number of trained personnel, just as a comparable British body did at the same time for its country. In each free country the persons in a position to know the facts were deeply concerned over the prospect of the Soviet dictators disposing of the services of scientific and technological personnel comparable or even superior in numbers and possibly in quality to that of the free countries.

Marxist Restrictions on Knowledge

Communist ideology contains such severe handicaps to the fulfillment of its own objectives that quantity has proved to be no guarantee of quality. Science was forced to conform to the Marxian dogmas. Marx and Engels had accepted the fact of evolution, but they had rejected the Darwinian concept of evolution through natural selection as not fitting their theory. The Communists have consistently had difficulty with genetics, for this subject since the time at least of Mendel has denied the inheritance of acquired characteristics. The Communists have maintained that man, animals, and plants could be made over quickly by changing the environment and that the new characteristics would then be inherited. In this way they expected to transform man to the communist pattern speedily and yet thoroughly. They regard the Mendelian-Morgan theories of the importance of both heredity and environment as reactionary and bourgeois; if one must wait for heredity to bring about the changes desired, one admits that change will occur very slowly and that it lies in large part beyond the power of man to influence the change. Hence the Communists condemn this theory as a weapon for the defense of bourgeois society againt the reform zeal of communism.

When the Nazis brought forth their racialist theories and placed emphasis upon heredity, the Communists in the person of the biologist Nikolai Lysenko reacted in 1936 with a politicoscientific denunciation of the Mendelian theory in favor of the discarded view of Lamarck (1744–1829) that acquired characteristics were capable of being inherited. Lysenko, a peasant in origin, succeeded in silencing his opponents and forcing Vavilov, the world-famous director of the Institute of Genetics, who could not accept Lamarck's views, into ignominy. Condemned as a British spy, Vavilov disappeared and Lysenko became his successor. In time Lysenko received the Order of Lenin, two Stalin prizes, the title of Hero of the Soviet Union, and was appointed president of the Lenin Academy of Agronomy and director of the Soviet Academy of Science.

When the Russian Revolution began, Lenin understood that the country needed the services of all the scientists it could muster. Communist dogma of class warfare, however, called for the elimination of the bourgeoisie, to which class all scientists belonged. The first interest of Communists being security against internal enemies, the suspect bourgeois scientists were ousted. Then scientists had to be trained from among the peasantry and the proletariat, classes without a tradition of scientific interests. The level of scientific teaching and study sank so low that the Communists devised a collectivist solution.

The students were divided into small groups that took their examinations in a body. They pooled their knowledge and, when a group was able to pass its examinations, the individuals who made up the group became scientists. . . . Thus it was not long before the Russian scientists were, literally, of all types, ranging from excellent to terrible, and the political authorities had a wide choice as to the kinds of scientists they could promote to positions of importance and influence. The political authorities were also uninhibited by any real scientific considerations in making their choices, for conditions in Russia are not such that the politicians prefer scientific standards to their own personal safety.[17]

Effects on Science and Technology

Scientists soon learned the behavior necessary in order to save their jobs and their lives. They endeavored to be on the winning political side and to supply the political leaders with pleasing information.

The road to safety was clearly not to be found by a careful and honest interpretation of experimental data but by preserving a rigid Communist orthodoxy, by endorsing just those doctrines which are compatible with the beliefs of the dominant clique.

It was more important to watch the opinions of the authorities, to take one's scientific line from *Pravda* and *Izvestia,* than to experiment and report accurately the results of one's research.

In a number of scientific fields her leaders have cut themselves off from the truth and, perhaps fortunately for the free world, they have no means for reestablishing the connections. Once the good scientists have been intimidated or disgusted, all the scientists are reduced to the same level, the level of the charlatans. Even if Stalin himself had wanted to know the truth about Mendel, he could not learn it. He could find no reason to believe what anyone would tell him.[18]

Not all branches of science have suffered to the same extent. In fields like engineering and applied physics the results of quackery are soon evident and can be corrected. In medicine and agriculture it is less possible to check the efficiency of work. "In spite of quacks and cultists, patients recover and crops grow. In medicine and agriculture only honest scientists can evaluate the current practices." [19] Most subjects fall between these two

[17] Conway Zirkle, "The Involuntary Destruction of Science in the U.S.S.R.," *Scientific Monthly,* May, 1953, p. 280.
[18] *Ibid.,* p. 281. [19] *Ibid.*

kinds. Some are too dangerous politically to attract capable scientists; they are the hunting ground of the mediocre and the charlatan. It has also been found that notwithstanding the ever-increasing interdependence of the sciences a scientist is safer who remains in one field. If he spreads over several subjects and in any one of them incurs the displeasure of the authorities, he will be discredited in all fields. In numerous subjects where results cannot be quickly tested by experience the scientists who have the ability to be original are held back by the fact that the mediocre majority may resist and force them to recant any important discoveries. Because of the limits set by these political considerations the record of achievement of the Communist scientists has been spotty. The following summary is based largely upon a symposium held in December, 1951, by a section of the American Association for the Advancement of Science.[20] There seems no reason to doubt that it is substantially accurate for the present day.

1. Genetics has been extirpated in Russia and its place taken by an archaic quackery.

2. Statistics has lost its basic honesty. It is now used to falsify data for propaganda purposes.

3. Psychology and psychiatry are practically dead, with little chance of recovery.

4. Biology and agriculture are so permeated by quackery that nothing of importance can be expected from them.

5. Physiology, pathology, and medicine are forced into a rigid and stupid orthodoxy which contains much quackery; their future development is inhibited, but some sound practices still survive. News from Moscow (January 12, 1953) shows that the high Soviet officials no longer trust their own physicians (Pravda). Their suspicions, of course, are justified, as the physicians dare not use methods in medicine incompatible with "Michurin science." (Michurin was a Lamarckian of this century in Russia and the scientist whom Lysenko used as an authority).

6. Geology is subjected to political attacks and pure research is discouraged.

7. Astronomy includes the amusing quackery of astro-botany, or the study of plant life on the planets. Certain theories as to the origin of the solar system are forbidden, but nevertheless much excellent work is being done by Russian astronomers.

8. In chemistry, certain theories, such as resonance, are forbidden, but much good chemical research is still being done.

9. The basic philosophical background of modern physics is labeled "idealistic" and is condemned. However, in physics, many of the words are separated from their meanings so that basic research is probably not hurt by its accompanying verbiage. Russian physics is definitely good.

10. Russian mathematics is truly excellent, a science of which any country might be proud.

11. Engineering in Russia is probably adequate for all military and civilian purposes.

[20] *Ibid.*

The results of nearly four decades of scientific research under communism appear, in short, to be uneven. Much practical work, in plant breeding and engineering, for example, has been done, as one would expect under the circumstances of the country's primitive economy. In fields like nuclear fission, of the utmost importance to military defense, the achievements have been comparable to those in Western nations. The basic contradiction between the freedom essential to science and the dictatorship essential to force communism upon society remains inhibiting. The scientists have had to learn the art of double talk; they pay lip service to communist dogmas in their science while continuing their researches. The handicap of hypocrisy and charlatanism will severely restrict science as long as the communist system lasts.

Effects on Historical Writing

Since the most objective of all branches of knowledge, namely science, is subject to dogmatic control, one would rightly expect history and the social sciences to be mere instruments of propaganda. That these are required to change with the party line may be illustrated in the case of any one of them; history will be selected for that purpose.

In the first decade of Soviet life Pokrovski, a Marxian historian but at least one who respected sources, dominated the field; and, although he forced a Marxian interpretation upon facts, he maintained some professional standards. After the death of Lenin, Stalin began to use historical writing as a weapon for gaining and keeping supreme power. From that time on the historian's profession became one of the most precarious. The historian was advised by those with power to destroy him that he should shun "objectivism" and "an exaggerated attachment to facts" and that he should cite and apply the "theoretical generalizations" of the party line. Historians received orders about what to write and how to write it; they were expected to produce like robots, to modify or reverse the views in their works according to dictates from Stalin. If the facts did not fit or did not exist, new ones were manufactured on the spot.

Thus Tarle was ordered to rewrite his work and prove that Napoleon had burned Moscow. Lenin's works were re-edited to omit all criticism of Stalin. Trotsky disappeared entirely from history, as did the Volga Germans. Stalin's own writings have had to be revised to bring his past statements into line with present ones. Stalin was glorified as the greatest Soviet historian, and his *History of the Communist Party: Short Course* went through numerous editions, "the greatest, dullest and most mendacious best seller in the history of literature," states Bertram D. Wolfe.[21] It has undergone constant revision as individuals have fallen into disfavor and been liquidated; but in this case the author survived and died in 1953, seemingly

[21] Bertram D. Wolfe, "Operation Rewrite: The Agony of Soviet Historians," *Foreign Affairs*, October, 1952, p. 47.

of natural causes. How effectively he has remade historical writing may be judged from the fact that in one of his volumes he took equal credit with Lenin for leading the October revolution in 1917.

Three successive Communist versions of the history of the Allied landing on the Normandy coast may be cited. A collective history of the U.S.S.R. published in 1945 quoted Stalin as saying, "A brilliant achievement. . . . The history of war knows no other enterprise like it for breadth of purpose, grandiose skill, and masterful execution." In the new edition of the next year the passage read, "On June 6, 1944, Allied forces accomplished a landing in Northern France. . . ." The recent prize-winning textbook by Shestakov describes the event as follows:

> England and the United States, in the course of three years of war, dragged out in every way the opening of a second front. . . . But when, after the gigantic victories of the Soviet Army, it became clear that the Soviet Union might alone defeat the enemy, occupy the territory of Germany and liberate all Western Europe, including France . . . in June 1944, the English and American Armies left England and landed on the coast of Northern France.[22]
>
> . . . . .
>
> It is suggestive [writes Mr. Wolfe] both of the hazards in the field and the real feelings of the historians that, despite urgings, dangled prizes and repeated threats, no one has yet been found to complete a single volume or a single serious article in the field of the history of the Party and the régime, though Stalin himself first suggested it in 1931, has ordered it at regular intervals since, and forced it into the place of top priority in the Five-year Plan for Soviet Historians adopted in 1946. Fifteen years after the task was first assigned by the Dictator, the lead editorial in *Voprosy istorii* (No. 8, 1949) warned that the failure to produce the ordered works creates a "completely impermissible situation" which "it would be completely wrong to look for objective circumstances to explain." This stubborn silence, continuing up to the moment in which I write, [1952] constitutes the most eloquent page in present-day Soviet historiography.[23]

When upon Stalin's death the Soviet government relaxed political control, intellectuals immediately began to plead for some freedom of thought and expression. They affirmed devotion to the régime but declared that communism would be furthered by independent activity of creative minds. The leading atomic physicist refused in 1956 to work on the production of atomic bombs. At a congress of scientists a minority advocated, unsuccessfully, the right of free election of officers, a move directed at eliminating domination by Communist party stalwarts over the choice of subjects for research, the allocation of research funds, and all other aspects of scientific work. Composers and writers joined the plea.

> It is impossible [Khachaturian, the composer, wrote] to imagine a work imbued with the drama of revolutionary romanticism, inspired by ardent love for the motherland, for the man of our socialist reality, yet written without

[22] *Ibid.*, p. 50. [23] *Ibid.*, pp. 41-42.

creative élan and with a cautious glance over the shoulder for fear that something untoward might happen. . . . I think the time has come to revise our established system of institutional guardianship over composers.

The slight amount of intellectual freedom became too dangerous for the Soviet leaders to bear: it might encourage the request for freedom in all lines. In 1956 the Politburo placed Molotov in charge of cultural affairs to restore discipline.

The French novelist Camus has asserted that "insecurity is what makes one think." Subject to the one condition that insecurity can be pressed to an extreme where thinking becomes impossible, the accuracy of Camus' assertion is proved by the enormous fruitfulness in all intellectual lines of this half century. World history must show few experiences which man in our period has not had at first hand, and the results have been an outpouring of knowledge and of creative aesthetic work too voluminous and too varied for us as yet to comprehend. Tragedy, heroism, martyrdom, pathos, life in death and death in life, the glory and the terror of science—millions and millions of individuals have personally gone through all of these. Good and evil and their multiple combinations have been the companions of our insecurity and have led us into the profoundest questions of the universe which we associate with metaphysics and theology. The writings on these subjects have come from scientists, poets, novelists, professional warriors, and other persons in activities which forced ultimate issues upon them. In the areas of political and social ideals we have had to wrestle with the relative values of the caste-state, liberal democracy, fascism, nazism, socialism, and communism, and we in the free countries of the West have had to justify our way of life once more, as we did in the eighteenth century. Faced with the moral defense of our freedom, we have learned that under totalitarian systems and under communism the dread of physical and spiritual oppression deadens the activity of the mind and reduces the masses to the dull routine of physical existence. Freedom has stirred the spirit and the mind to action and evoked the positive achievement of this century.

Suggestions for Further Reading

BARRACLOUGH, GEOFFREY. *History in a Changing World.* Norman: University of Oklahoma Press, 1956. Treats the relation between the study of history and the crisis of our civilization. Illuminates the character of the entire period and analyses much more than historical writing.

BERNAL, J. D. *The Freedom of Necessity.* London: Routledge & Kegal Paul, Ltd., 1949. Contains useful data on science in relation to government and education.

COUNTS, GEORGE S. *The Challenge of Soviet Education.* New York: McGraw-Hill Book Company, Inc., 1957. Basic work, by an American scholar.

———, and NUCIA LODGE. *The Country of the Blind.* See the Readings for Chapter 27.

CROWTHER, JAMES GERALD. *The Social Relations of Science.* New York: The Macmillan Company, 1941. Useful survey that attempts to live up to its title.

JONES, ERNEST. *The Life and Work of Sigmund Freud.* 3 vols. New York: Basic Books, Inc., 1953–1957.

MASON, STEPHEN FINNEY. *Main Currents of Scientific Thought.* New York: Henry Schuman, Inc., 1953. A general history with useful survey of the present century.

Preliminary Report on the World Social Situation. See the Readings for Chapter 6.

SAMUEL, RICHARD, and R. HINTON THOMAS. *Education and Society in Modern Germany.* London. Routledge & Kegan Paul, Ltd., 1949.

Social Science Encyclopedia. New York: The Macmillan Company, 1930. I, 172–349. Gives history of the social sciences during the past hundred years.

Index

Index

B

C

E

F

G

H

I

M

N

O

P

T

V

W

Y

Z

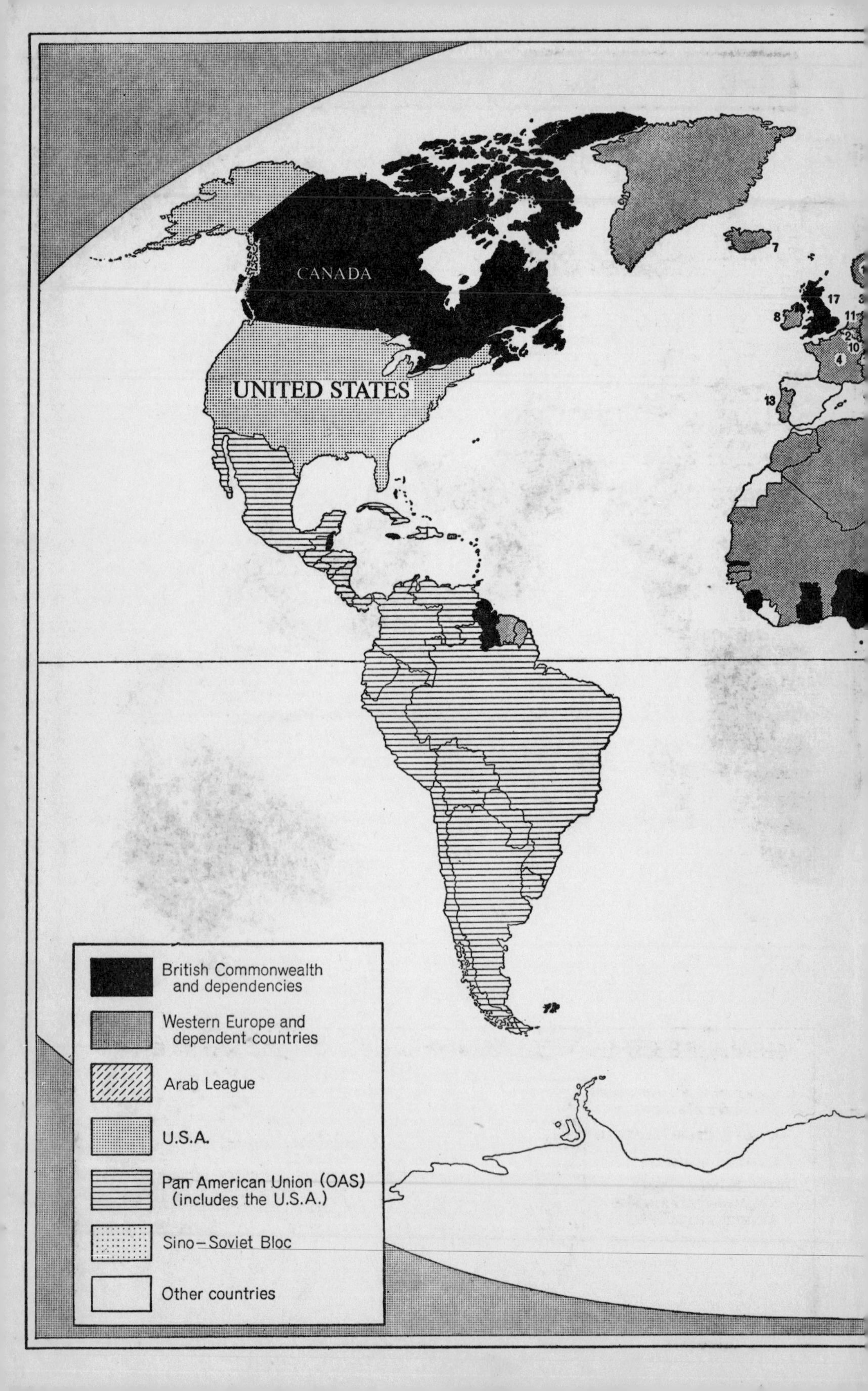

CANADA
UNITED STATES
7
17
8
11
2
10
4
13
British Commonwealth and dependencies
Western Europe and dependent countries
Arab League
U.S.A.
Pan American Union (OAS) (includes the U.S.A.)
Sino–Soviet Bloc
Other countries